Wordsworth
A Life

JULIET BARKER

VIKING

VIKING

Published by the Penguin Group
Penguin Books Ltd, 27 Wrights Lane, London W8 5TZ, England
Penguin Putnam Inc., 375 Hudson Street, New York, New York 10014, USA
Penguin Books Australia Ltd, Ringwood, Victoria, Australia
Penguin Books Canada Ltd, 10 Alcorn Avenue, Toronto, Ontario, Canada M4V 3B2
Penguin Books India (P) Ltd, 11, Community Centre,
Panchsheel Park, New Delhi – 110 017, India
Penguin Books (NZ) Ltd, Private Bag 102902, NSMC, Auckland, New Zealand
Penguin Books (South Africa) (Pty) Ltd, 5 Watkins Street,
Denver Ext 4, Johannesburg 2094, South Africa

Penguin Books Ltd, Registered Offices: Harmondsworth, Middlesex, England

First published 2000
1 3 5 7 9 10 8 6 4 2

Set in 10/13.5pt Monotype Janson
Typeset by Rowland Phototypesetting Ltd,
Bury St Edmunds, Suffolk
Printed in Great Britain by Clays Ltd, St Ives plc

A CIP catalogue record for this book is available from the British Library

ISBN 0-670-87213-X

For my parents,
Richard and Judith Bateson,
with gratitude
for a lifetime's support and encouragement

Contents

List of Illustrations

Illustration Acknowledgements

The author and publishers are grateful to the following for permission to reproduce illustrations:

Halftones

1, 41, John Garbutt; 2 from Marsh & Garbutt, *Wordsworth's Lakeland*; 3, 25, John Marsh; 4, 7, 8, 9, 32, Abbot Hall Art Gallery, Kendal, Cumbria, UK/Bridgeman Art Library, London, London; 5, Cornell University Library, USA; 6, 10, 14, 15, 19, 20, 22, 24, 27, 31, 35, 38, 39, 40, The Wordsworth Trust, Grasmere; 11, 13, 26, 36, 37, National Portrait Gallery; 12, Dorset County Council; 16, Pierpont Morgan Library/ Art Resource, NY; 17 from Martin, *In the Footprints of Charles Lamb, 1891*; 18, e.t. archive; 21, 30, from Blanshard, *Portraits of Wordsworth*; 23, University of Bristol; 28, Master and Fellows of Trinity College, Cambridge; 29 from The Masquerier Album (HCR VIII) Trustees of Dr Williams's Library, London; 33, Trustees of Rydal Mount; 34 from *LY*, iv.

Chapter heads

1, John Garbutt; 2, Trustees of Hawkshead Grammar School; 3, 22, St John's College, Cambridge; 4, 5, 6, 7, 10, 11, 13, 14, 15, 16, 18, 20, 21, 26, The Wordsworth Trust; 8, 24, Mary Evans Picture Library; 9, 17, National Portrait Gallery; 12, 25, Abbot Hall Art Gallery, Kendal, Cumbria, UK/Bridgeman Art Library; 19, Birmingham Museum and Art Gallery; 23, Paul Betz; 27, Trustees of Rydal Mount; 28, Cornell University, USA; Epilogue, John Marsh.

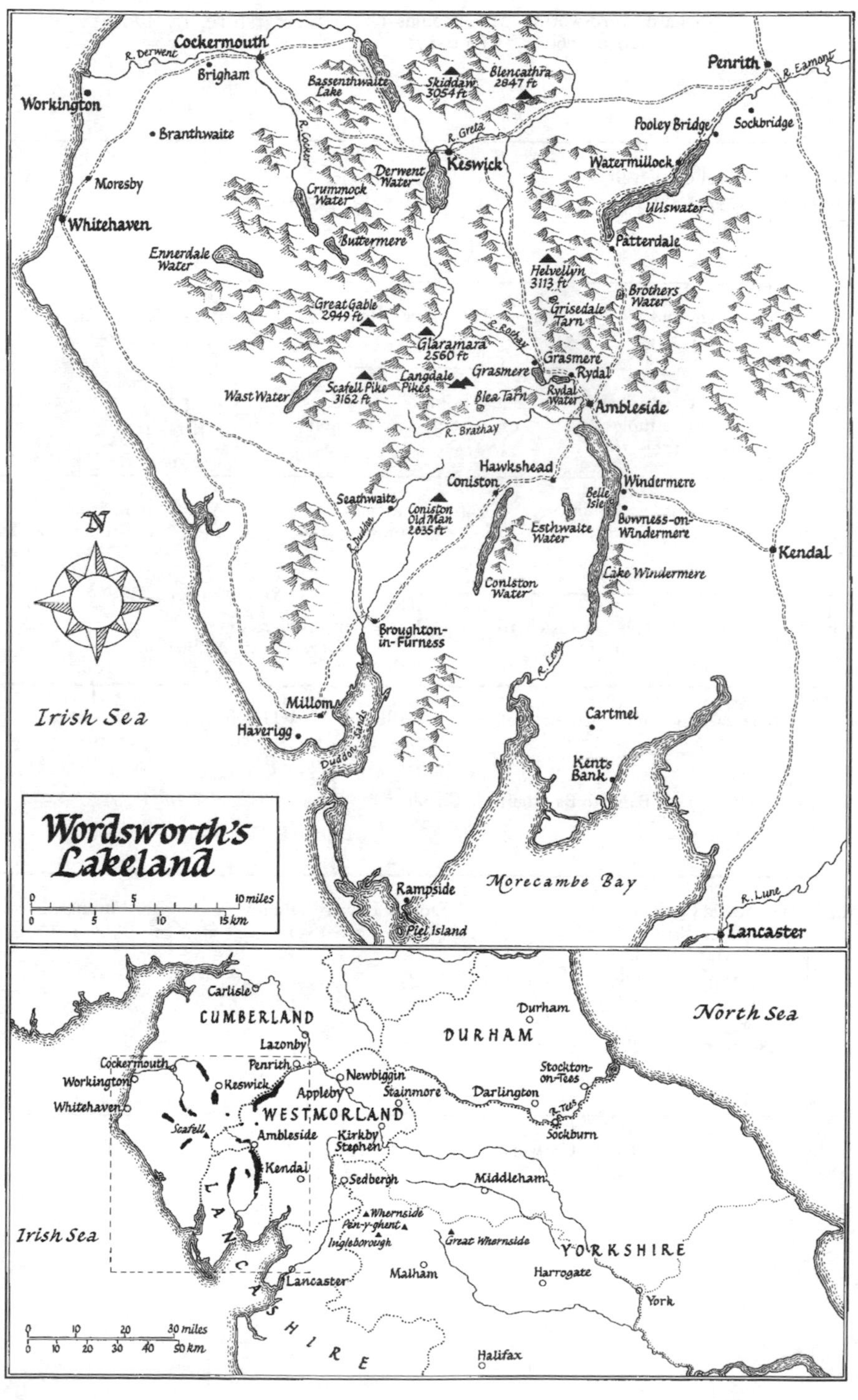

Wordsworth's Lakeland
Cockermouth
R. Derwent
Brigham
Workington
Branthwaite
Moresby
Whitehaven
Bassenthwaite Lake
Skiddaw 3054 ft
Blencathra 2847 ft
R. Greta
Keswick
Derwent Water
Crummock Water
Buttermere
Ennerdale Water
Great Gable 2949 ft
Glaramara 2560 ft
Scafell Pike 3162 ft
Langdale Pikes
Wast Water
Blea Tarn
R. Brathay
Grasmere
Rydal
Rydal Water
Ambleside
Helvellyn 3113 ft
Grisedale Tarn
Brothers Water
Patterdale
Ullswater
Watermillock
Pooley Bridge
Sockbridge
Penrith
R. Eamont
Hawkshead
Coniston
Seathwaite
Coniston Old Man 2635 ft
Esthwaite Water
Coniston Water
Windermere
Belle Isle
Bowness-on-Windermere
Lake Windermere
Kendal
Broughton-in-Furness
Millom
Haverigg
Duddon Sands
Irish Sea
Cartmel
Kents Bank
Morecambe Bay
Rampside
Piel Island
R. Lune
Lancaster
0 5 10 miles
0 5 10 15 km
Carlisle
CUMBERLAND
Lazonby
Penrith
Cockermouth
Workington
Keswick
Whitehaven
Appleby
Newbiggin
Stainmore
WESTMORLAND
Scafell
Ambleside
Kirkby Stephen
Kendal
Sedbergh
Middleham
Durham
DURHAM
North Sea
Stockton-on-Tees
Darlington
R. Tees
Sockburn
Whernside
Pen-y-ghent
Ingleborough
Great Whernside
YORKSHIRE
Harrogate
York
Malham
Lancaster
LANCASHIRE
Irish Sea
Halifax
0 10 20 30 miles
0 10 20 30 40 50 km

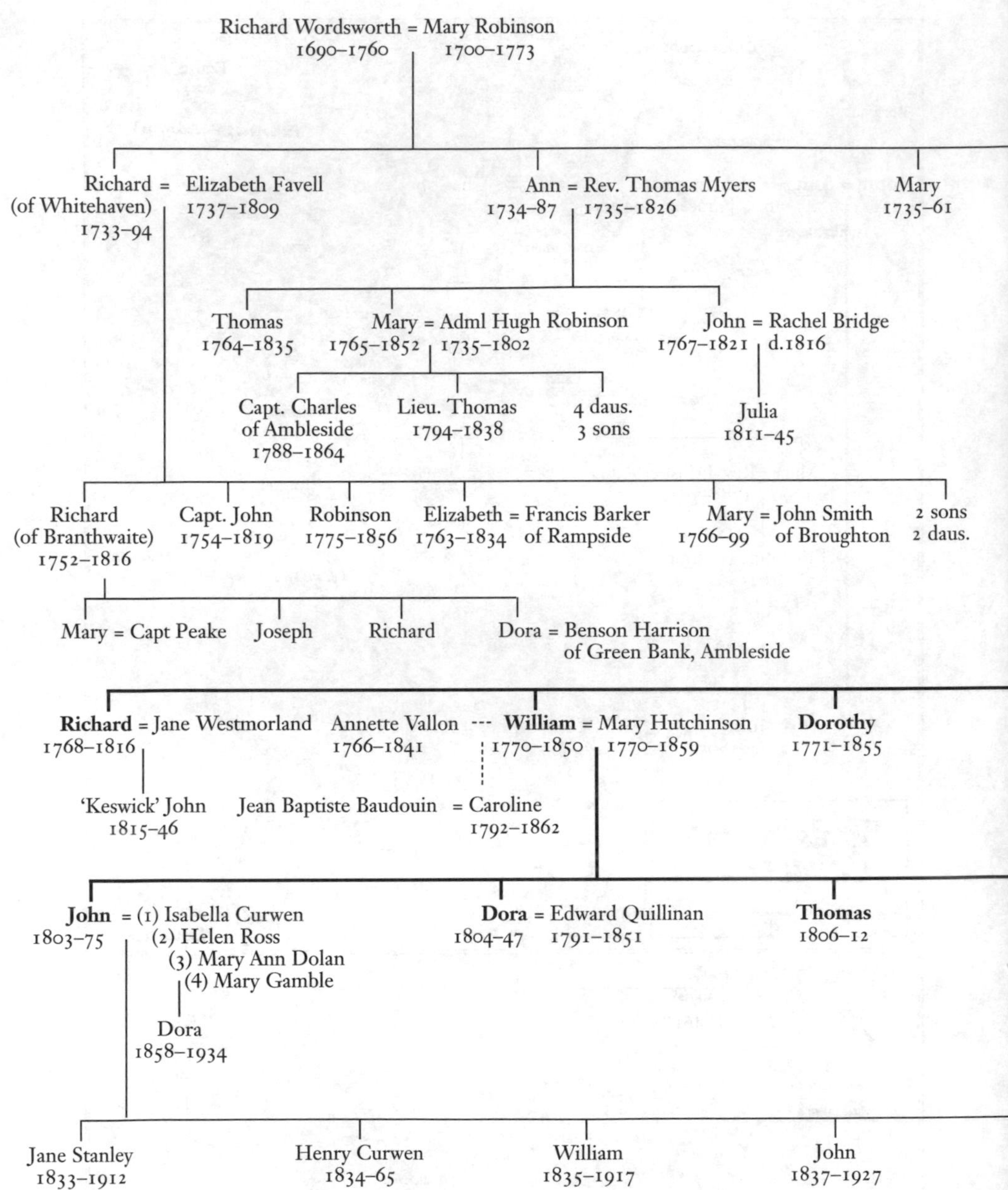

Wordsworth Family Tree

*After his mother's death in 1792, Christopher Cookson adopted her family name of Crackanthorpe, which descended to his children.

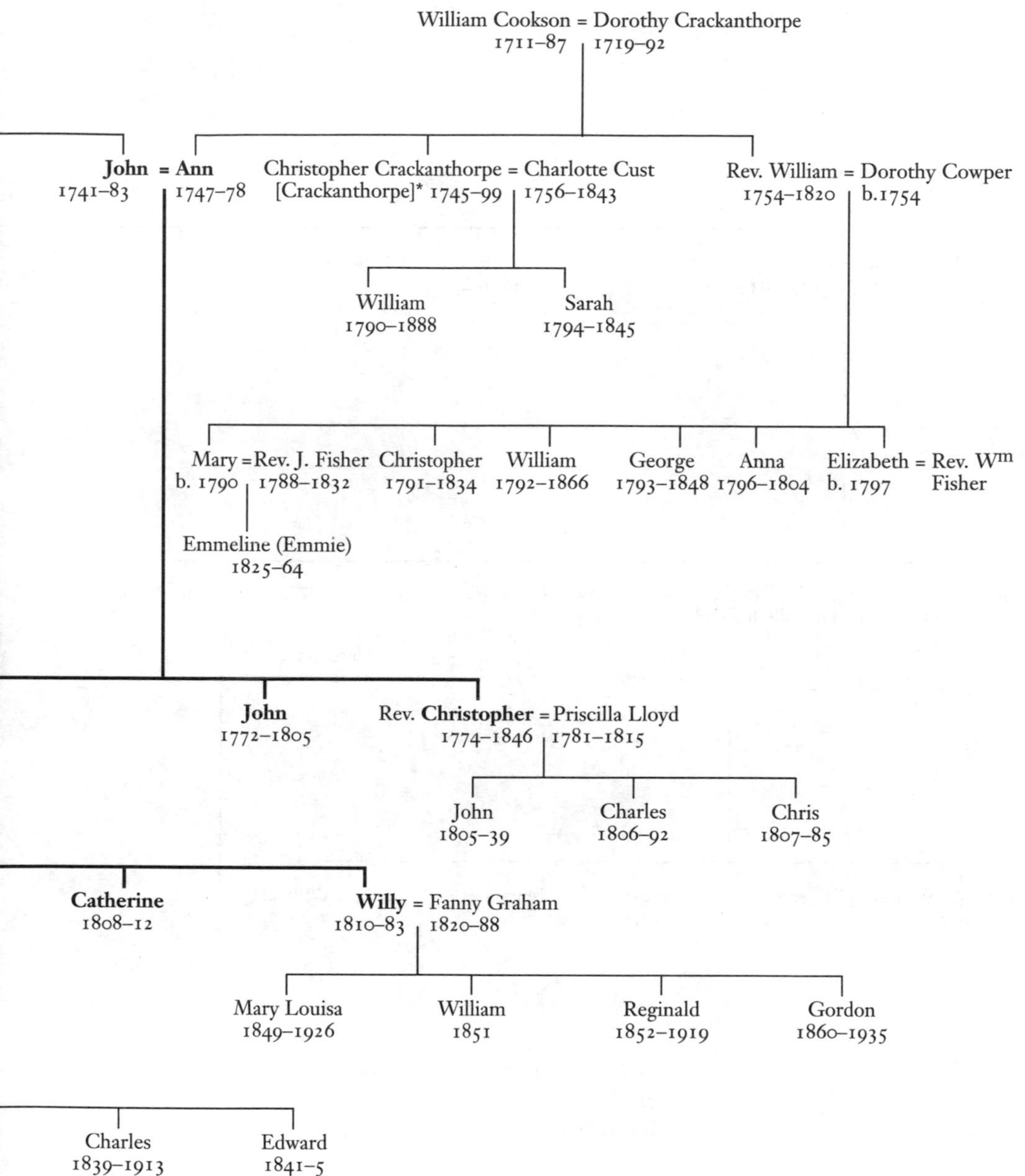
William Cookson = Dorothy Crackanthorpe
1711–87 1719–92
John = **Ann**
1741–83 1747–78
Christopher Crackanthorpe = Charlotte Cust
[Crackanthorpe]* 1745–99 1756–1843
Rev. William = Dorothy Cowper
1754–1820 b.1754
William
1790–1888
Sarah
1794–1845
Mary = Rev. J. Fisher
b. 1790 1788–1832
Christopher
1791–1834
William
1792–1866
George
1793–1848
Anna
1796–1804
Elizabeth = Rev. Wm Fisher
b. 1797
Emmeline (Emmie)
1825–64
John
1772–1805
Rev. **Christopher** = Priscilla Lloyd
1774–1846 1781–1815
John
1805–39
Charles
1806–92
Chris
1807–85
Catherine
1808–12
Willy = Fanny Graham
1810–83 1820–88
Mary Louisa
1849–1926
William
1851
Reginald
1852–1919
Gordon
1860–1935
Charles
1839–1913
Edward
1841–5

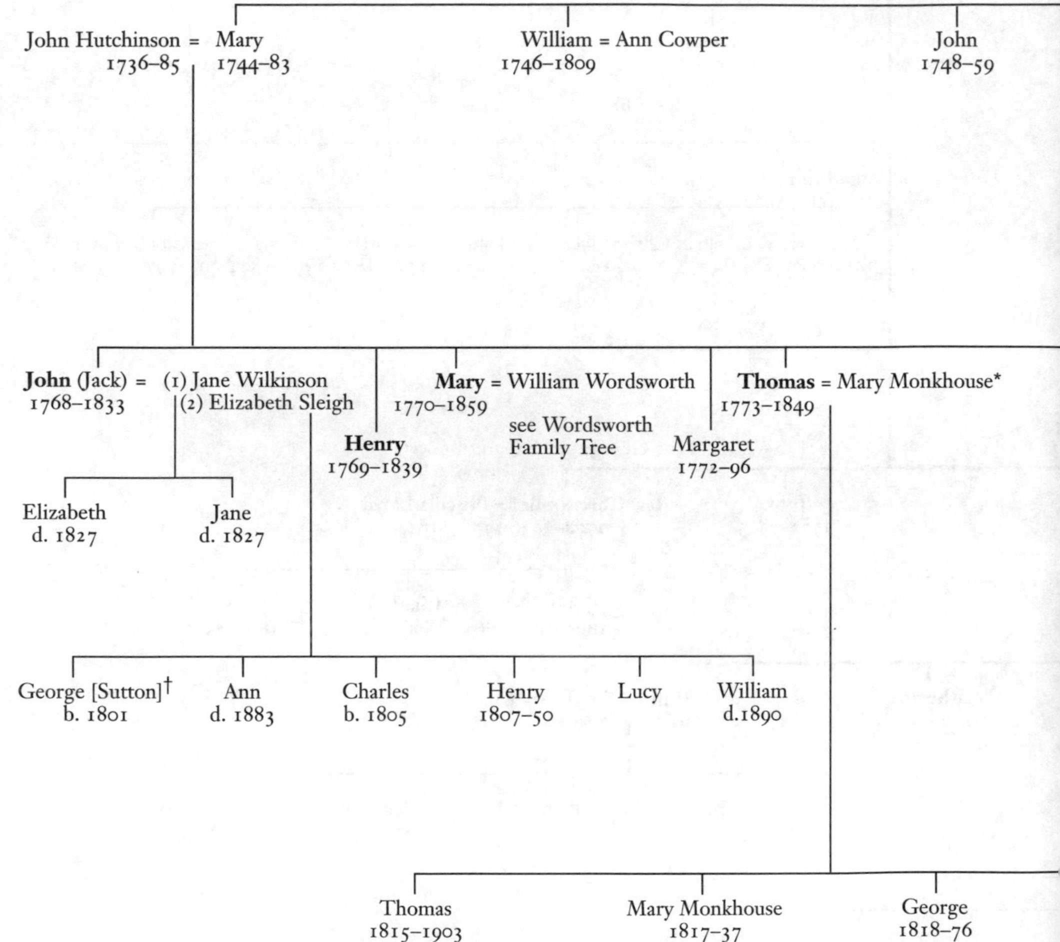

Hutchinson/Monkhouse Family Tree

*Mary Monkhouse married her first cousin Thomas Hutchinson.

†On inheriting maternal family estates, George Hutchinson took the surname of Sutton.

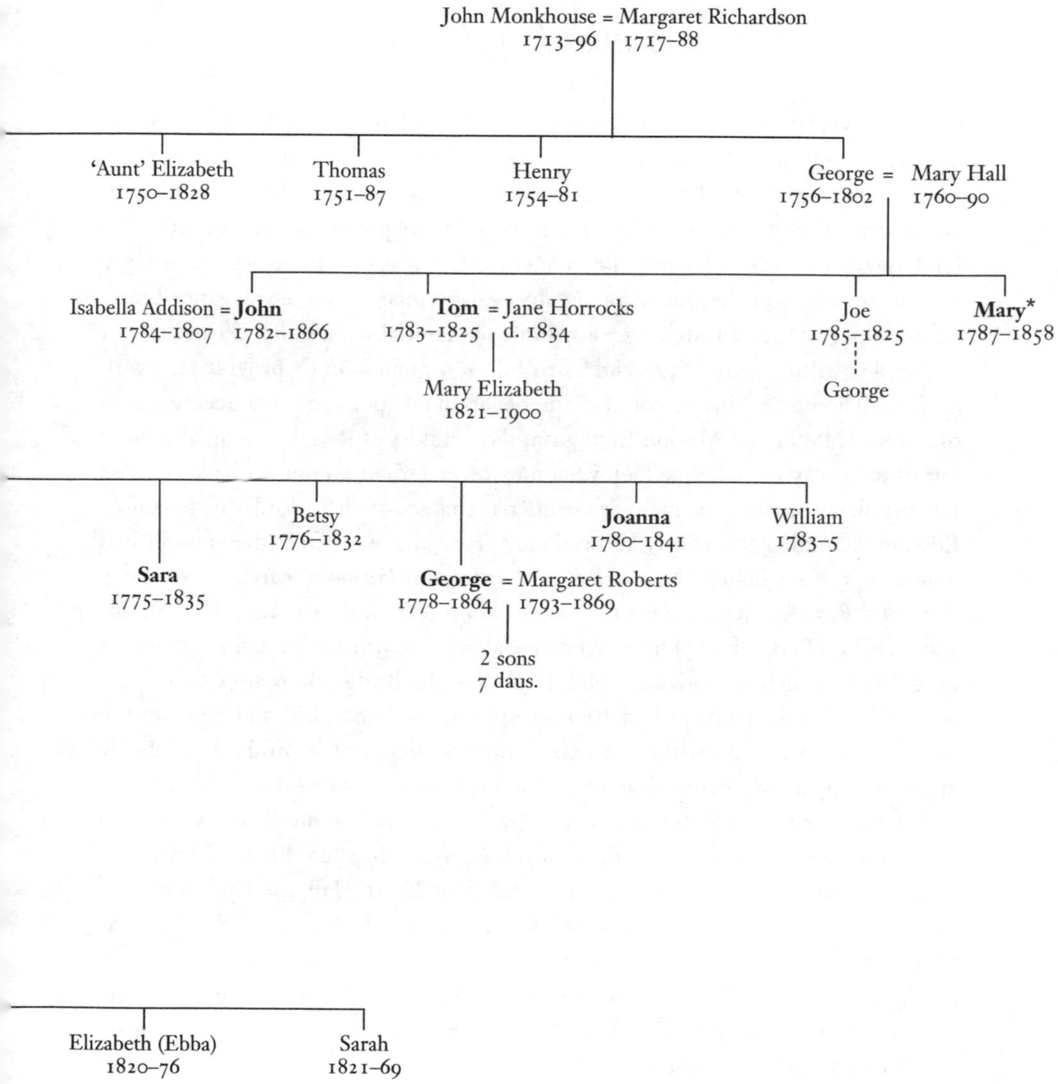

John Monkhouse = Margaret Richardson
1713–96 | 1717–88

'Aunt' Elizabeth
1750–1828

Thomas
1751–87

Henry
1754–81

George = Mary Hall
1756–1802 | 1760–90

Isabella Addison = **John**
1784–1807 1782–1866

Tom = Jane Horrocks
1783–1825 d. 1834

Mary Elizabeth
1821–1900

Joe
1785–1825

George

Mary*
1787–1858

Sara
1775–1835

Betsy
1776–1832

George = Margaret Roberts
1778–1864 | 1793–1869

2 sons
7 daus.

Joanna
1780–1841

William
1783–5

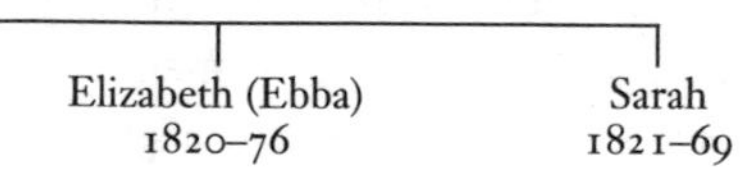

Elizabeth (Ebba)
1820–76

Sarah
1821–69

Acknowledgements

Over the years it has taken to complete a work of this scale, I have naturally incurred many debts. I am especially grateful to Marcus Ackroyd, who trawled the French archives on my behalf, discovering new material on Annette Vallon and guiding me through the complexities of Revolutionary politics with quiet authority. Jeff Cowton of the Wordsworth Trust at Dove Cottage, Grasmere, was unfailingly helpful and cheerful, despite my taking up semi-permanent residence in the library; I could not have got through such a volume of material without his aid and that of his band of willing helpers. Les and Chris Johnson-Senior kindly provided me with a second home at How Foot, Grasmere, at much personal inconvenience to themselves. Peter and Marion Elkington, the curators of Rydal Mount, also went out of their way to make me feel welcome; through their kindness I have enjoyed the privilege of meeting many charming members of the Wordsworth family. Edward Cumming generously allowed me to read and quote from the unpublished manuscript of his book, *The Wreck of the English East Indiaman, Earl of Abergavenny, Weymouth Bay, 1805*, and gave me the benefit of his technical expertise. The munificence of Paul Betz, who volunteered material from his private collections, deserves especial mention and gratitude. John Taylor, of the Bridge Bookshop, Grasmere, was an invaluable, efficient and friendly supplier of books, old and new, on the Wordsworth circle, but without access to the resources of the Brotherton Library at the University of Leeds this book could not have been written.

I would like to thank all those who allowed me to follow the Wordsworth trail on to private land, or even into their own homes, among them Joyce Cracknell of Sockburn Home Farm, the Misses Gatheral of Sockburn Hall, the Hunt family of Allan Bank, Grasmere, and the Rev. Bob and Celia Wilkinson of the Rectory, Grasmere. I am also grateful to all those who answered my queries: in particular, Michael Ball, Head of the Department of Printed Books, National Army Museum; Barbara and the staff of the Cumbria Record Office, Carlisle; Dr Sidney Chapman, to whose exhibition at The Penrith Museum, Robinson's School, Penrith, I also owe much information about that town; Stewart Eastwood of the King's Own Border Regiment Museum, Carlisle; Chris Evans of Brompton-by-Sawdon; Elspeth Griffiths, Librarian of Sedbergh School; Michael J. Harrison of Gallows Hill, Brompton; Ken Reeves of the Kington Museum, Herefordshire; Michael Richardson, Librarian of the Special Collections at the University of Bristol; Roger Sims of the Manx Museum, Douglas, Isle of Man; John Spedding of Mirehouse, Keswick; Malcolm Underwood, Archivist, St John's College, Cambridge; John West of Hawkshead Grammar School, who also drew my attention to the previously unpublished drawing reproduced at the head of Chapter 2; Harvey Wilkinson of the Abbot Hall Art Gallery and Museum, Kendal; and Derrick Woolf, curator of Coleridge's Cottage, Nether Stowey, Somerset, who kindly allowed me to visit out-of-hours.

Formal acknowledgment for permission to quote from manuscript material in their collections is due to the Archives Départementales of Loir-et-Cher, Blois; Archives Départementales of Loiret, Orléans; Archives Nationales, Paris; Carlisle Public Library, Cumbria; Cumbria Record Office, Carlisle; Dr Williams's Library, London; Pierpont Morgan Library, New York; Special Collections at the University of Bristol; Trustees of Hawkshead Grammar School, Cumbria; Trustees of Rydal Mount, Cumbria; Trustees of St John's College, Cambridge; West Yorkshire Archive Service at Calderdale, Halifax; Wordsworth Trust.

I have been fortunate in having the redoubtable Eleo Gordon as my editor. She and the team at Penguin have always been supportive and interested and I am truly grateful. Andrew Lownie has been an exemplary agent and I am indebted to him for his unstinting efforts on my behalf. Special thanks are also due to Stephen Gill, whose biograpy *William Wordsworth: A Life* (Oxford University Press, 1989) is a model of its kind; it first stirred my interest in the man and has been an unfailing source of reference ever since. Finally, I would like to thank all the long-suffering members of my family who have been forced to share their lives with the Wordsworths throughout the years this book has been in preparation. My brother, Tim Bateson, has repeatedly, if wearily, rescued me from the consequences of my own incompetence at word-processing. My husband, James, and children, Edward and Sophie, have all become reluctant experts, having given up their holidays and weekends to follow in the Wordsworths' (and Hutchinsons' and Monkhouses') footsteps. Though the children have complained unceasingly about this, we have all appreciated the excuse to acquire a more intimate knowledge of the Lakes. As my parents have not had this consolation, and yet have avidly read every chapter of this book as it was written, I think it only fair to dedicate *Wordsworth: A Life* to them.

1. *The Child is Father of the Man*

On a dark, stormy day in December 1783, a thirteen-year-old boy scrambled to the top of a rocky outcrop near the Lakeland village of Hawkshead. From this vantage point, half-sheltered by a dry-stone wall, and with only a sheep and a hawthorn tree for company, he sat on the damp grass, straining to see through the mist that intermittently shifted to reveal the woods and plain below. It was the eve of the Christmas holidays and William Wordsworth was waiting with mounting excitement and impatience for the first sight of the horses that were coming to bring him home from school. Not knowing which of the two roads they might take and afraid to miss them, he stubbornly maintained his post through the storm, watching so intently that his eyes swam with tears at the effort. It was an experience he would never forget:

> ... the wind and sleety rain
> And all the business of the elements,
> The single sheep, and the one blasted tree,
> And the bleak music of that old stone wall,
> The noise of wood and water, and the mist
> Which on the line of each of those two roads
> Advanced in such indisputable shapes –[1]

The turmoil of the scene, so perfectly mirroring that of his own mind, the symbolism of the two roads and, most of all, the intensity of his longing to be home would come back to haunt him. For the child waiting so anxiously was unaware that this would be the last time he would return to the home he was about to lose for ever. He did not know then that the whole course of his life was about to be changed and, with it, the history of English literature.

The Wordsworth family home lay on the western edge of the Lakes in the small Cumberland market town of Cockermouth, some thirty miles away by road from Hawkshead. William Wilberforce, visiting the town in 1779, had sniffily dismissed it as 'consisting chiefly of one very large wide street'. A more favourably disposed visitor, William Hutchinson, declared 'the situation . . . beautiful, in a country well cultivated, on the banks of two fine rivers, and in a climate tempered by the mountains which shelter the place from the north-east, and by a happy distance from the western ocean'. He admired the picturesque ruins of the medieval castle on an eminence above the town, the commodious church built in 1710 on the other, lower, hill and the 'pleasantly diversified' nature of the countryside, with its hills and dales, rocks, woodlands and waters, meadows and heath, which were seen to advantage from the public walk along the bank of the Derwent. The 'gloomy and antique appearance' of the moot hall, market house and shambles impressed him rather less and he wondered at the preference of the people of fortune for building their elegant houses on the short steep street leading up to the castle, but he had no hesitation in stating that 'the whole place bears the countenance of opulence'. He noted that, according to the 1785 census, there were 2,653 inhabitants, of whom about 500 were employed in the manufacture of hats, cloth and leather, upon which the prosperity of the town depended. Standing not only at the confluence of the Derwent and Cocker rivers, which provided power for the mills, but also on the main east–west route from Penrith to the prosperous ports of Workington and Whitehaven on the Atlantic coast, Cockermouth was ideally placed for the manufacture and distribution of goods. There were also weekly markets and a fortnightly cattle fair, held in the same 'spacious, open, and well built' street which had attracted Wilberforce's attention.[2] It was on this street, in the largest and most imposing house in the town, that the Wordsworth family lived.

Set slightly back from the street, with a small walled courtyard to the front and a large garden running down to the Derwent at the rear, it was an elegant Georgian building. It had been built in 1745 by the then sheriff of Cumberland with perfect symmetry: a pillared and canopied porch led to the hallway, on either side of which was a graciously proportioned room, each with four large sash windows and a plasterwork ceiling. Above, a row of nine identical windows filled the bedrooms with light. The back of the house was less distinguished, housing the kitchen and servants' quarters; there was also a stable in the rear yard. To all appearances, it was the town residence of a wealthy and influential gentleman.

Unfortunately for the Wordsworths, appearances were deceptive. The house, like Cockermouth itself, belonged to Sir James Lowther. Indeed, it might be said that the Wordsworths also belonged to him, for William's father, like his father before him, was law agent to Lowther. Whether they liked it or not, their family fortunes had been, and were to be, dependent on the grace and favour of the Lowthers throughout William's lifetime and beyond.[3] It was therefore doubly unfortunate for the Wordsworths that this particular Lowther was notorious for his ruthlessness in the pursuit of power and riches. 'Wicked Jimmy', the 'Tyrant of the North' and 'Jimmy Grasp-all', as he was variously known to his beleaguered tenants, started young. In 1751, aged fourteen, he inherited the title of Viscount Lonsdale and the vast Lowther estates; five years later, he added the highly profitable Whitehaven estates and collieries of a distant cousin, making him the greatest landowner in Cumberland and Westmorland. Before he reached the age of twenty-one, he had an annual income of £30,000 and was (illegally) a Member of Parliament for Cumberland. His ambitions did not stop there. His aim was to gain control of all ten parliamentary seats in the region and he set out to achieve this by a judicious mixture of buying votes, bribing officials and intimidating anyone who stood in his way. Even by the remarkably lax standards of the day, Sir James was a master of questionable electoral practices. He was also highly successful. In the general election of 1761, when he was still only twenty-four years old, his nominees were returned for eight seats, making him one of the most powerful men in the whole country.[4] When his father-in-law, the Earl of Bute, became Prime Minister and First Lord of the Treasury in 1762–3, Sir James milked the opportunity for all it was worth and acquired a stranglehold on public appointments and local government in Westmorland and Cumberland. In effect, it was impossible to obtain any sort of public office in the two counties without his nomination and approval. His officials, including the Members of Parliament, were expected to vote, and do, as he said, and put their master's interest before all others. Any show of independence, even by members of his own family, met with dismissal and persecution. Despotic, parsimonious, vindictive, litigious and corrupt, Sir James Lowther was not a man to be crossed lightly. The Reverend Alexander Carlyle was not alone in concluding that he was 'more Detested than any man alive as a Shameless Political Sharper, a Domestick Bashaw, and an Intolerable Tyrant over his Tenants and Dependants . . . he was truly a Madman, tho' too Rich to be confind'.[5]

In order to extend and maintain his authority, Sir James employed a network of agents, most of whom had a family tradition of such service and were lawyers by profession, which was undoubtedly an advantage in working for such a master. Richard Wordsworth, William's grandfather, was the first of the family to enter the Lowther service. A Yorkshireman by birth, he had practised as an attorney in London before coming into Westmorland as law agent and land steward to Sir James's father.[6] Not long afterwards, he married Mary Robinson of Appleby and purchased a small estate at Sockbridge, near Penrith. A Clerk of the Peace and Receiver-General for Westmorland, Richard Wordsworth's moment of glory came during the 1745 rebellion. Learning that Bonnie Prince Charlie's army of rebels was advancing over the Scottish border towards Penrith, he gathered up the county receipts and (being a lawyer) the account books, and fled into the mountains at Patterdale. The rebels entered Penrith in triumph, quartered themselves on the citizens and made off with their supplies and horses but, thanks to Richard's prompt action, did not get their hands on the county treasury.[7]

When Richard died, in June 1760, his wife's nephew, John Robinson, succeeded him as agent to Sir James Lowther. This was the eponymous 'Jack' Robinson, a rapidly rising star in the Lowther firmament. A former town clerk in his native Appleby, his financial and political skills, combined with his devotion to the Lowther interest, brought him swift reward. In 1764 he was nominated to one of the two county seats for Westmorland and duly took his place in Parliament. He remained a Lowther man through and through until they quarrelled, aptly enough, over an appointment they both wanted. Robinson had then to decide which way his loyalty and, more importantly, his own interest lay. As he was now enjoying a successful and lucrative career in the administration, Lord North having made him Secretary to the Treasury, there was little contest. At the next election in 1774 he became Member of Parliament for Harwich, thus severing his links with the man who had made him. His influence would become vitally important to all his dependants and relatives, not least because it was, to a large extent, independent of the Lowther interest.

Shortly after entering Parliament for the first time, Robinson resigned his land and law agencies in favour of his twenty-four-year-old cousin, John Wordsworth.[8] Sir James would later deny ever having formally made the appointment, but John entered upon his duties immediately. He moved to the Lowther pocket borough of Cockermouth, established himself in the grand Lowther residence and began administering the Lowther estates. As Sir James's law and land agent, he had to attend the manorial courts throughout the region to represent his master's interests and keep a record of the proceedings. He was also responsible for collecting rents, arranging mortgages and securities for investments, and making purchases of property. It was an ominous portent for the future that, in making up the accounts, he frequently paid out more than he collected, effectively making himself Sir James's creditor.[9] Most contentiously of all, as bailiff of Cockermouth, he was the returning officer of the borough, whose duty it was to scrutinize the claims of the electors that they held sufficient property to entitle them to vote. This was obviously a major advantage to the Lowther interest and, in election years, he became the borough paymaster, spending thousands of pounds in the pursuit of Sir James's parliamentary ambitions. In the three by-elections at Cockermouth and the single general election which fell between January 1767 and April 1769, John Wordsworth 'paid, laid out, and expended, and disbursed' almost £24,000 on election expenses alone. Out of this sum, £10,468 7s 4½d was assigned to the twenty-four taverns in Cockermouth as 'Cash paid publicans on account'. The money was intended to cover the costs of hiring rooms and horses, as well as providing beer for the electorate, which was just as well, given that the same public houses received a further £6,000 from Lowther's opponent, the Duke of Portland. One particular item in John Wordsworth's accounts is worth noting, if only for the light it sheds on Sir James's dubious electoral methods. The sum of £680 was lent in notes to the electors 'which after they were polled were ordered to be cancelled'. Whether this was because they had taken the money and then voted for Portland, or simply another example of Sir James getting the best value for his money (in his case, something for nothing), is not clear. Ultimately, the notorious Cumberland election of 1768 was a disaster for Sir James: though he and his supporter were elected, the corruption was so blatant that it could not be ignored. The sheriff was arrested and the election results were overturned on petition to Parliament.[10] The fall-out from this election was considerable. Though John Wordsworth was not the subject of investigation, as a loyal and active servant of the Lowther interest he could not have escaped the acrimony.

Financially, however, he was in a comfortable position. In January 1765, he had agreed with his mother that she would give up her life interest in the Sockbridge estate, in return for an annuity of £50. At the same time, he made legally binding settlements with his brother and sister that he would defer payment of the legacies due to them from their father's will until their mother died.[11]

A year later, he was sufficiently eligible to be accepted as the suitor of Ann Cookson, the only daughter of a wealthy mercer of Penrith. The Cooksons lived close to their shop, a grand drapery establishment on a prime site next to the George Hotel at the top of the Market Square, but they had pretensions to aristocracy. Ann's mother, Dorothy, was the daughter of Richard Crackanthorpe of Newbiggin Hall, an enchantingly pretty, if then somewhat dilapidated, miniature castle, hidden away in the folds of the wooded hills between Penrith and Appleby. Dorothy's brother had inherited Newbiggin in 1752, married a young bride the same year and then thoughtlessly died the next. The estate was left to his widow for life and then outright to his sister. To Dorothy's lasting chagrin and increasing irritation, the widow not only packed up and returned home to her parents in Durham, leaving Newbiggin Hall to the mercy of tenant farmers, but also declined to pay Dorothy's annuity and, worst of all, had the temerity to live to a ripe old age, excluding Dorothy from her family's estate for another thirty-seven years.[12]

Dorothy's temper was evidently soured by this grievance and it was perhaps the thought of welcoming a lawyer into the family that eased John Wordsworth's suit for her daughter's hand. Certainly, whatever their later attitude, both Dorothy and her husband, William, initially gave the marriage their blessing. Their approval was essential, for Ann, at sixteen, was legally a minor. Her parents not only gave their consent but also presented her with a generous dowry of £1,000, half of which was payable on the day of her marriage, the other half on her father's death.[13]

On 5 February 1766, a few days after her seventeenth birthday, Ann Cookson married John Wordsworth in the magnificent St Andrew's Church at Penrith. The ceremony was performed by the Reverend John Cowper and witnessed by the vicar's daughter, Mary Henrietta, and Ann's favourite cousin, Elizabeth Threlkeld.[14] The newlyweds then set off to begin their married life at Cockermouth.

It must have been a strange and unnerving experience for Ann. Little more than a child herself, she had left her lifelong home to become mistress of a grand house and wife to the most important man in Cockermouth. She must have been lonely, at least at first, as she knew no one in the town and her husband was often away on Lowther business. Like a dutiful wife, however, she applied herself to child-bearing and rearing. Her first son, Richard, named after his Wordsworth grandfather (and also his Crackanthorpe great-grandfather), arrived on 19 August 1768. He was followed, in quick succession, by William, born on 7 April 1770, Dorothy, the only girl, on Christmas Day, 1771, John, born on 4 December 1772 and, finally, Christopher, on 9 June 1774. Although all the other children were baptized at Cockermouth Church within a month of birth, William was the exception. According to the family Bible, he was baptized on 13 April, when he was six days old, but christened with his sister, Dorothy, on 18 January 1772, when he was twenty-one months old. One can only guess that he was a sickly baby and was therefore baptized privately at home, the ceremony being repeated in public at Cockermouth Church when the opportunity arose.[15]

'The time of my infancy and early boyhood was passed partly at Cockermouth, and partly with my mother's parents at Penrith', William would later recall. The casualness of this remark belies an important distinction, for William's memories of Cockermouth, unlike those of Penrith, were uniformly happy ones. His family were together, the household, taking its tone from John Wordsworth, a cheerful one, and the children close enough in age and sympathy to be natural playmates. Their favourite playground was the high terrace at the end of the garden, overlooking the broad, clear, fast-flowing waters of the River Derwent. Only a low wall separated the two; covered with closely clipped privet and roses, it made the perfect hiding place for birds, who built their nests in its most inaccessible depths. The river itself was a constant companion whose ceaseless music

composed my thoughts
To more than infant softness, giving me
Among the fretful dwellings of mankind
A knowledge, a dim earnest, of the calm
Which nature breathes among the fields and groves.

At four years old, William would make 'one long bathing of a summer's day', alternately basking in the sun and plunging into the silent pools beneath the castle;

or, when crag and hill,
The woods, and distant Skiddaw's lofty height,
Were bronzed with a deep radiance, stood alone
Beneath the sky as if I had been born
On Indian plains and from my mother's hut
Had run abroad in wantonness to sport,
A naked savage in the thunder-shower.

The banks of this 'fairest of all rivers' were an endless source of delight and, sixty years later, William could still vividly recall his boyish pleasure in collecting pebbles and gathering the wild flowers that grew there.[16] There were also, of course, the more robust pleasures of boyhood: running races with his brothers across the sandy meadows, fishing, bird's-nesting, exploring the hills, valleys and length of the river.

Cockermouth Castle, dominating the view from the Wordsworth's garden terrace, was naturally a potent draw for the children, who would play games in the sunny courtyard or dare each other to climb the dizzying heights of the ruined walls. On one occasion, William's spirit of adventure led to a terrifying experience. Like any small boy, he found the castle dungeons irresistible and decided to brave a descent. These were no ordinary dungeons, however, but *oubliettes*, accessible only through a small trapdoor in the vaulted ceiling. To get in, he must have persuaded his companions to let him down with a rope, leaving him trapped in the suffocating blackness and entirely dependent on them to get him out again. Not surprisingly, he was overcome with horror at the thought of being buried alive. To the hitherto blithe and unthinking boy, the 'soul-appalling darkness' of the dungeon was like an unexpected foretaste of the grave.[17] If, as seems likely, this happened not long after the death of his mother, who died when William was seven, the whole incident acquires an added resonance. Significantly, of all his many recorded recollections of his boyhood in Cockermouth, it was the only negative one.

This was in marked contrast to Penrith, where Ann Wordsworth and her children spent much of this period. The first long visit probably began in the middle of 1773 and, for some of the children, may have lasted for up to a year. Certainly it was long enough to require that the older ones should attend the dame school, for it was there that William, aged three, met his future wife, Mary Hutchinson, for the first time. Though it is next to impossible to work out precise details, there may have been a second extended visit to Penrith from the middle of 1775 to the middle of 1776 and a third over the winter of 1776–7.[18]

Such lengthy visits were understandable given that virtually all the family connections were with Penrith and that many of their friends, as well as relations, lived in the town. The distance between Penrith and Cockermouth was only some thirty-five miles, but the road passed right through the heart of the Lakes, along a wild and exposed route beneath Blencathra and Skiddaw, through Keswick, and along the shores of Lake Bassenthwaite. Though one of the better roads in the Lakes, it was not a journey to be undertaken lightly, especially in a carriage with small children. It is likely that the family had always passed the summer holidays at Penrith: it was an opportunity to see not only the Cooksons but also John Wordsworth's mother and his sister, Ann, who was married to the Reverend Thomas Myers, curate of Barton, a village close to Sockbridge. The Myers had three children, only slightly older than the young Wordsworths, so the two families had much in common.[19] As the main route from London into Scotland passed directly through Penrith, there were also opportunities for the Wordsworth parents to take one of the frequent stage coaches to visit their many Penrith friends who had settled in London.

The Wordsworth children's first long stay in Penrith may have been precipitated by the death of their paternal grandmother. She died on 3 September 1773, and the Sockbridge estate, which had been hers for life, now came into John's hands. There was much administration to do, necessitating John's presence at Sockbridge, so it was natural that his wife and children should accompany him. The lands and rather grand double-fronted house, dating from 1699, remained in the hands of tenant farmers but, now that he owned the estate outright, John took care to settle all the family legacies promptly and generously. He must have felt that an injustice had been done to his elder brother, Richard, who, in the normal course of things, should have inherited in preference to himself. For reasons which are not known, but possibly connected with his marriage, he had incurred his parents' disapproval. His father's will not only excluded him from the Sockbridge estate but also left him a legacy of only £300, compared to his sister's £500. John could not overturn the conditions of the will, but his first move on obtaining the estate was to make his brother a gift of the shortfall, so that he was at least on a par with their sister.[20]

While John sorted out the affairs of his mother, his family took up residence with his wife's parents in the centre of the bustling market town of Penrith. The Cookson household was nothing like the happy home at Cockermouth. In fact, it seems a curious place to have taken or sent such very young children. The Cookson grandparents, William and Dorothy, were elderly and their sons, Christopher and William, were already twenty-eight and nineteen when the Wordsworths made their first lengthy stay. Both sons were unmarried and, as Ann was their only sister, there was no bevy of aunts to shower the young Wordsworths with affection and share the responsibilities of looking after them. The burden therefore fell almost entirely on their grandmother. As she still took a lively interest in the shop, she had not much time to spare and the servants seem to have resented the extra work which devolved on them.

According to the young Wordsworths, who were by no means unbiased, the atmosphere was one of relentless disapproval. Grandmother Cookson may have resented her son-in-law's failure to obtain her Crackanthorpe legacy for her; Uncle Christopher (and probably his parents too) resented his loyalty to the Lowther interest, being of the opposite political persuasion.[21] The children could not have been unaware of these underlying tensions and the fact that their beloved father was the object of criticism. They found their grandparents' house restrictive, if not repressive, and there was certainly no condoning of the sort of carefree roaming about the countryside that characterized the Wordsworth home at Cockermouth. The children were obviously considered ill-disciplined and out of control: at the Cooksons', punishment for misdemeanours was swift and hard and there appears to have been much preaching about the perils of sin. One of William's earliest memories, as a child of four, was of lying awake at night, quaking under the bedclothes, 'in sharp conflict of spirit' at the idea that a good God permitted evil in His world.[22] Not, one would have thought, a subject which would have naturally occurred to a four-year-old.

A spirited, adventurous boy, William's instinctive response was to rebel, thus incurring punishment which only made him more defiant. On one occasion, he was with his oldest brother, Richard:

> we were whipping tops together in the large drawing-room, on which the carpet was only laid down upon particular occasions. The walls were hung round with family pictures, and

I said to my brother, 'Dare you strike your whip through that old lady's petticoat?' He replied, 'No, I won't.' 'Then,' said I, 'here goes;' and I struck my lash through her hooped petticoat, for which no doubt, though I have forgotten it, I was properly punished. But possibly, from some want of judgement in punishments inflicted, I had become perverse and obstinate in defying chastisement, and rather proud of it than otherwise.[23]

It was probably just such perversity that led to another frightening escapade William would never forget. Not yet six years old, he was learning to ride and, in company with his grandfather's servant James, had ventured out of the town. They made their way up the Beacon, the massive hill behind Penrith, which took its name from the distinctive stone edifice, shaped like a truncated church steeple, in which the beacon fires had been lit in 1715 and 1745 to warn the surrounding countryside that the Scots were advancing. Now heavily wooded, reducing its value as a vantage point, Beacon Hill was then a bleak and treeless common, pockmarked with dozens of small, unfenced stone quarries. To a small child, it had an element of danger, even threat, about it, which made it all the more exciting.

In his later account of what happened, William described his companion that day as 'honest James . . . my encourager and guide' and claimed that 'some mischance' separated them. He was being disingenuous. The young Wordsworths had all suffered at the hands of the Cookson servants, who treated them with an insolence bordering on contempt. 'Honest James' was the worst offender and cordially loathed by his young charges. Spurred on by either a sense of mischief or simply dare-devilry, William took the first opportunity to escape from his tormentor, who seems to have made little effort to recover his troublesome charge. Bravado soon gave way to panic as William became aware that he was lost. Afraid to ride on alone, he dismounted and, leading his horse, wandered into one of the quarries, only to realize that he had stumbled across the site of a notorious murder. The spot, marked by a stone carved with the murdered man's initials, was made even more ghastly by the knowledge that it was also the site of the gallows on which the murderer himself had been hung. To the terrified child, the long green ridge of turf appeared like a grave. He turned and ran. Regaining the summit, the first thing he saw was the strange juxtaposition of the beacon, a pool of water and a girl with a pitcher of water on her head struggling to walk against the wind.

It was in truth
An ordinary sight, but I should need
Colours and words that are unknown to man
To paint the visionary dreariness
Which, while I looked all round for my lost guide,
Did at that time invest the naked pool,
The beacon on the lonely eminence,
The woman and her garments vexed and tossed
By the strong wind.[24]

It was one of those recurring moments, a Wordsworthian 'spot of time', arising out of deep emotions, often (as in this case) guilt and fear, and fixed for ever in memory by the natural scene in which they had occurred.

William's mother was obviously troubled by her rebellious son, telling an intimate friend (but not William himself) that he was the only one of her five children about whose future life she was anxious. He would be remarkable, she pronounced, for either good or evil.

> The cause of this was, that I was of a stiff, moody, and violent temper; so much so that I remember going once into the attics of my grandfather's house at Penrith, upon some indignity having been put upon me, with an intention of destroying myself with one of the foils which I knew was kept there. I took the foil in hand, but my heart failed.[25]

William and his siblings may not have enjoyed staying with their grandparents, but Penrith itself had much to offer them. It was considerably larger than Cockermouth, with some 4,000 inhabitants, and its situation, straddling the Great North Road, led to a great deal of passing traffic. The town was built of the glowing red sandstone which is such a striking feature of the landscape in this corner of Westmorland: newly cut, it is the colour of raw liver, but with age and a patina of lichen it fades to a warm, greyish pink. Its castle, a square, bulky ruin in the centre of the town, is barely visible from the main thoroughfare, which was also the site of the Market Square. Here the great livestock markets were held, attracting drovers from throughout the county and as far afield as Scotland. Probably as a result of its thriving commercial interests, Penrith had a high proportion of professional inhabitants. William Hutchinson, visiting for his survey published in 1794, remarked approvingly on the good taste of the large number of modern well-built houses and of the townsmen, whom he considered 'wealthy, courteous, and well-bred'.[26]

The visible symbol of Penrith's wealth and influence was St Andrew's, a massive building of almost cathedral-like proportions, set in its own little close, just off the lower end of Market Street. Built in 1722 in the style of Nicholas Hawksmoor, it boasted a spacious gallery, supported on twenty spectacular pillars of solid stone, polished to look like marble, and two huge gilt chandeliers, purchased with the money given to the town by the Duke of Portland in recognition of their loyalty during the 1745 rebellion.[27]

Within the quiet precincts of this church, where John and Ann Wordsworth had married in 1766, was the dame school attended by their children. Only a few paces from the church tower, the school was housed in a higgledy-piggledy sixteenth-century building whose entrance was reached by a flight of steps four feet below the flagged pavement encircling the churchyard. It was run by an elderly lady, Ann Birkhead, 'a remarkable personage', who had taught three generations of the upper classes of Penrith. 'Tho' no bad teacher,' she 'was indifferent to method'. One of her most eccentric 'methods' was to allow her young pupils, the oldest of whom were only eight years old, to use Joseph Addison's periodical, the

Spectator, as a reading book. Rather more endearingly, she was a passionate follower of all the old local customs. May Day in particular was a high festival. The children gathered flowers from all the gardens and wove them into garlands; the girls were required to bring their dolls in on May morning and seat them amidst the garlands, which were then hung from the school windows.[28] It was also customary to go out on saints' days into the fields around Penrith to garland the springs and drink their waters. This practice, one can well imagine, would appeal to the young Wordsworth children. Certainly, as they grew older, they were more adventurous in exploring the neighbourhood. Brougham Castle, a vast medieval stronghold guarding the approach to Penrith from Appleby and the crossing of the River Eamont, was barely a stone's throw from the town. Nearby, on a wooded bluff and surrounded by battlemented walls, was the pretty toy-town castle of Brougham Hall, the antithesis of its older, more pragmatic neighbour. Further afield, but only a few miles away across the hills, were the strange legacies of an older world: megaliths and stone circles, such as Long Meg and her Daughters at Little Salkeld. Slightly further, but still only a pleasant day's excursion from Penrith, were the romantic riverside walks literally blasted out of the rocks in the grounds of his house, the Nunnery, by Christopher Aglionby. And, of course, dominating all, was Penrith Beacon, from which, looking westwards across the 'gleamy plain' and the distant grey glimmer of Ullswater, the blue-black mountains of the Lakes could be seen.[29]

The same mountains could also be seen from Cockermouth and it was here, despite the long periods at Penrith, that the Wordsworths spent most of their early childhood. William would later say that he owed much to his birthplace and its neighbourhood. 'They did not a little in making whatever of a Poet I may be.' Equally important at this period in his life, as it was to be again later, was the influence of his closest companion, his sister, Dorothy. Only twenty months younger than William, she shared his sensitivity to nature and his passionate love for it. What she had uniquely, however, was a sensibility so remarkable that it became a byword in the family. When she was less than six years old, the family paid a visit to Whitehaven, where their uncle, Richard Wordsworth, was Collector of Customs. William himself recalled being 'struck' by his first sight, from an eminence on the road, of the elegant seventeenth-century town and prosperous port, and the white waves breaking against its quays and piers. Dorothy's reaction was more dramatic. 'My Sister when she first heard the voice of the sea from this point & beheld the scene spread before her burst into tears'.[30]

Though Dorothy would join in her brothers' play, she was always happier observing than being actively involved. She would chase butterflies, but drew the line at capturing them, or, as they did, killing the white ones 'because they were frenchmen'.

> A very hunter did I rush
> Upon the prey: – with leaps and springs
> I followed on from brake to bush;
> But she, God love her! feared to brush
> The dust from off its wings.[31]

Similarly, though Dorothy would accompany William every day to the low terrace wall at the bottom of their garden to see the sparrow's nest with its clutch of bright blue eggs, she would look, but not touch.

> She looked at it and seemed to fear it;
> Dreading, though wishing, to be near it:
> Such heart was in her, being then
> A little Prattler among men.

It says something, also, of William's own sensitivity that, even as a boy, he recognized and respected this quality in his sister. As a man, he came to realize that she had fundamentally changed his view of the world.

> She gave me eyes, she gave me ears;
> And humble cares, and delicate fears;
> A heart, the fountain of sweet tears;
> And love, and thought, and joy.[32]

Had they remained together, secure in each other's affection and daily companionship, the course of both their lives might have been very different. At the very least, Dorothy's love for her brother might never have acquired the somewhat desperate quality of their later years which makes for such uncomfortable reading.

A parting was at hand, however, and not just between brother and sister. Ann Wordsworth had been to visit some friends in London. She returned with a heavy cold, caught, it was said, by her having been put into 'a best bedroom' which was not properly aired or heated. In fact, she had consumption and, as so often happened, the laryngitis and persistent cough, which appeared to be symptoms of the cold, were actually those of the fatal disease. By Christmas 1777 she was so ill that it was decided that she should go to Penrith, where she could be nursed by her parents. The children went with her, unaware that neither she nor Dorothy would ever return home. William's last memory of his mother was of passing the door of her bedroom at Penrith, during her final illness, and catching a glimpse of her as she reclined in an easy chair. She died, aged only thirty, on 8 March 1778 and was buried in Penrith churchyard three days later.[33] Her oldest child was nine, the youngest only three; William himself was not quite eight years old.

Extraordinary as it may seem, Ann's final resting place was never marked by any sort of memorial. Whether this was because her husband and parents disputed the right to do so, or because her parents hoped that they would eventually be buried in the same grave and share the same stone, we do not know. Whatever the cause, it was another grievance for their grandchildren to lay at the door of the Cooksons.[34]

The absence of a physical memorial seems almost symbolic, for, though clearly much loved, Ann Wordsworth remains a shadowy figure. 'Blessed be her memory!' Dorothy would write, adding the more prosaic, but equally unenlightening, 'From her I know that I received much good that I can trace back to her.' William was a little more forthcoming, describing her as his

... honoured mother, she who was the heart
And hinge of all our learnings and our loves;

He prefaced his eulogy of her with a curious comment: he had no wish to disturb the sanctity of her memory 'With any thought that looks at others' blame'. In the light of what follows, it is clear he was thinking, once again, of his Cookson grandparents and comparing them unfavourably to his mother. Her chief virtue was her piety: a serene faith that God would provide and that her children, left to His care and the natural instincts of innocent childhood, would grow in wisdom and strength.

This was her creed, and therefore she was pure
From feverish dread of error and mishap
And evil (overweeningly so called)
Was not puffed up by false unnatural hopes,
Nor selfish with unnecessary cares,
Nor with impatience from the season asked
More than its timely produce – rather loved
The hours for what they are, than from regard
Glanced on their promises in restless pride.
Such was she; not from faculties more strong
Than others have, but from the times perhaps
And spot in which she lived, and through a grace
Of modest meekness, simple-mindedness,
A heart that found benignity and hope,
Being itself benign.[35]

The unspoken implication of this passage was that his grandparents were all the things his mother was not.

It is Ann Wordsworth's piety that underscores the only two further recollections of her on record. William remembered, and celebrated in what is the only lively poem in his otherwise dreary collection *Ecclesiastical Sonnets*, how, one Easter, she had tied a nosegay of flowers, pinned it to his infant chest and stood by, heart a-flutter, as he made the customary public repetition of the catechism in church. On another occasion, he had told her that he had been to church on a weekday, to see a woman doing penance in a white sheet. Ann commended him for being present and expressed the hope that he should remember the circumstance for the rest of his life. 'But,' said I, 'Mama, they did not give me a penny, as I had been told they would.' 'Oh,' said she, recanting her praises, 'if that was your motive, you were very properly disappointed.'[36]

Ann's death placed John Wordsworth in a difficult position. What was he to do with his five motherless children? Not only was he a very busy man, but also he was often absent from home overnight. He could hardly leave them on their own and neither he nor Ann had one of those universal godsends, an unmarried sister, who could come to live with them and take charge of the household. The Cooksons probably made it clear that they did not want the responsibility or additional trouble. So John did the only thing he could; he did his best and muddled through.

Richard and William would return with him to Cockermouth, where they were already attending the local grammar school, and come back to Penrith for the holidays. John, aged five, and Christopher, aged three, are more likely to have remained at Penrith, where they were old enough to attend Ann Birkhead's dame school, though too young for Cockermouth Grammar.[37] The biggest problem was Dorothy. Only six years old, it was obvious to everyone that she could not remain in a house (at Cockermouth or Penrith) full of males. Her grandmother might have agreed to take her under her wing, but did not do so, earning another black mark in the Wordsworth account against the Cooksons. Instead, in an arrangement which must have seemed incredibly harsh to the little girl at the time, it was decided that she would go to live with her mother's cousin, Elizabeth Threlkeld, in Halifax, over seventy miles away, in the West Riding of Yorkshire. Having just lost her mother, she was now to lose her father and brothers as well. This second separation, only three months after the first, must have been heart-rending for a child of Dorothy's sensibilities. Ever after, she would regard the two events as the single great catastrophe of her life.

Elizabeth Threlkeld and her brother, William, drove up to Penrith in a chaise and, on Saturday 13 June 1778, after what one can only imagine was a traumatic parting, took Dorothy off to a new home and new life in Halifax. Her father, with prescient finality, noted her departure with an unusually precise and full entry in his account books.[38] However cruel the decision may have seemed at the time, even Dorothy soon came to realize that, in the circumstances, she could not have found a better home. 'Aunt' Threlkeld was, according to her obituary, 'a Woman of high natural Talent, and great energy'. She needed to be. Her sister had died in 1773, leaving five small children; Elizabeth went to live with them and, when her brother-in-law also died, only two years later, she took on the entire responsibility of bringing up the orphans and running their father's drapery shop in Halifax. Unfortunately for the young Wordsworths, she could not add another five chicks to her brood, but she was willing and able to take care of Dorothy. No greater tribute to the way she did this could be paid than Dorothy's simple statement: 'the loss of a Mother can only be made up by such a friend as my Dear Aunt'.[39]

Like Ann Wordsworth, 'Aunt' Threlkeld favoured a relaxed and loving regime for her adopted family. Though she was the youngest member of the household, Dorothy was soon made to feel at home. Her cousins, Martha (known as Patty), Edward, Ann, Samuel and Elizabeth (Betty) Ferguson, ranged in age from sixteen to seven, little Betty being only a few months older than Dorothy herself. William

Threlkeld, 'Aunt's' brother, lived nearby with his wife and twin four-year-old daughters, Elizabeth and Nelly, so, though far from home, Dorothy was still within the close family network. Indeed, she probably knew at least some of these relatives before she went to live in Halifax, for the Threlkelds were regular visitors to Penrith.[40] The family had many friends and a wide circle of acquaintance in Halifax, into which Dorothy was quickly absorbed. It is a measure of how successfully and happily she settled that the friendships she made at this period would last for life. Chief among these was her intimacy with Jane Pollard, the penultimate of the seven daughters of a wealthy merchant and banker, William Pollard, who lived just round the corner from 'Aunt' in Corn Market. Jane was a few months older than Dorothy and the two became confidantes, remaining on the closest of terms, despite a widening gap in their relative financial and social positions that would eventually become a chasm.

Halifax was in a period of great change. Formerly an agricultural market town, it was rapidly becoming one of the early centres of the Industrial Revolution. On New Year's Day 1779, only a few months after Dorothy's arrival, there was a procession through the town and fireworks in the evening to mark the grand opening of the Piece Hall. This massive, square amphitheatre, which had cost £10,000 to build, was to become the business centre of Halifax; each of its 315 rooms could be bought or rented for the display and sale of pieces of finished cloth. William Pollard was one of the subscribers and 'Aunt' Threlkeld, whose own home and shop were a few hundred yards away in Southgate, must have been a frequent visitor. The new Piece Hall was a sign of things to come, but Halifax was still predominantly composed of the gabled and half-timbered houses, shops and inns of the sixteenth and seventeenth centuries, a large number of warehouses and a smattering of new brick buildings, such as Square Chapel. Dissent was very much a feature of the town and, with her extended family, Dorothy attended the Unitarian chapel at Northgate End, where 'Aunt' Threlkeld's father had been the minister; her friends, the Pollards, were also part of the large and fashionable congregation.[41]

While Dorothy settled into a new life in Halifax, her brothers remained at home in Cockermouth. In an effort to make them more comfortable after the loss of their mother, their father had taken on two new servants, Betty, and Sally Lowthian, at the Martinmas hirings. Sally, who became nurse to the younger boys, was devoted to her charges, maintaining contact with them well into adulthood. Her affection was evidently reciprocated, for long afterwards William made it a point of honour to call upon her when visiting Cockermouth. He was not to enjoy her full-time attentions for long because, probably at his grandparents' insistence, he was about to be sent away to school. William had rather enjoyed the undemanding regime of Cockermouth Grammar School. The Reverend J. Gilbanks had not been an inspirational teacher, but neither had he imposed a stultifying curriculum enforced by undue discipline. His interest in local archaeology and geology may even have appealed to the boy who loved his birthplace so much.[42] Nevertheless, if the young Wordsworths were to receive the sort of education which would fit them for professional careers, as their grandparents undoubtedly insisted they should, then they needed to go to a better school.

The obvious choice was Hawkshead Grammar School, a charitable foundation established in 1585 by Edwin Sandys, Archbishop of York. A local man himself, Sandys had endowed twelve free places for Hawkshead boys, but the school was also open to outsiders. Its fortunes had been chequered, but under its current and aptly named master, James Peake, it was at the height of its reputation, attracting boys from all over the Lakes and beyond. The number of pupils had grown from around forty-five to over ninety, a very high proportion of whom went on to secure places at Cambridge. This was partly due to the excellence of the teaching in mathematics and partly, it has to be said, to the fact that a seventeenth-century patron of the school had left £250 to St John's College to fund closed scholarships available only to boys from Hawkshead and Kendal Grammar Schools.[43] Not surprisingly, St John's proved to be a popular choice of college among Hawkshead boys.

The academic reputation of the school was its chief recommendation, but its relative cheapness must have added to its advantages in the eyes of the Cooksons. Their own sons had been educated at the much more upmarket Sedbergh Grammar School, but their influence in choosing Hawkshead can be inferred from the fact that it was Mrs Cookson who paid the entrance fees for her two grandsons.[44]

Richard and William went to Hawkshead in May 1779, a few weeks after William's ninth birthday. Richard's reaction is not known, but, for William, the schooldays that lay before him would be among the happiest of his life. Their father had taken every care to ensure that they were well looked after. Most of the boys boarded with the master in the schoolhouse, but the Wordsworths were to lodge privately (and more expensively) with the Tysons, a childless couple in their sixties who lived in Hawkshead village. Hugh Tyson, himself a former charity pupil of the grammar school, was a master joiner; his wife, Ann, had kept a small grocery and draper's shop for twenty years before taking in boarders.[45] Richard and William were, apparently, her first charges and, for some time, her only ones, which perhaps partially accounts for the strong bonds of mutual affection that would rise between them. The Tysons lived in the centre of the village, in one of the typically shambolic Hawkshead cottages that now seem so picturesque: squat, low and angular, with no two windows the same size and tucked away down a narrow flagged alley. It also had all those vital defences against Lakeland weather: a little porch made from stone slabs, vast chimneys and a drip-course.[46] Having been accustomed to the grandeur and comforts of his birthplace at Cockermouth or his grandparents' house at Penrith, it might have been expected that William would be appalled at his new home. He was not; he revelled in it. A tiny artisan's cottage it might be, but it represented freedom from constraint and, in the motherly figure of Ann Tyson, emotional refuge. She practised economy and frugality because they were a practical necessity, not out of parsimonious habit or from an idea that they were good for the soul, as his grandparents did. Perhaps most important of all, lacking the Cooksons' 'feverish dread of error or mishap', she allowed them the freedom to roam wherever and whenever they liked outside school hours. It was a freedom that William was to use to the full.

Hawkshead lies in the Vale of Esthwaite in the heart of the less spectacular, but equally beautiful scenery which drives a wedge from the south of the Lakes into the centre of the mountains. Tucked away, high up in the hills between the great lakes of Windermere and Coniston, it has a hidden, secret quality about it which even the ravages of tourism have been unable to destroy. After a steep climb up from the ferry at Bowness-on-Windermere (which operated even in William's day) and over the lip of the hill, the vale is unexpected, a pastoral bowl set among wooded hillsides. The hills themselves are extraordinary: knobbly and lumpy, bare-topped, with craggy outcrops and, wherever the Forestry Commission has failed to erect its serried ranks of pines, the odd tree forced to its knees against the prevailing wind. The valley is tiny but open and almost filled with Esthwaite Water. Lacking a mountain setting to reflect, it is not the prettiest of the lakes, but the bays and little peninsulas of its western banks give it a peculiar charm. At its northern end and, again, tumbled upon unexpectedly is the village of Hawkshead.

The whole village is crammed into a very small space. Little cottages and inns jostle for elbow room in the alleyways and tiny courtyards, entered under archways leading off Market Square and the main street; in the struggle for extra room and light, some houses have a gallery along the upper storey. The whole village is built of the distinctive blue-grey Lakeland stone, much of which has been whitewashed. Dominating all is the low, squat church, dedicted to St Michael and All Angels, which perches on top of a high grassy knoll in the centre. The grassy knoll is actually the churchyard, which lies well above the level of the streets and houses surrounding it. From this vantage point, the vale of Esthwaite can be seen in its entirety and, on a rare clear day, the range of grey, green and russet mountains looming in the distance, so vast and alien to the immediate landscape that they appear unreal, like a painted backdrop in a theatre.

Just inside the churchyard, at the foot of the hill, stands Hawkshead Grammar School, a small two-storey building, little more than a cottage, which must have been crammed to the rafters when it had almost 100 pupils. An unsympathetic restoration of the late nineteenth century has given it pretensions it did not possess earlier, adding leaded lights, mullions and red sandstone architraves to the windows and a pediment over the doorway. In the Wordsworths' day, apart from Edwin Sandys's plaque over the door, it completely lacked distinction.[47] The windows were plain Georgian sashes and the whitewashed exterior was unadorned. Inside, there was a single large rectangular schoolroom. At one end, on a dais and next to the huge fireplace, stood the master's desk; at the other, and as far away from the warmth of the fire as it was possible to get, was the desk of the usher, his humble assistant. The boys sat on benches between them and along the walls, their desks a single simple ledge with a rest for pencils, quills and books at the bottom end and a hole for an inkwell at the top. It was evidently a tradition for the pupils to carve their names into these desks and William was no exception. W. WORDSWORTH is neatly inscribed into the wood of the desk nearest the door, where, for five years, he shared the hard bench with his friend John Spedding. The master's tiny study, the library and a room for older students, where William's brother John would later carve his name on the window-ledge, were housed upstairs. Outside was the little schoolyard, its grass worn down by the feet of the schoolboys as they ran about or played with quoits, marbles and balls. A corner of the yard was designated, in vulgar schoolboy parlance, 'the pissing corner'.

The school hours were laid down in its statutes and were designed to make the most of daylight hours. Between 25 March and 29 September, the day began between 6 and 6.30 a.m. and ended at 5 p.m., with a break from 11 a.m. till 1 p.m.; in winter it began an hour later and ended an hour earlier, with a break from 11 a.m. till 12.30 p.m. Prayers, written by the founder, were to begin and end all lessons. The pupils were supposed to use Latin and Greek 'as they shall be able' in lessons; there is evidence that this was encouraged but the practice seems to have been widely disregarded. Nevertheless, even for the youngest boys, there was a considerable emphasis on classical learning. William would later claim that he was much indebted to one of the school ushers, Joseph Shaw, who taught him more Latin in a fortnight than he had learned during the two preceding years at Cockermouth.[48]

Clever and interested, William had no difficulty with his lessons and made an apt pupil during the eight years he would spend at Hawkshead. He was also very happy, 'chiefly because I was left at liberty, then and in the vacations, to read whatever books I liked'. His taste was refreshingly unprecocious. He had a passion for fairy tales, his particular favourites being stories about Jack the Giant-killer, Robin Hood and St George, though he quickly progressed to more adult adventure fiction, such as *Don Quixote* and *Gil Blas*, and the novels of Fielding and Swift. Like most imaginative children he also adored *The Arabian Nights*. One of his most prized possessions was a small yellow canvas-covered edition which, on coming to Hawkshead, he was astounded to discover from his schoolfellows was 'but a block hewn from a mighty quarry'. To purchase all four volumes of the full edition was far beyond his means, but he made a pact with 'one not richer than myself' (probably his brother) to save every penny that came their way. For several months they hoarded their petty savings religiously, but the goal was too high and, in the end, they gave up. It is an irresistible temptation to attribute John Wordsworth's purchase of the four volumes of *Gil Blas*, during the Christmas holidays of 1781, to intensive lobbying by his impecunious son. William remained a stout defender of such reading all his life; it might not be 'improving literature' of the type favoured by moralists, but it fostered the imagination.

> The child whose love is here, at least does reap
> One precious gain – that he forgets himself.[49]

There was another gain for which William had reason to be thankful: reading about imaginary horrors took some of the terror out of real ones. Only a few weeks after his arrival at Hawkshead, as he was wandering alone after school along the banks of Esthwaite Water, he came across a heap of clothes. Thinking they had been left by a bather, he waited long and fruitlessly for the owner to return, but the next day they were still there. William joined the crowd watching from the shore as a boatload of villagers searched the lake with grappling irons and long poles. Suddenly, the naked corpse of the unfortunate bather, a young schoolmaster from Sawrey, rose bolt upright in the water. It was a ghastly and horrific sight by any standards.

> And yet no vulgar fear,
> Young as I was (a child not nine years old),
> Possessed me, for my inner eye had seen
> Such sights before among the shining streams
> Of fairyland, the forests of romance.[50]

Unusually for a boy of his age, William was equally drawn to more mundane stories about the everyday lives of the ordinary people around him. Ann Tyson had a fund of such tales. Born and brought up in Hawkshead, she knew everything about everyone there, but she had also been in domestic service at Coniston Waterhead with the family of George Knott. They had a house in Scotland at Bunawe, on Loch Etive, where Ann would accompany them on visits. It evidently made a great impression on her. Visiting the area in 1803, William and Dorothy found themselves 'among familiar fireside names', the places of which Ann Tyson 'used to tell tales half as long as an ancient romance'. One such dramatic tale, that of a Lakeland shepherd and his son searching the mountains above Brothers Water for a lost sheep, is retold in *The Prelude* and credited to Ann, 'my household dame'. In itself it was nothing: father and son search fruitlessly for sheep; son remembers sheep usually return to the place where they had grazed as lambs; son finds sheep but is stranded on rock in middle of brook; father rescues son. It was in the telling that it found its resonances and clearly, as William pauses in the midst of the story to repeat Ann's words verbatim, she had a poetic grasp of language which could hold her boyish audience spellbound. Significantly, too, this passage is also the one which interrupts the action to relate the local tradition.

> 'For take note',
> Said here my grey-haired dame, 'that though the storm
> Drive one of these poor creatures miles and miles,
> If he can crawl he will return again
> To his own hills, the spots where when a lamb
> He learnt to pasture at his mother's side.'

Such simple tales, imbued with homely wisdom and practical knowledge, were to be the raw material of the later poet; as a boy, listening entranced by Ann Tyson's fireside, they wove a magic as potent as that of the *Arabian Nights*.[51]

As William grew older, he grew more adventurous, ranging further afield in his expeditions. There were plenty of schoolfriends to encourage him. Indeed, because the school attracted so many boarders, there was an unusually high proportion of boys of the same age in the Hawkshead population. This accounts, at least in part, for William's sense of his schooldays being a golden age. Boyish pursuits were paramount, there was a strong identity of interests and, consequently, an unusual degree of companionship. Most of the boys came from a similar background to the young Wordsworths. They were the sons of professional men or small landowners and were intended for the law, the Church, the army, the navy or its more prestigious counterpart, the East India Company. The cleverer boys were expected to enter these careers after university, though not all could afford to do so. Like William, quite a few of his contemporaries were the sons of land agents: the fathers of William and Raisley Calvert, John Atkinson and John, Anthony and William Spedding, were respectively stewards to the Duke of Norfolk at Greystoke Castle near Penrith, the Duke of Montagu and Sir James Lowther.[52] William's younger brothers and the grandson and son of his uncle Richard Wordsworth of Whitehaven would also attend the school and share his lodgings with Ann Tyson.[53]

The charity boys, unless they were very clever, would normally attend only the writing class, in which they were taught the basics of reading, writing and arithmetic. One of these boys, Philip Braithwaite, was William's fellow lodger for a time. Though Philip was four years older and lame, the two seem to have become friends, exploring Windermere together and, carrying the school tradition a little further, jointly carving their names into Ann's bedroom window-seat. Philip's great attraction in William's eyes was the fact that he had been to London, a place so far away, and only read about in books and magazines, that it was like fairyland. It seemed impossible that he could return without being touched by the magic of such an experience, so William was cruelly disappointed in finding him not only unchanged but unimpressed. Philip, who long remembered his friend's repeated interrogations, also sheds one of the very few tiny shafts of light that illuminate William's brothers at school. Richard seems to have kept himself to himself and rarely conversed with Philip; John, who came to Hawkshead in January 1782, was 'the nicest' of the brothers.[54]

Whatever the origins of his schoolfriends, and however rosy the tinted spectacles with which he looked back, William was always at pains to point out that they were all ordinary schoolboys, 'a noisy crew' and

> A race of real children, not too wise,
> Too learnèd, or too good, but wanton, fresh,
> And bandied up and down by love and hate;
> Fierce, moody, patient, venturous, modest, shy,
> Mad at their sports like withered leaves in winds;

All the Hawkshead schoolboys were 'impassioned nutters', gathering the hazelnuts which grew in such profusion in the coppices along Esthwaite Water.[55] The lake itself was one of the few which was home to trout, so fishing was a popular pursuit – and, like nutting, a good way of supplementing the 'frugal, Sabine fair' of Ann Tyson's dinner table. In his first year at school, William was introduced to all the likeliest spots by Tom Park, son of the Hawkshead saddler, who was two years older than himself and a fellow pupil at the grammar school. Tempted by better prospects elsewhere and over-confident about his own strength, William once accompanied a local weaver on a fishing expedition up the River Duddon; it was a long walk over Langdale and Wrynose Pass before they started, then they spent the whole day angling, in torrential rain, with little success. Long before they reached Hawkshead on their return journey, William was so exhausted that he was in a state of collapse: 'and if the good man had not carried me on his back, I must have lain down under the best shelter I could find'. For years afterwards, he could never think of the Duddon without recollections of the disappointment and distress of that day.[56]

When they were not wreaking havoc on the fish population, the boys were after fowl. In the spring, they plundered birds' nests, challenging each other to dare the dangerous climb down the crags. William, perhaps remembering his gentle sister's response to the sparrow's nest, instinctively felt that stealing eggs was a mean and inglorious thing to do, but he could not resist the thrill of the climb and the sheer exultation of success against the odds.

Oh! when I have hung
Above the raven's nest, by knots of grass
And half-inch fissures in the slippery rock
But ill sustained, and almost (so it seemed)
Suspended by the blast that blew amain,
Shouldering the naked crag, oh, at that time
While on the perilous ridge I hung alone,
With what strange utterance did the loud dry wind
Blow through my ear! the sky seemed not a sky
Of earth – and with what motion moved the clouds!

William, with his cool head for heights, found the dizziness exciting, but one of his friends was not so fortunate. A party of Hawkshead schoolboys, which included William and two of his closest friends, Fletcher and William Raincock, had accompanied an older boy, John Benson, to Yewdale Crags, where there was a particularly inaccessible nest. The boy had tied a rope round his waist so that he could be hauled up afterwards, then climbed along the narrow ledge. As he did so, the overhang of the rock above became more pronounced, forcing him to lean outwards. Almost in sight of the nest, he lost his courage. He froze, unable to go forward, turn round or go back. William and the other younger boys ran off to fetch help and, after a lengthy ordeal, the boy was eventually rescued by a local waller and his son. It was a salutary lesson which cured John Benson and Fletcher

Raincock of any desire to go after ravens' nests again.[57] William, one can only assume, remained unrepentant.

In the autumn, when the frosts came, it was the turn of the woodcock, and William would spend half the night ranging over the fells alone to set his traps. Hurrying on from snare to snare to see what he had caught, he remained acutely aware that his anxious haste was at odds with the peace and stillness of the night. Sometimes he could not resist the temptation to bag a bird caught in someone else's trap, then paid for it with guilt-induced imaginings that he was being pursued.

> I heard among the solitary hills
> Low breathings coming after me, and sounds
> Of undistinguishable motion, steps
> Almost as silent as the turf they trod.[58]

Best of all, when winter came and the shallower lakes froze over, there was ice-skating, a sport at which William excelled and which, unlike some of his other youthful exploits, remained a life-long passion. (As an old man, he was observed skating on White Moss Tarn, at Grasmere, one hand tucked into his shirt front, the other into his waist band; his foot caught on a stone and he fell with a crash that starred the ice. Despite the assault on his dignity, he had the good grace to accept the accident cheerfully, merely sitting up and remarking to a watching child, 'Eh boy, that was a bad fall, wasn't it?') The schoolboy William and his friends would chase each other across the ice, pretending to be huntsmen after the fox or hare, and hallooing so loudly that 'the precipices rang aloud'. Sometimes he would retire from the throng to pursue the reflection of a star gleaming on the ice before him and, like a rainbow, always just out of reach. At others, for the sheer giddy physical excitement of it, he would give himself up to the wind and race round and round the frozen lake till the whole world was spinning. Then he would bring himself up short:

> yet still the solitary cliffs
> Wheeled by me – even as if the earth had rolled
> With visible motion her diurnal round!

On the rare evenings when it was raining too hard or the frost was too keen for the boys to go out, they would gather round Ann Tyson's cottage fire and while away the hours by playing noughts and crosses, loo or whist.[59]

What makes William's memories of his Hawkshead schooldays, as recounted in *The Prelude*, so extraordinary and compelling is not just the simple beauty of the poetry but also the contrast between the frenzy of youthful activity and the silent stillness of the setting. Whether scurrying between his snares and feeling himself to be 'a trouble to the peace' of the night, or playing noisy fireside games of cards, yet still hearing the echoes of splitting ice falling into the lake outside, the natural world impinged upon him.

> I held unconscious intercourse with beauty
> Old as creation, drinking in a pure
> Organic pleasure from the silver wreaths
> Of curling mist, or from the level plain
> Of waters coloured by impending clouds.[60]

Often these experiences would be almost revelatory, coming at moments when he was entirely self-absorbed. This is captured to perfection in *There was a Boy*, a poem describing how he had loved to stand on the lake shore at dawn or dusk and blow 'mimic hootings to the silent owls' through his cupped hands.

> And they would shout
> Across the watery vale, and shout again,
> Responsive to his call, – with quivering peals,
> And long halloos, and screams, and echoes loud
> Redoubled and redoubled; concourse wild
> Of jocund din! And, when there came a pause
> Of silence such as baffled his best skill:
> Then, sometimes, in that silence, while he hung
> Listening, a gentle shock of mild surprise
> Has carried far into his heart the voice
> Of mountain-torrents; or the visible scene
> Would enter unawares into his mind
> With all its solemn imagery, its rocks,
> Its woods, and that uncertain heaven received
> Into the bosom of the steady lake.

This 'shock of mild surprise', as William describes it, arose from his suddenly becoming aware of his surroundings; he had been so intent on producing his mimic hootings that he had forgotten where he was or even that there was anything outside himself and his preoccupation. 'I was often unable to think of external things as having external existence', he would later explain of this period in his life, '& I communed with all that I saw as something not apart from but inherent in my own immaterial nature. Many times while going to school have I grasped at a wall or tree to recall myself from this abyss of idealism to the reality.'

If it was difficult for William to distinguish between the 'dream-like vividness & splendour' of everything he saw around him and the equally vivid workings of his own imagination, it is understandable that he also struggled with the concept of death. 'Nothing was more difficult for me in childhood than to admit the notion of death as a state applicable to my own being . . . but it was not so much from animal vivacity that *my* difficulty came as from a sense of the indomitableness of the spirit within me.' He would brood over the biblical stories of Enoch or Elijah until he half-persuaded himself that, whatever might become of others (his mother, for instance), he would be carried bodily up into heaven like an Old Testament prophet and there would be no separation of body and soul.[61] He was about to learn, from bitter experience, that indomitableness of spirit was not enough to ward off death.

On 6 October 1783, his father rode the forty-odd miles from Cockermouth to Haverigg, on the southernmost tip of the Millom peninsula. He had been summoned in his capacity as Coroner of the Lordship of Millom to conduct inquests the following day on two bodies which had been washed ashore on the coast. Neither man could be formally identified, as they had been in the sea some time, but from papers found on one of them it was presumed that they were the captain and a crewman from the sloop *Industry*, which had foundered at sea after leaving Whitehaven.[62] After completing the inquests, John set off home. The previous Sunday had seen some of the worst flooding in the region for many years, the River Eden being particularly badly affected. Perhaps in an attempt to avoid the floods, John decided to stick to the higher ground and, in threading the mountain tracks over Cold Fell above Egremont, he lost his way. Darkness came on, compounding his problems. In the end, he spent the whole night wandering on the mountains, exposed to the wind and rain. When he eventually reached Cockermouth, he had no time to rest or recuperate, as he had to be in Penrith the following day to attend a manorial court at Newton Rainey.[63]

The outcome was predictable. At Hawkshead, his three eldest sons were preparing for the school ball, oblivious of their father's illness. They had been taking dancing lessons since August from Mr Mingay, the itinerant teacher of dancing and French, and the ball, on 20 November, was to be the showpiece of their newly acquired skills.[64] The end of term was approaching and they looked forward to the usual joyful celebration of Christmas at home in Cockermouth. William especially was in an agony of anticipation and, unable to wait patiently at his lodgings, ran out across the fields to the vantage point from which he could catch the first glimpse of the horses coming to take them home. He probably already knew that his father was seriously ill;[65] if not, the servant bringing the horses would have broken the news to him. By the time the three boys reached Cockermouth, John Wordsworth was on his deathbed. Ten days later, on 30 December 1783, only a month after his forty-second birthday, he died. On 2 January, the day of his funeral, a great quantity of snow fell in Cockermouth and the neighbourhood. Richard, William and John followed his coffin through the wind and snow to the churchyard at Cockermouth and, numb with cold and grief, stood by the side of his grave while he was buried. The next day, they left their beloved birthplace and were taken to their new home, their grandparents' house at Penrith.[66]

The death of John Wordsworth had far-reaching implications for his children. As a personal loss it is difficult to assess. He remains as shadowy a figure in the

Wordsworth story as his wife and oldest son, with not even a surviving portrait to put a face to the name. He is usually portrayed simply in terms of his job. This is an obvious and almost unavoidable temptation, given the notoriety of his master's career, but just because Sir James Lowther was a ruthless and manipulative man, it does not follow that his servants and agents were the same. Many of the latter were highly respected and well-liked members of the community. This seems to be true of John Wordsworth. His obituary in the *Cumberland Pacquet* contained a simple tribute: 'He lived deservedly esteemed, and died universally lamented.' This might be merely a glib platitude, but it was better than no tribute at all. Much has been made of Dorothy's mortification at finding that 'amongst all those who visited at my father's house he had not one real friend'.[67] Her test of real friendship, however, was the prompt payment in full of all debts to her father's estate. Her point of view was understandable, but it did not take into account the northerner's reluctance to be parted from his money or the standard business practice of discounting or making deductions from bills, a process which would have happened had her father still been alive. Certainly it cannot be taken as an indication that John was isolated and friendless – as indeed Dorothy's own statement refutes.

What little one can glean of his character requires a more subtle approach. That he was devoted to his wife is evident from William's comment that 'he never recovered his usual cheerfulness of mind' after her death. It is supported by the fact that, despite his wealth and the obvious advantages to him and his children, he never remarried. This was uncommon for the period. His 'usual cheerfulness of mind' and his affection for his children can be gleaned from his use of nicknames for them: even in his account books, Richard appears regularly as Dickie, Dorothy as Dolly and Christopher as Kit, and he called his son John, who from his earliest infancy had 'most lonely and retired habits', Ibex, the shyest of all beasts.[68] The children, in turn, inherited his sanguine disposition. He was also of a distinctly literary turn of mind. He wrote poetry, though the scraps which have been preserved do not say much for his talents, and had a passion for reading it. He instilled this love into his children at a very early age by teaching them to learn by heart large portions of Shakespeare, Milton and Spenser. It was an invaluable training for William, who retained for life not only an abiding love of these poets but also an extraordinary ability to commit poems to memory. One of William's great joys in the school vacations was to raid the large private library his father had built up over the years. It included the law books and reference works necessary to his profession but also a number of classical texts (Cicero, Horace, Cornelius Nepos, Florus' *History of Rome* and Euclid's *Elements of Geometry*) and the novels which William devoured so avidly as a child. More unusually for a private library of this kind, it also included a smattering of French books, including a dictionary and an old book of French plays. The biggest surprise of all is that John Wordsworth also had a copy of *Système de la Nature*, by the French philosopher Baron Holbach; one of the school of Diderot and D'Alembert, Holbach was a contributer to *L'Encyclopédie* with Voltaire, Montesquieu and Rousseau, and an advocate of religious scepticism and materialist, rationalist philosophy. It is not a book one would have expected to find in the library of a Lowther agent but it is one that his son William would have found provocative and interesting.[69]

John Wordsworth was therefore an educated man with literary tastes far more wide-ranging than the narrow limits of his profession. He was also, as his job implied, a good businessman whose personal accounts reveal a steady investment in mortgages and land as well as a speculation in the purchase of a thirty-second share of the brig, *Welcome*, of Maryport. His own accounts, as well as those he kept for Sir James Lowther, with the assistance of a permanent clerk, reveal him to be both tidy-minded and efficient.[70] Admirable though these qualities were, they would be of little service in the protracted battle for his children's rights which was about to ensue.

2. *A Poor, Devoted Crew*

John Wordsworth's death left his children destitute. They had no parents, no home and, because he left no will (which seems remarkably careless for a lawyer), no money. The forlorn little band, the oldest only fifteen, the youngest nine, were now dependent on their friends and relatives. And, as they swiftly found out, ties of friendship and blood are not necessarily strong enough to withstand financial pressures. As soon as the boys were safely packed off to school, the family set to and tried to sort out the mess.

The children's two uncles, Richard Wordsworth of Whitehaven and Christopher Crackanthorpe Cookson, applied to the ecclesiastical courts and obtained Letters of Administration which allowed them to settle John's debts and funerary expenses and to administer his estate for the benefit of his children. This would be no light undertaking, for many of John's clients took advantage of the situation to avoid paying for the work he had done on their behalf. Some of the debtors were still being pursued through the courts two years later. By far and away the biggest single debt, just over £4,625 (the equivalent of £250,000 today), was owed by Sir James Lowther; what made this particular debt most galling was that it included not just unpaid bills for work done for him but also actual cash expended on his behalf which ought to have been reimbursed. Sir James was determined to avoid payment and used every means in his power to do so, including denying that John Wordsworth had ever been appointed his agent. The litigation would drag on for decades and, ultimately, he obtained a Pyrrhic victory by dying without ever paying over a single penny. Had it not been for the unexpected generosity of his successor, the money would never have been paid at all, and what little capital the Wordsworth children had inherited would have been completely eaten up in legal costs.[1] The Lowther debt would hang over the whole family, to the Cooksons a festering source of reproach and resentment towards the children, and to the children themselves a blight on their lives and prospects. Had the money been paid promptly, the young Wordsworths would have been financially secure and comfortable. As it was, they were soon forced into a state of dependence on, and indebtedness to, their relatives, with increasingly remote prospects of ever being able to repay them.

At first things went well. John had £225 in cash and banknotes at the time of his death. By 5 May the fine house in Cockermouth had been stripped and its contents put up for auction. The sale included plate, mahogany furniture, looking glasses, a 'large and handsome Wilton carpet' and a great quantity of valuable prints, all glazed and framed, as well as more mundane household utensils. It raised £260, in addition to the £40 made by selling John's gold watch, rings, silver coffee pot, wines and, oddly in this context, his cow.[2] The key to the house was formally returned to Sir James's agent on 24 May. Ironically, this was the same day that Sir James was rewarded for giving William Pitt his first seat in Parliament by being created Earl of Lonsdale. To add insult to injury, as far as the Wordsworths were concerned, their birthplace was to be left empty for many years, falling into a state of neglect and disrepair.

The sum realized from selling off all John's personal assets grew slowly. There was a steady trickle of receipts from various debtors paying off the interest on their bills, if not the full amount. Additionally, there were the rents and income from John's properties, including the Sockbridge estate, which was close enough to Penrith for Christopher Cookson to oversee.[3] With this level of income, there was enough to provide for all the children's immediate needs and give each of them a small nest egg to start them up in their future careers. Payment of the Lowther debt meant the difference between being obliged to work for a living and gentlemanly independence. What no one could foresee, at this point, was that the cost of pursuing the Lowther debt would totally unbalance the equation.

Much has been made of the fact that the Wordsworths supposedly ended up in debt to their guardians, but this was only a very small part of the picture. When final accounts were drawn up, in 1812–13, Uncle Richard was indeed owed over £400, most of it for William's education. What is usually overlooked is that, at the same time, Uncle Christopher Cookson, on the other hand, actually owed almost £1,000 *to* his nephews and niece, which he had borrowed from their father's estate.[4] From the beginning, the guardians did very nicely out of their responsibilities. Every expense, no matter how small, from washing the children's clothes to the provision of schoolbooks, was duly noted and paid back from the estate. This was quite right and proper. Uncle Richard's making of a present of two guineas to Mrs Lowthian for the use of her parlour for two or three months prior to the household sale was defensible, as was his hiring of a chaise to attend the sale and charging the turnpike fees (together with the sum he was short-changed by the gatekeepers!): as the administrator of the estate, it was his duty to keep a close eye on his late brother's affairs. But there were other payments which seem at least questionable, such as the several sums, including one of over £71 'towards housekeeping', advanced to Uncle Christopher. Most dubious of all was the £930 lent in 1787 to Uncle Richard's son, Richard Wordsworth of Branthwaite, the lawyer who actually administered the estate. Though admittedly this was against the security of a mortgage, and charged at an annual flat interest rate of 4.5 per cent, the interest was paid only once and, ultimately, the loan was set off against Richard's expenses in pursuing the Lowther debt, so the capital was never repaid either.[5] The Richard Wordsworths also acquired the contents of John's library. Even if their original intention was to preserve the books for the children (which seems unlikely, given that items which would usually be handed down as personal mementoes, such as John's rings and watch, had already been sold off), they were still in the possession of Cousin Richard twenty-two years later. This was only discovered when Dorothy made inquiries about her father's family Bible; it was found in Cousin Richard's collection.[6]

As for the child Dorothy, the death of her father must have seemed an unreal and remote event; she could not even come from Halifax to attend his funeral. There is no positive evidence to suggest that she ever saw her father again after her mother's death, though an occasional meeting at Penrith would not have been impossible. Even so, it had repercussions for her as well as her brothers. In January 1781, just after her tenth birthday, she had been sent away to Hipperholme school, a few miles outside Halifax. The school took both girls and boys, taught separately by the usher, Dr Wilkinson, and his wife, 'a most excellent-tempered motherly and sensible woman', as Dorothy would later recall. Though close enough to 'Aunt' Threlkeld and her friends in Halifax to ensure frequent visits, she appears to have lodged in the village of Hipperholme with an elderly widow, Grace Simpson.[7] Dorothy had been very happy at the school but her boarding fees were higher than her brothers' at Hawkshead, so her guardians decided to make an economy. She was removed from Hipperholme and sent to a day school for girls in Halifax which had been opened two years earlier by a pair of spinster sisters, Martha and Hannah Mellin, who, like all 'Aunt' Threlkeld's extended family, attended Northgate Chapel.[8] This arrangement actually suited Dorothy better, because she could live with her 'Aunt' again and be in daily contact with Jane Pollard and her other friends. She settled blithely into the new routine, the least affected, as yet, by the change in her family's circumstances.

Richard, William and John, in the meantime, must have been overjoyed to get back to Hawkshead after their miserable Christmas vacation. Almost immediately, however, they were thrown into uncertainty again. The Tysons had moved out of the centre of the village the previous autumn and now lived in a larger cottage at Colthouse, a tiny hamlet 500 yards away across the fields. For the Wordsworths, the great advantage was that they now had a garden, with a seat and stone table under a spreading pine tree; under the garden, contained and silenced in a stone land drain, was the crystal-clear mountain stream which ran down through the hamlet. This cottage, looking out on to a mossy copse on the hillside, was to be their home for the remainder of their days at Hawkshead Grammar School.[9]

The newly orphaned Wordsworths were soon to receive another shock. They had been back at school for only a few weeks when Hugh Tyson, then seventy years old, fell ill. He had an inflammation of the chest which grew steadily worse. Ann, fraught with nursing him, had neither time nor energy to spare for her boys and, when one of her neighbours, Anne Rigge, offered to take them in, she accepted with alacrity. The few days turned into two or three weeks, for Hugh did not get better. He died on 1 March 1784 and was buried three days later in Hawkshead churchyard.[10] Though he had never been as important as his wife to William, his death, coming so soon after that of William's own father, must have been very distressing. It was hardly an auspicious start to the new term.

Fortunately for the young Wordsworths, Ann decided that she would continue to provide lodgings for Hawkshead schoolboys. For the next two years, they would be her only boarders, widow and orphans finding some comfort in their mutual need. In August 1785 they were joined by little Christopher, now eleven years old and soon to prove as good a scholar as his brother William. The following December, Richard left to take up residence and articles with Cousin Richard Wordsworth of Branthwaite.[11] As the oldest son, he had probably always been intended for the legal profession, following in his father's and grandfather's footsteps. At seventeen, he was now chosen by his guardians to take up the responsibility of pursuing the Lowther debt. It was a struggle that would last almost as long as his entire legal career.

Having successfully launched Richard on the path to independence, his guardians now turned their attention to William, the next in line. What would he do and what would he be? More importantly, when would he be in a position to earn his own living? As a second son, he had a number of options, the most obvious being the Church. To become a clergyman, William would have to go to university. His guardians had no intention of funding him and his own inheritance was so small and uncertain that it could not be relied upon. It was absolutely vital that he should win one of the free scholarships so conveniently attached to Hawkshead Grammar School. Whatever William's opinion of the Church as a career (and having no vocation was not a bar to success), at least going to university would give him a breathing space and allow him to put off the awkward moment when he would have to make choices. It now became crucially important that he should do well at school, a duty which was drummed into him during the holidays by his uncles and grandparents.

William had never had any trouble academically. A voracious reader since childhood, his companions on his walks had as often been books as other schoolboys. It was therefore no hardship to him to study and, increasingly, he had every incentive to do so. The Reverend James Peake had resigned as master in June 1781 and, for a short period, his place was taken by the twenty-three-year-old Edward Christian, fresh from a brilliant career as a Cambridge undergraduate. He would later become a fellow of St John's College and the Wordsworths' advocate in the

Lowther suit, though he is better known to posterity as the older brother of Fletcher Christian, of *Mutiny on the Bounty* fame. Even at this early stage, Christian was clearly destined for higher things. He too resigned the mastership after little more than a year in the post. He left no recorded impression on the young Wordsworths, despite the fact that they probably knew him before he came to Hawkshead, for his family lived at Maryport, not far from Cockermouth, and his father, like theirs, was an attorney.[12]

Christian's successor as master of the grammar school was the Reverend William Taylor, another brilliant young Cambridge graduate, but, unlike his predecessors, an inspirational teacher who, in four short years, would have a profound influence in forming and developing William's tastes. One of Taylor's intimate Cambridge friends, the poet George Dyer, described him as a man 'of extensive learning, a sound judgement, a modest demeanour and unblemished morals'; for William, he would become the 'honoured teacher of my youth'. Taylor taught the usual curriculum of the grammar school, Latin, Greek and arithmetic, but he had a passion for English literature and, in particular, poetry. His favourites were from what is known as the 'graveyard school', immensely popular eighteenth-century poets, such as Gray, Chatterton, Collins, Beattie, Young and Thomson, whose work was driven by an affectation of melancholy and musings on the grave. William was not alone in being influenced by Taylor's preferences. Edmund Irton, stepson of the vicar of Hawkshead, presented Taylor with a copy of Chatterton's *Miscellanies*, with an inscription which is testimony to his outstanding gifts: 'To the Revd. William Taylor, Master of the Free Grammar School at Hawkshead, to mark my appreciation of his luminous and pertinent reflections on the poets of our time, and especially the unhappy boy whose genius is evident in many of the pieces contained in this slender volume'.[13]

William himself would later call Chatterton 'the marvellous Boy, The sleepless Soul that perished in his pride', and would even offer to subscribe to a monument in memory of his 'transcendent genius'. He also retained a fondness for Collins and Thomson, considering that they had more 'poetic Imagination' than their contemporaries, though his appreciation was partly prompted by sympathy for their sufferings as individuals. Gray, however, went down in his estimation more than any of the poets he admired in his youth. 'He wrote English Verses, as he and other Eton school-boys wrote Latin', was William's scathing comment in 1816, 'filching a phrase now from one author, and now from another.'[14] This was a mature judgement from an established and confident poet; the impressionable schoolboy was different. Having lost both his parents, he was naturally inclined to identify with the morbid preoccupations of Taylor's favourite poets. He also saw nothing wrong in doing exactly as Gray had done, his earliest efforts at poetry being highly self-conscious imitations of, and borrowings from, the graveyard school.

This was probably inevitable, not just because most authors learn their trade in this way, but also because, as William later recognized, this was exactly what the classical curriculum trained its students to do. The study of Latin and Greek did not mean only translating classic authors into English but also the reverse; passages of prose and poetry by English writers had to be rendered into Latin or Greek in the style of one of the ancients. Political speeches, for instance, would be translated in the style of Cicero or Demosthenes, history in the style of Tacitus or Herodotus, and poetry in the style of Virgil or Homer. This meant 'filching phrases' as well as imitating construction and vocabulary. It was a system which favoured style over content and encouraged facility at the expense of originality. The poets of the eighteenth century had become trapped in their classical training. The poetry they wrote was not only full of arcane classical allusions comprehensible only to those with 'a gentlemanly education' but also drew heavily on ancient models for form. English poetry had been forced into the straitjacket of an alien language and metre and William Wordsworth would be the one to set it free.

As a schoolboy he had no such ambitions. Under Taylor's instruction,

> My ears began to open to the charm
> Of words in tuneful order, found them sweet
> For *their own sakes* – a passion and a power –[15]

With one of his schoolfriends, John Fleming of Rayrigg, he would get up at dawn and wander round Esthwaite Water, 'repeating favourite verses with one voice' or learning new ones. Twenty years later, William remembered the rapture of these moments and could only regret that the poems which had never failed to entrance him then should now be 'Dead in my eyes as is a theatre Fresh emptied of spectators'. What is more, he still understood quite clearly what had been the appeal of their overwrought sentiments and high-flown language:

> That wish for something loftier, more adorned,
> Than is the common aspect, daily garb,
> Of human life.[16]

Not content with merely providing his pupils with poetry to learn, William Taylor set them verses to write. The subject of their first exercise was that hardy perennial and stand-by of generations of teachers, 'The Summer Vacation'. Though the Cooksons and Penrith may well have inspired William with melancholic and graveyard thoughts, one could hardly imagine a topic less likely to stir him to poetry. The resulting lines, the first he ever wrote, he did not think fit to preserve. The writing of them, however, sparked his enthusiasm, prompting him to add voluntarily a companion set of verses, 'Return to School'. There was 'nothing remarkable' about either poem, according to their author, but he was one of the boys chosen in 1785 to write a celebratory poem for the bicentenary of the foundation of Hawkshead Grammar School. In an excess of enthusiasm, he composed 112 lines of precocious, scholarly verses which 'were but a tame imitation of Pope's versification, and a little in his style'. Nevertheless, they were widely admired (far more than they deserved, William admitted), so much so that his neighbour, John Spedding, who had been his contemporary at Hawkshead, could still remember and quote the opening lines almost sixty years later. Though William never chose to publish them, his schoolmaster insisted that they should be transcribed on parchment and kept for posterity.[17]

Perhaps it was the public success of this exercise which persuaded William that he could and should write verses 'from the impulse of my own mind'. He had reached the highest class at school in January 1785, before he was fifteen, and was soon churning out competent verse translations of Catullus, Callistratus and Anacreon.[18] He would always remain interested in translation, returning to it as a mental exercise and stimulus, but to the teenager it was unexciting. The more lugubrious delights of the graveyard school called. His first effort was *The Vale of Esthwaite*, 'a long poem running upon my own adventures, and the scenery of the country in which I was brought up'. That was how William remembered it, though an unkind (but accurate) modern scholar has pointed out that the twenty-five pages written at Hawkshead contain a dead starling, a dead dog, a dead wife, two dead girls, three dead boys, a ghost, a grisly phantom, a band of druids bent on human sacrifice, a sobbing owl, some ghosts of 'murtherers', a tall thin spectre, and two visions of William brooding over his own grave.[19] And this was an understatement, ignoring the clanking chains, haunted castle and iron coffer marked with blood. One wonders how the poor boy survived such excitements. Despite its Gothic terrors, *The Vale of Esthwaite* contained some glimmerings of the poet William would later become: the first account of his waiting for the horses coming to take him home, for instance, and some lovely lines descriptive of Lakeland scenery, including the earliest version of the last stanza of his poem addressed to his 'dear native regions', which would always stand first in William's collected editions of his poetry.

As Phoebus, when he sinks to rest
Far on the mountains in the west,
While all the vale is dark between
Ungilded by his golden sheen,
A lingering lustre softly throws
On the dear hills where first he rose.[20]

There were other poems along the same lines, such as the self-explanatory 'Dirge Sung by a Minstrel', which included three lines 'filched' from Chatterton's *Aella*. The best of them all was an untitled ballad, 'And will you leave me thus alone'. Though entirely derivative in style and unable to escape the thrall of 'woe and black despair', it is interesting for several reasons. It is the first of William's surviving poems to take an abandoned woman as its theme, to adopt everyday language instead of high-flown poetic rhetoric and to draw on the real sufferings of an ordinary local woman. William had been told the story by Ann Tyson. Mary Rigge, the daughter of the woman at Colthouse who had taken the Wordsworths in when Hugh Tyson was dying, had been seduced and betrayed by her faithless lover. She had borne him a child, whom she christened Benoni, or the child of sorrow, then died broken-hearted. Ann had been Mary Rigge's confidante, but William had known the boy, as well as his grandparents, so the tale had a peculiar interest for him; he would later rework it and publish it in another ballad, *Peter Bell*.[21]

William's great schoolboy triumph was to get one of his poems published. It was called *Sonnet on Seeing Miss Helen Maria Williams Weep at a Tale of Distress*, the title being the only part that is comprehensible to the modern reader. Miss Helen Maria Williams was not a Hawkshead resident. In fact she was personally unknown to William. She was a poetical Barbara Cartland of the late eighteenth century, admired (not just by adolescents like William) for her cloyingly romantic and sentimental lyrics. Her first volume of *Poems* was published in 1786 and William's dire sonnet was an apt response: quivering with emotion and full of 'dear delicious pain'. His friend, Robert Greenwood, who had lodged with the Wordsworths at Ann Tyson's since the beginning of 1786 and was, like William, destined for Cambridge, composed a companion sonnet, and the two poems were sent off to the *European Magazine* in London. Astonishingly, William's lines found favour, probably because the magazine was happy to publish a tribute to a popular contemporary poetess. They appeared in the issue of March 1787 under the pseudonym 'Axiologus', William's Greek translation of his own surname.[22] The decision to hide behind an assumed name was merely a convention and did not imply any wish to remain anonymous or to distance himself from the sonnet. Nevertheless, it was the first and last time the lines were to be published in William's lifetime, since they were the antithesis of everything he came to believe was important in poetry.

It is impossible to date precisely the poems of this period, many of which were reworked and fair-copied at later periods, but it is clear the initial impetus to write came from Taylor. It is tempting to think that it was also Taylor who presented William with a manuscript book in which to record his poetic efforts. The gift, William told a friend many years later,

> was the first *occasion* (I do not say *cause*) of his writing poetry. He thought it a pity, after filling up a few pages, to leave the remainder 'white and unwritten still,' and so got into the habit of reducing to shape the thoughts which had before been vaguely haunting his brain, like to body-waiting souls, which wandered by the Lethean pools.[23]

It was perhaps appropriate, given his tastes in literature, that Taylor himself should die young. Less than four years into his mastership, he fell seriously ill, and finally had the chance to play out for real the deathbed farewell scene so beloved by his favourite poets. A few days before he died, he summoned his favourite pupils to his room to give them his parting counsel. To William, knowing he would understand the reference, he added, 'My head will soon lie low!' He died on 12 June 1786, aged thirty-two, and was buried a few days later at Cartmel Priory, on the northern shores of Morecambe Bay. On his tombstone, in a final dramatic flourish, he ordered to be engraved the last stanza of the epitaph from Gray's *Elegy Written in a Country Churchyard.*

> No farther seek his merits to disclose,
> Or draw his frailties from their dread abode,
> (There they alike in trembling hope repose),
> The bosom of his Father and his God.

Eight years later, himself a much older, wiser and sadder man, William sought out this grave: reading the inscription brought back memories of Taylor so vividly that he was unable to hold back the tears. Returning across the sands of Morecambe Bay, he consoled himself with the thought that

> He loved the poets, and if now alive
> Would have loved me, as one not destitute
> Of promise, nor belying the kind hope
> Which he had formed when I at his command
> Began to spin, at first, my toilsome songs.[24]

William Taylor's early death did not spell the end of William's poetic endeavours. He was fortunate in Taylor's successor because, this time, the appointment was not given to an outsider. The Reverend Thomas Bowman, a fellow of Trinity College, Cambridge, had been the first assistant, or usher, at the school since January 1784. (The school also employed a second assistant and a writing master, as well as using the occasional services of Mr Mingay, the dancing and French master.) Bowman, who was still only twenty-five when he took over the mastership, had worked closely with Taylor and shared his enthusiasms, but in a different vein. He believed it was of 'infinite consequence' for young people to have 'access to a variety of useful books' and would later modestly suggest that he had done far more for William by lending him books than by his teaching. His most famous pupil had done 'well enough' under him at both classics and mathematics, 'But it was books he wanted,' Bowman's son remembered,

> all sorts of books; Tours and Travels, which my father was partial to, and Histories and Biographies, which were also favourites with him; and Poetry – that goes without saying. My father used to get the latest books from Kendal every month, and I remember him telling how he lent Wordsworth Cowper's 'Task' when it first came out, and Burns' 'Poems' . . . A story he used to tell about Wm Wordsworth is that he left him in his study once for what he thought would only be a minute or two, telling him to be looking for another book in place of the one he had brought back. As it happened he was kept half an hour or more by one of the school tenants. When he got back, there was W. poring over a book, so absorbed in it he did not notice my father's return. And 'what do you think it was' my father

would say, or 'you'll never guess what it was'. It was Newton's 'Optic[k]s', And that was the book Wordsworth was for borrowing next. He was one of the very few boys, who used to read the old books in the School Library, George Sandys' 'Travels in the East' and his Ovid's 'Metamorphosis' [*sic*], Fox[e]'s 'Book of Martyrs' & Evelyn's 'Forest Trees'.[25]

William would also acknowledge his gratitude to Bowman for lending him volumes of poetry which otherwise might not have fallen into his hands, naming specifically Langhorne's poems, Beattie's *Minstrel* and Percy's *Reliques of Ancient English Poetry*. These, with the poems of Cowper and Burns, were to be critically important to William's development as a poet and they shared important characteristics which are revealing about both William and Bowman. All, apart from Cowper, came from a northern tradition of writing: Burns and Beattie were Scots, Langhorne came from Westmorland and Percy was an adopted son of Northumberland. They were the antithesis of the urbane, satirical schools of Pope, Dryden and Swift. They celebrated the northern minstrels, composed ballads in the vernacular and wrote about the lives of ordinary people. According to William, John Langhorne's *The Country Justice* was 'the first Poem, unless perhaps Shenstone's Schoolmistress can be excepted, that fairly brought the Muse into the Company of common life'. When Burns died, he wrote:

I mourned with thousands, but as one
More deeply grieved, for He was gone
Whose light I hailed when first it shone,
    And showed my youth
How Verse may build a princely throne
    On humble truth.[26]

By introducing William to these contemporary poets, Bowman opened his pupil's eyes to new possibilities and helped him another step up on his way to becoming a poet.

In response to his reading, William's appreciation of the beauties of nature had taken a more contemplative turn as he grew older. The moments when he suddenly became aware of the vastness and stillness of the landscape in the midst of the frenetic activity of sports and games grew fewer. Now he actually sought solitude in order to become one with the landscape and to experience what he would later call 'the instincts of immortality'.

            For I would walk alone
In storm and tempest, or in starlight nights
Beneath the quiet heavens, and at that time
Have felt whate'er there is of power in sound
To breathe an elevated mood, by form
Or image unprofaned. And I would stand
Beneath some rock, listening to sounds that are
The ghostly language of the ancient earth,

Or make their dim abode in distant winds.
Thence did I drink the visionary power.
I deem not profitless those fleeting moods
Of shadowy exultation; not for this,
That they are kindred to our purer mind
And intellectual life, but that the soul –
Remembering how she felt, but what she felt
Remembering not – retains an obscure sense
Of possible sublimity, to which
With growing faculties she doth aspire . . .[27]

Despite his increasingly intellectual interests, William still delighted in the challenge of physical activity. With his schoolfriends, he would range far beyond the narrow confines of the Vale of Esthwaite. Lake Windermere, just to the east, was a frequent destination in summer. The boys would race along its length in rowing boats and then, victory or disappointment forgotten, enjoy a quiet picnic on one of its three islands; 'And I was taught to feel (perhaps too much) The self-sufficing power of solitude.'

Sometimes they would go to the grand inn on the eastern shores of the lake to play bowls and eat strawberries and cream. Perhaps inspired by the rich tourists who paid the innkeepers to fire cannons over the water or hired musicians to play from boats on the lakes, so that they could hear the sensational echoes, they would round off their day by playing the poor man's version. They would row one of their number, William's friend and fellow poet Robert Greenwood, out to an island and leave him alone on the rock, playing his flute, so that they could listen from the still waters of the lake.[28]

On at least two memorable occasions, in an excess of high spirits and funds after the holidays, they hired horses for the day from the local innkeeper. Though they persuaded him to agree by telling him they would not be going far, in fact their aim was Furness Abbey, on the most southerly point of the Furness peninsula. To add to the excitement of this deception, they had to race there and back, simply to ensure that they returned in time. By comparison with this strenuous activity, the brief period of stillness and quiet in the ruins of the old abbey assumed a special significance for William, especially when a wren sang in the nave:

though from recent showers
The earth was comfortless, and, touched by faint
Internal breezes – sobbings of the place
And respirations – from the roofless walls
The shuddering ivy dripped large drops, yet still
So sweetly mid the gloom the invisible bird
Sang to itself that there I could have made
My dwelling-place, and lived for ever there
To hear such music.

In *The Prelude*, William would claim that it was due to 'nature and her overflowing soul' that, by the age of seventeen, 'all my thoughts Were steeped in feeling'.[29] He would assign his wakening interest in the human condition to the French Revolution. This was true, as far as it went, but it did not go far enough. It is self-evident from the number of his later poems drawing on people he had met or known at Hawkshead that William was already an interested observer, even as a schoolboy. The frequent use of question and reply as a means of telling the story in these (and other) poems is partially a literary device, but it also suggests that he was insatiably curious and unafraid to interrogate even total strangers in pursuit of their stories. The old Cumberland beggar, sitting on a mounting block in the sun to eat the scraps given him on his round of the village, and involuntarily scattering the crumbs for the birds with 'palsied hand', was acutely observed '& with great benefit to my own heart when I was a child –'. The two thieves, Old Daniel and his three-year-old grandson, wandering through the streets and pilfering whatever came their way, yet tolerated and even pitied by their victims, who knew that Old Daniel's mind had gone and that his daughter would always reimburse them, were also described 'from the life as I was in the habit of observing when a boy at Hawkshead school'. The figure of the Wanderer in *The Excursion* was a composite one, as William himself would point out, but he identified one of the two main models as the packman who occasionally resided at Hawkshead, 'with whom I had frequent conversations upon what had befallen him & what he had observed upon his wandering life, &, as was natural, we took much to each other'. William's liking for itinerants was strongly influenced by what he called his own 'passion' for '*wandering*', adding that want of money alone prevented him from fulfilling his wishes. He went on to make the rather startling claim that 'had I been born in a class which would have deprived me of what is called a liberal education, it is not unlikely that being strong in body, I should have taken to a way of life such as that in which my Pedlar passed the greater part of his days'. On one occasion, William struck up a friendship with an Irish boy of his own age, the servant to a travelling conjuror. He led him from Hawkshead to the Station, a famous view point above Lake Windermere. 'My motive was to witness the pleasure I expected the boy would receive from the prospect of the islands below & the intermingling water', he explained, and, surprisingly, 'I was not disappointed.'[30]

William's preferred choice of company and his love of rambling at strange hours of the day and night were not calculated to appeal to his strait-laced Cookson relations. He was different; he was wild; he lacked the right sort of ambition. The summer holidays at Penrith became increasingly tense. Probably to the relief of both parties, William preferred to remain at Hawkshead, spending the minimum amount of time at Penrith. Even when he was there, he took care to keep out of the Cooksons' way as much as possible, making lengthy excursions overnight to the Nunnery Walks or to Ullswater. One such expedition ended in a typical Wordsworthian 'spot of time'. Rambling out alone one moonlit evening from the inn at Patterdale, at the westernmost extremity of Ullswater, he came across a boat hidden in a rocky cave under a willow tree. Such an opportunity was too good to miss. In an 'act of stealth And troubled pleasure', he 'borrowed' the boat and set out to row across the lake, taking his bearings by fixing his eyes on the ridge of the sheer rockface of Stybarrow Crag. Suddenly and unexpectedly, from behind the crag, loomed the vast naked summit of Glenridding Dodd 'As if with voluntary power instinct'. The further out he rowed, the greater it became, dwarfing the crag completely.

> And, growing still in stature, the huge cliff
> Rose up between me and the stars, and still,
> With measured motion, like a living thing
> Strode after me.

Overwhelmed, William turned the boat round and, with 'trembling hands', rowed back to the shore and returned the boat to its mooring place. For days afterwards, his thoughts and dreams were haunted by 'huge and mighty forms that do not live Like living men'.[31] No doubt the Cooksons would have had much to say about their nephew's theft of the boat and nocturnal ramblings.

Christmases were usually spent more cheerfully at Whitehaven with Uncle Richard Wordsworth, who had nine children of his own, though only the three youngest were exact contemporaries of their orphaned cousins. One of the older sons, John, was already a captain in the East India Company and therefore in a position to assist other members of the family. The choice fell on William's younger brother, John. Quiet and painfully shy, he was also bookish, but not as academically gifted as either William or their youngest brother, Christopher. 'Our poor John was called a dunce because, dear Boy, he loved his own solitary dreaming wanderings with his fishing rod, or social boyish sports, better than his master's Tasks', Dorothy wrote. Other than his self-sufficiency, he seems an unlikely candidate for the notorious brutalities of a career at sea. Nevertheless, beggars could not be choosers. John willingly accepted his cousin's offer, either from a sense of duty alone or, one hopes, because he found the prospect of foreign travel as exciting as William did. The decision meant that he would never proceed to the first class at Hawkshead and would be taken out of school as soon as he reached fifteen, in December 1787. After the Christmas holidays at Whitehaven, he would be presented with the sailor's stand-by, a leg of dried mutton and a bottle of rum, and packed off to attend navigation lessons with a Mr Wood.[32]

William and his brothers clearly found their Wordsworth relations more congenial than the Cooksons and would, whenever possible, try to stay at Whitehaven. There is evidence to suggest that William spent at least part of one summer there and the Administrators' Accounts reveal that some holidays were spent with Cousin Richard at Branthwaite.[33] The summer of 1787, however, had to be spent at Penrith and, for once, there was a reason to look forward to the visit. Dorothy had come to live with her grandparents and, for the first time since the death of their mother, just over nine years ago, the Wordsworth children would be together again.

Naturally, they were all beside themselves with excitement at the prospect. And then Uncle Christopher Cookson did the unforgivable. The boys had written from Hawkshead to tell him when the school would break up for the holidays, but had not specifically asked for horses to be sent for them. This had made no difference in the past, but now Uncle Christopher deliberately chose to regard the omission as meaning that horses were not required. For a whole week after the end of term, William, John and Christopher waited anxiously at Hawkshead while Dorothy, mortified, chafed at Penrith. In the end, William could bear the suspense no longer and, fearing someone must be ill, hired a horse for himself and rode over. His reaction on learning the reason for the delay is not recorded but is easily guessed. Belatedly, horses were now sent for John and Christopher and, at long last, brothers and sister were reunited.[34]

For all of them, it must have been almost like meeting for the first time; after so many years of 'separation desolate', Dorothy seemed to William like 'A gift then first bestowed'. She had been a child of six when they had parted and was now a young lady of fourteen and a half. She had come to live with her grandparents in May and had learned very quickly that she was the poor relation and expected to work. Having spent the intervening years so happily with 'Aunt' Threlkeld, she missed all her Halifax friends immensely. Her joy at meeting her brothers again was tempered only by the feeling that they were all unwanted residents in the Cookson household, and that their reunion could only be temporary. Writing to Jane Pollard, Dorothy could not resist singing her brothers' praises.

> I can bear the ill nature of all my relations, for the affection of my brothers consoles me in all my Griefs . . . They are just the boys I could wish them, they are so affectionate and so kind to me as makes me love them more and more every day. Wm and Christopher are very clever b[oys] at least so they appear in the partial eyes of a Sis[ter]. No doubt I am partial and see virtues in them that b[y every]body else will pass unnoticed. John, (who is to be the sailor,) has a most excellent heart, he is not so bright as either Wm or Christopher but he has very good common sense and is very well calculated for the profession he has chosen. Richard (the oldest) I have seen, he is equally affectionate and good, but is far from being as clever as William, but I have no doubts of his succeeding in his business for he is very diligent and far from being dull, he only spent a night with us.[35]

Dorothy's insistence on the affection of her brothers (at the expense of a more informative character appraisal) is indicative of the depth of her own emotional need. After all, the boys at least had enjoyed the consolation of growing up together; Dorothy had been excluded from that experience and she was understandably resentful. 'Many a time have Wm, J, C, and myself shed tears together,' she told Jane, 'tears of the bitterest sorrow, we all of us, each day, feel more sensibly the loss we sustained when we were deprived of our parents'. While this may be true, the conclusion is inescapable that the loss had been almost entirely Dorothy's.

What made this sense of a lost past almost unbearable was the humiliation of the present: it was now four and a half years since their father had died and the settlement of the Lowther debt was as far away as ever. Their dependent status was made absolutely clear to them:

each day do we receive fresh insults, you will wonder of what sort; believe me of the most mortifying kind; the insults of servants [who are] every one of them so insolent to us as makes the kitchen as well as the parlour quite insupportable. James has even gone so far as to tell us that we had nobody to depend upon but my Grandf[athe]r, for that our fortunes were but very small, and my B[rothe]rs can not even get a pair of shoes cleaned without James's telling them they require as much waiting upon as any *Gentlemen*, nor can I get a thing done for myself without absolutely entreating it as a [fav]our. James happens to be a particular favorite [with] my Uncle Kit, who has taken a dislike to my B[rothe]r Wm. and never takes any notice of any of us, so that he thinks [whi]le my Uncle behaves in this way to us he may do any thing, we are found fault with every hour of the day both by the servants and my Grandf[athe]r and Grandm[othe]r, the former of whom never speaks to us but when he scolds which is not seldom. I daresay our fortunes have been weighed thousands of times at the tea table in the kitchen and I have no doubt but they always conclude their conversations with 'they have nothing to be proud of'.

The children had discussed their prospects at length. Not surprisingly, if for once a little unfairly, they blamed Uncle Christopher for antagonizing Sir James into delaying payment of the Lowther debt by his disrespectful comments about the new Earl and by his having espoused the cause of Sir James's political rival, the Duke of Norfolk. If Sir James did not pay, and that was now becoming a distinct possibility, then they reckoned they would have £600 apiece. The self-effacing John was already offering to make sacrifices. 'John poor fellow! says that he shall have occasion for very little, two hundred pounds will be enough to fit him out, and he should wish Wm to have the rest for his education, as he has a wish to be a Lawyer if his health will permit, and it will be very expensive.'[36]

This is the first intimation we have that William was thinking of the law as a profession, rather than the Church, after university. The idea that someone with the robust constitution of William Wordsworth might be prevented from entering a career in the law by his health seems a little odd. According to Dorothy, he had been troubled with violent headaches and a pain in the side; these could be considered as laying the ground in preparation for a tactical withdrawal from the law at a future date, but were also undoubtedly the result of the stress of living in the Cookson household. Dorothy too suffered from pains in the head, 'but I think crying was the cause of it', she admitted. She had hoped that William might be permitted to stay with her at Penrith until October, when he would depart for Cambridge, but Uncle Christopher put his foot down. 'You may guess how much I was mortified and vexed at his being obliged to go away. I absolutely dislike my Uncle Kit who never speaks a pleasant word to one, and behaves to my B[rothe]r Wm in a particularly ungenerous manner.'[37]

On 5 August William was obliged to return to Hawkshead with John and Christopher to sit out the rest of the vacation at Ann Tyson's. Whatever one makes of the relationship between uncle and nephew (and there can be no doubt that William's defiance aggravated the situation), the decision seems harsh, especially as William could have employed his time more profitably in Penrith. His Uncle William Cookson had returned to his parental home the previous year and could have helped his nephew to prepare for his entrance to Cambridge. He was ideally suited for this as he had not only been a fellow of St John's College since 1776 but had also spent five years as a tutor to three of George III's sons at Kew.[38] Extra tuition of this kind would not have been strictly necessary, as Hawkshead had prepared William above and beyond the formal requirements of Cambridge entrance, but it would have been the sort of goodwill gesture which might have done much to ease tensions in the household.

Before they parted, her brothers made Dorothy a present of a little library of books which have a familiar ring to them: Homer's *Iliad* and *Odyssey* (probably in Pope's English translation), Fielding's works, *Gil Blas* in French, Milton's works and Goldsmith's poems. Richard also promised to send her the works of Shakespeare and the *Spectator*. Determined to keep up with her brothers, Dorothy had privately determined to pursue her education. Her grandmother spent the afternoons in the shop, so by working extra hard at her sewing and mending tasks for one hour, Dorothy thought she might be able to read for the second hour without being detected. With this scheme, and her early rising, she hoped to pursue her studies in English and French, despite the Cooksons.

Fortunately for her, she was about to find an advocate in the house. Uncle William, discovering her little library or catching her reading when she should have been sewing, realized that his niece was being starved intellectually as well as emotionally. He persuaded his parents to allow Dorothy to study with him and thereby earned her undying gratitude. In her eyes, he became the friend to whom, after 'Aunt' Threlkeld, she owed the greatest obligations; 'every day gives me new proofs of his affection', she enthused to Jane, using that word 'affection' again, 'and every day I like him better than I did before'. By November, she was having two hours of lessons a day with him, reading and writing French and learning arithmetic, with the promise of geography to come. They sat together in his room, they had a fire (a luxury not allowed Dorothy) and, knowing how rarely she found time to write letters to her Halifax friends, he would sometimes allow her to use the French lesson for that purpose. The contrast with the 'cold insensibility' of her grandmother and the 'ill-nature' of grandfather and Uncle Christopher could not have been greater. 'Never, till I came to Penrith, did I feel the loss I sustained when I was deprived of a Father', she told Jane.

One would imagine that a Grandm[othe]r would feel for her grandchild all the tenderness of a mother particularly when that Grandchild had no other parent, but there is so little of tenderness in her manner or of anything affectionate, that while I am in her house I cannot at all consider myself as at home, I feel like a stranger. You cannot think how gravely and silently I sit with her and my G[rand]f[athe]r, you would scarcely know me . . .[39]

Never remarkable for taciturnity, Dorothy now found herself sitting silent for hours on end, the only conversation occurring when she and her grandmother discussed how best to mend an old shirt. As Dorothy complained, it was futile labour, as the repairs usually took more time than the shirt was worth, but she was obliged to put on a '*notable* face' and pretend to be interested. 'Notability is preached up to me every day,' she remarked grimly, 'such an one is a very *sedate clever, notable* girl says my Gr[and]m[othe]r.' Not surprisingly, their ideas of what made a girl notable were poles apart. Dorothy's pet hate was the Cust sisters, Martha and Charlotte, of whom she waspishly remarked,

they are a mixture of Ignorance, Pride, affectation, self-conceit, and affected notability; I now see so many of those *useful* people, in their own imaginations, the *notables*, that I have quite an aversion to everyone that bears that character: Miss C.s are so ill-natured too; I could bear their ignorance well enough, if they did not think so exceedingly well of themselves; for it cannot be expected that those who have not had the advantages of Education can know as much as those who have.

Dorothy's view of the Custs was not without a tinge of jaundice. Miss Charlotte Cust was the chosen bride of hated Uncle Christopher, so it was a case of guilt by association. Uncle William's intended, Miss Dorothy Cowper, was, of course, all sweetness and light. No doubt her attractions were considerably increased in young Dorothy's eyes on learning that Miss Cowper had actually refused an offer of marriage from Uncle Christopher, before accepting Uncle William's.[40]

The Cowper household offered Dorothy a refuge and she often took advantage of it. The Reverend John Cowper was vicar of Penrith and knew her family well: he had married her parents and buried her mother. His wife, Mary, was even distantly related to her, on the Robinson side. Of their six children, only the three youngest, all daughters, were still at home; aged between thirty-eight and thirty-one, they could hardly be playmates to the teenager, but they were always kind and the household was a lively one.[41] More importantly, it was at the Cowpers that Dorothy renewed her friendship with Mary Hutchinson, who was only a few months older than her and had been her fellow pupil at Ann Birkhead's dame school. They had much in common, not least being that Mary, too, had lost both her parents at an early age. Her mother, Mary, had died giving birth to her tenth child in 1783, exactly nine months before John Wordsworth; her father, John Hutchinson, an importer and manufacturer of tobacco in Penrith, died two years later.[42]

Unlike the Wordsworths, the Hutchinsons had an embarrassment of relations ready and willing to give a home to the orphans. Their father, like John Wordsworth, was not a native of the town in which he died, but his parents, brother and sister still lived near Stockton in County Durham. As their son's family had grown so fast, his parents had made a practice of informally adopting the older ones for several years at a time. From the age of eight, Mary, the oldest daughter, had lived for three years with her Uncle Henry at Stockton, where she attended a ladies' school as a day pupil. Her holidays were spent with her beloved grandparents in the charming village of Bishopton. Her grandmother Hutchinson was 'a right-good-Spoiler of her Grand-children', but was also remarkable for energy and business acumen, having established a highly successful brewery as a diversion after the death of her daughter. Mary's twelfth year was spent idyllically in the quiet village; while her grandfather took his daily ride to oversee the family estate nearby at Whitton, her grandmother, 'the perfect housewife', taught her to make currant and cowslip wine and to cook, sew and spin.[43] Prior to this, Mary's oldest brother, John, had also lived for more than five years with these grandparents, before going away to school. When their mother died, in 1783, their Uncle Hutchinson took charge of the three oldest boys. John settled with him in Stockton, becoming an odd combination of farmer, meat and butter factor, and banker, and never returned to the family home in Penrith. The next brother, Henry, who was fourteen, was sent to sea. Like John Wordsworth, he was assisted in securing a place by family connections, but, unlike John, he never became an officer and remained a humble seaman throughout his career in merchant shipping and, later, the navy. The third brother, Thomas, became the protégé (and eventual heir) of his unmarried great-uncle, who farmed at Sockburn-on-Tees, a few miles south of Darlington, and had a reputation as one of the foremost innovators in breeding cattle and agricultural improvements.[44]

Like Mary herself, two of her younger sisters were sent to live with relations at an early age. Margaret, Mary's 'Companion-Sister', was 'detained', as Mary puts it, by her maternal grandparents, the Monkhouses, after spending a summer holiday with them at their pretty country residence at Sebergham, halfway between Penrith and Carlisle. The Monkhouses' main home was in Penrith, where Mary's grandfather, John, was the postmaster; though trained as an attorney, he had abandoned the law because 'the Profession often jarred with his Principles'.[45] Sarah, five years younger than Mary, was eight years old when her mother died and she was sent to live in Kendal. She went to the local day school there and lived with her mother's cousin, Margaret, and her husband, James Patrick.[46]

Mary had returned to her parents' home in 1782, to assist her mother with the youngest children, Elizabeth, George and Joanna. When her mother died, on 31 March the following year, Mary was not yet thirteen, and deemed too young to have sole responsibility for the children and the new baby. Her unmarried aunt, Elizabeth Monkhouse, and her widowed great-aunt, Mary Gamage, gave up their own homes in Penrith and came to live with the widower and his family. Both had already taken an active role in bringing up the Hutchinson children and were much loved by them all. Aunt Gamage had a store of nursery songs, hymns and prayers to teach them and a fund of fascinating stories about her own past. She had outlived two husbands, the second of whom was agent to Lord Lonsdale, the notorious Sir James's predecessor. As Mrs Gamage she had been in great request up at the Hall, joining the Lowther ladies to make up the numbers for dances and consoling one of them when her fiancé departed for Quebec with General Wolfe and again when he died. 'She used to dwell upon these sorrowful remembrances with an importance that was amusing to us.' On the other hand, her tales of the two rebellions, the '15 and the '45, were hugely exciting. She remembered the mothers, children and valuables being packed off to country friends as the Scots approached Penrith, the alarm bells being rung and the beacon set ablaze as they entered the town, the night-and-day cookings that went on to satisfy 'the hungry Rebels' and the rushing to catch a glimpse, or even shake the hand, of the triumphant Duke of Cumberland as he drove them back again. Aunt Gamage's servant, Old Barbara, and her husband had actually come to Penrith in the rebel train of 1715 and, after the rebellion collapsed, settled in the town as basket-makers; not surprisingly, Old Barbara was a 'cherished Visitant' to the children in the Monkhouse and Hutchinson households. Aunt Gamage's other great virtue was her passion for observing the traditional festivals and customs, so there were always special cakes at Candlemas, pancakes at Shrove-tide and pace eggs and new clothes at Easter. On holidays, she would also walk the children out into the fields to pick flowers and visit the different springs, though she refused to allow them to follow the ancient semi-pagan tradition of garlanding those dedicated to saints.[47]

After the death of John Hutchinson, on 19 May 1785, Aunt Gamage and Aunt Monkhouse decided to stay on in his house to provide a home for those of his children who yet remained. The baby, William, had been sickly since birth and had died a few months before his father, leaving only Mary, Elizabeth, George and Joanna. This was still a considerable responsibility, as the two youngest were only seven and five, and Elizabeth, known to the family as Betsy, was mentally retarded, which meant that she required special attention and had to be looked after all her life.[48] This, then, was the state of the Hutchinson household when Mary renewed her friendship with Dorothy Wordsworth in the summer of 1787. The two girls would seize every opportunity to be together, even after dark. Dorothy later recalled how 'Mary & her Sister Margaret, and I used to steal out to each other's houses, and when we had had our talk over the kitchen fire, to delay the moment of parting paced up one street and down another by moon or starlight.' Mary, too, recalled those early days of friendship with great affection: Dorothy 'was then as henceforth my chosen Companion[;] thro' life she continued to be'.[49]

The two girls must have made an odd contrast. Dorothy, small and thin, her brown hair worn in light curls, frizzed and turned under at the ends, and so determined to remain 'as Girlish as possible' that she refused to wear high-heeled shoes. Excitable, hyper-sensitive, romantic and passionate, she seemed constitutionally restless in both mind and body; even her eyes were 'wild and startling, and hurried in their motion'. Mary, thin too, but tall, with pale, clear skin, dark hair and dark eyes with, apparently, a pronounced squint in one of them. Observers were virtually unanimous in declaring her plain, in the conventional sense, but were almost always forced to admit that she exercised 'all the practical power and fascination of beauty, through the mere compensatory charms of sweetness all but angelic, of simplicity the most entire, womanly self-respect, and purity of heart speaking through all her looks, acts, and movements'.[50]

When Dorothy introduced her to William in the summer vacation of 1787, he was instantly bowled over.

> She was a Phantom of delight
> When first she gleamed upon my sight;
> A lovely Apparition, sent
> To be a moment's ornament;
> Her eyes as stars of Twilight fair;
> Like Twilight's, too, her dusky hair;
> But all things else about her drawn
> From May-time and the cheerful Dawn;
> A dancing Shape, an Image gay,
> To haunt, to startle, and way-lay.[51]

Mary soon joined the brother and sister on their walks along the banks of the Eamont to Brougham Castle and over the crags and exposed pools of Penrith Beacon. She lent a sympathetic ear to their tales of woe, shared their passion for the beauties of the landscape and, with her serene and sunny temperament, provided the perfect foil for their more highly charged ones. For William, this was 'a blessèd time of early love' and Mary

> . . . breathed
> A gladness o'er that season, then to me
> By her exulting outside look of youth
> And placid under-countenance first endeared –[52]

The exact period of this 'early love' is impossible to date, as William's references in *The Prelude* are vague and Dorothy makes no mention of Mary in her letters of this period, but it is most likely to have begun during William's first visit in July and August. (A burgeoning love affair, just before William was about to go off to college, might have been the reason why Uncle Christopher dispatched him back to Hawkshead so quickly.) If not, then it probably began in October, when William returned to Penrith without his brothers. Dorothy's letters give the impression that she was more settled and happier then than she had been earlier in the year, which suggests that she had found a congenial friend. William's second visit was intended for the last-minute preparations before he set off for Cambridge. It should have been brief, since term began on 10 October, but it dragged on for a full three weeks.

William had made his farewells at Hawkshead. There was doubtless an emotional parting from Ann Tyson, who had been more of a parent to him than any of the elders of his own family over the last eight years. He had also said his goodbyes to Thomas Bowman, the headmaster who had done so much to form his tastes in literature. All school-leavers going on to Cambridge were encouraged to present a book to the school library and William was no exception. With two other lodgers at Ann Tyson's, his friend and fellow poet Robert Greenwood and Thomas Gawthrop, together with another boy, John Millar, he presented the second edition of John Gillies's *The History of Ancient Greece, its Colonies, and Conquests from the Earliest Accounts till the Division of the Macedonian Empire in the East. Including the History of Literature, Philosophy, and the Fine Arts.* Just published in 1787, the book was as weighty as its title, running to four volumes. The same group also jointly presented another book newly published that year, John Hoole's two-volume translation from Torquato Tasso, *Jerusalem Delivered; An Heroic Poem.*[53]

At the end of October, William set off for Cambridge. He was in a state of high excitement. He had won the coveted sizar's place, which entitled him to pay reduced fees to both university and college and to take free dinners and suppers in hall. Ann Tyson and Dorothy had prepared a wardrobe of new clothes to match his new status.[54] He was in the first flush of love and he was ambitious for academic success.

His eagerness to go can only have been increased by the frustration of having to hang around in Penrith for a full two weeks after the usual date of the return to Cambridge. Certainly, there was no excuse for arriving late when Uncle William was obviously familiar with the routine, so the suspicion is unavoidable that Uncle Christopher was being difficult about the travel arrangements again. It was not until 20 October that Uncle Christopher finally gave him £15 10s (which he charged to John Wordsworth's estate), enabling him to leave Penrith by the London coach. Before he left, he went to the book-club, and secured a copy of one of his own favourites, Burns's *Poems*, for his sister.[55]

William's travelling companion was his cousin, John Myers, who was also going up to St John's College as a sizar. John had been at Sedbergh, rather than Hawkshead, and he was three years older than William, even though they were both entering university at the same time.[56] The journey itself must have been an exciting one for a seventeen-year-old boy who had never left his native Lakes before, and it took several days. On the way, they stopped for three or four days at York, where John's newly wed sister Mary, and her husband, Captain Robinson, lived in Micklegate. Trying to find the house, William inquired the way from a man in the street who offered to show them if they gave him sixpence. 'Well, John,' William remarked acidly, 'I can see that we are in Yorkshire now.' Captain Robinson (the brother of 'Jack' Robinson, MP) was thirty years older than his wife and obviously thought it incumbent upon him to address some words of paternal advice to his young relations. 'I hope, William, you intend to take a good degree', he lectured. 'I will either be Senior Wrangler or nothing', was the determined reply.[57]

On 30 October the chaise carrying William and his cousin rolled over the flat plains of Huntingdon and they caught their first glimpse of Cambridge on the horizon. In his imagination, William had probably thought that it would be bathed in celestial light, just as he had pictured London to be when he was a child. Instead, it was a dull, cloudy morning, with not a single shaft of sunlight to accentuate the soaring pinnacles and towers of the breathtakingly beautiful city. It was the vast, ethereal grandeur of King's College Chapel that first caught his eye, rising out of the dark groves and dull fens like some mythic palace. Magical though this must have seemed, it was William's first sight of a student, wearing his gown and tasselled cap, which really impressed him.

> He passed – nor was I master of my eyes
> Till he was left a hundred yards behind.
> The place, as we approached, seemed more and more
> To have an eddy's force, and sucked us in
> More eagerly at every step we took.[58]

Passing beneath the castle and over Magdalene Bridge, they finally alighted at the Hoop Inn. They had arrived.

Like anyone from a northern grammar school going up for the first time to Oxford or Cambridge, William was both overwhelmed at the sheer weight of history and erudition in which the universities are steeped and elated at the scarcely believable thought that he had earned a place there of right. Copying down a list of the freshmen at St John's in that October 1787, William could not resist underlining his own name and adding an exclamation mark. It was a totally unreal experience, and, like the schoolboy he had once been, he had to touch the walls and trees to convince himself that it was true: 'I was the dreamer, they the dream!'[59]

William's first task was to make his way round to the magnificent turreted entrance of his own college. Built in 1511 in mellow red brick, St John's was far and away the largest college in the university, with Trinity, next door, its nearest rival in size as well as academically. William's name was entered in the admissions and residence registers and he was allocated his rooms in the first of the three quadrangles at St John's. Though he was now admitted to the prestigious ranks of university men, he soon found out that, as a sizar, he was the lowest of the low. His rooms turned out to be 'a nook obscure' and noisy. They were immediately over the college kitchens, where the 'shrill notes Of sharp command and scolding' were intermixed with the general hum of activity; to make matters worse, they were also close to Trinity's 'loquacious clock', which chimed every quarter of an hour throughout the day and night, and to its chapel, with its pealing organ. One consolation was that, if he pushed his bed against the wall and stood on it, he could see only a few yards away the statue of his hero Isaac Newton,

> with his prism and silent face,
> The marble index of a mind for ever
> Voyaging through strange seas of Thought, alone.

The boy who had been absorbed in reading Newton's *Opticks* in his headmaster's study now found himself literally in the shadow of the great man, whose works were the basis of and underpinned Cambridge teaching. With hindsight, it seems significant that William had to make such an effort to see what was actually so close.

William spent his first few days wandering round Cambridge in a daze.

> I roamed
> Delighted through the motley spectacle:
> Gowns, grave or gaudy, doctors, students, streets,
> Lamps, gateways, flocks of churches, courts and towers –
> Strange transformation for a mountain youth,
> A northern villager.[60]

There were many former Hawkshead schoolboys in Cambridge and, in this world of strangers, every familiar face seemed like that of a friend. There was John Fleming from Rayrigg, on Windermere, the 'Friend of my soul!' with whom William had walked round Esthwaite Water reciting verses; he was now beginning his third year at St John's. Among the boys who were now entering their second year was William Penny, also a Johnian, and two of the friends who had shared the escapade at Yewdale Crags, Edward Birkett, at Christ's, and Fletcher Raincock, at Pembroke.[61]

These 'poor simple schoolboys, now hung round With honour and importance' were swift to offer the novice William the benefit of their wisdom and experience. The first thing he ought to do was to change his appearance. For all Ann Tyson's silks and velvets, the cut and make of his clothes marked him out as an uncouth northerner and therefore an object of amusement to the sophisticated gentlemen of the university. He was dispatched to buy something more appropriate to his standing and the Cambridge tailors were happy to offer him credit.

> To myself I seemed
> A man of business and expense, and went
> From shop to shop about my own affairs,
> To tutors or to tailors as befell,
> From street to street with loose and careless heart.
> . . . As if by word
> Of magic or some fairy's power, at once
> Behold me rich in moneys and attired
> In splendid clothes, with hose of silk, and hair
> Glittering like rimy trees when frost is keen –
> My lordly dressing-gown, I pass it by,
> With other signs of manhood which supplied
> The lack of beard![62]

Now that William also looked the part of a Cambridge gentleman, with his fashionable clothes and newly powdered hair, he was ready to embark on his academic career in earnest.

His hopes and spirits were high. After all, he had been one of the brightest boys at Hawkshead and a favourite of William Taylor, who had himself been Second Wrangler at Cambridge, having come second in the order of merit at the BA examinations in his year. Thanks to Hawkshead, William knew more mathematics than most of the public-school boys, which would give him a head start on his peers. And, thanks to his Uncle William Cookson, a fellow at St John's who had been Fifth Wrangler, he had every prospect of obtaining a fellowship himself on graduation. The college statutes did not allow more than two men from the same county to hold fellowships at the same time and these had to be vacated on marriage. Uncle William intended to marry Dorothy Cowper as soon as he found a living lucrative enough to allow him to resign his fellowship and support a wife; when this happened, William had every chance of stepping into the vacancy. A fellowship was the inevitable stepping stone to preferment in the Church, not least because the college had the right to appoint to a large number of livings and schoolmasterships and always filled these with Johnians. If William was serious in his expressed intention of going into the law, then the income from a fellowship would tide him over the years of reading for the bar at one of the Inns of Court. Should he need a helping hand, his former headmaster, Edward Christian, was now a lecturer in law at St John's and would soon become the University Professor of Common Law.[63]

William had every prospect of a successful career at Cambridge: he had academic talents, backed up by an excellent education; he had friends in the right places, with influence extending far beyond Cambridge; he had confidence in his own abilities, not only as a star in the Hawkshead firmament but also as a published poet; perhaps most important of all, as his proud boast to Captain Robinson had suggested, he was determined to succeed. And succeed he did. Despite his late arrival at Cambridge, he managed to impress his tutor, Edward Frewen (another friend of Uncle William), sufficiently to be awarded a Foundress Scholarship, worth between £23 and £26 a year, and two small exhibitions. The first term's syllabus was embarrassingly easy. Greek and Latin were represented by two basic texts, the last book of Xenophon's *Anabasis* and a work by Horace, either the *Ars Poetica* or one of the first two books of the *Epistles*. William undoubtedly knew them both well before he had even set foot in Cambridge. Beausobre's *Reading of the Scriptures* and Dodderidge's *Sermons on the Evidences of the Gospels* were probably new to him but hardly taxing to a young man of his ability. St John's, unlike the other colleges, set examinations for its students twice yearly, so that it could keep track of potential wranglers. In December 1787, William completed a flawless first term by winning a place in the first class. On 17 December he signed the matriculation register and was formally admitted to the University of Cambridge.[64] Everything was going according to plan and, back in Penrith, his Cookson relatives must have heaved a sigh of relief that the defiant and troublesome youth had acquired a sense of responsibility at last. William's future seemed set fair.

3. *Squandered Abroad*

Where William spent his first Cambridge vacation is a mystery. Given his recent successes, he might have felt justified in going to Whitehaven or Penrith to receive the family congratulations, but the cost of the journey was probably prohibitive. His brothers John and Christopher were at Whitehaven for the Christmas holidays, as usual, but they were about to go their different ways. Christopher was still at Hawkshead, but John had just left school; after attending navigation classes and 'much delighted with the profession he has chosen', he was about to sail to Barbados on his first voyage. Richard was still at Branthwaite, in articles to his cousin, Richard Wordsworth, and very busy preparing a decisive step in pursuit of the Lowther debt by issuing a summons against Sir James. Dorothy had been 'fully expected' at Whitehaven by her Wordsworth relatives, but had not been allowed to go, presumably because of the expense, so she remained, miserable and resentful, at Penrith. Even the winter assemblies in 'this petty little place', as she waspishly called it, brought her no pleasure: unlike the gay affairs in Halifax, there were not enough gentlemen to go round and the ladies were obliged to dance together. Her birthday, Christmas Day, which she now claimed had never been a joyous occasion since her childhood at Cockermouth, was even more depressing, for, on or about 19 December 1787, her grandfather Cookson died; he was buried in St Andrew's Church, Penrith, on 22 December. 'At first it was a great shock to us all,' Dorothy confided in her friend Jane, 'the suddenness of it was very terrifying, but I am now quite thankful that he did not linger any longer, for, poor man! he has for these two years been a burthen to himself and [his] friends'.[1] Though his death signalled a dispersal of the household, for the moment 'poor Dolly', as she called herself, continued to live with her grandmother and uncles.

William, far away from such traumas, had probably spent the brief month of his vacation in Cambridge, though, like many an undergraduate before and after him, the proximity of London may have tempted him to a visit. He certainly planned to go there for the equally short Easter vacation of 1788, because, in a letter he wrote ostensibly to inform his distant relative 'Jack' Robinson, who lived at Sion Hill, of his success in the December examinations, he asked for permission to pay a visit. Robinson's reply left him in no doubt that such distractions from his studies would not be countenanced. 'I was favoured with your Letter', Robinson wrote.

Believe me that I shall be truly glad to see you here, at all times, but my earnest recommendation to you is to stick close to College for the first two or three years; a little excursion now and then may be allowed, and in some of those I hope we may see you here. It will give me great pleasure to hear you go out high in your year, and I cannot by words alone express to you the satisfaction I shall feel in hearing you go out Senior Wrangler, strive for that, and establish a reputation at College which will go with you, and serve you thro' Life. To find this will give me much heartfelt Joy, for I most truly wish you well . . .[2]

After Christmas, the freshmen at St John's began to study the Roman historian Tacitus' *De Moribus Germanorum* and mathematics, which meant the study of algebra and the first three books of Euclid. It should have been as easy a syllabus as that of the previous term for William, especially as he had two full terms before the next college examinations in June. Instead, it proved fatal. In common with the other bright boys at Hawkshead, he had already studied all except the fifth of the first six books of Euclid and learned both simple and quadratic equations in algebra. 'This was for me unlucky,' William would later realize, 'because I had a full twelve-month's start of the freshmen of my year, and accordingly got into rather an idle way.' The Tacitus, too, whether it was new to him or not, should not have presented any problems; the Latin was not difficult and the subject, a eulogy on the simple manners and way of life of the German tribes, should have interested him. Over-confident in his own ability and knowledge, William obviously thought he did not need to make any great effort with his set books. Instead, he read nothing but 'classic authors according to my fancy, and Italian poetry'. The consequences became all too clear in the June examinations: he had slipped from the first into the second class. This need not have been disastrous. The first class was always whittled down in size over the years. In December twenty of the forty-two freshmen had been in the first class; in June 1788 there were only fourteen, including John Myers, who had come a respectable seventh and won a prize for maintaining his position. With application, it would not have been impossible for William to have regained the first class, as others in his year did. Unfortunately, his pride had taken not merely a bruising but a drubbing. It was bad enough to be in the second class but he had only just scraped that place. The men immediately below him in the order of merit had all been consigned to the third class.[3]

For some young men, such a drop in status would have been a challenge to reverse the trend, but for William, who had always had a streak of obstinacy and defiance, it simply meant that the system was wrong and should therefore be ignored. 'Some Persons decline to sit for University honours from pride fed by erroneous notions respecting the construction put upon what is called a low honour', he wrote in 1816, when he was older and wiser.

If they cannot obtain a high one they had rather have none, imagining that if they do not contend at all people will give them credit for ability to have succeeded, whereas if their names are found not high in the list, then it is to be presumed, from their having been there at all, that they have done their utmost, and may fairly be regarded as industrious and well-meaning dunces.

In 1788, William thought he had better things to do with his time. Though he is usually considered to be a silent, solitary figure by those who know him only from his poetry, William himself knew better. 'I only cleave to solitude', he wrote in *The Prelude*,

In lonesome places. If a throng was near,
That way I leaned by nature, for my heart
Was social and loved idleness and joy.
. . . Companionships,
Friendships, acquaintances, were welcome all;
We sauntered, played, we rioted, we talked
Unprofitable talk at morning hours,
Drifted about along the streets and walks,
Read lazily in lazy books, went forth
To gallop through the country in blind zeal
Of senseless horsemanship, or on the breast
Of Cam sailed boisterously, and let the stars
Come out, perhaps, without one quiet thought.

It is a picture any undergraduate of any generation will recognize immediately, but William was particularly unsuited to the rigours of academic study after the freedom of Hawkshead. He found the curriculum stultifyingly boring, or rather, as he put it more politely, he could have wished 'The river to have had an ampler range And freer pace'. Even so, he could not remain untouched by Cambridge's golden past.

I could not print
Ground where the grass had yielded to the steps
Of generations of illustrious men,
Unmoved. I could not always lightly pass
Through the same gateways, sleep where they had slept,
Wake where they had waked, range that enclosure old,
That garden of great intellects, undisturbed.

There were so many Cambridge associations with great men of the past that it was impossible to ignore them. William could ride out to Trumpington, for instance, on the outskirts of the town, with a copy of Chaucer's *Canterbury Tales* in his pocket. Then, *in situ*, by the 'pleasant mills' he could read *The Reeve's Tale*, laughing at the bawdy exploits of the two clerks revenging themselves on the miller of Trumpington. Two of his favourite poets, Edmund Spenser and John Milton, had both been Cambridge men. Edward Birkett, William's friend from Hawkshead, actually had the very rooms at Christ's College which had once been occupied by Milton. This was, of course, an excuse for celebration and, on William's first visit to this hallowed spot, he joined in the party with enthusiasm, drinking toasts to Milton's memory 'till my brain reeled'. Time slipped by and it was not until he heard the bell ringing that he realized he would be late for evening chapel, a punishable offence. He ran through the streets, 'ostrich-like' (a wonderful self-description for the gawky, long-legged boy), arriving after the bell had stopped and the organ had begun to play. A crowd of townsmen stood at the back of the chapel, not being permitted to enter because they were not members of the university. Still on a high with the drink and the knowledge that he too, like Milton, belonged to that élite, William ostentatiously flung his gown over his shoulder and 'clove in pride through the inferior throng'. Remembering this moment, in later years, he would feel only shame for 'the weakness of that hour' and his own 'unworthy vanity'.[4]

William's first year at Cambridge 'in submissive idleness ... rolled pleasingly away'. It had been marred only by the disastrous examination result and the inevitable feelings of guilt that he was letting his family down by failing to live up to his and their expectations. The long weeks of the summer vacation loomed and he knew he would have to go home and face the music. It is hardly surprising that he was in no hurry to get there, choosing instead to make a leisurely progress northwards through Derbyshire and the Peak District. Arriving at Ashbourne on the evening of Sunday 8 June, he hired a horse and made a short excursion to see Dovedale, a small, pretty valley at the southernmost tip of the Peak District which was not unlike Esthwaite. In doing this he was consciously following in the tradition of those seekers after the picturesque, William Gilpin, Thomas Gray and Thomas West, whose works had been so familiar to him at Hawkshead. Like them, he jotted down his impressions, striving to re-create the scene in terms of perspective as if describing a picture.

Dovedale is a very narrow valley somewhat better than a mile in length, broken into five or six distinct parts, so that the views it affords are necessarily upon a small scale. The first scene that strikes you upon descending into the valley, is the River Dove fringed with sedge, and spotted with a variety of small tufts of Grass hurrying between two hills ... The scene was pleasing – the sun was just sinking behind the hill on the left – which was dark – while his beams cast a faint golden tinge upon the side of the other. The River in that part which was streamy had a glittering splendor which was pleasingly chastized, by the blue tint of intervening pieces of calm water; the fringe of sedge and the number of small islands, with which it is variegated. The view is terminated by a number of rocks scattered upon the side of one of the hills of a form perfectly spiral –

The vocabulary is pure picturesque (though only William could describe a river as 'streamy'), but there is an effort and self-awareness about the description and, indeed, the whole excursion which bears out William's own claims in *The Prelude* that he was already conscious of a vocation to be a poet. He was certainly trying hard.

Before he left the Ashbourne area, and possibly on the same Dovedale excursion, he made a pilgrimage to Ilam, and was delighted to be shown a stone seat near the source of the River Manifold on which, according to local tradition, William Congreve had written his comedy *The Old Bachelor* almost a century earlier. 'One can scarcely hit on any performance less in harmony with the scene –' William would later remark, 'but it was a local tribute paid to intellect by those who had not troubled themselves to estimate the moral worth of that Author's comedies, & why should they? He was a man distinguished in his day – & the sequestered neighbourhood in which he often resided was perhaps as proud of him as Florence of her Dante.'[5]

Rather than go to either Penrith or Whitehaven, William chose to head straight for Hawkshead. By the time he reached Windermere, he could not control his excitement. He bounded down the hill to the ferry at Bowness in exultant mood, hailed the old ferryman on the opposite shore by shouting his name, and was relieved to find he had not been forgotten. It was the first of many happy reunions. Ann Tyson, 'my old dame, so motherly and good', gave him a rapturous, if tearful, welcome, unable to restrain her admiration at his improvement in appearance. Filled with 'a parent's pride' in her boy, she insisted on taking him round the village and showing him off to all her neighbours. William was more than willing to go with her; it was an opportunity to display the fancy new clothes and powdered hair that marked him out as a gentleman instead of the schoolboy he had been when he left Hawkshead. His newly assumed airs and graces did not last long, however, and he reverted to schoolboy behaviour. He could not resist hailing every familiar face he saw, interchanging 'unceremonious greetings', sometimes across the length of half a field. He rushed round the house and garden, ecstatic to discover that nothing had changed and that he would, once again, sleep in his old bed. Even the rough terrier, who had been the companion of his schoolboy walks, was still there. The dog had proved its worth many a time when William had been in his melancholic phase, composing his graveyard dirges aloud on their walks; trotting on before, the little dog had always warned him when someone was approaching so that William had time to compose himself and avoid arousing suspicions about his mental state. His youngest brother, Christopher, was probably there too, though, unlike the dog, he did not merit a mention in *The Prelude*.[6]

William's return to Hawkshead for this summer vacation was almost like his reunion with Dorothy the previous year. There was a sense of rediscovery so strong that it seemed like having his eyes opened for the first time.

When first I made
Once more the circuit of our little lake,
If ever happiness hath lodged with man
That day consummate happiness was mine,
... Gently did my soul
Put off her veil, and self-transmuted stood
Naked as in the presence of her God.
As on I walked, a comfort seemed to touch
A heart that had not been disconsolate;
Strength came where weakness was not known to be,
At least not felt; and restoration came
Like an intruder knocking at the door
Of unacknowledged weariness.[7]

The landscape may have been unchanged, but the people he had known and taken for granted since childhood were not. There were vacant places on the benches where the old men used to sun themselves, babies were now toddlers and some of the village girls had suddenly grown up to be rather pretty.

Apart from his admiration for Mary Hutchinson, this reference in *The Prelude* is the first indication that William had begun to take an interest in the opposite sex. It is perhaps surprising that this occurs in the vacation, rather than at Cambridge, which had an unenviable reputation as a hotbed of sin and iniquity. Cambridge was predominantly a male society. There were no female members of the university and, as senior members had to resign their fellowships in order to marry, the only women of their own class with whom most undergraduates ever came in contact (and even then rarely) were the wives and daughters of the few heads of colleges who were married. Feminine company therefore came from the lower ranks of society, college servants, the daughters of innkeepers and tradesmen in the town, actresses at the playhouses, and there was only one reason any gentleman of the university would wish to seek out women of this type.

Though exaggerated by the satirical writers of the day, whoring was commonplace. Many undergraduates frequented prostitutes, particularly fellow commoners who had the money to indulge in all the vices and, because they did not have to live in college, were not restricted by gate hours. Among William's contemporaries, both Samuel Taylor Coleridge and Thomas de Quincey are known to have done so. On the other hand, many northern boys were shocked and repelled by the sexual laxity. William's slightly younger friend Raisley Calvert was so disgusted by the 'excessive Drunkeness' and 'Whoring' when he came up to Cambridge in February 1793 that he abandoned university altogether after only a week. William Wilberforce, some ten years older than William, and a close friend of his uncle, William Cookson, refused to entertain prostitutes, even though he gambled regularly and heavily.[8] Christopher Wordsworth seems to have escaped all such temptations throughout a long and prestigious university career and it seems only reasonable to assume that his brother William did too. The only memorable incident he recalled from his first journey to Cambridge in 1787 was 'for the first time in my life' seeing a prostitute in the 'pride of public vice' and hearing her blaspheme. His reaction was a mixture of shock, disgust (he shuddered) and distress. There is no reason to suppose he sought a closer acquaintance then or at Cambridge. Indeed, he tells us specifically that he never participated in 'dissolute pleasure . . . and only now and then observed' it.[9]

Returning to Hawkshead, however, and fully aware of his own transformation from callow village schoolboy into suave sophisticate, he was more than willing to impress and be impressed by the female sex. The 'Frank-hearted maids of rocky Cumberland' were far more attractive than the painted ladies of Cambridge, and their boisterous, but innocent, society had much more to recommend it. William would later feel that he should have given up his vacation to solitude and study but, aged eighteen, social pleasures proved more exciting.

a swarm
Of heady thoughts jostling each other, gauds
And feast and dance and public revelry
And sports and games (less pleasing in themselves,
Than as they were a badge glossy and fresh
Of manliness and freedom), these did now
Seduce me . . .

He began a 'vague heartless chase Of trivial pleasures',[10] which was quite natural to his years, but would later come to seem a mere waste of time. First and foremost of these was undoubtedly the fairly recent innovation of a regatta on Windermere which was usually held in August. Yacht races and rowing competitions on the lake were followed by hunts, picnics, balls and parties at the Ferry Inn and in the houses of the local grandees on the lakeside. William was a participant in some of the sports and he certainly attended the balls. He had always loved dancing, but this summer vacation was probably the first opportunity he had to exploit his passion to the full. One ball lasted till dawn the following day.

I had passed
The night in dancing, gaiety, and mirth,
With din of instruments and shuffling feet
And glancing forms and tapers glittering
And unaimed prattle flying up and down,
Spirits upon the stretch, and here and there
Slight shocks of young love-liking interspersed
That mounted up like joy into the head
And tingled through the veins.

As he walked the two miles back to Colthouse, over Claife Heights, William watched the dawn break over the mountains. Revelling in the beauty of the landscape, the silence and the serenity, his heart was filled to the brim with thoughts and feelings he could not then articulate. Later, however, he remembered this moment of such emotional intensity that he came to see it as a turning point in his career as a poet, a symbolic rejection of social frivolity and acceptance of the eternal truths of nature. Like the heroes of antiquity, he did not seek to be a dedicated spirit, but passively accepted the role that was thrust upon him.

> I made no vows, but vows
> Were then made for me: bond unknown to me
> Was given that I should be, else sinning greatly,
> A dedicated spirit.[11]

Exhausted after another long evening of frenetic regatta entertainment, he enjoyed a similar moment as he walked home, late at night, along the silent public road. Drinking in the stillness of the starry night, he felt a 'restoration like the calm of sleep, But sweeter far'. This time, however, his musings were rudely interrupted when, round a corner, he suddenly came across a man of almost spectral appearance, gaunt, thin and seemingly of preternatural height, leaning against a milestone perfectly still. The shock of seeing this unexpected apparition, groaning quietly in the moonlight, was compounded for William because his imagination invested it with all the horrors of the graveyard school of poetry, to which he was still deeply attached. It took some courage (and some time) to approach the man, but his story proved real enough. He was a soldier who had been dismissed from the army on his return from service in the tropics, ten days previously, and he was making his way home. William offered to take him to a labourer's cottage nearby where he knew the man would receive food and lodging for the night. As they slowly made their way, William questioned the man intently about his experience of battle, hardship and pestilence. If he had hoped to hear blood-stirring tales of derring-do, he was mistaken; the man's replies were uttered in a tone of indifference, 'as of one Remembering the importance of his theme But feeling it no longer'. As he left the old soldier at the cottage, William begged him not to linger on the public roads in future, but to ask for assistance. He received an implicit reproof in return: 'My trust is in the God of Heaven, And in the eye of him that passes me!' It was the first of many memorable chance encounters with itinerants whose stories William would later immortalize in verse.[12]

Looking back on this summer, it seemed to William as if there had been a new contagion in the air at Hawkshead, one that was

> Unknown among these haunts in former days.
> The very garments that I wore appeared
> To prey upon my strength, and stopped the course
> And quiet stream of self-forgetfulness.

This was very much the view of the later poet of *The Prelude*, however, and at the time, he had no regrets at all. The later poet also exaggerated the 'vague heartless chase Of trivial pleasures' during this vacation, for it is clear from other sources that William had not entirely given up either his reading or his studies. He was still in regular contact with his old headmaster, Thomas Bowman, who continued to allow him to borrow books throughout all his college vacations, even though he was no longer a pupil at Hawkshead Grammar School.[13]

Through Bowman, or possibly Mr Bowstead, the writing master at the school, who was one of Ann Tyson's lodgers throughout 1788, William was reintroduced to Charles Farish, a former pupil who had returned to Hawkshead as first assistant. Farish had overlapped with William at both Hawkshead, where he had spent two years as a senior pupil in 1782–4, and at Cambridge, where his last year at Queens' College coincided with William's first at St John's. Despite their disparity in age and status, it is not unlikely that they had encountered each other at Cambridge, for both had been favourites of William Taylor and had written verses under his influence. The meeting during this summer vacation, after Farish had taken his degree, was an opportunity to pool experiences and ideas about writing poetry. William was no doubt already familiar with Farish's schoolboy efforts, which were not dissimilar to his own, but now Farish introduced him to the work of his brother. John Bernard Farish had been a pupil at Carlisle Grammar School and St Bees, before going up to Cambridge, where he died not long after taking his degree in 1778. His had been a precocious talent, made more poignant by his early demise. As a sixteen-year-old schoolboy, in 1770 (the year William was born), John Farish had written two versions of a poem he called *The Heath*, one in the style of Spenser, the other in that of Shakespeare. They described the body of a murderer hanging on a gallows on a lonely heath, with a raven flying round, and the appearance of the ghost of the victim opening his shroud to reveal the fatal wound. This macabre but virtuoso effort impressed William immensely. He borrowed the images for his poem *Guilt and Sorrow*, which he began to write in 1791, acknowledging his debt to the two Farishes in a footnote. He also attempted to do something similar himself, composing lines describing a woman crossing a heath in alternative Spenserian and Shakespearian stanzas.[14]

William spent most of his first long vacation at Hawkshead, but he could not avoid paying duty visits to his guardian uncles, especially if he wished to see his sister and brothers. He seems to have been in Penrith on 21 June, when his Uncle Christopher gave him £36 8s 6d in cash, a sum possibly designed to see him through the vacation, since he had already had £54 18s in February and would receive a further £35 in November for Cambridge expenses.[15] With Dorothy and her friend Mary Hutchinson, he again explored his favourite walks around Penrith, through narrow lanes, shady woods and over the Penrith Beacon, or sat in the ruins of Brougham Castle, dreaming of an earlier poet associated with that place, Sir Philip Sidney. Mary's presence this summer may have been less frequent, however, for her Aunt Gamage was growing less indulgent towards her older charges: 'to me & my

Friends, before I left Penrith, she was certainly often harsh in her manner,' Mary remembered, 'thwarting our schemes of pleasure &c.' This sounds like an attempt to curb any sort of relationship between Mary and William. If so, Aunt Gamage was right to wish to protect Mary's reputation by discouraging her from wandering the hills in the company of a young man whose prospects were by no means certain. Dorothy saw it differently, took offence and conceived a real dislike of the old lady.[16]

None of them yet knew it, but this second summer together would also be the last they would share for many a year, for the Cookson and Hutchinson households were both about to break up. The death of William and Dorothy's grandfather had given his older son the financial independence he needed to marry and, on 27 August 1788, Uncle Christopher finally led Miss Charlotte Cust to the altar. Coincidentally, at about the same time Uncle William had at last received his long-awaited promotion to a college living at Forncett, in Norfolk, resigned his fellowship and, two months after his brother, on 17 October, was married to his faithful Dorothy Cowper. William missed the first wedding as he was at Whitehaven, where his brother John, newly returned from his first voyage across the Atlantic, was staying briefly with Uncle Richard Wordsworth, before setting out again for Jamaica.[17]

It is possible, however, that William attended the second wedding, though his presence is nowhere noted. He always came to Penrith about this time to make the connection with the coaches for Cambridge and, the day after the marriage, Uncle Christopher gave him some small sums in cash, which indicates he was there in person. Another good reason for being in Penrith on the wedding day was to pay a final visit to his sister, who was about to leave the town for good. Only ten days earlier, Uncle William and his fiancée had taken Dorothy for a walk and shared their secret with her. Not only were they about to marry but they had decided to offer Dorothy a home with them at Forncett. 'My happiness was very unexpected', Dorothy gushed to Jane Pollard, '. . . when my Uncle told me I was almost mad with joy; I cried and laughed alternately'.[18] In the all too short interval between finding out and having to leave, Dorothy rushed around preparing her clothes and doing her packing. On the wedding morning, she attended the bridal couple to church and, with William Monkhouse, Mary Hutchinson's uncle, who was also brother-in-law of the bride, signed the register. If Mary herself did not attend the ceremony, she probably came to the wedding breakfast which followed at Mrs Cowper's. There was, no doubt, a tearful parting between Dorothy and Mary as neither of them had any idea when they would meet again.

Straight after the breakfast, the newlyweds and Dorothy set off for Newcastle, where both the Cooksons and the Cowpers had relatives. Dorothy had never expected to leave Penrith while her grandmother was still alive and she was wild with excitement. After a very agreeable fortnight at Newcastle, they set off for Norwich and their route naturally went through Cambridge, where William had already returned to college. For once, Dorothy seems to have paid more attention to a place than to her brother.

the buildings, added to the pleasure of seeing my Brother very well and in excellent spirits delighted me exceedingly; I could scarcely help imagining myself in a different country when I was walking in the college courts and groves; it looked so odd to see smart powdered heads with black caps like helmets, only that they have a square piece of wood at the top, and gowns, something like those that clergymen wear; but, I assure you, (though a description of the dress may sound very strange) it is exceedingly becoming.

After only a day in Cambridge, Dorothy was whisked off to Norwich. It was an auspicious moment to enter the town, which was deep in the throes of a double celebration, Guy Fawkes Night and the Centenary of the Glorious Revolution of 1688. The whole town was illuminated and the bells of all its many churches were ringing. To Dorothy, blossoming in the warmth of her uncle and aunt's affection, the general mood of exhilaration was the perfect expression of her own feelings. Nothing could disappoint her. Forncett, to which they made a day trip a couple of days later, proved to be 'a little village entirely inhabited by farmers, who seem very decent kind of people'; the house was very comfortable but would soon be excellent and the gardens were charming. 'I intend to be a great gardener', Dorothy announced proudly, 'and promise myself much pleasure in taking care of the poultry of which we are to have great abundance.' They were all busy making plans and had even sketched out a daily routine: prayers at nine ('it is *winter*', Dorothy apologized), after breakfast they were to read and write and Dorothy would improve herself in French; from twelve till three, which was to be their dinner hour, they would walk or visit the sick and poor; after tea, Uncle William would sit with them and read to them, if he, and they, felt so inclined. They were even planning to celebrate Dorothy's birthday and, after many consultations, decided that roast beef and plum pudding was the best Christmas Dinner. The comparison with the misery of the previous Christmas was unavoidable. 'I have now nothing left to wish for on my own account,' Dorothy acknowledged gratefully.

Every day gives me fresh proofs of my Uncle and Aunt's goodness, I am sure there is not a better man in the world than my Uncle, nor a more amiable woman than my Aunt; you know how partial I always was to a country life but I almost despaired of ever enjoying it; but to live in the country and with such kind friends! have I not every reason to be thankful?[19]

At Cambridge, William was equally blithe. He had come to an important decision which would have far-reaching implications for his future. As a result of his poor showing in the college's summer examinations and his increasing distaste for the sterility and restrictiveness of the university syllabus, he had decided that he 'wished to be a lodger in that house Of letters, and no more'. In other words, he would abandon all hope of becoming Senior Wrangler or, indeed, winning any honours, do only the minimum of set work required to prevent his being sent down and use the unrivalled facilities of the university to pursue a course of independent study. He was well aware that this decision was 'An act of disobedience towards them Who loved me, proud rebellion and unkind'; in retrospect it also seemed an act of cowardice which gave 'treacherous sanction' to his over-love of freedom and indolence.[20]

William was by no means unusual in his rejection of a formal university career. His friend Raisley Calvert, in seeking to justify his own decision to leave before he had even matriculated, declared that he would never enter the profession for which he was intended and so there was little point in his studying classics and mathematics. He had never met anyone who actually used their classical education in the social intercourse of ordinary life and, though mathematics was more obviously useful, to distinguish himself would require such intense application as would destroy his constitution.[21] This last argument is one which is heard over and over again; indeed, as we have seen, it had been suggested by William himself when he first considered the law as his profession. Robert Southey, William's contemporary and predecessor as Poet Laureate, wrote to offer words of wisdom and experience to a young friend who went up to Pembroke College in 1811.

> Do not be solicitous about taking a high degree, or about college honours of any kind. Many a man has killed himself at Cambridge by overworking for mathematical honours; recollect how few the persons are who after they have spent their years in severe study at this branch of science, ever make any use of it afterwards. Your wiser plan should be to look on to that state of life in which you wish and expect to be placed, and to lay in such knowledge as will then turn to account.[22]

This is exactly what William did, and many another young man like him. Of the forty-two freshmen, including William, who entered St John's in October 1787, almost a quarter had already dropped out before the end of the first year; by June of the second year, only twenty-one, half the original number, were still in contention. By the following December, William had joined the ranks of non-reading men. Robert Southey, whose career paralleled William's own in many ways, followed a similar route at university. Southey was at Oxford, which was then the only other university in England. The course there did not have the mathematical element which alienated so many Cambridge undergraduates, but both universities faced the same problems of moral laxity, academic absenteeism (most professors never lectured and college tutors, when they were there, had to lecture to up to eighty undergraduates at a time) and an appointments and honours system bedevilled by corruption. Southey was not only intellectually gifted but also fanatically hard-working by any standards, yet it was his own tutor who advised him to drop out: 'Mr Southey, you won't learn any thing by my lectures, Sir', he was told, 'so, if you have any studies of your own, you had better pursue them.' Southey accepted this offer 'thankfully' and eventually left Oxford without even attempting to take his degree.[23]

There were other disincentives to success at Cambridge, besides contempt for the syllabus, and William seems to have felt all of them in varying degrees. He hated the compulsory twice-daily attendance at chapel, which he felt was simply a hollow mockery of genuine piety. He objected to the examinations 'when the man was weighed As in the balance!' (and, in William's own case, found wanting), because they promoted all the deeper passions, excessive hopes, envy, jealousy, pride, shame and ambition. He had nothing but contempt for the entire academic system and its petty struggle for 'spurious fame and short-lived praise', attacking it in *The Prelude* with uncharacteristic bitterness.

> And here was labour, his own bond-slave; hope,
> That never sets the pains against the prize; . . .
> Honour misplaced, and dignity astray;
> Feuds, factions, flatteries, enmity, and guile;

Underpinning all these criticisms, though never explicitly mentioned, was William's own status as a university man. Like Dorothy, he had always been sensitive to personal slights, perceived or otherwise: as we have seen, when only a child at Penrith he had been ready to kill himself when 'some indignity' had been imposed upon him. And there is a very telling phrase in his description of being late for chapel after the drinking party at Christ's; running through the crowd of townsmen, he ostentatiously shouldered his gown which was both 'gloried in and yet despised'.[24] It is a throwaway line (William actually discarded it when he prepared *The Prelude* for posthumous publication) but it goes to the heart of William's disenchantment with Cambridge. His gown was the public symbol to the outside world of his membership of that élite band, the gentlemen of the university; to the gentlemen of the university it marked him out as the lowest of the low.

At that time there were three ranks of Cambridge undergraduates: fellow commoners, who were noblemen and plutocrats; pensioners (by far the largest class), who were younger sons of the aristocracy, the gentry and professional classes; and then there were the sizars, bright boys who could not afford the fees paid by their wealthier counterparts, but were expected to bring honour to their colleges by doing well in the examinations. William's closest friends among the Hawkshead boys already at Cambridge when he arrived, John Fleming, Edward Birkett and Fletcher Raincock, were all pensioners. William not only had less money than them in any case, but his inferiority was broadcast in the most humiliating of ways. He had to wear a different and distinctive gown so that he was instantly identifiable; he got the worst rooms in the college, as he had already discovered, and for his dinners and suppers he had to make do with whatever was left over from the fellows' table. William escaped one of the sizars' greatest indignities by the narrowest of margins; until only the year before he went up, sizars had been compelled to act as waiters at the fellows' table, where the undergraduate fellow commoners also dined, a practice that was abolished in St John's in 1786.[25]

Not surprisingly, many sizars chafed under these humiliations. Charles Lamb blamed Samuel Taylor Coleridge's sensitivity to his status for his bizarre decision to flee Cambridge and volunteer for the army under the delicious pseudonym, Silas Tomkyn Comberbache: he was, according to Lamb, 'ill-capable of enduring the slights poor sizars are sometimes subject to in our seats of learning'. John Scott, who was in the year above William at St John's, found the transition from Charterhouse to a sizarship unbearable because he was placed 'in a position so much beneath that to which all his former schoolfellows were admitted'. More than fifty years later, when conditions were much improved, Bulwer Lytton could still depict the sizar's lot as one of bitter degradation. 'Do you know what a sizar is? In pride he is a gentleman – in knowledge he is a scholar – and he crawls about, amidst gentlemen and scholars, with the livery of a pauper on his back!'[26]

Because they were so humiliatingly marked out from the other university men, the pressure upon sizars to prove themselves by doing well academically was immense. Many of them were dependent on college scholarships and exhibitions which could be, and were, withdrawn from those who failed to perform. William was fortunate in being at St John's, which had the largest number of sizars of any college; there were fourteen in his year alone. Additionally, the three Hawkshead boys who came up to Cambridge at the same time as himself, Robert Greenwood, John Millar and Thomas Gawthrop, were all sizars, as was his own cousin, John Myers. Though he was in a very small minority, William at least had the consolation of knowing he was among friends.

William's decision to abandon any pursuit of academic honours did not mean that he gave up reading and studying altogether. Quite the contrary, in fact. In *The Prelude*, he tells us that he now abandoned the gay round of parties, invitations and social pastimes of the previous year.

I lived henceforth
More to myself, read more, reflected more,
Felt more, and settled daily into habits
More promising.

Over the course of the next two winters, he 'devoured, Tasted or skimmed, or studiously perused' many books, but without any set plan in mind, other than the growing conviction that he wanted to be a poet. This sounds rather pretentious, but is borne out by the facts. It is clear from his examination records, for instance, that he did not completely sever himself from the university syllabus but carefully selected only those subjects which interested him. In December 1788, the set texts were the first six books of Euclid, Thomas Rutherforth's *Institutes of Natural Law* and Sophocles' *Oedipus at Colonus*, in the original Greek. Which of these texts he read (or remembered, in the case of Euclid), is not known, but his report indicated that he 'did not go thro' the whole of the examination & yet had considerable merit'. The following June, the men of William's year were examined in mechanics, the twenty-first book of Livy's *History of Rome* and Locke's *Essay on Human Under-*

standing. William took only part of the examination and, as a result, was unclassed, though he distinguished himself in the classics. Given his love of ancient history and interest in philosophy, it seems likely that he simply studied the Livy and completely omitted the mechanics.[27]

In place of the prescribed course of study, William decided to employ his time more productively in learning Italian. Though he gives the impression in *The Prelude* that this was simply following a whim, he actually set about it with great determination. His first step was to secure a private tutor and, by great good luck, one of the most famous Italian teachers of the day happened to live and teach in Cambridge. Agostino Isola, a refugee from Italy, had taught a number of eminent people, including the Prime Minister, William Pitt, and the poet Thomas Gray. He had also published in 1786 a translation of Tasso's *Jerusalem Delivered*, one of the books (though not the actual edition) William had given to Hawkshead Grammar School. Isola and his new pupil hit it off immediately. 'As I took to these studies with much interest,' William later recalled, 'he was proud of the progress I made. Under his correction I translated the Vision of Mirza, and two or three other papers of the Spectator, into Italian.'[28]

With Isola he also studied Italian poetry, for which he retained a lifelong affection, reading Tasso and Dante and translating Ariosto's *Orlando Furioso* and Michelangelo's sonnets. The sheer musicality of the language appealed to his poetic ear, though he later became convinced that 'an easy and mellifluous language was apt to tempt, by its facility, into negligence, and to lead the poet to substitute music for thought', whereas in struggling with words in the 'rugged language' of English 'one was led to give birth to and dwell upon thoughts'.[29]

William obviously flourished under Isola's guidance and it is interesting to see that, studying a subject he liked, for a teacher he admired, he fell victim to the prevailing competitive spirit at Cambridge for the first and only time. 'I never felt emulation with another man but once,' he told a friend when he was an old man,

> and that was accompanied by envy. This once was in the study of Italian, which I entered on at College with [blank]. I never engaged in the proper studies of the university, so that in these I had no temptation to envy anyone; but I remember with pain that I *had* envious feelings when my fellow student in Italian got before me. I was his superior in many departments of mind, but he was the better Italian scholar, and I envied him. The annoyance this gave me made me very thankful that as a boy I never experienced it.

Isola also taught Spanish, and William may well have studied this language with him. Though Spanish poetry never attracted him as much as Italian, he had loved Cervantes' *Don Quixote* since childhood, and always admired what he called the 'imagination' of the Spanish. Dorothy notes him reading in it extensively in a letter to Jane Pollard which, unusually, contains implicit criticism of her brother. She had pinned her hopes on his success at Cambridge; had he been like Uncle William, he could have secured a fellowship, a nice living and a parsonage in the country, where Dorothy could live without any sense of being the dependent relative. 'William you may have heard lost the chance, indeed the certainty of a fellowship', she wrote ruefully,

> by not combating his inclinations, he gave way to his natural dislike of studies so dry as many parts of the mathematics, consequently could not succeed at Cambridge. He reads Italian, Spanish, French, Greek and Latin, and English, but never opens a mathematical book . . . William has a great attachment to poetry . . . which is not the most likely thing to produce his advancement in the world; his pleasures are chiefly of the imagination, he is never so happy as when in a beautiful country. Do not think from what I have said that he reads not [at] all, for he does read a great deal and not only poetry and those languages he is acquainted with but history &c &c.

William's study of the romance languages was a deliberate attempt to gain access to some of the greatest poets of the past in their original tongue. It is clear from his percipient criticisms that he was also studying carefully the form and structure of the poetry, as well as the actual content, and the thoughts and feelings which had given rise to it. He could not completely escape the yoke of classical literature by widening his reading to include these languages, since it was a shared pan-European heritage, but at least different paths were opening before him. In English literature, too, the scale, if not the scope, of his reading expanded. He remained as enthusiastic as he had been when a schoolboy about the melancholics: Young, Collins and Gray were still his favourite poets. However, it seems that it was at Cambridge that he began to read far more poetry from earlier generations. His appreciation of Milton, Shakespeare and Spenser increased as he read more deeply in their work. He began to read more obscure authors too, such as Anne, Countess of Winchilsea, a poetess of the late seventeenth century, whose sensibility and simplicity of style he admired.[30]

His early love of Roman and Greek literature remained undimmed by his new enthusiasms. Throughout this period, he translated his favourite poets for his own personal pleasure. Interestingly, the ones which preoccupied him most (or, rather, which he considered worth preserving) are the ones which his great hero Milton drew on most heavily. We therefore find William translating Virgil's *Georgics*, for which he had an immediate and natural sympathy. Virgil, like William, had a rural upbringing and believed passionately in the virtues of a simple country life. His purpose in writing the *Georgics* was to revive a love of the land and agricultural pursuits in an urban age, not just from a sentimental attachment to the beauty of nature but from a deep conviction that country life was inherently more simple, pure and moral. It was the very same theory that would underpin all William's own poetry. Horace, another Roman poet of the first century BC, was far more sophisticated and urbane, but some of his lyrical poetry was exquisite; in his *Odes*, which William translated, he too celebrated the joys of retiring to the tranquillity of his country villa. Horace, unlike Virgil, had just the right tinge of melancholy, inspired by a sense of the brevity and futility of life, which appealed to William.[31] Significantly, neither Virgil nor Horace's poetry appeared on William's Cambridge syllabus, so his translations were part of his 'independent course of study' and reflected his personal preferences. The extent of William's indebtedness to classical literature in forming both his ideas and his poetical style has never been fully appreciated. It also accounts for the charges of paganism and pantheism levelled against him in later years which he struggled to deny, without, it has to be said, much success.

While he was studying poets of other lands and generations, William tells us that it was at this time he began to think that 'I might leave Some monument behind me which pure hearts Should reverence.'[32] The monument he had in mind was a major new poem which occupied much of his time throughout his first and second years at Cambridge. *An Evening Walk*, under which title the poem would be published in January 1793, drew heavily on verses William had written as a schoolboy, but began to take shape as an independent effort during his first summer vacation in Hawkshead. He worked on it at intervals throughout the autumn of 1788, finishing it off the following year, probably during his second summer vacation. The final version, after considerable revision in the interval, was 378 lines long.

'There is not an image in it which I have not observed', William later stated, adding that he even remembered the time and place he noticed most of them. He drew particular attention to two lines describing the effect of fading sunlight on an oak tree. 'This is feebly & imperfectly exprest', he admitted,

> but I recollect distinctly the very spot where this first struck me. It was in the way between Hawkshead and Ambleside, and gave me extreme pleasure. The moment was important in my poetical history; for I date from it my consciousness of the infinite variety of natural appearances which had been unnoticed by the poets of any age or country, so far as I was acquainted with them: and I made a resolution to supply in some degree the deficiency. I could not have been at that time above 14 years of age.[33]

Most of *An Evening Walk* was indeed both feebly and imperfectly expressed, but it did fulfil William's declared intention of describing the 'infinite variety of natural appearances' in rather a clever way. The poet's walk through the Lakes begins in the hazy heat of noon and ends in the light of a clear, bright moon, allowing him to note the progression of subtle effects caused by the changing light on the landscape and its inhabitants. Like *The Vale of Esthwaite*, William's earlier long poem, *An Evening Walk* 'filched' extensively from his favourite melancholic authors, Collins, Thomson, Charlotte Smith and Beattie, but his newer interests also left their mark in a phrase lifted out of Tasso and lengthy borrowings from both Milton and Horace. The poem was typical of the poetic conventions of the day in subject and in style. The allusions to, and quotations from, the work of other poets, which seem like mere plagiarism today, were not then seen as the result of mere lack of originality. Instead, they were regarded as a sort of dazzling display, a game in which the poet could show off his erudition and the reader could test his own skill by identifying them.

For the moment, however, the poem remained unpublished and its author's budding talents went unrecognized outside the small circle of his friends. This was still composed largely of Hawkshead boys but, significantly, nearly all those William called 'my *intimate* associates' at Cambridge were among the academic élite. John Fleming, the 'Friend of my soul!', with whom he had recited verses round Esthwaite Lake, was Fifth Wrangler in 1789; Fletcher Raincock, Fleming's brother, who had accompanied William on the Yewdale Crags escapade, was Second Wrangler in 1790. The following year, which was William's own graduation year, Robert Greenwood, with whom he had sent verses to the *European Magazine*, was Sixth Wrangler. Thomas Middleton, a future literary editor (of the *Country Spectator* and the *British Critic*) and Bishop of Calcutta, belonged to a brilliant circle of undergraduates who graduated in 1790. In William's own year at St John's, however, only one new friend was a high flier: William Terrot was eighth Senior Optime, effectively twenty-ninth in the order of merit in the final examinations. His two closest friends, his cousin John Myers and a jovial Welshman, Robert Jones, had careers as undistinguished as that of their friend. Myers, after a promising start in which he came in the first class in each of his first three examinations, sank to the third class in June 1790 and thereafter, like William, took only the subjects which interested him. Jones had dropped to the third class by the end of his first year and, disliking mathematics as much as William and Myers, opted only for the classical papers in future examinations.[34] Taken as a whole, however, William's group of friends were intelligent, academically inclined and comparatively sedate. They were certainly not idlers, profligates or even political activists. William's intimate association with them confirms that his own interests were still predominantly intellectual.

It is, therefore, a measure of how far William was determined to distance himself from the pursuit of academic honours that he refused to compete even in those areas of university life where he might well have been successful. There were a number of annual prizes for poetry, for instance, which would seem to have been an ideal opportunity to show off his skills and prove to his relatives that he was making some effort. He may have lacked the qualifying mathematical status to attempt either of the two Chancellor's Medals for Latin verses, but he could have entered for any one of the three Browne Medals. These were awarded for the best Greek ode in the style of Sappho, Latin ode in the style of Horace and the best set of Greek and Latin epigrams in the style of the *Anthologia* and Martial. As far as we know, William never even entered the competitions. Even more of a missed opportunity, at least in his Uncle William's eyes, was his blank refusal to write a set of verses when the Master of St John's, Dr Chevallier, died in March 1789.

According to the custom of that time, his body, after being placed in the coffin, was removed to the hall of the college, and the pall, spread over the coffin, was stuck over by copies of verses, English or Latin, the composition of the students of St John's. My uncle seemed mortified when upon inquiry he learnt that none of these verses were from my pen, 'because,' said he, 'it would have been a fair opportunity for distinguishing yourself.' I did not, however, regret that I had been silent on this occasion, as I felt no interest in the deceased person, with whom I had had no intercourse, and whom I had never seen but during his walks in the college grounds.[35]

In William's proud refusal to bow to convention or to seek advancement by judicious flattery, not to mention his haughtily dismissive tone, we get a rare first-hand glimpse of the stubborn and rebellious nature which was the despair of his Cookson relatives.

Uncle William had the opportunity to express his mortification in person. As the summer term of William's second year at Cambridge closed, he decided not to go north immediately, but to pay a visit to Forncett. It cannot have been an entirely comfortable time. He had to explain to his uncle not only his failure to write verses for Dr Chevallier but also his having been unplaced in the June examinations. It was all very well to have 'distinguished [himself] in the Classic' but his future career depended on him distinguishing himself in mathematics too. How long he stayed at Forncett is unclear but Dorothy was doubtless thrilled to show him her room, 'one of the pleasantest in the house', the garden and the beautiful views; they would also have walked together for hours on end, both in the garden and in the surrounding countryside. Most likely, too, Dorothy would have introduced him to her pet robins, which, through regular feeding, she had made so tame that they would hop about the room where she was sitting.[36]

When William left Norfolk, he went back to Hawkshead, where he spent a total of nine weeks this summer, boarding once again with Ann Tyson. This would be his last chance to stay with his 'grey-haired dame', for Ann was now seventy-six years old and had decided that she could no longer take boarders. For the moment, she still had a troop of Wordsworths, Christopher, his cousin Robinson (son of Uncle Richard) and his second cousin Richard (son of Cousin Richard), but after Christmas they would all have to find new lodgings. William's love for her was only increased by absence; he saw her again with 'new delight'.

Her smooth domestic life –
Affectionate without uneasiness –
Her talk, her business, pleased me; and no less
Her clear though shallow stream of piety
That ran on sabbath days a fresher course.
With thoughts unfelt till now I saw her read
Her bible on the Sunday afternoons,
And loved the book when she had dropped asleep
And made of it a pillow for her head.[37]

There seems to have been no visit to Penrith this summer. Perhaps William felt he had already done his duty to the Cooksons by staying with Uncle William but, in any case, he had little incentive to go there now. Not only had Dorothy left, but also Mary Hutchinson. Her grandmother Monkhouse had died on 27 December 1788 and the little Hutchinson household had been disbanded. Aunt Monkhouse felt obliged to return home to look after her father, taking the two youngest girls, Betsy and Joanna, with her. Aunt Gamage went back to her own lodgings in the town and Mary, with her youngest brother, George, left Penrith for good. They went to make their home with their brother, Tom Hutchinson, in County Durham, on the farm at Sockburn-on-Tees, near Darlington, which Tom was now managing for his great-uncle.[38]

Instead, he visited his more congenial Wordsworth relations at Whitehaven and, with little else to distract him, except for adding material to his *An Evening Walk*, he spent the summer making forays further afield, exploring the Yorkshire Dales and the more obscure and wilder parts of the Lakes.[39] Though this summer vacation had pleasures of its own, it was clearly not the heady experience of the previous year. The emotions which had been stirred so deeply by his return to the scenes of his childhood after his first prolonged absence could not be recaptured. On 16 October he returned to Penrith to catch the coach southwards and paid a fleeting duty visit to the Cooksons. 'Your Bro[the]r Wm called here on Friday last in his road to Cambridge', Uncle Christopher wrote to Richard, adding with a degree of asperity which reflects his frustration with his errant nephew, 'he looks very well, I should have been happy if he had favour'd me with more of his Company, but I'm afraid I'm out of his good graces'.[40]

Richard, unlike William, was very much in his uncle's good graces. He not only accepted all his uncle's advice willingly but actually appeared grateful for it. The contrast between his behaviour and that of his brother could not have been more marked. Since the beginning of 1789, Richard had been living in London and working in the offices of his cousin's London attorneys, Parkin & Lambert, at Gray's Inn. He was there specifically to keep an eye on the pursuit of the claim against Sir James Lowther which had, once again, ground to a halt. Uncle Christopher sent him regular admonishing letters, urging him to 'keep close at the Desk and make a good improvement of your time' and recommending that he 'pay attention to Mr Robinson, as much as you conveniently can, as he has it much in his Power to be of service to you in future'.[41] Uncle Christopher was still managing Richard's estate at Sockbridge, though not very competently, since he failed to get the rent raised and then, having agreed to accept a lower figure, lost the tenant. Richard, however, remained humbly grateful. He had just celebrated his twenty-first birthday and was legally of age to enter the estate in his own right, but, while he remained indefinitely in London, he had no one else to whom he could delegate the management. 'Though I have arrived at ye age at wch most young Men take upon themselve[s] ye entire managemt of their Affairs,' he scrawled hastily to his uncle, 'I shall consider myself part[icu]larly obliged to you for your assistance in future, which to this time you have alway[s] to this time [*sic*] been so ready to lend me. I shall always think it my duty to follow yr advice as those who have acted so friendly a part as y[ou] have done.'[42] The expression may have been incoherent, but the sentiment was clear.

William, the ingrate, meanwhile, was blithely compounding his sins at Cambridge by failing even to attempt the December examinations of 1789. The set texts were Joseph Butler's *Analogy of Religion, Natural and Revealed, to the Constitution and Course of Nature*, which was a defence of the Anglican Church on the grounds of its following natural laws, Mounteney's edition of the *Select Orations of Demosthenes*, Newton's *Opticks* and a book on hydrostatics. It seems odd that he should not have been interested in either the Butler or Demosthenes, since the former expressed ideas about nature which William himself would later endorse in his poetry and the latter, with its stirring attacks on the corruption of the Athenian state and its rallying call to truth and justice, should have appealed to his democratic instincts. Nevertheless, William did not offer himself for examination, the only occasion he failed to do so. In mitigation, it should be pointed out that this particular examination was clearly very unpopular; only twenty men in William's year actually entered for any part of it and eighteen, including William, boycotted it altogether.[43]

Now that his brother Richard was settled in London, it was easier and cheaper for William to spend time there. He almost certainly passed most of the Christmas vacation of 1789–90 in town, not least because this was a last opportunity to see their brother John before he set sail on his first voyage for the East India Company. John was now a relatively experienced sailor, with voyages to Barbados, Jamaica and America under his belt. Uncle Richard Wordsworth's second son, another John, had just been appointed captain of one of the largest ships in the Company's service, the *Earl of Abergavenny*, which was about to make its maiden voyage to India and China. Captain Wordsworth immediately offered his cousin a place on board as a midshipman and, since his return from America, John had been busy in London making his preparations, sparing only time for a brief visit, with Richard, to Dorothy at Forncett.[44] They hurried back for the start of the new law term, whereupon Richard discovered that some of the vital papers were at Branthwaite, causing yet another long delay and earning himself a stern rebuke from Uncle Christopher. There was also some sharp criticism of William: 'I am sorry to say that I think your Bro[the]r Wm very extravagant he has had near £300 since he went to Cambridge w[hi]ch I think is a very shameful sum for him to spend, considering his expectations.' It was not a remark calculated to ease tensions between the two. Indeed, the sting of 'considering his expectations' was just the sort of comment to irritate and infuriate his nephew – and, of course, to make him even more determined to pursue his own course. Bearing in mind these undercurrents, Uncle Christopher's remark at the end of the same letter, that their grandmother 'Desires her Love in the warmest manner both to you and John', seems very pointed in its omission of William's name.[45]

William even managed to irritate his sunny-natured brother John during this

Christmas vacation. On one of their walks through the streets of London, William had stopped to purchase a copy of William Lisle Bowles's newly published *Fourteen Sonnets.* Dipping into it as they walked along, he had gradually become more absorbed until, eventually, 'to the great annoyance of my brother, I stopped in a niche of London Bridge to finish the pamphlet'. At the beginning of January 1790, John went to Gravesend to join his ship; the *Earl of Abergavenny* left its moorings on 17 January and sailed for Bombay and Canton on the 30th. It would be eighteen months before John set foot in London again, but he wrote in 'excellent spirits' to his sister before they set sail and again, on 21 February, to Richard, to reassure him that he was 'perfectly contented & happy'.[46] The constant reiteration of these sentiments throughout John's sailing career cannot fail to instil some doubt as to their truth. Was he really happy? Or was he merely putting on a brave face for his loved ones who feared, perhaps rightly, that he was unfitted for the rigours of life at sea?

Dorothy, at Forncett, and Christopher, at Hawkshead, were genuinely content. 'I have every reason my dear Jane to be satisfied with my present situation', Dorothy assured her friend. 'I have two kind Friends with whom I live in that retirement, which before I enjoyed I knew I should relish. I have leisure to read; work; walk and do what I please in short I have every cause to be contented and happy.'[47]

The previous summer Dorothy had set up a little Sunday school to teach the local girls reading, spelling, prayers, hymns and catechisms; those who lived nearby came again every Wednesday and Saturday evening. The intention was that this would form the basis of a permanent school, employing a mistress who would teach the girls spinning and knitting during the week and, with Dorothy's assistance, reading on Sundays. Uncle William Cookson's old friend, William Wilberforce, who was now an MP and had already begun his parliamentary campaign against slavery, spent the Christmas holidays of 1789–90 with them and showed his approval of Dorothy's schemes in the most pragmatic way. He promised her ten guineas a year to distribute 'in what manner I think best to the poor', she proudly informed Jane, adding, 'I believe him to be one of the best of men'. Before he left, he presented her with a couple of Evangelical tracts, *A Practical Treatise on Regeneration* by John Witherspoon and Mrs Trimmer's *Oeconomy of Charity*, and suggested she read the New Testament with Dodderidge's exposition, the book to which he attributed his own conversion. Whether he made these gifts thinking Dorothy was in need of spiritual regeneration or because he wanted to encourage her in her good works, Jane Pollard immediately heard wedding bells for her old friend. Uncertain whether she was simply being teased, Dorothy felt it necessary to reject the suggestion with due solemnity. 'My heart is perfectly disengaged', she purred, 'no man I have seen has appeared to regard me with any degree of partiality; nor has any one gained my affections . . . believe me, *if ever I do* form an attachment it shall not long be a secret from you.' In any case, she added, rather spoiling her protestations of indifference, 'Mr W. would, were he ever to marry, look for a Lady possessed of many more accomplishments than I can boast'. Hastening to prevent similar wild speculations about the seal on her last letter, which had also attracted Jane's attention, she explained, rather more crisply, that it was a gift from 'a Penrith F[riend] Mary Hutchinson'.[48]

Dorothy was full of hope for her youngest brother, Christopher, who was still at school at Hawkshead and showing every sign of having a promising future. He had found new lodgings at Colthouse with a young farmer, John Rainforth, and his wife, where he was to remain until he left school. He was already planning to go to Cambridge but his ambitions, unlike William's, were much more in line with what his relations and guardians expected of him. Like dutiful Richard, he enjoyed a good relationship with Uncle Christopher, even going voluntarily to Penrith when an outbreak of fever caused the closure of the school for a month. His uncles considered him not only an excellent scholar 'for his years' but also, more crucially, 'a most amiable youth'. Dorothy, too, sang his praises in the same way she had once sung those of William. Christopher was 'a very modest gentleman' and 'from my own experience I know that he has the best of tempers'. She also thought him 'rather handsome; at least, there is some thing very interesting in his countenance'.

William, on the other hand, though still her 'Dear Wm.', was no longer immune from criticism. 'I am very anxious about him just now,' Dorothy confided in Jane, 'as he will shortly have to provide for himself: next year he takes his degree; when he will go into orders I do not know, nor how he will employ himself'. In what sounds like an echo of her Uncle William, she added the slightly desperate, 'he must, when he is three and twenty either go into orders or take pupils'.[49] Dorothy had begun to realize that her dreams of replicating her uncle's household idyll in a country parsonage shared with William were fast becoming unrealistic. Christopher might be a safer bet, but he was not her preferred choice of companion among her brothers.

Dorothy had every reason to be worried. William seemed set on a course which was not only at odds with every prospect of future success but even defied common sense. It is true that in June 1790 he made a partial return to the fold, taking (and doing well in) an examination in three of Juvenal's *Satires*, but he again ignored the greater part of the syllabus. Plane and physical astronomy had no attraction but Beausobre's annotated version of St Matthew's Gospel was an essential study for a future clergyman.[50] Worse still, with his crucial university examinations looming, instead of using the long vacation as an opportunity to catch up on his studies, formal or otherwise, he decided to take a holiday abroad.

It was, as William later boasted rather proudly in *The Prelude*, a deliberate act of defiance: 'An open slight Of college cares and study was the scheme'. Though he declared that it was not 'entertained without concern for those To whom my worldly interests were dear', at the time he took great care to ensure that none of his family knew about it. Not even Dorothy was allowed to share the secret, possibly because he feared she might confide it to Uncle William, but more probably because he knew she would give way to that 'feverish dread of error and mishap' which he found so irritating and claustrophobic. It was perhaps as well that he did not, for she shared in the general disapproval: 'had he acquainted me with his scheme before its execution I should (as many of his other friends did) have looked upon it as mad and impracticable.'[51]

The grand plan was that William, together with his college friend Robert Jones, would make a pedestrian tour of the Alps. This would be a herculean feat, for the journey would take them some 3,000 miles in less than three months. As if this was not a sufficient challenge in itself, the route presented enormous dangers. They would not only be walking and climbing some of the most inaccessible and perilous mountains in Europe but the easiest part of their journey, in terms of terrain, lay through France, a country which was still in considerable turmoil after a revolution not yet a year old. The French royal family were virtual prisoners in the Tuileries, the volatile citizens' army, which made up the national militia, paraded daily in Paris and at least four provinces were in a state of virtual anarchy due to price-fixing of bread and meat. Massive preparations were taking place throughout the entire country to celebrate the first anniversary of the Fall of the Bastille; 14 July 1790 had been declared a national holiday, the *Fête de la Fédération*, on which every French man and woman, from the king downwards, was to swear an oath of allegiance to the new constitution. Though these ceremonies were to take place in towns and villages throughout France, thousands of provincial delegates were travelling to Paris to witness the king taking his oath. In the first flush of enthusiasm for the dramatic birth of a democratic nation, large numbers of English men and women flocked to see these events for themselves and to take part in what they clearly recognized as history in the making.[52] William and Jones could hardly have chosen a more exciting time to travel to France.

But Switzerland, not France, was their destination. The object of their tour was to walk the Alps in search of the sublime and beautiful landscapes celebrated by the artists, poets and writers of the romantic movement, not to observe or participate in the political festivities of a people newly released from arbitrary rule. Their route was determined by authorities on the picturesque, most notably Thomas Gray and William Coxe,[53] and it would take them in a fairly direct line down the eastern side of France from Calais to Lyons, where they would branch off eastwards into the French Alps to see the monastery of the Grande Chartreuse and Mont Blanc, before entering Switzerland and reaching the Italian Lakes, which they would explore exhaustively.

Foolhardy though the scheme seemed, William was not so reckless as to attempt it alone. In choosing Robert Jones as his companion, he could not have found a more congenial fellow traveller. Jones was, like William, the second son of an attorney and destined for the Church. A few months older than William, he had entered St John's as a pensioner in June 1787 but academically was classed in the same year. His family home, Plas-yn-Llan, was at Llangynhafal, in Denbighshire, and the two young men shared a mutual passion for poetry, mountains and walking, which explains not only their friendship but also their plan for the pedestrian tour. What is perhaps more extraordinary is the fact that their friendship survived the tour. Some years later, William wrote a poem celebrating his friend's eccentricities:

I marvel how Nature could ever find space
For so many strange contrasts in one human face; . . .

This picture from nature may seem to depart,
Yet the Man would at once run away with your heart;
And I for five centuries right gladly would be
Such an odd, such a kind happy creature as he.

Perhaps fortunately for his friend, William did not identify the subject of his portrayal, but, in January 1793, when he published the poem, *Descriptive Sketches*, which was the result of the tour, he prefixed it with a touching public dedication to Jones.

In inscribing this little work to you, I consult my heart. You know well how great is the difference between two companions lolling in a post-chaise, and two travellers plodding slowly along the road, side by side, each with his little knapsack of necessaries on his shoulders. How much more of heart between the two latter!

The intrepid pair left Cambridge early in July 1790; they had about £20 each and were equipped with identical lightweight coats (for ease of walking), oak staffs and small bundles of 'needments' which, to the amusement of observers abroad, they carried, peasant-fashion, on their heads. They hurried through London, deliberately avoiding any contact with Richard Wordsworth, because they knew he would disapprove of their wild scheme. On 12 July they spent the night at Dover, then, the following day, they set sail for France.[54]

They arrived in Calais on the eve of the *Fête de la Fédération.* Most Englishmen would have made the effort to arrive earlier so that they could get to Paris for this unique occasion. The fact that William and Jones failed to do so speaks volumes for their lack of interest in contemporary politics. Indeed, though their route skirted right round the eastern edges of Paris, they were not tempted to make even the briefest of detours. They could not ignore the celebrations in Calais, however, for at eleven-thirty on the morning of 14 July, all the bells in the town rang out, guns were fired and, under the guidance of the mayor, in a public ceremony that was repeated at the same time throughout the kingdom, the populace took the oath of allegiance. William and Jones were undeniably present and actually deferred starting out on the first leg of their pedestrian tour till the afternoon so that they could see it,[55] but, astonishingly, this great exhibition failed to stir William's imagination. He made no mention of it in his letters home or in the *Descriptive Sketches.* Even when he came to write *The Prelude*, which contains some of the most famous and enduring images of revolutionary France ever written in English, his attitude seems remarkably subdued and the references almost incidental, as though they had been put in as an afterthought. This is easily explained by the fact that, at the time, he was simply not interested. Poetry, not politics, was his passion. 'I looked upon these things', he wrote apologetically in *The Prelude*,

As from a distance (heard, and saw, and felt,
Was touched, but with no intimate concern)

Writing in 1804, however, he had a different perspective. He was then highly politicized, having passed through a period of great enthusiasm for the French Revolution, followed by revulsion at its excesses and perverted aims. And, with the advantage of hindsight, he realized the importance of the events he had witnessed. He had first set foot on French soil at a time 'when Europe was rejoiced' and 'France standing on the top of golden hours'.

It was our lot
To land at Calais on the very eve
Of that great federal day; and there we saw,
In a mean city and among a few,
How bright a face is worn when joy of one
Is joy of tens of millions. Southward thence
We took our way, direct through hamlets, towns,
Gaudy with relics of that festival,
Flowers left to wither on triumphal arcs,
And window-garlands . . . .
Among sequestered villages we walked
And found benevolence and blessedness
Spread like a fragrance everywhere, like spring
That leaves no corner of the land untouched.[56]

These lines bear the unmistakable marks of having been written many years after the events they describe; beautiful though they may be, they lack immediacy, intimacy or any sense of personal involvement. Which, of course, was exactly how he felt in 1790.

In *The Prelude*, William noted, again merely in passing, that everywhere on their journey they saw dances of liberty, held in the open air to celebrate the *Fête de la Fédération* and lasting far into the night. When they joined a boat at Chalon to travel down the Saône, they found it full of southern delegates returning from the festivities in Paris.

In this blithe company
We landed, took with them our evening meal,
Guests welcome almost as the angels were
To Abraham of old. The supper done,
With flowing cups elate and happy thoughts
We rose at signal given, and formed a ring
And hand in hand danced round and round the board.
All hearts were open, every tongue was loud

With amity and glee. We bore a name
Honoured in France, the name of Englishmen,
And hospitably did they give us hail
As their forerunners in a glorious course –
And round and round the board they danced again!

What is particularly interesting about these impressions of France in 1790 is that they were only to emerge as distinct and important in retrospect. At the time, they did not even merit notice. Writing to his sister from Switzerland in September 1790, while he was still on his walking tour, William's only reflection on the French was that he found them much less imposing than the Swiss but their politeness, even in the lowest ranks of society, so engaging that he could only attribute it to real benevolence.

During the time which was near a month which we were in France, we had not once to complain of the smallest deficiency in civility in any person, much less of any positive rudeness. We had also perpetual occasion to observe that chearfulness and sprightliness for which the French have always been remarkable. But I must remind you that we crossed it at the time when the whole nation was mad with joy, in consequence of the revolution. It was a most interesting period to be in France, and we had many delightful scenes where the interest of the picture was owing solely to this cause.[57]

The flatness of this description is startling: it makes even the *Prelude* version seem comparatively warm and vivacious. It is even more startling and revelatory when laid side by side with other parts of the same letter describing the landscapes of Switzerland and the Italian Lakes. 'My Spirits have been kept in a perpetual hurry of delight by the almost uninterrupted succession of sublime and beautiful objects which have passed before my eyes during the course of the last month,' he wrote. Despite his determination to keep his description of their route to an absolute minimum, so as not to exhaust his supply of paper, he found it impossible to check his enthusiasm or his pen. Significantly, it was one of the lakes, Como, which sparked a digression as unstoppable as it was characteristically Wordsworthian. Having explained that the banks of many of the Italian and Swiss lakes are too steep to take roads, he described walking for thirty miles along a lakeside footpath between two villages.

We entered upon this path about noon, and owing to the steepness of the banks, were soon unmolested by the sun, which illuminated the woods rocks and villages of the opposite shore. The lake is narrow and the shadows of the mountains were early thrown across it. It was beautiful to watch them travelling up the sides of the hills for several hours, to remark one half of a village covered with shade, and the other bright with the strongest sunshine. It was with regret that we passed every turn of this charming path, where every new picture was purchased by the loss of another which we would never have been tired of gazing at.

The shores of the lake consist of steeps covered with large sweeping woods of chestnut spotted with villages, some clinging from the summits of the advancing rocks, and others hiding themselves within their recesses. Nor was the surface of the lake less interesting than its shores; part of it glowing with the richest green and gold the reflexion of the illuminated woods and part shaded with a soft blue tint. The picture was still further diversified by the number of sails which stole lazily by us, as we paused in the woods above them. After all this we had the moon. It was impossible not to contrast that repose that complacency of Spirit, produced by these lovely scenes, with the sensations I had experienced two or three days before, in passing the Alps. At the lake of Como my mind ran thro a thousand dreams of happiness which might be enjoyed upon its banks, if heightened by conversation and the exercise of the social affections.

Even at the age of twenty, William instinctively recognized that his own happiness was to be found in the solitude of a lakeland landscape, with the all-important proviso that his retreat should not be a hermitage. His delight was not confined to the immediate impressions preserved in this letter but led him to include a long and lyrical description of the same scene two years later in *Descriptive Sketches*, and, even when writing *The Prelude* many years later, he could still be seduced from his narrative by memories of the beauty of Como.[58]

The tour passed in a kaleidoscopic whirl of images: the 'awful solitude' of La Grande Chartreuse, where they spent the night in the monastery, which had not yet been desecrated by the Revolutionaries; the glaciers of the 'wondrous' vale of Chamonix, where 'winter like a tamèd lion walks, Descending from the mountain to make sport Among the cottages by beds of flowers'; most memorable of all, crossing the Alps by the Simplon Pass. In attempting to describe this to Dorothy a few weeks later in a letter from Switzerland, William was literally rendered wordless. 'The impressions of three hours of our walk among the Alps will never be effaced' was all he could say.

It would take him nearly fifteen years to find the words because, in 1790, he was still bound hand and foot by the metaphorical shackles of picturesque vocabulary. His is a textbook case of the dangers of using guidebooks: he saw what they saw and as they saw it. As he struggled to articulate his impressions for Dorothy, he inevitably fell back on the romantic conventions of his guides. 'Among the more awful scenes of the Alps,' he wrote, 'I had not a thought of man, or a single created being; my whole soul was turned to him who produced the terrible majesty before me.' While this was probably a genuine reaction, it was also a parroting of Thomas Gray's famous *dictum* on the Alps: 'Not a precipice, not a torrent, not a cliff, but is pregnant with religion and poetry. There are certain scenes that would awe an atheist into belief without the help of other argument.'[59]

As the mature poet of *The Prelude*, however, William could express what are still recognizably the same sentiments in a profoundly new and unique way: he had found his own voice because he had released his imagination and learned to invest the scene with his own personal experience. Crossing the Alps thus became the poetic climax of the sixth book of *The Prelude*, because it was a climactic moment, spiritually and emotionally, for William.

This was how he described it. He and Jones had joined a guided party crossing the Simplon but, because they lingered too long over their lunch, were accidentally left behind. In attempting to follow, they took the wrong path, veering off up the mountainside instead of following the stony bed of the stream. They thought something was wrong when they did not overtake the rest of their party, but it was not until they met a peasant who pointed out the right route that the terrible realization dawned. The moment which they had anticipated so eagerly – which was indeed the main reason for the tour – had passed unnoticed. They had crossed the Alps without knowing it.

Thoroughly disappointed, they were forced to retrace their steps down the mountain to regain their road, which, for several hours, lay through a narrow chasm, the Ravine of Gondo.

> The immeasurable height
> Of woods decaying, never to be decayed,
> The stationary blasts of waterfalls,
> And everywhere along the hollow rent
> Winds thwarting winds, bewildered and forlorn,
> The torrents shooting from the clear blue sky,
> The rocks that muttered close upon our ears,
> Black drizzling crags that spoke by the wayside
> As if a voice were in them, the sick sight
> And giddy prospect of the raving stream,
> The unfettered clouds and region of the heavens,
> Tumult and peace, the darkness and the light –
> Were all like workings of one mind, the features
> Of the same face, blossoms upon one tree,
> Characters of the great apocalypse,
> The types and symbols of eternity,
> Of first, and last, and midst, and without end.

Such an authoritative and resonant description was beyond the powers of the twenty-year-old boy walking the Alps and assailed on every side by overpowering images of grandeur. Even then, however, he was acutely aware that this whole experience would be of immense importance to him and he consciously tried to fix it in his memory. 'Ten thousand times in the course of this tour have I regretted the inability of my memory to retain a more strong impression of the beautiful forms before me,' he wrote wistfully to Dorothy,

> and again and again in quitting a fortunate station have I returned to it with the most eager avidity, with the hope of bearing away a more lively picture. At this moment when many of

these landscapes are floating before my mind, I feel a high [enjoyment] in reflecting that perhaps scarce a day of my life will pass [in] which I shall not derive some happiness from these images.[60]

These were prophetic words. Not only would he return to these scenes in his imagination and his poetry for years to come but, thirty years later, in 1820, he would return in person to retrace his route and to attempt to re-create the experience. It is a measure of how important Jones's role was in these memories that William actually invited his old friend to accompany him. Jones was still the same old poetry-loving genial Welshman he had always been, but he was also fat, unfit and a parson, so he regretfully declined. As a concession to age and the large family entourage, the second tour was made in a carriage, but, conscious of the almost ritualistic significance of the moment, William deliberately chose to take the same road he had trodden before and crossed the Alps on foot.[61]

Having dedicated two-thirds of their three-month tour to exploring Switzerland, William and Jones were now forced to draw it to a close. No doubt they were running out of money, though William had boasted to Dorothy that, between 14 July and 6 September, they had spent only £12 between them. More importantly, the new term at Cambridge would begin during the second week of October and they would have to get back to fulfil their residency requirements if they were to take their degrees. In a final gesture of bravado, they decided to buy a boat and sail down the Rhine from Basel to Cologne. 'The confidence of Youth [was] our only Art', William would later recall, 'And Hope gay Pilot of the bold design.' Youth and Hope were fortunately sufficient to keep them from harm and they arrived safely in Cologne, recovered their funds by selling the boat and set off on foot again to complete their journey home through Brabant.[62]

The tour of 1790 had taken in large areas of France, northern Italy, Switzerland, Germany and what is now Belgium. The two travellers had walked alongside Lakes Geneva, Maggiore, Como, Lucerne, Zurich and Constance, sailed down the Saône and up the Rhine. They had enjoyed uniform good health and become so inured to walking that they seemed incapable of fatigue; it was William's proud boast that they had several times walked thirteen leagues (almost forty miles) over the most mountainous parts of Switzerland without any more weariness than if they had been walking for an hour in a grove at Cambridge. This was undoubtedly an exaggeration, but thirty years later Robert Jones would recall, 'We were early risers in 1790 and generally walked 12 or 15 miles before breakfast and after feasting on the morning Landscape how we afterwards feasted on our Dejeuner of whatever the house might afford!'[63]

There had been some disappointments in addition to failing to recognize that they had crossed the Alps. Neither the summit of Mont Blanc nor the famed Falls of Schaffhausen lived up to its reputation as the height of sublimity, but William was the first to admit that he had been unrealistic in his expectations. Like all travellers, they had suffered some misadventures, or 'little disasters' as William called them. They had been misled by the chimes of the village clock at Gravedona into rising in the middle of the night, instead of at dawn, and so had to spend a miserable night in the open, stung by insects and fearful of the unfamiliar noises emanating from the woods. They had become separated and lost their way in a torrential downpour during one of those terrifyingly dramatic thunderstorms for which the Italian Lakes are notorious. William had almost been swept away when he crossed a rapidly rising river to view the magnificent waterfall at the head of the valley of Lauterbrunnen. Far from depressing them, these mishaps had simply added to the pair's resolution and spirits.[64] They had survived to tell the tale.

And what a tale it was! William could hardly contain his glee at the thought of returning to Cambridge and 'exulting over those of my friends who threathned [*sic*] us with such an accumulation of difficulties as must undoubtedly render it impossible for us to perform the tour.' His spirits were so high, he even fondly imagined that, on his return to England, he would be welcomed with open arms at Forncett – even though it meant deferring his return to university till 10 November, a month after term had officially begun (this in his final term before his degree examinations). 'You will remember me affectionately to my Uncle and Aunt', he blithely informed Dorothy, adding a hope so forlorn it could not have convinced even himself: '– as he was acquainted with my having given up all thoughts of a fellowship, he may perhaps not be so much displeased at this journey. I should be sorry if I have offended him by it.'

If William had persuaded himself that this was the case, he was soon to be disillusioned. His plea to visit Forncett received short shrift and, by the middle of October, he was back in Cambridge. The heady excitements of his continental tour were over. He had triumphantly fulfilled his declared intention of offering 'An open slight Of college cares and study'.[65] Now he would have to face the consequence.

4. *A Vital Interest*

The first thing William had to do on his return to Cambridge in October 1790 was to sort out his financial affairs. Uncle Richard, whatever he may have thought of his errant nephew, still sent him his autumn remittance on 19 October; at only £30, however, instead of the usual £35, it is tempting to see the reduction as a practical expression of disapproval. Perhaps that was why, when it came to paying five guineas he owed for his wine bills, William turned instead to his brother Richard in London.[1] There would be no point in appealing to the generosity of his guardians for such an extravagance.

What use William made of this, his last full term at university, is unrecorded. The liberating and mind-expanding experiences of his pedestrian tour can only have added to his sense of disillusionment with all the petty concerns of Cambridge. There were no college examinations in December, as the undergraduates were supposed to be studying for their final university examinations. These would be held in the Senate House at the beginning of January. It was perhaps with this in mind that Uncle William revoked his ban on his nephew visiting Forncett. At least if William spent the Christmas vacation there, his family could be sure he had not concocted another madcap scheme and gone gallivanting off to London or the Continent again. It was also an opportunity to exert some family pressure and ensure that he did some work.

To Dorothy's great joy, therefore, William was invited to Forncett for the vacation. For the first time since their childhood in Cockermouth, they would spend her birthday, Christmas Day, together. If Uncle William did insist on some work from his nephew, he had also the sense to allow William and Dorothy to spend some leisure time alone. The weather was 'uncommonly mild', according to Dorothy; 'we used to walk every morning about two hours, and every evening we went into the garden at four or half past four and used to pace backwards and forwards 'till six'. As they wandered along the gravel path, arm in arm, in the gloom of the winter evenings, they had 'long, long conversations', which were only interrupted by the unwelcome summons of the tea-bell. They talked not just about the past and William's travels on the Continent, but also about the future. Whatever doubts William may have had about the direction his life would take, Dorothy had still only that one object before her eyes: to live with him in a little cottage in the country, with a neatly furnished parlour, and a garden filled with roses and honeysuckle. It was to be '*our own*', but not exclusively, for even while building these cottages in the air, her happiness would only be complete if Jane Pollard, 'my earliest female Friend', could also live with them. Two and a half years later, having not seen William in the interval and with her cottage no nearer in reality than it had ever been, Dorothy would dwell forlornly on this visit and the happiness it had brought her: 'he is so amiable, so good, so fond of his Sister! Oh Jane the last time we were together he won my Affect[ion] to a Degree which I cannot describe.' Unable to stem her panegyric, she added,

> I am willing to allow that half the virtues with which I fancy him endowed are the creation of my Love, but surely I may be excused! he was never tired of comforting his sister, he never left her in anger, he always met her with joy, he preferred her society to every other pleasure, or rather when we were so happy as to be within each other's reach he had no pleasure when we were compelled to be divided.[2]

These seem curiously negative attributes to have been so valued by Dorothy; viewed dispassionately, they would seem to be little more than acts of common politeness. The fact that she read so much into her brother's patience and kindness towards her is an indication of her own depth of insecurity and that desperate longing for affection which had been so striking a part of her character since at least her residence in Penrith. It says much for William, as a man and as a brother, that he responded in such a kindly manner to her emotional dependency, which was a burden and a responsibility he would never lay aside. The shrewdness of Uncle William's forbearance in allowing the pair time alone together is immediately apparent. If his nephew could not be compelled by ambition or censure to strive for university success, perhaps the 'social affections' might do the trick.

William returned to Cambridge in time to sit his Senate House examinations on 17 January. Defiant and insouciant to the end, he apparently chose to spend the previous week reading a novel. Like most of William's acts of youthful rebellion, however, it was not all it seemed. The novel was Samuel Richardson's *Clarissa Harlowe*, an overpoweringly dull exposition of 'the Distresses that may attend Misconduct both of Parents and Children in relation to Marriage', in seven ponderous volumes. It says little for the quality of the Cambridge system at this time that William passed his examination and, on 21 January 1791, was awarded the degree of Bachelor of Arts. One hundred and forty undergraduates sat the examination and William, with his friend Robert Jones and his cousin John Myers, was among the *hoi polloi*, the seventy men who were unplaced in the order of merit and did not proceed to honours. So much for his proud boast on going up to Cambridge that he would be 'Senior Wrangler or nothing'. As his cousin Mary Myers remarked acidly, 'And he *was* nothing – at Cambridge'.[3]

Much has been made of the financial cost of William's Cambridge education, not least because, in retrospect, it seems to have been unproductive. After all, it did not set him on the road to a successful establishment career, as his family had so fondly hoped when he went there. Uncle Christopher's complaints about his extravagance seem entirely justified when set beside William's own portrayal of himself in *The Prelude* as idle and careless. As we have seen, however, it is clear from other sources that *The Prelude* greatly exaggerates William's indolence at Cambridge; and there can be no doubt that his experiences (including the extracurricular ones of the vacations), his reading and friendships, laid the ground for much of his own future success.

Just how extravagant was he? When Uncle Richard died in 1794, his widow claimed that the young Wordsworths owed his estate £430, 'the greater part of which was money advanced for my education', as William confessed. It was a sum which no one disputed, least of all William himself, and, as a round figure, it is borne out by the Administrators' accounts. It is usually forgotten that John Wordsworth's personal estate was still producing around £535 a year and Sockbridge, which now belonged to William's brother Richard, a minimum of £70 annually. Had there been no other costs, the young Wordsworths could each have counted on receiving an income of some £100, even before payment of the Lowther debt. And it was the Lowther debt that was the problem. The Earl of Lonsdale was still refusing to pay and the cost of legal proceedings and counter-legal proceedings was mounting. What is more, as the Administrators prepared for the case to come to the Carlisle Assizes in August 1791, the charges on the estate for preparing the documents, serving subpoenas and paying the expenses of witnesses spiralled. From a position where the estate had actually been in credit, it began the slide very gradually into debt.[4] The cost of William's university education therefore became a much more contentious issue.

From all the available evidence, it would seem that William was spending just under £100 a year, the maximum he could claim from his father's estate. This was a huge amount of money, especially at a time when (as no doubt all sizars were regularly reminded by those paying for their education) a sizar's annual college expenses were officially reckoned to be only £15, excluding tuition fees. This was true, up to a point. Patrick Brontë, father of the famous novelists, who from 1802 to 1806 was also a sizar at St John's, was a model example. His college bills amounted to between £12 and £15 a year. 'He came over from [Ireland], with 10£ in his pocket,' wrote Henry Kirke White, an admiring fellow sizar, to his mother, 'and has no friends, or any income or emolument whatever, except what he receives for his Sizarship; yet he does support himself, and that, too, very genteelly.' The difference between Patrick Brontë and William Wordsworth was that Patrick came from a humble Irish tenant-farming background, was used to poverty, had no prospect of any income at all, except what he could earn by his own efforts, and, as an Evangelical, was personally committed to entering the Church. He was also much older (twenty-five to William's seventeen on entering college) and more self-disciplined. Nevertheless, even Patrick could not survive on the income from his sizarship and his exhibitions. Less than eighteen months after entering college, he had to appeal for assistance, and was given £20 a year by no less a person than the ubiquitous William Wilberforce.[5]

John Jebb, who spent more than twenty years in Cambridge academic circles, was more realistic in assessing a sizar's expenses in 1775 at between £40 and £60 a year, without scholarships and exhibitions. William had incurred considerable expenses, not just in pursuing his social life but also in private tuition. Lessons with Isola cannot have been cheap. Henry Kirke White's private tuition in basic mathematics over the four months of the summer vacation of 1806 cost a minimum of twelve or fifteen guineas, and William cannot have expected to pay any less for the more esoteric subjects of Italian and Spanish.[6]

Comparisons with other contemporaries also suggest that William's expenditure was not immoderate. Samuel Taylor Coleridge, who went up to Jesus College in 1791, managed to find himself £150 in debt after only two years at the university, even though he held two college awards worth £70 annually and a scholarship from Christ's Hospital. Raisley Calvert's precipitous departure from Magdalene in February 1793 was prompted in part by his shock at the cost of living at Cambridge: 'I know of no satisfaction or enjoyment you can have at Cambridge for the Money custom calls upon you to throw away there,' he told his brother, adding that he knew one man at Cambridge who was generally considered careful with his money, yet could not live for less than £160 a year.[7] In the light of such examples, which were by no means unusual, William's own expenditure seems quite frugal and does not justify the opprobrium sometimes heaped upon him.

William's great dilemma now was what to do with himself. He no longer had any justification for staying in Cambridge, which was notoriously expensive, but he had no idea what he wanted to do with his life. Or rather, he knew what he did *not* want, which was to enter either the Church, as his friends Robert Jones, John Fleming, William Penny, Thomas Gawthrop, Robert Greenwood and William Terrot would do, or go into the law, like John Myers and Fletcher Raincock.[8] In the time-honoured fashion of undecided graduates everywhere, he decided to play for time. He allowed his family to assume that he would go into the Church – he may even have believed this himself. As he could not be ordained until he was twenty-three, this would give him two more years of freedom. In the normal course of things, he should have sought a fellowship, which would have provided him with an annual income for up to ten years to tide him over the transition. Robert Jones, for instance, was lucky in securing a Welsh fellowship, for which there were far fewer contenders than the highly sought after northern ones. He was also lucky in being able to return after graduation to his wealthy family home in Denbighshire, where he could comfortably sit out the intervening period until his ordination.

William had no such options. He had no wish to return to his grandmother or Uncle Christopher at Penrith; his 'old dame', Ann Tyson, could no longer provide him with a home at Hawkshead; and Forncett, where he might have been welcomed for the sake of his sister, would have stifled him. He chose therefore to go to London.

Quite what he intended to do there is not clear. Possibly, like Raisley Calvert, he simply thought he could live more to his satisfaction 'in every respect' in London than in Cambridge and at half the cost. This was not immediately apparent, however, as on 28 January 1791 Uncle Richard had to send him £60, almost double the usual remittance.[9] Coming a mere seven days after William had received his degree, this unexpected generosity might have seemed like a pat on the back or, more likely, an expression of relief that he had actually got his BA. (Neither Coleridge nor Southey did.) More pragmatically, it was intended to pay off all his Cambridge debts before he left for London.

For the next four months, William apparently lived quietly in London. The account he gives in *The Prelude* is a composite picture of different visits made over the next twelve years, and it is impossible to disentangle what actually belongs to this period. Many of the most striking incidents and events can be dated with certainty to later visits, particularly that of 1802, when Charles Lamb accompanied him and Dorothy. Lamb was also indirectly responsible for one of the liveliest passages, which seems to capture perfectly the bewildered first impressions of a country visitor:

> the Babel din;
> The endless stream of men, and moving things . . .
> The wealth, the bustle and the eagerness,
> The glittering chariots with their pampered steeds,
> Stalls, barrows, porters; midway in the street
> The scavenger, who begs with hat in hand;
> The labouring hackney-coaches, the rash speed
> Of coaches travelling far whirled on with horn
> Loud blowing . . .
> Shop after shop, with symbols, blazoned names,
> And all the tradesman's honours overhead –

Even this description is a paraphrase of a letter Lamb wrote to William in 1801, defending his love of city life against 'the mountaineers', as he called his poetical friends in the Lakes.[10]

If *The Prelude* is confusing, the only surviving letter William wrote at this period is downright mysterious. He was writing to William Mathews, a friend from Pembroke College, who had graduated at the same time as himself but, rather more responsibly, had taken up a temporary teaching post in Leicestershire before entering the law as a profession. On 17 June 1791 William apologized for neglecting to write for so long; two months previously, he explained, he had taken up his pen with the intention of beginning a letter but had been interrupted. He was then in London and too busy to write, but, just as he offered no explanation of who or what had interrupted him, so he offered only the most enigmatic description of his preoccupations. 'I quitted London about three weeks ago,' was the only fact he now volunteered,

where my time passed in a strange manner; sometimes whirled about by the vortex of its *strenua inertia*, and sometimes thrown by the eddy into a corner of the stream, where I lay in almost motionless indolence. Think not however that I had not many very pleasant hours; a man must be unfortunate indeed who resides four months in Town without some of his time being disposed of in such a manner, as he would forget with reluctance.

The obscurity of William's meaning in this passage has led to great speculation as to what he was doing and what he was trying to hide. The general consensus appears to be that this spring of 1791 was the period of his initiation into radical politics.[11] It was certainly a time when it was difficult to escape the radical agenda, which had been given new impetus in Britain by the successful, and hitherto comparatively peaceful, French Revolution. The London Revolution Society and the Society for Constitutional Information were both flourishing and eloquent in their demands for parliamentary reform and religious equality. The French Revolution had also provoked a war of words in pamphlet form. Edmund Burke's famously prescient denunciation of the inevitable bloody consequences of the fall of the Bastille, *Reflections on the Revolution in France*, had been published in 1790. It was answered in March 1791 (while William was in London) by Thomas Paine's equally passionate defence, *The Rights of Man*, and by James Mackintosh's *Vindiciae Gallicae*. As William himself would be in France before the end of the year, it is tempting to see his decision to go there as the result of his being drawn into the vortex of radical politics during the four months he spent in London. Attractive though this idea may seem, there is little evidence to support it. The rather more boring conclusion appears far more likely: that he spent the time as a tourist, visiting the sights and spending time with family and friends there. His mysterious letter to Mathews therefore becomes merely an attempt to avoid seeming provincial to his friend, who was himself the son of a London bookseller, rather than a deliberate covering up of more sinister activities.

The only indisputable fact is that William, possibly in the company of his brother Richard, paid a visit to 'Aunt' Threlkeld. Now in her mid-forties and having seen all her young charges safely through to adulthood and independence, Elizabeth had finally felt free to accept William Rawson, a Halifax mill-owner and banker. They married at Halifax Parish Church on 7 March 1791 and, as part of the customary round of bridal visits, travelled down to London. Dorothy, agog for details of this unexpected change in the fortunes of her 'aunt' (and it was a major change, as the Rawsons were among the wealthiest and most influential families in Halifax), longed to join the party in London, but it was not possible. Instead, she had to rely on second-hand accounts from Jane Pollard, her 'aunt' and, presumably, her brothers.[12]

Where William's meeting, or meetings, with the new Mrs Rawson took place is not known. One can guess, however, that it was Mrs Rawson who introduced William to Samuel Nicholson of Cateaton Street, Holborn. Nicholson was a haberdashery wholesaler who had, for many years, been the main supplier of her shop in Halifax. Like her, he was a Unitarian, but, more importantly for William, he was also a radical. He had been an early member of the Society for Constitutional Information, which campaigned for annual parliaments, full male suffrage and political rights for dissenters. He may not have been so active by 1791, when much of the middle-class dissenting support for reform had dropped away in the wake of repeated failures to persuade Parliament to revoke the Test Acts, which excluded them from the universities and positions of authority.[13] Nevertheless, he still had connections with radical and dissenting circles which were to become important to William in the future. Possibly during this spring of 1791, or, more likely, in 1793–4, Nicholson took pity on William 'at a time when I had not many acquaintances in London, [and he] used often to invite me to dine with him on Sundays'. On several of these occasions, William took the opportunity to go with his host to the famous dissenting house in Old Jewry to hear 'an able & eloquent man' preach. This was Joseph Fawcett, hailed by William Godwin as 'the first man [he] had ever known of great originality in thinking', and by William Hazlitt as 'one of the most enthusiastic admirers of the French Revolution'. Our William, however, was not particularly impressed by Fawcett's preaching. 'He published a Poem on War, [*The Art of War*, 1795] w[hic]h had a good deal of merit & made me think more about him than I should otherwise have done', he told Isabella Fenwick many years later. He also informed her that, in creating the disillusioned and misogynistic figure of the Solitary in *The Excursion*, published in 1816, he had drawn on Fawcett as one of his main models. This was well into the future, however, and what William then knew of Fawcett was influenced chiefly by information acquired in the intervening years from their mutual friend, Hazlitt. William's own personal knowledge of the man was confined to being a member of his congregation on several occasions; if he attended his sermons in 1791, his motive was probably nothing more than mere curiosity about the Unitarian faith, in which his sister had been brought up by their 'aunt'.[14]

It is impossible to compile a chronology or an itinerary for William at this period. We do not even know where he lived. He may have shared lodgings with his brother Richard, but he implies in *The Prelude* that he lived alone.[15] This seems more likely, for Richard was in the throes of preparing for the next crucial court battle with Lonsdale and would not have appreciated playing host to an idle younger brother. If *The Prelude* is to be believed, William spent most of his four months wandering round the capital, like any typical provincial tourist. He visited the great historic and national monuments, St Paul's Cathedral, the Tower, Westminster Abbey and Guildhall. He walked in London's celebrated pleasure gardens at Vauxhall, in Lambeth, and Ranelagh, in Chelsea, where there were fireworks, balls and masquerades. He went to the theatre, a lifelong passion, returning repeatedly to Sadler's Wells to watch with amusement, and occasional fits of irritation, the pantomime, burlesque and circus acts that were its staple fare. He probably attended one of the last performances at the old theatre in Drury Lane, which Richard Brinsley Sheridan had decided to close on 4 June, transferring the company and its star, Dora Jordan, to the Haymarket, while he rebuilt Drury Lane on a grand scale. Mrs Jordan was famous for her fine legs, which she displayed at every opportunity by playing gender-swapping roles, from Shakespeare to modern farce. She was about to become infamous for leaving her then partner, Richard Ford, son of the co-owner of Drury Lane and father of her three children, in favour of the Duke of Clarence. Both she and Ford would play curious cameo roles in William's later history.[16]

Much of the time, William claimed in *The Prelude*, he simply spent wandering the streets, just observing the crowds in what was, even then, a remarkably cosmopolitan city. He was, he said,

> At ease from all ambition personal,
> Frugal as there was need, and though self willed,
> Yet temperate and reserved, and wholly free
> From dangerous passions.

The most 'dangerous passions' of that time were those of radical politics, which were impossible to ignore. He read, 'eagerly Sometimes, the master pamphlets of the day', but he lacked that 'vital interest' which would later transform his political perceptions and commitment. He also went to listen to parliamentary debates. There he saw and heard the Earl of Lonsdale's former protégé, William Pitt the Younger, who had been Prime Minister since 1783. As Member of Parliament for Cambridge, Pitt was already a familiar figure to William, who had often seen him in the town. There were, however, many 'senators', as William deliberately called them, in imitation of the orators of the classical world, who were known to him by name alone. He was thrilled to see peers, such as Bedford, Gloucester and Salisbury, not just because of what they were saying, but because they were the living incarnations of lineages whose exploits were celebrated by Shakespeare.[17] He listened avidly to the flesh-and-blood orators of his own time: Edmund Burke, still a lone voice crying out, like Cassandra, against the 'radical and intrinsic' evils of the French Revolution which must inevitably lead to bloodshed; Charles James Fox, stout defender of the new French constitution as 'the most stupendous and glorious edifice of liberty, which had been erected . . . in any time or country'; and William Wilberforce, making his 'most impassioned and emphatic' but shamefully doomed appeals to end slavery in the British colonies. In the space of only sixteen days between the end of April and beginning of May, William had the chance to witness at least two momentous events: Pitt, Burke and Fox all rallying to support Wilberforce's bill against 'the dwarfs, [and] the pygmies' who would cause its ultimate defeat in a half-empty House, followed by the far more spectacular public breach between Burke and Fox in a packed Commons, when Burke declared, 'Our friendship is at an end', and Fox left the House in tears. The eloquence of such renowned speakers on such vital issues won William's admiration, but it could not hold his attention for long.

> Words follow words, sense seems to follow sense –
> What memory and what logic! – till the strain,
> Transcendant, superhuman as it is,
> Grows tedious even in a young man's ear.[18]

By the middle of May, William's enthusiasm for 'the Babel din' of London was growing thin. More importantly, his money was running out and, to justify asking for more, he would have to demonstrate that he had some plan in mind. He decided to visit his worthy friend Robert Jones, who was still biding his time until eligible for ordination at his family home in north Wales. To disapproving uncles, this could be presented as an economy: there were, after all, no theatres, pleasure grounds or shops in rural Denbighshire to encourage extravagance. It could also be seen as a staging post on his return journey to Cumberland. Dorothy cannot have been alone in assuming that he was on his way there and Christopher, who was on a walking tour of the Lakes, may have hoped that William would join him. The arguments must have been reasonably convincing, for Uncle Richard duly dispatched £20 on 19 May.[19]

William arrived at Plas-yn-Llan in holiday mood. He had no intention of doing any serious work and travelling light gave him the excuse to leave almost all his books behind, presumably in Richard's safekeeping. When questioned earnestly about the progress of his studies by his friend Mathews, he had to admit that he had not spent enough time reading recently to make any improvement; 'how desireable an attainment would Learning be, if the time exacted for it were not so great', he sighed, adding unconvincingly, 'Miserable weakness!' Since leaving Cambridge, he admitted that his sole reading in the field of modern literature comprised three of the nine volumes of Laurence Sterne's novel *Tristram Shandy* (he had not even reached the birth of the hero in the fourth volume), and two or three papers from Addison's *Spectator*. 'The truth of the matter is that when in Town I did *little*, and since I came here I have done nothing.' It was indeed 'A miserable account!' as he freely confessed, but he was unrepentant. 'I rather think that my gaiety encreases with my ignorance, as a spendthrift grows more extravagant, the nearer he approximates to a final dissipation of his property.'[20] William may have been trying to cheer up his overworked and miserable friend by exaggerating his own idleness, but his simile was ill-chosen, given that Mathews was deeply in debt and being hard-pressed by his creditors. It is difficult to believe, also, that in all the months since he left Cambridge he had not written any poetry.

At Plas-yn-Llan, William passed his time in a 'very agreeable manner'. The Jones family lived in the 'house by the church' in a glorious situation, halfway between Denbigh and Ruthin and high on the Clwydian range of mountains, with a seemingly endless prospect over the wide, fertile valley below. 'I often hear from my brother William who is now in Wales', Dorothy wrote to Jane on 26 June with more than a hint of envy,

> where I think he seems so happy that it is probable he will remain there all the summer, or a great part of it: Who would not be happy enjoying the company of three young ladies in the Vale of Clewyd and without a rival? His friend Jones is a charming young man, and has *five sisters*, three of whom are at home at present, then there are mountains, rivers, woods and rocks, whose charms without any other inducement would be sufficient to tempt William to continue amongst them as long as possible.[21]

Regardless of the inducements which may have been offered by Jones's sisters, the great object of William's visit was to plan a second pedestrian tour with their brother. This time they would not venture far afield, but would explore the northern counties of Wales. Their tour would last a maximum of six weeks, between June and August, and, just as they had done the year before, they went guidebook in hand. This time they used Thomas Pennant's *A Tour in Wales* and the climax of their tour, as of his, was to be a nocturnal ascent of Snowdon to watch the dawn break from the summit. The only indication we have of their route is given in William's dedication of *Descriptive Sketches* to Jones.

> With still greater propriety I might have inscribed to you a description of some of the features of your native mountains, through which we have wandered together, in the same manner, with so much pleasure. But the sea-sunsets, which give such splendour to the vale of Clwyd, Snowdon, the chair of Idris, the quiet village of Bethgelert, Menai and her Druids, the Alpine steeps of the Conway, and the still more interesting windings of the wizard stream of the Dee, remain yet untouched.[22]

Writing to Mathews on 3 August 1791, immediately after his return, he dismissed the tour in less than half a sentence: 'we visited [the] greatest part of North Wales, without having any reason to complain of disappointed expectations'. How different from his irrepressibly enthusiastic response to the Alps! Wales clearly suffered by comparison, and not just with the Alps. In 1809, compiling his own *Guide to the Lakes*, William claimed for his own native regions 'a decided superiority over the most attractive districts of Scotland and Wales, especially for the pedestrian traveller' on the grounds of what he called 'concentration of interest', meaning the immense variety of landscapes to be found in such a small area.[23] There was, however, one experience which left an enduring impression on William's mind. His ascent of

Snowdon came to assume almost mythical status for him, in much the same way as crossing the Alps the previous summer. Again, there was a palpable sense of expectation and excitement as they set out from Beddgelert on a close, warm night, wreathed with that 'dripping mist' which is a Welsh speciality. Collecting their guide, a shepherd who lived at the foot of the mountain, they began their climb. 'Hemmed round on every side with fog and damp', they could see nothing and, as the path became steeper and rockier, they were obliged to concentrate on where they put their feet.

With forehead bent
Earthward, as if in opposition set
Against an enemy, I panted up
With eager pace, and no less eager thoughts.

Suddenly William, who was at the head of the party, found himself unexpectedly bathed in light. Looking up, he discovered that he had emerged from the mist.

The moon stood naked in the heavens at height
Immense above my head, and on the shore
I found myself of a huge sea of mist,
Which meek and silent rested at my feet.
A hundred hills their dusky backs upheaved
All over this still ocean; and beyond,
Far, far beyond, the vapours shot themselves
In headlands, tongues, and promontory shapes,
Into the sea – the real sea, that seemed
To dwindle and give up its majesty,
Usurped upon as far as sight could reach.[24]

It was this moment of unexpected revelation which inspired the only incident from the walking tour of Wales to be included in *The Prelude.* The sunrise, which was the real purpose of their ascent of Snowdon, was forgotten.

There were two other incidents which, though totally different, were equally memorable in their own way. William and Jones made a detour to Holywell, on the coast of Flintshire, to visit Thomas Pennant, the author of the guide they had used so extensively. They spent several hours in his library and William was touched by the 'becoming pride' of this tall, erect man of seventy as he eagerly showed them the manuscripts of his forthcoming fourteen-volume *Outlines of the Globe.* One of Pennant's neighbours, William Thomas, had a house in a remote corner of Montgomeryshire which he invited them to visit. They spent several days with him and, in the course of dinner one evening, William managed to offend a pugnacious local parson who had joined them. The conversation had turned to the powers of the Welsh language. The parson, 'a bulky broad-faced man' who had been drinking heavily, boasted that the conciseness of Welsh was such that 'we can often express in one word what you can scarcely do in a long sentence'. When pressed to name an example, he triumphantly produced 'Tad', which, as William knew, meant 'Father'. William was unable to suppress a smile at such an inappropriate example, whereupon the touchy parson, sensing English superiority and smugness, leapt up, grabbed a carving-knife and brandished it over William's head, to 'the consternation of the Squire, the dismay of my friend, and my own astonishment not unmixed with fear'.[25]

Returning to Plas-yn-Llan after their tour, William showed a marked disinclination to uproot himself and make his expected journey to Cumberland. This is surprising, if only because the suit against Lord Lonsdale had now reached a critical point. The case was due to come before the Carlisle Assizes in August 1791 and there was the best possibility yet of a settlement, if not a decisive judgement against the Earl. That master of legal chicanery had employed every stratagem at his disposal to delay this moment, even insisting that the Administrators should authenticate the handwriting of every person signing vouchers in their claim before the court and, with supreme irony, pleading the Statute of Limitations. In the run up to the Assizes, difficulties multiplied. The Administrators had to serve a subpoena not only on their own supposedly friendly witness, 'Jack' Robinson, to force him to attend and give evidence, but also on the Earl's steward, Mr Arnott, who proved as evasive as his master. Five times the Administrators' lawyer went over to Lowther to serve the subpoena, only to be told that Mr Arnott was 'gone South' or 'off drinking' or some other equally implausible excuse for his absence.[26]

On 29 August, poor Richard, whose life revolved around the suit, wrote to his Grandmother Cookson from Carlisle to tell her that it was expected that the case would come before the Assizes the next day. As Counsel, they had retained Edward Christian, William's former headmaster at Hawkshead Grammar School, who was now Professor of Common Law at Cambridge. Robinson had arrived the previous night and spent the next morning closeted with the Earl. Quite what Robinson was up to is unclear, but his role in the whole affair was becoming increasingly opaque. Despite being the only living witness to John Wordsworth's appointment as agent in his own stead, he had consistently refused to give evidence against Lord Lonsdale unless formally subpoenaed to do so. Clearly, he had no wish to antagonize Lonsdale by voluntarily supporting the Earl's opponents. Now that he was legally obliged to give his evidence, he succeeded in avoiding doing this in open court by persuading both parties to accept a settlement. It may be unfair to Robinson, but it does seem odd that he could not have done this before and that he brokered an agreement only at the moment when Lonsdale faced actual defeat. Both parties consented that the disputed accounts between Lonsdale and John Wordsworth's Administrators should be referred to an independent arbitrator for a binding judgement. The suggestion apparently came from Lonsdale and was accepted only on condition that he admitted that the terms of John Wordsworth's appointment were that he 'was to be paid for all Law Business as other Gent[le]m[en] of the

Profession were paid' or provide documentary evidence to substantiate otherwise.[27] The court approved an award of damages in the region of £5,000 to John Wordsworth's estate, but referred the final figure to an arbitrator, Mr Burrow, who was appointed on Robinson's recommendation. Yet, less than a month later, when questioned by Richard, Robinson claimed to know nothing at all about the gentleman. It was unquestionably an ominous sign. And before the end of the year, the Administrators were beginning not only to suspect that Burrow was 'too much under the influence of his Lordship' but also to question openly his integrity. They were right to do so: Burrow was soon to be rewarded for his role in the affair by being presented to one of Lonsdale's pocket boroughs. It was possibly a sadistic little joke on the Earl's part that the borough in question was Cockermouth.[28]

Out of his depth among such experienced practitioners of deceit and hoping that his legal responsibilities on behalf of his family were coming to an end, Richard had decided to stay on in London. Perhaps he thought that he would be required to return to Branthwaite if the case against Lonsdale was decided at Carlisle, and could not face the prospect of losing the independence which living in London had given him. Whatever his reasoning, only days before the case came up at Carlisle, he transferred his articles from his cousin to Messrs Parkin and Lambert of Gray's Inn.[29]

The Carlisle Assizes had been an opportunity for a meeting of the extended Wordsworth clan, and it was no doubt in response to urgent requests by William's uncles that Robinson decided to see what could be done about their errant nephew. William's Welsh idyll was interrupted by a rude recall to reality: a summons from Robinson. The incumbent of Harwich, Uncle William Cookson's brother-in-law the Reverend William Cowper, 'from expensive habits, & other causes of improvident, & irregular conduct', had been obliged to flee his creditors and settle in Holland. The living, which was effectively in Robinson's gift, was not legally vacant, but as Cowper could no longer officiate, there was a desperate need for a curate to take his place. This post Robinson now offered to William.[30] Even had he been in a position to accept (which he was not, being still too young to qualify for ordination), William was being offered a poisoned chalice. As curate, he could never enjoy the full benefits of the very rich living, which belonged of right to the incumbent; even if Cowper resigned or died, there was no guarantee that his curate would succeed him in office. What Robinson was seeking was someone to do all his protégé's work without the reward. Fortunately for William, he had the perfect excuse; at twenty-one, he was still almost eighteen months short of the requisite age for ordination.

Nevertheless, even William could not afford to alienate such a powerful potential patron. Rather than simply write to reject Robinson's offer, he decided to return to London to plead his excuses in person. Time was running out for him and he knew he could not escape his fate much longer. At this important juncture in his career, he wrote a letter to his friend William Mathews which is extraordinarily self-revelatory of both his current attitude and his intentions. There can be no question of his sincerity. Mathews was in the depths of despair about his own prospects, and William himself was distressed beyond measure that his friend's letter had been delayed, preventing him from offering comfort sooner. Mathews was unable to reconcile himself to the tedium of his schoolmaster post or to the prospect of returning to a home that was riven by religious factionalism. He had been very disappointed that he had not been invited to join William and Jones on their Welsh tour, and now he proposed to William that they should take an extended tour abroad together. Tempting though the idea must have seemed, William had both the personal strength of mind and sufficient appreciation of his friend's character to resist. He set out his reasons in an impressively cogent and thoughtful letter which would probably have given his own guardians a pleasant surprise. 'I take it for granted that you are not likely to continue long in your present employment,' he wrote,

but when you leave it how you can put into execution the plan you speak of I cannot perceive. It is impossible you can ever have your father's consent to a scheme which to a parent at least, if not to every one else, must appear wild even to insanity . . . I do not think you could ever be happy while you were conscious that you were a cause of such sorrow to your parents, as they must undoubtedly be oppressed with; when all that they will know of you is that you are wandering about the world, without perhaps a house to your head. I cannot deny that were I so situated, as to be without relations to whom I were accountable for my actions, I should perhaps prefer your idea to your present situation, or to vegetating on a paltry curacy. Yet still there is another objection which would have influence upon me which is this. I should not be able to reconcile to my ideas of right, the thought of wandering about a country, without a certainty of being able to maintain myself, without being indebted for my existence to those charities of which the acceptance might rob people not half so able to support themselves as myself. It is evident there are a thousand ways in which a person of your education might get his bread, as a recompence for his labour, and while that continues to be the case, for my own part I confess I should be unwilling to accept it on any other conditions. I see many charms in the idea of travelling, much to be enjoyed and much to be learnt, so many that were we in possession of perhaps even less than an hundred a year apiece, which would amply obviate the objection I have just made, and without any relations to whom we were accountable, I would set out with you this moment with all my heart, not entertaining a doubt but that by some means or other we should be soon able to secure ourselves that independence you so ardently pant after, and what is more with minds furnished with such a store of ideas as would enable us to enjoy it. But this is not the case; therefore, for my own part, I resign the idea. I would wish you to do the same. What then is to be done? Hope and Industry are to be your watchwords, and I warrant you their influence will secure you the victory.

This letter was written from Cambridge, where William had returned after visiting Robinson at Sion Hill in London. While he might have hated the thought of 'vegetating on a paltry curacy', William had made up his mind that this was to be his fate. His Uncle William Cookson had suggested that he should embark on a study of Oriental literature. It was a typically astute idea, taking account of his nephew's evident preference for languages and holding out the prospect to him of distinguishing himself as a man of letters in a field which was not incompatible with a career in the Church. An additional advantage, at least in his uncle's eyes, was that the difficulty of obtaining books and tuition would effectively tie William to Cambridge for the foreseeable future.[31]

Unfortunately for everyone concerned, the plan went badly wrong. It made sense for William to begin his course of study with the start of the new term. Had he done so, he would almost certainly have met Samuel Taylor Coleridge, who entered Jesus College on 16 October 1791, and the course of both their lives might have been very different. Instead, towards the end of the month, William took himself off to London. He had some excuse in that it was an opportunity to see his brother John, who had returned to England in August after an absence of eighteen months on his first voyage for the East India Company. He was now 'a very tall handsome man' who, like his brothers, had acquired a taste for independence. Uncle Christopher was soon complaining that John had not written to either his grandmother or himself, which he considered 'a very great peice [*sic*] of Ingratitude'.[32]

John's presence alone cannot explain William's decision to go to London. It seems to have been an attempt to put some space between himself and his Uncle William, while they argued about how he was to spend the remaining time before he was of age to be ordained. William was not exactly entranced at the prospect of studying Hebrew and Aramaic: 'what must I do amongst that immense wilderness,' he asked Mathews, 'who have no resolution, and who have not prepared myself for the enterprise by any sort of discipline amongst the Western languages?' His own wish was to be allowed to go to France, with the object of polishing up his French, so that he could qualify as a travelling companion to a gentleman. Such a post was not unusual among ex-sizars and he could rely on St John's to recommend him to a suitably wealthy patron.[33]

For a month, there was some hard bargaining between uncle and nephew, but eventually they came to a compromise. William would be allowed to go to France for the winter but there were two important provisos. He would have to begin his study of Oriental languages as soon as he returned from the Continent and he was to live in 'some retired Place' in France. In other words, he was to avoid the excitements, political and otherwise, as well as the expense, of Paris. Having secured the consent of the one uncle who was not his legal guardian, William persuaded his brother to act as his intermediary with the others. Richard duly wrote a propitiatory letter to Uncle Richard, stressing that William had been 'advised' to spend some time in France before taking orders, that the experience would be 'less expensive and more improving' than being obliged to remain in England and, as a masterstroke, that the £40 he was now requesting would support him till next summer. Uncle Richard responded with admirable promptness, dispatching the full amount within three days.[34]

Events moved swiftly. Orléans, some eighty miles south and slightly west of Paris, was settled on as a suitably 'retired Place'. A medium-sized town on the Loire, with a population of something more than 30,000, it had the reputation of being a sleepy backwater and yet was also one of the towns always included by Englishmen on the Grand Tour. Temporary accommodation had been arranged at Les Trois Empereurs, the best hotel in the city.[35] By 22 November, William was at Brighton, waiting for a passage across the Channel. His anxiety to get to France 'immediately' was now thwarted by the weather. For five long days he was left kicking his heels, 'which time must have past in a manner extremely disagreeable, if I had not bethought me of introducing myself to Mrs Charlotte Smith'. This was a stroke of genius, for Charlotte Smith was not only a poetess whose works he had long admired (and imitated) but also a distant relative by marriage. 'She received me in the politest manner, and shewed me every possible civility', William reported with delight and pride to Richard. Flattered by her young admirer's enthusiasm for her poetry, Mrs Smith allowed him to read and copy some of her work in progress. She also gave him important letters of introduction to friends in Paris and Orléans, including one to Helen Maria Williams, the poetess to whom William had addressed his first published sonnet, who had been living in France since July and in Orléans since October.[36] It is tempting to think that she did so because William had admitted his authorship of the poem and recited it for her. Admiration for her poetry was the reason why William had sought out Charlotte Smith, but the introduction was to have significant repercussions, for she, like all her French contacts, was an enthusiast for the Revolution. Inadvertently, therefore, William had acquired a set of introductions to people within the most politically active and extreme revolutionary circles.

On the night of Saturday 26 November the adverse winds that had prevented William sailing from Brighton finally gave way to favourable ones, and he crossed the Channel, landing at Dieppe on Sunday morning. He made his way straight to Rouen, where he was again detained for two days, this time waiting for the public stagecoach, the diligence. On the night of Wednesday 30 November, he arrived in Paris.[37]

It was now almost two and a half years since the Fall of the Bastille and the revolution had proceeded with remarkably little bloodshed. Paris was still in a volatile state, not least because there were so many factions, revolutionary and counter-revolutionary, all plotting, spreading rumours and disinformation, and trying to win over the populace. With hindsight, it is obvious that there were signs, in the months before William's arrival, that extremism was increasing and mob violence was becoming more likely. At the time, however, this was not apparent, even to the most acute observers. There had been a few alarms, not least in June, when the royal family's abortive attempt to escape from effective imprisonment in Paris had ended ignominiously in their recapture at Varennes. This had played into the hands of the republicans, including Thomas Paine, who was just one of many English radicals residing in the city. They now began to demand that Louis

XVI should be dethroned and a republic set up in place of the mixed constitution which was then under discussion. Only two days after the annual *Fête de la Fédération*, a republican manifesto was read out at the 'altar of the country' in the Champ de Mars. Two spectators, hiding under the altar in order to get a better view, were seized by the crowd and brutally murdered as suspected counter-revolutionaries. The National Guard, called out to disperse the mob, fired on them, resulting in the deaths of some eighteen citizens. Alarmed at what was rapidly exaggerated into a massacre, the dominant party, the Jacobins, withdrew their support for the republican manifesto and things calmed down. The new constitution, which retained the king's right of veto, was approved by the National Assembly in September and the revolution seemed to have come to a suitably moderate and legitimate conclusion.[38]

William therefore arrived in Paris to find the city comparatively quiet, by its standards. He had only four days to spend before going on to Orléans, and he planned a longer stay in Paris on his return, so this time he confined himself to visiting the main sights. For the second time this year, he was a tourist in a capital city, hastily notching off 'each spot of old and recent fame'. Not surprisingly, given the brevity of his visit, it was the latter that chiefly interested him, and he followed a well-worn route familiar to all the Englishmen who had flocked to Paris since the revolution. The Champ de Mars was high on his list of priorities, not just because of the recent massacre but also because it was the symbolic heart of the revolution: it was here that king and people had sworn the oath on the *Fête de la Fédération*, the day after William and Jones landed at Calais the previous July. He visited the revolutionary districts of the Faubourg St Antoine and Montmartre and he went to the newly built Church of St Geneviève, erected as a pantheon 'to receive the ashes of great men belonging to the era of liberty'. Mirabeau had been buried there in April 1791. In July the body of Voltaire, who had died in 1778 and been denied Christian burial, was reinterred in the same church, after a nauseating triumphal procession of his corpse through the streets of Paris.[39]

Like most Englishmen visiting Paris at this time, he also attended the new National Assembly and the Jacobin Club in the Rue St Jacques, and was unimpressed by their disorderly proceedings. In their 'clamorous halls'

> I saw the revolutionary power
> Toss like a ship at anchor, rocked by storms;

Though he could probably have found someone to endorse his application to visit these places, simply because he was English Charlotte Smith's introductions enabled him to obtain the necessary passes speedily. The member who introduced him to the National Assembly would, William anticipated, be a useful contact on his return to Paris.[40]

He wandered round the Palais Royal, which was to remain one of his lifelong favourite haunts in Paris. Samuel Rogers, the poet, who later became William's friend, was also in Paris in 1791 and was similarly dazzled by this 'very elegant square, full of shops and coffee-houses, glittering with lights and crowded with belles and beaux who were taking their evening promenade'. A gracious room in the middle of the Palais Royal, designated the *cirque*, housed what he euphemistically called 'every species of entertainment', from gaming tables and fencing matches to dancing girls. William too, joining the crowds which thronged the arcades, was mesmerized by the sight of coffee-shop politicians in heated argument amidst the taverns, brothels, gaming-houses and shops:

> I stared, and listened with a stranger's ears
> To hawkers and haranguers (hubbub wild!)
> And hissing factionalists with ardent eyes,
> In knots, or pairs, or single – ant-like swarms
> Of builders and subverters, every face
> That hope or apprehension could put on –
> Joy, anger and vexation, in the midst
> Of gaiety and dissolute idleness.

The atmosphere was electrifying, its animation enhanced for William by the fact that his French was not yet good enough to follow all the arguments. 'The whole city is split into parties,' declared another English visitor at this time,

> and, at the corner of every principal street, the glaring letters of some inflammatory handbill invite the eye. All the coffee-houses are crowded with pretended politicians, who, according to their various prejudices, vent the noxious torrents of their fury; and groups of hirelings, half intoxicated, are everywhere bawling out their national airs.[41]

For William, the contrast between these noisy scenes of politics in action with the almost melancholy scene at the deserted Bastille became symbolic of the distance between the petty factionalism into which the revolution had descended and the great unifying cause in which it had begun. He sat among the ruins, where 'silent zephyrs sported with the dust', and 'in the guise Of an enthusiast' pocketed a stone to keep as a relic. It was an appropriate gesture, but it was an empty one. William 'in honest truth' was 'Affecting more emotion than I felt'. He was, he admitted, more genuinely moved by the celebrated painting by Charles Le Brun of Louis XIV's mistress Louise de la Vallière as the penitent Mary Magdalen than by anything else he saw in Paris at this time. Writing this section of *The Prelude* in 1804, he felt obliged to apologize for what then seemed his youthful 'indifference . . . strange'.

> I was unprepared
> With needful knowledge, had abruptly passed
> Into a theatre of which the stage

Was busy with an action far advanced.
. . . At that time,
Moreover, the first storm was overblown,
And the strong hand of outward violence
Locked up in quiet.[42]

On 5 December William left Paris, arriving at his ultimate destination the following day.

Orléans, a city with a venerable history, lies in the midst of a seemingly unending plain on a curve in the Loire. Surrounded on three sides by a medieval defensive ditch and city wall, fortified with towers at regular intervals, on the fourth it was protected by the broad waters of the river. The wharves and quays along the river frontage were the key to the city's economic success: they gave mercantile access to the Atlantic and the French colonies in the Caribbean. Sugar refining and cotton manufacture were the main industries dependent on this trade, which brought the region immense wealth. For centuries Orléans had been second only to Paris, enjoying royal protection and patronage, which was reflected in the large number of churches and convents crammed within its walls. It was also an outstanding intellectual centre. In early medieval times civil law and Greek were both taught there, even when banned in Paris, and one of its most famous scholars, Pope Clement V, founded its renowned university in 1306. It also had an equally prestigious medical school and an Académie Royale des Sciences. A monument to Joan of Arc, the 'Maid of Orléans', just off the main central square, commemorated her divinely inspired raising of the English siege of the city in 1429. Much of the medieval city, with its brick and timber houses, survived the siege and the depredations of the sixteenth-century Wars of Religion, but the fourth-century cathedral, where Carolingian and Capetian kings had been crowned, was blown up by Protestants and did not. Substantial rebuilding, funded by colonial wealth, began in the seventeenth century and continued well into the eighteenth, introducing new civic splendour to the city: a magnificent nine-arched bridge over the Loire leading to the grandly rebuilt Place du Martroy, in the heart of the city, and a vast Gothic-style cathedral. It was this cathedral, dedicated to the Sainte Croix, which, literally and metaphorically, dominated the whole city. Its great nave and towers soared above the surrounding buildings and, even today, are still visible for miles across the outlying plains. Orléans was devoted to throne and altar, and, as the revolution descended into extremism, became a centre of counter-revolutionary activity.[43]

Even at this period, English visitors with radical political views found the city disappointing. Felix Vaughan, who had graduated from Jesus College, Cambridge, the year before William, had visited Orléans in December 1790 and left after a single day, disgusted with the 'wretched inn, that afforded nothing, which an Englishman could eat', the '*caffés*' where there were no '*journeaux*' and the people, who talked about nothing but common occurrences, even though it was market day. 'The cathedral there is the only thing worth seeing', he complained. Helen Maria Williams, the poetess, had been similarly disappointed, dismissing the city as 'confined, illiberal, and disagreeable', a sure sign that its political conservatism, rather than the place, had disagreed with her.[44]

William was blissfully unaware of Orléans's lack of political credibility. 'I have every prospect of liking this place extremely well –', he wrote enthusiastically to Richard; 'the country thou' flat is pleasant and abounds in agreeable walks, particularly by the side of the Loire, which is a very magnificent river.' From his base at Les Trois Empereurs, he had quickly found lodgings which, he hastened to assure his brother, were both handsome and cheap. They were certainly handsome: a first-floor apartment over the arcades on the finest street in town, the newly built Rue Royale, which ran directly from the bridge over the Loire to the Place du Martroy. For this, his landlord charged him thirty livres a month, which was just less than £1. His board, which excluded breakfast, cost him an additional fifty livres a month. In an effort to be frugal, William had turned down alternative lodgings which he had liked 'extremely', because they were too expensive. He had even managed to negotiate a sliding-scale reduction in rent to only twenty-four livres and ten sous if he stayed eight months – an early indication that he was already considering the possibility of a longer stay in France than had originally been agreed.[45]

William's landlord, Jean Henri Gellet-Duvivier, a widower with three small children, was a silk merchant by profession. Although he is usually depicted as a rabid anti-revolutionary, this is not borne out by the evidence. It is true he was executed on 13 July 1793 for his part in an attack, four months earlier, on Léonard Bourdon, the Orléans deputy to the National Convention, but this, as we shall see, was not quite the anti-revolutionary gesture it has been blown up to appear. So far as it is possible to tell, in the murky political waters of revolutionary France Gellet-Duvivier, in common with most of the inhabitants of Orléans, was not always implacably opposed to the political developments that had taken place. He had, for instance, paid 100 livres as his *contribution patriotique*, a once-and-for-all voluntary tax assessed at a quarter of personal income decreed by the National Assembly on 6 October 1789. While the 'voluntary' nature of the tax might be queried, given the political pressures to conform, his children were also among the '*Citoyens Patriotes*' who offered their jewellery '*à la Nation*' the following December: eight- and six-year-old Pauline and Julie each offered a pair of gold earrings, and five-year-old Augustin, a pair of silver buttons.[46]

Nevertheless, among Gellet-Duvivier's other lodgers were a young gentleman from Paris and several cavalry officers, probably from the 5th Regiment of Dragoons, who had been stationed in the city since September. This latter group of men were certainly reactionary: they had been stoned on entering Orléans because their band had refused to play the revolutionary anthem *Ça ira*. It was perhaps his acquaintance with them which led William to the somewhat naïve judgement that 'almost all the people of any opulen[ce are] aristocrates and all the others democrates', adding,

'I had imagined that there were some people of wealth and circumstance favorers of the revolution, but here there is not one to be found.'[47]

William's greatest disappointment at Orléans was to find that his introduction to Helen Maria Williams was useless; she had already left the city before he arrived. With or, more probably, without a formal letter of introduction, William made the acquaintance of another fellow countryman, the Sheffield manufacturer Thomas Foxlow, who had set up a cotton mill in Orléans. Through Foxlow, whose business had been funded by the Duc d'Orléans and was dependent on the slave labour of the French colonies, William expected to mix in 'the best society this place affords'. Naturally, Foxlow's associates were mainly aristocratic and anti-Jacobin (the Jacobins were calling for the abolition of slavery), though they could not risk blazoning their sympathies abroad. All political discussion was studiously avoided and William passed the time attending their parties and card games, for all the world as though no revolution had taken place.[48]

In *The Prelude*, William says that he soon grew bored of this society and gradually withdrew into the noisier world of the revolutionary patriots. This is only partly the truth. What he does not say is that his main reason for withdrawing from this society – and indeed from Orléans itself – was that he had fallen head over heels in love. Marie Anne Vallon, or Annette, as she was always known, was the sixth and last child of Jean Léonard Vallon, a third-generation surgeon from Blois, who had died some years earlier. Both Annette's older brothers, Jean and Charles, had followed in his footsteps and were employed at the same hospital, the Hôtel-Dieu, a charitable institution where nuns provided nursing care for the indigent sick. Their mother had remarried and their stepfather, M. Vergez, was yet another Blésois surgeon. Annette's third brother, Paul, had broken the family tradition and was a lawyer who lived and worked as a notary clerk in Orléans. His employer, Maître Courtois, had an office in the Rue de Bourgogne, the main street which led to the eastern gate of the city.[49]

Why, how, where or even when William and Annette first met is a matter for conjecture, as is the progress of much of their affair. Any information not lost by chance, or deliberately destroyed by William and his widow, was suppressed in more recent years by his grandson, Gordon Wordsworth. Yet the liaison was of crucial importance in almost every aspect of William's life and its repercussions were still being felt decades later. It is therefore deeply frustrating that we know so little about this momentous relationship, particularly as the few surviving clues are so tantalizing.

We can surmise that the pair met in Orléans. William's sudden and unexpected removal to Blois, in contravention of his original plan to remain in Orléans, can be explained only by his desire to follow Annette home; he had no other reason to go. It is most likely that they met through either Paul or their mutual friends the Dufours family. The attraction must have been instant and overwhelmingly physical, for the one indisputable fact of the matter is that within weeks of their first meeting Annette was pregnant with their daughter, Caroline.[50]

Though a sister is not usually the best person to judge her brother's powers of attraction to the opposite sex, Dorothy's description of William at this time is all we have to indicate what drew Annette to the young Englishman. Dorothy described William's character as 'ardent' and 'highly touched'. In her eyes, he possessed, to an eminent degree, steadiness and sincerity in his attachments, but also what she curiously calls

> a sort of violence of Affection if I may so Term it which demonstrates itself every moment of the Day when the Objects of his affection are present with him, in a thousand almost imperceptible attentions to their wishes, in a sort of restless watchfulness which I know not how to describe, a Tenderness that never sleeps, and at the same Time such a Delicacy of Manners as I have observed in few Men.

Even this partial witness, however, could not persuade herself that her brother was handsome, 'his person is not in his favour,' she admitted, 'at least I should think not; but I soon ceased to discover this, nay I almost thought that the opinion which I first formed was erroneous. He is however, certainly rather plain than otherwise, has an extremely thoughtful countenance, but when he speaks it is often lighted up with a smile which *I* think very pleasing'.[51]

Of Annette, we know even less. She had been born at Blois on 22 June 1766 and she was a Roman Catholic. Given her family background, she was probably already conservative in her politics when she first met William, but it was not until the royalist rebellion in the Vendée, the area between Blois and the sea, that she became a committed and active counter-revolutionary. Her only surviving portrait does not indicate that she possessed any great beauty, though she was by no means unattractive: slight of figure, she had a mass of long curly hair, a long nose and dark eyes, her best feature, under delicately arched brows.[52]

What she lacked in conventional beauty, Annette more than made up for in personality. Guillemin de Savigny, who knew her at this period, described her as having been inculcated from childhood with the best principles and being always prepared to put the interests of others before her own. She had, he said, a great deal of sensibility, a very lively and very wild imagination and rare strength of character. In addition to her natural vivacity, ardour and gaiety, she had the frankness and freedom of manners which were typically French, but totally alien to young women of her class in England. Even so ingrained a puritan as Robert Southey found French women irresistible. They had 'something of Aspasia [a famous Greek courtesan] about them', he wrote, and were 'certainly more sensual than our country women' but also 'more intellectual'.[53] This was, one would have thought, just the combination to capture an ardent young poet's eye and heart. Certainly, if William was as naïve sexually as he was politically, he would not have been difficult to seduce. Annette was a very determined young woman; at twenty-five, she was also four years older than her lover. Though it is dangerous to draw conclusions from differences in age alone, it would be natural to assume that this would have its effect on the balance of their relationship, particularly in its early days. Nor can one ignore the fact that Annette's older unmarried sister, Françoise, also gave birth to an illegitimate child, a son, whom she did not acknowledge as hers for twenty years.[54] If nothing else, this suggests that the Vallons had a much more relaxed view of female morality than was customary in a comparable English family at the time. On the other hand, there was a different set of standards for men then, exemplified by the fact that, at about the same time, William's cousin Tom Myers, the son of a vicar, fathered an illegitimate half-caste daughter while living in India.[55]

Only one of Annette's letters to William survives out of all their long and frequent correspondence, together with two to Dorothy. All three were preserved accidentally; two of them never reached their destination but were held back by the French censor who, ironically, proved less efficient than the Wordsworth family in eradicating all evidence of the clandestine affair. Not a single letter to Annette, from either William or Dorothy, has seen the light of day.[56]

Annette's letter to William, written on 20 March 1793, almost six months after they parted, is revelatory: her passion fairly sizzles on the page as, in a flood of ill-spelt and ill-written words, with barely a punctuation or capitalization to indicate pause for breath, she assures him of her undying devotion. She is inconsolable not to have heard from him for eleven days; if her letters arrived as quickly as her thoughts she would not be troubled with painful fears; William is the best beloved of men, the tenderest of men. 'Come, my lover, my husband', she urges him,

> receive the tender kisses of your wife, your daughter[.] she is so pretty this poor little one . . . she resembles you more and more each day [–] I believe I hold you in my arms[.] her little heart often beats against mine[;] I believe I feel that of her father . . . always love your little girl and your Annette who kisses you a thousand times on the mouth on the eyes and [on] my little one that I love always[,] that I entrust to your safe-keeping [and then?] to God, I will write on Sunday. Adieu I love you for life[.][57]

Faced with such highly charged, even desperate appeals to one's sympathy, it may be cynical to point out that a three-month-old baby, however precocious, is unlikely to have borne much resemblance to its father or to have persuaded any mother that she was holding its father in her arms. While not doubting the genuine nature of Annette's feelings for William, both this letter and, perhaps even more so, the one to Dorothy are an eloquent form of emotional blackmail. Having been left, quite literally, holding the baby when William returned to England, Annette was understandably terrified that she had lost him for ever. Even if he had every intention of returning to marry her, their two countries were now at war. She was in an impossible position. 'I would be more comforted if we were married,' she wrote to him, 'but also I see it is almost impossible for you to expose yourself to [the danger]. If we have war you would perhaps be taken prisoner.'[58]

A year earlier, however, in March 1792, neither of them had any forebodings about their future. They seem to have given themselves up to the passion of the moment and, when Annette's visit to Orléans came to an end, William followed her to Blois.[59] How he explained this change of residence to his family at home is not known; it must have been difficult, especially as his 'winter' in France should have been drawing to a close. No doubt he did not give the true reason, but at least he could claim that Blois was also a 'retired Place'. In fact, it was an altogether smaller and quieter town than Orléans. Lying some thirty miles downstream on the Loire, Blois has repeatedly been compared to an amphitheatre, its terraces and higher levels being reached by tumbling narrow streets and laborious stone steps. Since early medieval times it had been the stronghold of the powerful Comtes de Blois (who included the English king Stephen among their number) but, from the end of the fourteenth century, it became a royal residence. The wonderfully eclectic château, a vast monument to the aspirations if not architectural taste of generations of builders, was the scene of the grisly murder of Henri de Guise in the sixteenth century. With only 12,000 inhabitants, clustered beneath the brooding presence of the château, the town enjoyed an influence out of all proportion to its size. It had given the events of 1789 a cautious welcome and its famous 'constitutional' bishop, Henri Grégoire, was elected president of the National Convention in November 1792. Unlike so many other prominent politicians, he managed to retain his power and influence in national politics throughout the worst excesses of the revolution.[60] Here was a supreme example of one of those 'people of wealth and circumstance' who were 'favorers of the revolution', whom William had so signally failed to find in Orléans. It was in Blois that his political education would begin.

Writing to Mathews on 19 May, William was as cheerful and sanguine as ever as he made his excuses for not replying earlier. 'Since my arrival day after day and week after week has stole[n] insensibly over my head with inconceivable rapidity', he explained, without alluding to the reason why, or indeed even hinting that he had acquired a French mistress. Unaware that Annette was pregnant, he was busy laying plans for his own future career. The world of literature still beckoned and he wrote with his usual robustness to encourage Mathews, who, having just lost his schoolmastering post, was more than usually inclined to depression and defeatism.

> You have still the hope that we may be connected in some method of obtaining an Independence. I assure you I wish it as much as yourself. Nothing but resolution is necessary. The field of Letters is very extensive, and it is astonishing if we cannot find some little corner, which with a little tillage will produce us enough for the necessities, nay even the comforts, of life.

Urging Mathews to use his enforced residence in London as an opportunity to look around for some literary project they could start together, William made the startling announcement that it was now his intention to take orders in the approaching winter or spring. This new determination, which flew in the face of his previous protestations that he could not do so until he was twenty-three, was the result of pressure from Uncle William. Fearing the worst from his nephew's reluctance to return to England and afraid Robinson's offer of the Harwich curacy might slip away, Uncle William, who had recently been appointed a Canon of Windsor, had offered to make him his own curate at Forncett. It was an offer that could not be refused. William allowed an uncharacteristic expression of gloom to escape him: 'Had it been in my power I certainly should have wished to defer the moment.'

In this letter, the first he had written Mathews since leaving Orléans, William gives the first indications that his political opinions were beginning to change. It is not so much what he actually said, but the way he said it. 'You have the happiness of being born in a free country,' he lectured Mathews, as if repeating a lesson given to himself,

> where every road is open, where talents and industry are more liberally rewarded than amongst any other nation of the Universe. You will naturally expect that writing from a country agitated by the storms of a revolution, my Letter should not be confined merely to us and our friends. But the truth is that in London you have perhaps a better opportunity of being informed of the general concerns of france, than in a petty provincial town in the heart of the kingd[om] itself. The annals of the department are all with which I have a better opportunity of being acquainted than you, provided you feel sufficient interest in informing yourself.

Nevertheless, William knew all about the recent rout of the French 'patriot' army by the Austrians, their 'ignominious flight' and their brutal murder of their own commander at Lille. 'The horrors excited by the relation of the events . . . is [*sic*] general', he assured Mathews. 'Not but that there are men who felt a gloomy satisfaction from a measure which seemed to put the patriot army out of a possibility of success.' Such a comment shows a totally new political awareness. It is enforced by the subsequent analysis, which is almost messianic in its language.

> The approaching summer will undoubtedly decide the fate of france. It is almost evident that the patriot army, however numerous, will be unable [to] withstand the superior discipline of their enemies. But suppose that the German army is at the gates of Paris, what will be the consequence? It will be impossible to make any material alteration in the constitution, impossible to reinstate the clergy in its antient guilty splendor, impossible to give an existence to the *noblesse* similar to that it before enjoyed, impossible to add much to the authority of the King: Yet there are in France some [?millions] – I speak without exaggeration – who expect that this will take place.[61]

This is such a different voice (and one with strong Gallic inflections) that the conclusion is inescapable: it was not William's own. If not his own, then whose was it? Certainly not Annette's: she was more likely to be numbered among the millions who expected the restoration of the *ancien régime*. Possibly Bishop Grégoire's, since he was resident in Blois for twelve months from September 1791, though William did not yet espouse his more extreme brand of republicanism. The voice is almost certainly that of Michel Beaupuy, a captain in the 32nd Bassigny regiment stationed at Blois, whom William identifies in *The Prelude* as his political mentor and credits with awakening his social conscience.

The portrait William draws of his friend is an extraordinarily romantic one, which (quite deliberately) owes more to Chaucer's 'verray, parfit, gentil knight' than to reality, for Beaupuy was the perfect example of an aristocrat who was also a fervent supporter of the principles of the revolution.

> Man he loved
> As man, and to the mean and the obscure,
> And all the homely in their homely works,
> Transferred a courtesy which had no air
> Of condescension, but did rather seem
> A passion and a gallantry, like that
> Which he, a soldier, in his idler day
> Had paid to women.

The fifth son of an aristocratic family from the Périgord to enter the army, Beaupuy had been actively involved in revolutionary politics since 1789. Now thirty-seven, he had, like so many others, become increasingly hardline and extreme in his views. The defeats suffered by the patriot army were of the deepest interest to him, politically and personally, as it was simply a matter of time till his own regiment was sent to the front. Nevertheless, it was Beaupuy's idealism that proved so inspirational to his young protégé – and, indeed, to others. His obituary described him as the personification of 'the religious spirit of the Revolution' and the 'Nestor and Achilles of our army'.[62] The latter description was particularly significant; Achilles was the pre-eminent Greek champion in battle, but Nestor was the aged statesman who counselled moderation in the quarrels of the leaders.

William spent many hours with Beaupuy, walking along the Loire and in the vast medieval forests surrounding Blois, which were (and still are) dotted with late-medieval châteaux and hunting lodges, Ménars, Chambord, Villesavin, Beauregard, Chevernay and Troussay, to name just those within a six- or seven-mile radius of Blois itself. There could be no more obvious and spectacular reminder of the wealth and power of the *ancien régime*. The poet in William responded to the physical beauty: this was the incarnation of the Arthurian world of Spenser, Ariosto and Tasso, haunt of damsels in distress and jousting knights. The nascent democrat saw them as symbols of a corrupt and profligate system of government.[63]

Against this emotive backdrop, William and Beaupuy discussed abstract ideas about the end and best forms of civil government, the nature of man and his capacity for both good and evil. Drawing on a mutual background of classical history, they painted for themselves the misery of royal courts,

. . . where the man who is of soul
The meanest thrives the most, where dignity,
True personal dignity, abideth not –

and then compared this with the democratic spirit that had brought about the greatness of Greece and Rome. It was this spirit, they agreed, that had inspired the citizens of France.

Elate we looked
Upon their virtues, saw in rudest men
Self-sacrifice the firmest, generous love
And continence of mind, and sense of right
Uppermost in the midst of fiercest strife.[64]

For the first time, William began to understand the idealism and commitment that had brought about the revolution. More importantly, he began to be enthused. Such discussions at Cambridge, or later in his native Lakes, were always an intellectual interest, sometimes even a passionate one. Now, in the literal and metaphorical heart of revolutionary France, with a sense of impending political crisis and talking with 'one devoted' in thought, word and deed to the cause of liberty, William found the 'vital interest' which would change his life. This was no longer a purely academic argument but a personal crusade.

One particular image came to symbolize the object of the revolution for William. Significantly, it was pointed out to him by Beaupuy, who also drew the moral from it. In itself it was a commonplace sight, and one which William must have seen time and again in both France and England. On one of their walks in the aristocratic playground of the forests of Blois, they came across 'a hunger-bitten girl' creeping along a lane. Attached by a cord to her arm was a heifer which, having no other means of providing for its sustenance, she allowed to graze on the wayside. Instead of idly tending the beast, the girl was busy knitting. At the sight, an agitated Beaupuy cried, '’Tis against *that* Which we are fighting!' For a man of William's natural empathy, it was an irresistible challenge.

I with him believed
Devoutly that a spirit was abroad
Which could not be withstood; that poverty,
At least like this, would in a little time
Be found no more; that we should see the earth
Unthwarted in her wish to recompense
The industrious and the lowly child of toil[65]

If that meant abolishing the monarchy and establishing a republic, then so be it.

On 27 July 1792, Beaupuy's regiment left Blois to defend the French frontier on the Rhine. William never saw him again. A misleading report in the *Moniteur* of December 1793 led him to believe that Beaupuy had been killed, ironically fighting a civil war against royalist rebels in the Vendée. In fact, though seriously wounded, he survived, became a general, and died fighting for France against the Austrians in October 1796.[66] For William, believing his friend had died for his cause rather than his country, the conversations with Beaupuy assumed a greater poignancy and importance. The man had lived and died for what he believed in; what sacrifice would he have expected of William?

Events in France were taking a dangerous turn in the summer of 1792. The constitution of 1791 was being undermined by extremists on every side. The disastrous prosecution of the war against Austria had inflamed republican sentiment, not least because the French émigrés, both aristocrats and clergy, were openly supporting the Austrians. A mob attacked the Tuileries in June, and only the personal bravery of the King prevented the seizure and massacre of his family. When, on the eve of the *Fête de la Fédération*, the National Assembly declared that the country was in danger, thousands of men throughout France volunteered for service in the army. The Duke of Brunswick's ill-conceived *Manifesto*, written by émigrés with the implied sanction of Louis XVI, was published in Paris on 28 July. Threatening vengeance on Paris if any harm came to the King, it simply fanned the flames of republicanism. On 10 August the situation exploded. In a carefully orchestrated campaign, an armed mob of citizens, supported by the National Guard, marched on the Tuileries in the early hours of the morning. The royal family escaped by taking refuge in the National Assembly, but hundreds of their loyal Swiss Guard were butchered in scenes of incredible barbarity. The practical deposition of Louis XVI would soon be followed by the formal abolition of the monarchy, proposed in the National Convention by no less a person than Henri Grégoire, the Constitutional Bishop of Blois.[67]

'William is still in France, and I begin to wish he was in England', Dorothy wrote gloomily to Jane. She heard 'daily accounts of Insurrections and Broils' and, though he had assured her he was 'perfectly safe', she could not help worrying. Her only reassurances were that she was expecting him to be back in London by August and she thought him 'wise enough to get out of the way of Danger'.[68] Little did she know that her brother's return would again be delayed and that he was actively seeking out the very dangers she most feared.

Since living in Blois, William had almost certainly attended the meetings of Les Amis de la Constitution, the provincial branches of the Jacobin Club in Paris. He may have been one of two Englishmen refused membership, but permitted to attend meetings, in February 1792. Alternatively, he may have attended under the aegis of Beaupuy. Undoubtedly, however, he was familiar with its proceedings, which included, that same February, amalgamating all the private book collections in the town into a single public library. Henri Grégoire had been elected president of Les Amis at Blois the previous November and he had a decisive influence on the political tenor of the meetings. By the summer of 1792 these were becoming markedly more republican. On the *Fête de la Fédération*, Grégoire gave a stirring speech to the society in which he predicted a golden future, not just for France but also for its neighbours.

Soon we shall witness the liberation of all humankind. Everything confirms that the coming revolution will set all of Europe free, and prove a consolation for the whole human race. Liberty has been fettered to thrones for far too long! She will burst those irons and chains and as she extends her influence beyond our horizons, will inaugurate the federation of all mankind![69]

If this was a missionary statement, then William was ripe to receive it. Though he had always had confidence in his own power to earn a living (as and when he chose to do so), the actual necessity had been forced on him by the arbitrary whim of the peer who held most of north-west England in his pocket. The Earl of Lonsdale was typical of the aristocrats condemned by Grégoire for jeering at the sufferings of the people and yet being protected by the laws of the land. Though personal resentment at the abuse of power might fuel William's revolutionary zeal, the example of Beaupuy was strong enough to inspire him with disinterested enthusiasm. He watched the departing army volunteers leaving Blois to defend their country and the revolution against a foreign enemy and the forces of reaction and they seemed to him 'arguments from Heaven' that the cause was just.[70] The example of Grégoire proved that it was possible to be both a radical and a clergyman, which was just as well, if William were to fulfil all expectations of him on his return home.

His thoughts were now turning that way. In May he had told Dorothy that he hoped to be back in London in August. In August he wrote to Richard, asking for £20 to be sent to him, presumably to fund his journey home. There were difficulties in sending the money, because Blois was not a commercial centre which could readily exchange bank bills. On 3 September, when he again wrote to Richard, William was still in Blois. He anticipated staying there until the money came through, but he expected to be in London some time in October and hoped to find a bed for a few weeks in Richard's lodgings.[71]

Despite these firm plans, and the necessity of waiting for his money to come through as arranged, William apparently left Blois immediately and unexpectedly. On the basis of his statement, repeated quite positively over fifty years later, in 1847 and again in 1849, that he was in Orléans when the September Massacres were committed in Paris,[72] it has been assumed that William was in Orléans by the 6th of the month. This seems unlikely: he was demonstrably still in Blois when they began, on 2 September, and the following day when he wrote to Richard, dating his letter from the town. The money could not have come through in less than three days (the post took at least five days and then he would have to wait for a reply)[73] and, having left for Orléans, he is unlikely to have wished to return to Blois to pick up his funds.

The only possible explanation which might have justified a precipitate departure from Blois before 6 September was the discovery of Annette's pregnancy. This cannot have been news to William. Even if his sexual relationship with Annette was restricted to a single encounter (which does not seem likely), she was anxious to marry him and knew he intended to return to England, so had every reason for telling him as soon as she was certain herself. She would clearly have had more cause to conceal her state from her relatives, though with three surgeons in her immediate family, it would have been increasingly difficult for her to have done so. She was now six months pregnant and her condition would soon be obvious even to the most casual observer. It was therefore decided that she should go back to Orléans, probably to the Dufours household, and remain there until her baby was born. Whether the decision was taken hastily, or even without William's knowledge, he decided to follow her.[74]

Where he stayed on his return to Orléans is not known, just as it remains a mystery whether he had lived in lodgings or with the Vallons in Blois. Other than to settle his affairs with Annette, it is not even clear why he should have gone to Orléans at all, as his plan had always been that he would return to London via Paris. Once in Orléans, there was no reason for him to linger, other than Annette. Yet linger he did, well into October. He might not have been there when the September Massacres took place, and up to 1,400 priests, nuns and monks, who refused to take the civil oath, were dragged from prison and brutally massacred by the Parisian mob. He might not have been there on 4 September, when fifty-three political prisoners from Orléans were butchered in the streets of Versailles on their way to Paris. But he was probably in Orléans in the middle of September, when there were bread riots, in which fourteen people were killed and martial law was declared in the city. According to the British spy in Paris, George Monro, Orléans was 'in an absolute state of civil war' and a deputation from the National Convention was sent to impose order. A 'stirring time' indeed for William and Annette to be in the city.[75]

On 21 September, while William was in Orléans, Henri Grégoire proposed the abolition of the monarchy to the National Convention. 'Morally speaking, kings have always been a grotesque freak', he declared to unanimous applause. 'The history of monarchy has been the martyrdom of entire nations'. The process of formally declaring France a republic had begun.[76] These events, and the fact that William knew at least one of the main instigators of them, were surely as good as any to persuade him to be in Paris. That he remained in Orléans can only be testimony to the strength of his attachment to Annette.

French historians are not alone in bemoaning William's infuriating failure to record life in Orléans at such a momentous time, to which one might add the equally maddening silence on Annette. For both these gaps in our knowledge, we can blame only the destruction of contemporary letters. There are just two things we know for certain: that he walked extensively along the banks of the Loire, as he had done all year, and explored again his favourite walks southwards along the

Loiret towards Orléans-La Source; and that he was writing poetry. Far from being love poems, as the more romantically inclined might have hoped, he was working on a Continental version of his *Evening Walk. Descriptive Sketches* was an account, in much the same form as his earlier poem, of his pedestrian tour through France and Switzerland with Robert Jones in 1790. Despite all that had happened in the interval, this tour still held him in its imaginative thrall, to the extent that he had even made plans for Jones to join him at Blois. The prospect of a walking tour on the Loire was dashed only when Jones prudently decided to take a teaching post at Bangor that would keep him in Wales till Michaelmas.[77]

William had been working on the poem (when his love affair and political interests permitted) throughout the year. By the time he left Blois, he was already planning to publish it on his return to England. The dramatic turn of events while he was in Orléans, however, inspired him to add a coda to *Descriptive Sketches* which is completely out of tune with the rest of what is, quite literally, a pedestrian poem. It is a rallying call to liberty, a song of praise to the French Revolution, a battle hymn of the republic.

> – Though Liberty shall soon, indignant, raise
> Red on his hills his beacon's comet blaze;
> Bid from on high his lonely cannon sound,
> And on ten thousand hearths his shout rebound;
> His larum-bell from village-tower to tower
> Swing on the astounded ear its dull undying roar:
> Yet, yet rejoice, though Pride's perverted ire
> Rouse Hell's own aid, and wrap thy hills in fire.
> Lo! from the innocuous flames, a lovely birth!
> With its own Virtues springs another earth:
> Nature, as in her prime, her virgin reign
> Begins, and Love and Truth compose her train:[78]

These were brave and defiant words, particularly after the September Massacres and the declaration of the republic, which alienated a large body of public opinion in France. What William had no notion of, as yet, was just how far out of step he was with public opinion in England.

Before he could leave France, William had to come to some arrangement with Annette. Had her pregnancy been the result of a passing infatuation or, indeed, a one-night stand, then he would not have been harshly judged by his contemporaries for abandoning her. Instead, he seems to have been determined to stand by her. He made arrangements to ensure that his name appeared on the birth certificate as the father, and for André Augustin Dufours to represent him at the baby's baptism. This was not simply a moral commitment, but a legal one, which would enable his child to claim maintenance from him in the future. That he was prepared to go so far and yet not marry Annette seems odd. All the obstacles which had stood in the way of their marrying before they consummated their relationship still remained in force and could never be removed.[79] Annette was a Roman Catholic and he an Anglican: if he still intended to enter the Church, a Catholic wife was an insuperable impediment to ordination and promotion. She was French and he was English: if he was to earn a living, in the Church or otherwise, then he was more likely to be successful in England, where he had contacts and family connections.

If he truly intended to marry Annette, as she clearly expected and the frequency of his own letters to her after his departure implies, then there was nothing to be gained by delay. William, with characteristic misplaced optimism, may have hoped that he might persuade his uncles to approve the match and a change of career, but there is no reason why he should have been more successful in person than by letter. He may, of course, have attempted to do so in letters which have been lost; his uncles may even have forbidden the match. But William faced no greater difficulty in persuading them to accept his wife and child than his intended wife and child. He was of age to marry without their consent and in the civil wedding ceremony, available in France since the revolution, he had the perfect means to overcome the problems caused by difference in religion.[80]

There was an additional obstacle to their union. Their affair had always been one of the heart, based on physical attraction. Intellectual sympathies, which were so vitally important to William, were simply not in the picture. Never once does Annette mention William's poetry in her letters, not even by way of interest or encouragement. And where they had a common interest, politics, their views were daily becoming more opposed. When they began their affair, they were both, if not indifferent, then at least not partisan. The momentous events of 1792 irrevocably changed that. The influence of Beaupuy and Grégoire on William ran directly counter to that of Annette. As William became more radical in his views, Annette became more reactionary. He became a committed republican and revolutionary; she became an active monarchist and counter-revolutionary. It is pure speculation but, in the circumstances, a justifiable suspicion that William had private reservations about the relationship which prevented him taking the step that would make them partners for life.

For whatever reason, William and Annette did not marry. To save face, and to enable her to keep her daughter, Annette called herself variously 'William Wordsworth Vallon', the '*f*[*emme*] William' and the '*veuve* Williams'. As late as 1816, her own family still believed that she had married the English poet and Annette was begging him not to endanger their daughter's prospects of inheriting from her uncles by revealing that they were not.[81] If William had balked at deceiving his own family by a secret marriage, he was later forced into colluding with Annette's deception that one had taken place.

Before he left Orléans, William and Annette had one last duty to perform together. Like any expectant parents, they went shopping for baby clothes and, in what must later have seemed a prescient gesture, Annette persuaded William to kiss every item. Intended as a tender fatherly blessing, it would become a symbol of farewell.[82]

William set off for Paris with the manuscript of *Descriptive Sketches* in his pocket, perhaps hoping it would solve all his problems. A successful publication might persuade his uncles that he had a future as a poet and provide the funds for him to bring Annette to England as his wife. He had always intended to return to Paris for an extended visit, but the city in October and November of 1792 was very different from that of a year earlier. Shocked by the September Massacres, many of the English residents, including Lord Gower, the British ambassador, and William Lindsay, his chargé d'affaires, had left. Other visitors were deterred from coming altogether. William Cobbett, who had spent 'the six happiest months of my life' in France since his arrival in March 1792, not only cancelled the coach he had hired to take him to Paris in September but fled the country. 'I did intend to stay in France till the spring of 1793 . . . But I perceived the storm gathering; I saw that a war with England was inevitable; and it was not difficult to see what would be the fate of Englishmen in that country, where the rulers had laid aside even the appearance of justice and mercy.'[83]

William was either oblivious or heedless. He arrived in Paris 'inflamed with hope' and set about seeing the sights again. This time he was in for a real shock, for what he saw was not some dignified re-creation of ancient Rome but the aftermath of mob violence. He saw the battle-scarred Tuileries, the Temple, where the royal family were now genuine prisoners, and the fire-blackened Carrousel, where the bodies of the Swiss Guard had been piled high and burnt. These were sights to shake his confidence in 'the lovely birth' of a republic, bringing love, truth and justice in its train. Not surprisingly, he spent a sleepless night. Nor was it much comfort the following morning to find the street hawkers in the Palais Royal bawling 'Denunciation of the crimes Of Maximilian Robespierre'. The pamphlets they were selling reported Jean-Baptiste Louvet's dramatic accusation in the National Convention the previous day. Robespierre, supremely arrogant as ever, had demanded that anyone who thought he was aiming at dictatorship should say so; in the silence that followed, Louvet had walked alone to face him and coolly said, '*Robespierre, c'est moi qui t'accuse.*'[84]

William clearly admired Louvet's courage and appreciated the drama of his gesture; whether he supported or even understood his attack on Robespierre at the time is another matter. Among the other pamphlets being hawked in the Palais Royal were a large number devoted to transcripts of the trial of Charles I and demands for the prosecution of Louis XVI. Henri Grégoire, elected president of the National Convention on 15 November, was one of those demanding that the King should answer for his crimes against the people. Robespierre, with his insistence that the King must die 'because the nation must live', was simply the most eloquent and ruthless of the anti-monarchists, among whose numbers one William Wordsworth must certainly be counted. He may have attended the meetings of the National Convention as the rowdy and ill-tempered debates raged and Jacobins struggled for supremacy over the more moderate Girondins; we simply do not know. Through Beaupuy and Grégoire, and possibly through Les Amis de la Constitution in Blois, he would have had introductions to any number of political figures in Paris. He later said he had met Jacques Pierre Brissot and Jean-Antoine Gorsas, both of whom were deputies, the former a Girondin, the latter a journalist and apologist for the September Massacres; both were to be executed only twelve months later, in October 1793.[85]

Even to a newcomer like William, who could not begin to understand the complexities of Parisian politics and was uncomfortably aware that he was out of his depth, it was immediately clear that the revolution was in danger, not just from émigrés and counter-revolutionaries, but also from demagogues and factionalists in the National Convention and from the volatile mob outside it. He even considered offering his services to the republic.

> An insignificant stranger and obscure
> Mean as I was, and little graced with powers
> Of eloquence even in my native speech,
> And all unfit for tumult and intrigue,
> Yet would I willingly have taken up
> A service at this time for cause so great,
> However dangerous.

There has been much speculation as to what role William envisaged for himself, but the only practical one open to him was that of a political pamphleteer.[86] This might have allowed him to influence the course of events and, as he well knew by the time he came to write *The Prelude*, had he been successful, he would undoubtedly have endangered his own life. In the Terror, journalists were as likely to be executed as politicians. This was only true, however, if he remained in France.

In England it was still possible for him to play an influential role as a political writer. Grégoire had scented the possibilities in his speech to Les Amis at Blois in the summer: 'the coming revolution', he had declared, 'will set all of Europe free'. On 19 November, while William was in Paris, the National Convention enacted a decree that the French Nation 'will offer *fraternité* and assistance to all peoples who wish to recover their liberty'. It was a provocative declaration of intent, made deliberately more so by being translated and printed into different languages. Here, then, was a way in which William could take up service in the cause: he could carry the revolutionary message back to England.

Though he was reluctant to leave Paris, he was compelled to do so 'by nothing less than absolute want Of funds for my support'. By early December he was back in England, lodging with his brother Richard in Staple Inn. On 15 December 1792, far away in Orléans, Annette gave birth to their daughter. She was christened the same day, in the Cathedral of St Croix, her absent father being represented by

André Augustin Dufours. Annette's brother Paul and her friend Mme Dufour stood as the baby's godparents. It somehow seems symbolic of the whole unhappy affair that no one knew how to spell William's surname and his daughter entered life inauspiciously named 'Anne-Caroline Wordswodsth'.[87]

5. *A Patriot of the World*

William's first priority on returning to England was to get his poem published, but *Descriptive Sketches* alone was a very meagre foundation on which to present himself to the world as a poet. Hurriedly scouting around for something to add to it, he settled on *An Evening Walk*, the poem he had written while a schoolboy and undergraduate. Despite being written so long ago, it needed little revision, but he did add a discordant and significant digression: a description of a poor woman, her two children clasped in her arms, found frozen to death on Stainmore, near Penrith, earlier in the year.[1] Beaupuy's lessons on the human face of poverty and suffering had not been forgotten.

William found a publisher almost immediately in Joseph Johnson of St Paul's Churchyard. It was an interesting choice, because Johnson was famous not only as the publisher of the poet William Cowper but also as a leading London radical. He was a member of the Society for Constitutional Information and Thomas Paine, William Godwin and Mary Wollstonecraft had all met at his house. As a Unitarian, he moved in the same circles as both Samuel Nicholson and Joseph Fawcett.[2] William may have met him during his previous visit to London; if not, his recent return from France and new radical credentials would have assured him of attention.

On 29 January 1793 two large but very thin volumes, bound in cheap brown-paper wrappers, were published by Joseph Johnson. They both boasted the snappy titles so beloved by eighteenth-century poets: *An Evening Walk. An Epistle; In Verse. Addressed to a Young Lady, from the Lakes of the North of England* and *Descriptive Sketches. In Verse. Taken during a Pedestrian Tour in the Italian, Grison, Swiss, and Savoyard Alps.* At least no disgruntled purchaser could pretend he had not known what he was getting. And this time there would be no hiding behind clever pseudonyms. Both books proudly proclaimed that they were by 'W. Wordsworth, B.A. Of St John's, Cambridge'. In an endearing confession to his friend Mathews, William later admitted that he had 'huddled up' these two little works and sent them out in such an imperfect state by way of an apology for his Cambridge career: 'as I had done nothing by which to distinguish myself at the university, I thought these little things might shew that I could do something. They have been treated with unmerited contempt by some of the periodical publications, and others have spoken in higher terms of them than they deserve.'[3]

The reviews (and there were not many) were, indeed, unkind. The *Critical Review* praised *An Evening Walk* for its 'new and picturesque imagery . . . which would not disgrace our best descriptive poets', but crushed *Descriptive Sketches* beneath the heel of its contempt.

The wild, romantic scenes of Switzerland have not yet been celebrated by an English poet; and its uncultivated beauties, which of themselves inspire the most sublime and poetical ideas . . . seem to have been surveyed by few of the poetic race . . . Mr Wordsworth has caught few sparks from these glowing scenes. His lines are often harsh and prosaic; his images ill-chosen, and his descriptions feeble and insipid.

The *Monthly Review* was, if anything, more contemptuous in ridiculing his imagery. 'How often shall we in vain advise those, who are so delighted with their own thoughts that they cannot forbear from putting them into rhyme, to examine those thoughts till they themselves understand them? No man will ever be a poet, till his mind is sufficiently powerful to sustain labour.'[4]

If William had hoped for indulgence from his family, he was swiftly disillusioned. Even Dorothy, the 'Young Lady' to whom *An Evening Walk* was dedicated, had cutting criticisms. She and Christopher, now in his first year at Trinity College, Cambridge, had amused themselves in the Christmas vacation at Forncett by 'analysing every Line' and preparing 'a very bulky Criticism', which they intended to send William as soon as Christopher's Cambridge friends had added their two penn'orth. Though William remained Dorothy's favourite, Christopher was now 'one of the dearest of my Brothers'. He was 'a most amiable young Man, sensible, affectionate, and engaging', who shared many of William's traits, including his passion for poetry, but in a less extreme form. Among his Cambridge friends, with whom he would soon found a literary society, was Samuel Taylor Coleridge, who would hail *Descriptive Sketches* as announcing 'the emergence of an original poetic genius above the literary horizon'. Coleridge possessed greater powers of perception than most critics (as well as having the useful gift of hindsight in this instance), but he would be one of William's earliest and most vociferous champions.[5]

Dorothy was less enthusiastic. While it is possible to hear the voice of Uncle William behind some of her remarks, particularly those relative to young poets, Dorothy was transparently offended that her brother had not seen fit to show her his poems before publishing them. 'The Scenes which he describes have been viewed with a Poet's eye and are pourtrayed with a Poet's pencil;' she declared with crisp authority, and the Poems contain many Passages exquisitely beautiful, but they also contain many Faults, the chief of which are Obscurity, and a too frequent use of some particular expressions and uncommon words for instance *moveless*, which he applies in a sense if not new, at least different from its ordinary one . . . I regret exceedingly that he did not submit the works to the Inspection of some Friend before their Publication, and he also joins with me in this Regret. Their Faults are such as a young Poet was most likely to fall into and least likely to discover, and what the Suggestions of a Friend would easily have made him see and at once correct.[6]

Though William might have been chagrined by the immediate reception of his poems, he was also well aware of the justice of the criticisms. 'They are juvenile productions, inflated and obscure', he wrote in 1801, 'but they contain many new images, and vigorous lines'. He regarded them chiefly as having curiosity value, evidence of how much his opinions on poetry had changed in the intervening years. Unless Johnson had sent them to be pulped for the trunk-makers, he admitted ruefully, copies must still be lying around 'in some corner of his Warehouse, for I have reason to believe that they never sold much'.[7]

It was not unrealistic of William to have hoped for a grand success with his first major publication. This had just happened to the equally unknown poet, Samuel Rogers, whose *Pleasures of Memory*, first published early in 1792, was now entering its fifth edition and was still selling 1,000 copies a year over a decade later.[8] Despite William's infinitely superior gifts as a poet, this sort of popularity would always elude him, even at the height of his reputation.

The poor sales of William's two books meant that he now had to look elsewhere for funds. Two small family bequests came at this opportune moment. His Penrith grandmother, Mrs Cookson, who had been failing since the beginning of the year, died on 11 June 1792. On inheriting the Crackanthorpe estate eighteen months earlier, she had generously promised to give £500 to each of her sons and a similar sum to be divided among her late daughter's children. Her sons had been given their share almost immediately, and Uncle Christopher's wife may even have received an additional £500 as a personal gift.[9] Nevertheless, only two of the dutiful grandchildren, Dorothy, the invaluable companion, housekeeper and nursemaid to a fast-growing band of baby Cooksons at Forncett, and John, struggling to raise the capital to invest in his next voyage to China, received their £100 each in the spring of 1792.[10] It is a telling insight into their respective characters and relationships with the young Wordsworths that Uncle Christopher, who inherited the estate, made no attempt to fulfil his mother's wishes. Uncle William, on the other hand, offered to rectify the imbalance by personally giving his niece and nephews £150, so that his share should be no larger than theirs. All that they got from Uncle Christopher, almost a year after their grandmother's death, was £166 13s 4d, their third share of a bequest from their great-grandfather, made before they were born, which was legally their due.[11] It is, incidentally, a reflection on the remarkable closeness and trust between the young Wordsworths that they always regarded these sums as a family pot and never queried its distribution among themselves.

Any hope that they might still win back their own family inheritance had now vanished. The supposedly independent arbitrator, Mr Burrow, had proved 'a very great Scoundrill'; no accounts had been agreed, and the case had ground to a complete halt. The Carlisle judgement against 'the Devil's likeness', as Uncle Christopher now termed the Earl, was effectively unenforceable: the Administrators could no longer afford to pursue the case in the courts and 'Wicked Jimmy' had won by default.[12]

Living with Richard in the winter of 1792, William no doubt had it thoroughly drummed into him that, though the Wordsworths' claim would never be dropped completely, he could not rely on getting his £1,000 from his father's estate and he must accept the necessity of earning his own living. It was not something William wished to hear, which accounts, in part, for the coolness that now arose between him and his brother. Richard, who had been hard at work as a lawyer since he was seventeen, and had dutifully forfeited a life of leisure on the Sockbridge estate so that he could pursue the family claim, had little patience with his wayward brother. 'Richard's disposition and his are totally different,' Dorothy helpfully explained to her friend Jane, 'and though they never have any quarrels yet there is not that friendship between them which can only exist where there is some similarity of taste, or sentiment or where two hearts are found to sympathize with each other in all their griefs and joys.' William's radical politics, not to mention the revelation of his mistress and child in France, can have done little to endear him to Richard. The atmosphere in the lodgings they shared at Staple Inn with their mutual friend Joshua Wilkinson from Cockermouth must have become increasingly tense over the coming months.[13]

Events had moved swiftly since William left France. On 21 January 1793 Louis XVI was guillotined in Paris. Having only recently returned from the city himself, William was more prepared than most for this latest act of violence; he considered it not merely justified by the circumstances but an absolute necessity for the survival and progress of the revolution. In this, he was out of step with the majority of English public opinion. In the general shock and revulsion, even those who had previously welcomed the French Revolution and argued for political and religious reform in England now backtracked furiously. Most notable among these was Richard Watson, Bishop of Llandaff, a former Professor of Divinity at Cambridge, who now lived on a grand estate on the shores of Lake Windermere. On 30 January, in an attempt to calm 'the perturbation which has been lately excited, and which still subsists in the minds of the lower classes of the community', he published a sermon he had given some years before, which preached the doctrine of divine will as the reason and justification for poverty. This was the usual response of establishment clergymen to fear of popular unrest; it made any attempt to overturn the preordained ranks of society an act of rebellion against God. To this he added a hastily compiled *Appendix*, protesting at the recent trend of violent events in France, culminating in the execution of the King, and extolling the virtues of the British Constitution.[14]

It was an obscure and rather ordinary publication which, in most circumstances, would not have merited any notice at all. In language and attitude it was oddly unprovocative, much less so than William asserted. What roused William to blazing indignation was the fact that its author had previously been renowned for his liberal views: 'While, with a servility which has prejudiced many people against religion itself, the ministers of the church of England have appeared as writers upon public measures only to be the advocates of slavery civil and religious, your Lordship stood almost alone as the defender of truth and political charity.'[15] Watson was now a political apostate and his defection might have serious consequences for the progress of reform in Britain.

Even this might not have tempted William to put pen to paper had it not been for the single event which, more than any other, was to shake him to the core. Two days after the publication of the *Appendix to a Sermon*, France declared war on England. It was not unexpected, but its effect on William was cataclysmic.

> No shock
> Given to my moral nature had I known
> Down to that very moment – neither lapse
> Nor turn of sentiment that might be named
> A revolution, save at this one time.[16]

William's natural and passionate love of his own country was now at odds with his equally passionate belief in the righteousness of the enemy's cause. By joining the alliance against France, Pitt's government had ranged itself alongside the powers of despotism against the defenders of democracy. Now, more than ever, there was need of someone to take up service 'for cause so great',[17] and William did so with a violence which did more credit to the ardour of his principles than to the persuasiveness of his arguments.

Just as he had done when publishing his poems, he set out his credentials in the title, *A Letter to the Bishop of L[l]andaff on the extraordinary avowal of his Political Principles contained in the Appendix to his late Sermon.* Lest there should be any doubt about his own political affiliations, he nailed his colours firmly to the mast: *by a Republican.*[18] In bold, vigorous prose, fuelled by his anger and punctuated with scathing sarcasm, he launched his attack on the Bishop of Llandaff by comparing him to Henri Grégoire, the Constitutional Bishop of Blois.

> At a period big with the fate of the human race, I am sorry that you attach so much importance to the personal sufferings of the late royal martyr and that an anxiety for the issue of the present convulsions should not have prevented you from joining in the idle cry of modish lamentation which has resounded from the court to the cottage . . . A bishop, a man of philosophy and humanity as distinguished as your Lordship, declared at the opening of the national convention, and twenty-five millions of men were convinced of the truth of the assertion, that there was not a citizen on the tenth of august who, if he could have

dragged before the eyes of Louis the corse of one of his murdered brothers, might not have exclaimed to him, Tyran, voilà ton ouvrage. Think of this and you will not want consolation under any depression your spirits may feel at the contrast exhibited by Louis on the most splendid throne of the universe, and Louis alone in the tower of the Temple or on the scaffold.[19]

Using the arguments of Jean-Jacques Rousseau's *Du Contrat Social* and Thomas Paine's *The Rights of Man* (for which Paine had been convicted of sedition by the British government the previous December), William demolished the case for monarchy, aristocracy and primogeniture. Virtue cannot be inherited, was his basic premise, nor can its continuance be guaranteed: 'a man's past services are no sufficient security for his future character'. Power corrupts and the office of king is inherently beyond the virtue of any man; the only sensible way of restraining a legislator is to appoint him for a limited period, since the knowledge that tomorrow he will be a private citizen again, and subject to the laws he has enacted, will restrain him from oppressive measures. A republic, based on universal suffrage, proscription of hereditary authority and the abolition of statutes limiting wages, is the only form of government which truly represents the general will.

In prosecuting his arguments William demonstrated an unexpected turn for the pithy phrase and incendiary political slogan: 'Government is, at best, but a necessary evil'; 'Is your lordship to be told that acquiescence is not choice, and that obedience is not freedom?'; 'You have aimed an arrow at liberty and philosophy, the eyes of the human race'. William's own experiences added particular venom to some of his criticisms. 'I congratulate your lordship upon your enthusiastic fondness for the judicial proceedings of this country', he remarked with the heavy irony of one who had spent futile years trying to regain his inheritance in the Lonsdale suit. 'I am happy to find you have passed through life without having your fleece torn from your back in the thorny labyrinth of litigation.' Looking forward to the establishment of a republic in Britain, and a resolution of inequality in wealth, he expresses the hope that 'the miseries entailed upon the marriage of those who are not rich will no longer tempt the bulk of mankind to fly to that promiscuous intercourse to which they are impelled by the instincts of nature, and the dreadful satisfaction of escaping the prospect of infants, sad fruit of such intercourse, whom they are unable to support'.[20] William could not have written this so soon after his separation from Annette and the birth of their illegitimate child without having himself and them in mind.

The most surprising element of his *Letter to the Bishop of L[l]andaff* is not so much his overt (not to say flaunted) republicanism, but his defence of the violence of the French Revolution. In doing so, he fell back on his usual catch-all explanation, which was its own justification: it was part of a natural cycle.

The coercive power is of necessity so strong in all the old governments that a people could not but at first make an abuse of that liberty which a legitimate republic supposes. The animal just released from its stall will exhaust the overflow of its spirits in a round of wanton vagaries, but it will soon return to itself and enjoy its freedom in moderate and regular delight.

He also put forward the dangerous argument so beloved of all revolutionaries: the end justifies the means. 'A time of revolution is not the season of true Liberty', he argued. 'Political virtues are developed at the expence of moral ones.' Compassion must be repressed when traitors are to be punished. Only afterwards can one afford to be more benign. Like all good revolutionaries, he also looked to education to solve the problems created in the wake of violent overthrow of government.

It is the province of education to rectify the erroneous notions which a habit of oppression, and even of resistance, may have created, and to soften this ferocity of character proceeding from a necessary suspension of the mild and social virtues: it belongs to her to create a race of men who, truly free, will look upon their fathers as only enfranchised.[21]

What William did to such great effect in this essay is harness emotion and reason. Every line thrills with the sincerity of youthful idealism and passionate conviction. The result is powerful, eloquent and authoritative. Comparing it with the dull and turgid *Descriptive Sketches*, with its tiresome affectation of melancholy, it is almost impossible to believe that both were written by the same man and within such a short space of time. If nothing else, *A Letter to the Bishop of L[l]andaff* is convincing evidence that William's heart was in politics, not poetry.

Had it been published in this spring of 1793, William would undoubtedly have been arrested, tried and found guilty of seditious libel; he would have faced the certainty of a lengthy prison sentence, possibly even transportation. Even as he was writing his pamphlet, the newspapers were full of reports of trials and convictions for sedition, so he cannot have been unaware of the dangers. The sole surviving manuscript is unfinished, which suggests that William himself may have begun to have doubts about the wisdom of publication. It was not just the personal risk involved, but the fact that, once again, the pace of events in France had outstripped him. By early April, news of the revolt in the Vendée had been confirmed and France was in a state of civil war, somewhat undermining his claims for the moral superiority of republican government. William's hesitation would have been increased by the advice of his friends. His publisher, Joseph Johnson, for instance, whose stable of radical authors included Joseph Priestley, John Horne Tooke and William Godwin, had shied away from Thomas Paine. After printing a few copies of the first part of *The Rights of Man*, he had taken fright and transferred the work to another publisher. *A Letter to the Bishop of L[l]andaff*, particularly after the outbreak of war with France, was an equally risky prospect.[22] William's brother Richard, with whom he was still living in the heart of the legal establishment at Staple Inn, would also have counselled caution. To publish a rabid republican tract now would be to play into the hands of the Earl of Lonsdale and prejudice still further the Wordsworth claim. Nor was it likely to impress their uncles, on whose goodwill Dorothy, John and Christopher were still dependent, as indeed was William himself. Richard might be prepared to overlook the offensive implications of William's tirades against 'the unnatural monster primogeniture', but Uncle Christopher, newly enriched by his inheritance of Newbiggin Hall and the Crackanthorpe estate, and Uncle William, royal protégé and Canon of Windsor, would be incandescent at his attacks on aristocracy, monarchy and the Church.

Even though wiser counsels prevailed and William decided to suppress his pamphlet, matters were coming to a head between him and his uncles. Since his return to England, the pressure on him to take orders must have increased substantially. Uncle William needed a curate and could not hold the place open indefinitely for his dilatory nephew. On 7 April William would be twenty-three, so he could no longer hide behind the excuse that he was under-age. Confrontation was inevitable.

It is worth pointing out that William could have taken the easy option. Uncle William knew nothing about either his revolutionary politics or his French mistress and illegitimate child. If William chose to keep silence, no one would be any the wiser. He could seek ordination and his future would be secure. He would have the certainty of a lifelong, comfortable and undemanding provision for himself in the Church. He would have leisure to pursue his vocation as a poet, without being dependent on precarious literary earnings. He could offer his sister the home she longed for in England and his mistress and child the financial support they needed in France. Though marriage with Annette would be out of the question, he could make amends by adopting Caroline: dependent female relatives of indeterminate status were so commonplace in England that he could bring her to live with him without provoking scandal. The same benefits were still open to him if he confessed all to his uncle. The war with France now gave him the ideal opportunity to renounce his republicanism, his mistress and his illegitimate child as 'juvenile errors'.[23]

To his eternal credit, William did neither, but stood firm by his principles. He could not be a hypocrite and he was debarred from ordination by his republicanism, which would prevent him swearing allegiance to the King, and by any thought of wishing to marry Annette. It was not the most sensible of decisions from a material point of view and the result was not unexpected. Uncle William refused to have anything more to do with him. From now on, he would have to make his own way in the world. And he was not welcome at Forncett.[24]

Of course, the person most affected by this ban was not William, but Dorothy. She had not seen her brother since the Christmas vacation of 1790 and now had little prospect of doing so unless, or until, the quarrel could be patched up. Her own loyalties were to be tested to the limits. William had always been her prime object of devotion, but she also sincerely loved and respected her uncle and aunt. He was 'one of the best of men' (but 'extremely indolent', she could not resist adding); she was 'without exception the best-tempered woman I know'. They had been unremittingly kind and generous to her since rescuing her from Penrith, and, consequently, had been responsible for subtle changes in her opinions which distanced her far more effectively from her brother than physical separation. She thought, for instance, it would be 'a charming thing' if William became curate to her aunt's debauched and disgraced brother, the incumbent of Harwich, because 'in the End [it would] be a certain Provision'.[25] She was 'charmed' with Windsor, where she had spent three months in the late summer of 1792. Thanks to Uncle William's appointment as a canon there, they had grace-and-favour apartments in the cloisters of St George's Chapel and were in daily contact with the royal family. She was equally enchanted with the royals themselves, fancying herself 'treading upon Fairy-Ground' when she walked on the castle terrace with them. Despite her denials, she was obviously dazzled by such proximity. She had never seen such a handsome family; it was impossible to see them informally at Windsor and not love them; the Queen and her train, driving in the park below, seemed like 'Fairies travelling on fairy Ground'. Regaling her friend with anecdotes and repeating herself in her excitement, Dorothy artlessly revealed her royalist sympathies. The King had played with the Cookson children,

who though not acquainted with the new-fangled Doctrine of Liberty and Equality, thought a King's Stick as fair Game as any other man's, and that princesses were not better than mere Cousin Dollys . . . I am too much of an aristocrate or what you please to call me, not to reverence him because he is a Monarch more than I should were he a private Gentleman, and not to see with Pleasure his Daughters treated with more Respect than ordinary People.[26]

These opinions, not to mention her contemptuously flippant use of revolutionary terminology, would be anathema to her republican brother, raising the question of just how much he confided in her at this time. Although he was writing to her 'regularly' from London, Dorothy was still looking forward 'with full confidence' to the happiness of receiving Jane Pollard 'in my little Parsonage' as late as the middle of February 1793, blissfully unaware that her 'charming' dream was nothing but a chimera.[27] Within weeks, if not days, however, Dorothy not only knew all about Annette but was actually in correspondence with her.

It was typical of Dorothy that she should respond so immediately and emotionally to the other woman's plight. She literally wept for Annette. So much so that the deserted mistress found herself having to comfort the sister. 'Your last letter gave me such a powerful feeling', Annette replied,

in every line I saw the sensibility of your spirit and that interest, so touching, you take in my sorrows, they are great my dear sister, I confess, but do not increase them, by distressing yourself too much[.] the idea that I am making you miserable is bitter to me, and that it is I who disturbs your rest, who makes your tears flow. Calm yourself o my dear sister[,] my friend[,] I have great need of this assurance so that I do not become more harassed. I wish I could offer you consolations but alas, I cannot[;] I have to find them from you. I find some relief in the assurance of your friendship and in the inviolability of my dear William's feelings . . . it is on the breast of friendship that the unfortunate find comfort[;] it is on that of my sister that I love to lean, but if you are moved by my fate, I share just as much in your annoyances, you do not have anyone in whom you can freely confide the painful state of your heart and you are forced to stifle the tears your sensibility causes [-] o my dear sister, how miserable I am to know how you have been, tell me[.] never no never can I ever make up to you all that you have suffered for me.

The two women were soon making common cause. Dorothy confided in Annette her dreams of the little cottage in the country (which could no longer be a parsonage), and willingly offered to share it with William's wife and child. Annette responded by filling in the picture: how happy they would all be when they were reunited! 'And you', she asked William,

do you long for that day as ardently as your Annette[?] when you will be surrounded by your sister your wife your daughter who will live only for you[,] we will have only one feeling only one heart only one soul and all will be offered to my dear Williams – our days will slip by quietly [-] I will at last enjoy the peace I can only feel near you and in telling you that I love you with my own *living voice.*[28]

Reading these letters 200 years after they were written is an uncomfortable experience. At a cursory level they appear to be those of a simple artless girl 'who not only loves but knows herself beloved'. For the romantically inclined, she is the model mistress, passively refraining from blame, reproach and selfish self-pity, while dashing off a heartfelt declaration of undying passion.[29] Tempting as this image is, it does not require much penetration to see that, beneath the surface, there is a subtle subtext which I have already described as emotional blackmail. The impression is unavoidable that Annette was beginning to doubt whether William would return to marry her, and that, using the only forces at her command, she cleverly and deliberately applied pressure on the most vulnerable feelings of both William and his sister. She astutely appealed to William's paternal responsibilities and his fraternal affection, telling him that their daughter was growing daily more like him, that she would be happier if they were married and praising his sister to the skies for her empathy with Annette's own plight. 'The earth could not produce two like her[.] she does honour to her sex. I truly want my Caroline to resemble her. How I have wept my dear Williams what heart [she has] what soul, how deeply she shares in the sorrows that overwhelm me but how distressed I am to see that she is so tortured because of us'.[30]

To underline the fact that she and Dorothy also now loved each other as sisters, Annette does not fail to mention Dorothy's enthusiasm in speaking of the little cottage, '*notre petit menage*', which they would all share one day. The message is clear, if not explicitly stated. Dorothy not only shared their secret but, like Annette herself, expected and longed for the marriage to take place. The pressure on William to fulfil his obligation to marry was being discreetly but relentlessly applied.

The letter to Dorothy herself was equally subtle, and more than twice the length of that to William. Annette was very careful to ensure that Dorothy should not feel excluded by their relationship. She looked forward to the day when William would be surrounded by sister, wife and daughter (in that order) and she hoped Caroline would know only love for her father, her aunt and her mother (in that order). 'My dear sister, you will be her second mother,' she assured Dorothy, 'and I am convinced that you will take great care to turn her into your second self.' There was a constant appeal to Dorothy's feminine sympathies: Annette had been parted not just from her lover but also from her child, whom her family had insisted should be entrusted to foster parents. Yes, of course, she missed William dreadfully, but her maternal sufferings at her enforced separation from Caroline were unbearable. The reproach is implicit: William had not only left her but also deprived her of her child. Justice demanded that he should return to France and marry her, not because she wanted to legitimize her own position, but only so that she and Caroline could be reunited permanently.

> then my daughter would have a father and her poor mother would enjoy the happiness of having her always with her. I would myself give her all the attentions I am jealous that she receives at the hands of strangers. I would not make my family blush in calling her my daughter my Caroline – I would take her with me and I would go into the country, there is no solitude where I would not find charms with her . . . I can truthfully assure you that if it were possible for *mon ami* to come and give me the glorious title of his wife, in spite of the cruel necessity which would compel him to leave his wife and child immediately, I would more easily bear an absence which is in truth painful but I would also find in his daughter a compensation which is now denied to me.[31]

No sister, however jealous of her brother's affections, could have withstood such a dignified and unselfish appeal to her compassion. In Dorothy, as Annette well knew, she would have a loyal and ardent advocate close to William. If he was, as she suspected, faltering in his resolve to marry her, there was no one better placed to keep him up to the mark than Dorothy. Annette's unerring instinct for addressing herself to the most vulnerable points in the Wordsworths' characters reveals her to be far more percipient and a better tactician than she is usually portrayed. And it says much for her persuasive skills that, although she never did marry William, she managed to achieve her aims without him: family, friends and neighbours were soon taught to accept her as Mme Williams and Caroline was restored to her care.[32]

Annette would need all her powers of tact and diplomacy in the coming months and years. Ironically, at the very time William was at his most fiery, inditing his republican tract, Annette was being drawn into an actively counter-revolutionary role. Only four days before she wrote to William and Dorothy, her brother Paul was involved in a fracas at Orléans. Léonard Bourdon, a deputy in the National Convention, attended a drunken banquet at *La Société Populaire* in Orléans on 16 March 1793. A lawyer by training, he had been sent to the city the previous autumn to investigate procedures against prisoners of the High Court, and was therefore implicated in their massacre the following month. Not unnaturally, he had many enemies in Orléans; his excess of revolutionary zeal and suspected corruption had even earned him the distrust of an extremist like Robespierre. Coming out of the banquet, he was jostled by the crowd, insults were exchanged and Bourdon was slightly wounded. He took refuge in the *maison de commune*, where a doctor confirmed his injuries were very slight and local officials pleaded with him to ignore '*une si petite affaire*'. Apoplectic with rage, Bourdon swore it was an assassination attempt by *aristocrates* and that he would be revenged: twenty-five Orléanaises heads would roll on the scaffold.[33]

Orders went out for the arrest of one woman, Angélique Legay, and twenty-six men, including Paul Vallon and Jean Henri Gellet-Duvivier, William's former landlord in Orléans. If ever there was a good time to attack one of the more combustible representatives of the National Convention, this was not it. Only six days earlier, a Revolutionary Tribunal for counter-revolutionary offences had been established as a response to French reverses on the front and to news of the revolt in the Vendée, just south-west of Orléans; three days afterwards, the Convention decreed the death penalty without appeal for rebels captured in arms.[34] Forewarned that he was about to be arrested, Annette's brother and ten other suspects left their homes and went into hiding; they were the lucky ones. Charges were laid against all the supposed *aristocrates*, who were tried before the Revolutionary Tribunal in June. Gellet-Duvivier was accused of calling Bourdon a *gredin* (a knave or blackguard), grabbing him by the throat and, when ordered not to attack a representative of the people, replying that he did not recognize the authority of the Convention; he had fired a shot in the Place de l'Etape and had been among those chasing Bourdon into the *maison de commune*. For these offences, he was condemned to death. Paul Vallon, in his absence, was indicted for being present in the armed 'mob' (like Gellet-Duvivier, he was armed because he was on duty at the *maison de commune* as a member of the *garde-nationale*), insulting Bourdon and having done everything possible to prevent an arrest. Because he could not be found, the charges lay on the file; should he emerge from hiding, he would be arrested immediately. To complete his retribution, Bourdon had a large number of public officials in Orléans, including the Vallons' friend André Augustin Dufours, sacked on suspicion of being '*fortement impregnés d'aristocratie*'.[35]

Twelve-year-old Pauline Gellet-Duvivier, the little girl who had voluntarily given up her gold earrings to the *patrie* in 1789, now made an agonized appeal to the nation for mercy. Her father had always been a loyal patriot, she declared, but his mind had been unbalanced since his wife's death. Confident in her father's innocence and the justice of his judges, she offered them her own liberty and life.

Her confidence was misplaced. On 13 July 1793, the same day that Charlotte Corday stabbed Marat to death in his bath, nine of the convicted 'assassins', including Gellet-Duvivier, were executed. Two years later, the judgements were to be revised in the light of evidence from the Dijon commune that Bourdon had boasted of provoking the incident.[36] It was too late for Gellet-Duvivier, but Paul Vallon had had a narrow escape. From this moment, the whole Vallon family, Madame Williams among them, would do all they could to assist the cause of 'throne and altar'.

The romantic imagination which so easily takes over when writing on the revolution tempts one to portray Annette, Orczy-fashion, as a glamorous female Scarlet Pimpernel, risking her own life to save émigrés and non-juring priests from the guillotine. It is therefore salutary to be reminded that, though the guillotine stood in the Place de la Liberté in Blois throughout the course of the revolution, it was never used.[37] This is not to say that Annette did not take risks, but the true extent of her activities is difficult to assess. The evidence can hardly be regarded as impartial: reports from surveillance committees and spies, on the one hand, and, on the other, royalist petitions for a pension as a reward for services rendered. What is interesting is that, though they come from different ends of the political spectrum, they are both agreed on two points: Annette was actively involved in counter-revolution and it was her diplomatic skills which made her so formidable. On 31 January 1801 the Minister of Justice gave an order to search her house for incriminating papers and arrest her if she was implicated in plots against the state. As she was not arrested, we can only assume she was tipped off by her friends in high places. The *préfet* of the Loir-et-Cher department in 1804 noted that the Vallon sisters had 'always' loved and served the royalists but he singled out Annette: '*La femme* Williams, notably, is known as *une intriguante decidée*', he declared. The police commission in Blois hastened to assure him that suspects were not meeting at her house, but the *préfet* himself was not convinced.[38]

The fullest and most interesting accounts of her activities in the 1790s, and beyond, come from two references provided in 1818 to substantiate her claims that she deserved a civil-list pension. Guillemin de Savigny, who had known her since childhood, declared that, like her parents, she had always been devoted to God and the Bourbons. She had scoured both town and country to find refuges for priests who had refused to take the civil oath and devoted herself to saving the lives of royalists. She had herself hidden M. Delaporte, the aged intendant of Roussillon and Lorraine, when he was denounced to the Revolutionary Tribunal, and she had got the Comte Dufort, M. de Montlivaut and others out of prison. In 1795–6, proscribed émigrés returning to France were sent to her for a safe haven at Blois; in 1799–1800 the royal armies of the Vendée and Brittany had relied on her for a supply of recruits. The *maire* of Blois added his own glowing reference.

> In the time of proscription, her house was the refuge and rendezvous of honest men and especially of those who were in communication with the Vendée; born with an enterprising

character, she undertook different missions and, amongst others, to treat with the merchants of this town for provisions for the royal army.

How did Annette get away with it? Guillemin de Savigny has a startling revelation.

She took it on herself to win the friendship of the accomplices of the ferocities of the [National] Convention who were at the head of the odious club at Blois [Les Amis de la Constitution] and the infamous revolutionary committees of that town and she knew how to soften them in favour of all the unfortunates that she knew.[39]

The conclusion is inescapable that, after the almost simultaneous attack on Bourdon at Orléans and outbreak of royalist rebellion close by in the Vendée, Annette used the connections she had made through her revolutionary English lover to further the counter-revolutionary cause. It was perhaps fortunate that William, whose fiery republicanism had taken him beyond even the notorious Thomas Paine, was unaware of what she was doing. Had the war between France and England, not to mention all their other difficulties, not intervened to separate them, surely their relationship would have foundered on the increasing polarization of their political opinions.

William was still trying to find a means of earning money. Writing had failed, he had rejected ordination, the war with France had deprived him of his preferred option of becoming a travelling companion to a wealthy gentleman touring the Continent. So he fell back on the usual options open to impoverished Cambridge graduates. He would become a private tutor or he would take pupils. He applied, through friends, for a position in Ireland, as tutor to the son of Lord Belmore, but the post was filled even before his application arrived.[40] Fortunately, at this juncture, another opportunity offered. One of his old schoolfriends from Hawkshead, William Calvert, had inherited a considerable fortune and an estate on Lake Bassenthwaite on the death of his father in 1791. He was therefore a man of independent means and leisure. Calvert decided he would like to make a tour of the West of England and Wales, but was averse to the idea of going alone. He invited William to accompany him, offering to pay all his travelling expenses; the trip would last till October, but William was free to leave whenever he wished, should a better opportunity arise. It was the perfect arrangement for William: he could indulge his wanderlust with a congenial companion, without incurring any cost or risking the loss of a permanent situation.

An added advantage was that, having got as far as North Wales, William could comparatively easily and cheaply make the journey up to Halifax, where, since the spring, he had had a standing invitation to visit Mrs Rawson (the former 'Aunt' Threlkeld). Dorothy, who had spent the last few years dreaming of just such a visit herself, had finally obtained permission from the Cooksons to pass the winter in Halifax. This was something of an achievement, as she had become indispensable to the household at Forncett, where she was 'head nurse, housekeeper, [and] tutoress of the little ones or rather superintendent of the nursery'. Writing in high excitement to Jane, she began her letter with the urgent warning, '*None of this is to be read aloud, so be upon your guard!*' Brother and sister had not met for over two and a half years; there was no prospect of them doing so at Forncett, since Uncle William would not invite his errant nephew. They therefore planned to meet in Halifax, without his prior knowledge, in case he withdrew his permission for Dorothy's trip.[41]

Dorothy, temporarily forgetting her tears for Annette, was beside herself with joy. She was about to be reunited with her favourite brother and Jane, 'the Friend of my Childhood, the companion of my pleasures "when Life reared laughing up her morning Sun". Oh Jane! with what Transport shall I embrace you! My dear Friend we shall live over again those Days, and we shall anticipate future joys, domestic felicity, Peace and retirement, when you visit me and find me united to my dear William.' To give Jane 'a faint idea' of her brother's affection for her and his desire to see her, she proudly copied out some passages from William's recent letters. 'Oh my dear, dear sister with what transport shall I again meet you,' he had written, 'with what rapture shall I again wear out the day in your sight. I assure you so eager is my desire to see you that all obstacles vanish. I see you in a moment running or rather flying to my arms.'[42]

Always excitable, the strain of keeping the secret of their planned meeting and the uncertainty attending the date of her own visit took their toll on Dorothy. She lost her purse containing the six sovereigns she had carefully hoarded for her trip to Halifax and she succumbed to an attack of worms.[43]

William and Calvert began their tour in leisurely fashion by spending a month on the Isle of Wight. For William it was an experience filled with contradiction. He loved that 'delightful island', particularly the walks along the seashore and in the woods. They enjoyed a succession of 'calm and glassy days', but the tranquillity of the natural scene was at odds with William's own emotional turmoil and the human activity in the Solent between the island and Portsmouth. The Royal Navy was assembling at Spithead in preparation for the war against France. Every evening, the stillness of the island was shattered by the thundering of the sunset cannon:

> at the sound
> The star of life appears to set in blood,
> And ocean shudders in offended mood,
> Deepening with moral gloom his angry flood.

There could hardly have been a more ominous daily reminder to William of his divided loyalties. For him, this gallant fleet, which could not fail to be an inspiring sight of itself, was 'doomed' upon an 'unworthy service', by 'The unhappy counsel of a few weak men'.[44] When they eventually left the island, probably early in August, William was filled with 'melancholy forebodings'.

The struggle which was beginning, and which many thought would be brought to a speedy close by the irresistible arms of Great Britain being added to those of the allies, I was assured in my own mind would be of long continuance, and productive of distress and misery beyond all possible calculation. This conviction was pressed upon me by having been a witness, during a long residence in revolutionary France, of the spirit which prevailed in that country.[45]

In his *Letter to the Bishop of L[l]andaff*, William had already attacked the war as an 'infatuation which is now giving up to the sword so large a portion of the poor and consigning the rest to the more slow and more painful consumption of want'. Watching the fleet gathering at Spithead, he saw the first signs that this was indeed happening. Many of the sailors had been forcibly conscripted into service, regardless of family or other commitments. Only two or three months earlier, while William was still in London, his brother John had seen the sailors from all the East Indiamen lying at Gravesend impressed into the navy, even though the company had written guarantees from the Lords of the Admiralty that this would not happen. The press gangs were out in all the Channel ports and, further inland, the recruiting sergeants were offering the king's shilling to any able-bodied man willing to accept it. Many were driven to do so by desperation, being unable to provide for themselves or their families in any other way. William, like his later friend Tom Poole, could not see this unmoved. 'I consider every Briton who loses his life in the war as much murdered as the King of France,' Poole wrote, 'and every one who approves the war, as signing the death-warrant of each soldier or sailor that falls.'[46]

As William and Calvert made their way towards Salisbury, Calvert's horse, which was not accustomed to pulling the light gig in which they were travelling, suddenly went out of control. Capering about the road, it dragged them into a ditch and smashed the vehicle beyond repair. The travellers were now in a quandary, as they had only the one horse between them and were reluctant to put it in harness again. William was anxious to continue and was quite willing to go on foot, but he could not keep pace with Calvert on horseback. The two friends therefore decided to part, Calvert riding back home on a more direct northern route and William keeping to their original plan of making a detour through Wales. Though he had received no salary from Calvert, William had five guineas, advanced to him by Richard before he left London, which would be sufficient to finance a pedestrian tour.[47]

For two or three days William wandered alone over Salisbury Plain. It was a period of intense introspection, heightened by the bleak aspect of a landscape which seemed like a metaphor for his own aimlessness. He roamed

There on the pastoral downs without a track
To guide me, or along the bare white roads
Lengthening in solitude their dreary line[48]

Fifty years later, he would declare, 'My ramble over many parts of Salisbury plain . . . left upon my mind imaginative impressions the force of wh[ich] I have felt to this day.' What he found so memorable was not just the emptiness of the swelling hills, rising one after another in seemingly endless succession, but the contrasting profusion of relics of ancient British civilization: white horses carved into the red earth, hill-forts, standing stones and stone circles. Gigantic in size and mysterious in origin and purpose, they were literally monuments to a lost past, when supposedly uncivilized men had worked with unity of purpose on a grand design. William could not help but contrast the strength, simplicity and grandeur of these images with the feverish, petty, selfish interests of the modern world. They led him 'unavoidably to compare what we know or guess of those remote times with certain aspects of modern society, and with calamities, principally those consequent upon war, to which, more than other classes of men, the poor are subject'.[49]

At Stonehenge, despite the solemnity of his surroundings, he was overcome with heat and fatigue and fell asleep in the stone circle. As he later remarked ironically to a friend, in such a place he ought to have been visited by the muse in his slumbers, but he was not. Nevertheless, landscape, antiquities and political conviction were all drawing together in his mind to produce a poem, *The Female Vagrant*, the object of which was, in part, 'to expose the vices of the penal law and the calamities of war as they affect individuals'.[50] The first of William's great didactic morality poems, it marked a clear break with the self-indulgent, insincere and derivative poetry he had written previously. Informed by personal experience, inspired by compassion and articulated by rage, he had found a voice at last.

The Female Vagrant told the story of the accidental meeting of two wanderers seeking shelter during a stormy night on Salisbury Plain. The woman explained how she came to be alone and destitute: her father had been evicted from his cottage in the Lakes by an acquisitive neighbour, she had married her childhood sweetheart but the advent of war had ruined them and, in a last desperate attempt to support her and their three children, he had volunteered for the army. Within a year, she was the sole survivor, having lost husband and children to sword and plague. This tale of human suffering is sandwiched between two powerful pieces of political invective. The introduction argued Rousseau's principle that the life of a savage, however hard, was better than that of modern man, because there were no distinctions in wealth or power to exacerbate suffering by comparison. The closing lines were a revolutionary rallying call, urging the 'Heroes of Truth' to 'uptear Th'Oppressor's dungeon from its deepest base', wield the Herculean mace of Reason over the towers of Pride and drag 'foul Error's monster race' from darkness into the light which would kill it. The poem was as violently radical and just as unpublishable in the current political climate as *A Letter to the Bishop of L[l]andaff*.[51]

Having crossed Salisbury Plain, William made his way through Bath to Bristol, then, crossing the Severn estuary by ferry, he landed at Chepstow and made his way northward up the River Wye. In taking a pedestrian tour up the celebrated Wye valley, William was following in the picturesque tradition. William Gilpin's *Observations on the River Wye*, first published in 1782, had become the bible of a generation of poets, artists and writers. Samuel Rogers had followed in Gilpin's footsteps and kept a journal of his tour in the summer of 1791; the next year, J. M. W. Turner, making the first of five tours in Wales, painted Chepstow Castle, Tintern Abbey and Llanthony Priory.[52] William was equally conscious that he was following in a literary and artistic tradition; indeed, that it is why he had decided to take that route. At the time he produced a few fragmentary verses, expressing suitably republican sentiments:

> In vain did Time and Nature toil to throw
> Wild weeds and dust upon these crumbled towers;
> Again they rear the feudal head that lowers
> Stern on the wretched huts that crouch below.[53]

Far more importantly, the tour laid the seeds for future poems: incidents and images which then impressed themselves on his mind would be mulled over in future years and subtly infused with his own imaginative colouring. At Goodrich Castle, for instance, he met a pretty little girl, about eight years of age, who insisted she was one of seven children, even though two of her siblings were dead. Her refusal to accept that she was now one of only five led William to write *We are Seven* several years later, as a graphic illustration of the inability of children to grasp the notion of death. Walking between Builth Wells and Hay-on-Wye, he fell in with a 'wild rover' who told him many 'strange stories' as they walked together; his 'countenance, gait and figure' would later supply those of Peter Bell. 'It has always been a pleasure to me through life', William would say, 'to catch at every opportunity that has occur[r]ed in my rambles, of becoming acquainted with this class of people.'[54] Most famously of all, however, the landscape a few miles upstream above Tintern Abbey would furnish calming images, 'beauteous forms' of peace and tranquillity, to bring solace to a troubled mind.

> . . . how oft –
> In darkness and amid the many shapes
> Of joyless daylight; when the fretful stir
> Unprofitable, and the fever of the world,
> Have hung upon the beatings of my heart –
> How oft, in spirit, have I turned to thee,
> O sylvan Wye! thou wanderer through the woods,
> How often has my spirit turned to thee![55]

In *Tintern Abbey*, written when revisiting the Wye valley five years later, William gives a wonderful description of his younger self, which perfectly captures his mood on this tour: his joy in his own physical prowess, his rapture at the beauty of the landscape and, more disquietingly, his sense that he was taking refuge in nature as a flight from his problems, rather than as an answer to them. The natural beauties of the Wye bewitched his physical senses; it did not, as yet, offer him a philosophy for coming to terms with the human condition. He describes how, 'like a roe',

> I bounded o'er the mountains, by the sides
> Of the deep rivers, and the lonely streams,
> Wherever nature led: more like a man
> Flying from something he dreads, than one
> Who sought the thing he loved. For nature then
> (The coarser pleasures of my boyish days,
> And their glad animal movements all gone by)
> To me was all in all. – I cannot paint
> What then I was. The sounding cataract
> Haunted me like a passion: the tall rock,
> The mountain, and the deep and gloomy wood,
> Their colours and their forms, were then to me
> An appetite; a feeling and a love,
> That had no need of a remoter charm,
> By thought supplied, nor any interest
> Unborrowed from the eye.[56]

How far William travelled up the meandering course of the Wye is not known, but by 30 August he was 'quietly sitting down in the Vale of Clwyd', awaiting his sister's arrival at Halifax. 'He is staying with his Friend Jones the companion of his continental Tour,' Dorothy wrote to Jane, 'and passes his Time as happily as he could desire; exactly according to his Taste, except alas! (ah here I sigh) that he is separated from those he loves. He says that "their House is quite a cottage just such an one as would suit us" and oh! how sweetly situated in the most delicious of all Vales, the Vale of Clwyd.' Dorothy herself was in a fever of anxiety and anticipation, waiting for the arrangements for her visit to be finalized. 'Oh count, count the Days, my Love', she urged Jane, 'till Christmas how slowly does each day move! and yet three months and Christmas will not be here. Three months! – long, long months I measure them with a Lover's scale; three months of Expectation are three Ages!'[57]

While Dorothy fretted in Norfolk, William appears to have sat out the interval till Christmas at Plas-yn-Llan. His brothers were both in the Lakes in August and September, Richard on business, Christopher on his summer vacation from Cambridge. John, who had sailed with the East India fleet under convoy from Spithead on 22 May, only a few weeks before William's residence on the Isle of Wight, was on his way to China as fifth mate under his cousin, Captain Wordsworth, on the *Earl of Abergavenny*.[58]

Four months was a long period for someone as constitutionally restless as William to 'quietly sit down' in Clwyd, but, until he reappears at Whitehaven on 26 December, his existence is totally uncharted. This has given biographers ample scope for varying degrees of wild speculation, based on a single, much-quoted passage in Thomas Carlyle's *Reminiscences*.

He had been in France in the earlier or secondary stage of the Revolution; had witnessed the struggle of *Girondins* and *Mountain*, in particular the execution of Gorsas, 'the first *Deputy* sent to the Scaffold;' and testified strongly to the ominous feeling which that event produced in everybody, and of which he himself still seemed to retain something: 'Where will it *end*, when you have set an example in *this* kind?' I knew well about Gorsas; but had found, in my readings, no trace of the public emotion his death excited; and perceived now that Wordsworth might be taken as a true supplement to my Books, on this small point.[59]

It seems inconceivable that Carlyle could be wrong. There was no one more likely to understand the references and the background than the great historian and author of *The French Revolution*. And he had the information direct from William himself. On these two premises alone, few have dared to challenge Carlyle's statement.[60]

Yet if Carlyle was right, some time between the end of August and the beginning of October William left North Wales, returned to the south coast, caught a boat to France and made his way to Paris. There, on 7 October, he was in the crowd and witnessed as Antoine Gorsas, a journalist of the Girondin party, was executed by the guillotine. He then scuttled back to England and the safety of his Wordsworth relatives in Cumberland, in time for a jolly Christmas reunion with his sister. This presupposes so many insuperable difficulties that it defies belief. Where did he get the money to finance his journey and bribe a ship's captain to take him to France, always assuming he could find one prepared to run the risk? How did he land at one of the French Channel ports, or travel to Paris without a French government passport or papers? How did he avoid the bands of armed royalist rebels and revolutionary guards roaming the countryside of Normandy? Or, for that matter, if he landed further east near Dunkirk, the triumphant French armies who had just trounced the English at the battle of Hondschoote on 8 September? How did he evade capture or arrest, given that, on 17 September, the National Convention had ordered the arrest of all foreign nationals from countries at war with France? How did he alone escape imprisonment in Paris, when such renowned English revolutionaries as Helen Maria Williams, her lover J. H. Stone and even the father of the revolution, Thomas Paine himself, were in detention? William's friends in Paris were chiefly drawn from the Girondin faction, so he could not have picked a worse time to rely on their assistance or protection. In May, they had been effectively evicted from power; on 3 October, they were proscribed and arrested. The execution of Gorsas was but the first of many in his party in the weeks that followed.

Viewed in such a light, William's return to France at this time would have been not just foolhardy but suicidal. Moreover, there is no reason, logical or otherwise, why he should have wished to go back. There had been no change in his circumstances which merited his risking his life to marry Annette; in any case, he supposedly went to Paris, not Blois, so that cannot have been his object. It is unlikely that the man who balked at publishing his *Letter to the Bishop of L[l]andaff* in England would have believed he had any contribution to make by throwing in his lot with any of the factions in France; if nothing else, such a quixotic gesture would have destroyed any chance he ever had of providing that cottage for his sister or, indeed, his mistress and child.

Quite clearly William lacked motive, money and contacts to enable him to return to France, however briefly. Had he done so, it is impossible that no reference to it should survive in his own writings or those of his family. Even the Wordsworth family were unable to suppress every single reference to Annette and Caroline, despite their existence being a far more potentially damaging revelation than that of another trip to revolutionary France. *The Prelude* makes no attempt to hide William's revolutionary sympathies; he even openly admits to rejoicing at the defeat of the English at Hondschoote and, when prayers for English victory were offered up in churches, sitting silent 'like an uninvited guest Whom no one owned'.[61] Quite apart from the obvious implication of these lines that William was still in England at this time, his declaration of such sentiments militates against any suggestion that he might have concealed a return to France for fear of being regarded as unpatriotic. Had he really been in Paris to witness the first public execution of a deputy to the National Convention, he would surely have recorded it in *The Prelude*. It would have been too significant an event, and too dramatically moving a moment, when Gorsas, in his final words from the scaffold, commended his wife and children to the pity of the republic, for anyone, much less a poet, to ignore. Nor could he have been unaware of the agitation in Paris which would lead, a week later, to Marie Antoinette being put on trial for her life and her execution on 16 October. It is worth noticing also that while William's poetry is littered with references to hangings, the scaffold and the rope, even to the point of obsession, there is nothing to indicate in any of his writings that he ever saw an execution by guillotine. Those Englishmen who did so were profoundly shocked and repelled by its brisk efficiency, the gore and the matter-of-fact disposal of severed head and torso. It was not surprising that '*Madame La Guillotine*' came to symbolize the French Revolution. It would be very surprising if witnessing it in action left no impression on William.[62]

Sadly, the inescapable conclusion is the boring, unglamorous one. Carlyle was simply mistaken. He was recalling a conversation which had taken place at least twenty-five years previously, with a man remembering events of almost fifty years before that. Carlyle did not think the conversation worth recording at the time: it does not appear in either his contemporary letters or his book *The French Revolution*. We can only conjecture that William talked about being present in Paris at the end of 1792, but, when the conversation moved on to Gorsas (whose execution

Carlyle himself had movingly described in the book), Carlyle assumed that William had been a literal witness of events which he had only read about in the newspapers.[63]

The likeliest scenario is that, in the autumn of 1793, William remained at Plas-yn-Llan for as long as he was welcome, writing his earliest version of *The Female Vagrant*, then moved on to visit his Wordsworth relations in Cumberland. Earlier in the year, he had said he wanted to visit Chester and Manchester at the latter end of the summer. As both towns lay on his route between Plas-yn-Llan and the Lakes, he may now have taken them in on the way.[64]

His decision to visit his Wordsworth relations seems to have been a diplomatic one, a case of building much-needed bridges with the side of the family that had always been less judgemental and more kindly disposed than the Cooksons. Uncle Richard had consistently forwarded funds whenever requested to do so, and William had obviously got on well with his cousin Captain John Wordsworth when they met in London. He could hardly be in the north and not visit them, unless he deliberately wished to cause offence, as it was now five years since William had last seen his uncle and other cousins. In the interval, one of his favourite cousins, Mary, had married Mr Smith, a brandy merchant of Broughton-in-Furness. They now lived in that pretty market town, close to the mouth of the beautiful River Duddon. The previous summer, they had welcomed John and Christopher, who had then moved on to stay with Mary's sister and her husband, Mr Barker, at Rampside, a tiny village on the furthermost tip of the Furness peninsula, overlooking Morecambe Bay.[65]

It seems likely that William now followed in his brothers' footsteps, visiting Broughton, and possibly Rampside, before travelling on to Whitehaven, where he spent Christmas with his Uncle Richard. Whether or not he confessed about Annette and Caroline, and despite his republican principles (even if he chose not to speak about them, they were obvious from his cropped and unpowdered hair), he still received a kindly welcome and left with £20 in his pocket and a new hat.[66] Before, or possibly after, Christmas William also paid a visit to his erstwhile travelling companion William Calvert at Keswick. From there he retraced his steps up the length of Lake Bassenthwaite to stay on its northernmost shores at Armathwaite Hall, with another old schoolfriend, John Spedding, his widowed mother and two sisters.[67]

By the middle of February, William was settled at the Rawsons' house at Millbank, just outside Halifax, and reunited with his sister for the first time in over three years. Writing to his college friend Mathews, he appeared as cheerful and casual about his own prospects as ever. 'I approve much of your change of profession,' he wrote, 'all professions I think are attended with great inconveniences, but that of the priesthood with the most.'

You have learned from Myers that, since I had the pleasure of seeing you, I have been do[ing] nothing and still continue to be doing nothing. What is to become of me I know not:

I cannot bow down my mind to take orders, and as for the law I have neither strength of mind purse or constitution, to engage in that pursuit . . . nor do I think it worth while to take my master's degree next summer. As an honour you know it is nothing, and in a pecuniary light it would be of no use to me, on the contrary, it would cost me a good deal of money.

Unlike his insatiable friend, he could not lay claim to having kept up his study of modern languages: he had read no Spanish for three years and little Italian, though he intended to resume his study of the latter immediately in order to teach it to his sister. Of French, on the other hand, 'I esteem myself a tolerable master.' The only subject which roused him to something like enthusiasm was politics. Mathews had just been to Portugal and William fired eager questions at him: 'have the principles of free government any advocate there? or is Liberty a sound of which they have never heard?'[68]

William's radicalism must have come as a profound shock to Dorothy, whose naturally aristocratic and conservative sympathies had been fostered by her five-year residence at Forncett and her proximity to the royal family at Windsor. Whatever reservations she may have had, she loved her brother too much not to enter into this passion as fully as she had his others. As they explored the beautiful Ryburn valley, with its tumbling wooded hillsides and vista of moorland beyond, he must have talked to her at length about France, his conversion to the republican cause, Annette and his unseen daughter and, perhaps most of all, his plans for the future. He could not continue 'doing nothing' for ever.

Brother and sister decided that they wished to be alone together. Having spent literally years longing for at least a six-month visit to Halifax, Dorothy now packed her bags after only half that time. At the beginning of April, she set off by coach with William for what turned out to be a very leisurely trip to Whitehaven. For once, they had money. In addition to William's £20, which must have been largely intact, in early March Dorothy had received five guineas from Uncle Richard and, at the same time, they had each received £28 14s 8d as their legacy from their Grandmother Cookson's personal estate, which Richard invested on their behalf at an advantageous rate of interest.[69]

At Kendal, they dismounted and walked the eighteen miles to Grasmere. It was a journey which would be forever etched in Dorothy's memory as her first introduction to the Lakes and the beginning of her 'pilgrimage' with William. They paused at a public house at Staveley to fortify themselves before tackling the mountains by drinking a basin of milk. Dorothy washed her feet in the brook and, on William's advice, put on a pair of silk stockings to prevent her shoes chafing. They walked the length of Windermere, stopping again to rest and refresh themselves by a little stream feeding into the lake at Lowwood. By the time they wound their way under the craggy heights of Nab Scar and Loughrigg Fell, the sun was just setting and pouring a rich yellow light on the still waters of Rydal and Grasmere, in which the islands were reflected.[70] They spent the night at Grasmere, before walking the next fifteen miles over Dunmail Raise and beneath the shadow of Helvellyn, to the far side of Keswick. The obliging William Calvert was in London and had offered to let them lodge at his house, Windy Brow, until his return. Dorothy was in ecstasies at her own wonderful prowess in walking, at the delightful manners of Calvert's caretaker tenants ('the most honest cleanly sensible people I ever saw in their rank of life') and, above all, the situation of the farmhouse itself. Standing at the top of a very steep bank rising 'nearly perpendicular' from the River Greta below, it looked out towards the little town of Keswick, over which towered the wooded steeps and silvery, rocky summit of Friar's Crag. About 100 yards above the house was a natural terrace along Latrigg Fell, the mountain under which Windy Brow sheltered, commanding a view of the whole Vale of Keswick. It was impossible, Dorothy declared, to describe the grandeur of this view over 'the vale of Elysium, as Mr Grey calls it', with Derwentwater lying in the lap of huge mountains to the south-west, the ribbon of Bassenthwaite to the north and Skiddaw's massive bosomy heights towering above the fields and cottages of the vale between. She had intended to stay for only a few days with William before travelling on to Whitehaven, but she could not tear herself away. A fortnight later, she had given up all thought of an early departure and was planning to stay for another month.[71]

This blissful existence was rudely interrupted by a stinging letter of rebuke from Uncle Christopher's wife. Dorothy's conduct was disgraceful, her reputation in tatters. Not content with rambling about the countryside on foot, instead of hiring a post chaise from Kendal like any proper lady, Dorothy was now living in lodgings at vast expense and, worse still, without any respectable guardian of her morals. To this shrill censure, Dorothy replied with admirable dignity and restraint. 'I am much obliged to you for the frankness with which you have expressed your sentiments upon my conduct', she wrote, 'and am at the same time extremely sorry that you should think it so severely to be condemned.' The walk from Kendal had given her pleasure and saved her thirty shillings. Her expenses were negligible, since they drank no tea, had bread and milk for breakfast and supper, and potatoes 'from choice' as their main dish at dinner. She considered 'the character and virtues of my brother' as 'sufficient protection' (one can just imagine the explosion at Newbiggin Hall on reading this) but, in any case, 'I am convinced that there is no place in the world in which a good and virtuous young woman would be more likely to continue good and virtuous than under the roof of these honest, worthy, uncorrupted people'. As proof that her reputation had not suffered, she made pointed reference to the friendly attentions she had received from several of her brothers' friends and Mrs Spedding, in particular, from whose house she had only just returned after a visit of three days and to whom she had promised further visits. Reiterating this at the close of her letter, Dorothy politely but implicitly snubbed her aunt: if Mrs Spedding of Armathwaite Hall chose to invite Miss Wordsworth into her house, who was Mrs Crackanthorpe to complain of ruined reputations and unprotected situation? Finally, with quiet emphasis, Dorothy informed her aunt that she intended to remain a few weeks longer at Windy Brow to cultivate these new acquaintances and, above all, enjoy the society of her brother.

I am now twenty two years of age and such have been the circumstances of my life that I may be said to have enjoyed his company only for a *very few* months. An opportunity now presents itself of obtaining this satisfaction, an opportunity which I could not see pass from me without unspeakable pain. Besides I not only derive much pleasure but much improvement from my brother's society. I have regained all the knowledge I had of the French language some years ago, and have added considerably to it, and I have now begun reading Italian, of which I expect to have soon gained a sufficient knowledge to receive much entertainment and advantage from it.[72]

Dorothy's intellectual hunger was a pleasant stimulus to William's own appetite for books and poetry. He wrote to Richard, asking him to forward to Keswick the Italian grammar and editions of Tasso and Ariosto he had left in his care after leaving Cambridge. Mindful of Dorothy's earlier criticisms and prompted by her presence, he began a thorough revision of *An Evening Walk* and *Descriptive Sketches*. In the case of *An Evening Walk*, this was a virtual rewriting, containing important additions which suggest that he was beginning to evolve his philosophy of 'seeing into the Life of things'. The sensitive heart, he now wrote, 'sees not any line where being ends' and 'Sees sense . . . Tremble obscure in fountain, rock and shade'; the unity and harmony of the natural world, of which man is an indivisible part, bear witness to man's potential for good and inspire 'Entire affection for all human kind'. Reviews of both poems were still appearing and William was hopeful that Johnson might be persuaded to publish a new edition. If he could be certain of earning some money by it, he intended to offer Johnson his Salisbury Plain poem, written the previous summer and now, neatly copied up by Dorothy, ready for the press. He even found time to write a new poem, an inscription for a seat by the pathway leading up to Windy Brow.[73]

William's new-found creativity and sense of purpose obviously owed much to Dorothy's presence but it had far-reaching consequences. Calvert's younger brother, Raisley, was one of the people who paid 'the friendliest attentions' to William and Dorothy. He was a remarkable young man, not yet twenty-one years of age, who had much in common with William, quite apart from a similar family background. He had been disenchanted with Cambridge, leaving before he had even matriculated, had a passion for travel and was a talented amateur sculptor. He was also in very delicate health and his chances of earning lasting fame were decidedly slim. It was perhaps for this reason that he now decided to offer William a share in his income. It is usually accepted that Raisley saw William's potential as a poet and wanted to free him from the necessity of earning his own living so that he could dedicate himself to writing poetry. This is undeniably true, but it cannot be the whole story. In acknowledging his debt to Raisley, William always couched his gratitude in specific terms. Just after the offer had been made, for instance,

William declared, 'he is . . . ready to support me in a situation wherein I feel I can be of some little service to my fellowmen'. In 1805, it is still the same story: 'the act was done entirely from a confidence on his part that I had powers and attainments which might be of use to mankind'.[74] Next to nothing is known about Raisley Calvert, but the implication of comments such as these is that he shared William's radical political beliefs.

Politics, more than poetry, were still uppermost in William's mind. In his *Letter to the Bishop of L[l]andaff* he had recognized that education was the key to bringing about change. Since then, he had read one of the most influential books of the day, William Godwin's *Enquiry Concerning Political Justice and its Influence on Morals and Happiness.* To account for the phenomenal impact of this book, not just on William but on a whole generation of young intellectuals and radicals, one has to realize that he offered them hope. The idealists who, in the name of republicanism, had welcomed the French Revolution, advocated the execution of the King and defended the massacre of counter-revolutionaries, found it increasingly difficult to justify the indiscriminate slaughter which resulted from warring factional interest. In the Terror that followed the fall of the Girondins and rise of Robespierre, literally thousands were executed: in Paris alone, 2,600 went to the guillotine, over 1,500 of them in the two months of June and July 1794. As William himself tellingly put it, the conservative cry now went up, 'Behold the harvest which we reap From popular government and equality!'[75] In the light of Godwin's arguments, the violence could be explained as the result of centuries of ignorance and repression. It was necessary to educate in order to bring about a social and cultural revolution. Man is, he argued, essentially a being whose actions are determined by reason. Once he has been rationally persuaded, it is impossible for him to act unreasonably. Reason teaches benevolence and, in a rational society, all institutions and laws would be unnecessary. It was a seductive philosophy, not least because it offered disillusioned revolutionaries an alternative to violence as a method of achieving change. They could become evangelists for education and reason.

William was actively searching out a way of putting these ideas into practice at the very time Raisley Calvert offered him a share of his income. 'It seems to me', he wrote to his friend Mathews at the beginning of June 1794,

> that a writer who has the welfare of mankind at heart should call forth his best exertions to convince the people that they can only be preserved from a convulsion [i.e. violent revolution] by oeconomy in the administration of the public purse and a gradual and constant reform of those abuses which, if left to themselves, may grow to such a height as to render, even a revolution desirable. There is a further duty incumbent upon every enlightened friend of mankind; he should let slip no opportunity of explaining and enforcing those general principles of the social order which are applicable to all times and to all places; he should diffuse by every method a knowledge of those rules of political justice, from which the farther any government deviates the more effectually must it defeat the object for which government was ordained. A knowledge of these rules cannot but lead to good; they include

an entire preservative from despotism, they will guide the hand of reform, and if a revolution must afflict us, they alone can mitigate its horrors and establish freedom with tranquillity.[76]

The best way of spreading this knowledge and educating the public was to set up a newspaper or journal. Many young radicals, including Southey and Coleridge in Bristol,[77] planned to do this, and William was no exception. He would publish a monthly miscellany, together with Mathews, and one of the latter's friends. At the very outset, William set out his creed: 'You know perhaps already that I am of that odious class of men called democrats', he wrote proudly to Mathews, 'and of that class I shall for ever continue.' In a work of the kind they were planning, it would be impossible 'not to inculcate principles of government and forms of social order', so his fellow writers needed to know what they were letting themselves in for. This was not an idle remark: only a few days before he wrote this letter, three prominent members of the London Corresponding Society, Thomas Hardy, John Horne Tooke and John Thelwall, had been arrested and charged with high treason. The same risk attended anyone planning to write for a radical journal.

William could not afford to help finance the setting up of their publication or to live in London, so he could not assist with the editing. Instead, he offered to contribute essays on morals and politics and 'critical remarks' upon the arts, which he defined as poetry, painting and gardening. (The last might seem an odd subject, but William was a passionate landscape gardener all his life, believing it to be an art determined by the same principles as poetry.) 'I should principally wish our attention to be fixed upon life and manners,' he thundered, 'and to make our publication a vehicle of sound and exalted Morality.'[78]

Ironically, the very day William wrote this outspoken declaration of his principles, his lawyer brother, Richard, wrote from London to warn him that the cornerstone of the English constitution, the Habeas Corpus Act, had been suspended. 'I hope you will be cautious in writing or expressing your political opinions ... the Ministers have great powers.' It would now be possible to be arrested on suspicion of fomenting political dissent and to be held indefinitely without charge. 'Tell me', Richard added suspiciously, perhaps having caught wind of the publication scheme, 'how you mean to dispose of yourself this summer.'[79]

By the time William got this letter he was in Whitehaven, where he had at last accomplished the plan agreed at Halifax of escorting his sister to her Wordsworth relatives. They had not been able to resist a detour on the way and had paid a nostalgic visit to their childhood home at Cockermouth. They had walked along the banks of the Derwent and been shocked to find the garden in ruins and their former playground, the terrace walk, 'buried and choked up' with the old privet hedge, which had been allowed to run wild.[80] There was another unpleasant surprise waiting for them at Branthwaite, the little village between Cockermouth and Whitehaven where their cousin Richard the attorney lived. His father, their guardian, Uncle Richard, was staying there and he was so seriously ill that he was not expected to live. In fact, he lingered till the middle of June, dying on the 16th, aged sixty-one; there was a gathering of the Wordsworth clan at Whitehaven on the 20th to witness the burial of the last of that generation.[81]

The illness and death of Uncle Richard added even greater urgency to the need for a grand sort-out of the family finances. Cousin Richard drummed this into Dorothy, who wrote in a state of alarm to her brother Richard, forcefully demanding that he should make a speedy settlement of their affairs. He should harry Uncle Christopher to draw up his accounts; he must consult with those 'most able to advise' him; he should go to the House of Lords; he should go to Lord Lonsdale himself. At least 'you might *gain something*'.[82] Dorothy's frustration was understandable, given her anxiety to have an income which would allow her to settle with William, instead of being dependent on visits to relatives, but Richard was clearly offended at this implicit criticism of his handling of the case. 'There is one circumstance which I will mention to you at this time', he replied with stiff dignity, '– I might have retired into the Country & I had almost said enjoyed the sweets of retirement & domestick life if I had only considered my own Interest.'[83]

Dorothy spent the summer making a round of all her Cumberland cousins. She stayed for several weeks with Mrs Wordsworth, the wife of Captain John Wordsworth, at Whitehaven, then with the Smiths at Broughton-in-Furness and the Barkers at Rampside. Whenever he had the opportunity, William rejoined her from Keswick, where Raisley Calvert was displaying all the classic signs of tuberculosis, alternately enjoying bouts of good health and spirits, followed by periods of extreme weakness and depression. In the light of Calvert's offer to share his income with him, William felt obliged to be there when required. This had become more necessary, because William Calvert had done his patriotic duty, volunteered as an officer in the Duke of Norfolk's militia and been posted to Tynemouth in Northumberland. Though he was under pressure to do this because his father had been the Duke's steward and he held his lands from him, the very act of enlisting, even in a volunteer militia, suggests that William Calvert's political sympathies were at odds with those of his friend and his brother. That the friendship survived to the end of their lives, and into the next generation, says much for the strength of their personal affection.[84]

Whether in Cumberland or in Keswick, William's mind was full of just one thing, his plans for the new journal. It should be called the *Philanthropist*, he suggested; each issue should begin with the topic of general politics, incorporating a commentary which would 'forcibly illustrate the tendency of particular doctrines of government'; then there should be essays on morals and manners, social and political institutions, all highly educational, followed by a blend of instruction and amusement in the form of biographies representing 'the advancement of the human mind in moral knowledge' and essays on taste and criticism. Reviews, particularly of works inculcating benevolence and philanthropy, poems (but not the 'trash' infesting current magazines), reports on parliamentary debates and, if they could get them, letters from foreign correspondents would end what would have been a highly educational and Godwinian, if boring, publication.[85]

The potential readership, William believed, would be found among university students, dissenters and the Irish. This last suggestion had come from Mathews, but was taken up with alacrity by William, who even offered to go personally to Dublin from Whitehaven to find an agent to disseminate the magazine. It was an astonishing plan and, had it been put into practice, one which would have been regarded as *prima facie* evidence of treasonable activity by the government. William's target readership in that country were the fiercely nationalist United Irishmen, who were not only stirring up rebellion all over Ireland but also openly advocating a French invasion to support their cause. So much for Dorothy's assurance to Richard that she could answer for William's caution about expressing his political opinions; he was, she said, 'well aware of the dangers of a contrary conduct'.[86]

William had indeed backtracked a little from his previous incendiary declaration that he was a democrat by hastily explaining to Mathews, 'I recoil from the bare idea of a revolution', but he remained defiant and explicit in his condemnation of monarchical and aristocratical institutions, 'however modified'. He attacked the government for its brutal suppression of free speech. 'Freedom of inquiry is all that I wish for; let nothing be deemed too sacred for investigation; rather than restrain the liberty of the press I would suffer the most atrocious doctrines to be recommended: let the field be open and unencumbered, and truth must be victorious.' He denounced the conduct of foreign and domestic policy over the previous two years as driving the country into inevitable rebellion. There was only one thing that could save the country from the coming revolution: 'the undaunted efforts of good men in propagating with unremitting activity those doctrines which long and severe meditation has taught them are essential to the welfare of mankind'.[87] William had no doubt that he was one of those good men. Whether his efforts would be undaunted remained to be seen.

6. Benighted Heart and Mind

In August 1794 William crossed the broad expanse of the River Leven estuary which divides the Furness peninsula from Grange-over-Sands. It was a bright sunny day, with glorious views of the mountains to the north and the great sweep of Morecambe Bay to the south. William was in serene mood: he was on his way back to his sister and cousins at Rampside, the tiny fishing village tucked into a fold of the southern extremity of the Furness peninsula, from an excursion that morning to Cartmel Priory. Wandering in the churchyard under its grey towers, he had accidentally come across the grave of his old schoolmaster William Taylor, whose love of poetry had been an inspiration to him as a boy. As he made for the rocky outcrop of Piel Island, with its little ruined chapel, just south of Rampside, the notoriously treacherous sands of the bay were thronged with guided columns of people on foot, on horseback and in carts and wagons, hastening across before the tide swept back in. Casually hailing one of the travellers, he asked if there was any news and received a thunderbolt in reply: Robespierre, the man of blood who had unleashed the Terror on France, was dead.

> Great was my glee of spirit, great my joy
> In vengeance, and eternal justice, thus
> Made manifest. 'Come now, ye golden times',
> Said I, forth-breathing on those open sands
> A hymn of triumph, 'as the morning comes
> Out of the bosom of the night, come ye!
> Thus far our trust is verified: behold,
> They who with clumsy desperation brought
> Rivers of blood, and preached that nothing else
> Could cleanse the Augean stable, by the might

Of their own helper have been swept away!
Their madness is declared and visible –
Elsewhere will safety now be sought, and earth
March firmly towards righteousness and peace.'[1]

It was an elation which could not survive for long. True, Robespierre's execution effectively ended the Terror, but it did not end either the war with England and her allies or the internal factional struggles in the new republic. And in October the French armies, which had hitherto been defending the republic against foreign invasion, became aggressors in their turn, invading and conquering their peaceable neighbours in the Low Countries. William, like most apologists for the French Revolution, would find himself once again trapped in the cycle of hope followed by disillusionment.

William spent about a month at Rampside, before returning to Windy Brow. He probably could not resist lingering with his cousin at Broughton on the way back, as the Duddon was one of his favourite rivers, by whose side he spent 'many delightful hours', 'With friends and kindred tenderly beloved'.[2] When he eventually got back to Windy Brow at the end of September, much later than he expected, it was to find Raisley Calvert 'worse than when I left Keswick, but a good deal better than he had been some weeks before'. Another winter in England would kill him, so Calvert had decided to go to Portugal, where the warm, dry climate offered at least a hope of recovery. William saw at once that there were major objections to this idea: Calvert was too weak to travel so far, and alone, to a country where he did not speak the language. Seeing how fragile he was, William may even have suspected that the scheme would come to nothing, but did not want to alarm or dishearten his dying friend by saying so. Instead, he decided to play along. If Raisley was determined to go, the obvious person to accompany him was William, who was at leisure to do so and knew Spanish, if not Portuguese. The problem was that William could not fund such a journey himself and Raisley, who was still under-age and living on an allowance, could not afford to pay for a companion.[3] The obvious person to whom they should appeal was William Calvert, but an already awkward situation was rendered many times more delicate by Raisley's second decision. Knowing that he might never return from Portugal, he had determined to make his will. His intention was to leave everything to his brother, with a legacy to William of £600. 'He would leave me this sum', William told his own brother, 'to set me above want and to enable me to pursue my literary views or any other views with greater success or with a consciousness that if these should fail me I would have something at last to turn to.'[4]

It was an incredibly generous offer and one that ensured William would continue to share Calvert's income after his death. (The statement that it would allow William to pursue 'literary views or any other views' is additional evidence that this was a gesture of political, not purely artistic, solidarity.) It was, however, beset with problems, the most pressing of which was how to tell William Calvert.

William insisted that this should be done immediately. The easier option would have been to allow Calvert to discover the fact for himself after his brother's death, but this would inevitably lead him to suspect William of underhand motives, or even of exerting undue influence on the invalid. It was better to have the matter out in the open at once, so William grasped the nettle and wrote the difficult letter to his friend. His discomfort is evident in his abruptness. He broke the news about Raisley's health first, and asked about the possibility of Calvert paying for him to go. 'This I think, if possible, you ought to do. You see I speak to you as a friend. But then perhaps your present expenses may render it difficult. Would it not exalt you in your own esteem to retrench a little for so excellent a purpose?' He then informed him of Raisley's intention with regard to the will. 'It is at my request that this information is communicated to you, and I have no doubt but that you will do both him and myself the justice to hear this mark of his approbation of me without your good opinion of either of us being at all diminished by it.' He ended with an appeal that 'it would be much the best' if Calvert could come over himself to discuss the matters face to face.[5]

Whether he did so or not, we do not know, but Calvert responded promptly and generously. Eight days after agonizing over this letter, William and Raisley set off together for Lisbon. They did not get far. They had completed only the first leg of their journey, as far as Penrith, when Raisley realized that he could go no further. His dramatic collapse, so soon after setting off, was sufficient justification of William's wisdom in insisting that Raisley needed a companion. It might also suggest that he had foreseen the futility of the whole travelling plan.[6]

They returned the next day to Keswick. They had intended to consult Richard and other lawyers in London; now it became necessary to execute the will locally. The biggest problem, as William had pointed out to Raisley, was that the young Wordsworths owed their recently deceased Uncle Richard something in the region of £460, most of which was the capital and interest on sums advanced by him to William for his education. Raisley was concerned that the legacy he intended to form a nest-egg for William's future should not be seized upon in payment of this debt. He therefore stipulated that William's brother Richard should personally enter into a legally binding agreement that the legacy would not be used for that purpose and that, if a claim should be made by Uncle Richard's estate, Richard himself would pay the sum. Having had to go cap in hand to William Calvert, William now found himself doing the same thing to his own brother. In an agitated letter, William sought to persuade him to agree to the arrangement and offered repeated assurances that, if ever he was worth more than the £600 of the legacy, he would immediately repay the debt to their uncle.[7]

Richard replied with irritating coolness. He had 'always most sincerely had my Sisters, yours & my younger Brothers Interest at Heart although I have not been fond of making professions which It could not be my intention to carry into effect'. He would 'readily' enter into the agreement and sent his sincere good wishes to 'Mr R. Calvert', but he could not resist a little amused irony at his and William's expense. 'I hope he will live to enjoy his Fortune. I suppose he has maturely weighed the matter and taken into consideration the claims of his Brother to keep any provision he may make for you alone.'[8] For almost another two weeks, the fate of the legacy hung in the balance. William chafed, torn between fear of losing the money which would make him independent and reluctance to harass his would-be benefactor for purely selfish reasons. Raisley dithered over whether to save a guinea and a half by not employing a lawyer from Penrith, but in the end he decided he could afford to be profligate. On 23 October 1794 he employed Mr Lough to draw up his will and he increased the legacy to £900. A codicil, added the same day, directed William to use the money to purchase annuities for himself and (which probably explains the increase in the amount) to lay out 'such part and so much of the said £900 as to him shall seem meet for the use and benefit of his Sister Dorothy Wordsworth'. William Calvert was to be his brother's sole executor.[9] Even now, as Richard had pointed out, William could not be sure of his legacy; if Raisley died before his twenty-first birthday in November, his brother could challenge and overturn the will on the grounds that it had been made by a minor.

Fortunately for William's future financial security, Raisley did survive, lingering painfully and distressingly into the New Year. Some time before Christmas, they removed to Penrith, probably for the sake of better medical care than Keswick could afford. They took up lodgings in the little Robin Hood Inn on King Street, just opposite the old dame school William had attended as a child. On 9 January 1795 Raisley Calvert died. Three days later, William saw him interred in the churchyard at Greystoke. It would be almost a decade before he considered that he had at last earned his patron's trust and felt able to write and dedicate a sonnet *To the Memory of Raisley Calvert.*

> . . . if in freedom I have loved the truth;
> If there be aught of pure, or good, or great,
> In my past verse; or shall be, in the lays
> Of higher mood, which now I meditate; –
> It gladdens me, O worthy, short-lived, Youth!
> To think how much of this will be thy praise.[10]

Cooped up in the sickroom for months on end, William had had plenty of time to consider his future. The grand scheme for the *Philanthropist* had come to nothing, thwarted not just by the obstacle of William's being in the Lakes, but by the impossibility of funding publication. William, like the good man he was, remained undaunted. If he could not publish a monthly miscellany himself, he would work for someone else who could. Mathews had already come to a similar conclusion and had accepted a post as parliamentary reporter on a new 'democratical' paper, the *Telegraph*, whose first issue was published on 30 December 1794. He now offered to help William find a similar post. Hastily claiming that he had 'neither strength of memory, quickness of penmanship, nor rapidity of composition' to enable him to report parliamentary debates (and besides, heated atmosphere and loud noises gave him nervous headaches), William instead proffered his services as a translator of French, Italian and Spanish gazettes. He was also prepared to write essays upon general politics and occasional commentaries on government measures, but only for an opposition newspaper.[11] Cheered by the recent acquittal and release of Hardy, Horne Tooke and Thelwall, a sign that the British Constitution was not entirely rotten, William longed to be in the thick of things. 'I begin to wish much to be in town', he had written to Mathews early in November;

> cataracts and mountains, are good occasional society, but they will not do for constant companions; besides I have not even much of their conversation, and still less of that of my books as I am so much with my sick friend, and he cannot bear the fatigue of being read to. Nothing indeed but a sense of duty could detain me here under the present circumstances. This is a country for poetry it is true; but the muse is not to be won but by the sacrifice of time, and time I have not to spare.[12]

Whether Raisley lived or died, there was only one place William wanted to be, and that was London. He could not leave the north without paying one last visit to his sister, who was now staying with their mother's cousins the Griffith family at Newcastle. She was quite happy with her 'very chearful, pleasant companions', but she must have been anxious about her future. She did not want to return to the domestic slavery of Forncett; the opportunities she had enjoyed over the last year of getting to know her brother (and his opinions), had made her aware that she could no longer be a compatible member of that household. Newbiggin Hall could not be contemplated. She even seems to have avoided paying her duty visit there, for the Misses Griffith had to broker a meeting between uncle and niece. To her great surprise Dorothy found Uncle Christopher was not the monster she believed him to be: 'I never saw a man so agitated in my life as he was at our meeting', she told Jane later. He had been kind and affectionate in manner and had made her a handsome present of ten guineas before they parted. Bemused, Dorothy could only attribute his faults to the influence of that 'proud and selfish woman', his wife, the former Miss Cust.[13]

Dorothy was temporarily saved from her dilemma by a timely invitation from her old Penrith schoolfriend Mary Hutchinson. For the last six years, Mary had been living Dorothy's own dream, keeping house for her brother. Tom had taken over his great-uncle's farm at Sockburn, in County Durham. Though three years younger than William, Tom was already providing a home not just for Mary, but for their sisters, Margaret and Sarah, and youngest brother George. He was, Dorothy noted enviously, 'a very amiable young man, uncommonly fond of his sisters, and in short, every thing that they can desire'.[14]

The Hutchinsons did indeed seem blessed. A close-knit and happy family, they lived in the large, elegant, red-brick house which their great-uncle had built, in a loop of the River Tees so pronounced that it almost made an island. It is, in fact, the last bastion of County Durham, for the river marks the boundary with Yorkshire. Accessible only over a narrow neck of land, Sockburn Farm still stands, its great sash windows facing out, over a small ha-ha, to lush flat meadows where Tom grazed his sheep. On every side there is the great circular sweep of the river, flowing broad and slow, round the edge of the property; beyond it rise the steep wooded banks of the opposite shore, enclosing Sockburn in an embrace which seems to protect it from the world outside. Though now uncomfortably close to Teeside Airport, it is still an oasis of calm which retains a sense of otherworldliness and magic. To add to its many charms, which completely seduced the Wordsworths and Coleridge, immediately in front of the house stand the grey stones marking the legendary spot where, in the year 1001, Sir John Conyers slew the local dragon, the Sockburn Worm, with his mighty falchion. Close by stands the Conyers family home, a remarkable seventeenth-century fantasy of gables and mullions, immured in woodland like Sleeping Beauty's castle, and, between the hall and the farm, what are now the picturesque ruins of All Saints' Church, where Sir John's effigy lies carved in stone, his feet resting on the slaughtered Worm. This was regarded by the Hutchinsons as their family church. Even when Dorothy made this, her first visit, the churchyard already contained the mortal remains of their great-aunt, Sarah Hutchinson, and Jane, the twenty-six-year-old wife of their oldest brother, John, who had died two years earlier. Almost exactly a year after Dorothy's visit, those of her friend, Margaret Hutchinson, who died of tuberculosis on 28 March 1796, aged twenty-four, were added. They would not be the last.[15]

Seeing the Hutchinsons so happily settled at Sockburn, Dorothy could not help but compare her fate with theirs: they too had lost their parents at an early age and been dependent on relatives but now 'have not a wish ungratified'. 'When shall I have the felicity of welcoming you my earliest friend to such a home?' Dorothy asked Jane mournfully. 'Would not you my dearest Jane be delighted beyond expression to be my guest? but these are airy dreams.'[16] The reason why these were still airy dreams, instead of solid realities, was now living in London. Here, for the first time in two years, William had the opportunity to see his brother John, who had returned from China on 20 September 1794. They had expected to meet in October, when William passed through London en route for Portugal, but Raisley Calvert's collapse prevented it. John's ship, the *Earl of Abergavenny*, was in the process of being purchased by the government for the navy; its replacement, a heavier vessel, was to be built in Northfleet in Kent and would not be ready for service until 1796. John was temporarily shipless, but, not being able to afford to remain idle, he accepted promotion to fourth mate on another East Indiaman, and sailed from London on 22 April. His new ship, the *Osterley*, was bound for Macao in south China, but would call at the Cape of Good Hope to land an English expeditionary force to help hold the Cape against the French.[17] John had therefore become an involuntary part of the British war effort of which his brother so strongly disapproved.

Great as his pleasure must have been at this brief reunion with John, William's main objective in coming to London was to see Mathews and immerse himself in radical politics. By the beginning of March he had taken up residence in lodgings at 15 Chalton Street, Somers Town. It was a significant address and deliberately chosen, for, literally a few doors away, at number 25, lived William Godwin, author of *An Enquiry Concerning Political Justice*.[18] The two men first met on 27 February, at the London house of William Frend, the Cambridge fellow who had been expelled from the university in 1793 for his radical views. This was another significant contact, for though Frend's name was a familiar one to William from his undergraduate days, there is no evidence that they were personally acquainted before this time. The same was true of almost the entire circle gathered in Frend's house that evening. Among them were George Dyer, the Unitarian, who had been a close friend of William Taylor, William's schoolmaster at Hawskhead; James Losh from Carlisle, an older brother of the boy who had lodged with William at Ann Tyson's; John Tweddell, the brilliant classicist of Trinity College, who had graduated the year before William; and Thomas Holcroft, the writer who had so narrowly escaped execution in the previous autumn's treason trials and had reviewed (patronizingly and unkindly) *Descriptive Sketches* and *An Evening Walk* for the *Monthly Review* in 1793.[19]

In this group of radicals, with a strong leavening of both Cambridge and literary men, William felt instantly at home. Nor was he afraid to argue with the Philosopher himself. Many years later, when he was a rather pathetic figure, rejected and even laughed at by most of the young men whom he had once enthused, Godwin claimed, 'I had the honour, in the talk of one evening, to convert Wordsworth from the doctrine of self-love to that of benevolence – ask him.'[20] (By the doctrine of self-love, Godwin meant the belief that self-interest determines all human actions.) William's writings reveal that he had been a convert since the previous summer, but Godwin's book, not his conversation, deserved the credit. Nevertheless, William was so impressed by this first meeting that he called on Godwin the following day and thereafter the two men visited each other regularly throughout the summer.[21] No doubt there were other meetings in general company, for William's circle of acquaintance among Godwin's disciples now expanded rapidly.

The most important of these was Basil Montagu, an illegitimate son of the Fourth Earl of Sandwich, with whom William had immediate and obvious reasons for empathy. They were the same age, shared the same politics and had been to the same university. In 1791, shortly after his twenty-first birthday, Montagu had married against his father's wishes; the Earl never spoke to him again. On 27 December 1792, only twelve days after Caroline Wordsworth was born in Orléans, Montagu's wife gave birth to a son, young Basil. A few days later, she died. Montagu was left with the difficult task of bringing up the boy unaided, while struggling to earn a living. By a curious coincidence, which must have struck William with peculiar force when he learned it, this child, so close in age to his own unseen daughter, was also called Caroline, after his mother. When William met Montagu, father and two-year-old son were living together in chambers in Lincoln's Inn. It was not an appropriate place to bring up a child, especially as Montagu was given to bouts of excessive drinking and wild behaviour. William, who always had a liking for small children, not only made friends with the father but also took the forlorn little boy under his wing. Montagu later paid tribute to his influence on them both.

By an accident I became acquainted with Wm Wordsworth. We spent some months together. He saw me, with great industry, perplexed and misled by passions wild & strong. In the wreck of my happiness he saw the probable ruin of my infant. He unremittingly, and to me imperceptibly, endeavoured to eradicate my faults, & to encourage my good dispositions. I consider my having met Wm Wordsworth the most fortunate event of my life.[22]

There could hardly have been a more practical expression of Godwinian benevolence and it resulted in a lifelong friendship.

Through Montagu, William was introduced to Francis Wrangham, a Yorkshireman, who would also become a friend for life. Though their careers at Cambridge had crossed (Wrangham had vied with John Tweddell and William's old friend Fletcher Raincock for the university prizes when he graduated from Cambridge in 1790), they had never been intimate. In 1793 Wrangham had lost an election to a fellowship because of his republican views, which, unlike William, he did not find incompatible with a career in the Church. When he and William met this summer, Wrangham was curate at the parish church of Cobham in Surrey and sharing pupils with Montagu. Visits to Cobham, which lay just south-west of London, made a pleasant excursion from the city.[23] William and Wrangham, who also had literary ambitions, embarked on a joint project, an imitation of the hard-hitting political satires of the Roman poet Juvenal. It probably began as an impromptu bit of fun, a scurrilous lampoon of the monarchy and aristocracy, but soon developed a momentum of its own. Of its very nature, it is full of topical references which are now obscure and humour which requires explanation to appreciate. What is still apparent, even for the modern reader, is the venom with which it was written. In lines not paralleled in the Juvenal original, for example, William and Wrangham employed their punning wit in pouring scorn on aristocratic titles.

Heavens! who sees majesty in George's face?
Or looks at Norfolk and can dream of grace?
What has this blessed earth to do with shame?
If excellence was ever Eden's name?
Must honour still to Lonsdale's tail be bound?[24]

The swipe at Lonsdale must have given William personal satisfaction, but the satire was also a republican manifesto. In what he claimed was 'A single word on Kings and Sons of Kings', but was in fact several dozen lines, he offered the rational argument against hereditary power.

– Were Kings a free born work – a people's choice,
Would More or Henry boast the general voice?
What fool, besotted as we are by names,
Could pause between a Raleigh and a James?[25]

Though ten guineas was offered for the work, plus half the profits should a second edition be required, the satire seems to have been left incomplete. The two friends ran out of steam and other work intervened.[26] As far as William was concerned, an opportunity had also arisen which could not be ignored.

Montagu and Wrangham had, between them, been tutoring two young men, John and Azariah Pinney. They were the twenty-two- and twenty-year-old sons of John Praetor Pinney, a wealthy Bristol merchant, who was a partner in the Bristol West Indies Trading Company. Despite the fact that their fortune was founded on the back of the slave trade – and that they still owned three sugar plantations and more than 200 slaves on the island of Nevis – the Pinneys were a liberal family. In an indefensible business, their father had sought to provide better conditions than many other plantation owners. His slaves never went without food, were allowed to own their own goats, pigs and poultry and, as Pinney pointed out in the argument always used by slavers, enjoyed better living standards than the free poor on the island. His son, John, however, to whom he had given the Nevis plantations as a twenty-first birthday present, was 'a rabid Whig'. He had been in Paris from May 1791 to April 1792 and, influenced no doubt by Montagu and Wrangham, was very much part of the radical Godwinian circle centred on both London and Bristol. Azariah was as active as, if not more so than, his brother.[27] Once again, political sympathies, rather than poetical promise, seem to have led a potential patron to take an interest in William.

The elder Pinney had built a country house in Dorset during the American War of Independence; the war threatened his sugar interests and the house was intended as a refuge in the event of financial ruin. In 1789 he had begun considerable alterations, including adding a third storey, and a complete refurbishment. On 1 May 1793 advertisements were drawn up for letting the property at £42 a year but no tenant had been found. Having no use for the place himself, since his business kept him in Bristol, Nevis and London, Pinney presented the property to his oldest son, expecting that he would either use it or derive an income from letting it out. This house, Racedown Lodge, John now offered to William with the casual generosity of a supremely rich young man who had been born to great wealth and saw no reason to doubt its continuance. William was to have it fully furnished and rent-free; the sole condition was that John was to be allowed, on occasion and only if convenient, to spend a few weeks there himself, paying for his own bed and board.[28]

Had there been no other incentive, William would have accepted with alacrity. Living in London was expensive and he had been unable to find a position on a newspaper, despite Mathews's offer and his own widening circle of political contacts.[29] The imitation of Juvenal remained unfinished and unpublished; if he had attempted to find a publisher for his Salisbury Plain poem, *The Female Vagrant*, he had failed. His one small success was the appearance on 21 August in the *Morning Chronicle* of a poem, *The Birth of Love*. It was not even an original or very recent composition, but a translation, made some time between 1792 and 1794, from the French allegorical poem *L'Education de l'Amour*.[30] A deeply contrived piece, even in the original, it had little to recommend it except that it probably earned William an urgently needed guinea or two.

This had now become critical, for, as yet, William had received nothing from Raisley Calvert's estate. Calvert had intended that the £900 legacy should be paid from a similar sum he had been left by his own father in cash, so that the paternal estates would not be affected and would remain within the family. Nevertheless, the money could not be handed over instantly, because it had been loaned out in order to pay Raisley an annual income of £100. Unravelling this would take time, and energy, and it is a credit to William Calvert that the first payment of £250 was made in September, with an additional £50 the following month. Investing the money to get the best return, and on sufficient security, would cause William and Richard considerable anxiety over the next few months, but they anticipated the same 9 per cent interest rate that Calvert had enjoyed.[31]

Even when all the legacy was paid, however, there would be only £100 a year to share between William and Dorothy. The offer of Racedown Lodge, rent-free, made all the difference. It also enabled William to offer a home not only to his sister but also to little Basil Caroline Montagu. The boy had been shuffled about between his father's chambers and various friends and William had persuaded Montagu that he needed a more settled home. There was a certain poetic justice in the fact that Montagu now asked William himself to take care of the child, offering him £50 a year for Basil's board, provided that Dorothy agreed to accompany them to Racedown. Indeed, the coming together of the offer of Racedown and the care of young Basil suggests that this was a concerted plan, and that John Pinney's generosity was as much a favour to Montagu, his tutor (to whom he had already made several loans), as to William.[32]

With the realization of her lifelong ambition for a cottage in the country with William so imminent, Dorothy was suddenly filled with qualms. She would be going to a place she did not know to take responsibility for a child who was a total stranger. Her years in charge of the Forncett nursery had equipped her for this sort of role, but Basil and his father were unknown quantities. The Fourth Earl of Sandwich had been a notorious hell-raiser: a gambler, adulterer, member of the Hellfire Club and so infamous for his corrupt management of the Admiralty that he was known as Jemmy Twitcher. Despite William's protestations that the Earl's illegitimate son had many 'amiable qualities', Dorothy and her friends were not convinced. Perhaps Montagu and young Basil would turn out to have inherited the Earl's taste for dissipation. An independent character witness was required and Christopher Wordsworth stepped into the breach. There could be no one more appropriate. Of unimpeachable morality and already determined to enter the Church, young 'Kitt' had immured himself in Cambridge after his summer visit to the north and was hard at work preparing for his final examinations. He knew not only Montagu but also young Basil, and he hastened to offer reassurance, speaking in the highest terms of the former as a man 'beloved and esteemed by all his acquaintance', who might 'be depended upon' for 'the strictest integrity'. The boy was 'a very fine healthy looking child'. Suitably reassured by this, and the Rawsons' emphatic insistence that she was quite equal to the charge, Dorothy gave her consent. Her reluctance to leave the Rawsons, who had been '*so very*, very kind to me, and my aunt, you know she has been my mother', was tempered only by the knowledge that a fifth baby was due at Forncett at Christmas and her presence had already been requested. It might be a struggle to part from the Rawsons, but it was a necessity. And better, far better, to go now to Racedown than in December to Forncett.[33]

About the third week in August, William left London for Great George Street, Bristol, where he had an invitation to await the arrival of Dorothy from Halifax and little Basil Montagu, both of whom were expected within a few days. In the end, however, Dorothy did not arrive until 22 September, allowing William to pass the time in the way he liked best. The weather was delightful and he was at liberty to walk where he pleased. He found the Pinneys an amiable family 'in all its branches' and 'my time slipped insensibly away'.[34] No doubt Mr Pinney would have appeared less amiable had he known the true state of his son's arrangements with William. Pinney the elder was under the clear impression that this was an ordinary tenancy agreement and he was anxious that his happy-go-lucky, unbusinesslike son should do everything by the book. He had fired off a series of diktats to John. Since Racedown was to be let furnished, he should make an inventory of every item in the place and give a copy to the new tenant: 'Let no article escape you, be it ever so trifling,' he urged, 'and let Mr Wordsworth understand I am to have liberty to remove any or all of the books, whenever I may please, though I have no reason at present, to suppose I shall touch them'. 'Tom Payne', however, was to be removed immediately: evidently Mr Pinney did not wish the new tenant to know he had a copy of the radical *Rights of Man.* Doors, window-frames, even the oak trees in the timberyard were to be listed: 'in short, let nothing escape you', he reiterated. As the orchard was not to be let with the house, John should ensure the gaps in the fencing were made up properly. He ended his letter with an admonition which explains his concern. In the circumstances, it is deeply ironic.

As our situation is so very critical, and it is possible nay probable at this moment your Estate [in Nevis] may be ruined and destroyed, I think it my Duty to remind you, once more, of your unthinking mode of conduct, by running into expenses you ought to avoid . . . Reflect a moment and say to yourself, that every sixpence you are now spending, is borrowed; and, of course, part of your Principal, and for which you are to pay five per Cent Interest. I am sure, if you have any feeling, you will act with more caution and not spend a Shilling, which may be saved until you have money in the hands of your Merchant.[35]

William took advantage of his residence in Bristol to cultivate his fellow radicals. Bristol had long been notorious as a centre of dissent, both political and religious. Earlier in the year, two fiery young democrats had leapt on to the centre of the stage with a series of public lectures. Robert Southey was almost twenty-one; his friend, Samuel Taylor Coleridge, two years older. The previous summer they had both abandoned potentially brilliant academic careers at Oxford and Cambridge respectively in order to put their republican ideals into practice by founding an ideal society, under a scheme which they called Pantisocracy. Twelve good men and true, with twelve ladies of similar principles, were to embark for America and found a self-governing and self-sufficient colony of philosophers on the Susquehanna River. 'When Coleridge and I are sawing down a tree we shall discuss metaphysics;' Southey had boasted, 'criticise poetry when hunting a buffalo, and write sonnets whilst following the plough.'[36] Everything that could be said about the practicality of the scheme can be summed up by their choice of location, which was dictated chiefly by its pretty name. Surprisingly, they had convinced a number of friends to accompany them, including Edith and Sarah Fricker, who were to be their brides. Unsurprisingly, the whole idea foundered even before these New Age pilgrims set sail.

Southey and Coleridge had also collaborated on a three-act drama, *The Fall of Robespierre*, published in 1794. Characteristically, though Southey had written two-thirds of the play, Coleridge managed to claim all the credit by putting his name alone on the title-page. Their plans in February 1795 to write and publish a monthly journal, the *Provincial Magazine*, had fallen through for the same reasons as William's and Mathews's for the *Philanthropist*. Instead, they had turned to a different arena and, in the spring of 1795, had each given a series of public lectures, Southey's ostensibly on historical subjects, Coleridge's on political ones, but all designed to promote the radical agenda. Both were lucky to escape prosecution, particularly when Coleridge's lectures were published in December as *Conciones ad Populum*. Coleridge would later backtrack furiously, defying his worst enemy to produce evidence that he had ever shown 'the least bias to Irreligion, Immorality, or Jacobinianism' in his writings. Southey, though not proud of his youthful republicanism, was more honest. If Coleridge was not a Jacobin in 1795, he wrote, 'I wonder who the Devil was. I am sure I was.'[37]

William did not arrive in Bristol in time to hear either of them lecture. He already knew both men, as they knew him, by reputation. He knew of Southey through Mathews, who was a fellow correspondent of the *Telegraph*, and of Coleridge through published reports of his lectures and through his own brother. Christopher Wordsworth, it will be remembered, had been a founder member, with Coleridge, of the literary society at Cambridge at which William's own poems had been so eagerly discussed. 'Coleridge was at Bristol part of the time I was there', William later told Mathews. 'I saw but little of him. I wished indeed to have seen more – his talent appears to me very great. I met with Southey also, his manners pleased me exceedingly and I have every reason to think very highly of his powers of mind.'[38]

Quite where they met is a mystery. An intimate friend of the Wordsworths and Coleridge asserted in 1810 that they had met at a political debating society, 'where on one occcasion Wordsworth spoke with so much force & eloquence that Coleridge was captivated by it & sought to know Him'. William himself said, in old age, that he had met both Coleridge and Southey 'in a lodging in Bristol'.[39] Whichever it was, and either, or even both, were possible, there was no indication at the time that the latent spark between William and Coleridge would soon ignite into a fire of friendship and creativity. Coleridge was preoccupied with his own problems and on the brink of a breach with Southey over his increasing reluctance to honour his obligation to marry Sarah Fricker. Southey, genuinely anxious to marry his beloved Edith Fricker, was under pressure from his guardian uncle to abandon his radical principles, go to Portugal and become a clergyman.

The three young men shared an instant attraction. William and Southey read their most recent poems to each other and Southey, always verbally acute, suggested two additional lines for William's *Imitation of Juvenal*. William could not return the compliment, but listened admiringly to some of Southey's epic poem *Joan of Arc*, which was about to be published.[40] Southey probably introduced William to his own publisher, Joseph Cottle, an enterprising young man of William's own age, who had the good fortune and perspicacity to publish Southey, Coleridge and, later, William himself. It is likely that it was Cottle who offered William ten guineas for the satire if he and Wrangham could complete it.[41] Most dramatically of all, William may have now read his Salisbury Plain poem to Coleridge, provoking a reaction which the latter would recall vividly more than twenty years later. 'I was in my twenty-fourth year, when I had the happiness of knowing Mr Wordsworth personally,' Coleridge would write in his *Biographia Literaria*, 'and while memory lasts, I shall hardly forget the sudden effect produced on my mind, by his recitation'. Coleridge was so impressed that he urged William to publish it as it stood. William was reluctant, feeling that he had not made the most of the different elements in the story, but this encouragement inspired him to make so many alterations and additions over the next couple of months that 'it may be looked on almost as another work'.[42]

The friendships which grew out of William's brief residence at Bristol were to be important and long-lasting; in the case of Coleridge, it was to be of profound significance on both a personal and literary level. For the moment, however, they parted, Coleridge to go to his future patron, Tom Poole, at Nether Stowey, Southey to resume residence in his native Bath, and William to Dorset.[43] Dorothy arrived late on the evening of 22 September: 'I like her manner and appearance extremely,' Eliza Pinney reported to her father, 'she is very animated and unaffected –' Four days later, William and Dorothy set off in a chaise for the fifty-mile drive down through Somerset and over the Dorset Downs to Racedown Lodge. It was almost midnight on 26 September when they arrived at their destination.[44]

Perhaps this was just as well, for they were spared the disappointment of their first sight of the ugly and forbidding exterior of what was to be their home for the next two years. Built of dark-red brick, Racedown stands on a bend in a narrow winding country lane, under the lee of a deceptively steep hill. Despite having three storeys and an unusually high-pitched grey slate roof, the house still appears squat and solid, an illusion fostered by the fact that it is sandwiched between two vast blocks of chimneys at each end. The frontage is uncompromisingly symmetrical, a sash window each side of the door, three similar ones above and another row of three smaller ones on the top floor, but there are not sufficient windows, and they are not big enough, to offset the blank expanse of brickwork. It is irredeemably a manufacturer's house, unlike any other in the area, and uncomfortably out of place in the soft, undulating landscape of the Downs.

Waking up the next morning, however, the Wordsworths would instantly see the best Racedown had to offer: long-distance views down the steeply shelving, narrow valley of the little River Synderford (a grand name for what is no more than a stream), over sinuous wooded hills and a lovely pastoral landscape, towards the Vale of Taunton Deane. Even better, when they scrambled up the hillside behind the house, they found themselves in the grassy bowl of the Iron Age fortress on top of Pilsdon Pen, at 909 feet the highest hill in Dorset, with magnificent views in every direction. They could see not only far into Somerset but, facing southwards, the glorious sweep of coastline from Torbay in the west to Weymouth in the east, with the Isle of Portland rising from the sea and clearly visible on the skyline beyond. Closer to home, looking over the rounded contours of gentle hills patched with woodland, broom, orchards and ploughed fields, and across the flat plain of the Vale of Marshwood, the land rises again into the distinctive contours of the cliffs at Lyme Regis, some ten or twelve miles away.

It is a landscape that invites one to explore on foot, and it is no coincidence that one of William's first priorities (second only to having his books sent on from Montagu's) was to order six pairs of shoes from his London cobbler. Four of these were to be William's own early version of the walking boot, made to his design and consisting 'of the very strongest kind double soles and upper leathers'. When he accidentally left a pair behind in London, some years later, Charles Lamb, who was commissioned to forward them, was vastly amused by these 'strange thick-hoofed shoes', declaring mischievously that they were 'very much admired at in London'.[45]

William was irresistibly drawn to the ocean. He often walked over the hills to Lyme Regis, delighting in hearing the murmur of the sea three miles before it was visible, though he also experienced its horrors when he watched the huge West Indies fleet setting out 'in all its glory', only to be wrecked in storms off the treacherous Chesil Beach. He also made regular forays to Crewkerne, which lay about the same distance away in the opposite direction. This big, bustling market town, built of glowing golden sandstone, with its narrow streets and abundant inns, was the nearest source of all supplies. The last place on the line for the public coaches, it was also the collection point for all the incoming and outgoing mail in the district. As Dorothy admitted, it was fortunate that William was so good a walker, for otherwise they would have been greatly inconvenienced by their isolation.[46]

Dorothy was in ecstasies, at last living out her dream and playing 'house' for real. Nothing could displease her. It was almost two months before she could tear herself away to write to her friend Jane Pollard, who, in very different circumstances, was just setting up house herself. Jane had recently married the enterprising and soon-to-be fabulously rich John Marshall, a cotton and flax manufacturer in Leeds. Dorothy was not in the least bit jealous, even though she knew her own household could not compare with that of Jane. It had not cost the Wordsworths ten shillings to fit out Racedown, for everything was in perfect readiness. They had two parlours, one a formal dining room with a best Axminster carpet, the other, smaller one being both a breakfast room and a library. On the shelves were 470 books, mainly early-eighteenth-century legal tomes, classical texts and commentaries, and histories, with a fair sprinkling of French and Italian works and, oddly out of place in an otherwise heavyweight collection, Henry Fielding's novel *Joseph Andrews* and Jonathan Swift's satire *A Tale of a Tub*. It comes as no surprise to learn that this latter room was their favourite, being 'the prettiest little room that can be; with very neat furniture, a large book[case?] on each side of the fire, a marble chimney piece, bath stove, and an oil cloth for the floor'. Upstairs, there were four 'excellent' bedrooms on the first floor, and a further four, also described as 'excellent', on the top storey; in addition to all the usual offices, including two outside 'Necessaries', there were a wash house, a brew house, a coach house and stabling for four horses.[47]

A month after their arrival, they managed to acquire a servant, Peggy Marsh, 'one of the nicest girls I ever saw', and a woman who came in once a month (for 9d a day) to do the washing. All the best linen, silver and glassware was locked away in an attic room, but the Wordsworths were more than adequately supplied, and could borrow from this store by arrangement. The manager, or caretaker, of the house and its extensive grounds, which included a fruit and vegetable garden, and a 'pleasure ground', with flowers, shrubs, fountains and statuary, was Joseph Gill. A cousin of the Pinneys, he had formerly managed their Nevis estates but, having acquired at least one of the island vices, alcoholism, he had proved financially incompetent and been hauled back to England in disgrace. He now lodged with the tenants of the neighbouring Pinney property, Harlescombe Farm. Apart from Gill, there were no close neighbours. The nearest villages were Blackdown, where some unsociable Pinney relatives lived, and, in the opposite direction, Birdsmoorgate; neither was much more than a cluster of two or three knapped flint and thatched cottages.[48]

While William walked the Downs, investigated the library at Racedown and worked hard on his revision of the Salisbury Plain poem, Dorothy devoted herself to the care of young Basil Caroline Montagu. He was now almost three years old, 'a charming boy, [who] affords us perpetual entertainment. Do not suppose from this that we make him our perpetual play-thing', Dorothy told Jane, 'far otherwise, I think that is one of the modes of treatment most likely to ruin a child's temper and character.' She had hoped to have a companion for him in a little girl, the illegitimate child of her cousin Tom Myers, who was now three or four years old. She had been expected in England in November, and her uncle, John Myers, had asked Dorothy to take charge of her. Perhaps she did not leave India, for her father was promoted to Accountant-General of Bengal the following year. In any event, she did not come to Racedown. William's hopes of being entrusted with the education of one of the younger Pinneys, a thirteen-year-old boy, were also dashed. This was a more severe blow, for Wrangham had earned £200 a year for tutoring one of his older brothers.[49]

Dorothy was convinced that little Basil flourished under her care. 'He is quite metamorphosed from a shivering half starved plant, to a lusty, blooming fearless boy', she wrote proudly to Jane after six months. When he first came, he was 'perpetually disposed to cry', a combination, they believed, of his petted upbringing and feeble physique. To rid him of this irritating habit, they devised a plan:

w[e]used to tell him that if he chose to cry he must go into a certain room where he cannot be heard, and *stay* till he chose to be quiet, because the noise was unpleasant to us; at first his visits were very long, but he alway[s] came out again perfectly good-humoured. He found that this mode was never departed from, and when he felt the fretful disposition coming on he would say, 'Aunt, I think I am going to cry' and retire till the fit was over. He has now entirely conquered the disposition.

They had no predetermined system of punishments, except that they tried, as far as possible, to make them the consequences of misdoing. When, aged four, he failed to get up when called two mornings in a row, the second time he found everyone too busy to help him dress, so he was obliged to go back to bed till four in the afternoon. Modern child psychologists might beat their breasts over this treatment of such a young child, but at least it was more enlightened than the whipping he would have received in most turn-of-the-century households. Plain victuals 'cooked tolerably well' by the willing Peggy Marsh and plenty of fresh air effected an equally remarkable physical change. 'He dreads neither cold nor rain. He has played frequently an hour or two without appearing sensible that the rain was pouring down upon him or the wind blowing about him.' Apart from teaching him his alphabet, they made no effort to instil 'book-learning' into him. 'We teach him nothing at present but what he learns from the evidence of his senses', Dorothy told Jane.

He has an insatiable curiosity which we are always careful to satisfy to the best of our ability. It is directed to everything he sees, the sky, the fields, trees, shrubs, corn, the making of tools, carts, &c &c &c . . . Our grand study has been to make him *happy* in which we have not been altogether disappointed; he is certainly the most contented child I ever saw; the least disposed to be fretful.[50]

In the light of Dorothy's obvious pride, pleasure and interest in her young charge, it comes as something of a shock to learn that William was altogether more sceptical about his progress. 'Basil is quite well *quant au physique*', he told Wrangham, '*mais pour le moral il-y-a bien à craindre.* Among other things he lies like a little devil.' What is more, William was quite right. Many years later, Basil's despairing father would feel obliged to write an account of his son to contradict all his lies. The one that had upset Montagu more than anything else was Basil's calumniation of the Wordsworths after he had left their care.

Basil had, day after day, vilified Wordsworth: he had stated, that when living with his Sister they had treated him with such cruelty that he was constantly employed in the most menial occupations: and, but for the pity of the poor Villagers, who privately supplied him with such pittance as they could ill share, he should have been starved. I had reason to suspect other calumnies.

There is no reason to believe these claims of deliberately inflicted cruelty. Basil made them in his early twenties, when he was about to be sent unwillingly to Ambleside, to resume his schooling within the Wordsworths' circle. He told similar lies about harsh treatment meted out to him by his father, stepmother, uncle and another family friend with whom he lived for a time. Basil deeply resented being shunted off by his father to a succession of relatives and, when stepbrothers and sisters arrived, was particularly jealous of them and his exclusion from their home. His lies were an understandable but clumsy attempt to secure sympathy by a deeply unhappy young man.[51]

Nevertheless, Basil may well have felt that he was not treated with the respect and attention which he seemed entitled to enjoy in the grand surroundings of Racedown. The education given to him may have been determined by the philosophy of Rousseau, but it owed more to William's memories of his own happy childhood. In re-creating those conditions for Basil, however, one essential ingredient was missing: the companionship of other children. This was a major stumbling block, particularly for a boy who was neither bookish nor interested in solitary pursuits. His complaints about being hungry may also have been true. As William had foreseen, the war had brought an escalation of prices. Meat could not be had for under 6d, and William himself would ruefully confess, 'I have lately been living upon air and the essence of carrots cabbages turnips and other esculent vegetables, not excluding parsely [*sic*] the produce of my garden'. Tea (the Wordsworths drank fine Souchong, bought in Bristol at 4s a measure) and sugar were their only luxuries, and these were rapidly becoming unaffordable.[52] This frugal diet was hardly an appropriate one for a growing boy, but it was one shared without distinction by the adults.

The Wordsworths' simple lifestyle was a personal preference, but major economies were also forced upon them by their lack of income. They had failed to secure additional pupils and Montagu was not exactly prompt in paying the annual £50 for his son. (Indeed, after two years, he failed to do so at all.) By January 1796 they had received only £500 out of the £900 due from Calvert's legacy. Of this £300 had been lent to Montagu 'in a sort of irregularly secured annuity', for which they received 10 per cent interest, and the remainder to Montagu's friend, Charles Douglas, a barrister and cousin of the future Marquess of Queensbury, on a promissory note at the same rate of interest. This was all well and good; the slightly higher than average interest represented the higher risk to which the capital was exposed by not having more formally secured loans. Even if the interest was paid regularly and in full (which it was not), the Wordsworths had only £50 a year to support themselves, with a further £50 for Basil. It was nothing like the joint income of 'at least 170 or 180£ per annum' they had anticipated.[53]

There were other problems, beside money, which insidiously poisoned the rural idyll the Wordsworths had hoped to create. The greatest of these, especially for William, was isolation. Dorothy had hoped that having their own home would enable them to offer their brothers John and Christopher 'a place to draw to', so that they could meet more often and as a family. This did not happen. John was on the *Osterley* in the Far East and, even before the ship reached its final harbour in February 1797, he had transferred to another East Indiaman, the *Duke of Montrose*, and set sail for India. Christopher had graduated from Trinity College, Cambridge, in January 1796 as Tenth Wrangler; having achieved such honours by dint of hard work as much as natural intellect, he had now set his heart on entering the Church and becoming a fellow of his college. A jaunt to Racedown was therefore out of the question.[54] It was, quite simply, too out of the way for visits to be made conveniently. A promised visit from Montagu failed to materialize, and William's invitations to John Myers, William Mathews and Francis Wrangham all went unanswered. He had to content himself with a brief exchange of visits with Nicholas Leader, a member of Godwin's circle, who was in Lyme Regis in October, and, at Christmas, a week-long visit from John and Azariah Pinney.[55]

The frustration of being out of the heart of events and cut off from all political discussion began to gnaw at William. He could not afford a London newspaper and Wrangham's vague hopes of securing him a free subscription to the *Morning Chronicle* fell through; the only paper he saw regularly, and that probably borrowed from Joseph Gill or the Pinneys of Blackdown, was the provincial weekly paper, the *Weekly Entertainer*.[56] Letters were a poor substitute for people, especially as the post was erratic, even at the best of times. Those that did arrive were full of gloomy news. At the end of October, the King's carriage was attacked en route for the opening of Parliament by a crowd chanting, 'No Pitt, no war, Bread, Bread'; the King himself narrowly missed injury from a stone which smashed through his window. The government's reaction was to introduce the Convention Bill, popularly known as the 'gagging acts', extending the definition of treason to include speaking or writing anything critical of the British Constitution (an offence of which William was frequently guilty), and prohibiting more than fifty people meeting together in public without the prior permission of local magistrates. The two acts met with fierce opposition, not least in Bristol, where Azariah Pinney reported the progress of events to William. He described how Coleridge had played a leading role in attempting to add an amendment to a public address congratulating the King on his escape. When this failed, Coleridge had helped organize a petition protesting against the acts, 'which I think you will agree was a very proper one', and, at a second public meeting, had moved its presentation to Parliament. 'I am afraid you will think me tedious in detailing the particulars of a meeting, the effective result of which is likely to be so nugatory', Azariah apologized, unnecessarily. This petition and the others like it flooding into Parliament were in themselves a hopeful sign, but if they were ignored,

> I dread the consequences – the murmurs of the people will for a time be suppressed by the military forces but whenever circumstances shall favour resistance, their complaints will burst forth with the whirlwind's fury – I have not yet heard one argument that I have even thought plausible in fav[ou]r of the Convention bill: all I can learn from its supporters and advocates, is, that the Times justify the measure. Pray let me know what you think of it, but I can almost anticipate your sentiments.[57]

Despite liberal protest throughout the kingdom, the acts were passed by a compliant and fearful Parliament, but not all radicals could be silenced. Coleridge, for instance, leapt to the challenge by launching a new periodical, the *Watchman*, which flagrantly defied the acts by demanding their repeal. William, entombed at Racedown, could only admire such activity from afar. 'Best comp[limen]ts to Coleridge,' he wrote wistfully to Cottle in the New Year, 'and say I wish much to hear from him.'[58]

Throughout the autumn of 1795 and the following spring, there is a distinct sense of disillusionment and depression in William's letters. Clearly he felt excluded from what was going on elsewhere and paralysed by his own inaction. Writing to Mathews, for instance, he began with an apology for writing at all, 'not that I feel myself able to say anything which is likely to be particularly interesting'. He assured his friend that he and Dorothy were 'both as happy as people can be who live in perfect solitude'. The importance of this statement is always overlooked, because it is misread. William is not saying that they *were* perfectly happy, only that they were 'as happy as people *can be* who live in perfect solitude'. The qualification is underlined by what follows. 'We do not see a soul. Now and then we meet a miserable peasant in the road or an accidental traveller. The country people here are wretchedly poor; ignorant and overwhelmed with every vice that usually attends ignorance in that class, viz – lying and picking and stealing.'[59]

Dorothy did her best to 'improve' herself so that she could be an intellectual companion. She studied Italian 'very hard' but, more importantly, she was obviously trying to understand William's experience in France. The books she read over the winter of 1795–6 are a fascinating and illuminating choice. Dr John Moore's *A*

Journal of a Residence in France, published in 1793–4, for instance, included an account of living in Paris between August and December 1792, the very period when William was in the city. The memoirs of Madame Roland, *An Appeal to Impartial Posterity* (1796), were equally significant. Her husband, Jean Marie Roland de La Platière, was one of the Girondin leaders and a minister of the interior; he had attacked Robespierre, tried to save Louis XVI's life and been forced to flee from Paris after the fall of the Girondins. Madame Roland had been a hugely influential figure in revolutionary Paris. From 1791 to 1793, her salon had been the headquarters for republicans, Girondins and sympathetic foreigners, including Helen Maria Williams, who had been a personal friend. After the fall of the Girondins, she was arrested, tried before the Revolutionary Tribunal (the same court which had tried and condemned William's landlord, Jean Henri Gellet-Duvivier) and guillotined on 8 November 1793. As she mounted the scaffold, she had said, 'O Liberty! What crimes are committed in your name'; her husband committed suicide on learning her fate. Given William's known associations with the Girondins, it is tempting to think that perhaps he had attended her salon; at the very least he knew many within her circle, and the lady herself by reputation. The third book Dorothy named as having read at this period was by another Girondin and associate of the Rolands, Jean Baptiste Louvet de Couvrai, *Narrative of the Dangers to which I have been Exposed* (1795). Louvet's great moment of fame had come in November 1792, when he had denounced Robespierre in the National Assembly; it was, as we have seen, an event which had thrilled William, who was in Paris at the time. Louvet, more fortunate than Madame Roland, had escaped Paris during the Terror and returned to government after the execution of Robespierre.[60]

This extraordinary choice of books Dorothy passed off with the brief, but hardly apt comment, 'very entertaining'. One longs to know what were the books she dismissed as 'some other french things', but among them was certainly Helen Maria Williams's *Letters Containing a Sketch of the Politics of France* (1795). It was another obvious text for Dorothy to study in order to learn about life in revolutionary France, but in it William found a little poem, purporting to be by two French prisoners awaiting the guillotine. Helen Maria Williams had offered her own translation of it, but William set to and composed his own. It was rather more than an academic exercise, for the prisoner's farewell words to his beloved wife could just as easily apply to William's parting from Annette. She cannot have been far from his thoughts as he translated, for at least one letter from Annette had arrived not long after the Wordsworths' removal to Racedown; all we know about its contents is that Annette mentioned having dispatched half a dozen letters to William, 'none of which he has received'.[61] While England remained at war with France, there was no possibility of a return to Blois or Orléans, and the unresolved problem of Annette and Caroline was yet another shadow on William's life.

The Pinney brothers were a life-line at this time. They sent or brought books, including the French ones Dorothy had devoured so avidly. At Christmas, when they stayed a week, they brought a gift from Joseph Cottle, the Bristol publisher, who had just brought out Robert Southey's epic poem *Joan of Arc.* Southey himself was in Portugal, forcibly extracted from Bristol politics by his concerned guardian uncle. Defiant to the last, he had secretly married Edith Fricker before sailing and set in motion the publication of the poem, whose radical subtext was immediately obvious to reviewers. William studied it eagerly, but was disappointed, as perhaps was only natural given its subject matter: how could he read about the 'maid of Orléans' without being reminded of Annette? Though there were some passages of 'first-rate excellence', he thought that, on the whole, it was of 'very inferior execution'. Southey's preface, which did more credit to his honesty than his common sense, was 'a very conceited performance'. It declared that he had 'run a race with the press'; the whole twelve books had been written in six weeks, and, on its improved plan of ten books, it had been virtually recomposed during printing. To William, who was mortifyingly slow in composition, worse in revising, and was still labouring over his Salisbury Plain poem more than two and a half years after he had begun it, this seemed like both boasting and treating the reader with contempt.[62]

Over the months at Racedown, William had virtually recomposed his Salisbury Plain poem. It was 'so much altered that I think it may in truth be called a new Poem', Azariah Pinney told their mutual friend James Tobin. William had transformed the role of the wanderer, to whom the female vagrant had told her own story, by giving him a life-history too. He was now a fellow victim of the war, a sailor from Portland (just visible down the Dorset coast from Pilsdon Pen), who had returned from war service only to be press-ganged into the navy again. This was a common enough fate, as William knew well enough from John Wordsworth, and the evidence of his own eyes and ears: the same thing had already happened to Henry Hutchinson, Mary's sailor brother, and would soon happen to him again.[63] William's fictional sailor, fleeced of his earnings by fraud and desperate to provide for his starving family, murdered and robbed a traveller on the plain, then fled when suspected, becoming a homeless vagrant. The full consequences of his crime were brought forcibly home at the end of the poem. The sailor accidentally came across another solitary outcast, a dying woman, who turns out to be his wife. She had been driven from her home by the parish overseers, who suspected her husband was the murderer. Having begged her forgiveness, the sailor gave himself up to the authorities and was hanged. The poem ends, as one expects a moral tale to end, with the grim image of his corpse hanging from the gibbet in an iron cage as a salutary warning to passers-by. But there is an unexpected twist in the final stanza which is far more shocking and memorable. The moral is lost on the passers-by, who care nothing for the sailor's fate.

> They left him hung on high in iron case,
> And dissolute men, unthinking and untaught,
> Planted their festive booths beneath his face;
> And to that spot, which idle thousands sought,
> Women and children were by fathers brought . . .[64]

It is perhaps the bleakest and most pessimistic ending to any of William's poems. It offers neither hope nor consolation; indeed, by suggesting that casual indifference is the basis of human nature, rather than rational benevolence, it undermines the essential Godwinian premise of the poem that the suffering individuals are the victims of government injustice. William's belief in the essential benevolence of humanity had been severely shaken, not just by the savagery of the warring factions in France but also, perhaps, by a closer acquaintance with those wretchedly poor, ignorant and vicious, miserable peasants of Dorset with their 'lying and picking and stealing'.

It therefore comes as no surprise to find that this uncharacteristic lack of optimism coincides with what amounts to a rejection of Godwin. Montagu had sent him a copy of the brand-new second edition of Godwin's *Enquiry Concerning Political Justice.* 'I expect to find the work much improved', William wrote to Mathews on 21 March 1796, adding that he had not been encouraged in this hope by looking through the new preface. 'Such a piece of barbarous writing I have not often seen. It contains scarce one sentence decently written. I am surprized to find such gross faults in a writer who has had so much practise in composition.' William's attack on the style of the preface was simply an expression of his increasing disillusionment with the substance of Godwin's philosophy. The new edition had retreated even further into philosophical obscurity, subjecting even central tenets of the original *Enquiry* to Godwin's own exasperating habit of demanding 'explanations, translations, limitations'. What had at first seemed like the declaration of universal truths derived from studying human nature had now become merely an egotistical exercise in academic analysis. Or as Coleridge put it, 'futile sophisms in jejune language'.[65]

The arrival in February of John Pinney, closely followed by his brother, proved a welcome diversion. 'While we were with him he relaxed the rigour of his philosophic nerves so much as to go a Coursing several times,' Azariah wrote in high glee to James Tobin, 'and I assure you did not eat the unfortunate Hares with less relish because he heard them heave their death groans, and saw their Eyes directed towards Heaven with that glare of vacant sadness which belongs to the expiring creature – for his usual Appetite shewed itself at the dining Table'.[66] Dorothy was captivated by John, as well she might be. He was two and twenty, with a 'charming countenance' and 'the sweetest temper I ever observed'.

He has travelled a good deal, in the way of education, been at one of the great schools, and at Oxford, has had always plenty of money to spend and every indulgence: all these things instead of having spoiled him or made him conceited have wrought the pleasantest and best effects, he is well-informed, has an uncommonly good heart, and is very agreeable in conversation.

Azariah, destined to be a merchant in the family firm instead of a gentleman of leisure, was naturally less attractive. He was merely 'much more pleasing in manners than the generality of young men'. Azariah's opinion of Dorothy was equally unenthusiastic. 'Miss Wordsworth has undoubted claim to good humour, but does not possess, in my opinion, that je ne sais quoi, so necessary to sweeten the sour draught of human misfortune and smooth the [rough?] road of this Life's Passage – '. The two young men entered fully into life at Racedown, on fine days walking with Dorothy and William, or riding out, hunting, coursing and even cleaving wood, which, as the pragmatic Dorothy pointed out, in a country where coal was so expensive, at least produced warmth both in and out of doors. In the evenings they would join the Wordsworths by the fireside, reading and conversing on politics and literature.[67]

When they left, on 6 March, Azariah took with him an invitation to Racedown for James Tobin (with William's caveat that he should not expect anything more than 'democratic' fare) and a copy of the Salisbury Plain poem, which he was commissioned to take to Bristol and deliver to Cottle, with a request that Coleridge might look it over before publication. It was almost three weeks before William heard from Azariah, and then it was a letter that brought mixed tidings. Coleridge had gone through it with considerable attention, interleaving it with blank sheets of paper on which to write his observations, and had pronounced it 'a very fine Poem'. Indeed, Coleridge even went so far as to assure William that publishing it would cost him nothing. The expenses could be taken out of the profits and the rest would go to William himself. Not only that, but he recommended printing 500 copies, instead of the 250 William had suggested.[68] As William would later learn to his cost, this was a typically Coleridgean reaction: extravagant, wildly enthusiastic and, since it was dependent on the cooler judgement of a publisher, unsustainable. Nevertheless, it was just the sort of response William needed at that time. If a poet, critic and radical with Coleridge's impeccable credentials was so impressed by his work, then perhaps this was a valid way he could contribute to the cause. Azariah had given Coleridge the Racedown address, and William waited to hear from him in a fever of hope and anxiety.

The second half of Azariah's letter brought less welcome news. Mr Pinney had found out about the Wordsworths' rent-free tenancy of Racedown. Canny businessman that he was, he had arranged that all his tenants paid their rent annually on the same day, 25 March, so that there was no room for confusion or dispute. He was expecting his sons to collect the Racedown rent and bring it to Bristol, so a confrontation was inevitable, as Azariah explained apologetically to William.

> We were obliged to let my Father into the knowledge of the whole transaction relative to the deficiency in the Cash I recd. for him at Race-down, as circumstances rendered it impracticable to conceal it effectually from him. – We did it as gradually as was possible, but all our precaution did not disappoint his anger – for some time he was so hurt that he determined to write to Mr Perkins [his land agent at Crewkerne] to desire he would call on you for the Money, but at our earnest request he relinquished the intention.

I assure you the change was not produced suddenly but required time and much solicitation – I have considered it proper to mention to you fully all that passed [upon?] the subject of that business – and it is written partly at my father's desire – I can only add that I am sorry it ever happened for it has caused us much uneasiness and my father still more –[69]

Quite how the Pinneys persuaded their father to allow the rent-free arrangement to continue is not recorded, but they informed him that John intended to use Racedown as an occasional residence and to make certain alterations, including adding a new kitchen, 'for the purpose of making it more comfortable for himself and my family when there in the Summer'. Letting the house would prove difficult if building work was taking place and, at least while the Wordsworths were there, it was being kept clean and aired. Additionally, William's passion for landscape gardening and his 'great dexterity' with the spade, of which Dorothy had boasted, were assets in his favour. The original letting agreement had allowed the tenant £12 out of his rent of £42 a year in return for fencing the vegetable garden and putting it, and the pleasure garden, in order.[70] These were tasks for which William was eminently qualified, and his industry in rooting up hedges and planting vegetables was not entirely due to the demands of self-sufficiency, but also, in part, to a sense of obligation to the Pinneys.

Compelled to accept the situation by his sons, Pinney the elder remained disgruntled. 'It is with real concern I view the conduct of you and your Brother', he wrote to Azariah two months later:

neither of you seem to pay the least regard to the value of property & I am afraid you will continue in the same unthinking way, untill you sensibly feel the ill effects of it, & then, in all probability, it will be too late to replace yourself in an eligible situation – I shall say no more on so unpleasing a subject but leave all matters to the cool operation of your own reason –

Nevertheless, he could not resist a sneer at the character of his son's tenant. He urged Azariah to become more prudent and businesslike, so that he might become a worthy and valuable member of society, 'free from those eccentrick Ideas which pervade the minds of our modern Philosophers, from whose opinions may the Almighty through his goodness preserve me and mine'. Matters were not improved by the emergence of a prospective paying tenant in September 1796. When Joseph Gill approached Mr Pinney for instructions, he received an abrupt and frosty response. 'I can say nothing in reply to Mr Egerton's application to rent the House &c as my Son [John] Frederick is to do with it as he pleases . . . He will also give Mr Hitchcock the directions respecting the cutting of Peat, as I shall not interfere about it.'[71]

After the departure of the companionable Pinney brothers, the sense of isolation at Racedown grew oppressive. Even Dorothy was affected, writing to Jane, 'We seem quite quiet now that we are alone again'. William, always more sociable, was even more depressed. 'Our present life is utterly barren of such events as merit even the short-lived chronicle of an accidental letter', he wrote bitterly to Mathews. 'We plant cabbages, and if retirement, in its full perfection, be as powerful in working transformations as one of Ovid's Gods, you may perhaps suspect that into cabbages we shall be transformed. Indeed I learn that such has been the prophecy of one of our London friends.'

With nothing else to do, he returned to his books, reading industriously 'if reading can ever deserve the name of industry'. 'As to writing', he added, 'it is out of the question.'[72] He vented his ill-humour in some desultory work on the satire he had begun with Wrangham, but neither man's heart was in the project. The few pieces William wrote at this time were equally mechanical: short alternative treatments of sections of the Salisbury Plain poem in blank verse and in Spenserian stanzas, for instance, and a dire *Argument for Suicide*. More interesting, though not for its quality, was an *Address to the Ocean*, an imitation of Ossian inspired by, and quoting as its first line, a poem by Coleridge, *The Complaint of Ninathona*, which had first appeared in *Poems on Various Subjects*, published in April 1796. William's acknowledged borrowing was simply returning the compliment, for in the same volume Coleridge had included *Lines Written at Shurton Bars*, which quoted a phrase from William's *An Evening Walk*. In a note to his poem, Coleridge had added a characteristically generous assessment of William as 'a Poet, whose versification is occasionally harsh and his diction too frequently obscure; but whom I deem unrivalled among the writers of the present day in manly sentiment, novel imagery, and vivid colouring'. William's decision to publish his *Address to the Ocean*, acknowledging his own debt to 'Mr Coleridge', in their local newspaper, the *Weekly Entertainer*, on 21 November 1796, must surely be seen as an attempt to express his gratitude publicly.[73]

The two men had been in correspondence since William's referral of the Salisbury Plain poem to Coleridge and had formed a mutual admiration society. Coleridge was basking in the fact that William had expressed his own approval of Coleridge's religious poetry. 'And this man is a Republican & at least a *Semi*-atheist', Coleridge boasted, though, as he also called William 'A very dear friend of mine' on the basis of one brief meeting and a very recent exchange of letters, his judgement with regard to William's faith, or lack of it, has to be suspect.[74]

By the end of May, Coleridge had sent the manuscript of the Salisbury Plain poem to London, even though Joseph Cottle had expressed keen interest in publishing it in Bristol. Whether this was simply so that Charles Lamb, Coleridge's old schoolfriend, fellow poet and most trusted critic, could read it or the intention was to obtain a London publisher is not clear. Lamb 'hurried thro' [the poem] not without delight', but, in what was perhaps a diplomatic move, declared himself too ill to return the manuscript to William in person.[75] William and Lamb may have met for the first time, however, because on 1 June William had left Racedown and returned to London.

Dorothy had deplored the 'unsettled way' in which William had previously lived in London as being 'altogether unfavourable to mental exertion', but since their removal to Racedown it had become evident that William needed more than rural solitude and reading to inspire him to write. The mental stimulation of like minds was a necessity and he returned to Godwin's circle with an avidity which suggests a man in search of answers or, at the least, reassurance. One of the first things he did on his arrival was to go with one of the Pinney brothers to call on Godwin himself, then take him back to Montagu's lodgings for dinner. They met several more times during the five weeks William remained in London, on each occasion as part of the group of Godwinian disciples centred round the Pinneys.[76] These included not only Basil Montagu (who had still not been to visit his son at Racedown) but James and John Tobin, the sons of Mr Pinney's partner in the Bristol West Indies Trading Company. James was three years older than William, John the same age. They both had literary aspirations but James had a degenerative eye condition which had already reduced him to virtual blindness, so it was John, an attorney by profession, who carried the standard as an aspiring dramatist. Robert Allen, an army surgeon who was about to be posted to Portugal, was a schoolfriend of Coleridge and Lamb, university friend and fellow Pantisocrat of Robert Southey, and a journalist. John Stoddart was a barrister at Lincoln's Inn, like Montagu, but also a journalist, who published translations of Schiller's works this year, 1796, and again in 1798, as well as a translation from the French, in 1797, of *An Account of the Committee of Public Safety*.[77]

In this small, closely knit world of Godwinian disciples, all radical and republican in politics and yet also passionately interested in literary matters, William could talk, theorize and dispute to his heart's content. Following Godwin's own example, they could subject all his theories to analysis and dissection in an attempt to come at the Truth. If nothing else, this period in London seems to have settled his own view on the impracticality of Godwin's ideas. In an ideal world, reason and benevolence alone might be sufficient to guide men's actions, without the need for government or institutions of authority. In the real world, it was all too apparent that mankind was simply not good enough to attempt such an exercise. Worse still, men like Godwin, who had indulged in, and encouraged, the dangerous habit of 'dallying with moral calculations', were capable of rationalizing any action and thereby justifying it. By the time William returned to Racedown, he was a man revitalized and determined to expose 'the dangerous use which may be made of reason when a man has committed a great crime'.[78]

To begin with, he embarked on a poem, now known as *Fragment of a 'Gothic' Tale*, describing a blind old sailor being led over chasms and up precipices towards a ruined castle, where his guide, having lodged him in the shelter of a dungeon, attempts to murder him for his little store of savings. This proved to be a false start: it was too simplistic to convey all the subtleties of motive and reasoning William had in mind. Instead, in a bold change of tack, he decided to write a play, or blank-verse drama, in which he could give each character a distinctive history and voice, allowing for greater interplay between them. *The Borderers* was his most ambitious project to date. It incorporated many strands of the Salisbury Plain poem, with which William was still dissatisfied and had decided to withdraw from publication. Again we have wanderers walking over an empty, wild and hostile landscape and an underlying theme of crime, guilt and retribution. Instead of coincidental meetings as the means of discovering the histories of the characters, however, there is a carefully structured plot, centred on the malevolent figure of Rivers, the incarnation of Godwinian thought, who drives the action forward. The play was deliberately set in the Middle Ages, in the Scottish marches, on the borders of Scotland and England: 'little more was required for my purpose than the absence of established Law & Government', William would later comment, 'so that the Agents might be at liberty to act on their own impulses'. Mortimer is the popular leader of a band of outlaws, a sort of Robin Hood figure, protecting the defenceless and dispensing justice in a lawless land. Rivers, seeing in Mortimer a reflection of his own youthful self, is determined to subvert him. He decides to do this in the same way as he himself has been subverted, by causing Mortimer to put to death a man who, to all appearances and rational argument, is guilty of heinous crimes, but is, in fact, innocent. Rivers has reasoned himself into justifying his own crime and, in a remarkable anticipation of late-twentieth-century chaos theory, has argued himself out of feeling remorse:

Remorse,
It cannot live with thought, think on, think on,
And it will die. – What? in this universe,
Where the least things controul the greatest, where
The faintest breath that breathes can move a world –
What, feel remorse where if a cat had sneezed,
A leaf had fallen, the thing had never been
Whose very shadow gnaws us to the vitals?[79]

Mortimer, unable to kill with his own hand, leaves Herbert, a blind old man, to die, alone and exposed to the elements, on a deserted moor. Rivers exultingly reveals Herbert's innocence and argues that, by passing through this initiation, he and Mortimer are now brothers bound 'by links of adamant':

To day you have thrown off a tyranny
That lives but by the torpid acquiescence
Of moralists and saints and lawgivers.
You have obeyed the only law that wisdom
Can ever recognize: the immediate law
Flashed from the light of circumstances
Upon an independent intellect . . .

Mortimer, however, appalled by what he has done, rejects both Rivers's philosophy and his offer of companionship, and condemns himself to the exile of Cain: 'No prayers, no tears, but hear my doom in silence!' he tells his men.

> I will go forth a wanderer on the earth,
> A shadowy thing, and as I wander on
> No human ear shall ever hear my voice,
> No human dwelling ever give me food
> Or sleep or rest, and all the uncertain way
> Shall be as darkness to me, as a waste
> Unnamed by man! and I will wander on
> Living by mere intensity of thought,
> A thing by pain and thought compelled to live,
> Yet loathing life, till heaven in mercy strike me
> With blank forgetfulness – that I may die.

Always powerful, alternately shocking and moving, *The Borderers* was a triumph of the sort that could not be foreseen in William's earlier work. It is still derivative, in the sense that the characters, passions, imagery and even the scenery owe much to Shakespeare: the influence of Lear, Hamlet and Iago is obvious, and there are deliberate echoes of, and borrowings from, *Macbeth*, *Julius Caesar*, *Hamlet* and *Othello*. What makes the play uniquely William's is his analysis of motivation and the influence of landscape. In his lonely wanderings, for instance, Rivers has perceived 'What mighty objects do impress their forms To build up this our intellectual being'. Mortimer, too, is prevented from murdering Herbert in the ruined castle when, like the boy William in the dungeon of Cockermouth Castle, he looked up and, through a crevice, beholds a star twinkling over his head.[80]

William was so enthralled by his creation, that he wrote a preface, dissecting minutely Rivers's character and his motives for committing what might appear a motiveless crime. It is an explicitly moral and didactic reading, accepting Godwin's insistence on benevolent intention as the foundation of all virtue, but rejecting his basic premise that reason teaches benevolence. Mortimer is persuaded by rational means that Herbert is guilty and, having been persuaded, cannot do anything but follow the logic and execute justice. The fact that Herbert is innocent and that Rivers has used 'perverted reasoning' to justify his own 'perverted instincts' strikes at the heart of Godwin's philosophy. William later claimed that he wrote this essay 'to preserve in my distinct remembrance what I had observed of transition in character & the reflections I had been led to make during the time I was a witness of the changes through which the French Revolution passed'.[81]

It was undoubtedly true that William had witnessed the growth of extremism in France and had seen many former liberals perverted by fanaticism, fear of failure, even political expediency. He had himself been an apologist for the September Massacres and the execution of Louis XVI, believing then that the end justified the means. The Terror and France's aggressive wars against her neighbouring states had led him increasingly to question his own judgement and his hitherto unwavering support for the revolution. Reading Louvet, Madame Roland and Helen Maria Williams with his sister in the spring at Racedown had forced him to re-evaluate his own perceptions of what had happened, both to him and to France. Godwin had offered him a welcome light to help him out of the darkness.

> . . . What delight! –
> How glorious! – in self-knowledge and self-rule
> To look through all the frailties of the world
> And, with a resolute mastery shaking off
> The accidents of nature, time and place,
> That make up the weak being of the past,
> Build social freedom on its only basis,
> The freedom of the individual mind,
> Which (to the blind restraint of general laws
> Superior) magisterially adopts
> One guide, the light of circumstances, flashed
> Upon an independent intellect.

It was no accident that in these lines from *The Prelude* William quoted Rivers's own words from *The Borderers.* Godwin's 'One Guide' had led Mortimer fatally astray. For William, it was a light that flared, flickered and then went out. By adopting Godwin's microscopic system of philosophic analysis and demanding, as he did, formal proof for every point, William had succeeded only in confusing himself.

> . . . I lost
> All feeling of conviction, and (in fine)
> Sick, wearied out with contrarieties,
> Yielded up moral questions in despair[82]

In *The Borderers* he resolved his own attitude towards Godwin and freed himself from the intellectual paralysis which had held him in its thrall for so long. Rationalism, he realized, provided 'a sophism for every crime'.[83] It was a decisive step forward. *The Borderers* offered liberation of another kind, less grand in scale, but equally significant in William's evolution as a poet. By reverting to Shakespeare as a model, he had thrown off the shackles of the Spenserian stanza and the eighteenth-century affectation of melancholy. He had discovered the power of blank verse.

7. *A Sett of Violent Democrats*

On 23 October 1796 William wrote to his local newspaper, the *Weekly Entertainer*, protesting at its publication of an extract from a work purporting to be by Fletcher Christian. 'I think it proper to inform you, that I have the best authority for saying that this publication is spurious', he wrote, adding somewhat magisterially, 'Your regard for truth will induce you to apprize your readers of this circumstance.' William was right to condemn the book as spurious, but it prompted him to include the story of the mutiny on the *Bounty* in *The Borderers*. Rivers, like Christian, would mastermind a ship's mutiny and abandon his captain, without victuals, to die on a bare rocky island. The threads of the play were coming together and, the day after writing to the newspaper, William was 'ardent in the composition of a tragedy'.[1]

Towards the end of November a new guest came to Racedown, the first of all those invited by the Wordsworths to accept their invitation. Mary Hutchinson arrived from Sockburn, after a long and arduous coach journey via York, London and Crewkerne. She was escorted by her sailor brother, Henry, who had just returned from a tour of duty in the Caribbean with Sir Alexander Ball, only to find his leave cut short by a summons to Plymouth. By great good luck, Racedown lay on the route to Plymouth. Mary had long wanted to see her friends again and was glad of an excuse to leave Sockburn for a while, after the death of her 'Sister-Companion', Margaret, in the summer. The two Hutchinsons arrived at half past five in the evening, to find the Wordsworths just sitting down to tea. Henry was due to leave early next morning but was persuaded, against his better judgement (which was never very strong), to take breakfast, and promptly missed his coach.[2]

Mary's visit, which thus began so inauspiciously, was to prove a momentous one, not because it was eventful, but because it laid the foundations for what was to become a lifelong companionship. Dorothy was 'very happy in her society';

Mary was 'one of the best girls in the world and we are as happy as human beings can be'. William did not declare his thoughts at the time, but later revealed how much Mary came to mean to him during this visit. In 'She was a Phantom of delight', he reveals that the girl who had seemed 'a lovely Apparition' to him at Penrith had grown 'upon nearer view' into 'A Spirit, yet a Woman too!' In *The Prelude*, he gave a subtle assessment of Mary's other attractions, which makes it quite clear why her presence made such an impact at this juncture in his life. It also explains why and how she became his sheet anchor. Like both the Wordsworths, she loved nature, but not with the intense craving for new sights and experiences, the emotional intensity, which afflicted William and Dorothy. And she was serenely content.

> Her eye was not the mistress of her heart;
> Far less did rules prescribed by passive taste,
> Or barren intermeddling subtleties,
> Perplex her mind; but, wise as women are
> When genial circumstance hath favoured them,
> She welcomed what was given, and craved no more;
> Whate'er the scene presented to her view,
> That was the best, to that she was attuned
> By her benign simplicity of life,
> And through a perfect happiness of soul,
> . . . God delights
> In such a being; for her common thoughts
> Are piety, her life is gratitude.[3]

What is fascinating about this description of Mary is that the quality which William most admired in her, 'she welcomed what was given, and craved no more', is such a contrast with Dorothy's famous sensibility. It is also a quality that was shared by two of the other most important women in his life: his mother, Ann, who was 'pure From feverish dread of error and mishap' and his old dame, Ann Tyson, who was 'affectionate without uneasiness'.[4] Annette, from what little we know of her from her letters, would appear to have been more like Dorothy, which raises an interesting question: what would have happened to William had he married her rather than Mary? Now, as they renewed their acquaintance after so many years of change and turmoil, his burgeoning love for Mary, and her quiet presence in the house, and his life, was a steadying influence. The 'barren intermeddling subtleties' of Godwinian philosophy, which he was exorcizing in his tragedy, would come to seem less important.

By the end of February 1797 the first draft of *The Borderers* was almost finished and it was as if the pent-up tide of William's poetic creativity had suddenly been released. Flushed with new-found confidence, the poems poured from him. They have two striking features in common: they are nearly all in blank verse, like *The*

Borderers, and they are all concerned with the poor. Most of them describe people and incidents William encountered on his daily walks round Racedown, like the woman and her five children unable to afford to buy bread and obliged to watch the baker's cart drive past their wretched hut, denied not just bread but also 'the common food of hope'. The sight and the woman's bitter comment, 'that waggon does not care for us', were a powerful reminder of the bread riots William had witnessed in France and a warning of the likely outcome of such poverty in England. His wonderful description of the patient old beggar walking slowly and steadily on his way, and so 'insensibly subdued To settled quiet' that he is ignored by the little hedgerow birds pecking in the road, also seems a response to personal observation. Even when he turned to an old poem, the *Inscription for a Seat* he had written at Windy Brow, he reworked and expanded it to include descriptions of a foot-worn soldier and his family whose eight-year-old son is already bound to his father's profession, taking advantage of the respite offered by the seat.[5]

The peasants and itinerants of Dorset, whom William had dismissed on his arrival at Racedown as 'lying and picking and stealing', were now an object of increasing interest and sympathy. Abstract philosophical concepts having failed to restore his faith in humanity, he now found answers in the sordid realities of the day-to-day struggle with poverty. Even in old age, William's predilection for walking along the highway, rather than randomly over the hills, would be a subject of local comment. In *The Prelude*, he explained his preference. 'I love a public road', he wrote, because the sight of it disappearing over the horizon had seemed to him, since childhood, like a guide into eternity, or at least to things unknown. The unknown it now led him to was his fellow traveller along the roads of Dorset.

> ... I began to enquire,
> To watch and question those I met, and held
> Familiar talk with them, the lonely roads
> Were schools to me in which I daily read
> With most delight the passions of mankind,
> There saw into the depth of human souls –
> Souls that appear to have no depth at all
> To vulgar eyes.[6]

What he learned was that 'books mislead us': they were written by, and for, those with wealth and education, therefore they ignored the vast majority of mankind. 'People in our rank in life', he would later declare in an uncharacteristic outburst of passion, 'are perpetually falling into one sad mistake, namely, that of supposing that human nature and the persons they associate with are one and the same thing. Whom do we generally associate with? Gentlemen, persons of fortune, professional men, ladies persons who can afford to buy or can easily procure books of half a guinea price'. The best measure of human nature, he argued, was to strip our hearts naked and look outwards, 't[owards me]n who lead the simplest lives most according to nature men who [h]ave never known false refinements, wayward and artificial desires, false criti[ci]sms, effeminate habits of thinking and feeling, or who, having known [t]hese things, have outgrown them'.[7]

It was a return to his roots, not just physically, in Hawkshead, but mentally, in the classics he had loved for so long, Virgil, Horace, Tacitus and their like, who had preached the virtues of simple country life against the corruption of city society. The men and women he met on the public roads of Dorset were 'obscure and lowly', but from them he learned 'truths Replete with honour', the simple virtues of courage, endurance, love, compassion and faith. They proved to him that the world was not rotten to the core, as he had come to believe in his disillusionment, but that the glory of humanity was its capacity to rise above self and suffering. He put this idea forward forcibly in one of his best poems to date, the haunting *Lines Left upon a Seat in a Yew-tree*, describing the character of the man who built the seat within the yew-tree bower. Like both Rivers and Mortimer in *The Borderers*, he had been a youth of 'No common soul ... A favoured Being' but, feeling neglected by a world which did not owe him the living he expected, he turned from it, 'And with the food of pride sustained his soul In solitude'. In drawing the moral, William explicitly attacked the egotism at the centre of Godwinism:

> Stranger! henceforth be warned; and know that pride,
> Howe'er disguised in its own majesty,
> Is littleness; that he who feels contempt
> For any living thing, hath faculties
> Which he has never used; that thought with him
> Is in its infancy. The man whose eye
> Is ever on himself doth look on one,
> The least of Nature's works[8]

William himself now chose to look outward, to the unsung individuals who formed the mass of humanity, and he appointed himself their champion.

> 'Of these', said I, 'shall be my song. Of these,
> If future years mature me for the task,
> Will I record the praises ...
> That justice may be done, obeisance paid
> Where it is due;

His theme, he declared would be 'No other than the very heart of man'. It was a bold decision, and one which would bring ridicule upon him from those (the vast majority of the reading public) who believed that pedlars and waggoners were not fit subjects for poetry. At the somewhat late age of almost twenty-eight, William had at last found his vocation in life. He even found the confidence to turn down an offer from Wrangham. 'As to your promoting my interest in the way of pupils', he wrote, 'upon a review of my own attainments I think there is so little that I am able to teach that this scheme may be suffered to fly quietly away to the paradise of fools.'[9]

With Mary as a willing secretary, making fair copies and transcribing his work, William rapidly completed *The Borderers* and embarked on a major new project, *The Ruined Cottage*, which would embody his new philosophy. Like most of his poetry at this time, it was a protest against the consequences of war. Unable to find employment to support his starving family, Robert cannot bear to witness their suffering, absconds, enlists as a soldier and leaves his bounty money to buy bread for his children. Margaret, his 'wife and widow', waits anxiously for his return. Her eldest child is sent to work on a distant farm, her baby, having caught from her 'the trick of grief . . . sighed amongst its playthings', drooped and died. After nine long years of fruitless waiting, Margaret herself dies, and her once cherished home falls into neglect and decay. It was a deeply affecting story, rendered more so because William presented it through the medium of a pedlar who has known the family for years and witnessed all the changes of fortune. In this earliest version it is a simple tale, simply told, but it had, as William quickly realized, the potential to become something much more.[10] Revising it would occupy him for many years to come, but, as with *The Borderers*, the intense effort of working on a grand project sparked off a number of shorter poems.

The sense that he was at last *doing* something transformed William. Writing to Jane on 19 March 1797, Dorothy declared him 'as chearful as any body can be; perhaps you may not think it but he is the life of the whole house'. A few days earlier, while the whole household was still in bed, Basil Montagu had called unexpectedly on his first visit to his son at Racedown. Dorothy was 'excessively pleased' with him, echoing her brother Christopher's judgement that he was 'one of the pleasantest men I ever saw, and so amiable, and so good that every body who knows him must love him'. Montagu was on his way to Bristol and William jumped at the chance of accompanying him. Though Dorothy still had Mary for company, she wrote gloomily, 'you cannot imagine how dull we feel and what a vacuum his loss has occasioned'. They occupied themselves in making shirts for William and Richard.[11]

William spent about a fortnight in Bristol with Montagu. It was an important foray from Racedown, not least because it was an opportunity for renewing old friendships and making new ones. They paid several visits to James Losh, brother of William's old schoolfriend and fellow lodger at Ann Tyson's. Losh had been in Paris during the revolution and become an active radical in London, where, like Montagu, he was a barrister at Lincoln's Inn and a member of Godwin's circle. Regarding Milton as 'one of the most illustrious friends of civil and religious liberty', he had provocatively published an edition of his *Areopagitica* in 1791, and, most recently, he had himself translated and published Henri Benjamin Constant's *Observations on the strength of the present government in France.* Overworked and, like many other English radicals, depressed by the course of the French Revolution, he had succumbed to pulmonary tuberculosis (and possibly a nervous breakdown) and was now living at Bath. Despite his ill-health, he was an active member of the Bristol radical circle, and was well known to both Southey and Coleridge.[12]

Losh had been in almost monthly correspondence with William since the previous summer and, the day after William set off for Bristol, had dispatched him a large parcel of books. Its contents were telling: Coleridge's printed version of his Bristol lectures on politics, *Conciones ad Populum* and his *Ode on the Departing Year*; Edmund Burke's *Letters on a Regicide Peace* and *Letter to the Duke of Portland*; Thomas Erskine's *View of the Causes and Consequences of the Present War* (Erskine had defended Paine, Hardy and Horne Tooke in the 1794 treason trials); *Evidences of Revealed Religion*, a collection of sermons against atheism, by Coleridge's Unitarian friend John Prior Estlin; and the March to December 1796 issues of the *Monthly Magazine*. A second parcel was sent off soon after William's return to Racedown.[13]

With Losh, William called on Dorothy's friends from Keswick, Mrs Spedding and her daughters, of Armathwaite Hall, who were on holiday in Bath. This was a purely social visit, but Montagu and Losh accompanied him to supper with John Wedgwood, son of the pottery magnate. The fact that Wedgwood was the elder brother of Coleridge's soon-to-be patrons, Tom and Josiah, and, indeed, the company all the Wedgwoods kept suggest the possibility that this was meant to be a potentially useful contact. Before he left Bristol at the end of March, William also called on Joseph Cottle. Resisting persuasion to publish his Salisbury Plain poem, William did, however, contribute his *Written on the Thames near Richmond*, a new revision of a poem he had written at Cambridge, to Cottle's personal Commonplace Book.[14]

Returning to Racedown, he could not resist the temptation to make a detour and pay a visit to Coleridge, who, disillusioned with politicians and politics alike, had 'accordingly snapped my squeaking baby-trumpet of sedition' and retired to contemplative treason in rural Somerset. Since 31 December 1796 he had lived with his wife and baby son at Nether Stowey, a pretty village a few miles west of Bristol, under the lee of the Quantock Hills. His patron, Thomas Poole, a wealthy tanner from the village, with radical sympathies and intellectual interests, had provided Coleridge with a tiny cottage in Lime Street. Their gardens interlinked, enabling Coleridge to avail himself of Poole's library and study whenever the cramped quarters of his own cottage became too much for him. Like Wordsworth, he could now boast, 'I raise potatoes & all manner of vegetables; have an Orchard; & shall raise Corn with the spade enough for my family.'[15] Unlike Wordsworth, and despite his own Pantisocratic dreams, Coleridge had neither interest in nor aptitude for his garden.

It was not a good time for a visit. Coleridge was miserable and depressed. The young man who lodged with him, Charles Lloyd, a Quaker and poet who was subject to occasional bouts of insanity, had suffered five serious fits in the space of ten days. Coleridge was physically and emotionally exhausted by the struggle of restraining him and harassed, as usual, by the need for money and a sense of failure. 'I am not the man I have been –', he wrote to a sympathetic Cottle, 'and I think never shall. A sort of calm hopelessness diffuses itself over my heart. – Indeed every mode of life which has promised me bread and cheese, has been, one after another torn away from me – but God remains.' It was a plight with which William was all too well qualified to sympathize, and his 'conversation, &c' had the effect of rousing Coleridge 'somewhat'. They consoled themselves for their own lack of productivity by attacking the prolific (and increasingly successful) Southey. William uttered the obviously heartfelt complaint that Southey wrote '*too much at his ease* – that he seldom "feels his burthened breast Heaving beneath th' incumbent Deity"'. Coleridge, who had quarrelled bitterly with his brother-in-law some fifteen months earlier, added the equally jealous observation that Southey would 'make literature more *profitable to him* from the fluency with which he writes, and the facility with which he pleases himself'.[16]

Having made common cause against poor Southey, they then discussed their own projects. By an extraordinary coincidence, Richard Brinsley Sheridan had just approached Coleridge and asked him to write a tragedy for his new Drury Lane theatre. Shortly before William's visit, Coleridge had sketched out a plan, 'romantic & wild & somewhat terrible'. Having reviewed a number of Gothic novels over the last few months, he declared himself surfeited with 'dungeons, and old castles, & solitary Houses by the Sea Side, & Caverns, & Woods, & extraordinary characters, & all the tribe of Horror & Mystery',[17] but this did not stop him using exactly the same scenario in his own tragedy, *Osorio.* The fact that he had embarked on his first drama and William had just completed his was an additional bond between the two young men.

Before William left Nether Stowey, Coleridge introduced him to the remarkable Tom Poole, a man who was 'never happy till he has introduced politicks' into the conversation, and whose robust republican views were the despair of his establishment cousins. 'He endeavours to load the higher class of people indiscriminately with opprobrium,' one of them wrote bitterly, 'and magnifies the virtues, miseries, and oppressed state of the poor in proportion. If he does not stand up as the advocate of the French enormities, he endeavours to palliate them, and I am sure, from his conversation and conduct, he would be glad to see all law and order subverted in this country.'[18]

Naturally, he and William found much in common. Poole was a fund of true stories about the rural poor. Walking with William and Coleridge out of the village, up to the top of an eminence overlooking Bin Combe and the Severn estuary, they came to a place named Walford's Gibbet. As a boy, Poole had known the man who was executed there; with the two poets hanging on his every word, he told them the dramatic and poignant tale. John Walford, a charcoal burner, had been prevented from marrying the woman of his choice by her mother. He had drifted into drunkenness and promiscuity, made a local idiot girl pregnant, been forced to marry her and, in a fit of self-loathing and disgust, killed her. On the gallows, he had an agonized reconciliation with the girl he loved, admitted his guilt and died expressing his remorse. Recognizing this as perfect material for William's poetry, he and Coleridge both begged Poole to write the story down.[19]

William returned to Racedown at the beginning of April, full of enthusiasm. He set to work immediately and began to revise and adapt *The Borderers* for the stage. This was a departure, for he had intended the tragedy to be read, rather than performed, but Coleridge had offered to forward it to Sheridan on his behalf and he could not pass up such an opportunity.[20] An irritated letter from Richard brought him down to earth again. Richard reproached him for not writing to their brother John, who, having failed to get a place on the new *Earl of Abergavenny*, was now stuck in the Downs, with a mutinous crew on a leaky ship, the *Duke of Montrose*, awaiting a passage to India. More seriously, he took William severely to task over his financial arrangements. He demanded a clear statement of how his affairs stood with Montagu and Douglas, told him it was 'absolutely necessary' that he should keep records of the accounts and, having pointed out his own expenditure on William's behalf, asked, 'How am I to be repaid these and other sums?' It was a fair question, to which William had no answer: 'you should have been repaid immediately if I had not been disappointed in my settlements with Calvert,' he pleaded, 'which has reduced my income much lower than I had reason to expect. If it were all properly settled my expenses would fall within my receipts.'[21]

To make matters worse, their cousin Robinson Wordsworth was about to be married and had therefore requested repayment of £250 from the Wordsworths' debt to his father. 'We are pestered with letters from every quarter upon this subject', Dorothy wrote miserably. Even Losh had reported hearing rumours in Cumberland that William had 'used his Uncle's children very ill' by not repaying the debt. They all looked to Richard to sort something out, preferably by extracting some of the money owed them by their Uncle Christopher. Though Richard was the only one in a position to do this, it was easier said than done. 'All these things are very unpleasant,' Dorothy admitted, 'besides their claims are so just that it is' (throwing Richard's own phrase back in his face) 'absolutely necessary that something must be done'. Just to remind Richard of their impoverished state she finished her letter with a tart request. 'Pray take care of your old cloaths. They will be of great use at Racedown.' Over a month later, William was writing with increased exasperation because he had not heard from Richard. 'What *is* to be done in this business? I cannot express my anxiety to see it brought to some sort of conclusion.'[22] No conclusion, however, was reached.

One of the coldest springs Dorothy could remember brought the whole household down with colds and coughs. Little Basil was very ill indeed, so much so that she feared he might die. By the end of May, however, the country had 'burst into beauty' and they had all recovered. A parting was now at hand. Mary Hutchinson's six-month visit to Racedown had come to an end. On 5 June she set off for London, carrying with her a letter to Richard and some of the shirts she and Dorothy had made for him: 'If you are at home when she calls you will walk out with her',

Dorothy ordered, 'and shew her the bridges and any thing you may have time for. Perhaps you may be able to go to St Pauls . . . Somerset Terrace or Temple gardens would be a good place.'[23]

Thirteen years later, seeing the Malvern Hills again, William was reminded of Mary's departure from Racedown, and was filled with anguish and regret.

I looked at them with a trembling which I cannot describe when I thought that *you* had not seen them, but *might* have seen, if you had but taken the road through Bristol when you left Racedown; in which case I should certainly have accompanied you as far as Bristol; or further, perhaps: and then I thought, that you would not have taken the coach at Bristol, but that you would have walked on Northwards with me at your side, till unable to part from each other we might have come in sight of those hills . . . and . . . I fancied that we should have seen so deeply into each others hearts, and been so fondly locked in each others arms, that we should have braved the worst and parted no more. Under that tree, I thought as I passed along we might have rested, of that stream might have drank, in that thicket we might have hidden ourselves from the sun, and from the eyes of the passenger; and thus did I feed on the thought of bliss that might have been, which would have [been] intolerable from the force of regret had I not felt the happiness which waits me when I see you again.[24]

As Mary left, Coleridge literally leapt into their lives. 'We have both a distinct remembrance of his arrival –', William would recall almost fifty years later, 'he did not keep to the high road, but leapt over a gate and bounded down the pathless field, by which he cut off an angle. We both retain the liveliest possible image of his appearance at that moment.'[25] Coleridge was in high excitement. Despite his scorn at Southey's speed in writing, he had completed two and a half acts of the tragedy which, when William had visited Nether Stowey two months earlier, had been only sketched in outline. The host having the honours, William first read his new poem, *The Ruined Cottage*, then, after tea, Coleridge read what he had written of *Osorio*. The next morning, William read *The Borderers*. It was a cataclysmic experience for them all. 'Wordsworth, who is a strict & almost severe critic, thinks *very* highly of [my Tragedy] – which gives me great hopes', Coleridge wrote proudly to his friends, adding a typically generous, but awed, tribute to William:

I speak with heart-felt sincerity & (I think) unblinded judgement, when I tell you, that I feel myself a *little man by his* side; & yet do not think myself the less man, than I formerly thought myself. – His Drama is absolutely wonderful. You know, I do not commonly speak in such abrupt & unmingled phrases – & therefore will the more readily believe me. – There are in the piece those *profound* touches of the human heart, which I find three or four times in 'The Robbers' of Schiller, & often in Shakespere – but in Wordsworth there are no *inequalities*. T. Poole's opinion of Wordsworth is – that he is the greatest Man, he ever knew – I coincide[26]

Dorothy, always predisposed towards people who admired her brother, was, quite simply, bowled over by Coleridge. Though she had never before shown any inclination to describe people in anything other than a few conventional phrases, she suddenly launched into a detailed description on Mary's behalf.

You had a great loss in not seeing Coleridge. He is a wonderful man. His conversation teems with soul, mind, and spirit. Then he is so benevolent, so good tempered and cheerful, and, like William, interests himself so much about every little trifle. At first I thought him very plain, that is, for about three minutes: he is pale and thin, has a wide mouth, thick lips, and not very good teeth, longish loose-growing half-curling rough black hair. But if you hear him speak for five minutes you think no more of them. His eye is large and full, not dark but grey; such an eye as would receive from a heavy soul the dullest expression; but it speaks every emotion of his animated mind; it has more of the 'poet's eye in a fine frenzy rolling' than I ever witnessed. He has fine dark eyebrows, and an overhanging forehead.[27]

The feelings were mutual. Dorothy and Coleridge were in instant sympathy.

She is a woman indeed! – in mind, I mean, & heart – for her person is such, that if you expected to see a pretty woman, you would think her ordinary – if you expected to find an ordinary woman, you would think her pretty! – But her manners are simple, ardent, impressive –.

In every motion her most innocent soul
Outbeams so brightly, that who saw would say,
Guilt was a thing impossible in her. –

Her information various – her eye watchful in minutest observation of nature – and her taste a perfect electrometer – it bends, protrudes, and draws in, at subtlest beauties & most recondite faults.[28]

A visit of a few days turned into one of several weeks. Coleridge discovered, to his relief, that on closer acquaintance William was 'more inclined to Christianity than to Theism'. He persuaded a willing Dorothy to copy out the last section of *The Ruined Cottage* for his friend John Estlin and worked hard on completing his own tragedy. At the end of the month, he reluctantly tore himself away, arriving back home on the evening of 28 June. A day or two later he returned over forty miles of 'execrable road' in a cart borrowed from Tom Poole, collected William and Dorothy, and bore them off in triumph to Nether Stowey.[29] They would not return to Racedown.

Dorothy was in ecstasies. 'There is everything here', she enthused, 'sea, woods wild as fancy ever painted, brooks clear and pebbly as in Cumberland, villages so romantic.' There was also, of course, Coleridge. And Mrs Coleridge, struggling to cope on straitened finances, in a cramped cottage, with not only her husband and ten-month-old baby, but also an influx of visitors. For, not content with inviting the Wordsworths, Coleridge had also invited Charles Lamb, whose place on departure was immediately taken by the radical lecturer and poet John Thelwall. There was a certain poetical justice in that, on the second day after the Wordsworths' arrival, Sarah spilt a pan of boiling milk on her husband's foot, confining him to the house and preventing him accompanying his guests on their walks.[30]

The Wordsworths evidently found Lamb a congenial companion, for this was the beginning of a lifelong friendship with this shy, charming, witty man. They had much in common. Lamb worked as a clerk in the East India House, so he knew their brother John and their cousin Captain John Wordsworth. He was unmarried and devoted to his sister, Mary, in circumstances which did him great honour. The previous September, on what Lamb would always call 'the day of *horrors*', she had murdered their mother in a temporary fit of insanity and been confined to an asylum. In an extraordinarily delicate gesture, Lamb had publicly dedicated the poems he had contributed to Coleridge's recent volume to Mary, 'The author's best friend and sister'. It was hardly surprising that Lamb was uncharacteristically subdued, but he was treated with tact and kindness, and clearly enjoyed the rural walks and poetry-reading sessions. Though he always affected to despise the country, he was quite capable of appreciating its beauties; 'besides', William would later point out, 'Lamb had too kindly and sympathetic a nature to detest anything'.[31]

Lamb stayed only a week at Nether Stowey but for him it was a restorative period. On his return to London, he begged Coleridge to send him a copy of William's *Lines Left upon a Seat in a Yew-tree.* 'I have some scattered sentences ever floating on my memory, teasing me that I cannot remember more of it.' He also asked Coleridge to send on his great-coat, which had 'so cunningly' lingered behind. 'But above all, *that Inscription!* – it will recall to me the tones of all your voices – and with them many a remembered kindness to one who could and can repay you all only by the silence of a grateful heart. I could not talk much, while I was with you . . . but company and converse are strange to me. It was kind in you all to endure me as you did.'[32]

To Lamb's innocent inquiry, 'Are Wordsworth and his sister gone yet?' there was a resounding denial. 'I have *settled them* –', Coleridge declared triumphantly. 'By a combination of curious circumstances a gentleman's seat, with a park & woods, elegantly and completely *furnished* – with 9 *lodging rooms*, three parlours & Hall – in a most beautiful & romantic situation by the sea side – 4 miles from Stowey – this we have got for Wordsworth at the rent of 23£ *a year, taxes included!!*' It was indeed a startling coup. William and Dorothy, 'in a wander by ourselves,' shortly after their arrival, had found 'a sequestered waterfall in a dell formed by steep hills covered with full-grown timber trees'. A few days later, they returned and 'pryed into the recesses of our little brook, but without any more fixed thoughts upon it than some dreams of happiness in a little cottage, and passing wishes that such a place might be found out'. The Wordsworths had fortuitously wandered on to the Alfoxton estate, which belonged to the ancient family of St Albyn. The house, which had recently been inherited by a minor, was empty. William and Coleridge immediately applied to Poole and affairs moved with bewildering speed.

Poole promptly drew up a lease in his own hand, witnessed it and offered to stand guarantor for the rent. On 14 July 1797 William therefore became the official tenant of Alfoxton House and Park and Dorothy, scarcely able to believe their luck, informed Mary that they were now 'in a large mansion, in a large park, with seventy head of deer around us'.[33]

Alfoxton was, and is, a lovely house in an exquisite situation.[34] Built on classical lines in 1710, it is elegant and simple, two storeys high, with large gabled attic windows set into the roof. The frontage, facing into the hills, is dominated by a central pedimented portico containing three large sash windows on the first storey and a single round ornamental window above. The ground level at the front of the house has been raised, but when the Wordsworths lived there a short flight of steps led up to the central door. The approach remains the same: a narrow, twisting, steeply embanked lane, winding for rather more than a mile up from the little village of Holford, through the gloom of acres of ancient oak woodland and groves of huge hollies, until it opens out into a pastoral landscape. The house lies above, snuggled into the hillside, with woods behind and above; it looks out on a panoramic view over gentle rolling hills, meadows and woods down to the grey streak of the Bristol Channel, with the hazy blue coastline of South Wales rising beyond. Wild deer are everywhere: casually strolling through the grounds, or gazing with unfazed contempt when caught in the dazzle of headlights. When they cannot be seen, they can be heard, coughing or lowing menacingly, like bulls, in the bushes and bracken. For these are not the tiny roe deer native to the Lakes, but the huge red deer of the Quantocks, which can be as big as cattle.

From the house there are walks of infinite variety and delight. Down through the woods of Holford Glen, where the very air takes on the hues of the dense leaves and moss and becomes bathed in greenish light, and, following the course of the river, through the downs to the shelving rocks and beaches of East Quantoxhead. Or, preferably, up the barely noticeable ascent of a narrow combe, where the stream is gradually reduced to a trickle, or a flash of water in a self-dug ditch, and the trees thin out until there is only an occasional stunted thorn or holly, bent into foetal position by the prevailing wind. A final scramble, almost on hands and knees, over the final bulwark of the combe head cannot prepare you for the surprise beyond. Suddenly, without notice, a huge vista of empty moorland opens out in every direction, riven with plunging valleys and scored by ancient pathways; the coastal plain below is scattered with villages and church steeples. On the coast itself, the dominant features are clearly visible: the stone arm of Watchet harbour, braced against wind and tide, the frowning grey towers of Court House, on the coast at East Quantoxhead, and the brutally minimalist boxes of Hinckley Point nuclear power station, which, fortunately for them, the Wordsworths did not have to see.

Alfoxton had all this to offer (apart from the power station, naturally), and the society of Coleridge, a mere four miles away, at Nether Stowey. This last was, as Dorothy admitted, the principal inducement for their move.[35] At Alfoxton they could have all the benefits of Racedown, without the drawback of its isolation. Bristol was close enough for comparatively effortless visiting and Coleridge himself was a magnet, drawing others to him besides the Wordsworths. The first of these visitors, arriving soon after Lamb left, was Citizen John Thelwall, a prominent and notorious radical. Trained as a lawyer, he had successfully bridged the gap between middle- and working-class protest, had been tried for his life, and acquitted twice, on charges of sedition and high treason, and was probably the most hated and feared of all radicals. His demagogic skills, which had earned him the nicknames 'John Bawlwell', 'Citizen Ego' and 'Mr Rant', and his courage in defying the government by continuing to lecture despite the 'gagging acts', even led to his public repudiation by Godwin, who feared another Robespierre in the making. Dogged by government spies and hounded by magistrates, who encouraged riots at his lectures and physical violence against him personally, he had finally decided to move from London and retire from politics.[36]

Thelwall, like William, was entranced by his visit to 'the enchanting retreat' (which he called 'the Academus of Stowey'), and by his first personal meeting with both William and Coleridge. 'We are a most philosophical party . . . [an] enthusiastic group', he reported excitedly to his wife, 'a literary and political triumvirate, [who] passed sentence on the productions and characters of the age, burst forth in poetical flights of enthusiasm, and philosophised our minds into a state of tranquillity, which the leaders of nations might envy, and the residents of cities can never know.' Finding Coleridge not at home, Thelwall followed him to Alfoxton, where he also became the Wordsworths' guest. 'He really was a man of extraordinary talent,' William would later write, and, despite being brought up in the city, 'he was truly sensible of the beauty of natural objects'. There were 'delightful' rambles through the woods and, naturally, to the Alfoxton waterfall, where the three poet-philosophers sat together on the turf on the brink of the stream 'in the most beautiful part of the most beautiful glen of Alfoxden'. 'This is a place to reconcile one to all the jarrings and conflicts of the wide world,' exclaimed Coleridge. 'Nay', said Thelwall 'to make one forget them altogether.' Coleridge remembered the same conversation, but with rather a different twist, believing he had said it was a place to make one forget *treason*, to which Thelwall had replied that it was 'a place to make a man forget there is any necessity for treason'. Though undoubtedly a better story, it sounds suspiciously like one of Coleridge's improved versions of events.[37]

Flushed with his recent success in securing Alfoxton for the Wordsworths, Coleridge now offered to find Thelwall and his family a suitable residence in the area. It was a big mistake. Thelwall's presence had already sent a *frisson* through the neighbourhood. The reaction of Tom Poole's stuffy cousin Charlotte was typical. 'We are shocked to hear that Mr Thelwall has spent some time at Stowey this week with Mr Coleridge, and consequently with Tom Poole. Alfoxton house is taken by one of the fraternity . . . To what are we coming?' It was a question William could well have asked himself, for out of his hospitality to Thelwall arose a most bizarre incident: what Coleridge gleefully called the 'Spy Nozy' affair.[38] The dangers of living in a closely knit community, instead of the isolation of Racedown, were suddenly brought home in the most startling manner.

It all began with servant gossip. Charles Mogg, who had been employed at Alfoxton by the recently deceased Rev. St Albyn, came back to visit his former friends. In the course of a conversation with Thomas Jones, who lived at the farm house, they naturally discussed the new tenants. Jones proffered the information 'that some French people had got possession of the Mansion House and that they were washing and Mending their Cloaths all Sunday'. Jones, like the good patriot and Christian that he was, 'did not like It', and intended to leave. Scenting a nice juicy scandal, Mogg called on the St Albyns' former huntsman, Christopher Trickie, who lived with his wife at the ancient Dog Pound, just outside the gates of Alfoxton Park. The Trickies were even more forthcoming. They told Mogg that

> the French people had taken the plan of their House, and that They had also taken the plan of all the places round that part of the Country, that a Brook runs in the front of Trickie's House and the French people inquired of Trickie wether the Brook was Navigable to the Sea, and upon being informd by Trickie that It was not, they were afterward seen examining the Brook quite down to the Sea. That Mrs Trickie confirmd every thing her Husband had said. Mogg spoke to several other persons inhabitants of that Neighbourhood, who all told him, They thought these French people very suspicious persons, and that They were doing no good there. And that was the general opinion of that part of the Country. The French people kept no Servant, but they were Visited by a number of persons, and were frequently out upon the heights most part of the night.[39]

Returning home to Hungerford, Mogg could not resist making a detour via Bath, to pass on what he had learned to another former servant of Alfoxton. In the best tradition of Chinese whispers, she duly reported all this to her new employer, Dr Daniel Lysons, who took it upon himself to inform the Duke of Portland, the minister in charge of the Home Office and, consequently, of both national security and espionage. Dr Lysons sent two letters, on 8 and 11 August, the latter adding even more juicy details. Not only were the new tenants Frenchmen but, even more sinisterly,

> the man of the House has no wife with him, but only a woman who passes for his Sister – The man has Camp Stools, which he & his visitors carry with them when they go about the country upon their nocturnal or diurnal expeditions, & have also a Portfolio in which they enter their observations, which they have been heard to say were almost finished – They have been heard to say they should be rewarded for them, & were very attentive to the River near them ... These people may *possibly* be under Agents to some principal at Bristol –[40]

Even before this second letter was dispatched, James Walsh, an experienced government agent, was on his way to Alfoxton, charged with investigating the story. This extraordinarily swift response is explicable only in terms of recent events. Since the rejection of British peace tenders the previous year, rumours of a French invasion had been rife. A landing had been attempted in Ireland but failed. In February 1797 three French frigates and a lugger had appeared off the north Devon coast near Ilfracombe. Even though they made no attempt to land, they scuttled several merchant ships and attempted to destroy shipping in the harbour before disappearing. This shock attack not unnaturally 'greatly agitated the Minds of all Ranks' and the local militia were called out. When the ships reappeared several days later, it was off the Pembrokeshire coast. They landed a small force of 1,200 Frenchmen, under the command of an American veteran, Colonel William Tate, which, two days later, surrendered to the local militia. Colonel Tate's orders were seized and it was discovered that the invasion of Wales was a fallback position: his prime objective had been to execute a *coup de main* on Bristol, 'which is the second city in England for riches and commerce; the destruction of Bristol is of the very last importance, and every possible effort should be made to accomplish it'.[41]

The Wordsworths were known to have Bristol connections; they were believed to have come from Devon. Their behaviour was suspicious: their night walks over the Quantocks, notebook in hand, and their interest in charting the brook from Alfoxton to the coast near Kilve could only have a sinister appearance to local minds. They had arrived suddenly, did not employ servants and had no obvious possessions; their visitors were all strangers to Alfoxton. William had a strange north-country accent, read French books and talked endlessly about French politics. Though there was a perfectly innocent explanation for all these things, it was not surprising that the government took the information seriously. If the new tenants of this secluded mansion were indeed Frenchmen, then they might be gathering information for another attempted invasion. On learning of their inquiries about the brook, the Home Office at once ordered Walsh to leave Hungerford, where he had been interviewing Mogg, and found him 'by no means the most intelligent Man in the World'.

> You will immediately proceed to Alfoxton or it's neighbourhood yourself, taking care on your arrival so to conduct yourself as to give no cause of suspicion to the Inhabitants of the Mansion house there – you will narrowly watch their proceedings . . . you will of course ascertain if you can the names of the persons, & will add their descriptions – & above all you will be careful not to give them any cause of alarm, that if necessary they may be found on the spot.[42]

It was a measure of how seriously the threat was taken that £20 – the equivalent of almost the entire annual rent of Alfoxton – was sent to Walsh to enable him to pursue his inquiries. He took up his headquarters at the Globe Inn at Stowey on 15 August and fortuitously found himself immediately on the case. A Mr Woodhouse asked the landlord 'If he had seen any of those Rascalls from Alfoxton' and if

Thelwall had gone. Walsh asked if they meant the famous Thelwall and, when they affirmed it was, needed no further inquiry to know what he had on his hands. For the last five years, he had followed Thelwall, reporting on his activities and lectures to the Home Office and, on at least one occasion, arresting him. 'I think this will turn out no French Affair', he wrote to the permanent under-secretary, 'but a mischiefuous gang of disaffected Englishmen.' His unwitting informants agreed. 'They are not French', was their opinion. 'But they are people that will do as much harm, as All the French can do . . .' Walsh ended his report with a significant bit of news. 'I have just procured the Name of the person who took the House. His name is *Wordsworth* a Name I think known to Mr Ford.'[43]

That evening, Walsh went up to Alfoxton and interrogated Jones, who confirmed all that he had said to Mogg. No doubt flattered by the stir he had caused, he added a few more interesting titbits. On 23 July, shortly after their arrival, the Wordsworths had thrown a dinner party at which Thelwall had been present. Poole's mother had provided a fore-quarter of lamb, as fourteen people were expected to sit down to dinner and Poole himself was urged to hurry over by eleven o'clock in the morning, so that 'we may have Wordsworth's Tragedy read under the Trees'. Apart from Poole, Thelwall, the Wordsworths and the Coleridges, the identity of the other guests remains a mystery, though they were probably members of Poole's circle at Nether Stowey.[44] As the Wordsworths still had no servant, Jones had been brought in to help with waiting on the table. After dinner, 'a little Stout Man with dark cropt Hair', who wore a white hat and glasses, had got up and talked 'so loud and was in such a Passion that Jones was frightened and did not like to go near them since'. This was, of course, Thelwall, a man whom Coleridge characterized as 'deficient in that *patience* of mind, which can look *intensely* and *frequently* at the *same subject.* He believes and disbelieves with impassioned confidence'.[45]

Jones also reported that William had lately been to Racedown and brought back a 'very Chatty' woman servant, the redoubtable Peggy Marsh, who had proudly informed Jones that 'Her Master was a Phylosopher'. William had also brought back little Basil and their personal possessions. John Perkins, the Pinney agent at Crewkerne, obviously suspected that the Wordsworths had done a moonlight flit and wrote in high excitement to the elder Pinney. No doubt he was disappointed to be reassured that, 'as Mr Wordsworth wrote to my Son and advised him of his intention of leaving Race-down, I have no doubt but he has left every thing in a proper state'. Mr Pinney perhaps took some small satisfaction for his disappointment over the rental arrangements by giving orders that William's carefully nurtured potatoes, 'wh[ic]h Mr Wordsworth writes he left growing for my Son', should be dug up, when ripe, and stored in the Racedown cellar. The arrival at Alfoxton on 14 August of Basil Montagu and Azariah Pinney was probably prompted by news of the Wordsworths removal from Racedown.[46]

By 16 August, only the day after arriving in the area, Walsh had convinced himself that the government had nothing to fear from the tenants of Alfoxton. He was clearly more troubled by what he found in Nether Stowey. Poole he described as 'a most Violent Member of the Corresponding Society' who had set up 'what He stiles *The Poor Mans Club*', with himself at the head of it: 'I am told that there are 150 poor Men belonging to this Club, and that Mr Poole has the intire command of every one of them', was his sinister analysis of poor Poole's efforts at practical philanthropy. Coleridge, he reported, was considered a man of superior ability and was 'frequently publishing': 'He has a Press in the House and I am inform'd He prints as well as publishes his own productions.' This was untrue, but Coleridge's supposed private press would have made him an instant suspect for printing and circulating seditious literature. As Coleridge later learned, the landlord of the Globe had been interrogated by both Walsh and a local magistrate: he had been asked if Coleridge distributed seditious papers and handbills, harangued the people or walked the seashore, charts and maps in hand.[47]

Coleridge dined out on the 'Spy Nozy' affair for years. William would simply dismiss the whole episode, declaring that the proceedings which inspired the investigation were 'such as the world at large would have thought ludicrously harmless'. Biographers have been divided into those who regard it as a hilarious case of mistaken identity and those who read into it every possible shade of sinister meaning. As usual, the truth would seem to lie between the two. There are unanswered questions. Walsh had shadowed Thelwall for years, for instance, yet it came as a surprise to him to find him at Nether Stowey and Alfoxton. Still more extraordinary is that Wordsworth's name should already have been known to both Walsh and his master, Ford, particularly as Walsh apparently knew nothing of either Poole or Coleridge, despite their very public activities in the West Country.[48]

One can only speculate on how, or why, Ford knew the Wordsworth name. There are two possibilities. William may have come to the attention of government agents while moving in radical circles in London, though this seems unlikely, given that they seem to have been unaware of such stridently active public figures as Coleridge and Poole. The most probable reason is the most mundane, but it is supported by the phrasing of Walsh's report. The personal identity of John Thelwall is unmistakable and needs no elucidation: he is '*Thelwall*' and 'the famous Thelwall'. William's personal identity, on the other hand, is not; it is the Wordsworth *surname* which is likely to be known to Ford. 'His name is *Wordsworth* a Name I think known to Mr Ford.' There were at least three reasons why Ford would know the Wordsworth surname. Captain John Wordsworth was a public figure in London, not just because of his East India Company connections but also because he moved in the same circles as Robinson and the latter's father-in-law, the Earl of Abergavenny. His brother, Robinson Wordsworth, had just been appointed Collector of Customs at Harwich under the aegis of 'Jack' Robinson. Finally, and most tellingly, because Ford was a lawyer and Bow Street magistrate, as well as a prominent member of London society, he could not have been unaware of the Wordsworth name in connection with the notorious Lonsdale suit.[49]

It may even have been that personal enmities played their part. Eight years afterwards, in August 1805, Lord Somerville declared he was sure that Southey (his rival for a disputed inheritance) and William 'were still Jacobins at heart', and claimed that he had been 'instrumental in having us looked after in Somersetshire'. Southey immediately understood this to mean the 'spy who was sent down to Stowey to look after Coleridge and Wordsworth'.[50]

Whatever the reasons prompting Walsh's commission, the most obvious one – that the initial reports suggested genuine fears that French agents might be preparing for another invasion – should not be underestimated. Walsh may have got drunk and revealed his mission, but not before he had satisfied himself that there was nothing to be feared. He departed as swiftly as he came. The consequences of his visit could not be so easily removed. 'The Aristocrats seem determined to persecute, *even Wordsworth*', Coleridge reported despairingly to Thelwall. Rumours about her tenant's alleged activities had reached the ears of Mrs St Albyn and she let her displeasure be known. William received notice to quit as soon as his lease expired in June 1798 and Mr Bartholomew, the unfortunate tenant who had sublet the house to him, bore the brunt of her anger. This was something the good Poole could not allow to happen. On 16 September he wrote to Mrs St Albyn, pleading William's cause and pointing out categorically that if anyone was responsible for William's tenancy it was himself. 'I believe him to be in every respect a gentleman', he affirmed, adding, by way of unimpeachable evidence, that their late vicar, a canon of Windsor, had been a particular friend of Uncle William Cookson. He feared the 'most infamous falsehoods' had reached Mrs St Albyn's ears about the company William kept. 'Mr Wordsworth is a man fond of retirement – fond of reading and writing', Poole argued, pointing out that Thelwall's visit had been unexpected and hospitality demanded that he should be received. Disingenuously, he claimed that no one at Stowey or Alfoxton had ever spoken to Thelwall before. This was true, but Coleridge had been in regular correspondence with him for some time prior to his visit. Poole ended his letter with a dignified but heartfelt plea.

> Be assured, and I speak it from my own knowledge, that Mr Wordsworth, of all men alive, is the last who will give any one cause to complain of his opinions, his conduct, or his disturbing the peace of any one. Let me beg you, madam, to hearken to no calumnies, no party spirit, nor to join with any in disturbing one who only wishes to live in tranquillity. I will pledge myself in every respect that you will have no cause to complain of Mr Wordsworth. You have known me from my youth, and know my family – I should not risk my credit with you in saying what I could not answer for.[51]

Perhaps because she had known Poole since his youth – and was therefore well aware of his radical politics – Mrs St Albyn was unpersuaded by his defence and refused to change her mind. Within two months of taking up residence at Alfoxton, the Wordsworths were already under notice to quit. In less than a year they would have to find an alternative home, though for the present they remained in undisturbed possession. Thelwall was less fortunate. Not for the first or last time,

Coleridge had to retract a rashly made promise. It was simply impossible for Thelwall to settle near them. 'Very great odium T. Poole incurred by bringing *me* here –', Coleridge wrote miserably,

> my peaceable manners & known attachment to Christianity had almost worn it away – when Wordsworth came & he likewise by T. Poole's agency settled here – You cannot conceive the tumult, calumnies, & apparatus of threatened persecutions which this event has occasioned round about us. If *you* too should come, I am afraid, that even riots & dangerous riots might be the consequence – *either* of us separately would perhaps be tolerated – but *all three* together – what can it be less than plot & damned conspiracy – a school for the propagation of demagogy and atheism?[52]

In a poem written as he was leaving Bridgwater, Thelwall had joyfully anticipated returning with his wife to join Coleridge's circle:

> . . . by our sides
> Thy Sara, and my Susan, and, perchance,
> Allfoxden's musing tenant, and the maid
> Of ardent eye, who, with fraternal love,
> Sweetens his solitude.

It was not to be. After a four-month search on foot, Thelwall eventually found his own rural retreat, a small farm at Llyswen on the Wye. Even this was not to be the idyll of his dreams: he was denounced from the local pulpit and became the victim of petty persecutions by his neighbours, his six-year-old daughter died and the failure of the harvests left him penniless. It would be many years before he regained his equilibrium and returned from 'his long exile'.[53]

Like all occupiers of large houses, William and Dorothy found that their supposed solitude was interrupted by a constant flow of guests, many of them overspill from Coleridge, whose tiny cottage could barely accommodate his own small family. In the middle of September, they were visited by Coleridge's young friend and lodger Charles Lloyd, who was anxious to hear the remaining acts of *The Borderers*, which William had been adapting for the stage. He found William 'ill & incapable of reading it', so was reluctantly persuaded to stay for a few days because the Wedgwoods were due to arrive for a short visit. 'This, as you may suppose was no great inducement', Lloyd wrote to Southey, but he could not think of an excuse to get out of the invitation.[54]

The Wedgwoods' visit was quite extraordinary, for they came with a purpose. John Wedgwood, with whom William had dined earlier in the year at Bristol, in company with James Losh, wanted to introduce his younger brother, Tom, who had just moved into the area in order to receive treatment at Dr Beddoes's Pneumatic Institution.[55] Tom Wedgwood was a committed philanthropist and Godwinian. Anxious to do his part for the furtherance of mankind, he had, in correspondence with Godwin, determined to devote a portion of his wealth to the education of a genius. One might wonder how he intended to identify a baby with such potential, but he had no such doubts. He believed, with Godwin, that there was no such thing as innate ability and that the source of all depravity was 'an erroneous and vicious education'. This Godwin basically defined as giving in to a child's demands any more than was absolutely necessary for its health and safety, for fear of allowing it to develop tyrannical tendencies. 'Empire in the infant over those who protect him is unnecessary', Godwin had stated, with the profundity one expects of a male philosopher who has had little to do with the nursery; 'if we do not withhold our assistance precisely at the moment when it ceases to be requisite, if our compliance or our refusal be not in every case irrevocable, if we grant any thing to impatience, importunity or obstinacy, from that moment we become parties in the intellectual murder of our children.'[56]

In order to prevent future mass murder, Wedgwood had come up with a scheme. The child was to be protected from contact with bad example and from sensory overload by never being allowed to go out of doors or leave its apartment. The nursery was to be painted grey, with only a couple of vivid coloured objects to excite its senses of sight and touch. It was to be surrounded by hard objects to continually 'irritate [its] palms' (a peculiarly Godwinian notion, lifted straight out of *Political Justice*). All this sensory deprivation was to be enforced by a superintendent, who was to ensure that the child connected all its chief pleasures with rational objects and acquired a habit of 'earnest thought'. Godwin himself had doubted the practicality of finding a preceptor sufficiently qualified to teach such a system; and even if such a paragon could be found, 'who will consent to the profanation of employing him in cultivating the mind of a boy, when he should be instructing the world?' Wedgwood's solution was that of the politician: he would establish a committee of philosophers, composed of himself, Godwin, Dr Beddoes, Holcroft and Horne Tooke, to devise the plan, and employ one or two superintendents to carry it into practice. For his superintendents, he told Godwin, 'the only persons that I know of as at all likely for this purpose, are Wordsworth and Coleridge'. He had qualms about Coleridge, as being 'too much a poet and religionist to suit our views', but of William he had no doubt: 'from what I hear of him, he has only to be convinced that this is the most promising mode of benefiting society, to engage him to come forward with alacrity'.[57]

William evidently disabused Tom Wedgwood pretty quickly. He quite agreed that an equable temper in dealing with children was an advantage, and might even agree with Dorothy that little Basil's solitary upbringing had prevented him learning habits of selfishness from other children. But there was not a chance that the writer of *The Prelude* could support the idea of shutting a child indoors and cutting him off from nature. Indeed, in a passage in that poem, contrasting his own upbringing among a race of 'real children', William launched into a startling polemic against this same Godwinian plan for educating a genius. The result would be not a child but a grotesque 'dwarf man . . . The noontide shadow of a man complete'.

He sifts, he weighs,
Takes nothing upon trust: his teachers stare,
The country people pray for God's good grace
And tremble at his deep experiments. . . .

Now this is hollow – 'tis a life of lies
From the beginning, and in lies must end.
Forth bring him to the air of common sense . . .[58]

The discussions at Alfoxton must have been intense. On the fifth day of the visit, the Wedgwood brothers agreed that the time had passed 'like lightning', but Tom's failure to persuade William rankled. Meeting Coleridge a few months later, Tom would express only 'a very indifferent opinion of his friend Wordsworth'. The full implications of this would not become clear until the following January, when Tom and his brother Josiah, prompted by Poole, offered a generous cash annuity to Coleridge but not to William.[59]

Early in November William, Dorothy and Coleridge walked westwards along the coast to Lynmouth, just over the Somerset border in Devon. It was a walk that took them from the relatively lush, small-scale landscapes of the Quantocks to the bleak grandeur and wilderness of Exmoor. From Porlock, a village of tiny cottages crammed into narrow streets, lying on the edge of a vast flat foreshore, they took the coast road up a vertiginous wooded gorge and over the dizzying pinnacles of the highest cliffs in England, before beginning the dramatic plunge of the descent into Lynmouth. Two rivers meet at Lynmouth at the bottom of a cleft in a rocky gorge, just before they empty into the sea, the noise of waterfalls and sea combining in uproar. Here they stayed the night to recuperate before the climb up what Southey, visiting a year later, aptly describes as 'a road of serpentining perpendicularity' to the object of their tour, the remarkable Valley of Rocks. Running parallel to the coast, this narrow, streamless valley cowers under ramparts of bare rock, 'the very bones and skeleton of the earth', as Southey described them, 'rock reclining upon rock, stone piled upon stone, a huge and terrific mass'.[60] Much beloved, then as now, by those of Gothic sensibilities, the desolation of the Valley of Rocks has inspired many an artist, and our poets were no exception. It was, they decided, the perfect setting for a description of the wanderings of Cain. Coleridge threw down a challenge: they would each write a canto, and whoever finished first would write the final one; the whole project was to be completed that night. It was a foregone conclusion. Thirty years later, Coleridge would still smile at the recollection.

Methinks I see his grand and noble countenance as at the moment when having despatched my own portion of the task at full finger-speed, I hastened to him with my manuscript – that look of humorous despondency fixed on his almost blank sheet of paper, and then its silent mock-piteous admission of failure struggling with the sense of the exceeding ridiculousness of the whole scheme – which broke up in a laugh: and the Ancient Mariner was written instead.[61]

While Coleridge may have confused this walk with others (as, indeed, did William), the two men occupied at least one pedestrian expedition towards Watchet in 'laying the plan of a ballad, to be published with some pieces of William's'. Their object was purely financial. The poems were to be published in the *New Monthly Magazine* and, from the profits, they hoped to finance another short excursion. The original idea for *The Ancient Mariner* had come from Poole's friend John Cruikshank, who had dreamt of a skeleton ship with figures in it. As they walked, they discussed the motivation and evolution of the plot. Once again, it was to be a joint effort, but this time there would be no artificial time limit. Even so, Coleridge was very much the dominant partner, inventing most of the story, though William's contributions were of central importance. Typically, for instance, he suggested that the Mariner should have committed some crime which brought about his spectral persecution. Having recently read a similar story in George Shelvocke's *A Voyage Round the World by the Way of the Great South Sea*, William also suggested that killing an albatross should be the Mariner's crime and that revenge should be sought by the tutelary spirits of the South Seas. Finally, he also put forward the idea of the dead men being reanimated to navigate the ship.

If some of the most crucial elements of the story came from William, the writing was almost exclusively Coleridge's. In the end, William contributed a mere ten or a dozen lines.

> As we endeavoured to proceed conjointly (I speak of the same evening) our respective manners proved so widely different that it would have been quite presumptuous in me to do anything but separate from an undertaking upon which I could only have been a clog . . . The Ancient Mariner grew & grew till it became too important for our first object which was limited to our expectation of five pounds, and we began to talk of a volume . . .[62]

And in this casual, almost accidental way, was born *Lyrical Ballads.* Some sort of collaboration between the poets was inevitable; that was the way Coleridge had always worked in the past, with Lloyd, Lamb and, most closely, Southey. Since their styles and method of writing were so dramatically different, it made sense to collaborate on a volume of poems rather than a single project. *Lyrical Ballads* did not take shape with either the foresight or the method which its authors later claimed for it. Indeed, apart from taking the decision that they wished to publish a joint volume around *The Ancient Mariner*, nothing more came of the plan for some time. It was not even clear what William's contribution would be. Should he offer his Salisbury Plain poem, for instance, or perhaps *The Ruined Cottage*? The whole idea had to be shelved for a while, however, when the real possibility emerged that *Osorio* and *The Borderers* might both be staged in London.

Coleridge had transmitted his play to Sheridan at Drury Lane, through his friend and fellow poet William Lisle Bowles, on 16 October. Shortly afterwards he procured an introduction for *The Borderers* to Thomas Harris of the Covent Garden theatre. The authors all affected an indifference they could not have felt. Coleridge's 'it does not appear to me that there is a shadow of probability that it will be accepted' was echoed by Dorothy's 'We have not the faintest expectation that it will be accepted.' At the beginning of December, Sheridan rejected *Osorio*, but Harris held out such hopes that a few alterations might make *The Borderers* feasible that William and Dorothy dropped everything and went straight to London.[63]

It was not appropriate for a woman to live in Richard's bachelor chambers, so they stayed with the Nicholsons at Cateaton Street, where, to add to the excitement of being in London again, Dorothy had the additional pleasure of meeting up with old Halifax friends. They received a hearty welcome and had an appreciative and encouraging audience for a reading of the play. Miss Nicholson reported back to Halifax that it had 'very great merit; the language is beautiful, and it is uncommonly interesting'. For the first week or so, William was kept fully occupied in rewriting and Dorothy in copying. The final draft was then presented and, while they waited for the verdict, they dreamt of all the possibilities a successful stage run might bring them. One of these schemes was a walking tour through Wales and Yorkshire into Cumberland. As their Halifax cousin Elizabeth Threlkeld tartly commented, 'This would *by many* be thought rather a *wildish* scheme, but by them it was thought very practicable'. Dorothy also made more practical plans for a family reunion. She had not seen Richard for five years and Christopher, at Cambridge, was within easy reach of London. She even hoped to persuade them to come back to Alfoxton for Christmas. John, of course, was still at sea. Had they remained only a few weeks longer at Racedown, they would have seen his latest ship, the *Duke of Montrose*, on which he was second mate, sail round Portland Bill to Torbay, where it was again held back for almost two months by unfavourable winds. He had finally sailed for India on 22 September.[64]

All these pleasant dreams were shattered when *The Borderers* was rejected. The metaphysical obscurity of Rivers was the stumbling block and Mr Harris pronounced it impossible that the play should succeed in the representation. William was disappointed, but bore his rejection philosophically; the problem was not his play, but 'the deprav'd State of the Stage at present'.[65] This may sound like sour grapes, but it was, in fact, quite true. Bowdlerized versions of Shakespeare and watered-down versions of Restoration comedy were staple fare, and the main performance of an evening was usually followed by a farce or even a pantomime. Actresses like Dora Jordan were equally at home playing Rosalind or Viola before the interval, and Priscilla Tomboy or Little Pickle after it. Even when the double bill was more serious, it still entailed drastic cutting (and even rewriting) of the plays to make them suitable for an evening's entertainment. This was perfectly illustrated in the productions that the Wordsworths themselves saw at Drury Lane while in London. On 2 December they saw *The Merchant of Venice* and Thomas Morton's opera *The Children in the Wood*; two days later it was the even more unlikely pairing of an adaptation, by the actor David Garrick, of Southerne's tragedy *The Fatal Marriage* and Milton's *Comus*.[66] One could hardly imagine a psychological thriller like *The Borderers* taking London by storm; nor can one imagine William accepting non-authorial interference in his work. 'William is not determined whether he shall publish it or no,' Elizabeth Threlkeld reported to Halifax, where everyone was agog with curiosity at this latest enterprise by the family black sheep.

> he expects a reform to take place in the Stage, and then it may be brought forward to great advantage. These are visionary plans the distant prospect of which may be very pleasant, but which on a nearer view, almost always disappoint one. However they are happy in having very fertile imaginings which are a continual source of entertainment to them, and serve to enliven many of their solitary hours . . . I wish we could send you a copy of it, for I dare say you will be as anxious as we are, to read the performance of our relation, and that of so excentic a young man.[67]

Before they left London, William and Dorothy paid a number of important visits. Southey, having determined to read for the bar, had been admitted to Gray's Inn at the beginning of the year and was now a resident in London. The Wordsworths dined with him three times during this brief trip and called there once or twice. Dorothy's opinion of him was decidedly cool, indeed almost frosty. The reason for this becomes clear in her description of him as 'a young man of rigidly virtuous habits and . . . I believe, exemplary in the discharge of all Domestic Duties', for she was merely parroting Coleridge. Only Coleridge could turn domestic virtues into a matter for blame; in Southey's case, they were the issue at the very heart of their bitter quarrel in 1795. Despite being (and probably because they were) brothers-in-law, Coleridge had never fully forgiven Southey. As his own marriage fell apart, he would unjustly blame Southey for forcing him into it, and make increasingly spiteful remarks about the Southeys' own wedded bliss.

In the last month, also, the uneasy truce between them had received yet another blow. For reasons best known to himself, Coleridge had published three parodies, *Sonnets Attempted in the Manner of Contemporary Writers*, in the *Monthly Magazine*, under the characteristically delightful pseudonym of Nehemiah Higginbottom. Less delightful was his choice of target: himself (fair game), but also his fellow contributors to his most recent volume of poetry, Charles Lloyd and Charles Lamb. This was singularly unkind, as both men were mentally and emotionally extremely fragile. Lloyd had only recently emerged from an asylum after his latest mental collapse and Lamb was still in the depths of depression after his sister's murder of their mother. Each of them, especially Lamb, Coleridge's friend from schooldays, had a special claim to Coleridge's friendship and support. This unprovoked attack was mortifying to them both; even Lamb, the slowest man on earth to take offence, was deeply hurt. Southey, too, with some justice, believed himself to be targeted in the sonnets. It is a measure of Coleridge's intellectual arrogance that he had thought his ridicule of 'infantine simplicity, vulgar colloquialisms, and lady-like Friendships' might 'do good to our young Bards'. Instead, it caused a breach between him and his victims which only Lamb had the generosity, eventually, to heal. Southey, always more robust, immediately demanded an apology and got one – of sorts. Coleridge was sorry he had written the parodies, not because they had hurt his friends, but 'because I am sorry to perceive a disposition in you to believe evil of me, and a disposition to teach others to believe Evil'.[68] As the Wordsworths would learn to their cost, it was Coleridge's instinct to rebuff even justified criticism of himself by turning it against his accusers: they were always the ones at fault, not him.

The quarrel was at full throttle while the Wordsworths were in London and, reluctantly, they were drawn in. Lloyd, who had been lodging with Southey, certainly tried to recruit Dorothy, for she would later tearfully show his abusive letter of Coleridge to Coleridge himself. Perhaps Southey also attempted to do so, though he secured a more apt revenge by parodying four of Coleridge's sonnets under the pseudonym 'Abel Shufflebottom'. If he did, he failed. Always the loyal partisan, Dorothy now simply dismissed Southey's abilities as 'very remarkable for his years', but 'much inferior to the talents of Coleridge'.[69]

A couple of days before they left London, William paid a visit to Godwin, with one of the Tobin brothers. It was an act of kindness rather than homage. Godwin must have learned from Tom Wedgwood that William had rejected his educational scheme and probably knew before then that he was losing his disciple. In September, however, Godwin's wife, Mary Wollstonecraft, had died giving birth to their daughter. Whatever his former disciples thought of Godwin, they all held her in universal esteem, if not veneration. She had worked for five years for the radical publisher Joseph Johnson, gone to Paris during the French Revolution, where she had borne an illegitimate daughter to her American lover, and, in 1792, published her courageous *Vindication of the Rights of Woman*. It was an indication of his respect for her that William, at her death, had given 5s he could ill afford to a subscription for her child. A visit to the widower, who must have known of his presence in town, was a duty he could not shirk.[70]

It was an unintentional act of sympathy but the following day one of William's most Godwinian poems, *The Convict*, appeared in the *Morning Post*. Written probably in 1796, it was William's affirmation of Godwin's argument that transportation was a preferable alternative to execution. Oddly enough, William may not even have known that it was to be published, for it had been sent in by Coleridge as part of his contract with the newspaper's editor, Daniel Stuart. There was no attempt to pass it off as his own, for it appeared under the pseudonym Mortimer, so it was either an 'in-joke' on Coleridge's part or a subtle attempt to publicize *The Borderers*.[71]

The possibility of publishing *The Borderers* rather than putting it on stage seems to have led the Wordsworths to go from London to Bristol, instead of straight back to Alfoxton. They stayed over Christmas and the New Year, probably with Cottle and his parents, returning to Alfoxton on the evening of 3 January 1798. A few days later they had to say goodbye to Coleridge, whose desperation at his financial affairs had prompted him to consider entering the Unitarian ministry. To see whether he was equipped for such a life, he had offered to act as a locum at Shrewsbury. For good or ill, his ministry was cut short by the offer of an unconditional annuity for life of £150 from Josiah and Tom Wedgwood. 'I accepted it on the presumption that I had talents, honesty, & propensities to perseverant effort', Coleridge informed William, with what would later come to seem painful irony. It would also enable him to stay near the Wordsworths, wherever they went when their lease ran out in June.[72]

In Coleridge's absence, and in the knowledge that their time at Alfoxton was drawing to a close, Dorothy felt the need to capture something of this beautiful place on paper. On 20 January 1798 she began to write a daily journal.[73] It was to become a lifelong, if irregular, habit and a useful tool for her brother. So much of his poetry was reliant on memory for its inspiration that her contemporaneous records of people and places were an invaluable *aide-mémoire* for details that might otherwise have been forgotten. Veering wildly from staccato lists of deeds and visitors to lyrical descriptions of landscapes and the tenderly observed minutiae of nature, Dorothy's journals have indisputably established her as a literary figure in her own right. The argument over how much she contributed to William's (and indeed Coleridge's) poetry is less easily settled, and it continues to rage. Was she simply William's amanuensis, tirelessly jotting down his observations? Or was she herself a poet, denied a voice by a misogynist age and selflessly feeding lines and images to her brother?

The most important point is that William was not a poet who composed in solitude, or on paper. Throughout his entire life, his preferred method of composition was to walk and talk. According to *The Prelude*, as we have seen, he had done this as a schoolboy at Hawkshead; and one of the most abiding impressions he left on the country folk in the Lakes was his habit of 'mumbling to hissel' along t'roads'. One of the Wordsworths' former servants, whose intimacy with the family gave her additional insight, gave a more explicit description: 'Mr Wordsworth went bumming and booing about, and she, Miss Dorothy, kept close behint him, and she picked up the bits as he let 'em fall, and tak' 'em down, and put 'em on paper for him.' For all the contrived quaintness of the dialect, this is a significant observation which goes a long way towards explaining the coincidence of vocabulary and imagery in William's poetry and Dorothy's journals. Dorothy's letters also reveal that she had a curious habit of unconsciously repeating words and phrases taken from her correspondents. Again, this has a bearing on her journal, as it reflects her ability to absorb and adopt the language of others, and explains Coleridge's description of her as 'a perfect electrometer'.[74]

And there is a major difference between the early and late journals which also sheds light on this question. The early ones, coinciding with William's most prolific years, have been extensively published and therefore trawled for evidence to support the argument that William simply turned Dorothy's prose into poetry. The later ones, particularly those of 1824–35, have not, and their significance remains unappreciated. For the clear impression of these journals is that they were of purely personal interest and written for Dorothy's eye alone. They are a brusquely efficient record of daily life and the descriptive passages, which are such a feature of the early journals, are few and far between.[75] It is true that, by this time, William was no longer in full creative flow, but he was still writing poetry, some of it as good as it had ever been. He was, however, no longer Dorothy's constant companion, particularly while walking, which had always been their main inspiration. Clearly, then, he was not totally dependent on the journals for his poetry.

On the other hand, William ceaselessly and publicly reiterated his debt to Dorothy, and there was no more obvious indication of the fact that 'she gave me ears, she gave me eyes' than her early journals. It was William's constant refrain that Dorothy reminded him of his younger self: someone with a physical appetite for nature and an exquisite sensibility. Their natural empathy makes it impossible to separate out what may or may not have been contributed by Dorothy: their reactions were the same and they drew on, and assimilated, each other's responses, so that these became indivisible. The difference between them, which is readily apparent in Dorothy's surviving poetry, was that her powers were purely observational; William was the poet because he had the ability to look beyond the stimulus of the physical senses and 'see into the Life of things'.

When she began her journal, Dorothy was self-conscious and determinedly poetic. Her entry for 20 January opens with a description of the view from Alfoxton: 'The green paths down the hill-sides are channels for streams. The young wheat is streaked by silver lines of water running between the ridges, the sheep are gathered together on the slopes. After the wet dark days, the country seems more populous. It peoples itself in the sunbeams.' It was not long before she began to acquire a more assured style. Returning to Alfoxton after sundown, she noted the crescent moon, Jupiter and Venus. 'The sound of the sea distinctly heard on the tops of the hills, which we could never hear in summer. We attribute this partly to the bareness of the trees, but chiefly to the absence of the singing of birds, the hum of insects, that noiseless noise which lives in the summer air.' Often, she encapsulates a scene or an image in a brief sentence. Sitting upon the heath on the tops above Alfoxton, she noted that its surface was 'restless and glittering with the motion of the scattered piles of withered grass, and the waving of the spiders' threads'. In addition to rhapsodic descriptions (and many a laconic 'an uninteresting evening'), the journal bears witness to the intimacy between the Wordsworths and Coleridge. Every few days they called on each other or walked together, regardless of the weather. Poole was frequently included, accepting and extending hospitality to them all. On one memorable occasion, he took his protégés to call on his disapproving relations at Marshmill. He begged his cousin Penelope to sing an aria for them from *Judas Maccabeus*, 'Come, ever smiling Liberty!', but she persistently selected another song. 'I *could* not sing it', she told her daughter years later. 'I knew what they meant with *their* liberty.'[76]

The one person who was consistently excluded from this charmed circle was Sarah Coleridge. Dorothy had conceived an aversion to her from the start, believing her to be an unworthy wife and helpmeet for the wonderful poet. The unavoidable suspicion is that her dislike and contempt sprang from jealousy: Dorothy could not be Coleridge's wife so she disliked the woman who was. For Sarah, it was particularly mortifying that Coleridge was equally besotted with William's 'exquisite sister'. With one small child already and another due in May, it became increasingly difficult for her to join in the walks, visits and excursions which were such an important part of the friendship. An already tense relationship between the women was driven to breaking point by what must have seemed like calculated provocation to Sarah, in her heavily pregnant state.

> Often it would happen that the walking party returned drenched with rain; in which case [Dorothy], with a laughing gaiety, and evidently unconscious of any liberty that she was taking . . . would run up to Mrs Coleridge's wardrobe, array herself, without leave asked, in Mrs Coleridge's dresses, and make herself merry with her own unceremoniousness and Mrs Coleridge's gravity.

It was an ominous indication of the state of affairs that, if Sarah expressed any resentment, Coleridge slapped her down for being narrow-minded.[77]

Since returning from London and Bristol in the New Year, William had been deeply engaged in composition. He had returned to *The Ruined Cottage*, determined to give it added depth and poignancy by developing the character of the Pedlar who tells Margaret's story. Instead of relating the bare facts, he would become a philosopher and draw out a moral from the tale. Coleridge's influence here was crucial, for the Pedlar became an embodiment of his philosophy of the 'One Life', which recognized the natural harmony and unity of the universe: ''tis God Diffused through all, that doth make all one whole'.[78] By the beginning of March, the poem had grown to 900 lines in length, of which the Pedlar's character made 'a very, certainly the *most*, considerable part of the poem'. He was now a Cumbrian who, despite his lack of schooling and lowly trade, possessed 'no vulgar mind'.

> He was a chosen son:
> To him was given an ear which deeply felt
> The voice of Nature in the obscure wind,
> The sounding mountain and the running stream.
> To every natural form, rock, fruit, and flower,
> He gave a moral life; he saw them feel
> Or linked them to some feeling.[79]

It was no coincidence that many of the lines now written for *The Ruined Cottage* would, the following year, be taken from the Pedlar, transferred to *The Prelude* and acknowledged as autobiographical. By the simple act of making the Pedlar a Cumbrian, William had finally tapped into the mainspring of his poetic power. 'His faculties seem to expand every day,' Dorothy wrote proudly to Mary Hutchinson, 'he composes with much more facility than he did, as to the *mechanism* of poetry, and his ideas flow faster than he can express them.'[80]

This revolution in William's writing habits was also prompted, in part, by the sense that he now had a mission in life. Dorothy had always encouraged him to believe he should be a poet, whatever the financial penalties or his impotent despair at the course of public events. Even through his darkest days at Racedown, when 'in search of knowledge desperate I was benighted heart and mind', she had,

> Maintained for me a saving intercourse
> With my true self...
> She, in the midst of all, preserved me still
> A poet, made me seek beneath that name
> My office upon earth.[81]

The months of almost daily contact with Coleridge at Alfoxton had stiffened William's resolve. That a man of Coleridge's dazzling intellectual gifts should be unstinting in his praise for William's work was, in itself, an affirmation of its worth. This brilliant, charismatic figure, with so many admirers and patrons of his own, had condescended to hero-worship of a virtual unknown, and William responded with a new confidence in himself and his abilities. Now Coleridge, in a gesture which was in itself a recognition of William's superior talents, handed over to William his own most cherished scheme: the idea of a great philosophic poem. 'I should not think of devoting less than 20 years to an Epic Poem', Coleridge had boldly declared to Cottle in April 1797, only a year previously, but before his friendship with William had blossomed.

> Ten to collect materials and warm my mind with universal science. I would be a tolerable Mathematician, I would thoroughly know Mechanics, Hydrostatics, Optics, and Astronomy, Botany, Metallurgy, Fossilism, Chemistry, Geology, Anatomy, Medicine – then the *mind of man* – then the *minds of men* – in all Travels, Voyages and Histories. So I would spend ten years – the next five to the composition of the poem – and the five last to the correction of it.[82]

William responded enthusiastically, though cynics might think it was hardly an act of friendship to pass on such a grandiose scheme, especially as Coleridge was, in Hazlitt's deliciously apt phrase 'a past master of the prospectus'. There is a remarkably similar ring to this plan, for instance, and the one he had hatched with Montagu, in December, for a three-year 'project of Tuition', going systematically through 'the mathematical Branches, chemistry, Anatomy, the laws of Life, the laws of Intellect, & lastly, thro' universal History', with 'constant reference to the nature of *man*'.[83]

In taking on Coleridge's idea of writing an epic poem, William accepted his premise that it would be 'of considerable utility'. He also accepted Lamb's considered judgement that nothing short of an epic poem 'can satisfy the vast capacity of true poetic genius. Having one great End to direct all your poetical faculties to, & on which to lay out your hopes, your ambition, will shew to what you are equal.'[84] Writing to James Tobin to explain his project at the beginning of March, William was able to announce that he had already written 1,300 lines (he did *not* mention that this included *The Ruined Cottage*, which would be subsumed into the new poem), and that his object was 'to give pictures of Nature, Man, and Society. Indeed', he added with Coleridgean grandeur, 'I know not any thing which will not come within the scope of my plan . . . the work of composition is carved out for me, for at least a year and a half to come.' William even had a title for his poem, *The Recluse or views of Nature, Man, and Society.*[85]

Coleridge was cock-a-hoop at William's decision to embark on this grand undertaking, and extravagant in his praise for what he had already written. 'The Giant Wordsworth – God love him! – even when I speak in the terms of admiration due to his intellect, I fear lest tho[se] terms should keep out of sight the amiableness of his manners – he has written near 1200 lines of a blank verse, superior, I hesitate not to aver, to any thing in our language which any way resembles it.' Even Poole, who was not given to hyperbole, gave grudging approbation, thinking it 'as likely to benefit mankind much more than any thing, Wordsworth has yet written'.[86]

There was only one obstacle in William's path: if he was to write a work on such a scale, he needed to have mastery of all the subjects he covered. In the first flush of enthusiasm, this did not seem to be an insuperable problem. Friends were simply asked to perform 'an essential service' and forward books. Cottle was asked to borrow John Wedgwood's copy of Erasmus Darwin's *Zoönomia* and Tobin to send any books of travels, 'as without much of such reading my present labours cannot be brought to a conclusion'.[87]

At the time, William did not appreciate the significance of this statement. For, ironically, his labours on *The Recluse* would never be brought to a conclusion. He would commit decades of his life to the project; it would entrance him and frustrate him, lead to periods of intense creativity and bring him to a complete standstill. Ultimately, it would become the bitterest disappointment of his whole poetic career, for he felt he had failed where it mattered most. This was odd, for, viewed with detachment, *The Recluse* was, like all Coleridge's other grandiose schemes, totally impractical. It was impossible for any one person ever to reach the point where he had sufficient knowledge to be able to expound a totally comprehensive philosophy to the world at large. Coleridge himself would suffocate in the attempt, unable to write because he was always in search of more complete knowledge. The confidence with which William set out his object, 'to give pictures of Nature, Man, and Society', obscured the fact that there never was a coherent plan on which it would proceed. As one scholar has so tellingly put it, it was the announcement of 'an ambition, not a poem'.[88]

8. *The Giant Wordsworth*

'It is decided that we quit Allfoxden – The house is lett', Dorothy wrote to Mary Hutchinson on 5 March 1798. Any cherished hopes that they might be allowed to stay, after all, had been crushed. Mrs St Albyn had proved obdurate and Poole's friends from Nether Stowey, the Cruikshanks, would take over the lease at midsummer. 'I am at present utterly unable to say where we shall be', William wrote the following day. If they could raise sufficient money they still hoped to make their projected walking tour through Wales and the north of England, taking in a visit to Mary at Sockburn. If not, they would have to return to Racedown.[1]

Less than a week later, there was a dramatic change in their plans. In the interval, the Coleridges had come to stay at Alfoxton, and there had been intensive discussion about their future plans. On 11 March William wrote in great excitement to the newly married James Losh.

> We have a delightful scheme in agitation, which is rendered still more delightful by a probability which I cannot exclude from my mind that you may be induced to join in the party. We have come to a resolution, Coleridge, Mrs Coleridge, my Sister and myself of going into Germany, where we purpose to pass the two ensuing years in order to acquire the German language, and to furnish ourselves with a tolerable stock of information in natural science. Our plan is to settle if possible in a village near a university, in a pleasant, and, if we can a mountainous, country; it will be desirable that this place should be as near as may be to Hamburg on account of the expense of travelling. What do you say to this?[2]

It was, of course, a Coleridgean idea, and bore all his hallmarks: the educational scheme (now reduced still further to a mere two years), and the 'little colony' of like-minded spirits, which he had been attempting to establish ever since dreaming up Pantisocracy with Southey. French aggression had made much of Europe inaccessible to English travellers, but the choice of Germany was not dictated solely by the constraints of Continental travel. Coleridge had been studying German daily in recent months and was already flirting with the German metaphysicians who would eventually tie his mind in knots.[3]

Switzerland, which would probably have been William's preferred alternative, and where they could have studied German, was out of the question, for the French had invaded this ancient bastion of independence only a few weeks earlier. Despite continued resistance from some of the more inaccessible cantons, Swiss liberties were abolished and a 'Helvetic Republic' would be proclaimed on 29 March. More than any other action committed by the French republic, it was this which alienated liberal, and even radical, feeling in Britain. One by one the nations of Europe had fallen to conquering French armies – Holland, Luxembourg, Belgium, Poland, the northern Italian nation states and now Switzerland. The rest had capitulated, some, like Austria, into armistice; others, like Spain, into active alliance. Only Britain remained resolute in opposition, no longer fighting an offensive, but a defensive, war. William was not alone in reluctantly coming to the unpalatable conclusion that the standard of liberty had now passed from the French to the British.[4]

The decision to go to Germany was easy: there was nowhere else the Wordsworths particularly wished to go, and their main objective was to remain near Coleridge. How to pay for it was another matter. Coleridge had his annuity from the Wedgwoods, but the Wordsworths were in more dire straits than usual. Montagu had abruptly left the legal profession the previous November and had remained unemployed since. He could not afford to pay his interest on the £400 he held on loan from Calvert's legacy; worse still, he was unable to pay the allowance for his son. The Wordsworths were therefore doubly straitened and having to support young Basil themselves, though Dorothy hastened to assure their aunt, Mrs Rawson, that 'we have lived upon our income'. Their total joint expenditure of the previous year, 1797, had been a mere £110 – not far off the sum William had spent annually on himself as a student at Cambridge. Even so, for some time past the Wordsworths had reluctantly been forced to rely on small sums loaned to them by Poole and Cottle.[5]

William's poetry was his only marketable commodity. Despite his recently expressed reluctance to go into print, 'a thing which I dread as much as death itself', within days of agreeing to accompany Coleridge to Germany, he had made an approach to Cottle.

What *could* you conveniently *& prudently*, and what *would* you, give for

1 Our two Tragedies – with small prefaces containing an analysis of our principal characters . . . To be delivered to you within a week of the date of your answer to this letter – & the money, which you offer, to be payed to us at the end of four months . . .

2 Wordsworth's Salisbury Plain & Tale of a Woman . . . with a few others which he will add . . . to be delivered to you within 3 weeks of the date of your answer – & the money to be payed, as before . . .

Coleridge, writing this letter on William's behalf, was evidently uncomfortable and begged Cottle to treat the matter 'merely as a bookseller' and not as a friend. William himself was determined to hold out for the thirty guineas he thought he needed to finance the trip to Germany; Cottle had first refusal, but if he could not offer so much, then William would approach other publishers. Cottle expressed interest in the volume of poems, so William set to work.[6]

'You will be pleased to hear that I have gone on very rapidly adding to my stock of poetry', William wrote to Cottle on 12 April. 'Do come and let me read it to you, under the old trees in the park.' William was not exaggerating. In addition to all those hundreds of lines written round *The Ruined Cottage* for *The Recluse*, he had produced a startling number of shorter poems for his projected volume. Of the nineteen poems William eventually contributed to *Lyrical Ballads*, virtually all were new compositions, written in a period of remarkable creativity, between November 1797 and July 1798. What is even more extraordinary is that eleven of them were composed between March and May 1798, and by the time *Lyrical Ballads* went to press William had almost enough poems in hand to furnish a second volume.[7] For a man who had spent literally years toiling over *An Evening Walk* and *Descriptive Sketches*, not to mention the still-unpublished Salisbury Plain poem and *The Borderers*, this was some achievement.

The poems William wrote in this period are among his most striking and original. Viewed as a body of work, they divide neatly into two: those which fulfil William's wish to give a sympathetic voice to the plight of the poor and those which are purely autobiographical. Rather more than half fall into the former category and these are the most radical in style, content and vocabulary. Several drew on real-life anecdotes. A Holford farmer, denied poor relief and obliged to sell off his flock, one by one, to feed his large family, was immortalized in *The Last of the Flock*. Christopher Trickie, the one-eyed former huntsman to the St Albyns, who lived on the common just outside the gates of Alfoxton, inspired *Simon Lee*. The contrast of his former strength and vigour with his feeble and impoverished old age was pathetically illustrated in a single incident. William had come across him one day tottering beneath the weight of a mattock as he tried to uproot a stump of rotten wood and, being young and healthy, had severed the root with a single blow. Trickie's tearful but profuse thanks led William to a reflective conclusion.

– I've heard of hearts unkind, kind deeds
With coldness still returning.
Alas! the gratitude of men
Has oftner left me mourning.[8]

(One wonders whether William would have been quite so sympathetic, or helpful, had he known of Trickie's role in the spying episode.) *The Idiot Boy* was composed 'almost extempore; not a word, I believe being corrected, though one stanza was omitted', in the woods of Alfoxton. 'I never wrote anything with so much glee',

William would later admit, adding that the tale had been wrought up out of the idiot boy's words, reported to him by Poole, 'The cocks did crow & the sun did shine so cold'.[9]

Madness, in less genial form, was represented by two powerful poems, *The Mad Mother* and *The Thorn. The Mad Mother* owed its origin to Coleridge's friend Mrs Estlin, who had observed the woman and her baby in Bristol. The story of *The Thorn* William devised himself, after noticing for the first time, on a stormy day, a thorn bush on a Quantock ridge which he had passed many times before. From this small beginning rose the moving tale of the woman who is daily seen at the thorn bush, repeatedly crying, 'oh misery! Oh woe is me!'; a small mossy hummock between the thorn and a pond (which William infamously describes as 'three feet long, and two feet wide') has led to local suspicion that this is the grave of her illegitimate child, whom she is believed to have murdered.

These two poems point us to another fascinating and familiar theme running through this poetry: abandoned women and children. *The Mad Mother*'s husband has deserted her and her child. The fiancé of the woman in *The Thorn* has jilted her on their wedding day, so that their baby is born out of wedlock. The wanderer in *The Female Vagrant* has lost her husband and children through poverty, disease and war. *The Complaint of a Forsaken Indian Woman*, though nominally about the Native American Indian practice of leaving behind the sick and dying, is actually about the woman's grief at having her child taken from her so that he can go on with the tribe.[10] Illegitimacy, abandonment and mental instability were commonplace among the poor and therefore demanded a place in William's work. His recent reading in Erasmus Darwin's *Zoönomia* and William Godwin's life of his wife was demonstrably the impetus behind these themes, but it is difficult to avoid the impression that they were close to the poet's heart. How could William have written so extensively, and so often, on the subject without thinking of the woman and child he had, himself, left behind in France? Or without wondering what had been the effect of his action on them?

On an altogether lighter note, several of the new autobiographical poems sprang directly out of incidents at Alfoxton. Again, there is a discernible theme, the competing claims on the poet's time of the study of books and nature. It did not bode well for William's grand scheme of reading in preparation for *The Recluse* that nature won every time. Addressing Dorothy on 'the first mild day of March', he urges her to put away her books, put on her woodland dress and give herself up to 'the hour of feeling'.

> One moment now may give us more
> Than fifty years of reason;
> Our minds shall drink at every pore
> The spirit of the season.

In *Expostulation and Reply*, he answered the criticism that he had spent half the day dreaming, instead of drinking 'the spirit breath'd From dead men to their kind' in books, by declaring that the mind could also be fed by 'wise passiveness'. Or, as he put it in *The Tables Turned*,

> One impulse from a vernal wood
> May teach you more of man;
> Of moral evil and of good,
> Than all the sages can . . .
>
> Enough of science and of art;
> Close up these barren leaves;
> Come forth, and bring with you a heart
> That watches and receives.[11]

William would always anxiously insist that he drew his inspiration from nature and personal observation, but books also made a vitally important contribution. Even in this collection, as he acknowledged, they had directly provided him with the subject matter for at least two of his poems. The ballad of *Goody Blake and Harry Gill*, for instance, told the story of a farmer who can never again feel warm, after being cursed by an impoverished old woman he had captured stealing twigs from his hedge to feed her meagre fire in the depths of winter. William had read this tale in Erasmus Darwin's *Zoönomia*, where it had been cited as an example of 'Mutable Madness', or mistaking imaginations for realities. No doubt remembering those 'lying and picking and stealing' peasants of Racedown, William set the poem in Dorset and turned it into a warning against lack of charity. *The Complaint of a Forsaken Indian Woman* was also, and more obviously drawn, from literature. As William pointed out in a head-note, the scenario came from one of the travel books he had lately been reading, Samuel Hearne's *Journey from Prince of Wales's Fort in Hudson's Bay to the Northern Ocean* (1795).[12]

Towards the middle of May, William took a short break from his studies. Together with Dorothy and Coleridge, he made an excursion to Cheddar Gorge, some twenty-five miles away from Alfoxton, in the Mendip Hills. They broke their journey at Bridgwater and spent a second night at Cross, a village just outside Cheddar. William then went on to Bristol, while Coleridge escorted Dorothy back to Nether Stowey. One can only imagine the seething resentment that met them there, for poor Sarah Coleridge had, as usual, been left behind. In fact, her husband had actually set out on this jaunt only two days after Sarah had given birth to her second son. Like his elder brother, Hartley, the unfortunate baby was named after a philosopher, Berkeley. Sarah, one would imagine, stood in greater need of a little philosophy than another little philosopher.[13]

William's involvement in this escapade was not entirely selfish. His trip to Bristol was on Coleridge's behalf. Coleridge's quarrel with Lloyd and Lamb was in danger of escalating out of all proportion to the perceived insults on each side, and William had taken on the role of peacemaker. He hoped to find Lloyd at Bristol and bring him back for a face-to-face meeting and reconciliation with Coleridge. In this he was disappointed. Lloyd had already left for his parental home in Birmingham. Unless William took the opportunity to visit Cottle to discuss his forthcoming publication, it was a wasted trip. Coleridge, at any event, was grateful for this intervention: 'I have now known him a year & some months,' he told Estlin, 'and my admiration, I might say, my awe of his intellectual powers has increased even to this hour – & (what is of more importance) he is a tried good man.'[14]

When William returned from Bristol, he found that Coleridge had a visitor, a new disciple, picked up during his brief residence near Shrewsbury earlier in the year. This was the artist, essayist and critic William Hazlitt, then an impressionable young man of twenty. The son of a Unitarian minister, he had been swept off his feet by Coleridge's eloquence and jumped at his invitation to visit Nether Stowey. The very day he arrived, Coleridge carried him off to the more gracious surroundings of Alfoxton, where Dorothy gave them what Hazlitt later grudgingly remembered as a 'frugal' meal and invited them to stay the night. Hazlitt slept 'in an old room with blue hangings, and covered with the round-faced family-portraits of the age of George I and II', and woke the following morning to hear the Alfoxton stag bellowing from the woods above the house. He was given free access to William's manuscript poems and, to ensure that he learned his lesson properly, Coleridge accompanied him into the park after breakfast and, in the Alfoxton tradition, sitting under the trees, read him *The Idiot Boy, The Thorn, The Mad Mother* and *The Complaint of a Forsaken Indian Woman.* It was, as Coleridge intended, a revelatory experience for the young Hazlitt: 'the sense of a new style and a new spirit in poetry came over me'. As they walked back to Nether Stowey, Coleridge expounded at length on William's merits and demerits as a poet. He regretted particularly that William did not share his own belief in the traditional superstitions associated with places, claiming, in an apt image, that 'there was a something corporeal, a *matter-of-fact-ness*, a clinging to the palpable, or often to the petty, in his poetry, in consequence. His genius was not a spirit that descended to him through the air; it sprung out of the ground like a flower, or unfolded itself from a green spray, on which the gold-finch sang.' This criticism applied only to his descriptive poetry (as exemplified by the poems which would appear in *Lyrical Ballads*); his philosophic poetry, on the other hand, 'had a grand and comprehensive spirit in it, so that his soul seemed to inhabit the universe like a palace, and to discover truth by intuition, rather than by deduction'.[15]

This was an analysis of immense significance, for it recognized and voiced William's rejection of Godwinian methodology in favour of the instinctive approach. The 'hour of feeling', the 'impulse from a vernal wood', were surer guides to moral truth than the chop-logic of the philosophers. This was the point at which Coleridge would always depart from William. Under the Wordsworths' influence, he had learned to 'love fields & woods & mounta[ins] with almost a visionary fondness'; like William, he had found 'benevolence & quietness growing within me as that fondness [has] increased'.[16] But, unlike William, he was never content to rest at that point, because he was instinctively more of a philosopher than a poet, and here the youthful Hazlitt stood with Coleridge rather than William.

The following day, William arrived at Nether Stowey on his way back from Bristol. Coleridge had created great expectations in Hazlitt's mind about this first meeting, and there is a palpable air of disappointment in Hazlitt's description of the encounter. Unlike Coleridge himself, William did not have 'the poet's eye, in fine frenzy rolling', which was the approved appearance for poets of the period. Instead, he was 'gaunt and Don Quixote-like', dressed 'quaintly' in a brown fustian jacket and striped pantaloons, which were probably his brother's cast-offs.

> There was a severe, worn pressure of thought about his temples, a fire in his eye (as if he saw something in objects more than the outward appearance), an intense high narrow forehead, a Roman nose, cheeks furrowed by strong purpose and feeling, and a convulsive inclination to laughter about the mouth, a good deal at variance with the solemn, stately expression of the rest of his face.

The overriding impression was one of a 'drooping weight of thought and expression'.[17]

Hazlitt's description is much, and reverently, quoted, both for its perceptiveness and because it is the first detailed word portrait of the poet. Coincidentally, however, not one but three portraits survive from this year. The other two, both pictures, were commissioned by Cottle, the only man of William's circle, other than Poole, sufficiently wealthy to afford such an extravagance. The first was an oil painting by a travelling artist, William Shuter, who had been at Nether Stowey only a few weeks before Hazlitt's visit. The second, a drawing in pencil and chalk, which was possibly intended as an illustration for *Lyrical Ballads*, was by Robert Hancock, a respected sixty-eight-year-old Bristol mezzotinter and engraver; it forms one of a set of four, Cottle also having commissioned Hancock to draw Lamb, Southey and Coleridge.

At first glance there is no obvious correlation between Hazlitt's description and Shuter's almost full-face portrait of a pleasant-looking, rather ordinary young man, with dark eyes and fine, dark hair worn loose at shoulder length. With the benefit of Hazlitt's analysis of his features, however, one perceives the distinctive vertical furrow in his right cheek, and a curiously coy half-smile, which was obviously meant to capture the 'convulsive inclination to laughter'. Hancock's altogether severer profile portrait gives a better idea of the Roman nose, and a receding hairline, which might indicate 'the worn pressure of thought about the temples'. Both portray William in what a later friend, Leigh Hunt, described as his 'habitual' pose, with one hand tucked beneath his jacket lapel. Neither portrait, however, supports Hazlitt's impression of either gauntness or 'a drooping weight of thought and expression', but one suspects that these, and indeed the other characteristics so graphically described, owe more to his later knowledge of the older William than to his first impressions in 1798.[18] The attitude of pained thought, which is so typical of the later, better-known portraits, is entirely absent. This, as we shall see, was an innovation consequent upon William's public elevation to the role of philosopher-poet, after the publication of *The Excursion* in 1814. In 1798 the painters simply depicted what they saw before them: an unremarkable and, as yet, unknown young man of twenty-eight.

If William's appearance was not impressive, his manners were equally informal. He sat down and instantly began to 'make havoc' with a piece of Cheshire cheese on the table. Among other humorous asides, William remarked that Monk Lewis's dreadful play *Castle Spectre*, which he had been to see while in Bristol, 'fitted the taste of the audience like a glove'. The irony was not lost on Hazlitt, even though he did not know of the recent rejection of *The Borderers*.

The following day, Coleridge and Hazlitt came over to Alfoxton for an open-air reading of *Peter Bell*, William's latest long poem. Begun on 20 April, it was intended for inclusion in the forthcoming volume, but its rapid expansion and its controversial subject led to its being omitted. Written in ballad form, it told the story of Peter Bell, a drunken, dissolute, itinerant potter, who tries to steal an ass he finds standing by a river. The ass refuses to move until Peter recovers his master's body from the water, then voluntarily carries Peter back to the widow and fatherless children. For Peter, the journey becomes a spiritual one, effecting a complete character reformation. As far as William was concerned, it was his greatest experiment so far in pushing back the boundaries of poetic taste: both subject matter and language were aggressively lower class. 'The *People* would love the Poem', he later wrote in its defence, 'but the *Public* (a very different Being) will never love it.'[19] He was wrong on both counts; but though the poem has its admirers, for most readers it is an experiment too far. Like much of the more accessible *Goody Blake and Harry Gill*, it teeters uneasily on the brink of doggerel, and occasionally slips over.

Hazlitt therefore found himself in the curious position of listening to William reading *Peter Bell* aloud 'in prophetic tones': 'and the comment made upon it by his face and voice was very different from that of some later critics!' he added unkindly. Whatever he thought of the poem, Hazlitt did have the perception to notice a key element in William's poetry. He attributed it to the hypnotic power of William's voice and intonation. 'There is a *chaunt* in the recitation both of Coleridge and Wordsworth, which acts as a spell upon the hearer, and disarms the judgment', he wrote. 'Coleridge's manner is more full, animated, and varied; Wordsworth's more equable, sustained, and internal. The one might be termed more *dramatic*, the other more *lyrical*.' Hazlitt could not resist an acerbic aside, 'Perhaps they have deceived themselves by making habitual use of this ambiguous accompaniment',[20] but he had a point. Unwittingly, he had put his finger on one of the main reasons for the declining popularity of William's poetry in the twentieth century. It was meant to be read aloud to an audience, not, as it almost always is, silently in books.

Well aware of the effect of the readings under the trees at Alfoxton, William became increasingly urgent in his invitations to Cottle. 'We look for you with great impatience,' he had written on 9 May, 'we will never forgive you if you do not come.' Before the end of the month, Cottle came to stay at Alfoxton for a week. He may even have brought William back from Bristol in his gig, though if this were so, it is odd that neither he nor Hazlitt mentioned the other's presence. Perhaps William walked over to Nether Stowey to meet him, for the gig played a vital role in Cottle's memories of this visit. Coleridge, Dorothy and the servant walked back to Alfoxton, while William accompanied Cottle in his gig. They carried with them a bottle of brandy, a loaf of bread and 'a stout piece of cheese' to enhance the table. When they drew up at Alfoxton, they discovered that the cheese had disappeared, presumably stolen by a beggar they had stopped to give alms to on the road. Coleridge, in a gesture of bravado, released the horse from the gig, causing it to lurch forward, and the precious bottle of brandy fell out and smashed to pieces. Dinner therefore consisted of the loaf of bread and a plate full of cos lettuces, freshly culled from the vegetable garden, washed down with water from the Alfoxton spring. An empty plate at the bottom of the table bore witness to the cheese that should have been. To add insult to injury, when someone asked for salt, the servant admitted she had forgotten to buy any. The philosophers comforted themselves, as one does, with the thought of those less well off than themselves.[21] Though Cottle's memoirs are notoriously inaccurate, one is irresistibly reminded of the frugal dinner offered to Hazlitt and, indeed, of little Basil and his complaints of being starved.

The highlight of Cottle's visit was another trip to Lynton, Lynmouth and the Valley of Rocks, but its real purpose was to determine the final form of the projected publication. There was some bargaining to be done. Cottle wanted to publish all William's unpublished poems in two volumes, a suggestion which to William was 'decisively repugnant & oppugnant'. Taken all together, he reasoned, they would lack variety, though he was prepared to consider publishing either *Peter Bell* or the Salisbury Plain poem separately. Coleridge was anxious to press ahead with publication of *The Rime of the Ancyent Marinere*, though Cottle does not seem to have been happy with its arch archaisms. Cottle was also opposed to the idea of a collaborative venture and, even more emphatically, to an anonymous one. Whatever the final configuration of the volume, or volumes, both poets were equally adamant that it, or they, should appear anonymously. Coleridge, still smarting from a personal attack in the *Anti-Jacobin*, explained why: 'Wordsworth's name is nothing – to a large number of persons mine *stinks*.'[22]

By the time Cottle left Alfoxton, he had come to an agreement, in principle, that he would offer William the thirty guineas he had demanded as his price. This was more a gesture of friendship than business, for he was anxious to assist William in any way he could. He carried away with him Coleridge's manuscript of the *Ancyent Marinere*, which was to form the centrepiece of the publication. Apart from this, its contents were as yet undecided. When they finally settled on a single joint volume, twenty-two of the twenty-three poems it contained had already been written.[23]

The midsummer deadline for the expiry of the lease on Alfoxton was fast approaching. If the scheme for going to Germany was to get off the ground, the

Wordsworths needed to sort out their finances. Cottle's accepted offer was precisely half the sum they had anticipated, but it more than covered the cost of the journey to Hamburg, which, they calculated, would cost them between twenty and twenty-five guineas. William was expecting the final payment on Raisley Calvert's legacy soon: by his calculations, he had received £585, so a further £315 was due. Additionally, he was due the tidy sum of £67 17s 3d, in the form of interest on the capital while it had remained in William Calvert's hands. Sending his brother Richard the release on the legacy in anticipation of the final settlement, William suggested that, if an advantageous annuity could not be purchased, then he would prefer the money to remain on loan to Calvert. In the event, it was 10 August before Calvert forwarded the full amount to Richard, including interest, and an extra half a crown 'to pay the postage of this letter'. And it was not until 4 December, by which time William had been out of the country for almost three months, that Richard finally invested the money in 3 per cent consols.[24] Richard might have cavilled at his brother's casual manner of loaning money to his friends, but at least William obtained a far better rate of interest.

The plans for travelling to Germany were also taking shape. The original intention was to settle immediately in the neighbourhood of one of the German universities, so that they could take full advantage of the opportunities for studying while they learned the language. Their optimistic belief that they could live more cheaply in Germany than England soon proved misplaced. On inquiry, they discovered that lodgings were more expensive, and all the other costs of living far higher, in university towns. Of necessity, therefore, they had to change their plans. They would reside in 'some small town or village' till they had acquired sufficient German for William and Coleridge to take up places in a university. Saxony was recommended to them as being both extremely beautiful and, more importantly, very cheap. The Wordsworths intended to board with 'some respectable family' so that they would be obliged to talk German constantly; the Coleridges, because of their children and the need to have a servant, would have to take a ready-furnished house. They would be able to augment their finances by translating from the German, 'the most profitable species of literary labour'. Dorothy even envisaged that, after a year, they might be able to make their way into Switzerland, if the state of Europe permitted it. If not, 'we shall travel as far as the tether of a slender income will permit'.[25]

It all sounded wonderfully pragmatic and organized. Friends and relatives were naturally horrified, and their cluckings of disapproval reverberated the length and breadth of the kingdom. Poole and Estlin both tried to dissuade Coleridge; Southey was simply contemptuous: 'a wilder and more ridiculous scheme was never undertaken than this – to go with a wife and two infants merely to learn a language which may be learnt by his own fireside!' It was a fair criticism, particularly as the Wordsworths had already reluctantly decided that they could not take five-year-old Basil Montagu with them 'as the experiment of taking a child of his age into a foreign country is at any rate hazardous'. Not until a month before their departure did Coleridge decide that it would be inappropriate for his wife and babes (Hartley almost two, Berkeley not yet six months old), to accompany him; even then, it was only on the grounds of expense. Not having consulted his wife, he could only guess that she would agree that this was the sensible thing to do. There was no question of his giving up the scheme: it was 'of high importance to my intellectual utility; and of course to my moral happiness'.[26]

William went to Bristol to supervise the final selection and printing of his poems. He carried with him the two latest ones, *Expostulation and Reply* and *The Tables Turned*, which had been written in response to a conversation with Hazlitt, who was 'somewhat unreasonably attached to modern books of moral philosophy'. While in Bristol, he took the opportunity to pay several visits to James Losh and his wife, perhaps in an attempt to persuade them to join the trip to Germany. They had recently taken a small house on the Avon at Shirehampton, just north-west of the city, where they had 'visions of a permanent and philosophical retirement from the world'. William read his poems to the couple and there was much conversation, in which Losh, rather wearily, noted that William was 'pleasant and clear but too earnest and *emphatic* in his manner of speaking'. Though William failed to persuade the Loshes to go to Germany, he was sufficiently happy in their company to decide that he would like to have more of it. There would be a hiatus between leaving Alfoxton and setting off for the Continent, and Shirehampton was as good a place as any to be. It had all the advantages of a pretty coastal village and yet was close enough to Bristol to allow him to supervise personally the printing of his poems. Lodgings for himself and Dorothy were engaged with a view to spending two or three months in Shirehampton before their final departure.[27]

He returned to Alfoxton a few days before they had to leave. Dorothy had been left to finalize the arrangements, including parting not only with little Basil, who would now be passed on to the care of an aunt, but also with Peggy Marsh, the faithful servant who had accompanied them from Racedown. On the morning of 25 June 1798, the day after their lease expired, the Wordsworths reluctantly left Alfoxton. It had indeed proved a place of enchantment for them. The seeds of William's talent, which had sprouted at Racedown, had blossomed at Alfoxton, and were about to bear fruit. For a week, they stayed with Sarah and the children in Coleridge's cramped cottage at Nether Stowey (Coleridge himself was away on a pedestrian tour), then they walked to Bristol, to spend a week with Cottle.[28]

Dorothy did not enjoy being in Bristol. A city 'in feeling, sound, and prospect is hateful', she informed Mrs Rawson. 'You can scarcely conceive how the jarring contrast between the sounds which are now for ever ringing in my ears and the sweet sounds of Allfoxden makes me long for the country again.'[29] This reaction owed more to her emotional state than to a genuine dislike for city life, for she had been happy enough in London just before Christmas. Despite the brave face she put on it, she was clearly upset at the departure from Alfoxton and anxious about the uncertainty surrounding their future residence.

Had there ever been any chance of the Loshes accompanying them to Germany, it was now at an end. Losh had taken a severe turn for the worse. Shirehampton 'decidedly disagreed' with him, his nervous complaint had returned and he had been carried off to Bath. On 8 July the Wordsworths went over to visit him there, and had a chance meeting which would have important consequences. They dined twice in company with Losh's friend the Reverend Richard Warner, whose book, *A Walk through Wales in 1797*, was hot off the press. The Wordsworths had long planned to take a walking tour through Wales and their conversations with Warner prompted them to take the plunge. Returning to Bristol, they caught the Severn ferry and, retracing William's own route in the summer of 1793, walked the ten miles upstream to Tintern Abbey. The next morning, they followed the Wye up, through Monmouth, as far as Goodrich Castle, where they again halted for the night, before retracing their steps back to Chepstow. There, however, instead of doing the expected thing and taking the ferry back to Bristol, they returned once more to Tintern Abbey. This time they went by boat, braving the muddy, swirling tidal waters of the Wye in one of the little coracles which plied the tourist route to Tintern from Chepstow and Monmouth. Landing at Tintern, they spent the night there, then returned the following morning to Bristol in a small vessel.[30]

Sketching out this bare outline of their tour, the Wordsworths gave not the slightest hint that it was anything more than a simple tourist jaunt. Nothing could be further from the truth, for out of it would be born *Tintern Abbey*, the giant of *Lyrical Ballads*. As soon as William set foot on the banks of the Wye, it became an act of symbolic significance. He knew immediately that he was not just introducing his sister to a particularly lovely part of the country, but also revisiting his own past. He was aware that this was a time for personal reassessment, for taking stock. And he did so triumphantly. The last five years had been comparatively uneventful, in terms of incident, but they had wrought immense changes in William himself. Then he had been an ardent young revolutionary firing off salvoes at the British establishment; now, like Coleridge, he had become a man of no party, someone who could not, in conscience, vote for the removal of the present ministry, even though he thought them 'weak & perhaps unprincipled men', because he could see no one better to replace them.[31] Then he had been a passionate lover of nature, constantly seeking the stimulus of new and different sights; now, 'with an eye made quiet by the power Of harmony, and the deep power of joy' he had learned to see 'into the life of things'. Then he had been in emotional turmoil, after leaving Annette and his unseen baby daughter behind in France; now, though still haunted by guilt, he had come to some sort of acceptance of the situation. Then he had been frustrated and purposeless: should he be a politician, a pamphleteer, a philosopher, a poet? How was he to earn a living? Now he had a vocation, which enabled him to combine all these things, but rendered him first and foremost a poet.

These reflections would probably have occurred to William had he returned to Tintern Abbey alone, but it was Dorothy's presence that brought them so forcibly home to him. For Dorothy, 'my dearest Friend . . . My dear, dear Sister!', who had loyally stood by him through thick and thin, was wild with delight and excitement. And she was the very image of his younger self.

> in thy voice I catch
> The language of my former heart, and read
> My former pleasures in the shooting lights
> Of thy wild eyes.

William was still a worshipper of nature, but his 'wild ecstasies' had been matured into 'a sober pleasure'. For him, that time, with all its 'aching joys' and 'dizzy raptures', was past, but other gifts had followed, which provided abundant recompense. He had learned to look on nature,

> not as in the hour
> Of thoughtless youth, but hearing oftentimes
> The still, sad music of humanity,
> Not harsh nor grating, though of ample power
> To chasten and subdue. And I have felt
> A presence that disturbs me with the joy
> Of elevated thoughts; a sense sublime
> Of something far more deeply interfused,
> Whose dwelling is the light of setting suns,
> And the round ocean, and the living air,
> And the blue sky, and in the mind of man,
> A motion and a spirit, that impels
> All thinking things, all objects of all thought,
> And rolls through all things. Therefore am I still
> A lover of the meadows and the woods,
> And mountains; and of all that we behold
> From this green earth; of all the mighty world
> Of eye and ear, both what they half-create,
> And what perceive; well pleased to recognize
> In nature and the language of the sense,
> The anchor of my purest thoughts, the nurse,
> The guide, the guardian of my heart, and soul
> Of all my moral being.[32]

Tintern Abbey was a mission statement by a mature and accomplished poet, confident in and at the height of his powers. It was William's equivalent of Martin Luther's 'Here I stand'. In the years to come, William silently acknowledged its perfection by refusing to alter it; it was one of the very few poems he ever wrote to escape his revision almost untouched. 'No poem of mine was composed under circumstances more pleasant for me to remember than this:' he would later say. 'I began it upon leaving Tintern, after crossing the Wye, and concluded it just as I was entering Bristol in the evening, after a ramble of 4 or 5 days, with my sister. Not a line of it was altered, and not any part of it written down till I reached Bristol.'[33] Once back in Bristol, William hastened to give the poem to Cottle. He knew instinctively that he had written something wonderful, but also that, being a summation of his own position, it was the perfect poem with which to conclude the volume.

Within five days of their return, *Lyrical Ballads* was in the press. Coleridge's *Rime of the Ancyent Marinere* was to take pride of place as the first poem in the book; at 658 lines, it was far and away the longest poem. Two extracts from his tragedy *Osorio* would appear in second and fourteenth place, as *The Foster-Mother's Tale* and *The Dungeon.* His fourth and last contribution, *The Nightingale*, was a last-minute substitution for *Lewti*, his reworking of William's juvenile poem *Beauty and Moonlight.* The replacement was probably dictated by the fact that *Lewti* had already appeared in the *Morning Post* on 13 April; it was one of six poems written by William but sent in by Coleridge in the first half of this year to fulfil his contract with Daniel Stuart.[34] It may, however, have been prompted by Coleridge's sudden realization that, despite his *Ancyent Marinere*, he was being relegated to the role of minor contributor, for all the remaining nineteen poems in the volume were by William.

What is more, it was probably William who wrote the advertisement, which appeared as a preface to *Lyrical Ballads.* It was an oddly defensive, even pugnacious document, which appealed to the intelligent reader over the heads of the critics. 'It is the honourable characteristic of Poetry that its materials are to be found in every subject which can interest the human mind', it began, promisingly enough.

The evidence of this fact is to be sought, not in the writings of Critics, but in those of Poets themselves.

The majority of the following poems are to be considered as experiments. They were written chiefly with a view to ascertain how far the language of conversation in the middle and lower classes of society is adapted to the purposes of poetic pleasure. Readers accustomed to the gaudiness and inane phraseology of many modern writers, if they persist in reading this book to its conclusion, will perhaps frequently have to struggle with feelings of strangeness and aukwardness: they will look round for poetry, and will be induced to enquire by what species of courtesy these attempts can be permitted to assume that title. It is desirable that such readers, for their own sakes, should not suffer the solitary word Poetry, a word of very disputed meaning, to stand in the way of their gratification; but that, while they are perusing this book, they should ask themselves if it contains a natural delineation of human passions, human characters, and human incidents; and if the answer be favorable to the author's wishes, that they should consent to be pleased in spite of the most dreadful enemy to our pleasures, our own pre-established codes of decision.

In other words, put aside your prejudices, gentle reader, and enjoy. Well aware that most readers would find 'many lines and phrases will not exactly suit their taste',

William attempted to forestall criticism by confessing that he might sometimes have gone too far; many of his expressions might appear 'too familiar, and not of sufficient dignity', but they were justified by the usage of centuries. 'An accurate taste in poetry . . . is an acquired talent,' was William's lofty pronouncement, 'which can only be produced by severe thought, and a long continued intercourse with the best models of composition.'[35] Though unintentional, the general implication of the advertisement was unfortunate: that the poet expected his offering to be disliked, and that the fault lay with the 'erroneous judgment' of the reader rather than the quality of the poetry itself. One is instantly reminded that William had blamed the rejection of *The Borderers* on 'the deprav'd State of the Stage at present'. Like many deeply private people, he was acutely sensitive to both criticism and rejection. Like them, too, his way of forestalling or dealing with it was to go on the attack, even when this was not necessary. He did this particularly in conversation, where, as his friend Losh had discovered, he could be 'too earnest and *emphatic* in his manner of speaking'.[36] It was an approach which antagonized and offended many of his contemporaries, who mistook his basic insecurity for mere egotism. And, of course, expressed in a preface to a book, it simply invited criticism. Reviewers might be able to ignore the poems, but they could not ignore the advertisement.

Even William's friends were uncomfortable with the inclusion of some poems. Cottle had succeeded in excluding *Peter Bell*, but James Tobin, who had seen some of the sheets as they were printing, came to see William one evening. With 'a grave face', he earnestly entreated William to leave out *We are Seven*, 'for, if published, it will make you everlastingly ridiculous'. William refused and Tobin left 'in despair'.[37] In this instance, William's instinct was right: it became one of his most enduringly popular poems. But faced with such contradictory opinions, even among people whose judgement he trusted, he had to cling to the belief that there was intrinsic merit in his work. Otherwise, there was no point in going on.

At the beginning of August, while the poems were printing, Coleridge persuaded William and Dorothy to join him in a brief excursion into Wales. As far as they were concerned, it was totally unplanned. Coleridge had intended to make his way along the southern coast to Swansea, but the Wordsworths easily persuaded him to walk up the Wye instead. This time they went much further, ending up on the northern side of the Brecon Beacons, between Builth Wells and Hay-on-Wye, at Llyswen, where John Thelwall had settled with his family. They received such a warm welcome that they stayed several days, then retraced their steps down the Wye and the Usk back to their lodgings at Shirehampton.[38]

A few days after their return, they set off again, this time on the first leg of their trip to Germany. Mrs Coleridge, Hartley and Berkeley remained at Nether Stowey, under the tender auspices of Poole and his mother, believing Coleridge would return in three or four months time, either to take them back with him or to stay. Coleridge and the Wordsworths arrived in London on 27 August, after a 'very pleasant' leisurely journey, via Blenheim and Oxford University, travelling on foot, by waggon, coach and post chaise. It did not augur well for the success of their emigration plans that, at the end of this short trip, their boxes had not arrived, a draft for £23 (possibly for the Alfoxton rent) had not been accepted and William had forgotten to bring a crucial letter from Cottle to Thomas Longman, asking him to undertake the London publication of *Lyrical Ballads*.[39]

By 13 September the book had been printed, but it was still unpublished. Cottle could not afford to take the entire risk himself and needed a second, preferably London, publisher. He optimistically printed up some title pages, giving his own name as printer and Longman's as publisher, but Longman refused to get involved. There was a very real danger that the whole venture would founder, particularly as Cottle seemed to be in some financial difficulty. William had committed too much to *Lyrical Ballads* to allow this to happen. On the other hand, he was uncomfortably aware that his own insistence on receiving thirty guineas for his contribution had persuaded Cottle to be over-generous, and added considerably to his unavoidable costs in printing, distributing and advertising. What is more, despite being urged to treat the matter merely as a bookseller, Cottle had repeatedly told William that he would publish the book as an act of friendship, and for William's benefit alone. It was intolerable that Cottle should suffer financially for his generosity to a friend.[40]

In an effort to sort the matter out to the benefit of all parties, William went to see Johnson, who had published *An Evening Walk* and *Descriptive Sketches* for him in 1793. He probably took Coleridge with him and introduced the two men. Given their radical past, they must have heard of each other before, but this was their first meeting. Coleridge, electric with charisma, immediately charmed the elderly publisher into undertaking a little collection of his own poems, *Fears in Solitude*, and giving him a credit note of £30 against the Hamburg bookseller, William Remnant.[41] Johnson proved equally amenable to publishing *Lyrical Ballads* and was apparently willing to offer more than Cottle. It was the perfect solution. The book would be published, William would get more than he had previously anticipated and Cottle would be relieved of an obligation which he was struggling to fulfil. The day before he set sail, William wrote to Cottle pointing out all the advantages of this arrangement and requesting him to transfer his interest in *Lyrical Ballads* to Johnson. He also wrote to Johnson, asking him to deliver six copies of the book to Richard for distribution among his friends. Having done all he could, William sailed for Germany, leaving Cottle to finalize all the arrangements in his absence.

It was a big mistake. From the best of motives, Cottle had no intention of giving up his interest in *Lyrical Ballads*. Over the years, he gave several conflicting accounts of what happened, culminating in the obviously tall tale that the reviews had been so bad and he had sold so few copies that he had been forced to dispose of almost the entire print run to another London publisher, J. & A. Arch. Had he done as William requested and transferred to Johnson, this would not have been necessary; what is more, the copies were with Arch before a single review appeared. From what one can glean from the muddle, it appears that Cottle took offence at William's assumption that he would not make a profit from the volume and at his making alternative arrangements with another publisher. He clearly believed that, without consulting him, William had entered into 'something like *an engagement*' with Johnson, whereas William thought he had left the decision in Cottle's hands. In any case, it appears that Cottle had already disposed of the copies (not the copyright) to Arch, so he was not in a position to sell to Johnson.[42]

The source of the misunderstanding was clearly William's letter, written in haste before sailing. In his absence, no one knew exactly what to do. There was a mildly acrimonious spat between Cottle and Johnson, but on 4 October 1798 *Lyrical Ballads* was finally published under the Arch imprint. A small, slim, insignificant-looking octavo volume, containing 210 pages of poetry and priced at 5s in boards, it bore neither Cottle's name nor those of William and Coleridge.[43] It could hardly have been more anonymous. Its authors, now resident in Germany, did not know of its publication and remained ignorant of its fate.

They had set off from London on 14 September, leaving Richard in charge of William's finances in his absence. The Wedgwoods, who had asked William to give them a copy of *The Borderers* before he left, were to be his bankers, since it was easy for them to transfer money abroad through their merchant contacts. William had been counting on Cottle's thirty guineas for his contribution to *Lyrical Ballads*, but so far had received only £9 13s. Richard would advance £13 but, in a last-ditch effort to raise cash, William prepared to sell his prized copies of Gilpin's tours in Scotland and the Lakes.[44]

Two days later, on 16 September, they sailed from Yarmouth. The little party included not just the Wordsworths and Coleridge, but also John Chester, a young man from Nether Stowey. Hazlitt unkindly described him as low in stature, bow-legged and with a drag in his walk like a drover. He worshipped Coleridge, hung on his every word and scarcely ever spoke himself. This unlikely companion had the advantage of being wealthy enough to subsidize Coleridge's expenses, which is probably why he had been invited along. They had what Coleridge sarcastically called 'an unusually fine passage of only 48 hours' to Cuxhaven at the mouth of the Elbe. To his evident glee, 'Chester was ill the Whole time – Wordsworth shockingly ill! – Miss Wordsworth worst of all – vomiting & groaning & crying the whole time!' Coleridge himself was 'gay as a lark'. Dorothy, emerging from her cabin for the first time in the still waters of the estuary, was surprised that she could not see the shores. Hamburg lay a further sixty-two miles further inland, and the captain agreed to take all the passengers there for half a guinea each.[45]

Sailing up the winding and narrowing waters of the Elbe, the passengers were all sufficiently recovered from their seasickness to emerge from the cabin and get to know one another. Dorothy seems to have kept herself to herself, unwilling or unable to speak French or German well enough to carry on a conversation. Instead, she began a new journal, recording, with typical English intolerance of dirty foreign habits, a catalogue of foul smells, filthy hotels and cheating locals preying on innocent tourists.[46] Coleridge had already attracted a motley party of rumbustious

Scandinavians and Germans, with whom he had caroused his way across the Channel. William found a more congenial acquaintance in an amiable fifty-year-old French émigré, Monsieur de Leutre, who 'appeared [to be] a man of sense, & was in his manners a most complete gentleman'. It was natural that William should gravitate towards the only Frenchman on board: it was an opportunity to speak French again, after a lapse of almost six years, and to pool experiences. They soon struck up what Coleridge called 'a kind of confidential acquaintance'. William discovered that de Leutre had managed to escape France with a large portion of his fortune intact and had settled happily in London, where his favourite niece had married an Englishman. Like many émigrés, however, he had been the victim of intrigues among his fellow countrymen and was now being deported by the Home Office, under the Aliens Act, on suspicion of being an agent of the French government. As Coleridge pointed out, de Leutre spoke 'with rapture' of life in Paris under the monarchy. Though he failed to convince his new friend on this, he did win him round to a conviction of his own innocence: 'I could dare warrant [him] guiltless of *espionage* in any service, most of all in that of the present French Directory.' De Leutre was also an intimate friend of the Abbé de Lille, whose poetry William had read and admired; indeed, William had actually cited his 'charming verses descriptive of the Seine' in a footnote to *Descriptive Sketches*. Literature was obviously much discussed between the men, for Coleridge was obliged to apologize for his own heated contribution to an argument on the merits of French poetry.[47]

At Altona, the busy port of Hamburg, they disembarked into smaller boats and, surrounded by a noisy flotilla containing people of every nationality, they were rowed up to the steps of the Customs House. There, on 19 September, they set foot on German soil for the first time. Leaving Dorothy, Chester and de Leutre's French servant to guard the luggage from rapacious German porters, William and de Leutre set out to find accommodation, while Coleridge rushed into town to present his letters of introduction from the Wedgwoods. After scouring the city (all 'Huddle and Ugliness, Stink and Stagnation!', in Coleridge's memorable phrase), the only place they could find any rooms was Der Wilder Man, 'an hotel not of the genteelest Class'. The difficulty of travelling with an unmarried woman was immediately apparent: she had to have a room of her own. De Leutre shared with his servant, and Coleridge with Chester, but there was nowhere for William. He was obliged to beg a bed off an old college friend, John Baldwin, who was in lodgings at the Duke of York's Hotel. Since de Leutre had the largest room, he agreed that they could all meet there for meals.[48]

The next morning, Dorothy and Coleridge were both woken by the noise of a market directly under their windows. While Dorothy, escorted by Chester, made a promenade of the town, William and Coleridge took advantage of Wedgwood's introduction to an English merchant, Mr Chatterley, to meet his German partner, Victor Klopstock. This was a means to an end. Klopstock was the proprietor of one of the Hamburg newspapers, but it was his older brother, the famous poet and dramatist Friedrich, who was the real object of their interest. Young Klopstock, as they jokingly referred to his younger, but elderly brother, proved kind and courteous. Speaking no English, he conversed with Coleridge in German and William in French, and took the two young men under his wing. He escorted them round the city in an effort to find them a carriage they could afford to buy, so that they could travel more cheaply, and he introduced them to some of his own friends, including the deaf Professor Ebeling. On this, the evening of their first full day in Germany, they decided to go French. They dined, with de Leutre, at the Saxe Hotel, because they thought it would be cheap, being French, and were 'detestably cheated'. Then they went off to the French theatre, for 'a mixture of dull declamation and unmeaning rant', which Coleridge dismissed as 'Execrable'.[49]

It was not a promising start to their life in Germany. The next afternoon, after another fruitless search for a carriage, Victor Klopstock took William and Coleridge to meet his brother, who lived just outside the city. 'In chusing his residence', William remarked with all the disapproval of a man who chose his own carefully, 'the poet does not seem to have been influenced by poetic ideas.' Friedrich Klopstock lived in a row of similar houses at the intersection of several roads on dull, flat land. Now seventy-four, his personal appearance was equally disappointing, for this legendary figure of German poetry was virtually toothless, had monstrously swollen legs and wore a ridiculous powdered and frizzled periwig of enormous proportions. William was unable to discover marks of either sublimity or enthusiasm in his countenance, but was favourably impressed by Klopstock's manner of speaking 'with the liveliness of a girl of seventeen'.

Unusually, Coleridge seems to have taken a back seat, allowing William to do most of the talking; French, again, had to be the medium of communication. They ranged over politics, including the recent French invasion of Ireland and rumours of Nelson's victory at the Nile. Klopstock had followed much the same path as our young poets. He had been a fervent Francophile, written odes in celebration of the French Revolution, and been sent gifts by the republicans; in the wake of French aggression against her neighbours, he had returned the presents with an ode of denunciation, and was now an equally fervent anti-Gallican. They also discussed the whole field of English and German literature. Unusually, again, Coleridge was severer in his judgement than William. 'He thought Glover's blank verse superior to Milton's – & knew nothing of the older German poets, & talked a great deal of nonsense about the superior power of concentering meaning in the German language.' William, noting the inconsistencies in Klopstock's statements, and disappointed by his obvious lack of knowledge, not only of English literature, but also the earlier German poets, came to the more succinct conclusion that his conversation was 'commonplace'.[50]

William, however, was sufficiently interested to return again several days later, bringing with him a gift, a copy of the *Analytical Review*, which he had bought specially at Remnant's, the English bookseller in Hamburg.[51] On this second occasion, without Coleridge's censorious presence, their conversation delved more deeply into the actual process of poetical composition and the role of the poet. Embarking on an epic poem himself, William was fascinated to learn that Klopstock had devoted three years to his *Messiah* without writing a single line, and then had taken thirty years to complete it. It was clearly a disappointment that Klopstock knew so little about English poetry and was disparaging about Schiller, whom William admired. Their most interesting disagreement, though, was about Wieland's *Oberon*, which William had just read in English. William thought the story flagged about the seventh or eighth book, and observed 'that it was unworthy of a man of genius to make the interest of a long poem turn entirely upon animal gratification'. Klopstock, however,

> seemed at first disposed to excuse this by saying that their [*sic*] are different subjects for poetry & that poets are not willing to be restricted in their choice. I answered that I thought the passion of love as well suited to the purposes of poetry as any other passion but that it was a cheap way of pleasing to fix the attention of the reader through a long poem on the mere sexual enjoyment. – Well but said he you see that such poems please every body – I answered that it was the province of a great poet to raise people up to his own level not to descend to theirs.

Later that same day they met again, when they dined together at Victor Klopstock's house. This time, they were in a party of nine, which included Dorothy, but the two poets spent all afternoon in 'animated conversation'. They talked of Kant, whom Klopstock found unintelligible, French comedy and tragedy. 'He seemed to rate too highly the power of exciting tears', William recalled, adding his own acerbic response, 'I said that nothing was more easy than to deluge an audience. That it was done every day by the meanest writers.' Dorothy, finding the strain of trying to understand, and be understood, in a foreign language too great, retired to bed early with a bad headache.[52]

Coleridge, meanwhile, was some thirty miles away in Ratzeburg, a pretty little red-brick town on an island in the middle of a lake, near Lübeck. He had gone there three days earlier, on the recommendation of Victor Klopstock, in the hope of finding cheap lodgings for them all. He was immediately undeceived, for Ratzeburg was a popular resort with the aristocracy and the cheapest to be had were twenty-one marks (£1 8s) a week, which was far more than the Wordsworths could afford. Seduced by the enchanting beauty of the place, however, Coleridge lingered on. The town was built on a hill, so there were lovely views over the lake on every side and delightful walks through groves on the shores. Almost equally attractive to Coleridge was the prospect of enjoying wealthy, and extremely Anglophile, German society, for there were concerts and balls every week. It all proved too much to resist. On the very day the Wordsworths were dining with the Klopstocks, Coleridge entered into an agreement with the local pastor for board and lodgings for himself and Chester at thirty-six marks (£2 8s) a week for both; on top of this, they were to find their own wine, tea and washing. There was no consultation with the Wordsworths, but Coleridge was obviously aware that they could not afford to join him in Ratzeburg, as he excluded them from his lodging arrangements.[53] Quite what he expected them to do, knowing that they had followed him to Germany principally for the pleasure of his company, is not clear.

Their first thought was to go to Weimar, which lay approximately 200 miles south of Hamburg, but Baldwin warned them that it would cost them a minimum of forty guineas to get there, and possibly as much as sixty. German friends, and the English bookseller Remnant, all assured them that this was an exaggeration, and they could expect to pay no more than £15 all told for all four of them. Who were they to believe? Staying in Hamburg was out of the question. Not only was it expensive, but they were cheated at every turn by the shopkeepers and inn-keepers, who took advantage of their ignorance of the language and customs. When William tried to pay 2s for four small rolls in a baker's shop, the baker struck the bread out of his hand, gave him two rolls and refused to return his second shilling. There were also a number of incidents which left them feeling concerned and vulnerable. They saw a man beating a decently dressed woman on the breast with a stick but, despite the fact that the man was a stranger and this occurred in a public street, no one attempted to intervene. Much to William's impotent anger, the onlookers seemed inclined to take the man's part. Another time, they saw a German swearing at and beating an unresisting Jew, again with a stick; a German bystander explained to them in broken English that this violence was quite legal, for 'the Jew had no right to *reign* in the city of Hamburg'. The Wordsworths were sickened, and Dorothy's headaches, not surprisingly, became semi-permanent.[54]

Coleridge's action in deciding to go immediately to Ratzeburg left them in a quandary. They had three options. They could go with him and try to find cheaper lodgings, but Coleridge assured them it was impossible. They could cut short their residence in Germany and return to England, but, in that case, all the money they had already spent on travelling, and living in Hamburg, would have been for nothing. The only other option was to revert to their original plan, conceived at Alfoxton, and this is what they did. 'Wordsworth & Sister determined to go on, & seek, lower down, obscurer & cheaper Lodgings without boarding', Coleridge recorded in his notebook. Two days after his return to Hamburg, they booked their places in the coach to Brunswick at twelve marks (16s) a head for the following Wednesday, and William personally carried their two trunks to the departure point rather than pay the exorbitant price demanded by a German porter. The next day Coleridge and Chester took the coach to Ratzeburg, and, after barely twelve days together in Germany, that was the last the Wordsworths saw of them for several months.[55]

The news of this unexpected separation was greeted with amusement and relief by their friends in England. 'I hear that the Two Noble Englishmen have parted no sooner than they set foot on german Earth,' Lamb wrote sardonically to Southey, 'but I have not heard the reason – Possibly to give Moralists an handle to exclaim "Ah! me! what things are perfect?"' Poole was, as usual, more down to earth. 'The Wordsworths have left you –', he wrote to Coleridge, 'so there is an end of our fear about amalgamation, etc.' This is often quoted as signalling Poole's disapproval of the relationship, but it is clear from what he goes on to say that this was not the case.

I think you both did perfectly right. It was right for them to find a cheaper situation; and it was right for you to avoid the expense of travelling, provided you are where *pure German* is spoken. You will, of course, frequently hear from Wordsworth. When you write remember me to him and to his sister, and thank him for his tragedy, which I am to receive from the Wedgwoods. Thank him in proportion as I value the present, which is indeed very highly . . .

Poole's great fear was that Coleridge would not make the best use of his time in Germany. 'Beware of being too much with Chester', he urged. 'Speak nothing but German. Live with Germans. Read in German. Think in German.' Amalgamation clearly meant nothing more sinister than being too close to other English speakers and therefore not needing to speak German. And, surprisingly, Coleridge did as he was told, making such rapid progress in his studies that within four months he was ready to put in place the second part of the original plan and enter a German university. The one he chose was Göttingen, some 140 miles due south of Hamburg, where the cost of living was less than half that of Ratzeburg.[56]

After Coleridge left, William and Dorothy took a final walk out of Hamburg towards Blankenese, returning along the river through Altona, where their enjoyment of the gay little houses was spoilt by the foul smells in the street. William called on Victor Klopstock to inquire the road to Saxony and paid an hour's visit, with Dorothy, to Remnant's, where they bought two books, Gottfried Bürger's poems, which both Coleridge and Klopstock had praised to William, and, more ominously for the future direction of William's studies, Thomas Percy's *Reliques of Ancient English Poetry*, a collection of ballads, metrical romances, songs and sonnets dating from the seventeenth century and beyond. Not knowing when they would have access to funds again, William drew the huge sum of £32 7s 3d from the Wedgwoods' bankers in the city. On the day they were due to leave, he hastily scrawled a letter to Poole informing him that they were leaving Hamburg, 'a *sad* place', and were going off 'to speculate farther up in the country'. A telling postscript asked Poole to keep an eye on Alfoxton. 'If any series of accidents should bring it again into the market we should be glad to have it, if we could manage it.' A second letter, written the same day, to a Bristol acquaintance, was equally downbeat.

We are now on the point of setting off to Brunswick whence we shall proceed into upper Saxony. The place of our destination is yet undetermined, but we intend to fix on some pleasant village or small town . . . We can scarcely say how we like Germany, Hamburgh is, I hope, a miserable specimen of what we are to find.

Every thing is very dear and the inn-keepers, shop-keepers &c. are all in league to impose upon strangers. We intend to apply with the utmost assiduity to learning the language when we are settled.

There was an equally telling postscript to this letter. 'I do not yet know what is become of my poems, that is, who is their publisher. It was undecided when I came off, which prevented my sending you a copy ... Lyrical ballads with a few other poems, is their title.'[57]

On the evening of 3 October they set off from Hamburg in the diligence, a slow, heavy coach which, despite being half-lined with leather inside, was so full of cracks and crevices that Coleridge described it as 'a Temple of all the Winds of Heaven!!' They had a miserable journey. Only four miles outside Hamburg, Dorothy began to vomit at the shaking motion. Hour after hour, they jolted along on 'miserably bad roads', pausing occasionally at 'wretched' public houses which grew 'more strange and more miserable' as they entered Hanoverian territory, and passing through Lüneburg, 'a wretched miserable place ... lifeless and dead'. After almost forty-eight hours of constant travel, they rolled into Brunswick and sank, with relief, into the unexpected comfort of the English Arms. With a schedule every bit as punishing as a modern coach tour, they were off again at eight o'clock the next morning, on the last twenty-five-mile leg of their journey. Between five and six in the evening on Saturday 6 October 1798 they finally reached Goslar.[58]

Though the Wordsworths had always intended to go to Saxony, their ultimate destination had been vague. Goslar had been mentioned by Victor Klopstock as a possibility, but Dorothy's travel sickness was probably as compelling a reason as any to take at least temporary residence in the city. 'You can have no idea of the badness of the roads', she wrote feelingly to a friend soon after their arrival. Yet Goslar was by no means ideal. 'Goslar is a venerable, (venerable I mean as to its external appearance) decayed city', William informed Josiah Wedgwood after they had spent eighteen weeks there. 'It is situated at the foot of some small mountains, on the edge of the Harts forest. It was once the residence of Emperors, and it is now the residence of Grocers and Linen-drapers who are, I say it with a feeling of sorrow, a wretched race; the flesh, blood, and bone of their minds being nothing but knavery and low falsehood.'[59]

It was impossible to find a family willing to take them in *en pension* as they had hoped. The Wordsworths innocently believed it was because the practice was rare and therefore very expensive in Germany; the more worldly-wise Coleridge realized it was actually because the Germans automatically assumed that 'sister' was a euphemism for 'mistress'. They found lodgings with Frau Depperman, widow of one of the wretched race of linen-drapers, at 107 Breitstrasse, the main street in the town. Despite being 'a civil and good kind of a respectable woman *in her way*', even she indulged in the national pastime and initially cheated her new lodgers out of petty amounts of cash. Neither she, nor her five children, spent much time with the Wordsworths, but a young apprentice from her shop came up to sit with them every evening. This was their only opportunity for daily conversation in German; shared meals, which William knew from experience were the best opportunity for learning the language, were 'utterly useless', as the Wordsworths were obliged to dine together alone. There was no society of the sort Coleridge was enjoying at Ratzeburg. The only person of any intellectual standing in the town with whom they had contact was a French émigré priest; as he merited a mere passing mention in their correspondence, he was clearly not on intimate terms with them and, in any case, conversing in German with a Frenchman was not the ideal way to learn the language. The only congenial German they met, a 'dear and kind creature . . . all kindness and benevolence', was unfortunately both deaf and toothless; 'so that with bad German, bad English, bad French, bad hearing, and bad utterance you will imagine we have had very pretty dialogues', William wrote with grim humour, adding an unusually ardent, 'I shall never forget him'.[60]

'We have not heard from the Wordsworths – to my great Anxiety & inexpressible Astonishment', Coleridge wrote on 8 November. 'Where they are, or why they are silent, I cannot even guess.' It was six weeks after taking up residence in Goslar before William wrote to Coleridge. When he did, it was to say that though provisions and lodgings were very cheap, there was no society, 'and therefore as he did not come into Germany to learn the Language by a Dictionary, he must remove: which he means to do at the end of the Month'.[61] The end of November came and went, as did December, January and most of February, but the Wordsworths were still in Goslar. What they had not foreseen was the ferocity of a German winter. 'For more than two months past we have intended quitting Goslar in the course of each week,' Dorothy wrote to Christopher on 3 February 1799,

> but we have been so frightened by the cold season, the dreadful roads, and the uncovered carts; that we needed no other motives (adding these considerations to our natural aversion to moving from a place where we live in comfort and quietness) to induce us to linger here. We have had a succession of excessively severe weather, once or twice interrupted with a cold thaw; and the cold of Christmas day has not been equalled even in this climate during the last century. It was so excessive that when we left the room where we sit we were obliged to wrap ourselves up in great coats &c in order not to suffer much pain from the transition, though we only went into the next room or down stairs for a few minutes. No wonder then that we were afraid of travelling all night in an open cart!

William's bedroom was particularly cold, because it lay over a passage that had no ceiling. This was a source of grim amusement to Frau Depperman and her family. 'The people of the house used to say, rather unfeelingly, that they expected I should be frozen to death some night.' Dorothy could not bear to leave the house, but William, wrapped up in fur gowns and caps, 'like any grand Signior', took his daily walk alone on the old city ramparts, or in the public gardens, where a kingfisher was his sole companion.[62]

The Wordsworths made the best of their enforced isolation. They might not get intellectual conversation in Goslar, but they corresponded regularly with Coleridge, discussing his latest grand project, a life of the German dramatist and critic Gotthold Lessing, to which he intended to add a survey of early German poetry. William could not share Coleridge's passion for Bürger, whose poems he had bought at Remnant's in Hamburg. Studying them now, he made perceptive criticisms which reflect his growing assurance in and understanding of his own role as a poet.

Bürger is one of those authors whose book I like to have in my hand, but when I have laid the book down I do not think about him. I remember a hurry of pleasure, but I have few distinct forms that people my mind, nor any recollection of delicate or minute feelings which he has either communicated to me, or taught me to recognise . . . It seems to me, that in poems descriptive of human nature, however short they may be, character is absolutely necessary, &c.: incidents are among the lowest allurements of poetry. Take from Bürger's poems the *incidents*, which are seldom or ever of his own invention, and still much will remain; there will remain a manner of relating which is almost always spirited and lively, and stamped and peculiarized with genius. Still I do not find those higher beauties which can entitle him to the name of a *great* poet.[63]

William could afford to speak with such authority because he was practising exactly what he preached. The social and physical isolation of Goslar had forced him back on to his own resources: he was living on his thoughts, feelings and memories, and the poetry simply poured out of him. In just four months he wrote some twenty short poems, including the *Lucy* and *Matthew* poems, and over 400 lines of what would become the earliest version of *The Prelude.* There was no question that what William now produced was indeed 'stamped and peculiarized with genius', but undermining its value, at least in the poet's eye, was the fact that it was not *The Recluse.* The whole point of coming to Germany had been to equip himself for writing that poem. He was feeling his way towards it, but he had made no concrete advance. That was why he felt obliged to offer some sort of justification to Coleridge for his own failure to implement the necessary scheme of study. 'As I have had no books I have been obliged to write in self-defence', he told Coleridge apologetically. 'Reading is now become a kind of luxury to me.' In attempting to explain, he revealed just how absorbed in his poetry he had become. 'When I do not read I am absolutely consumed by thinking and feeling and bodily exertions of voice or of limbs, the consequence of those feelings.' Dorothy was more prosaic: 'William works hard, but not very much at the German.' Coleridge, far away in the social whirl of Ratzeburg, found this strange. 'I work at nothing else, from morning to night –', he boasted to Poole; 'my progress is more rapid than I could myself have believed.'[64]

William's progress was of an altogether different kind. The poetry he was writing owed nothing to Germany, apart from the physical accident that Germany had separated him from Coleridge, books and social pleasure, and created the circumstances in which he was compelled to write. His fine ballad *Ruth*, for instance, could just as easily have been written at Alfoxton; indeed, it was actually suggested by the story of a Somersetshire vagrant, and told the now familiar tale of a woman, jilted by her lover and driven mad with grief.[65] The exquisite *Lucy* poems were similarly sparked by an actual incident. Dorothy related the true story of a little girl from Halifax who was lost in a snow-storm; her frantic parents traced her footsteps to the edge of the canal, where her body was eventually recovered. Out of these bare facts, William conjured up a haunting evocation of an unspoilt child of nature:

She lived among the untrodden ways
  Beside the springs of Dove,
A maid whom there were none to praise,
  And very few to love;

A violet by a mossy stone
  Half-hidden from the eye!
Fair as a star when only one
  Is shining in the sky![66]

Playing around with this theme in what would become a whole group of poems, William mourned her early loss in spare, elegiac lines that are all the more powerful for being so restrained.

A Slumber did my spirit seal,
  I had no human fears:
She seem'd a Thing, that could not feel
  The touch of earthly years.

No motion has she now, no force;
  She neither hears nor sees,
Mov'd round in Earth's diurnal course
  With rocks, & stones, and trees!

Coleridge, recalling this 'sublime Epitaph' when he belatedly learned of the death of his own infant son Berkeley, posed the question which has haunted biographers and critics ever since. Was there really a Lucy Gray in William's past? Or was she a figment of his imagination? Undecided himself, Coleridge came up with the only solution he could think of: 'Most probably, in some gloomier moment he had fancied the moment in which his Sister might die.'[67]

This reference, placed alongside Coleridge's comments about Dorothy being mistaken for William's mistress in Germany, has led to much prurient speculation about the relationship between brother and sister, particularly in the claustrophobic atmosphere of Goslar.[68] Was it merely 'intense', or was it incest? Coleridge himself suggested the latter, but only many years later, when he was estranged from the Wordsworths and felt excluded by the closeness of their family circle. For all Coleridge's multifaceted and undoubted genius, the one area of his life where he lacked any sort of perception was sexuality. When this was linked with his most emotional friendships, particularly those which included an element of jealousy, his judgement was completely unreliable. What one of his biographers has called his 'cuckoo in the nest mentality' would reassert itself every time: he would attach himself to the sister or sister-in-law of his friend, be it Southey, Morgan or, in this case, William, in an attempt to replicate the partnerships of his friends and their wives. When these attachments failed, or were rejected, he immediately perceived sexual relations between the relatives. He would do this twice with William, hinting at incest with Dorothy and, later, adultery with his sister-in-law Sara, which tells us rather more about Coleridge and his sexual hang-ups than about William and his relationships with the females in his family.

Coleridge's claims have been taken far more seriously than they deserve, not least because the post-Freudian world is incapable of believing that there could be anything innocent about intense sibling affection. The fact is that, before we were taught to see through Freud's distorting lens, such relationships were not only commonplace but also held up for admiration: Charles and Mary Lamb are typical examples, as are the Brontës. The latter, like the Wordsworths, have attracted this type of speculation because, unlike the Lambs, they did not live 'normal' lives, surrounded by London society, but alone in rural isolation. Inevitably that led to cosmopolitan suspicion about their motives for doing so. In William's case, it overlooks not only his compelling reasons for choosing to live in the country, but also the fact that he was already in love with Mary Hutchinson, and had been since she lived with them at Racedown. Though it is indisputable that much, if not most, of William's poetry owed its vital spark to incidents drawn from real life, this does not mean that there had to be literal originals behind every one of his poetic creations. As we have already seen, they were as often as not a fusion of different elements, and there is no reason to believe that Lucy, any more than Matthew, or the Pedlar, was anything other than an imaginary, composite figure.

In these winter months, frozen in at Goslar, William explored not only love and loss in his *Lucy* and *Matthew* poems, but also his own childhood in the Lakes. Looking back, he sought to distinguish those moments which had marked him out as a future poet: the boy blowing mimic hootings to the owls on the shores of Windermere, stealing the boat on Ullswater, skating on the ice on Esthwaite. Each one bore his distinctive hallmark: intense self-absorbed activity, followed by the shock of the intrusion of the outside world. Reading them for the first time, Coleridge could not suppress his excitement. 'I should have recognised [them] any where', he exclaimed, 'and had I met these lines running wild in the deserts of Arabia, I should have instantly screamed "Wordsworth!" '[69] Though not originally intended as contributions to the same poem, they would eventually coalesce into the earliest version of *The Prelude*. William might not be able to work on *The Recluse*, but he would at least explore what had made him fit to undertake the task.

Dorothy copied out these scenes for Coleridge, deliberately choosing those which would have most appeal for him. He had described his own thrill at learning to skate at Ratzeburg, for instance, so she transcribed the lines on skating on

Esthwaite and invited him to consider the greater pleasure of racing against William on his native Lakes. He had a beautiful German lake before him, so she offered him the description of Ullswater. William's recollections of his childhood had inspired both Wordsworths with a longing to return, they wanted Coleridge to go with them, and Dorothy was quite openly using these lines as lures to entice him up to the north of England. Wherever they finally settled, she told him, he must come with them at the end of the summer 'and we will explore together every nook of that romantic country'.[70]

On 6 February Coleridge and Chester left Ratzeburg for Göttingen, an ancient town with a splendid university, founded in 1734 by George II, in his capacity as Elector of Hanover, and therefore much favoured by Englishmen. Coleridge had fulfilled his ambition of learning enough German to equip him for entering the university as a student; he was soon roistering in the company of his fellow countrymen, the projected life of Lessing slipping gradually out of view. Living the high life in Ratzeburg had had its cost, at least £2 a week to be precise, and in reckoning over his expenditure at the beginning of January Coleridge realized he had already spent over £90 in just over three months. The Wordsworths' combined expenses had been less than half his alone. 'It would have been impossible for us to have lived as he does;' Dorothy told her brother Christopher, 'we should have been ruined.'[71]

Goslar certainly had the advantage of being cheap, but that was the only one it possessed. As the winter months dragged on, the Wordsworths became more and more frustrated. Coleridge's progression to university simply reinforced William's own failure. He had not even learned sufficient German to earn money by translation. 'We must pursue a different plan', William informed Coleridge.

> We are every hour more convinced that we are not rich enough to be introduced into high or even literary german society. We should be perfectly contented if we could find a house where there were several young people some of whom might perhaps be always at leisure to converse with us. We do not wish to read much but should both be highly delighted to be chattering and chatter'd to, through the whole day . . .
>
> My progress in German considered with reference to literary emolument is not even as dust in the balance. If I had had opportunities of conversing I should not have cared much if I had not read a line. My hope was that I should be able to learn German as I learn'd French, in this I have been woefully deceived. I acquired more french in two months, than I should acquire German in five years living as we have lived. In short sorry am I to say it I do not consider myself as knowing *any* thing of the German language. Consider this not as spoken in modesty either false or true but in simple verity.[72]

Determined to recoup something, William and Dorothy came up with a plan. They would walk the thirty or thirty-five miles over the Harz Mountains to Nordhausen, cutting twenty miles off the route taken by the public coach, which was an open cart. At Nordhausen, they had the option of taking covered diligences to any of the principal towns in Upper Saxony. As usual, they made no firm plans for a route, but intended to make a little circuit of towns, staying no more than a fortnight in each place. They had letters of introduction, presumably from the Klopstocks, to Weimar, the literary and intellectual centre of Germany, where the poet Goethe had lived since 1775. They also considered living in Erfurt or Eisenach, which would be cheaper, but did not think it likely they would be induced to spend more than a couple of months on their tour before returning to Hamburg, where they would take lodgings until they could sail home. Even if they did not acquire greater familiarity with the language, at least they would have seen something more of the country.[73]

Their baggage had been packed for several weeks before they were finally able to seize the opportunity of a break in the weather. At last, on 23 February, they set off on foot from Goslar with a guide to lead them over the mountains. William carried with him the equivalent of £40 in cash, drawn on the Wedgwoods' account with a business associate in Brunswick. Together with the £32 he had already drawn in Hamburg, this was the entire sum he had allocated for their residence in Germany, but he had no contacts in Upper Saxony and was anxious that they should not have to curtail their trip for want of money. Instructing Richard to reimburse the Wedgwoods immediately, William was aware that his income would not be sufficient to cover this withdrawal, leaving him in debt to them for some £15 or £20, which he would not be able to repay till the end of the summer.[74]

They made slow progress to Nordhausen. The first day they enjoyed a delightful walk through the pine forests of the Harz Mountains behind Goslar. Compared to the Lakes, or Wales, these mountains were merely high hills; even the waterfalls were 'kittenracts' rather than cataracts. They spent the night in the centre of the forest at Claustal, 'a large Hanoverian town cursed with the plague of a vicious population'; their inn, however, was excellent and cheap. Next morning, their eyes aching from the brilliance of the green moss beneath the trees after being so long accustomed to snow, they set off again. They had a glimpse of the Brocken, 'the Mont Blanc of the Hartz forest, and the glory of all this part of Germany', but 'it had nothing impressive in its appearance'. At four o'clock, they reached Osterode, another Hanoverian town, where they were stared out of countenance by the 'dirty, impudent, and vulgar' inhabitants and had a contretemps with some bloody-minded town officials who refused to allow them to proceed without a passport. This was not forthcoming till the following morning, when they were able to prove their identity by their letters of introduction, which were following behind in their trunk in the post waggon. Once off the hills, out of the forest and away from Osterode, the roads became increasingly impassable. Snow-melt had swept away the bridges and the ground, when it was not frozen, was waterlogged. They found themselves struggling up to their ankles in water and sometimes in clay. Nightfall caught them out before they reached their next destination and they might have been stranded had a waggon not stopped and given them a lift to Scharzfeld, the nearest town. The next day they made it as far as an inn ten miles from Nordhausen, where they spent the night, but as it was rainy the next morning, they gave up the unequal struggle and took places in the post waggon for the final leg of their journey. At the post house at Nordhausen, they found letters waiting for them from Coleridge. In her joy at seeing his handwriting again, Dorothy 'burst open the seals and could almost have kissed them in the presence of the post-master'. They responded immediately with a joint letter, Dorothy contributing an account of their journey, achieved, she noted, 'for a very trifling expense', and William a wide-ranging literary criticism, taking in the German poets, Bürger and his own favourite, Robert Burns. He had, he informed Coleridge, been hewing down *Peter Bell* for publication, as he was anxious not to be in debt on his return to England; he had also devoted two days ('O Wonder', he could not resist adding in self-deprecation) to the Salisbury Plain poem. It was their intention, he declared, to remain two or three days in Nordhausen and then, weather permitting, 'to saunter about' for a fortnight or three weeks before coming to pay a visit to Coleridge at Göttingen.[75]

In a repetition of what had happened at Goslar, the projected two or three weeks eventually turned into seven. It is possible that the weather delayed them and made travelling slower and more difficult than they expected. On the other hand, in the course of that time they managed to spend so much of their £40 that they were obliged to borrow three guineas from Coleridge to get to Hamburg, and draw a further £25 there for their passage home. This suggests that they had not found anywhere sufficiently attractive to take up lodgings again, and that they were travelling and staying in inns. The fact that no letters survive from this period also indicates that they were on the move, though Coleridge, their likeliest correspondent, preserved only a couple out of many from the Wordsworths during their entire seven months in Germany, so he may have lost or destroyed relevant material. The absence of a journal is more surprising, but Coleridge may again have been the culprit. The following year, when he was desperately trying to fulfil a contract with Longman for a publishable account of a German tour, William offered him 'the use of his Journal tho' not of his name'; Coleridge leapt at the chance to incorporate 'my friend's account of Germany farther south than I had been' but, in his usual dilatory way, failed to produce the promised publication.[76]

Faced with an absence of record, one can only assume that the Wordsworths made their intended tour of towns in Upper Saxony.[77] They are likely to have gone to Weimar, because they had letters of introduction there, but not to have met Goethe himself. William had a lifelong and violent antipathy to Goethe, whom he accused of 'wantonly outraging the sympathies of humanity' by an utter lack of moral sense;[78] had he met him in person, this would surely have been reported. They may also have visited Erfurt and Eisenach, as planned. We can only speculate where else they might have been. Blankenberg was a possibility: Louis XVIII had spent twenty-one months in exile there, though he and his court had departed for Livonia the previous February. It was certainly on Coleridge's itinerary a few weeks later. Jena, too, another famous university town, not far from Weimar, may also have been included. The only certainty is that on or around 20 April William and Dorothy arrived at Göttingen, 'burn[ing] with such impatience to return to their native Country'.[79]

Their object, of course, was to visit Coleridge, who, despite the death of his son and the pleas of his anguished wife, was remarkably reluctant to return home. The question of where they would all eventually settle in England had been much discussed in their correspondence over the last few months, but a decision was now necessary. All three assumed that they would wish to be near each other, but if nothing else the past few months had determined the Wordsworths that they wanted to go back to the north, and preferably to the Lakes. Coleridge wanted – and probably needed – to remain near Poole. They spent a day together, arguing the pros and cons, but it proved futile. Coleridge, relaying this news with an eye to how it would appear to Poole, declared the Wordsworths 'melancholy & hypp'd' (morbidly depressed) at his own fixed resolve '*not to leave you till you leave me!*' William, he said, was affected to tears at the thought of a prolonged separation, 'but he deemed the vicinity of a Library absolutely *necessary* to his health, nay to his existence'.[80]

William's sudden passion for a handy library was not just due to the book-deprivation of the last few months. In the white heat of poetic composition at Goslar he had discovered that only reading distracted him from thinking and feeling, the intensity of which had given him 'uneasiness at my stomach and side, with a dull pain about my heart'. Access to a library was also, of course, essential if William was ever to prepare himself properly for writing *The Recluse.* Nevertheless, for the rest of his life, including the immediate future, he would live miles from a major library; what is more, at Alfoxton he had enjoyed greater access to books than at any time previously, except at Cambridge. One cannot avoid the impression that Coleridge seized on this as an excuse to justify the separation to Poole. And he did not believe that the pull of the north would prove more powerful than that of his own society. 'I still think that Wordsworth will be disappointed in his expectations of relief from reading, without Society – & I think it highly probable, that where I live, there he will live, unless he should find in the North any person or persons, who can feel & understand him, can reciprocate & react on him.'[81]

It is a measure of how far apart the two friends had grown that Coleridge simply did not know, or perhaps could not admit, that William was quite capable of living without him. The pleasure of his company could not even detain the Wordsworths now. A day was all they could spare him, then they were off again. Coleridge accompanied them five miles along the road, then they parted. They would not see each other again for six months. The Wordsworths caught the diligence for Hamburg, pausing there only to draw on the Wedgwoods for £25. Then they took a boat upriver to Cuxhaven, where, after 'necessary refreshment', they set sail for England.

The German adventure was over. The Wordsworths had gone there to be near Coleridge and to learn enough German to be able to earn money by translating. They failed on both counts. On one level, Coleridge was right in believing William 'might as well have been in England as at Goslar, in the situation which he chose, & with his *unseeking* manners'.[82] On the other hand, William had made gigantic steps forward as a poet. For a year at Alfoxton he had been in almost daily contact with Coleridge, who had then been the assured and published poet, at the peak of his powers. In the year after parting at Hamburg, at the end of September 1798, they spent less than three days together.[83] In that time, the whole balance of their relationship shifted. William had indeed assumed the mantle Coleridge had bestowed upon him, but in doing so he had also stepped into Coleridge's shoes. There could be little doubt in future who was the master poet.

9. The Concern

'I dare say you will be surprised when I tell you William and Dolly Wordsworth are arriv'd at Sockburne', Joanna, Mary Hutchinson's youngest sister, wrote to their cousin John Monkhouse on 12 May 1799. Mary was delighted to see them (they had been promising to return her visit to Racedown for two years) but her uncle and youngest brother, on a visit from Penrith, were not too sure, as Joanna described.

I cannot help telling you how genteely your Pappa and Poet George behaved – you must know your father got a fall from his horse, and got very much wet so much as to be fors'd to have his Britches change[d], as soon as he he[a]rd William and Dolly was comming he said he must be off – and that he would not have time to come back to Sockburne but upon examination his small close was so wet he could not possibly put them on therefore he was obliged to stay; However he and George sat all the afternoon in the Kitchen enjoying the company of the Blacksmith and Tailor, at last however they were prevail'd on to go into the Parlor and upon Mary's asking them where they had been Geo: reply'd why you would not have had us so unmannerly as to have left the Tailor and the Smith.

In the general laugh that followed, Mary's family discovered that the Wordsworths might be intellectual giants with a reputation for doing the unconventional, but they were also pleasant and companionable people. William immediately acquired the family nickname 'the Great Poet', and he and Dorothy were welcomed into the extensive Hutchinson clan.[1] They were made to feel so much at home, that it would be the end of the year before they left Sockburn.

The Wordsworths had arrived in England on or about 1 May and travelled straight from Yarmouth to County Durham, in fulfilment of their long-intended plans to visit Mary. It was an indication of how much she now meant to both of them that they chose to go to her rather than any of their relations, though they did pay a fleeting visit to Christopher, at Cambridge, where they caught the coach to Darlington. In their absence, Christopher had been awarded the fellowship at Trinity College for which he had worked so long and hard, and in January he had become engaged to Priscilla Lloyd, the sensitive and deeply unhappy seventeen-year-old sister of Coleridge's troublesome protégé Charles. The Lloyds were Quakers and therefore would not, indeed could not, give their consent to a marriage outside the faith, and particularly to a future Anglican clergyman. Priscilla had been packed off to stay with the Clarksons, Quaker friends in the Lake District, and Christopher, as single-minded in his quiet determination to marry her as he had been to secure his fellowship, was ordained deacon on the day Joanna Hutchinson wrote of the Wordsworths' arrival at Sockburn.[2]

William's first priority was to sort out his financial affairs. He wrote immediately to Richard, asking for a statement of account, and to Josiah Wedgwood, informing him that he had had to draw the extra £25 in Hamburg but assuring him that he would reimburse this as soon as possible. Two days later, Richard dropped his bombshell. Instead of the £85 William had expected to come into his account during his absence, only £17 10s had been received. Douglas had paid £10 interest, disappeared to the West Indies and again defaulted on repayment of the capital of his loan. Montagu had not paid a farthing towards either repayment or interest, and had defaulted on a promissory note of £21 5s due in January: 'he might as well have given me a piece of blotting Paper' was Richard's understandably irritated retort. Matters had deteriorated to such a state that Richard was actually threatening Montagu with legal action for recovery of the money. Worse still, neither Cottle nor Johnson had paid a penny on account of *Lyrical Ballads* and it was not even clear who now owned the book. In the circumstances, Richard had not sent any money at all to the Wedgwoods. Heartily sick of dealing with William's affairs, he dumped them firmly back in his brother's hands. 'I expect to hear *from you* by the return of the Post', he ordered peremptorily, adding, 'I trust you will lose no time in endeavouring to effect a Compleat settlement.'[3]

William had no inkling that his affairs were in such a dire state. Instead of being a mere £15 or £20 overdrawn with the Wedgwoods, as he had expected, he now found himself owing them over £120, with no prospect of repaying them unless his own debtors paid him. A flurry of correspondence chasing these and a mollifying letter to Richard were immediately dispatched, but all to little purpose. Only the good-hearted Cottle, himself about to quit the book-selling trade because of his own losses, came up trumps, sending William £5 in June and a draft for £15 at the end of July. He even offered William interest, which was indignantly refused. 'I am not poor enough yet to make me think it right that I should take interest for a debt from a friend, paid eleven months after it is due.'[4]

He was poor enough, however, to have to think seriously about publishing more of his poetry. Repeated anxious queries to Cottle about the sale of *Lyrical Ballads* did not entirely reassure him, for he was all too familiar with Cottle's wish to please, which made him eternally over-optimistic. Southey, calling in to Arch's bookshop early in May, was told by Arch himself that he expected to lose on the book 'as they sold very heavily'.[5] A second edition was not a proposition but, in any case, William was not keen to commit himself to print again. His aversion to publication had been greatly increased by the reviews of *Lyrical Ballads*, which he now saw for the first time. The first had appeared in October 1798 in the *Critical Review* and it was by far the harshest. The *Ancyent Marinere* attracted particular contempt. 'We are tolerably conversant with the early English poets; and can discover no resemblance whatever, except in antiquated spelling and a few obsolete words.' It stood condemned as 'a Dutch attempt at German sublimity', *The Idiot Boy* as resembling 'a Flemish picture in the worthlessness of its design and the excellence of its execution'. There was high praise for *Tintern Abbey*: 'we scarcely recollect any thing superior . . .' to parts of it, 'in the whole range of English poetry', but even this compliment had a sting in its tail. 'On reading this production, it is impossible not to lament that he should ever have condescended to write such pieces as the Last of the Flock, the Convict, and most of the ballads.' The prefatory advertisement was skewered with clinical precision at the end. 'The "experiment," we think, has failed, not because the language of conversation is little adapted to "the purposes of poetic pleasure," but because it has been tried upon uninteresting subjects.' To add insult to injury, the author of this review was Robert Southey. Mortified, William could only affect an indifference he did not feel.

> He knew that I published those poems for money and money alone. He knew that money was of importance to me. If he could not conscientiously have spoken differently of the volume, he ought to have declined the task of reviewing it. The bulk of the poems he has described as destitute of merit. Am I recompensed for this by vague praises of my talents?[6]

Later reviewers unfortunately took their cue from Southey. In December the *Analytical Review* praised the simplicity and tenderness of the poems, but dismissed the *Ancyent Marinere* as 'the extravagance of a mad German poet'. To the critic writing in the *Monthly Review* of June 1799, the *Ancyent Marinere* was 'the strangest story of a cock and a bull that we ever saw on paper'. Going through the poems, one by one, he disapprovingly exposed every trace of radical sentiment and attacked the presumption of the advertisement. 'The author shall style his rustic delineations of low-life, poetry if he pleases, on the same principle on which Butler is called a poet, and Teniers a painter: but are the doggerel verses of the one equal to the sublime numbers of a Milton, or are the Dutch boors of the other to be compared with the angels of Raphael or Guido?' Despite this, he confessed, the author 'has had the art of pleasing and interesting in no common way by his natural delineations of human passions, human characters, and human incidents'. It was just that it was not poetry. Nevertheless, he ended on an encouraging note. 'So much genius and originality are discovered in this publication, that we wish to see another from the same hand, written on more elevated subjects and in a more cheerful disposition.'[7]

It was not surprising that William came to the view that the *Ancyent Marinere* had 'upon the whole' been an injury to the volume. 'I mean', he explained to Cottle, 'that the old words and the strangeness of it have deterred readers from going on. If the volume should come to a second Edition I would put in its place some little things which would be more likely to suit the common taste.' This was a far cry from his bold declaration to Klopstock that 'it was the province of a great poet to raise people up to his own level not to descend to theirs', but *Lyrical Ballads* was clearly not in the same category as *The Recluse*. William always claimed to regard the book solely as a money-spinner, though he never quite managed to remain emotionally disinterested about its reception, as his response to Southey's review suggests. 'My aversion from publication increases every day,' he wrote Cottle, 'so much so, that no motives whatever, nothing but pecuniary necessity, will, I think, ever prevail upon me to commit myself to the press again'.[8] Unfortunately for him, pecuniary necessity was to be the hallmark of most of his poetic career.

By August, he had succeeded in scraping together only £10 to set off against his Wedgwood debt. Anxious and depressed, he tried to forget his problems in poetry, writing, not for sale, nor even for *The Recluse*, but for the poem on his own life which he had begun in Germany. In many ways, it was a self-indulgence, but it had him in its grip and he could not escape. Now he was welding into a continuous narrative all the fragments he had written earlier about his childhood, adding and expanding his descriptions of the 'spots of time', and trying to identify what had made him a poet. By the beginning of September, he was again troubled with a pain in his side, a sure sign that he had been working intensively. Dorothy and Mary were also hard at work, transcribing (no mean feat given William's execrable hand and disjointed composition) and making fair copies of the poem.[9]

Coleridge, who had returned to Nether Stowey at the end of July, was concerned to learn that William was ill and apparently unhappy. He sought to rouse him in the only way he knew how. 'I am anxiously eager to have you steadily employed on "The Recluse" ', he wrote.

> My dear friend, I do entreat you go on with 'The Recluse;' and I wish you would write a poem, in blank verse, addressed to those, who, in consequence of the complete failure of the French Revolution, have thrown up all hopes of the amelioration of mankind, and are sinking into an almost epicurean selfishness, disguising the same under the soft titles of domestic attachment and contempt for visionary *philosophes*. It would do great good, and might form a part of 'The Recluse,' for in my present mood I am wholly against the publication of any small poems.

Instead of encouraging William, however, it reinforced his own sense of inadequacy for the task. And, living with the Hutchinsons, with Mary daily before his eyes, who was he to condemn the soft title of domestic attachment? Nevertheless, in a fitting tribute to the man who had instigated the whole project, he decided that he would end his poem on his own life by dedicating it to Coleridge. Under the misapprehension that William had actually completed *The Recluse*, not just a prologue to it, Coleridge was in ecstasies. 'I long to see what you have been doing', he wrote impatiently on 12 October. 'O let it be the tail-piece of the "The Recluse!" for of nothing but "The Recluse" can I hear patiently . . . To be addressed, as a beloved man, by a thinker, at the close of such a poem as "The Recluse," . . . is the only event, I believe, capable of inciting in me an hour's vanity'.[10]

A fortnight later, Coleridge arrived at Sockburn. He was in flight from his return to family life and responsibility, after the gaiety of student bachelorhood in Germany: the 'hovel' at Nether Stowey had flooded, Hartley had caught scabies so everything had to be fumigated and Sarah, obliged to part with her servant whom they could no longer afford, was tight-lipped and resentful. On the pretext of recovering his travel chests, he had abruptly left home and gone to Bristol; once there, he had discovered that Cottle was about to pay a visit to the Wordsworths. It was an opportunity not to be missed and he immediately decided to accompany Cottle, not bothering to inform his wife of his change of plans.[11]

There was a joyful reunion at Sockburn, marred only by an insignificant incident which later festered in Coleridge's mind. Mary had never met Coleridge before and, immediately after tea on their arrival, Cottle asked her, 'Pray what do you think of Mr Coleridge's [first: deleted] appearance?' Coleridge was sensitive to his unprepossessing exterior, and four years afterwards would recall that this remark had first made him laugh, then melancholy.[12] William had promised Cottle a tour into Cumberland and Westmorland, so, on the afternoon of 27 October, they set off on a leisurely amble, following the River Tees westwards. Cottle, who was lame from a childhood accident, rode a mare, while William and Coleridge walked by his side. The three young men made their way to Barnard Castle, taking in the churchyard at Gainford, where they lingered over the epitaphs, the grey ruins of Egglestone Abbey, set in rich woodland on a slope above the river, and the battlemented bridge over the Tees at Barnard Castle. William and Coleridge were impervious to weather and distance, but Cottle, never an instinctive countryman, soon found that the damp and riding brought on a convenient attack of rheumatism. Declining to accompany them into the Lakes, he parted from them at Greta Bridge, where he could catch the coach to London for a meeting with Thomas Longman, who was taking over his publishing business.[13]

The mists and rain were too much even for William and Coleridge to contemplate walking over the bleak heights of Stainmore, which separated Yorkshire from Westmorland. They were obliged to seek refuge in the mail coach from Greta Bridge. Instead of travelling all the way to Penrith, however, they stopped seven miles short at Temple Sowerby, probably in the hope of meeting up with William's brother Christopher, who had been staying with their Cookson-Crackanthorpe relatives at Newbiggin Hall. Christopher always spent at least part of his summer vacations there, but this year, he had gone to Birmingham instead, in pursuit of his Priscilla. As luck would have it, two days before he was due to set off back to Cambridge, he had received a reproachful letter from his aunt, informing him that his Uncle Christopher was dying and had been very hurt at his nephew's neglect. There was nothing for it but to go straight to Newbiggin. Just over a week later, Christopher Crackanthorpe Crackanthorpe died. He was buried in the pretty church adjoining the Hall on 17 October 1799. His brother, Uncle William Cookson, and his nephews attended the funeral. Either because they did not know or, more likely, because they chose not to go, only William and Dorothy were absent.[14]

Arriving at Temple Sowerby, only two miles from Newbiggin Hall, William clearly hoped that Christopher would still be there, and that he might be persuaded either to join or at least meet them. At the post office, however, he glimpsed a letter from his brother to their aunt, so he realized immediately that Christopher had returned to Cambridge. Disappointment turned to unexpected joy, however, for in conversation with the woman there he discovered that, although one brother had gone, another was still at Newbiggin. John, whom he had not seen for more than four years, had returned to England in August, after an abnormally long voyage to India, as second mate in the *Duke of Montrose*. Being a dutiful nephew, he had hastened to Newbiggin on learning of Uncle Christopher's perilous state of health, and had remained there to comfort their aunt and her children. There was no way William could bring himself to pay a visit to the former Miss Cust, whom, if anything, he disliked more than his uncle, but he immediately dispatched a note to John at the Hall and shortly afterwards the two brothers were reunited. Frustratingly, William's account of this momentous meeting has been cut from the letter describing it: all that is left is the bald comment that John 'looks very well'. Fortunately, Coleridge was on hand and, after a few days spent in the company of this shy, sensitive, self-effacing man, he delivered his verdict in terms of awed reverence. 'Your Br. John is one of you;' he wrote to Dorothy, 'a man who hath solitary usings of his own Intellect, deep in feeling, with a subtle Tact, a swift instinct of Truth & Beauty. He interests me much.'[15]

To the great delight of all concerned, John agreed to accompany William and Coleridge for a few days on their walking tour to the Lakes. Next day, they set off together on an arduous route criss-crossing the fells that William had carefully and deliberately designed for maximum visual impact. This was Coleridge's first trip to the Lakes. Just as Dorothy had sought to woo him with William's descriptions from the poem of his own life, now William tried to convince him that he should settle there by introducing him to the reality. They began, appropriately enough, at Barton. In the chancel of the squat little church, with its curious square central tower, the first of the Wordsworths to live in Westmorland, their grandfather, Richard, was buried. Sockbridge Hall, which he had purchased as the family seat, lay on the outskirts of the village. The Reverend Thomas Myers, William and John's uncle by marriage, still lived in Barton, and he provided them with dinner, before sending them on their way.[16] From the pleasantly rolling pastureland of Barton, they climbed up Walla Crag to Haweswater, then two smaller lakes joined by a river, but now unrecognizable as a reservoir. Descending mists prevented them from taking William's planned route over the tops to Ambleside; instead, they took the lower route down the precipitous heights of Long Sleddale to Kentmere, cutting across the lower fells to Bowness for the ferry to Hawkshead. Again, it was a significant choice of objective, for Hawkshead was central to William's development as a poet and therefore to *The Prelude.* William noted sadly a 'great change amongst the People since we were last there'; the greatest change was that AnnTyson, the old dame who had been a second mother to himself and John, had died three years previously and now lay in an unmarked grave in the churchyard.

Continually hampered by bad weather, the Wordsworths and Coleridge made their way up the western side of Windermere, where they roundly cursed the off-comers' new fashion for whitewashing their grand residences. Coleridge, William reported with obvious satisfaction to Dorothy, was 'enchanted' with the two vales of Rydal and Grasmere. For almost a week they made their headquarters at Grasmere, staying at Robert Newton's little inn, next to the church, and cradled on every side by soaring crags and sweeping fells. Bolstered by the approval of John and Coleridge, William began to think seriously about settling in Grasmere. 'You will think my plan a mad one,' he wrote to Dorothy, 'but I have thought of building a house there by the Lake side.' John, with typically selfless generosity, promptly offered to give his brother £40 to buy the land, but quite where William was to find the £250 he would need to build a house 'as good as we can wish' was anybody's guess. More practically, he had noticed a small, unfurnished house at Grasmere which was empty, 'which perhaps we may take'.[17]

A week after joining William and Coleridge, John felt obliged to return to Newbiggin. 'We accompanied John over the fork of Helvellyn on a day when light & darkness coexisted in contiguous masses, & the earth & sky were but *one*!' Coleridge told Dorothy. 'Nature lived for us in all her grandest accidents'.[18] It was the only fine day they had enjoyed so far and the three men seized the opportunity to head for the top of Helvellyn. Whichever route they took, it was literally a breathtaking climb, tearing at the calf muscles and bending the back double. They paused at the top, drinking in the glorious vista of a world in miniature below: ridges of rock clawed bare by the wind, encircling snow-capped mountains, the lead-grey flashings of half-glimpsed distant lakes and the expanse of sea beyond, before scrambling, half-sliding, down the dizzying slopes of Dollywaggon Pike to Grisedale Tarn. There, at the rock-strewn head of a deep cleft in the mountains, with the twin sentinel summits of Dollywaggon and Fairfield towering above them, they parted. William and Coleridge returned to Grasmere and John went forward alone to Patterdale and Penrith. It somehow seemed symbolic that, after he had gone, the clouds descended again.

Like every visitor to Lakeland in bad weather, William and Coleridge consoled themselves with the compensatory glory of the waterfalls. A trip to the spectacular Dungeon Ghyll over in Langdale had to be called off, but they visited the famous falls at Rydal in the gloom of an early November evening, incurring the wrath of one of the servants at Rydal Hall because they had walked in front of the house.

Their trespass on foot, Coleridge noted, was quite equal to the trespass on the eye inflicted by the 'damned White washing!' of the old Hall. From Grasmere, they went through the 'inverted arch' of Dunmail Raise to Keswick, from which centre they explored the northern lakes: Buttermere, where, at the humble cottage-inn, they were waited on by the soon-to-be-famous beauty, Mary, the Maid of Buttermere, and admired her grace and simplicity; Crummock Water; Ennerdale, where they learned the tragic story of James Bowman, who died after sleepwalking off a crag, leaving only his staff caught in a crevice on the cliff face; Wastwater, where the black screes plummet into the even blacker depths of the lake; Borrowdale, lake-less, but filled with angry brooks and waterfalls flashing through the mist; Derwentwater, where the Lodore falls thunder down a hidden, tree-lined crevasse; Aira Force, on Ullswater, where a permanent rainbow plays about the spray from the single cataract which plunges down a sheer rock face into the cupped hands it has itself worn out of the stone below. After more than a fortnight of such scenes, Coleridge's senses had taken such a battering that he was punch-drunk.[19]

They ended their tour quietly, spending a peaceful day with the great anti-slavery campaigner Thomas Clarkson and his wife, Catherine, at Pooley Bridge. Worn out with his efforts, Clarkson had recently retired to Eusemere, a pretty house they had built on an eminence at the northern end of Ullswater, facing down the length of the lake, towards the mountains jostling for position at its furthest end. Neither William nor Coleridge knew the Clarksons personally, but they had mutual friends (of sorts) in Charles Lloyd and his sister, Priscilla, who had been dispatched to the Clarksons when her engagement to Christopher Wordsworth was announced. 'I must tell you that we [had] a Visit from Coleridge and W. Wordsworth who spent a whole day with us', the gossipy Catherine informed Priscilla.

> C. was in high Spirits & talk'd a great deal. W. was more reserved but there was neither hauteur nor moroseness in his Reserve He has a fine commanding figure is rather handsome & looks as if he was born to be a great Prince or a great General. He seems very fond of C. laughing at all his Jokes & taking all opportunities of shewing him off & to crown all he has the manners of a Gentleman.

They might not have been so amused had they known that Coleridge, sitting in their garden overlooking the lake, was indulging himself by imagining that the combined effect of 'a round fat backside of a Hill' facing Eusemere, with a road running round its base, and its perfect reflection in the still waters of the lake, created an anatomically correct impression of the female pudenda. 'I never saw so sweet an Image!!' he wrote in his (secret) notebook.[20]

It was, unfortunately, an indication of how his mind was working. He left Pooley Bridge on the coach to Scotch Corner, where he should have taken a cold shower, but instead bathed his swollen and aching feet in a warm footbath. Then he made his way back to Sockburn. With William out of the way and Tom Hutchinson busy on his farm, Coleridge had exactly what he wanted but so seldom enjoyed: the cuckoo in the nest had the undivided attentions of the females of the household. There were three of them. William's sister, Dorothy, his future bride, Mary, and, last but not least, Sara, Mary's twenty-four-year-old younger sister. Part of William's intimate circle and yet also unattached, she had the misfortune to become the object of Coleridge's increasingly obsessive infatuation. Interestingly, she was physically more like Dorothy than Mary. She was later described as having 'fine, long, light brown hair, I think her only beauty, except a fair skin, for her features were plain and contracted, her figure dumpy, and devoid of grace and dignity'. This, however, was the not entirely unprejudiced judgement of Coleridge's own, stunningly beautiful, daughter, who harboured some natural resentment towards the woman she blamed for breaking up her parents' marriage. In 1799, Sara was little more than five feet high, pert and attractive, though not pretty. She had boundless energy, good-humour and quick wits, and, like all the Hutchinsons, the twin gifts of tact and delicate sympathy, which would make her an indispensable member of more than one household. As Coleridge's daughter gloomily put it, 'He much liked everything feminine and domestic, pretty and becoming, but not fine-ladyish.'[21] Sara was all those things, and what she lacked in looks Coleridge bestowed on her in his imagination. Increasingly frustrated and unhappy in his marriage with a real Sarah, he turned an equally real Miss Hutchinson into his ideal Sara, who was all the more desirable for being unattainable. It was symptomatic of his attitude towards her that, not content with dropping the final 'h' of her name to distinguish her from his wife, he also reinvented her as Asra, the more exotic anagram of her rather ordinary name.

In this visit of November 1799 there was only the tiniest hint of what was to come: an entry in Coleridge's notebook of the single enigmatic phrase 'The long Entrancement of a True-love's Kiss'. Four years later, reading this over in the depths of opium-addiction and depression, he would expand considerably on it. On the Sunday before he left, the oldest of the Hutchinson brothers, the jovial John, otherwise known as Jack, came over from Stockton. 'Conundrums & Puns & Stories & Laughter – with Jack Hutchinson – Stood up round the Fire', Coleridge now wrote in his notebook, adding guiltily in Latin 'and I held Sara's hand behind her back for a long time, and then, then for the first time, love pricked me with his arrow, poisoned, alas! & incurable'. Repeating his original phrase for the next day, Monday 25 November, he links it with taking leave of Sara and adds a cryptic, 'Ten Kisses short as one, one long as twenty'.[22] Sara would always maintain a discreet silence on every aspect of Coleridge's infatuation, so we have only Coleridge's own, later, account of what happened (or what he hoped, or imagined, had happened). Was there a flirtation or did he simply read greater significance into entirely innocent gestures? Did he hold her hand behind her back as part of a parlour game? He could hardly do so in company without some such excuse. Did he extract a true-love's kiss from her on parting or was it wishful thinking? Whatever the truth of the matter, there can be no doubt that Coleridge looked back to this point as the moment he fell in love, and Sara would have to bear the consequences for years to come.

Instead of returning to Bristol or Nether Stowey, Coleridge took the coach to London. There he found regular employment working for Daniel Stuart on the *Morning Post* as a leader writer; it was as if he had deliberately turned his back on all the allurements of the north. To complete his self-mortification, he summoned his wife and child to London, but had to ask Cottle where they were to be found.[23] The day after Coleridge left, William arrived at Sockburn, where he found Mary alone and overjoyed to see him. He had important news. The walking tour of the Lakes had failed in its objective of persuading Coleridge to settle there, but it had determined William. He had taken the lease on the little house at Grasmere at a princely rent of £8 annually. With hindsight, it seems inevitable that the Wordsworths would eventually return to live in the Lakes, but at the time it was not. At the end of June they had contemplated taking a house at or near Sockburn; in July Dorothy had asked Poole to keep his eyes and ears open for any place likely to suit them near Nether Stowey; and it was not until September, when it became clear that Montagu could not repay his debt, that they finally gave up all hope of returning to Alfoxton.[24]

In the early hours of 17 December William and Dorothy left Sockburn on two horses borrowed from the Hutchinsons. They crossed the Tees at the Neasham ford by moonlight and rode eight miles beyond Richmond into Wensleydale. There they parted with Mary's youngest brother, George, who had accompanied them to take back the horses, and set off on foot to follow the stately Ure westwards towards Kendal. At six in the evening, having paused to view Aysgarth Falls and walked three of the last twelve miles in the dark, they reached Askrigg. Next morning, with a keen frost, showers of snow threatening and twenty-one miles to cover before nightfall, they still found time to turn aside to view two more waterfalls, including the spectacular Hardraw Force, a ninety-eight-foot-high sheet of water cascading in a single drop over a limestone crag. The spray from the force had frozen on the nearby rocks, encasing them in ice, so the Wordsworths made their way cautiously up the narrow cleft until they found themselves standing in a cave directly behind the fall, which shot out over their heads. The roof of the cave was swagged like a drawn-up curtain and festooned with icicles; mosses and water-plants lent it brilliant hues. 'What would I not give if I could convey to you the images and feelings that were then communicated to me', asked William, before launching into an unusually long and lyrical description of the scene. They tore themselves away reluctantly and, with a following wind, travelled over the mountain road to Sedbergh. Next day, they walked the last eleven miles 'on a terrible up and down road' over the hills to Kendal. There, armed with £30 cashed for them by Jack Hutchinson, they bought and ordered the furniture they would need. On 20 December 1799 they hired a post chaise from Kendal and drove the final sixteen miles to Grasmere, drawing up, at half past four in the afternoon, at the door of the cottage which was to be their home for the next eight years.[25]

The cottage stood on the roadside at Town End, a hamlet half a mile south of Grasmere village, on the main thoroughfare between Kendal and Keswick. Built in the early seventeenth century, it had, until very recently, been an inn, the Dove and Olive Branch; now it was simply a nameless cottage, at the foot of the steep and winding road over White Moss Common. Tucked into the mountainside, with the vast heights of Heron Pike towering above and behind, it looked straight out over open fields to Grasmere lake, with its tree-covered island, and the craggy eminences of Silver How and Loughrigg Terraces. Apart from a cluster of four or five cottages at Sykeside, just below the Wordsworths', and two others just above, their nearest neighbour was How Top, a small farm squatting in a hollow on the road up to White Moss Common.

The cottage itself was tiny and shambolic; originally two up and two down, an extension round the back and side had added a wash kitchen and two tiny unceiled rooms above. Because it was literally carved out of the fellside, the ground-floor rooms at the back lay below ground level. Behind the cottage, extending up a steep bank, was a 'little Nook of mountain-ground', which William would celebrate as his

> Sweet garden-orchard, eminently fair,
> The loveliest spot that man hath ever found

Long neglected, it was now completely overgrown with brambles, shrubs and moss. The Wordsworths, with their passion for gardening, were more interested in the potential for the surroundings than the cottage itself. 'D is much pleased with the house and *appurtenances*', William told Coleridge four days after they had moved in,

> the orchard especially; in imagination she has already built a seat with a summer shed on the highest platform in this our little domestic slip of mountain. The spot commands a view over the roof of our house, of the lake, the church, helm cragg, and two thirds of the vale. We mean also to enclose the two or three yards of ground between us and the road, this for the sake of a few flowers, and because it will make it more our own.

It would take four years to realize the dream of the 'summer shed' or 'moss hut', but the need to separate the cottage from the dust and mud thrown up by passing waggons was more urgent. William erected a stone fence, or vaccary wall, made of huge upright slabs of slate, like the ones still in use round Hawkshead today. Then they filled the little garden with flowers and plants culled from the woods and mountains during their daily walks or donated by their kindly neighbours.

The cottage itself was like a doll's-house, especially compared to the grandeur of Racedown and Alfoxton. Thomas de Quincey, who would later take over the tenancy from the Wordsworths, described it on his first visit in 1807. Passing through the garden gate, ten paces (but he was very short) brought him to the main door:

A little semi-vestibule between two doors prefaced the entrance into what might be considered the principal room of the cottage. It was an oblong square, not above eight and a half feet high, sixteen feet long, and twelve broad; very prettily wainscotted from the floor to the ceiling with dark polished oak, slightly embellished with carving. One window there was – a perfect and unpretending cottage window, with little diamond panes, embowered, at almost every season of the year, with roses; and, in the summer and autumn, with a profusion of jessamine and other fragrant shrubs.

The combined effect of the panelling and luxuriant vegetation (planted by the Wordsworths) round the window was to make the room very dark. All the downstairs rooms had flagged floors, which contributed to the chill and damp which still pervade the cottage. The main room, which had been the public room of the inn, became the living room; the second room was turned into a lodging room, or bedroom, with matting on the floor and a bed large enough to sleep two when necessary. This was Dorothy's room. A little flight of fourteen stairs led up to the main sitting room of the house, which William also used as his study or library. 'It was not fully seven feet six inches high,' de Quincey reported,

and, in other respects, pretty nearly of the same dimensions as the rustic hall below. There was, however, in a small recess, a library of perhaps 300 volumes, which seemed to consecrate the room as the poet's study and composing room; and so occasionally it was. But far oftener he both studied, as I found, and composed on the high road.

The second, smaller, room upstairs served as William's bedroom; the fireplace smoked so badly that it was uninhabitable as a sitting room. Two single beds were placed in here, so that William could accommodate a male guest when necessary. The two remaining rooms were little more than walk-in cupboards. Dorothy papered one with newspapers and put in a small uncurtained bed, so that it could be used as an additional occasional bedroom; the other became a lumber-room.

To complete the idyll, the manners of the neighbouring cottagers 'far exceeded' the Wordsworths' expectations; the natives here were not like the 'lying and picking and stealing' peasants of Racedown, or even 'in league to impose upon strangers' like the Germans. 'The people we have uniformly found kind-hearted frank and manly, prompt to serve without servility', William declared with all the satisfaction of a man who has found his fellow northerners to be infinitely superior to the rest of the human race. They discovered that they could do without a live-in servant, which was fortunate, given the lack of accommodation. Sixty-year-old Molly Fisher, who lived at Sykeside with her brother and sister-in-law, agreed to come in for three hours daily to light the fires, wash the dishes and do the other hard work. On Saturdays, when she was employed in scouring, or if required to do extra work because of visitors, she was to receive her meals, in addition to her wage of 2s a week. 'We could have had this attendance for eighteen pence a week', William informed Coleridge, 'but we added the sixpence for the sake of the poor woman, who is made happy by it.' Dorothy soon discovered that Molly was not as useful as she might have been. 'She was very ignorant, very foolish, and very difficult to teach so that I once almost despaired of her,' she told Jane Marshall, 'but the goodness of her dispositions and the great convenience we knew we should find if my perseverance was at last sucessful induced me to go on.' Molly was eventually taught the basics of cookery and did all the washing for them and their guests, which was no small task. She also became a valued friend, who was 'much attached to us and honest and good as ever was a human being'.[26]

The Wordsworths' arrival at Town End was not propitious. No preparation had been made for them 'except beds, without curtains, in the rooms upstairs, and a dying spark in the grate of the gloomy parlour'. Dorothy had raging toothache, inflamed by walking over the Yorkshire Dales in the biting wind; they both developed colds, probably for the same reason. But they didn't care. 'We were young and healthy and had attained an object long desired, we had returned to our native mountains, there to live; so we cared not for any annoyances that a little exertion on our parts would speedily remove.' For once, their optimism was justified. Soon after their arrival, Molly Fisher popped round to see them. It turned out she had not known when to expect them and had come in daily for a fortnight to light a fire so that the cottage was dry and comfortable. Molly would never forget Dorothy's first appearance: six years later, on the anniversary of that event, she would solemnly come up to Dorothy, who was standing by the parlour fire, shake her by the hand and say, 'I mun never forget t'laal striped gown and tlaal straw Bonnet, as ye stood here.'[27] While Dorothy buried herself, her cold and her toothache under a mountain of needlework, making bedcurtains and the like, William established the pattern of his future life in Grasmere: he obtained a pair of skates, persuaded Dorothy to accompany him on a starlit walk up Easedale and he began to write *The Brothers*. The poem was a pastoral, based on the story he and Coleridge had been told of the Ennerdale shepherd who had fallen to his death while sleepwalking on the crags. It was a significant poem with which to begin his career as poet-in-residence of the Lakes.[28]

Equally significant was the second poem begun at Town End and completed on 28 December 1799. It was the first of what would become the wonderful series associated with Grasmere, *Poems on the Naming of Places*. Coleridge had commented in his journal of the walking tour, 'In the North every Brook, every Crag, almost every Field has a name – a proof of greater Independence & a society more approaching in their Laws & Habits to Nature'. What William did was take this a step further, renaming features of the landscape after members of his circle who were particularly associated with that place or who shared its characteristics. This very first poem belonged to the latter category and it was dedicated to Mary Hutchinson. She may have been left behind at Sockburn, but she was pre-eminent in William's thoughts. The place was a hidden pool, 'a calm recess', in the woods at Rydal. The message was obvious.

The spot was made by Nature for herself:
The travellers know it not, and 'twill remain
Unknown to them; but it is beautiful
And if a man should plant his cottage near,
Should sleep beneath the shelter of its trees,
And blend its waters with his daily meal,
He would so love it that in his death-hour
Its image would survive among his thoughts,
And therefore, my sweet Mary, this still nook
With all its beeches we have named from You.[29]

William would later claim that he had 'no thoughts of marrying' at this time; this may have been true, for he may still have considered himself bound in some way to Annette. It is perhaps a minor detail, but a relevant one, to note that, after a lapse in the records of a correspondence for more than four years, a small flurry of letters passed between William and Annette in the period November 1799–April 1800. A postscript to a further letter, from William to Dorothy, urged her, 'When you are writing to France say all that is affectionate to A. and all that is fatherly to C.' The postscript was destroyed by William's grandson, but it would appear to date from May 1800, when William was staying with the Hutchinsons at Sockburn.[30] The suspicion must be that the correspondence was reopened in order to come to some arrangement which would clear the way for William to marry Mary. If that was the case, he was disappointed. It would be two years before he would finally take her to the altar. The new century opened with what was to be an *annus mirabilis* for William. It began well enough, with the receipt on 1 January of an unlooked-for legacy of £100 to Dorothy from Uncle Christopher. She was the only one to benefit from his will, though John had received a loan of £100 for investment in his last voyage and Christopher had been generously supported through university by him. William, it was no surprise to learn, received nothing at all.[31]

Towards the end of January, the first of the many visitors who would cram themselves into the cottage at Town End arrived. He was one of the most welcome; indeed, William and Dorothy had been expecting him since before Christmas, but he seems to have shared their own dilatory habits. When they had almost given up looking for him, he arrived. Overcome with habitual shyness, fear of intruding and emotion at the thought of meeting the sister he had not seen for so many years, John twice made his way to the cottage door, put his hand on the latch and then walked away. In the end, his courage failed him altogether, he retreated to Robert Newton's inn beside Grasmere church and sent a message up to say that he had arrived. 'This will give you a notion of the depth of his affections, and the delicacy of his feelings', Dorothy proudly reported to a friend.[32]

John soon became an integral part of the little household at Town End. For eight 'blessed months' he lived with them, 'exulting within his noble heart that his Father's Children had once again a home together' and helping them turn the cottage into a home: 'he was so happy by the fire-side,' Dorothy remembered of this time, 'any little business of the house interested him, he loved our cottage, he helped us to furnish it, and to make the gardens – trees are growing now which he planted.' Every day, as they gradually came to know and love their reserved younger brother, they had abundant proof of Coleridge's judgement that he was, indeed, one of them. 'Of all human beings whom I ever knew, he was the man of the most rational desires, the most sedate habits, and the most perfect self-command', William would later say.

He was modest; and gentle: and shy, even to disease, but this was wearing off. In every thing his judgements were sound and original: his taste in all the arts, music and poetry in particular (for these he of course had had the best opportunities of being familiar with) was exquisite: And his eye for the beauties of Nature was as fine and delicate as ever Poet or Painter was gifted with; in some discriminations, owing to his education and way of life, far superior to any person's I ever knew.

Dorothy was equally captivated, reiterating that sensitivity to nature in her twenty-seven-year-old brother which had so impressed both William and Coleridge.

– he loved solitude and he rejoiced in society – he would wander alone among these hills with his fishing-rod, or led on merely by the pleasure of walking, for many hours – or he would walk with William or me, or both of us, and was continually pointing out with a gladness which is seldom seen but in very young people something which perhaps would have escaped our observation, for he had so fine an eye that no distinction was unnoticed by him, and so tender a feeling that he never noticed any thing in vain. Many a time has he called me out in an evening to look at the moon or stars, or a cloudy sky, or this vale in the quiet moonlight – but the stars and moon were his chief delight, – he made of them his companions when he was at Sea, and was never tired of those thoughts which the silence of the night fed in him –[33]

Unwittingly, John provided William with just what he needed to turn his pastoral, *The Brothers*, into one of his most moving poems. Its evolution was a perfect example of the way William composed his poetry. At its heart lay the true story of the shepherd boy who had fallen asleep on the fells and sleepwalked to his death. The earliest drafts show that it was a simple retelling of the tale by the village priest. What turned it from a pathetic incident into a genuine tragedy was the introduction of another figure, the man to whom the priest tells the story, not knowing that he was actually the dead boy's brother. This man, Leonard, was based on John. At the age of twelve, Leonard had been taken from the country life he loved by 'an Uncle . . . A thriving man [who] traffic'd on the sea', and sent to be a mariner, though 'his soul was knit to this his native soil'. Like John, who constantly reiterated his desire to work for William, Leonard had 'chiefly for his Brother's sake, Resolved to try his fortune on the seas'.

but he had been rear'd
Among the mountains, and he in his heart
Was half a Shepherd on the stormy seas.
Oft in the piping shrouds had Leonard heard
The tones of waterfalls, and inland sounds
Of caves and trees. . . .

Below him, in the bosom of the deep,
Saw mountains, saw the forms of sheep that graz'd
On verdant hills, with dwellings among trees,
And Shepherds clad in the same country grey
Which he himself had worn.

After an absence of many years, he returned to his native hills 'with some small wealth Acquir'd by traffic in the Indian Isles', determined to resume his former life with his brother. As he approached his paternal home, his heart failed him, just as John's had done, and, not daring to inquire tidings of one he so dearly loved, he had turned aside to the family plot in the churchyard. There he found a new, unmarked grave and discovered, through the priest, that it was indeed his brother who lay there. Not only that, but Leonard himself was indirectly responsible for his death: his brother had pined for him in his absence and, in dreaming that he was searching for him, had acquired the habit of sleepwalking. No longer able to bear the thought of living in the vale, Leonard returned to sea and became a grey-haired mariner. By this subtle change of emphasis and sympathy from one brother to the other, William transformed what might have been merely a voyeuristic account of an unusual accident into a deeply moving description of its effect on those left behind. It became the incarnation of one of William's most passionately held beliefs about his own poetry, which distinguished it from the popular poetry of the day: 'the feeling therein developed', William explained of his own poems, 'gives importance to the action and situation, and not the action and situation to the feeling'.[34]

John was determined to contribute to his brother's poetry more directly. Like Dorothy, he believed passionately that William should not be distracted from his vocation by petty worldly concerns. 'He encouraged me to persist, and to keep my eye steady on its object', was William's grateful testimony. 'He would work for me, (that was his language), for me, and his Sister; and I was to endeavour to do something for the world.'[35] Captain John Wordsworth had made his fortune in the East India Company and could afford to retire at the end of his current voyage in the *Earl of Abergavenny*. John had every hope that he would replicate his cousin's success and intended to apply for the vacant captaincy as soon as the *Abergavenny* returned to England. In the meantime, he was at liberty for the first time in his seafaring career. He gave himself up to the simple pleasures of living at Grasmere and waited for his ship to come in.

Not long after his arrival, another welcome visitor came to stay at Town End. Mary Hutchinson had spent the previous month at her grandfather's house in Penrith, with her sister Joanna, brother George and assorted aunts and uncle. She was escorted to Grasmere by William. 'Mr W. came for her,' the flirtatious Joanna informed her poetical cousin. 'I never was so much in love in my life, as I was with your Brother Poet'. With John sleeping in the little unceiled room upstairs, there was nothing else for Mary to do but share Dorothy's bed. Cramped quarters indeed, by modern standards. Nevertheless, Mary was 'very much delighted indeed with Grasmere, and the Wordsworth way of living, She says she never saw so compleat a Cottage in her life – and every thing [so] very comfortable as they have'.[36]

Mary and John, the two newcomers, struck up an instant friendship. 'John used to walk with her every where, and they were exceedingly attached to each other', Dorothy would later write, adding that Mary had a 'tender love of John and an intimate knowledge of his virtues'. Mary herself had a slightly different slant on this. 'He loved every thing about this dear spot, and John was the first who led me to everything that I love in this neighbourhood.'[37] This difference of emphasis is important, for there can be little doubt that John fell in love with Mary. He may have remembered her from his childhood when they went to dame school together in Penrith; he may even, indeed, have met her again during his regular visits to his Uncle Christopher; but this was the first time he had lived for so long, and so intimately, with her. There is no evidence to suggest that he ever declared himself. Mary may have broken through his natural reticence, but he may well have felt inhibited by the attachment between her and William. In any case, John was not in a position to marry. He could offer neither a home nor a secure income, and he would be away at sea more often than not.

After they parted, however, they kept up a regular correspondence. Mary's letters are unfortunately lost. At least some of John's have been preserved. At first glance these may not seem like love letters: they are frequently taken up with everyday matters, or discussion of William's poetry, and there is not a single overt declaration of love. John was never one to wear his heart on his sleeve, but he wrote to Mary with a tenderness that is unmistakable. He always addressed her, with old-fashioned intimacy, as 'thee' or 'thou', a term that never appears anywhere else in his letters, not even to his much-loved sister. He hated letter-writing, but always found time in the pressure of company business to scrawl a few lines to his 'dearest Mary'. 'As my time is precious I think I cannot do better than by writing to *thee*', he wrote in February 1801, ending his letter by begging her to write 'often and *long* letters': 'I make this request because my dear Mary there is nothing that thou canst write but what will give me pleasure & to be with *thee* I read thy letters over a *dozen* times in a day'.[38] He worried endlessly about Mary's lack of company, urging her to go visiting if only in order to make her appreciate her own home and advantages; he sent her little presents and offered his services in any way he could be useful; and he wrote often of his longing to be with her and back at Grasmere. Most telling of all is the way their correspondence ended. In September 1802, having just returned from his latest voyage, he met William and Dorothy in London, and his sister handed him a letter from Mary. It informed him of her forthcoming marriage to his brother. Dorothy had herself just written to Mary and, unaware of the impact of this news on John, gaily left him half a page to 'give you some account of his voyage'. John began his letter in his accustomed way, 'My dearest Mary', then, realizing that this was now an inappropriate form of address to another man's fiancée, he crossed it through. Even when he began again, he immediately slipped into the same error, but he had not the heart to erase it a second time. In a few brief lines, the most emotional he had ever penned, marred by many errors indicating his inner turmoil, he wrote his last letter to Mary.

> I have been reading your Letter over & over again My dearest Mary till tears have come into my eyes & I known [*sic*] not how to express my[s]elf thou ar't [a] kind & dear creature But wh<t>at ever fate Befal me I shall love to the last and bear thy<y> memory with me to the grave
>
> Thine affly
>
> John Wordsworth

William called John a '*silent* Poet', an epithet nowhere more justified than in this letter. Unable to find the words himself, John had been forced to borrow those of his more eloquent brother. The last two lines were a quotation from William's poem *Michael*.[39] John never wrote directly to Mary again, though he would always inquire tenderly after her in letters to Grasmere. Nor did he ever see her again. Though he could have visited Grasmere between voyages, like his *alter ego*, Leonard, in *The Brothers*, he chose not to do so. While he could not bear to see William and Mary as man and wife, he could take some comfort from the knowledge that, in committing himself to working for his brother, he was also providing for Mary.

All this was, of course, in the future. For the moment, in the early spring of 1800, John and Mary simply enjoyed each other's company and the blissful sense of being part of a closely knit group, bound together by deep affection and an identity of tastes, sympathies and interests. One person was excluded, however, and he felt his exclusion bitterly. Coleridge was accustomed to having a circle of his own admirers; he was therefore baffled that William refused to fall prostrate at his feet. What rankled particularly was that the one man whom he admired above all others should prefer the company of his family and native mountains to that of Coleridge himself. Towards the end of March, however, he had accepted the unpalatable truth, even if his pride would not allow him to admit why. He confessed to Poole that he was unable to persuade William to return to Alfoxton: 'he will never quit the North of England – his habits are more assimilated with the Inhabitants there – there he & his Sister are exceedingly beloved, enthusiastically.' Rather pettily, he ascribed this not to their character, but to northern exclusivity and his own friends' failure to appreciate William properly.

Such difference do small Sympathies make – such as Voice, Pronunciation, &c – for from what other Cause can I account for it [?] –. Certainly, no one, neither you, or the Wedgewoods, altho' you far more than any one else, ever entered into the feeling due to a man like Wordsworth – of whom I do not hesitate in saying, that since Milton no man has *manifested* himself equal to him.[40]

'Coleridge has left us,' Charles Lamb informed a friend on 5 April, 'to go into the North, on a visit to his God, Wordsworth.' If he could not persuade William to come to him, he would have to go to William. He arrived in Grasmere the next day, probably just missing Mary, who returned to Penrith about the same time, after a visit lasting five weeks. Coleridge stayed a month.[41] It was symptomatic of the alteration in their respective creativity that Coleridge was currently working on a translation of Schiller's *Wallenstein*, 'a *Bore*' which 'wasted and depressed my spirits', while William was in the full flow of original composition. He was already planning to publish a second volume of *Lyrical Ballads*, together with a series of *Pastorals*, inspired by the Lakes, of which *The Brothers*, although first written, had now become the conclusion. Remarkably, too, he was also contemplating writing a novel.[42]

Coleridge could not help but make comparisons. Perhaps a relocation to the Lakes might work wonders for him too? Instead of returning to London, where the daily grind of his journalism had become unbearable, he sought shelter once more under Poole's wing at Nether Stowey. But he had come to a decision: if a suitable house could not be found there, then he would uproot himself, and his family, and settle at Keswick.[43]

Within a few days of Coleridge's departure, William and John set off on a walking tour that would take them from one side of the country to the other. They had decided to visit Mary Hutchinson at Gallow Hill, a farm at Brompton-by-Sawdon, seven miles inland from Scarborough and the east coast of Yorkshire. Recent rent rises had made it impossible for her brother Tom to continue farming at Sockburn. At the beginning of the year he had sought, and found, the farm at Gallow Hill, where, for £120 a year he had more land (and better for growing corn) than the new tenant would have at Sockburn for an annual rent of £400. Their new neighbour, the biggest landowner in the area, was the youthful and enlightened eccentric, Sir George Cayley, who had diverted his energies from republicanism into agricultural reform, had already begun a drainage scheme for the area and was (less successfully) devising plans for man-powered flight.[44]

The Hutchinsons had left Sockburn regretfully for the more prosaic surroundings of East Yorkshire at the beginning of May 1800. They were determined to be cheerful. The country was 'very pleasant – the farm good & the house very convenient much better than the generality of farm Houses – tho' nothing like Sockburne but that was not to be expected'. In fact, the farmhouse was uncompromisingly functional, squarely built, of sand-coloured stone, with a pantiled roof. A range of outbuildings, with a distinctive dovecote in the end wall of the barn facing the side of the house, enclosed a large farmyard. What made it so different from Sockburn, however, was the position: Gallow Hill stood on a gentle incline facing south over the flat, featureless Vale of Pickering, towards the distant low hills of the Wolds on the horizon. Next to the house was a curious and deceptively steep wooded knoll, like a barrow in its distinctive shape. A few hundred yards away lay the main Pickering to Scarborough road, which, then as now, was always busy with tourists: during the season the '*spaers*', as Sara called them, were 'thronging past daily . . . we see Coaches *whirring* by for ever'.[45]

William and John set off for Gallow Hill on 14 May in high spirits and with a pocket full of cold pork each to sustain them on their journey. Dorothy accompanied them as far as Lowwood Bay, just beyond Ambleside. 'My heart was so full that I could hardly speak to W when I gave him a farewell kiss –', she wrote in the journal she now commenced.

I sate a long time upon a stone at the margin of the lake, & after a flood of tears my heart was easier – The lake looked to me I knew not why dull and melancholy, the weltering on the shores seemed a heavy sound . . . I resolved to write a journal of the time till W & J return – & I set about keeping my resolve because I will not quarrel with myself & because I shall give Wm Pleasure by it when he comes home again –

She arrived at Town End with a bad headache, the usual result of her overwrought emotions. That evening a young woman begged at the door. She had come from Manchester a few days earlier with only 2s and a slip of paper which she thought was a banknote but was in fact a fraud. With almost clinical detachment, Dorothy recorded the story of this female vagrant in her journal, knowing it would interest her brother. 'She had buried her husband & three children within a year & a half – All in one grave – burying very dear – paupers all put in one place – 20 shillings paid for as much ground as will bury a man's grave – a stone to be put over it or the right it will be lost; 11–6 each time the ground is opened'. Even this profoundly moving tale of real distress and suffering failed to distract Dorothy from her own grief. She ended her first day's entry with what would become a regular motif in the journal: 'Oh! that I had a letter from William!'[46]

In her brothers' absence, Dorothy settled into a routine to keep herself busy, reading Shakespeare's plays, working in the vegetable garden with the assistance of the Fishers, Molly, her brother, John, and his wife, Aggie, and walking the three and a half miles to Ambleside for the daily post. More often than not, she was disappointed of letters and moped all the way home; with the onset of bad headaches again, she took to retiring to bed for a few hours in the afternoon. The Sympson family, who lived further up Dunmail Raise, took pity on her evident loneliness. The Reverend Joseph Sympson, the eighty-five-year-old vicar of little Wythburn church, was as hale and hearty as a man of fifty. A fanatical fisherman, he regularly joined William and John on their fishing expeditions on Grasmere and, further afield, to the mountain-top tarns. His daughter, Margaret, who was only a few years older than Dorothy, became a good friend, as did his son, the unfortunately named Bartholomew. Taking Dorothy under their wing, they jollied her along by calling in unexpectedly, acompanying her on her walks, inviting her up to High Broadrain, their home, and even taking her out in a boat to fish on Grasmere.[47]

William, unaware of the trauma his absence was causing Dorothy, wrote only twice during the three and a half weeks he was away. For the last five days, she was on tenterhooks, lingering outside in the hope of hearing her brother's tread and staying close to the cottage in case she missed his return. On 7 June she sat up till past eleven at night, and her patience was at last rewarded. 'I heard a foot go to the front of the house, turn round, & open the gate It was William – – after our first joy was over We got some tea – We did not go to bed till 4 o clock in the morning so he had an opportunity of seeing our improvements'. John, almost completely overlooked in this account, did not return until the following evening.[48]

The brothers had lengthened the eighty-odd miles of their journey by making a detour through the Yorkshire Dales, visiting the gloomy depths of Yordas Cavern, so large the light from their candles could not penetrate to the walls and roof, Malham Cove, a spectacular natural semi-amphitheatre of sheer white rock, topped with a fissured pavement and a lonely tarn, and Gordale Scar, an inverted-funnel-shaped ravine, culminating in a sheer waterfall.[49] When William and John arrived at Gallow Hill, they found only three members of the Hutchinson family there: Mary, and her brothers Tom and George.[50] Inspired by the Wordsworths' example at Town End, Mary was hard at work creating a garden, a corner of which she would name after John. Touched though he was by the sentiment behind this gesture, John was distinctly unimpressed by Gallow Hill. He bluntly called it 'a vile abominable place' and conceived an immediate dislike to the (as yet unseen) Hutchinson landlord, Mr Langley, and his wife, who, as daughter of Lord Middleton, gave herself airs and graces. 'How does her honour & its honour behave to you[?]', John inquired of Mary, 'are they like the lords and ladies I have seen very proud[?] pray have you got any body that you can *speak* to[?]' William too worried about Mary's lack of company, asking his old friend Francis Wrangham, who lived only twelve miles away at Hunmanby, to perform 'a great kindness . . . to me' and call on her. William had hoped to introduce them in person, but when he and Tom Hutchinson walked over, they found Wrangham was not at home. Despite their reservations about Gallow Hill itself, William and John found the company of the Hutchinsons so beguiling that they left Dorothy solitary for longer than they had intended, extending their visit to three weeks.[51]

William returned to find good news awaiting him at Grasmere. Montagu's friend Charles Douglas had finally paid off his four-and-a-half-year-old debt; or rather, he had paid off £100 in capital, plus £4 17s in interest. The remaining £100 had been transferred to Montagu, from whom there was little or no chance of securing an early repayment. Richard was anxious to press Douglas for the full amount, but William, despite his own need for the money, was prepared to be quixotically generous. The previous December, William had written in desperation to John Pinney, asking him to exert pressure on Montagu to repay him. Coleridge had also hoped to persuade Pinney to intervene: 'He [Montagu] leaves Wordsworth without his Principal or Interest,' he wrote to Josiah Wedgwood, 'which of course he would not do, W's daily bread & Meat depending in great part on him, if he were not painfully embarrassed – Embarrassed I should have said: for Pinny tells me, that he suffers no pain from it.' Pinney, to whom Montagu also owed considerable sums, refused to pay his debt off for him, but did offer to take responsibility for the interest, thus considerably relieving William's very straitened means.[52]

More importantly, as far as William was concerned, the repayment of Douglas's loan enabled him to pay back the money he himself owed for his advances from the Wedgwoods in Germany. This unintentionally incurred debt had weighed heavily on his conscience and his relief was palpable as he wrote to Josiah Wedgwood on 13 July, apologizing for the delay, explaining the circumstances and authorizing him to call on Richard for immediate payment of the £110 13s he was owed.[53]

There was further good news from an unexpected quarter. Despite the reviews, the first edition of *Lyrical Ballads* had sold out and the booksellers were asking for a reprint. This was a far more valuable asset than it might have been, for Cottle had made William a gift of the copyright when he sold off his publishing business to Longman the previous autumn. Coleridge had approached Longman and negotiated an agreement which would give William £80 for two further editions of the original book, and two of the projected new volume. Writing to Richard, William said that he intended to accept this offer: 'if the books sell quickly I shall soon have the right of going to market with them again when their merit will be known, and if they do not sell tolerably, Longman will have given enough for them'. Anxious to avoid the confusion which had arisen over the publication of *Lyrical Ballads* on the eve of his departure for Germany, William spelled out his terms twice over in a letter to Longman.[54]

On 29 June Coleridge arrived, this time to stay. As hostages to his decision, he brought with him his long-suffering wife, who was well advanced in pregnancy, and his child, Hartley, and all three squeezed themselves into the cottage at Town End. Whether it was the stress of committing himself to a life in the north, a retreat into the opium-taking which had now become a habit or simply, as he claimed, a cold which the damp climate exacerbated, Coleridge did a Dorothy and retired to bed at Town End, overcome with rheumatic pains, weakness, listlessness and, for good measure, swollen eyelids.[55]

Despite Coleridge's illness, plans for the new edition of *Lyrical Ballads* proceeded apace. By the middle of July, Coleridge was writing to Cottle and his partner, Nathaniel Biggs, in Bristol, who were to print (but not publish) the poems, setting out the order for the edition. There were to be some significant changes. The Advertisement was to be dropped: in its place, at Coleridge's urgent request, William would prepare an expanded version of his poetic theory which would become the notorious preface. William would later claim that he 'never cared a straw about the theory' and that the preface was written 'out of sheer good nature'. 'I recollect the very spot, a deserted Quarry in the Vale of Grasmere where he pressed the thing upon me, & but for that it would never have been thought of.'[56] Like Topsy, however, once thought of, it just growed and growed. Almost as important as the introduction of a preface was the relegation of *The Rime of the Ancyent Marinere* from pride of place opening the volume, to second to last. What is more, Coleridge, bowing to universal criticism from friends and reviewers alike, had agreed to amend his obscure, pseudo-medieval vocabulary. The poem would now appear as 'The Ancient Mariner, a Poet's Reverie'. Coleridge's *Foster-Mother's Tale* and *The Nightingale*, which had stood second and fourth, were pushed back to seventh and seventeenth respectively. In their place, as William had decided after reading the reviews, were six of his own shorter poems. William's poem *The Convict*, which had incurred critical wrath for its overtly political message, was to be omitted altogether and replaced by Coleridge's *Love*, the only new contribution to the volume. One other poem by Coleridge, *The Dungeon*, was allowed to remain at fourteenth position. The rest of the volume was entirely William's composition, as it had been with the first edition, and, as before, he would close the volume triumphantly with *Tintern Abbey*.[57] This time, however, the change in order of appearance placed the emphasis squarely on William.

In the flurry of activity caused by the Coleridges' arrival at Grasmere, nursing Coleridge himself and making preparations for the new edition of *Lyrical Ballads*, Dorothy was too busy to keep up her journal. William was unwell, suffering from the pain in the side which afflicted him when hard at work composing or revising his poems; Coleridge, unkindly but amusingly, diagnosed it as a pain 'in the right hypochondrium'.[58] Nevertheless, it made a good excuse for turning down an offer from Daniel Stuart to write for the *Morning Post* on a regular basis. William was particularly anxious not to offend a man who had rendered him a considerable service by publishing seven poems from the original *Lyrical Ballads* between 2 April and 19 September. Their highly complimentary head-notes (which may have been written by Coleridge), as much as their republication to a wider readership, must have affected the level of sales and were probably responsible for it selling out. No doubt they also influenced Longman's decision to accept the new edition. William was the first to acknowledge his debt. 'Wordsworth requests me to be very express in the communication of his sincere thanks to you,' Coleridge wrote to Stuart, 'for the interest which you have been so kind as to take in his poems. We are convinced you have been of great service to the sale.' A further result of Stuart's interest in William's poetry was his referral of a request from Richard Brinsley Sheridan that William would send his tragedy, *The Borderers*, for possible staging at the Drury Lane theatre. Flattering though this interest was, William had no intention of undergoing that ordeal again; he made polite noises about allowing Sheridan to view his manuscript and point out the defects that made it untheatrical, so that he could write another play more suited to the stage, but he kept his manuscript safe at Grasmere. In any case, his energies were entirely taken up with his poetry: when he had *Lyrical Ballads* safely off his hands and in the press, he would return to his great project, *The Recluse*.[59]

On 23 July Coleridge left Town End for his new abode, Greta Hall, at Keswick; the next day he was followed by Sarah, Hartley, and the boxes containing their worldly goods. Coleridge was in hopeful mood. 'We drank tea the night before I left Grasmere on the Island in that lovely lake,' he wrote to Humphry Davy,

> our kettle swung over the fire hanging from the branch of a Fir Tree, and I lay & saw the woods, & mountains, & lake all trembling, & as it were *idealized* thro' the subtle smoke which rose up from the clear red embers of the fir-apples which we had collected. Afterwards, we made a glorious Bonfire on the Margin, by some alder bushes, whose twigs heaved & sobbed in the uprushing column of smoke – & the Image of the Bonfire, & of us that danced round it – ruddy laughing faces in the twilight – the Image of this in a Lake smooth as that sea, to whose waves the Son of God had said, PEACE![60]

Leaving Grasmere, Coleridge consoled himself with the delusion that William would probably leave Town End the following summer and settle near him in Keswick. In his heart of hearts, he knew it would not happen. 'His cottage is indeed in every respect so delightful a residence, the walks so dry after the longest rains, the heath and a silky kind of fern so luxurious a bedding on every hilltop, and the whole vicinity so tossed about on those little hills at the feet of the majestic mountains, that he moves in an eddy; he cannot get out of it.'[61]

Now that William, Dorothy and John had Town End to themselves again, work began in earnest on preparation for the second volume which was to be added to *Lyrical Ballads*. William revised, Dorothy transcribed and John kept the table going with a constant supply of fresh fish. By the end of July, Biggs and Cottle had printed the first volume and were ready for setting the proofs of the second. At Coleridge's suggestion, William decided to entrust the task of seeing the poems through the press to a man he had never met, Humphry Davy, Dr Beddoes's assistant at the Bristol Pneumatic Institution. This brilliant young chemist, who had discovered the laughter-inducing properties of inhaling nitrous oxide only the year before, hardly seems the most appropriate person to whom the task of proof-reading literary manuscripts should be delegated. Davy was, nevertheless, a Renaissance figure, equally at home with poetry as he was with chemistry; William even entrusted him with correcting his own punctuation, 'a business at which I am ashamed to say I am no adept'. Every three days, Davy received a set of sheets from Grasmere, checked them, then passed them on to the printer; as the proofs were printed they were returned to him for rechecking.[62]

As all William's subsequent assistants in this field were to discover, it was a thankless task. Experience had taught William to be a perfectionist, and he was determined not to repeat the mistakes of his earlier publications, which had been casually cobbled together at the last moment. He had learned the hard way that this was simply throwing away his work. If he was to give his poetry every possible advantage, he needed to control all aspects of the publication, from the layout of the page to the ordering of the contents. Delegation was anathema to him, but it was absolutely necessary. And even when he had appointed a deputy, he undermined his position by writing directly to the publishers countermanding previous instructions.[63]

Slowly, through the suffocating heat of early August, followed by a cold snap and the return of perfect summer weather, the second volume of *Lyrical Ballads* took shape. The Wordsworths walked almost daily, bathed, fished and sailed on the lake, tended their garden and interchanged visits with the Sympsons. They rarely passed more than a few days without Coleridge. If he did not come to stay, then they went to Keswick, where, for old times' sake, they visited their former home, Windy Brow, and called on the Speddings, who had been so kind to them when they lived there. From the end of August, they had a constant stream of visitors: Anthony Harrison, a contemporary at Hawkshead Grammar School, now a Penrith solicitor; James Losh and his wife, who, in her brothers' absence, Dorothy proudly showed round the cottage, 'which is remarkably neat tho very plain, as far as I cou'd judge, it being dark'; Thomas and Catherine Clarkson of Eusemere, with whom William and Coleridge had stayed briefly the previous autumn on their walking tour of the Lakes; John Marshall, husband of Dorothy's childhood friend Jane Pollard, whom William and John took on an extensive tour of the Lakes; perhaps most surprisingly of all, Robert Jones, William's college friend and companion of his walking tours in France and Wales, who brought rainy weather but stayed almost a week; the Wordsworths' uncle and cousin, Tom Myers, father and son; Christopher's future brother-in-law, Charles Lloyd and his wife, Sophia, who, much to the Wordsworths' dismay, had settled rather too close for comfort at Old Brathay, the other side of Ambleside.[64] It was demonstrable proof that Town End, unlike Racedown or Alfoxton, was well and truly on the tourist circuit: love it or loathe it, the season would bring an annual tide of visitors to the Wordsworths' door for the next fifty years and more.

And there was also a parting of the ways. For more than a month, John had been in daily expectation of the return of the *Earl of Abergavenny* to English waters. On 28 September, possibly while taking supper with the Lloyds, they learned that the ship had arrived. John had no option but to leave his Grasmere idyll and take himself off to London, there to begin the canvassing necessary to secure the captaincy of the ship for himself and, with it, the refoundation of the family fortunes. The following day was fine, but showery, with sunshine and clouds. William and Dorothy accompanied John up the stony beds of the precipitous becks leading up Fairfield and Seat Sandal to the eerie silence of Grisedale Tarn, clutched in the bony fingers of the unforgiving mountains. Loath to go their separate ways, they lingered by the still waters of the tarn, where the raucous cry of the raven and the plaintive bleating of a few scattered sheep echoed round the empty hills. Full of optimism, they talked over their plans for future happiness. John had even selected the field in which he intended to build his own house on the shores of Grasmere. As a pledge to the future, they agreed to lay the foundation stone of a little fishing hut by the side of Grisedale Tarn. Then they parted, John taking the plunging pathway down towards Patterdale, with Ullswater a dull gleam in the distance, and William and Dorothy retracing their route over the hills to Town End. 'Poor fellow my heart was right sad –', Dorothy recorded in her journal. 'I could not help thinking we should see him again because he was only going to Penrith.'[65] In fact, though none of them knew it at the time, he would never return to Grasmere again.

10. Home at Grasmere

In the autumn of 1800 William struggled to put the final touches to his second volume. Throughout the year, he had been constantly adding to his stock of poetry, and many of these new poems would be selected for inclusion. As the shape of the book emerged, it became obvious that it was something quite different from the first edition of *Lyrical Ballads*, and that the difference was the result of living at Grasmere. The poetic principle remained the same: simple tales about simple people, simply told. What had disappeared were the remnants of hyperbole. Instead of mad mothers, idiot boys and half-crazed peasants, the characters in these poems are the genuinely ordinary people who inhabited the Lake country, humble schoolmasters, shepherd boys and statesmen, living obscure lives, accepting and enduring their sufferings with quiet dignity. The result is both more lifelike and, consequently, more poignant. *The Childless Father*, for instance, depicts old Timothy, whose last child has died six months previously. Instead of giving himself up to extravagant grief, he keeps up the outward appearance of life. As he leaves his hut to join the rest of the villagers in coursing a hare and closes the door,

> Perhaps to himself at that moment he said,
> 'The key I must take, for my Ellen is dead,'
> But of this in my ears not a word did he speak,
> And he went to the chace with a tear on his cheek.[1]

Though many of the poems are formal, or informal, epitaphs and inscriptions, emphasizing the elegiac quality of the verse, they are suffused with a new mood of serenity. There is a sense of completeness, an acquiescence in the natural cycle of life, which culminates in the inevitability of death.

And, more than ever before, the people are a part of the landscape – one which is defiantly Lakeland. The names of mountains are invoked like a roll-call of ancient deities, Loughrigg, Fairfield, Helvellyn, Skiddaw, Glaramara and Kirkstone, and poems such as *The Idle Shepherd Boys* and *Michael* are as much an evocation of their settings, at Dungeon-Ghyll Force and at the top of Greenhead Ghyll, as of the people that inhabit them. The Wordsworths themselves had staked their own claim to belong by the series of *Poems on the Naming of Places.* William had added several more since his first, written immediately after his arrival in Grasmere, and addressed to Mary Hutchinson. Her sister, the flirtatious and merry Joanna, had one dedicated to her: curiously, despite its delightful and graphic description of her laughter echoing round the mountains, it was entirely a figment of William's imagination, for Joanna had not yet been to Grasmere. Dorothy, inevitably, had her place (if not her own name) in the poem describing Emma's dell, on the banks of the clear, pebbly brook running through Easedale. *Point Rash Judgement* commemorated a walk beside Grasmere Lake, taken by William and Dorothy with Coleridge, on his first visit to Town End. Seeing a man fishing in the lake, instead of joining his fellows in harvesting the fields, they leapt to the conclusion that he was an idle fellow. As they came closer, he turned and they realized he was mortally sick. Far from being idle, he was endeavouring to employ himself in the only useful activity he could, and his three observers were left to repent their hasty judgement.[2]

Appropriately, the best of all the poems in this series is the one inspired by the poet himself. If one needs an excuse for quoting such a characteristic and exquisite poem in full, it is for what it reveals about William's (and Dorothy's) perception of his character and vocation.

> There is an Eminence, – of these our hills
> The last that parleys with the setting sun.
> We can behold it from our orchard-seat,
> And, when at evening we pursue our walk
> Along the public way, this Cliff, so high
> Above us, and so distant in its height,
> Is visible, and often seems to send
> Its own deep quiet to restore our hearts.
> The meteors make of it a favourite haunt:
> The star of Jove, so beautiful and large
> In the mid heavens, is never half so fair
> As when he shines above it. 'Tis in truth
> The loneliest place we have among the clouds.
> And She who dwells with me, whom I have lov'd
> With such communion, that no place on earth
> Can ever be a solitude to me,
> Hath said, this lonesome Peak shall bear my name.[3]

It had always been William's intention to include some of Coleridge's work in this volume. Indeed, in the opening of his draft for the preface, he had actually declared that without *Christabel*, Coleridge's 'long and beautiful Poem', 'I should not yet have ventured to present a second volume to the public'. Unfortunately for both men, *Christabel* was incomplete and would never be finished. Coleridge had begun it in 1797 and, intending to include it in the new edition of *Lyrical Ballads*, had renewed his labours on it at Keswick, to the detriment of his contributions to the *Morning Post*. (To make up the deficiency, he had reverted to his earlier habit of sending in William's poems to be printed anonymously.) 'I tried to perform my promise', Coleridge told Josiah Wedgwood in November, 'but the deep unutterable Disgust, which I had suffered in the translation of that accursed Wallenstein, seemed to have stricken me with barrenness – for I tried & tried, & nothing would come of it.'[4]

A drinking session with a neighbouring clergyman helped clear the writer's block. Though he claimed to have written up to 1,400 lines by early October, Coleridge lacked the will-power or interest to complete the poem. William even suspected that he did not know *how* to end it. Something had to be done. Time was slipping by and, with it, all the advantages of publishing hot on the heels of the first edition. More than a fortnight after they had expected *Lyrical Ballads* to be published, Coleridge had still not produced his poem. William tried to play for time by sending in more of his own poems to be inserted before *Christabel*, but this was only a short-term solution. A revised deadline of the end of September came and went. William had completed the notes and the lengthy preface, Dorothy had transcribed them and they had been sent off, together with a letter to the printers asking them to change the title of the book. A new volume of poetry, *Lyrical Tales*, by Mary Robinson, had just been published. It was bad enough that Biggs & Cottle had printed it and Longman had published it, but William had an absolute horror of his poems being confused with the fashionable gushings of 'Perdita' Robinson, whose main claims to fame were that she had been both a successful actress and the Prince of Wales's mistress. He begged Biggs & Cottle to change his title-page to '*Poems in two Volumes* By W. Wordsworth'. Such a drastic change was not agreeable to Longman, and, in the end, they compromised. The title would now be '*Lyrical Ballads with other Poems in two volumes* By W. Wordsworth'.[5]

For the first time, therefore, William's own name would appear on the title-page of *Lyrical Ballads*. It was a significant change, reflecting the fact that this was emphatically William's work, and that he was proud to claim it as such. But where did it leave Coleridge? Only nine months earlier, William had urged him not to take any pains to contradict rumours that *Lyrical Ballads* was 'entirely yours. Such a rumour is the best thing that can befall them.' Now he was excluded. This was not unreasonable. Even if Coleridge had published a completed *Christabel* in the collection, he would still have contributed only six poems to William's fifty-nine. His contribution was also fully acknowledged and identified in the preface – which was more than Coleridge himself had done when publishing *The Fall of Robespierre* under his own name, despite the fact that Southey had written two-thirds of it. Both Coleridge's editions of his own *Poems* had included contributions from other poets whose names did not appear on the title-page; in 1796 Lamb had supplied four poems but, in 1797, he and Lloyd between them contributed almost 100 pages of poetry. At first Coleridge was unperturbed by the exclusion of his name. It was only later, when, frustrated by his own failures and increasingly jealous of William's sustained poetic power, he came to see this as a sinister denial of his abilities and of his own contribution to *Lyrical Ballads*.[6]

At the time, Coleridge also accepted, with perfect equanimity, the decision to leave *Christabel* out of the second volume. For those who believe Coleridge's later view of this event, that William had rejected him as a man and a poet, this is proof of the Wordsworths' selfishness and ruthless determination to wrest *Lyrical Ballads* from the man who had given his all to promote William's poetry. In fact, as the contemporary evidence proves, it was nothing of the sort. On 4 October Coleridge walked into the cottage at Town End and read the Wordsworths the second part of *Christabel*, with which they were 'exceedingly delighted'. He read it again the following morning, to their 'increasing pleasure'. Next day, 6 October, Coleridge put off his intended departure, presumably because they were deep in discussion about *Christabel*. After tea, William read his latest contribution to *The Recluse*, which he called *The Pedlar*. Dorothy noted with characteristic baldness, 'Determined not to print Christabel with the LB'. This sequence of events is important, because, as Coleridge himself cheerfully reported three days later, 'We mean to publish the Christabel . . . with a long Blank Verse Poem of Wordsworth's entitled the Pedlar'. William had 'so much admired' Coleridge's '1300 lines', 'he thought it indelicate to print two Volumes with *his name* in which so much of another man's was included'. This was surely right, though one wonders if Coleridge himself would have been so scrupulous had their relative positions been reversed. Additionally, as Coleridge himself was the first to acknowledge, his Gothic tale of 'witchery by daylight' was totally out of step with the rest of the poems in the second volume and the poetic principles set out in the preface. Far from excluding Coleridge, William did his utmost to keep him involved. He even suggested that Coleridge should write some *Poems on the Naming of Places* to replace *Christabel* in the *Lyrical Ballads*. Despite this proffered lifeline, Coleridge once again failed to deliver.[7]

A few days after he returned to Keswick, William and Dorothy took what they called a walk, but ordinary mortals would call a scramble, up Greenhead Ghyll, a precipitous path alongside a mountain stream which tumbled down a cleft between the swelling breasts of Stone Arthur and Heron Pike. Their object was to visit a ruined sheepfold which, they had learned from their neighbours the Fishers, had been built by a previous occupant of their own cottage. Whether it was the evocative shape of the sheepfold, 'in the form of a heart unequally divided', John Fisher's lamentations about the fate of the statesman (the local name for the Lakeland freeholder farmer), who was fast becoming an endangered species, or, more likely, a combination of both, William was instantly inspired. The next day he was out in the woods, walking and composing his sonorous and deeply moving pastoral poem *Michael*, which told the tale of an aged statesman forced to send his only son out into the world to earn a living.[8] Before leaving for the city, Luke, a child of his parents' old age, went up Greenhead Ghyll with his father to perform the symbolic gesture of laying the cornerstone of a new sheepfold, as a covenant for the future and

> An emblem of the life thy Fathers liv'd,
> Who, being innocent, did for that cause
> Bestir them in good deeds.

After making a promising start, Luke was gradually seduced into profligate ways and had to flee overseas to escape his creditors. For seven long years, his father daily toiled up the mountainside to continue building the sheepfold, but it was unfinished when he died. When his wife died three years later, the little estate was sold and went into a stranger's hand.

> The Cottage which was nam'd The Evening Star
> Is gone, the ploughshare has been through the ground
> On which it stood; great changes have been wrought
> In all the neighbourhood, yet the Oak is left
> That grew beside their Door; and the remains
> Of the unfinished Sheep-fold may be seen
> Beside the boisterous brook of Green-head Gill.[9]

William really struggled composing this poem, spending day after day toiling away, often unsuccessfully, and making himself ill in the process. Part of the problem seems to have been that he began to write it in rhyming stanzas and ballad form, like *The Idiot Boy* and *Goody Blake and Harry Gill*. Thankfully, however, he changed his mind, burnt the manuscript and returned to the blank verse of which he was an absolute master. *Michael* was not finished until 9 December, but by then William knew he had succeeded triumphantly. In Michael he had created a man 'of strong mind and lively sensibility, agitated by two of the most powerful affections of the human heart; the parental affection, and the love of property, *landed* property, including the feelings of inheritance, home, and personal and family independence'. It was a summation of his own first year at Grasmere, and, like *Tintern Abbey*, it made the perfect ending to the volume.[10]

Coleridge having failed to produce any *Poems on the Naming of Places*, despite the reprieve caused by William's lengthy struggle with *Michael*, the second volume, consisting of forty-one poems, would be entirely the work of William. As, also, was the preface, which began as an expansion of the advertisement but ended as a lengthy disquisition on the purpose and nature of poetry in general. For such an important and influential document, it is extraordinarily dense and obscure in its language and argument. Were it not for the fact that it effectively formed the taste and judgement of a whole generation in the nineteenth century, one might be inclined to dismiss it as an example of the emperor's new clothes. Time and again, struggling to understand some complex and grandiloquently expressed statement, one comes to the uncomfortable conclusion that it is either meaningless or blindingly obvious. The equally unpleasant alternative is that one is the only person in the world too stupid to understand its true meaning. It was this creation of an aura of élitism and exclusion that played an enormous role in spreading the popularity of William's poetry. The poems themselves are, for the most part, simple enough to understand. William's purpose in writing them is equally plain: his poems were intended to excite compassion and encourage benevolence. This is not a difficult concept to grasp, but it is nowhere stated in the preface.

Instead, we have an earnest and passionate defence of the style and subject matter of his poetry. Summarized, the arguments ran like this. William's poems needed some sort of introduction because they were 'materially different from those, upon which general approbation is at present bestowed'. The main 'mark of difference' was not, as one might expect, the lowly social class of most of the characters, but that each poem 'has a worthy *purpose*'. His object was to make 'the incidents of common life interesting by tracing in them . . . the primary laws of our nature'. 'Low and rustic life was generally chosen', he explained, '. . . because in that situation our elementary feelings exist in a state of greater simplicity and consequently may be more accurately contemplated and more forcibly communicated'. Simple countrymen spoke a 'more permanent and a far more philosophical language than that which is frequently substituted for it by Poets'; 'being less under the action of social vanity they convey their feelings and notions in simple and unelaborated expressions'.

In one of his least obscure (and therefore most often quoted passages) he blamed the current 'degrading thirst' for 'frantic novels, sickly and stupid German Tragedies, and deluges of idle and extravagant stories in verse' on 'the great national events which are daily taking place, and the encreasing accumulation of men in cities, where the uniformity of their occupations produces a craving for extraordinary incident which the rapid communication of intelligence hourly gratifies'. Hailed by modern academics as a radical new departure in poetical theory, this was in fact no more than an echo of those ancient Roman poets and historians whom William had loved since boyhood. Virtue was to be found in the simplicity of country life; unnatural vices, with fickle tastes and insatiable appetites, were the perversions caused by the unnatural way of life in cities. In 1800, when England was still a rural country, William's attack on city life must have seemed odd, exaggerated, even untrue, but as the Industrial Revolution gathered pace, it came to have a prophetic feel. It was no coincidence that the popularity of William's poetry increased in response to the swift progress of nineteenth-century urbanization and mechanization: his homely tales of rural virtue then seemed to hark back to a golden age and acquired the rosy blush of nostalgia.

More original was William's defence of his use of blank verse and everyday vocabulary. Rejecting the argument that poetry should have its own unique and elevated language, he argued convincingly, with an example quoted from Gray, that there 'neither is nor can be any essential difference' between the language of prose and poetry. He also remained impervious to the criticism that he had written on unworthy subjects in vulgar language which sometimes verged on the ludicrous. If he were convinced that he was mistaken, he would alter and correct.

> But it is dangerous to make these alterations on the simple authority of a few individuals, or even of certain classes of men; for where the understanding of an Author is not convinced, or his feelings altered, this cannot be done without great injury to himself: for his own feelings are his stay and support, and if he sets them aside in one instance, he may be induced to repeat this act till his mind loses all confidence in itself and becomes utterly debilitated.

It was a fair point, but in stating it with typical bluntness, William laid himself open to the oft-repeated charge of arrogance. Similarly his claim that, if his poetic principles were followed, 'a species of poetry would be produced, which is genuine poetry; in its nature well adapted to interest mankind permanently, and likewise important in the multiplicity and quality of its moral relations'.[11]

In writing his preface, William clearly felt himself to be on the defensive. He was afraid that the studied simplicity of his poetry meant that it would be dismissed as trivial, hence his need to offer a highly intellectual justification for his purpose and its meaning. The preface built up a mystique around it, and endowed it with a didactic purpose that would speak only to a cultural élite capable of receiving and benefiting from his lofty message. Put simply, if you liked his poetry, you were members of an exclusive club; if you did not, you were unworthy of membership. It is no coincidence that one of the two key phrases which appear repeatedly in the letters William received from his admirers in later years is gratitude for having their understanding enlightened, their taste exalted and their affections ameliorated by his poetry.[12] What is significant about these phrases is that they are lifted directly from the preface; by quoting them, his admirers could congratulate themselves on being among the select and chosen few.

Coleridge had suggested that it might be useful to the sale of the book to send copies to 'different people of eminence'. His idea of eminence was eclectic, if not bizarre. The actress Dora Jordan, who had expressed an intention of singing stanzas from *The Mad Mother* if she acted Cora again in Sheridan's *Pizarro*; the popular poetess Mrs Barbauld; the society beauty and hostess Georgiana, Duchess of Devonshire; the politicians and men of letters Sir James Bland Burges and William Wilberforce. While the Wordsworths were with him, on a visit to Greta Hall, Coleridge dictated the accompanying letters in William's name to Dorothy.[13]

Significantly, the only letter William composed and wrote himself was to Charles James Fox, the great Whig leader, who had been outspoken in his defence of the

French Revolution and of civil and religious liberties in Britain, to the detriment of his own personal career. Despite being 'utterly unknown' to Fox, William explained at length why he had chosen him to be a recipient of his poems. Throughout his political career, Fox had consistently displayed a 'predominance of sensibility of heart', an ability to see and treat men as individuals rather than simply a body or class of people, and had fought to protect 'the most sacred of all property ... the property of the Poor'. Such a man could not fail to be moved by the plight of the statesmen of the north of England, those 'men of respectable education who daily labour on their own little properties' whose 'little tract of land serves as a kind of permanent rallying point for their domestic feelings'. 'This class of men is rapidly disappearing', William bluntly told Fox. In words which recall the passion of his *Letter to the Bishop of L[l]andaff*, he argued that this was a national, and preventable, tragedy. Expanding on the hints he had given in the preface, he set out his political beliefs and purpose with a force and clarity totally lacking in that document.

It appears to me that the most calamitous effect, which has followed the measures which have lately been pursued in this country, is a rapid decay of the domestic affections among the lower orders of society. This effect the present Rulers of this country are not conscious of, or they disregard it. For many years past, the tendency of society amongst almost all the nations of Europe has been to produce it. But recently by the spreading of manufactures [factories] through every part of the country, by the heavy taxes upon postage, by work-houses, Houses of Industry, and the invention of Soup-shops &c. &c. superadded to the encreasing disproportion between the price of labour and that of the necessaries of life, the bonds of domestic feeling among the poor, as far as the influence of these things has extended, have been weakened, and in innumerable instances entirely destroyed. The evil would be the less to be regretted, if these institutions were regarded only as palliatives to a disease; but the vanity and pride of their promoters are so subtly interwoven with them, that they are deemed great discoveries and blessings to humanity. In the mean time parents are separated from their children, and children from their parents; the wife no longer prepares with her own hands a meal for her husband, the produce of his labour; there is little doing in his house in which his affections can be interested, and but little left in it which he can love. I have two neighbours, a man and his wife, both upwards of eighty years of age; they live alone; the husband has been confined to his bed many months and has never had, nor till within these few weeks has ever needed, any body to attend to him but his wife. She has recently been seized with a lameness which has often prevented her from being able to carry him his food to his bed; the neighbours fetch water for her from the well, and do other kind offices for them both, but her infirmities encrease. She told my Servant two days ago that she was afraid they must both be boarded out among some other Poor of the parish (they have long been supported by the parish) but she said, it was hard, having kept house together so long, to come to this, and she was sure that 'it would burst her heart.' I mention this fact to shew how deeply the spirit of independence is, even yet, rooted in some parts of the country. These people could not express themselves in this way without an almost sublime conviction of the blessings of independent domestic life. If it is true, as I believe, that this spirit is rapidly disappearing, no greater curse can befal[l] a land.

William drew Fox's attention specifically to *The Brothers* and *Michael*, poems which, he declared, were 'faithful copies from nature' and written 'to shew that men who do not wear fine cloaths can feel deeply'.

I hope, whatever effect they may have upon you, you will at least be able to perceive that they may excite profitable sympathies in many kind and good hearts, and may in some small degree enlarge our feelings of reverence for our species, and our knowledge of human nature, by shewing that our best qualities are possessed by men whom we are too apt to consider, not with reference to the points in which they resemble us, but to those in which they manifestly differ from us.[14]

One can only lament that this powerful and moving plea was for Fox's eyes only; though overtly political, rather than poetical, it would have made a far more eloquent introduction to his poems than the verbose and otiose preface.

Lyrical Ballads, with Other Poems. In Two Volumes by W. Wordsworth was finally published on or around 25 January 1801, though the title-page, due to all the delays, actually bore the date 1800. The first volume was effectively a reprint of the 1798 edition, with the addition of Coleridge's poem *Love* and the preface, which, after much indecision, appeared at the beginning. The second volume was entirely new. It was certainly an odd way to introduce a new collection of poetry to the world, though purchasers were able to buy the volumes separately for 5s each. Southey, for one, resented having to buy the first volume again: 'I am bitterly angry to see one new poem smuggled into the world in the *Lyrical Ballads*,' he complained to Coleridge, 'where the 750 purchasers of the first [edition] can never get at it.' John Wordsworth, visiting the London bookseller Arch, was told that, though the second volume sold well, the first did not, and customers complained of being 'cheated' out of the preface.[15]

In writing his preface, William had geared himself up for a reaction which he expected would be explosively hostile. In the end, it was a damp squib. There were only two reviews, one of them written by William and Coleridge's friend John Stoddart, who had visited the Wordsworths twice during their first year at Town End. Stoddart's review, in the February issue of the *British Critic*, was, as John declared, 'too flattering I mean too much of a panegyric they will see im[m]ediately that it has been written by a friend'. Stoddart had ploughed through the preface and accepted all its arguments at face value as proven by the poetry; the only hint of criticism was a rather weak and weary comment that it was written 'in some parts with a degree of metaphysical obscurity'. The poems themselves were treated favourably, but too briefly to give the readers any real idea of their merit or assist the sale. The *Monthly Review* gave the book only the shortest of mentions, declaring it unnecessary to enlarge on their review of the 1798 edition, except to say that 'the present publication [is] not inferior to its precursors [*sic*]'.[16] This was, no doubt, the reason why there were so few reviews, though the tone of the preface may also have antagonized potential critics.

So it was left to William's friends to deliver their verdict. By far the most acute observations came from the '*silent* Poet'. 'Most of Wm's poetry improves upon 2d 3 or 4th reading', John pointed out, quite accurately, 'now people in general are not sufficiently interested with the first reading to induce them to try a 2d'. In time, he thought, they would become popular 'but it will be by degrees – the fact is there are not a great many that will be pleased with the poems but those that are pleased will be pleased in a high degree & they *will be people of sense* this will have weight – & people who neither understand or wish to understand will buy & praise them'.[17]

Charles Lamb, who could not wait for his complimentary copy to arrive, borrowed the second volume and read it with mixed feelings. Though he had measured praise for some of the poems, he reserved most of his energy for a spirited defence of the *Ancient Mariner* against William's criticisms of it in a published note to the poem. 'To sum up a general opinion of the second vol.', he wrote to William, 'I do not **feel** any one poem in it so forcibly as the Ancient Marinere, the Mad mother, and the Lines at Tintern Abbey in the **first**.' Much to Lamb's amusement, this letter provoked an immediate response. 'All the north of England are in a turmoil', he told a friend.

> The Post did not sleep a moment. I received almost instantaneously a long letter of four sweating pages from my **reluctant Letterwriter**, the purport of which was, that he was sorry his 2d vol. had not given me more pleasure (Devil a hint did I give that it had *not pleased me*) and 'was compelled to wish that my range of **Sensibility** was more extended, being obliged to believe that I should receive large influxes of happiness & happy Thoughts' (I suppose from the L.B. –)

Coleridge was also galvanized into defensive action: 'four long pages, equally sweaty, and more tedious, came from him'. More seriously, Lamb privately expressed the opinion that the second volume 'too artfully aims at simplicity of expression. And you sometimes doubt if simplicity be not a cover for Poverty.'[18]

Equally disappointing for William was the response of Charles James Fox, which echoed Lamb's. He told William that *Lyrical Ballads* had given him the greatest pleasure, but the ones he singled out for praise were *Goody Blake and Harry Gill*, *We are Seven*, *The Mad Mother* and *The Idiot Boy*. In other words, all poems from the first volume, and, apart from the first, none with a social message of the kind William had so anxiously drawn to Fox's attention. 'I read with particular attention the two you pointed out', Fox continued, 'but whether it be from early prepossessions, or whatever other cause, I am no great friend to blank verse for subjects which are to be treated of with simplicity.' And that was that. The social and moral dimensions of the poetry, which were what William really cared about, passed unnoticed.[19]

Even Stoddart's flattering review turned out to be less than honest. His privately expressed opinions were scathing: he could make 'neither head nor tale' of *Nutting* and 'nothing' of *Joanna. The Idiot Boy* threw him into 'a *fit* almost with disgust', he could not '*possibly* read it'. The only consolation was that his views were diametrically opposed by other friends, and William derived some amusement in drawing up a little table of the contradictory opinions for Coleridge. John and Christopher were unswerving in their support, however, loyally proselytizing on their brother's behalf in London and Cambridge respectively, and reporting back (possibly selectively) plenty of favourable comments.[20]

The best answer to all the criticism, friendly or otherwise, was the level of sales. By June, only 130 copies remained in stock and Longman invited William to prepare a further edition. This should have been a simple enough exercise. A large number of printing errors had escaped Davy's less than vigilant eye. Some of them were horrendous: fifteen crucial lines describing Luke's childhood had been omitted from *Michael* and one ludicrous misprint made the sheep 'Panting beneath the burden of their wool' 'unborn' instead of 'unshorn'. No reissuing of his work was ever an easy task to William. He was constitutionally incapable of merely correcting errors; his perfectionism compelled him to re-examine every line of every poem, adding, deleting, relentlessly revising, until he made himself ill and drove his loved ones to distraction with what came to be known in the family as his 'tinkering'. It would be almost a year before he was well enough satisfied to submit his emended copy to the printers, but, for William, the process of revision would end only with life itself.[21]

In the circumstances, it was not surprising that, after a period of such intense creativity, lasting throughout 1800, the following year was poetically unproductive. The presence of the Coleridges at Keswick and the Lloyds at Ambleside added considerably to the Wordsworths' social circle. Despite Dorothy's initial doubts about being so close to the unpredictable Charles Lloyd, they were soon on friendly visiting terms, calling on each other several times a week. Towards the end of October, they had a reason for increased intimacy. Charles's sister, Priscilla, came to stay with the newlyweds for the winter. This was the first time William and Dorothy had had the chance to meet and get to know their brother's fiancée. What they thought of her is not recorded, but John, who met her a few months later in London, had strong reservations. 'I think I am sorry for this connection [with] Miss L.', he told Dorothy privately. Though he thought Priscilla a 'fine looking woman . . . upon the whole there was *that something* in her countenance that I could not bear to like'. Lloyd was equally unimpressed by a closer acquaintance with the Wordsworths: 'they are very unusual characters', he observed, 'indeed Miss Wordsworth I much like. but her Brother is not a man after my own heart. I always feel myself depressed in his society.'[22]

On 14 November 1800 two letters arrived from Coleridge, informing them that he was very ill. William responded immediately to what was obviously a personal summons, setting off on foot for Keswick the next day, as soon as the driving rain had cleared. By the time Dorothy arrived two days later, Coleridge was better, but it was a sign of things to come. At the end of the month he came to Town End, retiring to bed early with a great crop of boils on his neck. In the early hours, he had a screaming, opium-induced nightmare in which a woman 'whose features were blended with darkness' tried to pull out his right eye and he caught hold of her arm; William called out three times to him before he woke – and then Coleridge thought it cruel that his friend had not come to his bedside. He returned at Christmas, preceded by his wife and children, and, having been soaked through during his walk, again took to his bed, this time with a rheumatic fever. He remained there until the New Year, waited on hand and foot by his friends, and forcing Dorothy to abandon her daily journal. When he was eventually carried home in a chaise, he retired once more to his bed, this time with a swollen testicle which, astonishingly, responded to the application of three leeches and a home-made poultice of grated bread mixed up with a strong solution of lead.[23]

The nightmares, with their pursuing females, the increased opium consumption which accompanied (and caused) his illnesses and the swollen testicle were all symptoms of an acute underlying malaise. Coleridge was deeply unhappy. He owed money on all sides (including £20, soon to rise to £50, to William), he could not fulfil any of his literary engagements, even though he had received substantial advances for many of them and he was becoming increasingly disenchanted with his wife. When another bout of illness brought the Wordsworths scurrying over to Keswick again in April, Dorothy could no longer conceal her partisan dislike. Sarah Coleridge was entirely to blame: she was a bad nurse to her suffering husband and, worse still, enjoyed rude good health herself. She employed her time 'foolishly' with her children instead of tending Coleridge himself, and was such a 'sad fiddle faddler' that she spent three and a half hours on a Sunday morning just washing and dressing herself and her children. With spinsterish venom, Dorothy could not suppress the comment that, 'No doubt she suckled Derwent pretty often during that time.' Conveniently sweeping aside the happy early years of the Coleridge marriage, Dorothy put on the black cap and piously pronounced her verdict: 'She would have made a very good wife to many another man, but for Coleridge!! Her radical fault is want of sensibility and what can such a woman be to Coleridge?'[24] Dorothy, of course, was renowned for her sensibility.

But it was not Dorothy who was the object of Coleridge's increasing infatuation. It was Sara Hutchinson, who had inauspiciously begun her winter visit to the Wordsworths, by spending the first week with them at Greta Hall. At this stage, of course, no one, possibly not even Coleridge himself, knew that she was about to become the object of his monomania. Her presence, however, exacerbated the situation. While Mrs Coleridge fretted and nagged her husband about money, work and his hugely expensive opium habit, and had the temerity to put her children's needs before those of her spouse, the Wordsworths and Sara listened sympathetically, took his side and encouraged, rather than condemned, him. Believing Coleridge's own story, that his inability to write and his addiction were merely the result of his unhappiness in his domestic situation and his financial difficulties, they thought that these problems could be overcome by effort of will. William lent Coleridge a further £30 he could ill afford, in the hope that this would ease his mind. More importantly, he advised, or rather fervently entreated, Coleridge to abandon his distracting and futile studies of German metaphysics and urged him to apply himself to completing and publishing *Christabel.* 'The Poet is dead in me', Coleridge wailed to Godwin. '– my imagination (or rather the Somewhat that had been imaginative) lies, like a Cold Snuff on the circular Rim of a Brass Candle-stick, without even a stink of Tallow to remind you that it was once cloathed & mitred with Flame.' Ominously, Coleridge was already beginning to associate his own writer's block with a sense of his inferiority to William. Inquiring whether Godwin had yet read *Lyrical Ballads* (and generous as ever in his praise of William's poems) led him to the bitter conclusion which would become his constant refrain. 'If I die, and the Booksellers will give you any thing for my Life,' he added, 'be sure to say – "Wordsworth descended on him, like the Γνωθι σεαυτον [Know thyself] from Heaven; by shewing to him what true Poetry was, he made him know, that he himself was no Poet."'[25]

With William metaphorically standing over him, Coleridge wrote to Longman, asking whether he would publish *Christabel*, which he now claimed, with more optimism than accuracy, would be subtitled '*A Legend, in five Books*'. He intended to annex two essays, one on the preternatural and one on metre, and had also had the bright idea of commissioning an artist to draw scenes and places mentioned in the poem as head and tail pieces, all taken 'from the wildest & most romantic parts of this County'.[26]

Equally self-deluding were Coleridge's assertions that the Wordsworths might accompany him to America, where he believed he would find earning a living easier, or to the Azores, where the climate might restore his health. Much as they cared for him, they had no intention of uprooting themselves from the Lakes. They had even refused a tempting offer to relocate to Keswick. William Calvert had retired from the militia and was in the process of rebuilding his house at Windy Brow. In the New Year of 1801, while the Wordsworths were visiting Coleridge, Calvert had suggested that they should come and live with him again. According to Coleridge, William was 'strongly inclined to adopt the scheme', partly because they had lived with Calvert on the same footing before and were much attached to him, and partly because it would make them close neighbours of Coleridge himself. If the Wordsworths accepted his offer, Calvert, a 'man of sense, and some originality' as well as a good practical mechanic, would build a laboratory at Windy Brow. Though it conjures up a rather odd image, Coleridge was ecstatic at the idea of studying chemistry, together with William and Calvert, in their own little laboratory. A thorough knowledge of science had always been a vital part of Coleridge's plan for *The Recluse*, but William had never paid much more than lip-service to the idea. A few months earlier, he had acquired two microscopes and two copies of William Withering's *An Arrangement of British Plants . . . and an Introduction to the Study of Botany*, through Longman, for himself and Coleridge, but the prospect of studying chemistry in any depth had little appeal; it would be a distraction from his poetry. The Wordsworths made up their minds not to accept Calvert's kind offer. By way of a compensatory gesture, William sent him a copy of *Lyrical Ballads*, with a short but heartfelt note: 'I know that you do not set a very high value on the labours of the Muses; I cannot, however, refuse myself the pleasure of requesting your acceptance of these Volumes, which I offer to you from the sincere affection which I bear you, & from grateful remembrance of your Brother'.[27]

From Keswick, the Wordsworths, accompanied probably by Sara Hutchinson, made their way over to Eusemere in January 1801, where they spent more than three weeks visiting the Clarksons. They made a very favourable impression on their kindly hosts, even though Catherine Clarkson stood somewhat in awe of William, who read her some of his *Lyrical Ballads* in manuscript and told her of his plans for *The Recluse*. 'I am fully convinced that Wordsworths Genius is equal to the Production of something very great, & I have no doubt but he will produce "*something that Posterity will not willingly let die*", if he lives ten or twenty years longer.' The Clarksons also introduced William to a fellow Quaker and campaigner against the slave trade, Thomas Wilkinson, who lived at Yanwath, a little village in a loop of the River Eamont just outside Penrith. The two men had much in common: they were both poets and shared an enthusiasm for landscape gardening. Wilkinson found William 'very sober and very amiable' and the two became fast friends.[28] There were also meetings with Joseph Wordsworth, son of William's cousin Richard of Branthwaite, who came bearing a gift of bamboo fishing rods from John to his erstwhile angling companion, the Reverend Joseph Sympson; and with Joanna Hutchinson at Penrith, who was delighted to see the Wordsworths again. 'They are very nice folks – I love them dearly – ', she enthused to her cousin. 'I don't admire Mr Coleridge half so much as William Wordsworth – Sara thought I would have liked him better he is not half so canny a man, Dorothy is a sweet woman – is not handsome but has a[n] uncom[mon] good countenance – and is very lively.'[29]

Before they left the Clarksons, a letter arrived from their brother John, asking William to lend him the money he had invested in the funds. On 7 January 1801 he had been sworn as captain of the *Earl of Abergavenny*: 'the Ship is a very *noble ship* & I have every prospect of doing well & of being comfortable', he wrote proudly to Mary Hutchinson, 'indeed I do not know a man so lucky as myself'. It was more than just luck, or even family influence (though that played a part), since many of the shareholders in the ship were from Penrith. The East India Company could not afford to risk its astronomic investments in one of its merchant ships by placing it in unsafe hands. For a young man who had only just had his twenty-eighth birthday, it was an awesome responsibility, though John took it in his stride. His brother Christopher, who was in town as part of a Cambridge University delegation sent to congratulate the King on the passing of the Act of Union, bringing Ireland into the United Kingdom, was equally delighted. It was, he declared, 'a grand thing for him – effected without the expence of a farthing. If he is not unlucky, he may realize a handsome fortune out of the four voyages which the Ship has yet to run.'[30] But that was the crux of the matter, for the fortune to be gained was not from earning a captain's salary, but from private investment in trade. Having next to nothing of his own, John was compelled to raise money by whatever means he could. His family rallied round. Dorothy lent the £80 remaining from her Crackanthorpe legacy; William lent £277 10s of his meagre capital. In return, John arranged that Dorothy should be paid an annual allowance of £20 directly from his salary through East India House and gave William a legally executable bond and interest. By the time he sailed from Portsmouth, on 19 May, he had almost £10,000 personally invested in the voyage to China.[31]

Towards the end of March, Christopher Wordsworth paid his first visit to his brother and sister at Grasmere. His motives were not entirely dictated by fraternal affection. As William drily observed to Calvert, 'he lodges at Ambleside being violently in love with Mr Lloyd's Sister, so of course we see so little of him, that it will not be worth your while to come over to Grasmere on his account'.[32] His arrival coincided with the departure of Sara Hutchinson, who had been summoned to County Durham, where her youngest brother, George, at the age of twenty-three, had just taken his first farm and needed a housekeeper. He arrived at Town End at the end of March to escort Sara back to his vast but semi-ruined house, Middleham Hall, at Bishop Middleham, a pretty village which was little more than a few ancient houses clustered round a tiny hilltop church. Conveniently, it lay some ten miles north-west of Stockton-on-Tees, so his oldest brother, Jack, could keep a watchful eye on his proceedings. Within three months they would be joined by their sister Betsy, whose mental instability had apparently made her continued residence in Penrith impossible. Betsy could not go on her own, so Joanna was reluctantly and tearfully compelled to accompany her. It would not be long before Betsy would have to be consigned to the care of a nurse, but Joanna would never return to live in her beloved Penrith again.[33]

Throughout the spring, William had been working hard on his revisions for *Lyrical Ballads* and slowly adding lines towards *The Recluse*. He wrote only one new poem, unexpectedly reverting to the *Lucy* series and producing the delightful 'I travell'd among unknown men', which William himself transcribed immediately for Mary Hutchinson. 'How we long to see you my dear Mary', he wrote. 'God for ever bless thee, my dear Mary – Adieu'. Dorothy was more wistful. 'I wish from my heart that William and I could be with you'. The new poem had done William good. His health had improved: 'he is always very ill when he tries to alter an old poem – but new composition does not hurt him so much. I hope he will soon be able to work without hurting himself.' If that was an implicit wish that William would resume *The Recluse*, Dorothy was to be disappointed. His 'tinkering' with old poems accelerated to such a pitch, with such dire consequences for his health, that Dorothy eventually persuaded him to put aside all his manuscript poems: 'it is agreed between us that I am not to give them up to him even if he asks for them', she told Coleridge.[34]

If William's health was a cause for concern this summer, Coleridge's was a cause for great alarm. He had spent nearly half the previous ten months confined to bed, unable to write and, consequently, unable to earn. William could not rid himself of the guilty feeling that he was partially responsible: Coleridge had put himself to great expense in removing to the Lakes to be near him and it was the climate (so Coleridge claimed) which was responsible for his rheumatics and gout. The Wordsworths were deeply worried: even if the repeated bouts of illness did not kill Coleridge, as he feared, they must seriously undermine his constitution. There was nothing for it but to submit to his judgement that he needed to go abroad for at least six months to restore his health. Accepting this as fact, William did his utmost to facilitate his friend's wish. He applied to John for information as to the best, most salubrious and cheapest places abroad. When John suggested San Miguel in the Azores, William took it upon himself to write to Poole, the only one of Coleridge's intimate circle who could afford, and might be prepared, to fund such an expensive trip. Setting out the case as logically as he could, he took Poole into his confidence and made a straightforward appeal to his generosity. 'In short: I see it will be utterly out of his power to take this voyage and pass some time there without he can procure a sum amounting at the *lowest* to 50£. Further, it seems to me absolutely necessary that this sum should be procured in a manner the least burthensome to his feelings possible.' Coleridge had proposed his usual solution: selling a proposal to a publisher for an advance, with the additional (now unfortunately necessary) security of offering his friends as his guarantors. It was a plan William could not approve, knowing full well that 'ten to one' Coleridge would not be able to fulfil his engagement and, worse still, the obligation to do so would prevent him doing anything more useful. Instead, William placed Coleridge at Poole's mercy: 'My dear Poole you will do what you think proper on this statement of facts'.[35]

Poor Poole had had his fingers burned once too often where Coleridge was concerned. He did not reply to William but wrote to Coleridge himself, informing him that he had learned that Tom Wedgwood intended to spend the winter in Sicily for his health and had already suggested that Coleridge would be his ideal companion. If nothing came of this, he was prepared to lend £20, and he was sure other friends would do the same. And like Mrs Coleridge and the Wordsworths, he urged him to pull himself together. 'It seems to me impossible to imagine that you would not be well, if you could have a mind freely at ease', he wrote. 'Make yourself that mind. Take from it – its two weak parts – its tendency to restlessness and its tendency to torpor, and it would make you great and happy.'[36] He was wasting his ink. Coleridge had already flitted the nest, drawn inexorably by his almost pathological desire for self-destruction.

Even as Poole wrote, Coleridge was snugly settled at Bishop Middleham with George Hutchinson, 'a young farmer . . . [who] . . . makes very droll verses in the northern dialect & in the metre of Burns, & is a great Humourist', and, of course, Sara, 'so very good a woman, that I have seldom indeed seen the like of her'. Joanna, who was also there, did not merit a mention. His unconvincing excuse was that he wanted to consult the works of Duns Scotus, the medieval philosopher, which were to be found in the library of Durham Cathedral. There was only one there.[37] Nevertheless, he managed to extend his stay for over a fortnight, then fortuitously acquired a swollen knee which required horse-exercise and sea-bathing. There was nothing for it but to pay a visit to Tom Hutchinson at Gallow Hill, where he could avail himself of the sea-bathing and 'frolick in the Billows' at Scarborough. Sara, naturally, accompanied him. It was 9 August before he tore himself away from Gallow Hill, and even then it was only to return to Bishop Middleham, where he lingered a few days longer. By the time he arrived in Keswick, the damage had been done. His interest in Sara had turned to obsession and the first of many fantasizings about her and cryptic groupings of the Wordsworth circle initials, all excluding his own, would appear in his private journal.[38]

At the beginning of September, William set off on an expedition of his own. It was prompted by Basil Montagu, who at last seemed set fair on the road to success. He had returned to the bar, where he was a rising man in his profession, had paid off some £50 of the debt he owed to William within the last year, and was now about to marry the eighteen-year-old daughter of a wealthy Suffolk landowner, Sir William Rush. The marriage was to take place in Glasgow on 6 September and the wedding party, which William was invited to join, passed through the Lakes on their way to Scotland.[39]

It was not the sort of tour William liked to make, cooped up in carriages with Montagu, the Rushes and their six children, but it was an opportunity not to be missed. They probably took the direct route to Glasgow, through Carlisle, over the border at Longtown, up Annandale and Clydesdale to the city itself. After the wedding ceremony, the whole party explored the area round Glasgow. They visited the Duke of Hamilton's picture gallery at Hamilton, just to the south of the city, and travelled north to Loch Lomond, whose spectacular setting, amidst wooded shores and craggy mountains, comes as such a shock when one suddenly emerges from the sprawling urban dereliction of Glasgow and Clydesbank. Thereafter, their route remains a mystery, but it is likely to have been eastward, through the Trossachs, to Edinburgh, for by the middle of September they were in Northumberland, where they met Wedgwood's sister-in-law and her husband, Sir James Mackintosh, the formerly pro-revolutionary author of *Vindiciae Gallicae*, and, briefly, James Losh.[40]

When William returned to Town End in the last week of September, the first person to arrive on his doorstep was Coleridge. He had already decided in his own mind that he had to separate from his wife: 'we are not suited to each other'. He would leave her and his children at Keswick, and take himself off to London or Somerset, once he had borrowed enough money from his long-suffering friends to finance his plan. In the circumstances, it was appropriate that, before he returned to Keswick, he helped the Wordsworths finish what they called Sara's seat on White Moss Common. Sara herself had chosen the site and laid the first stone on 26 March; now it was completed as a memorial to her.[41]

On 16 October Sara's brother Tom Hutchinson arrived on a long-promised visit after the harvest at Gallow Hill. It was a much-needed distraction from Coleridge's woes, which had made Dorothy so sick and ill with worry that she too had resorted to laudanum. Tom was always a genial companion, cheerful and sociable. He enjoyed walking too, so they took him on a short circular tour, into Langdale, down the length of Windermere to Penny Bridge, where they spent the night, returning via Coniston to Grasmere. An enthusiastic admirer of William's poems, he did the now obligatory trip to the sheepfold up Greenhead Ghyll and even, one bright sunny day, climbed with the Wordsworths up Helvellyn. A week after his arrival, Mary Hutchinson came to Keswick and took up residence at Greta Hall. Quite what Mrs Coleridge thought about another of the Hutchinsons making free with her house we do not know. Mary was never an abrasive presence, but she was Sara's sister, and she did stay for more than two weeks, leaving only after Coleridge himself had departed.[42]

Coleridge spent his last few days in the Lakes not with his wife and children, but with the Wordsworths at Grasmere. Dorothy's journal is silent on what passed between them, but only because some officious censor has removed the relevant page, leaving just the words 'left us' still visible on the stub. The whole page was still there in 1850–51, when it was seen by William's nephew, Christopher Wordsworth, who published anodyne extracts in his *Memoirs of William Wordsworth*. One can only suspect the handiwork of Gordon Wordsworth, who, unlike his Uncle Christopher, destroyed primary evidence instead of merely editing it for publication.[43] This in turn leads one to suspect that the reason why the page was torn out is that it contained information the Wordsworth family wished to suppress. In which case, one can only presume it included the revelation of Coleridge's love for Sara. Why else select this particular page for destruction? Dorothy's extravagant grief after Coleridge's departure also becomes more explicable if she had only just learned of his infatuation.

On 9 November the three of them walked to Keswick. 'We enjoyed ourselves in the study & were *at home*', Dorothy recorded in her journal, while failing to point out that this was only possible because Mrs Coleridge and her children had already left for the Clarksons' at Eusemere. There was a joyful reunion with Mary, subdued only by the knowledge of Coleridge's impending departure the next morning. 'Poor C left us & we came home together', Dorothy noted on 10 November.

> we left Keswick at 2 o'clock & did not arrive at G[rasmere] till 9 o clock – drank tea at John Stanleys very comfortably I burnt myself with Coleridge's Aquefortes. Mary's feet sore. C had a sweet day for his ride – every sight & every sound reminded me of him dear dear fellow – of his many walks to us by day & by night – of all dear things – I was melancholy & could not talk, but at last I eased my heart by weeping – nervous blubbering says William – It is not so – O how many, many reasons have I to be anxious for him –[44]

The parting was not to be permanent. Coleridge hoped that a winter in the south would restore his health sufficiently to enable him to return to Keswick. By

15 November he was in London, where he described himself as like a fish panting and dying from excess of oxygen. 'A great change from the society of W. & his sister – for tho' we were three persons, it was but one God – – whereas here I have the amazed feelings of a new Polytheist, meeting Lords many, & Gods many'. Ten days' intended residence stretched to six weeks, but after a brief visit to Poole at Nether Stowey he returned to London on 21 January 1802 and took up residence in the bustle of Covent Garden.[45]

Life at Town End resumed its quiet outward tenor after Coleridge's departure, but significant developments were taking place. William had decided to ask Mary to marry him. There was no great fanfare or announcement; we do not even know when he proposed and was accepted. One can only pick up the nuances of Dorothy's journal which suggest that it happened on 12 November. On that Thursday, Dorothy lingered behind on their evening walk and returned to find William and Mary together at tea. The next day, they all three 'spent a happy evening' and went to bed late. Dorothy had a restless night and on Saturday 'lay in bed all the Day very unwell', which sounds like one of her typical nervous reactions. The following Monday, the servant, Molly Fisher, was 'very witty with Mary all day She says "Ye may say what ye will But there's no thing like a gay auld man for behaving weel to a young wife!"'[46] William was, in fact, exactly the same age as Mary, though he looked older than his years. At thirty-one, neither of them needed to seek family approval or permission to marry. Nevertheless, a few days later Mary wrote to her aunt, which suggests some sort of announcement; more importantly, William wrote to Richard, asking him to draw up an account of all the money he and Dorothy had received through his hands for the past two years. And crucially, on 21 December, a letter arrived from France which can only have been from Annette.[47] Viewed individually, these events seem insignificant, but as a body of evidence they point to the making of a formal engagement.

With marriage and future income in mind, William tried to kickstart himself back into a poetic routine. He had written nothing new for months other than a rather limp pastoral, *Repentance*, inspired by the complaints of their neighbour, Peggy Ashburner, whose statesman husband had sold their lands, leaving them with the unhappy thought, 'We've no land in the vale, Save six feet of earth where our forefathers lie!' This was surprising, for since the announcement of the truce with France in October, which would lead to the Peace of Amiens, there had been an influx of beggars and vagrants into the Vale. Many, if not most of them, were disbanded soldiers and sailors, returning to their native villages in varying degrees of poverty and disability. They all had a pitiful tale to tell and Dorothy recorded them faithfully in her journal for future use. For the moment, however, William occupied himself mentally, if not emotionally, in translating Chaucer into modern verse. It was a fairly futile task, but it fulfilled its purpose. Towards the end of December, he returned to the poem on his own life, which he had now decided to expand to include his Cambridge education.[48]

Heavy snow, followed by a rapid thaw made the roads impassable, so an invitation to spend Christmas and the New Year with the Clarksons at Eusemere had to be deferred. They were also short of money, having lent Coleridge £10 which he had not repaid. In the end, they could not afford to pay for places in the coach and had to walk the long way round, over Dunmail Raise to Keswick, then along the River Greta to Pooley Bridge. William occupied the first part of the journey composing his poem, becoming so absorbed that he left his Spenser at one resting place and his gloves at another.[49] At Keswick they had the good fortune to meet Joshua Wilkinson, the Cockermouth man who had shared Richard's chambers in London. He invited William to dine with him at the Royal Oak and they fell into conversation with a young man who was the heir to a marquisate. To the Wordsworths' evident pride, he not only knew all about *Lyrical Ballads*, but had even seen the Queen present a copy to Mrs Harcourt.[50] The next day, cutting over the fells lining the northern shores of Ullswater, in driving wind and hail showers, Mary fell several times and Dorothy was sometimes forced to crawl, literally on hands and knees. With the help of a few kind souls who redirected their path, they eventually arrived safe and sound to a hearty welcome at Eusemere.

On New Year's Eve, Mary went to Penrith to stay with her aunt, returning to spend a few days at Eusemere before the Wordsworths left on 23 January, then departing for Bishop Middleham.[51] William and Dorothy, with singular bravado, decided to risk going over the tops to Grasmere; Thomas Clarkson lent them horses as far as Grisedale, then they walked the rest of way, in conditions which would have appalled the Mountain Rescue Services. Grisedale Tarn was frozen solid, the ice cracked and split but waterless; they lost their way in the mists and snow and, by the time they reached Town End, it was dark.

It was a foolhardy and unnecessary escapade, and all their neighbours rightly censured them for it, but it prompted two poems, *To a Young Lady Who Had Been Reproached for Taking Long Walks in the Country* and *Louisa After Accompanying Her on a Mountain Excursion.*[52] Much ink has been wasted on trying to prove whether Dorothy, Mary or even Joanna was the subject of the poems. The image in the former poem of the 'Dear Child of Nature' become a 'Wife and Friend', with children round her knee, and subsiding into 'an old age serene and bright, And lovely as a Lapland night' seems more appropriate to Mary, but both poems are very much in the *Lucy* genre and are probably composite portraits. *To a Young Lady* would be published anonymously in the *Morning Post* on 12 February, the second of three of William's poems to appear that month, in repayment of a loan of £10 from Daniel Stuart, the editor.[53]

They were, in any case, unimportant poems as far as William was concerned, for, repeating a pattern of composition that had now become established, he had graduated from the poem on his own life to working on *The Recluse.* The section he was working on now, in the early months of 1802, was a development of the character of the Pedlar, the natural philosopher who would be the guide to the poem and link all the incidents and stories of rural life. In this he was considerably helped by a letter from Sara Hutchinson, containing her reminiscences of James

Patrick, the husband of her mother's cousin Margaret Robison. Sara had been sent to live with this couple after her mother's death, when she was eight years old. 'She went to School at Kendal – but the most important part of her education was gathered from the stores of that good man's mind.' Patrick, like his father-in-law, had begun life as a Scottish pedlar, before settling down in the hardware business at Kendal. 'My own imaginations I was happy to find clothed in reality & fresh ones suggested by what she reported of this man's tenderness of heart,' William wrote, 'his strong & pure imagination, & his solid attainments in literature chiefly religious whether in prose or verse.'[54]

William's preoccupation with his poem had all the usual results. When he wanted to break off composing, he could not do so, and 'did himself harm', as Dorothy darkly described it. A few days later, after a bad night and working away at his poem all day, 'We sate by the fire & did not walk, but read the Pedlar thinking it done but lo, though Wm could find fault with no one part of it – it was uninteresting. & must be altered – Poor William!' Driving himself on in this way, he was constantly tired and out of spirits. Like Dorothy, he suffered from bad headaches, minor bouts of illness and sleepless nights. These were not helped by 'heart-rending' letters from Coleridge, who, at the beginning of February, announced his decision to go abroad to the south of France for the sake of his health. What is more, displaying an incredible lack of sensitivity, he expected the Wordsworths (and Southeys) to accompany him. The news came as a considerable shock. 'I was stopped in my writing', Dorothy confided in her journal, '& made ill by the letters'. The very day Coleridge informed the Wordsworths of his plans, Southey repeated them to a friend as if everything had been settled and agreed between them. Always more robust in his opinions, Southey had no intention of going along with the scheme. 'I do not . . . wish that we should go abroad together. Our habits are not enough alike.'[55]

Clearly the matter needed to be discussed with Mary: how would she feel about emigrating to the country where William's former mistress and child were living? On 14 February William walked over to Penrith to see her, dressing up like a proper suitor in his blue jacket and 'a pair of <u>new</u> pantaloons fresh from London'. They had time only for the briefest of meetings, walking together for a couple of hours along the banks of the River Eden beyond Eamont Bridge. What Mary's answer was we cannot guess, but Coleridge, writing to his wife on 24 February, blithely informed her that the marriage would take place in March and that, in July, all three Wordsworths would set sail with him, and his family, from Liverpool. They would go to Bordeaux, in the south-west of France, and settle there, as 'companions, & neighbours', for a couple of years.[56]

Sarah Coleridge would have no say in the matter, but would William really have repeated the mistake of uprooting himself and his family to live in a foreign land, simply so that he could be near Coleridge? The Goslar experience surely militated against it. The scheme put all his loyalties, to Coleridge, to Mary, even to Annette and Caroline, in conflict. In the light of Coleridge's previous assumption that the Wordsworths would follow him anywhere he chose to go, it is tempting to dismiss the whole scheme as mere fantasy. On the other hand, Dorothy noted receiving a letter from 'the Frenchman in London' on 13 February and William writing to him on the 24th. Frustratingly, there is nothing to indicate who this Frenchman was, but, given the timing of the correspondence, it is likely that he was either connected with the emigration scheme or the bearer of letters from Annette.[57]

Whatever the Frenchman's role, or non-role, something had gone seriously awry with William's marriage plans. He would always look back to this period as one of acute misery. He was haunted by his longing to see Mary, 'when I am away from you I seem to have heart for nothing and no body else', and tortured by sleepless nights of sexual frustration.[58] Coleridge, as we have seen, expected the wedding to have taken place in March; in fact, it did not happen until October. What went wrong? It is pure supposition, but what little evidence there is suggests the possibility that Annette objected. It was only natural that she should do so. William's marriage to another woman ended any hope of his legitimizing her status, or that of their child. It also put her in a difficult position, since she had been passing herself off as William's wife and widow for almost ten years. Though they had kept up a correspondence throughout that time, which had been a momentous period in both their lives, their separation meant that they were effectively strangers to each other. Nevertheless, neither of them had married, and Annette was never to do so, which might indicate that she still carried a torch for William. Even if she did not, she cared passionately about her daughter's future, and that would be prejudiced by William's marriage and beginning a second, legitimate family. If nothing else, Annette would have wanted some sort of security for Caroline. That William did not ignore her letters altogether, or go ahead with his wedding when he had intended, suggests that he acknowledged the justice of her claims. It may even raise the possibility that he wanted Annette's approval of, or, at least, her consent to his marriage.

The indications we have that negotiations were taking place are few but significant. What had been an intermittent correspondence suddenly leapt to life, and thirteen letters are recorded passing between the Wordsworths and Annette between 21 December 1801 and 5 July 1802. The first was actually from Annette, though this does not preclude the possibility that it was a reply to one from William. Dorothy thought it important enough to notice in her journal, as she did the following letters, so it may have come out of the blue; in which case, it must have been a rude shock to William, who had just proposed to Mary. Recalling how Annette had enlisted Dorothy's sympathy and support on her behalf once before, it is interesting to see that her third letter, written only a week after her second, was a joint one, from mother and child, and it was addressed, not to William, but to his sister. After the receipt of a fourth letter from 'poor Annette', on 22 March, William and Dorothy had a serious discussion: 'we resolved to see Annette, & that Wm should go to Mary'.[59]

On 28 March they set off for Keswick to spend a few days at Greta Hall. Coleridge himself had returned to the Lakes only nine days before, shocking Dorothy by his 'half stupified' appearance. Though he had declared himself improved in health and prepared for a reconciliation with his long-suffering wife, it did not augur well that, when he left London, he headed straight for Gallow Hill, where all his good intentions evaporated. This was not a happy visit. Coleridge's passion for Sara was self-evident and the atmosphere was tense. Sara herself seems to have tried to put a distance between them: 'Sara Hutcheson's new gospel – alias – Honesty –', he wrote witheringly in his private journal, accusing her of making him 'feel uncomfortable'. 'You never sate with or near me ten minutes in your life without shewing a restlessness & a thought of *going*, &c – for at least 5 minutes out of the 10', he complained. He left Gallow Hill on 13 March, without Sara, though he had been expecting to escort her to Town End, where he arrived on the 19th and stayed till the 21st.[60]

At Keswick, the Wordsworths seem to have spent as much time with Calvert and his wife as with the Coleridges. Some sort of reconciliation had been patched up between husband and wife, for Sarah became pregnant about this time. It says little for Coleridge's loyalties that he was then employed in writing the first draft of his great poem *Dejection: An Ode*, which trumpeted his love for Sara Hutchinson, 'Thee, best belov'd! . . . O dear! O Innocent! O full of Love!', and his grief at having made her unwell and unhappy by his behaviour towards her. The poem was written in the form of a letter to Sara on 4 April, the day before William and Dorothy left Keswick.[61]

That night, despite being ill in bed, Coleridge 'continued talking with Wordsworth the whole night till the Dawn of the Day, urging him to conclude on marrying Mary Hutchinson'. Coleridge, it would seem, had fewer scruples about abandoning Annette than William, but he was unable to convince his friend.[62] The next day William set off for Eusemere, where he would leave Dorothy with the Clarksons, while he went on alone to Bishop Middleham, on a horse borrowed from Calvert, to tell Mary that, before he married her, he must have a personal meeting with Annette. Mary's reaction remains unknown, but one may guess it was not what the Wordsworths had hoped. William returned earlier than expected, on 13 April, retired early to bed and, when he finally rose at lunchtime the following day, his news made Dorothy 'ill – out of spirits – disheartened'. They returned to Town End, where it became Dorothy's first task to write a hearty admonition to Mary, who had, according to William, become very thin with anxiety: 'my dear Sister! be quiet and happy . . . do not make loving us your business, but let your love of us make up the spirit of all the business you have'. The correspondence with Annette continued.[63]

Extraordinary as it may seem, throughout all the uncertainties of this period, William was deeply engaged in one of his most prolific outbursts of poetry. As before, the poems were offshoots from his work on *The Recluse*. Between March and July, according to Coleridge's calculation, he wrote thirty-two poems, some of them of considerable length. Coleridge considered most of them were 'very excellent

Compositions', but the first seeds of doubt were beginning to gnaw at his mind. William had taken yet another step in his radical revision of what poetry should be, and Coleridge genuinely, or perhaps motivated partly by jealousy, could not follow him. There was, he complained,

> here & there a daring Humbleness of Language & Versification, and a strict adherence to matter of fact, even to prolixity, that startled me . . . and I have thought & thought again & have not had my doubts solved by Wordsworth On the contrary, I rather suspect that some where or other there is a radical Difference in our theoretical opinions respecting Poetry –[64]

Coleridge was uncomfortable with William's stubborn insistence on literalism of the kind displayed in one of his best poems written at this time, *Resolution and Independence.* The poet, meeting a leech-gatherer on a lonely moor, stops to inquire what he is doing and, while listening to the answer, drifts off into his own reveries and is obliged to ask the question and hear the answer again. Succinct and to the point the poem is not. But the repetition of question and answer reinforces the difference between the healthy young poet, preoccupied with imaginative fears for his own future, and the ancient, poverty-stricken leech-gatherer, 'carrying with him his own fortitude, and the necessities which an unjust state of society has entailed upon him'. Mary and Sara had the temerity to criticize the leech-gatherer's speech as 'tedious' (they were not alone in doing so), earning themselves a sharp reprimand: 'everything is tedious when one does not read with the feelings of the Author . . . It is in the character of the old man to tell his story in a manner which an *impatient* reader must necessarily feel as tedious. But Good God! Such a figure, in such a place, a pious self-respecting, miserably infirm . . . Old Man telling such a tale!' Warming to his theme in defence of *Resolution and Independence*, William went to the heart of what his object was in writing poetry.

> It is not a matter of indifference whether you are pleased with this figure and his employment; it may be comparatively so, whether you are pleased or not with *this Poem*; but it is of the utmost importance that you should have had pleasure from contemplating the fortitude, independence, persevering spirit, and the general moral dignity of this old man's character.[65]

William enlarged on this theme when responding to John Wilson, a young undergraduate at Glasgow University, who had written him a letter of enthusiastic praise, but criticized *The Idiot Boy.* Many people disliked the poem, William declared, many others preferred it above all the rest.

> This proves that the feelings there delineated [are] such as all men *may* sympathize with. This is enough for my purpose. [It] is not enough for me as a poet, to delineate merely such feelings as all men *do* sympathise with but, it is also highly desirable to add to these others, such as all men *may* sympathize with, and such as there is reason to believe they would be better and more moral beings if they did sympathize with.[66]

William's 'strict adherence to fact', which Coleridge had criticized, was very much an illusion. It was important to him that the characters he portrayed should seem real, and speak and act appropriately, but he was not therefore limited to what had actually happened. *Resolution and Independence* was again a perfect example of this. The Wordsworths had actually met the leech-gatherer who inspired this poem in September 1800, and learned his history from him. William's own feelings, and meditations on the sufferings of poets like Chatterton and Burns, which are central to the poem, do not relate to this meeting at all, but to another walk over Barton Fell, returning from Eusemere. Though correct for the scenario imagined in the poem, the supposed 'literalism' is a poetic device, not a truly literal account.[67]

It is an interesting illustration of the divide between fact and poetic fiction that the short poem William struggled most to write during this period was *The Beggars*. This was based on an unusually tall and striking woman who had begged at Town End while William and John were at Gallow Hill two years previously. Dorothy had given the woman money, then in a later walk encountered her sons, who tried to beg off her again, saying their mother was dead. As they bore a strong resemblance to her, Dorothy had known this was untrue and refused, so the children ran off. Since William could not recall the incident personally, she tried to help him by reading her journal account: 'an unlucky thing it was for he could not escape from those very words, & so he could not write the Poem he left it unfinished & went tired to Bed'.[68]

Though many of the poems William wrote in the spring and early summer of 1802 were about the beggars and itinerants who continually passed through the Vale of Grasmere, he also embarked on a whole new range of poetry, the short nature poems for which he is now best known. In a way, they were an extension of his earlier poetry: instead of celebrating the virtues of humble human life, he now chose to sing the praises of the lesser members of the animal and plant kingdoms. The robin, skylark, green linnet, cuckoo ('shall I call thee Bird, Or but a wandering voice?'), glowworm and butterfly each earned their own dedicatory poems. Withering's *Botany* was pressed into good service, with similar results for the daisy, barberry and, William's favourite, the small celandine:

Blithe of heart, from week to week
Thou dost play at hide-and-seek;
While the patient primrose sits
Like a beggar in the cold . . .[69]

What is self-evident in all these poems is the sheer delight which inspired them. Despite Coleridge's efforts to carry him off to France, his beloved vale was now his established home: in his second year of residence, the neat house and blooming garden could be enjoyed all the more since they were the creation of the Wordsworths' own hands. William was not yet a statesman, but he had made one corner of Grasmere his own.

For once, William's blithe optimism was justified. On 25 May, his cousin the retired Captain John Wordsworth, who was now living at Brougham Hall, just outside Penrith, sent a cryptic note to Richard. 'Lord Lonsdale is no more improve this Information if you can to your & your Family's Advantage.' Living close to Lowther Park, he had been quick off the mark with the news. 'Wicked Jimmy' had only died the day before, 'called to give an Account where his Knavery & his money will nothing avail him', as Uncle William put it, with evident satisfaction. The Earl had no sons, so his earldom and viscountcy of Lonsdale died with him. His heir was his forty-four-year-old cousin Sir William Lowther, whose reputation as an 'exceedingly just and honourable' man preceded him. The Wordsworths swung into action. William, in particular, was determined that their moral claim should be pursued, even if their legal claim had dragged on so long without active prosecution that it had fallen foul of the Statute of Limitations. He suggested that they should draw up a memorial stating their case and pointing out their sister's 'utter destitution' because of the affair. They could get some of Uncle William's, or even brother Christopher's, powerful friends to present it to Sir William. 'It can do no harm', he pointed out to Richard, 'and may do good.'[70]

On 18 June, as the Wordsworths were sitting after breakfast, one of their friends, Mr Luff, called in unexpectedly. He had ridden over the fells in haste from Patterdale to tell them that Sir William Lowther had placed advertisements in the local papers, stating his intention to pay all the Earl's just debts. Unbelievably, after almost twenty years, it seemed that the Lonsdale debt would be paid and the Wordsworths would come into their inheritance. Mr Luff brought with him a memorandum from Thomas Clarkson, drawn up in consultation with the Wordsworths' uncle, the Reverend Thomas Myers, and Dr Lowther, the rector of Lowther church, who knew that the debt was a just one and unpaid. It contained words of caution. 'It happens throughout Life, that People often lose their Object, by asking too much, when, had they ask'd in Moderation they might have obtained it'. The considered opinion of all three men was that the Wordsworths' claim was no longer recoverable by law, so they should only ask for payment of the principal and forget any demand for interest. The new Lord Lowther would have so many debts to pay that he could not afford to set the precedent of paying interest; as an added inducement to accepting this lesser amount, they were assured that an application for the principal only would be dealt with, and paid out, in a matter of weeks.[71]

Three days after receiving this opinion, William went over to Eusemere to consult his uncle, Clarkson and Dr Lowther in person. Their advice was straightforward: the Wordsworths should submit their claim immediately in writing to the new Lord Lowther's agent. With his marriage impending, William was more than prepared to settle for this, but he had reckoned without his brother Richard, whose whole life had been dedicated to recovering the debt. He was determined to demand interest. Fearing that the whole would be lost when part might be gained, William wrote anxiously to him. Had Richard considered that Lord Lowther would not pay interest unless forced to do so by law? What hope would the Wordsworths have of pursuing their claim against the new Lord Lowther and his immense fortune? Lowther himself might be a fair man, but what about his attorneys and advisers? 'In whatever manner you proceed in the business, let me earnestly exhort you to avoid every thing which may appear like a manifestation of a disposition to challenge Lord Lowther to try the affair in a court of justice', William advised his lawyer brother. 'Shun this as you would do the pestilence.'[72]

It was hardly surprising that Richard took offence. 'If I had the least doubt about the proper steps to be taken,' he informed his brother, 'I am sure I would instantly ask your advice . . . I fortunately have very favourable opportunities of procuring information on the subject.' Nevertheless, he sent the requisite letter to Mr Richardson, Lowther's agent, pointing out that he had personally delivered an account of the debt, amounting to £4,660 4s 10¾d, on 30 August 1786, and that the amount still remained due to his father's estate, plus interest and costs. He also wrote a justifiably indignant letter to William.

It is proper that one Person should take ye lead in the affair. If you can find any Person better qualified than myself I beg you will let me know. We must not have a number of meddlesome Persons concerned in it. I think I have seen enough of the world to have reapeatedly [*sic*] observed meddlesome interfering Persons though meaning well have often done immense mischief to their Friends . . . If we remain united we shall do well If your opinions & aim should be so much a[t] variance as to cause us to act not in concert our chance of success will be diminished if not destroyed . . . One would almost suppose from your Letter that you were apprehensive I was as it is vulgarly called wanting a Job. No believe me I have no such wish. You are now in possession of my Sentiments & I will be obliged to you [to] say wh[eth]er you approve or disapprove of my future Proceedings. For I have no desire to act in a Matter where my exertions are thought nothing of.[73]

Though William chafed at the delays, and huffed and puffed in righteous indignation at having his efforts and advice ignored, he had to bow to his brother's superior knowledge.

In the meantime, William had more immediate problems to overcome. On 9 July he and Dorothy left Town End for France and the prearranged meeting with Annette. Calais had been fixed as the rendezvous, not just because it was conveniently halfway between the Lakes and Blois, but also, one suspects, because no one knew any of them there. As a sort of reaffirmation of William's commitment to Mary, the Wordsworths travelled by Gallow Hill, even though it was an unnecessary detour which extended their journey by more than 100 miles. Coleridge was waiting for them at the Rock of Names, a wayside rock between Grasmere and Keswick on which Sara Hutchinson had carved her initials on her last visit. Since then Coleridge had returned several times to add further initials, which William had engraved more deeply. Now it bore those of not only Sara but William, Mary, John, Dorothy and Coleridge, a permanent reminder of the Grasmere power-house.[74]

This time, as always, however, Coleridge was to find himself an outsider. He escorted the Wordsworths to Keswick, but failed in his object of persuading them to give up Town End after William's marriage. He had hoped they might agree to settle in the other half of Greta Hall with him, but the Wordsworths were adamant, less from reasons of attachment to Grasmere, it has to be said, than from Dorothy's hostility to Mrs Coleridge. On 12 July, he accompanied them six or seven miles along their road, then, after sitting silently by the roadside together, they had a melancholy parting. It seems almost symbolic that Coleridge was left behind, alone and disconsolate, while William and Dorothy marched gaily and confidently forward towards Eusemere, Gallow Hill and, ultimately, a new life together with Mary.[75]

Having spent the night at the Clarksons, the Wordsworths caught the coach at Eamont Bridge and travelled as far as Thirsk in comfort. Then, much to the disgust of the landlady of the inn where they had spent the night, they left their baggage and walked the rest of the way, pausing only to admire the gracefully crumbling ruins of the Cistercian abbey at Rievaulx. At Gallow Hill, they had a fleeting reunion with Mary, Sara and Tom, then left for London, travelling through Beverley and Hull, 'a frightful, Dirty, *brick housey* tradesmanlike, rich, vulgar place –'. Their stay in London was equally brief. On 31 July they were off again, crossing Westminster Bridge very early in the morning, before the city was awake, and taking the coach to Dover. At four o'clock in the morning on Sunday 1 August they arrived at Calais. They stayed on board the packet till half past seven, then William went ashore for the letters that would inform him where Annette and Caroline were staying. His feelings can only be imagined as he set out in search of his former lover and the daughter he had never seen. Dorothy's journal, which had been prolix to the point of tedium, falls silent just when we really want to know details. What did William and Annette make of each other after a separation of almost ten years? Had they changed beyond all recognition, or were they still recognizably the lovers of 1792? And Caroline, what was she like, this living, breathing progeny of that ill-fated union? How did she feel towards this stranger, the father who had abandoned her before she was born, and was only come to see her now because he was about to marry a woman other than her mother?

From Dorothy all we learn are the barest of bald facts, written in retrospect, after her return to England. The momentous meeting took place between eight-thirty and nine o'clock in the morning on 1 August at Annette and Caroline's lodgings in the Rue de la Tête d'Or. The two odd couples walked together 'almost every evening' and William bathed often. Caroline was 'delighted' watching the boats sail out at sunset. The Wordsworths left Calais on 29 August, landing at Dover the following day, and Dorothy was sick all the way. And that is that. Had it not been for William's lovely sonnet, composed on one of the evening walks with Annette and Caroline along Calais beach, we would know nothing at all about his feelings.

It is a beautous evening, calm and free,
The holy time is quiet as a Nun
Breathless with adoration; the broad sun
Is sinking down in its tranquillity;
The gentleness of heaven broods o'er the Sea:
Listen! the mighty Being is awake,
And doth with his eternal motion make
A sound like thunder – everlastingly.
Dear Child! dear Girl! that walkest with me here,
If thou appear untouched by solemn thought,
Thy nature is not therefore less divine:
Thou liest in Abraham's bosom all the year;
And worshipp'st at the Temple's inner shrine,
God being with thee when we know it not.[76]

From this we can conclude that William's daughter was not the child of nature he had perhaps hoped to find. Caroline was no Lucy. Affectionate though the tribute is, it does not thrill with the recognition of a kindred spirit. They had met as strangers and they parted a month later, apparently without any burning desire to meet again. There is less passion in this poem, addressed to his daughter, than in another William wrote at the same time to the Evening Star, visible across the Channel, shining on England.

Blessing be on you both! one hope, one lot,
One life, one glory! – I, with many a fear
For my dear Country, many heartfelt sighs,
Among men who do not love her, linger here.[77]

Having done his duty, William returned to England with evident relief. Even Christopher, not noted for his sensibilities in such matters, noticed that his brother and sister 'seemed very glad to get home again' when he met them in London. Together, they paid a visit of a couple of days to Windsor, the first by William and Dorothy to the Cooksons for many a year. As far as Uncle William was concerned, he was quite prepared to let bygones be bygones: he had been interested in his nephew's poetic success and he could not but admire the determination with which he had pursued his chosen career. So this meeting, too, was a reconciliation of sorts, though it is unlikely to have happened had news not greeted the Wordsworths, on reaching London, that John had also arrived back in England. The *Earl of Abergavenny* was off the South Downs and they could not leave without seeing him. So they waited for him, spending the interval in visiting the Cooksons in their canon's lodgings at Windsor and seeing the sights of London, including the hurly-burly of Bartholomew Fair, in the company of Charles Lamb.[78]

On the evening of 11 September William and Dorothy returned to London from

Windsor and, as they crossed Temple Court, met Richard and John, pacing back and forth in the moonlight. They had much news to exchange, the good about the Lonsdale suit counterbalancing the bad about John's voyage, which had not been as successful as he had hoped. No doubt Richard had already informed John of their brother's forthcoming marriage, but when Dorothy put Mary's own letter into his hand the next day, John's usual self-control broke down. Overpowered by his emotions, he wrote her a brief but poignant farewell, to which he added the pragmatic gift of a new silk gown for Mary. It was the only wedding present the couple were to receive.[79]

For eleven days, the Wordsworths lingered in London, loath to part so soon from John after such a long separation. But Mary had waited long enough. On 24 September William and Dorothy returned to Gallow Hill. 'Never shall I forget thy rich & flourishing and genial mien & appearance', William later wrote of the moment when Mary appeared at the end of the lane to welcome him. 'Nature had dressed thee out as if expressly that I might receive thee to my arms in the full blow of health and happiness.' The whole Hutchinson clan gathered in force. Sara, Joanna and Tom, were already there; Jack and George arrived a few days later. Only Henry was absent, being now back at sea. Dorothy had to steel her nerves for the coming occasion. Ever since the engagement, she had been more than usually possessive about William, talking of him as if she, not Mary, were his lover. From plain 'William' or 'my dear Brother', he had been transformed into 'My Beloved'. When he was away for a couple of days at Keswick in March, she had confided in her journal, 'I *will* be busy. I *will* look well & be well when he comes back to me. O the Darling! here is one of his bitten apples –! I can hardly find in my heart to throw it into the fire.' 'I have long loved Mary Hutchinson as a Sister,' she now wrote to her erstwhile schoolfriend Jane, on the eve of her brother's wedding, 'and she is equally attached to me this being so, you will guess that I look forward with perfect happiness to this Connection between us, but, happy as I am, I half dread that concentration of all tender feelings, past, present, and future which will come upon me on the wedding morning.'[80]

She was probably not the only one dreading an outburst of emotion, though the preparations for the wedding went smoothly enough. William and Tom jointly signed a bond backing up William's affidavit that there were no impediments to the marriage, so that a licence could be obtained.[81] The wedding would be as quiet as possible. Wisely, it was decided that Dorothy should not attend, on the pretext that she, and Sara, should be responsible for the wedding breakfast. The night before the wedding, William brought the ring to Dorothy for safekeeping, and she slept with it on her forefinger all night. Early next morning, he came upstairs to collect it and say goodbye. In an oddly repellent gesture, which was clearly meant to be an endorsement of his continuing love for his sister, William slipped the ring back on her finger and blessed her 'fervently'. Just after eight o'clock, the little wedding party set off on foot from Gallow Hill to walk the mile over the fields to Brompton-by-Sawdon. There, on 4 October 1802, in the pretty twelfth-century church of All Saints, William and Mary were married by the Reverend John Ellis; the only witnesses to the ceremony were Tom, Joanna and Jack Hutchinson. Back at Gallow Hill, Sara had been left to prepare the wedding breakfast alone. 'I kept myself as quiet as I could,' Dorothy confided in her journal,

> but when I saw the two men running up the walk, coming to tell us it was over, I could stand it no longer & threw myself on the bed where I lay in stillness, neither hearing or seeing any thing, till Sara came upstairs to me & said 'they are coming.' This forced me from the bed where I lay & I moved I knew not how straight forward, faster than my strength could carry me till I met my beloved William & fell upon his bosom. He & John Hutchinson led me to the house & there I stayed to welcome my dear Mary.[82]

It was characteristic of both women that Dorothy managed to upstage Mary on her wedding day and that Mary bore it with perfect equanimity.

11. *The Set is Broken*

There was no honeymoon. The newlyweds could not afford one. Instead, accompanied by Dorothy, they made a leisurely journey by post chaise to Grasmere, revisiting some of their favourite places, including the ruins of Helmsley Castle and Rievaulx Abbey, and the waterfalls in Wensleydale. They arrived at Town End at six o'clock in the evening on Wednesday 6 October. 'Molly was overjoyed to see us,' Dorothy wrote in her journal, '– for my part I cannot describe what I felt, & our dear Mary's feelings would I dare say not be easy to speak of.' They explored the garden by candlelight and were astonished to find how much everything had grown in their absence. Next day, the two women unpacked the boxes, and, on Friday, having baked bread together, they performed another ritual in Mary's initiation to married life at Grasmere. 'Mary & I walked, first upon the Hill side, & then in John's Grove, then in view of Rydale, the first walk that I had taken with my Sister.' There were two more formalities to be observed: on 13 October Dorothy wrote to Annette, presumably to inform her that the wedding had taken place, and, more pleasurably, four days later, the Wordsworths held a celebratory tea-party for thirteen of their neighbours.[1]

It says much for Mary's tact and disposition that she was able to slip so unobtrusively into the established pattern of the Wordsworths' lives. It could so easily have become an unbearably fraught situation, since Mary was effectively usurping Dorothy's place as mistress of the household and, more importantly, ending her exclusive relationship with her brother. Mary succeeded in making a place for herself and did not alienate or antagonize Dorothy in the process. One might almost argue the reverse, for Mary's quiet presence seems to have been a calming factor, and Dorothy actually benefited from the company of another woman. Apart from exchanging bedrooms, so that the married couple now had the double bed in the larger room downstairs, there was no visible alteration to the routine at Town End. Mary had inherited a small property from her father, but the income from the rents was only in the region of £30 a year, so there was no gain to the little household from a material point of view.[2]

The only person who felt disadvantaged by the Wordsworths' marriage was not Dorothy but Coleridge, for whom William's domestic happiness was increasingly a matter of envy. Not only was William a more successful and productive poet, but now he was happily married as well. The night before the wedding, Coleridge had dreamt of William, Mary and a grotesquely transformed Dorothy in one of his nightmares about being pursued by a vengeful female. On the day itself, he published his poem to Sara as *Dejection: An Ode* in the *Morning Post*, addressing it deliberately to William as 'Edmund'. If this was not a sufficiently public hurling of a barbed spear, Coleridge also stooped to inflict a wound below the belt. The following week he published in the same paper a poisonous little satire, *Spots in the Sun*, which flaunted Annette's name and effectively accused William of being a hypocrite.[3]

William nobly ignored the public manifestations of Coleridge's jealousy, but the contrast between their respective lives was growing ever deeper. Coleridge was busy pouring out his woes to anyone who would listen, accusing his heavily pregnant wife of 'Ill-tempered Speeches sent after me when I went out of the House, ill-tempered Speeches on my return, my friends received with freezing looks, the least opposition or contradiction occasioning screams of passion' and much more. The friends were, of course, the Wordsworths, whom Sarah, not unnaturally, resented bitterly. They were deeply uncomfortable with the entire situation and could only be persuaded to visit Greta Hall in her absence. Once more, Coleridge decided to flee, taking up Poole's suggestion (which he had earlier spurned in vituperative terms) of acting as companion to the chronically ill Tom Wedgwood. William seems to have tried to dissuade his friend from this second separation, not least because Coleridge's baby was due in December, but he failed. On 4 November Coleridge left Keswick again and, being fortuitously unable to get a place in the London mail coach, was able to spend the day with Sara Hutchinson at Penrith. By the middle of the month, he was jaunting round Wales with Wedgwood, loftily informing his wife that she was his inferior 'in sex, acquirements, and in the quantity and quality of natural endowments whether of Feeling, or of Intellect', and demanding, as of right, that she should 'love, & act kindly to, those whom I deem worthy of my Love'. With incomparable insensitivity to his wife's plight, he also told her to ask Sara over to nurse her when she gave birth: 'you will hardly have another opportunity of having her by yourself & to yourself, & of learning to know her, such as she really is'.[4]

Sara had actually been on her way to Grasmere when Coleridge caught up with her at Penrith. She stayed at Town End for several weeks over the Christmas period, but apparently refrained from attempting to force her attentions on Mrs Coleridge, and left again soon after Coleridge's return.[5] The Wordsworths had all hoped that John would be able to join them, but this proved impossible. 'You do not say a word about coming to see us', Dorothy wrote plaintively. 'I look anxiously through all your letters to find out some hope that you will come.' John's excuse was that he was busy in London, trying to get the best price for the goods he had bought during his voyage, and indignantly (and ultimately unsuccessfully) fending off an attempt to fine him for breaches of East India Company rules on personal trade. He saw Coleridge briefly, when he passed through London, and thought that he looked poorly: 'he does not seem to have the life and spirits that he used to have – & yet he was *very* entertaining'. He paid his duty visits to the Cooksons at Windsor, where he was uncomfortable in the stiff and formal atmosphere, 'too much of the *Church* about it', and was 'a little shy' with his brother Christopher, who was quite obviously their uncle's favourite.[6]

John also saw a good deal of Richard, writing his own letters from Staple Inn and joining him in riding out into the country whenever his brother could spare the time from the throng of business. It was John who took the trouble to copy out Richard's letter to Sir William Lowther's solicitors, setting out the Wordsworth claim in full. The interest alone was now within £300 of the sum due for the original debt. In total, including legal costs, Richard was claiming £10,388 6s 8d. A vast amount in its own right, it paled into insignificance when compared to the full extent of the late Earl's debts, which now exceeded £200,000. Lord Lowther had made a point of including their cousin Captain Wordsworth and his wife among the first guests at Lowther, and had called on them himself. Such marks of respect, John and Richard were convinced, were ample evidence that the whole claim would be paid in full, and soon.[7]

Writing to them on Christmas Day, her thirty-first birthday, Dorothy was in buoyant mood. She assured Richard that she had fully recovered from the bouts of debilitating illness which had afflicted her for the last two months and joked about 'When I get *my fortune* Settled upon me'. She teased John with old Molly Fisher's doting affection for him: 'She is very loquacious when she begins to talk about "Maister John". She generally ends her discourse with "When you write to him mind you give my very best compliments to him, *poor* Maister John"!' Both brothers were urged to visit Grasmere, John most particularly; Dorothy ended her letter by wishing him 'many and many a happy year' from the bottom of her heart.[8]

John's forthcoming second voyage as captain of the *Earl of Abergavenny* provided the Wordsworths with the ammunition they needed to press home their claim to Lord Lowther. Richard had tried every other tack, writing to him personally on 4 February 1803 with an appeal to his sympathy: 'Your Lordship may possibly not be a stranger to the great difficulties our family have encountered; and we have long indulged the hope of having it in our power to repay those friends who have kindly contributed to our maintenance and education.' Richard clearly meant the Wordsworths, Cooksons and Crackanthorpes, but, only a fortnight earlier, he had paid £10 15s from William's account to James Wood, William's former tutor at St John's, as the ten-year-old arrears of his college expenses. A chance meeting with Sir William Lowther at the solicitor's office enabled Richard to make a personal plea, which he reinforced by introducing both Christopher and John to the solicitor himself. Now the prospect that John would be sailing to China in the course of a month or six weeks allowed him to be more urgent: 'It is very desirable that he should be furnished with money for his Investment', he wrote. 'If Lord Lowther could let us have 3000 or £4000, it would be of most essential service to my brother before he sails.'[9]

After much negotiation, Richard wrote privately to William, telling him that the most they could realistically expect to receive was between £8,000 and £8,500 and asking for his approval in accepting the offer. William had no hesitation in giving it and, in a transparent attempt to make up for his previous criticisms of Richard's handling of the affair, declared that he and Dorothy were 'so perfectly satisfied with your manner of conducting the business, that we leave the conclusion of it to your judgement entirely'. On 21 February Richard took out letters of administration enabling him to deal with his father's estate and, two days later, had the satisfaction of recording the receipt of £3,000 from Lord Lowther as the first instalment on the debt. A further £1,500 was handed over at the beginning of July, together with two promissory notes, worth £2,000 each, which were payable in twelve months' time, with interest.[10] It had taken just six months short of twenty years for the Wordsworths to extract the money owed to their father by the Lowthers and, ironically, they owed their success not to persistence, or legal right, but to quixotic generosity. For years they had railed against the tyranny of aristocratic power, wealth and influence; now they found themselves in the curious position of being the beneficiaries.

For William and Dorothy, the payment of the debt meant the difference between a life of scraping together every penny and having sufficient capital to be comfortable, if not rich. Their joint share eventually amounted to £3,825, but, at John's request, Lord Lowther's first payment was entirely appropriated by him for investment in his voyage. Curiously, this rather than the Lowther debt brought the Wordsworths to the brink of a family quarrel. William and Dorothy wanted Richard to stand security for what, in effect, was a loan to John, but their other brothers saw no reason why Richard should always stand all the risk. Dorothy was incandescent with rage:

> I am sure that William has never thought that it was fit you should *run all the risque*, only that it was *more* fit that John should call upon you to run a *further* risque rather than on him, for this plain reason that if you lost the whole of the money you would be, (taking in your profession) many, many degrees richer than he is, or has any grounds for hoping to be; and for me, I told you that I thought I ought not to be called upon to bear *any part* of the risque.

She explained to John that there were few sacrifices she was not prepared to make for him, but this was one of them. It was not a matter of affection, but of prudence. Old Molly Fisher was less cautious: 'if I could but see Maister John I would send all the money that ever I have for a venture with him!' she told Dorothy, who added wryly, 'you must know she has more than seven pounds'. William and Christopher gave their unconditional agreement to the loan, but Dorothy was moved to confront Richard again: 'as long as I am poor or in a state of dependence, I have claims upon you as your only Sister, and the only Daughter of my Father to which no other claims can be superior'.[11]

Dorothy was right to be concerned about her investment, for John's voyage was troubled from the start. Even before he left English waters, in May, his crew, the ragtag and bobtail who had escaped impressment into the navy, were mutinous and had to be punished. More worryingly, the Peace of Amiens had fallen through and war against France had resumed. East Indiamen were a valuable prize for any marauding Frenchmen and, on his return voyage the following year, John was involved in an action against the French Admiral Linois, who was waiting to intercept the fleet before they entered the Straits of Malacca. What could have been a disaster was averted by the cool heads of the British commanders, who, despite being outgunned, managed to get the French in their cross-fire and drive them off. A suitably grateful Board of Directors rewarded captains and crews generously, and John personally received 500 guineas, a piece of commemorative silverware, worth fifty guineas, and a beautifully ornamented ceremonial sword.[12]

All this was well into the future, however, and for the moment Dorothy had to be satisfied with her brothers' assurances that they would honour the informal promise they had made her when William announced his intention to marry: Richard, John and Christopher would each contribute £20 a year towards an allowance for their sister. It was just as well that they did, for she had gone on a spending spree in anticipation of her share of the Lowther claim and bought almost £20 worth of new clothes. Their new-found wealth also seems to have prompted the Wordsworths to consider moving from the tiny cottage at Town End. Mary was expecting a baby towards the end of July and it made sense for them to move into a larger house before the event. Quite where they intended to go is a mystery, but in March Coleridge (never the most reliable of witnesses) told Southey that they meant to reside half a mile from Keswick. At the beginning of June, Dorothy told Catherine Clarkson that they hoped to get into their new house the following week, then have an enormous wash so that everything was ready before the baby arrived.[13]

In the end, however, they were all taken by surprise, for just before six-thirty on the morning of 18 June 1803 Mary gave birth to 'a stout healthy Boy', whom they decided to call John. There was definitely something odd about the timing of his arrival. The Wordsworths were married on 4 October 1802, so in theory a full-term baby should not have been born until 16 July. Given that it was Mary's first child, a later date was likely, and was, indeed, clearly expected by the family. Despite arriving a full month before he was supposedly due, the baby was not undersized or weakly, but a large and thriving boy. The obvious inference is that he had been conceived before the marriage took place, which would not have been unusual at this period, when an engagement was commonly regarded as a licence for sexual relations to begin, but William was in Calais and London at the likeliest time of conception. He and Mary had parted on 26 July, which was too early for John to have been conceived, and William did not return to Gallow Hill until 24 September, a mere ten days before his wedding, which does not account for the disparity in dates. It is inconceivable (literally) that the child was not his, since there was never a breath of suspicion that Mary was anything other than totally loyal to William. She was also, it has to be pointed out, a month wrong in her dates for her second child, which was also born a month earlier than expected. Either Mary was careless in her computations, or she did not naturally carry babies full-term, in which case she was fortunate to have healthy children.[14]

Dorothy was ecstatic. 'The Babe is a true Representative of the Wordsworths,' she told Richard, 'for he is very like his Father and our Family.' Barely a week after his birth the infant prodigy was (according to his besotted aunt) sleeping sweetly all night through and both mother and baby were doing so well that the nurse who had been called in proved unnecessary and left after only three days' attendance. 'Oh my dear Friend', Dorothy sighed to Catherine Clarkson, 'how happy we are in this blessed Infant!' On 17 July a little party trooped into Grasmere church from Town End. Mary went through the old-fashioned ceremony of being 'churched', or purified after childbirth, and John was christened. Dorothy, of course, stood as godmother; the godfathers were Richard and Coleridge. As Richard could not be there in person, he was represented by one of the Wordsworths' earliest Grasmere friends, old Mr Sympson. A modest celebration was held afterwards at Town End, with tea, coffee and christening cake.[15]

The baby's early arrival had effectively put an end to any immediate plans to move house. Instead, William, Dorothy and Coleridge began to contemplate the possibility of making a tour of Scotland. It says much for Dorothy's devotion to 'our own darling child' that, whereas she would once have leapt at any chance to accompany her brother anywhere, she was now reluctant to go. 'William and C talk of it with thorough enjoyment, and I have no doubt I shall be as happy as they when I am fairly off, but I do not love to think of leaving home, and parting with the dear Babe who will be no more the same Babe when we return'. The idea for the tour had been prompted by Coleridge's recent return to the Lakes; it had been months, if not years, since he had spent any length of time with the Wordsworths. For most of the previous year he had been away, accompanying Tom Wedgwood in the hope of being taken abroad. On 24 December he had breezed unexpectedly into the cottage at Town End, with Tom Wedgwood 'worn to Skin and Bone' in tow, and it fell to the Wordsworths to inform Coleridge that he was now the father of a daughter, little Sara, born the previous morning. Before the end of January, he had gone again, and though he wrote confidently about taking up residence in Italy, Sicily, the Canaries, the South of France or even Madeira, nothing came of his plans. Much to John's consternation, he had even begged a passage to China on the *Earl of Abergavenny*. Ultimately, however, Wedgwood shook Coleridge off: he needed a companion who would look after him, not a liability for whom he did not wish to be responsible. He went abroad without Coleridge, who, deprived of his meal ticket and alarmed by the outbreak of war with France again in May, was forced to return to Keswick.[16] A six-week tour of Scotland with William and Dorothy was not in the same category as a couple of years on the Continent with Wedgwood, but it was better than nothing.

William had more serious reasons for wishing to have a change of scene. For several months he had written nothing at all. This was not surprising, given his productivity the previous year, but the longer his fallow period dragged on, the more it became a matter for concern. His last great surge of creativity had been associated with his trip to France. This seems odd, as one would have expected all his emotions to have been focused on and absorbed by Annette and Caroline. Instead, he produced at least nine poems, beginning with his wonderful hymn to a still and silent London, viewed from the roof of the stage coach driving over Westminster Bridge in the early morning, on the way to France.

> Earth has not anything to show more fair:
> Dull would he be of soul who could pass by
> A sight so touching in its majesty:
> This City now doth, like a garment, wear
> The beauty of the morning; silent, bare,
> Ships, towers, domes, theatres, and temples lie
> Open unto the fields, and to the sky;
> All bright and glittering in the smokeless air.
> Never did sun more beautifully steep
> In his first splendour, valley, rock, or hill;
> Never saw I, never felt, a calm so deep!
> The river glideth at his own sweet will:
> Dear God! The very houses seem asleep;
> And all that mighty heart is lying still![17]

It was inevitable that William should contrast his first, hopeful visit to France at the dawn of the French Revolution with this, altogether sadder, occasion. The Peace of Amiens had been made possible by Napoleon Bonaparte's elevation to the office of consul for life; the great struggle for liberty had ended, as Burke had predicted it would, in substituting one tyranny for another. William was sickened at the sight of so many English tourists (who included Poole) pouring over the Channel to 'bend the knee . . . before the new-born Majesty' and scathing in his contempt for the 'men of prostrate mind . . . to slavery prone!' All his political instincts were also outraged by a different kind of slavery, that of the African negroes, whom the French republic refused to set free. He dedicated one great sonnet to Toussaint L'Ouverture, the former Haitian slave who had been an early supporter of the French Revolution, established free government on the island and, in resisting Napoleon's efforts to re-establish slavery there, had recently been captured and brought back to France as a prisoner. 'Thou hast left behind Powers that will work for thee . . .' William comforted him,

There's not a breathing of the common wind
That will forget thee; thou hast great allies;
Thy friends are exultations, agonies,
And love, and man's unconquerable mind.[18]

On a more humble variant of this same theme, he wrote sympathetically of one of their fellow passengers from Calais, a negro woman expelled from France by decree of the government, contrasting her downcast, hopeless manner with her spotless white clothes and her eyes which still retained their 'tropic fire'. More than once he drew the obvious comparison between the spontaneous popular joy and 'faith . . . pledged to new-born Liberty' which had greeted himself and Jones in 1791 with the servile pomp that was now displayed in Napoleon's honour. The contrast was all the more forcible on returning to England, 'Europe is yet in bonds . . . Thou art free, My country!', but perhaps the finest of the series was not a triumphal celebration of England and all things English. It was written in London, after his return from France, and it invoked William's greatest hero, John Milton, the blind poet who had dedicated his life and work to the cause of liberty.

Milton! thou shouldst be living at this hour:
England hath need of thee: she is a fen
Of stagnant waters: altar, sword, and pen,
Fireside, the heroic wealth of hall and bower,
Have forfeited their ancient English dower
Of inward happiness. We are selfish men;
Oh! raise us up, return to us again;
And give us manners, virtue, freedom, power.[19]

After this outpouring, occasioned by a deep sense of political grievance, William had fallen silent. Over the Christmas period he had marked time by translating sonnets from the Italian, but had not engaged in anything new. In the past, this pattern had resulted in renewed effort on *The Recluse*, but this time it did not work. He simply did not know where to take the poem and, when he wrote for advice to Coleridge as the instigator of the work, he got nowhere. 'I made the attempt –', was Coleridge's forlorn response, 'but I could not command my recollections. It seemed a Dream, that I had ever *thought* on Poetry – or had ever written it'.[20]

William may not have been writing new poetry in 1803, but he was publishing extensively through the medium of Daniel Stuart's newspaper, the *Morning Post*. Over the course of that single year, at least fifteen of his poems appeared. More than half of them were published under an editorial banner which said that they were 'Sonnets of a Political nature, which are not only written by one of the first

1. An early view of Cockermouth, painted from a point close to the Wordsworths' house, which stands just outside the picture on the right bank of the River Derwent. The smaller River Cocker flows into the Derwent from the right and the town is dominated, as it still is today, by its medieval castle.

2. An Edwardian photograph of the Market Place, Penrith. The Cooksons' drapery shop (with awning) stands at the top, facing into the square.

3. A photograph of Hawkshead Grammar School, taken by Herbert Bell of Ambleside before the 'restoration' of 1891 which completely altered its appearance. Note the typical Lake District round chimney pot and the plaque commemorating the school's foundation in 1585 by Archbishop Sandys of York.

4. *Belle Isle, Windermere, in a Calm*, painted in 1786 by Philip de Loutherbourg. The Windermere ferry, which provided the only lake crossing, ran just in front of the island and was often used by the boys from Hawkshead. In later life, the Wordsworths often visited Belle Isle as guests of their son John's wife's family, the Curwens, who owned the unusual round house, with its dome-shaped roof, built in 1774. This picture hung in the Curwens' main residence, Workington Hall.

5. William Wordsworth, aged twenty-eight, by William Shuter, 1798.

6. Dorothy Wordsworth, an anonymous and undated silhouette portrait.

7. *The High Sheriff of Lancashire Crossing Morecambe Sands*, undated watercolour by Thomas Sunderland (1744–1823). Travellers wishing to cross the treacherous sands of Morecambe bay were taken in convoy at low tide by experienced local guides. It was from just such a cavalcade as this that William learned the dramatic news of Robespierre's death in 1794.

8 and 9. John Harden of Brathay Hall, near Ambleside (1772–1847), was a talented amateur artist whose intimate portrayals of social life and the ordinary occupations of those around him form a unique record of the period. His pictures of the itinerants and poor of the Lakes complement those drawn by William in his poems. (*Above*) Beggar. (*Below*) Peasant women and children.

10. Mary Wordsworth, an anonymous and undated silhouette portrait.

11. Samuel Taylor Coleridge, aged twenty-four, by Robert Hancock, 1796.

12. The *Earl of Abergavenny* sank in only forty fathoms of water in Weymouth bay in February 1805. Ingenious attempts to salvage the treasure were made by divers wearing Mr Tonkin's patent diving machine (illustrated here), but the bulk of the cargo was recovered by the professional Braithwaites, who were employed by the East India Company. The three masts and their rigging were clearly visible from the shore, making the wreck a macabre but popular tourist attraction.

13. Sir George Beaumont, William's friend and patron, drawn by another of his protégés, the artist and architect George Dance (1741–1825), in October 1807.

14. Anonymous undated silhouette of Sara Hutchinson.

15. Grasmere, by Fennel Robson, 1830. The artist has omitted the island so that the village can be seen across the lake. Three Wordsworth homes are identifiable: Allan Bank, on the left-hand slope, the Vicarage to the left of the church, and Town End on the extreme right.

16. (*Opposite*) William's plan for the winter garden at Coleorton, Leicestershire, drawn upside-down in a letter from Dorothy to Lady Beaumont, 23 December 1806.

No 6

My dear Lady Beaumont Coleridge & his son Hartley arrived on Sunday afternoon the pleasure of welcoming him to your house mingled with our joy, & I think I never was more hap-py in my life than when we had had him an hour by the fire-side; for his looks were much more like his own old self, &, though we only talked of common things & of our friends, we perceived that he was contented in his mind & had settled his affairs at home to his satisfaction. He has been tolerably well & cheerful ever since, & has begun with his Books. Hartley (poor Boy!) is very happy & looks uncommonly well but we are afraid of the hooping-cough, for there is now no doubt that the cough which our young ones have is the hooping-cough. Thomas is better than when I wrote on Saturday. I long to know your opini-on & Sir George's of my Brother's plan of the winter garden. Cole-ridge (as we females are also) is much delighted with it, only he doubts about the fountain; & he thinks it is

Plan
of garden

possible that an intermingling of Birch trees somewhere on account of the richness of the colour of the naked twigs in winter might be of advantage. I may add also, from myself, that we have often stood for half an hour together at Grasmere on a still morning to look at the raindrops or hoar frost glittering in sunshine upon the birch twigs, the purple colour & the sparkling drops produce a most enchanting effect. All our family except the three children (for Hartley is of their party) are gone to Grace Dieu with one ass to help Mrs W. & my sister over dirty places, the fineness of the morning tempted them & I hope they will not be much fatigued as they will

17. No. 20, Great Russell Street, Covent Garden, by Herbert Railton. Charles and Mary Lamb lived in these rooms over an ironmonger's shop on the corner of Great Russell Street from 1817 to 1823. Looking down to Covent Garden theatre at the rear and Drury Lane at the front, Lamb told Dorothy, 'We are in the individual spot I like best in all this great city.'

18. Breakfast party at Samuel Rogers's, 1815, engraved by Charles Mottram. Portrait pictures of this type enjoyed great vogue in the nineteenth century and were compiled by the artist from extant images of famous men rather than from life. Rogers was unique in his ability to attract literary and artistic men to his breakfast parties, but this gathering is purely imaginary. (*Seated, l. to r.*) Sheridan, Moore, Wordsworth, Southey, Coleridge, Rogers, Byron, Kemble. (*Standing, l. to r.*) Flaxman, Walter Scott, Mackintosh, Lansdowne, Sydney Smith, Washington Irvine, Francis Jeffrey, Stothard, Lawrence, J. M. W. Turner, Tom Campbell.

Poets of the age, but are among his best productions. Each forms a little Political Essay, on some recent proceeding.' In order to make them appear as a body, and in sequence, the *Morning Post* even went to the unusual lengths of reprinting on 29 January 1803 'I grieved for Buonaparté' and *Calais, August 1802*, which had already been published on 16 September 1802 and 13 January 1803. Although the editor had promised twelve of these poems, only seven eventually appeared, all of them under the initials WLD, which may have stood for something like 'Wordsworth libertatis defensor'. Apart from a single short epitaph and 'I find it written of Simonides', published on 14 January and 10 October respectively, the rest of the poems were translations from the Italian. All appeared without signature.[21] Other than the political sonnets, which had a serious purpose, William considered most of them ephemera and did not republish them in his lifetime. What he needed was something new to stimulate his interest and feeling, hence the Scottish tour.

The original plan was to walk, but Coleridge's uncertain state of health persuaded them to purchase what they called a jaunting car, but Samuel Rogers said 'looked very like a cart'. It was a low open vehicle, with a dicky box for the driver, hanging seats down each side capable of taking six people in all, and a space in the middle for luggage; to pull it, they purchased an 'aged but stout & spirited' horse. The tour seems to have been doomed from the start. Sara could not come, as expected, to stay with Mary and little Johnny, and Joanna, 'a good hearted girl with a large share of the Hutchinson generosity and disinterestedness about her', had to step into the breach at the last minute. The evening before they were due to set off from Grasmere, Rogers and his sister, who were also on their way to Scotland on a tour, called for tea. The poet had met the Wordsworths before, in June 1801, when he and Richard 'Conversation' Sharp had called with a letter of introduction from Josiah Wedgwood. Though William greatly liked Rogers, Coleridge had thought him a 'drivelling Booby' then, and was now disposed to be outraged by the 'envy, the jealousy, & the other miserable Passions, that have made their Pandaemonium in the crazy Hovel of that poor Man's Heart'. William was simply amused by this display of pettiness, but Coleridge became 'melancholy', which was always a bad sign, indicating a resort to opium. Dorothy, nerves on edge at the thought of leaving home, fell victim to one of her bilious attacks, delaying their departure from Grasmere. Not to be outdone, as soon as they reached Keswick, Coleridge diagnosed himself as suffering 'a compleat & almost heartless Case of Atonic Gout' and declared himself in imminent danger of a paralytic stroke.[22]

At this point, most sane individuals would have abandoned the whole idea of going on a six-week tour of Scotland in such company, but William was not to be put off so lightly. When they eventually set off from Keswick, at twenty past eleven on the morning of 15 August, they must have made a hilarious sight: William up on the dicky box of the cumbersome cart, driving the ancient nag, like some nineteenth-century Don Quixote, and a miserable Dorothy and Coleridge hunched up in the rear, determinedly scribbling their notes for their journals of the tour. 'I never yet commenced a Journey with such inauspicious Heaviness of Heart before',

Coleridge moaned to Southey. Less than four years later, he would complain that he could not recall a single image or conversation of the first week or more of the tour.[23]

If true, this was extraordinary. Their route took them through Carlisle, where they arrived on 16 August, the very day on which the notorious bigamist and forger John Hatfield was sentenced to death. Coleridge had played a personal role in exposing Hatfield by writing a series of articles for the *Morning Post*, describing how he had passed himself off as Colonel Augustus Hope, MP, and bigamously married Mary Robinson, the beautiful Maid of Buttermere, in October 1802. The three travellers not only attended the assizes to see him condemned (Coleridge alarming the whole court by shouting 'Dinner!' to William who was on the other side of the hall), but also went to the gaol where he was being held. At Dorothy's ghoulish instigation, Coleridge obtained an interview with Hatfield, coming away with the impression that he was vain and a hypocrite: 'It is not by mere Thought, I can understand this man', was his conclusion. By a curious coincidence, Dorothy, waiting outside, fell into conversation with a debtor at the prison, only to discover he had been a fellow sailor with John under their cousin Captain Wordsworth. William needed no persuasion to give him a shilling when they left.[24]

From Carlisle they travelled to Longtown, where they took the left fork in the road which led to Glasgow. William was thus retracing his route of 1801, when he had accompanied Montagu and the Rushes to Scotland, and he took pleasure in revisiting the highlights of his former tour. At Dumfries, they unexpectedly found themselves staying in the same inn as Rogers and his sister; William and Dorothy called on them briefly but Coleridge remained aloof. 'Wordsworth and Coleridge were entirely occupied in talking about poetry', Rogers noted; 'and the whole care of looking out for cottages where they might get refreshment and pass the night, as well as of seeing their poor horse fed and littered, devolved upon Miss Wordsworth. She was a most delightful person, – so full of talent, so simple-minded, and so modest!'[25]

Coleridge remained behind at the inn, presumably keeping out of the way of the Rogerses, while William and Dorothy went to pay homage to Robert Burns. William had loved Burns's poetry from being a very young man and had introduced his sister to it. Now they went together and, with the help of a friendly bookseller, sought out his unmarked grave in a churchyard ironically full of expensive and fantastically wrought memorials. Afterwards, they called at Burns's house. Mrs Burns and her children were at the seaside, but the maid let them in and they viewed with approval its austere simplicity and cleanliness, which contrasted with the meanness of its external appearance. The fate of Burns and his children preoccupied and troubled them throughout the next day, as they travelled through his old haunts in the Vale of Nith. Coleridge, significantly, had other thoughts: the vale reminded him of Gallow Hill, 'every feature greatly magnified'. This disparity in interest between Coleridge and the Wordsworths would only increase as the tour went on. By the evening of the fourth day, Coleridge declined to accompany them on their evening walks, claiming to be ill. When they were forced to dismount by the steepness of the rough road between Leadhills and Crawfordjohn, the three of them walked 'chearfully' along in the sunshine, but 'each of us alone'. As tension between them increased, so did the length of Dorothy's entries in her journal, as she chattered to herself rather than to her silent companions.

Just as William had done two years earlier, they visited the Falls of the Clyde at Corra Linn, where Coleridge observed with amusement the 'droll dissonance' between the bored yawns of the little girl sent to accompany them and Dorothy's 'Raptures'. At Hamilton, however, they failed to gain admission to the Duke of Hamilton's picture gallery. Oblivious of the different circumstances, William had led Coleridge and his sister on foot straight to the front door of the house. The porter, observing their shabby appearance, refused to admit them and told them it would not be agreeable to the Duke's family if they walked in the grounds either. Their humiliation was completed when the waiter at their inn informed them that 'it was not usual to refuse admittance to strangers'.[26]

Hastening through a busy, noisy and dirty Glasgow, they made their way up the west bank of Loch Lomond (which continually reminded them of Ullswater), through Luss to Tarbet, at the northern extremity of the lake. As they set out to explore the Trossachs, the weather became increasingly cold and wet. The Wordsworths took every opportunity to travel by boat, but Coleridge preferred to walk on alone rather than face such exposure to the cold. There was clearly little point in going on together, so William suggested that perhaps they should part: the Wordsworths would continue with their tour and Coleridge could walk the twenty or so miles across the Trossachs to Stirling, where he could catch a coach to Edinburgh. 'I eagerly caught at the Proposal;' Coleridge told his wife, 'for the *sitting* in an open Carriage in the Rain is Death to me, and somehow or other I had not been quite comfortable.' The two poets and erstwhile friends both had an interesting gloss on their separation. 'Poor Coleridge was at that time in bad spirits, & somewhat too much in love with his own dejection', was William's analysis; Coleridge blamed William's 'Hypochondriachal Feelings' which 'keep him silent, & [self]-centered'. Dorothy pretended that nothing had happened. They divided their money, the Wordsworths, who had the longer journey and the expense of the horse, as well as themselves, to consider, taking twenty-nine guineas, Coleridge six, and on 29 August they went their separate ways.[27]

That it was only the company which had been ungenial became immediately transparent. Instead of heading straight for Edinburgh, 'poor Coleridge' decided to explore the Highlands, travelling 263 miles of mountainous terrain on foot in the space of a mere eight days. Much to their surprise, as they advanced deeper into the Highlands, the Wordsworths discovered that they had been anticipated by Coleridge; he had even stayed in some of the same inns and cottages. If they thought this was odd, they kept it to themselves. The Wordsworths' route took them through some of the loneliest and most spectacular scenery in central Scotland and was determined by their desire to see the lakes. They walked, rode and sailed along Lochs Awe, Etive, Linnhe, Tay and Tummel, travelling as far north as Fort William and as far east as Blair Atholl, before returning through the Trossachs to take the road they had themselves suggested to Coleridge, to Stirling and Edinburgh. Dorothy's response to the grandeur of the landscape was understandably rapturous: she saw everything with fresh eyes, and became neither jaded nor blasé. Again and again she declared she had never seen anything finer, more delicious or more delightful, reminding one of William's description in *Tintern Abbey* of 'the aching joys' and 'dizzy raptures' of his own youthful 'appetite' for nature, which

> . . . had no need of a remoter charm,
> By thought supplied, nor any interest
> Unborrowed from the eye.

Dorothy's *Recollections* of this tour are ample evidence that she still retained this appetite, but she had also learned the lesson underpinning *Tintern Abbey.* On returning to the Trossachs, she noted, 'I felt that it was much more interesting to visit a place where we have been before than it can possibly be the first time, except under peculiar circumstances.'[28]

At Edinburgh, the Wordsworths visited all the usual tourist sights, but apparently made no effort to be introduced to any of the literary society already flourishing there. On leaving, however, they made a detour eastwards to visit Walter Scott at his cottage in Lasswade. Having walked down Roslin Glen in the early morning, they arrived before Scott and his wife had risen. 'We were received with that frank cordiality which . . . always marked his manners', William later told Scott's son-in-law and biographer, J. G. Lockhart.

> . . . indeed, I found him then in every respect – except, perhaps, that his animal spirits were somewhat higher – precisely the same man that you knew him in later life; the same lively, entertaining conversation, full of anecdote, and averse from disquisition; the same unaffected modesty about himself; the same cheerful and benevolent and hopeful views of man and the world.[29]

William and Scott shared a mutual friend in John Stoddart, who supplied the introduction for this first meeting, but, more importantly, Scott, like William, was devoted to the land of his birth, knew all the local people, places and histories, and was the ideal guide to the borders. A practising barrister, Scott was busy performing his duties as sheriff, but he agreed to meet them again, two days later, at Melrose. There, on 19 September, he conducted them round the town and the beautiful pale-red sandstone ruins of Melrose Abbey, pointing out much that would otherwise have escaped them and regaling them with tales of its venerable history.

The Wordsworths were reluctant to part so soon from their new-found friend, who was on his way to the assizes at Jedburgh, so he agreed to meet them again, but begged that they would not enter the court, 'for I really would not like you to see the sort of figure I cut there'. Accidentally catching sight of him later, wearing a cocked hat and sword and marching in the judge's procession to the sound of a single cracked trumpet, they understood his embarrassment. After the business of the day was over, he joined them and greatly delighted them by partly reading and partly reciting, 'sometimes in an enthusiastic style of chant', the first four cantos of his as yet unpublished ballad the *Lay of the Last Minstrel.* Though after Scott's death William would say that 'the novelty of the manners, the clear picturesque descriptions, and the easy glowing energy of much of the verse, greatly delighted me', he was then being kind to his friend's memory. At the time, he found himself in a very awkward position indeed, for he immediately recognized that the poem was an imitation of Coleridge's *Christabel*, and included at least one phrase lifted straight from it. 'We were both equally convinced from the frankness of Walter Scott's manner that it was an unconscious imitation,' Dorothy wrote later. What is more, they understood how it happened. John Stoddart had 'a very wicked memory' and had repeated various passages from the then-unpublished *Christabel* to Scott. For years afterwards, William would reproach himself for not having said anything at the time, not least because the prior publication of the *Lay of the Last Minstrel* would pre-empt Coleridge's poem and steal its thunder. 'I did not expect that it [the *Lay*] would make much sensation', William admitted, 'but I was mistaken; for it went up like a balloon.'[30]

With Scott as their guide, the Wordsworths explored up the River Teviot to Hawick, scarcely passing a house for which he did not have some story and in which he did not find a hearty welcome. On 23 September they were obliged to part from their genial friend and they turned their faces homeward. At Carlisle they paused to view the site of Hatfield's execution, and on 25 September, between eight and nine o'clock, they arrived at Town End, 'where we found Mary in perfect health, Joanna Hutchinson with her, and little John asleep in the clothes-basket by the fire'.[31]

William and Dorothy had been away almost exactly six weeks. They returned in good health (though both whinged about minor ailments) and in high spirits, with a fund of material and memories from which they would both profit over the coming years. What William had not succeeded in doing was adding to his stock of poetry. Perhaps the sheer physical exertion and constant travel had made this impossible, for he returned with only one completed sonnet, *Composed at [Neidpath] Castle*, attacking the Marquis of Queensbury for cutting down the ancient trees adorning the gorge of the Tweed below his castle, and three lines addressed to Kilchurn Castle.[32] The images, thoughts and feelings needed to mull quietly in his memory until the vital spark of inspiration came.

There was no need of such delay when it came to politics. Rumours of a French invasion of Britain had followed the Wordsworths even to the remoter regions of Scotland; at Peebles their unusual method of transport had even led to William being questioned on suspicion that they might be connected with the invaders. Returning to Grasmere, he found the whole vale literally up in arms. Lord Lowther had sent out a circular calling all loyal subjects to volunteer for the local militias in preparation for the defence of their country. On 3 October William 'with the greatest part of the Men of Grasmere' went to Ambleside to enlist. Ten years earlier he would have thought it impossible that he could ever contemplate fighting for England against the French, but France under Napoleon was not the same as France in the early days of the revolution. Mary and Dorothy tried to dissuade him, pointing out the inconvenience and fatigue of being called upon to be exercised in arms two or three times a week, but William was implacable: 'surely there never was a more determined hater of the French', Dorothy wrote proudly and with unconscious irony, 'nor one more willing to do his utmost to destroy them if they really do come'.[33]

The threat of invasion stirred William to poetry and he immediately dashed off a couple of sonnets, which did more credit to his patriotism than his talent. One he addressed to the 'Vanguard of Liberty, ye men of Kent', to assure them that

> We all are with you now from shore to shore:
> Ye Men of Kent, 'tis victory or death!

The best one can say about both sonnets is that they suited the mood of the country, and quickly found a place in more than one publication.[34]

One of the most urgent calls on William's duty was not connected with the war against France. Thank-you letters are never the easiest to write, but this one was particularly difficult. Just before he had set out from Keswick on the Scottish tour, Coleridge had presented him with an extraordinary gift. It was the title deeds to a little estate at Applethwaite, gloriously situated on the lower slopes of Skiddaw, just outside Keswick. The donor was Sir George Beaumont, a wealthy baronet, who was a talented amateur painter himself and a generous patron of artists and writers of every kind. With his wife, Lady Margaret, he had spent the summer lodging at Greta Hall with Mr Jackson, the owner and co-resident with the Coleridges. His object had been to sketch and paint in the Keswick area, but, like so many others, he had fallen under the spell of Coleridge's brilliant conversation. His wife was even more enthusiastic. Coleridge, as always, had been generous in his praise of William's poetry and had lent the Beaumonts copies of the 1802 edition of *Lyrical Ballads*. By the end of July, they were 'half-mad' to meet William too. 'Lady B. told me, that the night before last as she was reading your Poem on Cape Rash Judgement, had you entered the room, she believes she should have fallen at your feet'. Even before the meeting came about, Beaumont decided that he had to make a practical gesture to show his appreciation of the two poets and encourage their respective careers. Discussion with Coleridge had led him to the conclusion that the best thing he could do was to bring the two men closer together: 'I thought with pleasure on the encrease of enjoyment you would receive from the beauties of nature', he told William, 'by being able to communicate more frequently your sensations to each other, & that this would be a means of contributing to the pleasure & improvement of the world by stimulating you both to poetical exertions'. Applethwaite was less than two miles from Greta Hall; it was worth £100 and consisted of a few old cottages and two small fields. An additional benefit was that ownership of a freehold estate in Cumberland also conferred the right to vote. Beaumont's intention was that William would 'patch up a house there if I liked to be near Mr Coleridge', as his recipient somewhat ungraciously phrased it.[35]

It was an extraordinarily generous gesture, not least because the purchase was a *fait accompli*, made before Beaumont had even met William. Unfortunately, it was entirely misdirected. Had he consulted William, his family or even the unfortunate Mrs Coleridge, he would soon have discovered that living in closer quarters was not something anyone but Coleridge himself wanted. There was the added difficulty that William felt great reluctance to accept such a valuable present from someone he barely knew. What should he do? His indecision, combined with his incurable habit of putting off an unwelcome task, meant that it was 14 October, two months after he had received the deeds, before he wrote his acknowledgement. It was an awkward letter, struggling both to justify the delay by implausible accounts of ill-health, and to reject the proffered kindness without causing offence. 'It is a most delightful situation,' he told Beaumont,

> and few things would give me greater pleasure than to realise the plan which you had in view for me of building a house there. But I am afraid, I am sorry to say, that the chances are very much against this, partly on account of the state of my own affairs, and still more from the improbability of Mr Coleridge's continuing in the Country ... what I sh[ould] wish is, that I might be considered at present as Steward of the land with liberty to lay out the rent in plant[ing] or any other improvement which might be thought [advi]sable with a view to building upon it. And if it should [be] out of my power to pitch my own tent there, I would then request that you would give me leave [to] restore the property to your own hands, in order tha[t] you might have the opportunity of again present[ing] it to some worthy person who might be so fortu[nate] as to be able to make that pleasant use of it which it was your wish that I should have done.

Beaumont was having none of it: 'talk no more of obligations', he roundly declared, 'plant it, delve it – & build upon it or not, as it suits your convenience, but let me live & die with the idea the sweet place, with its rocks, its banks, & mountain stream are in the possession of such a mind as yours'. He ordered William to keep the entire transaction a secret and forbade him to mention a word about it again. Applethwaite was his and so, in this most unexpected way, William had finally become a member of that class he so admired, a statesman of Cumberland.[36]

Beaumont was not offended by William's refusal to build a house at Applethwaite, but Coleridge was, and his private comments about his old friend were becoming increasingly venomous. To Poole, he confided that he thought William was becoming more 'self-involuted': 'I saw him more and more benetted in hypochondriacal Fancies, living wholly among *Devotees* – having every the minutest Thing, almost his very Eating & Drinking, done for him by his Sister, or Wife'. This blatant jealousy he endeavoured to pass off as pious fears 'lest a Film should rise, and thicken on [William's] moral Eye'. Not even William's frequent appearances in the *Morning Post* escaped Coleridge's acerbic comment. The habit of writing such a multitude of small poems was 'hurtful to him' and only a return to *The Recluse* would restore him to his natural element. 'I have seen enough, positively to give me feelings of hostility towards the plan of several of the Poems in the L.Ballads:' he wrote, '& I really consider it as a misfortune, that Wordsworth ever deserted his former mountain Track to wander in Lanes & allies.' The canker of jealousy was growing steadily, but at least Coleridge still had sufficient shame to ask Poole to destroy this letter.[37]

His relationship with the Wordsworths was not helped by the unexpected news that Sara Hutchinson was about to take up residence in the Lakes. Her brother had been given notice to quit Gallow Hill. The Hutchinsons were particularly distressed because their landlord was renowned for never dismissing a tenant without good reason, yet they were being evicted because his wife had taken a fancy to Tom's improvements and wanted 'a little Rural place to carry her fine Ladies to drink tea at'. Encouraged by the Wordsworths, as much as by his own links with Penrith, Tom came over to find a farm and by 22 October he had agreed to take Park House, on the Dalemain estate, overlooking Ullswater. Intimacy with the Wordsworths must have warped his judgement, for, though the house was gloriously situated, high on the silent fells, beside a noisy tumbling brook, with the empty moorland of Barton Fell rising behind and a vista of mountains across the lake below, the farm itself would never be particularly successful. His lease would not begin until March, so he returned to Gallow Hill for the winter, taking Joanna back with him as far as Penrith, where he left her staying with old family friends.[38]

As the late autumn slipped away there was much excitement at Keswick. William Hazlitt, Coleridge's former disciple, who had visited them at Alfoxton in 1798, had come to the Lakes in July to paint portraits of William and Coleridge. At the end of October he returned to complete them. They were both dolorous and funereal efforts, which made the poets look twenty years too old. William's, as Southey humorously pointed out, looked like a man 'at the gallows – deeply affected by his deserved fate – yet determined to die like a man'.[39] Coleridge had taken a dislike to the young man: 'he is jealous, gloomy, & of an irritable Pride – & addicted to women, as objects of sexual Indulgence'. It was this last quality which got him into trouble. He made a number of 'gross attacks' on women at Keswick, even whipping one for not yielding to his advances, and brought the wrath of the town on him. He narrowly escaped being ducked, or even sent to prison, and only got away by slipping out under cover of darkness, arriving at midnight at Grasmere, where he threw himself on William's mercy. Hazlitt was lucky not only to find a refuge, but also to be given clothes and several pounds to make good his escape. No doubt he did not tell the full story, for, remembering William's reaction to the men who had publicly beaten women in the streets of Germany, it is difficult to imagine he would have assisted had he known. As it was, the incident did nothing towards improving the relationship between them, which was already under strain due to Hazlitt's hero-worship of Napoleon.[40]

Another visitor from the Alfoxton days also made a reappearance this winter. Towards the end of November, John Thelwall, the radical demagogue, whose arrival at Alfoxton had attracted the suspicions of the Home Office, paid a visit. Unable to support himself and his family on his little farm in Wales, he had embarked on a new lecturing career, this time avoiding politics and advocating an uncontentious system of elocution. He was in Kendal to give his public lectures, and drove out to see his old friends at Grasmere and Keswick. He arrived at an inopportune moment. Mary, Dorothy and baby Johnny were alone at Town End. Alarming reports of Coleridge's health had compelled William to hurry over to Greta Hall. There he found his friend 'SO VERY VERY ill, with such a complication of bodily miseries', as Coleridge himself put it, that it was evident something would have to be done about him. Coleridge had no doubts about what he wanted to do. 'I have a Persuasion, strong as Fate, that from 12 to 18 months' Residence & perfect Tranquillity in a genial Climate would send me back to dear old England, a sample of the first Resurrection.' There was little point in arguing with him; he was in no state to earn a living for himself, let alone provide for his wife and children. His drug-taking had reached such heights that he slept half the day, was awake half the night and suffered regular screaming nightmares, none of which was conducive to normal family life. His brother-in-law, Southey, and his wife, who had lost their much beloved only child while the Wordsworths and Coleridge had been on their Scottish tour, now agreed to take up at least semi-permanent residence at Greta Hall. This meant that Coleridge could leave with a clear conscience, knowing that his family would have the Southeys' support in his absence.[41]

All that remained was to find the money. William was understandably reluctant to lend anything, at least until he had recovered the sums invested in John's voyage, but this last bout of illness convinced him that it was necessary. Change of climate and country offered perhaps the only chance for Coleridge to pull himself together, throw off his opium dependency, recognize his obsession for Sara as the chimera it was and sort himself out completely. With a generosity he could ill afford (he had just received another demand for payment of college debts), William offered Coleridge a loan of £100.[42]

On 20 December Coleridge and his younger son, three-year-old Derwent, arrived in a post chaise at Town End. It was supposed to be a farewell visit, for Coleridge had determined to go to Madeira. He intended to stay a single day, then walk on to Kendal for the coach to London. In the event, he stayed almost a month, reluctant to leave the genial atmosphere of the Wordsworths' home. Now that he was about to part from them for eighteen months or two years, he relearned to appreciate their virtues and temporarily forgot all his jealousies. For much of the time (three-quarters, he claimed) he was ill and, despite the inconvenience in the tiny household, made sure he was the centre of attention. His bed was moved into the sitting room and Mary and Dorothy nursed him 'with more than Mother's Love', sitting in turn by his bedside, ready to wake him whenever the first symptoms of 'distressful Feeling' appeared. With one of those flashes of endearing self-knowledge that were his saving grace, Coleridge admitted that the Wordsworths were 'in too great Sympathy with my Ill health' for his own good. On this occasion, however, he tried even the patience of Dorothy, for whom he could usually do no wrong. Most of the additional work had fallen on her, as both Mary and the servant, Molly Fisher, were unwell. With unaccustomed asperity, she noted that Coleridge had been 'lame with the gout, stomach-sick, haunted by ugly dreams, screamed out in the night, durst not sleep etc etc' and been 'continually wanting coffee, broth or something or other'.[43]

On the days he was not ill, Coleridge retraced their favourite walks round Grasmere, Rydal and Easedale, writing exquisite and acute observations in his notebooks with all the sensitivity and emotion of a man who expected not to return. On 31 December, the last day of the old year, the two poets made a symbolic pilgrimage to Greenhead Ghyll together, and there 'On this blessed calming Day – sitting on the very Sheepfold dear William read to me his divine Poem, Michael.' A few days later, as a second earnest for the future, 'in the highest & outermost [part] of Grasmere Wordsworth read to me the second Part of his divine Self-biography'. On 14 January 1804 he set off on foot for Kendal. William accompanied him the first six or seven miles, almost as far as Troutbeck, then the two friends parted. It would be more than two and a half years before they met again.[44]

The visit may have tested the Wordsworths' friendship for Coleridge, but they emerged unscathed, and Coleridge, after a long period of increasing disenchantment, left with a new appreciation of his old friends. He could even regard William's domestic happiness without jealousy: 'his is the happiest Family I ever saw', he wrote. Were he only in good health and their neighbour, he believed that 'the Cottage in Grasmere Vale would be a proud sight for Philosophy'. He had learned to recognize his own importance to them, even if his reasoning was suspect: being so very happy within themselves, he declared, they needed a friend and common object of love as a sort of outside interest. He was on surer ground when he analysed the reason for William's happiness (and, by inference, his own unhappiness).

he both deserves to be, and *is*, a happy man – and a happy man, not from natural Temperament – for therein lies his main obstacle – not by enjoyment of the good things of this world – for even to this Day from the first Dawn of his Manhood he has purchased Independence and Leisure for great & good pursuits by austere frugality and daily Self-denial – nor yet by an accidental confluence of amiable and happy-making Friends and Relatives, for every one near to his heart has been placed there by Choice and after Knowledge and Deliberation – but he is a happy man, because he is a Philosopher – because he knows the intrinsic value of the Different objects of human Pursuit, and regulates his Wishes in Subordination to that Knowledge – because he feels, and with a *practical* Faith, the Truth

... that we can do but one thing well, & that therefore we must make a choice – he has made that choice from early youth, has pursued & is pursuing it – and certainly no small part of his happiness is owing to this Unity of Interest, & that Homogeneity of character which is the natural consequence of it –

The drift of these observations was readily apparent. Coleridge had no doubt that, in the future, William would be regarded as 'the first & greatest philosophical Poet': 'and I prophesy immortality to his *Recluse*, as the first & finest philosophical Poem, if only it be (as it undoubtedly will be) a Faithful Transcript of his own most august & innocent Life, of his own habitual Feelings & Modes of seeing and hearing'.[45]

Whether it was the result of Coleridge's urgent demands during his visit or the effect of his departure, which they all, Coleridge included, half-suspected might be to his death, William now returned to the project of *The Recluse* with a vengeance. He walked out every morning, during a spring which Dorothy described for its mildness as 'perfect South of England', and, on his return, dictated another large section of *The Prelude*. By 5 March he had written 1,200 lines, completing another book, and anticipated completing the final one in two or three days' time. As the autobiographical poem neared completion, William became increasingly anxious to have Coleridge's long-promised notes containing his outline of how *The Recluse* was to take shape. 'I cannot say how much importance I attach to this,' he wrote to Coleridge, 'if it should please God that I survive you, I should reproach myself for ever in writing the work if I had neglected to procure this help.'[46]

At Coleridge's request, Mary and Dorothy began to transcribe all William's manuscript poems, so that he could take a complete copy with him on his voyage. It was a thankless and time-consuming task, particularly when it came to the autobiographical poem and the sections of *The Recluse* already written, which were 'scattered about here and there in this book and in that, one Stanza on one leaf, another on another which makes the transcribing more than twice the trouble'. The manuscripts were in such wretched condition that William's almost constant superintendence was required, so Mary and Dorothy wisely took the precaution of making a second copy for themselves as they went along, knowing that William was unlikely ever to repeat the exercise solely for his own benefit. It says much for the stamina and determination of the two women that they managed to transcribe about 8,000 lines in something under six weeks, and Coleridge had his own copy of William's entire unpublished opus before he set sail from Portsmouth on 9 April. William had his own reasons for being grateful for the request: '[It wa]s an intricate and weary job;' he acknowledged, 'but I do believe that one half of those last 3 books [has b]een preserved by it.'[47]

This spring, which saw one of William's most sustained efforts on *The Recluse* and what would become *The Prelude*, also witnessed the creation of about a dozen shorter poems which are among the most famous he ever wrote. Several of these were connected with the Scottish tour, such as *To a Highland Girl* and *Yarrow*

Unvisited, but out of the former developed the lovely lines which became the poem addressed to Mary, 'She was a Phantom of delight':

> A perfect Woman, nobly planned,
> To warn, to comfort, and command,
> And yet a Spirit still, and bright
> With something of angelic light.[48]

It comes as something of a surprise to learn that Mary, who is not usually credited with poetic insight, contributed what William considered the two best lines to perhaps his most famous poem. 'I wandered lonely as a cloud' was probably prompted by a visit he paid at the end of April to Gowbarrow Park, on Ullswater. His object was to see his friend Charles Luff, who was a captain in the Loyal Wedgwood Volunteers at Patterdale, exercising his militia in a 'Grand field day' at Gowbarrow. The site was renowned throughout the Lakes for its profusion of wild daffodils, which are much smaller, paler and more delicate than the cultivated varieties best known today. It was by no means the first time William had seen them, stretching in a golden band along the bay and fluttering and dancing in the breeze, and the poem celebrates not just the daffodils themselves, but also the power of memory:

> For oft, when on my couch I lie
> In vacant or in pensive mood,
> They flash upon that inward eye
> Which is the bliss of solitude;
> And then my heart with pleasure fills,
> And dances with the daffodils.[49]

Two other important poems were written about this time. *Ode to Duty* was, as William admitted, modelled on Gray's *Ode to Adversity*, which was itself an imitation of the Roman poet Horace's *Ode to Fortune*, but it clearly arose from conversations with Coleridge on his last visit. Both men had reason to lament their lack of commitment to their work. Despite all his grandiose schemes and prospectuses, Coleridge had never yet written the great work which everyone expected of him; his mind, as Southey pointed out, 'is in a perpetual St Vitus's dance – eternal activity without action'. William, as friends and family continually reminded him, was supposedly dissipating his talents on small poems instead of dedicating his life to the completion of *The Recluse*. 'Mortal Life seems destined for no continuous Happiness save that which results from the exact performance of Duty – ', Coleridge wrote sadly after his departure, 'and blessed are you, dear William! whose Path of Duty lies thro' vine-trellised Elm-groves, thro' Love and Joy & Grandeur'. In his poem, which he addressed to Duty as the 'Stern Daughter of the Voice of God', William acknowledged his besetting sins of idleness and procrastination and effectively dedicated himself to *The Recluse*.

. . . oft, when in my heart was heard
Thy timely mandate, I deferred
The task, in smoother walks to stray;
But thee I now would serve more strictly, if I may.

He was, of course, making himself a hostage to fortune; the *Ode to Duty* became a family joke and William was frequently teased by wife and sister for having forgotten this dedication of himself to the 'Stern Lawgiver!'[50]

The second ode, *Intimations of Immortality*, was, quite simply, the greatest William ever wrote. So many of its lines and phrases have been used as titles for books and films, or become part of the common vocabulary, that it is difficult to come to it fresh. Reading it for the first time is like going through a dictionary of quotations. And yet it is impossible not to be impressed with its sheer grandeur and authority; it is emphatically the philosopher-poet speaking. The first four stanzas lamented the passing away of 'a glory from the earth' as we move from childhood to adulthood.

Whither is fled the visionary gleam?
Where is it now, the glory and the dream?

These lines had been written two years earlier, in March 1802, and then William had not known the answer. Coleridge, however, had characteristically reworked them and turned them into the self-explanatory *Dejection: An Ode*. Now William returned to his original lines and transformed the poem into a positive, if thoughtful rather than joyous, celebration of human nature. Taking his cue from Platonic philosophy, he argued for the pre-existence of the soul as the reason why childhood is 'apparelled in celestial light'.

Our birth is but a sleep and a forgetting:
The Soul that rises with us, our life's Star,
  Hath had elsewhere its setting,
    And cometh from afar:
  Not in entire forgetfulness,
  And not in utter nakedness,
But trailing clouds of glory do we come
  From God, who is our home:
Heaven lies about us in our infancy!

This verse, in particular, would cause endless controversy because pre-existence is not a tenet of the Christian faith. William was always highly sensitive to criticism on this point, but he flatly refused to withdraw or alter the lines. They were, indeed, central to the poem, for they conjured up the boy William, who could not believe in his own mortality, but expected, like Elijah, to be physically translated to heaven, and whose imagination was so strong that he could not conceive of external things having a separate existence from himself. Just as in *Tintern Abbey* the adult William had found compensation for the loss of childish glory.

> Though nothing can bring back the hour
> Of splendour in the grass, of glory in the flower;
> We will grieve not, rather find
> Strength in what remains behind;
> In the primal sympathy
> Which having been must ever be;
> In the soothing thoughts that spring
> Out of human suffering;
> In the faith that looks through death,
> In years that bring the philosophic mind.

He ended the poem with four deceptively simple lines which were the summation of his philosophy.

> Thanks to the human heart by which we live,
> Thanks to its tenderness, its joys, and fears,
> To me the meanest flower that blows can give
> Thoughts that do often lie too deep for tears.

It was no accident that William chose to end every future edition of his poems with these lines.[51]

By the end of April 1804 William had added almost 3,000 lines to his poem on his own life. 'I am at present in the 7th book of this work,' he wrote, 'which will turn out far longer than I ever dreamt of: it seems a frightful deal to say about one's self, and of course will never be published, (during my lifetime I mean), till another work has been written and published, of sufficient importance to justify me in giving my own history to the world.' But the fit of creativity which had held him in its grasp since the beginning of the year gradually petered out. In Coleridge's absence, the Wordsworths felt an increased sense of responsibility towards his family, so there were regular visits to Greta Hall. An added bonus was the presence of Southey, to whom William, rather to his own surprise, took a liking. They had much in common: a shared republican past which had given way to a less radical stance in domestic politics, a commitment to their work as poets (and in Southey's case, as a historian and essayist as well) and a devotion to their families. That they had been wary of each other was principally due to Coleridge, whose bitter quarrels with his brother-in-law had drawn in their mutual friends. An uneasy truce now existed between the two men: 'my inclination to like him', Southey wrote of Coleridge, 'has always got the better of [my] judgement'. William, who had previously dismissed Southey as a coxcomb, was now forced to re-evaluate and discovered Southey was not only 'very pleasant in his manners' but also a man of 'great reading, in old books, poetry, Chronicles, memoirs, &c., particularly Spanish and Portuguese'.[52]

Another shared bond, though not one that either man accepted, was that, with Coleridge and Lamb, they were now being classed as the 'modern school of poets', soon to be labelled, even more inaccurately, the 'Lake School of Poetry'. The man who coined these descriptions, and would be their scourge for years to come, was Francis Jeffrey, an Edinburgh lawyer, who had co-founded the *Edinburgh Review* in October 1802 and was its principal literary critic. Famed for his corruscating attacks on contemporary poets, his reviews made highly entertaining reading, unless you were the unfortunate author whose work was under scrutiny. In the very first volume of the new periodical, Jeffrey turned all the savagery of his undoubted wit on the '*sect* of poets, that has established itself in this country within these ten or twelve years'. The article purported to be a review of Southey's *Thalaba*, published the previous year, but almost half was dedicated to a scathing attack on the poetic principles of 'the modern school'. Almost as his starting point, Jeffrey took the much-enlarged preface to the 1802 edition of *Lyrical Ballads*, describing it as 'a kind of manifesto that preceded one of their most flagrant acts of hostility'. Without actually naming William anywhere, he tore him apart: 'It is absurd to suppose, that an author should make use of the language of the vulgar, to express the sentiments of the refined'. He attacked William's central thesis, that 'we have all of us one human heart'.

> The love, or grief, or indignation of an enlightened and refined character, is not only expressed in a different language, but is in itself a different emotion from the love, or grief, or anger of a clown, a tradesman, or a market-wench. The things themselves are radically and obviously distinct . . . The poor and vulgar may interest us, in poetry, by their *situation*: but never, we apprehend, by any sentiments that are peculiar to their condition, and still less by any language that is characteristic of it . . . After all, it must be admitted, that there is a class of persons (we are afraid they cannot be called *readers*), to whom the representation of vulgar manners, in vulgar language, will afford much entertainment. We are afraid, however, that the ingenious writers who supply the hawkers and ballad-singers, have very nearly monopolized that department, and are probably better qualified to hit the taste of their customers, than Mr Southey, or any of his brethren, can yet pretend to be.

William dismissed the review with lofty disdain, 'the Fellow was a Blockhead and knew nothing about the Business', but he read it in a country bookseller's shop, where he was not permitted to cut the pages of the periodical, so the full force of Jeffrey's splenetic contempt was probably lost on him. Nevertheless, he was wrong to be unconcerned. Jeffrey was being deliberately contentious and excessive, but his entertaining style quickly won him an enormous readership and a proportionately powerful influence on critical opinion.[53]

Much of the summer of 1804 was taken up with visits to Greta Hall, and to Park

House, where Tom, Sara and Joanna had been living since the beginning of April. Dorothy went over to help them settle in and, a few weeks later, the jaunting car was put into service once again to carry William, Mary and little Johnny there for a visit. One of the major disappointments was that the Clarksons were no longer at Eusemere: the idea of being their neighbours had been one of the attractions of moving to Park House. Catherine had gone to Bristol the previous year to receive treatment from the ubiquitous Dr Beddoes, leaving her husband at Eusemere to complete his book, *A Portraiture of Quakerism*. The Wordsworths had hoped and expected that she would return, but when the anti-slavery movement demanded his presence in London Thomas, too, had left, and in July 1804 Eusemere was sold to Lord Lonsdale.[54]

The Wordsworths remained for three weeks at Park House, where Jack Hutchinson's two little daughters, Bessy and Jane, with their governess, Miss Weir, were also visitors. Dorothy, who remained at Grasmere, had dreaded the separation, but it was little Johnny, not her brother, for whom she pined: 'I shall be very lonely – at home without John – home without him will seem more lonely than it could possibly have been before his birth.' Dorothy had devoted herself, heart and soul, to her nephew. Her letters now were a continuous eulogy of this passionate child: even his fits of temper, when neither his mother nor his aunt could hold him, were recounted with admiration as proof of his remarkable strength. Nor could she quite hide her satisfaction that he had also suffered greatly from the separation, refused to be pacified by his maternal aunts at Park House and returned more passionate than ever due to not being 'so *regularly* attended to as at home'.[55]

The Wordsworths had not been home long when Mrs Coleridge and her three children descended on them for a visit. Even though they managed to farm some of the children out to a neighbour, it must have been a trying time for Mary, who was heavily pregnant. At least they now had more active assistance in the form of a fifteen-year-old servant girl who had come in May to take old Molly Fisher's place. Molly's sister-in-law had died suddenly, so she had been promoted to the 'high office of her Brother's Housekeeper and attendant upon his single Cow'. This enforced departure came as a great relief to the Wordsworths, for Molly, or 'the drollery belonging to the Cottage', as Coleridge called her, had been unfit for her duties for at least the previous six months. By rights she should have been dismissed, but the Wordsworths knew that this would break her heart, so they had struggled on. Entering on her third life, as Dorothy put it, Molly astonished them all by the transformation she wrought in the cleanliness of her brother's cottage; it was her great pride to be continually bearing little gifts from her garden and dairy to the Wordsworths. The new servant was active and strong (though nameless), and fortunately she loved children.[56]

The Coleridges were still with them when Mary unexpectedly went into labour. She was delivered of her second child, a girl, whom they had already decided would be named Dorothy, on 16 August, which was her own birthday. Despite the fact that the baby was named after her, Dorothy could not conceal her preference for Johnny. 'She is a nice Baby, healthy enough – stout enough – pretty enough', she damned with faint praise, 'but in nothing *extraordinary*, as John certainly was . . .' Johnny, barely fourteen months old, was equally unimpressed, taking every opportunity to hit his new sister and make her cry, but William was besotted with his daughter: 'She is her Father's darling', Dorothy remarked, 'I think he is more tender over her than he ever was over her Brother.'[57]

This time, they did not bother to get a nurse. Sara came over the day after the birth and Mrs Coleridge and her children departed two days later, easing the cramped conditions in the cottage. It was only a short breathing space, however, for less than a month later Mary's aunt and cousin, Elizabeth and Mary Monkhouse, arrived on a visit from Penrith and stayed a week. Little Dorothy, whom the family would later call Doro, or Dora, to distinguish her from her aunt, was christened on 16 September in Grasmere church, like her brother. Sara stood proxy for her godmother, Lady Beaumont, who, though a virtual stranger to the entire family, had been in regular correspondence with Dorothy since her husband had presented William with Applethwaite. As a christening gift, Lady Beaumont sent her god-daughter £10, which, in a typically Wordsworthian gesture, they decided to lay out in planting trees on a small plot of ground, to be called 'Dorothy's Grove': 'They will grow up *with her* at first, as brethren, with whom she may measure and compare herself from year to year, but if sun and wind prosper them they will be a shelter and a shade for her by the time she has lived twenty years, and who knows but they may be the nursery of her tenderest and best thoughts!'[58]

Sara and the Monkhouses left Town End on 23 September, and on the first fine autumnal day that followed, William and Dorothy set off in the jaunting car for a short tour of Ennerdale and Wasdale. At Keswick they were waylaid by the Southeys (whose own daughter, Edith May, had been born on 30 April), Mrs Coleridge and Mrs Lovell, who persuaded them to take them all on a day trip to Buttermere. The next day, the Wordsworths left Keswick for a second time, making their way over the wild and remote mountains of the Whinlatter Pass to the Vale of Lorton, where they visited the solitary and patriarchal yew tree, whose 'vast circumference and gloom profound' proved an inspiration to William. Ennerdale, enveloped in mist and rain, was a disappointment, but Wasdale was gloriously stark and bare, a complete contrast to the pastoral Vale of Duddon, through which they completed their tour.[59]

They returned to find yet more visitors. Staying at the Grasmere inn were the perennial bad penny Basil Montagu and his friend George Dyer, the Cambridge man, who had once been a friend of William Taylor, William's headmaster at Hawkshead Grammar School. Montagu still owed William £160, on top of the annuity he was supposed to pay him, but this was no bar to their friendship. He was a regular visitor to the cottage at Town End, more so than Richard Wordsworth, who, having received the final payment of the Lowther debt in July, had returned to the Lakes in August, for the first time in many years, for what should have been a triumphal tour. His visit was marred only by the claims of his cousin Richard

Wordsworth of Branthwaite, who, in the wake of the settlement with the new Lord Lowther, sought repayment of all the money advanced by his father to the young Wordsworths, in addition to all his own legal expenses in the case. Richard paid a brief visit to his brother and sister at Grasmere (his first) but most of his time was spent at Allonby, Penrith and Newbiggin. By the beginning of October, Dorothy was writing peevishly to him, 'How can it possibly be that you can not find time to come over, if but for one day[?] . . . Mary and I are grieved to the heart – we had counted up[on your] spending some quiet time with us'. Whether he was present for the christening of his niece at Grasmere on 16 September or at the long-delayed marriage of his brother Christopher to Priscilla Lloyd at Birmingham on 6 October is not recorded, but seems unlikely in both cases.[60]

Someone who would have been more than welcome at Grasmere but did not come, pleading pressure of business in London, was John. He had returned from China at the beginning of August after an eventful voyage that had included the engagement with the French off Malaysia. He arrived in the Northfleet docks outside London on 14 August and the next morning was closeted with the managing owner of the *Earl of Abergavenny*, lobbying hard for one of the more profitable voyages which went to China via India. John's cachet with the East India Company had evidently risen, thanks to his role in protecting their ships from Admiral Linois. As a result of his reputation, and some power-brokering by a few of Uncle William Cookson's influential friends, particularly William Wilberforce, by 15 September John had succeeded in his wish. He was promised the fifth choice in the forthcoming voyages on offer and was therefore assured of one combining India and China. John was now free to travel to Grasmere. An added incentive was that Richard, with whom he usually spent much of his time in London, was himself in the Lakes. What more sensible than that he should pay a visit now? He had not seen his brother and sister for two years and had never seen either of the children. Despite pressing invitations from both William and Dorothy, he did not come, and one is forced to the conclusion that he could not face the prospect of seeing Mary as his brother's wife.[61]

Christmas passed quietly at Grasmere. Once the flood of visitors had slackened off, William returned to composition. At the special request of one of them, Southey's friend Richard Duppa, an engraver who was preparing a life of Michelangelo, William had undertaken to translate some of Michelangelo's sonnets for inclusion in the work. It proved to be a more difficult task than he expected and the work progressed very slowly.[62] He had also more important matters on his mind. Writing to Sir George Beaumont on Christmas Day, William could report that he had written 'upwards of 2000 verses during the last ten weeks', mainly for *The Prelude.* He now hoped to have completed it by May and then he intended to 'fall with all my might' on *The Recluse*, which he expected to be up to 12,000 lines in length. So far he had only some 2,000, most of them relating to the Pedlar, and composed long ago. He had also written 'a dwarf inscription' for a little circular summer-house which they had recently built at the top of the garden. Lined with moss inside 'like a wren's nest', and with heather outside, the 'Moss Hut', as the family called it, commanded wonderful views over the lake and valley, marred only by the church, which had just been whitewashed and disturbed the proportions of the entire vale by standing out so incongruously. The moss hut was an ingenious solution to the lack of space in the cottage, serving as a refuge where William could retire for quiet (the cries of the children could be heard all over the house, and Johnny, in particular, had a 'thundering voice when he roars'), and a pleasure-house where the Wordsworths and their guests could take tea. They could get to it easily for, earlier in the year, at Catherine Clarkson's suggestion, they had replaced the window on the landing with a door, so that they could go straight out from the house into the back garden.[63]

The New Year was ushered in by a series of sparkling days, brilliant sunshine, clear skies and keen frosts. Grasmere lake froze over and, with the help of Mary's energetic youngest brother, George, William took the entire family out on the ice, the two men on skates pushing chairs in which Mary and Dorothy sat, each holding a child in her arms. The next day, New Year's Day, they all packed into the jaunting car and, with George as their intrepid charioteer, drove over Kirkstone Pass to stay with the Hutchinsons at Park House. It proved to be a foolish escapade, for the severe cold and the strenuous exercise of having to walk up the hills carrying the children left Mary with toothache, Dorothy a bad cold and William an inflammation of the eyes. Almost the entire Hutchinson clan was waiting to greet them, only Jack, the oldest, being absent. Little Hartley Coleridge was there too, so the New Year began with a joyful family reunion.[64]

John Wordsworth spent his thirty-second birthday and Christmas on board the *Earl of Abergavenny*. He had sailed from the company docks early in November and had orders to be at Deal by 21 December. He was full of hope and enthusiasm, for everyone assured him that he would make 'a very good voyage ... if not a *very great* one'. Not only would the Wordsworth family fortune be made, but John himself would be able to retire from the service. He had been assigned a new route to China which would take him to Bengal rather than Bombay and, so long as his was among the first ships to reach Canton, he stood to make immense profits in the way of trade. The cargo alone, which included £67,000 worth of dollars, packed in sixty-two chests, 200 tons each of copper, tin, lead and iron, and a vast quantity of cloth, haberdashery, millinery, glass, Wedgwood ware and military supplies, was valued at £200,000 (the equivalent of £7,046,000 today). John's personal investment amounted to some £20,000 in goods and money. He had thirty-five passengers dining at his table, nine of them civilians, the rest officers and cadets from the King's and the Company's own militia. There would have been more, but John had been obliged to ask the Court of Directors to remove some of them before he set sail, because he could not provide so many with food and accommodation on such a long voyage. This must have been rather galling, for as captain he was personally entitled to all the fees charged the passengers, including those for dining rights at his table.[65]

John's crew numbered 164. His petty officers were all younger than himself, but were tried and trusted men with whom he had sailed before. They included, as third mate, his own twenty-three-year-old second cousin Joseph, the son of Richard of Branthwaite. The ordinary seamen were, in John's characteristically blunt words, 'only *trash*': slightly more than half were English, the rest, because of the shortage of experienced sailors caused by the war, a motley collection of Portuguese, Irish, Italians, Scandinavians and Germans. Thirty-two Chinese sailors, who were not allowed by Company law to crew an outward-bound ship, were returning as passengers, and there were approximately 156 soldiers, the majority of them little more than boys, cadets and recruits for the army and East India Company. Altogether, there were almost 400 people on board.[66]

There was an unfortunate incident even before they set sail for China. During a gale off the Downs, another East Indiaman in the convoy, the *Warren Hastings*, drifted into the *Earl of Abergavenny*, damaging the starboard bow and carrying away the anchor fixings. It was a lucky escape, necessitating only minor repairs at Portsmouth while they waited for the passengers to arrive and board the ship. Contrary winds and heavy gales, with hail and sleet, delayed their departure, while John fretted and fumed in his anxiety to get off and be the first ship in Bengal. William Jerdan, later to become famous as a journalist and editor of the *Literary Gazette*, spent several days on the *Earl of Abergavenny* while it was in harbour. It was the first East Indiaman he had ever seen, and he was deeply impressed by the 'splendid ship' and its 'noble' sailors, who were 'full of every hopeful prospect and generous feeling'. (One assumes he talked to the officers, not the men.)[67]

On 1 February the convoy finally put to sea, under the escort and overall command of HMS *Weymouth*. The orders were to sail through the Needles, 'a passage I do not like much but I hope will be attended with no accident'. In the hurry of departure, the first mate, Samuel Baggot, Joseph Wordsworth and two of the soldiers had to be left behind; so determined were they to reach their ship that they paid the master of an open boat forty guineas to follow and overtake the vessel, which, ironically, he succeeded in doing. Having safely navigated the Needles, off the Isle of Wight, the weather deteriorated fast and the slower merchant ships were in a quandary, for they lost sight of the *Weymouth*. The storms grew more violent and, at ten o'clock on the morning of 5 February, the signal was given to turn back and run for safety into Portland Roads, the natural harbour between Weymouth and the Isle of Portland. The *Earl of Abergavenny*, no doubt as a result of John's anxiety to be first out, was the furthest ship from shore. The three other East Indiamen managed to get the obligatory local pilot on board in order to negotiate the Shambles, a notorious shoal of shingles and rock to the south of the island, before the tides turned. John was not so lucky. It was three in the afternoon before his pilot came on board, and by then they had lost the benefit of a flood tide. To clear the Shambles the pilot should have taken a more southerly course than the one he chose, but he seems to have underestimated the clearance needed for the fully laden ship. John was aware of the danger and clearly distrusted the pilot, but having received an assurance in answer to his questioning, there was nothing he could do. They were in the pilot's hands.[68]

At five o'clock disaster struck. The wind suddenly dropped and the strong ebb tide drove the ship straight on to the Shambles. For two and a half hours, they battled to get her off again, but when the wind veered round to the north-west, it was clear that she was doomed. The distress signal guns were fired to alert those on shore and the rest of the convoy to their plight. Every time the wind drove them off the rocks, the tide drew them on again. Under this battering, the hull was irreparably damaged; even with all hands manning the pumps, the leaks continued to gain on them. By seven o'clock, no assistance had arrived, so John gave the command for the distress signal guns to be fired continuously. With great presence of mind, he also sent off one of the ship's boats to fetch help. Aware this might be the only chance of escape from the wreck, he sent a crew of six and only two officers, the purser, Mr Stewart, who carried the ship's log and all her documentation, and Joseph Wordsworth.

About seven-thirty in the evening the ship finally got clear of the Shambles, but it soon became clear that she was waterlogged. The best hope of saving all on board was to hoist all sails and run for the nearest shore. There were several sloops in sight, but only one sent a small skiff to assist. It was too small to make any effective rescue, so John ensured that the few available places went to the civilian passengers, two Bengal merchants, John Routledge and Thomas Evans, the latter's daughter and niece, and two of the military officers. Mrs Blair, the only other woman on board, refused to go in the boat, too afraid of the darkness and mountainous seas to leave the ship. Evans would later recall how, as the little boat departed, John leaned over the ship's rails and said 'emphatically', 'God bless You!'[69]

With the aid of his officers, John managed to maintain an air of calm and purpose on the sinking vessel. The exhausted cadets who manned the pumps, many of them only boys in their early teens, were encouraged by their superiors to keep up their efforts and, when this failed, were issued with rations of grog. At around eleven o'clock, the chief mate, Samuel Baggot, came to John, who had stayed on deck throughout, and informed him, 'We have done all we can, Sir – she will sink in a moment'. John replied, 'It cannot be helped – God's will be done'. They were his last known words. The *Earl of Abergavenny* sank only a mile and a half from the safety of Weymouth sands, in a mere sixty feet of water. The vast size of the ship meant that between a third and a half of the upper rigging, top masts and yardarms were above the level of the water. Some 180 survivors clung to them in the hope of rescue, but though boats were heard paddling round in the darkness, it was between midnight and two in the morning before any sort of attempt was made. Less than half of them survived that freezing February night; benumbed by the bitter cold, many fell insensible from the rigging, or were swept away by the huge breakers of the winter storm. As always in such desperate circumstances, there were individual acts of heroism. Baggot died trying to save Mrs Blair, and the sixth mate, Herbert

Mortimer, left the safety of one of the boats to climb up the rigging and carry down, on his back, Sergeant Heart of the King's Infantry. Thomas Gilpin, the twenty-four-year-old fourth mate, made equally heroic efforts to save his captain, but they were in vain. John was last seen clinging to the ropes of his lost ship, impervious to Gilpin's pleas that he would save himself.[70] No one would ever know whether he had been overcome by the cold or had simply lost the will to live. Like the proverbial good captain, he went down with his ship.

12. *Acquiring the Quiet Mind*

First reports of the disaster reached London on the morning of 7 February and it fell to Richard to inform the rest of the family. He wrote identical short notes immediately to both William and Christopher:

> My dear Brother,
> It is with the most painful concern that I inform you of the loss of the Ship Abergavenny off Weymouth last night.
>
> I am acquainted with but few of the particulars of this melancholy Event. I am told that a great number of Persons have perished and that our Brother John is amongst that number. Mr Joseph Wordsworth is amongst those who have been saved – The Ship struck against a Rock & went to the Bottom.

Knowing their sister's likely reaction, Richard added helplessly to William, 'You will impart this to Dorothy in the best manner you can'.[1] The following day, *The Times* carried the first of many long and detailed accounts of the wreck which would appear in the press. And yet, unbelievably, the Wordsworths at Grasmere remained in ignorance of John's death until 11 February, six days after his ship went down.

It was Sara Hutchinson who brought the news. She was staying in Kendal with an old schoolfriend, saw the newspapers and came straight over to Grasmere to offer what comfort she could. Fortunately, she had the foresight to call at Rydal and intercept Richard's letter. When she arrived at Town End, William and Mary were out walking, and only Dorothy was at home. Realizing that they did not yet know, Sara had the unenviable task of breaking the news first to Dorothy alone, and then again to William and Mary. It requires little imagination to appreciate its devastating effect. Shocked and distraught, the Wordsworths could only weep together. 'I have done all in my power to alleviate the distress of poor Dorothy and my Wife', William wrote later that night, 'but heaven knows I want consolation myself.'[2] Sara agreed to stay for as long as was necessary and, the next morning, a letter arrived from an unexpected quarter. Southey, belying his reputation for coldness, was swift to sympathize. 'I scarcely know what to say to you after the thunderstroke', he wrote,

> – nor whether I ought to say anything. – Only – whenever you feel – or fancy yourself in a state to derive any advantage from company – I will come over to you, – or do you come here. It has been my custom when in affliction to force myself to mental exertion, a difficult thing – but possible. – but it made my sleep dreadful. – for grief – as far as it is a bodily feeling like disease will have its course . . . Come to me or send for me whenever you think society will not be impertinent.

'If you could bear to come to this house of mourning to-morrow,' William replied by return, 'I should be forever thankful.' Southey came, stayed two days, and left promising to return again before the week was out: 'he comforted us much, and we must for ever bear his goodness in memory'.[3]

By 16 February some semblance of calm had descended. 'I will not harrass your feelings with an account of what we have endured, or what we have yet to go through;' William wrote to another concerned and distressed friend, Thomas Clarkson.

> Dorothy's health I am afraid will suffer much in the end; though she has yet had no bodily illness but sickness of the stomach. Both Mary and she look ill, but not worse than might be expected. But I fear for Dorothy's health in the end. Sarah Hutchinson for ever bless her! has done us much good; and I have borne up as well as I could; but oh my dear Friends! what have we not endured! But the will of God be done. . . . We shall endeavour to be resigned: this is all I can say; but grief will have its course. Our loss is one which never can be made up; had it come earlier in life or later it would have been easier to bear; we are young enough to have had hope of pleasure and happiness in each others company for many years, and too old to outgrow the sorrow.

It was no accident that William quoted his brother's last words, for they had all seized on them as a crumb of comfort in this most bitter loss. 'A thousand times have I repeated to myself his last words "The will of God be done," and be it so', Dorothy wrote to Christopher at the end of the month. 'I trust I shall always be both better and *happier* too because he has lived; though I seem to myself as if I never more could be as *chearful* as heretofore.'[4]

Further comfort came from a host of unsolicited testimonials to John, all testifying to the love and respect he had inspired. Thomas Clarkson, who had been among the first to hear the news of the wreck and had fluctuated in hope and fear until John's death was confirmed, described how he had seen Wilberforce weep at the news and extol John's character at every opportunity. 'I mourn for my lost friend,' Clarkson himself wrote,

> not only on account of his Loss to you, but of his Loss as a Man. I believe, that if he had returned, and settled in Life, he would have been useful in his Day, by the practical Duty of Benevolence, and by his Example to others. But it has so pleased Providence; and if we cannot call him back, we must reverence his Memory, by the Imitation of his Virtues.

His wife, he informed them, had been made ill by the news, as had Charles Lamb. 'We loved and honoured your Brother', Lamb wrote, as his sister wept beside him, 'as long as we remember any thing, we shall remember your Brother's noble person, & his sensible manly modest voice'.[5] Coleridge, far away in Malta, heard the news by chance in a social gathering in the drawing room of the governor, Sir Alexander Ball. He staggered to the door, almost fainting with shock, and gave way to his anguish in private.

> O William, O Dorothy, Dorothy! – Mary – & you loved him so! . . . O dear John! and so ended thy dreams of Tairns & mountain Becks, & obscure vales in the breasts and necks of Mountains! So thy dream of living with or among thy Brother & *his* – O Heavens! Dying in all its Shapes; shrieks; and confusion; and mad Hope; and Drowning more deliberate than Suicide; – these, these were the Dorothy, the Mary, the Sara Hutchinson, to kiss the cold Drops from thy Brow, & to close thy Eyes! – Never yet has any Loss gone so far into the Life of Hope, with me. I now only fear.[6]

Far more moving, in their simplicity and obvious sincerity, were the tributes paid by those who survived the wreck. From Thomas Evans, the wealthy Bengal merchant whose family owed their lives to John's ensuring that they had places in the rescue boat, down to the humblest, barely literate seaman, they one and all paid tribute to his kindness, cheerful disposition and calm authority in his final hours. His shipmates, the Wordsworths discovered, had called him 'the Philosopher'.[7]

These were but small crumbs of comfort, however, in the face of the press reporting of the wreck. The scale of the disaster – one of the largest merchant ships in the country, laden with valuable cargo, not to mention the loss of some 300 lives – captured the public imagination. The wreck became a macabre tourist attraction: summer visitors to Weymouth (including the royal family) could see the masts of the sunken ship from the esplanade and were ferried out in small boats to view it at close quarters.[8] Newspapers and a flurry of opportunistic pamphlets cashed in on the disaster, with increasingly lurid speculation about its cause. Nowhere was John's personal courage doubted, but questions were asked about his judgement. Why had he delayed firing the signal guns for an hour and a half after they first struck? Why had he not ordered the ship's boats to be cut free? Possibly even more distressing was the almost universal consensus that John had effectively committed suicide, rather than face the consequences of losing his ship and his fortune.

William was desperate for reassurance that his brother had died the hero, not just for his own satisfaction but because he could not bear the thought that the relatives of those lost would blame John. The *Earl of Abergavenny* was a Penrith ship and there was not a family in the town untouched by the tragedy. William knew he would never be able to look these people in the face again if he could not clear John's name. He plagued Richard with requests for the minutest details of the wreck, until his anguished brother was finally goaded to respond: 'It is impossible for me to enter into particulars of the melancholy catastrophe. It will be enough to say that our dear Brother, did Every thing that Man could do on so trying & arduous an Occasion. This must be a great consolation to us all. . . . You will excuse me for not writing sooner, for the truth is, I have had no relish for writing.'[9] The Wordsworths of Grasmere did not have a monopoly on grief. Unable to get anything more out of Richard, William turned to Charles Lamb, who was a clerk at East India House, and his own cousin Captain Wordsworth, who had been a major investor in the voyage. Both of them made enormous efforts to track down survivors and provide William with the answers he wanted. Unfortunately, this was not the same as the truth.

It proved impossible to scotch rumours that John had not wished to survive the wreck. He had, after all, had at least five hours, between six o'clock, when the extent of the damage was discovered, and eleven o'clock, when the ship finally sank, to contemplate the fact that he had lost everything: reputation and fortune, as well as the woman he loved. As Lamb pointed out, all accounts agreed that, just before the ship went down, John 'seemed like one overwhelmed with the situation, & careless of his own safety'. Realizing afterwards how much this was likely to upset William, the next day he recanted, adding that he had since seen Thomas Gilpin, who 'assured me that your Brother did try to save himself, and was doing so when Gilpin called to him, but he was then struggling with the waves & almost dead'. This was still not good enough for William, who wrote directly to Gilpin himself. Replying from his new ship at Portsmouth, Gilpin described how he got within ten or twelve feet of his captain, who was holding on to a rope on the mizzen mast. He had hailed him and thrown him a rope, but John was 'motionless & insensible he did not katch the rope or answer'.[10] With this, William had to be content, persuading himself and his sister that John had simply been overwhelmed by the elements.

At least there was no question of misconduct. There was a logical, nautical, explanation for each of the decisions queried by the amateurs of the press, and, in any case, an investigation by the Committee of Shipping reporting to the Court of Directors unanimously resolved 'that the Commander, Officers & Ship's company of the Earl of Abergavenny be fully acquitted of all Imputation of neglect or misconduct in respect to the Loss of that Ship'. The owners were also cleared of any neglect or misconduct in supplying and equipping the ship. All the evidence vindicated John and put the blame squarely on the pilot, 'if he may so be call'd' (as

Gilpin bitterly put it), who not only survived the wreck he had caused, but somehow managed to remain anonymous. The local community closed ranks. The suspicion must remain that the men of Portland and Weymouth also deliberately refrained from assisting the survivors. Indeed, they had an unenviable reputation for exactly that. Shipwrecks were commonplace on that notorious stretch of coastline but it was not often that the rich pickings of a fully laden East Indiaman were to be had. Many of the survivors reported hearing boats in the darkness after the ship went down, but their cries for help were ignored, because, it was later improbably claimed, of fears that they would be swamped in the rush for safety. Though there were important exceptions, boxes of personal belongings washed up on shore in the weeks that followed were plundered and left empty; no doubt valuables also went missing from the unidentifiable corpses.[11]

For this reason, at Captain Wordsworth's instigation, a reward of £200 was offered for the recovery of John's body and, six weeks after the ship down, it was found by dragging the wreck site. His sword, presented by the East India Company after the engagement with Admiral Linois the previous year, was missing; a reward was offered and, lo and behold, it too was recovered. Mr Stewart, the purser of the *Earl of Abergavenny*, who had been appointed an agent to the underwriters and thus remained in Weymouth, was on hand to identify the body. On 21 March John was buried in the churchyard at All Saints' Church, Wyke Regis, overlooking the bay where he had lost his life. His funeral was attended by twelve mourners, including the mayor of Weymouth and representatives of the Company; 'by particular desire', presumably of the Wordsworth family, the burial arrangements were made by the widow of Thomas Fowell Buxton, whose country house, Bellfield, was just outside Weymouth in the parish of Wyke Regis. Mrs Anna Buxton, a Quaker, was a cousin of Christopher's wife, Priscilla, and her own son, Edward, was a midshipman in the service of the East India Company.[12] John was interred next to the Buxton vault by the south door of the church; a large stone was laid on the grave, but was removed on the authority of a later bishop, who identified it as an altar table and removed it to the sanctuary. The daughter of John's cousin Robinson Wordsworth wrote to William in 1846 to point this out and suggest that it should be replaced. William refused: 'if another Stone were put up what assurance could be had that it would not shortly meet with the same fate?' He thought a brass plaque within the church, recording the fate of the *Earl of Abergavenny* and pointing out the location of John's grave, might be more appropriate, but added, 'I should be somewhat more desirous of this being done if my own Poems had not widely spread the knowledge of my poor Brother's fate.' No plaque was put up so the silent poet, whose physical image was not preserved in either words or picture during his life, now sleeps anonymously in an unmarked grave.[13]

His lasting memorial was, as William rather egotistically claimed, the poetry his life and death inspired in his brother. 'For myself I feel that there is something cut out of my life which cannot be restored,' William wrote to James Losh.

I never thought of him but with hope and delight, we looked forward to the time not distant as we thought when he would settle near us when the task of his life would be over and he would have nothing to do but reap his reward. By that time I hoped also that the chief part of my labours would be executed and that I should be able to shew him that he had not placed a false confidence in me. I never wrote a line without a thought of its giving him pleasure, my writings printed and manuscript were his delight and one of the chief solaces of his long voyages. But let me stop – I will not be cast down were it only for his sake I will not be dejected. I have much yet to do and pray God to give me strength and power – his part of the agreement between us is brought to an end; mine continues and I hope when I shall be able to think of him with a calmer mind that the remembrance of him dead will even animate me more than the joy which I had in him living.[14]

In the first shock of bereavement, William could write no poetry at all, but by 11 April he had begun work on a memorial poem. 'Till he has unburthened his heart of its feelings on our loss he cannot go on with other things,' Dorothy told Lady Beaumont, 'and it does him good to speak of John as he was, therefore he is now writing a poem upon him. I should not say a *poem* for it is a *part* of the Recluse.' Once this labour of love was finished, Dorothy had every confidence William would return to his great task with renewed vigour. Inspiration was certainly not lacking, but it was too soon. William was overpowered by his own feelings and had to stop. Unfortunately, he had composed so much so fast that he had been unable to remember, or record, more than a few lines, and 'the subject was such, that I could not employ Mrs Wordsworth or my Sister as my amanuensis'. The work would therefore have to be set aside until he was calmer, but, he added, 'I shall . . . never be at peace till, as far as in me lies, I have done justice to my departed Brother's memory.'

Instead, he returned to *The Prelude*, adding a further 300 lines in the course of a week. The poem was now so long that William was rather embarrassed. 'It will not be much less than 9,000 lines, not hundred but thousand lines, long', he admitted to Beaumont; 'an alarming length! and a thing unprecedented in Literary history that a man should talk so much about himself.' It was not self-conceit that led him to this, however, but real humility. As he only had to describe his own feelings and thoughts, he was sure of success, unlike *The Recluse*, for which he still felt unprepared and diffident of his powers. To Beaumont he also made a rare admission of his own failing as a poet, his inability to cut down his work. Redundancies ought to be 'lopped off', he knew. 'But this is very difficult to do when a man has written with thought, and this defect, whenever I have suspected it or found it to exist in any writings of mine, I have always found incurable. The fault lies too deep, and is in the first conception.'[15]

By the middle of May, William had put the finishing touches to *The Prelude*. It was a moment he had long anticipated as a joyous one, but it proved to be the inevitable anticlimax.

When I looked back upon the performance it seemed to have a dead weight about it, the reality so far short of the expectation; it was the first long labour that I had finished, and the doubt whether I should ever live to write the Recluse and the sense which I had of this Poem being so far below what I seem'd capable of executing, depressed me much: above all, many heavy thoughts of my poor departed Brother hung upon me; the joy which I should have had in shewing him the Manuscript and a thousand other vain fancies and dreams. I have spoken of this because it was a state of feeling new to me, the occasion being new.

John's unexpected death had forced William to re-evaluate his own life and define its purpose. Finishing the poem on his own life was merely the first stage of what had now become a three-part plan. 'This work may be considered as a sort of portico to the Recluse, part of the same building, which I hope to be able erelong to begin with, in earnest; and if I am permitted to bring it to a conclusion, and to write, further, a narrative Poem of the Epic kind, I shall consider the *task* of my life as over.'[16]

To begin properly on *The Recluse*, however, he needed Coleridge's notes and detailed plan of the poem. These were still not forthcoming, despite all William's pleas, but Coleridge now had a splendid excuse. He had indeed written the notes and a complete account of his travels for publication in the *Morning Post*, but he had entrusted them to Major Ralph Adye, who was returning to England. Adye had the temerity to catch the plague on the way home and died in Gibraltar; all his papers were burnt by the authorities for fear of contamination. And so perished the precious notes for *The Recluse*. Or so Coleridge claimed. The loss was not as irretrievable as might have been feared, for the Wordsworths were convinced that Coleridge himself was about to return to England at any moment. They had heard that he intended to leave Malta in March, but, as William confidently assured Beaumont, 'I am sure he will return the first minute he can after hearing the news' of John's death. 'I am as sure of this as if I heard him say so.' It was not the first or the last time that such confidence would be misplaced. Coleridge had an almost pathological fear of facing up to the bereavements of those he loved: he had not returned home from Germany when his own son died and he did not come back now. He lingered at Malta until September, then set off for Italy, where he spent almost a year playing the gentleman of leisure in Rome and Naples. He did not set off for England until 23 June 1806.[17]

At Grasmere the Wordsworths slowly picked up the shattered pieces of their lives without Coleridge. Sara Hutchinson had stayed with them only a week after breaking the news of John's death: 'they thought it was better she should leave them, and then they would be obliged to exert themselves more'. On 18 March she returned to stay for a month, her second departure being 'a great loss to us'. Southey also paid several visits and presented them with a copy of his newly published poem *Madoc*. It lay unread for more than a fortnight because the three adults wanted to read it aloud quietly together, and could only do this when the children were asleep. Like Walter Scott's *Lay of the Last Minstrel*, which they also read in this way, they found the poem entertaining and full of lively description, but in criticizing *Madoc* to Beaumont, William pointed out that it lacked what he considered the two most important elements of poetry, imagination 'in the true sense of the word' and knowledge of human nature and the human heart.[18]

They had long neglected the garden, unable to bring themselves to work in it because it was so closely associated with John. It was three months after his death before they could summon up the courage to finish off the moss hut they had begun before Christmas, and set the garden itself to rights. They also made some necessary improvements to the little cottage, easing the cramped conditions by raising the roof of the peat store, which created space for another bedroom, and by taking over another cottage at Townhead, which belonged to the Keswick carrier, where they could do all their cooking and provide a bedroom for Sally Ashburner, who was now their servant.[19]

There were other hurdles to be surmounted. On 8 June William and a neighbour went up to Grisedale Tarn to fish. It was the first time William had visited the place since John's death and he was so overcome he had to leave his companion in tears. Grisedale had been one of John's favourite haunts, 'for the pleasure of angling in part, but still more, for his love of solitude and of the mountains'; significantly, it was also the scene of the brothers' last parting in the Lakes, and it was this that William memorialized in the *Elegaic Verses* he composed as he wept.

– Brother and friend, if verse of mine
Have power to make thy virtues known,
Here let a monumental Stone
Stand – sacred as a Shrine;

A couple of days later, with Mary and Dorothy to support him, William returned to the tarn and, taking leaving of them there, walked in his brother's footsteps to Patterdale, where he intended to spend a few days fishing and relaxing before he embarked on *The Recluse.* 'You will judge that a happy change has been wrought in his mind', Dorothy observed, 'when he chuses John's employments, and one of John's haunts (for he delighted in the neighbourhood of Patterdale) for such a purpose.'[20] Before the end of the month, he had written two more memorial poems. One was the famous and beautiful poem inspired by, and echoing, a rare descriptive passage in one of John's letters. It was addressed to the daisy, John's favourite flower, and in appropriately simple and poignant lines it celebrated both John's life and death.

Six weeks beneath the moving sea
He lay in slumber quietly;
Unforced by wind or wave
To quit the Ship for which he died,
(All claims of duty satisfied);
And there they found him at her side;
And bore him to the grave.

Vain service! yet not vainly done
For this, if other end were none,
That He, who had been cast
Upon a way of life unmeet
For such a gentle Soul and sweet,
Should find an undisturbed retreat
Near what he loved, at last –

That neighbourhood of grove and field
To Him a resting-place should yield,
A meek man and a brave!
The birds shall sing and ocean make
A mournful murmur for *his* sake;
And Thou, sweet Flower, shalt sleep and wake
Upon his senseless grave.

The second poem, though inferior in every respect and never published by William in his lifetime, is important in a different way. It was prompted by the now redundant manuscript book of William's latest poems, which John had intended to carry with him on his voyage. Looking at it, with a heart oppressed by pain and grief, William was driven to cry,

gracious God
Oh grant that I may never find
Worse matter or a heavier mind,
Grant this, and let me be resigned
Beneath thy chastening rod.[21]

It is hardly startling stuff, but it is the first explicit statement of belief in God in William's poetry. Conventional religion had clearly meant little or nothing to him. There is no evidence, for example, that he had attended church regularly as an adult, or that he had any deeply held religious beliefs. Coleridge, in the early days of their friendship, had suspected him of the atheism which usually went hand in hand with revolutionary politics; though this was not true, his poetry had veered between vague utterances on the eternal verities and outright pantheism (the worship of nature as the manifestation of God), and he was not yet a Christian. In the wake of John's death, he was forced to re-examine his spiritual beliefs in a way he had never done before. In an anguished letter to Beaumont, written a month after hearing the news, he asked the questions most of us ask in the bitterness of bereavement.

Why have we a choice and a will, and a notion of justice and injustice, enabling us to be moral agents? Why have we sympathies that make the best of us so afraid of inflicting pain and sorrow, which yet we see dealt about so lavishly by the supreme governor? Why should our notions of right towards each other, and to all sentient beings within our influence differ so widely from what appears to be his notion and rule, if every thing were to end here? Would it be blasphemy to say that upon the supposition of the thinking principle being destroyed by death, however inferior we may be to the great Cause and ruler of things, we have *more of love* in our Nature than he has? The thought is monstrous; and yet how to get rid of it except upon the supposition of *another* and a *better world* I do not see.

William might have been arguing himself into an intellectual acceptance of faith, but in his wife, her family and Southey he had support from those with a more instinctive and emotional belief. By 16 April he could write to Richard to say how much comfort he derived from the idea that their brother had done his duty not only to his ship but also to himself: 'he went a brave and innocent Spirit to that God from whom I trust he will receive his reward'.[22]

There was also comfort of a less elevated kind in learning that they were no worse off financially because of the shipwreck. With that delicate tact which marked all his dealings with the touchy members of the arts fraternity, Sir George Beaumont had conjured William 'by the obligation of our love, by the rights of our fellowship', to tell him if he had ventured his capital on the voyage. William was able to reassure him: John was well insured and Richard did not expect that any of the family would lose anything. Nevertheless, Beaumont insisted on sending William a gift of money by way of compensation: 'you may be suddenly called to town, expensive business you do not at present expect may arise, – at all events I do not want it, & I am sure I cannot dispose of it with equal satisfaction to myself'. If nothing else, it might finance a future tour. 'You have done me infinite service', he explained. '– I have lived many years in the world, & I began to think, that all is selfishness was at least as true an axiom, as all is vanity – I fear they in a great measure divide it betwixt them – but I now have the satisfaction of knowing there are exceptions.'[23]

The summer brought the distraction of the usual flood of visitors. Mrs Coleridge and her daughter came on 18 June and stayed for between two and three weeks, enabling Dorothy to record with satisfaction that the two-and-a-half-year-old Sara was greatly altered for the worse, no longer a meek and exquisitely beautiful baby, but 'a Snarler – a little vixen'. They were followed immediately by two of the Halifax Threlkelds, the sister-in-law and niece of Mrs Rawson, who were on their way to Newbiggin Hall. Not having seen Dorothy for many years, they were shocked at her changed appearance: she was 'grown so thin and old that they shou'd not have known her, – lost many of her teeth and her cheeks quite sunk that it has entirely alter'd her profile, – yet she looks healthy'. They got over their revulsion pretty quickly, for a two-day visit turned into one of a fortnight.[24]

It was difficult enough catering for visitors to the cottage at the best of times, but the Wordsworths had an additional responsibility throughout the late summer. Towards the end of July, the Clarksons came to Grasmere, taking up lodgings in a house belonging to Robert Newton close to the village inn. Catherine had been away from the Lakes for more than two years and was now a confirmed invalid, but, having known John well, she insisted on coming to Grasmere to lend the Wordsworths her support. Despite her fragility, she was a cheerful and lively companion who brought some much needed merriment to the mourning household.[25]

It cannot have been long after the Clarksons' arrival that a gruesome discovery was made by a shepherd on Helvellyn. Hearing barking, he went to investigate and found a small dog alone on the rocks at the head of Red Tarn. She led him to the headless corpse and bleached bones which were all that remained of her master. From a pocket book found in his clothes, Clarkson discovered that the unfortunate man was Charles Gough, a young artist from Manchester, who had fallen to his death from Helvellyn while on his way to fish in the tarn. As the dead man was a Quaker, it fell to Clarkson to arrange his interment in the Friends' burial ground at Tirril, and send news of his demise to his mother. The discovery caused a brief sensation, not least because of the loyalty of the dog in maintaining her lonely vigil beside the corpse for three long months. It was just the sort of pathetic incident to appeal to William, who set about commemorating it in verse. The resulting poem, *Fidelity*, is marred only by the rhetorical question at the end: how was the dog nourished 'through such long time'? – which invites the irreverent but obvious rejoinder, how was the corpse stripped of flesh in just three months? The more kindly disposed of the Lakers decided it ate grass.[26]

Another visitor, in August, was Walter Scott, who had at last yielded to William's entreaties to visit the Lakes. William went to Keswick to meet him and repay his courtesy two years previously by giving him a guided tour. It turned into quite a party, for they were joined by Southey and his brother Harry, Humphry Davy, the friend from Bristol who had seen *Lyrical Ballads* through the press, and Southey's friend Charles Danvers. From Greta Hall they had an expedition to the Lodore Falls, Watendlath and the Bowder Stone, the vast boulder resting in splendid isolation on the lower slopes of Borrowdale, returning to Keswick over Castle Crag. The following day, William, Scott and Davy went to Patterdale, spent the night (uncomfortably deprived of their room till after midnight by a party of ladies) at the inn there, then, bright and early, climbed Helvellyn together. It was a day they would always remember. Their progress was slow, for Scott was lame from birth, but this did not deter him, and he beguiled the time by telling stories and amusing anecdotes. Over thirty years later, William remembered with admiration the vigour with which Scott had then scrambled along the treacherous horn of Striding Edge:

> Where once together, in his day of strength
> We stood rejoicing, as if earth were free
> From sorrow, like the sky above our heads.

No doubt William pointed out the place where Gough's body had been found, for Scott too, quite independently, wrote his own poem on the subject of the devoted dog. Davy grew impatient with the two dawdlers, and, having reached the summit, set off on his own to the rendezvous at Town End. The little party were then joined by Mrs Scott, dined together and, next day, sailed on Windermere, before going their separate ways. Scott left the Lakes with a profound admiration for both Southey and William.

They are certainly men of very extraordinary powers, Wordsworth in particular is such a character as only exists in romance virtuous, simple, and unaffectedly restricting every want & wish to the bounds of a very narrow income in order to enjoy the literary and poetical leisure which his happiness consists in.[27]

Richard paid a fleeting visit to Grasmere this summer too. His reason for visiting the Lakes this time was not social but business, for he had decided to purchase some tenanted land on Ullswater to add to his Sockbridge estate. Dorothy's appearance shocked him as much as it had her Halifax cousins. He was convinced she was doing too much walking for her own good, so, before he left, he made arrangements for the purchase of a pony for her, adding, at her request, a bridle and side saddle. It proved an invaluable gift and the pony was pressed immediately into service by all the family.[28]

Even after the last visitors departed, in mid-October, William still could not settle to any serious employment: the expectation that Coleridge might arrive any day 'not a little unhinges me'. He did some desultory work on Michelangelo's sonnets, but, despite attempting fifteen, succeeded in translating only one: 'so much meaning has been put by Michael Angelo into so little room, and that meaning sometimes so excellent in itself that I found the difficulty of translating him insurmountable'. It was, he concluded, just what you would expect from such a man, 'shewing abundantly how conversant his soul was with great things'.[29]

On 9 October *Lyrical Ballads*, a reissue of the 1802 edition, was published by Longman. Five hundred copies were printed, anticipating a steady, if not high-volume, sale. Even for what should have been a reprint, William could not resist tinkering with both poems and preface, though his changes this time were restricted to punctuation and odd words. The reprint of his most successful publication to date set William thinking. Perhaps he should publish another volume of small poems? He had enough in hand to do so, and throughout the late autumn and winter continued adding to his stock. *Fidelity* prompted two more poems on canine devotion, both inspired by Music, a favourite companion of the Hutchinson family, who had accompanied them from Sockburn-on-Tees to Gallow Hill, where, old and blind, she had fallen into a well and drowned. The Scottish tour of 1803 was still proving fertile ground for poetry, not least because William was continually reminded of its salient images by Dorothy's recent completion, and multiple copying, of her journal. *Rob Roy's Grave* and *To the Sons of Burns, after Visiting the*

Grave of their Father were both rather dull meditations arising out of visits to the graves of two famous Scotsmen during the tour.[30] A third, lovely poem, *The Solitary Reaper*, which bears all the hallmarks of William's art of recalling and investing an image with later meaning, was deceptive. Though the Wordsworths had seen, and commented on, many striking instances of solitary figures in otherwise empty landscapes, they had not seen this Highland lass, whose sweet and plaintive song filled the vale and was borne away in the poet's heart long after he had last heard it. She had actually been seen and described by Thomas Wilkinson, the Quaker poet of Yanwath, in his manuscript journal of his own tour of Scotland in 1787, which William had just read.[31]

By the beginning of November, William had 'entirely given up the idea' of publishing some of his smaller poems. It was not just that he had a great dislike to the whole business of publishing: 'that is not his reason –' Dorothy informed Lady Beaumont, 'he thinks that having been so long silent to the world he ought to come forward again with a work of greater labour'.[32] In other words, the elusive *Recluse*. Instead he went on a short tour. This was neither the grand scheme he had concocted before John's death of going to Norway, nor even the longed for tour of Scotland with Mary, but a three-day exploration of the tributary vales of Ullswater, which he had never visited before. He set off on 7 November, walking beside Dorothy, who rode her new pony. They were dogged from the first moment by bad weather; mists and rain followed them over Kirkstone Pass, and, though they had assured accommodation with their friends, the Luffs, at Patterdale, their wanderings were curtailed to the lake shores. Dorothy minutely recorded descriptions of everything they saw in a journal dedicated to the 'tour', probably written for Lady Beaumont. It was while staying with the Luffs at what is now Side Farm that William found what he considered the perfect spot for building a cottage. It lay quarter of a mile from the village of Patterdale, across the deep, wide, clear, slow-running waters of Goldrill Beck, which bisects the broad vale, and it is surrounded by the fells, which rise sheer and bare and crested with rock. With views up the valley to Kirkstone Pass, across to the heights of Helvellyn and down to the waters of Ullswater, with the shadowy fells looming beyond the lake, it was indeed a perfect setting. What distinguished this particular spot, Broad How, from those around it, was the large wooded and rocky knoll, dominated by a great yew tree, which was a vantage point for the whole vale.[33]

On the last morning of their visit, as they sat at breakfast, the maid-servant 'with an uncouth stare and grin of pleasure' announced that there had been a great British victory at Trafalgar and that Lord Nelson was dead. Dorothy immediately burst into tears, but William refused to believe it, 'and forced me to suspend my grief' till they had made further inquiries. Rushing over to the village inn, they learned that it was indeed true and were shocked to hear that there had been great rejoicings at Penrith; for Dorothy at least, the loss of Nelson outweighed the joy of victory. Returning to the Luffs' house, they made a detour to walk by 'William's rock & grove', and William came to an uncharacteristically swift decision. Perhaps the shock of the news of Nelson's death at sea brought back thoughts of that similar, yet so much more personal, 'thunderstroke' earlier in the year, reinforcing the knowledge that John had particularly loved Patterdale, but William decided to buy Broad How. Though they were already overdue at Grasmere, the Wordsworths set off immediately to see Wilkinson, hoping that he might know the owner and negotiate a deal on William's behalf. Having begged beds for the night from the Hutchinsons at Park House, William called on Wilkinson that very evening and authorized him to offer up to £800 for the site.

Next morning was fine, so they decided to go to Lowther. The bad earl had left both house and grounds to fend for themselves, but Sir William was determined to repair the neglect of decades. Tactfully, he had appointed his neighbour, Wilkinson, as his 'Arbiter Elegantiarum, or Master of the grounds at Lowther'. Wilkinson was an 'amiable inoffensive man, and a little of a Poet too', as William rather patronizingly, if aptly, described him. He had earned something of a reputation for the way he had laid out his own little estate at Yanwath, on the banks of the Eamont, with paths and bowers, 'all very pretty', for each of which he had written his own inscription. Now he was busily at work, transforming the grounds at Lowther, for which he received a half-hearted endorsement from William: 'what he has done hitherto is very well', he told Beaumont, 'as it is little more than making accessible what could not before be got at'. Where the two men parted company was Wilkinson's manufactured riverside walk. William admitted it was 'absolutely necessary in many places', but what he lamented was that it would efface a natural forest pathway, which he had loved since childhood.

> This Path winds on under the trees with the wantonness of a River or a living Creature; and even if I may say so with the subtelty of a Spirit, contracting or enlarging itself, visible or invisible as it likes. There is a continued opening between the trees, a narrow slip of turf besprinkled with Flowers, chiefly Daisies, and here it is, if I may use the same kind of language, that this pretty path plays its pranks wearing away the turf and flowers at its pleasure.[34]

They found Wilkinson at work with his spade in one of his own fields, and, with him as their guide, the Wordsworths, accompanied by Sara and Miss Green, one of the new tenants of Eusemere, explored the length of the new riverside path. Dorothy, oblivious to the devastation Wilkinson had wreaked on the ancient woodland, recorded 'three delightful hours [spent] by the River-side' in her journal, and later described it as 'a marvellously beautiful walk'. The next day, she and William retraced their steps through Patterdale and over a starlit Kirkstone to Grasmere, where they found Mary and the children all retired to bed.[35]

The exposure to the rain and cold brought on one of Dorothy's chest infections, 'a slight attack of *Peripneumony*', but she was sufficiently recovered by 25 November for Mary to leave her in charge of the children while she went on a fortnight's visit to Park House. William joined his wife a few days later, and Dorothy was left alone with the children and her own thoughts. William had deliberately left her with an important task to complete: the transcription of the entire *Prelude*, but it failed to keep her thoughts from John. 'The Children are now in bed', she wrote to Lady Beaumont on 29 November.

The evening is very still, and there are no indoor sounds but the ticking of our Family watch which hangs over the chimney-piece under the drawing of the Applethwaite Cottage, and a breathing or a beating of one single irregular Flame in my fire. No one who has not been an Inmate with Children in a *Cottage* can have a notion of the quietness that takes possession of it when they are gone to sleep. The hour before is generally a noisy one, often given up to boisterous efforts to amuse them, and the noise is heard in every corner of the house – then comes the washing and undressing, a work of misery, and in ten minutes after, all is stillness and perfect rest. It is at all times a sweet hour to us; but I can fancy that I have never enjoyed it so much as now that I am quite alone – yet it is a strange kind of pleasure for the Image of our departed Brother haunts me with many a pang in the midst of happy recollections of him . . .[36]

Christmas Day, Dorothy's thirty-fourth birthday, was a particularly sad occasion. Not only were they haunted by memories of John, but, once again, they had been disappointed of Coleridge's return, despite letters which had led them to believe he would arrive any day. They were still bereft of Mary, who had been obliged to remain at Park House, so William, Dorothy and the children shared their Christmas dinner, two plum puddings 'rumbling in the Pot' and a sirloin of beef 'smoking at the Fire', with old Molly Fisher and her brother. On Boxing Day, with wind, rain and snow driving down the vale, the little cottage at Town End came briefly to life as the Grasmere fiddler did his annual round, and half a dozen little children danced wildly round the kitchen. Dora was in ecstasy, Johnny too shy to dance with anyone but 'Anny', as he still called his aunt Dorothy. Looking back over the six Christmases she had spent at Grasmere, and aware that this was likely to be her last, Dorothy had time for reflection:

though the freshness of life was passed away even when we came hither, I think these years have been the very happiest of my life, – at least, they seem as if they would bear looking back upon better than any other, though my heart flutters and aches striving to call to my mind more perfectly the remembrance of some of the more thoughtless pleasures of former years, and though till within this late time I never experienced a real affliction.[37]

Deliberately, or unwittingly, Dorothy was echoing her brother's lines in *Tintern Abbey*. In coming to terms with her own most bitter loss, she too had acquired the quiet mind.

As the winter progressed, William became increasingly anxious to get on with *The Recluse*, but he was at a loss how to proceed. He was reading extensively, 'for the nourishment of his mind, preparatory to beginning', but, as Dorothy wisely observed, 'I do not think he will be able to do much more till we have heard of Coleridge.' William had begun to build up a collection of his own books in the autumn of 1804, commissioning Lamb to purchase for him 'as complete a library of old Poets & Dramatists as will be prudent to buy'. To this, a year later, he added all the books from his father's library at Cockermouth, which had been sitting on Cousin Richard Wordsworth of Branthwaite's shelves for more than twenty years.[38]

It was in his reading that William found a model for his next poem, *Character of the Happy Warrior*, but the idea came from contemplating Nelson's death. Unlike Dorothy, whose views were representative of the popular feeling in the country, it was an event William was able to view quite dispassionately. 'Few men have ever died under circumstances so likely to make their death of benefit to their Country', he told Beaumont; 'it is not easy to see what his life could have done comparable to it.' The loss of men such as Nelson was great and real, but it was not irreparable. For every man like Nelson, there were 500 as good as he who had not been fortunate enough to have come to their country's attention. Men, for instance, like John Wordsworth. And it was John's virtues, as much as, if not more than, Nelson's, which contributed to answering the question posed in the opening lines of the poem:

> Who is the happy Warrior? Who is he
> That every man in arms should wish to be?[39]

William was never satisfied with the poem, which he felt was unworthy of its subject. (He had succeeded in putting the same view forward far more succinctly and effectively in his sonnet 'I grieved for Buonaparté'.) Even when it predictably became one of Victorian England's favourite poems, he felt that it was flawed as a composition: 'it does not best fulfil the conditions of poetry:' he later told the poisonous Harriet Martineau, who could not resist mocking what she saw as the odd mixture of the old man's pomposity and northern accent, ' "but it is" (solemnly) "a chain of extremely valooable thoughts" '.[40]

The same could not be said of the other poem he wrote in the first two weeks of the new year. *Benjamin the Waggoner* would always be a personal favourite in much the same way, and for much the same reasons, as *The Idiot Boy*. His own note on the poem, dictated in old age to Isabella Fenwick, was grumpy and brief, 'The character & story from fact', but this was a response to the critical mauling the poem received on publication. At the time he wrote '*con amore*' and the whole was 'thrown off under a lively impulse of feeling'. It was not surprising that *Benjamin the Waggoner* offended the sensibilities of the reviewers, for it was diametrically opposed to the high-flown, earnest, moral didacticism of *Character of the Happy Warrior*. A light-hearted narrative poem, it tells the tale of Benjamin, driver of the great waggon, pulled by a team of eight horses, between Kendal and Keswick, whose soft-heartedness and fondness for drink cause his downfall. Having withstood the temptation of the various inns along his route, he stops to offer a lift to the wife and child of an unemployed sailor and ends up on a two-hour drinking-spree with the sailor. Approaching Keswick, he finds his employer out on the road to meet him and is dismissed, even though he is the only man who can manage the team. It was, William insisted, 'purely fanciful': there was no moral message, nor even the sort of social commentary which had underpinned so much of his earlier poetry. But, as his friend Robinson later said, it is told with grace, has delightful descriptive passages, informed by William's intimate knowledge of the setting, and is written with elegant playfulness. Benjamin, for all his faults, is portrayed affectionately and his changing moods are brilliantly captured in the pace of the poetry itself, particularly the alteration from the ebullience of the convivial drinking in the inn to the languor and sickliness of hangover.[41] It was fun, but it was hardly *The Recluse.*

The non-appearance of Coleridge had left them all in limbo. As the vale was battered by one winter storm after another, and the anniversary of John's death came and went, Dorothy spent sleepless nights conjuring up images of shipwrecks and imagining that Coleridge too had drowned at sea. Even if he escaped such a fate by travelling overland, there was every possibility that he might be captured by the French. The news from the Continent was so depressing that she dreaded the arrival of the newspapers. Napoleon's armies were sweeping across Europe: French victories at Ulm and Austerlitz were followed by his dictating the terms of offensive and defensive alliance treaties with Prussia and Austria. In March his brother Joseph Bonaparte was crowned King of Naples and Sicily. In the midst of this crisis, William Pitt, the Prime Minister, died. As the nation mourned the loss of the man who had kept Britain at the forefront of opposition to French aggrandizement, William, his radical sympathies rising to the fore, offered only muted praise.

> I have never been able to regard his political life with complacency: I believe him, however, to have been as disinterested a Man, and as true a lover of his Country as it was possible for so ambitious a man to be. His first wish (though probably unknown to himself) was that his Country should prosper under his administration; his next, that it should prosper: could the order of these wishes have been reversed, Mr Pitt would have avoided many of the grievous mistakes into which, I think, he fell.

William was indifferent to which administration would succeed Pitt's, believing there was no true honour or ability among any of the contending politicians. He did think, however, that all the people of England should be instructed in the use of arms.[42]

'We are crammed into our little nest edge-full', Dorothy told Catherine Clarkson at the beginning of March. They had taken on an additional temporary nursemaid while Mary visited Park House, but she had been so useful that they had kept her on. Mary had brought Sara back with her and she too was still with them. All three women were hard at work, transcribing copies of William's poem on his own life. Every bed in the house was shared by two people, and the cause of Mary's ill-health before Christmas was now clear: she was pregnant again, and, as usual, casually unaware whether the baby was due in May or June.[43]

William decided to get out from under everyone's feet. The Beaumonts had repeatedly offered him the use of their house in Grosvenor Square and, with nothing better to do, it seemed like a good time for a visit to London. It required a couple of letters to Montagu to extract the necessary funds, even though he still owed William considerable sums. The second carried a pained postscript: 'We have been entangled by your assurances into making promises which we have been unable to fulfill, especially one to our Landlord to whom we owe two years rent, and whom we have disappointed.' Montagu duly responded and on 29 March William set out on his first trip to London in two and a half years. Southey was his travelling companion for the first part of the journey and was much amused by William's difficulties. At Penrith, he picked up the wrong key, leaving behind the one for his own trunk and taking one belonging to the Monkhouses. Unable to change his clothes, he had flattered himself that his breeches were 'very genteel', until the invariably dapper Southey pointed out that he had torn a hole in them and that the buttons needed covering.[44]

William arrived in town at the beginning of April and went immediately to Lambeth, to stay with his brother Christopher, who was now chaplain to the Archbishop of Canterbury. It was an unsalaried appointment, lasting seven years, but at the end of it his prospects for rapid and substantial advancement within the Church were excellent. This was William's first visit to his brother's home since Christopher's marriage; he already had one son, like William's named John, after their lost brother, and Priscilla was expecting a second child in August.[45]

As William informed Mrs Clarkson soon after his arrival, 'I am here to see everything and every Body good bad great little &c &c that I can.' Old friends and new were on his agenda. Having stayed with Christopher, he paid visits to both the Montagus and the Lambs, probably saw his brother Richard, and the Clarksons, and paid a three-day duty visit to the Cooksons at Binfield, where his uncle now had a rich living in addition to his canonry at Windsor. William Godwin, another figure from his past, soon found him out, and there were regular calls on, and from, him. Through Godwin and Sir George Beaumont, William met once again the radical lawyer Horne Tooke, and a host of up-and-coming artists: James Northcote, the historical and portrait painter, who had been an assistant to Sir Joshua Reynolds; Henry Edridge, the brilliant society miniaturist, who had called at Town End in the late summer of 1804; Richard Duppa, Southey's friend, who had accompanied Edridge and to whom William had promised the translations of Michelangelo; David Wilkie, the young Scottish artist and portrait painter; Joseph Farington, an artist-friend of Uncle William Cookson, now probably better known for his voluminous and splenetic diaries than his landscapes. Southey too brought his friend John Rickman, the statistician and founder of the decennial census, and Lamb his friend Thomas Manning, the mathematician and linguist, who was on the point of departure for Canton, where he would practise as a doctor.[46]

It was a glittering array of the brightest and best London had to offer. And what did they make of William? The general opinion (as reported by the arch-gossip Farington) was that he was considered a better poet than conversationalist. Northcote whispered that Godwin, considering the relative merits of William and Coleridge, preferred the poetry of the former and the conversation of the latter. John Taylor, who had just started his own publishing business, invited William to dine and was startled to find him 'strongly disposed towards Republicanism. His notions are that it is the duty of every Administration to do as much as possible to give consideration to the people at large, and to have *equality* always in view; which though not perfectly attainable, yet much has been gained towards it and more may be.' Most of William's time was devoted to the Beaumonts, where he was a welcome guest at any hour of the day. To their great delight he had brought them many of his unpublished poems, which he read aloud to them in his incomparable manner. He also read a couple written by Dorothy which, to her chagrin, he had insisted should be included among the number. The Beaumonts professed to admire these too, but Dorothy was under no illusions about their quality, insisting, quite rightly, that they had all allowed their affection for her to interfere with their judgement.[47]

At the beginning of May, Beaumont acquired tickets for the Royal Academy exhibition, where three of his own paintings were on show. Showing yet again that delicacy of feeling which made him such a genuinely good man, Beaumont showed William the one inspired by his own poem from *Lyrical Ballads*, *The Thorn*, but did not draw his attention to one of Piel Castle, near Rampside, even though he must have known that William would be familiar with the place. The reason was that the painting depicted a storm and a ship about to be wrecked beneath the castle, which Beaumont feared 'might raise painful sensations in your mind'. This was exactly what did happen, but it proved to be an unexpectedly positive experience, for out of it came *Elegiac Stanzas suggested by a Picture of Peele Castle.* A measured, multi-layered poem, it contrasted William's memories of the calm, glassy sea he had witnessed daily while staying near Piel Castle in 1794 with the storm painted by Beaumont. At its core lay William's abiding grief for John, and the fact that it had permanently altered his outlook on life. It was a moment of self-recognition comparable to that in *Tintern Abbey* and the *Ode: Intimations of Immortality.*

> A power is gone, which nothing can restore;
> A deep distress hath humanized my Soul.
>
> Not for a moment could I now behold
> A smiling sea, and be what I have been:
> The feeling of my loss will ne'er be old;
> This, which I know, I speak with mind serene.[48]

While he was in London, William sat for his portrait to Henry Edridge, who had recently drawn Charles James Fox, Lord Nelson and the King. The delightful little pencil drawing, only six by five inches, was probably commissioned by Beaumont. It represents the thirty-six-year-old William in solemn pose, the half-turned face giving peculiar prominence to the heavy-lidded eyes and thoughtful expression. His hair is still worn democratically short and unpowdered.[49]

The highlight of William's visit was his attendance at a ball given by Mrs Charles James Fox. He was taken there by his friend Rogers, whose wealth, as much as his literary reputation, opened every door in London. It was the first and last time William would ever meet Fox, the man to whom he had so hopefully sent *Lyrical Ballads* with such disappointing results. Fox had not forgotten. When Rogers introduced William to him, he said '"I am very glad to see you, Mr Wordsworth, though I am not of your faction," . . . meaning', as Rogers explained, 'that he admired a school of poetry different from that to which Wordsworth belonged.' Southey, who was also in London, but not invited to Mrs Fox's ball, remarked sourly, 'Wordsworth flourishes in London, he powders and goes to all the great routs. No man is more flattered by the attentions of the great, and no man would be more offended to be told so.'[50] Allowing for exaggeration (William is unlikely to have powdered his hair), there is more than a grain of truth in this. William had always been sociable and, for someone who lived and wrote in the comparative solitude of the Lakes, it was thrilling to come to the centre of literary life and find everyone knew his name and his work. He would have been less than human had he not been flattered.

William returned to Grasmere on 25 May in great spirits and much improved in health. He had spent twice as long as he had originally intended in London and yet had been so busy he had not had chance to read for more than five minutes the entire time he was there. The cottage at Town End was in chaos. They were without a servant, both Johnny and Sara Hutchinson, who had come to assist her sister at the birth, were ill, and Mary showed no signs of going into labour. The one bright spot was little Dora, now twenty-one months old, who had grown into 'the most delightful Chatterer ever seen', as her proud father noted, 'all acquired in two months; nor is it the least of her recommendations that she is more delighted with me than with a new Toy; and is never easy, if in my sight, when out of my arms'. Even Dorothy was won over: 'she is so full of life and sensibility and has so many pretty tricks'. She called William 'Dear 'Ather', and he could refuse her nothing. All the neighbours were equally enchanted with the little girl, though they, and Dorothy, muttered darkly about her being 'too wise for this world'. Even at this age, it was obvious that she was much cleverer than Johnny, a stolid little boy, who had been slow to walk and speak; but she did not enjoy his robust constitution, having been subject to croup since birth.[51]

Four days after William's return, Johnny was sent over to Park House for two months, to be out of the way when his mother was confined. That childless household had become something of a convenient nursery, for both Hartley and Derwent Coleridge had separately enjoyed lengthy visits there during their father's absence. Unfortunately, Park House had little else to recommend it and Tom was already looking for a new farm. William had made extensive inquiries on his behalf with Montagu, the Clarksons and Beaumont while in London, without success. It was Tom who arranged the sale of Dorothy's pony, which was now badly lame, and the purchase in its place of a cow, to supply the growing family with milk and butter.[52]

Thomas Wordsworth made his belated appearance on 15 June, just three days short of three years since Johnny's birth. It was a coincidence they all found peculiarly affecting, and Dorothy immediately felt 'a double rushing-in of love' for the new baby, 'as if I had both what had been the first-born infant John's share of love to give it, and its own'. At first they decided to call him William, but Southey, who called two days later, was decidedly against it: there should not be two *William Wordsworths.* On reflection, they agreed, neither Mary nor Dorothy wishing to start calling William 'Mr Wordsworth' or 'Brother' to distinguish him from his son. As Tom was to be his godfather, they therefore settled on Thomas. He was christened at Grasmere church on 13 July in the presence of his godfather and godmother, Mary's cousin Mary Monkhouse. The latter, and Joanna, who had also come over for the christening, stayed on at Town End till the beginning of August.[53]

William had hoped to go on a tour of the Scottish borders with Walter Scott once the baby arrived, but an anguished letter arrived from Montagu, informing them that his second wife, like his first, was dying in childbed: 'without your love and support', he wrote to William, 'I shall be bereft of my senses'. Not knowing whether Montagu would come to him or he would have to go to Montagu, William was forced to cancel his planned tour.[54] It was just as well, for Mary was slow to recover from Thomas's birth and, just after his christening, there was an outbreak of whooping cough in Grasmere. Alarmed that Dora, with her delicate health and tendency to croup, might be at risk, William, Dorothy and the nursemaid, Hannah Lewthwaite, carried her off to the safety of Park House. For fear of infection, she was not allowed to see Johnny, who was asleep in bed when they arrived, and the next morning, before she woke, William spirited Johnny off to Penrith, to stay with Mary's cousin John Monkhouse and his new bride.[55]

At the beginning of August, William was startled to get a letter from Wilkinson informing him that he had come to an agreement with the vendors of Broad How and, on William's behalf, had agreed to purchase the nineteen-acre estate in Patterdale for £1,000. William had given the idea up completely before he went to London, knowing that £800 was the most the estate was worth and having failed to persuade the wealthy rector of Patterdale, who owned the adjoining land, to give up his interest in it. He had thought no more about it, but Wilkinson had been so grieved at his failure that he poured out the whole story to Lord Lowther, who immediately offered to make up the difference, with or without William's knowledge. Wilkinson had insisted that William had to know, but had gone ahead and signed the agreement, at the asking price. William was thus in a quandary. 'This good Quaker for an excellent simple-hearted man he is, no doubt is eagerly waiting for a Letter of thanks and joyful congratulation from me, and alas! I know not which way to turn me in the affair.' He could not undo the agreement, which was legally binding; he did not wish to pay more than he could afford out of his own pocket, which would, in any case, appear to be an ungracious rejection of Lord Lowther's generosity; yet he did not wish to be under obligation to Lowther, especially unnecessarily. 'Strange it is that W[ilkinson] could not perceive, that if I was unwilling to pay an exorbitant price out of my own money, I should be still more unwilling to pay it out of another's', William fretted to Beaumont, who hastened to reassure him. 'I know no man to whom I would sooner be under obligations than Lord Lowther – he is candid, he is sincere, & generous – he esteems worth, & he admires genius'. If William could not bear the thought of accepting the money as Lowther's gift, Beaumont suggested he might consider it as a loan or even sell the Applethwaite property he had himself presented to William to make up the shortfall.[56]

William swallowed his pride. In offering the money, Lowther had expressed a wish to meet him, so, taking Mary and the baby to Park House for a reunion with Johnny and Dora, who had both escaped whooping cough, William called on Wilkinson, and together they went to Lowther. Sir William was not at home. They had to make do with escorting the Lowther daughters as far as Yanwath, where William showed his appreciation of his friend's efforts by assisting him in building one of his beloved riverside paths. He also seized the opportunity to tell Wilkinson, frankly but gently, that he would not have accepted Lord Lowther's offer had he been consulted. Wilkinson not only accepted the implied rebuke 'very well', but also seemed quite happy that he had *not* consulted William. When William returned home, he wrote a surprisingly gracious letter of grateful acceptance and thanks to his new benefactor.[57]

It had been an unusually quiet summer at Grasmere. There were fewer tourists than usual, though annual visitors, like Sharp, called in as they always did. With the two children away at Park House, the cottage was also 'strangely dull' and quiet. For once, therefore, William was able to work, and this time he turned to *The Recluse*. By 1 August, he had written 700 additional lines. 'Should Coleridge return, so that I might have some conversation with him upon the subject,' he informed Beaumont, 'I should go on swimmingly.'[58]

Exactly a fortnight later, 'the blessed news' arrived: Coleridge was in English waters, confined to his ship by quarantine restrictions, but within sight of Portsmouth. Ominously, the tidings came not from Coleridge himself, but from one of his fellow passengers. Once the quarantine was over, he went straight to London, took up residence with the Lambs and began working for Stuart again. He was, he said, 'shirtless, & almost penniless'. He had nothing to show for his two years abroad. The manuscripts and letters which had survived burning as plague-papers had, he said, been thrown overboard by his ship's captain when they were boarded by a privateer. The Wordsworths had had only a single letter from him since John's death, and his wife not many more, but they all excused him. 'I have no doubt (as Mrs Coleridge thinks also) that he is afraid to inquire after us lest he should hear of some new Sorrow.' They were wrong. Coleridge had decided to separate permanently from his wife but lacked the courage to tell her in person or by letter. The Lambs, miserably caught up in the middle, walked a tightrope. Coleridge persuaded Mary to ask William and Southey to do his dirty work for him, but having done so she received Mrs Coleridge's letter telling her 'as joyful news' that her husband was home and retracted her request. It was Mary Lamb also who eventually persuaded Coleridge to write his first letter to his wife, a month after his arrival. Even then, he wrote as if nothing had changed between them. He made no mention of separation and talked of bringing her to join him in London.[59]

The Wordsworths had seen much of Sarah Coleridge and her children during their friend's long absence and had come to appreciate her worth. Even Dorothy realized that if Coleridge would just accept his wife for what she was, instead of what he wanted her to be, they ought to be able to live together in peace and quiet. But on such things many a marriage founders and, in the meantime, William lost patience. He wrote a brief note expressing his disappointment at not hearing from, or seeing, Coleridge, offered to go to London 'if a meeting there would be more acceptable to you' and championed the abandoned wife. 'This is absolutely necessary either that you should decide upon something immediately to be done; or that Mrs Coleridge should be furnished with some reason for your not coming down as her present uncertainty and suspense is intolerable.' William's letter probably crossed in the post with the one Mary Lamb had compelled their friend to write, but it did no good. Coleridge remained paralysed in London, refusing to write or answer letters, to the great distress of many old friends. Josiah Wedgwood had no reply to a request for material for a life of his brother, Tom, Coleridge's friend and patron, who had died the previous year. William tried to counsel patience: 'he believes, if the state of [Coleridge's] mind was known, his friends would be more inclined to pity than to blame him, which I daresay is true;' Wedgwood remarked to Poole, adding bluntly, 'but though they may pity him, I suspect their regard for him is likely to be diminished, judging of others by what I feel myself'.[60]

All this could not have come at a worse time for William. The children had succumbed to whooping cough, despite all their precautions, and the family were preparing to leave the cottage at Town End. In the summer months they could manage by using the moss hut at the top of the garden as a sanctuary and additional room for visitors, but it was not practical to do so in winter. The three permanent adult members of the household could not face the prospect of being cooped up in the confined quarters of the cottage throughout the long dark days which lay ahead, especially with three children of whom the oldest was just three and a half. No other house in the area being available, William had gratefully accepted the Beaumonts' offer of the use of the Hall farmhouse on their Coleorton estate in Leicestershire. Though Sir George had described the situation as 'bleak', it was much larger than the Wordsworths' tiny cottage and could accommodate them all comfortably.[61]

In the midst of all this domestic upheaval, William had serenely continued to add to *The Recluse* and, having read in the papers that Charles James Fox was on his deathbed, had composed his wonderful poem while walking that evening at Grasmere.

> A Power is passing from the earth
> To breathless Nature's dark abyss;
> But when the great and good depart
> What is it more than this –
>
> That Man, who is from God sent forth,
> Doth yet again to God return? –
> Such ebb and flow must ever be,
> Then wherefore should we mourn?[62]

Such lines could not have been written before John's death.

At the end of October, the Wordsworths set out for Coleorton. Their reluctance to leave was exacerbated by the fact that Coleridge had not fulfilled his much reiterated promise to come to see them before they left. They had arranged to meet Sara, who was to accompany them, at Kendal, where they stayed overnight with her friends the Cooksons. Sara brought news that they had only just missed Coleridge: he had arrived at Penrith half an hour after she left it, but said, in his letter to her, that he could not come to meet them at Kendal if it was only to part again immediately. Nevertheless, the Wordsworths sent a special messenger over to Keswick, begging him to come and telling him they would delay their departure for another day. Coleridge had second thoughts, and at seven o'clock in the evening he arrived at the inn and summoned William to him. Dorothy, Mary and Sara had no intention of being left behind, so it was a joyful party that descended on Coleridge at the inn. 'Never, never did I feel such a shock as at first sight of him', Dorothy later confided to Catherine Clarkson. Physically, he had changed almost beyond recognition: lack of exercise and an increased dependency on opium had made him so grossly fat that his eyes were lost in flesh. Worse still was his mental state.

> We all felt exactly in the same way – as if he were different from what we have expected to see; almost as much as a person of whom we have thought much, and of whom we had formed an image in our own minds, without having any personal knowledge of him . . . He is utterly changed; and yet sometimes, when he was animated in conversation concerning things removed from him, I saw something of his former self. But never when we were alone with him. He then scarcely ever spoke of anything that concerned him, or us, or our common friends nearly, except we forced him to it; and immediately he changed the conversation to Malta, Sir Alexander Ball, the corruptions of government, anything but what we were yearning after. All we could gather from him was that he must part from her or die and leave his children destitute, and that to part he was resolved.[63]

The Wordsworths were bewildered and distraught. All they could extract from him was a promise that he would join them at Coleorton as soon as he had come to an arrangement with his wife.

Having delayed their journey twenty-four hours, Mary, Dorothy, the servant and the three children were packed into a post chaise and set off for Coleorton. They had a fraught journey: they were three days on the road, Thomas was miserable with his lingering cough, Johnny was 'unmanageable' and Dora 'cross'. William and Sara, who remained at Kendal for another day with Coleridge, fared better in the public coach. The two parties arrived within twenty minutes of each other on the evening of 30 October. The Beaumonts were waiting to greet them and, though they had met only William before, they gave all his family a kind and affectionate welcome. Nothing was too much trouble. 'They are the best of people,' William told Coleridge, 'and their kindness to us most delicate and unbounded'. To Beaumont himself, William was quite candid: 'I esteem your friendship one of the best gifts of my life . . . I speak of soul indebted to soul.' The feeling was genuine and mutual. 'Were I to express to you how much our interest & if possible our regard is encreased by a personal knowledge of your family of Love, it might appear like affectation', Beaumont wrote shortly after he and his wife departed for London. 'I never see you, or read you but I am the better for it – & at least make resolutions which I hope in time I shall perform.'[64]

The farmhouse at Coleorton was to be the Wordsworths' home for more than seven months. It lay two miles east of Ashby de la Zouche, in the midst of what would have been pleasant, rolling Leicestershire countryside, had it not been for the open-cast coal-mining surrounding it. The coal pits were the main source of Beaumont's wealth and, in 1804, he had begun to build a vast mock-baronial castle on his estate, just a mile outside the village of Coleorton; unlike the Lowthers, he had not seen fit to move the village itself, but he had decided to redevelop all his grounds to make an apt setting for his grand new house. William had strong views on landscape gardening and he did not fail to make them known to his patron. He believed passionately, with Coleridge, that a house should belong to the country and that the country should not be an appendage to the house. He deplored the recent fashion for formal gardens, with their topiary, exotic trees and plants, and pristine pathways: 'let nature be all in all,' he urged Beaumont,

> taking care that every thing done by man shall be in the way of being adopted by her . . . all just and solid pleasure in natural objects rest upon two Pillars, God and Man. Laying out grounds, as it is called, may be considered as a liberal art, in some sort like Poetry and Painting; and its object like that of all the liberal arts is, or ought to be, . . . to assist Nature in moving the affections . . . No liberal art aims merely at the gratification of an individual or a class, the Painter or Poet is degraded in proportion as he does so; the true Servants of the Arts pay homage to the human kind as impersonated in unwarped and enlightened minds.

He was, he told Beaumont, glad to learn that he did not intend moving the village: 'for my part strip my Neighbourhood of human beings and I should think it one of the greatest privations I could undergo. You have all the poverty of solitude, nothing of its elevation.' Having set out his views so forcefully, and at such length, William ruefully concluded his letter was 'something like [a sermon], upon the subject of taste in natural beauty'.[65]

With the Wordsworths living at Coleorton, it was natural that the Beaumonts should ask William to advise them on laying out their grounds. He had already volunteered the suggestion that they should plant thickets of underwood, hazels, wild roses, honeysuckle, hollies, thorns and trailing plants, such as Traveller's Joy (clematis), beneath the old trees near the house. When Lady Beaumont asked him to plan and supervise the planting of her latest scheme, a winter garden, William was in his element. It was a practical opportunity to put into practice his belief that laying out gardens was a liberal art and to prove that a poet was the best person 'to assist Nature in moving the affections'.

He was full of ideas. The winter garden should be enclosed by a double fence of evergreen shrubs and trees to create depth, shelter and seclusion, and the '*feeling* ... of a Spot which Winter cannot touch, which should present no image of chillness, decay, or desolation, when the face of nature everywhere else is cold, decayed and desolate'. Taking his inspiration from Thomson's *Ode to Solitude*, there should be a single break in this 'fence', opening out on to a view with a distant object as its focal point, to remind the visitor of the crimes, cares and pains of the outside world and encourage him to 'shield me in the woods again'. The purpose of William's detailed plan was to draw the visitor into different walks, each with its own distinct character: a formal border, edged with boxwood, full of colourful spring- and autumn-flowering plants and shrubs, and centred on a fountain or *jet d'eau*; an open forest glade strewn with wild flowers; a cloistral alley-walk, on a mossy path, lined with laurels, 'soothing and not stirring the mind or tempting it out of itself'; a blind path leading to a bower, inspired by a poem by Chaucer, paved with different-coloured pebbles, mainly white, with a stone table in the middle and a mossy seat round it; a small secluded glade, belted with evergreens, in which there should be only a basin of water, inhabited by two gold or silver fish, 'these little creatures to be the "Genii" of the Pool and of the place'. Concluding a letter which he admitted was the longest he had ever written in his life, William urged Lady Beaumont to be patient:

> I am sensible that I have written a very pretty Romance in this Letter, and when I look at the ground in its present state and think of what it must continue to be, for some years, I am afraid you will call me an Enthusiast and a Visionary. I am willing to submit to this, as I am seriously convinced ... less than six years would transform it into something that might be looked at with pleasure. Fifty would make it a paradise. O! that I could convert my little Dorothy [Dora] into a Fairy to realise the whole in half a day.[66]

From the extant letters of this period, one might be forgiven for thinking that William had abandoned poetry in favour of gardening, but this was not the case. In June he had told Walter Scott that he had 'some thoughts of publishing a little Volume of miscellaneous Poems, to be out next Spring'. Immediately after his arrival at Coleorton, he began to put the collection together, assisted by Sara, who did all his transcribing for him. 'I publish with great reluctance,' he told Scott on 10 November,

> but the day when my long work will be finished seems farther and farther off, and therefore I have resolved to send this Vol: into the world. It would look like affectation if I were to say how indifferent I am to its present reception; but I have a true pleasure in saying to you that I put some value upon it; and hope that it will one day or other be thought well of by the Public.[67]

Just as had happened in 1800, the process of selecting poems for publication seems to have ignited a spark. New composition flowed from revising the old, and a dozen or more short poems were written, all but two of which found their way into the new book. Among them were two short ballads, *The Horn of Egremont Castle* and *Song at the Feast of Brougham Castle*, both tales of medieval chivalry, based on local Cumberland tradition. Though it was not William's first attempt at this type of verse (*Hart-Leap Well*, for instance, had been written for the 1800 edition of *Lyrical Ballads*), he may have written with an eye to its current popularity, thanks to Scott's immense success with *The Lay of the Last Minstrel*.[68]

More characteristically Wordsworthian were two wonderful sonnets he wrote in reaction to the desperate state of affairs on the Continent, where, in October, Napoleon's armies had crushed the Prussians at the battles of Jena and Auerstadt, and added Prussia and its dependencies to an increasingly long list of annexed territories.

> Another year! – another deadly blow!
> Another mighty Empire overthrown!
> And We are left, or shall be left, alone;
> The last that dare to struggle with the Foe.
> 'Tis well! from this day forward we shall know
> That in ourselves our safety must be sought;
> That by our own right hands it must be wrought;
> That we must stand unpropped, or be laid low.

Having taken up this determinedly patriotic stance, William ended the sonnet in distinctly downbeat fashion. Victory would be won only if Britain's leaders were

> Wise, upright, valiant; not a servile band,
> Who are to judge of danger which they fear,
> And honour which they do not understand.

The second sonnet was a more oblique reflection on the same subject.

> Two Voices are there; one is of the sea,
> One of the mountains; each a mighty Voice:
> In both from age to age thou didst rejoice,
> They were thy chosen music, Liberty!

The voice of the mountains, Switzerland, had been silenced by the French, so William appealed to Liberty to 'cleave, O cleave to that which still is left' – that is, to Britain, the voice of the sea.[69]

In such elevated mood, it was scarcely surprising that William gave short shrift to his old friend Francis Wrangham, who had written asking him to contribute to a volume of political satires. 'I have long since come to a fixed resolution to steer clear of personal satire', he said,

> in fact, I never will have anything to do with it as far as concerns the *private* vices of individuals on any account; with respect to public delinquents or offenders I will not say the same; though I should be slow to meddle even with these. This is a rule which I have laid down to myself, and shall rigidly adhere to; though I do not in all cases blame those who think and act differently.

The poet who preached 'that we have all of us one human heart', and tried to inspire universal benevolence in his readers, had no wish to return to the splenetic, futile and ultimately self-destructive arena of personal satire. He even asked Wrangham to destroy those vicious imitations of Juvenal he had written in the 1790s; neither true fame nor profit could come from them and, having chosen a different path himself, he did not wish them to be preserved as reminders of a past aberration.[70]

On 21 December Coleridge arrived at Coleorton to 'an uproar of sincere Joy'. He brought with him his eldest son, Hartley, now aged ten, and the news that he had persuaded his wife to accept that their marriage was over. They had agreed to separate permanently: for the moment, Coleridge and Hartley would live with the Wordsworths, while his wife would remain at Greta Hall, under Southey's protection, with Derwent and little Sara.[71] Coleridge had been telling everyone for years that all his troubles, the inability to write, the heavy drinking, opium-taking and ill-health, were the result of his unhappiness in his marriage. Whatever their private reservations about ending the marriage, now that it was finally over the Wordsworths were naïvely convinced that Coleridge would be transformed back into the creative, charismatic figure of the Alfoxton days. William had blithely assured Coleridge that he and Hartley could live with them as long as they liked, free of all expense but washing, that he would be 'altogether uninterrupted' and could proceed as rapidly as he liked with the book of travels he intended to write. Dorothy was just as optimistic, believing that 'William's conversation and our kind offices may soothe him, and bring on tranquillity', so that Coleridge could embark on a great work of his own. With the confidence born of ignorance, she gaily declared to Lady Beaumont that Coleridge would be 'tolerably safe' with them: 'I think, if he is not inclined to manage himself, *we* can manage him'.[72] She could not have been more wrong.

They soon discovered that he was incapable of leaving off all stimulants. Unable to drink brandy, because there was none in the house, he drank strong beer at night, mid-morning and dinner-time. While the Wordsworths congratulated themselves that at least he was taking nothing stronger, they were apparently unaware that he had a supply of opium. What they did not know, because they did not have access to his private thoughts recorded in his journal, was the perverted turn his drug-induced fantasies had taken. His obsession with Sara had, if anything, grown stronger. When he had first embarked on his voyage for Malta in 1804, one of his earliest recorded entries had been what even he admitted were 'SICKLY Thoughts', the panic-inducing idea that if Mary died, William would marry Sara. With John Wordsworth safely dead and out of the way, it had been possible for Coleridge to conjure up the comforting image that he might have approved of John marrying Sara. Now, at Coleorton, faced with a living, breathing Sara who was determined not to encourage him, he could not face the reality that she did not return his feelings. 'I know, you love me! – My reason knows it, my heart feels it', he confided in his journal. 'Do you command me to abide Asra's neglect?' he wrote in an accusing poem, written in Latin, and addressed to William as 'Vilmum Axiologum',

> and submit to the sight of Asra's estranged eyes? and know for certain that she who was – and always will be – dear to me is false and cruel? And you bid me endure the daylight when I am crazily in love with an empty woman and my whole wide world quivers and totters? Why not, William, order me – with mock grief – to let my guts be pierced with a knife? Why not tear out my heart, or my eyes, or whatever – if possible – is more precious! I shall command my failing spirit to observe your wish – though I am dying – as long as faith in Asra lingers . . . My life is finished; yet Asra lives on, heedless of me.[73]

William's kindly meant warnings served only to divert Coleridge's warped imaginings into new channels. On 27 December Coleridge wrote in his journal '**The Epoch**.' in large, bold lettering centred on the page, adding beneath it the cryptic comment, 'Saturday, 27th December, 1806 – Queen's Head, Stringston, 1½ a mile from Coleorton Church, 50 minutes after 10'. Three subsequent pages recording what had happened (or, rather, what he imagined had happened) have been torn from the journal, but later entries make it all too clear what this was. 'But a minute and a half with ME – and all that time evidently *restless & going* – An hour and more with [Wordsworth] *in bed* – O agony!' for years afterwards he was haunted by the image of Sara, her breasts exposed, in bed with William. Some biographers have chosen to regard this as proof that William had an adulterous relationship with his sister-in-law, but this is simply not credible. If William had wanted a secret tryst with Sara, the local inn was hardly the place to do it. Coleridge's presence there is more suspect; he can only have been there to buy drink or take opium. In any case, Coleridge later admitted that the whole scenario was simply a lurid product of his own imagination. 'Yes! Yes! I *knew* the horrid phantasm to be a mere phantasm: and yet what anguish, what gnawings of despair, what throbbings and lancinations of positive Jealousy!'[74]

Instead of confronting his friend, as honesty demanded if what he had seen was real, Coleridge kept his gnawings, throbbings and lancinations (shooting pains) to himself. What is even more peculiar is that he was able to maintain such a convincing façade of ordinary life that no one had the slightest inkling of the suspicions and jealousies festering in his heart. And, ironically, when the family gathered round for a ceremonial reading by William of *The Prelude*, which was dedicated to Coleridge himself, he was moved to write a generous tribute in some of the finest lines he had ever composed.

And when – O Friend! my comforter and guide!
Strong in thyself, and powerful to give strength! –
Thy long sustainèd Song finally closed,
And thy deep voice had ceased – yet thou thyself
Wert still before my eyes, and round us both
That happy vision of beloved faces –
Scarce conscious, and yet conscious of its close
I sate, my being blended in one thought
(Thought was it? or aspiration? or resolve?)
Absorbed, yet hanging still upon the sound –
And when I rose, I found myself in prayer.[75]

It should have been one of the happiest evenings of their lives, a joyful celebration of mutual achievement. Instead it was symbolic of all that had gone wrong in their relationship.

13. The Convention of Cintra

William's new book progressed slowly, not least because he insisted on correcting the proofs himself this time. The projected single volume had become two smaller ones, each containing miscellaneous poems and sonnets. A thousand copies were to be printed by Longman, the publisher of *Lyrical Ballads*, for which William was to receive 100 guineas.[1] It was hardly a princely sum for the product of more than six years' labour.

William was also hard at work on the winter garden at Coleorton, visiting the workmen twice a day to supervise their efforts, and accompanying Mr Craig, who was nominally in charge of laying out the grounds, on expeditions as far afield as Nottingham to purchase plants. Sir George Beaumont began to be concerned that it was proving a distraction from his poetry. 'I hope Wordsworth is not engaged <u>too</u> deeply in gardening', he wrote to Coleridge.

> when Lady Beaumont first applied to him, I was fearful it might interrupt his pursuit in which all mankind are interested, but on considering that it might possibly induce him to take exercise in the open air, gently amuse him & enable him to relax from that intenseness of thought, which must sooner or later affect his health, I was induced to give my consent to the application ... certainly the advantage I expected to receive from his taste was a pretty potent bribe & I confess his plan has far exceeded my expectation –

Dorothy immediately sent reassurances. Her brother was 'very happy in his employment'; his poetical labours 'will and must go on when he begins' and the interruptions caused by attending to the garden were actually useful to him; 'for after a certain time the progress is by no means proportioned to the labour in composition, and if he is called from it by other thoughts, he returns to it with ten times the pleasure, and his work goes on proportionally more rapidly'.[2]

Of greater concern to them all was the problem of where they should live. Coleridge had decided to make his home permanently with the Wordsworths, a decision which gave his brother-in-law a certain grim satisfaction: 'It is from his idolatry of that family that this has begun –', Southey told Rickman, 'they have always humoured him in all his follies, listened to his complaints of his wife, and when he has complained of his itch, helped him to scratch, instead of covering him with brimstone ointment, and shutting him up by himself.' With rather less justice, he accused William and Dorothy of being the 'most intensely selfish' people he had ever known. They had only offered Coleridge a home because it suited William.

> The one thing to which W would sacrifice all others is his own reputation, concerning which his anxiety is perfectly childish ... and so he can get Coleridge to talk his own writings over with him, and criti[ci]se them, and (without amending them) teach him how to do it – to be in fact the very rain and air and sunshine of his intellect, he thinks C is very well employed and this arrangement a very good one.[3]

It was hardly fair comment, but then Southey had every right to feel bitter, having had Coleridge's wife and children dumped on him.

Providing Coleridge with a home also meant providing one for his sons, and the Wordsworths were in despair. Where could they find a house sufficiently large to take them all? The Beaumonts were happy for them to remain at the Hall farm but William, already labouring under an uncomfortable sense of obligation, was unwilling to trespass further on their kindness. Coleridge suggested Greta Hall, under a misapprehension that Southey and his extended family were about to leave it, but neither Mary nor Dorothy relished the prospect of living in his former marital home. They were hugely relieved to discover that Southey had no intention of moving. On 25 March William completed the purchase of his little estate at Patterdale. It might have been possible to build there, but he had neither the money nor the time to do so.[4]

Such was his determination to offer accommodation to all his entourage and to return to the north that William submitted to the mortification of taking a lease of Allan Bank at Grasmere. It was a house that flew in the face of all the principles he had so proudly espoused for so long. Standing on 'that beautiful ridge that elbows out into the vale (behind the church and towering far above its steeple)', Allan Bank was, in William's own phrase 'a temple of abomination'. It had been built by a Liverpool attorney, 'A wretched Creature, wretched in name and Nature, of the name of *Crump*, goaded on by his still more wretched Wife', who had bought the site early in 1805. A year later, to Dorothy's undisguised glee, it had become a 'ruinous mansion' when a third of it collapsed while being built. A year further down the line, it was still not ready for habitation, but the plasterers and painters were putting the finishing touches, and Crump turned to William for advice upon planting the grounds. In agreeing to do so, William was performing something of a public service: it was his opportunity to reduce the impact of the stark new house on the bare ridge dominating the whole vale.[5]

In April William, Mary and Sara accompanied Coleridge and Hartley to London, leaving Dorothy in charge of the children at Coleorton. The Wordsworth contingent took up residence in Thornhaugh Street, with the recently widowed Basil Montagu, moving, at the beginning of May, to stay with Christopher and Priscilla at Lambeth. From a social point of view, it was a relatively quiet trip. Mary and Sara were eager to play the tourist and declined to join the dinner party circuit, but they breakfasted twice with Walter Scott, who was also in town, and persuaded him to return to Coleorton with them on his way home. They were also, of course, regular visitors to the Beaumonts in Grosvenor Square. William accompanied the Beaumonts on a visit to the artist Joseph Farington, and all four returned together to view a picture, *The Hermitage*, by Richard Wilson, which Beaumont was considering purchasing. It led to an inevitable discussion about painting, William arguing that historical figures should never be introduced into landscapes, unless they were the main subject of the painting, because they were a distraction, or, as he put it, injurious to the effect which the landscape should produce 'as a scene founded on an observation of nature'. A few days later, Farington met William and Mary (or Sara) at the Royal Academy: 'He thought it a poor exhibition, & she said it was the worst she had ever seen.' William and Coleridge dined with Godwin before the party split up and went their separate ways, Coleridge to visit his brother George and Poole in Devon, Sara to stay with the Clarksons in their new home at Bury St Edmunds, and William and Mary to Coleorton.[6]

The main purpose of the visit, however, was business. On 28 April 1807 Longman published William's new book, succinctly titled *Poems, in Two Volumes*. The title-page bore his name as 'William Wordsworth, Author of *The Lyrical Ballads*', a significant association, since it reminded purchasers of the success of the earlier work, which was now in its fourth edition, and of the pioneering nature of that publication. This latter was particularly important, because *Poems, in Two Volumes* had nothing to prepare the reader for its contents: there was no advertisement, no preface, no attempt to explain or justify William's poetic theory or method, just the poems themselves. This was quite deliberate. William had originally written some introductory remarks, explaining that he had been long engaged on a 'work of length and labour', but, as he could not even begin to guess when this would be completed, he had been compelled to overcome his reluctance to publish more short poems. Just before publication, he withdrew the statement, primarily, it would seem, because he realized that it was an apology for something of which he had no need to be ashamed. Friends and relations might be disappointed that it was not *The Recluse*, but *Poems, in Two Volumes* was still a significant body of work, containing some of his finest poems. What is more, despite Southey's sniping, it had been achieved almost entirely without Coleridge. *Lyrical Ballads*, *The Recluse*, even the poem on his own life, all owed their inception to Coleridge. *Poems, in Two Volumes* did not. The very fact that William chose to publish it at all was a repudiation of

Coleridge's insistence that writing so many small poems was 'hurtful' to his poetic genius. It was a sign of his confidence in his own powers. As one modern critic has put it, '*Poems, in Two Volumes* presented [William's] claim to be the most original, copious, and various lyric poet since the seventeenth century.'[7]

William had chosen the poems, and their order of appearance, with his usual care. The first volume contained sixty-nine poems, beginning with *To the Daisy* and ending with the sonnet *November, 1806*; the second, forty-six, opening with *Rob Roy's Grave* and closing with *Ode: Intimations of Immortality*. The publication therefore began and ended with lines celebrating the humblest of flowers. William had also given much thought to the grouping of the poems, introducing for the first time a system of categorization which would become increasingly complex with the passing years. In 1807 it was simple, logical and self-explanatory: 'Poems, composed on a tour, chiefly on foot', 'Miscellaneous sonnets', 'Sonnets dedicated to liberty' (which, interestingly, included the largest number of poems), 'Poems written during a tour of Scotland' and 'Moods of my own mind'. William arranged for copies to be sent to Scott, Coleridge, Southey and Duppa, and collected additional ones for personal distribution, the Beaumonts being at the top of his list.[8]

Almost before they left London, the adverse criticism of *Poems, in Two Volumes* began. Even William's friends showed no mercy. Rogers declared it a pity that so many 'trifling things' should be allowed to obscure the poems that had real merit. Sharp was scathing, saying, 'He had carried His system of simplicity too far, and had proceeded to puerility.' Beaumont, who had been present at the gathering where Sharp made his comments, remarked gloomily afterwards that, 'He supposed the Blood Hounds would now be upon Wordsworth.' Lady Beaumont was so upset on his behalf by the virulence of the mounting tide of criticism that William had to reassure her. 'It is impossible that any expectations can be lower than mine concerning the immediate effect of this little work upon what is called the Public.' He looked to future reputation, not current reception, trusting that the destiny of his poems would be 'to console the afflicted, to add sunshine to daylight by making the happy happier, to teach the young and the gracious of every age, to see, to think and feel, and therefore to become more actively and securely virtuous; this is their office, which I trust they will faithfully perform long after we (that is, all that is mortal of us) are mouldered in our graves'. How could fashionable society possibly understand his poems: 'the thoughts, feelings, and images, on which the life of my Poems depends . . . what have they to do with routs, dinners, morning calls, hurry from door to door, from street to street, on foot or in Carriage[?]'

> These people in the senseless hurry of their idle lives do not *read* books, they merely snatch a glance at them that they may talk about them. And even if this were not so, never forget what I believe was observed to you by Coleridge, that every great and original writer, in proportion as he is great or original, must himself create the taste by which he is to be relished; he must teach the art by which he is to be seen;[9]

In the short term, William failed to create the taste or teach the art. The reviews were venomous. Having no introductory remarks to attack in this publication, they fell like a pack of ravening dogs on the preface to the 1800 edition of *Lyrical Ballads* and tore it to shreds. William's poetic theory was attacked and then turned against him. He had claimed, for instance, in his preface that all his poems had 'a worthy purpose'. 'Of the pieces now published he has said nothing', wrote James Montgomery in the *Eclectic Review*; 'most of them seem to have been written *for* no purpose at all, and certainly *to* no good one.' Lucy Aitkin, in the *Annual Review*, agreed. 'Mr W. piques himself upon having had in view an end, a purpose, in all his narratives; but we confess if he has had one here, it is more than we can discover.' *The Redbreast and the Butterfly* was dismissed as 'downright raving', *To the Small Celandine* as 'a piece of namby-pamby', *Yarrow Unvisited* 'a very tedious, affected performance', *Resolution and Independence* 'feeble, unimpressive, and intolerably prolix', *Ode* (printed without its explanatory sub-title: *Intimations of Immortality*) 'illegible and unintelligible' and 'a wilderness of sublimity, tenderness, bombast, and absurdity'. Francis Jeffrey summed up the reaction in the *Edinburgh Review*: 'If the printing of such trash as this be not felt as an insult on the public taste, we are afraid it cannot be insulted.'[10]

Had the reviews been unmitigated spite, it might have been easier to dismiss them. What complicated the picture was the constant refrain that *Poems, in Two Volumes* did not live up to the expections created by *Lyrical Ballads.* William had promised to be 'the poet of the heart', and instead had become 'the capricious minion of a debasing affectation'.

> But when the man to whom, in early youth, Nature 'was all in all: who cannot paint what then he was . . .'; when that man is found in his riper years, drivelling to the redbreast . . . and to a common pile-wort . . . , how can we sufficiently lament the infatuation of self-conceit and our own disappointed hopes?
>
> Is it possible for Mr Wordsworth not to feel that while he is pouring out his nauseous and nauseating sensibilities to weeds and insects, he debases himself to a level with his idiot boy . . . [?][11]

Again and again, the reviewers insisted that 'on worthy subjects this man can write worthily'; what held him back was his adherence to his poetic theories, set out in the preface of 1800, what they called his system. Even the rottweiler Jeffrey was moved to quote in full three of William's Miltonic sonnets as proof that 'he does always write good verses, when . . . he is led to abandon his system'. 'When we look at these, and many still finer passages, in the writings of this author,' he lamented, 'it is impossible not to feel a mixture of indignation and compassion, at that strange infatuation which has bound him up from the fair exercise of his talents, and withheld from the public the many excellent productions that would otherwise have taken the place of the trash now before us.' One and all, they expressed the hope that *Poems, in Two Volumes* would be rejected by the public and fail to sell. William would then be forced to realize the 'lamentable consequences of [his] open violation of the established laws of poetry' and abandon 'a system which appears to us so injurious to its author, and so dangerous to public taste'. He was urged to stop starving his mind in solitude, which caused him to attach 'undue importance' to 'trivial incidents' and 'exquisite emotions to objects which excite none in any other human breast', and to return to his books.[12]

To a certain extent, William was shielded from the full force of the critical onslaught by the very isolation which the critics so despised: most of the periodicals simply did not make their way to Grasmere unless specifically requested. And the Wordsworths were, at last, on their way back home. On 6 May William and Mary left London for Coleorton, accompanied by Walter Scott. He spent only two nights with them, and parted from William and Dorothy at Lichfield, where he wished to visit his friend Anna Seward, the poetess known as the 'Swan of Lichfield'.[13] The Wordsworths had hoped to set off almost immediately for Grasmere, but they were detained by the Beaumonts, who were anxious to visit Coleorton on their own way to the Lakes and wished to be escorted round the winter garden by William in person. In the end, they did not arrive until 3 June and then they pressed the Wordsworths to remain longer. It would have been churlish to refuse, after all their kindness, so the departure was again deferred. Before they left, William and Beaumont planted a cedar tree together, a symbolic gesture of the enduring nature of their friendship.[14]

It was 10 June before the Wordsworths finally left Coleorton, and they had another horrendous journey, for little Thomas was teething and unwell, and cried continuously all the way from Nottingham to Huddersfield. Despite being only eight miles from their destination, they were obliged to stay the night there. Next morning, they reached Halifax, where they were rejoined by Sara and spent a fortnight very happily, staying with the former 'Aunt' Threlkeld, Mrs Rawson, and her husband, who had moved into the town the previous year. Mr Rawson, 'a truly liberal pious and affectionate-hearted man', had a carriage, enabling them to ride out frequently: '*I* had great pleasure in the revival of many old recollections and in finding every favourite valley more beautiful than I had ever imagined', Dorothy told Catherine Clarkson. It was indeed a trip down memory lane for Dorothy, because they then went on to spend a long weekend with her old schoolfriend Jane Pollard, now Mrs Marshall, and her family at New Grange, near Leeds.[15]

On 6 July Mary, Sara, the servant, Molly, and the children went off in a post chaise to Kendal to stay with the Cooksons, while William and Dorothy, Mrs Rawson and the Marshalls took an excursion up to Bolton Abbey, a ruined Augustinian priory standing meditatively on a lazy loop in the broad sweep of the River Wharfe. It was a site well known to lovers of the picturesque; it had been painted in 1800 by Thomas Girtin and would be painted again in 1809 by J. M. W. Turner. Dorothy was enchanted by the beautiful situation, 'a retired woody winding valley, with steep banks and rocky scars', and (unlike Tintern or Kirkstall) 'no manufactories – no horrible Forges'. William was equally impressed, admiring, with the eye of a fellow practitioner, the laying out of the grounds by the Reverend Mr Carr, 'who has here wrought with an invisible hand of art, in the very spirit of Nature'.[16]

From Bolton Abbey, William and Dorothy walked up Wharfedale as far as Gordale Scar and Malham Cove, then rode to rejoin the rest of the family at Kendal. On 10 July they all returned together to Grasmere. It was an unexpectedly melancholy homecoming, for much had changed in the eight and more months they had been away. Mary's cousin at Penrith John Monkhouse had lost his young bride of less than a year; one of their earliest friends at Grasmere, the ninety-two-year-old Reverend Joseph Sympson, had also died, as had young George Dawson, leader of the Grasmere Volunteer Militiamen, Jenny Hodgson, the Wordsworths' washerwoman, and a host of other characters from the vale. The trees at Bainriggs, below Sara's Wishing Gate, had been cut down, as had the giant sycamore near the parsonage and all the fir trees that overtopped the church tower. To add to their disappointments, Allan Bank was not yet ready for them and they would have to manage in the cottage at Town End a little longer. All they could do was hope for fine weather.[17]

Fortunately, it was an unusually quiet summer. The Beaumonts arrived at Keswick a few days after the Wordsworths at Grasmere, and much of the time was spent in their company. Thomas Clarkson called several times, having just completed his latest book, a history of the abolition of the African slave trade, which Dorothy declared was more interesting than anything she had ever read before. The wretched Crump arrived, and turned out to be a most kind-hearted and good-natured man who was quite prepared to leave all the planting of trees and laying out of grounds at Allan Bank entirely in William's hands.[18]

It was an indication of how firmly William was already identified with the Lakes that he had become something of a tourist attraction himself. On 26 August he was summoned as 'one of the Lake poets' to dine at the Lowwood Inn with an aristocratic party led by Lord Holland, the nephew of Charles James Fox, and his wife, Elizabeth, the beautiful society hostess. It was a perfect example of the gulf that William had recognized as existing between his own life, sympathies and tastes, and that of fashionable London society. Lady Holland was suitably condescending. 'He is much superior to his writings,' she wrote in her journal,

> and his conversation is even beyond his abilities . . . He holds some opinions on picturesque subjects with which I completely differ, especially as to the effects produced by *white* houses on the sides of the hills; to my taste they produce a cheerful effect. He, on the contrary, would brown, or even black-work them . . . His objection was chiefly grounded upon the distances being confounded by the glare of white . . .

William refused to be intimidated, maintaining his opinion 'with a considerable degree of ingenuity'. 'He seems well read', Lady Holland added, 'in his provincial history.' Lord Holland was equally scathing. The Wordsworths' cottage at Town

End was dismissed as 'such as the peasants inhabit'. 'His Sister, who is full of Romance, is quite in despair . . . at leaving her cottage. Their notions of the picturesque . . . are rather extravagant; the comforts of life, such as a warm house with doors & windows, &c., are monstrous and unpoetical – and a dry walk, monotonous and disgusting, in the extreme.'[19]

William was received with rather less condescension and amusement by his benefactor Sir William Lowther, newly created Earl of Lonsdale. The first meeting between the two men took place in August or September, possibly in company with the Beaumonts, when William and Mary were staying for twelve days at Eusemere, the Clarksons' old home. The new Earl had great plans for the family estate. Not only had he employed Wilkinson to lay out the grounds, but he had begun to rebuild the dilapidated house. The bad old earl had often talked of doing this himself, but never had, because, as William informed Lord Holland, with pardonable bitterness, 'Stones were not Stubborn enough for him, and timber and quarries offer'd no conflict, and gave no handle for Tyranny and oppression.' The new Lowther Castle would be a fantastic fairy-tale creation, with soaring turrets and battlements, and the Earl was anxious that it should have an appropriate setting. William's new-found status as landscape gardener made his advice indispensable.[20]

Once their last visitors, the Beaumonts, had gone, towards the end of the second week in September, William and Mary seized the chance to make a three-day tour of the north-western corner of the lakes, visiting Wasdale, Ennerdale, Whitehaven and Cockermouth. The object was probably partly business, as the Wordsworths were still negotiating a settlement for the debts they owed their late uncle's estate, but it was also pure nostalgia for William. They visited Sally Lowthian, William's old nurse and his father's former housekeeper, and made a pilgrimage to the house in Market Street where William, his brothers and his sister had all been born. They were delighted to find the terrace walk unspoilt and the old privet hedge still as full of roses as it had been thirty years before.[21]

Returning to the cottage at Town End, William threw himself into composition. He had an entirely new subject, inspired by the summer visit to Bolton Abbey, and, for him, an equally new way of handling it. The project was *The White Doe of Rylstone*, a narrative poem in cantering octosyllabics, almost 2,000 lines in length. It neatly interwove what William took to be historical fact, the tragic story of Emily Norton's father and nine brothers, who were all killed in the futile northern uprising of 1569, with the legend of a white doe which, after the rebellion, frequented the churchyard of Bolton Abbey. William would always indignantly deny that it was an attempt to cash in on the lucrative seam of medieval romance opened up by Scott's *Lay of the Last Minstrel*. He pointed out, with some justification, that Scott's poems were purely concerned with action, whereas *The White Doe* began and ended with the spiritual. The stirring events of the uprising are not an end in themselves, but merely a backdrop to the state of mind of the heroine of the tragedy, who is entirely passive in the midst of action. She knows

> *Her duty is to stand and wait*;
> In resignation to abide
> The shock, and finally secure
> O'er pain & grief a triumph pure.

The white doe, which becomes the companion of her solitude in bereavement, has 'a tender & humanizing influence' upon her. The twin points at which the poem aimed were the 'anticipated beatification . . . of her mind' and the 'apotheosis' of the doe. The comparison with Scott was 'inconsiderate': the true subject of William's poem was not the fate of the Nortons, but Emily's struggle over and conquest of her own sorrows. 'How insignificant a thing, for example, does personal prowess appear compared with the fortitude of patience & heroic martyrdom, in other words with struggles for the sake of principle, in preference to victory gloried in for its own sake.' It is unfortunate, therefore, that *The White Doe* invites, and suffers from, comparison with Scott's *Lay of the Last Minstrel*, and his *Marmion*, which would appear in 1808. Even the secondary title, *The Fate of the Nortons*, appears calculated to mislead the reader into thinking that this is a tale of chivalric derring-do.[22]

William composed with a rapidity and fluency that were unusual in his longer poems. He was helped by the arrival, on 16 October, of two mighty tomes which had been procured for him by Dorothy's friends the Marshalls from their author, the antiquarian Dr Whitaker. One of the books, *The History and the Antiquities of the Deanery of Craven*, related the legend of the white doe, providing William with just the information he needed. Within two months, he had written over half the poem; by 16 January 1808 it was finished.[23]

This was despite a number of distractions, the most important of which was the much anticipated meeting with Thomas de Quincey on 4 November. Four and a half years earlier, in May 1803, de Quincey, then a troubled young man about to go up to Oxford, had written an extraordinary fan letter to William in which he expressed his fervent admiration, literally on bended knee, for *Lyrical Ballads* and 'earnestly and humbly sue[d]' for William's 'friendship'. William was touched by the youth and ardour of his correspondent. He replied tactfully and with just the right amount of encouragement and reserve. He pointed out that de Quincey had already achieved his main aim: how could William feel anything but kindly feelings towards one who had written so enthusiastically about his work? 'My friendship', he added more sternly, 'it is not in my power to give: this is a gift which no man can make, it is not in our power: a sound and healthy friendship is the growth of time and circumstance, it will spring up and thrive like a wildflower when these favour, and when they do not, it is in vain to look for it.' He ended the letter with a casual, if sincere, invitation: 'I shall indeed be very happy to see you at Grasmere; if you ever find it convenient to visit this delightful country.'

De Quincey was overwhelmed. 'Henceforward I shall look to that country as to the land of promise', he replied. When he went up to Oxford, William, remembering the frantic and dissolute manners of university undergraduates in his own day, was moved to write words of fatherly advice to his young protégé. 'I need not say to you that there is no true dignity but in virtue and temperance,' he warned de Quincey, 'and, let me add, chastity; and that the best safeguard of all these is the cultivation of pure pleasures, namely, those of the intellect and affections . . . I do not mean to preach; I speak in simplicity and tender apprehension as one lover of Nature and of Virtue speaking to another.'[24]

Ironically, William thought he had recognized in de Quincey a version of his youthful self, a comparison that was inevitably strengthened when the latter's beloved younger brother was apparently lost at sea. In fact, de Quincey might more aptly be likened to Coleridge: he was also an opium addict, with all the delusions and paranoia which that induced, he had the same desperate need to be loved by those whom he admired and he was promiscuous as Coleridge had been in his youth. Like Coleridge, too, he was acutely aware of his lack of physical attractiveness (de Quincey was small to the point of dwarfism), but he lacked the compensatory charisma, personality and verbal fireworks of Coleridge on a good day. Quiet, observant, shrewd and well read, he was willing to please and desperate for admission to what Coleridge called the Concern, the magic circle of William's devoted family and friends. Several times over the intervening years he had made arrangements to meet William, but his courage had always failed him at the last moment. Now he had a legitimate reason to do so, having offered to escort Mrs Coleridge and her children from Bristol back to Keswick, enabling Coleridge to go to London alone as he wished and relieving him of an uncomfortable duty.[25]

On 4 November a trembling de Quincey finally accomplished his dream and found himself face to face with William, 'a tallish man, who held out his hand, and saluted me, with the most cordial manner, and the warmest expression of friendly welcome that it is possible to imagine'. Entering the cottage, he encountered Mary, 'a tall young woman, with the most winning expression of benignity upon her features that I had ever beheld', and Dorothy, shorter and slighter, whose unladylike 'determinate gypsy tan', glancing quickness of motion and ungraceful 'even unsexual' deportment, startled him.[26] De Quincey was one of the few people who knew the Wordsworths well in this early period to attempt to describe them fully. His account has to be treated with some caution. It was written as a piece of journalism, with an eye to the sensational, and long after he had become disenchanted with the whole Wordsworth circle, and most of all with William, who had not made 'those returns of friendship and kindness' to which de Quincey felt himself entitled by his own personal devotion to the poet. Nevertheless, despite its jaundiced colouring, it is a fascinating insight by an intelligent and perspicacious observer.

De Quincey described William as being 'upon the whole, not a well-made man', five feet ten inches tall, thick-limbed, with legs that were 'serviceable beyond the average standard of human requisition . . . [but] certainly not ornamental'. A narrowness of chest and a droop about the shoulders added to what de Quincey called the 'absolute meanness' of his figure, especially when viewed from the back and not counteracted by his countenance, which 'was one which would have made amends for greater defects of figure; it was certainly the noblest for intellectual effects that, in actual life, I have seen . . .' It was a variety of the indigenous face of the Lake District, like that of a courtier in a painting by Titian or Van Dyck, not oval, but long, with a broad and expansive forehead, large, rather arched nose, eyes which, after a long walk, assumed the most solemn and spiritual expression possible, and a prominent mouth. Both he and Dorothy always looked fifteen or twenty years older than they were, because they shared 'the secret fire of a temperament too fervid; the self-consuming energies of the brain, that gnaw at the heart and life-strings for ever'.

For Mary, so often overlooked or ignored by observers, de Quincey immediately conceived, and (unusually) preserved, profound respect and admiration. Physically, she was tall, with a good figure, though too slender for de Quincey's taste, and possessed of natural dignity: 'she furnished a remarkable proof how possible it is for a woman, neither handsome nor even comely, according to the rigour of criticism – nay, generally pronounced very plain – to exercise all the practical power and fascination of beauty'. Her 'sunny benignity – a radiant gracefulness – such as in this world I never saw equalled or approached' transformed her. (Sir George Beaumont had been equally struck by this, telling William that no one could be more sensible of Mary's 'angelic kindness & goodness of heart . . . indeed it is not possible to be two minutes in her company without perceiving it, it beams from her countenance & shines out in all her actions & expressions'. If all men and women were like her, there would be something approaching perfect happiness in this world. 'This is not a compliment –', Beaumont assured William, 'I seriously declare it to be the conviction of my heart & I have repeatedly said the same thing to Lady Beaumont who feels exactly as I do upon the subject'.) Intellectually, de Quincey described her as 'inactive'; blue-stocking loquacity, discussion and analysis were not her natural *forte.* Indeed, she talked so little that Clarkson used to say of her that she could only say '*God bless you!*' What she did have was 'a luxurious repose of mind', 'a quiescent, reposing, meditative way' which was perfectly suited to the needs and tastes of her husband.[27]

Having described Mary as a paragon of femininity, de Quincey rounded on Dorothy with a brutality which is all the more shocking for the contrast. It was a deliberate juxtaposition, for the whole thrust of his portrayal was that Dorothy was 'unfeminine'. The italics in the following descriptions are mine.

Her manner was warm and even ardent; her sensibility seemed constitutionally deep; and some subtle fire of impassioned intellect apparently burned within her, which, being alternately pushed forward into a conspicuous expression by *the irrepressible instincts of her temperament, and then immediately checked, in obedience to the decorum of her sex and age*, and her maidenly condition, (for she had rejected all offers of marriage, out of purely sisterly regard to her brother and his children,) gave to her whole demeanour and to her conversation, an air of embarrassment and even of *self-conflict*, that was sometimes distressing to witness ... At times, the *self-counteraction* and *self-baffling* of her feelings, caused her even to stammer, ... The greatest deductions from Miss Wordsworth's attractions ... was the glancing quickness of her motions, and other circumstances in her deportment, (such as her stooping attitude when walking,) which gave an *ungraceful*, and even an *unsexual* character to her appearance when out of doors. She did not cultivate the graces which preside over the person and its carriage ... she ought to have been the more polished of the two; and yet, from greater natural aptitudes for refinement of manner ... Mrs Wordsworth would have been pronounced the more *lady-like* person.

Writing in 1839, in *Tait's Edinburgh Magazine*, de Quincey could do no more than hint that Dorothy was a lesbian, by suggesting that she had a masculine mind and spirit trapped in a female body. It was almost as an afterthought that he paid tribute to her 'very remarkable' intellectual endowments, and her 'sympathizing attention', 'by which she made all that one could tell her, all that one could describe, all that one could quote from a foreign author, reverberate as it were, *à plusieurs reprises*, to one's own feelings, by the manifest impression it made upon her'. Dorothy's sexuality would always intrigue her male friends, just as it does modern commentators, but de Quincey was the only one to postulate the possibility of lesbianism. At the time, however, it did not lessen her personal interest in de Quincey's eyes, for it seems that he was one of those rejected suitors for her hand in marriage.[28]

Welcoming de Quincey to their cottage, the Wordsworths had no idea that he would one day expose them to the prurient gaze of magazine readers. For the moment, they were completely taken up with the Coleridges. Sarah brought news that nothing had changed: her husband had parted from her, just as he had done before, assuring her that he would never live with her again, but he did not have the courage to make the separation public knowledge. This suited Sarah, who was afraid that a formal separation would bring disgrace on herself and the children, but, as the Wordsworths feared, the uncertainty was not in Coleridge's interest. Accusations that he had forsaken his family would be made and, while his marital affairs remained unsettled, he would be unhappy, and therefore unable to fulfil the promise of his great genius. In the meantime, he had gone to London, to undertake a series of twenty lectures on poetry for the Royal Institution. 'I will not say, how dearly I love you all;' he now wrote to Dorothy, 'as perhaps it is a misfortune, that so enormous is the difference between my Love of you & of others, that it seems as if I loved nothing & nobody else. O God! has there been a single hour of my Life, even in sleep, in which I have not been blending with you in my Thoughts!' To his private journal, he was confessing something quite different: 'It is not the W's knowlege of my frailties that prevents my *entire* Love of them No! it is their Ignorance of the Deep place of my Being – and o! the cruel cruel misconception of that which is purest in me', which was, of course, his love of Sara. Even now he was still haunted by jealousy of William, whom he held responsible for teaching Sara 'to pity & withdraw herself from my affections – Whither? – O agony! O the vision of that Saturday morning – of the Bed – O cruel! is he not beloved, adored by two – & two such Beings – and must I not be beloved *near* him except as a Satellite?'[29] It was perhaps just as well that he was safely out of the way in London and that the Wordsworths had no inkling of his true feelings towards them.

De Quincey stayed with the Wordsworths for five days; they showed him the sights, walked him up Easedale and round the lakes of Grasmere and Rydal, and took him to Keswick by the picturesque route over Kirkstone Pass and round Ullswater. De Quincey had already been unnerved by the Wordsworths' 'modest hospitality': he woke to find he was sharing a room with Johnny and, at breakfast, Dorothy herself boiled the kettle on the fire in the little sitting room. 'I had never seen so humble a *ménage*', he admitted. He was in for another shock when they went to Eusemere, for they travelled not on foot, or in a carriage, but in 'the common farmers' cart of the country'. A further one was in store at Greta Hall, where he listened with horror as William and Southey casually revealed their republican sympathies by suggesting that Britain would never come to any good till the royal family should be 'expatriated'. As if this was not 'absolutely disloyal' enough, Southey, who had a gift for witty impromptus, amused himself and William by improvising verses suggesting that the royals should be transported to Botany Bay. De Quincey returned to Oxford with all his preconceptions challenged, his ideas in turmoil and his admiration for 'the Lake Poets' greatly increased by personal acquaintance. He left a good impression at Grasmere, as 'a remarkable and very interesting young man; very diminutive in person, which, to strangers, makes him appear insignificant; and so modest, and so very shy that even now I wonder how he ever had the courage to address himself to my Brother by letter'. Dorothy thought of him with particular pleasure, proudly believing de Quincey to be 'a remarkable instance of the power of my Brother's poems, over a lonely and contemplative mind, unwarped by any established laws of taste'.[30]

Soon after de Quincey left, there was one of the greatest falls of snow in living memory. The mountains were impassable and all the roads were blocked for weeks on end. Mary, whom Joanna had persuaded to accompany her to Stockton, to visit their brother Jack, was stranded there. It was 1 December before the roads were clear enough for William to join her and 23 December before they returned home. At Penrith, they chanced upon a copy of the *Edinburgh Review* and there read Jeffrey's scathing criticisms of *Poems, in Two Volumes*. The Wordsworths maintained an air of calm indifference. 'There is nothing to say,' William wrote, 'for there is nothing in it that bears the least upon the question'; 'it is so senseless, so contradictory, and plainly so spiteful, that it can do no harm with any wise and feeling mind', was Dorothy's response. Their only fear, a justifiable one, was that it would affect the sale of the book. As Southey neatly put it, reviews of this kind 'cannot *blast* our *laurels*, but they may *mildew* our *corn*'.[31]

This mattered more than ever, for William was putting the finishing touches to his new poem, *The White Doe of Rylstone*, and he was determined that it should be a financial success. It was ironic that he was spurred on to this by Scott, who had informed Southey, 'I do not think Wordsworth and you understand the bookselling animal well enough', and suggested they both take their next works to his own publisher, Archibald Constable, who 'would give any terms for a connexion with you'. Neither Southey nor William had the slightest intention of taking the second part of Scott's advice, for Constable was the co-founder of the despised *Edinburgh Review*, but William had taken the first part to heart. He knew exactly what he wanted. He had laboured long and hard throughout a winter so long and severe that they had often been unable to use the facilities of the neighbouring cottage. For the most part, he had been confined to the sitting room, and had had to compose with the children playing at his feet and visitors wandering in and out at will. He had made up his mind that his poem was to be published in quarto (unlike his previous two publications, but, significantly, like Scott's *Lay of the Last Minstrel*) and that he would accept nothing less than £100 guineas for an edition of 1,000 copies.[32]

Southey, to whom William read the completed poem, was all encouragement. 'The story affected me more deeply than I wish to be affected . . . nothing was ever more ably treated', he reported to Scott. William had already decided that he would go in person to London to sell his book for the best possible price when news came that Coleridge was so seriously ill that he had had to give up his lectures at the Royal Institution after delivering only two. Coleridge informed his friends that he could not live many months, but he had cried wolf once too often, even for the Wordsworths. 'We gather consolation from past experience;' Dorothy remarked; 'he has often appeared to be dying and has all at once recovered health and spirits.' They were equally convinced that, unless, and until, he left off opiates, he would never be well again. On the other hand, unless he had some cheering society, he would become more depressed, resort to more opiates and the cycle would become unbreakable. William decided to go to London immediately. Coleridge was lodging in a pair of rooms above the *Courier* office; the state of his bowels was such that, as Lamb put it, he 'receives visitors on his close-stool'.[33]

By the time William arrived in town, on 27 February, Coleridge had rallied a little, having been drawn out of the contemplation of his own miseries by those of Henry Hutchinson. The Hutchinson name 'would be a Spell to recall me for the time even from the verge of death . . . he is the Brother of the two Beings, whom of all on Earth I most highly honor, most fervently love'. Henry had had a disastrous seafaring career. He had been captured at sea, held prisoner in Guadeloupe, released, become a successful privateer, been impressed (and relieved of his winnings) by HMS *Fortunee*, recaptured and held prisoner for twenty-two months in Mexico, released again in a second exchange of prisoners and sent back to Plymouth, where, as his impressment was still in force, he was expected to rejoin the *Fortunee*. 'He has done enough – he has suffered enough', Coleridge pleaded, as he enlisted Beaumont and Clarkson to lobby all their Admiralty contacts on Henry's behalf. By 3 March he was able to announce triumphantly that he had secured Henry's immediate discharge and earned the undying gratitude of all the Hutchinsons for his prompt and energetic intervention.[34]

The effort of this campaign probably did as much to revive Coleridge's flagging spirits as William's presence. Though Coleridge did acknowledge his friend's role as 'a Comforter', he kept him waiting for daily admittance to him, till four o'clock in the afternoon. William himself 'saw no appearance of disease which could not have been cured, or at least prevented by himself'. By 30 March, Coleridge had recovered sufficiently to resume his lectures, after a break of two months, and William was able to attend two of them before returning to Grasmere.[35]

As usual, William packed as much into his visit as he possibly could. The two men took advantage of an introduction from Beaumont to Sir Thomas Lawrence to visit John Julius Angerstein's collection of old masters and William attended a debate in the House of Commons. There was the usual round of breakfast, dinner and tea parties. They spent a dull evening dining with William's publisher, Longman, and his partner, Rees, in a company which included an antiquarian friend of Scott's, Richard Heber, and the historian Sharon Turner; Coleridge was in belligerent mood and gave them all 'some good haranguing, talk I cannot call it' in denunciation of the clergy, for which he later had to apologize. There was a tea party in the office of the *Courier*, attended by its editor, Daniel Stuart, Lamb and Godwin, as well as Southey and de Quincey, who were both visiting London. William went out to Lambeth several times to stay with his brother Christopher, and his family; they were treated to readings of his poem on his own life and *The Brothers*, but not *The White Doe*.[36]

The Lambs played host to several gatherings. On the evening William finally yielded to their entreaties and brought *The White Doe* to read, he was disconcerted to find that Hazlitt and his fiancée, Sarah Stoddart, were fellow guests. William's personal dislike of Hazlitt had intensified since they last met; the latter had published a political pamphlet in 1806 denouncing as 'apostates' those who, like William, Southey and Coleridge, had changed their attitude towards France as Bonaparte rose to power. In the circumstances, William at first refused to read his poem, but then grudgingly relented and read a single canto. He had not expected a rapturous reception, and he did not get one. Lamb complained that the principal characters 'did nothing'. It was an understandable complaint, given the expectations roused by the form and title of the poem, but if friends like Lamb so completely missed the point, then how would the public react? William's frustration boiled over: in another of those long, sweating letters he poured out his defence of the spiritual object at the heart of the poem, and urged that Lamb should 'learn to be ashamed of himself in not taking some pleasure in the contemplation of this picture'. Poor Lamb was roundly condemned for having the temerity to dislike the poem (or rather, as William would have said, to misunderstand it): 'of one thing be assured,' William wrote Coleridge, 'that Lamb has not a reasoning mind, therefore cannot have a comprehensive mind, and, least of all, has he an imaginative one'.[37]

It was comments like these – sadly all too frequent when William felt driven to justify his poetry in both his conversation and his correspondence – which so often provoked charges of arrogance and egotism against him. Southey regarded this unlikeable trait with amused contempt. 'It would amuse you to hear how he talks of his own productions, – his entire & intense selfishness exceeds anything you could have conceived.' Hazlitt suggested that William's temper had been soured by a 'sense of injustice and of undeserved ridicule'.

To have produced works of genius, and to find them neglected or treated with scorn, is one of the heaviest trials of human patience. We exaggerate our own merits when they are denied by others, and are apt to grudge and cavil at every particle of praise bestowed on those to whom we feel a conscious superiority. In mere self-defence we turn against the world, when it turns against us; brood over the undeserved slights we receive; and thus the genial current of the soul is stopped, or vents itself in effusions of petulance and self-conceit.[38]

The most perceptive response, however, came from Henry Crabb Robinson, to whom William was introduced by the Lambs during this visit to London. Robinson was a barrister, five years younger than William, and an intimate friend of the Clarksons. He had long been an admirer of William's poems and would become a lifelong friend. 'Wordsworth quotes his own Verses with pleasure', he told his brother after he had enjoyed two têtes-à-têtes with the poet, but he had an unfortunate habit of judging the moral worth of his audience by their reaction to his poems. As Robinson observed, there were many who could fully appreciate the moral truths and sentiments of the poetry, but could not overcome their dislike of his style; William did not make any allowance for the influence of 'conventional & habitual taste'.[39]

That there was this confusion in William's mind is evident from his barely suppressed anger at Lamb's reaction to *The White Doe.* Anyone who appreciated the moral truths at the heart of the poem *must* like the poem itself was his argument; it therefore followed that disliking the poem could result only from moral ignorance or turpitude in the reader. It was a logical extension of his belief that 'Every Great Poet is a Teacher: I wish either to be considered as a Teacher, or as nothing',[40] and also that his works would never be appreciated until the depraved tastes of his generation had been reformed. Such a view was undoubtedly comforting for William, in the face of rejection and ridicule, but, as Robinson said, it failed to take into account that it might be possible to approve of the moral message of the poetry while still disliking the poetry itself.

Lamb was not alone in being critical of *The White Doe.* Lady Beaumont and her sister, Frances Fermor, 'liked' it (not a good sign, as they were both noted enthusiasts), but 'it did not much interest Sir George'. Coleridge also had considerable doubts, objecting to the sudden and entire transference of interest, three-quarters of the way through, from the Norton father and sons to Emily; he found the battle scenes and Francis's delivering up of the family '*comparatively* very heavy' going, and, in terms of Francis's motivation, 'quite obscure'. These were significant censures, particularly coming from a critic as astute as Coleridge.[41] William's confidence faltered. He had carried out his intention to offer Longman the right to publish a first edition of 1,000 copies of *The White Doe* in return for 100 guineas, but when Longman (not unreasonably) insisted on having the manuscript referred to an independent editor for approval before he agreed to accept it, William seized on this as an excuse to back out and refused. 'I do not chuse to send it to be thumbed by his criticasters', he informed the family at Grasmere. 'I do not think it likely I shall publish it at all – indeed I am so thoroughly disgusted with the wretched and stupid Public, that though my wish to *write* for the sake of the People is not abated yet my loathing at the thought of publication is almost insupportable. – Therefore trouble yourselves no more about it.' William might have been prepared to abandon the project out of principle, but his wife and sister had more pragmatic concerns at heart, as Dorothy did not hesitate to remind him.

We are exceedingly concerned, to hear that you, William! have given up all thoughts of publishing your Poem . . . without money what *can* we do? New House! new furniture! such a large family! two servants and little Sally! we *cannot* go on so another half-year; and as Sally will not be fit for another place, we must take her back again into the old one, and dismiss one of the Servants, and work the flesh *off our poor bones*. Do, dearest William! do pluck up your Courage – overcome your disgust to publishing – It is but a *little trouble*, and all will be over, and we shall be wealthy, and at our ease for one year, at least.[42]

Coleridge came to the rescue. He suggested that William leave the manuscript with him and authorize him to make what arrangements he could for its publication. On 3 April William left London, ironically recalled home early by news that Sara was seriously ill. He parted from Coleridge at seven o'clock in the morning and walked towards the City

in a very thoughtful and melancholy state of mind; I had passed through Temple Bar and by St Dunstan's, noticing nothing, and entirely occupied with my own thoughts, when looking up, I saw before me the avenue of Fleet street, silent, empty, and pure white, with a sprinkling of new-fallen snow, not a cart or Carriage to obstruct the view, no noise, only a few soundless and dusky foot-passengers, here and there; you remember the elegant curve of Ludgate Hill in which this avenue would terminate, and beyond and towering above it was the huge and majestic form of St Pauls, solemnised by a thin veil of falling snow. I cannot say how much I was affected at this unthought-of sight, in such a place and what a blessing I felt there is in habits of exalted Imagination. My sorrow was controlled, and my uneasiness of mind not quieted and relieved altogether, seemed at once to receive the gift of an anchor of security.

It was the perfect subject for a poem, yet another of those 'moments of time' when the outside world suddenly and unexpectedly impressed its presence on a preoccupied mind. The resulting blank verse lines, 'Pressed with conflicting thoughts of love and fear', drew heavily on the imagery and vocabulary of this prose description to create a wonderful meditative poem. Despite its obvious quality, William deliberately suppressed it during his lifetime, for reasons which remain obscure.[43]

He returned home to scenes of more than usual chaos. They were all still 'sadly cooped up' in the little cottage at Town End, though living in hope that Allan Bank would be ready in May. Sara was in a very delicate state, though no longer in danger, but Johnny, who had been ill with influenza, suddenly developed alarming symptoms of meningitis on the very day of William's return. For more than a week his parents and aunts were frantic with worry; doctors were brought in from Ambleside and Keswick and, despite their best efforts (purgatives, bleeding and blistering) Johnny recovered.[44] The burden of the nursing fell on Mary, who was herself unwell, being in the fourth month of pregnancy; their servant had left to get married and she had only two young girls to help her, one of whom, Sally Green, had just suffered a terrible bereavement. On the night of 19 March her parents had been caught in a snowstorm returning over the tops from Langdale to their isolated cottage in Easedale, where they had left their six youngest children in the care of the oldest, a girl of eleven. For two days the children waited for their parents to return, thinking that they had stayed in Langdale, so the alarm was not raised till the oldest went to borrow a cloak so that she could go out to look for them. Realizing what must have been their fate, between fifty and sixty men turned out and began an organized search; the bodies were found, forty-eight hours later, lying at the foot of the precipice from which they must have fallen. They were buried in a single grave in Grasmere churchyard on 25 March. The Greens had been typical Lakeland statesmen, fiercely independent, struggling to provide for themselves and their family on a small, heavily mortgaged farm and refusing to go to the parish for assistance. 'See them when you would,' Dorothy remarked, 'they were always chearful, and when they went from home they were decently dressed. The children, too, though very ragged, were clean; and are as pure and innocent, and in every respect as promising children as I ever saw.'[45]

It was not until after their deaths that the full extent of their poverty became known. Mary and Dorothy, who visited the orphans almost immediately, were shocked and distressed to find that there was virtually no food in the house. They determined that something would have to be done. There were twelve orphans: the five oldest were already in employment and one of them could take a younger brother into his house and business. The Wordsworths offered a home to Sally. She had been with them as a nursemaid to the children since their return from Coleorton, but, before the tragedy, they had decided that she would have to be replaced at Whitsuntide by someone older and more authoritative. Now they volunteered to keep her, not as a servant but as a member of their household, sending her to Grasmere school and teaching her sewing to enable her to go out and earn her own living in due course. Only the five youngest children were left without any means of support. Their plight could not fail to move the Wordsworths, who knew all too well what it was like to be penniless orphans. It was decided to raise a public subscription to enable the Greens to be boarded with families in the vale, sent to school and trained as servants and apprentices. Mary joined a committee of local ladies at Ambleside to supervise the care of the orphans and personally took charge of keeping the accounts. William, immediately on his return from London, drafted a short account of the fate of the Greens and circulated it among his rich and powerful friends, appealing to them to assist this 'cluster of little orphans, who have been left such in a most afflicting manner'. He was phenomenally successful. As the result of his efforts, over a third of the total sum of £500 was raised. Wrangham alone raised £41, Rogers £31 8s and Lady Holland, to whom William applied only after some hesitation, £32 10s.[46] After visiting the new grave, William composed a poem which he dismissed as 'a mere pouring out of my own feeling', but nevertheless asked Coleridge to utilize for 'any profit for the poor Orphans' by reciting, circulating or publishing it. He even contemplated inserting an account of the tragedy in the *Courier* to aid the subscription, but changed his mind when it became apparent that it was unnecessary. In less than a month, they had collected over £300; to raise much more, in such a public manner, would excite envy among other poor families in the neighbourhood, who considered themselves equally deserving, and jealousy among the older children, who were not to benefit from the subscription. William was justifiably proud of the way the whole vale had united to help the orphans, suggesting to Dorothy that she should make 'a minute narrative' of all the circumstances. It would, he said, 'throw much light upon the state of the moral feelings of the inhabitants of these Vales'. To those who complained that his own poetry celebrated a way of life and a spirit of benevolence long since passed away from the Lakes, Dorothy's *A Narrative Concerning George and Sarah Green* furnished a practical example that they had not.[47]

At the beginning of May, Henry Hutchinson paid his first visit to Grasmere. His discharge from the navy had come through at last and he was a free, if impecunious, man. His arrival stirred memories of the Wordsworths' other sailor brother, who had also walked up the vale to the little cottage at Town End seven years earlier and busied himself in the family's domestic concerns. Henry proved to be not only a raconteur who had them all hanging on his every word, but also 'the handiest creature in the world – can sew, cook, wash dishes – put up beds – any thing that you can name'. What is more, from enforced abstinence during the years of his imprisonment, he had also been weaned entirely off the grog, which had been the cause of so many of his past misfortunes. He stayed only for a few days, but long enough to make himself so indispensable that they all begged him to return to help them make the long-awaited move to Allan Bank.

It was fortunate that he did, for Sara was too ill to do anything other than a little light sewing, Mary had sprained her wrist in a fall just before the move and William was generally regarded as useless in such situations: he was not expected to do anything and was, whenever possible, dispatched safely out of harm's way. The whole burden of packing and unpacking papers, linen, books and all the paraphernalia of daily life fell on Dorothy. She and Henry worked body and soul, determined to save as much money as possible by making their own carpets and curtains;

fortunately, Sailor Harry was as good as a tailor. Reluctant as Dorothy had been to move from the cottage, she, and indeed all the family, felt the advantages of Allan Bank immediately. The children thought they were in Paradise: they were free to play all over the surrounding fields without fear of being run over by the horses, waggons and carriages which daily passed the old cottage door.[48]

Allan Bank, which was to be the Wordsworths' home for the next two years, was unquestionably a gentleman's house. Externally it was imposing, if brutally symmetrical, with large sash windows and semicircular bays to take full advantage of the views offered by its elevated situation. Internally, a surprisingly modest entrance porch gave way to a vast, square hall, with a highly impractical glass roof. From this central hallway opened out a series of huge, ornately plastered reception rooms, each one large enough to swallow the cottage at Town End whole. Up a sweeping staircase, a rabbit warren of bedrooms led off the galleried landing which ran right round the upper floor. For the first time in years the Wordsworths had space and privacy. They each had a room of their own and the views from every window were spectacular: Dunmail Raise passing through Helm Crag, Seat Sandal and Fairfield mountains to the east; the length of Grasmere lake, with Loughrigg Terraces stacked behind, to the west; the dark cleft of Greenhead Ghyll facing them, above the rocky knolls which hid the village from view, to the south.[49]

Now that the Wordsworths had room to accommodate any number of guests, they were inundated. Mary's family descended *en masse* from Penrith: her sister Joanna, aunt Elizabeth Monkhouse and cousins John and Mary Monkhouse were their first guests, and an invitation was also offered to de Quincey.[50] There were visits to the Lloyds at Old Brathay, a disastrous picnic party to the island on Grasmere lake as guests of Crump, which was rained off, and a renewal of an acquaintance struck up the previous year with John Wilson, a wealthy young Scotsman who was building a new house, Elleray, on Orrest Head, overlooking Windermere. Wilson, like de Quincey, had been drawn to the Lakes by his personal admiration for William. As a young man at the university in Glasgow in 1802, he had written him a long and appreciative letter, full of discerning criticism of *Lyrical Ballads*, to which William had responded in similar vein. Still only twenty-three, this 'very amiable young man' had become a friend, as well as an '*adorer* of William and his verses'; he had contributed five guineas to the subscription for the Greens and, as Dorothy said, 'It seems as if he, and his whole family, thought they could hardly do enough to express their liking to us all'. The friendship was to prove enduring, though it was not without its difficulties once Wilson was drawn into the ambit of *Blackwood's Magazine*.[51]

Summer brought the usual influx of Lake visitors, among them the crass and self-important vicar of Kildwick and Skipton, the Reverend John Pering, who bore letters of introduction to Dorothy from the former Margaret Spedding. He was clearly impressed with Allan Bank, 'the edifice itself is almost new, and handsome, and the rooms far superior to the lot of most Poets', and, surprisingly, admired the way William deferred to his sister for opinions, 'which she expressed with readiness, generally decisive, with good sense, and always unassumingly'. Being a good tourist in the late-eighteenth-century mode, he had been thoroughly indoctrinated with what he ought to see and how: unable to remember accurately two views pointed out to him on a walk by William, he described one in his journal as being 'adapted to the taste of Salvator, and the other that of Claude'. It was hardly surprising that he could not agree with William's political or poetical views; he was nonplussed by William's vehemence in attacking the government-backed lotteries as 'a ruinous mode of gambling' by those who could least afford to risk their money, and dismayed by his attack on the 'vitiated Taste' of even the best Augustan poets. The high point of his visit came when Dorothy related the story of the Greens, which he resolved to include in his journal. It seemed perfectly 'reasonable' to him to write to William several months later, asking him for a detailed account of the melancholy story and hinting strongly that, if William could, without much trouble, add an account of his neighbouring mountains, 'either Philosophical or otherwise', it would render the pages of his journal 'more acceptable'. It says much for William's amiable qualities that he sent Pering a copy of the duplicated account of the Greens' fate and merely declined, graciously, to write his description of the Lakes for him, declaring himself to be a writer of impulse, who had been unable to oblige his own wife by writing an account of their own Lake tour the previous autumn. 'I must be my own Task master or I can do nothing at all.'[52]

The one visitor who was most anxiously expected did not make his appearance at Allan Bank till 1 September. Coleridge had pleaded ill-health to cut short his series of lectures in London in June, but instead of coming straight to Grasmere, as planned, had gone with Stuart to Margate, then to stay with the Clarksons at Bury St Edmunds. Both Coleridge and the Wordsworths looked forward to their reunion with mixed feelings. The previous December, Dorothy had confided her fears to Catherine Clarkson:

> we had long experience at Coleorton that it was not in our power to make him happy; and his irresolute conduct since, has almost confirmed our fears that it will never be otherwise; therefore we should be more disposed to hesitation; and fear, of having our domestic quiet disturbed if he should now wish to come to us with the Children. I do not say that we *should not consent*; but it would be with little hope; and we shall never *advise* the measure.[53]

Since then, relations between Coleridge and William had hit a new low. The ostensible cause was William's sudden decision in May to cancel publication of *The White Doe.* Coleridge had fought long and hard on his friend's behalf to secure the terms he wanted from Longman and had succeeded where William himself had failed. On 1 May Dorothy had written to Coleridge, saying,

> *We are very anxious* that 'the White Doe' should be published *as soon as possible*... Our main reason (I speak in the name of the Females) for wishing that the Poem may be *speedily* published, is that William may get it out of his head; but further we think that it is of the

> *utmost importance*, that it should come out before the Buz of your Lectures is settled [Coleridge's emphases].

Coleridge naturally took this to be an authorization to send the manuscript immediately to the publisher, not realizing that when Dorothy said she spoke for the 'Females', she spoke for them alone. They were certainly pushing William to go ahead, but he proved obdurate, being increasingly convinced by the reaction of those permitted to read the poem that it would neither sell nor add to his reputation. When he learned that Coleridge had given the go-ahead to Longman's, he wrote at once to countermand the order, suggesting that Coleridge had exceeded his authority.[54]

There had been a perfectly genuine misunderstanding which, in normal circumstances, would not have mattered at all. But Coleridge was not in a normal state of mind: the stress of delivering weekly lectures, a run-in with the *Edinburgh Review* and being 'on show' in London society had driven him to drinking and opium-taking of heroic proportions. As a result, he was both paranoid and psychotic, believing that he had been 'Cruelly' treated by 'almost every one', a list which included his greatest benefactors, Poole and the Wedgwoods, as well as the usual suspects, his own family, Southey and the Wordsworths. The suggestion that he might have exceeded his authority was the catalyst to ignite all his festering grievances, both real and imagined. He wrote William a long and bitter letter, articulating for the first time all the complaints which he had previously confided only to his private notebooks. William was accused of 'cowardly Mock-prudence relatively to his Friends' because he had not defended Coleridge against Stoddart's charges of plagiarism with sufficient warmth, and of cultivating friendship with Charles Lloyd, whom Coleridge regarded almost as a mortal enemy. William's 'High Self-opinion', Coleridge declared, had been 'pampered in a hot bed of Dor[othy's] & Mrs W's Ideal moral & intellectual Sympathy'. Worse still – and here lay the heart of the poison which so ignominiously ate away at Coleridge's great soul – he charged the Wordsworths with turning Sara against him. Her letters to him had been written under their censoring eye, but 'the keystone' of their 'offences' was their 'cruelty' in instilling into Sara's mind the notion that his attachment to her had been 'the curse' of all his happiness.[55]

William must have been both shocked and hurt to receive such a letter, but he refused to take offence: he understood that it was not the true Coleridge speaking, merely 'a man in a lamentably insane state of mind'.

> There is more than one sentence in your letter which I blushed to read, and which you yourself would have been unable to write, could never have thought of writing, nay, the matter of which could never even have passed through your mind, had you not acquired a habit, which I think a very pernicious one, of giving by voice and pen to your most lawless thoughts, and to your wildest fancies, an external existence . . .

Though he considered all the accusations 'utterly unworthy of notice', he would not have been human had he not wished to refute them. One by one, he dealt with and dismissed each claim. He tried hard to remain both calm and reasonable, drafting the letter twice, but it was an effort that could not be sustained, particularly when it came to Coleridge's 'unmanly and ungentlemanly' accusation that he censored Sara's correspondence. 'She is 34 years of age and what have I to do with overlooking her letters!' As for trying to make her believe she was the curse of Coleridge's happiness, 'the very reverse is the truth'. Mary and Dorothy had told Sara that it was in Coleridge's nature to conceive such an infatuation; she was therefore not the cause of his unhappiness, but the innocent occasion of it. What is more, she could congratulate herself, for *his* sake, that she was the object of his passion. Had he fixed on a less virtuous woman, what might his sufferings then have been?[56]

What the Wordsworths believed was true, but then Truth is not always comfortable or acceptable, especially when preached to the suffering. Having given vent to his own feelings, William did what Coleridge should have done and did not send his letter. Coleridge also seems to have realized that he had gone too far. When he went to stay with the Clarksons, they found him a Quaker doctor and, not for the first or last time, he made a serious attempt to overcome his addiction. By the time he arrived at Grasmere, he had reduced his opium intake to a sixth of his former consumption and, as a result, was in better health and spirits than he had been for years. He arrived on 1 September, making a spectacular entrance at half past eleven at night, which roused the whole household from their beds.[57]

Coleridge would share the Wordsworths' home at Allan Bank for the next two years. Despite the undercurrents and tensions which would soon rise to the surface, the co-residence began well enough. A few days after his arrival, William accompanied Coleridge to Keswick, where, to universal relief, there was an amicable meeting with his wife. She not only agreed that her two sons should live with their father at Allan Bank during school terms and with her during the holidays, but also that little Sara should pay him an extended visit. Sara was now almost six and barely knew her father, who was determined to win her affection. She returned with him to Allan Bank, where her delicate beauty and quiet manners won all hearts – and provided a striking contrast to naughty Dora, with her long blonde ringlets, wild eyes and even wilder motions. Johnny was instantly smitten and, to the amusement of all the adults, the pair decided that he would be her future husband. The relationship with her father proved less successful. When her mother arrived to carry her back home, Sara flew to her and 'wished not to be separated from her any more'. Her father could not hide his annoyance at this understandable preference and, more than forty years later, Sara could still recall vividly both her distress at his accusing her of 'want of affection' and her jealousy when he contrasted her coldness towards him with the childish caresses which the young Wordsworths lavished on him.[58]

The new house filled up rapidly. On 6 September, while William was at Keswick with Coleridge, Mary gave birth to her fourth child and second daughter, Catherine, who was named after her godmother, Catherine Clarkson.[59] At the end of the month, Hartley and Derwent Coleridge, aged twelve and eight, arrived. They were to go to Mr Dawes's school at Ambleside as weekly boarders, but would spend every weekend at Allan Bank. At the beginning of November, they were joined by another permanent guest, de Quincey, who had thrown up his studies at Oxford in the middle of taking his examinations. As Dorothy wearily pointed out to Catherine Clarkson, they regularly had thirteen people in the household, rising to fifteen at weekends.[60]

Given the size of Allan Bank, this should not have been a problem. Unfortunately, the autumn closed in cold, wet and windy. Not only were they all confined to the house, but they now discovered the fatal flaw in its design: the chimneys did not work. 'You can have no conception of the uncomfortableness, not to say *misery*, of this House in these storms –', Sara complained to her cousin; 'not a chimney will draw the smoke! and one day we could not have a fire except in the Study; & then you could not *see* each other. In the rest of the rooms the fire was actually blown out of the Grates'. The combination of cold and smoke was so great that they were forced to go to bed in the middle of the day with the baby, just to keep her warm. Poor Dorothy was kept continually on the trot, scouring and cleaning away the soot which covered every surface in the house. A chimney doctor was summoned, worked for a month and did no good. 'We females wish to quit the Premises immediately but the Men will not hear of it', Sara sighed. The Men were hard at work and happy. The grounds were taking shape rapidly under William's eye; he had planted trees and shrubs around the house, to screen its impact on the otherwise empty eminence on which it stood, and had created a terrace, with gravelled walks, to the front and side, separated from the surrounding park by an iron railing.[61]

More importantly, he had become caught up in the latest political controversy. British troops, under the command of Sir Arthur Wellesley (the future Duke of Wellington) had landed in Portugal at the beginning of August and inflicted a crushing defeat on the French army of occupation. Instead of insisting on an unconditional surrender, his superiors agreed that the French could retreat, with their arms, honour and plunder from Portuguese palaces, museums and churches completely intact, and French collaborators in Portugal were guaranteed immunity from prosecution and persecution. The blindingly obvious outcome was that the retreating French army was free to reinforce Napoleon's armies in Spain and assist in crushing the native Spanish revolt against the imposition of Joseph Bonaparte as their king. The terms were set out in the notorious Convention of Cintra on 30 August 1808, which was widely regarded as a betrayal of Britain's Portuguese allies and the Spanish resistance.

William was mortified. 'We are all here cut to the heart', he declared; '. . . for myself, I have not suffered so much upon any public occasion these many years.' Coleridge, Southey and de Quincey were equally incensed: little Sara Coleridge would never forget how the four men 'gravely and earnestly' paced the room, discussing the affairs of the nation 'as if it were their private concern'.[62] William was determined that something should be done. With his old schoolfriend John Spedding, he visited Southey at Keswick and had a council of war. Together they would raise the county by writing to local newspapers and calling a public meeting which, they agreed, William, as a freeholder, would address. The meeting would avoid prejudging the military inquiry into the matter and would not be party-political, but it would make the county's feelings plain by asking the King to appoint a day of national humiliation 'for this grievous national disgrace'. The Earl of Lonsdale's support was crucial: when it was not forthcoming, they were obliged to abandon the idea, but William could not let the matter drop entirely. Reverting to the idealism of his radical youth, he decided to turn political pamphleteer.[63]

By the beginning of December, he was 'very deep in this subject' and believed he would soon be ready to publish, 'first, I believe in a newspaper for the sake of immediate and wide circulation; and next, the same matter in a separate pamphlet'. He even had a title, *The Convention of Cintra brought to the Test of Principles; and the People of Great Britain vindicated from the Charge of having prejudged it.* Coleridge wrote to Stuart, offering him William's 'series of most masterly Essays on the affairs of Portugal & Spain' for the *Courier.* Stuart, who was himself so indignant about 'our military affairs' that he did not trust himself to write on them, was delighted. 'The subject is extremely important; the present situation of Spain abounds with new & important subjects for reflexion ... Never did I hear any Measure so universally execrated as the Cintra Convention.'[64]

Fired with enthusiasm for his project, William would frequently stay up into the early hours, writing or talking with Coleridge, with shy little de Quincey a rapt and silent auditor. Anxious for the latest news from the Peninsula, he would leave the house at midnight and walk up the Keswick road to meet the carrier bringing the *Courier* from London. Despite the acrid smell of smoke pervading the house, and the fact that the study fire had frequently to be used for cooking and heating water, William composed rapidly. With Coleridge's assistance and Mary as his amanuensis, five instalments were sent off to London before Christmas, and the first, some 2,500 words long, appeared in the *Courier* on 27 December. There was a short delay, caused when the manuscript of the next essay was lost in London and had to be completely rewritten, then it was followed, on 13 January 1809, by a further 4,250 words.[65]

At this point it must have been obvious to Stuart that he was not getting what he had anticipated. Instead of a hard-hitting *exposé* of the military and administrative failings which had led to such a shameful episode, he had received two essays which, despite their length, were merely introductory and mentioned the Convention only four times in passing. Had there been no other news, Stuart would have continued the series, but a sensational investigation by a House of Commons Committee was about to begin. Mrs Clarke, the mistress of the Duke of York, was accused of accepting bribes to influence military appointments by the Duke, who was Commander-in-Chief of the army. It was not merely hot news, unlike the Convention of Cintra, but it went to the heart of what was wrong with the British administration and its handling of the war. Reports of the committee proceedings filled the *Courier* throughout February and the newspaper serialization of William's pamphlet ended before it had properly begun.

There were no hard feelings on either side. William was rather relieved, as his style and method of writing were not adapted to the pressures of meeting newspaper deadlines; now he could afford to take a more leisurely approach. He decided to widen his reading and eagerly accepted Stuart's offer to find him both relevant reports and pamphlets and a publisher for his own work. Nevertheless, he was still acutely aware that the pamphlet had to be published as soon as possible if it was to be relevant and effective. Sheets of copy were duly dispatched in batches to the printers as soon as they were written, but the post was so dilatory and haphazard that direct supervision of the proofs from Grasmere proved impractical. De Quincey, delighted to have an opportunity to render practical service to his hero, volunteered to go to London to see the pamphlet through the press. William accepted gratefully: it would save him time and expense, and Stuart the trouble which had, by default, fallen to him.[66]

De Quincey arrived on 25 February to find London agog with the news that Sheridan's splendid new Drury Lane theatre had burnt down in the night. In his anxiety to please, he sent long chatty letters, full of all the latest gossip, every few days to Allan Bank. They were clearly designed to entertain the Grasmerians, but ultimately led to (unfounded) suspicions that he had not dedicated himself to the task in hand.[67] The printers had already received between a half and two-thirds of William's text, most of which had been seen and approved by the author. The tasks of punctuating the rest of William's manuscripts, as they arrived, passing them on to the printer and correcting the proofs would fall to de Quincey. It was a grave mistake. Though scholarly and conscientious, he had no practical experience of proof-reading or editing, and would often fail to pick up misprints until printing was far advanced. He was too young, stood too much in awe of William and lacked the self-confidence to take decisions without referring to Grasmere, which rather undermined the whole purpose of his being there. Like everyone who had ever undertaken the thankless task of seeing William's work through the press, he was also deluged with last-minute emendations, cancellations and second thoughts, all of which caused delay and confusion.[68]

His problems were aggravated by the fact that this was not a volume of poetry, but a commentary on contemporary politics, which was inherently liable to be wrong-footed by the pace of events. The appearance in March of the official Report of the Board of Inquiry on the Convention of Cintra meant that the Appendix, which had been compiled from newspaper reports, had to be completely remodelled. The fall of Saragossa under a second siege, after a successful resistance to a first, necessitated comment or changes. De Quincey provided a lengthy and painstakingly compiled footnote, which, to his mortification, William cancelled as unnecessary. The death of the British commander Sir John Moore at Corunna on 16 January and his widely publicized aspersions on the Spanish also had to be taken into account.[69] Nevertheless, by the end of March de Quincey had received all the copy, and corrections, and William confidently expected the pamphlet to be published within the next fortnight. In the event, it was not published until eight weeks later, by which time the French, under Marshal Soult, had reinvaded Portugal, a revolution in Sweden had led to the abdication of the monarch, France and Austria were at war and Napoleon had annexed the Papal States. The Convention of Cintra was no longer a topical subject.

What caused the delay? De Quincey laid the blame squarely on the printers and a drunken compositor. Stuart blamed de Quincey, saying that the printers had never known 'so much chopping & changing, so much cancelling & correction'. 'I wish Mr Wordsworth had trusted to himself to send the Pamphlet to Press', he wrote glumly to Coleridge. 'We got on much faster when it was in his own hands. I am quite satisfied of Mr de Quincey's amiable character & kind intentions; – but these are nothing on such an occasion.' Coleridge, who seems to have taken a certain malicious and jealous delight in fomenting trouble for de Quincey, encouraged both the Wordsworths and Stuart to believe that it was entirely de Quincey's fault, declaring that the latter's turn of mind, 'anxious yet dilatory, confused from over-accuracy, & at once systematic and labyrinthine', would make him a great 'plague' to 'a London Printer'.[70]

William himself was unconcerned, and, indeed, contributed to the delay by a last-minute panic of his own. He suddenly realized that he might be fined or imprisoned for remarks which might be construed as libellous, particularly against Arthur Wellesley, who had just been sent back to Portugal as Commander-in-Chief of the British forces there. Stuart and de Quincey were urgently requested to read the pamphlet through before publication and cancel any defamatory passages. 'We Females', as Dorothy, Mary and Sara had taken to calling themselves, thought the whole notion extremely funny. 'We Females . . . have not the least fear of Newgate', Sara informed de Quincey; '– if there was but a Garden to walk in we think we should do very nicely – and a Gaol in the Country would be quite pleasant'. Taking his tone from her letter, de Quincey replied that there was 'no hope of Newgate', but rather spoilt the joke by admitting that he and Stuart could not agree which passages might be libellous.[71]

William tried hard to keep his nerve and his temper, but admitted to being 'ruffled . . . not a little' when he learned that all 500 copies of the pamphlet had been run off before Stuart had completed his read-through for libel; worse still, after all the delays, the completed pamphlet then lay for ten days at the printers instead of being forwarded to Longman's for publication. Belatedly, William realized that de Quincey was temperamentally unsuited to the task he had been given; he had been 'the *occasion*', if not the 'necessary *cause*' of most of the problems. 'But it avails nothing to find fault, especially with one [who] has taken such pains (according to the best of his judgment) to forward this business', he admitted. To de Quincey himself, William could not bring himself to give the heartfelt thanks and unqualified approval which the young man believed he had earned and deserved for his selfless labours. His praises were at best half-hearted – 'I am surprized how you have been able to get it done so correctly'; his most fulsome compliment was a congratulation 'on your escape from so irksome an employment and . . . my sincere thanks for all the trouble you have undergone'. When Mary chivvied him into expressing 'stronger language of approbation', he had the grace to repeat her rebuke to de Quincey, but followed it with a string of regrets about misprints which negated its value. It was hardly surprising that de Quincey would later publicly complain that William had never made 'those returns of friendship and kindness [to] which most firmly I maintain [I was] entitled'.[72]

And what of the pamphlet itself? It was finally published on 24 May 1809 by Longman, who set the price at 5s. Unlike any of his other publications, William personally bore the entire cost of printing and publishing, a sure indication of how much the pamphlet meant to him. He had not been sanguine about its prospects, even before publication. 'What I have written has been done according to the best light of my Conscience;' he told his old friend Wrangham; 'it is indeed very imperfect, and will I fear be little read, but, if it is read, it cannot I hope fail of doing some good – though I am aware it will create me a world of enemies, and call forth the old yell of Jacobinism.'[73]

He had every reason to be wary, for in its own way the pamphlet was as radical as his unpublished *Letter to the Bishop of L[l]andaff*, written fifteen years earlier. He accused the government of preparing to lay further restraints upon freedom of speech and of the press 'in contempt of the rights of the nation'. He declared that the purpose of his pamphlet was to instruct men in authority, who, 'if they possess not talents and acquirements, have not title to the high stations which they hold', and 'to assert the sanctity and to display the efficacy of principles and passions which are the natural birth-right of man'. He attacked the self-serving, place-seeking spirit of those in Parliament, who had refused to bow to popular demand and censure or condemn the Convention of Cintra. 'If the People would constitutionally and resolutely assert their rights, their Representatives would be taught another lesson; and for their own profit', he thundered. And, though speaking of Spain, the lesson for British politics was implicit when he asserted that a nation 'determined to be free' could overcome the mightiest power which a foreign invader might bring against it: 'the cause of the People . . . is safe while it remains not only in the bosom but in the hands of the People; or (what amounts to the same thing) in those of a government which, being truly *from* the People, is faithfully *for* them'.[74]

William aptly prefaced his pamphlet with a quotation from Lord Bacon: 'Bitter and earnest writing must not hastily be condemned; for men cannot contend coldly, and without affection, about things which they hold dear and precious.' No one could doubt what he held dear and precious on reading his pamphlet, or, to give it its proper title, which was an essay in itself: *Concerning the Relations of Great Britain, Spain, and Portugal, to each other, and to the Common Enemy, at this Crisis; and Specifically as Affected by the Convention of Cintra: The whole brought to the test of those Principles, by which alone the Independence and Freedom of Nations can be Preserved or Recovered.* (William remarked, with typically wry humour, 'This is less a Title than a Table of Contents'.)[75]

After a rather wearisome introduction on general principles, 'the long Porch [that] may prevent Readers from entering the Temple', as Coleridge described it, the pamphlet took fire when William turned his blazing indignation on what he termed 'the moral depravity' of the Convention itself. 'What an outrage!' he cried.

– We enter the Portugueze territory as allies; and, without their consent – or even consulting them, we proceed to form the basis of an agreement, relating – not to the safety or interests of our own army – but to Portugueze territory, Portugueze persons, liberties, and rights, – and engage, out of our own will and power, to include the Portugueze army, they or their Government willing or not, within the obligation of this agreement.

In just over 200 pages of sizzling prose, he lambasted the British generals for exceeding and perverting their powers by pretending to be diplomats, and the injustice and consequent evil of the Convention itself. 'The evil is incalculable; and the stain will cleave to the British name as long as the story of this island shall endure.'[76]

They were fine words, and the reviewers responded with surprising sympathy. The *Eclectic Review* could not resist a snide comment on the style, which, it said, 'resembled nothing so nearly as the blank verse of the Westmoreland triumvirate of Bards', but went on to praise the pamphlet.

In these Sibylline leaves, (full of portentous and awful denunciations,) snatched from the winds, and stitched loosely together to make a pamphlet of only one day's longer life than a newspaper, there is more of the spirit and fire of geniune poetry, than we have found in many a cream coloured volume of verse . . . there is a pulse of philanthropy, that beats through every page (though not through every line), and a soul of patriotism that breathes through the whole body of this work, which raises it, as an off-spring of intellect; far above the political ephemera, quickened from the carcasses of transient events which Time leaves behind him in his devastating march to Eternity.

The *British Critic* was equally enthusiastic: 'Upon the whole, the generous spirit which this pamphlet breathes, and the knowledge of human nature, which in many passages, it evinces, claim attention and applause; although the Author's enthusiasm is not, we think, void of extravagance . . . although his style, though it often interests by eloquence, as frequently fatigues by prolixity.' It was left to Robinson, in his first published review of William's work, to point out that the pamphlet confounded ordinary expectations.

It is not a political pamphlet, but an essay on a political subject, in which the philosophy of human nature, and the principles of an high-toned and pure morality, are applied to the conduct and fate of nations . . . he who sits down to the perusal of this pamphlet, with the feelings with which we all read, for instance, those of Burke, less for the political matter they treat of, than the great philosophical truths with which they abound, and the spiritual eloquence with which they have adorned and elevated our language, will not fail to enjoy a kindred satisfaction from it.[77]

Stuart, an experienced journalist and political commentator, had every confidence that the pamphlet would be a success 'in all ways, – in political influence – in popularity & in money'. He was wrong on every count. It sank, virtually without trace. William needed to sell all 500 copies to recoup his costs. There was an initial flurry of interest and, by 7 July, 170 copies had been purchased. Two years after publication, the remaining 178 copies were sold as waste paper.[78]

14. *The Blessedest of Men!*

Throughout the winter and spring of 1808–9, William had been engaged 'head, heart, soul, and fingers in the Spanish Business'. Not only had he composed his *Convention of Cintra* pamphlet, but also some ten sonnets celebrating the struggle of the Spanish patriots against the French, which would later be published among his 'Poems Dedicated to National Independence and Liberty'. Since then, he had done some desultory tinkering with *The White Doe*, but his heart was not in it, and he did not allow it to go to press.[1]

Much of his work was done against a domestic background that was both unsettled and unsettling. In February, there were three departures from the household at Allan Bank. De Quincey went off to London to deal with William's proofs, Coleridge set out on what was supposed to be a short visit to the Lloyds which turned into an absence of four months, and little Dora, just four and a half years old and the apple of her father's eye, was carried off to Penrith by her Aunt Sara and John Monkhouse. It was not the first time she had been away from home without her parents or brothers. The previous April, she had spent some time at Brathay, staying with the Lloyds, where she was in high spirits, 'inchanted with all the novelties that are about her and declar[ing] that she will never come home again'; nevertheless, she had been shy of the family, and had clung to the gardener and the cook, Molly Dawson, who had formerly been the Wordsworths' servant. Now she was taken to Penrith to stay with her great-aunt, Elizabeth Monkhouse, who had brought up all her own orphaned nephews and nieces and was about to be left bereft by the departure of her two youngest charges, Joanna Hutchinson and Mary Monkhouse: 'if she is any comfort & gratification to my Aunt we shall think ourselves well repaid for the want of [Dora]', her mother wrote. When Aunt Monkhouse was ready to part with her, Dora was to go to Appleby to visit her cousins from Stockton, Bessy and Jane Hutchinson, who were at Miss Weir's school there, and bring them back to Grasmere for the summer holidays. 'She . . . is the sweetest little creature in the world', her besotted Aunt Joanna declared, 'is so tractable, & behaves to admiration.' William, however, missed his daughter so much that he suffered severe headaches after her departure and seized any opportunity to visit her.[2]

Joanna and Mary's departure from Penrith was part of a major change of circumstances which would permanently break up the extended Hutchinson clan. They were going to join their respective brothers Tom and John in the Welsh borders. Both men had been unhappy for a long time. Since giving up Park House, Tom had acted as a carrier between Penrith and Stockton, then taken a situation as steward to Sir Francis Blake, which he left after only a few months. The Bishop of Llandaff had offered him a farm at Windermere, but refused to grant him a lease, leaving him vulnerable to rent rises and eviction, so he had reluctantly turned it down. John had been depressed and ill since the death of his wife so soon after their marriage and had sold his father's wine business, intending to go to Portugal; prevented by the Peninsular War, he agreed to throw in his lot with Tom. Efforts to find a farm near the Clarksons, in Suffolk, proved futile, but a trip down 'the *Sylvan Wye*', as John pointedly called it (quoting *Tintern Abbey*), was more successful. John found a farm belonging to the MP, Sir Frankland Lewis, at Hindwell in Radnorshire (now Powys), and was immediately offered a sixteen-year lease at a reasonable rate. By the middle of April 1809 the four cousins were settled in their new home, or, as Mary and Sara complained, were '*buried* in Wales'.[3]

Amidst all these comings and goings, William was also heavily caught up in Coleridge's plans for a revival of his youthful scheme to write and publish his own weekly newspaper. This new venture was different from the *Watchman* in that it was aimed only at those 'who either by Rank, or Fortune, or Official situation, or by Talents & Habits of Reflection, are to influence the multitude'. Its object was philosophical rather than rabble-rousing. 'I write to found True PRINCIPLES,' Coleridge declaimed. 'To oppose false PRINCIPLES in Legislation, Philosophy, Morals, International Law.' His record was not such as to inspire anyone with confidence that he would be able to carry out his scheme, but, as Dorothy pointed out, he would never embark upon it unless and until he committed himself. The Wordsworths therefore set to and circulated his prospectus to all their friends and acquaintances, as did Southey and Coleridge himself, building up a list of 500 subscribers so that the venture could be launched. Inevitably, the fact that this was done under the auspices of the Wordsworths raised the expectation that William would also be a contributor, which had never been his intention.[4]

The prospectus promised the opening issue of the *Friend* for the first Saturday in January. As delay succeeded delay (not all of them Coleridge's fault), his friends became increasingly pessimistic. Publicly, they did all they could to support and encourage him. William and Southey both accompanied him and his printer to Appleby to sign the bonds and securities required for issuing a newspaper, but privately they had reservations. Only the day before, 30 March 1809, William had confessed to Poole that he had not 'much hope' for the project, as Coleridge was not 'managing himself well'; 'do not hint a word of this to any body,' he added, 'as any thing of that kind should it come to his ears would completely dash him'. Two months later there was still no sign that the *Friend* would appear. For the first time, writing to Poole 'in the most sacred confidence' and bound only by 'a strong sense of duty', William admitted his despair.

I am sorry to say that nothing appears to me more desirable than that his periodical essay should never commence. It is in fact *impossible* utterly impossible – that he should carry it on; and, therefore, better never begin it; far better, and if begun, the sooner it stop, also the better – the less will be the loss, and not greater the disgrace ... I give it to you as my deliberate opinion, formed upon proofs which have been strengthening for years, that he neither will nor can execute any thing of important benefit either to himself his family or mankind. Neither his talents nor his genius mighty as they are nor his vast information will avail him anything; they are all frustrated by a derangement in his intellectual and moral constitution – In fact he has no voluntary power of mind whatsoever, nor is he capable of acting under any *constraint* of duty or moral obligation. Do not suppose that I mean to say from this that The Friend may not appear – it may – but it cannot go on for any length of time. I am *sure* it cannot.

It was a terrible indictment – William ended the letter by begging Poole to burn it – but it turned out to be all too prescient.[5]

Against all the odds, the first issue of the *Friend* appeared on 1 June 1809; it had been written at Yanwath, where Wilkinson had taken Coleridge in, deprived him of spirits and opium, and urged him to work. It was ironic that a Quaker thus became 'the Father of *The Friend*'. Having published his first two editions, and left the third with the printer at Penrith, Coleridge returned to Allan Bank, not only sober and on restricted use of opium, but resolved to remain so. He seemed determined to confound all criticism. Reading the first issues, the Wordsworths were distressed to discover that he had referred to William as 'the *one* poet of his own time', which they knew would hurt Southey's feelings, and that he had stooped to deny ten-year-old accusations about his Jacobinical past again; they also thought the first number 'very obscure' and lacking *joie de vivre.* On the other hand, they had to admit that 'everywhere the power of thought and the originality of a great mind are visible'; almost more important, from a purely personal point of view, was their delight in his achievement. 'I cannot enough admire his resolution in having written at all', was Dorothy's heartfelt comment, and William happily retracted the pessimistic forecast he had felt duty-bound to utter only a fortnight before. 'I now think it right to say that such appear to be the present dispositions, resolutions, and employments of Coleridge that I am encouraged to entertain more favourable hopes of his exerting himself steadily than I ever have had at any other period of this business.'[6]

The *Friend* turned out to be Coleridge's most sustained literary achievement. It ran for twenty-eight weekly issues, contained over 140,000 words of his own composing and gave voice to some of his most brilliant insights. It was, as he declared towards the end, 'the History of my own mind'. And therein lay the problem, for it was also chaotically organized (some issues ending mid-paragraph, mid-argument and even, on occasion, mid-sentence!), full of disproportionate digressions and convoluted footnotes and, finally, so densely and obscurely written that most readers were simply left bewildered.[7] Anything more different from the pellucid lyricism and teleological focus of William's poem on the history of *his* own mind could not be imagined.

The women had rather hoped that William would return to his poetry once he had exhausted his enthusiasm for the *Convention of Cintra.* Instead, he had rediscovered his raw passion for politics which, for many years, had been, if not exactly dormant, then at least diverted into poetic channels. Even before his pamphlet was published, he had startled them all by announcing that he had decided to write upon 'publick affairs' in the *Courier*, or some other newspaper. His excuse was that, unlike his poetry, this would be a profitable way of employing his pen, though he knew that he could not write unless his heart and mind were also engaged. Both Scott and Southey had recently criticized him for living 'too much for the lyre', not just because poetry failed to produce enough income for comfort, but because it restricted his faculties: 'the study of poetry however delightful in itself is so warped & woven in with the desire of fame that it engages the student too far in pursuit of that most capricious of all fantasms'.[8] Coleridge's presence and preoccupation with political affairs could not fail to give impetus to William's own interest, though the two men did not always see eye to eye.

'Two things are absolutely wanted in this Country;' William announced to Stuart at the end of March; 'a thorough reform in Parliament and a new course of education.' In the cause of reform, he was prepared to support even a violent democrat like Sir Francis Burdett, whose inflammatory oratory at public meetings had drawn condemnation from both the *Courier* and Coleridge. 'If we, who work for a temperate reform, are utterly to reject all assistance from all those who do not think exactly as we do, how is it to be attained?' William argued. 'For my part I see no party with whom in regard to this measure I could act with entire approbation of their views, but I should be glad to receive assistance from any. If I have a hill to climb and cannot do it without a walking-stick, better have a dirty one than none at all.' Reform, he thought, would never be effected unless the people took up the cause in public meetings. It was natural at such gatherings that the most violent men should be the most applauded, but it did not necessarily follow that their words would be realized in action.

> The misfortune of this question of reform is, that the one party sees nothing in it but dangers, the other nothing but hopes and promises. For my part I think the dangers and difficulties great but not insurmountable, whereas, if there be not a reform the destruction of the liberties of the Country is inevitable.

Such views seem moderate enough now, but they were radical by the standards of the day. So much so, indeed, that Sir George Beaumont felt obliged to caution his visitors against William's 'terrific democratic notions'.[9]

William was equally passionate on the subject of educational reform, believing that it should be preceded 'by some genuine philosophical writings from some quarter or other, to teach the principles upon which that education should be grounded'. There is no indication that he saw himself as being the quarter in question, but it was about this time that, through Coleridge, he became a disciple of Dr Andrew Bell. While Coleridge had been lecturing in London in the spring of 1808, he had been drawn into the debate then raging between two new rival systems of education. Both relied on the use of 'monitors', older pupils who supervised the efforts of younger ones, to maximize the effectiveness of the teacher, and there was some controversy as to who had first invented the idea. Bell, a Scottish clergyman, had successfully pioneered his scheme in an Indian orphanage (hence its name, the Madras System), and saw its potential for making a national system of education available even in the poorest districts of Britain. Joseph Lancaster, a Quaker, had also introduced similar ideas (the Lancasterian System), but, being a dissenter, wished the schools to remain independent of any establishment control. Coleridge and William both believed that education should be the responsibility of the state and should be conducted under the banner of the Anglican Church. For this reason, they supported the Madras System: 'Next to the art of Printing it is the noblest invention for the improvement of the human species' was William's considered opinion. Where he and Coleridge also parted company with Lancaster was over the Quaker's enforcement of learning and discipline by punishments of extraordinary ferocity and humiliation.[10]

William had philosophical and personal reasons for supporting Bell. As we have seen, he had long believed that education was the vital means by which the moral state of society could be transformed, and in his own way, in his poems, he had sought to assist the process. 'I am a teacher or I am nothing', he had insisted. Since the cataclysm of his brother John's death, he had been forced to re-examine his religious beliefs and had become a committed deist and practising Anglican, though the emphasis was definitely on practice rather than commitment. William had always been eclectic in his choice of church. As a boy at Hawkshead, he had attended the Quaker meetings at Colthouse whenever it had been too wet or hot to trail across the fields to the village church. (He later remarked drily that his chief recollection was 'that they were always telling God Almighty of His Attributes, rather than seeking Spiritual Communion with Him for themselves'.) In his radical youth he had attended dissenting chapels when in London and, even now, when staying in Kendal with the family of Sara's former schoolfriend Elizabeth Cookson, he would accompany them to worship at the Unitarian chapel.[11]

There had been little incentive to attend the Anglican church at Grasmere. The rector, John Craik, had been insane for sixty-three years until his death in 1806. His curate, Edward Rowlandson, who officiated in his stead for forty years, was if anything even more infamous. William was unusually caustic in his judgement. 'Two vices used to struggle in him for mastery, avarice & the love of strong drink: but avarice as is common in like cases always got the better of its opponent, for though he was often intoxicated it was never I believe at his own expence. As has been said of one in a more exalted station he could take any *given* quantity.'[12] Craik's successor, Thomas Jackson, was inevitably an improvement, but it was at Coleorton that the Wordsworths began to attend church regularly, more from a desire to set a good example to the children than from personal preference. The adults took it in turns, two by two, to do their duty. Yet even at Coleorton William was scathing about the quality of Anglican clergymen, reporting of the local incumbent to Sir George Beaumont that,

> His sermon was, to be sure, as Village sermons often are, very injudicious; a most knowing discourse about the Gnostics, and other hard names of those who were '*h*adversaries to Christianity and *H*enemies of the Gospel.' How strangely injudicious this is! and yet nothing so frequent . . . I don't know that I ever heard in a Country pulpit a sermon that had any especial bearing on the condition of the majority of the Audience.

Even in old age, despite a revolution in the quality of Anglican clergymen, thanks to the Evangelical and Puseyite movements, he remained unimpressed by most village sermons, confiding to an amused Moravian minister, 'with a peculiar expression of countenance & intonation, "Ah, well! I go to church for the sake of the Prayers – the Sermon you know is an Accident."' Whatever the failings of its ministers, and indeed his own reservations about its doctrine, William supported the Anglican Church because, unlike its sectarian opponents, it was comprehensive, inclusive and tolerant. It was therefore a unifying force for moral good nationally and, in its parish system, a focal point and exemplar for benevolence, even in the remotest regions.[13]

But William had more personal reasons also for supporting the Madras System. Despite his insistence that young Basil Montagu should not begin formal learning too early, all his own children began school at the age of three – indeed, little Thomas was a couple of months short of his third birthday when he went for the first time after Easter this year. They all attended the village school in Grasmere, at the gate of the churchyard. Clever, wilful Dora was a great favourite with the schoolmaster, but poor Johnny, who struggled with his alphabet and was slow to learn to read, was beaten regularly. (The family did not discover this punishment until a new master came and Johnny revealed that, since then, he had only been beaten once.) His Aunt Sara was indignant: 'He is not to be dealt with by severity – it would make him quite obstinate and stupid.' In sharp contrast, he made great progress over the summer, motivated solely by the desire to be an assistant to de Quincey, who was thinking of setting up a private press at Grasmere. De Quincey had tactfully encouraged and enthused him by pointing out that, if he wanted to be a printer, he would first have to be a good scholar. As Sara observed, 'the hope of being with Mr de Q. would stimulate him to any thing – for he loves him better than anything in the world!'[14] In the circumstances, it was not surprising that William favoured the Madras above the Lancasterian System.

After his labours on William's behalf in London, de Quincey did not return to Grasmere until the autumn. In his absence, there was a host of visitors. Sara's friend Mrs Cookson and her son came from Kendal to stay for a week. They were followed by Dora, who returned home at the end of June after an absence of four months, accompanied by Miss Weir and her niece, but not her Hutchinson cousins, who had gone back to Stockton. Her return was celebrated with a grand party on Windermere, John Wilson providing the boats and all the family and friends sailing out on the lake.[15] Mary's brother, the unlucky George, arrived about the same time. Once again, he was without employment, owing to the failure of the manufacturer in whose counting house he had worked. William wrote to Wilkinson on his behalf, hoping that a stewardship at Lowther might be available. It was not, but other overtures were more successful and, before he left Grasmere in August, George had been engaged as a land steward in the south of England, through the influence of the MP for Carlisle, Mr Curwen.[16]

In addition to the family visitors, who each spent more than a month at Allan Bank, Southey came with a party of his friends and Sharp paid his annual visit. Clarkson arrived with his son Tom and his friend Samuel Tillbrooke, who would later become a friend and neighbour of the Wordsworths at Rydal. They stayed only a few days, but were followed by Catherine Clarkson's aunt, uncle and cousin, the Hardcastles, who arrived at the worst possible time. An army of workmen had descended on the house, determined to eradicate the problem of the smoking chimneys before the onset of winter. They were assisted by the gift of a 'patent *Smoke-Dispenser*', purchased in London by de Quincey as 'my offering to Allan Bank'. Under Crump's instructions, they were also adding a bow window to William's study.[17]

In the circumstances, the Wordsworths seized every opportunity to get away. In June William went off on a week-long fishing expedition organized in the grand style by Wilson, 'a nice creature for all his follies', according to Sara; the party, or 'Wilson and his Merry Men', as William called them, were to go from tarn to tarn and sleep under canvas on the mountains. Dorothy escaped to the Cooksons at Kendal for a week in July, and, at the beginning of September, Mary, Sara and Johnny paid a more sedate visit to Wilson, his mother and sister, at Elleray.[18] William had hopes of an autumnal tour of Wales and Scotland, in company with Wilson and de Quincey, but his plans were thwarted when Wilson decided to go off to Spain, and Sara, whom he was supposed to escort to Hindwell, put off her visit to the following year.[19]

Towards the end of October, to the great delight of the Wordsworth children, de Quincey returned to Grasmere. It had been agreed that he should become the new tenant of the cottage at Town End; a six-year lease had been granted and Dorothy, Mary and Sara had jointly taken on the task of redecorating and refurnishing it to his requirements. With new wallpapers, a ceiling in the kitchen and mahogany furniture (mainly bookshelves to contain de Quincey's vast library), it was unrecognizable as the Wordsworths' former home. Sally Green had been commissioned to provide his breakfasts until the end of November, when the new housekeeper, Molly Dawson, would have worked her notice at the Lloyds and could take up her duties. Whether Sally was inadequate or de Quincey was reluctant to move out of the heart of the Wordsworth circle, he managed to inveigle his way back to Allan Bank until Molly's arrival made his own removal necessary.[20]

As the frosts and snows returned to the vale with the approach of winter, a financial crisis threatened the Wordsworths. William had lost money on his *Convention of Cintra* pamphlet and the sale of his poems was so meagre as to bring him virtually no income. Coleridge could contribute nothing to the household as he was heavily in debt: until the twentieth issue of the *Friend* had been published, he could not call in the subscriptions and was having to fund the production costs personally. William was therefore having to subsidize not only Coleridge's living expenses but also those of his children, as well as to support his own extended family. To add to their problems, Mary was pregnant with her fifth child, due in May, and living at Allan Bank was once again intolerable as the winter storms proved that the workmen had failed to cure the smoking chimneys.[21]

The need to earn money had become pressing. There was little prospect of doing so through poetry and William's plan to write political essays for the *Courier* had come to nothing. Instead he embarked on another prose work, which was commissioned from him by the Reverend Joseph Wilkinson, former rector of Ormathwaite, near Keswick. Now resident in Norfolk, Wilkinson was an amateur artist much admired by his friends Coleridge and Southey for his fidelity in depicting landscapes. In the summer, he had asked Coleridge to write a text to accompany the publication of forty-eight engravings of his drawings of the Lakes. Fully occupied with the *Friend*, Coleridge had declined, but suggested William in his stead. William had been reluctant from the start. His own friend William Green of Ambleside (a far more talented artist) was about to publish a similar volume of his own work and William did not wish to contribute to a rival project. Wilkinson assured him there would be no clash of interest: his engravings would be published by subscription and in serial form, four prints appearing each month for a year.[22]

It is an indication of how desperate the Wordsworths were for money that William agreed to the undertaking at all. Though he had toyed with the idea of producing his own 'manual to guide travellers' for at least two years, he had never found sufficient motivation to do so. The previous summer he had rejected Pering's request for a formal delineation of 'this sublime & beautiful region', saying, 'I must be my own Task master, or I can do nothing at all.'[23] Now, however, for the first and last time in his life, he hired out his pen and submitted to the drudgery of writing on commission.

What Wilkinson expected from William is not clear. We have only his vague statement that the text was intended 'to enable me to make my work more perfect and acceptable to the public than it otherwise would be'.[24] Undoubtedly, he wanted something along the well-worn lines already established by the likes of Gray, Gilpin and West: an appreciation of the scenery and instructions to the traveller on how to find the best vantage points from which to see the sublime and beautiful vistas depicted in his prints. What he cannot have expected was the idiosyncratic document he eventually received as the introductory essay to open the series.

It began, uncontentiously enough, with a general topographical and historical description of the Lake country, which Dorothy proudly declared to be 'the only regular and I may say *scientific* account of the present and past state and appearance of the country that has yet appeared'. As it progressed, however, it turned into a lengthy lamentation for the passing of a 'perfect Republic of Shepherds and Agriculturists' and a diatribe against inappropriate development by wealthy incomers. William pinpointed the date when the old ways ended – small, self-sufficient estates, 'perfect equality' among the inhabitants, even transportation by packhorse instead of on carriage roads – very precisely, though the significance of this is not immediately apparent until one sees that in subsequent editions of the work the date was altered. In 1810, for example, when it was first published, it was 'within the last forty years'; in 1820 it became 'within the last fifty years' and, subsequently, 'within the last sixty years'. In other words, William felt that the golden age had ended with his own birth in 1770. This was clearly poignant symbolism rather than historical fact, for some of William's strictures on the changes which had taken place, such as denuding the lake shores of their mature native trees, which read as though he had personally seen them take place, actually occurred when he was too young to observe them or even long before he was born.[25]

It would be wrong, however, to dismiss this introduction as just a misty-eyed exercise in nostalgia, for what William was attempting to do was as revolutionary as anything he had ever done in his poetry. Once again his aim was to change and educate prevailing tastes. In doing so, he rejected the perceived wisdom of a generation of topographical writers who judged landscapes solely in accordance with their own preconceived images of what constituted perfection. 'What I wished to accomplish was to give a model of the manner in which topographical descriptions ought to be executed', he told Lady Beaumont privately, expressing quiet satisfaction with his own wonderfully apt, yet totally original, simile, comparing the eight main valleys stretching out from a central point between Great Gable and Scafell as 'like spokes from the nave of a wheel'. William described this comparison as being both 'useful' and 'intelligible'.[26] Just as he had done in his poetry, he was applying the simple language and homely imagery of everyday life to a literature which had developed its own highly specialized and esoteric vocabulary.

In the late eighteenth and early nineteenth centuries, the fashion was for the 'picturesque', a word which then meant, quite literally, 'like a picture', and specifically the idealized landscape paintings of the schools of Claude Lorrain, Gaspard

Poussin and Salvator Rosa. No self-respecting tourist in search of the picturesque travelled without his Claude-glass, a plano-convex mirror of convenient pocket-book size through which he would view the scenes and objects to be admired. It seems wholly appropriate that to do so he had to turn his back on the real living landscape in order to see its image reflected in miniaturized form and neatly contained within the mirror's frame. In other words, reduced to a picture. Not surprisingly, the devotees of the picturesque rarely saw '*real views* from Nature in this country . . . equal to the poorest imitations of Gaspar or Claude'. (A statement, astonishingly, made by Thomas Gainsborough, one of the most evocative of English landscape painters.) Gilpin, whose works William had admired as a young man, not only expounded the view that purely natural scenes were seldom 'correctly picturesque' but suggested that the 'practised eye would usually wish to correct' the 'deformities' of nature; he even recommended judicious use of a mallet to 'improve' the ruins of Tintern Abbey.[27]

The tourists who flocked to the Lakes came clutching their guidebooks, Claude-glasses and preconceived ideas: they came, to quote West's *Guide to the Lakes* of 1778, to see the 'delicate touches of Claude' at Coniston, 'the noble scenes of Poussin' at Windermere and the 'stupendous romantic ideas of Salvator Rosa' at Derwent Water. If they used their own eyes at all, it was only to make the obligatory (and usually denigratory) comparison with the Alps. It was against this fashion that William took up cudgels. 'My object is to reconcile a Briton to the scenery of his own country', he proclaimed, explaining with all the passion of personal conviction, 'Nothing is more injurious to genuine feeling than the practice of hastily and ungraciously depreciating the face of one country by comparing it with that of another'. To do so inevitably led to disappointed expectations: '. . . the best guide to which, in matters of taste we can entrust ourselves, is a disposition to be pleased'. He illustrated this with an example that will strike a chord with the modern visitor to the Lakes. The perceived wisdom was, and is, that waterfalls are scarcely worth seeing except after much rain, and that the more swollen the stream, the more fortunate the spectator. This is a fallacy, as William argued;

what becomes, at such a time, of that sense of refreshing coolness which can only be felt in dry and sunny weather, when the rocks, herbs, and flowers glisten with moisture diffused by the breath of the precipitous water? But, considering these things as objects of sight only, it may be observed that the principal charm of the smaller waterfalls or cascades consists in certain proportions of form and affinities of colour, among the component parts of the scene; and in the contrast maintained between the falling water and that which is apparently at rest, or rather settling gradually into quiet in the pool below. The beauty of such a scene, where there is naturally so much agitation, is also heightened, in a peculiar manner, by the *glimmering*, and, towards the verge of the pool, by the *steady*, reflection of the surrounding images. Now, all these delicate distinctions are destroyed by heavy floods, and the whole stream rushes along in foam and tumultuous confusion.[28]

What this perceptive comment (one of many) illustrates so beautifully is William's instinctive belief that nature cannot be improved: beauty is there to be seen by the discerning eye and feeling heart. The fashionable habit of comparison and demand for spectacle and sensation, fed by more conventional guides, served only to obscure the genuine 'spirit of the place'.

This blindness among tourists was bad enough, but among the new inhabitants of the Lakes it was unforgivable. In the longest and most important section of his introduction, 'Changes, and Rules of Taste for Preventing their Bad Effects', William launched a blistering attack on unsympathetic development in the Lakes. He did not mince his words: '. . . in truth, no one can now travel through the more frequented tracts, without being offended, at almost every turn, by an introduction of discordant objects, disturbing that peaceful harmony of form and colour, which had been through a long lapse of ages most happily preserved'. He attacked the 'gross transgressions' and the 'disfigurement' which incomers had inflicted on this 'country so lavishly gifted by nature': their 'immoderate' 'craving for prospect' which led them to build on 'the summits of naked hills in staring contrast to the snugness and privacy of the ancient houses'; their affectation and pretension which dictated that every new house should be a mansion sufficiently grandiose to attract comment; their anxiety to sweep away ancient woodlands and introduce 'the whole contents of the nursery-man's catalogue', foreign plants and exotic trees all 'jumbled together – colour at war with colour, and form with form . . . everywhere discord, distraction, and bewilderment!' These people were, as William pointedly reminded them, 'liable to a charge of inconsistency, when they are so eager to change the face of that country, whose native attractions, by the act of erecting their habitations in it, they have so emphatically acknowledged'. Worst of all, because their impact was so visually intrusive, were the plantations now springing up over the Lakeland hills: serried ranks of larches and firs marching inexorably and indiscriminately over all terrain, lacking variety of shape, colour, size or movement.[29]

This was not just a negative and reactionary piece of what might now be called 'Nimbyism', for what William sought to do was to re-educate the perpetrators. Mansions are inappropriate in mountain regions, he reasoned, because they can never have sufficient dignity or interest to become the focal point of the landscape and must always be subordinate to the view. In building houses, one should consult antiquity, 'the co-partner and sister of Nature'. In laying out grounds, 'The rule is simple . . . work, where you can, in the spirit of nature, with an invisible hand of art.' Houses, grounds and, most of all, plantations should be so constructed as 'to admit of [their] being gently incorporated into the scenery of nature'. He ended his introduction with a heartfelt plea to the new proprietors who, within the next few years, were likely to acquire all the ancestral lands yet remaining in the hands of statesmen. They should strive for better taste and better understanding and should not deviate from 'that path of simplicity and beauty along which, without design and unconsciously, their humble predecessors have moved'. In simple but stirring words which would make him the spiritual father of not only the National

Trust, founded eighty-five years later in the face of more significant threats to his beloved Lakes, but also the modern conservation and ecology movements, he prophesied: 'In this wish the author will be joined by persons of pure taste throughout the whole island, who, by their visits (often repeated) to the Lakes in the North of England, testify that they deem the district a sort of national property, in which every man has a right and interest who has an eye to perceive and a heart to enjoy.'[30]

By 18 November William had completed the introduction and Sara, taking a brief respite from her labours on Coleridge's behalf, transcribed a fair copy to send to Wilkinson. Dorothy, ever mindful of the Wordsworths' precarious financial position, was convinced that William should now apply himself to writing a proper guide of his own, prefixing this introduction: 'it would sell better, and bring him more money than any of his higher labours', she claimed, quite rightly as it proved. William demurred. Wilkinson's publication ought to have its fair run before he attempted anything independently.[31]

While he waited for the arrival of the first batch of Wilkinson's plates, so that he could embark on the accompanying text, William found himself temporarily at leisure. He occupied himself, as he usually did at such moments, by translating eleven epitaphs from the Italian of the poet Gabriello Chiabrera. Six of these he allowed Coleridge to print in the *Friend*, even though, in doing so, he lost the opportunity of earning any money for them. Coleridge, however, was beginning to flounder. For six months he had confounded all expectations and, almost single-handedly, kept the *Friend* afloat, supplying the material, the editorial and even the finances, but his enthusiasm and energies were beginning to flag and he had begun to solicit contributions from some of his friends. William supplied not only the epitaphs but also hitherto unpublished extracts from *The Prelude* and *The Recluse*, as well as seven of his latest sonnets written in the autumn of 1809. These were inspired by the heroic resistance of the shepherd patriots of the tiny Tyrol, who, led by a charismatic innkeeper, Andreas Hofer, repeatedly defied the might of Bavarian and French armies in a doomed struggle to retain their liberty. For William, this unlikely hero was a 'godlike Warrior' who embodied the spirit of William Tell and had fought, with his humble compatriots, for 'a *moral* end' which had not been vainly sought.

> For in their magnanimity and fame
> Powers have they left, an impulse, and a claim
> Which neither can be overturned nor bought . . .
> And when, impatient of her guilt and woes,
> Europe breaks forth; then, Shepherds! shall ye rise
> For perfect triumph o'er your Enemies.[32]

Less successful was a prose essay, written at Coleridge's request, in response to a letter published in the *Friend* from three of William's own devotees, Wilson, his friend Alexander Blair and de Quincey, under the pseudonym Mathetes. The letter was a painfully contrived effort by three young men who obviously thought themselves very clever. Posing the hypothetical moral dilemma that the optimism of youth led to an unjustified admiration for the present degenerate age, Mathetes (meaning 'pupil' in Greek) suggested that the only remedy was for a 'Teacher [to] stand up . . . conspicuous above the multitude in superior power, and yet more in the assertion and proclamation of disregarded Truth'. It was transparently designed to elicit an answer from William, whom they designated the 'one such Teacher who has been given to our own age . . . there are many to whom the name of Wordsworth calls up the recollection of their weakness, and the consciousness of their strength'.[33]

Flattering though such comments might be in private correspondence, they were injudicious, to say the least, in a public journal conducted by one of William's closest friends. Even Lamb could not resist the gibe that the *Friend* was 'chiefly intended to puff off Wordsworth's poetry'. The delicacy of William's position, and his embarrassment with it, are reflected in his *Reply to Mathetes*, which, in typical Coleridgean muddle, was published in two very unequal parts in the seventeenth and twentieth numbers, with a three-week gap between. The temptation was to be dismissive, since the hypothesis was so contrived. 'I do not see why a belief in the progress of human Nature towards perfection should dispose a youthful Mind however enthusiastic to an undue admiration of his own Age, and thus tend to degrade that mind.' William might have left it at that, but as an essay was required to fill Coleridge's empty pages, he rather wearily expanded, arguing that the present age was no more degenerate than previous ones; we simply forget the 'overbalance of worthlessness' which has been swept away in the past when looking at the excellence of what remains. The need for a 'Teacher' he rejected outright, for even if such an exalted being could be found, reliance on his judgement would produce only 'passiveness and prostration of mind' on his pupils.

> Protection from any fatal effect of seductions and hindrances which opinion may throw in the way of pure and high-minded Youth can only be obtained with certainty at the same price by which every thing great and good is obtained, namely, steady dependence upon voluntary and self-originating effort, and upon the practice of self-examination sincerely aimed at and rigourously enforced.

If we do not recognize this primary duty of being accountable to ourselves, 'to our Conscience, and, through that, to God and human Nature', then 'all secondary care of Teacher, of Friend, or Parent, must be baseless and fruitless'.[34]

Having performed his own, somewhat dreary duty, William was free to enjoy an unusually social Christmas. The whole household decamped to Elleray to join the Kendal Cooksons for two days of 'merriment and thoughtful discourse', hosted by the combined forces of 'Mathetes', Wilson ('the Beau', as the Wordsworths teasingly called the eligible bachelor), Alexander Blair and de Quincey. From

Elleray they all proceeded to Brathay to dine with the Lloyds, then on to Town End, where de Quincey entertained them to a New Year dinner and the entire village to a firework display.[35]

It was a short respite, because it was increasingly clear that Coleridge could no longer sustain the *Friend*. 'My own hopes concerning *The Friend* are at dead low water', he wrote to Lady Beaumont in January 1810. 'Of the small number, that have payed [*sic*] in their Subscriptions, two thirds nearly have discontinued the work.' He was already considering giving up altogether and returning to settle in London. Sara, who had worked tirelessly as his amanuensis and exerted all her influence over him to the full, bullying and harrying him to keep to his deadlines, was exhausted and ill. They were all well aware that if the journal folded, Coleridge would once again face total mental and physical collapse, and London was the last place he ought to be, so they rallied round to support him. William contributed another essay on 22 February, this time prompted by his translations from Chiabrera. He had not planned to publish it at this point, probably intending it to be a commentary for *The Recluse*, but Coleridge was 'in such bad spirits' and so 'utterly unprovided' for that he allowed it to be used. It was the first, and dullest, of a series of three *Essays on Epitaphs*, which laboriously investigated the nature and purpose of the epitaph and came up with the hardly startling conclusion that it was 'a record to preserve the memory of the dead, as a tribute due to his individual worth, for a satisfaction to the sorrowing hearts of the survivors, and for the common benefit of the living'.[36]

Six days after this essay was published, William hastily completed the second two so that they could be held over in reserve for a similar emergency. They would not be needed, for the last issue of the *Friend* appeared on 15 March. This would become apparent only in retrospect, for Coleridge blithely continued to speak of it 'as if it were going on, and would go on'. The Wordsworths had no such delusions, though they continued to hope against hope that he might surprise them once again. His habits of composition had always been erratic. 'The fact is that he either does a great deal or nothing at all' was Dorothy's tart but accurate assessment. The sheer volume of material he had produced for the *Friend* belied the fact that there had been weeks on end when he had not written a line, for he would suddenly compose a whole issue in two days, drawing on his prodigious stores of knowledge and relying on his facility in conversation to dictate verbatim to Sara. It was a matter of wonder among the Wordsworths, who were used to William's finicky rewritings, that Coleridge's contributions were never retranscribed.[37]

The pressure had told, however, particularly on Sara. Her situation was bizarre. Not only was she living in the same house as the married man who loved her, but for hours on end she was cooped up with him, acting as his secretary, and effectively at his beck and call. She could not have been unaware of his feelings towards her and his private notebooks reveal that their enforced intimacy had done nothing to stem the passion which consumed him. He was still haunted by his fantasy that he had seen William and Sara in bed together three years previously at Coleorton. 'Did I *believe* it? Did I not even *know*, that it *was* not so, *could* not be so?' he asked himself, while admitting that 'even to this day' the very thought could still inspire unbearable anguish and jealousy. He was racked by sexual torment, forced to acknowledge that Sara was strictly off-limits: '*a mother of my children*', he wrote in cipher, '*how utterly improbable* – how utterly improbable dared I hope it! How impossible for me (most pure indeed are my heart & fancy from such a thought) even to think of it, much less desire it!' Yet he still wanted more than she could give: 'O so very deep & strong & vehement is my *love* that it requires all the accompaniments of *love* in its utmost – all but its utmost – *blessedness*, all its *smiles*, its *embraces*, its most genial pledges of unalterable *reciprocity* to make it compatible with the full possession & exercise of *reason*'.[38]

It was an impossible situation and when, in the new year, Coleridge became tired of his work, depressed by his loss of subscribers and reverted to his usual comforter, opium, it became intolerable. Sara finally decided she could bear it no longer and took the first opportunity to flee. She had a standing invitation to visit her brother and cousins at Hindwell, their new farm in Radnorshire, and had, indeed, put off a visit there the previous autumn, for fear of disrupting Coleridge's labours on the *Friend*. This she now accepted and, in the middle of February, her cousin John Monkhouse came to collect her. An accident delayed their departure. As John was walking his horse between Allan Bank and the blacksmith's shop, it lashed out, knocking him unconscious and giving him a suspected fractured jaw. Perhaps because Sara was anxious to be gone, John defied the surgeon's orders that he should rest for a month and on 5 March, with his brother-in-law Henry Addison, who was about to embark on a farming apprenticeship at Hindwell, whisked her away to Wales.[39]

Sara had been a vital part of the Wordsworth household for more than four years and she would be sadly missed. That she chose to leave so soon before her sister was due to give birth is an indication of how desperate she was to get away from Coleridge; that the family were relieved by her decision also speaks volumes. 'I need not tell you how sadly we miss Sara', Dorothy confided in their mutual friend, Catherine Clarkson, on 12 April,

> – but I must add the truth that we are all glad she is gone. True it is she was the cause of the continuance of The Friend so long; but I am far from believing that it would have gone on if she had stayed. He was tired, and she had at last no power to drive him on; and now I really believe that *he* also is glad that she is not here, because he has nobody to teize him. His spirits have certainly been more equable, and much better. *Our* gladness proceeds from a different cause. He harassed and agitated her mind continually, and we saw that he was doing her health perpetual injury. I tell you this, that you may no longer lament her departure.

Having unburdened her heart thus far, Dorothy could no longer hold back the pent-up frustration, bewilderment and despair, which had clearly been building for months.

As to Coleridge, if I thought I should distress you, I would say nothing about him; but I hope that you are sufficiently prepared for the worst. We have no hope of him – none that he will ever do anything more than he has already done. If he were not under our Roof, he would be just as much the slave of stimulants as ever; and his whole time and thoughts, (except when he is reading and he reads a great deal), are employed in deceiving himself, and seeking to deceive others. He will tell me that he has been writing, that he *has* written half a Friend; when I *know* that he has not written a single line. This Habit pervades all his words and actions, and you feel perpetually new hollowness and emptiness. I am loth to say this, and burn this letter, I entreat you. I am loth to say it, but it is the truth. He lies in bed, always till after 12 o'clock, sometimes much later; and never walks out – Even the finest spring day does not tempt him to seek the fresh air; and this beautiful valley seems a blank to him. He never leaves his own parlour except at dinner and tea, and sometimes supper, and then he always seems impatient to get back to his solitude – he goes the moment his food is swallowed. Sometimes he does not speak a word, and when he does talk it is always very much and upon subjects as far aloof from himself or his friends as possible.

In a final, bitter coda, she entirely (and surely unfairly) rejected the idea that Sara's departure had in any way contributed to the demise of the *Friend*.

With respect to Coleridge, do not think that it is his love for Sara which has stopped him in his work – do not believe it: his love for her is no more than a fanciful dream – otherwise he would prove it by a desire to make her happy. No! He likes to have her about him as his own, as one devoted to him, but when she stood in the way of other gratifications it was all over. I speak this very unwillingly, and again I beg, *burn* this letter. I need not add, keep its contents to yourself alone.[40]

The Wordsworths were obviously hurt and bewildered by Coleridge's conduct, even though no facet of it was news to them. What lies unspoken at the heart of this indictment, and explains its bitterness, is that they had always believed that, once he had separated from his wife and come to live with them, they would be able to restore him to his former glory. That they had failed to do this must have seemed like a rejection of them personally – particularly as Coleridge seemed to wish to avoid their company and conversation, even while living in their midst. All the habits which Dorothy complained of had been known to them of old, but it was a different matter having to deal with their consequences on a daily basis, particularly in such a large household, full of children, where every penny counted.

Since the beginning of the year, Dorothy had been making repeated, and increasingly desperate, efforts to secure a statement of their accounts from Richard. They had no regular memoranda of the sums they had drawn since the payment of the Lowther debt and were not even sure how much they were entitled to draw. All they knew was that they had certainly far outrun their income – they had, in fact, spent just over £400 in 1809, more than twice their expenditure the previous year. 'We are resolved to meet this evil and to remedy it; by reducing our expences by every possible means', she declared. 'For instance we intend to give over drinking tea, and if possible, to take a house where coals are cheaper.' Economies had been implemented immediately, and it must have been yet another source of aggravation that Coleridge did not play his part. 'We drink (*none of us*) any thing but water', he feelingly informed Poole, admitting, however, that he could not give up tea at breakfast: 'it is, for *me*, an absolute necessary, if not of Life, yet of literary exertion'. And he still had a daily fire in his study.[41]

Coleridge's self-centredness must have grated particularly in the crisis which occurred a few days before Dorothy let slip her criticisms. On 7 April little Catherine, who was eighteen months old, was suddenly taken seriously ill with a brain seizure. A fit of vomiting led to a series of violent convulsions affecting her face, body and limbs. In the panic that followed, Richard Scambler, the apothecary from Ambleside, was called, and the poor infant was subjected to warm baths, blistering, lancing of her gums and half-hourly doses of purgatives. Seven hours later, the convulsions ceased, and she fell into a deep and continual sleep. When she eventually woke, her distraught parents discovered that she was paralysed down the right side of her body. In the days and weeks that followed, she gradually recovered movement in her arm and leg, but her right hand remained useless and she was unable to walk without limping. Afraid Mary would go into premature labour with the shock and distress, Scambler assured the Wordsworths that Catherine's prognosis was bright; what he did not tell them, because he knew nothing could prevent it, was that another similar seizure would probably kill her.[42]

The imminent arrival of the new baby finally persuaded Coleridge to do what Catherine's illness did not. At the beginning of May he left Allan Bank to pay a ten-day visit to his wife and daughter at Greta Hall. Though Dorothy suspected that his 'irresolute habits' would detain him longer, not even she suspected that he had left for good. It is not even clear whether Coleridge himself knew it, but the longer he stayed at Keswick, the more difficult it became to return to Grasmere, for then he would have to face the Wordsworths in the full knowledge that he had abandoned the *Friend* and, once more, become a slave to opium. And facing up to his own failings, let alone admitting them to those he loved, was something he was unable to do. Instead, he shut himself up in his study at Greta Hall and nurtured a growing sense of grievance against the Wordsworths, convincing himself that they had conspired to remove Sara out of his clutches. Opium-induced dreams and reality once again began to fuse: Sara, he dreamt, was about to marry John Monkhouse, and William and Dorothy had left for Wales to give her away. 'I am persuaded, that the Sharpness of Sense will not, cannot, be greater in the agony of my Death, than at the moment when the insufferable Anguish awoke me', he confided in his notebook, before giving way to hysterics at the idea that this might have been a prophetic dream. 'O no! no! no! let me die – tho' in the rack of the Stone – only let me die before I suspect it, broad-awake! *Yet*, the too, too evident, the undeniable *joining* in the *conspiracy* with M[ary] & D[orothy] to deceive me, & her *cruel neglect & contemptuous Silence* ever *since!*' Bored she might have been by the talk of sheep and farming at Hindwell, but it was undeniably better for Sara to be away from Coleridge.[43]

On Saturday 12 May, at quarter past two in the morning, Mary gave birth to her fifth child, 'a fine Boy', who looked just like Johnny and was 'stout and healthy with the Wordsworth nose'. Despite the objections raised when Thomas had been born, the Wordsworths were determined to call this son William; the name was decided on by the end of the month and on 24 June a second William Wordsworth was christened at Grasmere church. His godparents were Joanna and two of his father's young admirers, Wilson and de Quincey.[44]

A few days after the christening, William and Dorothy left for Coleorton. They were both reluctant to leave Mary, especially with five children to look after, the oldest of whom was only just seven, and the hay harvest to supervise. But she had the assistance of three servants and she was insistent that they should go. William needed a holiday and a change of scene after his labours over the winter and spring. In addition to his contributions for the *Friend*, he had been producing copy for Wilkinson's prints and managed to complete three books of *The Recluse*. More importantly, the Beaumonts had asked them, were indeed anxiously awaiting their arrival, and the Wordsworths were duty-bound to oblige the friends who had been so kind to them. Lady Beaumont had even offered to pay Dorothy's travel expenses, but it still required all Mary's powers of persuasion to make her go. 'I *knew* that she would enjoy herself, and that she would have been most cruelly disappointed if she had stayed behind & I was also sure that her heart was set upon going forward, in spite of her wishing to persuade herself & you to the contrary all this I *knew*, which made me unwilling to hear of your going without her', Mary told William triumphantly, upon learning of Dorothy's happiness at Coleorton.[45]

Brother and sister set off at the end of June, spent a few days with the Cooksons at Kendal, then made their way by coach to Derbyshire, where they had arranged to meet Alexander Blair. Together they walked to Dovedale, and visited Lord Scarsdale's magnificent Georgian mansion and park at Kedleston Hall; at Derby William called on, and monopolized, the attention of John Edwards, a minor poet and subscriber to the *Friend* who had enthused about William's poetry and *The Convention of Cintra*. They arrived at Coleorton, with Blair in tow, so late in the day that the Beaumonts had given them up and they were mistaken for wandering troopers. Their days passed in leisurely fashion: they breakfasted between eight-thirty and nine, William rode out with Beaumont from eleven till two-thirty, they dined at three, had tea between six and seven and then walked till nine. A couple of times, they had a little reading in the afternoon.[46]

It was an undemanding routine which suited Dorothy, whose health and appearance improved dramatically. William, however, pined for home and found the absence from Mary particularly trying. A series of seven letters passed between husband and wife this summer. Unlike all previous extant letters, which were usually joint efforts with Dorothy, they were entirely private and written for each other's eyes only. And they are revelatory. For, aged forty, and after eight years of marriage and five children, their passion for each other shines out with all the ardour of a pair of teenage lovers. What is more, this rare expression of their love is convincing proof that, however deeply William cared for his sister, his love for her was altogether of a different kind. Had these letters been available to earlier biographers, it would have been difficult for them even to have posited the case for an incestuous relationship between brother and sister.

William wrote the first letter on 22 July, seizing the opportunity while Dorothy was at church to address Mary, 'my dearest Love', 'sweet love', 'my joy, my repose, my hope, and my support in every good thought or profitable feeling that enters my spirit'.

We have now been here a fortnight and every thing has been done which kindness could do to make us happy ... For my own part though I should feel it a disgrace to be discont[ent]ed to any oppressive degree, with so much affectionateness, & tranquil and innocent pleasure about me, yet I do feel, that to no place where I am stationary some time can I ever be perfectly reconciled, even for a short time. When I am moving about I am not so strongly reminded of my home, and you and our little ones and the places which I love. Therefore I must say[,] though not without regret do I say it, that I cannot help being anxious that I were gone, as when I move I shall feel myself moving towards you; though by a long circuit. O my beloved how my heart swells at the thought; and how dearly should I have enjoyed being alone with you so long!... How do I long to tread for the first time the road that will bring me in sight of Grasmere, to pant up the hill of Allan bank to cross the threshold to see to touc[h] you to speak to you & hear you spea[k] ...

Alluding delicately to his overwhelming physical desire for her, which had been increased by the necessity to abstain from sexual relations prior to, and immediately after, the baby's birth, he compared his sufferings during this separation to those he had endured while she was at Middleham and Gallow Hill before they married, made heavier and more uneasy by 'a thousand tender thoughts intermingled, and consciousnesses of realized bliss and happiness'. All his pleasures were marred by his inability to share them with Mary. 'I am never instructed, never delighted, never touch[e]d by a tender feeling but my heart instinctively turns to you. I never see a flower that pleases me but I wish for you.' The Beaumonts were already talking about a repetition of the visit next year, but William would not even consider it. 'I cannot think of any thing of the kind; nor will I ever, except from a principle of duty, part from you again, to stay any where more than one week. I cannot bear it.' He ended the letter with a passionate appeal. 'Fail not to write to me with out reserve', he begged her; 'never have I been able to receive such a Letter from you, let me not then be disappointed, but give me your heart that I may kiss the words a thousand times!'[47]

Receiving this letter at Allan Bank, Mary was overwhelmed. She literally shed tears of happiness, much to the puzzlement of little Dora. 'O My William!' she replied, it is not in my power to tell thee how I have been affected by this dearest of all letters – it was so unexpected – so new a thing to see the breathing of thy inmost heart upon paper that I was quite overpowered, & now that I sit down to answer thee in the loneliness & depth of that love which unites us & which cannot be felt but by ourselves, I am so agitated & my eyes are so bedimmed that I scarcely know how to proceed... Indeed my love it has made me supremely blessed – it has given me a new feeling, for it is the first letter of love that has been exclusively my own – Wonder not then that I have been so affected by it.

Despite constant interruptions from the children, she managed to pour out her heart to her husband. 'I am SORRY for what causes in me such pious and exulting gladness –', she told him, 'that you cannot fully enjoy your absence from me – indeed William I feel, I *have felt* that you cannot, but it overpowers me to be told it by your own pen'. She responded with equal ardour and modesty to his expressions of sexual longing. 'I did not *want thee* so much *then*,' she wrote, referring to an earlier letter where he had spoken of coming home, 'as I do now that our uncomfortableness is passed away – if you had been here, no *doubt* there would have existed in me that underconsciousness that I had my *all in all* about me – *that* feeling which I have never wanted since [I slept with: deleted] the solitary night did not separate us, except in absence.'

Having filled many pages with the news and anecdotes about his children which she knew he longed to hear, Mary made a telling reference to Dorothy, to whom she had written only a short letter: 'do not give her to understand that you have recd. a longer one – this would make her uneasy – and I have not had it in my power to do any better'.[48] Allusive though the remark is, it is an indication of some of the difficulties inherent in the Wordsworth relationships. It is a tribute to Mary's remarkable generosity of spirit that she not only understood her sister-in-law, but was constitutionally incapable of feeling jealousy or resentment towards her.

William and Dorothy spent just over a month at Coleorton before going their separate ways. William and Beaumont travelled together to Birmingham, where they visited the Leasowes, former home of the poet William Shenstone, and attended a performance of Thomas Otway's tragedy *Venice Preserv'd*, abominably performed by a troupe of starved actors to an empty house. Despite this disappointment, Beaumont would look back on the three days he spent in William's company as 'amongst the whitest of my life'. He had taken great delight in introducing William to scenes familiar from his own youth, '& to have all your observations upon them which I felt flattered by finding consequent with my own, together with your remarks on other subjects & your instructive conversation in general – together produced an effect upon my mind, which I cannot expect to have often repeated during the remainder of my life'. Having parted from his generous host, William joined his brother Christopher and his family for dinner at the Lloyds', before setting off on the final leg of his journey to visit Sara at Hindwell. He went with the utmost reluctance, since it delayed his return home, but it was a sacrifice he felt he had to make for both Sara and Mary. 'You often laugh at me about Duty,' he told Mary, 'but this [is] a pure march of duty, at vast expence of inclination if ever one was made by man.'[49] Why should William feel that he was duty-bound to visit Sara? One can only surmise that he wanted to reassure her that she had not suffered in his estimation by running away from Coleridge and that he did not hold her responsible for the stoppage of the *Friend.*

William arrived at Hindwell on 11 August and, having quickly ascertained that all were well, wrote immediately to his wife. 'We have been parted my sweet Mary too long, but we have not been parted in vain, for wherever I go I am admonished how blessed, and almost peculiar a lot mine is. –. . . O Mary I love you with a passion of love which grows till I tremble to think of its strength'. He described the situation of Tom's new farm to her as standing in the longest and widest vale of 'a Country of many Vales', in a comparatively naked landscape of 'large fields and poor Hedgerows'. Though surrounded on all sides by low hills of erratic, knobbly shape, the width of the flat valley bottom makes Hindwell feel as though it stands on an empty plain. The house itself was, and is, an unpretentious, solid, four-square, red-brick farmhouse, its one redeeming feature being that it faced on to a three-acre pool. Its purpose was purely pragmatic – water was in short supply in the vale and it also provided a seemingly inexhaustible source of fresh fish – but it transformed the appearance of the place. 'The view from the windows is truly delightful,' William enthused, 'and shews beautifully the great importance of still water in Landscape.' Having only just arrived at Hindwell, he was already making plans to depart. 'I shall move heaven and earth to be with you by this day three weeks', he reassured Mary. How wrong Coleridge was in his belief that William was 'by nature incapable of being in Love, tho' no man more tenderly attached' is manifest in the private outpourings of husband to wife.

Every day every hour every moment makes me feel more deeply how blessed we are in each other, how purely faithfully how ardently, and how tenderly we love each other; I put this last word last because, though I am persuaded that a deep affection is not uncommon in married life, yet I am confident that a lively, gushing, thought-employing, spirit-stirring, passion of love, is very rare even among good people.

Mary's response was equally joyful and passionate.

O William! I really am too happy to move about on this earth, it is *well* indeed that my employments keep me active about other things or I should not be able to contain my felicity – Good Heavens! that I should be adored in this manner by thee thou first & best of Men, is a lot so far beyond, not only all my hopes but all my desires & the blessing is so weighty it is so *solemnly great* that it would be even *painful* were I left to brood much upon the thought of it.

On 16 August she celebrated her fortieth birthday, noting, as one does, with some dismay that, though she still felt as though she were twenty, she was beginning to lose her teeth and her hair was becoming grey: 'these, the two great ornaments my Youth had to boast of, (my hair especially I prized, because thou once ventured to speak in admiration of it) I must own are *upon the wain*'. William was undismayed. As soon as he had fulfilled his promise to take the Hutchinsons and Monkhouses on a short tour up the Wye as far as Rhayader, he would be home. 'I am giddy at the thought of seeing thee once more', he wrote.[50]

Dorothy, by contrast, had prolonged her absence from home. She left Coleorton a few days after William and travelled alone to Cambridge, where Clarkson was waiting to carry her off to Bury St Edmunds. Before they set off, they packed in a crammed sightseeing schedule, attending Trinity College chapel, taking a brief glance at William's old college, St John's, walking in the groves to identify William's favourite trees, dining at Peterhouse with Clarkson's friend Tillbrooke and paying a visit to King's College Chapel. Dorothy left Cambridge feeling more impressed than she had ever been before. She put it down to her advancing years, which made her appreciate buildings more than formerly, but as she now had the benefit of seeing everything through the medium of her brother's account of his college days in *The Prelude*, it was clearly this which gave added meaning to her visit. At Bury, she was welcomed with open arms by Catherine Clarkson, and the friends spent the ensuing two months quietly and happily enjoying each other's company.[51]

When she finally left Bury, it was in the company of William's recent acquaintance Robinson, who was an old friend of Catherine. He had visited the two ladies several times at Bury and now offered to escort her to London, where the Lambs had offered her accommodation (unwittingly sparking off another of poor Mary's mental breakdowns). Robinson waited on her daily, taking her to see Westminster Abbey and the British Museum, and, on her last evening, to Covent Garden.[52] There was a second joyous reunion at Binfield. The Cookson children had all come home from university and school to see her, Uncle William was all affection and his wife still the same admirable, cheerful woman who had been so kind to Dorothy in her youth, though, as the latter could not forbear remarking, 'she would look as if she were dead if her eyes were shut'. Christopher and his family were all there too, but Dorothy's plans to return with them to her brother's new country parish of Bocking were pre-empted when a letter arrived from William, informing her that the children had all taken the whooping cough and little Catherine was dangerously ill. She packed her bags and left immediately for London, but then persuaded herself that William had probably exaggerated the case and resolved to stay there a couple of days before catching the mail coach to Kendal. It was an opportunity to see Mary's cousins John and Mary Monkhouse, and accompany them to a consultation with a London specialist on Mary's apparently consumptive symptoms. On Monday morning, Dorothy got a seat on the coach to Kendal, spent the night at the Cooksons, and arrived in style, by gig, at Grasmere on Thursday 25 October.[53]

She received a terrible shock. Johnny came bounding down the field to greet her, followed by the two Williams and then Mary, bearing Catherine in her arms.

The child, who was never fit and well at the best of times, was worn to a skeleton: constant coughing and vomiting had reduced her to a sickly pale, hollow-cheeked shadow of her former self. In Dorothy's shocking phrase, 'She looked to me – when I could *think* at all – like a child bred and born in a Gin-Alley.'[54] The next morning, the entire family packed their bags and decamped to stay with the parents of one of their servants, Sally Yewdale, who lived at High Hacket, an ancient, rambling, cottage-style farmhouse clinging precariously to the rocky ridges high on the fells above Little Langdale. Dora and Thomas had been sent to recuperate there a fortnight earlier, on Scambler's advice, and the sunny, sheltered location, fresh air and kindly attentions of their hosts had gone some way to restore them.

The family were fortunate in glorious weather. The morning after their arrival, they sat out on a crag twenty yards from the house, in hot sunshine, watching the mists evaporate from the floor of the valley below while William read Milton's *Morning Hymn* from *Paradise Lost* to them. When he left that evening to return to Grasmere, Dorothy accompanied him for part of the way, but when she attempted to retrace her route across the peat moss and trackless fields, she became lost. It was a nightmare situation. Stumbling alone through the thickening darkness, often up to her knees in mud, she managed to keep panic at bay and tried to think what she would do if she had to stay out all night. It was pure chance that brought her to an isolated cottage. As she laid her hand on the latch of the door, her courage suddenly deserted her and she burst into fits of weeping, much to the bemusement of the cottagers. So concerned were they that not only did the husband escort her safely back to High Hacket, where she found Mary and the children distraught and the Yewdales gone out to seek her, but his wife called the next day to make sure that she had recovered. It was a grim lesson which Dorothy duly took to heart: 'I shall never again go alone in rough places and on unknown ground late in the evening.'[55]

They had not been back home for long when a second, deadlier disease struck the vale. Scarlet fever made its way insidiously towards Allan Bank. When it reached the two houses next to them and a previously fit and healthy man died of it, they knew that they would have to leave immediately. In their weakened state, the children were desperately vulnerable. But where to go? Sockbridge was considered, but rejected in favour of Elleray. William set off at once to see Wilson and, less than a fortnight after their return from High Hacket, the Wordsworths were established at Elleray. Wilson, who was in hot pursuit of Jane Penny, his bride-to-be, had temporarily left off his drinking, cock-fighting and wild ways. He proved to be a genial host who took evident pleasure in the Wordsworths' company. His servants were kind, good-natured and fond of the children, the situation of the house, on the shores of Windermere, was 'enchanting' and, as Dorothy noted with satisfaction, 'we could not have been so well off anywhere.'

The children escaped the scarlet fever, but they could not shake off the whooping cough, which still had them in its thrall six months after its first appearance. As soon as one child seemed to improve, another took a turn for the worse. While they were at Elleray, Tom became so ill that Mary took him, and the baby, who was still at the breast, into lodgings at Ambleside, simply so that they could be near Scambler. Thomas and Catherine were the worst sufferers, coughing and vomiting day and night until they were both weak and undernourished. Catherine, in particular, gave cause for concern. Her right hand was still useless, despite rather clumsy attempts to make her use it by binding her left arm to her side, and she continued to limp. A semi-permanent invalid, she had become so dependent on her mother that she refused to allow anyone else to nurse her and would not let Mary out of her sight. Fortunately, the baby, though suffering from whooping cough himself, was not so 'very troublesome' and, apart from feeding him, Dorothy was able to assume all responsibility for his care.[56]

Frantic with worry about their precious children, and worn out with the constant nursing and broken nights, it was not surprising that the Wordsworths had little thought for anyone or anything outside the family. It explains, at least in part, why they remained oblivious for so long to a second catastrophe that struck them in the autumn of 1810.

At the time, there was nothing to alert them to anything unusual. William and Mary had been alone together for a mere three weeks after his return from Hindwell when Montagu and his third wife, the former Anne Skepper, arrived at Allan Bank. The ostensible reason was to visit Algernon, Montagu's oldest son by his second wife, Laura Rush, who, at the beginning of May, had been sent to join Hartley and Derwent Coleridge at Mr Dawes's school in Ambleside. It had been left to the Wordsworths – in practice, Mary, who had been about to give birth – to find him lodgings with Mrs Ross at Ambleside and to manage the boy's finances. Like the Coleridge boys, he would also become a regular weekend visitor at Allan Bank.[57]

The new Mrs Montagu was as much an admirer of William as her husband, but for different reasons. A self-important woman, she was something of a trophy hunter and liked to be seen to be on intimate terms with the poets. 'Our Children are brought up with the highest reverence for Mr Wordsworth,' she wrote soon after her marriage in 1808, 'and I hope that one day they will be nearer to him.' Having achieved this aim, she was now seeking to accomplish her second, which was to lure Coleridge within her ambit, by offering him 'a quiet Bed room whenever you choose to occupy it' at their house in Frith Street, London, and suggesting that he submit himself to the latest fashionable doctor, Sir Anthony Carlisle. William positively loathed the new Mrs Montagu: 'the Creature is utterly odious to me', he confessed to Mary, adding that he had persuaded Dorothy to prolong her absence from home, simply to avoid having to meet her. 'I so exceedingly despise [Mrs Montagu] that I did not wish that D – who has never seen her, should have that disagreeable business to encounter.'[58]

Despite William's prophecy that they would not be troubled with a long visit, because Mrs Montagu would want to go 'jaunting off' to Keswick to see Southey and Coleridge, the Montagus stayed almost a month at Allan Bank. They were still there in October, when the Wordsworth children became seriously ill with whooping cough, and when Dora and Thomas were sent off to High Hacket, and even when a distraught William wrote to tell Dorothy that Catherine was at death's door. It was not until a few days later, on 18 October, that they finally took their leave, and when they did so they took Coleridge with them. He had never returned to Allan Bank since his departure at the beginning of May, but his self-incarceration at Greta Hall had weighed heavily with him, making Mrs Montagu's offer increasingly attractive. 'I do not know any other motive that he has for going to London,' Southey wrote despairingly, 'than that he becomes daily more and more uneasy at having done nothing for so long, and therefore flies away to avoid the sight of persons, who he knows must be grieved by his misconduct, tho they refrain from remonstrances.'[59]

Coleridge's decision to go to London placed his friends in a dilemma. It was patently obvious that the Montagus had no idea what they were letting themselves in for; like the Wordsworths before Coleridge moved in with them, they thought that Montagu's own industrious habits and spartan regime (he rose early and worked late, drank no alcohol and had an almost vegetarian diet) would inspire a reformation in Coleridge himself. Well aware that any disruption of his orderly existence would cause Montagu severe problems, and that the two men would inevitably quarrel, since Montagu was the last person to tolerate habits so discordant to his own, especially in an inmate of his house, William felt duty-bound to warn him. His friendship with Montagu pre-dated that with Coleridge by many years, and he could not allow him to make the same mistake as himself, simply through ignorance of the true state of things. Some time before Coleridge arrived at Allan Bank to join the travel party, William took Montagu on one side and suggested that it would be better for them both if Coleridge did not take up residence at Frith Street. His arguments were in vain. Montagu 'was resolved. "He would do all that could be done for him and would have him at his house."' In the circumstances, William felt that he had no other option but to speak the plain truth.[60]

Quite what that truth was remains a matter of dispute to this day, dividing Wordsworthian and Coleridgean sympathizers as effectively as it divided the two men themselves. Given the tenor of William's recent letters to Poole, and Dorothy's to Catherine Clarkson, it is likely that William said that the Wordsworths no longer had any hope of Coleridge either reforming his habits or producing anything more, or better, than he had already done. He undoubtedly described Coleridge's antisocial and disruptive habits: his turning night into day by lying in bed till the early afternoon, then demanding fires in his rooms and gruel, toast and water, and eggs at unreasonable hours of the day and night; his long fits of depression and silence and his screaming nightmares; his daily petty deceptions of himself and others about the progress of his work and his reliance on stimulants. Coleridge's opium addiction was an open secret, but William pointed out that, in his current state, he would not be able to sustain the sort of severe regimen which Carlisle proposed to put him on immediately, and that he would therefore be driven to deception. As proof of this, he cited the fact that, though Coleridge had not drunk spirits with the Wordsworths, they had suspected, and he had admitted, that he had secretly obtained 'a very small supply' from the public house. As Dorothy indignantly complained to Catherine, this was a private conversation between mutual friends who were both anxious to do their best for Coleridge. What William had confided was nothing more than common local knowledge: 'If he [Coleridge] were to be told what was said at Penrith after he had been at Anthony Harrison's, then he might be thankful to William', she added bitterly.[61] Nevertheless, a monstrous spectre had unwittingly been conjured up which would tear open a breach in the friendship between Coleridge and the Wordsworths, and destroy their intimacy for ever.

At the time, there was no indication at all that anything out of the ordinary had happened. Montagu gratefully accepted William's warning and his advice that, rather than actually live with them, Coleridge should be found lodgings nearby. William had intended to speak privately to Coleridge and make the same suggestion, but in the bustle between his arrival and departure there was no opportunity to do so. Coleridge therefore left Grasmere under the impression that he was going to stay with the Montagus. If Montagu had suspected William had exaggerated Coleridge's faults, then he was swiftly disillusioned. Only a few days on the road served to convince him as he saw, with his own eyes, 'confirmation of all that W. had said'. Instead of seeking a diplomatic way of informing Coleridge that he no longer wished to offer him a home, or taking responsibility for that decision on his own shoulders, Montagu took the easy option, used William's warning as his excuse and repeated his comments verbatim to Coleridge. What poisoned an already unpalatable draught was that Montagu told Coleridge (or Coleridge believed Montagu had told him, which distressed him no less) that William had 'commissioned' or 'authorized' him to repeat these comments to Coleridge himself.[62]

Coleridge was understandably devastated. 'W. authorized M. to tell me, he had no Hope of me!' he wept into his notebooks. 'No Hope of me! absol. Nuisance! God's mercy is it a Dream!' Instead of confronting William to ascertain the truth and express his anger and dismay, Coleridge did what he always did. Just as at Coleorton, when he had imagined William and Sara in bed together, he pretended that nothing had happened. Only in his notebooks did he admit his distress, and, repeating a now familiar pattern, lapsed into accusation and self-pity.

> How perceptibly has [Wordsworth's] love for poor C lessened since he has procured other enthusiastic admirers! – As long as C. almost all dissenting, was the *sole* Admirer & Lover, *so long* was he loved. – But poor C. *loved*, truly loved! . . . W. once – was unhappy, dissatisfied, full of craving, then what Love & Friendship, now all calm & attached – and what contempt for the moral comforts of others –[63]

To the Wordsworths, he maintained a pained and prolonged silence for eighteen months. That he did not write caused no surprise at first, for it was a familiar trait, and they were so harassed by anxiety for the children that Dorothy even forgot to tell Catherine Clarkson that Coleridge had gone. Soon after his arrival in London, Montagu wrote to confess what he had done and revealed that Coleridge had been 'very angry', but Mrs Montagu assured them that he was well, powdering his hair (a sign that he was enjoying an active social life) and 'talked of being busy'. Confirmation of this came from the Lambs: 'if I had not known how ill he is I should have had no idea of it,' Mary wrote on 13 November, 'for he has been very chearful'. He had not yet begun Carlisle's regimen, as Lamb mischievously informed them.

Coleridge has powdered his head, and looks like Bacchus, Bacchus ever sleek and young. He is going to turn sober, but his Clock has not struck yet, meantime he pours down goblet after goblet, the 2d to see where the 1st is gone, the 3d to see no harm happens to the second, a fourth to say there's another coming, and a 5th to say he's not sure he's the last.[64]

Relying on reports like these, it was not surprising that the Wordsworths had no intimation of the true nature of Coleridge's feelings towards them. Oblivious of the storm brewing, they returned to Allan Bank from their self-imposed exile at Elleray on 18 December preoccupied with their own problems. The sick children demanded constant attendance, in addition to which Mary dedicated two hours a day to rubbing Catherine's paralysed limbs, in the vain hope of restoring some movement. Southey walked to Ambleside to collect the Coleridge boys for the holidays, but though the adults dined with him at de Quincey's, he wisely preferred to keep away from the children, for fear of carrying their infection back to his own. Others were less cautious. On Christmas Eve Jane and Mary Hutchinson, daughters of Mary's oldest brother, Jack, came to stay for the holidays, and there was a large party in the kitchen for all the children and local friends, including the three servants from Elleray who had been so kind to them. A week later, they were joined by Miss Weir, who would stay until it was time to escort the Hutchinson girls back to her boarding school at Appleby.[65]

The new year brought no relief from sickness. William suffered a recurrence of the trachoma – a disease of the eyelids causing painful swelling and affecting his vision – which had afflicted him the previous summer on his way to Coleorton, and the children could not rid themselves of whooping cough. Now it was the two youngest who were the most severely affected: Mary and Dorothy were confined to the warm parlour for days on end, each nursing a child in her lap who was too ill and distressed to be removed. By the middle of February, Catherine was so reduced and feeble that change of air again became imperative. At this crisis, one of their friends, Miss Knott, came to the rescue, sending her carriage round to fetch the little girl and her aunt to stay at her house in Ambleside. Against the odds, Catherine rallied once more.[66]

In the circumstances, it was not surprising that William's literary activities were at a standstill. Since going to Coleorton, he had produced almost nothing. Even if the harassing anxiety he suffered over the children had allowed him to write, he was hampered by the fact that neither Mary nor Dorothy had time to spare to act as his amanuensis. As his sister ruefully admitted on Willy's first birthday in May, she had not opened a book since her return to Grasmere, except on a Sunday and when all the family were in bed, and had managed to read only one through.[67]

Writing the text for Wilkinson's prints had theoretically been a continuing project throughout 1810, but William had composed the bulk of it before leaving for Coleorton, including a detailed itinerary and advice to tourists on the best approaches to and viewing points for the Lakes. Again, however, his approach to the work did not suit Wilkinson, who seems to have thought the text too long. As a result of this disagreement, William refused to waste any more time or energy on work. 'D– has been so good as to abridge the sheets I wrote for Wilkinson', he told Mary in July, 'for my own part I have no longer any interest in the thing; so he must make what he can of them; as I can not do the thing in my own way I shall merely task myself with getting through it with the least trouble.' He was as good as his word. By November, when the final sheets were being prepared for publication, he had farmed out the composition of some of the descriptions to Dorothy. 'It is a most irksome task to him, not being permitted to follow his own course,' she explained, adding, quite correctly, 'I daresay you will find this latter part very flat.'[68]

It was no doubt the frustrations of working for Wilkinson which led William, the following spring, to reject outright a proposal from Godwin that he should produce an English version of the French fairy-tale 'Beauty and the Beast', for a series of illustrated children's books which he and his wife were editing. Godwin wanted a poem, written 'in a sort of smooth and flowing rhyme', and containing 'nothing abstruse'. Ignoring the implicit criticism in this comment, William merely announced, 'I cannot work upon the suggestion of others however eagerly I might have addressed myself to the proposed subject if it had come to me of its own accord.' Trying to soften the refusal, he admitted that he found the subject unedifying: 'there is to me something disgusting in the notion of a human Being consenting to *Mate* with a Beast, however amiable his qualities of heart'. Godwin's thoughtlessness in sending the little booklet containing the tale earned him a reproof which was only semi-jocular.

> You live and have lived long in London and therefore may not know at what rate Parcels are conveyed by Coach. Judging from the diminutive size of yours, you probably thought the expence of it would be trifling. You remember the story of the poor Girl who being reproached with having brought forth an illegitimate Child said it was true, but added that it was a very little one; insinuating thereby that her offence was small in proportion. But the plea does not hold good. As it is in these cases of morality so is it with the Rules of the Coach Offices. To be brief, I had to pay for your tiny parcel 4/9 and should have no more to pay if it had been 20 times as large.[69]

William's resentment at having to pay such a huge sum for a worthless trifle was exacerbated by the family's precarious financial situation. A year after her first asking for a statement of their accounts, Dorothy was still rather wearily pleading with Richard to comply with her request. Even without the written evidence, however, it was plain that they were in difficulties. William's obstinacy in refusing to publish his poems did not help. His more practical womenfolk tried to persuade him to send fifteen of his 'political sonnets' to the *Courier*, 'both in order that they might be read, and that we might have a little profit from his industry', but they could not prevail against his disgust with 'critics, Readers, newspaper-Readers – and the talking public'.[70]

This was an old complaint, but, probably as a result of having to live so many months with the daily prospect that one or more of his children would die from the whooping cough, William was suffering from a new malaise in the spring of 1811. 'I am shocked to find how indifferent I am becoming concerning things upon which so much of my life has been employed', he wrote to Edwards in March. 'I am not quite 41 years of age, yet I seem to have lost all personal interest in everything which I have composed.' When he read his own poems, he explained,

> I often think that they are such as I should have admired and been delighted with if they had been produced by another, yet, as I cannot ascertain how much of this approbation is owing to self-love, and how much to what my own powers and knowledge supply to complete what is imperfect in the poems themselves, upon the whole my own works at present interest me little, far too little . . .[71]

He would not write another poem for many months to come.

15. Suffer the Little Children

William may have become indifferent to his poetry, but politics still had the power to fire him. The fate of the Peninsula hung in the balance. In the summer of 1810 the French had seemed supreme. The whole of central Spain was heavily garrisoned with French troops and from this secure base Marshal Masséna had invaded Portugal. Knowing that the French relied on local requisitions to supply their armies, Wellington had organized that all the inhabitants from the invaded areas should destroy their crops and stores and abandon their homes. Forced to move further into the interior to replenish his dwindling supplies, Masséna was surprised and defeated at Busaco. Stranded in the heart of Portugal over the winter of 1810–11, disease and starvation wiped out a third of his troops. By the beginning of May 1811 Wellington had succeeded in retaking every French foothold in Portugal and given the Emperor Napoleon his first serious check.

William followed these events avidly. He and de Quincey, who shared his passion, were in a state of torture awaiting the arrival of each *Gazette* with the latest news from the Peninsula, and would sometimes walk by starlight up the Keswick road in the hope of meeting the carrier.[1] Towards the end of March, he received a copy of Captain Charles Pasley's *The Military Policy and Institutions of the British Empire*, read it through twice immediately, and composed a long and thoughtful letter in response. Reiterating the central thesis of his *Convention of Cintra* and his sonnets dedicated to national liberty, he argued that the moral character of a nation – what he called 'the *mind* of the Country' – was more important in determining victory than sheer force of arms: 'highly as I rate the importance of military power, and deeply as I feel its necessity for the protection of every excellence and virtue . . . I . . . rest my hopes with respect to the emancipation of Europe more upon moral influence, and the wishes and opinions of the people of the respective nations'. The might of French armies was supported by plundering conquered nations, but conquest could not continue indefinitely and, under the iron yoke of an arbitrary government, the enslaved peoples had neither the spirit nor the incentive to create wealth. British forces, on the other hand, were supported by a surplus of wealth created by domestic agriculture, trade, commerce and manufacture, which flourished precisely because its inhabitants enjoyed liberty and security. Echoing the philosophers of ancient Greece and Rome, he declared,

> Woe be to that country whose military power is irresistible! . . . If a nation have nothing to oppose or to fear without, it cannot escape decay and concussion within. Universal triumph and absolute security soon betray a State into abandonment of that discipline, civil and military, by which its victories were secured . . . England requires, as you have shown so eloquently and ably, a new system of martial policy; but England, as well as the rest of Europe, requires what is more difficult to give it, – a new course of education, a higher tone of moral feeling, more of the grandeur of the imaginative faculties, and less of the petty processes of the unfeeling and purblind understanding, that would manage the concerns of nations in the same calculating spirit with which it would set about building a house.

The statesman ought to proceed, he argued, in a final, grand (though unhelpful) analogy, upon calculations and from impulses similar to those of a great artist preparing a picture, or a mighty poet planning a poem. 'Much is to be done by rule; the great outline is previously to be conceived in distinctness, but the consummation of the work must be trusted to resources that are not tangible, though known to exist.'

Convinced of the importance of his arguments – but unable to afford to publish them – William persuaded a willing de Quincey to transcribe the letter neatly for him, so that it was legible, appended a couple of sonnets on liberty and enclosed the whole as an open letter to his friend the Whig MP Richard Sharp. His reason for doing so was that he had learned 'from a private quarter of unquestionable Authority' that the Whigs intended to recall the army from Portugal if they came to power. 'If they sincerely believe in the omnipotence of Buonaparte upon the Continent, they are the dupes of their own fears and the slaves of their own ignorance', he bluntly informed Sharp. 'We have destroyed our enemies upon the Sea, and are equally capable of destroying them upon land.'[2]

At the beginning of April, the Hutchinsons descended on Allan Bank for a family reunion and conference. Jack came from Stockton, Tom and Joanna from Radnorshire and Aunt Elizabeth Monkhouse from Penrith. Henry Hutchinson, their wealthy bachelor uncle, had died on 28 January, leaving his vast estates to be divided among his nephews and nieces. Jack, Tom and their three male cousins were each to receive between £8,000 and £10,000; Mary and Joanna were to share the income of an estate near Stockton let at £100 a year; and a similar arrangement was put in place for Sara and Betsy. Their youngest brothers, Henry and George, were comparatively hard done by, being left only the interest on £500 each. For the Wordsworths, an additional £50 a year was more than welcome.[3]

Joanna's presence and nursing skills freed Mary and Dorothy to do some urgently needed sewing, for on 25 May they were due to move house. The lease of Allan Bank had come to an end and they were to move into smaller, cheaper quarters at the Parsonage in Grasmere. The incumbent, Thomas Jackson, lived at Langdale and had agreed, the previous year, to create a library out of the adjacent barn and build a back kitchen before the Wordsworths entered the house. Despite Mary and Dorothy's determination not to move in until all the work had been completed, the workmen were dilatory and much remained to be done.[4]

The Parsonage could not have been more different from Allan Bank. Built in 1687, it lacked all pretension and, even with Jackson's improvements, was nothing more than a traditional Lakeland farmhouse. Long and low, with thick walls and cottage windows, it stood in the bottom of Grasmere Vale, only yards from the church, and close to Robert Newton's lodgings, where so many of their family and friends had stayed. Downstairs there were two parlours (the smaller one, assigned to William as a study, was a mere 'cabin', but the larger one was bigger than that at Town End), two good kitchens with a back porch, a dairy and large storeroom, a small cellar and a good pantry; upstairs there were four bedrooms, including one assigned to Sara, a maids' room and a lumber room. The barn was at least as large again, attached to the southern end of the house, but set back from it. Though partially filled with the parson's tithe hay, there were stalls for the Wordsworths' two cows. To the front of the house lay a small rectangular courtyard, enclosed within ugly white walls, but otherwise the property was unfenced. Though the Wordsworths were more comfortable with the idea of living cottage-fashion than in the empty grandeur of Allan Bank, they soon discovered that the location of the Parsonage left much to be desired. It lacked privacy, because it stood in the fork of the roads into Grasmere village and over Red Bank into Langdale, but this they planned to remedy by planting shrubs and trees. Irremediable, however, was the fact that one end of the property was bounded by the River Rothay, running crystalline clear over its stony bed in good weather, but apt to rise and flood its banks after heavy rains or snow-melt. The field in which the Parsonage stood was therefore a permanent bog, delightful for the children, but not conducive to health or cleanliness.[5]

By early June the Wordsworths were firmly established in their new home. The children were all better, even the three youngest, who had been most ill. Five-year-old Thomas was well enough to go off to Keswick to stay for a month on his own at Greta Hall, where little Herbert Southey was a playmate of the same age. The Coleridge boys and Algernon Montagu were still regular weekend visitors, even though the comparatively cramped accommodation of the Parsonage meant that they could no longer stay overnight.[6]

There was now only one cloud on the horizon and that was Coleridge himself. The Wordsworths had heard nothing from him since his departure for London, but, as they knew he had not written to Southey or his own children, they had not been worried by his silence. They all knew his habit of keeping letters he received unopened, for fear of learning bad news or being reproached. It was, as Southey said, the least pardonable of all his wretched practices, for it was 'a sort of wilful outlawry; or excommunication of himself'.[7] The first intimation that something was wrong came from Mary Lamb, who wrote to say that she knew that 'a coolness' existed between the two men, and urged William to come to town immediately, as Coleridge's mind was seriously unhinged. (Coleridge had visited her that day, burst into tears and declared, between sobs, 'Wordsworth – Wordsworth has given me up. *He* has no hope of me – I have been an absolute Nuisance in his family'.) Dorothy had replied, denying any coolness on William's part and telling her what had passed between her brother and Montagu. She, or perhaps her brother himself, also reported William's remark which, according to Coleridge, who learned it only from an indiscreet third party, 'amounted in substance to a Sneer on my reported high Spirits & my wearing Powder'. (Coleridge's hilarious excuse for adopting powder was to prevent his catching cold because his hair was thinning.)[8]

The fact that a third person saw the letter to the Lambs, and reported its contents to Coleridge, is symptomatic of the whole affair. It is ironic that the indiscreet repetition of comments made in a private conversation should have caused the quarrel, for it was envenomed and prolonged by similar revelations from both William's and Coleridge's private correspondence to third parties. It was Mrs Coleridge, for instance, who revealed to the Wordsworths that her husband blamed his mental collapse in London on William's 'cruel or unjust conduct' towards him, quoting, without Coleridge's knowledge, his own letter to her as proof. Dorothy tried hard to be magnanimous, claiming that her initial indignation had given way to pity for Coleridge's 'miserable weakness', but she could not hide the hurt or bitterness. 'It is certainly very unfortunate for William that he should be the person on whom he has to charge his neglect of duty', she confided in Catherine Clarkson, '– but to Coleridge the difference is nothing, for if this had not happened there would have been somebody else on whom to cast the blame.' William himself refused to be drawn, neither justifying his own conduct nor complaining of Coleridge. 'Time will remove the cloud from his mind as far as the right view of our conduct is obscured,' Dorothy hoped, 'and having deserved no blame we are easy on that score. If he seek an explanation William will be ready to give it, but I think it is more likely that his fancies will die away of themselves – Poor creature! unhappy as he makes others how much more unhappy is he himself!'[9]

Believing that Coleridge would eventually come to his senses and preoccupied with the approaching departure of Dora, the Wordsworths dismissed him from their thoughts. Dora, who was a month short of her seventh birthday, was about to go away to school. With her brothers, she had been attending the village school at Grasmere, but while Johnny and Thomas plodded through their lessons, she was quick, clever and easily bored. No other school was available for her locally, and neither Mary nor Dorothy had sufficient time to keep her 'regularly and steadily to work, which is absolutely necessary for a learner of her airy dispositions'. Reluctantly, therefore, they had decided that she should join her cousins at Miss

Weir's school in Appleby, at least until September, when her Aunt Sara would return and more time and attention could be devoted to her. It was perhaps the knowledge that her absence would be only a short one which reconciled them to it, for Dorothy, who had suffered bitterly from her own banishment from the family home as a child, was among the most earnest in persuading William to part with his precious daughter. Dora would not be going among strangers. She had visited the school before and, in addition to her cousins, she knew Miss Weir, an old friend of the Hutchinsons, who had also been a recent visitor at Allan Bank. The school was small, only nine boarding pupils, so it was more like a large family than an institution, and they were all young girls about Dora's own age. This last was the deciding factor. 'There never was a Girl in the world who would more easily be led to industry by following others, or to whom it would be more difficult to learn to sit still when she has no companions.' Dora herself had no qualms. She left Ambleside in great glee, perched on top of the coach with Miss Jameson, one of the Wordsworths' friends, who taught at Miss Weir's school. She was followed by a box containing spice cake, tea, sugar and a letter from Johnny, the first he had ever written. Two days later they heard that she had arrived safely and in good spirits.[10]

Shortly after Dora's departure, William, Mary, Thomas and Catherine, accompanied by one of their servants, Fanny Turner, set off to spend six weeks by the sea, leaving the oldest and youngest children at Grasmere in Dorothy's care. Thomas and Catherine were still delicate after their whooping cough, and it was hoped that sea-bathing would restore their health and even relieve the little girl's lameness. Though unacknowledged by any of them, this was a significant step. William had deliberately avoided the sea ever since his brother's death and only his concern for his children could persuade him to go there now. This perhaps explains why they first established themselves at Duddon Bridge. Lying at the point where the River Duddon opens out into the long flat sands of the estuary, it was the nearest they could get to the sea without having to face the open ocean. After four or five days there, however, it was apparent that the waters were not salty enough for their purposes, so they removed to Bootle, on the Cumberland coast, and took up residence in a cottage seven minutes' walk from the seaside. It was a 'dreary' place, bleak and treeless, but abounding in cornfields, miles of empty beach and ravishing views of the Isle of Man, whenever it fleetingly emerged from its bed of clouds. They had typically English weather, but this did not prevent them walking as far as Muncaster Castle, where William was distinctly unimpressed to find every estate entrance locked up and the castle itself invisible behind impenetrable plantations. He consoled himself with the companionship, and library, of James Satterthwaite, one of Christopher's closest friends both at Hawkshead and at Cambridge, who was then the rector of Bootle.[11]

From Bootle, William wrote his first letter to Sir George Beaumont in almost a year, enclosing a transcript of his latest poem as a peace-offering for his silence. It was a sonnet, inspired by one of Beaumont's own pictures, which now occupied pride of place over the mantelpiece of the parlour in their new home at Grasmere. In a graceful and subtle tribute to his friend and patron, William praised the power of the art which could capture 'one brief moment caught from fleeting time' and cast over it 'The appropriate calm of blest eternity'. Apart from a short burst of enthusiasm for *The Recluse*, which had ended almost as soon as it had begun, this was all he had written since the spring of 1810. The holiday proved to be just the incentive William needed to return to composition – though boredom seems to have been the catalyst rather than inspirational sights and experiences. The prose letter to Beaumont prompted a verse *Epistle* describing their journey, and the vicinity of Black Combe, the lofty mountain whose brooding heights dominate the upper Furness peninsula, inspired two shorter poems.[12]

At the beginning of September, they returned to Grasmere, William and Mary seizing the opportunity for a quiet and leisurely digression on foot up the Duddon valley, while Fanny drove the children home through Coniston. Husband and wife lingered for a couple of hours in the beautiful churchyard of Ulpha Kirk, looking at epitaphs, then made their way to Seathwaite, whose exquisite tiny chapel had earned fame far beyond its size by the ministry of the Reverend Robert Walker, curate of the parish for more than sixty years. They arrived at home to find Dorothy and Johnny at church. A silver teapot and a writing desk were on display in the parlour, which turned out to be gifts from Sara Hutchinson, in anticipation of her return from Hindwell. At the end of the month, William rode over to Warrington on a Kendal hack to meet her and escort her back to Grasmere, riding on her pony. It was now eighteen months since she had parted with the Wordsworths and her delight in her return was palpable. She plunged into a whirl of social activity: walks, rides, excursions and parties with de Quincey's mother and sisters, who were on a visit to Grasmere; exchanging visits with the Luffs at Patterdale and the Southeys at Keswick. Casting an acerbic eye over the scarlet cloaks and silk pelisses of the grand summer visitors, arriving at Grasmere church in their landaus and carriages, she could not resist reporting Peggy Ashburner's comment that, surely, 'Miss Joanna' would like Grasmere now that there was so much visiting; 'I never expected to see Grasmere come to sic a pass.' William, Sara noted, 'is always the soul of the Parties – the Ladies say they are nothing without him'.[13]

Rather more surprising was the fact that William was now involved in the village school on a daily basis. A new curate, William Johnson, had arrived the previous summer and made an immediate impression with his 'jingling' sermons, good plain discourses of the kind William advocated for country churches. He had also endeared himself to Mary by the eagerness with which he accepted a proffered volume of William's poems, 'went smiling off like a shot with the book open, & ere he crossed the threshold to which I followed him he had begun to read'. Young and ambitious, he was determined to transform the school and, probably at William's suggestion but certainly with his assistance, was in the process of introducing the Madras System. 'It is impossible to over-rate the benefit which might accrue to humanity from . . . [its] universal application', William wrote enthusiastically. Not content with being merely a theorist, he spent two or three hours in the school every morning and evening, teaching and helping to set up the system. He was justifiably proud of this achievement and when, in the middle of October, Southey brought Dr Bell himself to call, William instantly rushed him off to the school to hear the children at their lessons and give Johnson and himself the benefit of his advice. Despite the brevity of the visit, Bell was sufficiently impressed to declare that he would like to steal Johnson from them. The following spring, he was as good as his word, offering Johnson the post of headmaster of his newly established Central School in London. This was done not only through William but with his active support. It was, he admitted, one of the most disinterested acts of his life. 'For besides his general usefulness to the parish, I feel how much my own children will lose in him.'[14]

In addition to his voluntary labours in the school, which would soon involve all the female members of the family,[15] William was hard at work on his poetry. This, however, was a chore, for he was belatedly responding to a request from Sir George Beaumont that he would write some inscriptions for decorative features in the gardens at Coleorton. William could hardly refuse his friend and patron, but his distaste for the task was self-evident. Not only was he having to write to order again, but the Beaumonts were surprisingly indifferent to his artistic integrity and politely insistent on certain changes. The reference to 'Female and Male' in one poem, for instance, 'some would find ludicrous'. A rewrite was also sought for the final lines of the inscription for an urn dedicated to Beaumont's old friend Sir Joshua Reynolds. To Beaumont it appeared a relatively simple matter to transpose these lines from the first person to the third, but to the author it was almost impossible. 'I tried a hundred different ways, but cannot hit upon anything better.' As for the 'Female and Male', 'I know not how to get rid of it', he wrote miserably, adding that these lines would have to be suppressed, 'for it is not improbable that the altering of them might cost me more trouble than writing a hundred fresh ones'. William then had the frustration of finding that Lady Beaumont, from what her husband apologetically called 'redundancy of care', had lost the first versions of his poems, so he could not compare them with the alterations he had laboured so long and hard, and against his better judgement, to produce. Worse was to come, for by the end of November the Beaumonts had changed their minds once more and decided that, on the whole, they preferred the first versions after all.[16]

In the circumstances, it was remarkable that the finished inscriptions were so good. They were all, as William himself admitted, too long for their intended purpose, 'but I was unable to do justice to the thoughts in less Room'. Each was intended for a specific location in the gardens: the cedar 'Planted by Beaumont's and by Wordsworth's hands', the memorial urn to Reynolds, a seat looking towards the ruins of Grace Dieu, birthplace of the poet Francis Beaumont, and a niche carved out of the sandstone in the winter garden. Considered both individually and as a body, the poems illustrate perfectly the principles William had set out in his *Essays on Epitaphs.* There he had declared that the 'primary requisite' of an epitaph was that it should contain 'thoughts and feelings which are in their substance common-place, and even trite', but that these truths should be expressed in such a way that they should strike the reader as having the freshness and clarity of original intuition. In style and sentiment, the poems for the gardens at Coleorton were inscriptions masquerading as epitaphs.

> ... 'tis a common ordinance of fate
> That things obscure and small outlive the great:
> Hence, when yon mansion and the flowery trim
> Of this fair garden, and its alleys dim,
> And all its stately trees, are passed away,
> This little Niche, unconscious of decay,
> Perchance may still survive. And be it known
> That it was scooped within the living stone, –
> Not by the sluggish and ungrateful pains
> Of labourer plodding for his daily gains,
> But by an industry that wrought in love; ...[17]

Beaumont was too generous-spirited not to feel at least a twinge of guilt about his imposition on William's time and good-nature. At the end of one of his letters containing emendations, William casually mentioned that he was about to go to Lowther to seek a personal interview with Beaumont's friend, Lord Lonsdale. The purpose of his journey was an embarrassing one: he would go as a suppliant in the hope that Lonsdale might be able to offer him one of the thousands of posts, many of them sinecures, within his extensive patronage. 'In fact, whatever sacrifice it cost me,' a chagrined William wrote to Beaumont, 'a considerable portion of my time *must* in some way or other be devoted to money-making. The expences of living encrease so fast, and my family necessarily as the Children grow up requires more to support it.' Beaumont's response was typical. He immediately dispatched a letter wishing William success in his application and enclosing a banknote from himself. William was mortified that his words should be so misinterpreted. He refused the money immediately, and, anxious not to appear ungrateful, assured Beaumont that if he ever found himself in real financial difficulties, he would not hesitate to inform him. The tact which both men displayed in handling such a delicate matter was a tribute to the genuine friendship between them.[18]

Towards the end of November Sara and her sailor brother, Henry, who had been staying at Grasmere for a month, went to visit Miss Weir and their three nieces at Appleby. They found all three girls well, happy and delighted to see them, but it was Dora who entranced Sara. 'I thought her the most beautiful Creature I ever saw in my life ... *bewitchingly* so – for your life it seemed impossible not to admire her – there is such a life and variety in her countenance as I never saw – then she was so modest & pretty-behaved that it gave her face a milder & sweeter expression than I thought it capable of'. Aunt and uncle stayed a week at Appleby to attend the school ball, for which they had brought Dora a new dress. Miss Weir had employed a dancing master for eleven weeks in preparation for the great event, but it was, in Sara's opinion, 'abundant in *bad* dancing'. When Dora herself returned to Grasmere for the Christmas holidays, the general opinion of her progress was more favourable. According to her Aunt Dorothy – her severest critic – Dora 'reads very tolerably – spells well – writes decently and sews as well as one could expect'. Another half-year at school, it was decided, would set her well and truly on the path of regular advancement in learning and, with good habits thus established, there was every prospect of her becoming what Dorothy called 'a useful Girl in the family'.[19]

Writing her usual end of the year summary for Catherine Clarkson, Dorothy reported that Johnny had made some progress with his books in recent weeks, but to the family's lasting regret his 'duncery' was unconquerable; Thomas was also slow, but lack of inclination rather than intellect was his problem; Catherine, 'almost as broad as she is long', was 'uncommonly good-tempered', but at three years old was hardly more articulate than her eighteen-month-old youngest brother. Dorothy herself was in fine fettle, walking between ten and twenty miles daily without the least fatigue, and William had at last resumed work on his 'great poem'. After the trials and tribulations of the last eighteen months, the outlook now seemed bright. 'We had the finest Christmas day ever remembered, a cloudless sky and glittering Lake; the tops of the higher mountains covered with snow.' The Wordsworths celebrated, as usual, with roast beef and plum cake; William walked with his sister in the morning, while the rest of the family were at church, then by moonlight with his wife. Dorothy played cards with the children, a treat she promised to repeat on New Year's Day, and there was dancing in the kitchen when the Grasmere fiddlers arrived on their annual round.[20]

At Keswick the new year was greeted with alarms and fears of an uprising among the manufacturing population. 'Half the people in Keswick sat up on Thursday night last', Southey reported, 'because two "ugly fellows" had been seen in the town. I have been obliged to load an old Spanish fowling piece to keep up the courage of the family, and to write to London for a brace of pistols and a Watchmans rattle.'[21] Grasmere remained tranquil, but courage of a different kind was required, for William addressed himself to Lord Lonsdale. His own instinct had been to make the first approach informally in person, but he had been thwarted by Lonsdale's absence from Lowther for the winter. The letter he now wrote, though seasoned with a little judicious flattery of His Lordship's 'gracious manners' and 'attachment to Literature', was remarkably frank and to the point. 'Literature has been the pursuit of my Life', he wrote,

> . . . I long hoped, depending upon my moderate desires, that the profits of my literary labours added to the little which I possessed would have answered to the rational wants of myself and my family. But in this I have been disappointed; and for these causes; 1st the unexpected pressure of the times falling most heavily upon men who have no regular means of increasing

their income in proportion; and 2ndly I had erroneously calculated upon the degree in which my writings were likely to suit the taste of the times; and, lastly, much the most important part of my efforts cannot meet the public eye for many years through the comprehensiveness of the subject. I may also add (but it is scarce worth while) a fourth reason, viz. an utter inability on my part to associate with any class or body of literary men, and thus subject myself to the necessity of sacrificing my own judgement, and of lending even indirectly countenance or support to principles either of taste, politics, morals, or religion, which I disapproved; and your Lordship is not ignorant that except writers engaged in mere drudgery, there are scarcely any authors but those associated in this manner, who find literature, at this day, an employment attended with pecuniary gain.

Having established himself firmly on the moral high ground, William then proceeded to the main thrust of what was, after all, a begging letter. He had just learned of the death of John Richardson, Lonsdale's principal agent, and the opportunities thus created for new appointments:

if any Office should be at your Lordship's disposal (the duties of which would not call so largely upon my exertions as to prevent me from giving a considerable portion of time to study) it might be in your Lordship's power to place me in a situation where with better hope of success I might advance towards the main object of my life; I mean the completion of my literary undertakings; and thereby contribute to the innocent gratification, and perhaps (as the Subjects I am treating are important) to the solid benefit of many of my Countrymen.

Lonsdale replied that he had no suitable vacancies available on this occasion, but assured William of his respect for his talents and character, and urged him to get in touch again 'whenever you think I can be of use to you'.[22]

There was nothing William could do but return to his poetic labours. A smoking chimney in the larger parlour gave him the excuse to leave off his work on *The Recluse*, but he did take the time to revise *Peter Bell*. That he did so now, and that Sara made fair copies of it, and of *Benjamin the Waggoner*, suggests that he was considering the possibility of raising some money by their publication. This view is supported by the fact that he took the manuscripts with him to London later in the year and gave the latter well-received public readings at both the Lambs' and Sergeant Rough's. In vain, however, for his reluctance to publish soon overwhelmed him, the manuscripts were again returned to the drawer and neither poem saw the light of day for another seven years.[23]

William was restless and uncharacteristically edgy in these early months of 1812. There were a number of factors: the departure from Grasmere of Johnson, for example, and from Patterdale of their old friends the Luffs, whose financial problems had forced them to sell up their much-loved cottage and accept a posting to Mauritius;[24] and the Wordsworths' own money problems and the increasing pressure to find a resolution of them. Dwarfing all these was the quarrel with Coleridge. The Wordsworths had long known that their old friend was angry with them, and unhappy, but they had not appreciated how deep these feelings ran. It was brought home to them in the most dramatic manner. On 19 February Coleridge called at Ambleside to collect Hartley and Derwent from school and carry them home to Greta Hall. 'I passed thro' Grasmere; but did not call on Wordsworth', he airily informed his friend Morgan. What he did not say was the effect that this omission had on his children, who, though still in the habit of paying weekly visits to the Wordsworths, had no idea that anything was amiss. 'Poor Hartley sat in speechless astonishment as the Chaise passed the turning to the Vicarage where W. lives,' his mother told Poole afterwards, 'but he dared not hazard one remark and Derwent fixed his eyes full of tears upon his father, who turned his head away to conceal his own emotions.' It was left to Mrs Coleridge to explain their father's conduct, and the reason for it, to her sons.

When the Wordsworths learned what had happened, they were deeply hurt, particularly on Dorothy's behalf. Whatever Coleridge's quarrel with William, she had played no part in it. She had confidently looked forward to Coleridge visiting them on his return and was completely bewildered by his refusal to do so. 'Numerous were the letters and messages I received from Miss W. to urge C. to write to her and not to leave the country without seeing them;' Mrs Coleridge told Poole, 'but he would not go to *them* and *they* did not come to him'. This was something of a simplification, for, as Coleridge himself declared at the time, what he wanted from William was not just a visit but an apology for his remarks to Montagu. 'I have refused to go over,' Coleridge wrote on 24 March, '& Wordsworth has refused to apologize and has thus made his choice between me and Basil Montagu, Esqre'. The affair, he prophesied, 'will end in complete alienation'.[25]

For six weeks, there was an *impasse*. Both men had friends in both households and efforts were made on each side to effect a reconciliation, but to no avail. Then, as suddenly as he had arrived, Coleridge left, not having seen any of the Wordsworths, nor, indeed, Sara. What none of them knew was that he would never return to his home or the Lakes again. From Penrith, on the eve of his departure, he wrote bitterly to Morgan, complaining that he had received four letters in the last three days

> about my not having called on Wordsworth as I passed thro' Grasmere – & this morning a most impassioned one from Mrs Clarkson – Good God! how could I? how can I? – I have no resentment – and unless Grief & Anguish be resentment, I never had – but unless I meet him as of yore, what use is there in it? What but mere pain? I am not about to be his Enemy – I want no stimulus to serve him to the utmost whenever it should be in my power. – And can any friend of mine wish me to go without apology received, and as to a man the best-beloved & honored, who had declared me a nuisance, an absolute nuisance – & this to such a Creature as Montagu?

A well-meant intervention by Southey only added to Coleridge's misery. Relying on William's own word, as well as 'on the common sense of the thing', Southey had 'denied most peremptorily' that William had ever commissioned Montagu to tell Coleridge that he had no hopes of him. This meant only one thing to Coleridge: William believed Montagu in preference to him and was therefore accusing him of being a deliberate liar as well as an absolute nuisance. On 27 March the Wordsworths learned from Mrs Coleridge that her husband had gone. It clearly came as an unwelcome surprise. 'We are all very sorry that his visit has ended so;' Sara reported, 'being persuaded that he never would have come down at all but in the hope of a reconciliation.'[26]

A fortnight later, William also left for London. The visit had been planned since the beginning of the year and was originally a purely social one, but it had now assumed a more immediate importance. He was determined to 'confront' both Coleridge and Montagu 'upon this vile business'. He took his time, however, for his first duty was to escort Mary and five-year-old Thomas to Chester to meet Tom Hutchinson. Mary and Thomas would then go on to Hindwell, where they would stay for the next two or three months, while William made his way to London. He travelled via Birmingham, staying overnight there with the Lloyds, to Oxford, 'an enchanting place', where he spent thirty-six hours exploring everything but the museum. He called on his cousin William Cookson, a student at Brasenose, and on William Jackson, son of the rector of Grasmere, who was an undergraduate of Queen's College; with Jackson, he attended the examination schools and, by chance, heard Coleridge's nephew, John, give an impressive performance. Wishing he could spend another day in Oxford, he reluctantly left for Binfield, to spend a few days with the Cooksons, before travelling up to London, where, on 27 April, he took up residence with the Beaumonts in Grosvenor Square.[27]

William's first priority on arriving in town was to get to the bottom of the whole affair with Coleridge. This had now become urgent, for reports had already begun to reach him that the quarrel was the subject of dinner and tea-table gossip. Coleridge was constitutionally incapable of keeping his own counsel and, since his return from the Lakes, had lost all sense of proportion and discretion. Sharp had received a letter informing him that William, 'whom to that very moment I had cherished in my Heart's Heart', was now Coleridge's 'bitterest Calumniator'. The Beaumonts had received letters and a visit from Coleridge himself in which he had tried to enlist their sympathy by telling his side of the story, with 'plentiful abuse' of William, to which they refused to listen. As William had carefully refrained from confiding in Sir George, because he was a mutual friend and he had not wanted to cause him pain, this was particularly hard to bear. 'This conduct is insufferable', William complained to Mary, 'and I am determined to put an end to it.'[28]

The indiscreet revelations by Coleridge and the Montagus had been improved upon by scandalmongers in London society. Southey's friend, Sharon Turner, availed himself of a dinner at Longman's (William's own publisher) to regale the party with gossip about the quarrel in a way which outraged at least one of his auditors: William, it was said, had accused Coleridge of being a '*rotten drunkard*' and 'rotting out his entrails with intemperance'. On another occasion, Godwin's wife told Henry Crabb Robinson that Montagu had brought Coleridge to London on the pretext of seeking medical advice for him 'but in reality by W[ordsworth]'s desire in order to get rid of C[oleridge]' and that Montagu had been 'commissioned by W[ordsworth] to say that C[oleridge] c[oul]d no longer remain with him!!!'[29]

Catherine Clarkson, a friend of Robinson, Coleridge and, of course, William himself, was horrified that matters had come to such a pass. 'I hope you will either see [Coleridge] or at least take some measures to put a stop to the reports which are in circulation respecting your conduct towards him', she urged William. 'My dear friend! There has been downright lying somewhere not mere misrepresentations & dressing up of facts but inventing against you – and if I were in your place I would take Mr Montagu & C Lamb with me & force an interview with C.' This was precisely what William decided to do. It was hardly subtle, but at least it was honest. His first call was on Montagu, but no opportunity presented itself for raising the matter. He therefore wrote instead to Coleridge's oldest friend, Lamb, asking to see him alone at home: 'as I wish to have the business sifted to the bottom, and will take his opinion how it may be done in the most unexceptionable manner'.[30] Lamb thus became the unofficial go-between, carrying verbal and written messages between the two men in a way that was distasteful to himself and did little to appease either of the aggrieved parties.

Coleridge's reaction to William's suggestion of a meeting was to point out, quite rightly, that it would turn into a confrontation. Only one version of events could be true: either William had indeed said what Montagu had told Coleridge he had said, or Montagu, or Coleridge, was lying. Faced with one man's word against the other, what could be achieved? A duel was the only possible outcome. Though he did not decline to attend such a meeting, he suggested that William should first read his own statement which he had begun to prepare for Sara, but had left unfinished 'in consequence of understanding that she had already decided the matter against me'. This merely poured oil on the flames. Why, William declared, should he read a paper whose object was to win an opinion against himself from the sister of his own wife? No doubt fearing that the paper would also contain protestations of love for Sara, William declined to read it and returned it unopened. Nevertheless, he recognized the justice of Coleridge's objections to the proposed meeting with Montagu and suggested that the two men should prepare a written statement of what they each believed had been said. The two could then be compared and William would write his own, adding 'under what circumstances I spoke, with what motive, and in what spirit. And there, I believe, the matter must end'. Once such documents had been produced, they would provide an authoritative statement which would put an end to the lies and half-truths then circulating; 'only I shall admonish Coleridge to be more careful how he makes written and public mention of injuries done by me to him'.[31]

The feelings of both parties had only been exacerbated by the exchanges between them, and there was now every possibility that the breach would become irreparable. Both men were becoming intransigent. Coleridge was convinced that William's 'commissioning' Montagu to make his criticisms for him was 'an intentional means of putting an end to our long Friendship'; William was equally convinced that Coleridge was 'glad of a pretext to break with us, and to furnish himself with a ready excuse for all his failures in duty to himself and others.' At this crucial point, a cool head was desperately needed, and fortunately for everyone concerned one was found. Henry Crabb Robinson was the epitome of discretion, and motivated by liking both parties. He had a genuine desire to bring the quarrel to an end, but he needed all his considerable diplomatic skills, as well as his legal training, to do so. Robinson's diary, which details the delicate path he had to walk in these negotiations, is frustratingly discreet. Many of the entries are in code and a number of the conversations with William are simply noted as being 'confidential', 'of a kind not to be repeated' or 'I ought not to put in writing what he said'. As an insight into the quarrel, however, it is unique, for the admirable Robinson managed not only to remain impartial, and to perform his task as intermediary punctiliously, but also to ensure that anything inflammatory was quietly suppressed.[32]

It was Coleridge who first involved Robinson by relating his grievances and giving him permission to repeat them to William, probably because William had refused to open letters from him on the subject. Robinson duly conveyed the message, and in return was asked to give William's verbal answers to Coleridge's charges. There were three absolute denials: he had never 'commissioned' Montagu to say anything, used the expression '*rotten drunkard*' or said Coleridge himself was a 'nuisance', only that some of his habits were. He admitted that he had expressed no hopes of Coleridge, but indignantly repudiated the suggestion that he would ever have said so, directly or indirectly, to Coleridge himself. He did, however, blame himself for forgetting that Montagu 'was not a man whose discretion could be safely trusted with even so much as he did say'. He no longer wished to confront Coleridge and Montagu and was content to leave undetermined who was at fault, but he expected Coleridge to give him credit for the truth of this declaration, 'And not continue to use that langu[age] abo[u]t him which he had done'. These points Robinson duly repeated to Coleridge, 'Except perhaps the conclusion of the last which I might not distinctly state to C– W added other remarks which I was careful not to repeat as they co[ul]d not tend to the reconciliation so desireable, [*sic*] And perhaps so important to the future happiness of C.'[33]

Coleridge's immediate reaction was simply to reiterate all his complaints, but Robinson, though 'apprehensive of saying too much', would not allow him to dwell on them.

> I endeavoured to draw C's attention *from* words w[hi]ch are so liable to misrepresentation – And w[hi]ch in repetition so entirely change their character, to the fact so positively denied by W that he ever intended (least of all commissioned) M to repeat what W stated to him – This in my mind is the only material fact. Every thing else admits of explanation. This does not.

And so a compromise was finally beaten out. Coleridge wrote out his statement which, 'tho' not elaborately drawn up, or artfully written' contained 'the most indubitable internal evidence of truth'. As such, it had its due effect on William. Convinced now that Coleridge had genuinely believed William's reported comments to be true, and of the sincerity of his unhappiness, William drew up his own statement. It proved a difficult task, 'because he had to reconcile things very difficult to unite – The most exact truth & sincerity with the giving his friend the least possible pain'. What facilitated the writing of a conciliatory letter was William's bad opinion of Montagu and his wife. Robinson seems to have asked the obvious question. Why was William so reluctant to put an end to his friendship with Montagu, if he believed Montagu was responsible for causing the quarrel between himself and Coleridge? William's answer impressed him: he 'spoke eloquently of the difficulty of breaking off an intimacy early formed, more especially where a benefit is conferred by that intimacy And where by the influence of friendship characters are preserved from lapses that might otherwise prove their shipwreck'.

In the end, 'the great part' of William's statement was actually written by Robinson, who found him 'willing to say anything he could truly, to give Coleridge satisfaction'. No doubt this explains why it bears more resemblance to a legal document than a letter to a friend. 'The conversation that accompanied the writing it was highly interesting & exhibited W in a most honourable light', Robinson noted in his diary on 11 May. 'His integrity his purity, his delicacy alike are eminent'. Having carefully preserved his impartiality throughout the affair, Robinson now let slip that, as far as conduct went, he had learned to admire William more than Coleridge: 'How preferable is the *coolness* of such a man to the heat of C.'[34]

Having drawn up at least two drafts of his statement, a shorter final form was agreed with Robinson, written out by William and delivered to Coleridge the same day. That evening, when Robinson called on Coleridge, he had the immense satisfaction of learning that it was considered 'perfectly satisfactory'. Reporting the glad news to Greta Hall, a jubilant Coleridge announced that William had given him an 'unequivocal denial of the Whole *in spirit &* of the most offensive passages in letter as well as Spirit', and that, in response, he had 'instantly informed [Wordsworth] that were ten thousand Montagues to swear against it, I should take his word not ostensibly only but with inward Faith!' The level-headed Robinson, who was overwhelmed at the thought of having brought about a reconciliation between 'two *such men*', was rightly more sceptical: 'the Wound is healed,' he wrote in his diary, 'but . . . probably the Scar remains in Coleridge's bosom'.[35]

When the two men finally met, face to face, it was something of an anticlimax. William called on Coleridge at the Morgans', where he had taken up residence since coming to town. 'I felt no awkwardness at the meeting,' William told Dorothy, 'nor was he much agitated.' Both behaved as if nothing had happened. At neither this meeting nor the ones that followed did either of them touch upon the subject of quarrel which had consumed so much of their time and energy and caused them both so much pain. They met frequently on social occasions, even at each other's residences, and William attended Coleridge's lectures, but the old intimacy had gone for ever.[36]

The very day of the reconciliation, 11 May, a shocking event took place which threw the whole country into a state of panic. The Prime Minister, Spencer Perceval, was shot dead in the lobby of the House of Commons by John Bellingham, a Liverpool merchant. William was at a dinner party at Rogers's house when the dramatic news was announced by no less a person than Lord Byron. William's first thoughts were for his family, for the murder had been greeted with joy by the lower orders; in the streets and in the pot-houses they were toasting the radical Francis Burdett as 'the People's Champion', who would rid them of all sufferings, real and imaginary. It was revolutionary France all over again and William's blood now ran cold at the thought. 'Oh my Joy & my comfort, my hope & my repose,' he wrote to Mary, 'what awful thoughts passed through my mind of thee & Dorothy and home'. Only ten days earlier, he had seen Perceval in the House of Commons 'and admired the spirit and animation with which he suppressed & chastized that most dangerous & foolish Demagogue Sir Francis Burdett . . . The country is no doubt in a most alarming situation; and if much firmness be not displayed by the government confusion & havoc & murder will break out & spread terribly.'

It was a sobering thought that Bellingham had probably also been in the Commons that same day, for he had stalked his victim for a fortnight before murdering him. In the debate William had heard, Burdett had vigorously opposed the building of army barracks in Liverpool, Bristol and London, on the grounds that they were part of a system to enslave and murder the people. William was convinced that this speech must have influenced Bellingham and been a 'determining motive' to his act. Repeating these thoughts at a dinner party in the presence of Robinson on 13 May, he was rudely and offensively contradicted by a young Liverpudlian who claimed Burdett's speech was 'constitutional' and asked what the people were to do who were starving. 'Not murder people', was William's laconic response, 'unless they mean to eat their hearts'.[37]

Having 'settled the business with Coleridge', as he always referred to the reconciliation, William now found himself more at liberty to enjoy all London had to offer. The rest of his visit passed in a hectic round of social engagements. His brother Christopher and the Beaumonts were in regular attendance, as was Robinson, who took particular pride in introducing William to his own circle of friends. He breakfasted, dined, went to the theatre and partied with many old friends, including the Lambs, Rogers, Sharp, Stoddart, Davy and Stuart, but his circle of acquaintance was expanding rapidly. Through Rogers, he met Lord Byron, whose recent publication of *Childe Harold* had made him all the rage. William admitted the power of his writing, but dismissed his style as un-English and the man himself as 'somewhat cracked'. Rogers also introduced him to the poet William Lisle Bowles, whose works William had long admired: though unimpressed by his 'mean appearance' and lack of 'strength in his conversation', William was delighted with his simple, frank and ingenuous manners.[38] Robinson took him to meet the

Aitkin family, editors of and contributors to the *Annual Review*, which had so viciously reviewed *Poems, in Two Volumes*. There he met the 'old snake' Mrs Barbauld, whose poetry he despised almost as much as her political opinions, and the poet James Montgomery, who appeared feeble but amiable. At Beaumont's many grand dinners he met a wide range of people, from artists such as the American, Washington Allston to the highest in the land. On one occasion he was even introduced to the Princess Regent, the notorious Caroline of Brunswick. It was, as William cheerfully admitted, 'an empty honour, for her RH– was at some distance from me, and I had no conversation with her. She is a fat unwieldy Woman, but has rather a handsome & pleasing Countenance, with an expression of hilarity that is not however free from Coarseness.' (At this particular party, William was obviously fascinated by a woman with a 'huge & tremendous' bosom: 'Her Breasts were like two great hay-cocks or rather hay-stacks, protruding themselves upon the Spectator,' he told Mary, 'and yet no body seemed to notice them'.)[39]

With such a busy social calendar, it was not surprising that William occasionally found himself double-booked: he was only half-joking when he told Robinson that he would have to get 'a regular card to minute down my engagements, or I shall be getting daily into scrapes of this kind'. But after a while it began to pall. He had to spend £8 12s on a new suit, hat and silk stockings, an enormous sum to lay out for a man who was usually to be found wearing the cast-off clothing of his brothers and brothers-in-law. He was also increasingly frustrated and bored by the constant round of engagements.

> I am quite tired of these things; If you happen to fall into conversation with a person at all interesting, on an interesting subject, it is impossible to prosecute it; for either some body comes in between; or inclination of variety prompts or an obligation of civility enjoins, an attention to some other individual, and the conversation is immediately broken off. I have already neglected several invitations of this kind, and shall in future attend to still fewer; so that I believe that I should soon slip into as deep a solitude in London as in Grasmere.[40]

Despite all the claims on him, William found time to perform a number of quiet kindnesses. He went several times to visit the former Grasmere curate William Johnson and was somewhat dismayed to find him 'in a nasty Dirty place' which was the temporary school. 'Johnsy' was also having difficulties with Dr Bell, who, though an 'excellent Creature', had frequent changes of mind and 'something of a plaguy manner'. In an effort to ease tensions, William agreed to undertake a most disagreeable chore: 'viz to select and compose with Mr Johnson's assistance 20 pages of monosyllabic lessons for Children.' He also offered his services in a different capacity to Charles Pasley, author of the book on British military policy which he had read earlier in the year and so much admired. Having sought him out and arranged to visit him at Chatham, where he was to set up an officer training unit for the ordnance department, William discovered that Pasley had not yet received his promotion and could do nothing till Lord Mulgrave, the Master

General, issued his warrant. As William had dined with Mulgrave only a few days earlier and knew that Beaumont was among his intimate friends, he immediately begged to be allowed to use these contacts on his behalf.[41]

William also spent considerable time and effort in trying to secure the release of a French prisoner-of-war. It is a very odd story, made all the more strange by the fact that it can only be pieced together from scattered and allusive references which raise more questions than they solve. The Frenchman was Eustace Baudouin, whose elder brother, Jean Baptiste, married William's daughter Caroline in 1816. It has been assumed that the Baudouins and Vallons became acquainted because, after his release, Eustace carried messages from the Wordsworths to the Vallons. In fact, this is an inversion of the true order of events, for it is clear that the Baudouins were already friends of the Vallons, and Eustace's plight was brought to William's attention by a letter from Annette in the spring of 1812. (This is also the first indication we have that there was still a correspondence with Annette. There are no known references to letters to or from her after 13 October 1802 until now; whether this letter broke a ten-year silence or was simply the first to register in the wider correspondence remains a mystery.)

The first reference to Eustace Baudouin appears in Mary's letter to William, written from Hindwell on 23 April. Describing her journey after she and Thomas had parted from William at Chester, she says they dined at Oswestry in Shropshire. 'Oh with what a fervent heart did I greet the river Wye for thy sake & for its own loveliness!' she wrote. 'I looked for our friend in the face of every Frenchman we met, & never before was sorry that I could not speak their language I was sorry for his sake that you had not come so far with us – for I dare say he has never recd. his father's . . . letters.'

By 29 April William had received a letter 'from the French Prisoner at Oswestry', forwarded from Grasmere, 'telling you that he has no present want of money having received a supply – that he wished much that by applying to the Transport office you could assist him in obtaining his release but seemed to have little hope; and requested to hear again, telling him your address – where he might *always* find you, and saying you might write in English'.[42] 'I wish you may be able to serve Annette's friend', Mary responded, and William did attempt to do so, seeking the advice of Daniel Stuart, 'a most able man' whose 'good sense & knowledge of things are consummate', and whose contacts, through his editorship of the *Courier*, were second to none. Having made his inquiries, Stuart informed William that nothing could be done, and advised him to let the matter drop. Unable to secure Baudouin's release, William sent him £20, half of it borrowed from Mary's cousin Tom Monkhouse.[43]

The correspondence with Annette continued, however, for in bringing Baudouin to their attention she had also referred to her own straitened circumstances. The Wordsworths were determined to assist her and wrote to ask her for a detailed account of her situation. Throughout most of May, they waited anxiously for her response. The letter they eventually received was written jointly by Annette and

Caroline, who was now almost twenty years old. It described how their days were confined to an office, where Annette had managed to secure some sort of official post which required their constant attention. They could not take holidays and had no time for exercise or recreation; all their pleasure in life they found in each other. They had supported themselves, however, had no present need of money, and Caroline's devotion to her mother was a credit to the way she had been brought up. It was, the Wordsworths agreed, a deeply affecting letter. 'Does not Annette appear to have behaved well (& even in a dignified manner[)?];' William asked his wife. 'I shall be happy if it appears so to you'. Mary responded with her usual generosity. 'I do indeed think Annette's conduct very dignified & most heartily wish we were rich enough for you to settle something handsome upon dear Caroline . . . God bless her I should love her dearly & divide my last with her were it needful – God bless them both & thee my best beloved'.[44]

Throughout the eight weeks of their separation, William had belied his reputation as a poor correspondent by writing almost daily to his wife. Twenty-four letters passed between them, every bit as ardent as the ones of the previous year. 'My sweet Love how I long to see thee;' he wrote on 13 May; 'think of me, wish for me, pray for me, pronounce my name when thou art alone, and upon thy pillow; and dream of me happily & sweetly. – I am the blessedest of Men, the happiest of husbands'. 'Oh William I can not tell thee how I love thee,' Mary replied, '& thou must not desire it – but feel it, O feel it in the fullness of thy soul & *believe* that I am the happiest of Wives & of Mothers & of all Women the most blessed.' 'Oh my Mary!' he rejoined; 'my own Darling, one thought one wish, one longing for thee such as now pervades my Soul & every particle of my Frame, turns human existence with all its cares & fears into a heaven of heavens. I am as a Husband, and a Father, and a Brother, the blessedest of men!'[45]

On 2 June Mary set off with her brother Tom and sister Joanna on a short tour down the Wye to Tintern Abbey and Chepstow. For all of them it was a journey undertaken almost in a spirit of pilgrimage, but Mary especially was haunted by the sense of how important this same journey had been to her husband. 'O William what enchanting scenes have we passed through', she wrote from Tintern, '– but you know it all – only I must say longings to have you by my side have this day been painful to me beyond expression'. The idea of Mary wandering in his own footsteps by his beloved Wye gave William an erotic charge: 'the fever of thought & longing & affection & desire is strengthening in me,' he wrote,

> and I am sure will be beginning to make me wakeful and to consume me. Last night I *suffered*; and this morning I tremble with sensations that almost overpower me. I think of you by the waters & under the shades of the Wye, and the visions of nature & the music of [ ] raptures of love . . .

Over and over again, he dwelt on the phases of his love for Mary: the silent lover who had not dared to tell his passion, the suitor, the husband, the father.

& thy past self also, participating every sentiment of thy heart & being, as far as Nature would allow what thou hast been, from the hour of our first walks near Penrith till out last parting at Chester, and till thy wanderings upon Wye, & till this very moment when I am writing, & Thou most probably art thinking of me and losing all sense of the motion of the horse that bears thee, in the tenderness & strength of thy conceptions and wishes, & remembrances. Oh my beloved – but I ought not to trust myself to this senseless & visible sheet of paper; speak for me to thyself, find the evidence of what is passing within me in *thy* heart, in thy mind, in thy steps as they touch the green grass, in thy limbs as they are stretched upon the soft earth; in thy own involuntary sighs & ejaculations, in the trembling of thy hands, in the tottering of thy knees, in the blessings which thy lips pronounce, find it in thy lips themselves, & such kisses as I often give to the empty air, and in the aching of thy bosom, and let a voice speak for me in every thing within thee & without thee. Here I stop & wherefore, – Oh what an age seems it till we shall be again together under the shade of the green trees, by the rippling of the waters, and in that hour – which thou lovest the most the silence the vacancy & the impenetrable gloom of night. Happy Chamber that has been so enriched with the sweet prayers of thy pure bosom; with what gratitude shall I behold it! Ah Mary I must turn my pen from this course.[46]

On 4 June he wrote to tell Mary that his visit to London was at last drawing to a close. He had only duty visits to pay to Christopher at Bocking and the Clarksons at Bury, then in a month's time he would meet her at Hindwell and, together with Thomas, they would return home for a grand family reunion. It was not to be.

The very day he wrote, tragedy struck at Grasmere. Little Catherine died. It was as much a shock to her aunts Dorothy and Sara, who had been looking after her in her parents' absence, as it was to William and Mary. 'For several days the Child had been in the most joyous spirits', wrote Dorothy.

On the Sunday afternoon and the Monday I had been for several hours with Willy and her in the Churchyard and they had run races and played on the very ground where now she lies. I then particularly noticed how little was to be seen of her lameness, and several persons who came up to speak to us while we were there observed how trifling the lameness was, and how thriving and healthy she looked.

Sara had noticed a corresponding improvement in her paralysed hand. The afternoon before she died, Catherine had surprised Sara by turning over a playing card with it and had eaten her dinner with a fork 'as steadily as any Child'. After a supper of porridge, she had run up to bed, 'in such glee striving to get before William, and proud that she was going to sleep in her *Mother's* bed, an unusual treat'. It was not until Johnny went up to join her later that anyone realized anything was wrong. He found that she had been sick and was lying with her eyes fixed. Sara thought she was simply overpowered by the sickness, but Dorothy, who had been present when Catherine had her last seizure, instantly knew what was to come.[47] Fanny, the servant, galloped off immediately on Sara's pony to fetch Scambler, and while they waited his arrival, they tried all the remedies they had applied before. Scambler arrived an hour later, by which time Catherine was completely convulsed down her right side. He examined her eyes, which were also turned towards the right, and announced that the brain was 'very much affected'. When Dorothy asked him if it was more dangerous than the previous attack, he simply replied 'undoubtedly', '& by his manner we saw that he had no hope'.

For hour after hour through that terrible night, Sara, Dorothy and the two servants took turns to nurse the dying child on their knees. As death approached, Sara could bear it no longer and had to leave the room.

> I went down stairs & could hear her moaning & could even fancy she spake – once after she begun she said Aunt Ant or something like it but it was mechanical for she had no sense. I stayed down stairs & walked in the court knowing I could do nothing & fearing to witness the change but at last my anxiety got the better of my fear & I went up & looked at her & saw the film was spread over her eyes D felt that her feet were growing cold & I bade the old woman raise her head a little higher & soon after the noise of phlegm in her chest & her moaning ceased D got up & gave her place to Fanny & the Angel breathed about 20 times after this every breath lower till it died away & seemed to have no struggle at the last her face did not the old woman said move. I have not seen her since but she is beautiful they say as an angel her own sweet countenance with something more heavenly . . . D has had much comfort in looking at her in her present peaceful state. I cannot bear to see her for I hope to forget all but her own dear sweet living face but the countenance of death would I know be never forgotten.[48]

Catherine died at quarter past five on the morning of 4 June 1812. She was three months short of her fourth birthday. Four days later, she was buried in the quiet north-east corner of Grasmere churchyard, beside the river, and under the hawthorn tree where she had played so happily only three days earlier. The little coffin was carried by the mothers of four of the Wordsworths' past and present servants, and followed by Dorothy, Sara and Johnny, the two servants, Fanny and Sarah, and Hartley and Derwent Coleridge. In Dorothy's opinion, 'All who attended her Remains . . . were sincere mourners.'[49]

Somehow the news had to be broken to the bereaved parents. Dorothy and Sara talked the matter over, realized that neither William nor Mary could get to Grasmere in time for the funeral and decided that Mary would be better able to stand the shock if the news was broken to her by her husband. Dorothy wrote to William that afternoon. Forced to keep her own emotions on a tight rein, her letter was brutal in its baldness. 'My dearest Brother,' she began, 'Sara and John and William and I are all in perfect health, but poor Catherine died this morning . . .' Scambler fulfilled his promise and wrote by the same post, briefly describing Catherine's symptoms and the treatment he had applied. 'I hope it will be some consolation to you to know,' he ended his letter, 'that from the first she appe[ared] quite insensible to her sufferings; & that every attention was paid to her that possibly could be'. Sara did her part, writing a long and detailed description of Catherine's last hours. Nominally, it was addressed to Tom Hutchinson, but it was meant for Mary; once she had recovered from the shock of hearing the news, Sara knew her sister would want to know exactly what had happened.[50]

Unfortunately, the thoughtfully laid plans went awry. Dorothy's letter reached the Beaumonts' an hour after William had left and had to be forwarded to Bocking, so it was not until 11 June, a week after Catherine's death and three days after her funeral, that he finally learned the dreadful news. His first impulse was to rush straight to Hindwell, but on his return to London the next day, he realized that it was probably too late. He was right. Sara's letter had already arrived at Hindwell and Mary had been in the room when it was handed to Tom. There was, of course, no way that the news could be kept from her and her reaction was everything they had most feared. Racked with guilt that she had not been there when she was most needed and tortured by the belief that, had she been there, a mother's instinct might have enabled her to save her child, Mary's grief was unassuageable. The terrible irony also now struck her that, when she had written so joyously to William on learning such glowing accounts of Catherine's improved health, her child had already been dead four days.[51]

In London, William had consoled himself with the thought that having his arrival to look forward to would be of far more use to Mary than his actual presence, at least in the first instance. Several days after his arrival, he had to admit that she was

> yet little recovered from the deploreable dejection in which I found her. Her health has suffered: but I clearly see that neither thought nor religion nor the endeavours of friends, can at once quiet a heart that has been disturbed by such an affliction. We must wait patiently and do what we can . . . She suffers more than in the ordinary course of nature from the tender connection and dependence in which this child has long existed with her, or hung upon her maternal care; and I feel that the privation will be a sorrow for life; though I hope at some future period she will be able to draw consolation from her very source of encreased suffering.[52]

The whole family now rallied round the afflicted mother, finding some relief for their own grief in their attempts to help her. Dorothy began her next letter to Hindwell with a reassuring 'We are all well', heavily underlined; Sara was dispatched to Ambleside with a long list of Mary's questions for Scambler; and again and again they all assured her of their unalterable conviction that nothing more could have been done for the child and that, had she survived, she would not have recovered her mental or physical faculties. William tried to persuade Mary to take a tour of Wales to improve her health and spirits before she had to face a return to Grasmere, but she was so afraid she might lose another child in her absence that he could not do so. William struggled hard to maintain at least a façade of calm and resignation. 'I have yet not felt my own sorrow, only I know well that it is to come. – But . . . I do not mean to yield to the emotions of my heart on this sad and unexpected privation', he wrote to Dorothy and Sara, before yielding to fatherly anxiety. 'I long to hear how little Dorothy is and how she is looking – take care of the water, and of fire, and of all dangers; especially for William.'[53]

It was the beginning of July before Mary was well enough to make the journey home. It could not, of course, be a happy homecoming, but it was some comfort to be reunited with her remaining children. Six-year-old Thomas returned with his parents. Living on the farm at Hindwell had suited him down to the ground; he had fished in the pool, ridden in the carts and even helped shear the sheep. Though the suggestion had been made that he should stay on after his parents left, his sister's death made this unthinkable. Dora had returned from Appleby a couple of weeks earlier, and both aunts expressed themselves indebted to Miss Weir for her care. Dora, now almost eight, was still as wayward as ever, but she read prettily, sewed well and was industrious with her lessons. Since her return she had become an inseparable companion to her brothers, looking after Willy and encouraging Johnny in his lessons. Johnny himself had left Grasmere school and on 9 June, just before his ninth birthday, had joined Hartley and Derwent Coleridge and Algernon Montagu at Mr Dawes's school at Ambleside. Instead of being a weekly boarder, however, he walked happily to and from school each day, with his tin bottle over his shoulder and his basket in his hand. Though deeply distressed by Catherine's death, his sensitivity and good sense in his affliction were a great comfort to his aunts. Two-year-old Willy, whose most recent illness had been kept from his mother (though it had been sufficiently alarming to send Dorothy scurrying off to Ambleside to see Scambler), was fully recovered and as lively as ever.[54]

The Wordsworths tried hard to pick up the threads of their life. A couple of days after William and Mary's return, Dorothy went off to Eusemere to spend four days with her cousin Captain John Wordsworth and almost a fortnight with her 'aunt', Elizabeth Rawson, who was visiting the Marshalls at Watermillock, their new country home on Ullswater. Only a couple of days after Dorothy's return to Grasmere, Mary Monkhouse arrived from Hindwell on a visit that would last three months. Her presence was a comfort to them all. She was 'a *perfect Woman*', Dorothy said admiringly, 'the only one I ever knew – except Mrs Rawson. I *know* not one fault she has'. Mary brought good news to cheer the mourning family. She was engaged to be married to her cousin, Mary's brother Tom, and the wedding would take place at Grasmere in October.[55]

There was the usual influx of annual summer visitors: Samuel Tillbrooke and his friend Charles Blomfield, from Cambridge, who stayed at Robert Newton's lodging house next to the Parsonage, shared the usual round of tea-drinkings, dinners and excursions. Blomfield, a future bishop of London, also provided them with a rare treat by taking duty at Grasmere church in place of the incumbent, Thomas Jackson, who, in Dorothy's acerbic phrase, 'is a worthy man – very good as a Steward or a Farmer; but totally unfit to preach or read prayers'. When they left, Dr Bell took over their lodgings. Taking swift advantage of the Wordsworth secretarial pool, he soon had Dorothy constantly employed in helping him to arrange and correct his various publications for reissue as a single work. On 8 August Bell carried William, Mary, Dorothy, Dora and Johnny off to Keswick to pay a visit to Greta Hall. They left Dora there, wild with joy at the prospect of staying with her friends Sara Coleridge and Edith Southey, and brought Herbert Southey back to stay with Thomas, who was his great friend. This summer, too, Rogers accompanied Sharp on his annual visit to the Lakes; they stayed at Low-wood, but were frequent and welcome visitors at the Parsonage.[56]

Despite all these distractions, and the need to exert herself with all the household concerns, Mary's spirits did not improve. She flatly refused to go on a family excursion to High Hacket with Tillbrooke, Blomfield and Sharp, preferring to remain alone at home, because High Hacket was where Catherine had first begun to recover from the whooping cough. Every day she could not fail to be reminded of her loss: not only were the house and garden full of memories of the child, but from them she could see the corner of the churchyard where the small grave, with its simple headstone, lay. William and Dorothy were deeply concerned that Mary's usually sunny nature failed to reassert itself. 'I would give the world that she had been at home –', Dorothy wrote miserably to Catherine Clarkson, 'for I am convinced that she would have felt very differently . . . If she had been here I think that she would have had more power to exercise her reason in looking at her loss.'[57]

At the end of October, the Monkhouses and Hutchinsons gathered at Grasmere for what was truly a family wedding. At the last minute, there was a crisis. The bride's brother Tom, who was to give her away, was recalled to London by his partner because of a threatened bankruptcy. It proved to be a false alarm, but the bride was naturally disappointed. 'I was grieved on your account, as well as mine,' she told him,

> because if you had staid you would have seen so much of William's goodness, and how nice and entertaining he can be some times, and I fear from what you saw of him you will have rather an unfavourable impression upon your mind – he apologized to me for his strange behaviour on the day of your first arrival at Grasmere, and said he had been very uncomfortable about it ever since –

By way of compensation, on the eve of the wedding William presented Mary with 'too valuable a present for any body to share in', a sonnet he had written specially for the occasion, praising the quiet simplicity of the wedding and the bride herself. The torrential rains which had completely flooded the vale miraculously ceased on the morning of the wedding and on 2 November Mary and Tom were married in Grasmere church by the curate, Thomas Powley. John Wilson represented Tom Monkhouse, and he and William witnessed the signing of the marriage register. The newlyweds, accompanied by Joanna, then set off for Hindwell, leaving the Wordsworths to enjoy a wedding dinner with the Wilsons, followed by tea with the Crumps and the Kings.[58]

William's unexplained 'strange behaviour' might have been the result of his struggle to compose the sonnet, but it is more probably attributable to his preoccupation with his financial affairs. At the beginning of September he had received an unexpected letter from Sir George Beaumont. Lord Lonsdale was anxious to assist William in securing a suitable post, but was concerned that the opportunity of doing so might be very distant. Until that moment arrived, it was his wish to offer William an annuity of £100. Knowing how proud William was about accepting anything that smacked of charity, he had made his proposal through their mutual friend, who proffered his 'sincere opinion that you may accept it without degradation, circumstanced as you are'. To sugar the pill, Beaumont also suggested that a refusal would give Lonsdale 'more pain than you would be willing to inflict'.[59]

It was a subtle argument, not to mention a tempting offer, but Beaumont was wasting his time. William would not even consider it, though he was grateful for this evidence of Lonsdale's willingness to help him. An explanation that the sum had been carefully fixed upon as being large enough to add to the Wordsworths' comfort, but small enough not to make William feel obligated or dependent, did nothing to change his mind. He might need Lonsdale's help to obtain an office, but he was determined that he should earn his own income from that office. It was a measure of how serious his intentions were that he now wrote to Stuart, asking to be informed of any likely vacancies and assuring him that, if the salary were adequate and the duties 'what I am equal to, without being under the necessity of withdrawing myself wholly from Literature', he had no objection to leaving the Lakes. 'Of course', he added, 'all this is *between ourselves*.'[60]

Stuart identified several possibilities, so, early in November, William decided to go over to Lowther to seek Lord Lonsdale's assistance in applying for them. Hoping that a short excursion might benefit Mary, he took her, and Dora, with him as far as Keswick, where they all stayed together for a few days. It proved to be a pleasant visit, 'parties for ever visiting all the gentry round', but it failed to raise Mary's spirits. As soon as she returned to Grasmere, she went straight to the churchyard 'to throw herself upon the poor Child's grave –', Sara sadly noted, 'so that we had no cheerful meeting'.[61]

Worse was to come. The Wordsworths' third child, Thomas, had always been delicate and whooping cough had left him with a permanent weakness in the chest. Indeed, the previous year, when Sara saw him for the first time in eighteen months, she had observed that 'he looks so weak and feeble that I often fancy he will not live'. Nine days after his parents' return, Thomas developed a cough and showed all the symptoms of measles, which were rife in Keswick and Kendal. For several days he ran a high fever, but on the morning of 1 December, when Richard Scambler called, his temperature had returned to normal and he was thought to be going on as well as possible. An hour after the apothecary left, Thomas was seized with a violent coughing fit and sickness. Shaking with fear and panic, he cried out to his mother, 'I shall die, I shall die'. William rushed off to fetch Scambler back; in his absence, his son grew calmer and declared that he was getting better, but it was obvious he was failing fast. When William returned from Ambleside, Sara met him at the door to tell him that there was no hope. The little boy died just before six in the evening.[62]

After a sleepless night, William rose early next morning and set off to intercept Dorothy, who was on her way to Keswick from Watermillock, where she had spent the previous fortnight with the Marshalls. He met the coach at Threlkeld, broke the news to her and brought her straight home in a state of collapse. This time it was Mary who displayed what her husband admiringly called 'striking fortitude'. 'She received me with the calmness of an Angel –', Dorothy wrote; 'she comforted me, – and in truth I was ashamed of my own weakness; and bitterly reproached myself that I could not bear the sorrow as she did.' That evening, William somehow found the strength to write brief businesslike notes to their closest friends informing them of this second tragic loss. Only to Southey, who had been such a comforter in the dark days after John's death and was himself the father of Thomas's best friend, could William betray a glimpse of the emotion he was struggling to keep at bay.

For myself dear Southey I dare not say in what state of mind I am; I loved the Boy with the utmost love of which my soul is capable, and he is taken from me – yet in the agony of my spirit in surrendering such a treasure I feel a thousand times richer than if I had never possessed it. God comfort and save you and all our friends and us all from a repetition of such trials – O Southey feel for me! If you are not afraid of the complaint, I ought to have said if you have had it come over to us![63]

On 5 December Thomas Wordsworth was buried beside his sister in Grasmere churchyard. All the family attended the coffin to the grave, except his Aunt Sara, who could not face a second funeral in six months and was literally ill with grief. 'Nothing . . . can sustain us under our affliction but reliance in God's Goodness,' William wrote the next day,

and a firm belief that it is for *our* Good, as we cannot doubt it was for his, that he should be removed from this sinful and troublesome world. He was too good for us; we did not deserve such a blessing – and we must endeavour to correct and amend every thing that is wrong in us and our bitter sorrow will in time become sweet and kindly, and never such, at no moment such, as we should wish to part with –[64]

William's hard-won resignation to the will of God was about to be tested to the full. No sooner had he penned this statement of faith than all three of his remaining children were struck down with measles. Determined to take no risks, the entire family packed their bags and left immediately for Ambleside, so that they could be near Scambler. For the rest of the month, they lived in an agony of hope and fear, as they had to contemplate losing first one child, then another. Just when it seemed that they had weathered the storm, and were about to return to Grasmere for

Christmas, Willy had a relapse. As Johnny and Dora were both recuperating, it was thought better to keep them out of the way of the sick child and give them a change of air, so Sara and Dorothy took them home. William and Mary were therefore left to spend an anxious and exhausting week in lodgings, nursing a desperately ill toddler.[65]

While they were at Ambleside and Willy was at the height of the measles, William received a letter from Lord Lonsdale informing him that there was no prospect, within any foreseeable period, of obtaining any of the offices suggested by Stuart. The new Tory Prime Minister, Lord Liverpool, had expressed 'the strongest inclination' to assist William, but candidly said he saw no means of doing so, except by presenting him with a pension. Lonsdale's own offer still remained open 'which you can revert to whenever you think proper, or find occasion'. William was too distraught even to consider the matter. 'Were I to trust to my present feelings I should indeed have no difficulty,' he explained, 'but oppressed with sorrow and distracted with anxiety as I am, I fear that in a calmer state of mind I might hereafter disapprove of a determination formed at once under such circumstances.' Once Johnny and Dora were on the mend, William turned again to Lonsdale's letter. Though he nominally canvassed the opinions of his friends, his own preference was obvious, for as early as June he had identified what seemed to him to be the ideal government office. The post of Distributor of Stamps for Westmorland, based at Appleby, was held by one of his own distant relatives, a seventy-year-old man who had recently suffered a paralytic stroke. Death, or incapacity, was certain to ensure a vacancy sooner or later. '400£ per ann. in Westmorland would be to me more desirable than 800 in London, and I must rest content with that expectation; for as to the pension, I do not see how I can accept it'.[66] His friends were less scrupulous. Stuart sent a typically robust response.

> You hesitate more at taking a Pension, I think, than is reasonable. What is the difference between a Pension & such a Place as you describe? The one would lay you as much under an obligation to the Government or the Ministry as the other but the pension would be more honourable to a literary man, I think, & more consistent with his character & pursuits. Surely, surely a Literary Man might most honorably deserve a Pension for his writings?. . . If you dread the reproach of a certain class of scandalous writers and politicians, that would meet you on the ground of Place quite as much as Pension. If a man does nothing dishonorable to obtain a Pension I have no objection to his taking it . . .

Beaumont had a less forceful argument, but one that spoke to the heart. Were he in William's position, he would accept Lonsdale's offer without hesitation: 'I had far rather receive it from him than from government'.[67]

Battered and beaten by the events of recent months, and cowed by the threat to what remained of his family, William gave up the fight. On 27 December he wrote to Lord Lonsdale and accepted the proposed annuity, until the Distributorship became available. He would, he declared, 'rather . . . owe any addition to my income, required by my present occasions, to your Lordship's friendship than to the Government, or to any other quarter where it was not in my power to return what in the common sentiments of men would be deemed an equivalent'.[68]

For the second time in six months, William and Mary had to face a dismal homecoming to Grasmere. Dorothy and Sara did everything they could to make it more cheerful, but their efforts were in vain. Mary's courage and strength, which had borne up under her son's death and throughout the children's illnesses, now deserted her completely. 'She is as thin as it is possible to be except when the body is worn out by slow disease, and the dejection of her countenance is afflicting', Dorothy wrote miserably; 'wherever we look we are reminded of some pretty action of those innocent Children – especially Thomas whose life latterly has been connected with the church-yard in the most affecting manner – there he played daily amongst his schoolfellows, and daily tripped through it to school, a place which was his pride and delight'. The unaccustomed stillness of home and the unavoidable view of the churchyard oppressed all their spirits. William grew 'very thin, and at times I think he looks ten years older since the death of Thomas', but Mary seemed to have given herself up to her grief. 'I feel that it knits about the heart strings and will wear her away if there is not a turn in her feelings.'[69] It was obvious to them all that they would have to leave Grasmere.

16. *The Excursion*

On 8 January 1813 William received a letter from Lord Lonsdale, enclosing a draft for £100. It could not have come at a more opportune moment, and it was to transform the Wordsworths' lives in ways far beyond its material value. In writing to thank Lonsdale (and also to reject his offer to double the amount by backdating the gift to the previous January), William explained that 'you have been the means of relieving my mind, in a manner that, I am sure, will be gratifying to your Heart . . . I have found it absolutely necessary that we should Quit a place, which, by recalling to our minds at every moment the losses we have sustained in the course of the last year, would grievously retard our progress towards that tranquillity of mind which it is our duty to aim at.' The money would enable them to move 'to a most desirable Residence soon to be vacant at Rydale' in the certain knowledge that they could now afford the higher rent. The residence was Rydal Mount, 'a place that ten years ago I should have almost danced with Joy if I could have dreamed it would ever be ours', according to Dorothy. The current owners, the Norths, had sold it to their wealthy aristocratic neighbours, the Le Fleming family of Rydal Hall, and would ever leave in February. As it would then stand empty until May Day, the Wordsworths hoped to be allowed to move in immediately, 'and if our pleadings for an afflicted Mother do not avail', Dorothy added, much to her brother's disapproval, 'I shall give them up as reprobate spirits'.[1]

Lonsdale's money would also allow William to return to his poetry, 'that species of intellectual exertion which only I find sufficiently powerful to rouze me'. Until his son's death, William had been working rather half-heartedly on what he called 'a task undertaken for profit', which was probably his expanded guide to the Lakes. He had even sought the assistance of his friend, Rogers, in finding an appropriate publisher. Now he could set aside that work and return, with a clear conscience and palpable relief, to his unprofitable poetry.[2]

It is significant that, at this juncture, he went back to *The Recluse*, perhaps hoping to find some consolation for himself in his great philosophical poem. While Mary wept inconsolably from morning to night and Dorothy poured out her grief uncontrollably in page after page to her friends, William retreated into himself. His own sufferings were still too raw to commit to paper, so instead he explored them at one remove, adding a large section to the autobiography of the Solitary, describing the deaths of his son, daughter and wife, and his subsequent retreat into the mountains to live a hermit-like existence, which excluded not only all human contact but also all human emotion. Much of this section was eventually omitted from publication within the long poem – it was too personal and painful and therefore emotionally out of step – but it was reshaped into, and inspired other, shorter poems, which were to form a lasting memorial to his lost children. Included for the first time were the lovely lines he had written about Catherine, after her return from the seaside holiday, *Characteristics of a Child Three Years Old.*

> Loving she is, and tractable, though wild;
> And Innocence hath privilege in her
> To dignify arch looks and laughing eyes;
> And feats of cunning; and the pretty round
> Of trespasses, affected to provoke
> Mock-chastisement and partnership in play.
> . . . this happy Creature of herself
> Is all-sufficient; solitude to her
> Is blithe society, who fills the air
> With gladness and involuntary songs.[3]

In describing the response of the Solitary's wife to the loss of her children, William drew a touching portrayal of Mary's initial 'striking fortitude', followed by her collapse.

> The eminence whereon her spirit stood,
> Mine was unable to attain. Immense
> The space that severed us!
> . . . overcome with speechless gratitude,
> And, with a holier love inspired, I looked
> On her – at once superior to my woes
> And partner of my loss. – O heavy change!
> Dimness o'er this clear luminary crept
> Insensibly; – the immortal and divine
> Yielded to mortal reflux; her pure glory,
> As from the pinnacle of worldly state
> Wretched ambition drops astounded, fell
> Into a gulf obscure of silent grief,

And keen heart-anguish – of itself ashamed,
Yet obstinately cherishing itself:

William's own fears for Mary were reflected in the fate he assigned the Solitary's wife, who, consumed by her sorrow, 'melted from my arms; And left me, on this earth, disconsolate!' In lines which were an offshoot of these, but were, as he later admitted privately, a faithful portrayal of Mary's 'feelings & habits after the loss of our two children within half a year of each other', he gave a sensitively observed and deeply felt description of the effect his wife's grief had on their remaining children.

. . . Full oft the Boy,
Now first acquainted with distress and grief,
Shrunk from his Mother's presence, shunned with fear
Her sad approach, and stole away to find,
In his known haunts of joy where'er he might,
A more congenial object. But, as time
Softened her pangs and reconciled the child
To what he saw, he gradually returned,
Like a scared Bird encouraged to renew
A broken intercourse;[4]

The greatest of all the poems William wrote as a result of his children's deaths – in fact, one of his finest by any standards – was the exquisite sonnet he wrote about Catherine 'long after her death'. It stands in sharp contrast to the histrionics of de Quincey, for instance, who burst into tears on seeing William for the first time after Catherine's death '& seemed to be more affected than the father'. William had always found such public displays of emotion distasteful and had a healthy contempt for what he called the 'false sensibility' of the age. In this sonnet, more perhaps than any other, he gives us a poignant glimpse of a heart that was no less feeling for not being worn on his sleeve.

Surprised by joy – impatient as the Wind
I turned to share the transport – Oh! with whom
But Thee, deep buried in the silent tomb,
That spot which no vicissitude can find?
Love, faithful love, recalled thee to my mind –
But how could I forget thee? Through what power,
Even for the least division of an hour,
Have I been so beguiled as to be blind
To my most grievous loss! – that thought's return
Was the worst pang that sorrow ever bore,
Save one, one only, when I stood forlorn,

> Knowing my heart's best treasure was no more;
> That neither present time, nor years unborn
> Could to my sight that heavenly face restore.

The loss of two of his beloved children in such a short space of time, and so unexpectedly, affected William profoundly at the time, but it was to be an abiding and ineradicable sorrow. Forty years later, he would describe to Aubrey de Vere 'the details of their illnesses with an exactness and impetuosity of troubled excitement, such as might have been expected if the bereavement had taken place but a few weeks before'.[5]

One of the immediate consequences of the bereavement was that they all became understandably over-anxious. Dorothy wrote to Richard, entreating him to visit. 'Human life is short – year passes on after year and we do not meet, and I wish you to see and know your Nephews and Niece. The late warnings make us feel daily, the uncertainty of their life and ours'. William ended a letter to Montagu, 'God preserve [you] and all yours, and leave me what I now possess though I feel by a slender hold.' As a consequence, they also became over-protective of the remaining children. Johnny was removed from Mr Dawes's school at Ambleside and sent back to the greatly inferior village school across the churchyard. Dora too became a pupil there. Every ailment, however minor, became a cause for panic, and Willy, being the youngest, was particularly mollycoddled. 'It would distress you to see how a pale look of that childs has the power to disturb his father', Sara wrote more than two years later; '... he will scarcely suffer the wind of heaven to come near him & watches him the day through.'[6]

A more insidious trait, of which they were completely unaware, was that the adults, particularly Dorothy, could not forbear making comparisons between the living and the dead. Catherine and Thomas became apotheosized into perfect children, their faults (of which she had complained frequently when they were alive) forgotten, their undoubted virtues magnified into saintliness. Dora's thoughtless, wilful ways would be contrasted with Catherine's affectionate, sunny nature and poor Johnny's duncery with Thomas's belatedly discovered book-learning and quickness of intellect, which had manifested itself only in the last six months of his life.[7] Both children grew up to feel instinctively that they had somehow let the family down by living when their 'better' siblings had died. This was by no means intentional. It was not even completely true, for they were both deeply loved for themselves. Nevertheless, the feeling was there and the Wordsworths were at fault in failing to eradicate it. Johnny would never completely rid himself of the belief that his failure to shine intellectually was a disappointment to his father, and would become a sullen, jealous and dissatisfied man. Dora reacted by trying to become the perfect dutiful daughter, even to the point of sacrificing her own happiness by refusing to marry the man she loved, so that she could stay at home with her parents.

A further, indirect, consequence of the bereavement was that it became clear that the previous year's reconciliation with Coleridge had merely papered over irreparable cracks in their friendship. William had written to him immediately after Thomas's death and had received a confused and self-involuted, but well-meant, reply, the gist of which appeared to be that he would come to them as soon as possible. Rehearsals for his play *Remorse*, a reworking of *Osorio*, the tragedy he had written some sixteen years earlier, were about to begin and 'upon this depends my best Hopes of leaving Town after Christmas & living among you as long as I live'. In January Dorothy was 'confident he will come', but the weeks stretched into months and he did not. Both William and Dorothy wrote again, saying that nothing would do William so much good as his company and conversation. Their pleas went unheeded. When they finally learned that he had left town and gone to the seaside, they knew he would never come.[8]

Catherine Clarkson was incensed at this insensitivity to the Wordsworths' plight. 'If I do not hear better accounts from Grasmere soon – I shall make an effort to go & see them,' she wrote to Robinson.

> I think they will be better when they get into their new house & perhaps better than if they had moved into it immediately – Indeed I see in the effects of these losses upon them the evil of living so entirely out of the world . . . If human life cd be an uninterrupted scene of Happiness – then retirement in a beautiful country with books & a few friends & inmates wd be enough & more than enough – But . . . Our friends have no *acquaintances* – They have neighbours – But in their present circumstances they need the sight of *equals* who are not intimate friends – in whose company they must put some restraint upon themselves and in return they wd be won from their sadness by hearing of other things.

The move to Rydal Mount would supply just that need Catherine had so perceptively identified. Just as Dorothy feared, however, the 'rancorous' Norths indeed proved to be reprobates, refusing to allow the Wordsworths to move in after their own departure, and it was probably 12 May before they were at last able to leave Grasmere and enter the house which was to be their home for the rest of their lives.[9]

Rydal Mount was, and is, a lovely house, with a delightful split personality. The oldest part is a simple sixteenth-century farm cottage, little more than one-up, one-down, with three-foot-thick stone walls and what might politely be called random mullioned windows. In the mid-eighteenth century it was transformed into a gentleman's house by its owners, the Knotts, who added a west wing twice as large as the original building. This wing, facing due south, was typically Georgian: neat and symmetrical, with two large sash windows either side of the central glazed folding doors, which opened out on to a terrace, and five identical ones above. By thus reorienting the house, the Knotts took full advantage of the incomparable view. The house stands on the lower slopes of Rydal Fell, a few hundred yards from the road from Ambleside to Grasmere, which snakes along the valley bottom. All the main windows therefore look out over the beautiful little

Vale of Rydal, towards Ambleside, which is hidden behind the fold in the hills, where the craggy peaks of Wansfell Pike and Loughrigg Fell fall away to reveal the distant grey glimmer of Lake Windermere. Immediately in front of the house, across the terrace, is an ancient mound of indeterminate age and origin, which was traditionally believed to be a ninth-century Northumbrian observation post.[10] From this spot, which was William's pride and joy, there is a panoramic view over the ancient woodlands of Rydal Hall to the east, the parkland and lush pasture running down to the sparkling waters of the River Rothay and, to the west, one of the most beautiful of all the lakes, Rydal Water, a limpid pool reflecting in mirror image the precipitous slopes of the fells which cradle it and scattered with tiny rocky islands. (Grasmere lake, which lies just beyond Rydal Water, is clearly visible only from the westernmost end of the garden.) Looming above and around on every side are the fells, dwarfing the scenes below. If one imagines them as a giant clawed hand poised above Patterdale, then Fairfield, rising to 2,864 feet high, would be the back of the hand, from which extend the crooked thumb, Wansfell Pike, and the four fingers of Red Screes, High Pike, Heron Pike and Stone Arthur. Kirkstone Pass, the main route to Ullswater, lay between thumb and first finger, Rydal Mount between second and third, and the cottage at Town End between third and fourth. Facing Rydal Mount was Loughrigg Fell, standing in moated isolation, with its distinctive grey rocky outcrops, almost 2,000 feet high; walking out on to the terrace after tea to watch the sun set and the evening star rise behind its parapets would become a daily ritual for William which never lost its potency to move him.

The move from the Parsonage at Grasmere to Rydal Mount was both literally and metaphorically one from darkness into light. 'I was the last person who left the [Parsonage] yesterday evening', Dorothy wrote. 'It seemed as quiet as the grave ... the house only reminded me of desolation, gloom, emptiness, and chearless silence.' Next morning at Rydal Mount, however, the weather was 'delightful, and the place a paradise'. As Sara smugly commented a few weeks later, 'It is the admiration of every body – the *crack* spot, and the envy, of the whole neighbourhood.'[11] Curiously, the Wordsworths had never seen the inside of the house until they moved into it and, though they were mildly disappointed that it did not quite live up to their expectations, everything was neat and comfortable.

Eager for an outlet for their pent-up energies and a distraction from their personal sorrows, they flung themselves into home-making. William wisely decided that it was time for a little extravagance. 'We are going to have a *Turkey*!!!! carpet – in the dining-room, and a Brussels in William's study', Dorothy reported in high glee to Catherine Clarkson. 'You stare, and the simplicity of the dear Town End Cottage comes before your eyes, and you are tempted to say, "are they changed, are they setting up for fine Folks?"' Thrift was the useful excuse: a Turkey carpet would last four times longer than a Scotch one, so would be cheaper in the end. Even Mary and Dorothy balked at the idea of buying a Brussels carpet as well, but William had a fancy to make his study smart: 'Our Master was all for the Brussels and to him we yielded'. With a bookcase, some chairs from Allan Bank, newly painted black, a writing table, new curtains and Sir George Beaumont's pictures on the walls, it looked 'very neat'. Economy was satisfied by purchasing the carpets cheaply in London, through Tom Monkhouse, and the furniture at local sales. The excitement of attending the auctions and bidding for bargains against the wealthy John Harden and the acquisitive Miss Green was in itself a tonic to them all. They stayed till the bitter end, walking home by moonlight from Dove Nest proudly carrying their breakable purchases, a decanter and glass and a gilt-framed mirror, while Fanny, their servant, drove a full cart-load home. Though they tried not to get carried away, like most bidders they ended up with far more chairs than they knew what to do with. Dorothy's pleasure in these activities is evident in her racy accounts, very differently written from the tearful outpourings of earlier in the year. Mary benefited too. At the end of August she was still only 'at times in tolerable spirits i.e. when she is obliged to exert herself – but when she is alone she seems to have gained nothing towards subduing her affliction'. A month later, Dorothy observed, she was looking better and in good spirits, 'the sales were the very thing for her'.[12]

The Wordsworths were able to justify their unusual profligacy by the fact that William had, at last, secured the post he had earmarked as the most suitable for his purposes. Wilkin, the current Distributor of Stamps, had been unable to resume his duties after his stroke; when he discovered that his clerk was a drunkard who had been neglecting the business, he agreed to retire, on the customary understanding that he would receive, as a pension, an annuity for life of £100 from his successor. There was no official salary, but William had been led to believe the annual profits would be between £400 and £500, so he accepted Wilkin's terms. On 27 March the Treasury approved William's appointment, on Lord Lonsdale's nomination, as Distributor of Stamps for Westmorland, Whitehaven and the Penrith area of Cumberland. William signed a personal bond on 26 April for £15,000, forfeitable for malpractice or maladministration, and, with Lord Lonsdale and Sir George Beaumont as his sureties for a further £8,000, he officially assumed his duties.[13] These were not particularly onerous, for the stamps were not postage stamps but sheets of stamped paper, issued by the Treasury, upon which legal documents were written and newspapers printed. The day-to-day business of issuing them and receiving payment was handled by sub-distributors throughout the area. William was required to act as an intermediary between them and the Treasury, overseeing his subordinates, ensuring that they had an adequate supply of stamped papers and accounting for the money raised to the Board of Stamps. He had to make a quarterly return, which entailed visiting each of his sub-distributors, auditing their accounts and forwarding the receipts to London. Legacy receipts, which often involved large sums of money, had to be made up monthly. The accountancy side of the business could all be safely delegated to a clerk and William was extraordinarily fortunate, right at the outset, in finding John Carter. Competent and entirely trustworthy, he remained in the Wordsworths' employment for forty-three years, becoming such a trusted friend and intimate of the family that he was even appointed executor of their wills. Bizarrely, he combined his Stamp duties with the role of gardener and general handyman at Rydal Mount, as well as acting as an amanuensis for William's poetic output.[14]

It would have been all too easy for William to have turned the post into a sinecure, and it is to his credit that he did not. He took both his duties and his responsibilities very seriously. Obliged to keep a supply of stamped paper and money at Rydal Mount, he ensured that it was kept locked in a designated chest and that it was never left unattended. If he had to be absent, he made sure that a member of the family was in his place, refusing even to leave Carter in sole charge without prior authority from the Stamp Office. Sixteen years after taking up office, William was able to boast that '24 hours have not elapsed, save once, for a very few days, without myself, or one of my nearest connections being present'. He was equally scrupulous in ensuring that his sub-distributors were as conscientious as himself, taking particular care over their appointment. If necessary, he was prepared to defy even the mighty Lowthers, to whom he owed his own post, by sacking one of their candidates, whose expensive habits and disposition 'rendered it very improbable that he could resist the temptation of public money, passing through his hands', and substituting his own choice.[15]

The erstwhile poet thus became a government tax collector. It was an irony that William himself was the first to acknowledge, referring sarcastically to himself in a letter to Wrangham as 'your *esteemed* friend Mr Wordsworth, that *popular* poet, Stamp-Collector for Westmorland &c.'[16] While he was able to see the humour in the situation, many of his idealistic young admirers could not. Keats, Byron, Shelley, the rising generation of poets, regarded it as an act of betrayal: they accused him of being a political turncoat, abandoning his youthful radicalism and becoming a Tory hireling. As Stuart had prophesied, few could see the difference between accepting a government place and a government pension. Even today it is still used as a stick with which to beat his reputation. But what else could he have done? He was no longer the young man who could cheerfully accept privation and difficulty for himself and a sister who willingly shared them with him. He had a wife and dependent children to support and, however high his poetic calling, he believed it was 'his duty to turn to some meaner employment' to provide for them. That he chose to earn money rather than live on the bounty of politicians or private patrons ought to be a matter for congratulation, not reproach. The Wordsworths themselves were 'not much rejoiced' about the appointment, fearing that the duties might prove a distraction from William's poetry, but they accepted it as a practical necessity. Their friends, however, were delighted. 'It will relieve the females from a good deal of hard work which they have performed most cheerfully – but wh[ich] has certainly at times been prejudicial to them . . . and what is the greatest good of all it will release Wordsworths mind from all anxiety about money', was Catherine Clarkson's over-optimistic verdict.[17]

Throughout the spring and summer, William was constantly occupied in 'dancing about the Country' in the performance of his new duties. By the middle of

September, Dorothy was complaining that he had done nothing else for weeks and had been away from home two-thirds of the time. Fortunately, both she and Mary were too busy to repine, for they were inundated with visitors. In addition to all the Ambleside gentry coming to pay their house-warming visits, there was the usual flood of summer visitors. 'Were I to give you a list of the folks we have had & our consequent engagements it would make a list as long as that of Crossthwaite's Museum', Sara told her sister-in-law. Among them were many old friends: from London came Stoddart and his wife, Sharp, Stuart and his eighteen-year-old bride ('more like Father & Daughter than Husband & Wife' was Sara's acerbic comment); from Cambridge Tillbrooke; from Keswick the Calverts, the Coleridges, Southey's friend Miss Barker and his sister-in-law Eliza Fricker; and from Leeds the Marshalls. Rather less welcome were the first-time visitors, Lord Lonsdale's younger son, Henry Lowther, and his bride, who dined at Rydal Mount; Robert Blakeney, 'a mountain of vanity' cordially loathed by the Wordsworth women, who was Secretary and Treasurer to the Whitehaven Harbour Trustees, and therefore one of William's new business acquaintances; and Dr Henry Parry, the Inspector of the Stamp Office, who stayed several days and turned out to be a perfectly pleasant man, though he confirmed the Wordsworths' worst suspicions, that Wilkin had inflated the value of the Distributorship. Already it looked as though William would clear only £100 a year, after paying Wilkin's pension and Carter's salary, instead of the £200 or £300 he had expected.[18]

Family visitors were also very much in evidence. Twenty-three-year-old William Crackanthorpe, son of the hated Uncle Christopher, came to stay in July with his sisters. Much to everyone's surprise, the younger generation of 'Cousin Cracken crokes', as Willy called them, proved very likeable. 'I was as much prejudiced against them all as any body could be before they came –', Sara confessed, 'but it is entirely removed'. The purpose of the visit was not entirely social, though it did coincide with the Regatta. Crackanthorpe was about to go abroad and was anxious to settle his late father's debts to the Wordsworths, incurred during the years he had acted as their guardian and administrator of their father's estate. As a result of this visit, both Dorothy and William wrote to Richard, urging him to send a statement of the account. For once they got a swift reply, possibly because the debt now amounted to almost £1,000 and most of it was due to Richard personally. A final settlement was reached by the end of the year.[19]

Early in September Elizabeth, the wife of William's cousin Richard Wordsworth of Branthwaite, her son, John, and three daughters came to stay. The Wordsworths had a particular liking and empathy for one of the latter, Mary Peake. She had visited them earlier in the year, when they were still at Grasmere, and had been full of hope and joy because her husband, captain of the Royal Navy frigate *Peacock*, had just received a posting which would enable him to spend several years on shore. Before he could get home, his ship was destroyed in enemy action, and the same cannonball which killed him wounded Mary's fifteen-year-old brother, the same John Wordsworth who now visited Rydal Mount. It could not be anything but a painful visit for all concerned, reviving memories of the death at sea of their own John, but it was a salutary reminder that others had suffered as much, if not more, than themselves. Mary and her siblings stayed a fortnight, but Dorothy, the youngest sister, became a member of the Rydal Mount household till the following summer. 'A good girl' of whom they all became very fond, she seemed like an older sister to the Wordsworth children. Though very backward in her books, she proved to be a steadying influence on Dora, and Dorothy found the two girls far easier to teach than she had ever found her restless niece alone.[20]

The frenetic activity of this first summer at Rydal Mount proved beneficial to them all. 'My employment I find salutory to me,' William told Wrangham, 'and of consequence in a pecuniary point of view, as my *Literary* employments bring me no emolument, nor promise any.' This did not prevent him writing poetry, however, for Sara complained at the end of August that he was 'over head & ears in his verses, so what with them, & company, & stamps, he is more busy than agreeable'. Dorothy, too, while admitting that the 'bustling summer' had been better for them all, especially Mary, than 'perfect stillness would have been', could not help regretting that she had been too busy to read.

> I feel that much of the knowledge which I had formerly gained from Books has slipped from me, and it is grievous to think that hardly one new idea has come in by that means. This in itself would be no great evil, but the sorrows of this life weaken the memory so much that I find reading of far less use than it used to be to me, and if it were not that my feelings were as much alive as ever there would be a growing tendency for the mind to barrenness.[21]

By the beginning of October, however, they were able to look forward with some relief to 'long evenings and winter's quiet'. The women had comparatively few domestic chores. The house was fully fitted out and, as they were now so much closer to Ambleside, Johnny had returned to Mr Dawes's school with Hartley and Derwent Coleridge and Algernon Montagu. Willy, now three years old, had also begun to attend school; like his sister, he proved to be quick and clever, but not fond of his books. Only Dora and Dorothy were still being taught at home, spending four hours a day in lessons with Sara and the elder Dorothy. The Coleridge boys were regular weekend visitors, but Algernon's elder brother, Basil, was 'a constant dish with us every evening'. Basil was now almost twenty-one. After leaving school, he had become a midshipman in the navy, but hated every minute of the two years he served at sea. In May, after months of importuning his father, he had obtained his discharge on the grounds of ill-health, leaving 'with an excellent character from his officers, but with scarcely any hope of life'. Having exhausted the goodwill of all the friends and relatives to whose care he had since been dispatched, Basil was sent back to his old lodgings at Ambleside, intending to renew his classical studies under the watchful eye of the Wordsworths. Basil gave his father the impression that he would 'atone' to William for the malicious stories he had spread about the way he had been treated by the poet and his sister as a boy, which may account for his daily visits. If so, either he must have been a consummate actor or he failed, for his letters home reveal that he had nothing but contempt for the Wordsworths and their friends, and preferred the company of the Lloyds.[22]

At the end of November Sara returned to Rydal Mount, after an absence of three months at Stockton. Mary had been loath to part with her. 'Death has made such a coward of my poor sister that she cannot hear [bear?] the notion of any one of us leaving her for any length of time', Sara had written a few days before her departure. Only a sense of duty to her brother Henry had dragged Sara away, but her absence made them all realize how much she had become part of the family. Their sufferings had brought them together in a way nothing else could. The two aunts had become fast friends. Sara had been an 'inexpressible comfort . . . to all of us, but to me especially', Dorothy wrote. 'I know not how I could have borne up if I had not had her when Catherine died – and I could never have kept up without her against Mary's depression of mind'. On their wedding anniversary, William and Mary both wrote to her: 'every year whether fraught with joy or sorrow has brought with it additional cause why I should thank God for my connection with your family', William wrote, ending his letter, 'wishing ardently to have you here again'. Sara herself was miserable at Stockton, declaring that she had caught the '*indifferentism*' which affected everyone in that corner of the world.

I fancy that all people here are affected with it and that it is contagious – but perhaps the cause exists in myself; for living as I do with those who think and feel exactly as I do upon most subjects and are interested by the same things no wonder when I get among another set that I should fancy that they are interested about *nothing* when I find them actually dead to all that concerns me –[23]

Glad though they were to see her again, when they discovered that she had stayed with Miss Weir at Appleby, where there had been an epidemic of scarlet fever, she was made to perform quarantine by living temporarily with their old friend Miss Green, who lived nearby. They could take no risk with the health of the children. Christmas seems to have been an understandably subdued affair. Dorothy took the children to Ambleside, to see Mr Polito's wild beasts and a Punch and Judy show. As it rained, they were obliged to spend the night at Basil's lodgings, an experience he did not relish: 'I contrived to be gracious all the time', he told his stepmother, 'tho' Miss Wordsworth (that is old Dorothy) contrived to fidget most amazingly'.[24]

A few weeks later he had cause to be deeply grateful to Dorothy. Mary Barker, who lived in the half of Greta Hall not occupied by the Southeys and Coleridges, had invited him to stay. He disliked the woman, 'she talks too much about eating and drinking and dear Sir Edward', but he was tired of his lodgings and wanted a change. While there, he suffered a serious relapse, vomiting so much blood that he was not expected to live. Dorothy went immediately to his assistance and, as he was too weak to be moved from his bed, she agreed to stay and help nurse him. Three months later, to her great frustration, she was still there. Basil had recovered.

He rode out daily on horseback, but he was, she remarked with pardonable asperity, 'loth to remove from good quarters where he lives *Scot Free*'. The reason Dorothy herself had not gone home was that she had become indispensable to Mary Barker, who was desperately lonely after a quarrel with Southey's womenfolk had left her cut off from their company. Wisely refusing to be drawn into openly taking sides, Dorothy nevertheless felt she could not leave her friend alone.[25] So she stayed on at Keswick, homesick and heart-sore in the knowledge that, by this self-exile, she was denying herself a part in William's most important publishing project to date.

'*Now* above all other time I should have wished to be at home,' she confessed miserably to Catherine Clarkson, 'for William is actually printing 9 books of his long poem.'[26] That William should have decided to publish part of *The Recluse* at this point in his life is astonishing. Everything militated against it. He had been working on it for sixteen years and it was meant to be the goal and summation of his poetic career, yet it was unfinished. He had long believed that he would gain nothing financially by it, and had convinced himself that it would be badly received, because the world was not yet ready for his work. So why did he decide to lay part of it before the public now? It is a question William did not address in his preface to the published poem, despite the fact that he felt obliged to explain the circumstances of its composition. Nor did he ever offer an explanation afterwards.

Two possibilities present themselves. First that William felt it necessary to respond to the derogatory comments of the literary critics. Despite the fact that he had not published any poetry for the last six years, they still continued to ridicule the childishness, vulgarity and affectation of his verse. That this was done simply by coupling any passing mention of his name with a contemptuous reference was probably more damaging than a full-frontal assault, because it implied a consensus of critical opinion. The main offender was Francis Jeffrey, who had been nipping at the heels of the 'Lake Poets', as he called them, for the last ten years in the *Edinburgh Review*, but he was not alone.[27] Publishing part of *The Recluse* would be an emphatic answer to these critics, proving that William was capable of writing not just short poems on what they considered trivial and inappropriate subjects but a grand philosophical poem 'containing views of Man, Nature, and Society'.

Had this been William's sole reason, one would have expected to see in his correspondence prior to his decision to publish an increasing irritation with the critics, perhaps even a developing sense of being persecuted, and a desire to respond. That is not the case. Indeed, it would appear that, unlike all his other publications, except for the first edition of *Lyrical Ballads*, the project was conceived and executed within a very short space of time. One can even pinpoint it to the three months of Dorothy's absence at Keswick, for the first mention of it is in her letter of 24 April, by which time it was already a *fait accompli*, the manuscript having been revised, 'greatly altered', fair-copied, sent to the printers and reached proof stage.[28]

There is, however, a key phrase in Dorothy's letter which suggests a more powerful motive than simply a desire to confound the critics. 'We are all most thankful that William has brought his mind to consent to printing so much of this work;' she wrote, 'for the MSS. were in such a state that, if it had pleased Heaven to take him from this world, they would have been almost useless.' The uncertainty of life, the suddenness with which it can be cut off, *is* a new and constantly reiterated theme in the Wordsworth correspondence. It had arisen as a natural consequence of the deaths of Catherine and Thomas, and all the Wordsworths dwelt on it.[29] The fact that both children had appeared well and happy only a few hours before they had been so unexpectedly snatched from life forcibly impressed on the survivors the insecurity of their own existence. There had been no time to prepare for death. William's decision to publish part of *The Recluse* at this point bears all the hallmarks of having been forced upon him by the fear that he might die with the greatest part, in every sense, of his work unpublished. Without dwelling morbidly on his own mortality, it was a practical precaution to safeguard his work in case of his own early demise. 'I am about to print – (do not start!) eight thousand lines, which is but a small portion of what I shall oppress the world with,' he told Samuel Rogers, 'if strength and life do not fail me.'[30]

The suggestion that this was the compelling reason is reinforced by the surprisingly ambitious nature of William's publication scheme, which did not stop at *The Recluse*, but embraced a new, two-volume, edition of his shorter poems, and also the hitherto unseen *Peter Bell*, *Benjamin the Waggoner* and *The White Doe*. In other words, before the end of the year William expected to see his complete works in print, leaving only his autobiographical poem (*The Prelude*) to languish in his desk until he had completed *The Recluse*. He was determined to proceed in grand fashion; critics might ridicule the style and subject of his verse, but they could not fault the exquisite presentation of his latest offering. *The Excursion*, as he now grandly named the nine books of *The Recluse*, was to be published in an edition of 500 copies by Longman in two magnificent quarto volumes, costing the princely sum of two guineas.[31] Appropriately, it was dedicated to the man to whom he owed so much, William, Earl of Lonsdale. It was a belated homage, for he had wanted to dedicate his poems to the Earl ten years earlier, when Lonsdale first agreed to pay the Lowther debt. Then he had been restrained by the more cautious Richard, who had urged him to wait till the money had actually been paid. Now, however, having benefited so much more from Lonsdale's goodwill, he was able to acknowledge publicly his own 'high respect and gratitude sincere' in a dedicatory sonnet. Surprisingly, it was here that William came closest to admitting why he now published only part of *The Recluse*.

> Gladly would I have waited till my task
> Had reached its close; but Life is insecure,
> And Hope full oft fallacious as a dream:[32]

After the dedicatory sonnet there followed another of William's combative prefaces. As he himself admitted there, *The Excursion* was a self-contained unit which was perfectly capable of standing alone. Nevertheless, in both the title (*The*

Excursion, Being a Portion of The Recluse, A Poem) and at length in the preface William unnecessarily advertised to the world that it was just 'a portion of a poem'. As this 'portion' was just short of 9,000 lines long, his admission was a gift to hostile critics. Conversely, it raised expectations among his well-wishers that the remainder of the poem would follow, putting him under intolerable pressure to do the impossible. Why did he do it? Partly honesty – it was the simple truth, after all – but partly from a desire to prove that he was a poet of far greater vision, depth and power than his published works had so far indicated. Just as he had done in the preface to *Lyrical Ballads*, he set out a chronology of his composition which was not strictly accurate, but suggested that his whole life and all his poetic labours had been dedicated to the fruition of a single grand plan. He claimed that when he retired to his native mountains, 'with the hope of being enabled to construct a literary Work that might live', he had undertaken a review of his own mind to see how far Nature and Education had qualified him for this purpose. The result of this review was a determination to write *The Recluse*, which he described once again, repeating the usual mantra, as 'a philosophical poem, containing views of Man, Nature, and Society', with a significant addition, '... having for its principal subject the sensations and opinions of a poet living in retirement'. *The Prelude* (which he had, in fact, begun in Germany before returning to the Lakes) he now claimed was a subsidiary outcome of the review, but it was inextricably linked with *The Recluse*, as he explained in a magnificent analogy:

> the two Works have the same kind of relation to each other ... as the ante-chapel has to the body of a gothic church. Continuing this allusion, ... [the] minor Pieces, which have been long before the Public, when they shall be properly arranged, will be found by the attentive Reader to have such connection with the main Work as may give them claim to be likened to the little cells, oratories, and sepulchral recesses, ordinarily included in those edifices.

Without stooping to debate with his critics, William thus dismissed their accusations that his published poems were trite, silly and puerile. He ended his preface with an earnest for the future, offering an extract 'from the conclusion of the first book of The Recluse ... as a kind of *Prospectus* of the design and scope of the whole Poem'. Speaking in his own voice as the poet, he invoked the Muse, Urania:

> ... upon me bestow
> A gift of genuine insight; that my Song
> With star-like virtue in its place may shine,
> Shedding benignant influence ...

Deliberately echoing Milton, he claimed that Paradise was not lost, but could be regained if the 'discerning intellect of Man' were 'wedded to this goodly universe In love and holy passion'. In describing the subjects he would cover in *The Recluse*, William again reverted to Milton, this time actually quoting *Paradise Lost*:

Of Truth, of Grandeur, Beauty, Love, and Hope,
And melancholy Fear subdued by Faith;
Of blessed consolations in distress;
Of moral strength, and intellectual Power;
Of joy in widest commonalty spread;
Of the individual Mind that keeps her own
Inviolate retirement, subject there
To Conscience only, and the law supreme
Of that Intelligence which governs all –
I sing: – 'fit audience let me find though few!'[33]

Though this '*Prospectus*' applies to the whole of *The Recluse*, it is equally applicable to *The Excursion* alone. Indeed, it is perhaps the best summary of a poem which is impossible to summarize, for *The Excursion* is very much more than the sum of its parts. The plot is easily sketched. The poet accompanies the Wanderer, the 'intellectual Pedlar', on a pedestrian tour of the Lakes. Together they visit the Wanderer's friend, the Solitary, a pessimistic misanthrope living in self-imposed isolation by Blea Tarn, and endeavour to persuade him that his unhappiness is caused by want of faith in religion and in the virtue of humanity. The three men then visit another friend of the Wanderer, the Pastor, who, in a series of oral epitaphs of the dalesmen buried in his village churchyard, gives practical examples of the importance of religion and virtue in daily life. The poem ends with a visit to the Pastor's house, and a sail on the lake, while the Wanderer draws together the threads of their discussions, lamenting the ignorance and degradation brought about by excessive industrialization, advocating a system of national education as the solution and ending with a joyful prayer of thanksgiving to the Almighty.

Such a summary can be nothing more than the sloughed skin of a snake: the bare dry outline which retains the shape, but gives no idea of the colour, vitality and movement of the living creature which has emerged. *The Excursion* is formidably long, often obscure in meaning, and has many a dull moment, but it is one of those rare books which rewards persistence. It improves out of all proportion to the initial struggle and yields new treasures on every reading. The language is sonorous, majestic and hypnotic, carrying the reader irresistibly forward; there are touching stories of human suffering told so tenderly that they cannot fail to move; and above all broods what can only be called the gigantic spirit of Wordsworth, patient, wise, empathic, sympathetic, suffering, yet sustained by faith. This is not the appropriate place for extensive quotation, but two passages, both from the fourth book, *Despondency Corrected*, are fundamental. Not only do they go to the didactic heart of the poem, but also to the core of William's own philosophy, for they are the hard-won result of his personal experience in trying to come to terms with the trials of his own life. Having heard the Solitary's tale of bitter disillusionment and personal loss (not unlike William's own), the Wanderer says:

One adequate support
For the calamities of mortal life
Exists – one only; an assured belief
That the procession of our fate, howe'er
Sad or disturbed, is ordered by a Being
Of infinite benevolence and power;
Whose everlasting purposes embrace
All accidents, converting them to good.
– The darts of anguish *fix* not where the seat
Of suffering hath been thoroughly fortified
By acquiescence in the Will supreme
For time and for eternity.

The second extract is the famous analogy of the child, who puts a shell to his ear and hears the sea from which it came.

Even such a shell the universe itself
Is to the ear of Faith; and there are times,
I doubt not, when to you it doth impart
Authentic tidings of invisible things;
Of ebb and flow, and ever-during power;
And central peace, subsisting at the heart
Of endless agitation. Here you stand,
Adore, and worship, when you know it not;
Pious beyond the intention of your thought;
Devout above the meaning of your will.
. . . the Man –
Who, in this spirit, communes with the Forms
Of nature, who with understanding heart
Both knows and loves such objects as excite
No morbid passions, no disquietude,
No vengeance, and no hatred – needs must feel
The joy of that pure principle of love
So deeply, that, unsatisfied with aught
Less pure and exquisite, he cannot choose
But seek for objects of a kindred love
In fellow-natures and a kindred joy.
. . . he looks round
And seeks for good; and finds the good he seeks:[34]

Even before the poem was published, William was deliberately steeling himself for failure. 'I shall be content if the Publication pays its expenses,' he told Rogers, adding with grim humour, 'for Mr Scott and your friend Lord B[yron] flourishing at the rate they do, how can an *honest* Poet hope to thrive?' To Beaumont, he professed faith in the notion that he would eventually win over his critics, but admitted his conviction that 'the herd of minute critics will be astounded and thrown upon their backs, from which shock they will recover only to vent their malice more bitterly'.[35]

The Excursion was published in August 1814, while the poet was taking his own excursion in Scotland with his wife and sister-in-law. As a gesture of lofty indifference to the fate of his poem, this was somewhat spoilt by the way he rushed straight to a bookshop the moment they reached civilization 'with a sneaking hope that I might hear something about the Excursion'. Not only was there 'not a word' about his own poem, but he had the additional mortification of hearing the bookseller in rhapsodies over the latest publishing sensation, a joint publication of Byron's *Lara* and Rogers's *Jacqueline*, which sold faster than copies could be obtained. 'Now dont you think I am quite a hero not to be envious[?]' he inquired, pointing out what a blow this would have been to 'poor me if I had been of the commonly supposed poetic constitution'.[36]

The trip to Scotland had been planned for many months. Mary had long dreamt of making such a tour with her husband, but had always been prevented, first by child-bearing and rearing, then by fear of what might happen if she left her children again. William was determined that she should go this summer, in an effort to restore her health and spirits. His own inclination was to go to London, not just because his book was printing there, but mainly because he longed to see all the festivities in the wake of the Armistice with France. After his disastrous march on Moscow in 1812 and consequent retreat, with enormous losses, from Russia, Bonaparte had suffered a further humiliating defeat at the hands of the Allies at the battle of Leipzig in October 1813. Wellington had then crossed the Pyrenees into France and the Prussians and Russians, advancing from the east, had entered Paris in March 1814. They established a provisional government and, much to the disgust of the Wordsworths, allowed Bonaparte to abdicate on a fat pension and go into exile on Elba. Following the First Peace of Paris, signed on 30 May, Field Marshal Blücher, the Prussian King and his two sons were among the Allies to come to London, where they were showered with honours. As an active member of the war faction, as he called himself, William would have loved to see Bonaparte's conquerors, but he could afford neither the money nor the time to go to London and Scotland, and therefore sacrificed the former for the sake of his wife.[37]

'It is like a dream', Dorothy wrote of this sudden ending to a war which had lasted most of her adult life; '– peace peace – all in a moment – prisoners let loose – Englishmen and Frenchmen brothers at once!' One of the immediate personal consequences to the Wordsworths was the arrival at Rydal Mount in June of Eustace Baudouin, newly released from prison and come to pay his respects before returning home to France. It is inconceivable that the Wordsworths made no comment on his visit, so it must have been a significant one, prompting the later destruction of the evidence. Were it not for the fact that Baudouin accompanied

Sara on a visit to Southey at Keswick, we would not know that it had taken place. Southey found the young man 'apparently one of the best of these Frenchmen' who had the grace to admit that the war in Spain had been an unjust one, despite his complaint, which greatly amused Southey, that the Spaniards were 'very hard-hearted' towards their conquerors.[38]

Before departing on the Scottish tour, William sent out a flurry of notes to his patrons and friends, informing them that he had ordered copies of *The Excursion* to be delivered to them as soon as it was published. He also dispatched a brusque note to Richard, asking him 'for heavens sake' to send the statement of their accounts for which they had been waiting, quite literally, for years. 'We wish to know what we have, and are most uneasy that we do not know; and it is just and reasonable that we should have command of our money.' The Wordsworths set out on 18 July, armed with a copy of *The Traveller's Guide through Scotland*, presented the day before by John Marshall. They travelled in the old jaunting car which had served William, Dorothy and Coleridge so well on the Scottish tour of 1803. To begin with, they were quite a large party, for in addition to William, Mary and Sara they had Johnny, who was now a sturdy eleven-year-old, and a friend of the Lloyds, Miss Alms, who had begged a lift home to Carlisle. They travelled via Sebergham, where Mary and Sara had spent so many happy childhood holidays on their grandfather Monkhouse's estate, and when they got to Carlisle were joined at Miss Alms's sister's house by two old friends, James Losh and Anthony Harrison. Losh noted that William seemed 'chearful and less affected than formerly', so one assumes they did not discuss poetry![39]

For William, this third tour of Scotland was a reprise of his earlier ones, with a northern detour after Longtown to Burnfoot, where they were to leave Johnny with the Misses Malcolm until their return to England. Their brother was an old friend of Christopher Wordsworth and they had a school of their own in a thatched hut in the woods on their estate. After a 'highland' welcome, with a houseful of company, plentiful hospitality and dancing in the evening, William, Mary and Sara turned westward to rejoin the main route to Glasgow at Moffat. They paid the now obligatory visits to the Falls of Clyde and Hamilton House, but also spent two nights at the country house of Clarkson's friend Robert Grahame, who loaned them a landau so that they could travel in style to see 'the curiosities' of the new industrial age: steam-powered looms with their flying shuttles in the weaving sheds, steam-driven circular saws at the coopers and a packet boat 'come up the Hill'.

From Glasgow, they wound their way up Loch Lomond, with detours to the west to Lochs Gare and Long, and to the east into the Trossachs as far as Callander, before setting out from Tarbet on a northern loop that would take them, via Inverary, to Loch Linnhe. Instead of turning southward at Ballachulish, as William and Dorothy had done in 1803, they continued north-east, travelling up the banks of the natural straight line formed by Lochs Linnhe, Lochy, Oich and Ness, leading from Fort William to Inverness on the Moray Firth. This was the most northerly point of their tour, from which they turned south-east to Aviemore and Blair Atholl, picking up the route of 1803 through Perth, Stirling, Edinburgh and Kelso, and, after collecting Johnny from Burnfoot, back into England through Longtown.[40]

Throughout the seven and a half weeks of the tour, Sara jotted down notes which were intended to form the basis of a journal similar to Dorothy's *Recollections.* Though it was a self-conscious exercise, the notes she made were little more than an *aide-mémoire* and were never worked up into the finished article. Even in this form, Sara's pungent sense of humour and sharply observant eye produced some characteristic vignettes of Scottish life: the 'screaming minister' of the Established Kirk at Lanark, for instance, who screamed 'with his whole might . . . & seemed not the least fatigued by it', in contrast to the '*grunting* Priest' of the old Kirk at Perth; the mother of seventeen children living at the toll-bar house at Garelochhead 'in the midst of dirt & wretchedness scarcely to be met with in an English cottage', yet wearing 'silver rimmed spectacles', possessing ladylike manners and conversation, and paying £30 a year to educate each of her sons; the disagreeable inn at Luss, where the waiters ran around as if they were cracked in the head, the baker called once every ten days '& the possibility of making bread at home never entered their heads'; the 'horrid dirty Inn' on Loch Dochart, where they were served 'Whisky Pudding & a grey Chackin' and Sara drily noted 'M[ary] sick of Chacken'. Twice they were mistaken for itinerant showmen, partly because of their shabby appearance, but mainly because of the jaunting car, resulting in their being refused admittance to the inn at Fort William until Mary managed to convince the owner that they were respectable travellers.[41]

Just as William and Dorothy had been in 1803, Sara was struck by the contrast between the poverty of the Scots and their innate intelligence and good breeding. 'Men living in such hovels as you would not think good enough for Cattle you will find far more intelligent & expressing themselves much better than any person you can meet with in England who has not had, as I may say, an *university* Education or one as liberal.' It was not surprising that these encounters should revive memories of James Patrick, the Scottish former pedlar who had provided William with the model for his 'intellectual Pedlar' in *The Excursion.* As they asked directions on the road to Aberfoyle, they were told that 'awa' to the east' lay Buchlyvie and Campsie, 'names made familiar to me in my childhood by my good Friend Mr Patrick – the latter being his Birth-place'.[42]

Having completed their tour of the Highlands, the party arrived on 25 August at Edinburgh, where they were immediately drawn into literary circles. They dined out every evening, twice with their friend Mrs Wilson, mother of John, of Elleray, once with Mrs Taylor and, on their final evening, with a new acquaintance, Robert Pearce Gillies. William was particularly drawn to this young man, who was twenty-six years old and, despite having just lost much of his fortune in a rash speculation, was rapidly squandering the rest in extravagant living. What interested William was that Gillies seemed to be a version of his younger self. He was a struggling poet who believed that originality was all-important and, failing to achieve this, was subject to overpowering fits of depression. William befriended Gillies and took him under his wing. He attempted to persuade him that morbidity and peculiarity should never be the chosen material of poetic composition, and urged him to imitate Cowper, who was constitutionally morbid but 'wisely *tried* to help it by looking abroad on nature and society, by endeavouring to do good, and in that pursuit to lose himself'. Though William attributed this formula to Cowper, it was the very same one which had so successfully dragged him out of the depression he had suffered at Racedown. Before he left Edinburgh, William composed a sonnet to Gillies, assuring him there was 'immortal seed' in his mind, and exhorting him to free himself from the chambers of dejection and trust to his youth, genius and ambition:

> A cheerful life is what the Muses love,
> A soaring spirit is their prime delight.

Later in the year, when he learned that Gillies was still suffering from morbid feelings and regarded them as incurable, William offered a more forthright opinion:

> poetry and the poetic spirit will either help you, or harm you, as you use them. If you find in yourself more of the latter effect than of the former, forswear the Muses, and apply tooth and nail to law, to mathematics, to mechanics, to anything, only escape from your insidious foe. But if you are benefited by your intercourse with the lyre, then give yourself up to it with the enthusiasm which I am sure is natural to you.[43]

The kindly interest William had shown and Gillies's gratitude for his concern would ripen into a friendship that would last many years.

Another poet who was introduced to William at Mrs Wilson's was the remarkable James Hogg, whose life was a romance in itself. There was something of both Burns and William's own Pedlar of *The Excursion* in 'the Ettrick Shepherd', as he was commonly known. Hogg had been snatched from obscurity as a shepherd in his native Ettrick Forest by Walter Scott, who had recognized his poetic gift and published his ballads. He now lived in Edinburgh, where he had found fame as a poet and contributor to the *Edinburgh Review.* William would remain ambivalent about both the man and his work. Soon after meeting Hogg and, as a result, reading his poems for the first time, he described him as 'too illiterate to write in any measure or style that does not savour of balladism', sugaring the pill by adding 'this is much to be regretted; for he is possessed of no ordinary power'. Many years later, he reaffirmed that Hogg 'was undoubtedly a man of original genius, but of coarse manners & low & offensive opinions'. (William was offended by Hogg's 'self-conceit' in pronouncing judgements on classical literature about which he knew nothing, but was also not best pleased to see himself parodied by Hogg in the *Poetic Mirror.*) Hogg himself was overjoyed to meet William and listened to his conversation 'as to a superior being, far exalted above the common walks of life. His sentiments seemed just, and his language, though perhaps a little pompous, was pure, sentient, and expressive.'[44]

From Edinburgh William, Mary and Sara went in search of several of the leading literary figures of the day. At Traquair, near Peebles, they were rejoined by Hogg, who had offered to escort William on what they all knew would be an emotional journey: his first visit to the River Yarrow, which demanded an answer to *Yarrow Unvisited.* They were joined by Dr Robert Anderson, the sixty-four-year-old clergyman who, in 1795, had published *A Complete Edition of the Poets of Great Britain* in fourteen volumes. It was a work of immense significance to William: he was indebted to it intellectually because it had introduced him to many of the Elizabethan and early Stuart poets, and emotionally because his own copy had accompanied his brother John on his voyages to India, and had been given to him by John when he left Grasmere for the last time. William was delighted to have the opportunity to acknowledge his debt to Anderson, and, as Hogg commented, 'it was delightful to see the deference which Wordsworth paid to that venerable man'. Anderson accompanied them part of the way, but age and infirmity prevented him following the river from its source down to St Mary's Loch with the rest of the party. It was a day none of them would ever forget. For once they had perfect weather, and William 'was in great good-humour, delightful, and most eloquent'. They took refreshment at the cottage of Hogg's father, himself a Yarrow shepherd, described by Sara as 'an Old Man upward of 80 – a fine old Creature'. By the evening of the next day, Sara was confidently able to predict 'we shall soon have a poem *Yarrow Visited*'.[45]

Having parted from Anderson and Hogg, William, Mary and Sara made their way to Abbotsford, Scott's home since 1812, but not yet the elaborate Gothic fantasy it became. To their disappointment, Scott was not there, but they were hospitably received by his wife, and their daughter Sophia showed them round all her father's favourite haunts with bounding step, bright eyes, animated tones and a 'confiding simplicity that was quite enchanting'. The Scotts accompanied them to Melrose Abbey and to lunch with Lord Buchan at Dryburgh Abbey, before seeing them off on their return to England.[46]

The tour had been a great success. It had provided material for new poetry, but this was almost incidental: 'dearest Mary is much improved by her journey', Sara wrote a fortnight after they set out; 'she truly enjoys herself; & William is happy that the journey has accomplished this his chief aim'.[47] They returned to Rydal Mount on 9 September to find that Dorothy and the children were well and nothing of note had occurred in their absence. There was, however, a curious coda to the Scottish tour. James Hogg had anticipated them by a couple of days and, while he awaited their arrival, Dorothy had made an immediate conquest of him by her kindness and conversation, 'a true mental treat'. Hogg became a regular visitor during his stay in the Lakes. One evening a comet blazed across the sky, creating a lingering trail of light that arched from horizon to horizon. According to Hogg, there was a large party of literary gentlemen at Rydal Mount that night, including de Quincey, and the poets, Wilson, Lloyd and himself. On being told of the phenomenon, they all went out on to the terrace in front of the house to observe it, and Dorothy, who was walking arm in arm with Hogg, expressed the fear that it might prove an ominous portent. Hogg gallantly declared that it was nothing more nor less than a triumphal arch, raised in honour of the meeting of the poets. Wilson was gratified and laughed, but William, who had overheard the remark, apparently turned on his heel and disdainfully asked de Quincey, 'Poets? Poets? – What does the fellow mean? – where are they?' 'Who could forgive this?' Hogg asked, when he published the story in 1832; 'for my part, I never can, and never will!' Apocryphal as William's words probably are – even Hogg admitted he did not hear them personally – it is indicative of William's reputation for egotism that they were, and are, widely believed to be true.[48]

When he left Rydal, Hogg took with him a copy of William's verses *Yarrow Visited*, which William had agreed he could publish in an anthology intended to include a poem from every living author in Britain. 'Nothing but a wish to show to Mr Hogg that my inclination towards him, and his proposed work were favourable, could have induced me to part with it in that state', he wrote to Gillies in November, as he substituted a virtual rewrite for the original poem. Even then, he was still unhappy with it; 'we think it heavier than my things generally are', he confessed. 'Second parts if much inferior to the first, are always disgusting', he wrote later. '. . . I was anxious that there should be no more falling off; but that was unavoidable perhaps, from the subject: as Imagination almost always transcends reality.'[49]

Hogg also took with him a letter from William to Anderson, suggesting that he should add a few volumes to his edition of *British Poets*. In consultation with Southey, William had drawn up a list of the most notable omissions from the work, which included thirty-seven individual authors and three miscellaneous volumes of 'Ballads and state Poems', 'Metrical Romances' and 'Miscellanies of the age of Tudor'. It was an ambitious project which Anderson had neither time nor energy to undertake, though he seems to have suggested that William and Southey might do so in his stead.[50]

The flurry of enthusiasm for expanding Anderson's *British Poets* was merely a temporary distraction from the main concerns of the autumn, which were the reception of *The Excursion* and the preparation of the new edition of William's poems in two volumes. The first copies of *The Excursion* had been released during the second week in August. Robinson actually stole out of the theatre to see an early copy and, after hastily scanning the preface and a few extracts, proffered a hesitant, but all too accurate, verdict.

> It is a poem of formidable size, and I fear too mystical to be popular. But it will, however, put an end to the sneers of those who consider him or affect to consider him as a puerile writer [who] attempts only little things. But it will draw on him the imputation of dullness possibly. Still it will, I trust, strengthen the zeal of his few friends.[51]

The first review was by Hazlitt, who carried off Lamb's complimentary copy and rushed into print on 21 August. It was, as one would expect from Hazlitt, a beautifully written, clever and discerning critique, which both eulogized and as heartily damned. 'In power of intellect, in lofty conception, in the depth of feeling, at once simple, and sublime, which pervades every part of it, and which gives to every object an almost preternatural and preterhuman interest, this work has seldom been surpassed', it began. Having defined *The Excursion* (inadequately) as 'a philosophical pastoral poem . . . a scholastic romance', Hazlitt launched a thinly veiled attack on the egotism of its poet, who could not paint a scene, delineate a character or tell a story, either ordinary or remarkable, without clothing it in his own thoughts, recollections or imagination.

> It is less a poem on the country than on the love of the country. It is not so much a description of natural objects as of the feelings associated with them; not an account of the manners of rural life, but the result of the poet's reflections on it. He does not present the reader with a lively succession of images or incidents, but paints the outgoings of his own heart, the shapings of his own fancy. He may be said to create his own materials; his thoughts are his real subjects.

Though some would feel that this is William's greatest attribute, for Hazlitt it was detrimental to the poetic process: 'The image is lost in the sentiment, as sound in the multiplication of echoes.' 'An intense intellectual egotism swallows up everything', he complained. 'Even the dialogues introduced in the present volume are soliloquies of the same character, taking different views of the subject. The recluse, the pastor, and the pedlar, are three persons in one poet.' Seizing upon the preface, Hazlitt cleverly turned the argument against William in a way that would be repeated by future reviewers. The 'poet living in retirement', far from being a seer who could view the world dispassionately, was his own worst enemy. 'The power of his mind preys upon itself. It is as if there were nothing but himself and the universe. He lives in the busy solitude of his own heart; in the deep silence of thought. His imagination lends life and feeling only to the "bare trees and mountain bare," peoples the viewless tracts of air, and converses with the silent clouds.'[52]

Hazlitt's review was bad enough, but Jeffrey's in the *Edinburgh Review* would have destroyed a lesser man than William. Jeffrey adopted an air of amused contempt, as if he were a rather superior and sardonic teacher reproving a foolish child. The infamous opening sentence, 'This will never do.', launched thirty pages of criticism of the poet, his 'system' and his poem, which is all the more devastating for making the reader smile guiltily in recognizing the undoubted truths behind the malice. William's 'imprudent candour' about *The Recluse* in the preface was a gift to Jeffrey. 'What Mr Wordsworth's ideas of length are, we have no means of accurately judging; but we cannot help suspecting that they are liberal, to a degree that will alarm the weakness of most modern readers.' If the 9,000 lines of *The Excursion* covered a period of precisely three days, Jeffrey argued, tongue-in-cheek, 'by the use of a very powerful *calculus*, some estimate may be formed of the probable extent of the entire biography'. More seriously, he too attacked 'the poet in retirement' as being, not above society, but out of touch with it.

> Long habits of seclusion, and an excessive ambition of originality, can alone account for the disproportion which seems to exist between this author's taste and his genius ... if Mr Wordsworth, instead of confining himself almost entirely to the society of the dalesmen and cottagers, and little children, who form the subjects of his book, had condescended to mingle a little more with the people that were to read and judge of it, we cannot help thinking, that its texture would have been considerably improved: At least it appears to us to be absolutely impossible, that any one who had lived or mixed familiarly with men of literature and ordinary judgment in poetry, (of course we exclude the coadjutors and disciples of his own school), could ever have fallen into such gross faults, or so long mistaken them for beauties.

The Excursion, Jeffrey declared, was 'a tissue of moral and devotional ravings' which displayed the author's talent for 'enveloping a plain and trite observation in all the mock majesty of solemn verbosity'; it might contain 'salutary truths' but these were inculcated 'at far greater length, and with more repetitions, than in any ten volumes of sermons that we ever perused'. Where the moral was not trite, it was so obscurely phrased that 'if our readers can form the slightest guess at its meaning, we must give them credit for a sagacity to which we have no pretension'. Like Hazlitt, Jeffrey revived the old complaint about William's poetry and objected to the choice of a common pedlar as the Wanderer.

> Why should Mr Wordsworth have made his hero a superannuated Pedlar? What but the most wretched and provoking perversity of taste and judgment, could induce any one to place his chosen advocate of wisdom and virtue in so absurd and fantastic a condition? Did Mr Wordsworth really imagine, that his favourite doctrines were likely to gain any thing in point of effect or authority by being put into the mouth of a person accustomed to higgle about tape, or brass sleeve-buttons?

The odd thing about this review is that, despite the relentlessly hostile tone, it is clear to the dispassionate reader that Jeffrey was not entirely convinced by his own arguments. Having quoted some of the single lines and images 'that sparkle like gems in the desart, and startle us with an intimation of the great poetic powers that lie buried in the rubbish that has been heaped around them', Jeffrey suddenly admitted, 'we feel half inclined to rescind the severe sentence which we passed on the work at the beginning'. Loath to spoil his demolition at this stage, however, he hastily reassured himself, 'But when we look into the work itself, we perceive that it cannot be rescinded ... while we collect the fragments, it is impossible not to lament the ruins from which we are condemned to pick them.' Nevertheless, by his extensive quotation from *The Excursion*, Jeffrey inadvertently undermined his own stance. The influential blue stocking and evangelical Hannah More cannot have been alone in deciding that she would purchase the book even though she had never seen the poem or any other review except Jeffrey's.[53]

Most of the later reviews were paler versions of the two first trend-setters. The *Monthly Review* rather pompously blamed most of William's 'errors and eccentricities' on his unbounded indulgence in his excessively poetic feelings in solitude; habitual mixing with society was 'absolutely requisite to keep an enthusiastic mind within the confines of sound and temperate judgment'. The *British Critic* lamented that he had not 'sufficiently distinguished between the common feelings of mankind and the wanderings of his own solitary spirit ... He listens to a lamb bleating, or gazes on the flight of a bird, and the visionary associations which spring up within him he takes for the ordinary stirrings of the heart, which all men who have leisure to feel at all, must feel as well as himself at the like objects.'[54]

Both the reviewer in the *British Critic* and James Montgomery, who wrote an otherwise enthusiastic piece in the *Eclectic Review*, raised the question of the religious orthodoxy of the poem. Depending on one's viewpoint, this is either the greatest strength or the greatest weakness of *The Excursion*. The poem is saturated with the spirit of religion – but quite which religion is never made explicit. It is therefore either ecumenical, embracing all Christian sects (and some paganism and pantheism besides), or doctrinally unsound. Robinson's perceptive comment about William himself, that his religion 'would not satisfy either a religionist or a sceptic', was equally applicable to his great poem. The reviewer in the *British Critic* was unhappy with what it saw as William's 'firm belief' in the Platonic idea of pre-existence of the soul, 'a doctrine, more poetical, perhaps, than either philosophical or Christian'. Montgomery also lit on this point, though more charitably referring to it as a 'brilliant allegory, (for such we must regard it,)'. More seriously, while speaking in the highest terms of the poem, Montgomery managed to convey the implicit criticism that its author was a pantheist, worshipping God in everything, and everything in God. 'He loves nature with a passion amounting almost to devotion; and he discovers throughout her works an omnipresent spirit, which so nearly resembles God in power and goodness, that it is sometimes difficult to distinguish the reverence which he pays to it, from the homage due to the Supreme alone.'[55]

Even Charles Lamb could not resist a gibe, 'Apropos, are you a **Xtian**? or is it the Pedlar & the Priest that are?', but at least he confined it to a private letter. Lamb's own public critique, which appeared in the *Quarterly Review*, was the first he had ever written. To his great indignation, the editor cut more than a third of his article and altered the language throughout. 'Every warm expression is changed for a nasty cold one', Lamb protested, as he disowned it, '... but if they catch me in their **camps** again let them spitchcock me.'[56]

William was bitterly disappointed by the critical reception of his great poem, but, once again, he tried to hide the hurt behind a cloak of dignified indifference. 'As to the Excursion I have ceased to have any interest about it, since I read Lamb's Letter,' he told Southey; 'let this benighted age continue to love its own darkness and to cherish it. I shall continue to write with I trust the light of Heaven upon me.' With almost the same breath, however, he revealed that the unconcern was entirely feigned. A Unitarian friend of Catherine Clarkson, Patty Smith, had written to her, criticizing *The Excursion* forcibly for not distinguishing between nature as the work of God and God himself. It was, according to Robinson, 'an exceedingly sensible letter' and it was hardly worth a response, but it touched a raw nerve and William launched into a furious rebuttal. It was just like the 'sweating pages' Lamb had received when he had dared to criticize *Lyrical Ballads*. In page after page of indignant argument, which consumed several pens and wore out both Mary and Dorothy in transcribing it, he demanded to know where Smith had gathered that he looked upon Nature and God as the same and accused her of 'reading in cold-heartedness and substituting the letter for the spirit'. 'One of the main objects of the Recluse is, to reduce the calculating understanding to its proper level among human faculties –' he thundered, 'Therefore my Book must be disliked by the Unitarians, as their religion rests entirely on that basis; and therefore is, in fact, no religion at all – but – I won't say what.' As a rather touching illustration of instinctive religion, he described a conversation he had had in bed the other morning with Willy, who was now four and a half. Willy had said, 'How did God make me? Where is God? How does he speak? He never spoke to *me*.' William had replied by saying that God was a spirit, not like Willy's flesh, which he could touch, but like the thoughts in his mind, which he could not. 'The wind was tossing the fir trees, and the sky and light were dancing about in their dark branches, as seen through the window – Noting these fluctuations he exclaimed eagerly – "There's a bit of him I see it there!"' Even then, he could not leave it, but returned to write a lengthy and telling postscript in his own hand, in which he explained that what he had found 'so monstrous' was that Smith had talked of 'the offense [*sic*] of writing the Exn and the difficulty of forgiving the Author'. These words had wounded him to the quick – and he could not forget them. That is why he refused to read Jeffrey's review. 'His impertinences, to us[e the] mildest te[rm,] if once they had a place in my memory, would, for a [time] at least, [sti]ck there. You cannot scower a spot of this kind ou[t of] your mind as you may a stain out of your clothes.'[57]

It was only human of William to feel bitter about the derision and criticism heaped upon his life's work. Fortunately, he had the unwavering support not only of 'the Concern', his family circle, but also a much wider group of devotees, who were growing in number and importance. All these converts were themselves keen proselytizers, spreading the word among their friends and publicly reading William's poetry aloud at every opportunity, so, like the ripples from a stone flung in a pool, his work was gradually reaching a wider audience. Neither Lamb nor Southey had been uncritical in the past, but both were now ardent in his defence. Lamb thought *The Excursion* 'the best of Books'. Southey openly declared his 'full conviction that posterity will rank [Wordsworth] with Milton', and ridiculed Jeffrey's claim to have written a '*crushing* review'. Though he had just published his own *Roderick* and had every reason to fear the same treatment, Southey wrote to Hogg, '*He* crush the *Excursion*!!! Tell him that he might as easily crush Skiddaw.' Robinson and the Beaumonts were particularly active, though Lady Beaumont's zeal often outran her discretion and could be counter-productive. Through them, and others like them, the Wordsworths were informed of favourable opinions: the Bishop of London was 'in raptures', Sergeant Rough thought there had been nothing to equal it since Milton and young Tom Clarkson had stayed up all night to read it.[58] Particularly gratifying were the unsolicited letters which now began to arrive from 'ordinary' people who had no contact with the Wordsworth circle, such as the Liverpool Quakeress Abigail Hodgson, whose fervently expressed admiration prompted a graceful tribute to her own 'comprehensive thought, and feelings at once deep and delicately discriminative' from William. Even Uncle William Cookson was moved to write a sincere appreciation, though, remembering the battles with his nephew over his youthful refusal to enter the Church, there was perhaps a touch of irony in his declaration that he was 'peculiarly gratified with it on Account of the amiable and cheering Light in which you have represented revealed Religion, and of the Respect which you have every where shewn for the religious, and, especially, the clerical character'.[59]

There was one opinion, however, which mattered more than any other to William, and from that quarter there was a deafening silence. The Wordsworths had heard nothing from Coleridge for many months. Rumours were rife that he was about to publish a review of *The Excursion*, but nothing appeared. By New Year's Eve, William had given up hope, telling Catherine Clarkson, 'I much doubt whether he has read three pages of the poem'.[60] It was not until some eight months after the publication of *The Excursion* that Coleridge broke his silence. Even then, it was only to make a passing remark in a letter to Lady Beaumont that he did not think *The Excursion* equal to *The Prelude*, followed by perhaps the most cutting criticism he could make of what was, after all, the second book of William's great philosophical poem.

> I have sometimes fancied, that having by the conjoint operation of his own experiences, feelings, and reason *himself* convinced *himself* of Truths, which the generality of persons have either taken for granted from their Infancy, or at least adopted in early life, he has attached all their own depth and weight to doctrines and words, which come almost as Truisms or Common-place to others.[61]

However hurtful this disclosure must have been, William managed to keep his feelings in check, writing a pleasant if somewhat formal letter directly to his old friend, admitting perplexity at Coleridge's '*comparative* censure'. 'One of my principal aims in the Exn: has been to put the commonplace truths, of the human affections especially, in an interesting point of view; and rather to remind men of their knowledge, as it lurks inoperative and unvalued in their own minds, than to attempt to convey recondite or refined truths.'[62]

Whatever the original schematic for *The Recluse* had been, it was certainly not this, as Coleridge rightly reminded him. Putting commonplace truths in an interesting point of view was all very well for the *Poems, in Two Volumes*, but *The Recluse* was to have been 'the *first* and *only* true Phil[osophical] Poem in existence'. It should have been a profound insight into the whole truth, bottomed in human nature, not an assertion of mere commonplace truths. The greatest irony of the entire history of *The Recluse* is that it was only now, when William had spent sixteen years of his life working on the poem, and a portion of it was irrevocably in the public demesne, that Coleridge at last produced the coherent, cogent and detailed plan for which William had so long and so fruitlessly begged him. As a description of the poem that never was (or could have been), it is fascinating. As an indication of how far apart the minds, as well as the hearts, of the two men now were, it is heartbreaking.

I supposed you first to have meditated the faculties of Man in the abstract, in their correspondence with his Sphere of action, and first, in the Feeling, Touch, and Taste, then in the Eye, & last in the Ear, to have laid a solid and immoveable foundation for the Edifice by removing the sandy Sophisms of Locke, and the Mechanic Dogmatists, and demonstrating that the Senses were living growths and developements [*sic*] of the Mind & Spirit in a much juster as well as higher sense, than the mind can be said to be formed by the Senses –. Next, I understood that you would take the Human Race in the concrete, have exploded the absurd notion of Pope's Essay on Man, Darwin, and all the countless Believers – even (strange to say) among Xtians of Man's having progressed from an Ouran Outang state – so contrary to all History, to all Religion, nay, to all Possibility – to have affirmed a Fall in some sense, as a fact, the possibility of which cannot be understood from the nature of the Will, but the reality of which is attested by Experience & Conscience – Fallen men contemplated in the different ages of the World, and in the different states – Savage – Barbarous – Civilized – the lonely Cot, or Borderer's Wigwam – the Village – the Manufacturing Town – Sea-port – City – Universities – and not disguising the sore evils, under which the whole Creation groans, to point out however a manifest Scheme of Redemption from this Slavery, of Reconciliation from this Enmity with Nature – what are the Obstacles, the *Antichrist* that must be & already is – and to conclude by a grand didactic swell on the necessary identity of a true Philosophy with true Religion, agreeing in the results and differing only as the analytic and synthetic process, as discursive from intuitive, the former chiefly useful as perfecting the latter – in short, the necessity of a general revolution in the modes of developing & disciplining the human mind by the substitution of Life, and Intelligence (considered in it's [*sic*] different powers from the Plant up to that state in which the difference of Degree becomes a new kind (man, self-consciousness) but yet not by essential opposition) for the philosophy of mechanism which in every thing that is most worthy of the human Intellect strikes *Death*, and cheats itself by mistaking clear Images for distinct conceptions, and which idly demands Conceptions where Intuitions alone are possible or adequate to the majesty of Truth. – In short, Facts elevated into Theory – Theory into Laws – & Laws into living & intelligent Powers – true Idealism necessarily perfecting itself in Realism, & Realism refining itself into Idealism. – Such or something like this was the Plan, I had supposed that you were engaged on –.[63]

Though Coleridge said nothing about *The Excursion* itself, only attacking what it was not, his criticism was absolutely devastating. It went far beyond the mere sniping of Jeffrey, for it cut the ground from under William's feet as a man, as a philosopher and as a poet. Quite simply, it told him that he had failed in the most important work of his life. And reading this critique, this prospectus for a poem of which a third was already written, William must have been forced to accept his failure. If he responded, or made any sort of protest, the letter has been lost. But it was the end of the dream which had motivated almost the whole of his literary life. *The Recluse*, whose future completion he had so confidently announced a few months earlier in his preface to *The Excursion*, was quietly abandoned.[64]

17. *Increasing Influence*

Throughout the autumn and winter of 1814 William was hard at work preparing a new edition of his shorter poems for the press. This was not to be merely a revision of *Poems, in Two Volumes* of 1807, but a radical overhaul and rearrangement of all the poetry he had written since 1793. A copy of *Descriptive Sketches* was found, after much searching, and Mary transcribed the description of Como for the new book,[1] together with extracts from *An Evening Walk*, *The Female Vagrant* and even the schoolboy lines 'Dear native regions, I foretell'. To these were added most of the critically despised poems published in 1807, including William's contribution to *Lyrical Ballads*, but also virtually all that he had written since then. In this latter category were the important and substantial body of 'Poems Dedicated to National Independence and Liberty', the sonnet to Catherine Wordsworth (but not *Maternal Grief*), and *Yarrow Visited*, the only poem prompted by the Scottish tour to have been completed.

As so often happened when revising his work, William was inspired to compose at least one wholly new poem. Unusually for him, its origins were purely literary, for it was a reworking of the classical legend of Laodamia, cribbed from Virgil's *Aeneid.* It was in some ways an unfortunate departure, because it encouraged William to go reading and hunting through his old books in the hope of further inspiration, 'for no *good purpose*', as his wife noted. As usual, also, he made himself ill with the stress, suffering night sweats and a painful boil between his thumb and forefinger, which infected his arm to his armpit and crippled his right hand.[2]

The burden of preparing the text for the printers now fell entirely on Mary. Dorothy and Sara had gone on a long visit to Hindwell in the middle of September, expecting to be back around Christmas. Much to Mary's distress, Tom had bought an estate in Wales, so it was obvious he did not contemplate a return to the Lakes;

his brother-in-law John Monkhouse, with whom he was in partnership, had also established himself on a farm of his own, the Stow, twelve miles south of Hindwell, looking over the flat Wye valley to the Black Mountains beyond. Dorothy was delighted with her first visit to Hindwell; 'it is a thousand times more beautiful than she expected & as she has become a compleat horsewoman since she came', Mary Hutchinson wrote. 'I hope she will see every thing that is worth seeing before she leaves us.'[3]

It was not to be. At the beginning of December she received a carefully written note from William which opened with the words, 'At the sight of this short Letter do not be alarmed'. Little Willy had been seriously ill with what Scambler diagnosed as inflammatory croup and her presence was needed urgently at home, 'solely to relieve Mary from fatigue', as William reiterated. Only after Dorothy had set off and Willy was pronounced out of danger could William admit that neither he nor Mary had slept for the previous five nights: 'oh dearest Sara what an anxious, and for some hours, what a wretched time have we passed. The time since Thursday night has appeared to me as long as half a century.' Dorothy was back at Rydal Mount by 15 December, and was thrown straight into nursing duties, for Dora too was ill, and neither child recovered as quickly as they had hoped. 'Our own anxieties have been dreadful,' William wrote to Catherine Clarkson on New Year's Eve,

> and I seem to possess all my children in trembling, the youngest in particular after so narrow an escape. The ordinary health of them all is excellent, but they are all subject occasionally as all my Father's family were to bad Catarrhs. Wm is a charming Boy; beautiful and animated; I wish you could see him, he is the delight of my eyes; pray heaven that I may not have to say with Ben Jonson, 'My sin was too much hope of thee loved Boy.'[4]

The same could not be said of Johnny, who was still at Mr Dawes's school and 'for book-attainments the slowest Child almost I ever knew', according to his father. 'He has an excellent judgment and well regulated affections; but I am much disappointed in my expectations of retracing the Latin and Greek classics with him. Incredible pains has [*sic*] been taken with him, but he is to this day a deplorably bad reader of *English* even.' Dora was quick and clever, but as careless and inattentive as ever, despite the fact that she had been attending a school at Ambleside since April. The school had been set up by a friend of Miss Barker's, Miss Fletcher, who was a former governess, qualified to teach German, French, Italian and music; as they soon discovered, she was also deaf, which was something of a handicap in teaching. Among her pupils were the Lloyd girls, Jane Harding and Richard Scambler's daughter, but Dora had not benefited from their companionship. William said she knew no French and only half the Latin she had learned the previous winter. 'I have not the least hope that any regular progress, (let what pains there may be taken with D.) will be made', her mother wrote despairingly, 'until her own sense and pride bring her to it – her temper is so much against her improvement.'[5]

William had hoped that the new edition of *Poems* would be ready for publication by the beginning of January, but he was to be disappointed. The printing proved slower than expected, but the main cause of delay was his decision to include an engraving as the frontispiece to each volume. This was an attempt to make the books more attractive and elegant, but also a compliment to Sir George Beaumont, to whom *Poems* would be dedicated. Beaumont had painted several pictures inspired by William's poems and it seemed appropriate that these should now adorn the new publication. Two were chosen, a representation of Piel Castle and an illustration of Lucy Gray's cottage, but Beaumont rejected the first engravings as inaccurate and they had to be redone.[6]

The other cause of delay was that William belatedly decided he would have to include a preface to the *Poems*. As late as 22 December he had told Gillies that 'my indolence will prevent me from prefixing any prose remarks to my poems' and that he would reprint the old preface to the 1800 edition of *Lyrical Ballads* as an appendix. For once, however, a preface was essential to explain the innovatory system under which William classified his poems. He had introduced a rudimentary categorization in 1807, dependent on subject matter, but now he implemented a far more complex system, which he had been meditating upon for many years. What he wanted to do was to break away from the idea of chronological progression. He would blend together all his poems, irrespective of their dates of composition or publication, and then redivide the whole body into groupings dictated principally by their subject matter. The basic scheme had been outlined to Coleridge in 1809 and consisted of allocating the poems into categories roughly equating to the periods of human life. By 1812, when William expounded his theory to Robinson, it had become more complicated and involved a psychological approach: the poems would also be arranged 'with some reference either to the fancy, imagination, reflection or mere feeling contained in them'. That the two methods of classification were incompatible, logically and in practice, did not matter to William, but, as Robinson admitted to his diary, it made explanation and justification difficult.[7]

Nevertheless, in his preface, William tried to explain as logically as he could. Six powers were requisite for writing poetry: observation and description, sensibility, reflection, imagination and fancy, invention and, finally, judgement. There were also six types of poetry: narrative, dramatic, lyrical, 'the Idyllium', didactic and philosophical satire. It therefore followed that 'poems, apparently miscellaneous, may with propriety be arranged either with reference to the powers of mind *predominant* in the production of them; or to the mould in which they are cast; or, lastly, to the subjects to which they relate'. As far as possible, he also tried to place the poems in order of time, beginning with Childhood, and ending with Old Age, Death and Immortality. The result was a grouping of poems under such headings as 'Poems referring to the Period of Childhood', 'Poems Founded on the Affections', Poems of the Fancy', 'Poems of the Imagination' and 'Poems proceeding from Sentiment and Reflection'. 'My guiding wish', William declared in the preface, 'was, that the small pieces of which these volumes consist, thus discriminated, might be regarded under a two-fold view; as composing an entire work within themselves, and as adjuncts to the philosophical Poem, "The Recluse." '[8]

The problem with the new arrangement was that it was almost entirely subjective. And as William not infrequently moved poems from one category to another in future editions, it would appear that it was neither obvious nor definitive, even to the author himself. Though one might not wish to go as far as the critic in the *Monthly Review*, who declared the system 'a pompous classification of trifles', it is impossible not to feel some sympathy with his bewilderment: 'in the present volumes we have a poem belonging to the class of "Fancy", with no possible distinguishing characteristic from another in the class of "Imagination"; the "Affections" lay claim to a third, which might as well have been ranked under the head of "Sentiment and Reflection" '.[9]

William's classification of his poems might have exposed him to ridicule, but it was hardly contentious. Unfortunately, once again he could not leave it at that, but felt obliged to hit back at his critics, and more specifically at one critic in particular. Francis Jeffrey's review of *The Excursion* had been the final straw. Not only was it likely to damage the sales of the book, which mattered financially to the Wordsworths, who had the expenses of the Scottish tour to repay, but also it threatened to undermine William's poetic reputation permanently. William had written to Stuart, asking him to print in the *Courier* a series of letters from de Quincey 'upon the subject of the stupidities, the ignorance, and the dishonesties of the Edinburgh Review; and principally as relates to myself, whom, perhaps you know, the Editor has long honored with his abuse'.[10]

Perhaps because Stuart declined, William decided to retaliate himself, in an 'Essay, Supplementary to the Preface'. Written in magisterial prose, far removed from the 'sweating pages' of his private letters defending his poetry, it was a covert attack on all his critics. The Unitarians, though not named, were implicitly taken to task as being 'men who read from religious or moral inclinations'. They were therefore 'prone to over-rate the Authors by whom those truths are expressed and enforced' and could not enjoy poetry which seemed to them to endorse doctrinal errors; 'at all seasons, they are under temptation to supply by the heat with which they defend their tenets, the animation which is wanting to the constitution of the religion itself'. The real enemies of poets of original imagination, however, were 'critics too petulant to be passive to a genuine poet, and too feeble to grapple with him . . . men of palsied imaginations and indurated hearts . . . judges, whose censure is auspicious, and whose praise ominous!' Citing a long list of major poets whose works had not achieved immediate popularity, such as Spenser, Shakespeare and Milton, he compared them with their ephemeral contemporaries, who had blazed into fame but then left scarcely a trace behind them. Naturally, William placed himself in the former category. 'Grand thoughts', he wrote, '. . . as they are most naturally and most fitly conceived in solitude, so can they not be brought forth in the midst of plaudits, without some violation of their sanctity.' He ended by assuring his readers that he would immediately destroy 'the contents of these

Volumes, and the Work to which they are subsidiary', were he not convinced that they revealed something of the 'Vision and the Faculty divine'.[11]

Robinson thought the publication of the 'Essay, Supplementary to the Preface' an error of judgement which would 'afford a triumph to [Wordsworth's] enemies. He betrays resentment and that he has suffered pain', he noted. 'His reproaches of the bad taste of the times will be ascribed to merely personal feelings, and to disappointment.' When he repeated the criticism to William's face, he was amused that the poet denied that there were any expressions of anger in the preface, 'though he has nothing but contempt, etc . . .'! Both men were right. The preface and the essay were remarkably free from bitterness, but as a defence of William's poetry they were a pointless exercise. His enthusiasts did not need one and his critics could not be converted by one. Indeed, it played into the latter's hands by inviting a response to it, instead of to the poetry. The *Quarterly Review* was comparatively polite.

> For a writer to protest that he *prides* himself upon the disapprobation of his contemporaries, and considers it as an evidence of the originality of his genius, and an earnest of the esteem in which he will be held by succeeding generations, is whimsical enough, to say the least of it . . . He should remember, moreover, that the public, and those who profess to be the organs of the public voice in these matters, have at least as much right to dislike *his* poetical taste, as he has to dislike *theirs*.

The *Monthly Review* was less restrained, adopting a note of facetious contempt worthy of Jeffrey himself.

> We are so thoroughly overwhelmed by the high and mighty tone of this author's prose, that we really must have immediate recourse to his verse, in order to get rid of the painful humiliation and sense of inferiority which he inflicts on his readers. There, (Dieu merci;) we are comforted by silliness instead of system; by want of harmony instead of abundance of pride; by downright vacancy instead of grandeur and presumption.[12]

By the end of February the two volumes were nearly through the press and the Wordsworths believed it would be possible to publish by the second week in March. At the same time, however, the first proof sheets were beginning to arrive for *The White Doe of Rylstone*. It had originally been William's intention to go to London in April to bargain with his publisher about this book in person and then see it through the press. When or how he changed his mind is not clear, but it was a deeply significant decision. Longman would, as usual, be the publisher of the poem, but, for the first time, it would be printed by James Ballantyne of Edinburgh. Ballantyne was, first and foremost, the printer of Scott's work, including his immensely popular ballads *The Lay of the Last Minstrel*, *Marmion*, *The Lady of the Lake* and *Rokeby*. Scott had been a secret partner in Ballantyne's printing business since 1805 and, in 1809, had joined him and his brother, John Ballantyne, in setting up as publishers and booksellers. To have Ballantyne's name on the title page of *The White Doe* was therefore to identify with a distinctive and highly successful genre of book-production. It was William's one act of cynical and naked literary ambition: perhaps the Ballantyne name might do for *The White Doe* what his own could not and make his poem sell like Scott's. The Wordsworths were delighted with Ballantyne. 'Never more would I have a Book printed in London –', Dorothy declared. 'Ballantyne goes on like Buonaparte in his march to Paris, and the White Doe will, if they do not make haste in London, beat the Poems.'[13]

The reference to Bonaparte was portentous. On 25 February he had escaped from Elba and on 8 March he landed at Cannes. On 17 March he was at Fontainebleau, just outside Paris, and it became public knowledge that Marshal Ney had deserted to him. On the evening of 19 March Louis XVIII slunk quietly out of Paris, abandoning the city and country to its returned emperor. The spectre of war loomed large over Europe once more. The Wordsworths, who had stopped taking a newspaper after peace had been declared the previous year, became subscribers again. 'We could not exist without one sent directly to us;' Dorothy explained, 'and every post-day . . . we are full of anxiety and catch at every favourable omen.' They had more reason than most to be deeply concerned at this unexpected turn of events. The previous autumn, the Vallons had announced that a marriage treaty was under discussion between Caroline, then twenty-one, and Eustace Baudouin's brother, Jean Baptiste, a thirty-three-year-old government officer. Caroline needed her father's permission to marry and the settlement of an annuity upon her in order to do so. William willingly consented, but only on the understanding that the marriage would bring an increase of income to the Vallons. Annette and Caroline were anxious that there should be a representative of the Wordsworth family at the wedding and Dorothy was the obvious candidate. Dorothy herself was equally keen to go.

> I desire exceedingly to see the poor Girl before she takes another protector than her Mother, under whom I believe she has been bred up in perfect purity and innocence, and to whom she is life and light and perpetual pleasure; though from the over-generous dispositions of the Mother they have had to struggle through many difficulties . . . the reports . . . we receive from Caroline's Mother and Mr Beaudouin [*sic*] of her interesting and amiable qualities . . . both say that she resembles her father most strikingly, and her letters give a picture of a feeling and ingenuous mind. Yet there must be something I think very unfavourable to true delicacy in French manners.[14]

As Dorothy clearly could not travel so far unaccompanied, it was arranged that either Joanna or Sara Hutchinson would go with her, and the wedding was tentatively fixed for April 1815. They could not have chosen a worse time. Bonaparte's resurrection put an end to all their plans. 'For the sake of our Friends I am truly distressed', Dorothy wrote as the news filtered slowly through to Rydal.

> [Annette] from the first was a zealous Royalist [who] has often risked her life in defence of adherents to that cause, and she despised and detested Buonaparte. Poor Creature! in the last letter which we had from her she spoke only of hope and comfort; said that the king's government was daily gaining strength and Buonaparte's friends were daily coming over in their hearts to the other side.

The Wordsworths were in a fever of anxiety. The next letters from Annette and Caroline contained high drama. They were written on the eve of Bonaparte's entry into Paris. Eustace Baudouin had set off to join the royalist forces, but his old loyalty to the emperor had overcome his new to the king and he returned without striking a blow. As Annette finished her letter at midnight, she heard troops advancing which she guessed were the vanguard of Bonaparte's army. The last words of her letter were, 'Good God what is to become of us?'[15]

'I utterly despair of ever seeing peace again in our days', Mary wrote to her cousin Tom Monkhouse. 'But for this out-break, you would have seen Dorothy and Sarah in London where they were to have met in the course of a month, with an intention of taking a trip to Paris. Our great comfort is that the Arch-fiend made his incursion before they actually got there.' William's own desire to be in London at this time of political crisis can only have been sharpened by a first visit from Charles Pasley, now a colonel, who stayed three days at Rydal Mount in the last week of March. With the renewal of war, Pasley's visionary training college for officers at Chatham was now to prove its worth, the colonel himself retaining his station there, instead of being sent abroad on active service. The Wordsworth women did not immediately warm to this shy, grave man whose wife had died of consumption the previous year, but the children broke through his reserve and he won all hearts before he left.[16]

At the beginning of May William and Mary set off on the long-projected visit to London, leaving Dorothy in charge of the children and the Stamp office. They were accompanied by Hartley Coleridge, who was now eighteen and about to take up a place at Merton College, Oxford. This was something of a personal triumph for William and Southey, because it was almost entirely due to their efforts that Hartley had secured a place at university. A year earlier, Coleridge had been living in Bristol with his friend Josiah Wade, and Cottle had written to Southey, suggesting that a subscription should be solicited on his behalf. In one of the most painful letters he ever had to write, Southey vetoed the proposal. He pointed out that Coleridge's wife and three children were totally dependent on an annual income of £67 10s, which was Tom's half of the Wedgwood annuity and only covered the expenses of the boys. (Southey himself supplied the shortfall, though he did not say so.) Coleridge was capable of working, if he chose, but he did not do so. Opium was a hugely expensive drug and in the quantity Coleridge consumed it and spirits, the cost of his addiction would more than absorb the whole of the annuity Cottle proposed to raise. So what was the point? A more valuable exercise would be to raise funds to support Coleridge's family, particularly to secure the children's future. What they most needed was an education which would enable them to support themselves as adults, and time was fast running out, especially for Hartley. A brilliant but eccentric young man of odd appearance (he was very short, with thick black eyebrows and 'a beard which a Turk might envy'), he was already showing signs that he was his father's son: he had 'overwheening confidence in his own talents' and, more dangerously, 'a perilous habit of finding out reasons for whatever he likes to do'.[17]

William therefore wrote to Poole, asking him to approach Coleridge and secure his blessing for the raising of an educational fund for his children. As there was no response from Coleridge, William and Southey consulted together, decided the children's needs came before their father's approval, and set out to get the money together. One by one they approached Coleridge's relations and old friends. Hartley's Coleridge uncles offered £40 a year, Lady Beaumont £30, Poole £10 and Cottle £5. William himself was prepared to contribute, though he could not afford much from his own limited income. With the assistance of a college office, worth £50 annually, it was hoped that Hartley would do well, but William was not confident: 'he is too much inclined to the eccentric'. Was William aware of the irony, bearing in mind his own youthful rebellion, as he now lectured his friend's son just as his own uncles had once lectured him? 'I have done all in my power to impress upon H.'s mind the necessity of not trusting vaguely to his talents, and to an irregular sort of knowledge, however considerable it may be, in some particulars; and of applying himself zealously and perseveringly to those studies which the University points out to him', he told Poole. 'His prime object ought to be to gain an independence.'[18]

The Wordsworths left Hartley at Oxford in the care of his cousin, William Hart Coleridge, on 6 May, then travelled on to London, where they were to rendezvous with Sara. William usually stayed with the Beaumonts or Montagus, but Mary could not face all the hectic socializing which this inevitably involved, so they went into private lodgings at 24 Edward Street, Cavendish Square. This was fortunate, because the guards on the coach lost most of their luggage and they were stranded in town at a weekend without any appropriate clothes. William's first priority was to pay a personal call on the Earl of Lonsdale, who had just offered him the post of Collector of Customs at Whitehaven. This was a much more valuable office than the Distributorship, but would mean that the Wordsworths would have to move to Whitehaven. This they did not wish to do, not just because they were reluctant to leave Rydal Mount, but because the idea of living in the busy seaport which John had sometimes sailed from would constantly revive memories of his last fatal voyage. It was, however, easier to say this and more courteous to refuse the post in person than by letter.[19]

Lady Beaumont had expressed the hope that they would meet 'in a quiet way', knowing large parties did not suit Mary, but for William this London visit was as busy as ever. There were several dinners at the Beaumonts', to the first of which, with his hosts' permission, he invited John Taylor Coleridge, Hartley's cousin, whom William had seen acquit himself so well in his Oxford *viva voce* examination three years earlier. Scott was also in town, and the two poets made a pilgrimage with the Beaumonts and Richard Heber, the antiquarian, to view a newly discovered portrait of Milton. Scott, not unnaturally, thought *The White Doe* 'the most beautiful thing' his friend had ever written. He and William attended several 'pleasant parties' together, 'though not so many as I could have wished', and when he left London, his wife and daughter parted from Mary and Sara with equally genuine regret. William, who revelled in his occasional dips into London social life, was, according to Scott, 'flourishing like a green bay tree'.[20]

It was through the Beaumonts that William had his first introduction to William Wilberforce, the anti-slavery campaigner and friend of his Uncle William Cookson. Lady Beaumont invited Wilberforce to choose his day to dine with them to meet William, but prior engagements and his ill-health prevented this happening. Instead, claiming 'what I hope you will admit as the right (grounded on our many common friends) to become acquainted with you by the earliest practicable means', Wilberforce offered William an open invitation to breakfast. The two men were in instant sympathy on at least one issue which dominated home politics. They were both in favour of the Corn Laws, which protected the market of English farmers by prohibiting the importation of foreign corn, if the price at home was less than 80s a quarter. With hindsight, it seems obvious that such a measure would cause immense hardship among the poor by keeping the price of bread artificially high at a time of falling wages and rising unemployment. At this time, however, when the new laws were being introduced, the issue was by no means clear-cut. Having witnessed bread riots in revolutionary France, William was all too well aware of the dangers of an inadequate supply. He was therefore convinced that, without some form of protectionism, no native corn would be grown: unless farmers were assured of a decent return on their crops they could not afford to pay their rents, which had risen 'unnaturally' in recent years. (He knew from personal experience that farmers were suffering; his brothers-in-law were all fearful of losing their farms because they could no longer afford the rents.) If Britain became reliant on foreign imports, then corn would become insupportably dear and perhaps could not be got at all. Conversely, with protection in place, once the price had reached the ceiling where foreign imports would be allowed, the resulting influx would immediately and inevitably drive down the cost of corn and bread. 'The advocates for the Corn Laws are in fact the friends of the poor', he declared, and, having read one of Wilberforce's speeches in favour of the Bill, it was 'almost word for word what I had said by our fireside before'. Like Wilberforce, William had one serious reservation: that the ceiling price had been fixed too high. So they had much to talk about on their first meeting, which turned out to be a long one, and Wilberforce was 'much pleased' with his new acquaintance.[21]

William, Mary and Sara spent much of their time with the hospitable Lambs and Robinson. The new edition of *Poems*, which had been published in April, was much discussed, as were the reviews. Knowing how sensitive William was to criticism, Robinson was pleasantly surprised to find that the poet agreed with their preference for the earlier versions of some of his verses and even talked of restoring the epithets 'fiery' and 'laughing' to the poems on the nightingale and the daffodils, in place of the 'ebullient' and 'jocund' which he had substituted. Robinson had not met either William's wife or her sister before and was initially disappointed. Mary appeared to be 'a mild and amiable woman, not so lively or animated as Miss Wordsworth'; several weeks later, he began to feel 'quite cordial' with her and decided she was emphatically 'an amiable woman'. Sara was 'a plain woman, rather repulsive at first, but she improves on acquaintance greatly. She is a lively, sensible little woman.' With the Lambs, they made up several parties for the theatre, seeing the celebrated Miss Eliza O'Neill in *Romeo and Juliet* and sitting at the front of the new Drury Lane theatre for a production of *Richard II*.[22]

At both the Lambs' and Robinson's, the Wordsworths attended many small, informal gatherings and were introduced to a number of young men who counted themselves among William's small but growing band of devotees. These young men were the seed-corn of William's future reputation, for they would all achieve eminence in their chosen fields, and possess power and influence which they would exert on his behalf. They included Thomas Alsager, a musician and scholar who wrote for *The Times*, Thomas Noon Talfourd, a fledgling writer and barrister, and the unfortunately named Barron Field, also a barrister, who, rather touchingly, showed the Wordsworths his copy of the *Poems*, which he had interleaved with his own handwritten transcripts of William's unpublished poems, copied from Lamb's manuscripts.[23]

One person who was deliberately excluded from these gatherings was Hazlitt. When William attended, Hazlitt was not invited, and, when Lamb knew Hazlitt was likely to call, he warned William, so that he could absent himself. William explained to Robinson that he never refused to meet or speak to Hazlitt when they met accidentally, but he had not been in his company voluntarily since Hazlitt's escapade in the Lakes in 1803. This was undoubtedly the root cause of the snub, but it cannot explain why it suddenly became an issue now. The key factor was Hazlitt's review of *The Excursion*. Hazlitt himself expected gratitude for what he considered a laudatory piece; when William did not visit him to proffer thanks, he was deeply offended. For William, Hazlitt's sneering remarks about, and abuse of, the natives of the Lakes in his review had been a forcible reminder of the whole degrading episode, which had caused him so much embarrassment. Perhaps, too, because the Wordsworths spent so much time with the Lambs, William's decision to avoid Hazlitt became more pointed and obvious than it had been on previous visits. Unfortunately, Hazlitt's 'acid feelings' were roused by what he regarded as this public and deliberate snub, and William would bear the consequences for years to come. Hazlitt had never missed an opportunity to snipe at William's politics. Now he would turn a stream of vitriolic and belittling comment on his poetry as well, and it would have a corrosive effect on public opinion. Even while William was in London, he launched the attack by publishing an article in the

Examiner on 11 June which honoured Milton as a consistent patriot and disparaged William as the author of 'paltry sonnets upon the royal fortitude'. Hazlitt even insinuated that William, now being of the war party, had not published *The Female Vagrant* simply because it described the miseries caused by war to the poor.[24]

Leigh Hunt, the editor of the *Examiner*, disclaimed the article when William called on him the day it was published, but his attitude towards the poet was always what one mutual friend aptly described as 'weathercock'. The two men had never met before but in 1811, Hunt had satirized William in his *Feast of Poets*, having him driven from the feast for 'gath'ring the refuse that others reject'. William comforted himself with the knowledge that Hunt had not actually read any of his verse when he gave vent to these sarcasms. After the publication of *The Excursion*, Hunt privately retracted his opinion, and when William learned from Henry Brougham that Hunt admitted 'valuing' his poetry, he sent him a complimentary copy of *Poems*.[25] Thanking him for it in a letter written on 28 May, Hunt declared himself 'one of the most ardent of your general admirers' and, when they met again on 13 June, he paid William 'the highest compliments' and told him that 'as he grew wiser & got older he found his respect for his powers & enthusiasm for his genius encrease'. In a facetious account of his distinguished visitor, written many years later, Hunt described the poet as having a dignified manner, 'a deep and roughish but not unpleasing voice, and an exalted mode of speaking'. He noted William's habit (captured in his portraits) of keeping his left hand tucked into the bosom of his waistcoat while he sat, 'dealing forth his eloquent but hardly catholic judgments'. Though Hunt gently mocked William's manners and opinions, he was mesmerized by his eyes: 'certainly I never beheld eyes that looked so inspired or supernatural', he wrote. 'They were like fires half burning, half smouldering, with a sort of acrid fixture of regard, and seated at the further end of two caverns. One might imagine Ezekial or Isaiah to have had such eyes.'[26]

Another new acquaintance of this London visit who was also impressed by William's physical appearance was Benjamin Robert Haydon. A twenty-nine-year-old artist who famously quarrelled with almost everyone he met, including, and especially, his patrons, he shared with William an exalted sense of his vocation. Unfashionably, and much to the detriment of his purse as well as his career, Haydon painted huge historical canvases in which he struggled for anatomical accuracy. He had been an admirer of William's poetry for many years and had written to him as an eighteen-year-old student to praise his 'sublime, enthusiastic hymn' and assure him 'if you never write again, this will immortalize you'. The two men met, possibly not for the first time, at one of William's literary breakfasts, where Haydon spent a 'delightful two hours'. He recorded only one snippet of conversation, but it was a characteristic Wordsworthian pronouncement: talking of his youthful attendance at parliamentary debates, he said, 'You always went from Burke with your mind filled, from Fox with your feelings excited, & from Pitt with wonder at his making you uneasy at his having had the power to make the worse appear the better reason. Pitt preferred power to principle.'[27]

Three weeks later William returned to Haydon's studio to sit for the artist. Haydon did not paint a picture, however, but took a 'life mask', a plaster cast of William's face. It was an uncomfortable, lengthy and undignified process, but as Haydon wrote in his diary, 'He bore it like a philosopher.' John Scott, who was to meet William at breakfast, arrived while the plaster was still in place, so his head was wrapped in cloth and straws were sticking out of his nostrils to enable him to breathe. Haydon invited Scott 'as a curiosity to take a peep, that he might say the first sight he ever had of so great a poet was such a singular one as this'. William was sitting, in Haydon's dressing gown, 'with his hands folded, sedate, steady, & solemn . . . there he sat innocent & unconscious of our plot against his dignity, unable to see or to speak, with all the mysterious silence of a spirit'. When it was all over, he came into breakfast 'with his usual cheerfulness, and delighted & awed us by his illustrations & bursts of inspiration'. The conversation was principally about William's plans for *The Recluse* and he so enthralled both his auditors that, eighteen months later, they were still talking about it, and Haydon begged him to 'write me, what you then said. It appeared to me at the time as grand an intention as ever entered the conception of any Poet, and it would be a memento, I would keep as long as I breathed.'[28]

John Scott's enthusiasm for William's poetry was new and important. He too was young and influential, for, at the age of thirty-two, he was already editor of the *Champion.* He had been what William called 'a desperate Enemy of mine', but after reading *The Excursion* he had undergone a Damascene conversion. Just before William came to London, Scott had sent him a complimentary copy of his newly published book, *A Visit to Paris in 1814*, which gave a highly unfavourable account of the French. More importantly, only a fortnight after his first meeting with William, he published a review of the new edition of *Poems* and *The White Doe* which he had personally written for the *Champion.* It was a significant moment, for Scott was a poacher turned gamekeeper and was determined to recruit an audience for William's poetry. Quoting eight lines from *A Poet's Epitaph*, he declared, 'We doubt not that many of our readers will be startled to find that eight lines so simply beautiful, so chastely sublime, can be taken from the works of an author whose writings they have never read, but have seen quoted in broken lines to be ridiculed for their quaintness and vulgarity.' While not falling into the trap of eulogizing, which would have been as counter-productive as Jeffrey's hostilities, Scott ended his review with the first published acclamation of William's right to be considered the greatest living poet.

> He is now before the public in a variety of works, – of unequal merit certainly, – but in their collective testimony proclaiming him the greatest poetical genius of the age. It may be a question how far he is right and how far he is wrong; critics may employ themselves and amuse their readers in picking out what they think objectionable passages, – but his heavenly faculty raises him above the application of their rules, and even (which is the privilege only of the few first rates) places him out of the reach of being substantially injured by his own defects.[29]

When William left London, on or about 19 June, he could do so secure in the conviction that he had indeed found 'fit audience ... though few' for his poetry. He had been introduced to a whole new range of people, principally young men, who were fervent in their admiration. (Two of them, Talfourd and Haydon, would even name their sons after him.) He had won over two more editors of influential journals, Hunt and, more particularly, Scott, to add to the faithful Stuart. The reviewers might, and would, continue to pour scorn on him, but now William had conclusive evidence to prove that his poems were valued outside the tight-knit loyal band of relatives and friends. 'I can assure you I find in Society your <u>understanders</u> (if I may say it) encrease,' Haydon assured him in November 1816, 'and I think if you live ten years, you will see your genius, my dear Sir, triumph over all the petty ignorances of cursed reviews'. There were still many impediments to his popularity, and it would continue to be an uphill struggle to establish his reputation, but he was at last, in his own phrase, beginning to create the taste by which he would be enjoyed.[30]

Before the Wordsworths left London, William's latest book, *The White Doe of Rylstone, or The Fate of the Nortons*, was published by Longman. Like *The Excursion* and *Poems*, it was printed in large quarto size, though it constituted a much thinner volume and was optimistically priced at one guinea. An engraving of Beaumont's painting graced the frontispiece, and the volume was dedicated to Mary, 'Beloved Wife!', in a poem describing how they had loved to read together the story of Una, in Spenser's *Faerie Queene*, in the early years of their marriage. Una, like the heroine of *The White Doe*, was 'a bright, encouraging, example' of 'female patience winning firm repose; And of the recompense that conscience seeks'. This time there was no preface to aggravate the critics, only an uncontentious introductory sonnet on the sacred power of imagination, 'the glorious faculty assigned To elevate the more-than-reasoning mind', and a quotation from Francis Bacon's *Of Atheism*. There were, however, a large number of notes to the text, rooting it in its historic, geographic and balladic setting.[31]

The reviews trickled out over the next six months and were a mixed bag. Hot on the heels of Scott's praise in the *Champion* came a similar review in the *New British Lady's Magazine*, which began by pointing out that it seemed 'strange that the works of the author now before us should have met with such unmerited obloquy'. Declaring *The White Doe* 'almost entirely free' from all William's 'peculiarities', the critic opined, 'we think [it] will be perused by all classes, by all poetical sects, with a pleasure that experiences no drawback by the insertion of passages for which the reader's mind is not prepared'. The review ended on a curiously humble note entirely alien to all William's previous critics. Only an imperfect sketch of the poem had been given,

> partly from want of room, and partly (with unfeigned diffidence we say it) from incapacity to estimate worthily a man of Mr Wordsworth's mind. This feeling is, we are happy to say, becoming more general; and although perhaps the poem now before us will not contribute

to raise him in the admiration of his friends, we doubt whether it will not render him more popular.[32]

If William had hoped that such a favourable reception marked a turning point in his relationship with the critics, he was to be greatly disappointed. Jeffrey, of course, led the attack, with an opening sentence almost as memorable as 'This will never do.' 'This, we think, has the merit of being the very worst poem we ever saw imprinted in a quarto volume', he began. When he first started to read it, Jeffrey said, he thought it was a cruel parody of William's style, until he realized that 'nothing in the nature of a joke could be so insupportably dull'. In the hands of a Scott or Byron, the story would probably have made an interesting ballad (*not* a quarto volume); in William's, it was a vehicle for 'low and maudlin imbecility'. The fun had clearly gone out of the persecution, however, for the rest of the review was a rather limp summary of the poem, lacking Jeffrey's usual bite.

This same feeling of merely parroting hackneyed old criticisms afflicted other reviewers. The only novelty the *Eclectic Review* could devise was that the dedicatory poem touched 'the fancy and . . . the heart' and 'afforded us, after all, more pleasure than anything in the volume'. The *Monthly Review* frankly admitted it was tired of pointing out William's incurable errors, all of which were to be found in the current poem, and therefore resigned 'the wearisome office of censure'. Had William overwhelmed his severest critics by the sheer volume of his output? Unfortunately not. The reviewer in the *Gentleman's Magazine* identified the reason for this abatement of hostilities when he pointed out that *The White Doe* had neither the homeliness of diction nor want of dignity in its characters which had always been the focus of critical censure in the past; without them 'the ingenious severity of criticism will not easily find matter for ridicule'.[33]

Instead of returning home after their six weeks' residence in London, William, Mary and Sara travelled by coach to Bury, to pay a visit to their friends the Clarksons. While they were there, the stunning news of Bonaparte's defeat at Waterloo on 18 June was announced, followed shortly afterwards by that of his abdication and recapture. Amid all the rejoicing, Sara could not resist a smug boast that William had been a true prophet in foreseeing that Bonaparte was not the French people's chosen leader. Leaving Sara with the Clarksons, William and Mary went to visit Christopher and his family at Bocking. Christopher was always busy: the day after their arrival there was the Charity sermon to preach for the school, with a large party to entertain. Christopher's friend Dr Satterthwaite and Priscilla's father, old Mr Lloyd, were also staying and it was probably a chaotic visit. According to Dorothy's somewhat jaundiced view, Priscilla had always been 'helpless' in the house and a 'wretched manager', but she now had three children and was heavily pregnant. So it was probably with some relief that, on 3 July, William and Mary left for Coleorton, to rejoin the Beaumonts on their country estate and, a month later, to accompany them to the Lakes.[34]

Dorothy had had a miserable time of it in their absence. 'It has been the sickliest season in the North that was ever known –', she told Catherine Clarkson, 'and none of my Flock were spared.' They had all had coughs and fevers, including Dorothy herself, and Scambler had been called in more than once to administer blisters to Willy and Dora. All this she had kept from William and Mary, knowing that they would have come racing home in panic. 'I was glad that they were spared the anxiety, . . . I always suffer a thousand times more from my Brother's unconquerable agitation and fears when Willy ails anything than from any other cause.' By the end of June they were all well again, though delicate, and the arrival of glorious summer sunshine promised to restore them to better health.[35]

A placard on the Ambleside coach bearing the slogan 'Great News. *Abdication of Buonaparte*' brought the first tidings of this event to Rydal. It revived all Dorothy's hopes of going to France for Caroline's wedding, and Annette, writing in great joy after the return of Louis XVIII, urged her to come immediately, saying all was safe and quiet. Nevertheless, Dorothy demurred, preferring to wait until she could be certain that peace and stability had been re-established. A proposal that Caroline should come over also foundered, as they could find no one to escort her to England or to whom they could 'with propriety' entrust her once she arrived in London.[36]

On 21 August there was a huge bonfire on the top of Skiddaw to celebrate the victory at Waterloo. William, Mary, Dorothy and Johnny went over to Keswick to join Southey, his wife and children, and Miss Barker, who were the instigators of the event. Together with a huge party of neighbours, 'some adventurous Lakers', including the son of James Boswell, the biographer of Johnson, and 'Messrs. Rag, Tag, and Bobtail', they made their way up the mountain. They roasted beef and boiled plum puddings on the bonfire and drank hot rum punch – until William, who was notoriously clumsy, tripped over the kettle and spilt all the boiling water. The irrepressible Southey immediately set about exposing the culprit and punished him by singing a parody, which all the party joined in, ''Twas *you* that kicked the kettle down! 'Twas you, Sir, you!' They sang 'God save the King' round the bonfire, fired cannons at every toast and rolled blazing balls of tow and turpentine down the steep side of the mountain. 'The effect was grand beyond imagination', Southey enthused. 'We formed a huge circle round the most intense light, and behind us was an immeasurable arch of the most intense darkness, for our bonfire fairly put out the moon.' Without water to let down their grog, the 'Rag, Tag, and Bobtail' were soon heartily drunk, and it must have been an entertaining sight to see the column of revellers staggering down the mountainside, a wavering line of fire marking the progress of their torch-lit procession.[37] It was an event which, not surprisingly, entered the folklore of the Lakes.

Less memorable, but equally special in its own way, was a personal memento of Bonaparte which found its way to the Wordsworths. Henry Parry, the Inspector of Stamps who had stayed at Rydal Mount two years earlier, had found himself on board a ship moored alongside that in which Bonaparte was imprisoned, before his exile to St Helena. The former emperor's chamberlain cut a profile portrait of the prisoner. Parry obtained permission to trace it, and sent it to William, 'thinking it might be acceptable'. As William had been disgusted by the crowds flocking to see David's portrait of Bonaparte in London, this was debatable, but he nevertheless preserved the profile among his letters.[38]

There was the usual influx of summer visitors. The Beaumonts spent nine 'delightful summer days' at Rydal Mount, walking daily in the park of Rydal Hall, 'which is as good as our own', and professing themselves enchanted with the Wordsworths' home and surroundings. Despite this, when they decided to take a small house for the summer months of the three ensuing years, they chose to be at Keswick. Samuel Tillbrooke made a welcome return from Cambridge for his annual visit to the Lakes; despite being badly lame, after an accident in his gig in Scotland in 1813, he was as cheerful and uncomplaining as ever. At the end of September John Monkhouse escorted Sara back from Hindwell to Rydal Mount, and in October his brother Tom came from London to stay for a few days on his way to the Penrith races.[39]

As the summer drew to a close, the Wordsworth circle was hit by a series of tragedies. Charles Lloyd's mental derangement had become significantly worse. For three months he had been confined to his room and would allow no one except his wife near him; it was only at the end of September that he allowed her to have some relief from her constant attendance, but even then he could not bear to have anyone near him, except Mary or Dorothy. The two women therefore took it in turns to go to Brathay on a daily basis, taking over Sophia Lloyd's nursing duties, or looking after her eight children for her. It was clear that things could not continue in this way, so Sophia decided that she would take her husband to his native Birmingham, where there were medical men devoted to the management of insanity in whose care he could be placed. On 12 October William escorted the afflicted husband and his wife as far as Manchester, leaving Dorothy in charge of their children at Brathay. The night before they set off, the shocking news arrived that Priscilla Wordsworth had died. A fortnight earlier, she had given birth to a still-born baby; she had appeared to be recovering, though deeply unhappy at the loss of a much wanted daughter, but had died unexpectedly on 7 October, probably from septicaemia. Lloyd was in no fit state to learn of his sister's death, so his wife and William had to keep the news to themselves. As soon as he returned from Manchester, William wrote a note of sympathy to his brother, offering to dispatch Dorothy immediately to Bocking, if Christopher wished for or needed her assistance. 'Heaven preserve you, and what remains to you on earth of yours:' he wrote, 'for her who is gone she is among the blessed – . . . for myself as a Husband I feel for you to the utmost – I would write more could I suggest any consolation; I only can assure you, of what you well know, our heart-felt sympathy and our wish to relieve you, in any way you can point out'.[40]

As Priscilla had no unmarried sisters, Dorothy was the obvious choice to look after her widowed brother and three nephews, the oldest of whom was not yet eight. Though she was prepared to do this on a temporary basis, she had no intention of doing so permanently. 'I have no thoughts of residing with him', she wrote to Jane Marshall, eight days after her sister-in-law's death. 'I could not give up my present home for any other.' She was equally dismissive about the unfortunate Priscilla. With terrible irony, bearing in mind what she herself would one day become, she described Priscilla's tendency 'if not to insanity, to that excess of nervous irritability which puts our feelings and actions almost as much out of our own power as if we were actually what is called insane' and Christopher's tenderness and patience in looking after her as 'almost beyond belief'. Her conclusion? A crisp 'Priscilla might have suffered less if she had had a less indulgent Husband.' It was perhaps fortunate that Christopher decided he did not wish to bring Dorothy from home 'unless absolutely necessary'; his father-in-law had come to him immediately, and Sophia offered to visit when the doctors decided it would be expedient for her to be separated from Charles for a while. Thereafter, he would manage on his own. He never married again, devoting himself instead to his three young sons and his career. The following year, he accepted a transfer to the vast suburban parish of Lambeth, where there was much for a conscientious clergyman to do and he could try to forget his own sorrow in hard labour for others.[41]

Hard on the heels of these calamities came news that Mary Lamb had suffered another mental breakdown and again been confined. 'She has left me very lonely and very miserable', her brother wrote. 'I stroll about, but there is no rest but at ones own fireside, and there is no rest for me there now.' And then, from Catherine Clarkson, they learned that William's old and dear friend from Patterdale, Captain Luff, had died in Mauritius. 'We are truely afflicted by the event;' William told Catherine, 'as he was much valued by us all; and we looked forward to their resettling themselves in our neighbourhood as one of the pleasantest hopes that this Family entertained.' William felt strongly that there should be a memorial of some kind: 'Luff was a genuine lover of his Country, and a true and enlightened Friend of Mankind.'[42]

In the midst of all these sorrows, William had little time or inclination for poetry. The sales of *The Excursion*, *Poems* and *The White Doe* had all been very poor. Only 300 of the 500 copies of *The Excursion* had been sold. There was no doubt that this was principally because of the cost, but, as Lady Beaumont pointed out, many people balked at buying what William himself had described in the preface as only part of a work. The supposedly more popular *White Doe* was equally slow-moving and Dorothy now resigned herself to the idea that her brother's poetry would never sell.

> I once thought *The White Doe* might have helped off the other, but I now perceive it can hardly help itself. It is a pity it was published in so expensive a form because some are thereby deprived of the pleasure of reading it; but however cheap his poems might be I am sure it will be very long before they have an extensive sale – nay it will not be while he is alive to know it.[43]

There was clearly no point in proceeding with the plan to publish *Peter Bell* and *Benjamin the Waggoner*, so this part of William's grand scheme for laying his works before the public was shelved once more.

There were crumbs of comfort, not the least being a small but steady stream of poems dedicated to William himself, suggesting that he was beginning to win approval among his peers. His Edinburgh protégé Robert Pearce Gillies, Keats's and Haydon's friend John Hamilton Reynolds and the Quaker poet Bernard Barton all sent him poems and letters detailing their indebtedness. Barton was prompted to write his poem after reading Jeffrey's review of *The White Doe*, earning himself a mild rebuke from William for allowing himself to be so provoked. His letter is particularly interesting because he revealed he had been an admirer of William's poetry since childhood, had been shamed out of his early allegiance when he began to mix in the world and then returned with renewed pleasure to it. It was, he said, 'the chosen and endear'd companion of my hours of retirement . . . I believe I may say not in flattery but in sober simple truth that few Poets will in the Hour of Affliction be oftener recurred to than thyself'. In reply, William confessed that his best assurance that his work would live came from hearing of people like Barton who, having once learned to enjoy his work, never ceased to value it.[44]

It was just such a letter from Haydon which sparked William's first creative effort of the winter. The two men had kept in touch since their meeting in the summer. Haydon wanted to include William's portrait among the crowd in his ambitious project to paint a vast picture of Christ's entry into Jerusalem and he was also, at Keats's request, trying to get a bust made of William. Beaumont had been commissioned to draw a sketch and take measurements, which William relayed back to Haydon, not omitting to draw attention to the bald patch on his crown. Writing to thank William for the gift of a pencil case, Haydon had been embarrassingly grateful: 'I have the highest enthusiasm for your genius & purity of mind –', he wrote. 'I have benefitted & have been supported in the trouble of life by your Poetry.' William was equally convinced of Haydon's genius. *Christ's Entry into Jerusalem* would, he believed, 'do you huge credit; and raise the Reputation of Art in this Country'. In a moment of artistic solidarity, William composed his sonnet addressed to Haydon, 'High is our calling, Friend!', which urged faith 'in the whispers of the lonely Muse, While the whole world seems adverse to desert' and ended with the triumphant rallying cry, 'Great is the glory, for the strife is hard!' It was not a poem of which William was particularly fond or proud, but to Haydon it became a talisman: it was 'the highest honor that ever was paid or ever can be paid to me'. His first instinct was to ask if he could give it to John Scott to publish in the *Champion* '& might he say it was written by you to me [?]', but over the coming years, as his own fortunes declined, he would quote it with monotonous regularity, until William must have been heartily sick of hearing it.[45] William reluctantly gave his permission to publish on condition it was made clear that his sonnet to Haydon was a private tribute and had not been written for the papers. 'I naturally shrink from solicitation of public notice', he told Haydon. 'I never publish any thing without great violence to my own disposition which is to shun, rather than court, regard.' The sonnet, with two others enclosed in the same letter, was duly published in both Scott's *Champion* and Hunt's *Examiner* the following spring. The three sonnets had been written on three consecutive days, but the last proved to be more prophetic than the first, for it welcomed the first blasts of winter air which

> Announce a season potent to renew,
> 'Mid frost and snow, the instinctive joys of song,
> And nobler cares than listless summer knew.

Sending these off to Haydon on 21 December, William confessed, 'I am grieved to think what a time has elapsed since I last paid my devoirs to the Muses, and not less so to know that now in the depth of Winter when I hoped to resume my Labours, I continue to be called from them by unavoidable engagements.'[46]

The most urgent of these engagements was a final settling of the accounts between himself, Dorothy and their brother Richard. Both William and Dorothy had been pressing for this for years, but it had become imperative for two reasons. While in London, William had obtained confirmation from Richard's partner, Richard Addison, that, as he had long suspected, his brother had invested all his and Dorothy's money in purchasing land. Rents were low, as the Wordsworths knew all too well from the tales of woe coming from the Welsh borders, and neither he nor Dorothy had any legal security for their money. This was a particular worry for Dorothy, who had no capital or income other than that in Richard's hands.

To add to their problems, Richard was now the father of a son, John, born in January 1815, to whom his estate would pass on his death. After years of leading an entirely dutiful and respectable life, Richard had scandalized all his acquaintance by suddenly marrying, at the age of forty-five, his twenty-two-year-old servant at Sockbridge, Jane Westmorland. The Wordsworths could not help but disapprove of him marrying one so young, and one of his own servants to boot, but when they actually met her they were won over. William thought her 'very decent and comely' on their first meeting; Dorothy was more disapproving. She liked Jane 'very well – the circumstances of her education – her rank in Society – her youth etc being got over . . . She is not vulgar, though she has nothing of the natural gentlewoman about her.' At least she was 'kind and attentive to her Husband'. Their little boy, who would be known as 'Keswick' John, to distinguish him from his cousin at Rydal Mount, was a different matter: 'he is indeed a sweet creature,' his aunt enthused, 'very pretty, and most intelligent and engaging. This in an extraordinary degree, for he forces every one to admire him.'[47]

On 8 December William and Dorothy set off to walk over Kirkstone Pass to visit Richard at Sockbridge. They broke their journey overnight at Patterdale and paused to breakfast at Hallsteads, John Marshall's new house on Ullswater, admiring the rising sun as it tinged the snow-capped mountains pink. Dorothy then went on to stay with Captain Wordsworth and his wife at Penrith, while William made his way to Sockbridge to spend several days negotiating the accounts. A week after getting back to Rydal Mount, William was due to return again, this time with Mary. They had planned to share a chaise to Keswick with Mrs Lloyd and Miss Alms, but the heaviest snowfalls in sixteen years closed all the roads and they had to postpone their departure till Christmas Day. As Sara was also stranded by the weather at Penrith, on her way back from a visit to the Cooksons at Kendal, Dorothy's forty-fourth birthday was spent (not unhappily) as the lone adult in charge of a large party of children – three Wordsworths, six of the Lloyds and Sophia Crump. The little Lloyds, like the Coleridges before them, were to become part of the extended family at Rydal Mount. Their mother had returned to the Lakes only to prepare for the family's final removal to Birmingham after Christmas; the house at Brathay had to be emptied and a sale would be held before the end of January. Dorothy was full of admiration for Sophia Lloyd's fortitude in the face of her afflictions. 'I should be utterly incapable of doing as *she* does and bearing what *she* bears.' Not the least of her sorrows was a parting from her boys, who would remain at Ambleside at Mr Dawes's school, where Johnny too was now a weekly boarder, in the hope that this change would rouse him out of his habitual laziness.[48]

By the time William left Sockbridge early in January, he had not achieved a final settlement but had obtained a bond for £3,000 as security for his and Dorothy's money invested in Richard's land. What he still needed was Christopher's approval for their decision to set off the debt paid by William Crackanthorpe to the estate against that due to Uncle Richard. The latter debt had almost wholly been incurred by William's own education, but, as he pointed out, it was hardly fair that he should have to repay it personally, as Christopher's had been entirely paid for by the Crackanthorpes. 'This is the *only* point in which you are concerned in the account between us –', William wrote in some irritation, when Christopher queried this. 'If you could conceive a hundredth part of the obstacles, which I have had to get over from my Brother's procrastinating habits, and knew the time which I have sacrificed in this business, which I really never would have done on my own account merely, I am sure that you would acknowledge the reasonableness of this determination.'[49]

Despite all these harassments, William found that the winter had indeed been a 'season potent to renew . . . the instinctive joys of song'. On 29 January he wrote to John Scott, offering him three new sonnets, belatedly inspired by the Allied victory at Waterloo. The last six lines of the third poem were intended to stand alone, if required, as an inscription for a memorial to the English who had fought there.

> Heroes! – for instant sacrifice prepared;
> Yet filled with ardour and on triumph bent
> 'Mid direst shocks of mortal accident –
> To you who fell, and you whom slaughter spared
> To guard the fallen, and consummate the event,
> Your Country rears this sacred Monument!

England did not take the hint, but Scott was thrilled to be offered the first chance to publish the sonnets: 'to have the country's finest Victory celebrated by her finest Poet in my Journal, I certainly regard as the most honorary thing that has yet happened to me'.[50]

It was no accident that William's poetic response to Waterloo was so tardy, for the sonnets marked the beginning of a whole series of poems, mostly odes, written in the spring of 1816, which would reflect on the victory. William claimed that they owed their existence to patriotism, but they were by no means jingoistic or triumphalist. In fact, they were rather subdued. 'Have we not conquered? – by the vengeful sword?' he asked in one. 'Ah no, by dint of Magnanimity . . . Say not that we have vanquished – but that we survive'.[51] It is almost as if, having written his splendidly stirring 'Sonnets dedicated to National Independence and Liberty' out of conviction, he now felt simply duty-bound to celebrate the victory that had been achieved. Then, and in the *Convention of Cintra*, he had urged that victory would not be won by strength of arms alone, but by superior moral virtue. This was the theme he again adopted in these celebratory odes, suggesting that God had conferred eventual success on the nation which had deserved it. The problem, as William tacitly admitted in the prefatory advertisement, was that it was hard to see any superior moral virtue in a post-war Britain, where much of the populace was starving, the mills were idle, Luddites were smashing machines and even the countryside was subject to riots. Everywhere one looked there was poverty, distress and discontent.

In the circumstances, it is not surprising that William's odes strike a wrong note, for they seem out of touch with reality. It is as if the poet is disengaged from his subject. His critics had often complained that he invested every image of every poem with his own feelings, but it was certainly not true of this body of work. Even the way they were written, though appropriate to the subject, seems the antithesis of everything William had made his own. They are full of classical and biblical allusions, elaborate imagery and hyperbolic language, trussed up in an inelegant format which William called 'dramatised ejaculation', but was really modelled on the Pindaric ode loathed by every schoolboy classicist. William was not unaware of the incongruity at the heart of his poems. In his advertisement he went to some lengths to refute the charge he knew would be made against him, that of 'insensibility' to the 'present distresses'. These, he said, should not be allowed to obscure the great moral triumph that had been won. The present sufferings, he believed (wrongly), would be transitory; Britain had wisely poured out her treasures for the deliverance of Europe and, trusting in the same national wisdom and energy which had brought victory, he confidently expected that her prosperity would be restored. These poems looked beyond immediate and transitory distress to commemorate 'that course of action, by which Great Britain has, for some time past, distinguished herself above all other countries'.[52]

William completed the odes by 11 March, admitting privately that he feared he had laboured too long and hard on the style, at the expense of the spirit. Taken together with the handful of sonnets which also belonged to the collection, he had written just over 700 lines of poetry, his most sustained effort for several years. The manuscript was parcelled up and posted off to Longman, with instructions that it should be printed in the same size and style as the 1815 edition of *Poems*, so that the two could be bound up together by collectors. Three weeks later, when his publisher had still not even acknowledged receipt of the manuscript, he permitted himself a wry comment to Gillies: 'from this you may judge of the value which the Goods of the author of the Excursion at present bear in the estimation of the Trader'.[53]

The slim volume appeared in May, with a price tag of 4s on its sixty-one pages, and a title out of all proportion to its size: *Thanksgiving Ode, January 18, 1816: With Other Short Pieces, Chiefly Referring to Recent Public Events.* The reaction was predictable. A few weary reviews, reiterating the old complaints about William's 'peculiarities', and a sale so poor that he was driven to declare 'as to Publishing I shall give it up, as no-body will buy what I send forth: nor can I expect it seeing what stuff the public appetite is set upon'.[54]

A second publication by William appeared at the same time as the *Thanksgiving Ode.* This was his *A Letter To A Friend of Robert Burns.* The 'Friend' was James Gray, an admirer of *The Excursion*, who had visited the Wordsworths at Rydal Mount the previous summer. William had obviously expatiated at length on one of his favourite hobby-horses, his dislike of intrusive biography.

> I have found nothing more mortifying in the course of my life than those peeps behind the curtain, that have shown me how low in point of moral elevation stand some of those men who have been the most efficient instruments and machines for public benefit that our age has produced. We live in inquisitive times, and there is but too little reserve in gratifying public curiosity.

Having reported his host's views to Gilbert Burns, who was preparing a vindication of his brother's life and character against the reviewers in a new edition of the works, Gray wrote to William in November 1815, saying that Burns would appreciate his advice on how to proceed.[55]

William leapt to the challenge but his practical suggestions, such as attaching notes to correct misrepresentations and prefixing a concise life, were merely an excuse for what was really a blistering attack on biographers in general, more specifically on biographers of authors and most specifically of all on Francis Jeffrey and the *Edinburgh Review.* Biography is an art, he thundered, not a science. 'Truth is not here, as in the sciences, and in natural philosophy, to be sought without scruple, and promulgated for its own sake, upon the mere chance of its being serviceable; but only for obviously justifying purposes, moral or intellectual.' While admitting that biographers might sometimes be justified in prying into the private lives of some active figures on the world's stage, he did not extend the same licence to biographers of authors. (Though his argument, that revelations about the private lives of the former might help explain their public conduct, seems equally applicable to both categories.) Authors, and poets particularly, were a special case. 'Our business is with their books, – to understand and to enjoy them . . . if their works be good, they contain within themselves all that is necessary to their being comprehended and relished.' The attack on 'the Edinburgh reviewer' at the end of the *Letter* was as irrelevant as it was transparent and ill-judged. 'It is notorious that this persevering Aristarch, as often as a work of original genius comes before him, avails himself of that opportunity to re-proclaim to the world the narrow range of his own comprehension.' Jeffrey was accused of writing with 'happy self-complacency', 'unsuspecting vain-glory' and 'cordial *bonhommie*', and betraying a mind at once 'obtuse, superficial, and inept'. In a final flourish, William compared this 'anonymous conductor of a perishable publication' to those twin enemies of mankind, Bonaparte and Robespierre.[56] That William had taken such a mighty tumble from his pedestal of lofty disdain was a matter of great glee to his critics, who pounced upon it as soon as it was published in May. 'The world is not to be gulled by his hypocritical zeal in the defence of injured merit', Wilson wrote in *Blackwood's Edinburgh Magazine.* 'It is not Robert Burns for whom he feels, – it is William Wordsworth.' The *Letter* also provided perfect ammunition for Hazlitt, who was so contemptuous in speaking of William in one of his public lectures that the normally placid Robinson was betrayed into hissing his disgust.[57]

Life at Rydal Mount continued on an even tenor throughout the spring of 1816. The education of the children was still a priority. Dora was introduced to music, a subject in which she would excel, during a two-month visit to Keswick with her Aunt Sara. No one else in the family had musical skills, so it was Miss Barker who began to teach Dora to play the harpsichord. Johnny was still boarding at Mr Dawes's and improving steadily. Willy too, who had proved as inattentive and easily bored as Dora when taught by the Wordsworth women, began to take lessons from John Carter and, to everyone's delight and astonishment, made rapid progress. Dorothy's comment about Dora, that she would have done much more for herself if they had all been less anxious about her and taken less pains with her, began to seem applicable to all the children.[58]

Dorothy herself was still hoping rather forlornly that she might get to Paris to see Caroline, but William and Mary were unwilling to let her go until France was more settled. The main reason for the trip had been removed, for in February Caroline had married Jean Baptiste Baudouin. Despite the family's straitened circumstances, the wedding was a glittering occasion at which Annette's royalist friends turned out in force. Among the guests were the widow of the Prince de Craon, the wife of the Duc de Montmorency, the Vicomte de Montmorency and the Baron de Tardif, as well as the Comte de Salaberry, who was the deputy for Loir-et-Cher, and both Baudouin's superiors at the Mont de Piété bureau. They witnessed the civil marriage contract, which was signed by the groom, his bride as 'A. C. Wordsworth' and her mother as 'M. A. Vallon *dite* William', and specifically stated that the marriage had the consent of 'M[onsieur] W. Wortsworth'.[59] Annette was determined to see her daughter married in style, providing a dinner, ball and supper for thirty people, even though, as Dorothy remarked, she would feel the financial penalty for months to come. Thanks to the efforts of a number of the guests, Annette herself had secured the promise of a royal pension or place, as soon as one became available. The financial future of the newlyweds did not look as promising. By living with Annette, they had enough income to support themselves but not a family, though Caroline's first child would be born before the end of the year. William's annuity of £30, rising to £35 the following year, would be an important part of his daughter's future income, and a millstone round his neck.[60]

William's own financial situation was still far from secure. Richard's health had been giving cause for concern for many months. In February he and his wife went to London, partly on business but partly to consult doctors about his continuing bilious attacks. They proved to be the symptoms of fatal liver disease. In the confined quarters of their lodgings, he became so seriously ill that Montagu, redeeming himself for his former mischief-making, took pity on him and carried the couple off to his own house. When he discovered that Richard, like his lawyer father before him, had not made a will, or appointed guardians for his child, he made haste to report this to William. At first William was concerned only about his infant nephew, but, consulting an attorney in Kendal a couple of days later, he discovered that, if Richard died intestate, his bond would be unenforceable during the twenty-year minority of his son. The only remedy would be chancery proceedings, but the Wordsworths had had more than enough experience of them for one lifetime. It was therefore imperative that Richard should be persuaded to make a will. William wrote immediately to Montagu, begging him, 'as a friend and a man of business acting as my *representative*', to put the matter to Richard. 'Do think of my poor sister's situation at present,' he pleaded, 'forty-four years of age, and without the command of either principal or interest of her little property'.[61]

A similar letter went to Christopher, who, having taken possession of his new rectory at Lambeth a fortnight earlier, was now in a position to offer his brother and sister-in-law a home. They arrived on 1 May and it was obvious that Richard's case was hopeless. On 6 May he formally executed his will, appointing his widow, his brothers and Thomas Hutton, his Penrith lawyer, as his executors. His widow and brothers were also to be guardians of his one-year-old son.[62] For a few days it looked as if Richard would rally and his doctor, the same Anthony Carlisle whom Coleridge and Mary Monkhouse had consulted, was hopeful, but the end came fairly quickly. Christopher sent daily bulletins to Rydal Mount, in answer to their anxious queries and expressions of love to Richard and his wife. Like the Rydalians, Christopher was impressed with his sister-in-law. 'His Wife watches and nurses him most attentively – and shews him all possible tenderness', he wrote, adding that he feared her own health would be undermined by her devotion. Richard died at five in the morning on 19 May; he was forty-seven years old. As he had never expressed any opinion about where he wished to be interred, he was buried in the chancel of Christopher's new church at Lambeth. William offered to go to London for the funeral on 24 May, but it was decided that his presence was more useful in the north, so there was only one carriage containing three mourners to accompany the body to the grave. Though 'the contemplation of the death of a *Brother* was solemn and distressing', Richard's passing was not the devastating blow to his surviving siblings that John's had been. 'We have seen very little of Richard for many years', Dorothy explained, 'therefore as a companion his loss will not be great; but when we did meet he was always amiable and affectionate; and there has been in all our connections with him a perfect harmony.'[63] The consequences of his death, however, were to reverberate for years to come.

Both William and Christopher feared that Richard's affairs would turn out to be in a worse state than he himself had believed, but even they were not prepared for what they found. Their first intimation came when Hutton refused to act as a trustee of the will. On 31 May William went over to Sockbridge to see him and to meet the widow, who had returned that day from London. Neither Hutton nor his suggested alternative, Wilkinson, could be persuaded to accept the responsibility of the trusteeship, though both were happy to offer informal advice and help, and Hutton to carry out the legal work on a professional basis.[64] The inability to find a third trustee would delay the administration of the will for months, causing great frustration to Richard's many long-standing creditors, who included not only his business partner, Addison, but also Lord Abergavenny. It was not until the autumn that steps could finally be taken to put Richard's lands on the market, and the following spring before they could rent out the Sockbridge estate and hold a sale of his effects.[65]

By this stage, Lord Abergavenny, who was owed over £4,500, lost patience and threatened the estate with a suit in chancery. 'If this cannot be put a stop to', Dorothy wrote gloomily in March 1817, 'farewell to every farthing of the property I got from my Father (I have none else) and in the meantime we touch no Interest.' The direct personal intervention of Christopher prevented the suit going ahead, but the threat was only suspended, since his sole bargaining counter was that they would pay as soon as possible.[66] Probate was finally granted on 24 April 1817, but it was the end of the year before the trustees were in a position to offer any payment to creditors. Richard's simple contract debts then amounted to almost £12,500 pounds, but the sale of his effects had grossed less than £10,000. The immediate objective of paying off the creditors 'of any material importance' could therefore be achieved, but Christopher balked at William's suggestion that they should contribute to the shortfall, because he was himself in debt to the tune of £500. In the end, all that was left to Richard's son and heir was a very uncertain £300 a year in rents, half of which would pay the widow's annuity, the rest the interest on William and Dorothy's bond. Their capital, to all intents and purposes, was irrecoverable.[67]

Richard's death was followed by that of two local grandees. The Bishop of Llandaff, whose lamentations on the execution of Louis XVI had inspired William's first political pamphlet, died at his estate on Windermere and was buried at Bowness. His death created a vacancy in Professorship of Divinity at Cambridge, which he had held since 1781. Christopher was an obvious candidate, but he declined to stand, probably because his duties at Lambeth were too arduous for him to contemplate adding to them. The second death was more regretted: Lady Diana Le Fleming of Rydal Hall died in London, but her remains were brought back to be buried next to those of her husband. 'Poor Lady F[leming; the daughter] has lost her *only* Friend –', Sara wrote, 'the Poor a most benevolent one – and we, and the country round, an excellent neighbour.' The cortège was a fortnight on the road and the funeral was conducted with great pomp. Much to the Wordsworths' amusement, the master-undertaker in charge of the proceedings brought his wife with him, all the way from London, not as an indispensable part of the ceremony, but simply to show her the Lakes.[68]

August brought the true Lakers out in force. The Beaumonts came to stay at their house in Keswick for the season, and Samuel Tillbrooke, for whom the Wordsworths had secured Ivy Cottage at the foot of the hill leading to Rydal Mount, came in July. 'We expect to have a treasure of a neighbour in him;' Sara wrote, 'for he is an honest, worthy, preacher and free from all affectation, and overflowing with the milk of human kindness.' He was also a congenial companion for William, and the two men got along famously. William nicknamed his friend 'the knight of the white stockings', because he always wore these distinctive cotton garments, whatever the weather, and Tillbrooke has left a delightful vignette of their evenings together in a joke-ballad, describing how

> . . . Willy's fire and wit shone bright,
> And foot to foot beside the grate
> Like story-telling Boys we sate. –
> With many a joke, and many a rhyme,
> We killed the hoary rogue old Time.

More importantly, Tillbrooke's messianic zeal for William's poetry was beginning to bear fruit. No fewer than fourteen 'Cantabs', as the Wordsworths called the members of the University of Cambridge, took up residence in Ambleside and Bowness for three months during the summer. 'Some have been introduced,' Sara noted in July, '& I suppose most of them will find means to get a sight of the Poet before the summer is past.' The Wordsworths were in no doubt that, though William's poems did not sell, his reputation was growing.[69]

Among the visitors who came to stay at Rydal Mount was Southey. He brought with him his friend the artist and miniaturist Edward Nash, who produced such delightful portraits of the Southey children, and also a telling pencil sketch of William. Southey himself looked like a ghost. His beloved nine-year-old son Herbert, 'the very heart and life of my happiness and my hopes', had died on 17 April. With his usual self-command, he had buried himself in his work, but it was clear to him, and to all who knew him, that he was no longer his old cheerful self. The Wordsworths, whose own dead son had been Herbert's best friend, knew better than most what he was suffering and were quietly, but steadily, supportive.[70]

Young visitors were also much in evidence. Elizabeth Cookson came over from Kendal to stay for the summer and Jack Hutchinson's oldest son, fifteen-year-old George, also became a resident of the neighbourhood. A 'nice boy' but with 'a little too much of the bear', George had been placed, at the Wordsworths' suggestion, as a pupil for a year with the Reverend William Jackson, son of the vicar of Grasmere, who was a Fellow of Queen's College, Oxford, and currently acting as his father's curate. William thought so highly of him that he had recommended him to his brother.

He is without exception one of the most admirable Clergymen for his years that I have known. He is very clever, very zealous, an excellent Scholar, has no discernible northern dialect or pronuntiation [*sic*] . . . and in my opinion reads the Liturgy most impressively. His sermons likewise, which are of his own composition, are exceedingly good. – I therefore think it my duty to point him out to you as a man in every respect deserving of regard.

The enthusiasm was general and Grasmere church was enjoying a renaissance in popularity, though as Sara remarked, with characteristic acerbity, young parsons tend to attract young ladies and their beaux.[71]

One of the most welcome visitors of the late summer was Robinson, for whom William had drawn up a detailed itinerary for his first tour of the Lakes. On his way there, Robinson had fallen in with a twenty-year-old Italian, Count Torlonia, and his tutor, a Mr Walter, who seized the opportunity of an introduction to William with alacrity. The three men enjoyed a convivial evening at Rydal Mount, in which Walter sang Scottish airs, accompanied by Tillbrooke on the flute, and the poet took them on a personal guided tour of Rydal, Grasmere and Patterdale. After visiting both de Quincey and Southey, Robinson accompanied William on a five-day tour from Keswick to Cockermouth, Calder Bridge and Ravenglass. It was, as Robinson gloomily noted, 'uninterruptedly rainy. So that excepting the pleasure of his company they were unpleasant [days] as well as laborious.' Part of the time was spent inspecting Richard's lands which were to be sold, and attending the auction, in company with Hutton, who unintentionally provided the one bright spot in this little tour. Taking Robinson confidentially on one side, Hutton had asked him, 'Is it true – as I have heard reported – that Mr Wordsworth ever wrote verses?' When Robinson finally parted from the Wordsworths, on 24 September, he left with an introduction from William to the Reverend William Carr at Bolton Abbey in his pocket, and 'under the impression of thankfulness for personal attentions in addition to the high reverence I felt for his character before'. Mary Lamb reported in November that Robinson still spoke 'in raptures' of the days he had spent with the Wordsworths, adding, 'He says he never saw a man so happy in *three wives* as Mr Wordsworth is.'[72]

Less happy had been Robinson's meeting with de Quincey, whom he found 'very dirty and even squalid' in appearance, and bitter against the Wordsworths, from whom he was estranged. It was a re-run, on a smaller scale, of the affair with Coleridge. The Wordsworths had known that de Quincey was an opium addict for at least two years. His health had suffered in consequence, but he was still capable of rabble-rousing with the best of them. 'He doses himself with Opium & drinks like a f[ish]', Sara had commented the previous autumn, observing his painful determination to match Wilson in his debaucheries. Worse still, he had notoriously acquired a mistress in Margaret Simpson, who was only just seventeen when she caught his attention. The daughter of a local statesman, who lived at Nab Cottage on Rydal Water, a stone's throw from Rydal Mount, she was barely out of childhood, uneducated and statuesque, a potent combination for de Quincey. Rumours that they were to marry had reached the Wordsworths as early as November 1815, but a year later, when Margaret produced their first son, the parents had still not made it to the altar. The Wordsworths, particularly the women, did not approve of this conduct, and had left de Quincey in no doubt of their opinion, so he had broken off all contact with them.

The fastidious Robinson was repulsed by de Quincey's appearance and was only persuaded to accept an invitation to walk with him by the Wordsworths, who still retained kindly feelings towards de Quincey, and thought the exercise and company would be good for him. It was a kindness Robinson came to regret, for he had to spend the day listening to a torrent of abuse of William, whom de Quincey accused of being very 'secular', loving 'no one but his own family', being 'incapable of friendship' and 'weak to be delighted with the notice of great people'. While acknowledging the justice of some of these claims, Robinson was sufficiently disgusted by de Quincey's bitterness and resentment to wish that he could avoid all future acquaintance with him.[73]

William greeted the birth of William de Quincey on 15 November with heavy irony which, as the father of an illegitimate child himself, was inexcusable. 'Such, in these later times, are the fruits of philosophy ripening under the shelter of our Arcadian mountains', he informed Lamb. 'A marriage is expected by some; but, from the known procrastination of one of the parties, it is not looked for by others till the commencement of the millenium.' Confounding these expectations, the marriage did take place, ten weeks later, on 15 February 1817, in Grasmere church. Dorothy was so vitriolic that one is inclined to suspect some jealousy of the woman who had won de Quincey's affections. 'Mr de Quincey is married; and I fear I may add he is ruined', she wrote. 'He utter'd in raptures of the beauty, the good sense, the simplicity, the "angelic sweetness" of Miss Sympson, who to all other judgments appeared to be a stupid, heavy girl, and was reckoned a Dunce at Grasmere School; and I predict that all these witcheries are ere this removed, and the fireside already dull.'[74]

She was quite wrong. Margaret was to prove a devoted wife and mother, enduring much unhappiness and abject poverty in her marriage, as well as regular abandonment by her erring husband. It was not long before the Wordsworths realized her value, and, having done so, they did everything in their power to assist her and her children.

The year ended with two unsolicited, and very different, tributes to William's growing reputation as a poet. The first was the anonymous publication of Hogg's *Poetic Mirror*, which contained parodies of the poetry of Byron, Scott, Southey, Coleridge, Wilson and William himself, as well as a self-parody. William's three 'contributions', the *Stranger*, the *Flying Taylor* and *James Rigg*, each mischievously purporting to be 'a further portion of *The Recluse*,' were all in blank verse. William at first suspected Lamb might have had a hand in this, but then, realizing that Scottish poets were disproportionately represented, he guessed that it probably originated over the border. For all that it mocked his style, the fact that it was so instantly recognizable to the reading public as to be an appropriate subject for parody was in itself a compliment, of sorts.[75]

The second tribute was sincere and significant. It came from the pen of a new disciple, a man who, at twenty-one, was younger than William's eldest daughter, had published his first poem in the *Examiner* only in May and, before his death less than five years later, would leave behind a body of poetry which would establish his reputation as one of the greatest of all lyric poets. The man was John Keats and the tribute was a sonnet, written on 21 November and forwarded to William by their mutual friend the artist Haydon, on 31 December. 'The Idea of your sending it to Wordsworth put me out of breath', Keats wrote to Haydon; '– you know with what Reverence – I would send my Wellwishes to him'.

The sonnet itself is an exquisite work of art in its own right but it is also important because, at every level, it reveals Keats's debt to William. Not only is he obviously familiar with all William's poetry, but he has adopted his mentor's style and language, and, most important of all, his philosophy.

Great Spirits now on earth are sojourning
  He of the Cloud, the Cataract, the Lake
  Who on Helvellyn's summit wide awake
Catches his freshness from Archangel's wing
He of the Rose, the Violet, the Spring
  The social smile, the Chain for Freedom's sake;
  And lo! – whose stedfastness would never take
A meaner sound than Raphael's Whispering.
And other Spirits are there standing apart
  Upon the Forehead of the age to come;
These, these will give the World another Heart
  And other Pulses – hear ye not the hum
Of mighty workings? –
  Listen awhile ye Nations and be dumb![76]

18. Bombastes Furioso

William, Mary and the children spent Christmas alone at Rydal Mount. Dorothy was on a visit to her 'aunt', Elizabeth Rawson, at Halifax. Month after month had slipped by, but whenever Dorothy brought up the subject of leaving, Mrs Rawson begged her to stay a little longer. By the time she returned home, on 15 February 1817, she had been away for five months. 'I could not have believed it possible that my Friends could have prevailed upon me, or that I could have possibly had a desire to stay so long from home', she confessed to Catherine. The days had been spent very pleasantly in a quiet routine of social visiting, walking and reading. With only two elderly people in the house, servants to perform the work 'as if by magic' and no children's voices disturbing the perfect stillness, it was a complete and, for a time at least, not unwelcome contrast to Rydal Mount. 'I was very happy there', she wrote, 'yet now that I am placed again in the perfect freedom of home, I rejoice many times in every day that I am here saying, "how glad I am that I am among you once again"!'[1]

Sara had also been away since the middle of December, staying with Mary Barker at Greta Hall, but spending most of her time with the Southeys. 'I could not live at this place for worlds –', she told her cousin Tom, 'notwithstanding it is one of the pleasantest *in doors* residences in the Island; for we have good apartments, good fires, plenty of nice books, music, painting, and excellent company with now & then a pool at Quadrille – Yet one "*would*" die for want of exercise – it is impossible to stir to the door without danger of being blown away'. Sara was devoted to Southey's five little daughters, who ranged in age from eleven to four, loving them almost as much as the Wordsworth children. Like Dorothy, she prolonged her stay far beyond her original intention. Southey was preparing to write a history of the Peninsular War and Wellington had lent him all his personal papers, including officers' letters, secretarial journals and memoranda. He asked

Sara to transcribe them and she was in her element. 'We have had the secret history of all these affairs', she confided with glee, '. . . and it has given us not only a greater general but even a personal interest in the war.'[2]

The bustle of literary activity round Southey was in stark contrast to the atmosphere at Rydal Mount, where, in Sara's typically pithy phrase, William was 'doing nothing'. This was undoubtedly true in the sense she meant it, for William had not touched poetry in a long time, but his time was fully occupied. 'W[illiam] is so little fit for business that it worries him beyond all measure –', Sara observed. 'These affairs of his Brother and some plaguy Stamp concerns have deranged him in a piteous manner – when he is thus employed – he is in a fever the whole time and unable to sleep.' The 'plaguy Stamp concern' had the potential to be critical. One of William's sub-distributors, John Hall at Kirkby Stephen, had stolen almost £300 from legacy receipts, which he had not recorded in his returns. The money was legally due to the government, but as William had no sureties from him William himself was personally liable for the whole sum. He therefore had the distasteful duty of going over to Kirkby Stephen, seizing all his sub-collector's movable goods and selling them to raise the amount due. Just to complicate matters, Hall was then arrested for other debts and all William's prompt and diligent efforts to procure the money were threatened by the demands of other creditors. 'I heartily wish I were at the end of this troublesome concern', he wrote miserably on 24 January, but it would be more than three weeks before he knew for certain that the government's money had been secured and he would not have to reimburse the sum from his own pocket.[3]

Financial insecurity once more threatened all the Wordsworths' plans. Richard's embarrassments and demise had long deprived his brother and sister of part of their income, so the long-talked-of trip to Paris by Dorothy and Sara was now impracticable, as the money could not be found. William too had to give up a projected trip to London. 'I should like much to come to Town this Spring;' he informed Haydon, 'but I dread the expence. My family consists only of Three children but their education is becoming more costly every year; and my income is barely sufficient for my outgoings.' 'Prudential considerations' demanded that he stayed at home. For Haydon, this created a practical problem. He was anxious to complete William's portrait in his *Christ's Entry into Jerusalem.* He had finished the face from the life-mask he had taken, but he wanted William to be standing in an attitude of reverence, with his right hand across his breast. Insistent on purity of anatomical detail, he wanted to paint it from life, but this was now impossible. William's pragmatic (if unpoetic) response was to have a plaster cast taken of his hand and charge Southey with delivering this disembodied member to the artist on his next trip to London. It served its purpose, but it has to be said that Haydon's much-vaunted portrait resembles nothing so much as a plaster mask and hand, muffled up in a cloak, rather than the living poet.[4]

Southey, in flight from his inextinguishable grief for the loss of his only son, had decided to take a trip to the Continent. William wanted to go with him, but could not afford to do so. Instead he charged Southey with a commission to do what none of the Wordsworths had been able to do, visit his daughter in Paris. The ostensible reason for calling on Caroline was to inquire after Eustace Baudouin, whom Southey had met after his release in 1814, but in giving his daughter's address William 'told me what I knew before', adding 'that it would not be necessary nor pleasant to myself to appear to be acquainted with it'. On 16 May Southey called at 47 Rue Charlot, 'small lodgings, pleasantly situated', only to find Caroline alone with her daughter. She spoke no English, his French was halting, but as soon as he mentioned that he had met Baudouin in William's company Caroline said that William was her father 'and we had a tete-a-tete of about an hour long, much like a scene in sentimental comedy', during which Caroline wept copiously and appeared 'much affected'. Southey's eagerly awaited impression of Caroline was that she was 'a very interesting young woman, with much more of natural feeling than of French manners, and surprizingly like John Wordsworth, much more so than his own sister. The little French Dorothy is very like her mother, a sweet infant, in perfect health and good humour.'

Southey arranged to call back the next morning to meet Annette and Baudouin, neither of whom spoke English. Perhaps diplomatically, he did not even attempt to describe Annette. Baudouin was like his brother, but taller, and 'very fond of his child, a fair presumption that he is not less fond of his wife'. Both Caroline and Annette spoke of him as the best of husbands. 'We parted sworn friends,' Southey told his own wife, 'and I was stopt on the way down stairs to take leave of the baby, who had been pleased to smile very graciously upon us and take me into favour.' Perhaps the most revealing incident of the whole episode occurred at breakfast. Annette may not have been able to speak English, but she thought she knew English customs. After breakfasting, French-fashion, on meat pie, Gruyère cheese and white wine, Annette 'made me drink coffee, would have made me drink tea also if I had not obstinately refused, and proposed *punch*'.[5]

One longs to know how William reacted to this account. He was, after all, a grandfather of a child he had never seen, as well as father of a girl he had known only for less than a month when she was eleven years old. His passionate love for his other children is well documented. Even now, in the fifth year after the loss of Catherine and Thomas, he could not bear to look at John Scott's newly published poem about the death of his own son, *The House of Mourning*, because the subject was too painful to contemplate. Catherine and Thomas 'are perpetually present to my eyes –', he admitted to Haydon. 'I do not mourn for them; yet I am sometimes weak enough to wish that I had them again.'[6]

A similarly poignant, reflective mood pervades the poetry that William wrote this spring and summer. It was in many ways an unexpected return to verse, which Dorothy hailed with heartfelt relief and delight. 'To-day he has composed a Sonnet,' she observed on 13 April, 'and in our inner minds we sing "Oh! be joyful!" It has indeed been most melancholy to see him bowed down by oppressive cares, which have fallen upon him through mismanagement, dilatoriness, or negligence.'

The poems he wrote, however, were anything but joyful. Like those he had written the previous spring, they were principally odes, but the new ones were less strictly constrained by classical models. Instead, they referred back, quite consciously and deliberately, to the great ode, *Intimations of Immortality*, he had written in 1804. While echoing both its sentiments and its language, the new mood is altogether less optimistic. *Vernal Ode*, for instance, has a lovingly and wonderingly observed description of a bee, but ends by looking back sadly to the golden age, when all creatures met in peace and the bee itself did not need its sting.

> We were not mocked with glimpse and shadow then,
> Bright Seraphs mixed familiarly with men;
> And earth and stars composed a universal heaven![7]

Composed upon an Evening of Extraordinary Splendour and Beauty is more explicit in its borrowings from *Intimations of Immortality*, particularly in the final stanza. The poem is a wonderful evocation of a sunset, observed from the mount in front of the house. These are the closing lines.

> Such hues from their celestial Urn
> Were wont to stream before mine eye,
> Wher'er it wandered in the morn
> Of blissful infancy.
> This glimpse of glory, why renewed?
> Nay, rather speak with gratitude;
> For, if a vestige of those gleams
> Survived, 'twas only in my dreams.
> Dread Power! whom peace and calmness serve
> No less than Nature's threatening voice,
> If aught unworthy be my choice,
> From THEE if I would swerve;
> Oh, let Thy grace remind me of the light
> Full early lost, and fruitlessly deplored;
> Which, at this moment, on my waking sight
> Appears to shine, by miracle restored;
> My soul, though yet confined to earth,
> Rejoices in a second birth!

Had the poem ended there, it would have struck the same note of renewed optimism as *Intimations of Immortality*, but it does not. The final two lines are a claustrophobic return to the 'prison-house' of mortal flesh.

> – 'Tis past, the visionary splendour fades;
> And night approaches with her shades.[8]

The same sense of time running out for the poet haunts the first *Ode to Lycoris.* This draws on William's own youthful preference for twilight rather than dawn, and autumn rather than spring, and suggests that as we age, or 'downward tend', a counterbalancing principle leads us to prefer dawn and spring instead, because they seem 'to recall the Deity Of youth into the breast'. Two other poems written at this time are also retrospective, but in a different way. The second *Ode to Lycoris*, celebrating an ascent of Helvellyn with Dorothy in June, ends with a version of lines he had written as long ago as 1798 and last revised in 1802. *Sequel to 'Beggars' Composed Many Years After* was a new poem, but, as its title suggests, referred to the fate of the two little beggar boys whose antics he had described in 1802.[9] The very fact that he was drawing on material dating from the spring of 1802 in these poems is significant, for this was also when *Intimations of Immortality* was conceived.

Should we look at the poems of 1817 and see them as a poet coming to terms with the idea that his best work is behind him? With the benefit of hindsight, we know that this was true, on the whole. William would never recapture the vitality, originality or prolific output of his earlier years. We know that he would never write the rest of *The Recluse.* On the other hand, William could not know this, and did not. He had always found revision of his work a fruitful source of inspiration for new poetry and, as late as October, he was planning 'to work hard at the Recluse in Winter'. In the meantime, what was left of the summer after the demands of business was given up to social pleasures. The catalyst was the arrival of Joanna Hutchinson at the beginning of May. For two years, she had acted as housekeeper to her brother George, who had taken a small farm, the Porth, at New Radnor, not far from Hindwell and the Stowe. His affairs had gone from bad to worse. He was considerably in debt to his brother Tom, even after his landlord agreed to reduce his rent by a third. Worse still, he had had at least two liaisons with different maids working for him. Joanna was 'heartily sick' of his conduct towards her, which their cousin described as 'unkind and ungrateful as it is mean & unprincipled', and had decided to leave him to his own devices.[10]

She decided to make her home with her brother Henry, the former sailor, who, despite a lingering fondness for drink, was an altogether better character than his scapegrace youngest brother. 'He seems so gentle and affectionate that you forget his faults when he is with you or regret that he should have any to remember', John Monkhouse stated, '& he lives so respectably upon his little Income that I cannot but admire him for it.' Henry too had been working on a farm, acting as his brother Jack's steward on land at Stockton. Jack had promised to allow Henry a certain income from their uncle's inheritance, on condition that Tom did the same for George. Tom had fulfilled his part of the bargain, but Jack had reneged on his, reducing Henry's annuity by half. Not wanting to quarrel with his brother, Henry had simply run off, arriving at Rydal at the end of April 1815. Having spent the summer at Hawkshead, where he could indulge his love of fishing to the full, he talked of buying a cottage there, but nothing came of it. Now, however, he had rented a cottage and he and Joanna were to settle there, to the great delight of the Wordsworths.[11]

Within days of Joanna's arrival, she and Sara were off to Penrith to sell up the worldly goods of their aunt Elizabeth Monkhouse, who had decided to make her home with Tom and Mary at Hindwell. On 23 June the two sisters set off again, this time for a three-week holiday on the Cumbrian coast, taking Dora, who had not been well, with them. On their return, Joanna and Sara joined a large party of Rydal and Grasmere neighbours for the Regatta gaities: with four of the Crumps of Allan Bank, George Gee, Samuel Tillbrooke, William Jackson and his charge, young George Hutchinson, and Elizabeth Cookson, they spent a whole day on Lake Windermere, dining, gypsy-fashion, on a rock. Joanna was deprived of the Regatta ball, not having an escort, but in September, when Tom Monkhouse was a guest at Rydal Mount, he and William accompanied her to the Book Club ball in Kendal and, two days later, to an evening ball at Ambleside.[12] Tillbrooke and Gee organized a public breakfast at the Lowwood Inn on Windermere, which even Mary was persuaded to attend, and on 13 September the Regatta party got together again for an expedition into Langdale to meet Dorothy and Willy, who had been staying with Mary Barker at her new house in Borrowdale, and the Crackanthorpes, who had been at Coniston. 'We had a famous large party', Joanna happily informed her cousin, for at Dungeon Ghyll they were joined by eight friends of Tom Monkhouse. With some on horseback, some on asses, some in carts and some on foot 'you may guess what a cavalcade we were down the Vale of Langdale'; they picnicked on the green and returned to Rydal for tea.[13]

Among the guests to stay at Rydal Mount this summer were William Crackanthorpe, who, according to the forthright Joanna, was 'very conceited [and] at times talks so fine there is scarcely any understanding him – & yet he is so polite & good tempered that you cannot help liking him', and his sister, Sarah, 'very plain but very agreeable'. 'No doubt we see the best of them', Joanna added, 'for as they know WW dislikes affectation they will be upon their guard'. Lamb's friend Thomas Alsager also called and the notoriously susceptible Joanna almost lost her heart to him. The Wordsworths themselves were on a continuous cycle of visiting. Dorothy went to stay first with the Marshalls at Hallsteads, then with Willy to Borrowdale and finally, in October, with William and Mary to Eusemere to see Captain John Wordsworth and his new second wife, Elizabeth Littledale.[14] William and Mary climbed Helvellyn together in June and had an excursion to Coniston and Furness in September; William also paid his annual duty visit to Lowther. 'The general complaint in this house is that there is no Letter writing', Sara wrote on 16 September; '– there is certainly no settling to anything – the only leisure one has is when off on an excursion for there is constant company to [attend?] at home.'[15]

The most important visitor to Rydal Mount this summer was a completely unknown northern artist, just twenty-five years old, called Richard Carruthers, whom Tom Monkhouse had commissioned to paint a portrait of William. It was Carruthers's first major commission and it would make him famous because it was the first of all William's portraits to be engraved, and every picture of the poet published in the next fourteen years would be based on it. As much as the likeness, it was the pose which made this portrait famous. Carruthers was determined to capture not just the man but also the poet. He painted him sitting under a tree and leaning on a boulder, against a backdrop of mountains and cloud on one side and a river, with tumbling cataracts, on the other. While his left hand is tucked into his waistcoat, his right props up his head, the hand being carefully placed so that the fingers rested on the part of the forehead which, according to the popular pseudo-science of phrenology, was the seat of poetry.

The importance of this pose was recognized by both the Wordsworths and the artist himself. Carruthers's first attempt was almost completed when it was abandoned by mutual agreement. 'He erred in chusing the attitude – one in which William is never seen – and the face is too fat & the expression unnatural – but this was not the artist's fault for Wm himself sate, as Joanna told him, in "*a perpetual smirk*" – and would not put on one Schedoni glance'. The 'Schedoni glance' was all-important, for this was the impressively blood-chilling look cast by the monk in Ann Radcliffe's romance *The Italian*, improbably set during the Inquisition. The second portrait, with its look of pained world-weariness and heavy-lidded eyes, was judged a great success. Tom Monkhouse was 'quite charmed', Mary and Dorothy were 'perfectly satisfied' and Joanna thought there could not be a better likeness. Indeed, catching sight of it for the first time through an open door at the end of a long corridor as it stood propped up on the end of the sofa, Dorothy exclaimed, 'why William has got *laid* up on [the] Sofa already!' Old Betty Yewdale, on a visit from High Hacket, disliked the portrait intensely because she found the resemblance unnerving. 'God bless us!' she said when she saw it. 'It comes ower naar'.[16]

The Wordsworths had looked forward to a quiet winter in the Lakes once all their visitors had gone, but towards the end of November William, Mary and Sara suddenly packed up and rushed off to London. Christopher had been pressing William to come for some time as he was reluctant to take the decision about settling Richard's debt to Lord Abergavenny alone. William had some business affairs of his own to sort out, and Sara had promised to spend the winter with Catherine Clarkson at her new house, Playford Hall, near Ipswich. They arrived in London around 26 November and divided their time between Christopher's house in Lambeth, his 'nice old-fashioned crincum-crankum' country parsonage twenty-two miles away at Sundridge, near Sevenoaks, Tom Monkhouse's lodgings in Mortimer Street and his house at Hampstead.[17]

William had brought with him the poems he had written earlier in the year, planning to publish them, 'as it is the fashion to publish small volumes now', but with the intention that they could ultimately be bound together with the *Thanksgiving Ode* to form a third volume of *Poems*. The idea was abandoned, probably because of William's reluctance to go into print and the exorbitant cost of publishing such a small collection. There was little hope of even recovering his expenses: his income from Longman the previous year had amounted to the princely sum of £17.[18]

Publishing and executorship business aside, William had to settle his own affairs with Montagu, which had taken an unexpected and unpleasant turn. Montagu still owed William £7 13s 1d as the outstanding amount due on the loan of 1795, but the question of what should happen to the contingent life insurance policy, which was now worth over £100, had become a matter of dispute. According to Montagu, William insisted that it was legally his property, because he had paid the premiums. Montagu claimed he had a right to it in equity because he had paid higher interest than was necessary, and was now threatening to file a bill in chancery against William. 'I would gladly interfere in this business, but I fear to attempt it', Robinson admitted, after hearing Montagu on the subject on 2 November. 'The parties are too much irritated against each [other]. I should offend both, I have no doubt.' Robinson clearly believed Montagu's story. The fact that Montagu paid the final amount due, and William gave him the policy on 27 December, would also appear to bear it out. The mystery is that William had told his brother Richard four years earlier that he believed Montagu was entitled to the policy and asked him to sort the matter out. He had clearly not done so, but there is no indication that William had changed his mind on the subject, and he had been anxious for a settlement. 'I wish that you would conclude your little affairs with me', he had written to Montagu in May 1816. 'I am heartily sick of all long-pending accounts, whether small or great'. One can only assume that because the policy had been in Richard's possession, its retention had been caused by the difficulties of administering his estate, rather than any ill-will on William's part.[19]

While in London, William met Coleridge several times at the Lambs' and at Tom Monkhouse's. They had not seen each other since they had patched up their quarrel in the summer of 1812. Since then, Coleridge had been living in Bristol and Wiltshire and their paths had not crossed. The only member of the family who had seen him had been the redoubtable Joanna. In 1813 she had called on him in London, refused to accept his servant's claims that he was not in and stormed the citadel. Coleridge had appeared 'with his Pensive face' but had cheered up after a chat. His hair, she noted, had gone 'quite gray – & he looks quite an old man'. Eighteen months later she had been less successful, attempting another surprise call when she was staying near him at Bath; this time the bird had flown, so she had to make do with interrogating his landlady. In the spring of 1816 Coleridge had returned to live in London, taking up residence as a paying lodger-cum-patient in Highgate with Dr James Gillman. Lamb had sarcastically informed William that Coleridge 'plays at leaving off Laud[anu]m', and it was true that he was soon deceiving his host by surreptitiously acquiring opium, but Gillman was able to enforce a regimen which kept his patient's consumption down to manageable levels – and kept him alive for another eighteen years.[20]

The meetings between Wordsworth and Coleridge witnessed by Robinson were not entirely comfortable. In the summer Coleridge had published his *Biographia Literaria*, which purported to be his autobiography, but was actually his most important work of literary criticism to date. The book had not pleased William:

'he finds just fault with Coleridge for professing to write about himself and writing merely about Southey and Wordsworth', Robinson observed. 'With the criticism on the poetry too he is not satisfied. The praise is extravagant and the censure inconsiderate. I recollected Hazlitt say that Wordsworth would not forgive a single censure mingled with however great a mass of eulogy.' Conversely, Coleridge was piqued that William, in his 'Essay, Supplemental to the Preface' of 1815, had credited the Germans, instead of himself, with introducing a correct appreciation of Shakespeare. He resented this particularly because he blamed William indirectly for the reviewers' hostility towards himself. He had, he said, fought for William's poetic fame 'with an ardour that amounted to absolute Self-oblivion'. This was entirely true, but it did not follow, as Coleridge claimed, that this had caused the 'ranco[u]r of the Edinburgh clan and ... the coldness, neglect, and equivocal compliments of the Quarterly Review' towards himself.[21]

With both men harbouring these resentments, and on opposite sides on the burning political issue of the day, the prosecution of William Hone for blasphemy, it was not surprising that the conversation was 'not altogether as it ought to have been'. On 27 December Robinson dined at Tom Monkhouse's with William, Mary, Sara, Coleridge and his son Hartley and Samuel Tillbrooke. Charles and Mary Lamb joined them after dinner. 'I was for the first time in my life not pleased with Wordsworth, and Coleridge appeared to advantage in his presence', Robinson wrote.

> Coleridge spoke of painting in that style of mysticism which is now his habit of feeling. Wordsworth met this by dry, unfeeling contradiction. The manner of Coleridge towards Wordsworth was most respectful; but Wordsworth towards Coleridge was cold and scornful. Coleridge maintained that painting was not an art which could operate on the vulgar, and Wordsworth declared this opinion to be degrading to the art. Coleridge illustrated his assertions by reference to Raphael's Madonnas. Wordsworth could not think that a field for high intellect lay within such a subject as a mother and child, and when Coleridge talked of the divinity of those works, Wordsworth asked whether he thought he should have discerned those beauties if he had [not] known that Raphael was the artist; and when Coleridge said that was an unkind question, Wordsworth made no apology.

While one might not agree with Robinson that William was 'substantially wrong' in his opinion on art, one cannot quarrel with his verdict that William's conduct had been at fault. Perhaps he felt this himself, for when they met again three days later at the Lambs', he was content to remain tête-à-tête with Talfourd for the evening, leaving Coleridge to hold the floor to an admiring crowd.[22] Catherine Clarkson thought it a pity that the two friends had met in company. 'Men of the world have a certain tact by which they regulate their conduct in society & which seems to have been wanted upon the occasion to which you allude', she wrote to Robinson. 'A man of the world in W's place would have been kind before strangers cold in private. W's better nature I have no doubt would make him affectionate in private & only cold before strangers because his whole mind could not be expressed before them.' The justice of this remark soon became apparent. Before he left London, William wrote privately to a mutual friend, John Payne Collier, asking him to attend Coleridge's new series of lectures and help make them a success. His sympathy for Coleridge was explicit, generous and warm.

He talks as a bird sings, as if he could not help it: it is his nature. He is now far from well in body or spirits. The former is suffering from various causes, and the latter from depression. No man ever deserved to have fewer enemies, yet, as he thinks and says, no man has more, or more virulent. You have long been among his friends; and as far as you can go, you will no doubt prove it on this as on other occasions.[23]

The Wordsworths' visit passed swiftly in a round of entertainments, parties, plays, operas, dinners and breakfasts. Tom Monkhouse held open house for artists and writers, and Carruthers's portrait was on constant display. The likeness did not impress as much in London as it had done in the Lakes, though this was not entirely the artist's fault: 'here your Father is not in his thoughtful way and therefore the picture is not lively enough –', Sara explained to Dora, 'indeed it does not seem half so like him as it did, even to me – beside your father looks so well & rosy, that the picture appears sickly'. Robinson, too, thought the likeness and expression 'strong', but complained that there was 'a languor approaching to disease in the countenance'. Carruthers tried his hand at a pencil portrait of Mary on 3 January, but this was even less successful and the attempt was abandoned.

The argument surrounding his portrait of William prompted two other artist friends to see what they could do. Edward Nash's miniature pencil sketch was simply a sleepier, hairier version of Carruthers's painting, but Haydon (who did not usually condescend to the humble life-portrait) produced something strikingly different. A pencil and chalk study of William's head, it needs only a bolt through its neck to complete a more than passing resemblance to Frankenstein's monster. This is no effete gentleman philosopher weighed down by great thoughts, but a strong-featured, almost ugly man, with piercing eyes staring boldly out beneath a massive domed brow and over a hawk-like nose. His receding hair, like his dress, is dishevelled and unkempt, and his collar, like a Venetian merchant's, stands open at his throat. Dorothy was dismayed by this portrait: 'all that there is of likeness makes it to me the more disagreeable'; William himself preferred the Carruthers, prompting a characteristic sarcasm from Sara: 'The Painters who flatter are quite in the right – Truth gives no satisfaction.' Within the family, it was aptly known as 'the Brigand'.[24]

Haydon was also responsible for the highlight of this winter visit to London. On 28 December he held his 'Immortal Dinner' in his studio, with his vast painting of *Christ's Entry into Jerusalem* towering behind as a backdrop. It was a small and select party, all friends and all at ease with each other: William, Monkhouse, Lamb, Haydon himself and Keats, for whom Haydon had organized the event, so that he could meet his fellow poet. 'Wordsworth was a fine cue, and we had a glorious set-to, – on Homer, Shakespeare, Milton and Virgil', Haydon wrote in his *Autobiography*. 'Lamb got exceedingly merry and exquisitely witty; and his fun in the midst of Wordsworth's solemn intonations of oratory was like the sarcasm and wit of the fool in the intervals of Lear's passion.' Lamb was the life and soul of the party, teasing everyone mercilessly and contributing to the general tipsiness by offering toast after toast. 'Now, you old lake poet, you rascally poet, why do you call Voltaire dull?' he demanded of William. He then attacked Haydon for including Newton in his picture, agreeing with Keats that Newton had destroyed all the poetry of the rainbow by reducing it to the prismatic colours, and proposing that they drank a health to Newton 'and confusion to mathematics'. Lamb was irresistible and William laughed as heartily as the rest. When they retired to tea, however, they found an intruder, a self-confessed enthusiast for William's poetry, who had begged Haydon for an introduction on the basis that he had corresponded with the poet. What Haydon 'forgot' to tell William was that this admirer was John Kingston, Deputy Comptroller and Accomptant General of the Stamp Office in London.

Kingston was stone-cold sober, prosaic, self-important and completely out of his depth, but he tried to make appropriate conversation. 'Don't you think, sir, Milton was a great genius?' he asked William. Keats looked at Haydon, William looked at the comptroller. Lamb, who was dozing by the fire, turned round and said, 'Pray, sir, did you say Milton was a great genius?' 'No, sir; I asked Mr Wordsworth if he were not.' 'Oh,' said Lamb, 'then you are a silly fellow.' William remonstrated in vain, 'Charles! my dear Charles!' After an awful pause, the comptroller broke out again. 'Don't you think Newton a great genius?' While Keats and Haydon struggled to keep their countenances, William stared at Kingston as if asking himself, 'who is this?' The irrepressible Lamb, however, got up, seized a candle and advanced on the poor man, saying, 'Sir, will you allow me to look at your phrenological development?' All further attempts at serious conversation were interrupted by Lamb singing nursery-rhyme ditties and begging, 'Do let me have another look at that gentleman's organs'. Keats and Haydon hurried Lamb out into the painting room, shut the door and collapsed with laughter. While William, who had just made the alarming discovery that Kingston was his superior, tried to smooth the ruffled man down, Monkhouse managed to spirit Lamb away, though his struggles and cries of 'Who is that fellow? Allow me to see his organs once more' were all too embarrassingly audible. 'It was indeed an immortal evening', Haydon reminisced many years later. 'Wordsworth's fine intonation as he quoted Milton and Virgil, Keats' eager inspired look, Lamb's quaint sparkle of lambent humour, so speeded the stream of conversation, that in my life I never passed a more delightful time.'[25]

Kingston's discomfort was amusing, but it was also highly embarrassing, not only to him, but also to William. In front of a crowd of literary people, including some of his young admirers, he had been unexpectedly confronted with a man who clearly expected the deference due from a government official to his superior. The dead silence with which he greeted Kingston's complacent announcement that he was a comptroller of Stamps was surely an indication of his embarrassment. Haydon did not realize this, but the more sensitive Keats did. He refused Kingston's invitation to meet William again at his own house, 'not liking that place', and when he called on the poet on 3 January he was mortified to find him dressing formally for the occasion. It was anathema to Keats to see the 'great spirit' whose poetry he worshipped in worldly bondage to a humble tax collector. The two men dined together at Monkhouse's two days later, on 5 January, in company with Mary and Sara, whom Keats described as William's 'beautiful Wife and his enchanting Sister'. Again there was a small incident which irritated Keats. When he tried to intervene in one of William's lengthy disquisitions on poetry, Mary laid a restraining hand on his arm and murmured, 'Mr Wordsworth is never interrupted.'[26]

The two men met again several times, but Keats could never quite forgive or forget his idol's feet of clay, which made him all the more susceptible to Hazlitt's jaundiced views of William's politics and character. So much so that, after attending Hazlitt's lectures, he remarked to his brothers, 'I am sorry that Wordsworth has left a bad impression wherever he visited in Town – by his egotism, Vanity and bigotry'. In justice, he could not refrain from adding, '– yet he is a great Poet if not a Philosopher'. And only a few days earlier he told Haydon, 'I am convinced that there are three things to rejoice at in this Age – the Excursion Your Pictures, and Hazlitt's depth of Taste.'[27]

Keats's image of William would have been dented even further had he known of the correspondence then under way between the poet and the Lowthers. Astonishingly, despite this encounter and his unpleasant experience with the sub-distributor at Kirkby Lonsdale earlier in the year, William was anxious to expand his income by acquiring more Stamp distributorships. Just as he had done with the office he now held, he had earmarked the one he thought most suitable. It was that of Carlisle, which was said to be worth £600 a year to the current distributor, Mr Ramshay, who was seventy-one years old. With the backing of the Lowthers and Parry of the Stamp Office, William had entered into negotiations with Ramshay, but before these could be brought to a conclusion they were overtaken by events.[28]

In 1818 there was to be a general election and, for the first time in many years, there was to be a contest in Westmorland, where both seats were held by the sons of Lord Lonsdale. Neither was as young or as feckless as the opposition portrayed them. The elder, thirty-year-old William, Viscount Lowther, was a career politician who had entered Parliament in 1808, when he was three weeks short of his twenty-first birthday. The younger, twenty-seven-year-old Henry Cecil Lowther, had performed distinguished service in the army, fighting under both Sir John Moore and the Duke of Wellington in the Peninsula, and had risen to the rank of Lieutenant Colonel in the 12th Foot; he had joined his brother in the House of Commons in 1812.[29]

Rumours that a contest was likely began to circulate in December 1817. Tom

Monkhouse learned that there had been a meeting in the name of Westmorland Freeholders on 10 December at the City of London tavern; £3,000 had been subscribed to support a candidate against the Lowthers and no lesser person than William Crackanthorpe had agreed to stand. 'Surely he can have no hope of success, therefore where is his motive?' Dorothy asked, as William hastened to relay the news to Lord Lonsdale. A few days later, William offered his services to the Lowther cause. 'I need not say how happy I should be if I could be of any use', he informed the Earl; '... your Lordship has only to point out the way in which you wish me to exert myself.'[30] His ink was hardly dry before his offer was accepted and he was swept up into the maelstrom of an election campaign which, even in those days of entrenched interests and minority representation, was distinguished for its bitterness and violence.

The enthusiasm with which William flung himself into the Lowther cause was, and remains, a matter of acute embarrassment to his apologists. Quite apart from the fact that he had once been an ardent republican, who had railed against the establishment and urged greater democracy, here he was actively supporting hereditary wealth and power in the face of popular demand. The poet who had championed the common man, the pedlar, tinker, shepherd and beggar, was now on the side of aristocratic reaction and conservatism. He was a hypocrite and a turncoat, a government hireling and an aristocratic toady. Or, at least, so said the likes of Hazlitt; and, as we are all democrats now, we are inclined to agree.

Yet this is a distortion of both the truth and the truth as William saw it. We should not judge the past by the standards of today. There are two keys to understanding William's stance in 1818 and beyond. The first is his belief that, though his opinions had changed, his *principles* remained the same. The second is his personal experience of the French Revolution, which led him to fear the mob (as opposed to the people) above all else. 'A representative legislation is still in my opinion the best of political blessings when a Country has materials fit to compose it', he wrote in 1816. Though most people would put the emphasis on the first half of this sentence, the second half was just as important, if not more so, to William. That was why he had always been a fervent advocate of national education, believing that it was the means by which the 'fit materials' could be created for greater representation. As a young man, he had believed it 'derogatory to human nature to set up Property in preference to Person, as a title for legislative power'. He still believed it would be better to widen the franchise, but only so long as it remained in the hands of those with property. 'I should think that I had lived to little purpose if my notions on the subject of Government had undergone no modification –', he wrote to Losh in 1821.

My youth must, in that case, have been without enthusiasm, and my manhood endued with small capability of profiting by reflexion. If I were addressing those who have dealt so liberally with the words Renegado, Apostate etc, I should retort the charge upon them, and say, *you* have been deluded by Places and Persons, while I have stuck to Principles – I abandoned France, and her Rulers, when they abandoned the struggle for Liberty, gave themselves up to Tyranny, and endeavoured to enslave the world.[31]

Ever since the end of the war with France, poverty among the rural and urban poor had escalated, bringing with it the threat of disaffection and even riot. Though the Wordsworths read about such things in the papers, even heard first-hand reports from Wales, the Lakes seemed impervious to such problems. 'In this part of England we are happy –', Dorothy wrote in May 1816, 'no public disasters seem to touch us. Labourers find the benefit of the cheapness of corn; and their wages are not much reduced'. This was echoed by Sara a couple of months later. 'We see nothing of the distresses so prevalent in the Island; except in the encreased number of travelling beggars, there is nothing like *poverty* among us'. It was only when Dorothy went to stay with the Rawsons at Halifax that she began to appreciate the enormity of the problem among the manufacturing population. 'The wealthy keep their mills going, chiefly for the value of employing workmen', she observed,

– and few get more than *half* work – great numbers none at all, so that really a great part of the population is reduced to pauperism – a dreadful evil. Things cannot go on in this way. For a time whole streets – men, women and children may be kept alive by public charity; but the consequence will be awful, if nothing can be manufactured in these places where such numbers of people have been gathered together.

She could not help but contrast the situation of the urban poor of the industrial towns of the West Riding with that of the rural poor in the Lakes. 'It is a great comfort to me that my home is out of the way of these dismal sights and sounds. We see little of distress in our neighbourhood that we cannot in some degree diminish – either by sympathy or help, but if one lived here it would be far otherwise.'[32]

William, like most of his friends of his own age and class, was full of fears. 'A Revolution will, I think, be staved off for the present,' he wrote to Stuart.

Nevertheless I am like you, an alarmist, and for this reason, I see clearly that the principal ties which kept the different classes of society in a vital and harmonious dependence upon each other have, within these 30 years either been greatly impaired or wholly dissolved. Everything has been put up to market and sold for the highest price it would bring. Farmers used formerly to be attached to their Landlords, and labourers to their Farmers who employed them. All that kind of feeling has vanished – in like manner, the connexion between the trading and landed interests of country towns undergoes no modification whatsoever from personal feeling, whereas within my memory it was almost wholly governed by it. A country squire, or substantial yeoman, used formerly to resort to the same shops which his father had frequented before him, and nothing but a serious injury real or supposed would have appeared to him a justification for breaking up a connexion which was attended with substantial amity and interchanges of hospitality from generation to generation. All this moral cement is dissolved, habits and prejudices are broken and rooted up; nothing being substituted in their place but a quickened selfinterest, with more extensive views, – and wider dependencies, – but more lax in proportion as they are wider. The ministry will do well if they keep things quiet for the present, but if our present constitution in church and state is to last, it must rest as heretofore upon a moral basis; and they who govern the country must be something superior to mere financiers and political economists.

In this penetrating and perceptive analysis of the problems facing post-war Britain, William obliquely explains his own fervent attachment to the Lowther cause. If there was anywhere in the country where the 'moral cement' was still effective in binding society together, it was the Lakes, and it could only be attributed to the pervasive influence of the Lowthers, and, more particularly, of the 'Good Earl' himself, Lord Lonsdale. 'I find it difficult to speak publicly of good men while alive,' William confessed to Wrangham,

especially if they are persons who have power; the world ascribes the eulogy to interested motives, or to an adulatory spirit, which I detest. But of Lord Lonsdale I will say to you that I do not think there exists in England a man of any rank more anxiously desirous to discharge his Duty in that station of life to which it has pleased God to call him. His thought and exertions are constantly directed to that object, and the more he is known the more is he beloved and respected and admired.

It was no coincidence that there was less disaffection among the labouring classes now, when conditions were worse, than in 1794–5, when 'Wicked Jimmy' had wielded his power so arbitrarily and despotically. It was logical to suppose that this corner of England had been least touched by the misfortunes of the times because of the Lowther influence. 'What else but the stability and weight of a large Estate with proportionate influence in the House of Commons can counterbalance the democratic activity of the wealthy commercial and manufacturing Districts?' William argued. How else could the republican principles which had brought such havoc to France and, indeed, to Europe be resisted?[33]

The news that Henry Brougham, owner of Brougham Castle, near Penrith, and a leading Whig, had accepted the invitation to stand against the Lowther brothers sent the Wordsworths racing back home. This was an altogether more serious challenge than that posed by young Crackanthorpe. 'William continues to imagine that he can be of use in Westmorland', his wife wrote indulgently, as they cut short their remaining duty visits to Uncle William Cookson at Windsor and the Beaumonts at Coleorton. By 29 January they were in Kendal, and William immediately set about investigating the loyalties of the freeholders and compiling lists of lawyers whose assistance would be essential in deciding who was eligible to vote. 'I do not like the appearance of things in this Town', he wrote the day he arrived. 'If your Lordship fails, it will be owing to the hostility of little people; blind in their prejudices and strong in their passions.'[34]

Kendal was to prove a thorn in the flesh of the Lowthers throughout the campaign, not least because it was a manufacturing town (its main industries were the production of snuff and 'Kendal Green' cloth) with a high proportion of dissenters among its population. William was on good personal terms with many of these men, but it was difficult for him to intervene too openly because, as the holder of a government office, he was officially disbarred from canvassing. '*We* do nothing, you know', Mary wrote, warning Tom Monkhouse not to say a word about William's activities behind the scenes. Yet these were substantial and influential. William was, in effect, like his father before him, acting as the Lowthers' political agent, albeit unpaid. Every few days he would send bulletins on the state of local political feeling, analysing the changing situation and making intelligent and informed suggestions for the Lowther campaign. It was William, for instance, who urged them to change the second part of the 'Lowther and Loyalty' slogan from 'Church and King' to 'King and Constitution', so as not to exclude or offend dissenting voters.[35]

Again and again, throughout the election campaign, William drew parallels with his own experience of revolutionary France. Brougham, for instance, immediately assumed a Robespierre role. 'Mr B. may at this moment be regarded as the most prominent Demagogue in the Kingdom', William wrote in March.

> I am convinced, at this moment there is such a hostility among the lower Ranks, including servants, day-labourers, handicraftsmen, small shopkeepers, to whom must be added many who from education and situation in life ought to know better, that if it went by counting heads Mr B. would sweep all before him, and be triumphant to a degree which I fear to contemplate.

These fears seemed to be justified by the reaction of what William significantly referred to as 'the Mob', who rioted violently in Kendal when Viscount Lowther made his first attempt to canvass the town. When 'the great Demagogue', Brougham himself, appeared in Westmorland, he reinforced these fears by refusing to address the freeholders, who were the only men entitled to vote. Instead, he always made a play for the sympathies of the wider, unenfranchised, audience. Dorothy's account of his first speech at Kendal is significant in its terminology. 'I could have fancied him one of the French Demagogues of the Tribunal of Terror at certain times, when he gathered a particular fierceness into his face. He is very like a Frenchman', she wrote. 'Oh! he looked ready to lead a gang of Robespierrists set to pull down Lowther Castle and tear up the very trees that adorn it.'[36]

William was less hysterical, but he was deeply concerned at Brougham's attempts to pressurize the electorate by means of the unenfranchised crowds who followed him from hustings to hustings. 'There are instances in which Mr B. has harangued to hundreds, and not above three or four Freeholders there; in Patterdale there was only one', he informed Lord Lonsdale. 'Yet his words were not thrown away; if the Father was not there, two or three of his Sons were, the Mother also, probably;

– these catch the infection, and uniting their forces they become too strong for the old Man. I do not say that many votes have been lost to us in this way, but to my certain knowledge some have, and the work is going on'. Well aware of the role journalists and pamphleteers had also played in inciting violence in France, William had quickly identified the Kendal newspaper, the *Westmorland Advertiser and Kendal Chronicle*, as a source of much anxiety. Even before the campaign began, he thought it propagated 'Jacobinical principles', and it became increasingly and more openly anti-Lowther. 'This Paper as now conducted reminds me almost at every sentence of those which I used to read in France during the heat of the Revolution', he wrote in March; 'there is a *ferment of disaffection* in the County – excited by these Libellers and others who talk as prompted by them.'[37]

To counteract its inflammatory rhetoric, William first of all attempted to persuade the editor, his friend the Unitarian minister John Harrison, at least to be even-handed; when that failed he urged the Earl to buy it, and when that proved impossible, he recommended, and assisted in, setting up a rival newspaper, the *Westmorland Gazette*. Stuart advised him to secure a writer as editor, preferably a man of 'good sense, steadiness & integrity, he having been bred a Printer & having a common Education'. Unfortunately, William ignored this voice of experience. When de Quincey wrote asking for the post, promising that he was now a reformed character as far as 'punctuality . . . and power of steady perseverance' went, William backed his appointment. He gave de Quincey a glowing reference, 'a most able man; one of my particular Friend . . . [whose] attainments and abilities are infinitely above such a situation', admitting reservations only on the score of his punctuality.[38]

William was also actively involved in writing, printing and circulating pro-Lowther literature. Unable to write under his own name, he chose a variety of pseudonyms. As 'A Friend to Consistency' he appealed to voters not to split their votes by choosing between one of the Lowthers and Brougham; as 'A Friend to Truth' he defended Viscount Lowther against accusations that he lived off government sinecures and Colonel Lowther against insinuations that he had not earned his military rank. These letters were published in the *Kendal Chronicle*, but were also circulated in their thousands by the Lowther committee as handbills. (Ironically, they achieved a far higher print run than any of William's poetry.)[39] As 'A Freeholder', he also wrote two lengthy *Addresses to the Freeholders of Westmorland*, extolling the virtues of the Lowthers and the Tory government and lambasting the Whig record in opposition. 'To have hoped too ardently of human nature, as they did at the commencement of the French Revolution, was no dishonour to them as men', he wrote of the latter, 'but *politicians* cannot be allowed to plead temptations of fancy, or impulses of feeling, in exculpation of mistakes in judgement.' These were also published, in part, in the *Kendal Chronicle*, and then, when it became clear the paper had gone over entirely to Brougham, in full as a pamphlet in April.[40]

Despite his strenuous efforts for the Lowther cause, William was not blind to its failings. 'The more I see of this Contest the more I regret that circumstances should have thrown the representation upon both your Sons', he wrote to the Earl.

'This is unpalatable to many respectable people wellwishers to your Lordship's family . . . "Two Brothers, and these Sons of a Peer, for one County!" is a frequent exclamation from quarters entitling it to regard.' He was similarly outspoken in his relief when the Earl refused to support the government's proposal to pay a huge annuity to the German princeling who was the widower of the late Princess Charlotte. 'There is scarcely any part of the conduct of Government which I have found so difficult to defend (or indeed which I have been so little inclined to defend) as the grant to Prince Leopold.'[41] Lord Lonsdale would have pushed on with securing the annexation of the Carlisle Stamp Distributorship for William, but William would not hear of it. 'Do not think of me at this crisis', he urged. 'It would grieve me to the heart, should your Lordship be prejudiced by any act or exertion of Patronage at this moment.'[42]

By the third week in February, William's role in the campaign was already an open secret. In a speech at Ambleside, James Brougham, the opposition candidate's brother, publicly threatened to have him fined £100 for 'having intermeddled'. His authorship of the *Two Addresses* was also swiftly detected, earning him the soubriquet 'Bombastes Furioso' in the *Kendal Chronicle*. Worse still, it was also known in London, where Clarkson heard it, and wrote post-haste to warn William, in case he was unaware that he should remain neutral as a government official, '& knowing that both gratitude & conscience would induce him to take an active part'. Clarkson found himself in a very difficult position. He admired the Earl personally, but Brougham had been such an active opponent of the slave trade, even to the point of introducing one of the anti-slavery bills, that he could not, in conscience, vote against him. More importantly, he carried with him the votes of the large Quaker community in Kendal, so his intervention could have been a decisive factor. Ultimately, he decided to play a low-key role, writing a couple of letters in support of Brougham, but refusing to campaign more actively or in person. This was fortunate for Sara Hutchinson, who was in the even more embarrassing position of being a guest in the Clarkson household throughout the election campaign. They resolved the difficulty by setting up a good-humoured wager of two pounds of snuff to one, on Sara's part, that Brougham would lose.[43]

Election fever had certainly seized the entire household at Rydal Mount. Dorothy went over to Kendal several times, and, having been an eye witness of Brougham's first entry into the town, wrote a heated and partisan account of his speech for circulation among their friends. Her letters, Sara complained, were all full of election matters. The children were equally excited. Johnny accompanied Dorothy to Kendal to see Brougham, but Dora was such a '*decided Yellow*' that nothing would induce her to see the arch-enemy. Even little Willy entered into the spirit, as his father joked to Viscount Lowther. 'My youngest Son is a complete Yellow, having got the jaundice, poor Lad, so that he has no *occasion* for Ribbons, though he wears them.' Surrounded by so many enthusiasts, and constantly employed in transcribing William's propaganda, it was not surprising that Mary was 'heartily sick' of the whole business. 'I wish it were over', Sara echoed, 'for they are all possessed by it – and, as Mary says, it is pitiable that William should be thus diverted from his natural pursuits.'[44]

It would be many months before William returned to his poetry. All the family, except Dora, were in Appleby, the county town, for the closing of the polls on 4 July, when both Lowthers were returned to Parliament by a substantial majority, but the after-effects of Brougham's campaign continued to reverberate. The next day there were riots in Kendal and troops had to be called out to restore order; it seemed likely that they would have to remain there all winter to keep the peace, since the magistrates could not do so and Brougham had announced his intention to stand at every future election until 'the independence of Westmorland' had been attained. It was essential, as William advised the newly returned MPs, that they should do everything in their power to conciliate the disaffected and make themselves personally known to their electorate. 'I confess that I am at present utterly unable to recommend any course of parliamentary conduct which would appease, much less satisfy the different descriptions of Dissenters who have so much influence in Kendal', he wrote. 'Oppose jobs [i.e. sinecures], and lavish expenditure, and be as careful of the public purse as the carrying on of affairs will allow – this is a *duty* of a member of parliament, and with respect to the people of West[morla]nd and of Kendal in particular, who are frugal and economical, it would be *politic*.'[45]

Though William was convinced of the necessity of conciliation, others were not. De Quincey, who took over the editorship of the *Westmorland Gazette* just as the election ended, was determinedly combative and took every opportunity to score points against Brougham's supporters and, especially, his own rival, the *Kendal Chronicle*. William was concerned that this was getting out of hand. 'Two rules *we* ought to lay down;' he told Viscount Lowther, '*never* to retort by attacking private character; and never to notice the *particulars* of a personal calumny; or any allegation of a personal nature proceeding from an anonymous quarter.' The Lowthers agreed, but they could not dampen the ardour of their supporters. One of the worst offenders was William's old schoolfriend John Fleming of Rayrigg, who contributed weekly letters full of personal abuse of Brougham, which de Quincey printed. Lowther was irritated beyond measure, but he was reluctant to be seen to be controlling the *Gazette*, preferring to act through William, who thus acquired an unwanted supervisory editorial role. 'Let the editor refuse all the trash signed Loelius &c . . .', Lowther ordered, 'Really if he puts in all that is sent to him every Clergyman and Schoolmaster in the County, will become an author . . . If this scurrility could be dropped, it would be far better for both parties.' 'We are only putting ourselves in the wrong', he added a few days later. William hastened to apologize for the *Gazette*'s failings, urged de Quincey not to accept any more letters from Fleming and, when he proved irresolute, went to see Fleming himself. This was a last resort, for, as William knew all too well, Fleming was a prickly character, irritable of temper, 'and somewhat headstrong and unmanageable'. The result was predictable. Fleming took offence at both the message and the messenger, and told everyone that he had been silenced by William. 'I am much hurt', William admitted, 'for he is both an able and excellent man.'[46]

At the Appleby poll, Brougham had threatened that, to strengthen his hand for a future election, the Whigs would make a concerted effort to purchase and create freeholds in the county. There could be only one response to this, and once again William led the van in identifying potential freeholds and persuading friends to buy them. Within a month of the closing of the polls, he was in negotiation for an estate which could be divided into twelve freeholds. This sale seems to have fallen through, but on 15 November he agreed the purchase of Ivy How farm, 'a sweet sunny place with beautiful rocks. Yew trees and hollies around two comfortable dwellings', just below High Hacket, in Little Langdale. 'Already we see in imagination Betty [Yewdale] an inhabitant of one of these Cottages', Mary wrote, as William tried to set up a syndicate of Lowther supporters to put up the money. Southey could not afford to join them, but Christopher Wordsworth, Jack, Tom and Henry Hutchinson, Tom and John Monkhouse, Eldred Addison (son of Richard's business partner) and George Gee, the Wordsworths' neighbour at Rydal Mount, all contributed to the 700 guineas, and eight freeholds were squeezed out of the little property.[47]

Not everyone entered into these arrangements with equanimity. Christopher considered it his duty to become a freeholder of Westmorland, but in joining the syndicate he could not help feeling it might be discreditable to purchase a property for 'the mere purpose of giving a vote'. William had no such qualms. 'I cannot but be of opinion that the feudal Power yet surviving in England is eminently serviceable in counteracting the popular propensities to reform which would unavoidably lead to revolution', he thundered. 'The People are already powerful far beyond the encrease of their information, or their improvement in morals.'[48]

Despite the disruption caused by the election, the summer saw an endless stream of visitors to Rydal Mount. In addition to all the usual faces, such as the Beaumonts, and the extended family coming for Penrith races, there were new and interesting ones. John Keats's first and only visit was a disappointment. When he called on 27 June everyone was out, and all he could do was leave a note, tucked behind a portrait which he 'knew must be' Dorothy's. Learning from a waiter in Bowness that William had been canvassing for the Lowthers, Keats was roused to indignation, which the sight of Rydal Mount fuelled. 'Lord Wordsworth, instead of being in retirement, has himself and his house full in the thick of fashionable visitors quite convenient to be pointed at all the summer long.'[49] On 25 August the Wilberforce family arrived in style for a visit that would last two months. As there were nineteen in their party, planning for their accommodation proved a major headache for Dorothy, as there was nowhere big enough for them all. Most of them were put up in the two houses at the foot of the hill, but five people had to be boarded out in different houses in the village, and there was panic when the inns at Ambleside refused to take all their horses. Though the servants were disdainful about their accommodation, the Wilberforces were easier to please, delighted with the houses, the situation and their 'Mountain mutton and Westmorland Beef'. Dorothy, who had not seen Wilberforce since they met at Forncett in 1789, was shocked by his feeble appearance, but his mind was as lively and his disposition as sweet as ever.[50]

On 28 August Thomas Arnold, the future headmaster of Rugby school, but then a twenty-three-year-old graduate of Oxford, called at Rydal Mount. Arnold immediately fell in love with the house and the vale, 'one of the most beautiful Situations I ever saw'. More fortunate than Keats, he found Mary and Dorothy at home, received directions for a walk round Rydal, Grasmere and Easedale, and an invitation to dinner the next day. It was, as he commented, a tolerably large party, but oddly compounded of visitors to and inhabitants of the Lakes. The star turn was Viscount Lowther, whom William had brought back with him from 'some Festivity in honour of the Election' at Kendal. Lowther stayed three days at Rydal Mount and made a good impression on the Wordsworth women. 'He has very good sense and was pleasant and chearful in a quiet way', Dorothy reported. 'If he did not know it before he must now perceive that much will be and is already required of him,' she commented, adding that he seemed disposed to live up to the character his rank and profession demanded of him. On 15 September his brother and sister-in-law also called. 'He is a fine brave Fellow and has seen much of active service abroad', Dorothy wrote admiringly. After his electioneering, he was no longer so painfully shy as at their first meeting, when 'he seemed quite daunted – like a Rustic from one of our mountain vales'.[51]

As the winter closed in, comparative peace and quiet returned to the Wordsworth household, and William was suddenly seized with the desire to write. 'W is at this moment sitting, as he has been all the morning, except while he dashed off a letter to Till[brooke] with his feet on the Fender, and his verses in his hand –', Mary wrote with pride and delight on 1 December; 'nay now they have dropped upon his knee and he is asleep from sheer exhaustion – he has worked so long. He has written 21 Sonnets (including 2 [o]ld ones) on the river Duddon – they all [to]gether comprise one Poem'.[52] Over the years William had written a number of sonnets inspired by the River Duddon, which had been a favourite haunt since childhood. Now he had had the idea of drawing these together, adding more and creating a single body of work.

Strictly speaking, as William was uncomfortably aware, it was not his idea at all. Coleridge had first suggested writing a poem about a river twenty years ago at Alfoxton. (It was the explorations along Holford beck for this poem which had roused suspicions about Alfoxton being a nest of spies.) More importantly, only eighteen months previously he had referred to it in his *Biographia Literaria.* There he explained that he had intended to call his poem 'the Brook', and trace its route from its source among the lonely hills, through farms, villages, market towns and manufactories, to a great seaport. The river image was the perfect vehicle for a poet, Coleridge added, offering a unifying theme with 'freedom for description, incident, and impassioned reflections on men, nature, and society'. This familiar phrase was, as we know, shorthand for *The Recluse* – and William himself had used it in his preface to *The Excursion.* Anticipating both the obvious inference that he was also indebted to Coleridge for the concept of this new work, and Coleridge's inevitable criticism that, like *The Recluse*, it did not live up to the grandiose philosophical ideas proposed for 'the Brook', William wrote a characteristically aggressive postscript to accompany the final published text. The sonnets were 'the growth of many years', he stated; as he had added to them, he had 'proceeded insensibly, without perceiving that I was trespassing upon ground pre-occupied, at least as far as intention went, by Mr Coleridge'. Acknowledging that Coleridge had described his scheme in 'a recent publication', William went on the offensive.

> a particular subject cannot, I think, much interfere with a general one; and I have been further kept from encroaching upon any right Mr C. may still wish to exercise, by the restriction which the frame of the Sonnet imposed upon me, narrowing unavoidably the range of thought, and precluding, though not without its advantages, many graces to which a freer movement of verse would naturally have led.

He concluded by expressing the hope that his own publication would spur Coleridge to fulfil his 'own more comprehensive design'.[53]

Despite these protestations, it is impossible to avoid the suspicion that reading about 'the Brook' in the *Biographia Literaria* planted the seed in William's mind for *The River Duddon.* Only a handful of the thirty-three sonnets were old ones, and at least nineteen were demonstrably written this winter. What is more, linking them together created a poem that was much more than the sum of its parts. This was very important to William, for he was sensitive to the criticism that he had done nothing towards *The Recluse* since publishing *The Excursion.* 'How do you get on with the Recluse?' Haydon had asked in September. 'I am very anxious that this Poem should be all arranged and put out of the way of accident or Death'. 'I long to hear of your getting on with the Recluse', Christopher echoed in the spring, while Dorothy's reproach was implicit in her comment, 'William has written some beautiful sonnets lately. That is all he has done.'[54] Though his family considered the sonnet beneath William's powers, it was eminently useful to him: it was more easily and quickly written than a longer poem (a crucial factor in his increasingly busy life), and it had been repeatedly singled out by his critics as his most successful poetic form. A series of sonnets based on a single theme was therefore likely to be a winning combination.

A sustained return to poetry was under threat from a new quarter in the winter of 1818–19. The problem was Johnny. He was now fifteen and, if he was to go to university, as the family hoped and planned, he needed to have a better education than that afforded by Mr Dawes. The brilliant Hartley Coleridge had just taken his degree at Oxford, but had only been placed in the second class, a failure which was generally attributed to the defects in his early education. The Wordsworths were anxious to avoid the same mistake with their son and, having consulted widely, they determined to send him immediately to public school. Charterhouse was chosen for three reasons: it operated the Madras System, there was a chance of Johnny getting a scholarship on the foundation and, lastly, Christopher and Monkhouse gladly undertook to look after him in London. The former Grasmere curate William Johnson, of the Central School, also offered to devote all his spare time to helping Johnny with his studies.[55]

Johnny himself was quite distraught at the very idea of leaving home: 'a diseasedly shy creature', he knew all too well that his academic attainments were not adequate for the rigours of public school. Mr Dawes suggested that his eyesight was at fault, but it is clear from his father's description of his inability to read even English accurately that he suffered from dyslexia, a condition unrecognized at that time. 'I am sure that he is not of "slow faculties"', his aunt Sara wrote; '– He is only slow at his Book.' Fortunately for Johnny, the headmaster of Charterhouse was not prepared to take on such an unpromising pupil and, though his bags were packed and his journey booked, the plan had to be abandoned. '*I* am much disappointed that John was not admitted into the Charterhouse –', Mary admitted to her cousin, 'though his Father does not appear to be in the least so.'[56]

The only option now open was for William himself to teach Johnny, and, as everyone but William recognized, this could not fail to have a detrimental effect on his poetry. 'It is very unfit that his Father's time should be consumed in a task that an inferior Person could perform much better', Sara complained. Even Christopher added his voice: 'I hope you will not think of preparing him for College yourself. You have be[en] already too much and too long separated from the Recluse, by executorship & election matters.' Determined to do the best for his son, William ignored this advice, preferring instead to consult the founder of the Madras System, Dr Bell, and Johnson, both of whom visited Rydal Mount in the new year.[57]

Bell arrived just as the Wordsworths were decorating Rydal Mount with evergreens as they prepared to host a grand ball on 7 January 1819 for Dora and her friends. Mrs Coleridge had brought her daughter, Sara, and niece, Edith Southey, to stay on New Year's Eve and, on the day of the ball, they were joined by Dora's fellow pupils from Ambleside. Miss Fletcher's little boarding school had been taken over by a friend of Sara Hutchinson, Miss Dowling, a former governess, who ran it on the Madras System and had rapidly achieved excellent results. Dora had recently been joined there by Mary Calvert, the daughter of William's old friend from Keswick, and Sophia Crump, from Allan Bank, both of whom were to be among her closest confidantes for the rest of her life.[58]

Much to the bemusement and amusement of the party, William received a letter from the Lord Chancellor informing him that he had been appointed a Justice of the Peace for Westmorland. Johnny, 'a very good, sweet-tempered lad, but without one spark of imagination, or the slightest feeling for the importance of his father's studies', was anxious that he should accept it, but William's womenfolk were wiser, knowing 'that whatever pursuit I direct my attention to, is apt to occupy my mind too exclusively' and that 'my literary exertions will suffer more than I am aware of from this engagement'. William dithered, anxious 'to discharge my obligations to society' and not to offend Lord Lonsdale, who had obviously put forward his name. When both Beaumont and Christopher added their objections to those of the females, and for the same reason, William bowed gracefully to the inevitable and allowed the commission to lapse without ever taking up office.[59] It was just as well that he did so, for, despite Carter's wonderful efficiency and reliability, William was still involved to a distressing degree in the minutiae of Stamp Office business, trying to maximize his income by actively ensuring that payments were made in his district rather than elsewhere.[60]

Against the odds, literary matters did take precedence throughout the spring of 1819. Much to William's impotent fury, three sonnets he had written in the winter appeared without his prior knowledge or permission in the January edition of *Blackwood's Magazine.* The poems had been inspired by William Westall's recently published *Views of the Caves near Ingleton, Gordale Scar, and Malham Cove in Yorkshire.* William had presented Westall with copies of the sonnets when he stayed at Rydal Mount the previous November and Westall had passed them on to Wilson, the editor of *Blackwood's.* This was a significant coup for Westall and, more especially, the magazine, for William loathed *Blackwood's* heartily. 'I have seen in it articles so infamous that I do not chuse to let it enter my doors', he told Wrangham, who had foolishly admitted to sending some pieces for it. 'The Publisher sent it to me some time ago, and I begged (civilly you will take for granted) not to be troubled with it any longer.' To vent his indignation a little, William sent newly revised and updated versions of the poems to de Quincey, suggesting he might like to include them in the *Westmorland Gazette,* where they duly appeared, with his letter, on 6 February.[61]

The same month, an engraving of William's portrait by Carruthers appeared in the *New Monthly Magazine* as part of a series of literary profiles. Southey remarked that William had got off lightly, for it was 'a respectable likeness', but the accompanying brief memoir was so extravagantly laudatory as to be embarrassing (and unrecognizable). It read more like Squire Wordsworth than Wordsworth the revolutionary poet, describing him as 'a good husband, father and friend, esteemed in his neighbourhood . . . a loyal subject of the King, and a sincere member of the Church of England'. The mystery becomes a little clearer when we discover that the information had been supplied by Scambler, the well-meaning Ambleside physician, who shared William's enthusiasm for the Lowther cause, but was not best known for his literary taste.[62]

Oddly, Scambler's opinion was borne out by a distinguished visitor to the Lakes in March, the American George Ticknor, who had just been appointed Professor of Belles Lettres at Harvard University. 'He is about fifty-three or four,' Ticknor noted in his journal (William was actually forty-eight), 'with a tall, ample, well-proportioned frame, a grave and tranquil manner, a Roman cast of appearance, and Roman dignity and simplicity.' Having 'scrambled up the mountains' and dined on a simple meal together, Ticknor felt that he was among friends. 'His conversation surprised me by being so different from all I had anticipated. It was exceedingly simple, strictly confined to subjects he understood familiarly, and more marked by plain good-sense than by anything else.' It was, Ticknor added, with evident feeling, only when he talked poetry that he became metaphysical and extravagant. 'It was best of all, though, to see how he is loved and respected in his family and neighbourhood . . . The peasantry treated him with marked respect, the children took off their hats to him, and a poor widow in the neighbourhood sent to him to come and talk to her son, who had been behaving ill'. In the evening, William showed Ticknor the manuscript of *The Prelude* and read to him *Peter Bell* and *Benjamin the Waggoner*.[63] The choice of these two poems, rather than any of the Duddon sonnets he was then writing, was significant, because William was, at long last, about to publish them.

Peter Bell had, quite literally, come of age; it was now twenty-one years old. Why William decided to publish it at this point is unclear: other than wishing to have as much as possible of his work in print, there could be no other motive, for its reception was entirely predictable. The poem was duly advertised to be published early in April, but before it reached the shops an extraordinary thing happened. Keats's friend Reynolds, who had once addressed an admiring sonnet to William, hastily composed a parody of the as yet unseen poem and got it into print a week before the genuine article. *Peter Bell, A Lyrical Ballad* is a very funny romp through a graveyard where all the characters of the *Lyrical Ballads* lie buried. Even funnier is the accompanying prose, for Reynolds decked the poem out complete with Wordsworthian Preface, Supplementary Essay and Notes, which are wickedly accurate in lampooning William's style. 'Out of sparrows eggs I have hatched great truths, and with sextons' barrows have I wheeled into human hearts, piles of the weightiest philosophy', the preface intoned;

> to a man of my inveterate morality and independent stamp, (of which Stamps I am proud to be a Distributor) the sneers and scoffings of impious Scotchmen, and the neglect of my poor uninspired countrymen, fall as the dew upon the thorn, (on which plant I have written an immortal stanza or two) and are as fleeting as the spray of the waterfall, (concerning which waterfall I have composed some great lines which the world will not let die.) – Accustomed to mountain solitudes, I can look with a calm and dispassionate eye upon that fiend-like, vulture-souled, adder-fanged critic, whom I have not patience to name, and of whose Review I loathe the title, and detest the contents.

There was much more in the same vein, revealing Reynolds's intimate knowledge of William's published work and hitting the target so often that Sara, for one, was convinced that the parody was by Hazlitt: 'there are some expressions & rhymes . . . that occur *only in Peter Bell* which Hazlitt saw many years ago'.[64]

Published anonymously, but with the initials 'W. W.' appended to the preface, the parody caused a flurry of excitement. Coleridge, who was unaware that the real *Peter Bell* had been advertised, wrote in high dudgeon to the publishers, Taylor and Hessey, accusing them of a base breach of trust in publishing a skit on a manuscript poem. They replied by presenting him with a copy of the parody. When he read it, he laughed out loud, though he felt honour-bound to defend William by pointing out that he had been 'worried at last into a semblance of Egotism' by the unremitting hostility of the reviewers over sixteen years. Reynolds's witty parody enjoyed great success: it was reviewed in at least thirteen journals and went into three editions.[65] Against the odds, William also benefited. The first edition of *Peter Bell* sold out within a fortnight and a second one had to be printed to meet the demand. It was a popular success of a kind William had never before experienced. What is even more striking about the reviews which followed is that, although they were almost universally condemnatory, the tone changed from bitter invective to what one can only describe as good-humoured indulgence of the poet's foibles.

This is all the more extraordinary because *Peter Bell* is one of the most defiantly mould-breaking of all William's poems, with an ass and a womanizing, heavy-drinking, thieving potter as its subjects, and a belligerently 'unpoetic' vocabulary. William was equally confrontational in his dedication of the poem. Instead of the Earl of Lonsdale or Sir George Beaumont, to whom the last volumes had been inscribed, *Peter Bell* was dedicated to the beleaguered Poet Laureate, Robert Southey. This was undoubtedly a public gesture of political solidarity, for Southey had been under sustained and bitter attack in the press since the publication (without his consent or knowledge) of his radical drama *Wat Tyler* in 1817. Written in 1794, when Southey had been an ardent apostle of the French Revolution, the poem was used as a stick to beat all those who, like Southey, Coleridge and William himself, had turned from youthful republicanism to middle-aged Toryism. Coleridge had reacted by blustering denials of his past, but both Southey and William (whose radicalism had not been as public or well documented as that of his friends, and was therefore less open to attack) candidly acknowledged it. *Peter Bell*, as William unnecessarily pointed out in his introductory remarks, had been written in 1798. By dedicating it to Southey, he effectively stood up to be counted alongside his friend.

Had *Peter Bell* been published before *The Excursion*, it would have been greeted with howls of derision, but since then there had been a sea-change in opinion. The *Eclectic Review*, for instance, mocked the name and subject of the poem, but closed with the telling comment, 'he is a poet that, after all, cannot be laughed down'. Reviewing the poem in greater depth a couple of months later, the critic explained, 'In spite of the imbecilities of style which run through the narrative, and in spite of our determination not to allow *Peter Bell*, the potter, to gain upon our feelings, the Poet got the better of us, and we closed the Tale resolved, even at the imminent risk of being set down for *Lakers* ourselves, to do its Author justice.' Some reviewers were as acerbic as ever. Leigh Hunt, in the *Examiner*, proved his weathercock reputation once more by denouncing the poem as 'another didactic little horror of Mr Wordsworth's', while the *Monthly Review* challenged, in mock despair, 'Can

Englishmen write, and Englishmen read, such drivel, such daudling, impotent drivel, – as this?'[66]

Though the comments are familiar (and William himself was convinced that the reviews were as bad as ever), it is significant that they defy the trend. Perhaps the most perceptive appreciation came in a long, dull and deeply earnest review in the *British Critic.* Though it took issue with William's 'system' and made many criticisms, it made two important points. If readers had formed their opinions of his poetry 'from public reputation, from illiberal and unjust criticism, from any thing but an attentive and impartial study of his writings, they ... have done the poet great wrong, and themselves yet greater'. The anonymous reviewer then went on to make a public confession. He had read *Peter Bell* in a hurry in the midst of business and had been disappointed; he had then read it again, at a more leisurely pace, 'and with a total change of opinion'. Its 'unobtrusive beauties' more than counterbalanced its 'staring defects' which had first influenced his judgement. 'What has happened to ourselves, we shall venture to think may happen to other, and even wiser men; and we hope we may without presumption, urge upon them the propriety also of doing as we did, the giving the poet a second and more attentive consideration.'[67]

William naturally felt the criticisms more than the appreciation. 'Peter Bell has furnished abundant employment to the Witlings and the small critics, who have been warring with me for more than 20 years, and seem more bitter than ever', he wrote miserably to Lord Lonsdale. The females of his household were a little more clear-sighted. They could see that the reviews indirectly admitted the importance and pervasiveness of William's influence on contemporary poetry, and therefore urged him to publish *Benjamin the Waggoner* with the second edition of *Peter Bell*, 'just to give them another bone to pick'.[68]

Benjamin the Waggoner made his public début in May, thirteen years after his private one. The poem was inscribed to its champion, Lamb, who wrote a typical letter of thanks, complaining of a mechanical fault in the binding which made the book 'always to open at the dedication'. Something of Lamb's wit seems to have rubbed off on William, for the poem bore as its motto a quotation from *Julius Caesar*, '"What's in a Name?" "Brutus will start a Spirit as soon as Caesar!"' which cocked a snook at the critics who complained about his use of plebeian names. 'Beautiful reasoning!' the *Monthly Review* remarked sarcastically, 'and beautifully illustrated in the poem itself'. The reviews were a mixed bag. Some liked its light, playful mood and simple, unaffected lyrics; others could not resist the opportunity to mock. Benjamin's waggon was said to carry heavy loads from the Lakes to London, 'Mr W's own works included', and the accuracy of William's description of the drinking scene in the inn prompted tongue-in-cheek insinuations that he was drawing on personal experience.[69]

Letters arriving at Rydal Mount suggested a happier reception among the reading public. De Quincey wrote a graceful tribute: 'In common with all Englishmen who know anything on the subject of Poetry, – I feel more and more how great a debt of gratitude is owing to you for the vast services which you have rendered to the literature of the country and eventually to the interests of Human Nature.' William Pearson, a friend from Kendal, was more forthright. 'You may not dislike to hear the real opinions of some of your less learned admirers', he wrote. The Waggoner, he declared, was the most lively and humorous of all William's poems, and therefore more accessible: 'it comes more home to the business and bosoms of every-day Man'.[70]

The summer of 1819 was unusually quiet. Sara returned to Rydal Mount in April, after an absence of eighteen months. She brought with her, from Hindwell, her sister-in-law, Mary Hutchinson, and her three children, all under four years old, Thomas, Mary and George. Such little children were a delight to all the Wordsworths and, when they left, three months later, the house appeared as still as death for days. Later in the summer, they were followed by the usual family visitors, Joanna and Henry Hutchinson and Tom Monkhouse, but, as Dorothy complained, other than Christopher's friend William Howley, then Bishop of London, they had no 'remarkable persons'.[71]

There were a few young admirers of the author of *The Excursion*, such as the Quaker poet and schoolmaster Jeremiah Wiffen, and his brother Benjamin, who called on 6 July, having visited Southey at Keswick. The reverberations from the blasting in the slate quarry between Grasmere and Rydal failed to dim their enthusiasm for William as the 'spirit who pervades the spot'. He welcomed them affably, suggested they visit Blea Tarn, where the Solitary of *The Excursion* lived, and invited them back to tea. Jeremiah's admiration was then somewhat chastened by hearing William's caustic comments on other contemporary poets, but, after tea, as he stood watching William standing 'with folded arms in a reverie', 'absorbed' in the view from the mount, his veneration returned. In a final kindly gesture, the poet and his family accompanied the Wiffens on a glorious sunset walk back to Ambleside. 'I shall never revert to the day, without a feeling of serene pleasure', Jeremiah wrote gratefully. It was the sort of experience literally hundreds of strangers visiting Rydal Mount would enjoy, though they had no other claim on William's time or attention than simple admiration of his poetry.[72]

As Sara pointed out, they had had 'fewer visitors than I ever knew at this Season'. Many of the former Lakers were now abroad, enjoying the first opportunity to travel in comparative peace and security in Europe for many a long year. William had been sorely tempted by the idea of a trip to the Continent, or even to Norway, but he was obliged to conceal his disappointment as best he could. His self-imposed task of teaching Johnny effectively tied him to home. The difficulty of fulfilling this commitment as he wished was now forcibly brought home to him when he suffered another severe bout of trachoma. He could neither read nor write, let alone supervise his son's studies; any sort of strain on his eyes aggravated the condition. His eyelids were so painful and swollen that he could not appear in public and he was even obliged to give up an invitation to meet Prince Leopold at Lowther on 23 September.[73]

Reluctantly, William allowed himself to be persuaded that both Johnny and Willy should go away to school. As Johnny was supposedly too old for entrance at Charterhouse, the Wordsworths decided that he should go to Sedbergh, a grammar school of sixteenth-century foundation which, like Hawkshead, had strong links with Cambridge University. The appointment of the master and the control of the school's income were all in the hands of William's own *alma mater*, St John's College. The Wordsworths had family links with the school. Uncle William Cookson was one of its distinguished old boys, their cousins John Myers and William Crackanthorpe less so. Just ten miles east of Kendal, the school was gloriously situated in the pretty market town of Sedbergh, at the confluence of the lush pastoral dales which lie in the shadow of the tumescent Howgill Fells. The problem, as the Wordsworths discovered when they went over to visit in October, was that the school was in sharp decline. There were no longer any boarders, only eight day pupils, and William Stephens, the headmaster, whose wife had died giving birth to her twelfth living child in August, was obviously at death's door himself.[74]

The Wordsworths characteristically took it upon themselves to sort the matter out. As soon as they left the school, William immediately sent the Kendal doctor over to see Stephens and, when he died a week later, the whole family were active in seeking donations towards a private subscription to support his destitute orphaned children.[75] William also enlisted Lord Lonsdale's support in pressurizing St John's into appointing a more able successor. When the twenty-seven-year-old Henry Wilkinson, a Second Wrangler and fellow of St John's, took up the post, Johnny entered the school in April 1820. This time he went fearlessly, secure in the knowledge that his academic studies had blossomed under his father's tuition.[76]

Six months earlier the decision to part with Willy, who was almost nine and a half, was less easily taken, but acted upon with less difficulty. His aunts were anxious to prise him away from his father, who, they were convinced, was spoiling the boy, and to get him into Charterhouse before it was too late. Johnson, the former curate of Grasmere church who was now the headmaster of the Central School in London, willingly agreed to admit Willy immediately and prepare him for entrance to Charterhouse in six months' time. Tom Monkhouse, who paid his annual autumnal visit to Rydal Mount on his way to Penrith races, volunteered to take charge of the boy and deliver him safely into Johnson's hands. Despite his youth, Willy was far more able and sociable than his elder brother. He settled quickly into his new school, piously informing his sister by letter that, 'for my own credit and your satisfaction, I mean to do my utmost that not one defect may be left and that I may get to the top of the Tree'.[77]

Any hopes that he would be less indulged at boarding school proved ephemeral. His father's friends and relations fell over themselves in the mad scramble to entertain him. Tom Monkhouse, Christopher Wordsworth, the Lambs, the Lloyds, who had moved from Birmingham to London, Mrs Hoare, who had taken Willy's motherless cousins under her maternal wing, all invited him to their homes, took him out to see the sights, fed him treats and gave him pocket money. Knowing how the Wordsworths worried about the boy, Lamb sent them a droll letter giving a mock character assessment and relating all Willy's *bon mots* in response to Lamb's inveterate teasing. He seemed, Lamb said, to remain purposely ignorant of what mighty poets had done before him. 'For being asked if his Father had ever been on West[minste]r Bridge, he answered that he did not know.' 'He has been so much noticed & invited out that he has had far too much pleasure', his Aunt Sara scolded. Nevertheless, despite his junketings and his fondness for over-eating and visiting the zoo at the Exeter Change, Willy did well enough at the Central School to secure a place at Charterhouse, to which he transferred at the beginning of April 1820.[78]

For the first time, the Wordsworths could congratulate themselves on the fact that all three children were placed in good schools, doing well and promising better. The drawback was the financial cost. Though only Dora's school was fee-paying, 'customary fees' were demanded for both boys, and there were the additional heavy expenses of boarding out each child to be taken into consideration. Unable to risk losing any of his small capital, but anxious to secure the best return for it, William sold off one of his small estates for £2,000, sought Lord Lowther's advice and invested the money for his children's education in the French Funds.[79]

Having done his duty by his children, it was now high time that William should return to his own poetic labours and do his duty by himself. 'O for a potent voice to call forth the Recluse from his profound dormitory, where he sleeps forgetful of his foolish charge, The World', Lamb had lamented earlier in the year. 'William has done nothing lately except a few Sonnets,' Dorothy apologized to Catherine Clarkson on 1 August, adding defensively, 'but these are exquisitely beautiful.'[80] The sonnets were the final contributions to the River Duddon series, which William intended to publish the following spring. Together with *The White Doe*, *Benjamin the Waggoner*, *Peter Bell* and the *Thanksgiving Ode*, they would form a third volume to add to the *Poems, in Two Volumes*, which formed his collected works. It was expected that a new edition of this last publication would be needed within the next few months and, in another attempt to gain a wider readership, William intended to republish the three volumes in a smaller, cheaper form. 'Then, *he says*', Sara wrote with an emphasis which all too clearly indicated her disbelief, 'he will never trouble himself with anything more but the *Recluse*'.[81]

19. *A Tour of the Continent*

On 29 January 1820 King George III died. His reign had been distinguished by its length, the loss of the American colonies and the struggle against, and final defeat of, Bonaparte. For the last nine years, he had been a pitiable figure, blind and insane, a 'dread Shadow of a King! Whose realm had dwindled to one stately room'. A couple of days after his death, nine-year-old Willy, agog with excitement, watched as the Lord Mayor of London led a solemn parade through the streets to the Temple Bar, where he proclaimed the Prince Regent, who had long been king in all but name, George IV.[1] According to the Constitution, the death of the reigning monarch demanded an immediate dissolution of Parliament and the calling of a general election. After a lull of only eighteen months, William would again be dragged from Parnassus into the muddy waters of politics.

Brougham lost no time in announcing his intention to stand again for Westmorland, but he wrong-footed himself at the outset. His advertisements were dated the day after the King's death and, in an unfortunate phrasing, declared that 'this event is, on every account a subject of sincere congratulation'. He meant the opportunity caused by the dissolution of Parliament for Westmorland to assert its independence from the Lowthers, but one did not have to be an ardent monarchist to feel, with the Wordsworths, that he appeared to welcome the king's death and that this was 'a shocking indecency'. Brougham may have been first off the starting-block, but William was close at his heels. He dispatched a swift letter to the *Westmorland Gazette*, denouncing the tone of the advertisement. On 4 February he wrote to the Earl of Lonsdale to inform him that his neighbourhood was '*decisively* in favor of your Lordship's Sons being proposed again', following it up the next day with a list of the new pro-Lowther freeholders he had helped to create since the last election. These now included the Ambleside physician, Richard Scambler, the curate of Grasmere, William Jackson, and William's cousin John Myers. The last, who had acquired a freehold in Grasmere, had done little to endear himself, or the Lowther cause, to the inhabitants of the vale, with whom he immediately began a dispute over rights of enclosure. Even the Wordsworths began to dread his occasional appearances at Rydal Mount. Since the death of his wife, he had gradually sunk into alcoholism, and he would arrive half-tipsy, 'all dirt and snuff', and belligerently demand their sympathy in his quarrels.[2]

Once again William found himself in almost daily correspondence with one or other of the Lowthers, reporting local sentiments, drawing attention to dissatisfaction among the voters and identifying attempts by Brougham's supporters to create more freeholds. As Mary's brothers and cousins were now Westmorland freeholders, he was also legitimately able to bring their concerns before the candidates. Farming was, once again, in such dire straits that emigration seemed like the only solution to their woes. Even the prudent, hard-working and economical John Monkhouse had to borrow £500 from his brother in February, to tide him over until he could sell his cattle at Easter. When he did sell them, they only raised nine-tenths of their value. 'Parliament must do something for our relief', he begged. His cousin George Hutchinson, an altogether more feckless character, plunged from disaster to disaster. Even though he was struggling to survive at Porth Farm, he had, like Richard Wordsworth, at the age of forty-one, secretly married his twenty-two-year-old servant, Margaret Roberts, whom he had made pregnant. Though John had bailed him out by taking over the farm and its remaining stock, and Tom stood surety for him, they discovered that George owed the Kington Bank £500 and had twice been arrested for debt. William put the problems of the farmers as forcibly as he could to his Lowther candidates and urged John, as the most literate and intelligent of the farming relations, to set out their case in a letter and in person.[3]

This attempt to influence government policy, in however small a way, was symptomatic of William's attitude towards this election. The Lowthers had his unwavering support, but not so the Tory government to which they belonged. In the wake of 'Peterloo', or the 'Manchester Massacre', in August 1819, when the Manchester magistrates had overreacted to a massive demonstration by radicals agitating for reform by sending in the cavalry, killing at least one man and wounding forty others, the ministry had clamped down ferociously on civil liberties. The notorious 'Six Acts', extending the measures taken in 1817, restricted the right to assembly, introduced Stamp Duty on all pamphlets and empowered magistrates to prevent the publication of seditious and blasphemous libels. Though the Wordsworth women were wholeheartedly behind these measures – Sara even thought Habeas Corpus should be suspended again – William was not. He criticized the 'mismanagement' of the Manchester magistrates to Viscount Lowther, welcomed and encouraged the enrolment of Whigs among the Kendal Yeomanry so that it was not simply a Lowther corps, and was forceful in his condemnation of the act to restrict the freedom of the press. 'William always dreads any measures that may be necessary to strengthen Govt', Sara observed. A temporary restriction might be justified, but 'I cannot reconcile myself to the notion of this being made permanently part of the Law of this Country', he wrote to the Earl.

Every body rejects with horror the idea of a government licence for the circulation of thought; and surely this regulation is of the same character; it *prejudges*, it presumes that the circulation of the opinions or reasonings of *poor* men must upon the whole be *unavoidably mischievous*. This is surely an unpalatable doctrine; I like it neither as a man nor an Englishman . . .[4]

Fortunately, there was not the same need to become a propagandist in this election. De Quincey's dilatory habits had forced his resignation from the editorship of the *Westmorland Gazette* on 5 November 1819, so the paper had become less controversial, and William's intervention was no longer required. Nevertheless, much of his time was taken up with visits to the hustings throughout the county, leading Sara to complain in April, 'This work will never have an end – Poetry & all good & great things will be lost in Electioneering.' When the poll finally did close, the Lowther brothers retained their seats and Brougham was discomforted once more.[5]

Throughout this winter and spring, William was putting the finishing touches to the River Duddon volume. This would not be just another book of poetry, but a celebration of the Lakes in prose and verse. There were now thirty-three sonnets on the Duddon. As a note to that on Seathwaite Chapel, William added a twenty-page memoir of 'Wonderful Walker', the humble pastor who had faithfully served his flock there for sixty-six years and whose memory was still revered in the Duddon valley. The book closed with a revised version of William's *Guide to the District of the Lakes*, now published independently of Wilkinson's plates for the first time. The inclusion of these two long prose digressions from the poetry was important, for together they proved a potent combination. They not only staked William's claim to be the Poet of the Lakes (rather than just one of the Lake School, as Jeffrey had so often taunted him), but each piece underpinned and reaffirmed his profound belief in the unique moral character of his corner of England. Like *The Excursion*, which he reissued at the same time, in a second, smaller-format edition, the *River Duddon* was imbued with William's politics. The memoir of Walker was simply a historic example of the independent rural virtues of the Lakeland statesmen. The dedicatory poem to Christopher Wordsworth emphasized this point.

Hail, ancient Manners! sure defence,
Where they survive, of wholesome laws . . .
Hail, Usages of pristine mould,
And ye that guard them, Mountains old!

In the final sonnet of the series, which is incomparably the best, William assumed an elegiac note in bidding farewell to the Duddon as it reached the sea.

I thought of Thee, my partner and my guide,
As being past away. – Vain sympathies!
For, backward, Duddon! as I cast my eyes,
I see what was, and is, and will abide;
Still glides the Stream, and shall for ever glide;
The Form remains, the Function never dies;
While we, the brave, the mighty, and the wise,
We Men, who in our morn of youth defied
The elements, must vanish; – be it so!
Enough, if something from our hands have power
To live, and act, and serve the future hour;
And if, as toward the silent tomb we go,
Through love, through hope, and faith's transcendent dower,
We feel that we are greater than we know.

The air of finality which pervades this poem was indicative of William's own mood. *The River Duddon, A Series of Sonnets: Vaudracour and Julia: and Other Poems. To Which Is Annexed, a Topographical Description of the Country of the Lakes, in the North of England* was printed and published by Longman in April 1820.[6] Purchasers were informed that it completed 'the third and last volume of the Author's Miscellaneous Poems'. The implication, as the *Eclectic Review* was quick to point out, was that the poet would write no more. What William actually meant was that there would be no more miscellaneous poems because from now on he intended to work solely on *The Recluse.* Having learned the lesson of raising public expectation in his preface to *The Excursion*, however, he did not intend to advertise the fact to the world again. It would be time enough to talk of *The Recluse* when – if – it was completed.

In what was probably intended as a final clearing of the decks in preparation for embarkation on *The Recluse*, William also performed a complete overhaul of all his published work, reissuing it in July in what Sara described as '4 nice pocket volumes – far more agreeable to my mind than the last ones'. This was not simply a cynical exercise in commercialism, but a comprehensive revision, re-editing and, in some cases, rewriting of all his poems which had ever appeared in print. What is more, many of the changes were a response to criticism, particularly by Coleridge, whose judgement in such matters was incomparable. Some, like *Alice Fell*, were dropped altogether. Others, like *Peter Bell*, had many 'offensive' passages removed. Nothing was considered too unimportant – or too sacred – for revision, though William remained stubbornly attached to the idiosyncratic system of categorization he had introduced in 1815.[7]

All this was achieved despite continuing trouble with his eyes which prevented him reading or writing by candelight. The recurrence of the trachoma had raised a very real fear in William's mind that, like his hero, Milton, he might be going blind. This was an added incentive to get his poems republished in what might be regarded as the definitive version, though labouring over the proofs aggravated the condition. William's anxiety to get the books out as soon as possible became more pressing as time went by. In January he had decided that he would go to London in May and, if possible, spend the summer in Switzerland. The necessity of seeing his work through the press and the election both delayed his departure, and it was not until the end of May that he and Mary left Rydal Mount. Sara had nobly volunteered to stay behind in charge of the Stamp Office, since Dorothy was determined to accompany her brother and Mary too had a rare opportunity to go, with all three children away at school.[8]

Dorothy had gone to London at the beginning of April, partly to take personal charge of the printing at Longman's, but mainly to see a London dentist. She was now forty-nine years old and, though remarkably fit for her age, she had 'a true old woman's mouth and chin' because she had just six teeth left. She had long contemplated acquiring false ones but had balked at the hazards of provincial dentistry and the cost of a London orthodontist. Emboldened by the imminent departure for the Continent, she took the plunge. She paid fifty guineas (more than six times the annual rent she had paid for the cottage at Town End) to a Mr Dumergue, had her remaining teeth pulled and, while she waited for her gums to heal and the new set to be made, took refuge with Christopher at Lambeth. Only 'particular friends' were permitted to see her in her toothless state, including Willy, now happily settled at the Charterhouse, and his cousin, Jack's son Henry, who was at Westminster school.[9]

William and Mary made their way slowly to London, taking a detour at Manchester to see the site of 'Peterloo' and seeking details from a talkative eyewitness. It was a miserable journey at first, for William, preoccupied with his painful eyes, was silent and looked ill; however, as his wife observed, with admirable restraint, when they were joined in the coach by a Manchester magistrate 'of the right sort of principles' and the two men fell into conversation, William 'cheered up . . . and . . . his eyes now began rapidly to improve'. Their first port of call was Souldern, Robert Jones's 'happy model of a Country Rectory', halfway between Banbury and Bicester. Jones was still the same 'good kind creature' he had been at St John's College thirty years ago, and he was 'rejoiced' to see his old friend. William had hoped to be able to persuade Jones to accompany him in retracing their tour of 1790, but even if corpulence and indolence had not disinclined him to attempt it, the arrival of news that his mother had died meant that he had to abandon his guests and set off immediately for Plas-yn-Llan.[10]

When the Wordsworths arrived in London, their plans for going abroad had to be put on hold. Christopher was dangerously ill and it was impossible for Dorothy to leave him until he was at least convalescent. Overworked and disinclined to pamper his own ailments, his recovery was slow, but towards the end of June he went to Hampstead to stay with the Hoares, and Dorothy, sporting her new set of false teeth, was free to join the touring party.[11] This had now grown considerably in size. Tom Monkhouse had long been included in their plans, but at the beginning of June he announced his engagement to Jane Horrocks, sister of the MP for

Preston, and, according to Robinson, 'a young and very beautiful woman'. The bride and one of her sisters would accompany them, and the Wordsworths' Continental tour was thus transformed into the Monkhouses' wedding tour. Dorothy had also invited Robinson, who had kindly squired her about London while her brother was ill. Much as he wished to go, the enforced delays and his own circuit commitments prevented him setting out with them, but it was agreed that, if possible, they would meet in Switzerland.[12]

The month that the Wordsworths spent in London prior to their departure was quieter, from a social point of view, than usual. William and Mary divided their time between Tom and Christopher, and spent several evenings with the Lambs and Robinson. Keats was invited to supper but was 'too careful of my health to risk being out at night'. As Haydon had all too accurately prophesied, his friend was 'very poorly, & I think in danger'.[13] Haydon himself was keeping a low profile, from a mixture of mortification and pique. A few weeks earlier, he had written to William asking for a loan to tide him over one of his recurrent cash crises. 'I am sure you are little aware of my pecuniary resources, or you could never have thought of me in your difficulties; which I do earnestly wish I could remove. –' William had replied, 'But it is some time since I have been impelled to lay down a rule, not to lend to *a Friend* any money which I cannot afford *to lose*... I could not be easy were you to repay the money to your own inconvenience and I could not at the same time spare it without embarassment.' Anxious to help his friend, however, he tried to set on foot a subscription to purchase his *Christ's Entry into Jerusalem* as an altarpiece for one of the new London churches; unfortunately not everyone shared his opinion of Haydon's talents, artistic or personal, and the scheme came to nothing. Even Beaumont was prepared to offer only £50.[14]

He was rather more generous where William was concerned, for he now paid between 100 and 120 guineas for a marble bust of the fifty-year-old poet for his gardens at Coleorton. The sculptor was the highly successful Royal Academician Francis Chantrey, who also produced busts of Scott and Southey. Sitting for Chantrey occupied much of William's time in London, but the finished article was remarkable, not least because it is his only three-dimensional likeness. There was some dispute at the outset between Mary, who wanted an accurate depiction of her husband, and Chantrey, who wanted to portray the poet. To do this, he wished to minimize the furrows down William's cheeks, thinking they would be so striking as to detract artistically from the overall resemblance. Chantrey prevailed, with William's backing (on artistic grounds), and the result, as Robinson observed, was 'a good likeness' with 'a delicacy and grace in the muscles of the cheek which I do not recollect in the Original'. William himself came to believe it was his finest image: far more sophisticated than the Carruthers, and superbly executed as a work of art, it expressed his vocation in a way that his own face did not. Or, as Coleridge put it, 'Chantrey's bust of Wordsworth was more like Wordsworth than Wordsworth was like himself.'[15]

When he was not preoccupied with sitting for Chantrey, William was busy putting the finishing touches to his four-volume *Miscellaneous Poems*, and Robinson, for one, was impressed by what he saw as William's determination to make concessions to public taste and cut out or amend the passages which had most attracted criticism. 'I never before saw Wordsworth so little opinionated, so willing to make sacrifices for the sake of popularity as now', he wrote in his journal. 'He is improved not a little by this, in my mind.' The final proofs would be left with Christopher, convalescing at Hampstead, to steer through the press in William's absence.[16]

After a final consultation with a London oculist, to ensure that William's eyes would be up to the journey, the Wordsworths finally left Lambeth for Dover on 10 July. There they were joined by the newlyweds, who had married on 8 July, and Miss Horrocks. Next day, after a swift passage of less than four hours, they landed at Calais on the first stage of a tour that was to last four months and take them through France, the Low Countries, Germany, northern Italy and Switzerland. Had the Wordsworths been able to do as they wished, they would probably have gone straight to Paris to visit Annette and Caroline, but the presence in their party of two new relatives who were, as yet, total strangers made it impractical. This was an early intimation of the problems that would dog the entire trip, for, as they soon discovered, the Wordsworths and the Horrockses were chalk and cheese. The Wordsworths, and Dorothy in particular, were on a pilgrimage to re-create William's tour of 1790; they wanted to see all he had seen, stay where he had stayed and literally walk in his footsteps. Jane Monkhouse and her sister (plus maid) were on a fashionable Continental tour. They wanted to visit all the usual places frequented by English society travellers, do it as easily as possible and mix only with their fellow countrymen. Poor Tom was torn between the two, with unfortunate consequences for his marriage and his future happiness.

As Dorothy noted with some amusement, 'Journals we shall have in number sufficient to fill a Lady's bookshelf', for everyone in the party kept a travel diary, apart from William. Three survive, Dorothy's, Mary's and Robinson's, and of the three only Mary's has not been published. This is unfortunate. It is every bit as observant and perceptive as her sister-in-law's, but spiced with her own brand of mordant humour, and William himself placed them on a par, expressing a wish that they might some day be published together. When he wrote his own record of the tour in a series of poems which would be published in 1822 as *Memorials of a Tour on the Continent, 1820*, he would turn as often to Mary's journal as to Dorothy's for inspiration.[17]

At Calais, they bought two second-hand travelling carriages and set off at a cracking pace through what is now Flanders and Belgium as far as Cologne, where they turned southwards and followed the Rhine for almost 280 miles before entering Switzerland. Despite rising at five every morning, there was only time to visit the cathedrals and great churches before moving on to their next destination. Brussels alone merited more than a single night's stay, significantly because, in a rare moment of unanimity, all the party wished to visit Waterloo. 'Oh! this is a wondrous place', Dorothy enthused of Brussels. 'We have seen the gay Ballroom where our heroes danced before the day of Quatre Bras – and heard details from the mouths of living witnesses of the horrors of the return of sick and wounded'. On the field of Waterloo itself, they were fortunate to encounter a man who had been compelled to act as Bonaparte's guide on the battlefield and had been at his side until he fled in defeat. He escorted them round, as he had Southey some time before, pointing out to them all the memorable places where the action had taken place. For the Wordsworths it was the equivalent of a trip today to the killing-fields of the Somme. 'We stood upon grass, and corn fields where *heaps* of our countrymen lay buried beneath our feet', Dorothy wrote in her journal. 'There was little to be seen; but much to be felt; – sorrow and sadness, and even something like horror breathed out of the ground as we stood upon it!' William worked this moment up into one of the best of his sonnets memorializing this tour. It opens with an image of the goddess of victory hovering above the 'far-famed Spot' and bestowing her crowns and garlands, but ends on an altogether more sombre note.

She vanished; leaving prospect blank and cold
Of wind-swept corn that wide around us rolled
In dreary billows, wood, and meagre cot,
And monuments that soon must disappear;
Yet a dread local recompense we found;
While glory seemed betrayed, while patriot-zeal
Sank in our hearts, we felt as men *should* feel
With such vast hoards of hidden carnage near,
And horror breathing from the silent ground!

William's occasional fits of poetic inspiration on the tour were not always welcome, for he became morose and introverted until he had finished to his own satisfaction. 'He has been the very reverse [of merry]', Mary complained when he had been 'sonneteering' at Bruges, 'but it is now written out and as our affairs have suffered by his remissness I trust he will now cease'.[18]

After only eighteen days of this hectic pace, the cracks began to show. Mrs Monkhouse was a delicate flower, unused to robust Wordsworthian ways. She had been constantly 'unwell' with headaches and sickness, retreating early to her bed and opting out of the daily pedestrian exploration of the towns in which they stayed. As they made their way to the borders of Switzerland, she decided she wanted to go to Baden-Baden, the fashionable spa in the foothills of the Black Forest. Tom was determined to humour her, so the party went their separate ways: the Monkhouses, Miss Horrocks, the maid and Dorothy making a three-day detour to Baden-Baden, and William and Mary travelling on to Schaffhausen alone. This was a considerable sacrifice on Dorothy's part, for she was longing to get to Switzerland, 'our end and aim . . . the accomplishment of wishes cherished from the days of youth', but none of the Monkhouse party could speak sufficient German, so Dorothy's services were required as interpreter. 'D is an adept in making her way, for she never hesitates – going into the Kitchens, talks to everybody there – and in the villages, on the roads, and makes friends and gains information and gabbers German everywhere', Mary wrote admiringly. 'She astonishes us all.'[19]

As they crossed over from Germany into Switzerland, Dorothy abandoned the carriage and walked. It was a symbolic gesture, a conscious re-enactment of her brother's pedestrian tour of 1790.

This first sight of that country so dear to the imagination, though then of no peculiar grandeur, affected me with various emotions. I remembered the shapeless wishes of my youth – wishes without hope – my brother's wanderings thirty years ago, and the tales brought to me the following Christmas holidays at Forncett; and often repeated while we paced together on the gravel walk in the parsonage garden, by moon or star light.

The Wordworths took on a new lease of life in Switzerland. 'Poor W is no longer the active traveller he used to be', Mary had sighed at the outset of their tour. Dorothy too had bewailed the carriages that were a concession to their age, 'often did I wish that I were a youthful traveller on foot'. Now, they rediscovered their lost youth. The carriages were abandoned and they took to their feet, determined to cross and recross the Alps with all the vigour of people half their age. The problem, once again, was the Monkhouse party. It was not to be expected that the ladies would be capable of such exertion and another parting of the ways was inevitable. What was unexpected, and deeply shocked everyone who found out, was Tom's decision to go with the Wordsworths. For all her selfish and self-pitying behaviour, it is impossible not to feel sorry for Jane Monkhouse, married for only a month and then abandoned by her husband in a foreign country while on her bridal tour. With her sister and maid she would take up residence in Geneva, where there was a large expatriate English community, and await the return of her husband and the rest of the party. It was an obvious solution to the problem, but such early evidence of incompatibility did not augur well for the future of their marriage.[20]

The carriages were disposed of at Berne and a large portion of their luggage was forwarded to Geneva, in the care of John Wedgwood, whom William had not seen for twenty-one years and unexpectedly bumped into at the Staub-back falls. At Lucerne (where they found a German magazine in a milliner's shop with a review of William's *River Duddon*) they were joined by Robinson, and the Wordsworth party took to the hills. They climbed every mountain, forded every stream, visited the waterfalls, traversed the glaciers and sailed on the lakes. Everywhere they went, they constantly compared all the sights to those of their own lakes and mountains – despite William's strictures against tourists doing the reverse in his *Guide to the Lakes*. They observed with passionate interest every place associated with the gallant Swiss resistance to the French invaders. Most of all, they saw everything through the filter of William's earlier experience, as portrayed in *Descriptive Sketches* and *The Prelude.* It was almost a pleasure when the border guards between the cantons of Berne and Unterwalden stopped them to demand taxes for repairing the road, for instance, because the same experience had befallen William and Jones in 1790. They identified, sometimes fancifully, the paths which the two younger men had walked, and made repeated efforts to retrace William's adventures on the shores of Como, when he had become separated from Jones and spent a night lost in the woods between Gravedonna and Chiavenna. Indeed, Dorothy's persistence in attempting to do this led to the only serious falling-out of the tour, when the Wordsworths took advantage of an offer from a fellow traveller to return to Como, and Monkhouse and Robinson, who had not wanted to go back, were left behind at Milan.[21]

After visiting the wonderful Ambrosian Library at Milan, where they were privileged to see Petrarch's copy of Virgil and a book of Leonardo da Vinci's mechanical sketches, exploring the Italian Lakes and considering, and deciding against, an excursion to Venice (much to Mary and Dorothy's disappointment), the party returned to Switzerland.[22] After the experiences of Como, there was only one way this could be done and the Wordsworths duly walked over the Simplon Pass, deliberately choosing the old road in preference to Bonaparte's new improved one, which the rest of their party took. When they rediscovered the track which had misled William and Jones into crossing the Alps without knowing it, even Dorothy was lost for words to describe William's emotion. Surprisingly, neither this moment, nor that when they first came upon the 'aboriginal vale' of *The Prelude*, merited commemoration in verse. 'I find that my remembrance for thirty years has been scarcely less vivid than the reality now before my eyes!' William declared on the latter occasion.[23]

It is significant that, though all their minds were constantly recurring to that earlier, profoundly important tour, not a single poem in *Memorials of a Tour on the Continent, 1820* would look back or refer to it. For a poet whose work was built upon the subtle fusion of past and present experience and remembered emotions, this was extraordinary. It was as if he deliberately excluded from his verse the most important part, imaginatively and creatively, of the entire tour. This no doubt explains why the *Memorials* are, upon the whole, a disappointingly pedestrian performance, but why he failed to engage at that level is inexplicable.

They were reunited with Mrs Monkhouse, her sister and maid at Geneva, where they also met again a young Scotsman who had turned aside from his own tour to accompany them from Lucerne to Zurich. His companion, a twenty-year-old American, Frederick Goddard, had been drowned on Lake Zurich only three days after parting with the Wordsworths, an event which cast something of a cloud over the final days of their Swiss adventure. From Geneva, the entire party made a swift dash through Dijon and Sens to Paris, where it was now possible for them all to go their separate ways without inviting comment. The Monkhouses and Robinson found accommodation in hotels, while the Wordsworths stayed in Rue Charlot, taking lodgings next door to Annette and Caroline. 'Mr Eustace Baudouin met us at the door of our lodgings; –', Dorothy wrote for her entry on 1 October, 'and here ends my Journal.'[24]

Her discretion is infuriating, for one longs to know how they all reacted to this long-anticipated meeting between William's two families. There are hints in Dorothy's sketchy notes of this period, which she did *not* write up for the journal, and from Robinson's diary that it was not without its emotional cost. Nor is it surprising that the person who suffered most was Mary, who found it hard to come to terms with meeting William's first family face to face. In her notes, Dorothy reveals that the Wordsworths actually spent the night of their arrival in Paris at a hotel. It was the next morning that she and William went to Rue Charlot and met Caroline's husband at the door of his house; Mary stayed behind alone at the hotel until Robinson thoughtfully joined her for breakfast, and the Wordsworths removed to Rue Charlot later that same day. Indeed, Robinson consistently showed a delicate sympathy for Mary's plight, visiting her and chaperoning her round Paris while her husband and sister-in-law were with the Baudouins. Meeting them himself, he found Caroline 'a mild amiable little woman in appearance' and liked everything about her, 'except that she called Wordsworth "father" which I thought indelicate'. What Robinson found 'indelicate' must have been painful to Mary, and perhaps explains why, for the first time in four months, she became 'poorly'.[25]

Both Eustace Baudouin and his brother, the Colonel, escorted the Wordsworths round the sights of Paris: they went to Fontainebleau, Versailles, the Palais Royale, the Père Lachaise cemetery, Notre-Dame, the Louvre and the Jardin des Plantes. 'I miss many antient Buildings,' William confessed to Lord Lonsdale, 'particularly the Temple, where the poor king and his family were so long confined. That memorable spot where the Jacobin Club was held, has also disappeared.' Helen Maria Williams was still a resident of Paris and Robinson, who was involved in her latest publication, effected the introduction which had eluded William in 1791–2. Then it had been the young unknown poet, whose sole publication had been his sonnet to Miss Williams, who sought the introduction; now it was she who anxiously and rather touchingly assured him 'how deeply she has felt the power of his compositions' and 'how much she would regret losing an opportunity of being introduced to him'.[26]

There were plenty of other compatriots in Paris, including Lady Mary Lowther, newly married to Lord William Frederick Cavendish-Bentinck, George Canning, the former editor of the *Anti-Jacobin*, MP for Liverpool and soon to be Foreign Secretary, and Tom Moore, the Irish poet, who had been forced to live in retirement on the Continent since 1818, when his deputy as Admiralty Registrar in Bermuda embezzled £6,000 while Moore was absent on foreign jaunts. Moore was a friend of Byron and shared the latter's virulently hostile feeling towards William's poetry and politics. No doubt this accounted for his jaundiced view of the Wordsworths. Meeting poor Mary for the first time, he snidely remarked that she 'requires all the *imaginative* powers of her husband to make anything decent of her – I mean *personally*, for she seems otherwise a comfortable sort of person enough'. He was amused by William's indecision over whether to accept an invitation from Lady Mary to her box at the theatre, which clashed with his own arrangement to take his wife and sister there. Moore chose to see this as a struggle between 'nobility & domesticity', snobbery and family duty, whereas William was simply anxious not to offend. The next evening, William dined at Canning's, in company with Moore and the Bentincks. Moore, who was rather too much in love with his own powers of dazzling conversation, found William 'rather dull'. Their differences were accentuated when they breakfasted together on the day before William's departure from Paris. William 'Talked a good deal so very smugly', attacking Byron's plagiarisms from his own work, asserting (against Moore's opposite opinion) his conviction that Scott was the author of the Waverley novels, and declaring Burke to be 'by far the greatest man of his age – Not only abounding in knowledge himself but feeding, in various directions, his most able contemporaries'.[27] Morally and politically, as well as poetically, the two men were too far apart ever to become friends.

The Wordsworths left Paris at the end of October and made their way to Boulogne, where they were to spend a few days with another expatriate living in France to escape her creditors in England. Mary Barker had poured her entire fortune into building her house in Borrowdale, only to find that she could not afford to live there and enjoy it. With her uncle Sir Jere Homfray, she had settled in the English community at Boulogne the previous summer and looked set to remain there.[28] There was a happy meeting between the old friends, but the Wordsworths were eager to be back in England. When the packet boat could not sail on the day appointed for their departure, they foolishly took passage on a smaller boat which, alone of all the ships in harbour, was willing to defy the contrary winds and huge breakers. It was then that they had an unwelcome adventure which inescapably conjured up visions of John's fate. Ten minutes after leaving harbour, their boat struck the rocks, water began to pour in and it looked as if they would all be lost. Fortunately, the tide was running in their favour, the boat was soon left stranded high and dry, and the Wordsworths had an undignified return to Boulogne in the carts sent across the bay to rescue them. It was 7 November before they finally set foot on English soil again, prompting not one but two heartfelt sonnets from William addressed to Dover.[29]

It is possible, but unlikely, that they arrived in London in time for William to attend the final day of Queen Caroline's trial for adultery, as his portrait was included in a curious picture depicting this scene in the House of Lords. There is no doubt that he took a lively interest in the trial. At Lugano they had actually stayed in the same rooms occupied by Caroline and her alleged paramour, Count Bergami. As Robinson then observed, she had exchanged a magnificent lake-view room for one which had no view, was close to the toilet and whose only advantage was an internal connecting door with Bergami's bedchamber; though not evidence of adultery, it suggested 'mala condutta'. As the painter James Stephanoff also included a number of other celebrities, including Byron and Moore, who were demonstrably unable to attend, William's inclusion was not so much a record of fact, or even a statement of sympathy, as simply a recognition of his growing public reputation.[30]

This was immediately apparent during this visit to London. The reviews of the *River Duddon* had been uniformly the best William had ever received, though one or two critics could not resist the gibe that it was a 'practical recantation' of his 'system'. On 1 December Talfourd sent him a copy of the *New Monthly Magazine*, which contained an essay he had written on William's poetry. It was a deliberately evangelical piece, but even so it did not express all that Talfourd felt. 'I might have said with truth, what I must deeply feel, that there is no writer who has ever lived to whom I personally owe the obligation which I owe to you, whose verse has so slid into the very current of my blood, and has so mingled with all my thoughts, hopes, and joys', Talfourd wrote privately to William. 'There is no sympathy of my nature which you do not enoble nor any day of my life which you do not make happier.'[31]

Though Mary was 'painfully anxious to be at home' and Sara, who had been left holding the fort at Rydal Mount, was now 'quite *angry*' with them for prolonging their absence, the Wordsworths lingered almost a month in London. The excuse was the need to resume sittings for Chantrey, so that he could finish his bust, and, of course, it was a rare opportunity to spend time with Willy, but most of their time seems to have been spent, as usual, in social parties with their closest friends, the Lambs, Robinson and Monkhouse, and attending exhibitions. Robinson was gratified to find that the Wordsworths 'duly appreciated' the private collection of his friend Charles Aders, but, when they visited the British Museum, 'I did not perceive that Wordsworth enjoyed much the Elgin Marbles'. As this seemed incomprehensible to Robinson, he could only suggest that William was 'a still man when he does enjoy himself and by no means ready to talk of his pleasure except to Miss Wordsworth'.[32]

At the end of November, the Wordsworths left London for Cambridge, where they were to spend a fortnight with Christopher, who had just taken up residence in the magnificent Master's Lodgings of Trinity College. With his usual talent for finding work, Christopher had not only taken on the mastership but also the vice-chancellorship of the university, and he was determined to reform and liberalize the Cambridge syllabus. William was impressed with what he now saw of a Cambridge which was very different from that of his youth. Observing the 'great ardour of Study among the young Men', their more temperate habits, and the zeal with which their masters, tutors and lecturers discharged their duties, he could not but augur well for the rising generation. 'What with the company (but by the bye I saw very little of him) of my dear brother, our Stately appartments with all the venerable Portraits there that awe one in to humility, old Friends, new Acquaintances, and a thousand familiar remembrances, and freshly conjured up recollections, I enjoyed myself not a little', William wrote the following spring.[33]

Dorothy would remain in the south until the end of January, dividing her time between her brother and his three sons at Cambridge and the Clarksons at Playford Hall. William and Mary left Cambridge for the north on 6 December, breaking their journey at Coleorton, where Lady Beaumont wanted William's advice on replanting some of the winter garden. The Beaumonts were always congenial hosts and the intended week-long visit turned into a fortnight, so it was 20 December before the Wordsworths finally turned their faces towards home.[34]

William and Mary had been away for six long months and much had happened in their absence. Their old friend and trusted physician in so many times of need, Richard Scambler, had died, leaving a widow and nine children in straitened circumstances. John Wordsworth, the younger brother of Mary Peake, who had visited Rydal Mount with his mother and sister in 1813, after so narrowly escaping death on the *Peacock*, had fallen victim to the sailor's scourge, yellow fever, and died on board ship. On a lighter note, Carter had displayed a hitherto unsuspected talent for philandering. He had been engaged to one of the servants, Mary Bell, but when his ardour cooled, he did not have the courage to break off the affair himself. Instead, he had conducted a flirtation with the cook under his fiancée's nose, driving poor Mary to resign rather than live in the house with her rival. Faced with sorting out this mess, Sara had taken a brusquely spinsterish view of the pulsating emotions below stairs. She allowed Mary six months to lick her wounds, rehired her and dismissed the cook. Carter himself was indispensable. The districts of Maryport, Cockermouth and Workington had all been added to William's Stamp Distributorship in his absence, and Carter had assimilated them smoothly and without difficulty.[35]

There were some things Carter could not do, however, and within days of his return William had to go off to Appleby to dismiss the sub-distributor and inform the Stamp Office of his new appointments to this office and the three new districts. He had barely returned home again when he had to go chasing off to Millom, on the Duddon estuary, on distressingly personal business. John Myers, his cousin and inseparable friend at university, had been found dead on the floor of his bedroom. The news was not unexpected to the Wordsworths, who were all too aware of his intemperate habits since the death of his wife, but it was a profound shock to his father, the eighty-five-year-old Reverend Thomas Myers. It fell to William to break the news to John's only child, nine-year-old Julia, who was Dora's fellow pupil at Miss Dowling's school at Ambleside. He also had to organize the funeral at Millom and, in March, a sale of his cousin's household effects and livestock.[36] Myers's death was the fourth in the Wordsworth family in just over twelve months. Another cousin to whom they had been very close, Captain John Wordsworth, had died in December 1819, after falling while trying to carry out repairs on the roof of his house at Penrith. And on 23 February 1820 Uncle William Cookson had died after a lingering illness.[37] William was rapidly acquiring the unwanted position of head of the family.

Two more deaths in February 1821 affected William deeply, but in a profoundly different way. Both were young men who had been his disciples and had paid tribute to him in their own work. On the 23rd, twenty-five-year-old John Keats coughed his last in Rome, his early demise attributed by common report to his sensitivity to the hostile reviews. Four days later, John Scott, the youthful editor of the *Champion*, died of wounds received in a duel over a literary squabble with Lockhart. 'God forgive those who have been the hasteners of their untimely fate!' Mary wrote feelingly, happy in the knowledge that her own husband was made of sterner stuff. William had liked Keats and admired his talent, believing him to be 'a youth of promise too great for the sorry company he keeps', but Scott's unnecessary and futile death was more distressing. 'I do not recollect any other English Author's perishing in the same way', William observed. 'It is an Innovation the effect of others which promise no good to the Republic of Letters or to the Country.' And, as always, he was among the first to make discreet inquiries about the financial circumstances of Scott's bereaved family.[38]

William's own work progressed swiftly this spring, despite recurrent problems with his eyes. His first priority was not poetry, however, but a new edition of his *Guide to the Lakes.* This had long been on the cards, but the moment had never seemed right. The decision to expand and publish it separately was prompted by the commendation of this section in at least four important reviews of the *River Duddon.* Westall, too, was trying to persuade William, or Southey if William would not, to write an accompanying text to his views of Windermere. And every visitor to Rydal Mount, friend or stranger, wanted the benefit of William's advice on how to make the best of their tour of the Lakes. There was clearly a demand for such a publication, and in fulfilling it there was a chance of recovering some of the cost of the Continental tour.[39]

The direction of his poetic endeavours surprised even his sister. 'William is quite well, and very busy,' she informed Catherine in March, 'though he has not looked at the Recluse or the poem on his own life; and this disturbs us. After fifty years of age there is no time to spare, and unfinished works should not, if it be possible, be left behind. This he feels, but the will never governs *his* labours.' With an unintentional pun, she announced, almost apologetically, to her Quaker friend that William was now composing a series of sonnets on a subject 'which I am sure you would never divine, – the Church of England, – but you will perceive that in the hands of a poet it is one that will furnish ample store of poetic materials'. Southey was also struck by William's choice of subject. 'Wordsworth was with me last week', he wrote on 15 April.

> Oddly enough, while I have been employed on my Book of the Church, he has been writing a series of historical sonnets upon the same subject, of the very highest species of excellence. My book will serve as a running commentary to his series, and the one will materially help the other; and thus, without any concerted purpose, we shall go down to posterity in company . . .[40]

The coincidence was not as remarkable as either man supposed, for they were both reacting to one of the burning political issues of the day, the perceived threat to the Established Church from the relaxation of constitutional rules excluding Roman Catholics from positions of secular authority and power. William's *Ecclesiastical Sketches* were begun in response to the setting up of a Parliamentary Committee to consider the Catholic claims and the consequent introduction, at the beginning of March, of the Roman Catholic Disability Removal Bill. If this measure went ahead, William argued, it would not only lead to further demands from the Catholics, but also be followed inevitably by a repeal of the acts which similarly excluded dissenters. And dissenters, as William knew all too well from his experience in the elections at Kendal, were 'to a man hostile to the Church'. 'I cannot but tremble at the prospect of introducing men who *may* turn, and (if they act consistently with the spirit of their Religion and even with its open profession) *must* turn their mutual fidelity against our Protestant Establishment', he wrote to Viscount Lowther; 'till in co-operation with other Dissenters and Infidels, they have accomplished its overthrow'.[41]

As long ago as 1812, William had declared that he would shed his blood in defence of the Church of England. (He rather spoilt the effect by confessing 'he knew not when he had been in a church at home "All our ministers are such vile creatures" '.) Ink was a more appropriate commodity for a poet than blood, and William shed a great deal of it, writing 102 sonnets descriptive of the history of the Church in England, neatly subdivided into three sections, 'From the introduction of Christianity into Britain to the consummation of the Papal dominion', 'To the close of the troubles in the reign of Charles I' and 'From the Restoration to the Present Times'. The subtext was a celebration of the Church of England as a unifying force for moral good and its clergymen – men like the Pastor of *The Excursion* or Robert Walker of the *Duddon* sonnets – as a civilizing and elevating influence, particularly in rural communities. Its doctrines were, in some senses, irrelevant. William did not believe it was necessary to define dogma 'with precision', complaining privately that 'the Church of England has encumbered itself by needless and mischievous attempts at explanation' and that the Athanasian Creed was one such 'unhappy excrescence'.[42] Nevertheless, it was still literally a broad church, encompassing many shades of opinion. As an institution, it remained a bulwark against sectarianism and factionalism, a final defence against anarchy.

The poems were much admired in their day, but even then it was their pious sentiment, rather than their poetical quality, which drew approval. They are not the sort of work which a modern reader, however religiously inclined, would choose to read voluntarily. What is lacking is not so much engagement with the subject as William's emotional presence, through which all his best poems are filtered. He did a huge amount of research and historical reading for the series, and it shows. The *Ecclesiastical Sketches* are, for the most part, worthy but dull. The few exceptions are those which touch William's personal experience: the vignette of his mother in *Catechizing*, for instance, or the lovely sonnet describing a vision of

Dora, which was based on an actual dream and composed on a single walk between Rydal and Grasmere.[43]

William was conscious that the execution of *Ecclesiastical Sketches* did not equal the grandeur of its conception. In two brutally honest criticisms, he summarizes why it fails to fire the imagination. 'The Ecc. Sketches labour under one obvious disadvantage, that they can only present themselves as a whole to the reader, who is pretty well acquainted with the history of this country;' he told Sharp; 'and, as separate pieces, several of them suffer as poetry from the matter of fact, there being unavoidably in all history . . . something that enslaves the Fancy.' In a second letter, written a few days later to another poet, Walter Savage Landor, he defended the sonnet form for its 'harmony', 'gravity' and 'republican austerity'. Then he admitted that his facility in writing sonnets was not always in his own best interests as a poet. Since writing his first three sonnets inspired by Milton, 'from want of resolution to take up anything of length, I have filled up many a moment in writing Sonnets, which, if I had never fallen into the practice, might easily have been better employed'.[44]

It was not just the Church of England that was under threat in the spring of 1821. On 22 March Joseph Hume, a radical MP, made a speech in the House of Commons proposing the abolition of the posts of Receiver-General and Distributors of Stamps, on the grounds of economy and a reduction of the influence of patronage. Distributors, he argued, were sinecurists who received too high a percentage of the public money passing through their hands and earned interest on it too. 'The distributors of stamps did not discharge their duties in person, but by deputy, and the consequence was, that when an idle poet (Mr Wordsworth) was appointed one of their number, he minded little in what manner his deputy made his profits, provided he received his share of them.' Viscount Lowther leapt to William's defence, armed with a list supplied by the 'idle poet' of his duties and responsibilities and a candid account of his profits. Recently, he had been collecting £18,000 a year, of which more than half was always forwarded direct to the Stamp Office; the remainder was sometimes banked, but rarely earned interest because it was mostly paid in provincial and Scottish notes, on which the banks refused to pay interest until they had been in their hands for six weeks. From interest he therefore received next to nothing; from the 4 per cent he was allowed to deduct for his own profit (£720 in total out of the £18,000), he had to pay a pro rata percentage to each of his sub-distributors. Despite the Solicitor-General being favourably impressed with William's submission, Hume succeeded in getting his motion referred to an investigative Commons committee, changes would become inevitable and William would never again be able to view his government office as a certain source of income.[45]

The summer proved to be one of the busiest in many years and there was not a spare bed in the house for months on end. Sara, who had left for Stockton as soon as William and Mary returned from the Continent, came back in May, bringing her oldest niece, Bessy, with her for the grand Ambleside ball, though bad weather frustrated the usual picnics and excursions. Henry Hutchinson paid his annual visit, but he was the only other member of Mary's family to do so.[46] The farmers among them were all in dire straits. John Monkhouse had secured another rent reduction from his sympathetic landlord and it was an indication of the harshness of the times that he was now paying 30 per cent less than in 1813; by the following year it had been reduced again, to £600, from the £3,000 he had contracted for in his original lease. As he acknowledged, this generosity caused his landlord considerable financial hardship: 'with these specimens of the Condition of the Country Gentlemen what can you expect of the farmers[?]' John asked; '– the situation is deplorable and it appears that the ministers will not or can not grant them any effectual relief'. Tom Hutchinson was less fortunate in his landlord and was therefore in greater difficulties. A man of 'few words and still less of a complainer', he was now resolved that, if times did not improve, emigration was the only option open to his family at the expiration of his lease. As for George, who had lost his own farm, though now nominally employed as a steward, he was little better than a labourer. He lived in a 'wretched hovel', performed drudgery 'like the meanest of our work men' and earned £20 a year (less than half the amount Dorothy had paid for her false teeth), with which he had to support his pregnant wife and child.[47]

Tom Monkhouse had problems of a different kind which prevented him making his annual visit to the Lakes and Penrith races. His wife, who had already suffered one miscarriage, seemed likely to lose her next baby and was therefore sent to Hindwell to be nursed through her pregnancy by his sister.[48] And to the initial joy of the entire family, Joe Monkhouse suddenly announced his intention to pay them a visit. Joe, the youngest of the three brothers, had lived for many years in the West Indies, where he was the manager of sugar plantations on Jamaica. Henry Hutchinson had spent a couple of days with him on one of his voyages in 1808–9, and he had himself come to England on a visit in 1816, but had not yet earned enough to retire permanently to his homeland. In the meantime, according to Henry, he had become a 'staid Bashaw! With slaves attentive to his wish'; this was the problem, for he had made money not only by slave labour on the plantations, but also by speculating in selling them.[49]

As his shocked family were about to discover, he had also used them in other ways, having fathered several children, all by different slave women. One of these, his three-year-old son George, he now brought with him to England, with the obvious intention of leaving him in the care of his relations. 'I am not partial to such like progeny', his sister wrote coldly, 'and shall feel great reluctance to have it introduced amongst mine which I suppose he will expect.' The ban did not extend to the errant father, who was in a very precarious state of health, virtually paralysed from 'a long continued cold', as he called it, though his family rightly suspected the West Indian planter's vice, alcoholism, which would soon kill him. 'Most happy shall we all be to see Joe,' his sister wrote, with careful emphasis, 'and I trust that the pure welch air and this fine weather will soon restore him to perfect health'. When brother and sister finally parted in October, knowing well that they were unlikely ever to meet again, Mary hoped Joe would take the child back with him. 'It seems most absurd to have so young a child here when we none of us have shewn any inclination to take charge of it.'[50]

Needless to say, Joe had no intention of taking his son home, placing him instead at a school in London, apparently with Tom's collusion. Whether it was the thought of little George's illegitimacy, his slave descent or his negroid blood which had so alienated his English relations, when Joe died, on 2 September 1822, leaving him penniless, they all rallied round. His Uncle John offered him a home at the Stow, Tom undertook to pay for his clothing and education and Mary, in a sudden sympathetic return of maternal feeling, welcomed him into the bosom of the family. 'He is a sweet little fellow as can be –,' Tom wrote with surprise and delight, 'of a mild disposition & very interesting & pensive Countenance'.[51]

Rydal Mount was, as usual, a refuge for waifs and strays this summer. Richard's widow (now also thoroughly rehabilitated, despite initial prejudice) and her six-year-old son came to stay for five weeks. 'Keswick' John was 'a pretty genteel looking child – but when he speaks the revolution is astonishing! he has the very worst and most barbarous of all the dialects of Cumberland'. It was hoped that sending him to Sedbergh the following year would prove an effective cure. The orphaned Julia Myers also spent her summer holidays with the Wordsworths, before returning to Miss Dowling's with Dora, who was entering upon her last term at the school. Julia's cousins and their mother, the Robinsons of York, came to see her in August and, naturally, they too made Rydal Mount their headquarters.[52]

Among the Lakers this year were many old friends, including Robinson, Kenyon and Losh. (The last, like Robinson, thought William had mellowed with age: 'I think his manners are improved and that he displays less than he used to do, of a desire to give a kind of mysterious importance to common sentiments and common trains of reasoning merely because he considered them to be his own.') Making their first visits to Rydal Mount were two distinguished scholars, Christopher's friend William Whewell, a fellow of Trinity and brilliant scientist, and Sir Henry Holland, author of *Travels in the Ionian Isles, Albania, Thessaly, Macedonia etc, during 1812 and 1813*, who, less agreeably, as physician to Queen Caroline, had testified to her innocence during her trial.[53] The most significant newcomer, however, was not a grandee or an eminent academic but a half-pay Irish dragoon who had retired from the army and taken up residence in the Lakes. Edward Quillinan was thirty-one years old, a veteran of the Peninsular War, a minor poet and a fervent admirer of William's work. He was, quite literally, to become one of the Wordsworth family, but no one could have guessed it from their first disastrous encounter.

Quillinan was stationed at Penrith and rode over to Rydal three times before he finally plucked up the courage to call. He caught William during one of his composing fits, in which he was always inclined to be irritable, and he aggravated the situation by refusing to hand over his letter of introduction from their mutual friend Gillies, because, he said, it was too flattering. William seemed 'quite angry', 'hurled a chair about' and made 'short and stiff remarks'. Quillinan, who was just as proud and touchy, was beginning to think his hero 'most disagreeable' when the door opened and a tall young lady, not handsome but with a 'most engaging innocence & ingenuousness of aspect', walked in. It was sixteen-year-old Dora, who, on seeing a stranger, turned to flee. 'Then it was that I saw the Poet's countenance to advantage – ', Quillinan declared. 'All the father's heart was thrown into his eyes & his voice as he encouraged her to come . . . It was a most timely interruption I have loved that sweet girl ever since.' Dora refused to stay, but, assessing the situation rapidly, ran off to fetch Aunt Sara to sort out the belligerent pair, who had resumed their stand-off. 'I was about to retire much disappointed,' Quillinan remembered,

> when in came Miss Hutchinson, who saw at once that there was some awkwardness between us: she relieved me in a moment, with that fine tact & benign politeness thoroughly understood only by women. She civilly accosted me, rallied the poet for twirling the chair, took it from him & appropriated it to her own use; made herself mistress of the cause of our restraint, laughed him into good humour, & sent him out to shew me the garden & the terrace.[54]

It worked like a dream. The two men rambled together for hours, talking of poetry, and Quillinan returned in triumph to share the poet's dinner. Within a matter of weeks, Quillinan had left the army for good and taken up residence with his wife, Jemima, and their eighteen-month-old daughter, Mima, at Spring Cottage, under Loughrigg Fell in the Vale of Rydal. The two families were instantly on intimate terms. Jemima was the daughter of Sir Egerton Brydges, whom William had met only once but with whose publications he was familiar. Her sister, and brother-in-law, who visited in August, were as sociable as her husband, and the Quillinan party was soon cutting a dash at the Ambleside balls. Quillinan almost succeeded in persuading William to accompany him on a five-week tour of his native Ireland that summer and, though this project fell through, he did join him on a short excursion into the Yorkshire Dales at the beginning of November. Quillinan drove in his gig. They called on John at Sedbergh and walked with his headmaster, visited Hardraw Force and Aysgarth Falls, glimpsed Mary Queen of Scot's prison at Bolton by the light of a 'watery moon', passed Richard II's stronghold, Middleham Castle, and explored the gardens at Studley Royal and the ruins of Jervaulx Abbey and Fountains Abbey.[55]

Quillinan was an intelligent and agreeable companion for William, but he secured a lasting hold on the entire family's sympathies and affections by the sufferings which the autumn and following spring would inflict. In September, his wife gave birth to a second daughter, whom, at William's suggestion, they named Rotha, after the river flowing through the Vale of Rydal. A proud and delighted Dora was invited to join her father in standing as the baby's godparents, but they had to enter on their duties sooner than expected when Jemima failed to recover from the birth. Suffering from what would now be diagnosed as postnatal depression, she became so ill that Mary, her constant nurse, could do nothing for her, and she had to be removed to Lancaster for mental treatment. When Mary took her babes over to see her in the new year, she seemed to be making an excellent recovery, and the Wordsworths all looked forward to their return in April. 'They have been most agreeable neighbours to us', Sara wrote then, '– and but for the prospect of their return our neighbourhood would seem very forlorn'.[56]

Throughout the year, Mary and Dorothy had been employed in writing up their journals of the previous summer's Continental tour. With typical self-deprecation, Mary dismissed hers as 'a mere transcript' of her notes, copied at her daughter's 'earnest request', because Dora could not read the hastily scribbled originals. Her transcript was ready by May, but she was 'so very shy of exposing it' that Sara made a fair copy of her own, 'that I might lend to whom I liked'. Their fellow traveller, Robinson, read the journal during his brief stay at Rydal Mount in August, and was 'greatly delighted with its minuteness and faithfullness; and liveliness of observation.' He was also permitted to read Dorothy's journal, as far as it went. It was a chastening experience for the habitual diarist. 'They filled me with shame at the comparison with my own . . . [they] drew my attention to a great and unobserved distinction. The ladies' journals abound in observations, and contain no reflexions.'[57]

Anxious not to be influenced by Mary's work, Dorothy refused to read Mary's journal until she had completed a first draft of her own. This proved to be a far more laborious task. 'Had not my Brother so very much wished me to do my best,' she explained to Catherine Clarkson, 'I am sure I should never have had the resolution to go further than just re-copy what I did by snatches, and very irregularly, at the time; but to please him I have amplified and arranged; and a long affair will come out of it, which I cannot think any person can possibly have the patience to read through'. Had it not been for William's encouragement, the journal would never have been completed. Dorothy had started to write it while at Playford Hall in the new year, thinking that the quietness of the place would be conducive to her work, but she swiftly discovered that she lacked the self-discipline to sit and write steadily for hours on end. At Rydal Mount there were so many visitors and other distractions, even during the supposedly quiet time of the year, that progress was minimal. 'I am sorry to find [her journal] is little advanced', William informed Kenyon, adding a little sarcasm at his sister's expense, 'talking being, as you know, a much more easy, and to one party at least a more pleasant thing than writing.'[58]

The most effective way William found of motivating his sister to complete her work was to offer to write poems for her to intersperse with her text, just as he had done with her *Recollections of a Tour in Scotland.* The poems he now wrote were not of the same quality as those inspired by the earlier tour. As with *Ecclesiastical Sketches*, it is as if his head, rather than his heart, was engaged in the work. Dorothy's comment on her own journal, 'you will be frightened when you see so many pages – all written about the outside of things hastily viewed!', is also a peculiarly apt description of the poems, though William worked diligently and with interest. The few poems intended for the journal soon swelled into thirty-eight, to which would be added a dedicatory poem to the fellow travellers, and a concluding poem, written when William received the proof sheets. As late as the end of November, when William was still trying to complete his sonnets for *Ecclesiastical Sketches*, which he intended to publish in the spring, there were no plans to publish the tour poems. Sara then made a fair copy of them for Tom Monkhouse specifically because 'you are not likely to see them in print – having been written for the purpose of *ornamenting* "the *Journals*"'. Tom was strictly prohibited from giving a copy of the poems to anyone else, even Robinson, though he was to be allowed to read them, if he wished. By the middle of January, Dorothy for one was convinced that they should be published: 'his work has grown to such importance (and has continued growing) that I have long ceased to consider it in connection with my own narrative of events unimportant, and lengthy descriptions'.[59]

The conviction of all those of his fellow travellers who read the poems was that they ought to be published. 'I think of their kind he never wrote anything that was more delightful' was Dorothy's opinion. Robinson too was enthusiastic, though he advocated the idea of printing one of the journals with the poems intermixed, believing this would be more popular. It was a suggestion which had been mooted at Rydal Mount, as Mary admitted: 'we sometimes jestingly talk of raising a fund by such means for a second and a further trip into Italy!'[60] Both women were diffident about their journals, believing that they would be of no interest to anyone except their friends, and once William had decided to publish his poems as an independent collection, such a joint venture could not go ahead. Nevertheless, Dorothy could not quite let go of the idea. The thought that publishing her journal might raise enough money for her to afford a second tour was too alluring. In September William, who was even more anxious to see the journal in print than his sister, wrote to Rogers on her behalf, taking him up on his offer to assist in securing her a London publisher. Dorothy would not sacrifice her privacy by becoming a published author, she told Rogers, for less than £200. Whether he was unable to secure such a sum or her doubts finally got the better of her, the journal did not appear in print until long after the reluctant authoress was dead and buried.[61]

Throughout January William revised his poems and added new ones. By the beginning of February *Memorials of a Tour on the Continent, 1820* was in the press and *Ecclesiastical Sketches* about to join it. Before the end of the month, the printing was almost complete and final proofs of both works had arrived at Rydal Mount. As Sara accurately foresaw, however, the *Memorials* would be finished only when they were 'bound up *tight in boards*' and could no longer be 'tinkered'. A last-minute suggestion by Robinson sent William scurrying back to composition, and *Desultory Stanzas, upon Receiving the Preceding Sheets from the Press* were added, no doubt to the despair of the printers. William's customary generosity in handing out complimentary copies of his books now had to be severely reined in. His account for the previous year with Longman revealed he had given away £60 worth of books – far more than he had actually earned from his writings in the same period. Gifts of the new publications were to be made to only two friends, both of whom had contributed indirectly to the poems: Southey, to whose forthcoming *Book of the Church* he had made graceful reference in the preface to *Ecclesiastical Sketches*, and Richard Sharp, whose detailed itinerary for the Continental tour the travellers had followed almost to the letter.[62]

The two little books were published by Longman in March to reviews which generally acknowledged William's staying power as a poet, if they did not wax lyrical about the poems now laid before them. Only two reviews struck a discordant note. The *Literary Gazette*, which paradoxically was part-owned by Longman, dismissed the *Memorials* with the pungent phrase 'there is hardly one ... worth reading at all' and took William severely to task over *Ecclesiastical Sketches*. 'It is astonishing to see a man of genius so far delude himself as to fancy he can render any thing popular, no matter how untractable the subject, how prosaic the verse, and how absurd the plan.' And in November the acrid giant of the *Edinburgh Review* waded in with his customary arresting opening sentence: 'The Lake School of Poetry, we think, is now pretty nearly extinct.' William, Jeffrey went on, had 'exchanged the company of leech-gatherers for that of tax-gatherers' and had fallen into a distasteful way of writing, which was 'a sort of prosy, solemn, obscure, feeble kind of mouthing'.[63] As both reviews were so obviously dictated by political enmity rather than literary judgement, they could be dismissed out of hand, more particularly as they were so out of tune with the general reception accorded the poems.

A third volume completed the trilogy of William's publications in 1822. This was his *Guide to the Lakes*, which he now republished as a separate volume for the first time. Substantial revision had taken place. The work had been divided into three sections and there were some major additions: a comparison of Alpine scenery with that of the Lakes, inspired by the Continental tour; a revised version of Dorothy's account of her excursion up Scafell Pike with Mary Barker; and a final chapter setting out the route of a recommended tour. Newly retitled with one of those comprehensive titles so beloved by the youthful William, *A Description of the Scenery of the Lakes in the North of England. Third Edition, (Now First Published Separately) with Additions, and Illustrative Remarks upon the Scenery of the Alps*, it too was published by Longman. Unlike William's poetry, it was to prove a great success, the 500 copies of the first edition selling out within the year, and double that number being printed for the next edition of 1823.[64]

The publication of the three volumes of 1822 was to become a milestone in William's literary career. Everything he had ever written and wished to preserve for posterity was now in print, except for *The Prelude* and *The Recluse*. Once again, he was ready for a fresh start on his life's work. '*The Recluse* has had a long sleep, save in my thoughts;' he confessed to Walter Savage Landor in April; 'my MSS. are so ill-penned and blurred that they are useless to all but myself; and at present I cannot face them.'[65] He never would. And as far as the public were concerned, he now ceased to be a writing poet. It would be thirteen years before his name again appeared on the title-page of a new work.

This withdrawal into a silence of such duration was neither premeditated nor intentional. It simply arose from circumstances. Domestic concerns were at the forefront of William's mind throughout most of 1822. Dora had left Miss Dowling's school at Christmas, having regularly carried off prizes for her application and attainments. Her departure, after three years at the school which had transformed her, was marked by a splendid ball, attended by 'all the Beauty and Fashion of the neighbourhood'. She was now almost eighteen: her education was complete, a career was out of the question and, like most girls of her age and class, she would remain at home until she married. In the summer she was joined by Willy, whose career at the Charterhouse was unexpectedly and ignominiously cut short by the discovery that despite the 'enormous expense' lavished on his education, he had made very little progress. 'It does not appear to me –', wrote his Uncle Christopher, after examining him during the Christmas holidays, 'that his being at the Charter house hitherto has been very profitable: and yet I am far from seeing any natural deficiency about him.' Johnson concurred. It was clearly folly to keep him at the school: 'if he will be idle he must be idle at less cost!' Sara declared, feeling sorry for his elder brother. 'What would [Johnny] not give now for the advantages that this little *Monkey* has thrown away!'[66]

At the beginning of May Willy was dispatched to join his brother at Sedbergh, but within weeks of his arrival he had to be sent home again. He was clearly very ill, dropsical as his anguished father described it, and for three weeks his family despaired of his life. Scambler's replacement, Thomas Carr, and a physician from Kendal were both brought over to treat him, and gradually he recovered his health and spirits, though he remained so delicate that he would not be sent away to school again. For the rest of his life William would be tortured with guilt, blaming himself for destroying Willy's health and education by sending him to the Charterhouse so young, and doing his best to compensate for what he considered the irreparable wrong he had done his son.[67]

For the Wordsworths, Willy's brush with death was just the latest in a series of calamities. The Quillinans had returned to Rydal from Lancaster in March, taking up residence at Tillbrooke's Ivy Cottage, at the foot of the hill to the Mount. Jemima was apparently quite recovered but, a few weeks later, she accidentally set her clothes on fire and was horribly burnt. The Wordsworth women nursed her devotedly, day and night for a fortnight, but other than change her dressings there was little they could do to ease her suffering. Then Mary and Dora were suddenly called away to Lowther by the news that William had had an accident. Riding near Lowther with Tom Monkhouse and George Gee, his horse had taken fright and thrown him against a stone wall, gashing the back of his head. In this crisis, Dorothy was worse than useless: she simply took to her bed until reassurance arrived from Mary and Dora that her brother was on the mend.[68] William's accident detained the family several days at Lowther rectory, where James Satterthwaite had kindly offered them all accommodation until the invalid was fit to travel home. As Sara was away sampling the waters at Harrogate, Dorothy was thus alone with Jemima when she died, and it fell to her and Gee to arrange the funeral on behalf of Quillinan. With strange prescience, Dorothy chose a site adjoining the graves of the Wordsworth children as the place where Jemima would lie in Grasmere churchyard. William, Mary and Dora did not return to Rydal till the day after the funeral, so were spared the painful memories which a burial at this sacred spot would inevitably cause them. On 12 June Quillinan left Ivy Cottage, his dreams of settling permanently in the Lakes shattered by this unforeseen tragedy. Leaving Mima and Rotha, who had been cared for at Rydal Mount since their mother's death, with his wife's family at Lee Priory, in Kent, Quillinan embarked on a series of lengthy Continental tours in a fruitless flight from guilt and grief.[69]

It was unfortunate that Thomas and Catherine Clarkson arrived only two days after Jemima's death. Their visit had been long planned and greatly anticipated, but as they could not stay longer than a fortnight, the general chaos prevented the old friends spending as much time together as they would have liked. Perhaps it was just as well, for they were now poles apart politically. Having heard William Jackson give what she called a 'bombastical' funeral sermon, in which he had pointedly referred to Jemima's (very remote) royal ancestry, Catherine was shocked to hear William declare him to be 'the *model* of a parish priest'. 'It is curious to me to find them so thoroughly torified', Catherine admitted to Robinson. 'Though I *will* not acknowledge it to my Husband it is a little drawback upon the pleasure of our intercourse even to me'.[70]

The summer saw an unusually large family gathering at Rydal Mount. This was occasioned, in part, by the christening of Tom Monkhouse's baby daughter, Mary Elizabeth, who had been born the previous December. Jane had been slow to recover from the birth and it was thought she might benefit from a change of air; they were also about to move house and would have to go into temporary lodgings until the new one was ready. It therefore made sense to do as Sara suggested and take a cottage at Rydal from April till October. Tom would have to spend a couple of months in London on business, but Jane and the baby would not be lonely, sheltering under the Wordsworths' wing. The christening was to be held on 9 August and the family gathered in force. Mary Hutchinson, who was to be godmother, and her aunt, Elizabeth Monkhouse, who would remain at Rydal for the winter, came up from Hindwell, Joanna, with Mrs Ellwood, from Penrith.[71]

Coincidentally, too, Christopher Wordsworth and his three boys, aged seventeen, sixteen and fourteen, were taking their first ever holiday in the Lakes. It was in fact their first proper holiday together as a family. Christopher had never had time to spare before taking up the mastership of Trinity, and now, having settled into the post, he could legitimately use at least part of the long vacation for his own pleasure. Despite seven weeks of incessant rain, and the restrictions that imposed on their occupations, both families took great delight in each other's company. Christopher's boys were immediately enslaved by their lively, affectionate cousin Dora, and when they parted in September it was with genuine regret. The youngest, Charles, was even prompted to verse.

> Fare thee well! Dear couzin Dora
>   And believe me when I tell
> That my heart was never sorer
>   Than at bidding thee Farewell –

Their father was equally smitten, this being the first chance he had ever had to get to know his goddaughter, but he was constitutionally incapable of complete relaxation. Even before he left in September, he was enlisting the services of his powerful friends to help raise money to build a National School for girls and a new church at Kendal.[72]

As the Wordsworths left, Jack Hutchinson came, escorting two of his sons to Sedbergh, where they were Johnny's fellow pupils, and taking Dora and her Aunt Sara back with him to Stockton on a visit that would last till Christmas.[73] They were accompanied over Kirkstone Pass by William, who was on his way to Lowther, and Dora's aunts Dorothy and Joanna. These two middle-aged ladies, in an unlikely pairing and even more unlikely mood of adventure, were embarking on a tour of Scotland together, without the benefit of masculine company or escort. For Dorothy, it was mainly a reprise of her earlier trip, except that, as a concession to age and gender, the travelling would be mostly by coach and steamboat. Their tour would take them to Edinburgh, Stirling, Glasgow, Inverary, as far north as Skye, then back down the western coast by steamboat to Glasgow and home by the Lanark road.[74]

Dorothy was, once again, assiduous in writing notes for her journal. Age had not diminished her powers of observation. At the inn at Tarbet, for instance, she detected that Cambridge students had been there 'by mathematical papers that had been thrown out of the windows', and there are entertaining glimpses of the other tourists 'doing' the sights. Dorothy and Joanna congratulated themselves on their superiority in not accompanying the tourist herd to view 'Rob Roy's Caves', especially as the only motive for doing so was 'to *say* they have been in . . . because Sir Walter Scott has made them so much talked about; and, when they come out, dashing the dust off their cloaths, the best they can say is "Well! there is nothing to be seen; but it is worth while, if only to *say* that one has been there!" '[75] Despite these occasional lively moments, Dorothy's journal of this tour is a comparatively dull performance. The most interesting thing about it is not what it actually says, but what it suggests about the composition of her journals. The obvious inference is that her more successful efforts were indebted to the stimulation of her brother's company. Without him to draw attention to striking images, particularly in scenery, her own description was less vivid and less original. As both Coleridge and de Quincey had recognized, her greatest gift was to empathize and respond. It was essentially reactive. And without William to evoke a response, her journal lacks its usual sparkle.

It was probably predictable that Dorothy would wear out the less active Joanna, who had long suffered from occasional bouts of rheumatism. The Scottish weather, relentless sightseeing and a frightful day and night inadvertently spent in the wilds near Moffat, when they missed a coach connection and hourly thought they were about to be murdered by every stranger they met, began to take its toll. By the time they reached the Malcolms' welcoming home at Burnfoot, Joanna was too ill to continue. They remained there several days, then backtracked to Edinburgh, so that Joanna could have the benefit of the baths there. When they eventually returned to Rydal Mount early in November, they had been absent seven weeks.[76]

Dorothy's return coincided with an unexpected and severe recurrence of Willy's summer illness. For ten days he stared death in the face, but once more he recovered. This illness was decisive, however, for it determined the Wordsworths not to send him away to school again. Carter had been giving him lessons at home but, much to idle Willy's delight, the doctor ordered a complete rest from all application to books and said that, for the next few months, he was to be watched over and treated like an invalid.[77]

In the circumstances, it was not surprising that William found it hard to settle to poetry, though Quillinan's request that he would write an epitaph for his wife weighed heavily on his conscience. In addition to the difficulty he always felt at writing to order, anxiety about Willy and the discomfort of his own eye problems meant he could do nothing but what Dorothy called 'vagrant reading by day light'. Mary had prepared Quillinan as best she could for a long wait, reminding him of the years it had taken William to write the six simple lines on their own son's gravestone, 'Yet he could not give it up.' A month later, she tactfully suggested to Quillinan that, 'judging from many of your own elegant verses', the best and speediest solution would be if he wrote a draft himself, which would either give William something to work on or prompt him to write new verses of his own. She was right, as usual. William gratefully seized on Quillinan's thirteen lines, reduced them to ten, added an introductory six lines of his own and made several emendations. His comments on why he made these changes are more interesting than the finished lines. He thought that the cause of Jemima's death (which Quillinan had not mentioned) should be specified, and he substituted 'patient' for 'lovely' in the description of her virtues, because he did not think personal beauty should be dwelt on in an epitaph. It was a measure of how seriously he had taken his task that, when Quillinan responded with a letter of fervent thanks, expressing his sense of obligation, William was affected 'to tears'. The lines would be engraved in marble by Chantrey for a memorial in Grasmere church.[78]

Apart from these lines, and a couple of other short poems, written in December, William's poetry was at a standstill. As Christmas approached and the family gathered together at Rydal Mount, he and Dorothy embarked on a revision of the *Guide to the Lakes* in preparation for a second edition. It was the only one of William's

1822 trilogy of publications to have been a commercial success. 'He is now giving his mind to Poetry again,' Dorothy wrote on 21 December, 'but I do not think he will ever, in his life-time – *publish* any more poems – for they hang on hand – never selling'.[79]

20. *Idle Mount*

In January 1823 William sent Lady le Fleming a peace-offering. Relations between landlady and tenant had become increasingly strained over the preceding year. Ever since moving into Rydal Mount, the back rooms of the house had been so damp as to be uninhabitable in winter, and sometimes during wet seasons in the summer. A new roof had been promised time and again, but had never materialized. Just as workmen were about to arrive, William discovered, almost accidentally, that in return for the repairs he was expected to hand over some of his barns and outbuildings to a local farmer. 'The character of the place would be entirely changed and vulgarized, were these premises turned into a common farmer's yard', William had complained to Lady le Fleming. So once again the repairs had not been carried out.[1]

Rumours had also come to the Wordsworths' ears that Lady le Fleming intended to build a new church at Rydal – right in front of their house. The plans had been carried out with the greatest secrecy, not for sinister reasons, but because Lady Ann had an ostentatious dislike of appearing ostentatious. Unlike the kindly and sociable Lady Diana, she was a reclusive, deeply pious, but decidedly odd, woman who shut herself up in her 'winter quarters' every year at Rydal Hall, rarely saw anyone and discouraged any sort of contact with her neighbours. When the Wordsworths learned that she intended to build a church in the village they welcomed the idea: it would be a convenience to them and an invaluable asset to the neighbourhood. What concerned them was the precise location and, more particularly, the style to be adopted, particularly as the matter was entirely in the hands of Lady le Fleming's agents, who were not renowned for their appreciation of the finer arts. 'We are very anxious that nothing should be done to disfigure the Village –', Mary explained to Lady Beaumont, 'they might, good taste directing them, add much to its beauty.' Unfortunately, 'good taste', that is, William Wordsworth, was not to be consulted. Instead, he could only stand by and watch helplessly as the foundations for the new chapel were laid in the orchard below Rydal Mount, opposite the door leading to the lower waterfall. Perhaps, Mary asked hopefully, the Beaumonts might send some hints, or sketches, for a chapel appropriate to this setting which might influence the final design?[2]

William's 'peace-offering' to Lady le Fleming was a poem in praise of her decision to build the chapel.

> How fondly will the woods embrace
> This daughter of thy pious care,
> Lifting her front with modest grace
> To make a fair recess more fair;[3]

He received what Mary politely called 'a very proper reply', written in the third person, thanking him for 'his most friendly wishes' for the future of the chapel and his 'interesting' verses. Ironically, given Dorothy's decided opinion that he would never publish again, William was extremely anxious to publish this poem, but Lady le Fleming would have none of it. She 'decidedly declined' to have her name associated with the project and did not wish 'to be thus obtruded on the public'. William tried again. 'The purpose of the verses being to support however humbly and feebly the cause of religion and piety especially as connected with the ordinances and institutions of the Church of England', he urged upon the retiring benefactress, 'Mr W is desirous that they should be published at this time when the Church is assaulted openly and unceasingly by enemies in all orders of society from the highest to the lowest.' His perseverance paid off, and when he had removed her name and altered the verses to exclude any localized references which might identify the place, he finally received a frosty permission to publish.[4]

On 18 February William and Mary left Rydal Mount to pay a three-week visit to the Beaumonts at Coleorton. Sara accompanied them as far as Derby, then went on to London, to stay with Tom Monkhouse, whose wife was confined to the couch by that affliction beloved of Victorian ladies, 'spinal weakness'. The Wordsworths' visit to Coleorton was 'of *infinite service*' to William: the stimulus of the Beaumonts' society was even more valuable to him now, when his eyes were so weak and easily irritated by light and heat that he was unable to read for himself. For Mary too, though she did not say so, it came as a considerable relief, releasing her from 'those everlasting Newspapers!' which she was duty-bound to read aloud to her husband for hours on end.[5] As usual, the three weeks turned into four, and on 19 March they left Coleorton to meet their son John at Birmingham.

After all his years of schooling at Sedbergh, John was now, aged almost twenty, at last about to achieve his own, and his parents', dream of going to university. Cambridge had been the natural choice, not least because of his Uncle Christopher's presence and influence there, but the great stumbling block was the mathematics, which still formed the core of the curriculum. At John's own request, therefore, his admission to his father's old college was quietly set aside, and he applied instead to Oxford. His father's contacts did much to smooth the way. John Keble, soon to be famous as a founder of the Oxford Movement, had long been a devotee of William's poetry and, having been introduced to him by Coleridge's nephews in 1815, admired the man as much as the poet. Now a fellow and tutor of Oriel, he willingly gave his advice on where and how to apply.[6] Augustus Hare, a fellow and tutor of New College, who had been a regular summer visitor at Rydal Mount since 1819, lent his support and was a decisive influence in the ultimate choice of New College for John. What is more, he volunteered his services as a tutor above and beyond those provided by the college itself, ensuring that, despite John's many difficulties, he would emerge with a creditable degree to his name. Unlike his father, John would enter university with every possible advantage. Not for him the lowly status and despised gown of a sizar; this Mr Wordsworth would be a true gentleman of the university, a gentleman commoner, wearing a silk gown, and costing his father more than half his annual income to support.[7]

Having seen John safely matriculated at Oxford, the Wordsworths travelled on to London to join Sara at the Monkhouses' new home in Gloucester Place. It was a fleeting visit, packed with the usual socializing, viewings of paintings and a visit to the Beaumonts to see Sir George's latest acquisition, a fragment of a sculpture of the Holy Family by Michelangelo. The highlights were two dinners. The first, at Rogers's on 1 April, reunited the Wordsworths with their old friend Sharp and a more recent acquaintance, the poet Tom Moore. There were also two new faces at the table: the historian Henry Hallam and the translator of Dante Henry Cary, whose work William greatly admired.[8] Cary was impressed with William, noting how his general appearance was much more benevolent than the impression created by the Chantrey bust, and that he was both engaging and amiable in manners and character. Moore, however, found the experience 'dull enough', presumably because his fellow guests failed to respond appropriately to his various provocatively 'electrifying assertions' on Shakespeare, Racine and Voltaire. Nevertheless, he was interested enough to note William's admission that he completely lacked an ear for music and that he had, for a long time, been unable to distinguish one tune from another. When the subject turned to Coleridge's *Christabel*, which both William and Cary praised 'far beyond my comprehension', Moore was clearly out of his element.[9]

This was also the case at the second dinner, on 4 April, hosted by a proud Tom Monkhouse, who could scarcely contain his glee when Rogers described it as 'the *most brilliant Thing* this Season'. It was quite a coup for a humble London vintner, whom Moore, with customary acerbity, described as the Maecenas of the Lake poets, 'contributing nothing but good dinners and silence'. The Beaumonts and Lord Lowther were unable to come, but '*five of the most distinguished Poets of the Age*' were present: William, Coleridge, Lamb, Moore and Rogers. Coleridge, who was in fine health and spirits, dominated the conversation, talking mainly metaphysical criticism to William. Lamb was on his best behaviour, did not get drunk and 'was only cheerful at last'. How Sara must have laughed inwardly when all five poets concurred in Robinson's gallant, but all too true, diagnosis that Jane Monkhouse was 'an Imposter . . . she looks so well it is impossible that she can ail anything'.[10]

From London, William and Mary travelled to Lee Priory, in Kent, to stay briefly with Quillinan and his family, before embarking on a short tour of the Low Countries. From the outset, the journey was dogged by ill-luck. Bad weather and a virulent attack of William's trachoma delayed their departure for five long weeks. When they did set off, on 16 May, the sea was so rough that they both began vomiting before they even got on board the steam packet, then lay in their bunks, rigid with fear and sickness, throughout the crossing. Mary tried valiantly to be positive. Though she could not sit upright in the boat taking them ashore at Ostend, she marvelled at the beauty of the phosphorescent waters sliding off the oars, the pillar of light streaming across the bay from the lighthouse on the pier, and the brilliant glow of the tar being burnt from the keel of a ship on the beach, as it faded among the dim stars in a grey mottled sky. 'I thought if we were to see nothing more, this exhibition repaid us for [our] day of suffering.'[11]

As she compiled her journal of the tour, Mary more than once lamented that she had not a painter's skill to delineate the scenes that passed before them, yet the word-pictures she conjures up are highly effective. Travelling on the barge along the canal between Bruges and Ghent, for instance, they were detained in the cabin after dinner by a heavy shower. 'A grand subject for a dutch or flemish Painter to look from the door of the first room after dinner is over, along the three tables in the second;' Mary observed;

> all are, or seem to be happy – some too much so to keep awake spread their jolly arms & rest their head upon the table – others thrown back & fast asleep, amid a rare din – some drinking &, of course, many smokeing [*sic*] – the variety of pipes curious – Scarcely one old flemish female cap to be seen   worked net ones most common & lace of english manufacture universal –

At other times, she recorded simply because William told her to do so. At Rotterdam, for example, she wrote,

> Here it is impossible to find time for description, nor is it needed. Dutch Towns are so much alike & the Guide Book tells it all . . . only certain things Wm says I must put down – for instance a picturesque groupe of Men on board a vessel in one of the Water Streets – 3 in scarlet & one in drab costume – caps of different forms – a rich treat for the eye, or for the memory of a Painter – but no idea of the effect can be given in words.[12]

Somewhere in Leiden, Mary (or, more likely, William, who was notoriously careless) lost the guidebook lent them by Captain Barrett Brydges, Quillinan's brother-in-law, in which she had conscientiously scribbled her notes. This was an immense frustration to her. 'I have not the power to recollect many things that I should have wished to record', she confessed, adding later that she did not remember anything at all about the Michelangelo monument they twice visited the church at Breda to see. 'All my notes which were of any value are gone for ever –', she mourned, 'for they were dates & positive information as far as they went – & without my book – & with a worthless tongue I have been travelling – not in the dark – but without ears.'[13]

Travelling mainly by barge, but also by road, the Wordsworths made a circular tour through Bruges, Ghent, Antwerp, Dort, Rotterdam, Delft, The Hague, Leiden, Haarlem, Amsterdam, Utrecht and Brussels. They visited churches, looked at paintings and walked quietly round the streets of the towns, but their activities were curtailed by the state of William's eyes. The eastern wind and sands of Ostend and the bright lights in the shimmering canals all irritated them and brought back the inflammation; they were obliged to go to bed early and even, in Amsterdam, to shut out the view from a window overlooking a canal because of the glare. Mary bore these deprivations with her customary good humour. 'Adventures we had had few –', she wrote in the final entry of her journal. 'William's eyes being so much disordered & so easily aggravated naturally made him shun society – & crippled us in many respects, but I trust we have stored up thoughts & Images that will not die.' And with a not unnatural pride in her managing skills, she added, 'It is worthy to record that our travelling expences, from our departure to our return to Lee Priory, inclusive of washing &c did not quite amount to 24 English pounds. A cheap Excursion!'[14]

A cheap excursion it may have been, but, as Robinson observed when the travellers returned to London on 17 June, William had not 'laid in many poetical stores'. They made a leisurely progress northwards, visiting Christopher at Cambridge and then joining Dora at Harrogate for three weeks, before returning together to Rydal Mount in the early hours of 15 July.[15] They arrived to find Dorothy and Willy well, and John returned from Oxford for the vacation. Hartley Coleridge, who had been staying at Rydal Mount with his mother and sister, was unimpressed by the Wordsworth children. 'John is laborious as an Ass', he told his brother. 'Dora is a sweet, good humour'd girl. Little Will is a bore.' His venom was understandable, given that laborious John was likely to make a success of his Oxford career, whereas brilliant, eccentric Hartley had been expelled from his fellowship at Oriel, for allegedly heavy drinking and bringing the college into disrepute by his erratic behaviour. Now, aged twenty-seven, he was reduced to the position of master in the school at Ambleside where he had once been taught himself, tutoring young Willy Wordsworth, and being lectured like an errant child by Dorothy for his sudden and unexplained absences from Rydal Mount.[16]

The summer of 1823 was one of the quietest the Wordsworths remembered; few friends came to visit them and the bad weather deterred the usual crop of Lakers. Mary's brother Henry arrived in July for the fishing on Lake Coniston, but Tom Monkhouse had to cut short his annual trip to the Penrith races, his wife's supposed ill-health requiring that they should spend the summer at Ramsgate instead. The best he could do to escape the matrimonial thumb was a brief excursion to France, squiring Sara on a duty visit to Mary Barker at Boulogne.[17] When they returned to Ramsgate, Sara found herself in the odd position of being constantly in the company of her erstwhile would-be lover, Coleridge, though she appears to have carried off the difficulty with more presence of mind than he did. Though Coleridge lavished attention and kisses on Mary Elizabeth, the Monkhouse baby, it did not escape her mother's waspish attention that, even now, Sara was the real object of his passion. The Wordsworths were in high hopes that Tom would purchase Fox Ghyll, the pretty cottage in Rydal Vale built by Robert Blakeney, with considerable input from William, but terms could not be agreed and the opportunity was lost.[18]

There was only one memorable visitor to Rydal Mount this summer, the actor William Charles Macready, who had made his name playing Shakespearian characters on the London stage. A long-standing devotee of William's poetry, he had been introduced to the poet and his wife at a breakfast at Talfourd's in June, a fleeting encounter which provided him with an excuse to present himself at Rydal Mount a few weeks later. William received him cordially, if gloomily, in the dining room, where the blinds were pulled down to exclude the painful daylight from his sensitive eyes. Finding an avid listener in Macready, William soon perked up, reciting his poetry sonorously and impressively. He and John accompanied the actor back to his lodgings in Ambleside that evening, took him on an evening excursion on Lake Windermere and sat with him while he ate his dinner. Like the pastor in his *Excursion*, Macready commented, William held their attention with his comments on the beauty of the evening and the scenery.[19]

In the autumn, they were visited by Thomas Clarkson, whose health and spirits had been greatly restored by the unopposed passage through the House of Commons, in May, of a motion in favour of a gradual abolition of slavery. The Wordsworths rejoiced with him, and William urged him to complete his literary labours by writing a history of Africa as 'the most appropriate one for him who has so nobly spent his life in the service of the poor natives of that country'. He was premature in thinking Clarkson's labours were over, for the planters rejected the government's demands for immediate reforms, prompting a slave uprising on Demerara and Essequibo, which was put down with extraordinary ferocity. In the aftermath, 1,000 rebels were executed as an exemplary punishment. This had a profound effect on William, who had hitherto been an abolitionist. When Clarkson sought William's aid in raising yet another anti-slavery petition the following spring, William demurred. 'Anxiously as I desire to see the condition of the Negroes improved, and slavery abolished, I feel the Question involved in so many difficulties, that I am inclined to leave it to the discretion of the Government', he wrote. 'The Petitions you are so desirous of obtaining may be of use in giving Ministers courage to act up to their own wishes; but is it not possible that those very petitions may make the Negroes impatient under their present condition; and excite them to disturbance[?] I should like much to have the benefit of your knowledge on this subject.'[20]

In October, the whole family accompanied Tom Monkhouse to Penrith for the races, William, Mary and Dora staying on for the balls and entertainments. For Dora, this was a hugely exciting time, her first appearance at a public ball, but, as she noted with sly humour, she was not the star of the ball. '"Father" was the gayest of the gay in spite of his eyes –', she told Sara, 'made the agreeables to every Lady in the Ball room, & notwithstanding the *lights* was all the better for his exertions.' On their return, Dorothy went over to the Marshalls at Hallsteads to stay with her 'aunt', Mrs Rawson, whom she had not seen since her visit to Halifax in 1816. Now seventy-eight, the old lady was 'as chearful and gay as if only 16', walked regularly in the gardens, despite her lameness, and looked set to outlive them all. Once Mrs Rawson left, Dorothy went to Penrith, to visit another venerable relative, her ninety-year-old uncle, the Reverend Thomas Myers, and stay with her sister-in-law, Richard's widow, Jane. 'She is a good creature, and I have a great affection for her – which grows every time I am with her'; her son, little 'Keswick' John, was 'a mild and amiable child', still delicate, but growing stronger with the passing years.[21]

Throughout the winter William worked 'very hard' at his latest project, a translation of Virgil's *Aeneid.* It was something he had stumbled on accidentally, probably when he had been helping John with his classical texts in preparation for his next term at Oxford, but what began as a merely technical exercise soon absorbed him. 'When I read Virgil in the original I am moved,' he told Lord Lonsdale, 'but not so much by the translations'. What he wanted to do was to be much more literal than Dryden, who had simply paraphrased Virgil's Latin to get its sense, but also to capture the high poetic passion of the original.[22] Two books were complete by 23 January 1824, and these he forwarded to Lord Lonsdale, with an apologetic note, stressing the 'good deal of pains' he had taken over the work.

> If [a translator] wishes to preserve as much of the original as possible, and *that* with as little addition of his own as may be, there is no species of composition that costs more pains. A literal Translation of an antient Poet in verse, and particularly in rhyme, is *impossible*; something must be left out and something added; I have done my best to avoid the one and the other fault.

The versification also called for an apology, or at least, an explanation. William found 'long narratives in couplets . . . very wearisome', so he had run them together freely, in an effort to recapture the movement of the Virgilian original. 'I have long been persuaded that Milton formed his blank verse upon the model of the Georgics and the Aeneid,' he explained,

> and I am so much struck with this resemblance, that I should have attempted Virgil in blank verse; had I not been persuaded, that no antient Author can be with advantage so rendered. Their religion, their warfare, their course of action and feeling, are too remote from modern interest to allow it. We require every possible help and attraction of sound in our language to smooth the way for the admission of things so remote from our present concerns.

William's answer to this intractable problem was what Hartley aptly called 'a sort of confluent couplet – or if the phrase be not a bull, rhyming blank verses'. It was not, as William came to realize, a happy experiment. 'It is certainly, from the sample I have seen, a powerful work,' Hartley commented diplomatically, 'but between Wordsworth's republican Austerity, and the courtly pomp of Virgil, the contrast is so wide, that I doubt, whether the more perfect correctness of sense, can atone in a translation for such disparity of mode.' William evidently agreed. He suppressed the translation during his lifetime, allowing fewer than 150 of the 3,000 lines he wrote to be published in a scholarly classical journal, the *Philological Museum*, in 1832. Even then, they appeared with a prefatory letter admitting that the experiment was a failure.[23]

In the middle of February William and Dorothy left Rydal Mount for Coleorton, where they were to spend a month, before calling in at Oxford on a 'very very industrious' John for a couple of days and then travelling on to London. There they were to meet Dora, who, in a first attempt at independence, had gone to London in December to stay with her friends the Gees at Hendon. William had been especially reluctant to part with his daughter, having seen so little of her the previous year. Within days of his own return after a five-month absence from home, Dora had gone to Ambleside as a teacher at Ann Dowling's school. This was purely as a favour to her beloved Miss Dowling, who had been left temporarily without teachers while her two sisters were in Paris 'for pleasure and improvement'. As the Wordsworths persisted in treating Dora as a child, it had come as something of a surprise to find how well she performed her duties and how much she enjoyed them. Jane Dowling had then offered to chaperon Dora from Rydal Mount to London, where she would meet her friend Edith Southey and the two girls would go on to Hendon together.[24]

As usual, the Wordsworths stayed at Gloucester Place with the Monkhouses. 'I wish you could be with us now . . . when the Wordsworths are here –', Tom wrote to his sister at Hindwell, on 26 March:

> you would find more Entertainment in a Week – than a Month at another Time – They are such seekers out of Pleasure – & you would see also so many interesting people – They are in the full Tide of Enjoyment from Morning to Night – it is quite delightful to see how compleatly happy Miss Wordsworth seems to be – she is an excellent Creature – & deserves to be happy – The Poet is in high Feather – never more agreeable – & Dora is of so contented a Nature – that she is always happy among her friends – she has grown a fine Girl & is much admired by every Person –[25]

Every night they dined with innumerable old friends: Coleridge, Rogers, the Lambs, the Beaumonts, Quillinan, Robinson, Christopher's sons. Every day they were out seeing the sights, from exhibitions of old masters and modern painters to panoramas and dioramas of Switzerland, Mexico (ancient and modern) and Pompeii, and even the Swiss Giantess, 'a strapping wench of six feet two inches . . . But she was not worth paying money to look at'. Dorothy was indefatigable: she 'trudged' the streets, sometimes with Robinson, sometimes without, 'thro' the rain just as in Westmoreland'.[26]

Despite all the gaiety, the Wordsworths were deeply concerned about their genial host. Even Dora had swiftly realized that all was not as it should be in Gloucester Place. 'Mrs M is on the Sofa –', she wrote to Quillinan the day she returned there from Hendon, 'she looks very well & is in excellent spirits. Mr M looks miserably ill but says he is better.' While he (and everyone else, including the susceptible Robinson) danced attendance on the beautiful pseudo-invalid, the Wordsworths could not fail to see that Tom was genuinely ill. They tried, and failed, to get him out of the smoky air of London to Lee Priory, Wales or the Lakes, but his wife preferred the fashionable society of Ramsgate and Tom had no say in the matter.[27]

On 23 April William, Dorothy and Dora set off for Lee Priory to see Mima and Rotha Quillinan for the first time in almost two years. They could stay only a week, for Dorothy had promised to return home before the end of June, so that Mary could pay a long-promised visit to her brother and cousins in Wales. A tearful Dora had then to be parted from her goddaughter so that the Wordsworths could visit Christopher and his sons at Cambridge before setting off homeward. It was at this point that Dora staged a quiet rebellion. Her father and aunt had intended that she should return to London and accompany the Monkhouses to Ramsgate. 'It will be a most uncomfortable disagreeable visit as I plainly saw that neither Mrs M. nor Miss H[orrocks] wished me to go –', Dora confessed miserably to Quillinan; 'the truth is I suppose She & Miss H. think I shall be a Spoil Sport in their contrivances – I know nothing more disagreeable than to feel yourself where you know you are not wanted – indeed where you are I may say a complete Nuisance'. Dorothy was adamant that she should go and was thoroughly exasperated to find that William was entirely on his daughter's side: 'The point he most dwelt upon was, that her absence from home and from her Mother and himself would be too long – more than could be afforded – "nine or ten months being a long portion of human life after 53 years of age" '. The combined forces of father and daughter were enough to carry the day and they 'absolutely made an elopement', riding off in triumph and leaving a disgruntled Dorothy to write Dora's apologies alone in Trinity Lodge with her nephew John. Her own arrangements could not be so easily abandoned: she had to go to Playford Hall to meet her friend Mrs Luff, who was returning to live in the Lakes, bringing with her two cart-loads of goods and her African menagerie.[28]

Mary's visit to Wales was now deferred till the autumn, and it was agreed that both William and Dora would accompany her. The Wordsworths spent the interval pleasantly enough, surrounded by family and friends. All the Robinsons came over from York and there were regular musical parties at the Mount. They were often joined by the summer tenants of Spring Cottage, a likeable pair of sisters from Sussex, Frances and Emma Ayling, with their clergyman brother and Frances's intended, 'an antiquated Baronet', Sir William Ashburnham. The two Miss Aylings charmed everyone and were soon on intimate terms with the Wordsworths: 'they play and sing beautifully – ', Mary enthused, 'come here every morning to practice, and poor Willy is half in love – cannot sleep for making rhymes about his own happiness, ventures to rally the Ladies on the old Gentleman, all which is taken in good part – and they never tire of his company'. On 3 August one of Dora's closest friends, Mary Calvert, married her neighbour Joshua Stanger at Keswick. Dora, Sara Coleridge, Mary's cousin and Isabella Curwen, a young woman who was to play an important future role in the Wordsworth family, were her bridesmaids. As Sara commented, somewhat bitterly, few of her circle would be so fortunate in their love affairs as Mary.[29]

The Wordsworths were now free to plan their trip to Wales. William's old friend Robert Jones had long been pressing them to visit him there and this proved to be the ideal opportunity. On 24 August William, Mary and Dora set off from Rydal Mount for Liverpool, where they stayed with the Crumps, the owners of Allan Bank. The Crumps and William Jackson, the former curate of Grasmere, accompanied them on the first stage of their journey, by steamboat under Penmaenmawr and by Puffin Island to Bangor, where they admired the 'stupendous preparations' for Thomas Telford's great suspension bridge linking Anglesey to the mainland across the Menai Straits. The next day they spent three hours exploring Conwy Castle, 'which I think the King of castles', Dora wrote. 'All that I have heard of it, all that I have seen – even Sir George's picture – nothing gives one a sufficient idea of its grandeur . . . The longer I stayed the longer I wished to stay.'[30] Her father was equally entranced by the journey from Conwy to Llanberis. 'A little before sunset we came in sight of Llanberris Lake, Snowdon,' he informed Beaumont,

> and all the craggy hills and mountains surrounding it; the foreground a beautiful contrast to this grandeur and desolation – a green sloping hollow, furnishing a shelter for one of the most beautiful collections of lowly Welsh cottages, with thatched roofs, overgrown with plants, anywhere to be met with: the hamlet is called Cwm-y-Glo. And here we took boat, while the solemn lights of evening were receding towards the tops of the mountains.

There was no carriage road from Llanberis, so the Wordsworths took to their feet and walked the eight miles to Capel-Curig, along the Pass of Llanberis, with the Snowdonian range of mountains towering above them. They had arranged to meet Jones at Llanrwst, in the Vale of Conwy, but it was symptomatic of William's growing reputation that, before they did so, they had a prearranged meeting with John Hobart, Bishop of New York. A leading reformer in the Protestant Episcopalian Church in America, he had visited Rydal Mount just before the Wordsworths' departure, and had been invited to join them at Llanrwst. 'The day when you honored me with your attentions at the Lakes and that which I subsequently passed with you in Wales, I shall always look back to with pride & with the highest pleasure', he wrote afterwards, with all the enthusiasm of one of William's young university disciples.[31]

It was a great pleasure to see Jones again, particularly in his native element, for once again, just as he had done on the Continental tour of 1820, William was consciously retreading old ground. Jones brought his carriage and a servant, which made travelling more comfortable, but he was an altogether more agreeable companion than the Horrockses, and he was quite happy to set a leisurely pace far different from the frenetic sightseeing of 1820. 'Jones was the best of companions,' William told Christopher, 'being master of the language, very extensively known in the Country, a most affectionate Man, and, I verily believe, the best-tempered Creature imaginable; to me, who am apt to be irritable in travelling, an inestimable qualification.' Jones introduced them to his friends in the Vale of Clwyd and to the famous 'Ladies of Llangollen', Lady Eleanor Butler and the Hon. Sarah Ponsonby, the aristocratic eccentrics whose dedication to reclusiveness, celibacy and Rousseau (not necessarily in that order) had ironically made them a tourist attraction. More importantly, they retraced together their earlier steps across what is now the Snowdonia National Park towards the Welsh coast, revisiting Beddgelert, from where they had made their midnight ascent of Snowdon thirty-three years earlier, Cader Idris, Barmouth and Aberystwyth, finally parting, after thirteen days, at Devil's Bridge. 'I had seen these things long ago,' William confessed, 'but either my memory or my powers of observation had not done them justice.'[32]

Mary could scarcely contain her joy at the success of this tour – so different from their most recent jaunts on the Continent. William had been well and in excellent spirits for the three weeks they had been away, Dora had been 'enchanted' with everything they had seen, '*I* could not therefore but be happy'. To crown her pleasure, this tour had at last awakened the poet: her husband had been 'murmuring verses' throughout their wanderings. From Ruthin he addressed a sonnet to the Ladies of Llangollen, christening their Dee-side home 'the Vale of Friendship'.[33] Exploring the ruined castles of North Wales, with their 'shattered galleries, 'mid roofless halls', inspired a characteristic meditation on the changes wrought by passing years:

> Relic of Kings! Wreck of forgotten wars,
> To winds abandoned and the prying stars,
> Time *loves* thee! at his call the Seasons twine
> Luxuriant wreaths around thy forehead hoar;
> And, though past pomp no changes can restore,
> A soothing recompense, his gift, is thine!

At the Devil's Bridge, where they parted from Jones, the waterfalls were 'in perfection', after heavy overnight rains. William 'poured out' a sonnet 'in the chasm there, during a heavy storm, while Dora was at my side endeavouring to sketch the body of the place, leaving, poor Girl! the soul of it to her Father'. As in most of William's better poems, it was a coming together of past and present, interfused with his own personal memories. The rocky chasm with its raging torrent reminded him of the infant Rhine he had seen in the ravines of Viamala in 1790.[34] It was, as Mary said, 'a sublime finale' to the tour.

Except that it was not the end, only the beginning, for the main object of this absence from home was to visit Mary's brother and cousins in Radnorshire. It was a last chance to do so, for Tom had lost hope of ever making a success of the farm at Hindwell, given notice on his lease and engaged to take a new one just outside Hereford. Looking at the magnificent Brinsop Court today, with its fourteenth-century great hall, mellow golden stone, half-timbering and encircling moat, it is difficult to imagine it being the residence of a penurious farmer obliged to give up his former property because he could not afford the rent. It is emphatically a gentleman's residence, an ancient manor house set in a natural bowl amidst gently rolling hills which are crowned with woodland. Secluded but not isolated, it is surrounded by cereal fields so rich and productive that the gorged pheasants stagger drunkenly under their own weight, barely able to strut, let alone fly. In 1824, however, the estate had recently been purchased by David Ricardo of Gatcombe Park, its manorial rights granted to Sir Uvedale Price, and the house and farm were suffering from years of neglect. It was, as they say, a place with potential.[35]

One of its advantages was that it was still less than ten miles from the Stow, where John Monkhouse, thanks to his more amenable landlord, was at last beginning to see an improvement in his farming concerns. Unfortunately, this was counterbalanced by his failing eyesight: aged forty-two, he was gradually going blind, a particular problem for him, since he lived alone. He had never remarried after losing his young bride, Isabella Addison, and his greatest pleasure in life was reading. Sara, always desirous to make herself 'useful as well as ornamental', had been his guest at the Stow since the spring, helping to train his servants for him and acting as his amanuensis and reader. As she remarked somewhat pointedly to Tom Monkhouse, his brother was a model sufferer. 'He really is the most truly *satisfied & chearful* Person I ever met with – He is a daily source of wonder and admiration to me – I never hear any allusion to his affliction except in thankfulness for what he *can enjoy*.'[36]

When the Wordsworths arrived at Hindwell for a grand family reunion, however, it was not John but Tom himself whose appearance shocked them. His foray to Ramsgate had done nothing for him, and he had prevailed on his wife to try a visit to his family in Wales. Sara, who was devoted to her cousin, was determined to believe that he was 'killing himself with *anxiety*', but the Wordsworths were under no such illusions. It was obvious that he was suffering from pulmonary tuberculosis and 'travelling slowly, but I fear surely, to the grave'. In the circumstances, there was nothing any of them could do, except help make that journey as easy as possible. William was at his best at times like these. According to Sara, 'nobody ever saw him in better plight – & he was the life of our party – doing always his utmost to amuse & keep up our spirits – which he always does God bless him! when there is a real necessity for his exertions'. The Wordsworths extended their stay as long as they could, leaving only when Jane Monkhouse finally succeeded in carrying her husband off to Torquay for the winter, even though she knew he was happier with his brother and sister in Wales than anywhere else. He 'will scarcely be *permitted* to stay quietly – ', Sara wrote, with pardonable venom, 'for it is evident that either upon the plea of his own or his wife's health he will never have any rest in this world'. Sara was determined to prevent her beloved cousin being left to the not-so-tender mercies of his wife, and, when the Monkhouses left the Stow on 18 October, she went with them, devoting herself for four long and miserable months to the dying man.[37]

The Wordsworths left Hindwell on the same day. Instead of going straight home, however, they went to Coleorton, 'to secure to ourselves a long sojourn when we do arrive [at Rydal Mount] – thinking it better to lengthen our long absence, than be called upon in the early spring by our Friends here to perform Wm's *half* promise of making our annual visit to them'. Mary's contrivance to obtain a long period at home was a little wifely plot, inspired by William's recent return to verse. 'I trust after we feel ourselves settled at Rydal, he will be able seriously to address himself to the Recluse – ', she confided to Quillinan, 'but I do not mention this hope, lest he should be scared by the prospect.' It was a fallacious hope, even though Dorothy colluded. On 13 December Dorothy had to admit that her brother had not yet looked at *The Recluse*: 'he seems to feel the task so weighty that he shrinks from beginning with it – yet knows that he has now no time to loiter if another great work is to be accomplished by him – I say another – for I consider the Excursion as one work though the Title-page tells that it is but a *part* of one that has another Title'.[38]

What William had written was a number of small poems, for the poetic mood which had overtaken him in North Wales had never left him. Most of them were associated with Tom's approaching death, some by a more tenuous thread than others. *The Contrast: The Parrot and the Wren*, for instance, was composed at the Stow as much for Tom's amusement as Dora's, to whom it was nominally addressed. Contrasting one of Mrs Luff's feathered menagerie, an

Arch, volatile, a sportive bird
By social glee inspired;
Ambitious to be seen or heard,
And pleased to be admired!

with the 'self-contented Wren', which lived in the moss-lined summer-house between the two terraces at Rydal Mount, the poem posed Dora the leading question:

Which would you be, – the bird of the saloon,
By lady-fingers tended with nice care,
Caressed, applauded, upon dainties fed,
Or Nature's Darkling of this mossy shed?[39]

Another poem, which was deliberately written to please Tom, was one in praise of his little daughter, Mary Elizabeth, who was now three years old and the light of her father's life. 'Our little Darling grows sweeter as she grows older –', Tom had proudly informed his sister, 'so happy in herself – so lively, & such an amiable docility, & such pretty ways . . . Mr & Miss Wordsworth think her incomparable'. Unlikely though this seems, it was quite true. Dorothy, who had met 'Good-good', as the family called her, in London in the spring, simply marvelled. 'She is a child by herself – Such an one as was never born before and never will be again. There seems to be no seed of evil in her . . . She is constantly happy – and everything that is new and everything that is old affords her amusement.' William's tribute, highly prized by Tom, was a lovely sonnet, beginning with the memorable lines, 'Unquiet Childhood here by special grace Forgets her nature, opening like a flower', and ending by comparing Mary Elizabeth's placid innocence to that of the infant Virgin.[40]

Less elevated in sentiment, but no less sincere, were two poems William addressed to his own Mary, which reveal that twenty-two years of marriage had done nothing to diminish his love for her. Even after all these years – perhaps, indeed, because of them – Mary still needed reassurance about her lack of conventional beauty. 'Let other bards of angels sing, Bright suns without a spot;' William wrote, adding honestly, if ungallantly,

> But thou art no such perfect thing:
>   Rejoice that thou art not!
>
> Heed not though none should call thee fair;
>   So, Mary, let it be
> If naught in loveliness compare
>   With what thou art to me.
>
> True beauty dwells in deep retreats,
>   Whose veil is unremoved
> Till heart with heart in concord beats,
>   And the lover is beloved.[41]

The second poem is the other side of the coin, for it reveals William's emotional dependence on his wife. Though not one of William's better-known poems, it is fascinating on many counts, not least because it is a rare and uncharacteristic admission in verse of religious doubt. William had never scrupled to raise this in private conversation. Earlier in the year, for instance, he had met, for the first time, Edward Irving, the charismatic Scottish preacher, and had immediately brought up what he called 'the great difficulty which had always pressed on his mind in religion', his inability to reconcile the concept of divine omniscience and foreknowledge with that of accountability in men. At other times, in discussion with Robinson, he had admitted that, like Coleridge, he found it hard to believe in the central doctrine of Christianity, the Atonement. 'The thought that an infinitely pure being can receive satisfaction from the sufferings of Jesus Christ and accept them as a satisfaction for the sins of the guilty is declared by Coleridge to be an outrage on common sense . . . I leave this as an awful mystery I am not called to solve.' Perhaps most significantly of all, when Robinson said that he personally '*tried* to believe', William had agreed, 'That is pretty much my case'.[42]

The poem he now addressed to Mary was a similar admission, but, as it would be published, it was a public one. As Tom began to spit blood, and was reduced to speaking in a whisper, 'dying very, very slowly', William found himself

> Trembling, through my unworthiness, with fear
> That friends, by death disjoined, may meet no more!
> Misgivings, hard to vanquish or control,
> Mix with the day, and cross the hour of rest;

For Mary, secure in her faith, there was no such uncertainty, and William, in his anguish, appealed to her for reassurance, and through her for unquestioning belief for himself. 'Yet bear me up', he begged,

> – else faltering in the rear
> Of a steep march: support me to the end.
>
> Peace settles where the intellect is meek,
> And Love is dutiful in thought and deed;
> Through *Thee* communion with that Love I seek:
> The faith Heaven strengthens where *he* moulds the Creed.[43]

That the author of *The Excursion*, one of the greatest affirmations of faith, could be so stricken with personal doubt is ironic and instructive.

The uncertainties of human life were reinforced by changes in the vale. In the Wordsworths' absence, there was a freak storm which wreaked havoc on the ancient woodlands of Rydal. Sixty trees were completely uprooted and scarcely one was left undamaged. As both William and Mary commented, it looked as if there had been a war among giants in that quarter, though, miraculously, Rydal Mount had escaped untouched.[44] What threatened to change totally and permanently the whole character of the vale was enclosure. As still happens with such high-impact planning applications, there was no prior consultation or warning. A notice in the Kendal newspapers and on the church doors simply announced that a bill would be introduced into the next session of Parliament to enclose the wastes and commons of Grasmere and Loughrigg. The scheme had been initiated by Lady le Fleming, or rather her agents, in response to what William admitted were encroachments and abuses committed by many who had an interest in these commons. William was now a seasoned campaigner and he leapt into action in defence of his beloved mountains and the dwindling band of small statesmen whose livelihoods would most be threatened by enclosure. He went to see Thomas Jackson, Lady le Fleming's agent, and secured a hint that the measure might be abandoned if the abuses could be prevented; he helped organize, and attended, meetings, where he secured resolutions that the proposed enclosure was financially unviable and that measures would be taken to resolve the problem of abuses; and he wrote to Lord Lonsdale, as Lord of the Manor of Grasmere, pleading that the opponents should be given a fair hearing before he consented to the application. 'My own conviction is, that if carried, it would displace, and that very speedily, the greatest part of the present valuable race of inhabitants, who are already too much supplanted by other causes –', he urged, 'and this probably will be done without advantage to any; for the Ground, if enclosed, would be of little use but for planting, and situations much more favourable, might be had for that purpose elsewhere.' It was almost as an afterthought that he pointed out that enclosure would be an 'irreparable injury . . . to the beauty and dignity of the Vales of Grasmere or Rydal'.[45] The threat was beaten off for the time being, but it was not the last time William would have to be an active and vocal champion of the silent fells.

A second violent storm, the worst William ever remembered, struck on Christmas Day. In some ways this was unfortunate, for it was the day Rydal Chapel opened its doors for the first time. 'I never was out in such a storm', Dora declared, but, with some sixty or seventy other worshippers, she and her family struggled through the wind and rain to attend the service. 'The sight must have been highly gratifying to the munificent Foundress', William remarked, adding somewhat crisply that the cost of building the church had 'much exceeded what was needful'. Nevertheless, the Wordsworths were almost entirely reconciled to the new chapel. William was still somewhat grudging, 'when time has softened down the exterior a little it will prove a great ornament to the Village', but both Mary and Dorothy were enthusiastic. 'Nothing can be more lovely than the prospect from the "red room window" at which I write', Mary told Quillinan; '. . . the frosty mist glistening and curling over the rich tawny hillsides and the *steeple tower* gleaming between the branches of the laurel upon the Mount'. Dorothy thought the outside of the church 'very pretty' in itself, but 'you can have no idea how beautiful in connexion with the village, especially seen from the other side of the lake'. Even the clergyman was more than satisfactory. Fletcher Fleming was only distantly related to Lady le Fleming, but he was the son of William's old school and college friend John Fleming of Rayrigg. The Wordsworths were unanimous in declaring the young man 'a Treasure in these parts where, as my Father says, we are so ill parson'd'; he was 'very earnest', gave 'beautiful' sermons and his only fault was that he read too slowly.[46]

The opening weeks of the new year were marred by news of Tom's worsening health and increasing depression of spirits. He loathed Torquay and daily regretted having left the Stow. Sara's reports were so heart-rending that John, despite his blindness, could bear it no longer. He went in person to Torquay and organized

Tom's immediate removal. The journey had to be taken in easy stages, but by 9 February they had reached Clifton, on the outskirts of Bristol. Another fashionable society resort, Clifton suited Mrs Monkhouse very well, and it was agreed that they should spend a month there, before moving on to the Stow. 'I trust nothing will prevent our return to Stow for nothing else will satisfy [Tom]', Sara wrote anxiously to her confidant, Quillinan, '& truly it is most desirable that he should be with his brother whose society is an unspeakable support & comfort to him'. In the end death cheated them all. Tom died suddenly, but peacefully, at Clifton on 26 February. Only his wife, Sara and a friend from Penrith, Major Bleamire, were present at the end, though John arrived in time for the funeral on 4 March, and carried the bereaved family home with him to the Stow.[47]

Writing to thank Bleamire for his letter informing them of Tom's death, William had 'an unsteady hand & a full heart. The loss which we have sustained cannot be supplied – He was a man of perfect integrity, as you well know – of refined honor, the most gentle manners, & a sincere humble-minded Christian.' To Rogers, William added a more personal note, which went beyond the usual platitudes of obituary: 'he was not bright or entertaining, but so gentle and gracious, and so much interested in most of what ought to interest a pure mind, that his company was highly prized by all who knew him intimately'. His death removed not only 'one of my most valued friends' but 'one of the strongest of my inducements, and the most important of my facilities for visiting London, and prolonging my stay there'.[48] It was some small comfort that he had left his widow and daughter well provided for. Technical problems with the will deprived John of the family estate at Sebergham which Tom had left him, but he, his sister and even little George Monkhouse, the half-caste son of their late brother Joe, each benefited by legacies of several thousand pounds. As Tom's executor and guardian of little Mary Elizabeth, John was also presented with the *de facto* and unwelcome legacy of the merry widow. Mrs Monkhouse had, in Sara's sarcastic phrase, borne her loss 'with wonderful fortitude', and scampered off to the delights of Clifton as soon as she was able to escape the mourning household at the Stow. Within two years she had married again, to the bizarrely named Dr Paris Dick, but her unconscionable demands for money and, worse still, her refusal to allow Tom's family to see his daughter were a constant source of aggravation and worry for years to come.[49]

Tom was thirteen years younger than William and his death, at the age of only forty-two, affected the poet profoundly. It effectively put an end to the stream of poetry which had flowed slowly, but steadily, since the tour of North Wales. William now had some 500 or 600 lines of verse in hand and once again he began to consider publishing a new edition of his poems. Since 1798 his poetry had been published exclusively by Longman, but, comparing his reputation to the profits from his sales, William could not help but feel that he might do better elsewhere. Longman had refused to alter his usual terms of publication, so, emphasizing that he had 'no *positive* ground for complaint', William wrote to his old (and highly successful) friend Rogers to ask for his advice. Was there any publisher 'more liberal, more adventurous, or more skilful in pushing off unfashionable books than Messrs Longman'? The new poems could not make a volume of themselves, but they could be incorporated into a new edition of his *Miscellaneous Poems.* And, he suggested, it might be possible to rearrange these in a new way which would be more attractive to purchasers: a volume of local poetry, for instance, and a volume of sonnets.

Now you may think that I ought to undertake this disagreeable business myself, and so I should think, if I had not so kind a Friend who has 50 times the talent for this sort of work which I possess, and who besides could say 100 handsome things, which, egotist as I am described to be, and as *in verse* I am *willing* to be thought – I could not say of myself.[50]

Rogers could not refuse, but he did dare to suggest that perhaps the best way to achieve a profit was to publish a selection 'of the most admired, or the most popular' of his poems. This seems such an obvious solution that William's rejection of it out of hand appears incredible. Yet reject it he did, not just because he had 'insuperable objections to it in my own feelings' but because he was, quite genuinely, 'utterly at a loss how to proceed in that selection'. This smacks of the notorious Wordsworthian arrogance, but since *Lyrical Ballads* in 1798 opinion among professional, and even friendly amateur, critics had been sharply divided: the same poems were loved and loathed in equal measure, and often for the same reasons. As William had observed only a few weeks earlier, anticipating the accusation that he could not accept critics finding fault with his own work, 'Did you ever know a critic who suspected it to be possible that he himself might be in the wrong? – in other words, who did not regard his own impressions as the test of excellence?'[51] How then could it be possible to make a *popular* selection?

As always, the desire to earn a just financial reward for his poetical labours conflicted with William's high-minded notions of the integrity of his work. He did not scruple to reject the increasing number of requests which were now being made for him to contribute poems to the new monthly magazines and annuals, simply because these were ephemeral publications deliberately aimed at the popular market and he did not approve of their partisan attitudes.[52] The very fact that his contributions were being sought at all was an indication that astute editors and publishers recognized his importance as a poet, and thought his name would sell their titles, but this in itself was objectionable to William. He wanted his work to sell on its own merit, not because it was being puffed in fashionable magazines. The same notion underpinned his idea of his relationship with his publisher, which should be that of enabler not patron. 'I assure you that I would a thousand times rather that not a verse of mine should ever enter the Press again, than to allow any of them to say that I was to the amount of the strength of a hair dependant upon their countenance, consideration, Patronage, or by whatever term they may dignify their ostentation and selfish vanity.'[53]

The negotiations for a new publisher would drag on tediously, and ultimately unsuccessfully, for almost two years. Rogers succeeded in obtaining a verbal offer from John Murray, which would give William two-thirds of the profit if he took two-thirds of the risk and expense, but it never proceeded to a formal contract. William (and his womenfolk more especially) were not predisposed in Murray's favour. He was the friend and publisher of Byron, who had christened William 'Turdsworth' and written about him in terms of scurrilous abuse. Murray had founded and published the *Quarterly Review*, which had been less than complimentary in its criticism of William's poetry. As he also declined to answer William's letters, the poet took offence at 'his high Mightiness' and, with his women cheering on the sidelines, withdrew from the negotiations. Writing to thank Rogers for his efforts, William explained, 'I am persuaded that he is too great a Personage for any one but a Court, an Aristocratic or most fashionable Author to deal with.'[54]

William spent the spring 'tinkering' with his poems in preparation for the new edition, which had already swollen to six volumes by April. Imaginatively, however, he was still captivated by his tour of North Wales. He was already planning to return there,

> not with any view to writing a Tour thro' the Country but of giving an analysis of Snowden, Cader Idris and their several dependencies, with a sketch of the characters of the principal rivers . . . my wish being to teach the *Touring World*, which is become very numerous, to look thro' the clear eye of the Understanding as well as thro' the hazy one of vague Sensibility.

This idea gave way almost immediately to another, to make Snowdon 'the scene of a Dialogue upon Nature, Poetry, and Painting – to be illustrated by the surrounding imagery'.[55] This sounds suspiciously like a portion of *The Recluse* – which perhaps explains why it was never written.

Mary might not have succeeded in encouraging William to return to *The Recluse*, but she did achieve her objective of obtaining a more settled period at home. This year there would be no lengthy absences for any of them, except Sara, who had been persuaded to stay on in Wales while the Hutchinsons made their move to Brinsop Court. 'The House is full of Workmen Masons – Carpenters – Painters – Glaziers – Paperers – Upholsterers &c but we should soon finish, within doors, if they would but be constant to us –', she wrote in June, 'but they run off & leave me in the lurch when I least expect it – I advise you, if you wish to preserve your sweetness of temper, never to build or alter a House.'[56]

There were great temptations to go off on another tour. Beaumont's sister-in-law, Frances Fermor, had died the previous December and, though the Wordsworths barely knew her, she had read *The Excursion*, derived great pleasure from it and unexpectedly left William a legacy of £100 'as a small mark of her esteem and regard'. Informing him of this, Beaumont had dropped a hefty hint, 'O for a Muse to consecrate her Memory', to which William had dutifully responded by writing not one but two poetic tributes, whose fulsomeness was proof of his gratitude, if nothing else. Beaumont was delighted, however, and promptly offered William

£100 of his own, in the hope that the two sums would enable William, Mary and Dorothy to finance a tour of Italy. 'I trust you will not be offended at this offer, when you consider of what use you have been to my mind by your poetry & by your friendship & kindness of various occasions to my body –', he wrote, with his usual delicacy of feeling. 'Your friendship has been one of the chief blessings of my life & I shall remain deeply in arrears'. It was an offer that William could not, and did not refuse, but simply put on hold. He could not think of going to Italy until John was nearer the end of his university career.[57]

As they sacrificed current pleasures, the Wordsworths anticipated future ones. John would graduate at the end of 1826. There would then be nothing to prevent them taking another tour, and they dreamt of making this the grandest yet – 'no less than spending a whole winter in Italy, and a whole summer in moving from place to place – in Switzerland and elsewhere, not neglecting the Tyrol', Dorothy excitedly confided in Robinson, whom they wanted to be one of the party. William even fancied that making a two years' residence abroad would cancel out the cost of the journey, while Dorothy was convinced that between them they ought to be able to produce a journal that would at least be original enough to ensure them a profit.[58] It was, of course, a pipe-dream, a revival of the schemes they had planned so long ago with Coleridge, but it was a good excuse for saving their money and forgoing the pleasure (and expense) of a tour this year.

Instead of travelling to foreign parts, the Wordsworths had to make do with a trip to the English seaside, and, as is the way with such things, it turned into one of their happiest ever holidays. This was in no small part due to a young lady who, until May, had been a complete stranger to them all. Maria Jane Jewsbury was twenty-five, the oldest daughter of the large family of a widowed Manchester merchant and a budding authoress. The previous year she had published her first work, *Phantasmagoria, or Sketches of Life and Literature*, which she had dedicated (without his permission) to William. In an accompanying note, sending a copy of the first volume to him earlier this year, she begged to be excused this unpardonable liberty, which was 'the honest expression of youthful enthusiasm', and confessed that she had felt obliged to dedicate her first work 'to him whose works occasioned whatever merit this possesses'. William had been deeply touched, not least because his own problems in finding an appropriate publisher had left him feeling vulnerable. 'I am not altogether free from reflections natural to my time of life,' he replied, 'such as, that I have lived and laboured to little purpose, – assurances like yours are correctives of this mistake, for how can it be other than one, when I receive blossoms of such promise with declarations so fervent, yet evidently sincere!' Incapable of telling an untruth, William had to admit that he preferred Miss Jewsbury's prose to her poetry, and cautioned her 'not to rest your hopes or happiness upon Authorship'.[59]

Miss Jewsbury was not the fragile flower she liked to paint herself, and less than three weeks after receiving this letter, she had inveigled her way into Rydal Mount. Dora spoke for the whole family when she declared their visitor 'a most enthusiastic

& interesting creature' who had 'run away with all our hearts'. So much so that she was invited to join them a few weeks later at Kents Bank, on the northern coast of Morecambe Bay, where they rented lodgings for six weeks. The ostensible reason for going to the coast was to secure a change of air for Dora, but it turned into quite a party. The Wordsworths all paid visits in turn, including John, newly returned from Oxford, Dora's aunt Mary Hutchinson, from Brinsop Court, the Cooksons of Kendal and a seventeen-year-old heiress, Miss Barlow, 'who by John's manner I do suspect he has some notion of;' Sara confided to her cousin, 'but this is entre nous'. Love had wreaked its magic on dull John. 'I never saw any one so changed as he – ', his aunt marvelled, 'no lark can be more lively & agreeable.'[60]

The undoubted life and soul of the party was Maria Jewsbury, who chose to commemorate the holiday in the most delightful way, drawing up a miniature newspaper, set out in the proper format, including columns of Local and Foreign News, and print-style script. Dora thus became 'our beloved Queen', William 'the poet laureate' and Dorothy, who had stayed at home, 'regent of Rydal Mount'. Everything was drolly reported in its appropriate place: the 'straw hats of Mambrino shape' under the Fashions and Willy's acquisition of sea shells and seaweed for the Literary and Scientific Intelligence. Willy was also the butt of one of the advertisements: 'Wants a Situation A youth of about fifteen years of age, He is able to do any kind of work, but prefers sitting to standing, riding to walking, and lying in bed to any thing in the world.' Rather more respectful was a reported 'Philosophic Remark' during a 'conversazione' at the 'Kents Bank Saloon', when a 'celebrated belle' made a lively remark on a well-known gentleman's equally well-known susceptibility:

> 'You are too severe on the gentleman' said an illustrious poet then present with an emphasis which shewed him sensible of the worth of words, 'you ladies are often infinitely more susceptible, your hearts very often resemble looking-glasses, not in their capability of being broken but in that of receiving every impression and retaining none!'

Flirtation was clearly the order of the day, though a silhouette portrait of William, with a Roman nose and peaked Popeye hat, which ends the little paper, is hardly flattering. The poet's considered judgement, that Miss Jewsbury's natural bent was 'more decidedly toward life and manners than poetic nature', seems entirely justified.[61]

Learning of William's difficulties in finding a new publisher for his work, Maria Jewsbury got in touch with her friend and fellow Wordsworthian enthusiast Alaric Watts, whose annual, the *Literary Souvenir*, like her own *Phantasmagoria*, was published by Hurst & Robinson. Watts leapt at the chance to obtain a better deal for William, pouring such scorn on both Longman's and Murray's 'preposterous', 'very mean' and 'disgusting' conduct that William immediately broke off his negotiations with Murray and placed himself in Watts's hands. A joyful Dora spoke for all the Wordsworth women when she wrote to Miss Jewsbury, 'we shall be for ever obliged to you for being the means of my Father's having *naught* to do with that vile John Murray'.[62]

William left the happy party at Kents Bank on 7 August to pay his annual visit to Lord Lonsdale at Lowther Castle, and to attend some splendid festivities at Storrs, the grand house on Windermere belonging to John Bolton, a Liverpool merchant and prominent Lowther supporter. The celebrations were in honour of the Foreign Secretary, George Canning, and a great assembly turned out to fête him. Lonsdale's daughter Lady Mary and her husband, Lord Frederick Bentinck, headed the aristocrats; William and John Wilson, now the Professor of Moral Philosophy at Edinburgh University (a post he had secured in 1820 with the help of a 'Jesuitical' letter of recommendation from William), headed the local intelligentsia. The arrival of Sir Walter Scott and his son-in-law, J. G. Lockhart, who had just toured Ireland and North Wales together, was the icing on the cake. Lockhart (who had not known Tom Monkhouse) commented loftily, 'It has not, I suppose, often happened, to a plain English merchant, wholly the architect of his own fortunes, to entertain at one time a party embracing so many illustrious names.' Lockhart, who seems to have been under the impression that the annual Windermere Regatta had been laid on especially for his father-in-law and Canning, was impressed.

> The weather was as Elysian as the scenery. There were brilliant cavalcades through the woods in the mornings, and delicious boatings on the lake by moonlight; and the last day, 'the Admiral of the Lake' [Wilson] presided over one of the most splendid regattas that ever enlivened Windermere. Perhaps there were not fewer than fifty barges following in the Professor's radiant procession, when it paused at the point of Storrs to admit into the place of honour the vessel that carried kind and happy Mr Bolton and his guests. The bards of the Lakes led the cheers that hailed Scott and Canning; and music and sunshine, flags, streamers, and gay dresses, the merry hum of voices, and the rapid splashing of innumerable oars, made up a dazzling mixture of sensations as the flotilla wound its way among the richly-foliaged islands, and along bays and promontories peopled with enthusiastic spectators.[63]

On 23 August Scott, Lockhart and Wilson accompanied William home to breakfast at Rydal Mount, then Dora and her father, 'spouting his own verses very grandly all the way', escorted Scott and Lockhart to Keswick. Scott, more gracious than his acerbic son-in-law, was troubled to find his friend looking so old, but described his conversation as being 'like a fountain in the desert', 'as much distinguished by manly sense and candour as by talent and principle'. Sara Coleridge, observing William, Scott and Southey together, could not forbear to comment that Scott was the least 'bard-like' in appearance: 'he is more like an old Admiral than a romance writer & poet'. From Greta Hall, William accompanied Scott and Lockhart to visit his friends the Marshalls at Hallsteads, on Ullswater; here they parted, the two visitors going on to Lowther Castle, while William escorted Dorothy and Cordelia Marshall home from Hallsteads in time for the consecration of Rydal chapel. This was carried out by no other than the Wordsworths' old friend Charles Blomfield, now no longer a simple Cambridge graduate but Bishop of Chester, in whose diocese Rydal lay.[64]

'We have had the finest weather, and the most bustling summer ever remembered', Dorothy wrote breathlessly in October. 'We never in our lives had so many visitors.' For three months there had never been fewer than ten people at dinner, and usually thirteen or fourteen. Now, as the last of the Lakers departed, the Wordsworths decided to pay an autumnal visit to the Beaumonts. Mary and her sister-in-law Mary Hutchinson, who had spent three weeks together, taking the waters at Harrogate, joined William and Sara at Derby, and the whole party proceeded to Coleorton, where Tom Hutchinson was waiting for them. It was not a particularly happy visit. William's eyelids were inflamed and painful, so he was not in the liveliest of spirits, and Mary and Sara, between them, managed to overturn the garden chair, bruising Mary's leg and spraining her sister's ankle. There was an unseasonable fall of snow and, as Sara complained, it was 'cold beyond all endurance', despite the coal fires. Had it not been for the Beaumonts, it could well have been a disaster. 'Never was there such a well assorted pair – or one so full of enjoyment at such an advanced period of life', Sara wrote admiringly. Fortunately, too, they were joined for a few days by Christopher, who brought news of his brilliant sons' latest prize-winning exploits.[65]

The Wordsworths left Coleorton on 9 October, Mary and Sara travelling by coach and William, at fifty-five, a somewhat elderly charioteer, driving in a pony chaise which Sara had bought at Ashby de la Zouche. They reunited, briefly, at Manchester, where they stayed with Miss Jewsbury, and though they missed Alaric Watts, who was currently negotiating on William's behalf with Hurst & Robinson, they were introduced to his wife. So proud was Mrs Watts to meet the great poet that she had the foresight to take notes of their conversation, which was by no means one-sided. At her request, William recited some of his sonnets, speaking of his own poems with a confidence and authority likely to be 'misunderstood by strangers' who were unaware of the 'entire singleness and sincerity of his nature'. He rather shocked her by his admiration for Burns and his comment that Coleridge's *Christabel* was 'an indelicate poem', but in the end she was won over. Interestingly, he reminded her of the older Quakers she had known in her youth.

> I was much struck by the spirit of rectitude which seemed to animate the expression of every opinion he uttered. He spoke always as though he were upon oath. He was a patient and courteous listener, paying the most scrupulous attention to every word, never interrupting, and with a certain fixedness of his clear grey eyes which made one feel that, whatever one's opinion might be, one must be prepared to give a substantial reason for it, and, in doing so, to discard all that might appear fanciful, and not to be readily explained.

On their way back home, the Wordsworths made a final overnight stop at Preston, where they hoped to see Tom Monkhouse's daughter, but the '*brisk* Widow' declined to allow her to see them. As Sara bitterly remarked, Mrs Monkhouse had taken up residence with her family only 'till she meets with another husband'.[66]

Dorothy, Dora and Willy had been left alone at Rydal Mount while William, Mary and Sara had been away. They had anticipated a quiet time, but the Lakers were merely exchanged for friends and neighbours who called, or were called upon, on a daily basis. On 21 October Bertha and Kate Southey came to stay. All the young people at Greta Bank had been struck down with whooping cough, Sara Coleridge particularly badly, and it was thought wise to send her two cousins out of the way for a time.[67] It is only thanks to this coincidence that a momentous event in the Wordsworth household was preserved from oblivion. One of the most assiduous visitors to Rydal Mount at this time was a thirty-one-year-old Royal Navy Lieutenant, Tom Robinson, who was Dora's second cousin. He arrived at Rydal on 8 October and left on 23 November, staying with his widowed mother and his many siblings in Ambleside – when he was not having breakfast, dinner or tea at Rydal Mount, accompanying Dora to visit 'Cousin Dorothy' at Coniston, walking with her to the waterfalls or to pay local visits, or playing cards with the young ladies in the evenings.[68]

Tom was quite the dashing naval lieutenant. Mary Wordsworth, who was not usually susceptible, had thought him a 'beau' when he visited her at Harrogate, and even Bertha Southey, who was only sixteen at the time, remembered him almost half a century later as 'a very handsome & delightful man'. Dora, at twenty-one, was far more innocent than young Bertha. She treated Tom just as she treated every other member of the family, admitting him to a degree of intimacy which was both flattering and misleading. No one, except Dora, could have failed to see what Tom's intentions were, Bertha remarked indulgently. Fail she did, however, and, after her parents' return, the smitten young man made a formal application to William for his daughter's hand in marriage. William replied instantly, and in a kindly manner, but with a decided negative. 'My answer must be unfavourable to your wishes, as it would be to those of any one similarly circumstanced', he wrote. In a rather clumsy attempt to lighten the mood, he added this advice.

> If you have thoughts of marrying, do look out for some lady with a sufficient fortune for both of you. What I say to you now I would recommend to every naval officer and clergyman, who is without prospect of professional advancement. Ladies of some fortune are as easily won as those without, and for the most part as deserving. Check the first liking to those who have nothing.

Tom behaved impeccably. He neither made a parade of his feelings nor tried to wound Dora in any way. As Bertha put it, he behaved under his trial like a gentleman ought. What did Dora think about her first romantic encounter? As she had never considered the possibility that Tom could be interested in her, she emerged heart-whole, though deeply grieved at unintentionally causing her would-be lover pain. 'There are few young women of my acquaintance whose situation & circumstances are exactly to their mind;' Sara Coleridge wrote wistfully; 'few are so fortunate in their love affairs as my cousin Fanny & my friend Mary [Stanger] – few so free from vexation & disturbance in a single state as dear Dora – long may she retain her present peaceful state "fancy-free" as her father exultingly declares she is.'[69]

It was not Dora, but John, whose future was uppermost in William's mind at the end of 1825. In twelve months' time he would be a graduate, and he would have to decide what career he wished to pursue. 'Under any consideration it would be most satisfactory to us if John's thoughts should rest upon the Church;' Mary confided in Lady Beaumont, 'but this is a delicate subject, and unless his own mind – in conjunction with our own wishes, which are not unknown to him – led him thither, we should think it wrong to *press* him into the sacred profession merely to gain a worldly maintenance.' John, like his father before him, had a romantic hankering to be a soldier, but he was left in no doubt that the army was 'out of the question'. His father could not afford to purchase a commission for him and no one, least of all John himself, wished him to enter the army without one.[70]

When John decided he would like to become a fellow at Merton, William was overjoyed. He pulled every string he could, firing off letters indiscriminately to any, and every, friend and acquaintance who might be able to influence the election. The list was impressive, reflecting William's far-reaching contacts within political, academic and religious circles. It included the Foreign Secretary, George Canning, the MP for Oxford, Richard Heber, and the Bishop of London, William Howley, as well as all the usual suspects, including the Earl of Lonsdale, his daughter Lady Mary Bentinck and his son, Viscount Lowther.[71] It was a family joke that William was famous for 'providing opportunities for his Friends to do him a service', but this was the most important 'opportunity' he had ever presented to them. It was to no avail. The quirks in the university patronage system, which had previously worked in his favour, were now against him, he discovered: as a resident of the diocese of Chester, John was debarred from holding a fellowship at Merton. 'You have no reason at any rate to be uneasy at having troubled your friends', the Bishop wrote gallantly. 'If I may judge of their feelings by my own they will be those of concern at being deprived of the opportunity of being of use to you, as far as their interest could prevail.'[72]

The bitter disappointment the Wordsworths felt at this blow to John's career prospects was rendered insignificant in the scale of the disasters which overtook them this autumn. The lease of Rydal Mount was fast running out. Earlier in the year, Lady le Fleming had granted an extension until May 1827, but rumours began to circulate that she intended to install her widowed aunt in the house. The Wordsworths knew Mrs Huddleston had no wish to move from Temple Sowerby, but they had reckoned without Lady Ann's autocratic determination. When the Crackanthorpes wrote to warn them that Mrs Huddleston had given up the fight to stay in her own home, a remote threat suddenly became reality and William reacted with remarkable speed and decisiveness. He went straight to James Backhouse, owner of the Rash, a field which lay in front of Rydal Mount, between the house and the church, and agreed to buy it for £300. Next morning, he wrote to Lady le Fleming, asking to know if the rumours were true, and informing her of his purchase and his intention to build a house upon it, if he were forced to vacate Rydal Mount. 'He then told her he should much prefer staying here, apologised for applying so long before the time, and added that his excuse must be the necessity for making preparations for building – that his family might not be without a house to remove to. Lady Fleming's answer was a verbal one, that Mrs Huddleston was coming in 1827.'[73]

As if it was not bad enough to lose their beloved home, the Wordsworths also faced the prospect of losing everything else they had. At Christmas there was a national financial crisis which, in the way such panics feed on themselves, was caused by, and caused, a run on the banks. This was the period before the Bank of England: all the banks were privately owned, most of them an extension of a business or manufactory, and many were simply overwhelmed. Among them was Jack Hutchinson's Tees Bank, in which every member of the extended family was involved to a greater or lesser degree. John Monkhouse and his late brother's estate were major investors, but Mary, Tom and Sara – and more importantly, Henry, Joanna and their elderly aunt, Elizabeth Monkhouse, who had no other source of income – were dependent on the bank for the payment of their annuities. All of them would suffer losses, but Jack, as one of the partners, was ruined. 'After having stood all shocks, & enjoyed, most deservedly, the confidence of the public for 45 years they are become Bankrupt', Sara wept, '– but heaven be praised no dishonourable conduct has brought them to this; & if they can pay every one their own all the partners *bearing our name* will retire to comparative poverty without a blush'. Lands which had been in the family since the time of Henry VIII would have to be sold, but the haunting fear was that they might not be able to raise the £100,000 necessary to cover their losses. And then what would happen to them all? It was hardly surprising that Sara literally became ill with worry and, for three weeks, could not venture from her room.[74]

At precisely the same time, and for much the same reasons, William's new-found publisher, Hurst & Robinson, also collapsed. Only a few days earlier, on 30 December, Alaric Watts had finalized a deal with them, contracting for an edition of 1,000 copies of William's complete poems, to be published entirely at Hurst & Robinson's risk and expense, allowing William twenty-five copies for personal distribution, and paying him £300, half on receipt of the manuscript, half on publication. John had carried the first volume ready for the press to Manchester on 18 January and on the very next day William read in *The Times* that Hurst & Robinson were stopping payments. He wrote a letter of controlled desperation to Watts, seeking to prevent the manuscript being handed over, and waited in an agony of suspense to learn his fate. Watts had had his own suspicions that all was not well, had not forwarded the manuscript and, by the grace of God, William escaped unscathed. His old friend Scott was not so fortunate. The collapse of Constable's publishing house in Edinburgh left him personally bankrupt, and, in his determination to pay back his creditors, he worked so hard that he ruined his health and shortened his life.[75]

'My Brother hitherto has been most fortunate –', Dorothy wrote at the end of February. 'While people are suffering losses on all sides he has wholly escaped'. It was not quite so simple. William had already spent the £300 he was to receive from Hurst & Robinson in buying the Rash. Somehow or other, he would have to raise the money from an alternative source if Lady le Fleming's plans were to be thwarted. The obvious thing to do was to find another publisher for his poems. It was an added consideration, and one of increasing weight, that these had now been out of print for some time. *The Excursion* had sold out almost three years earlier and the four volumes of *Miscellaneous Poems* within the last eighteen months. Yet another friend, Robinson, was now provided with an opportunity to assist the poet. His protestations about his unfitness for the task were dismissed out of hand as 'a degree of modesty – rare in all men of these days – and singularly rare in men of your profession – and', William added with a smile, 'of mine'.[76]

Though the Rash still had to be paid for, the Wordsworths hoped against hope that it would not be necessary for them to build on it. Mrs Huddleston, 'who we know must have unwillingly yielded to importunity in giving her consent', might change her mind, her son might dissuade her or something might happen to prevent her coming. 'We think that in such case Lady Fleming can not be so cruel as to turn us away: besides, even if she has a particular dislike to us as tenants, it would not be less disagreeable to have us as neighbours, in a house of our own, so close to her Chapel and her Hall.' Dorothy was simply clutching at straws, but her brother proceeded resolutely with his determination to build, summoning George Webster, the architect who had designed Rydal chapel, from Kendal in February to draw up the plans. Remembering William's scathing comments and earnest advice about new building in his *Guide to the Lakes*, it is not surprising to find that the new house, which now took shape on the drawing board, was very much in the vernacular, though grandiose, style. Lady le Fleming might object strenuously to the erection of 'another "genteel Cottage" a thing very obnoxious to the dignity of the Lady of the Manor', but there was nothing she could do.[77] The Wordsworths would not be bullied into leaving Rydal.

Though forewarned and forearmed, it was still a profound shock when, in May, the unbelievable happened and Lady le Fleming served them with a legal notice to quit Rydal Mount. William mourned in verse.

The doubt to which a wavering hope had clung
Is fled; we must depart, willing or not,
Sky-piercing Hills! must bid farewell to you
And all that ye look down upon with pride,
With tenderness imbosom; to your paths,

And pleasant Dwellings, to familiar trees
And wild-flowers known as well as if our hands
Had tended them:

Rydal Mount had come to assume an almost symbolic importance for the Wordsworths. It had been a refuge in the days of their greatest suffering, had exerted its healing power and, together, they had made it into a family home. In the thirteen years they had lived there, they had shaped the house and, more particularly, the garden. The lower terrace, which William had carved out of the mountainside, was inextricably associated with everything that mattered most to him.

A Poet's hand first shaped it; and the steps
Of that same Bard – repeated to and fro
At morn, at noon, and under moonlight skies
Through the vicissitudes of many a year –
Forbade the weeds to creep o'er its grey line.
No longer, scattering to the heedless winds
The vocal raptures of fresh poesy,
Shall he frequent these precincts; locked no more
In earnest converse with belovèd Friends,
Here will he gather stores of ready bliss,
As from the beds and borders of a garden
Choice flowers are gathered! But, if Power may spring
Out of a farewell yearning – favoured more
Than kindred wishes mated suitably
With vain regrets – the Exile would consign
This Walk, his loved possession, to the care
Of those pure Minds that reverence the Muse.[78]

21. *Shades of the Prison-house*

At the beginning of 1826 Robinson wrote a mock obituary for William, anticipating the comments of future generations of literary critics with uncanny accuracy.

This great poet survived to the fifth decennary of the nineteenth Century, but he appears to have dyed [*sic*] in the year 1814 as far as life consisted in an active sympathy with the temporary welfare of his fellow creatures – He had written heroically & divinely against the tyranny of Napoleon, but was quite indifferent to all the successive tyrannies which disgraced the succeeding times – The Spaniards the moment they were under the yoke of the most odious & contemptible tyrant that ever breathed – ceased to be objects of interest – The Germans who emancipated themselves were most ungratefully neglected by their sovereigns & the poet – The Greeks began a War as holy as that of the Spaniards He was silent – He had early manifested a feeling for the negroes & the poet did honour to his friend Clarkson – That source of sympathetic tears was dried up – A new field of enterprise was opened in America – The poets eye was not a prophetic one – There is proof that he was alive abo[u]t 1823–4 when new churches were built in London but otherwise he took no care about any of the events of the day –[1]

It was not meant to be entirely serious, and Robinson had not intended that William himself should read it. Nevertheless, he did so, and it touched a nerve, though he put a brave face on it. 'Your supposed Biography entertained me much', he informed Robinson, adding drily, 'I could give you the other side.' His poems were all out of print, no publisher seemed eager to take them on and now he was about to lose his much-loved home. It was hardly surprising that William felt his whole life was crumbling to the touch. And, as he had already confessed to Maria Jewsbury the previous year, he had reached the age when he had begun to think 'I have lived and laboured to little purpose'. When his friend Kenyon inquired after his poetry, William could only say that he had made little progress, confessing, 'I cannot get over the idea which long ago haunted me, that I have written too much in common with almost every writer of our time.'[2] The seeds of self-doubt, which had been sown by his inability to come to grips with *The Recluse*, were beginning to take root.

There was little to cheer him at home. Dorothy had left for Brinsop and the Stow on 8 February, and William was supposed to join her in May, to fulfil his dream of making another tour of North Wales, culminating in an ascent of Snowdon. The notice to quit put paid to these plans, as William sorrowfully informed Jones. 'Do come and see *us*,' he begged, 'we are growing old and ought to make the best of our time to keep up long tried affections.' As if to underline the uncertainties of life, news arrived that his brother Christopher was seriously ill, having overworked himself into a state of collapse. A brief note, tacked on to one from his son John, asked William to take care of his boys if he should not recover. William replied by return. 'Depend upon it, my dear Brother, that if it should please God I should survive you, I shall not be wanting in rendering every service in my power to your Sons. It would be no less my duty than my Gratification to do so. They are fine young Men and I feel strongly attached to them.'[3]

The election of June 1826 provided a welcome relief from personal troubles. For the first time in many years, the result was a foregone conclusion. Brougham had antagonized many of his supporters by his reforming agenda: not only had he been prominent in campaigning for Roman Catholic emancipation, but he had placed himself at the forefront of demands for secular education. Both of these were anathema to William, and his was the more representative view among the Westmorland electorate. On 10 June a number of Brougham's former supporters announced their defection on these grounds in a Declaration published in the *Westmorland Gazette.* The election itself passed off relatively peacefully, the general feeling that Brougham was fighting a lost cause depriving the proceedings of their anticipated sparkle. William performed his by now customary role of sending daily reports to Lord Lonsdale from the hustings, but even the presence of his old foe Jeffrey of the *Edinburgh Review*, newly elevated to a Westmorland freehold by the Whigs so that he could vote for Brougham, failed to arouse more than passing indignation. His heart was not in it.[4] Dorothy's enthusiasm for electioneering had also died a natural death; though she should have been back at home, she preferred 'to avoid the bustle' and remained at Brinsop. It somehow seemed a fitting close to the campaign that, when Lord Lowther called to see Lady le Fleming, to plead on William's behalf that he might be allowed to remain at Rydal Mount, her Ladyship claimed to be indisposed and refused to see him. There were still some things even the mighty Lowthers could not have their own way.[5]

There were only a couple of bright spots during the election. Tom Hutchinson and John Monkhouse were obliged to make a welcome visit to the Lakes, in order to place their votes, and, more divertingly, Southey returned from a Continental tour to find that, in his absence and without his knowledge, he had been returned as a Member of Parliament for Downton. Lord Radnor, who 'owned' the rotten borough, had conferred this honour on him because he approved of Southey's *Book of the Church*. 'Keswick was in an uproar when I arrived', Southey told his brother. 'The Band had assembled to salute the Member for Downton, the people here having agreed that my election is greatly to the credit of the place; and a crowd of men women and children among whom I have lived three and twenty years were collected to see me in my new character! There was music on the lake in the evening!' At any other time, Southey would have been hugely amused, but he had returned to find his youngest daughter, Isabel, who was not yet fourteen, seriously ill. A week later, she was dead. Her suffering parents were outwardly the 'pattern of resignation and patience', but Kate, her inseparable companion, was desolate, and Sara Coleridge affirmed 'we shall miss her merry voice & sparkling face sadly in our circle'.[6]

The Wordsworths could not fail to be moved by their friends' affliction, knowing from bitter experience how much it cost to maintain a façade of composure. Writing a poem a few days later, William felt obliged to apologize for its melancholy tone, protesting a little too much that this was simply caused by his fellow-feeling for Southey, rather than any deeper cause.[7] A sure sign that he was unsettled was that he was suffering from his eyes again (they had been very bad 'since *the election*', Sara pointedly remarked, 'during which time luckily they were uncommonly well'). There were few Lakers to distract him and even their summer guests were not the usual cheerful crowd. Foremost among them were Joanna and Henry Hutchinson, who spent six weeks at Rydal Mount, by way of saying farewell. The collapse of the Tees Bank had reduced their tiny income even further and, like many others in financial difficulties, they had decided to move to the Isle of Man, where they could live respectably, but cheaply, on their combined income. Poor Jack, meanwhile, had literally fled the country. Afraid of being arrested for debt in England, he had gone into lodgings in Edinburgh, and, when that danger disappeared, returned to them 'to be out of the way of all reports & comments'. Sara and Mary had both escaped without loss, as had Tom Monkhouse's estate – though, in the last case, only through the 'over liberality of his high-minded Brother, who means to bear the loss himself'. As William remarked, this was all the more admirable in view of the fact that John Monkhouse had been deprived of his own legacy through a technical fault in the will. The '*brisk* Widow' was unappreciative of this sacrifice, however, informing the family in a 'hoity-toity' letter that she was off to the Continent; she seemed, Sara noted bitterly, to be 'in the height of enjoyment'.[8]

All William's own travel schemes this summer were thwarted by uncertainty over the future of the tenancy of Rydal Mount. At the end of July, he was obliged to give up a long-cherished project of going to Ireland with Robinson, 'as I cannot get my Neighbour Lady le F. to assure me that in the event of her Aunt not coming to Rydal Mount which the aunt does not wish to do, we may be permitted to remain'. Everything was ready to build, the plans had been drawn up, the site surveyed, even the timber had been bought, but the final decisive step had not yet been taken. It was not just the problem of financing the building work, though anyone with any experience of building advised against it: the Beaumonts urged that it would be 'ruinous' and none of them could forget that building her house in Borrowdale had cost Mary Barker her fortune. The family themselves were deeply divided over whether they should build, or simply find somewhere else: William, Dora and Willy were all in favour, Dorothy, John and Sara, still smarting from overseeing the workmen at Brinsop, against, Mary undecided. The main reason for hanging back, however, was the hope that Lady le Fleming might change her mind. If they were allowed to stay, and had already built in front of Rydal Mount, they would have destroyed much of the charm of their old home.[9]

September saw a belated flurry of social activity. The '*comers & goers*', as Sara called them, 'have crammed our rooms & occasioned parties by Land & water innumerable'; there was a Crump wedding at Allan Bank, a christening at Ulverston at which William and Mary stood godparents for 'Cousin Dorothy's' third child, and numerous routs at Rydal. Among the semi-permanent house-guests were Mrs Coleridge, who had at last allowed her daughter, Sara, to slip from her ample grasp and escape to her pining cousin-fiancé, in London, and Elizabeth Cookson, still a cheerful invalid waiting patiently at death's door as she had been for the previous three years. Beaumont and Rogers were among the more welcome Lakers, William accompanying them to Keswick, Lowther and on a short tour of Buttermere. Hard on their heels came Robinson, fresh from his tour of Ireland, and Poole, William's friend from Somersetshire days, making an unexpected and much appreciated call on his way back from holidaying in Scotland. Mrs Luff, who had now taken up residence at Fox Ghyll, had her friends from Mauritius, the Farquhar family, staying with her. Sir Robert had soon tired of the Lakes and escaped back to Town, but his wife and their sons were enchanted with the scenery and the company. Lady Farquhar and Sara were soon fast friends: 'She has won all hearts by her simple manners, & accommodating disposition –', Sara enthused. 'Always ready to enjoy whatever was proposed – never making any difficulties, & contented with all things – just like dear Dorothy!'[10]

Someone else who stole all hearts this autumn was Miss Emma Ayling. She and her brother had returned to Spring Cottage, bringing with them a young friend, Lionel Fraser, who was a grandnephew of William's acquaintance the poetess Charlotte Smith. The rapport the Aylings had enjoyed with the Wordsworths on their previous visit, two years earlier, was instantly re-established. 'She is certainly a charming person . . . such delightful spirits I never before saw – nor any one who was so *instantaneously* attractive', Sara mused. Beautiful, accomplished and yet also 'a truly useful female of the old-fashioned kind', Dora's '*Syren* friend' had at least two old bachelors, Tillbrooke and Rogers, eating out of her hand. 'Our Dora is more bewitched than any one –', Sara observed, 'she has neither eyes nor ears for anything else – and her Mother sometimes says, in spite of her own love, "I wish this Miss Ayling had never come hither."' It was a lament in which they would all soon join.

The fascinating Emma succeeded in catching one of her matrimonial prizes, Samuel Tillbrooke, but her brother, the Reverend William Ayling, did not. A thirty-three-year-old clergyman, without a benefice but with an independent income, Sara thought him 'a very agreeable Person – of mild manners with a spice of humour'. Dora thought differently, merely tolerating his presence for the sake of his sister, an interpretation of appearances which never crossed the unfortunate clergyman's mind. When the lease of Spring Cottage came to an end, he escorted his sister down to Leicestershire, but unexpectedly reappeared at the beginning of November, announcing that he intended to stay for the winter in Tillbrooke's Ivy Cottage.[11] At what point William Ayling proposed to Dora is not clear. On 1 October she was taken 'very ill' with an attack of biliousness and nerves, which lasted several weeks. This might pinpoint the date, for Ayling unfortunately chose not to accept Dora's word for it that she could not return his affection. On the other hand, he is more likely to have proposed after his return, for Dorothy's journal records him coming to tea on 26 November, supper two days later (when Dora was 'very nervy'), walking with William, Dorothy and Dora to Grasmere on 30 November and 2 December, and dining with the Wordsworths at Ivy Cottage on 3 December. The following day, he abruptly left Rydal for good, despite his stated intention of remaining there for the winter.

What made this affair so unpleasant was Ayling's response to his rejection. He simply refused to believe that Dora was not interested in him. Almost fifty years later, Bertha Southey's blood still boiled whenever she thought of what happened next. Ayling 'went about & told every one that Mr W would not let his daughter marry him & that she was breaking her heart in consequence'. His sisters sided with him and, according to Bertha, 'turned against her also and behaved shamefully – no wonder poor Dora was made really ill by such base conduct on the part of friends'. Letters were exchanged between Dora and Emma for 'a little while' after the refusal, until it became clear to the Wordsworths that the Aylings were spreading malicious gossip about them. The most regrettable casualty of the whole sorry business was the Wordsworths' long-standing friendship with Tillbrooke. Forced to choose between friends and future wife, the 'Knight of the White Stockings' naturally sided with the latter.[12]

Dora's health continued to give cause for concern throughout the winter. She began a regular regime of warm bathing and, when she was well enough to do so, took daily exercise riding on her pony. There were no consumptive symptoms, her aunt explained defensively, she was just 'debilitated'. Dora's brother John was also 'debilitated'. As his university examinations loomed ever nearer, he suffered 'a rush of blood to the head', which a doctor conveniently diagnosed as the result of too much study. The remedy was even more convenient: he was to lay aside his books for a month and then read only in moderation. For a young man who did not stand a chance of winning the honours his family hoped for, it was a timely rescue from disappointment and shame. John's health was far more important to them than academic glory. He went into the examinations secure in the knowledge that his father would be satisfied with a common degree and that he would not be expected to read for honours. He took his degree in December and, having crushed a wayward ambition to join the army, dutifully returned to Oxford in January to read divinity and prepare himself for ordination.[13]

Dorothy was in better health than any of her nephews and nieces. She had arrived home on 4 November, having spent seven months at Brinsop and the Stow, and two more on the road to the Lakes. She had visited, and exhausted, Maria Jewsbury, who took to her couch while the indefatigable Dorothy played the tourist and got to know Kenilworth 'by heart', 'absolutely digested' Warwick, and 'swallowed whole' Stratford and Charlecote. She had also paid a quiet visit to Coleorton, spending her time reading and walking, when she was not lecturing Lady Beaumont over the changes she planned to make to the winter garden.[14]

William, too, was enjoying a sudden resurgence of health and purpose after a year of somewhat aimless drifting. One of his summer visitors, the editor of the *Keepsake*, Frederic Reynolds, had suggested that he should rub his eyes with the blue stone (copper sulphate) to cure the trachoma. Miraculously, it worked. Within weeks they were better than they had been for years, and as good as any eyes in the house. This remarkable recovery just happened to coincide with the joyful news that Lady le Fleming had abandoned her determination to force the Wordsworths out of, and her aunt into, Rydal Mount. Always the mistress of the understatement, Mary informed Kenyon that they now looked forward 'to a quiet and industrious winter – without any harassing fears that we are to be turned [out] of our favoured Residence'.[15]

Relieved of two of his long-standing problems, William now turned his attention to his third. His poems had been out of print too long and none of his negotiators had succeeded in finding him a publisher. It was time to take matters into his own hands, and he did so decisively. He asked Watts to return the manuscript of the first volume and offered John Murray first refusal of the complete poems, on the same terms as Rogers had agreed the previous year, with the proviso that, if Murray did not reply '*immediately*', his silence would be interpreted as a rejection. Staying true to type, Murray did not respond, so William offered the same terms to his old publisher, Longman, who promptly accepted. His perseverance had paid off: from now on, he would meet two-thirds of the expense and risk of publishing (which, as William had learned from his dealings with other publishers over the past year, was no risk at all), and would receive two-thirds of the profit. By 2 January 1827 the first volume was winging its way to London on the Manchester Mail, and the first proof sheet arrived ten days later.[16]

As if to make up for lost time, the new edition proceeded by leaps and bounds. 'W's eyes are famous', Mary wrote in high delight on 15 January 1827, '– and I hear his voice below murmuring over the work he is about to forward to the press; but tho' able to read himself he still requires a help-mate – and as soon as I have done scribbling to you I must join him.' Despite repeated criticisms from his friends, he was determined to stand by his unique system of classifying his poems. Lamb had observed that 'there is only one good order – And that is the order in which they were written – That is a history of the poet's mind'.[17] Though he never admitted as much, this was precisely what made such an order unpalatable to William. There could be no surer method of drawing attention to his declining powers than to print his poems in the order in which they had been written. If *Ode: Intimations of Immortality*, which he believed his finest poem, appeared in historic sequence, it would suggest that he had composed nothing of equal importance for almost a quarter of a century. Additionally, as he pointed out to Lamb and Robinson, it would lose its effect.

Miscellaneous poems ought not to be jumbled together at *random* – were this done with mine the passage from one to another would often be insupportably offensive; but in my judgement the only thing of much importance in arrangement is that one poem should shade off happily into another – and the contrasts where they occur be clear of all harshness or abruptness.

This very valid point was perfectly illustrated by *Friendship's Offering*, one of the new annuals whose editors so frequently, and vainly, sought contributions from William. 'The arrangement of miscellaneous poems is of consequence', he informed its publisher; '– it either may greatly aid or much spoil their effect – For instance, Mr Montgomery's serious and even solemn Lines are unluckily followed by a smart jeu d'esprit . . . and the two poems, though both very good in their several ways, strangle each other.'[18]

On 10 May William received a parcel from Longman containing six copies of the new edition, in five volumes, grandly titled *The Poetical Works of William Wordsworth*. 'I am pleased with the appearance of the books', he informed Longman, 'except an error in apportioning the matter in the third vol. which is too large, the miscalculation was my own fault.' Complimentary copies were scattered with his usual prodigality: Watts, Robinson and Rogers were all rewarded for their efforts on his behalf, while his growing army of female fans was recognized in the sending of copies to Lady Beaumont (his earliest and most loyal), Maria Jewsbury and her friend the poetess Felicia Hemans (the latest addition to the coterie). 'No one I am sure will enjoy it more than I do –', Robinson responded.

My first act was to finger it as a child does a new toy – I soon made the discovery by the simple operation of counting pages that the new edition has 264 more pages than the corresponding volumes of the last – And that it has much less *fat* In the work of collation I have yet been able to make but little progress But I have seen enough to rejoice both in the quantity of the new and the quality of the alter[e]d

Rogers was equally enthusiastic: the volumes 'are full of Virtue, full of Piety, full of Wisdom, the Wisdom of the heart, & must console you under any circumstances . . . Of the Genius I need say nothing.'[19]

Rogers's comment about consolation was prompted by the knowledge that one of William's closest friends, his earliest patron, Sir George Beaumont, had not lived to see the publication of the new edition. He had suffered a seizure while standing at his easel and died eight days later, on 7 February, aged seventy-three. Beaumont's death struck William hard. It was not just his friend's unstinting support and many tactful kindnesses over the long period of their intimacy, but the intensity of the artistic sympathy between the two men. A perfect example of this occurs in an anecdote William himself told Scott to illustrate the poet George Crabbe's lack of imagination. The three men had been sitting together when Beaumont blew out a candle, 'and exchanging a look with Wordsworth began to admire in silence the undulating thread of smoke which slowly arose from the expiring wick'. Crabbe, however, put on the extinguisher. 'In two other men I should have said "this is affectations," with Sir Hugh Evans', Scott remarked, quoting from *The Merry Wives of Windsor*, but in this case he knew it was sincere.[20] It was typical of Beaumont's modesty that, despite decades of patronage of the arts, he declined any personal ostentation in death, requesting only a simple marble tablet with nothing but his name, dates and the legend 'Enter not into judgement with thy servant, O Lord!' engraved upon it, to commemorate his long and useful life. In a final act of generosity, he left William a legacy of £100 outright, together with a life annuity of £100.[21]

The Wordsworths' columns of births, marriages and deaths filled up rapidly. A third daughter, Sarah, was born at Brinsop Court in January, bringing the number of little Hutchinsons to five, while poor Jack, still reeling from his bankruptcy, lost not one but two daughters within a month to consumption. Bessy and Jane, the only children of his first marriage, were buried together in the little churchyard at Sockburn-on-Tees, close to their mother and aunt. Not one of them had reached her thirtieth year.[22] The 'Ephesian Matron' as William called Mrs Tom Monkhouse, referring to a character in a farce who married her second husband while mourning in the tomb of her first, announced that she intended to marry Dr Paris Dick at the beginning of April; her fondness for Clifton, it was now obvious, had more to do with the living than the dead, for it was where her new husband had his practice. It was also rumoured that Owen Lloyd, Christopher's nephew, who had just been ordained curate to Mr Dawes at Ambleside, was on the brink of marriage with Jane Harden, of Brathay Hall, much to Dora's delight; 'they are as nice a pair as I could wish to see'. Theirs was to be a long, star-crossed and ultimately doomed affair, but Owen, bright, cheerful, affectionate, and a regular visitor at Rydal Mount since childhood, was the 'delight of all this household'.[23]

'Sickness is an humbling thing', Dora wrote to her old schoolfriend Mary Stanger; '– it shows one what poor weak mortals we are'. She had never recovered from the Ayling débâcle and, throughout the winter and spring, had been confined to the house, even, at times, to her room. Edith and Bertha Southey both came to cheer the invalid and keep her company in the sickroom, but she remained delicate, with a cough and cold that she could not shake off.[24] Reluctantly, the Wordsworths came to the conclusion that she should not spend another winter at Rydal. The Southeys hatched a plot to carry Dora, and her Aunt Sara, who, in Southey's own words, was 'one of the persons whom we all – young and old alike – like best', off with them to Harrogate in May. It was not entirely successful – the Southeys had to content themselves with Sara – but on 2 June Dora joined them, her father having driven her over by slow stages in the pony chaise. She returned 'a new creature!', ready to enjoy the social delights of a Lake summer. Her cousin Richard's son, now twelve years old, was to spend his holidays at Rydal Mount, and all three of Christopher's sons were expected as part of a Cambridge reading party, based in Ambleside. Unlike poor dull John, this side of the Wordsworth family carried all before them. As Mary, in great excitement, informed John Monkhouse, they were coming fresh from their latest triumphs at university, which were unparalleled; 'three brothers bearing off so many honours in the same year' was news to bring 'unmingled exultation' to every member of their proud family.[25]

On 15 August they were joined by Edward Quillinan, returning to Spring Cottage for the first time since the death of his wife five years earlier. Having paid a pilgrimage to her grave in Grasmere churchyard, and been joined by his Portuguese half-brother, he flung himself wholeheartedly into all the gaieties, including a grand picnic under Raven Crag, near Wythburn, where the families of Greta Hall and Rydal Mount, with assorted hangers-on and 'vagrants', made a merry party of thirty as they sat round a gypsy fire on the rocky shore of the lake. Dora was in her element, 'is become as strong as I ever remember her to have been', her mother noted, but she was a complete barometer, her state of health depending on the weather. Before the next rainy season began, she would have to be out of the weeping climate of the Lakes.[26]

On 4 September Dora and Mary left for Brinsop, their journey brought forward by the news that Mary's aunt, Elizabeth Monkhouse, a creaking gate who was at last genuinely drawing to the close of her long life, was 'diseasedly anxious lest she should die before their arrival'. They had barely time to say hello and goodbye to Dorothy, who had returned the day before after a ten-week visit to the Rawsons in Halifax, and they missed John Monkhouse altogether. He arrived the day after their departure, just in time to join the Southey and Wordsworth households in an assault on Blencathra, in which they were accompanied by their old friend Blomfield, the Bishop of Chester, and three not-so-young American visitors. The summit accomplished triumphantly on foot or horseback, seventeen or eighteen of the intrepid mountaineers celebrated with a second picnic by the side of Scales tarn.[27]

The Americans caused much amusement and interest at both Keswick and Rydal. They were two brothers and a sister, William, George and Harriet Douglas, whom Southey nicknamed '*Hic, Haec* and *hoc coelebs*', a punning reference to the elder brother and sister, who, like characters out of a novel by Trollope or James, were intent on marrying and marrying well: Harriet, a thirty-seven-year-old heiress, declared that nothing less than a duke would do. The '*hoc coelebs*', as befitted his neuter appellation, was 'silent & innofensive [*sic*]'. Harriet was not just in search of a title. She was a determined 'lionizer', or what would now be called a groupie, collecting literary men as some people collect autographs or entry visa stamps. She informed Southey she would like to run off with him to Rome and William that she would like to 'domesticate' at Rydal Mount. 'She is a most ingenuous & enthusiastic creature –', Sara commented, 'but the oddest manners, & such a speech!!' William was concerned enough about her welfare to write her a letter of fatherly advice after her departure, urging her to ensure that she knew her intended thoroughly before she married him, and recommending (in the kindliest way!) that she should observe more, read more and talk less.[28]

'The dissipation of our family since the departure of Mary & her Daughter has exceeded all former dissipations of the kind', Sara proudly reported, as the whole household, young and old, trooped gaily from one ball to another and attended races not only at Penrith but even as far away as Doncaster. Idle Mount well and truly lived up to its reputation. This was all very well for Christopher's sons, who were enjoying a well-earned vacation, and even for young Owen Lloyd, who was already on the ladder of ecclesiastical preferment, albeit on the first rung. It was not so healthy for John and Willy, neither of whom revealed any real sense of purpose. John was supposed to be on the point of ordination, but he showed a marked reluctance to do anything about it. 'I should like to see him more earnest than he is in <u>preparation</u> for his profession – he is reading but slackly', his mother fretted. His parents had been determined from the start not to push him into any career, particularly not the Church, which demanded at least some sense of vocation, merely to gain a worldly maintenance. Yet John seemed quite happy to sit back and let his father do everything for him. He could not be ordained until he found a curacy and, as with the Merton fellowship, it was William who had to do the hustling, asking his friends to alert him if a suitable vacancy occurred. Such was his anxiety on behalf of his son that, when his old friend Satterthwaite, rector of Lowther, died, he wrote with unseemly haste to Lord Lonsdale to ask if there was an opening for John.[29]

In the end, John had to swallow his pride and accept the only curacy which had been offered to him, that of Whitwick, in Leicestershire. The greatest objections to the place were the fact that John would have to furnish part of the rectory there and keep house for himself, but Whitwick itself was not attractive, especially to a young clergyman in his first post. A grim village in the industrial desolation of the coalfields on the edge of Charnwood Forest, his parishioners would be miners and stocking weavers, impoverished, illiterate and stridently Nonconformist. Though beggars could not be choosers, there were also advantages to the position. John's rector would be the Wordsworths' old friend Merewether of Coleorton, and the hospitality of his house, and Lady Beaumont's, both less than three miles away, would constantly be open to him. As none of William's friends among the Church grandees – Wrangham, Blomfield, even his brother Christopher – could come up with anything better, Whitwick it had to be. John was packed off to his uncle for last-minute cramming for his examination before the bishop and, on 2 March 1828, he was ordained deacon. A few weeks later, his father accompanied him to Whitwick, leaving him in his new home with Mary, one of the Wordsworths' own Rydal Mount housemaids, now elevated to the rank of housekeeper.[30] Short of performing John's duty for him, there was little more William could do for his son.

John had been satisfactorily settled but Willy was, if anything, more of a problem than his elder brother. He was now seventeen and, for the last two years, had been studying at home with the indispensable Carter, preparing to follow John to Oxford, but he had little inclination for university, and even less for study. 'His thoughts turn (I fear constantly) on the Army', Dorothy wrote to Quillinan in November. William admitted he was sadly at a loss what to do with his younger son: he 'is bent upon being a beggar either in the honourable character and profession of a Soldier or of a Farmer', he told Rogers. 'Could you suggest to me anything better for this infatuated youth – any situation in a Counting-House or a public office? He dislikes the thought of the University because he sees nothing afterwards open to him but the Church; which he does not think himself fit for, or that he ever can be made so.'[31]

All the arguments of the elders failed to quell Willy's '*Army mania fever*'. Like many a teenager, he thought they were trying to stop him doing what he wanted for their own reasons, and when they raised the spectre of money, he dismissed the need for it as outdated and uninformed. Without his parents' knowledge or permission, he wrote to Harriet Douglas, who was now in Dublin, asking her to intercede for him with Lady Wellesley to secure him a commission by favour instead of purchase. 'Pray do not fail to let the Marchioness know that my son's application was made wholly unknown to me; and if you choose to, add the fact that I was truly thankful it failed', William wrote to Miss Douglas, when he learned what his son had done. 'Had the commission been obtained I should have been greatly embarrassed, for everything would have been done on my part to prevent my son's accepting it.' Willy was now forced to accept that an army career was out of the question and his family vainly hoped that he would reconcile himself to a mercantile life. For the time being, until something could be found for him, he would have to continue his studies at home.[32]

Willy's little rebellion had occurred in his parents' absence, for on 13 November William had left Rydal Mount to join Mary at Coleorton, where they were to spend three weeks with Lady Beaumont, before going on together to Brinsop Court. Their route took them through Birmingham, where, as usual, they stayed with the Lloyds. Christopher's father-in-law was now in his eightieth year, and too unwell to put his own house at their disposal, but he suggested they stay with his daughter, Sophia, who lived opposite. Having seen his letter, Sophia remarked that it sounded more like an offer of accommodation than an assurance of welcome, but the old Quaker merely said, 'Will[ia]m Wordsworth understands me perfectly, & I am persuaded such a thing will never come into his head, but if thee thinks so, thee mayst tell him how it is.'[33] Christopher himself, just disappointed of his ambition to become Regius Professor of Divinity at Cambridge, joined them for Christmas at Brinsop Court. 'We are very quiet sober folk, scarcely see a soul from one week to another, a great contrast to the idle bustle of a Rydal Mount summer, & we enjoy the contrast', Dora had written, when inviting him. Wherever the Wordsworths went, however, there was always bustle. The Christmas party included not just the seven resident Hutchinsons and two Monkhouses, but William, Mary and Dora, Christopher and Edith Southey. Even the fact that Mary's seventy-seven-year-old aunt, Elizabeth Monkhouse, was now genuinely dying did not put a damper on the party: she herself was always cheerful and sometimes 'as merry as her *great-nieces*'. Dora, too, was fully restored to health and happiness, writing cheekily of her father's saying 'in his pompous way' that he did not like the weather because it had 'none of the dignity of rain or the beauty of sunshine'.[34]

Satisfied that it was in his daughter's best interests to see out the winter at Brinsop, William returned alone to Rydal Mount on 29 January. 'You, I hope, are now seriously set down to the Recluse', Christopher wrote sternly a few days later, but, of course, he was not. Instead, after years of implacable resistance to the idea of writing for periodicals, he had finally succumbed to the siren call. He had, quite simply, been made an offer he could not refuse. Reynolds (he of the blue stone cure for trachoma) came to beard the lion in his den, calling on William at home in early February and offering him the princely sum of 100 guineas for just twelve pages of verse to be published in the *Keepsake*. William always found it more difficult to refuse an application face to face, but the offer was very timely, since he was now faced with 'formidable' bills for John. In addition to more than £60 owed to his college, excluding tailor's bills, there was money to find for his new furniture at Whitwick, his journey there and his other incidental expenses on taking up his living.[35]

Just before accepting Reynolds's offer, William had rather grandly informed one editor who applied to him for a contribution that he had 'never *composed* a line for the sake of pelf [i.e. money] – though I *some*times *published* from that immediate motive'. Now, however, he could not afford to be so high-minded. 'It is a matter of trade', he admitted. 'All my natural feelings are against appearing before the Public in *this* way.' It was, as Dora commented to Maria Jewsbury, 'degrading enough I confess but necessity has no law, and galling enough but we must pocket our pride sometimes and it is good for us.' Within days of agreeing to contribute William was hard at work, and by the end of the month had produced three of the five poems which would appear in the *Keepsake*.[36] The best of them was a sonnet as good as any he had written. It was based on a story told him by the coachdriver as they were passing through Derbyshire, but what makes it so successful is that it was informed by William's own feeling for the brother he had lost so long ago. Even now, John's death had power to move him.

'Tis said that to the brow of yon fair hill
Two Brothers clomb, and, turning face from face,
Nor one look more exchanging, grief to still
Or feed, each planted on that lofty place
A chosen Tree; then, eager to fulfil
Their courses, like two new-born rivers, they
In opposite directions urged their way
Down from the far-seen mount. No blast might kill
Or blight that fond memorial; – the trees grew,
And now entwine their arms; but ne'er again
Embraced those Brothers upon earth's wide plain;
Nor aught of mutual joy or sorrow knew
Until their spirits mingled in the sea
That to itself takes all, Eternity.[37]

Dorothy, it would seem, did not approve of the *Keepsake* contribution. 'My Brother is writing verses – but has not yet turned to the Recluse – and we shall lose him again so soon that I fear this winter will produce nothing – and how years roll away!' It is significant that William deliberately did not show his sister the alterations he had made to a fourth poem, and actually took pains to conceal them from her. The poem was *The Triad*, which he had promised Dora and Edith he would write several years previously. As in all such requested poems, he had difficulty engaging with the subject, a celebration of the close friendship and differing characters of the three poets' daughters, Dora Wordsworth, Edith Southey and Sara Coleridge, but the fancy now seized him and the poem was 'thrown off rapidly – and afterwards revised with care'. Of all the poems he contributed to the *Keepsake*, this was William's particular favourite: 'I think [a] great part of it is as elegant and spirited as any thing I have written – but I was afraid to trust my judgement – as the aery Figures are all sketched from living originals that are dear to me.'[38]

On 17 April, having completed something above 300 lines of verse for the *Keepsake*, William left Rydal Mount for Cambridge, where he was to meet Mary and Dora. John went with him as far as Whitwick, having practised for his new role by reading prayers at Grasmere and Rydal, to his father's satisfaction and even greater pride. John had wanted his Aunt Dorothy to come with him, but she declined, promising instead to come in the autumn, when he would need a fireside companion to cheer his solitude.[39] After a series of grand dinners in the lodge at Trinity College (meals being the only time they saw Christopher, who was always fully occupied), the Wordsworths went up to London for what William had said would be 'a short, very short, visit'. As usual, it turned out to be nothing of the kind. The object of the visit was supposed to be to find a mercantile situation for Willy. Determined not to spend the rest of his life behind a desk, young Willy, who was now eighteen, had bowed to the inevitable, given up his '*Army mania fever*' and agreed to be a merchant – but on condition that he could do so abroad. Once they had reached

London, however, where they stayed with the hospitable Quillinan in Bryanston Street, their good intentions soon went by the board.[40]

Scott, Lockhart, Southey and the American Douglases were all in town, and there were innumerable other friends to see. 'Breakfast, dinner, and evening engagements are overwhelming us', Dora wrote; '*truly*, I am sighing for Rydal rest.' Humphry Davy's wife whisked William and Dora off to the opera to see Madame Sontag; Reynolds offered his new contributor four tickets to Drury Lane and Robinson took them all to the French theatre. The Lambs, Coleridges, Rogers, Kenyon, even that figure from the past Godwin, 'grown old and thin', were all on the visiting list. Talfourd hosted a dinner for lawyers, Quillinan one for the military. Scott formed an excursion party to Hampton Court and proudly carried off all three Wordsworths, Rogers and Moore to walk and dine with his tall son, Major Walter Scott.[41]

By the beginning of June, Mary had had enough. She was also anxious to fulfil her promise to visit John at Whitwick. William saw her on to the stagecoach on 3 June and she drove off, expecting that her husband and daughter would join her before the end of the month. They, however, had other ideas. 'You will be not a little astonished at our plans –', Dora wrote to Mrs Hoare on 16 June. 'We are going up the Rhine the *We*, Mr Coleridge my Father & myself – going to visit a Lady who lives in the most interesting part of that interesting country.'[42] It was an improbable scheme and the choice of companion even more so. The intimacy of the old friendship between the two poets had never been restored: though relations were now cordial, and they always met when William was in town, they were not even on letter-writing terms. What is more, apart from an annual trip to the seaside at Ramsgate, Coleridge had not left London since taking up residence in Highgate. And he had never gone anywhere without his minders, the Gillmans, who controlled his opium habit, as far as anyone could do so.

The unlikely trio set off on 21 June for Margate, where they were to take the steam packet to Ostend. Dora was beside herself with joy at the thought of her first Continental tour, and determined to maintain the female family tradition by keeping a journal. Her father, without his 'three wives' to run round after him, was in an almighty panic, firing off a last-minute letter to Reynolds telling him not to publish his poems in the *Keepsake* until his return, and trying desperately to borrow a carpetbag from Robinson for his luggage. Coleridge, serenely indifferent, floated along in a drug-induced haze, the personification of benevolence. Poor Mary, stranded for she knew not how long at Whitwick, was reduced to writing exasperated letters to Quillinan, asking to be enlightened as to how, when, where and with whom her 'Vagabonds' were travelling.[43]

The travellers took the shortest route across the Low Countries to Cologne, where they joined the Rhine, and followed it southwards for some twenty odd miles to Godesberg, where they stayed a week with Robinson's friend Mrs Aders, before proceeding down the Rhine as far as Bingen and then retracing their route home. During the seven weeks they were away, Dora faithfully kept her journal and, though she frequently deferred to her mother and aunt when attempting scenes they had already described, her ready wit, sense of fun and sheer sense of enjoyment shine through on every page. The poets were her 'tutors', pointing out the best pictures in the Dutch galleries and churches, but her own views were pungently matter-of-fact. Viewing a celebrated statue of the Virgin and Child in the Church of St Salvador in Bruges, she was unimpressed, noting indignantly, 'they have given the Virgin a double chin'! An equally celebrated Bruges pulpit, carved from marble and dark wood, was dismissed as having 'somewhat of a ginger-breadish effect'. No man is a hero to his daughter, even if he is a romantic poet. Driving to Waterloo on the coach, she observed that William and Coleridge were 'perched on the roof exactly like a pair of monkies', and she recorded without scruple how they had all laughed when, William having offered one of the men selling souvenirs on the battlefield two sous, instead of the two francs he was asking, the man had turned to her and said, 'Ah Mademoiselle you have a very miserly father'. As Dora mischievously noted, having two elderly poets as guardians gave her plenty of opportunity for flirtation with fellow travellers: Coleridge preferred to remain in his canal boat cabin (his excuse being that the portholes provided free picture frames for the scenes they were passing through), and her father was 'often asleep or lost in his own meditations'.[44]

At Brussels, they were introduced to Thomas Colley Grattan, a novelist and travel-writer most famous for his popular series *Highways and Byways, or Tales of the Roadside, picked up in the French Provinces by a Walking Gentleman.* Not for the first or last time, meeting Coleridge and William together, an observer was swept off his feet by the former and disappointed by the latter. 'He was a perfect antithesis to Coleridge – tall, wiry, harsh in features, coarse in figure, inelegant in looks', Grattan complained of William. 'He was roughly dressed in a long brown *surtout* [i.e. frock coat], striped duck trousers, fustian gaiters, and thick shoes. He more resembled a mountain farmer than a "lake poet". His whole air was unrefined and unprepossessing.' By comparison, Coleridge held instant court wherever he went, talking so constantly that he seemed to 'breathe in words'. While William hustled Dora through the streets, trying to arrange accommodation and transport, Coleridge wandered dreamily along, 'in a total abstraction of thought and feeling', indifferent to where they went, but finding something to admire in every glance of moonlight or effect of shade. Though he never got over William's northern accent, Grattan was forced to revise his first opinion of the man.

> But, on after observation, and a little reflection, I could not help considering that much that seemed unfavourable in Wordsworth might be really placed to his advantage. There was a total absence of affectation, or egotism; not the least effort at display, or assumption of superiority over any of those who were quite prepared to concede it to him. He seemed satisfied to let his friend and fellow-traveller take the lead, with a want of pretension rarely found in men of literary reputation far inferior to his; while there was something unobtrusively amiable in his bearing towards his daughter.[45]

Much the same conclusion was drawn by another young man, Julian Young, son of the actor Charles Mayne Young, who was their fellow guest at Godesberg. He, however, was not predisposed towards Coleridge, whose slovenly appearance, with his breeches unbuttoned and slippers 'much trodden down at the heel', only served to exacerbate the fact that he completely ignored Young on their first meeting. It was not a deliberate unkindness, he was entirely preoccupied and anxiously waiting for William to return from a walk. William made his appearance, dressed *à la mode*, in a 'brown-holland blouse; he held in his left hand an alpenstock (on the top of which he had placed the broad-brimmed "wide-awake" [i.e. soft felt hat] he had just taken off), and in his right a sprig of apple-blossom overgrown with lichen'. He had barely time to give Young a 'kindly smile, and courteous recognition of my bow', before he was grabbed by Coleridge, who pushed him back into an armchair, stood over him so that he could not escape and proceeded to expound one of the fallacies he had just discovered in Bishop Berkeley's propositions. After several days of their company, Young observed that,

> as a rule, Wordsworth allowed Coleridge to have all the talk to himself; but once or twice Coleridge would succeed in entangling Wordsworth in a discussion on some abstract metaphysical question; when I would sit by, reverently attending, and trying hard to look intelligent, though I did not feel so; for at such times a leaden stupor weighed down my faculties . . . If Wordsworth condescended to converse with me, he spoke to me as if I were his equal in mind, and made me pleased and proud in consequence. If Coleridge held me by the button, for lack of fitter audience, he had a talent for making me feel *his* wisdom and my own stupidity: so that I was miserable and humiliated by the sense of it . . . when he gave tongue on 'a priori knowledge and a posteriori knowledge' and spake of 'modality' and of the 'paralogium of pure reason', my feeble brain reeled.

(Had he but known it, William sometimes felt the same, for he and Rogers once spent two hours listening 'uninterruptedly' to one of Coleridge's 'harangues', during which William had listened with 'profound attention, every now and then nodding his head as if in assent'. As they walked away afterwards, Rogers said, 'Well, for my own part, I could not make head nor tail of Coleridge's oration: pray, did you understand it?' to which William had replied, with his usual honesty, 'Not one syllable of it.')[46]

William invited Young to walk with him to the ruins of a Cistercian abbey across the Rhine at Heisterbach, and, in Coleridge's absence, Young discovered for the first time that William's reticence was not constitutional but self-imposed. Nothing could stop Coleridge in full flow, but William would break off in the middle of an argument to observe the scenery. He would

> dilate with exquisite sensibility and microscopic power of analysis on the construction of the humblest grasses, or on the modest seclusion of some virgin wild flower . . . In that same stroll to Heisterbach he pointed out to me such beauty of design in objects I had used to

trample underfoot, that I felt as if almost every spot on which I trod was holy ground, and that I had rudely desecrated it. His eyes would fill with tears and his voice falter as he dwelt on the benevolent adaptation of means to ends discernable by reverential observation.

That same evening, 6 July, Young was present at the meeting of Titans organized by Mrs Aders. Among the illuminati of Bonn invited to meet William and Coleridge were the classical scholar and historian Barthold Niebuhr and the scholar and critic Augustus Schlegel, who was a leading light in the German school of romantic writers. Unfortunately, in the presence of such an eminent gathering, neither Young nor Dora felt able to do justice to the conversation. Only Schlegel spoke English, and his remarks, Young said, were not worth preserving. Schlegel spent the evening admiring his own reflection in the mirror, boasting of his success with the opposite sex and competing with Coleridge to be the centre of attention. Despite having spent a lifetime plagiarizing Schlegel's work, Coleridge stubbornly refused to defer to the older man, who was determinedly provocative. He praised Byron, abused the English through thick and thin, claimed that Coleridge's German, which he had learned 'grammatically, critically and scientifically' at Göttingen, was 'unintelligible', and begged him to speak English. Coleridge retired hurt, before the dinner, so it was left to William to uphold his country's honour at the table. When their hostess asked Schlegel to repeat some lines in honour of the occasion, Schlegel deftly passed the honour on to William, who, like the forthright northerner he was, declared he preferred 'good plain prose on such occasions' and proposed a toast in a few words. After this evening, it was perhaps not surprising that Mrs Aders reported that William was 'not liked' in Germany, 'he was too haughty and reserved'.[47]

Coleridge had often been 'ill' on their travels, complaining of the food, the heat and the pace. Dora, in a letter to her mother, confided that, though they '*get on* famously . . . Mr C. sometimes detains them with his *fiddle faddling*, and that he likes *prosing* to the folks better than exerting himself to see the face of the Country and that Father with his few ½ dozen words of German makes himself much better understood than Mr C. with all his weight of German Literature'. Such are the minor irritations of travelling, but, in the light of this comment, and the observations of both Grattan and Young, it comes as something of a shock to see what Coleridge himself confided to his private notebooks. From Bruges to Godesberg to Bingen and back, he said, he had 'never on earth known such hard, rigid, continual, in all points despotic Egotism' as that displayed by William. His commonplace talk, his 'coarse concern about money . . . In short, all the failings which characterised him in early manhood have grown astonishingly – the grandiose gigantic flowers of his philosophical and poetic genius are faded and withered.'[48] It says much for their relationship that now, as ever, the Wordsworths had no idea how he *really* felt about them.

While William and Dora had been touring on the Continent, Dorothy had completed a tour of her own and on her own. On 28 June she set sail from Whitehaven for the Isle of Man. Her object was twofold: to visit Joanna and Henry in Douglas, where they were living in lodgings, and to explore this most beautiful and unsung of British islands. Like Dora, she kept a journal, from which it is clear that, like many a visitor before and since, she arrived with few expectations and left with a lifelong passion for the island. It is one of the chief charms of the Isle of Man that many of her descriptions are as relevant today as they were in 1828: the people and language may have changed, but the place and spirit remain identifiably as she saw it. It is amusing, for instance, to find that she shared the modern visitor's perception of a place where time had stood still: Douglas reminded her 'of gentry life at Penrith 40 years back'. After spending nine days there, enjoying the busy social life of the eclectic expatriate community, she set off on a pedestrian circuit of the island. Her companions were Henry and Willy, who had also come across for a holiday. Joanna, who had dislocated her hip in a fall on the quay in December 1826, was too lame to accompany them, but Dorothy, despite her fifty-six years, was in fine fettle. 'I can walk 15 miles as briskly as ever I did in my life', she had boasted in February, and now she would prove it, completing her circuit of the island in only four days. Unaccustomed to the sight of a woman pedestrian, the Manxmen were 'astonished', and Dorothy noted with great pride that the wife of a pot-house keeper at Dalby Glen had remarked, 'that woman steps so light she's made for walking'. Peel, on the west coast, with its romantic, rose-hued castle on an island severed from the mainland cliffs by a sliver of wild sea, was her favourite place, despite the sickening sight and smell of the herring catch, but she was 'bewitched' by the little thatched cottage, tucked away in a quiet glen leading down to the sea, where she stayed at Ramsay. Her visit to the Isle of Man was all too brief, a mere month, but she returned with such favourable impressions that it would not be long before her brother followed in her footsteps.[49]

'The two Poets and their amiable Daughter', as Dora put it, returned to England a month after Dorothy, arriving on Quillinan's accommodating doorstep in London on 6 August. As a result of having mischievously persuaded her father that he had taken an ague during a day of pouring rain in Rotterdam, Dora was able to brag, 'I have made the best travellor of the trio'. Tempting though it was to linger in London, Mary had been stranded so long at Whitwick that her husband and daughter did not dare to leave her there any longer. The day after their return, they sent notes to the Aders, thanking them for their hospitality at Godesberg, and to Robinson, telling him his carpetbag was at the Custom-House, and called at Blomfield's London address to congratulate him on his elevation from the bishopric of Chester to London. William also had to fend off William Jerdan, editor of the *Literary Gazette*, who wanted him to contribute a piece about his Continental tour. The two men had met some weeks earlier and Jerdan had been both surprised and impressed by William's lively and entertaining description of his visit to the Italian opera the night before.

His remarks on the singing and his limning of the limbs of the dancers, were as replete with shrewdness and pleasantry as anything I ever heard from the most witty and graphic lips. I was so charmed with both the matter and manner, that I wrote immediately to offer *carte blanche* for his correspondence, from the continent . . . Had he complied with my wish, and written letters in the tone and spirit of the criticisms on the opera, I am sure the public would have had a variation in the style of Wordsworth which would greatly have surprised it, little anticipating that the tender poet could also be the grotesque delineator of individual peculiarities, and humorous caricaturist of social anomalies.

Despite the *carte blanche*, William could not be persuaded. 'You over[r]ate my powers of amusing and my opportunities in supposing any thing observed by me, could have interested your Readers'. When Jerdan persisted, William good-humouredly put him in his place. 'There is an obstacle in the way of my ever producing any thing of this kind, viz – idleness, – and yet another which is an affair of taste. Periodical writing, in order to strike, must be ambitious – and this style is, I think, in the record of Tours or Travels intolerable – or at any rate the worst that can be chosen.'[50]

After a fortnight spent at Whitwick, where they were reunited with Mary, and found John happy in the discharge of his duties, the travellers returned to Rydal Mount on 27 August. It was almost exactly a year since Mary and Dora had left home. They arrived just in time for the annual Keswick and Windermere regattas, with all the balls and fêtes attendant on them. Nor were they too late for the summer visitors who flocked to Rydal, the most eminent of whom was Andrews Norton, Professor of Sacred Theology at Harvard, and brother-in-law of an earlier American visitor, George Ticknor. Dr Bell, founder of the Madras System, also made an appearance and, personally, was as welcome as ever. William, however, had undergone a profound change of opinion with regard to the Madras System, probably as a result of Willy's experiences at Charterhouse. It was supposed to encourage moral discipline, and it clearly taught reading and writing more quickly than the old dame schools. Where it failed, he now believed, was in promoting rote-learning at the expense of understanding. 'Wherein does it encourage the imaginative feelings, without which the practical understanding is of little avail, and too apt to become the cunning slave of bad passions?' he asked. His objections were particularly strong where the pupils were girls. Anticipating the heated debate of 'the Woman Question' by twenty years, William foresaw the problem of educating girls so that they acquired skills and knowledge which the current state of society debarred them from using.

What is the use of pushing on the education of girls so fast, and mainly by the stimulus of Emulation, who, to say nothing worse of her, is cousin-german to Envy? What are you to do with these girls? What demand is there for the ability that they may have prematurely acquired? Will they not be indisposed to bend to any kind of hard labour or drudgery? And yet many of them must submit to it, or do wrong.

The old-fashioned dame school, for all its faults, was better than 'all Dr Bell's sour-looking teachers in petticoats that I have ever seen'.[51]

The great error of all such systems, William believed, was to confuse education with tuition, sacrificing all that life and nature teach to the little that could be learned from books and teachers. 'What more sacred law of nature, for instance, than that the mother should educate her child?' he argued. 'Yet we felicitate ourselves upon the establishment of infant schools which is in direct opposition to it.' No wonder the streets of a certain Lancashire town at about nine in the morning 'resound with the crying of infants, wheeled off in carts and other vehicles . . . to their school-prisons'. Why sharpen the intellect, he asked, if, in the process, the affections were blunted?

> In the present generation I cannot see anything of an harmonious co-operation between these schools and home influences. If the family be thoroughly bad, and the child cannot be removed altogether, how feeble the barrier, how futile the expedient! If the family be of middle character, the children will lose more by separation from domestic cares and reciprocal duties than they can possibly gain from captivity, with such formal instruction as may be administered.[52]

The Madras System had clearly failed Willy. All his father's attempts to find him a situation had been fruitless; there were no opportunities in business, though William tried as far afield as America, and even the mighty Lowthers could not identify a suitable opening in a government office. There was nothing for it but to fall back on the idea of sending him to university. 'He *must* go somewhere, and where could he be better; whether as qualifying him in a general way for the world, and for any office that might prove vacant; or in the end for the Church[?]' William was not unaware of the irony that he was now considering a career in the Church as a last resort for his son, but he vainly hoped that John's example might encourage his brother to undergo a change of heart.[53]

Before Willy could go to university, however, he required a more intensive course of study than his father, brother or Carter could offer him. To Willy's delight, a foreign education proved more easy to find than an opening in foreign commerce. Just before Christmas, the Wordsworth network managed to locate a Mr Papendick, the British vice-consul in Bremen, a town in the north-west corner of Germany. Not only was he the English master in a school, but he took a few boarding pupils himself; Willy would have the opportunity to learn both the classics and modern languages. The Wordsworths jumped at the opportunity, and it was agreed that when Papendick came over to England in April, Willy would return with him for two years. In the meantime, like Mr Micawber, they hoped something would turn up.[54]

Something had turned up for John. At the beginning of December, Lord Lonsdale offered him the living of Moresby, a small village on the coast between Whitehaven and Workington. It was an infinitely preferable posting to Whitwick, despite the fact that a new coalfield was planned there, and John had no hesitation in accepting. His rector, Merewether, graciously agreed to allow him to give up his curacy on condition that he remain at Whitwick for a further six months, until a replacement could be found. His Aunt Dorothy, who had been with him since the middle of November, was happy to stay. 'In fact, if he had continued here another winter, I should have done so also; as, in the first place, I am more useful than I could be anywhere else, and, in the second, am very comfortable.'[55] It was a long time since Dorothy had been in sole charge of a household, and she clearly relished this Whitwick reincarnation of keeping house for her brother at Town End. One wonders if it ever occurred to her that she was now, at the age of fifty-seven, finally realizing her youthful dream of living in a country parsonage, albeit with her nephew, rather than her brother.

Sara, too, had left Rydal Mount for the winter. After recurrent attacks of spitting blood, it was thought wise that she should take advantage of the milder climate of Herefordshire. As one invalid left, her place was taken by another, her sister Joanna, who was still very lame two years after her accident, and had great hopes that Carr, the Ambleside physician, might be able to cure her.[56] Amidst all these comings and goings, and the uncertainties over his sons' futures, William's poetic confidence also deserted him. 'I have not written a verse these 9 months past –', he wrote miserably on 11 November, 'my vein I fear is run out.' What was almost worse was that the sale of his new edition of *Poetical Works* was now threatened from an unexpected source. A Parisian publisher, Galignani, had taken advantage of the absence of international copyright law to print a pirated edition of William's own five volumes, reduced to a single volume, for which the author received nothing. Selling at only twenty francs, it was a mere third or quarter of the price of Longman's edition. It was not the first time that this had happened. A publisher in Boston, Cummings, Hilliard & Co., had printed a pirated copy of William's works in four volumes in 1824. America was too far away to influence the sale of the legitimate edition, but, as the disconsolate poet gloomily remarked, 'Everybody goes to Paris nowadays', and not everybody was as high-minded as Robinson, who declined to purchase a copy on principle. When William's nephew John inquired in a couple of Parisian bookshops, he was told that it sold 'Etonnament'.[57] Galignani did send a beautifully got-up presentation copy, which William was forced to admit had been printed with admirable accuracy, but it was 'a poor Compensation for his Piracy'.

> But how can we expect that foreign Nations will respect our literary property when our laws of copy right are so shamefully unjust. – Hereafter – a remedy must be applied to this grievance – the law as it now stands, as to the point of duration of copy right is a premium upon bookmaking and mediocrity. My own Poems have been thirty years struggling up hill . . . Were I to die tomorrow, my Mss – whatever might be their advantage to Booksellers, would in 28 years time be of no value to my Children or their descendants.[58]

Urging Robinson, as a lawyer and a man of letters, to reflect and write in the periodicals on this subject, William sounded the first clarion-call in a campaign to rectify the injustice to authors. He could not have foreseen that it would take fourteen years of intensive lobbying to achieve any satisfaction.

William's engagement with the *Keepsake* was also proving troublesome, not least because Watts, disappointed of a contribution for his own *Literary Souvenir*, had accused him of publicly recommending the *Keepsake* and running down other annuals. 'I never wrote or said a word in depreciation of any particular Annual in my life', William responded indignantly. 'How he could think me capable of anything so presumptuous, so ungentlemanly, and so *ungenerous*, I cannot conceive. I was offended – and did not reply.' William had another, more serious, reason to regret his engagement to the *Keepsake*. In December Reynolds wrote to inform him that the poems he had supplied fell '*very short*' of the stipulated agreement for between twelve and fifteen pages. William hastened to assure him he would have no cause for complaint, the deficit would be made up. He was therefore not best pleased to discover, when he at last saw a copy (two months after publication), that Reynolds had printed only five of his poems, rejecting four sonnets which would have brought his contribution well within the contract limits. In the circumstances, he showed remarkable restraint. 'Now I care nothing about my Contributions being inserted – I mean on the score of personal vanity – but I certainly don't expect that a claim for more should be grounded upon rejection, for you clearly see, if this principle be admitted – I might write on for ever, before my part of the Contract were fulfilled.'[59]

With this experience in mind, William tried hard to impress upon Hartley Coleridge, who was a constant visitor to Rydal Mount in the winter of 1828–9, the importance of making sound business arrangements with his publishers. Hartley had given up his school at Ambleside and, for the past three years, had been struggling to earn his living as a writer for the magazines. Mary was uncharacteristically harsh in describing him as 'doing nothing', but William was more supportive. He could not condone Hartley's predilection for getting drunk in local pot-houses, disappearing for weeks on end and failing to keep his engagements, but insisted, 'I believe he writes a good deal, and always what is clever and interesting'. He tried to help the young man by recommending him to editors of the annuals, but Hartley suffered exactly the same fate as himself, having three of the four sonnets he wrote for the *Gem* rejected. As William observed to the young man, editors should not have this power of selecting and rejecting: they should agree for a certain number of sheets and pay for what they received. He also passed on another useful piece of advice, founded on experience. Hartley should stop writing poems in albums on request; it was wasted labour. While he had 'a debt unpaid or any hesitation about a new suit he must be economic in this way'.[60]

After a long fallow period – and indeed within weeks, if not days, of bemoaning the fact that his 'vein had run dry' – William suddenly embarked on a new poem. It was new in every sense, for it was his first (and thankfully his last) excursion into Arthurian romance. *The Egyptian Maid; or, The Romance of the Water Lily*, described how a fair Egyptian princess, shipwrecked through the malevolence of Merlin, is brought back to life by the touch of Sir Galahad. His ability to do this, where other knights had failed, identified him as the one chosen, by divine will, to be her husband. 'It rose from my brain, without let or hindrance, like a vapour', William wrote happily on 25 November, when he had completed all 360 lines, though he would later admit that its halting metre was not well suited to narrative poetry. William intended the poem for the *Keepsake*, to make up the supposed shortfall in his contribution, but, having made his discovery about the rejected sonnets, he declined to send it, or indeed any further verses to Reynolds.[61]

Though *The Egyptian Maid* is not one of William's most memorable poems, it broke through his writer's block and prepared the way for what he considered one of his most important poems. This was his ode *On the Power of Sound*, which he began to compose in December, though it was not completed until some nine or ten months later. The high opinion William entertained of it was undoubtedly due to the fact that, from its inception, it was intended as part of *The Recluse*. 'During the last week I wrote some stanzas on the Power of Sound which ought to find a place in my larger work – if aught should ever come of that', he informed one friend on 15 December. A fortnight later Dora could boast that her father had done 'pretty well for a Man in his 59th year', having composed nearly 1,000 lines in the previous six or seven weeks.[62]

This sudden outpouring of poetry was brought to an abrupt end by a nasty accident. Running down from the mount, where he had been entertaining a small party of visitors, he caught his toe in the turf and was thrown head-first down to the bottom of the hill. 'He fell like a log of wood', his daughter observed; 'having one hand in his breast & the other in his Trowser's pocket he had no power of balancing or saving himself'. He landed on his head, gashing the bridge of his nose, giving himself a black eye and straining the muscles in his neck, which altered his voice, so that he sounded as if he had a cold. The leather front of his cap was broken in two by the force of the fall, but fortunately William himself was made of hardier stuff.[63]

Forced to withdraw temporarily from his books, William had time to contemplate what he would do next. He had plenty of ideas. He still felt 'inclined' to publish a short life of the poet James Thomson, prefixed to an edition of his works, an idea he had first conceived more than twenty-five years ago. He also wanted to publish what he rather grandly called 'an Account of the Deceased Poetesses of Great Britain – with an Estimate of their Works', a book which would have remedied what he perceived to be a great wrong. 'Neither Dr Johnson, nor Dr Anderson, nor Chalmers, nor the Editor I believe of any other Corpus of English Poetry takes the least notice of female Writers – this, to say nothing harsher, is very ungallant.' Regrettably, this remarkably modern idea remained only an idea: 'I still am of opinion that something is wanted upon the subject', he now told the editor to whom he had suggested it, '. . . but, for myself, I could not venture to undertake the employment, two requisites being wanting – Books (I mean access to Libraries) and industry to use them.'[64]

Increasingly, William had also to reject other people's ideas. Barron Field, about to leave England for a legal posting in Gibraltar, was anxious that he should write an Oriental poem 'as unlike "Lalla Rookh" as possible'. At William's request, he supplied him with a suitable story, that of a Brahmin who smashed a microscope rather than accept that it overturned traditional Hindu teaching about nature. William politely demurred. 'I have always thought that stories, where the scene is laid by our writers in distant climes, are mostly hurt, and often have their interest quite destroyed, by being overlaid with foreign imagery; as if the tale had been chosen for the sake of the imagery alone.' Another of his disciples, a young American schoolmistress, Elizabeth Peabody, begged him to do what 'no-one but yourself has power to do – write a volume for children'. Such a volume, she explained, would be the best means of developing the nobler side of children's nature. William again declined, pointing out, 'if I am to serve the very young by my writings, it must be by benefiting at the same time, those who are old enough to be their parents'.[65]

The idea that some of his existing poetry would be valuable for practical teaching purposes was continually urged on him from different quarters. William had nothing against this in principle; he had always believed that his poetry had a didactic moral purpose. The objections were twofold: first, publishing his poetic plums cheaply and separately from the rest would be the final kiss of death to his already beleaguered *Poetical Works*, and, second, as always, how to make the selection. An Edinburgh schoolmaster, James Dyer, succeeded in persuading William to sanction a selection he had made for schoolchildren, but the publisher wanted the right to all future editions of the work in perpetuity, which was completely unacceptable to the poet. The project fell through, though William suggested to Dyer that he would have no objection to his printing such an edition privately, for use at the Edinburgh Academy, and would happily forgo any financial claim himself to make it viable. Another attempt was made by Allan Cunningham, secretary to Francis Chantrey, and a poet and editor in his own right. Cunningham argued for a cheap edition to circulate among the Scottish peasantry and, like Dyer, was prepared to make the selection for William. Once again, however, the idea appears to have foundered on a failure to agree terms with a publisher – which was perhaps not surprising, since Cunningham approached the same Edinburgh house as Dyer. What is interesting about Cunningham's proposal is that he sketched out a preface, explaining exactly why he thought such an edition was necessary. William's poetry had been too long withheld 'from the lower classes of the community whose feelings and sympathies it appeared so well calculated to awaken'.

It is the object of this selection to place his poetry within the reach of the more simple and unsophisticated classes of the People – to lay before them a series of verses full of social and philosophical feeling – exhibiting manifold images of domestic love and home-bred enjoyment and counting nothing too humble in which the hand of God is seen and poetic emotions called forth.

Cunningham's actual selection, as revealed in his proposed table of contents, can have done little to reassure a poet who feared that his powers were declining. Out of thirty-eight poems, the vast majority were from *Lyrical Ballads*, and only three post-dated the 1807 edition of *Poems, in Two Volumes*. William's lack of enthusiasm for the project seems understandable: his entire poetic output of the last twenty years had been reduced to just two poems.[66]

Throughout the spring of 1829 William watched, with increasing dismay, as a Tory government, led by the Duke of Wellington and Sir Robert Peel, pushed the Roman Catholic Emancipation Act through stormy sessions in both Houses of Parliament. The act, which secured its final passage in June, allowed Catholics to vote, sit in Parliament and hold civil office, provided that they met the necessary property qualifications and took an oath of loyalty to the Constitution. It was undoubtedly an act of expediency, designed to alleviate the rising demands for Catholic equality, behind which loomed the spectre of rebellion in Ireland. This made it seem even more of a betrayal to those, like William, who opposed it root and branch, on moral, as well as practical, grounds. At the heart of his argument was his fear that the act would lead to the disestablishment of the Church of England. Rather touchingly, William naïvely believed that, because a Catholic's first duty was to obey the Pope, every Catholic was therefore absolutely committed to the restoration of papal supremacy in Britain. To ask a Catholic to take an oath to protect the Church of England was therefore '*monstrous*' and immoral, because it forced him to prefer a civil duty above a religious one. The proposal that the government would pay the salaries of Irish Catholic priests was similarly immoral, because it was a disingenuous attempt to bribe men of sacred calling to act contrary to their sense of duty. Sincere priests would find it impossible to accept such a salary, knowing it was granted with that expectation; the more worldly minded would simply take it, and continue to undermine the government, while pretending to support it. Once Catholics were admitted to civil office themselves, they would be morally obligated to disestablish the Church of England. All William's experience of travelling on the Continent, he declaimed, had taught him that it was impossible for the Catholic and Protestant Churches to share power in a free country and preserve Christian belief as a vital principle of action.[67]

As for the very real threat of civil war in Ireland (a country he had never visited), William argued that making concessions to the Catholics would not solve the problems there. 'The chief proximate causes of Irish misery and ignorance are twofold – Papacy and the tenure and management of landed Property'. His answer was simple, as those of theorists usually are. The Catholic clergy should be prevented from punishing any of their flock found in possession of the Bible or attending Protestant churches, and the consolidation of Protestant parishes should be reversed, so that Protestant clergymen were more in evidence throughout the country. First and foremost, however, the security of person and property should be re-established, if necessary by military force, so that absentee landlords would return, rents would be kept within the country and a flow of 'English Arts, Manners, refinements and aspirations' into Ireland would be encouraged. In time, William believed, 'the grovelling Peasantry' of Ireland would realize the 'Social blessings which Protestants have acquired by being delivered from Spiritual thraldom', be encouraged to accumulate property and therefore be less liable to become the tools of political and religious agitators.[68]

There was little William could do to oppose the Catholic Emancipation Act, but that little he did, to his utmost. He wrote to his old friend Blomfield, Bishop of London, for instance, putting his case as strongly as he dared, and entreating the bishops to stand firm in the House of Lords. And, in common with Anglican clergymen and laymen throughout the country, he was personally responsible for organizing a local petition against the passing of the act. 'I cannot . . . conceal from you, that during this Spring I have been in very bad Spirits for what has been done,' he told John's vicar, Merewether,

> and still more [is it inexcus]able for the manner in which it has been done – it has been utterly without candour and dignity . . . Every day brings additional proof that the Institutions of the Country are losing ground in the favour of those who are the most ready to meddle with public business. And it seems to me next to impossible that the now existing order of Society can be preserved in Great Britain, unless our public Schools and Universities pursue a course of education more adopted to the exigencies of the times. We go on at full speed, teaching the Poor gr[ammar] as if there could be any Security for a State in that, while the Rich are no better taught – I mean not more wisely taught than they now are.

To an older friend, Basil Montagu, he confided similar fears, adding that the Liberals in his neighbourhood told him that the mind of the nation had outgrown its institutions: 'rather say, I reply, that it has shrunk and dwindled from them, as the body of a sick man does from his clothes'. Quillinan, a Catholic, and naturally a supporter of the act, could not resist teasing his gloomy friends at Rydal Mount and Brinsop Court.

> I am sorry you are such an intolerant set . . . but you will learn charity from the papists in time; especially after we have had a few holy bonfires on Penenden Heath near Maidstone, & Martyr's Field near Canterbury, where the chiefs of the Brunswick Heresy [i.e. Protestants] are to be boiled, broiled, grilled, roasted, or stewed, according to the pleasure of His Holiness the Sovereign Pontiff.[69]

It was not a happy spring in other respects. William was very anxious about Dora, who, having spent the winter at Rydal Mount, had been afflicted with persistent colds. As Sara Coleridge observed, she had also an 'unpleasant, obstinate cough' which 'often drives him out upon the terrace when he would otherwise make one of the social circle: I suppose this cough has an ominous sound to him but I trust his apprehensions will prove ground less'. After a trouble-free two years, and more, William also suffered three consecutive attacks of trachoma, of increasing severity, within two months, culminating in a large abscess on his eyelid. Unable to read or write, and forced to leave off composition, he tried to bear his privations patiently, but the same east wind which he believed had caused the initial inflammation claimed another victim.[70]

On 3 April Dorothy, who had never suffered a day's serious illness in her life, was suddenly struck down with one of those irritatingly vague nineteenth-century illnesses which William described as an 'internal inflammation' and Dorothy, probably more accurately, as 'Cholera morbus'. She and John had both had influenza, but a week before her attack Dorothy had paid a round of visits to the parish sick of Whitwick, including a poor woman and a child, both of whom she described as 'very ill'. Whether she caught something from them or had some chronic illness of her own, for forty-eight hours she suffered agonies of griping pain in her bowels, sickness and violent perspirations, both hot and cold. 'The old women at my bedside talked to each other as if quite sure I *must* die', she later recalled. Fortunately, Willy had been at Whitwick since 6 March and, according to his grateful aunt, he proved 'the tenderest nurse possible'. By the time Mary arrived, on the first available coach, the crisis had passed, but Dorothy was left so weak she could scarcely speak, let alone stand, and it was a full month before she was able to do anything more than potter round the house and garden. 'I never can forget what I suffered myself nor the anxiety of those around me', she wrote at the beginning of May; 'I never before had an opportunity of knowing how much some distant Friends care about me – Friends abroad – Friends at home – all have been anxious – and more so, far more I am sure, than I deserved; but I attribute much of this to my having been so remarkably strong and healthy, it came like a shock to every one, to be told of a dangerous illness having attacked me.' It was a sentiment her brother echoed feelingly. 'What a shock that was to our poor hearts. Were She to depart the Phasis of my Moon would be robbed of light to a degree that I have not courage to think of.'[71]

The doctors assured them that relapses in this kind of illness were rare and, by the second week in May, Dorothy was well enough for Mary to feel able to return home. Willy had departed the day before, to visit his uncle and cousins at Cambridge, and spend a few days in London with Quillinan, before embarking for Bremen.[72] Ominously, he spent this time partying, ran up a bill of more than £20 on clothes, borrowed £5 from Quillinan and assured his father that George Huntly Gordon, through whose good offices the Bremen place had been obtained, agreed that he should not study Greek, 'as it will be entirely a waste of time unless I had made great progress indeed & unnecessary if I do not go to the University'. Arriving in Bremen on 4 June, he immediately sought permission to buy a coat and boots and to hire a horse, 'it is such wretched work walking'. There was no fear of his losing his heart in Germany, he informed his Aunt Sara shortly afterwards, as there were no pretty faces and the ladies there were all 'sad unlicked cubs'; in fact, 'as Father would say, I have not seen one kissable Lady since I left England'. His progress was slow –'I still find much difficulty in reading German from my excessive want of breath' – but he was proud and pleased to be pointed out, wherever he went, 'as the Poet Wordsworth's (the pronunciation of this darling word they can't get for their lives) son'.[73] His letters are extremely entertaining, as, indeed, they were meant to be, but they do not suggest the sort of single-minded application to study which would justify the expense of his residence in Germany.

On 22 June John and Dorothy said their farewells to their kind friends the Merewethers and Lady Beaumont and set out for Halifax, where Dorothy had reluctantly agreed to pay a visit to her 'aunt', Elizabeth Rawson. Only the knowledge that her 'aunt' was so old, and had been newly widowed, persuaded Dorothy to relinquish her intention of going straight to Rydal, for she was longing to be home after such a long absence. She was also in a very delicate state of health. Lady Beaumont was so concerned that she wrote to warn William that he would have to watch his sister carefully, as she could not bear any excitement or fatigue. Earlier in the month (despite the doctors' assurances), she had suffered a severe relapse, brought on by taking too long a walk in cold weather and Lady Beaumont had had to carry her off to Coleorton Hall to be nursed back to strength again. Exactly the same thing was to happen in Halifax, for, as Lady Beaumont warned, when Dorothy was cheerful she was apt to forget her changed state of health. The social life of Halifax was too enticing to be ignored, and after a month of daily visiting and a walk up on to the moors to the reservoir, she collapsed with another 'severe tho' short' bout of illness.[74]

It was not Dorothy, however, but Lady Beaumont herself who died, suddenly, a mere three weeks after they had parted at Coleorton. It was a painful shock to the Wordsworths, as William wrote in his letter of condolence to her husband's cousin and heir, the new Sir George. 'It is seven and twenty years since I first became acquainted with the lamented Pair whom we have lost. We soon became united in affectionate intercourse, which has known no abatement, but our friendship rather strengthened with time, and will survive in my heart till it ceases to beat.' It went without saying that everyone expected a suitable poetic tribute from William: 'I have only to say that to make any promise of the kind would be the surest way of defeating the object altogether –', William responded. 'You may be assured however generally that if I live and have health and spirits to write verses, a tribute will not be wanting, some where or other, among my works to the Memory of so dear a friend and so excellent a person'.[75]

Dorothy returned to Rydal Mount on 8 September, just in time to welcome Sara Coleridge's bridal party from Keswick. The 'Celestial Blue' was now 'quietly *happy* and chearful – and not abstracted as she often used to be'. Five days earlier, she had at last become Mrs Henry Coleridge, marrying her cousin after a lengthy engagement. Dora, and Sara's three Southey cousins, Edith, Bertha and Kate, were among the eight bridesmaids, and John Wordsworth officiated at the ceremony. The newlyweds, accompanied by an uncomfortable Dora, who did not appreciate playing gooseberry, honeymooned in the Lakes and stayed twice at Rydal Mount. The second visit was a momentous one, for it closed another chapter in the Coleridge family's life in the Lakes. With both Sara and Derwent married, there was no longer any reason why their mother should remain at Greta Hall. She had come to Keswick most reluctantly, and would leave it with even deeper regret, but her home in the future would lie with her son, in Cornwall, and, ultimately, her daughter in London. Only one Coleridge would remain in the Lakes, 'li'l Hartley', gifted but flawed, son of a gifted but flawed father. And like his father, he could not face an emotional parting from his mother, disappearing before she arrived at Rydal Mount and not reappearing till she had gone. Deeply sensitive to his own failings and peculiarities, he concluded, 'I remain alone, bare and barren and blasted, ill omen'd and unsightly as Wordsworth's melancholy thorn on the bleak hill-top. So hath it been ordain'd, and it is well.' It was not well, for he would never see her again, and the knowledge that he had avoided this chance to say goodbye would haunt him for the rest of his life.[76]

Within a month of returning to Rydal, Dorothy had again to take to her bed with a recurrence of all the symptoms which had first attacked her at Whitwick. 'There *were* times when I could neither read nor listen to reading – much less employ my hands in sewing or any thing else – and I could not stand for a minute together even leaning upon another.' It would be a fortnight before she would be fit enough to walk around the house, fighting against weakness and 'unconquerable stiffness', and she could not go outside, unless she was pushed in a bath-chair, or driven in a carriage by family or friends.[77] As she approached her fifty-eighth birthday, it was apparent to them all, Dorothy herself included, that her constitution was shattered. There would be no more foreign tours, no more excursions and no more walking fifteen miles a day. William's 'exquisite sister' had become a permanent invalid.

22. *Furiously Alarmist*

Dorothy's illness prevented William fulfilling a promise, made more than thirty years earlier, that he would take her on a tour of North Wales. Even when she recovered, she was obviously not physically capable of the exertion of a Wordsworthian tour. He toyed with the idea of accompanying Joanna and Henry Hutchinson to Norway. 'As far as I look back I discern in my mind imaginative traces of Norway:' he told Robinson; 'the people are said to be simple, and worthy, the *Nature* is magnificent'. With the passage of the Roman Catholic Emancipation Act, however, there was only one place he felt he should go, and that was Ireland.[1]

Two years earlier he had met a young Irishman, William Rowan Hamilton, a brilliant mathematician, polyglot and poet who, at twenty-two, was already Professor of Astronomy at Trinity College, Dublin. With two friends, Alexander Nimmo, a civil engineer, and Caesar Otway, a Church of Ireland clergyman, Hamilton had visited Rydal Mount in September 1827 and struck up an instant rapport with William. Despite the disparity in their ages, each man was dazzled by the talents of the other. They had spent all evening together conversing, then, reluctant to part, took a midnight walk together, 'for a long, long time, *without any companion* except the stars and our own burning thoughts and words', as Hamilton put it. William afterwards wrote, 'Seldom have I parted – never I was going to say with one whom after so short an acquaintance, I lost sight of with more regret. I trust we shall meet again'. On his return to Dublin, Hamilton sent William a poem he had written at Ambleside, prompting an intelligent and sympathetic critique from the poet which ensured that the correspondence would continue.[2]

When William decided to go to Ireland, he immediately turned to Hamilton for advice: 'I am ignorant of so many points, as where to begin, whether it be safe at this *rioting* period, what is best worth seeing, what mode of travelling will furnish the greatest advantages at the least expence.' A prompt and helpful reply encouraged him and he laid tentative plans to go with Dora in August, but, at the last minute, he got cold feet. 'I dread the risks as to health, the fatigue, and the expenses of taking Dora and the long sea sickness.' Luckily, his old friend John Marshall, of Hallsteads, had planned a visit to Ireland himself, with his son, James, and offered William a place in his carriage.[3] The little party set off from Kendal on 25 August, travelling on a nostalgic route through North Wales to Holyhead, where they took the ferry across the Irish sea to Dublin. For several days before they sailed, there had been terrific storms and at least two ships were wrecked at Whitehaven, but William was blessed with a calm voyage, arriving in Dublin on 30 August. While the Marshalls spent a leisurely three days exploring the city, William took up residence with Hamilton at the Observatory, just outside Dublin, and embarked on a whirlwind series of social engagements and tourist visiting, 'all the public buildings inside and out; Trinity College its Hall, Library Various MSS – etc., including the Fagel collection 20,000 Volumes for which during the French Revolution the College gave between 8 and ten thousand pounds – the Bank formerly the Parliament House etc., etc.'[4]

It was a visit that was even more exhausting mentally than physically. 'Mr Hamilton is a most interesting person quite a man of Genius and always very lively – but I was over stimulated; and could not have stood it long.' The over-stimulation did not make itself apparent to his host's family, who were charmed with the poet's 'slight touch of rusticity and constraint about his perfect gentlemanliness of manner ... everything he said and did had an unaffected simplicity and dignity, and peacefulness of thought that were very striking'. Once again, by reading his poems aloud, in his sonorous voice and dignified manner, he succeeded in winning over an audience which, if not actually hostile, had not been predisposed in his favour. Eliza, Hamilton's sister and a poetess herself, commented, 'everything of his I had thought silly took the beautiful colouring of a wondrous benevolence, that could descend through love to the least and most insignificant things ... I think it would be quite impossible for anyone who had once been in Wordsworth's company ever again to think anything he has written silly.'[5]

On the third day William rejoined the Marshalls and they set off, in their private carriage, on a five-week clockwise tour of Ireland, which would take them through 'all the crack places of the Wicklow Mountains and Country – the Devils glen excepted', Wexford, Waterford, Cork, Limerick, Sligo, Londonderry, the Giant's Causeway, Antrim and Belfast. 'You cannot guess how hard I work to see and hear all I can', William wrote from Enniskillen. 'I am never in bed later than half after five, and often rise at five.' On one occasion, he and James Marshall

> breakfasted at 5, set off from Kenmare at half past, rode 10 Irish miles, took to our feet, ascended nearly 15,00 feet, descended as much, ascended another ridge as high, descended as much, and then went to the top of Carrantuohill, 3000 feet, the mountain being the highest in Ireland, 3410 feet above the level of the sea. We then descended, walked nearly two hours, and rode on bad horses an hour and a half or more, and reached Killarney at ten at night, having

eaten nothing but a poor breakfast of spongy bread without eggs and one crust of the same quality, and drank milk during the whole day. I reached Killarney neither tired nor exhausted after all this. We were richly recompensed by a fine day, and most sublime views.

This was by no means an untypical day, as William's purpose in rising early was to explore the country on foot before the Marshalls set off on the next stage of the journey in their carriage. Not only was this a preferable way of seeing the scenery, but it gave him a much-needed opportunity to meet and converse with the Irish people, for, despite his prejudice against Catholicism, he was anxious to see and learn for himself. And he was pleasantly surprised. At St Kevin's Pool, in County Wicklow, he was deeply moved by the sight of a peasant woman bearing her sickly child in order to dip him nine times in the holy waters in the hope of a cure. 'It would have affected you very much to see this poor confiding creature – and to hear the manner in which she expressed her faith in the goodness of God and St Kevin', William told his brother. 'What would one not give to see among protestants such devout reliance on the mercy of their Creator, so much resignation, so much piety – so much simplicity and singleness of mind, purged of the accompanying Superstitions[?]' Talking to the ordinary people, he discovered that the Catholics among them believed that Protestants were attached to their religion by personal interest, not genuine conviction. Much to his surprise, he also discovered that they spoke well of their priests; 'this was not so in Italy where the commonalty treated them with derision'. When he asked them what they hoped to gain from Catholics being eligible to sit in Parliament, the universal response was to be relieved of Church rates and for tithes to be apportioned between the two churches. After mixing with many Catholics among the wealthy, educated classes, he was also forced to the conclusion that he had overestimated their desire to exalt their Church at the expense of the Protestant establishment. When he reported home comments by Lord Lorton's brother, that 'the country [was] more unquiet than ever, and [that he] forbode the very worst from Catholic bigotry and intolerance in alliance with political Demagogues', William added an important caveat: 'But remember Lord Lorton and his family are Brunswickers [Protestant hard-liners] of the first water.'[6]

William returned to Rydal Mount on 11 October with much matter for thought, but none for poetry. Out of all the sights he had seen, only one, admittedly magnificent, image, that of a pair of eagles off Fairhead Promontory, in County Antrim, found its way into a poem (on Scotland!) two years later.

> The last I saw
> Was on the wing; stooping, he struck with awe
> Man, bird, and beast; then, with a consort paired,
> From a bold headland, their loved aery's guard,
> Flew high above Atlantic waves, to draw
> Light from the fountain of the setting sun.

William was later ashamed of 'this want of notices, in my verse, of a country so interesting', ascribing it to lack of time, due to the shortness of the autumnal days and speed at which he had travelled. This was not true, as is clear from his enthusiastic and detailed observations of both people and scenery in his letters home. What is undoubtedly true is that politics, rather than poetry, had always been uppermost in his mind, and above all else the apparently insoluble problem of Irish poverty. 'The subject of the Poor Laws was never out of my sight whilst I was in Ireland', he admitted on his return. Though it was a system he favoured in principle, he now realized that it simply would not work in Ireland: there were too many poor with equal claims for relief, and not enough people of sufficient income to support or administer it.[7]

As usual after a tour, he had some thoughts of composing a guidebook, because the existing ones were 'sorry things, and mislead by their exaggerations'.

> If I were a younger man and could prevail upon an able Artist to accompany me, there are few things I should like better than giving a month or six weeks to explore the County of Kerry only. A judicious topographical work on that district would be really useful both for the Lovers of Nature and the Observers of manners. As to the Giants Causeway and the Coast of Antrim you cannot get wrong; there the interests obtrude themselves on every ones notice.

This was just an idle dream, however, for he had more important things to do. His spat with Reynolds over his contributions to the *Keepsake* had turned into a full-scale war, which William was also fighting on behalf of others, most notably Southey. Reynolds had not responded to his repeated requests for the return of his unpublished sonnets. Not only was he holding them over, claiming the right 'to spread a *one* years contribution over *two* or *twenty* if he pleases', but he refused to pay William, on the grounds that he had not fulfilled his contractual obligation.[8] 'I am properly served for having had any connection with such things –', William admitted. 'My only excuse is that they offered me a very liberal sum, and that I have laboured hard through a long life without more pecuniary emolument, than a Lawyer gets for two special retainers, or a public performer sometimes for two or three songs.' Though he was resigned to his own folly, and the loss of the 200 guineas he had expected for two years' contributions, William would not give up the battle for his precious manuscripts. He applied polite, but unrelenting, pressure until Reynolds finally cracked. All the manuscripts, apart from two sonnets which had been 'mislaid', were returned at the end of October. William would have nothing more to do with the 'venal' trade of writing for annuals, letting slip a bitter tirade to his friend and fellow sufferer, Rogers, against 'those greedy receptacles of trash, those Bladders upon which the Boys of Poetry try to swim'.[9]

As Quillinan, the last of the summer visitors, took his leave, the annual cry went up from Rydal Mount. 'He does intend to fall to the "Recluse" being seriously impressed with the faith that very soon it must be too late (His next Birth day will be his 60th)', Dorothy wrote hopefully to her Cambridge nephews,

– but, in the mean time he has been busy with less important matters, polishing the small poems he wrote last year, and actually he has written another *Sonnet*! This we were not glad of, fearing it might be but the beginning as heretofore, of a *Batch*: he has, however, promised that he will write no more. Now I should have little faith in this promise, if it were not plain that his mind is set upon doing its best at the great Work.[10]

William began by altering and, ominously, completing *On the Power of Sound.* 'We all think there is a grandeur in this Poem', Dora wrote, 'but it ought to have been in the "Recluse" & Mother on that account but half enjoys it'. The frustration of all the Wordsworth females would only increase, as Dora explained, a month later.

Aunt & I are exceedingly anxious something were done towards forwarding the printing of these small Poems, for till they are out of the way we feel convinced, his great work will never be touched & every day he finds something to alter or new stanzas to add – or a fresh Sonnet – or a fresh Poem growing out of one just finished – which he always promises shall be the last –.

Even Dorothy – especially Dorothy – was perplexed by William's failure to engage with *The Recluse.* 'He is still the crack skater on Rydal Lake,' she boasted on 9 January 1830,

and, as to climbing of mountains, the hardiest and the youngest are yet hardly a match for him. In composition I can see no failure, and his imagination seems as vigorous as in youth; yet he shrinks from his great work, and both during the last and present winter has been employed in writing small poems . . . in the course of man's life, but a few years of vigorous health and strength can be allotted to him. For this reason, my sister and I take every opportunity of pressing upon him the necessity of applying to his great work, and this he feels, resolves to do it, and again resolution fails. And now I almost fear habitually, that it will be ever so.[11]

It was the first time any of the Wordsworths had voiced the fear that *The Recluse* might never be written. Even William had not yet admitted this to himself, though in his heart of hearts he must have known that he no longer had the necessary energy, or, indeed, poetic powers.

Christmas at Rydal Mount was a relatively quiet affair this year. Sara and Joanna, who were expected on Christmas Eve, did not arrive until New Year's Eve. John could not be spared from his duties at Moresby and Willy was still in Germany, where he had taken up smoking (not *much*, he hastened to assure his father, who loathed the habit), playing billiards 'a gentlemanly game', and had generously reconciled himself to his greatest expense, attending the theatre, because he learned 'a great deal of german there'. He had abandoned the classics, and, at his father's suggestion, was now studying mathematics, drawing and architecture, in addition to modern languages, in preparation for a career as a landscape gardener. Willy had been honest enough to admit he did not particularly like the proposal, as there was not much prospect of making money, and he felt it was 'somewhat beneath' him, but Papendick agreed with William that it was the only respectable profession where Willy could enjoy the outdoor life he craved.[12]

Unfortunately, it was a profession better suited to his father, who, as soon as the winter snows had cleared, threw aside his poetical labours with obvious relief and began 'draining a bit of spungy ground' to build a new terrace at Rydal Mount. This would be a third terrace, below the two in front of the house and at the top of the Rash field, which he had bought when he thought he might have to build. 'I am making a green Terrace, that commands a beautiful view over our two Lakes Rydal and Windermere, and more than two miles of intervening vale with the stream visible by glimpses, flowing through it', he declared, with evident pride. The principal object was to create additional, accessible walks within the grounds for the family invalids, in particular Dorothy, so that she could enjoy 'a very great length of walk with constant variety of slope and level, and prospect'.[13]

Supervising the workmen, and sometimes wielding a spade himself, were therapeutic employments for William as, on 7 April, he reached the milestone of his sixtieth birthday. 'I have given over writing verses till my head becomes stronger or my fancy livelier', he informed his daughter a few weeks later. A new edition of his poems would soon be needed and William could not decide what to do. Dorothy had no doubts. 'We females wish him to publish the numerous poems now in store immediately, in one small volume, that they may have a Boom, and the Edition get sold off before the 5 vols. are again printed'. The new volume could then be incorporated with the complete poems, like the *River Duddon*, *Ecclesiastical Sketches* and *Memorials of a Tour*. William was not convinced. 'Now in his heart, he approves of our plan;' Dorothy added, 'but his aversion to publication at all, is so great that he *will not* resolve to do it, and would much rather smuggle the new ones in among the rest, as he did before, and thus get nothing for them.' There was also a third way. 'A much better plan than this would be to publish nothing new, and let the whole remain for the benefit of his Family after death.'[14]

William dithered, deciding first of all that he would go ahead with a single volume, then, much to Dora's frustration, as her father had promised that she could be the sole amanuensis for this publication, that it would be more prudent to wait until the *Poetical Works* was almost sold out.[15] His reluctance to publish was not just for the usual reasons, dislike of the trouble and fear of critical reaction. Since publishing his last edition, he had come to realize that public taste was changing. Books, even books of poetry, were no longer the preserve of a minority of wealthy purchasers. The runaway success of the cheap pirated copies of his works in France and America, combined with that of the annuals, which Southey wittily called 'picture-books for grown children', had shown that there was a voracious market for poetry. When yet another reader, a complete stranger, John Gardner, wrote to inform him that the pirated Galignani edition was being widely sold in England, and urged him to publish a cheap edition of his own, he merely confirmed what had already become a growing conviction. 'I am inclined to think with my Friend Mr Southey that shortly few books will be published except low-priced ones, or those that are highly ornamented, for persons who delight in such luxuries.'[16]

Inquiries at Longman's revealed that they had little enthusiasm for the idea of a cheap edition, maintaining the traditional line that purchasers of poetry were 'of that class who do not regard prices'. William's experience had taught him otherwise – and he had been listening to what his readers told him. 'My Poetry, less than any other of the day, is adapted to the taste of the Luxurious, and of those who value themselves upon the priviledge of wealth and station', he observed. 'And though it be true that several passages are too abstruse for the ordinary Reader, yet the main body of it is as well fitted (if my aim be not altogether missed) to the bulk of the people both in sentiment and language, as that of any of my contemporaries.' With or without his publisher's support, William had already decided that his next edition would have to be compressed into four volumes, simply to make the price more affordable. And when the young and enterprising Edward Moxon wrote, at the beginning of June, to inform him that he had left Longman's to set up on his own, William not only offered his active support for the venture but immediately inquired about the potential for a cheap edition of his poems.[17]

Early in June John sprang a surprise on his unsuspecting family by announcing that he was engaged to be married. It was, as his father commented laconically, a bold step, for John's income as rector of Moresby was a mere £100 a year. (What he did not say was that John was already living beyond it, having just purchased a horse, which he considered a necessary luxury 'for various reasons'. He had also cost his father more than £255 in the past two years, despite being employed for most of that period at Whitwick.) Fortunately, John's preference for heiresses had not deserted him and his intended bride was Isabella Curwen, oldest daughter of Henry Curwen, of Workington Hall and Belle Isle, on Windermere. 'The Father's allowance to his Daughter is so liberal as to remove every objection upon prudential grounds', William assured his brother. 'The young Lady is in her 23d year, bears the highest character for feminine virtues, and in her demeanour and appearance is truly engaging, but her health is, I grieve to say, delicate.'[18]

Dora, who knew Isabella from their schooldays at Miss Dowling's and had stayed with John at Moresby in the spring, had suspected an attachment, but William, who had dined and slept at Workington Hall only a few days before the announcement was made, had not. Given that Isabella's grandfather, John Curwen, had been an outspoken political opponent of the Lowthers for many years, it was something of a relief to find that her father had no taste for active politics. After only a couple of meetings, William's verdict on his new relation was positive: 'he is a man of extensive reading, accurate memory, and very intelligent: His habits are those of a retired Man, and I like him the better on that account.' The two men exchanged cordial letters agreeing the match, met again on Belle Isle, and the wedding was arranged for October.[19]

Isabella herself came to stay at Rydal Mount in July, giving the Wordsworths their first opportunity to get to know their future daughter-in-law. Predisposed in her favour as they all were, she did not disappoint them. 'She gains daily and hourly on our affections', Dorothy reported, '. . . in every thing she does or says, you can trace the best of dispositions.' The engagement naturally led to intimacy with all the Curwen family, who were frequent visitors over the summer months. They were not alone. 'The house has been more like an Inn, for the last six weeks, than a private one', Sara pretended to complain to Quillinan. She was not exaggerating, for thanks to the Rydal Mount Visitors' Book, which was started in May of this year, we know that more than 166 people crossed the Wordsworths' threshold before the end of the year.[20] Bertha Southey, her brother Cuthbert and fifteen-year-old Tom Hutchinson from Brinsop were guests throughout the summer, but most simply passed through. There were Americans: 'an irruption of all the Douglases', led by the dashing 'Red Harriet', was followed by the Reverend John MacVickar, Professor of Moral Philosophy at Columbia College, New York, with his wife and daughters, and two Bostonians. There were 'Cantabs', mostly, it has to be said, from Trinity College, including the Master himself, who had been lured to 'Idle Mount' with the promise of his own quiet sitting room and bedroom upstairs, well away from the bustle of visitors, and the use of the libraries at Rydal Hall, Hawkshead Grammar School and Greta Hall. The youthful Professor Hamilton came to stay, bringing his sister, Eliza, with him. 'She has been all the morning with Wordsworth, shut up in a summerhouse which nobody dares to approach. It is rumoured that they are engaged in a critical discussion of her poems', her brother wrote jealously, adding that he had had more time to admire the scenery this visit, since he was less engaged with William than on his last.[21]

And there was Mrs Felicia Dorothea Hemans, popular authoress of such gems as 'The boy stood on the burning deck', who owed her introduction to her friend Maria Jewsbury, but behaved as though she were bestowing the favour. 'For one *long* fortnight we had Mrs Hemans & one of her boys –', Sara wrote feelingly to Quillinan.

> He was a sweet interesting creature – but she tho' a good-natured person is so spoilt by the adulation of '*the world*' that her affectation is perfectly unendurable – Don't say this to Miss Jewsbury who idolizes her – Mr W *pretends* to like her very much – but I believe it is only because we do not – for she is the very opposite, her good-nature excepted, of anything he ever admired before either in *theory or practice.*

Eliza Hamilton, Sara added tartly, had ten times the feeling, and wrote ten times better poetry, than Mrs Hemans, 'tho' *she* would be shocked if she thought *the world* should ever know that she had written a line'. They were not to get rid of Mrs Hemans so easily. When she left Rydal Mount on 2 July it was only to go as far as Dove Nest, on Windermere, where she took up residence for the summer, happy in her conviction that she had conquered the poet with her charms and taking a malicious glee in his foibles. 'Imagine my dear – a Bridal present made by Mr

Wordsworth to a young lady in whom he is much interested – a poet's daughter too!' she confided in a letter, later published in the *Athenaeum*, which reveals as much about her as it does about William.

You will be thinking of a brooch in the form of a lyre or a butterfly shaped [aigette?] or a forgetmenot ring, or some such 'small gear'. Nothing of the sort – but a good, handsome, substantial, useful-looking – pair of scales to hang up in her storeroom! 'For you must be aware, my dear Mrs Hemans' added he gravely 'how necessary it is for every lady to see things weighed herself!' Poveretta me! I looked as good as I could, & happily for me the poetic eyes are not very clear sighted, so that I believe no suspicion derogatory to my notability of character has yet flashed upon the mighty master's mind; indeed I told him that I looked upon scales as particularly graceful things & had great thoughts of having my picture taken with a pair in my hand.

It does not seem to have occurred to Mrs Hemans that the 'poetic eyes' were indeed clear-sighted, and that the poet himself was having a little private joke at the expense of a 'literary lady'. 'She is a great Enthusiast both in Poetry and music,' William commented drily, 'and enjoys this beautiful Country as much as any one can do who is new to such scenery.'[22]

One visitor to the Lakes who was not invited into Rydal Mount this summer was a precocious eleven-year-old, John Ruskin. Anxious to get a glimpse of the poet, Ruskin and his parents developed a sudden urge to attend Rydal chapel, and were rewarded by sitting only a couple of pews away from him. Ruskin was not impressed. 'He appeared asleep the greatest part of the time', he noted in his journal. 'He seemed about 60 This gentleman possesses a long face and a large nose with a moderate assortment of grey hairs and 2 small grey eyes not filled with fury wrapt inspired with a mouth of moderate dimensions that is quite large enough to let in a sufficient quantity of beef or mutton & to let out a sufficient quantity of poetry.'[23]

On 4 August William had to go to Lowther Castle to meet Lord Lowther and accompany him to the polls at Appleby, a general election having been called in the wake of the death of the unlamented George IV. After three defeats in three Westmorland elections, Brougham had taken himself off to stand as a candidate in Yorkshire, leaving Lord Lowther and Colonel Lowther to be returned unopposed. An event which would formerly have aroused great passions at Rydal thus barely merited a passing reference. In any case, the Wordsworths were now exchanging one kind of bustle for another, as preparations were set on foot for the first family wedding since 1814. There were all the usual fallings-out, in which it rapidly became apparent who was the dominant partner. The Wordsworths wanted Christopher to conduct the marriage, but were pre-empted by Mrs Curwen, who asked her brother, the rector of Plumbland, to do the honours. The Wordsworths had arranged for John to move from his lodgings and rent a house at Moresby, and had half completed furnishing it when the Curwen family doctor pronounced it much too cold for the bride and they had to start from scratch again. The wedding was celebrated with great panache on 11 October. Dora, the eternal bridesmaid, did her duty once more, accompanying the bride and her father in the first of five carriages which carried the wedding party from Workington Hall to the church. The whole of Workington turned out to cheer the bride to and from church, and when the newlyweds emerged, they scattered silver among the crowds, guns were fired and all the ships in the harbour hoisted their flags. Fifty guests sat down to the wedding breakfast, after which the married couple set off for a honeymoon in Scotland.[24] It was a far cry from the walk across the fields and quiet village church ceremony which had marked the start of William and Mary's married life together, twenty-eight years earlier.

The bridegroom's parents and sister returned briefly to Rydal Mount, where Dorothy and Sara had remained in companionable seclusion during the wedding festivities, before setting out again, on 1 November, to spend the winter in Cambridge. Throughout the year, Dora's health, or lack of it, had been a cause of deep concern. While staying with her brother in his bachelor lodgings at Moresby in the spring, she had been taken seriously ill and the after-effects – violent pains in her head, weakness and fainting fits – lingered with her throughout the summer. Afraid that she would not be able to withstand the usual winter coughs and colds in her weakened state, her parents were determined that she should stay in the south, at least until the spring. As they thought it would be useful if Dora could ride her pony regularly, they decided to take it with them, her sixty-year-old father undertaking 'very valiantly and economically' to ride it all the way to Cambridge himself, while Mary and Dora travelled by more conventional means.[25]

It was just the sort of eccentric gesture William loved. Ambling along, with only the silent pony for companionship, he made his way through Lancashire and the Peak District, revelling in this rare chance for unhurried observation, exploration of enticing vales, streams and village churchyards, and conversation with chance-met strangers. By the time he reached Chatsworth, he was beginning to murmur verses for the first time in twelve months. He broke his journey, as in the old days, at Coleorton. The new baronet and his wife were both quite charming, but William could not visit the place he had done so much to shape without thinking of his departed friends. 'When I sate down in Lady B's grotto near the fountain I was suddenly overcome and could not speak for tears.' The day after he left, riding thirty-seven miles through tempestuous rain, he found himself pouring out the tributary verses he had long wished to write for Sir George. Mary forwarded a revised version of the poem to Lady Beaumont on 21 December, apologizing for its length, which made it unsuitable for the inscription they had sought, and explaining, 'I do not like to mention the subject to Mr W at present – but I should rather wish him to recast something shorter, than attempt to reduce the verses which, as they stand, appear to me to be so happy.'[26]

The poetic spirit fled as soon as William reached Cambridge, for the whole university was abuzz with the news that Wellington had resigned as Prime Minister and that Lord Grey had formed a ministry committed to parliamentary reform, with Brougham as his Lord Chancellor. From the sanctuary of Trinity Lodge, William watched in dismay as the fires of reform, both metaphorical and literal, began to blaze in the surrounding countryside.[27] Everywhere he looked, it seemed as if the old order was being destroyed. In the space of just a few months, there had been popular revolutions in France, Belgium and Poland, which were now spreading to Germany and central Italy. The king of France had been deposed and the king of Holland ousted from a Belgium which now claimed its independence. The new king of England, William IV, had refused to go to Guildhall for fear of riots on the streets of London, and Ireland, tinder-dry, was awaiting the explosion.

At such a crisis, William could not return to the Lakes for Christmas, as he had intended to do. Instead, when the university broke up for the vacation, he allowed Christopher to persuade him to go to his country parsonage at Buxted, a village just outside Uckfield, in Sussex. This was a convenient place to leave Mary and Dora, while he took advantage of an open invitation from Quillinan to make frequent excursions into London. 'He is dreadfully engaged, both at breakfasts, luncheons, dinners – & evening parties –', Dora told her cousin at the beginning of March. 'Employed chiefly as he tells us – in conversing with men of all ranks & parties hearing their opinions & endeavouring to correct the bad ones – he is very busy is he not?' For all Dora's apparently innocent sarcasm, it was entirely true. At Cambridge William had been invited by the son of his old friends the Speddings to take coffee with a group of student admirers in his rooms and had stayed up till one o'clock in the morning, 'in good talking mood but furiously alarmist, nothing but revolutions, [and] reigns of terror' and defending the idea of passive obedience by quoting Scripture. Not having lived through the French Revolution themselves, the undergraduates were amused, rather than convinced, by his eloquence.[28] In London, however, his audience was in an altogether different league, reflecting once again the fact that, through his brother's contacts and his own friendships, he now had a voice in the highest and most influential circles in the land. He dined several times with the Bishop of London and the Archbishops of Canterbury and York, who could be expected to lead the opposition to reform in the House of Lords. He was continuously in the company of the new Lord Liverpool, half-brother of the former Prime Minister, who was also opposed to reform. 'Five times have I dined while at Buxted at the table of an Earl – and twice in the company of a Prince. Therefore let you and Mrs Kenyon prepare yourselves for something stately and august in my deportment and manners,' he wrote joking to his friend, but the very fact that he was so often in such company reflected the respect in which his opinions were held.[29]

What comes as more of a surprise is to find that he was also mixing regularly with radicals and reformers. Henry Taylor, a poet and playwright, who worked in the Colonial Office and had met William on earlier visits to London, hosted at least four breakfasts to which William was a welcome guest. 'Though he was old, and the rest so young, and he was opposed to them in politics, yet the force and brightness of his conversation, his social geniality, and the philosophic, as well as imaginative largeness of his intellect, delighted them all', Taylor wrote afterwards. Both Taylor and a young John Stuart Mill were flattered to receive an invitation to call at Rydal Mount, and another radical, Charles Greville, was won over by William's 'chearful', 'courteous' behaviour and his generous tributes to Brougham's talents and moral virtues, particularly his devotion to his family.[30] That William was capable of distinguishing between Brougham's personal attributes and his politics, at a time when the latter seemed about to triumph over everything he believed in, is a remarkable instance of his generosity of spirit.

William was also invited to dine and sleep at Holland House, a significant invitation as it came from the most influential of all Whig salons. Unabashed, he proceeded to have a fierce argument with Lord John Russell, one of the chief proponents of parliamentary reform, which came to assume almost legendary status in London circles. 'Your admirers say [you] gave it him', Haydon wrote some weeks later. 'You ask my opinion about the Reform Bill', William replied.

> I am averse (with that wisest of the Moderns Mr Burke) to all *hot* Reformations; i.e. to every sudden change in political institutions upon a large scale. They who are forced to part with power are of course irritated, and they upon whom a large measure of it is at once conferred have their heads turned and know not how to use it . . . My admirers, as you call them, must have been led (perhaps by myself) to overstate what I said to Lord John Russel[l]. I did not conceal from him my utter disapprobation of the Bill; and what I said principally alluded to its effect upon the Aristocracy. I remember particularly telling him that the middle and lower classes were naturally envious haters of the Aristocracy – unless when they were *proud* of being attached to them – that there was no *neutral* ground in these sentiments – the Mass must either be your zealous supporters, said I, or they will do all in their power to pull you down.[31]

William's letter to Haydon was but one of many which poured from his pen over the next eighteen months, as the Reform Bill struggled slowly through both Houses of Parliament. Through thick and thin, William clung to the belief that the bill was morally and politically wrong. Morally, because it was unjust, allowing the bare 5,000 inhabitants of Cockermouth to retain a Member of Parliament, but granting Manchester, with all its hundreds of thousands, a mere two. Politically, because it was the first step on a road which would lead inevitably to universal suffrage and annual elections. 'In the present stage of our affairs,' he wrote in December, 'the class that does the most harm consists of well-intentioned men, who, being ignorant of human nature, think that they may help the thorough-paced reformers and revolutionists to a *certain* point, then stop, and that the machine will stop with them.' William's own experience of the French Revolution had taught him otherwise. 'You mistake in supposing me an Anti Reformer –', he corrected Robinson, '*that* I never was – but an Anti-Bill man; heart and soul. – It is a fixed judgement of my mind, that an unbridled Democracy is the worst of all Tyrranies.'

It was obvious to him, as to many of his contemporaries, that the equally inevitable result of universal suffrage and annual elections would be a government dependent on the whim of the mob and at the mercy of the popular press. 'I have witnessed one revolution in a foreign Country,' he wrote with sad dignity, 'and I have not courage to think of facing another in my own.'[32]

Christopher, Lord Liverpool, and indeed many others, urged him to write publicly against the Reform Bill, but he could not be persuaded to do so. 'Your exhortations troubled me in a way you cannot be in the least aware of; for I have been repeatedly urged by some of my most valued friends, and at times by my own conscience, to undertake the task you have set before me', he answered one Cambridge friend.

> But I will deal frankly with you. A conviction of my incompetence to do justice to the momentous subject has kept me, and I fear will keep me, silent. My sixty-second year will soon be completed, and though I have been favoured thus far in health and strength beyond most men of my age, yet I feel its effects upon my spirits; they sink under a pressure of apprehension to which, at an earlier period of my life, they would probably have been superior.[33]

It was ironic that William's sense of impotence was increasing at a time when, to all outward appearances, his influence was gaining ground every day. During his visit to London this spring, he had accepted not one but four separate requests to take his portrait. Francis Wilkin, a fashionable draughtsman and lithographer, produced a delightful chalk drawing which, more than any other portrait, except perhaps the very first, reveals the man, rather than the poet. There is no affectation of pose, poetic or otherwise. William simply looks into the distance, his thin face remarkable only for a great expanse of forehead, receding almost to his crown, set off by an abundance of soft, fluffy grey hair and those famous grey eyes, which are mesmerizing in the intensity of their gaze. He looks exactly as he was so often described: pleasant, good-humoured and intelligent, without being oppressed by weight of thought. As Dorothy put it, 'I value it much as a likeness of him in company, and something of that restraint with chearfulness, which is natural to him in mixed societies. There is nothing of the poet . . .' Or as William himself commented drily, when being congratulated on its likeness, it was indeed a correct likeness – 'if you suppose all the finer faculties of the mind to be withdrawn: that, I should say, is Wordsworth the Chancellor of the Exchequer, – Wordsworth the Speaker of the House of Commons'. For all the lack of supposed poetic spirit in the portrait, it is significant that Wilkin reproduced it as a lithograph for one of the first in a series 'of the most eminent men in literature, art and science'.[34]

The second portrait was by William Boxall, a young artist who selected William for his first attempt at portrait painting. The result is a moon-faced caricature, in oils, of the Wilkin portrait, with added poetry (one might say, added poetic licence). The poet sits with folded arms and downcast eyes, with one side of his face bathed in a strong light which shines off his domed forehead and casts peculiar shadows on the side in darkness. It was admired by contemporary critics for 'the presence of poetry', but William did not like it and was 'much mortified' when it was engraved: apart from Dorothy, his friends all thought it 'much too dark and gloomy, and they do not think the likeness happy.' Quillinan was more forthright, calling it 'an engraving from Boxall's imagination of what William Wordsworth Esqre, bad poet, worse stamp-controller, and worst man, of the county of Westmoreland, ought to look like'.[35]

The third portrait was by John Gardner, who had written to urge him to publish a cheap edition of his poetry and now met the poet for the first time. An amateur effort – Gardner was a surgeon – it is not known to have survived.[36] A similar fate awaited the fourth, a bust by a young Scotsman, Lawrence Macdonald, who had made Walter Scott's the previous year and appears to have been introduced to William when they dined together at the Marshalls' London home.[37]

Perhaps more flattering than any of these attempts at portraiture was an extraordinary visit William paid, by invitation, to a Brixton school on 1 March. 'On Tuesday Captain Todd and I accompanied him to Brixton, not to the tread-mill, but to see a mad Schoolmaster named Hine or Hind', Quillinan informed Dora.

> Now listen. This broad shouldered muscular Theban had one advantage over us besides his learning. His eyes are so arranged that you never know when he is looking at you; so that he may be staring hard at you all the time that he seems to look quite the other way. I shouldn't like to have such a cunning-eyed Schoolmaster. He received us all three with the most earnest cordiality, and gave us glasses of sherry, and pound-cake. But to Mr Wordsworth he was crushingly affectionate. I wouldn't have had my hand in those brawny fingers so long and often for something . . . we were ushered into the School-room. There were 54 boys at desks in rows of 8; as in the pit of a theatre. We were on the stage: viz. Poet, Pedagogue, Captain of Dragoons & I. – the boys rose and bowed; sate and gazed: one made a speech of welcome after formal introduction of Poet – Poet replied –: pencils and slates were brought out at word of command; pedagogue gave out, line by line, the Sonnet supposed to be written on Westminster Bridge. All the Boys wrote it, one echoing the Master, as the clerk in certain cases, does the clergyman. When finished, several boys in turn, read it aloud: very well too. They were then called upon to explain the meaning of 'the river glideth at its own sweet will.' One boy . . . made a dissertation on the influence of the moon on the tides &c &c, and seemed rather inclined to be critical; another said there was no wind; another that there were no water breaks in the Thames to prevent its gliding as it pleased; another that the arches of the bridges had no locks to shut the water in or out: & so forth. One Boy said there were no boats – that was the nearest – Poet explained: was then called on by Pedagogue to read his sonnet himself: declined. Ped. entreated: Poet remonstrated: Ped. inexorable: Poet submitted. I never heard him read better. The Boys evidently felt it; a thunder of applause; Poet asked for a Half Holiday for them – granted – thunders on thunders Seriously speaking, the whole scene was indescribably animated and interesting.[38]

For all his droll account, Quillinan had evidently been moved. How much more so, then, must William have been, hearing his poem discussed with such lively and intelligent interest, and being cheered to the rafters by boys who had responded so positively to his poetry? To a man who loved children, was passionately interested in education and yet was riven with doubt about his own poetic powers, there can have been no more powerful, or touching, affirmation of his own achievement.

Which, of course, was precisely what Joesph Hine wanted him to feel, for despite his clumsy frame and crossed eyes, Hine was a teacher committed to the idea of reading poetry aloud to his pupils 'as a mode of culture profitable to health, to manners, to the understanding, and the social affections'. Having given William such a practical example of the effectiveness of this method, he succeeded where everyone else had failed. He persuaded the poet to sanction the publication of a not-so-slim volume, *Selections from the Poems of William Wordsworth, Esq. Chiefly for the Use of Schools and Young Persons.* Equally important, he also persuaded another Wordsworthian disciple, Edward Moxon, to print and publish it. The selection William left entirely to Hine. Quillinan tried to have *The Idiot Boy* removed, but William backed Hine: 'it was precisely for his perception of the merit of this Class of Poems that I allowed Mr Hine to make the Selection. You would find no two Persons agree what was best; and upon the whole tell Mr H. that I think he has succeeded full as well if not better than most other Persons could have done.' For a poet who had been painstaking, to the point of obsession, in the arrangement of his editions of his poetry, this was a rare tribute. William was prepared to abrogate responsibility for the selection, and even to forgive some embarrassingly 'injudicious' editorial comments: 'Mr Hine is an original person, and therefore allowance must be made for his oddities. He feels the poetry, and that is enough.' What William could not, and would not, cede to anyone was the right to edit the poetry. The proof sheets would be sent to him, scrutinized with his usual meticulous eye for detail and returned to Moxon suitably corrected. The pocket-sized volume, just over 380 pages long, contained 'I should suppose, at least 1100 verses', cost just 5s 6d, fully bound, and, as William remarked, 'would be found a good travelling companion for those who like my poetry'. Within days of publication, in June, Rogers wrote to tell William that the little book was selling fast '& giving an animation to Moxon which he has not known for some time'. And, within months, its success would encourage Southey to embark on a similar experiment with his own poetry.[39]

By this time, the Wordsworths were back at Rydal Mount. They had left London on 21 April, taking William and Dora's goddaughter, Rotha Quillinan, with them, but they had been forced to halt at Nottingham, when Mary was struck down by so severe an attack of lumbago that she could not get up from bed, dress herself or be moved without fainting. Fortunately, William's poetical reputation saved the day. He remembered that William and Mary Howitt, the Quaker poets who had presented him with a copy of their first publication, lived in the town. Though he had never met them personally, he sought them out and asked them to recommend a doctor. Not only was their brother a physician, but they gladly offered Mary, and Dora, who stayed behind with her mother, accommodation in their own house. 'We fell among good Samaritans', Dora wrote with relief, '... [They] took us in & nursed her most tenderly for ten days.' The awkwardness of the situation was increased by the discovery that their kind hosts were radicals and actively involved in the election which was about to take place. They had landed 'in a hot bed of Reformists – in a wasps nest positively, & it drives me mad to hear of the "enlightened mob" – "the poor neglected" "their rights trampled upon" – "laws made for the rich & not for the poor" ...' Mrs Howitt was 'a red hot Reformist', but she was also 'a charming Creature much the most fascinating of the Authoresses I have seen', and when they parted, twelve days after the Wordsworths' arrival in Nottingham, it was with genuine regret on both sides. William ordered a copy of his *Selections* to be sent to the Howitts' daughter and invited them all to Rydal Mount in the autumn; Howitt 'consoled himself' with writing a sonnet to Dora. Another unlikely friendship across the political divide had been established.[40]

William had been forced to abandon his wife and daughter, as it was imperative that he return to Westmorland immediately. Not only was he anxious to be there for the general election, but he had to attend to urgent Stamp Office business. One of the reasons he had been called to London in the first place was that the long-threatened changes in the administration of Stamp duty were taking place. As Dora remarked at the time, 'this reform bill has quite driven that & every other private concern out of his head', but the changes were significant. The districts of Cumberland and Westmorland were to be amalgamated, under William's sole distributorship, and his sub-distributors were to have their salaries doubled, though their responsibilities remained unchanged. In other words, she complained on her father's behalf, 'my Lord Althorp has been most liberal, just given him double risk, double duty, & no more pay'.[41]

The Stamp Office reforms provided William with the opportunity he had been looking for to place his second son in employment. Willy had returned to England in March, his sojourn on the Continent cut short by the revolutions sweeping Europe. He had left Bremen the previous June, telling his parents that because the Papendicks spoke English in the house and had taken another English boarder, he was not getting enough practice in speaking German, and that his studies were making him ill. The Wordsworths agreed that he should go to Godesberg, where he could be under Mrs Aders's wing, and then to Heidelberg. This last was a far more congenial place for a charming and sociable young man like Willy. He enrolled at the ancient university, renowned for its hard-drinking students and duelling societies, and spent much of his free time in the company of Mrs Tobin, the widow of William's old friend from Bristol, and her three sons. Despite his high-living and spending, Willy was not entirely feckless. 'Oh I pray try to get a something for me ere I enter upon my 21st [year]', he wrote anxiously before leaving Bremen. 'I can not bear the thoughts of year after year slipping away without the faintest idea of what I am to be or to do!!'[42]

William's first idea was to dismiss his clerk, Carter, and employ Willy in his place, 'which I believe the youth does not consider a very dignified employment'. But Carter had been with him from the beginning, and William simply could not bring himself to dismiss someone who had served him so long and so well, just to find a job for his own son. Besides, Carter was indispensable. Not only did he single-handedly run the office, but he was always willing and able to lend a hand around the house, even though he had officially given up his gardening duties in 1824. His services would be vital in amalgamating the administration of the huge new district with that of the old, and, as William and Carter did their annual round together, William realized that there was a better opening for his son as a sub-distributor in Carlisle. His duties would be less complicated than Carter's, he would earn in the region of £180 a year, and he would enjoy all the benefits of city life in Carlisle without being banished from the bosom of his family.[43]

William had been depressed by his tour of his new district, 'which I heartily wish I was rid of – seeing nothing but confusion and disorder, and being dismayed with the responsibilities of the situation. I have no less than 21 Agents to look after, whose circumstances must more or less be thrown into confusion by the revolutionary dis[as]ter impending over us'. He was even more depressed by the result of the general election a few days later. Another Lowther, Sir John, who had sat for Cumberland for thirty-five years, had declined to stand again. At the last minute, his place had been taken by Lord Lowther and, in a shock result, the Cumberland electors rejected him and returned two radical Members of Parliament. A radical also replaced the sitting Tory M P at Carlisle. Even in Westmorland, the Lowthers avoided outright defeat only by coming to an arrangement with their opponents, whereby a single candidate from each party was put forward for unopposed election. Embarrassingly, John's father-in-law, Henry Curwen, had contributed to the Lowther defeat by putting up £500 to support the radical candidates. 'We are all in the Dolefuls –', Sara told Quillinan after the results were known. 'Miss W & I [were] dolor[o]us enough before [William's return] – but he has made us ten times worse.'[44]

'Poor Father is quite overpowered by the horrors & sorrows which seem to him hanging over this hitherto favo[u]red spot of earth', Dora wrote at the beginning of June, '. . . he can neither think nor write nor talk on any other topic.' With the return of a Parliament committed to reform, however, there was nothing more he could do, except resign himself to the inevitable passage of the bill. He tried to find occupation for mind and body in the garden, where he and Willy became fellow labourers, chopping down trees, making seats for sunshine and shade and a pool at the end of the terrace for the fish Maria Jewsbury had given them.[45] Though he complained that his Muse had forsaken him, 'being scared away by the villainous aspect of the Times', he made a great effort on behalf of his old friend Haydon, who had requested a sonnet to his picture of 'Napoleon on the Island of St Helena'. Knowing that Haydon was in dire financial straits, William sent him the sonnet 'not "warm" but piping hot from the brain, whence it came in the wood adjoining my garden not ten minutes ago, and was scarcely more than twice as long in coming', and gave him permission to publish it wherever he wished. This was generous, for Haydon immediately offered it to Samuel Carter Hall for his annual, the *New Monthly Magazine*, where it appeared in the July issue as a splendid piece of publicity for the picture.[46] A few days later, William composed a second short poem, which he intended as an inscription for a stone in 'a hazel nook' in the garden, but was more like an epitaph for himself.

In these fair Vales, hath many a tree
At Wordsworth's suit been spared,
And from the builder's hand this Stone,
For some rude beauty of its own,
Was rescued by the Bard;
Long may it rest in peace! and here
Perchance the tender-hearted
Will heave a gentle sigh for him
As One of the Departed.

In stark contrast to the doom and gloom pervading spirits at Rydal Mount, the summer proved a brilliant one for weather and 'unexampled gaiety in Regattas, Balls, Dejeuners, Picnics by the Lake side, on the Islands, and on the Mountain tops – Fireworks by night – Dancing on the green sward by day'. Even the Wordsworths were not immune, holding a dance for 'forty beaus and belles, besides Matrons, ancient Spinsters, and Greybeards' and a 'Venison feast' at the beginning of September.[47]

Among the summer visitors was the young Utilitarian philosopher John Stuart Mill, whom William had met at Henry Taylor's radical breakfasts in the spring. Despite being poles apart from his mentor in politics, Mill was then a devoted Wordsworthian, attributing to William's *Poems, in Two Volumes* his own salvation from a depression so deep it threatened to overwhelm him. Analysing why they had succeeded where everything else had failed, Mill concluded that the poems spoke to his own love of rural objects and natural scenery, but also (and here he paraphrased that all-important preface to *Lyrical Ballads*), they expressed, 'not mere outward beauty, but states of feeling, and of thought coloured by feeling, under the excitement of beauty'.

They seemed to be the very culture of the feelings, which I was then in quest of. In them, I seemed to draw from a sense of inward joy, of sympathetic and imaginative pleasure, which could be shared in by all human beings; which had no connexion with struggle or imperfection, but would be made richer by every improvement in the physical or social condition of mankind. From them I seemed to learn what would be the perennial sources of happiness, when all the greater evils of life shall have been removed. And I felt myself at once better and happier as I came under their influence.

In other words, they restored a sense of the importance of imagination and feeling to a young man who had been brought up in the Gradgrind tradition of facts, leavened with the application of logic, reason and more facts. At the beginning of August, he spent four days at Ambleside, 'chiefly for the purpose of seeing Wordsworth'. The two men walked, talked and dined together, and Mill left feeling 'amply repaid both in pleasure, intellectual excitement, and instruction'.[48]

On 13 September William, Dora and Sara went over Kirkstone Pass in a little four-wheeled open carriage, pulled by a horse purchased by William and Willy against the advice of Dora and Sara, who thought it too young for the task before it. Sara was bound for Patterdale, to stay with the Marshalls, but father and daughter were setting out on a tour of Scotland together. To their frustration, they were delayed for several days, both at Rydal Mount and at Patterdale, by a severe recurrence of William's trachoma, but they could wait no longer, for it was imperative that they should reach Abbotsford before the end of the month. William had been summoned by Scott, who had sent 'an affectionate message' saying that 'if I did not come soon to see him it might be too late'.[49] For months they had heard reports of his declining health; now he was so ill that he was about to leave for Italy, in the fragile hope of prolonging his life beyond the winter. Even before William set out, therefore, he and Scott both knew that this would be the last time they would meet.

This knowledge imbued the whole visit with a poignancy that at times became unbearable. The Wordsworths found all Scott's family gathered at Abbotsford, together with Sir William Allan, the Scottish historical painter, William Laidlaw, Scott's steward and secretary, and the eldest son of Lord Ravensworth, Henry Liddell, his wife and brother-in-law. They were also joined, at William's invitation, by his own nephew, Charles Wordsworth, who was on a walking tour of Scotland. The highlight of the visit was an emotional trip to the Yarrow, so that the two poets could retrace their footsteps one last time in one of their favourite haunts. As they crossed the Tweed in their carriages on the way back to Abbotsford, a setting sun bruised the clouds above the Eildon Hills with a purple light. It was a moment when the elegiac moods of poet and nature synthesized, prompting William to begin his sonnet *On the departure of Sir Walter Scott from Abbotsford, for Naples*, which mourned the departure of a 'kindred Power' and assured him that 'the might Of the whole world's good wishes with him goes'. He was also, of course, duty bound to produce the inevitable *Yarrow Revisited*, which became a tribute to his old friend, the 'last Minstrel'.

For Thou, upon a hundred streams,
   By tales of love and sorrow,
Of faithful love, undaunted truth,
   Hast shed the power of Yarrow;
And streams unknown, hills yet unseen,
   Wherever they invite Thee,
At parent Nature's grateful call,
   With gladness must requite Thee.[50]

One evening passed pleasantly enough: the Liddells sang, Mrs Lockhart 'chaunted old Ballads to her harp' and Allan told and acted odd stories in a humorous way, but the evening before the Wordsworths' departure, the two poets, one dying, the other half-blind, sat quietly together in the library. In the course of their conversation, Scott dwelt at length on the singular fact that both Fielding and Smollett had been driven abroad by declining health and had never returned. William was equally struck that neither of these authors had inspired due marks of respect at the close of their lives. It was, undoubtedly, these remarks which lent a sense of urgency to the composition of the tributes to Scott; both poems were sent to him personally, as he was *en route* to Italy, and William had the satisfaction of learning that he had been 'delighted' with them. Not content with this purely personal compliment, William overcame 'an aversion little less than insurmountable to having any thing to do with periodicals' and sent the sonnet to Watts for publication, 'if you choose to insert it', in the *Literary Souvenir.* Watts not only chose to insert it, but gave it pride of place on the first page of his next volume.[51]

On the final morning before their departure William and Scott said their farewells in private, and Scott wrote a faltering few lines of verse in Dora's album. 'I fairly broke down', he admitted later, and, as William noted, the uncharacteristic mistakes, particularly the omission of the initial S in his own name, revealed all too clearly what it had cost him to write them. Handing the album back to Dora, in William's presence, he told her, 'I should not have done any thing of this kind but for your Father's sake; they are probably the last verses I shall ever write.'[52]

While Scott and his family made their way slowly southwards to embark for Italy, William and Dora parted from Charles and took the road to the Highlands. They had to go slowly, for it soon became obvious that the horse was, in Dora's apt phrase, 'a Child [put] to Man's work'; more often than not, William had to walk, and eventually they had to part with him altogether, leaving him to pasture out the winter at Bunawe, while they hired replacements to get them home. Nevertheless, the enforced slowness of the pace proved a blessing. Dora had to thank it for 'an impression which must be more lasting than my first introduction to the Rhine', her arrival in complete darkness at the Macnabs' burial place at Killin. For William, it was the ideal pace for unhurried contemplation of the scenery and poetic composition. 'From Abbotsford we went to Roslin, Edinburgh, Sterling, Loch Kettering, Killin, Dalmally, Oban, the Isle of Mull – too late in the season for Staffa – and returned by Inverary, Loch Lomond, Glasgow, and the falls of the Clyde', William reminisced to another poet, Rogers, after their return.

> The foliage was in its most beautiful state; and the weather, though we had five or six days of heavy rain, was upon the whole very favourable; for we had most beautiful appearances of floating vapours, rainbows and fragments of rainbows, weather-gales, and sunbeams innumerable, so that I never saw Scotland under a more poetic aspect. Then there was in

addition the pleasure of recollection, and the novelty of showing to my Daughter places and objects which had been so long in my remembrance.[53]

For William it was that most potent of mixtures, past and present, combined with a state of heightened feeling, brought on by the emotional parting from Scott. He forgot, or laid aside, all his troubles and gave himself up to sheer enjoyment. 'I set off with a severe inflammation in one of my eyes, which was removed by being so much in the open air; and for more than a month I scarcely saw a newspaper, or heard of their contents', he told Lord Lonsdale's daughter.

During this time we almost forgot, my daughter and I, the deplorable state of the country. My spirits rallied, and, with exercise – for I often walked scarcely less than twenty miles a day – and the employment of composing verses amid scenery the most beautiful, and at a season when the foliage was most rich and varied, the time fled away delightfully; and when we came back into the world again, it seemed as if I had waked from a dream that was never to return.

On 7 October Dora was able to send her mother six new poems her father had composed in the eight days since they had parted from Charles at Callander, adding that he was, even as she wrote, 'hammering at a horrid sonnet & he cannot give me his ear at the moment'.[54] The momentum did not leave him once they returned home and before the end of the month he had added several more, including *Yarrow Revisited* and the wonderful sonnet *Eagles*, contrasting an imprisoned eagle seen at a castle near Oban with the freewheeling birds he had watched off Fairhead in Ireland. 'You say your disinclination to move encreases every year –', he observed to Montagu,

it is not so with myself – travelling agrees with me wonderfully. I am as much Peter Bell as ever, and since my eyelids have been so liable to inflammation, after much reading especially, I find nothing so feeding to my mind as change of scene, and rambling about; and my labours, such as they are, can be carried on better in the fields and on the roads, than any where else.

Reinvigorated by his Scottish tour, William promised his daughter that *The Recluse* would be this winter's employment, but 'entre nous', Dora whispered to Maria Jewsbury, 'I think his courage will fail him when winter really arrives.'[55]

The females were taking no chances. They had invited William's oldest nephew, John Wordsworth, twenty-six years old, a fellow of Trinity and a brilliant scholar, yet also a shy, eminently likeable young man in delicate health, to spend the winter at Rydal Mount. The unspoken hope was that his companionship would provide William with the intellectual stimulus he needed to go on with *The Recluse*. It was too much to ask of anyone, but the four months John spent at Rydal Mount were both productive and important: 'having John to talk to in his walks', Christopher proudly reported, William 'was very industrious through the whole winter at all other times of the day – and worked very hard, specially in the revising and finishing of his long autobiographic poem'. Mary was a willing amanuensis, helping William to make out his 'mangled and almost illegible MSS'; the two of them, their daughter reported, were 'busier than 1000 bees', working 'like slaves from morning to night – an arduous work – correcting a long Poem, written 30 years back . . . and not to be published during his life'. The contribution of 'Cambridge John' in helping to secure this important stage in the growth of *The Prelude* for posterity would soon be forgotten, but he won all hearts at Rydal Mount. Even Quillinan, who came to collect his daughter Rotha in the spring, was deeply impressed, after only a month's acquaintance. 'I like him much', he confided to his diary. 'What a contrast are his modesty & courtesy to the manners of that little queer will o the wisp of conceit Hartley Coleridge. Yet John W has more learning than HC & perhaps as much natural aptitude if not more.'[56]

For five weeks over Christmas, the Wordsworths also enjoyed the daily society of the Arnold family, who were staying in the cottages at the foot of the hill. Thomas Arnold, who had first paid homage to William at Rydal Mount in 1818, was now headmaster of Rugby school, married, with seven children of his own and another due in May. The little Arnolds were as taken with their neighbours as their parents: the Wordsworths were themselves so fond of children, and knew so well how to amuse them, their mother affirmed, that she had never seen the four eldest in such high spirits. There were tea-drinkings and parties, presided over by Dora and her great Newfoundland dog, Neptune, and the little Arnolds made lively companions for the Wordsworths' own winter house-guests, their niece Mary Hutchinson and Rotha Quillinan.[57] More importantly, Thomas Arnold and William delighted in each other's company, despite being diametrically opposed in politics. 'My almost daily walks with him were things not to be forgotten', Arnold recalled several months later.

> Once, and once only, we had a good fight about the Reform bill during a walk up Greenhead Ghyll to see the 'unfinished sheepfold' recorded in 'Michael.' But I am sure that our political disagreement did not at all interfere with our enjoyment of each other's society; for I think that in the great principle of things we agreed very entirely – and only differed as to the τα καθ' 'εκαστα [things individually].

So inclined was Arnold to 'rave about Rydal' and 'our little Pet Rydal Society', declaring it a 'perfect Marvel in Man's Life to have every Thing that one would most wish for in neighbourhood combined with such perfect Peace & Beauty', that he determined to buy or rent a house, so that the family could spend all their holidays there.[58]

William had cause to be thankful for the companionship of both Arnold, and his neighbour, Captain Thomas Hamilton, the new winter occupant of Ivy Cottage, who was known to the Wordsworths as 'Cyril Thornton', because he was the author of a novel of that name. Just before Christmas, Dorothy suffered another serious seizure; for a fortnight, they were all in acute anxiety about her. Once again, she rallied, but so slowly that on 1 April William's bulletin to his brother was the least hopeful it had ever been.

> Our dear sister makes no progress towards recovery of Strength. She is very feeble, never quits her room, and passes most of the day in, or upon, the bed. She does not suffer pain except now and then from wind and stitches. She is very chearful, and nothing troubles her but public affairs and the sense of requiring so much attention. Whatever may be the close of this illness, it will be a profound consolation to you, my dear brother, and to us all, that it is borne with perfect resignation; and that her thoughts are such as the good and pious would wish. She reads much, both religious and miscellaneous works.[59]

What Dorothy did not do – or rather, what someone did not wish future generations to know that she *did* do – was keep a journal. Unless intervening manuscripts have been lost (which is quite possible, as Dorothy was remarkably careless with them), she had begun to keep a daily journal again on 1 December 1824, after a lapse of more than twenty-one years. Little more than a list of her engagements and record of her visitors, she had nevertheless kept it up regularly for seven years, with a few lapses when too busy, idle or, latterly, ill to do so. Her last entry was on 14 December 1831, when an entry at the bottom of a left-hand page reads 'all day rain – copied Virgil &c – Southey's Selections from Keswick'. The next entry, at the top of the facing page, is an incomplete one, carried over from a preceding page, which obviously refers to the spring: '[birds] are singing – & all is wrapped up in happy brightness – but the grass with hardly a tinge of greenness – & even larches & lilacs are but just shewing green'. The following entry, immediately beneath it, but written in a different pen and almost in a different hand, is dated 16 July 1833, and begins 'What a pause! – during all this time have been convalescent but so slowly I hardly knew it except by looking back – & have been very helpless as to reading & working'. The entries then continue until November 1835.

At a casual glance, the reader of the manuscript, and more especially a printed transcript, might be forgiven for thinking that the 'pause' for convalescence covers the nineteen months between 14 December 1831 and 16 July 1833. Closer scrutiny reveals that eighteen leaves – containing thirty-six pages of diary entries – have been cut out from the journal, leaving only the smallest of stubs, on which the ends of words are just visible.[60] Who would wish to censor Dorothy's journal, and, more importantly, why? Clearly not Dorothy herself, as the '1833' is written in a different hand and in pencil, not her usual ink. It is a possibility that it was done by a member of the immediate family: Mary and Dora, for instance, did not scruple to erase a paragraph Dorothy had added to a joint letter, because they felt it gave an alarming and unjustifiably gloomy picture of her own and Dora's health. They did, however, explain what they had done, and their reason for it, unlike the phantom journal editor, who went to remarkable trouble to conceal his handiwork.

The finger of suspicion points firmly in one direction, that of Gordon, Willy's youngest son, who was born in 1860, after all his grandfather's generation were dead, and died in 1935. Never having known William, Mary or Dorothy personally, he became the guardian of the flame, collecting, preserving and annotating Wordsworthiana. An insatiable and meticulous scholar in his own research, he did not hesitate to shape the legend for others. In particular, as we have already seen with regard to Annette, he had no qualms about destroying evidence of anything he considered likely to damage or discredit his family. As this evidence has been removed, one can only guess what he might have discovered in his great-aunt's diary and felt obliged to suppress.

The likeliest possibility – and it is only a possibility – is that he found entries relating to his father's tangled love affairs. These can only be pieced together from tangential references in unpublished sources, but a crisis occurred which clearly dates to the missing period in the diary. Willy had long carried a torch for Bertha Southey; the feeling was mutual, and on his return from Germany, Bertha's sister Edith had said to him, 'You'll go to Carlisle for a few years, then something will occur & you & B will marry'. Something had indeed occurred, but it was not what Edith (or, indeed, Willy or Bertha) expected. He had met, and fallen in love with, Mary Cust, who was tenuously related to him through the Crackanthorpes. When he paid a visit home from Carlisle in April 1832, Dora expected him to be cross with her for being a 'cold calculating old maid', and sending Bertha home the day before. Willy, however, was 'happy & merry & pleasant as possible – & has two cards ("Miss Cust") in his pocket book, wh[ich] he made a great fuss about shewing to me wishing me all the time to see them – alas! alas! I thought he was faithful', Dora teased. Returning with him to Carlisle, Dora was determined to see 'his reigning love', and noted, with great amusement, that Willy had two 'Penguins' by his fire, one made by Bertha, the other by Miss Cust, 'he first looks at one & then the other & cannot tell wh[ich] is the more charming'. At some point, he shared his dilemma with his Aunt Sara, who knew the Southey girls better than anyone outside the family. She seems to have assured him that Bertha did not expect them to marry, an impression that was confirmed when Willy visited her several times at Keswick 'with a view to have an explanation'. The moment they were left alone together, Bertha retired, which he interpreted as her delicate way of avoiding having to give him a direct refusal. As his mother remarked, this was probably his fancy, but it suited his own inclinations, as he now felt free to propose to Mary Cust, which he had done by October of that same year, 1832. 'Master Willy is still in happy uncertainty about his Mary –', his sister then reported; 'at present she is from home but I trust on her return it may be settled without loss of time.'[61]

It was not to be. Mary's mother would not accept any suitor for her daughter who did not have a minimum of £400 a year and Willy could not raise 'that unromantic unpoetical yet indispensible wherewithall'. Though not formally engaged, Willy considered himself to be so in spirit. In October 1834 Dora told Quillinan '"oh no we never mention her" but I believe he is constant to his Mary

& she to him'. The quotation from the popular ballad suggests that the marriage had not been approved by Willy's parents either, a hypothesis supported by a remark from Sara Coleridge in 1843: 'Willy deserves to have a nice girl with money, because he was very constant to one who was poor and plain and sickly, till her death released his friends rather than himself, for such freedom was unwelcome to him at the time, from a miserable engagement.' One can well imagine that Willy's engagement to a girl without fortune would not be welcomed by his family on purely pragmatic grounds and more so because they would have preferred him to marry Bertha. The Southeys, Bertha included, all felt that he had treated her badly, though Willy remained oblivious of this until she married her cousin, Herbert Hill, in 1839.[62] As the confidante of both Sara and Willy, Dorothy may well have recorded these transactions in uncontrovertible detail in her journal, which Willy's son might have found discreditable and wished to suppress.

Whatever the dark secret removed from Dorothy's journal, 1832 was not to be a happy year for any of the Wordsworths. For William, it was dominated by the passage, in June, of the Reform Bill, an event he had opposed and dreaded in equal measure. All his worst fears for the preservation of the Constitution were realized, in that it required the threat of a mass creation of peers to force the House of Lords to allow the bill through. Advising Lord Lonsdale to trust to his principles rather than expediency in determining how to vote, William asserted that, in the Earl's position, he would vote against the bill, 'tho' with my eyes open to the great hazard of doing so'.

> Our Constitution was not preconceived and planned beforehand – it grew under the protection of Providence – as a skin grows to, with, and for the human body. Our Ministers would flay this body, and present us, instead of its natural Skin, with a garment made to order, which, if it be not rejected, will prove such a Shirt as, in the Fable, drove Hercules to madness and self-destruction. May God forgive that part of them who, acting in this affair with their eyes open, have already gone so far towards committing a greater political crime than any recorded in History.[63]

Yet again, he circulated a petition against the bill, sending it to be presented by Sir Robert Inglis, who had visited Rydal Mount the previous October. When Southey called, at the end of March, he found William 'more out of heart than I am', which he attributed to his lacking 'constant employment to relieve him from the thoughts of impending evils'. As he still refused to publish on public affairs, the females, who 'cannot bear to think that his voice should never be raised in a cause which he has so much at heart', seized on a sonnet he had written, and secured his reluctant permission to 'newspaper it', so long as it appeared without his name or initials. Once the bill was passed, William's anxiety was succeeded by 'dejection to despondency'. Parliament, he declared, had given birth to a monster. Accurately predicting that out of nine members to be returned by Cumberland under the new arrangement, only two would be Tory, the rest 'down right Jacobin Republicans' or, more dangerous still, 'rash or complying Whig Innovators', he waited impotently for the coming revolution.[64]

Had all been well at home, his spirits might have rallied; instead he felt under siege. James Hogg had just published his highly coloured account of the celestial 'triumphal arch', containing the unkind words de Quincey had attributed to William, and everyone was talking about it. 'The reviving this business in this formal way after a lapse of nearly 18 years does little credit to Mr Hogg & affords another proof how cautious one ought to be in admitting to one's house trading Authors of any description', William retorted bitterly. (Dora, typically, used the anecdote to tease her Aunt Dorothy about her moon-lit walk, arm in arm with 'the pet pig'.)[65] It was the first of several hurtful betrayals of his privacy and confidence.

Far more serious, however, was the state of Dorothy's health. Still confined to her room after her last attack, before Christmas, she had another relapse at the end of April. 'I cannot conceal from you that this last attack has alarmed me much more than any other –', William told Christopher, 'not for its violence – for it was less violent much than the others she has had; but her recovery from each attack is slower and slower – indeed, except that her pain is only occasional, proceeding from extreme flatulence, she can yet be scarcely said to have rallied at all.' What frightened William most was that there was no apparent cause for his sister's relapses. And if a cause could not be identified, then they could not be prevented. The only consolation was that Dorothy herself remained cheerful, even when unable to leave her room. When Dora carried up the first spring flowers, it prompted her aunt to compose what Dora rightly called an 'affecting poem', despite its 'limping measures'.

> I felt a power unfelt before
> Controlling weakness, languor, pain,
> It bore me to the terrace walk,
> I trod the hills again.
>
> No prisoner in this lonely room
> I saw the greens [*sic*] banks of the Wye
> Recalling thy prophetic words
> Bard! Brother! Friend from infancy!
>
> No need of motion or of strength
> Or even the breathing air
> I thought of Nature's loveliest scenes
> And with Memory I was there.[66]

While Dorothy was in her most precarious state, news came from Stockton that Mary's younger sister, Betsy, had died. 'She has always been of weak faculties; and latterly her mind was disordered; so that it is a happy deliverance', William commented. Nevertheless, it was a breaking of the Hutchinson circle; the first death among Mary's siblings since that of Margaret, thirty-six years earlier.[67]

In June 1832 a new edition of William's *Poetical Works* was published by Longman. This was the long-heralded, cheaper edition of his poems, which, by dint of printing the lines closer together and two sonnets a page, instead of one, had been compressed from five volumes into four. Despite these economies, the price could not be reduced below the magic figure of £1 without incurring a loss to both publisher and author. It would therefore sell for £1 4s, which was almost half the price of the last edition. Prudence dictated that the new edition should not appear until the last copies of the old had been sold, and that no new, unpublished, poems would be included, these being reserved either for separate or posthumous publication. It was characteristic of William's thoughtfulness in these matters, that he did not forget to send a complimentary copy to John Gardner, the London surgeon who had written to him two years earlier, suggesting he should publish a cheap edition.[68]

Gardner had proved himself useful in other ways. Knowing his occupation, William had written to him earlier in the year, asking his advice on how to place his nephew, 'Keswick' John, on a medical apprenticeship. John was now seventeen, so shy that he was still called 'Dora's child', because she was the only one who could get him to speak, and eager to do something for himself. Though he had spent two years at Hawkshead Grammar School, the quality of the teaching was not what it had been, and even his uncle had to admit that he was not a good scholar. Gardner, who was already training his own nephew, offered to take John himself. William, with some embarrassment, insisted on checking Gardner's medical credentials, ensured that John could live with the family, so that he would not be alone in London, and arranged for a month's trial. As his father's estate could not stand the costs, his guardian uncles had to find the money for John's maintenance, and the £200 indenture fee. No doubt remembering their own miseries when they had been in the same dependent position, both William and Christopher were generous, ensuring that the indenture was paid for out of their own pockets as a gift to the young man. Fortunately, the amenable John was happy in his new-found profession, liked all the Gardners, and, as Quillinan observed, with a new London haircut, he already looked 'sharper'.[69]

William's own son John also had a stroke of luck. In May Lord Lonsdale and Lord Lowther offered to present him to the living of Brigham, two miles from Cockermouth, on the River Derwent. It was a huge parish, including part of the town of Cockermouth itself, as well as several chapelries, worth £190 a year to its vicar, who would be able to hold it jointly with Moresby. It was a considerable advance for John, but there was no doubt at all on whom the Lowthers were conferring their favour: the letter offering the presentation was addressed to William.[70]

In normal circumstances, William would have been happy in the knowledge that his sons and nephews were all provided for, and making a success of their careers, but he could not rid himself of a depression he had not felt so strongly since his late twenties at Racedown. Then he had sought to come to terms with political disillusionment in the wake of the French Revolution, his guilt about Annette and Caroline, and his growing love for Mary. Now he had to face his fears about the consequences of the Reform Bill and the realization that Dorothy, if not actually dying, would never be restored to health and strength. An uncharacteristically flat letter to Hamilton is eloquent proof of what he there asserted. 'I have for some time from private and public causes of sorrow and apprehension been in a great measure deprived of those genial feelings which thro' life have not been so much accompaniments of my character, as vital principles of my existence.'[71]

He went through the motions of a bustling Rydal summer, but his heart was not in it. At sixty-two years of age, and half blinded with eye disease, he was still able to accompany his friends Julius Hare, Thomas Arnold and Captain Hamilton to the top of Helvellyn, 'and had as pleasant a day as any middle-aged Gentlemen need wish for', except that 'certain sad recollections ... weighed upon my heart. Once I was upon this summit with Sir H. Davy and Sir W. Scott; and many times have I trod it with my nearest and dearest relatives and friends, several of whom are gone, and others going to their last abode.' The Arnolds had taken up residence for the summer at Brathay, having closed the entire school down when cholera struck the neighbourhood. William was not to enjoy the benefit of Arnold's company for long, for at the end of July he and his wife were called to the deathbed of his sister, leaving the children, with their governess, at Brathay. The Wordsworth women, as usual, rose to the challenge, and the little Arnolds were gathered under their collective wing. Before they left, Arnold decided to buy the Fox How estate, high on the shoulders of Loughrigg Fell, overlooking the Vale of Rydal and across to Rydal Mount, where, with William as his foreman in charge of works, he would build his holiday home in the Lakes.[72]

The summer saw literally hundreds of visitors (more than 267, according to the Rydal Mount Visitors' Book, of whom at least 192 came in the four months of July to October). 'Father's popularity is amazingly on the increase if we may judge from the odd & queer indeed impertinent I had almost said expedients that have been resorted to this summer by strangers high & low to have a sight of him or his dwelling.' A travelling carriage drove round the front to take a closer look at the poet's residence, and was duly noted by Dora in the Visitors' Book. Others were even bolder. 'One Man sent in a note well written with some needles to sell price 3d – "as a Lover of Poetry the Author of the Excursion would confer an additional great obligation by paying the bearer in person["]. We have had two or three other notes quite as funny', Dora observed.[73]

There was the usual crop of Americans, 'Cantabs' and relations,[74] but also a first-time visitor who came with an important mission, which proved indisputably that William's poetic reputation had risen to hitherto unimagined heights. Henry Pickersgill was an artist and Royal Academician who had been commissioned to paint William's portrait for St John's College, Cambridge. It was a signal honour. William's undistinguished university career, his youthful republicanism, his years as the butt of literary critics' contempt were all forgotten. James Wood, who had been a fellow of the college when William was an undergraduate there, and was now its Master, wrote a flattering letter in June 1831. A 'numerous body of our Fellows', he informed William, had expressed an 'earnest wish' that the college should have a lasting memorial of a quondam member whose literary character stood high 'and whose writings have uniformly and essentially tended to the promotion of virtue and religion'. Wood himself heartily coincided with this wish, requested William to pick the painter of his choice and informed him that the portrait would be placed in the Old House 'in token of the high opinion they entertain of your Merits and of the honour which the college derives from being able to reckon Mr W. Wordsworth among its worthies'.[75]

William had selected Pickersgill rather by default; there was no one else he preferred, and his friends, particularly Quillinan and Rogers, had recommended him. 'I saw Pickersgill's Pictures at his own house, but between ourselves I did not much like them', William admitted to Rogers. The females, however, were enraptured with the idea and determined to like whatever the artist painted. William insisted that Pickersgill was to be his guest at Rydal Mount. At first the Wordsworths found him 'so odd & pompous', but they soon warmed to him, to the point where Dora jokingly threatened to reveal the 'flirtation' between him and Sara to Mrs Pickersgill. 'The 10 days Mr Pickersgill was with us were the happiest and most memorable I had well nigh said, of my life', Dora enthused.

> Our garret was the only corner of the house that afforded a high light so there the picture was painted, and as Mr P. liked to have people with him to keep the Poet from thinking of where he was and what he was doing everyone that came was introduced into the garret and great fun we had. The Fox Ghyll ladies [Mrs Luff, Lady Farquhar, Mrs and Miss Hook] were daily visitors and Miss Hook and I, or 'Hook and Eye' as we call ourselves ... fairly quarrelled for Mr Pickersgill, alias 'Pick', as I call him. At first we scarcely knew what to make of him, but ere he had been two days with us we cd. not make enough of him – one and all – and such a picture or rather head – for only the head is finished – he has made of Father!

There were the usual battles – to wrinkle or not to wrinkle – which Pickersgill clearly won, as neither the preliminary chalk drawing nor the finished portrait bear the tell-tale furrow down his cheek. Looking at the latter, which still hangs in St John's College, it is hard to see why the Wordsworths were all so pleased with it. William sits, in the half-reclining pose only poets in portraits adopt, on the green terrace with Rydal lake beyond. He is swathed in what Quillinan describes as a 'dandy military sort of cloak', clutches a cap in his right hand and, improbably, a pencil and paper in his left. Given the unnaturalness of the pose and background, the head looks as though it has been grafted on to a mannequin, and, unlike the chalk drawing, which is both dignified and powerful, the face is that of a weak and senile old man. Nevertheless, in the first flush of enthusiasm, they all felt 'deeply grateful to Pickersgill for giving us such a likeness of such a Father! We all agree that Rotha's . . . picture & this are the only perfect likenesses that is living likenesses, we ever saw.' Dora declared she could not look at it for five minutes without tears welling up, a reaction with which one cannot fail to agree, though for entirely different reasons.[76]

Dora's tearful enthusiasm, combined with a feeling that this first public honouring of William's poetic career ought to be recognized by the poet himself, led to the obligatory sonnet: 'Go, faithful Portrait! and where long has knelt Margaret, the saintly foundress, take thy Place'. A workmanlike effort rather than an inspired piece, it centred around the appropriate image of the poet, immutably fixed on the canvas by his hills and streams, 'tho' Kingdoms melt Before the breath of Change', and referred to Dora's tears. Quillinan, in particular, had strong reservations about William publishing a sonnet to his own portrait: 'they seem to be lines purely domestic, and not proper, as yet at least, for the eye of the public: it would be impossible to explain to Strangers their full meaning, and many are the ungenerous who would pretend to find in them matter for sarcasm.' The sonnet was not intended for publication Dora replied, 'but more copies have been given than my Mother & I like – my Father as you know in such matters – is all dove no serpent. We are truly obliged by your hint for he will not always give ear to our notions but you have put him on his guard as to whom & where it is repeated.'[77]

As one of the most momentous years in parliamentary history drew to a close, William was more than ever convinced that the country was on the brink of disaster. 'A spirit of rash innovation is every where at war with our old institutions', he wrote in October,

> and the ardor of those who are bent upon change is exactly according to the measure of their ignorance. – Where men will not, or through want of knowledge, are unable to, look back they cannot be expected to look forward; and therefore, caring for the present only, they care for *that* merely as it affects their own importance. Hence a blind selfishness is at the bottom of all that is going forward – a remark which in other words was made by Mr Burke long ago –

Two months later, he wrote to urge all those members of his family with votes to come to Westmorland to support the Lowther cause: 'having spent nearly 160,000 pounds in resisting the enemy in this County they deserve the generous support and the personal exertions of all friends to good order and the British Constitution'.[78] This personal plea and a signature on a petition requesting Lord Lowther to stand again for Westmorland, rather than Cumberland, was the extent of William's involvement in this election. The Lowther brothers were duly returned, but this was no cause for rejoicing, for all the towns in both counties returned reformers to a man, and the tidal wave of reform would continue. As the old year passed away and a new one dawned, William felt tired, defeated and depressed.

I have been so dejected in mind, by some private distresses, and still more by the alarming State of public affairs . . . that I have not been able to take the least pleasure in Poetry, or in my ordinary pursuits. – In my Youth I witnessed in France the calamities brought upon all classes, and especially the poor, by a Revolution, so that my heart aches at the thought of what we are now threatened with –'.[79]

23. *Falling Leaves*

'You will grieve to hear that our dear Sister is very poorly and seems to grow weaker every day', William informed Christopher on 29 January 1833. Dorothy had suffered another relapse, this time accompanied by alarming new symptoms, swelling in her legs, blackness about her ankles and distressing spasms. 'Alas! my dear Friend, I fear she will not be long with us', Sara wrote to Mrs Coleridge; '. . . her weakness & languor are truly deplorable – indeed without the help of stimulants you could scarcely believe her alive – but with these she is kept at times tolerably easy – & even comfortable & *cheer*ful – which is always the case when free from pain & languor'. Entirely confined to her bed, Dorothy amazed them all with her patience and gaiety, greeting everyone who entered her sick chamber with her usual 'bright smile so full of love & tenderness'. The Ambleside surgeon, Carr, warned them there was no hope, so it came as no surprise when, at the beginning of February, she suffered another attack. Everyone, including Carr, thought her last hour had come, but still she clung to life. 'I wash her face as she used to do mine some thirty years ago', Dora wrote, 'she dear creature not having the power to do so much for herself without great exhaustion – but she is happy & contented & only has one regret – that she cannot read or even bear to be read to & as she cannot gain new ideas she knows she must lose some old ones – so she tells us'.[1]

It seemed that everyone was ill. Dora had had another of her severe winter colds and ate so little that her parents could not help being anxious about her. 'Keswick' John was reported to have suddenly grown extremely thin and was suffering from a return of his cough, symptoms which did not bode well to a concerned guardian uncle's ear. Most dramatically of all, however, a series of shocking revelations about Tom Monkhouse's widow, Mrs Paris Dick, reached the Wordsworths from unimpeachable quarters. First of all, she wrote to inform Richard Addison, the

London solicitor who had been Richard's business partner, that due to a 'long continued series of Injuries & provocations', she had separated from her husband. Towards the end of November Addison discovered that she was 'a confirmed Drunkard', a fact which her family knew, but refused to acknowledge or do anything about. Her daughter, who was not quite eleven years old, was said to appear 'low-spirited'; she was living in lodgings in Blackpool with her mother and a governess who was nearly as bad as her mistress. It was an intolerable situation and, as the Horrockses refused to intervene, it was left to Tom's family to act to save his child. At the suggestion of Mrs Dick's own solicitor, they therefore kidnapped her. Mary was invited to Brinsop Court for the Christmas vacation and simply not returned, a place being found for her at boarding school, a solution which the Wordsworths, applauding from the sidelines, welcomed with relief.[2]

Happier news came from Moresby, where on 7 March the first Wordsworth grandchild, Jane Stanley, made her appearance. 'Her father thinks it the prettiest little thing that ever was', Dora reported, 'but if the truth were known I dare say it is a perfect little fright.' The proud grandfather was persuaded to pay her a brief visit, and ended up staying three weeks, executing family shopping commissions and paying visits to the Curwens at Workington Hall, Lord Lowther at Whitehaven and the theological training college at St Bees. As the baby's other grandfather, Henry Curwen, had stood as a reforming candidate in the recent election, Lord Lowther was full of gloomy predictions of 'an explosion and the entire overthrow of the Institutions of the Country', and St Bees was up in arms at the government's proposal to reform the Church of Ireland, beginning with the abolition of ten bishoprics, it is not surprising that William's spirits did not revive. He tried hard. He threw himself into his son's plans to build a rectory at Brigham, accompanying John and the architect to the chosen site on the banks of the Derwent. He walked twelve miles a day, and discovered, for the first time, that the sea, which he had shunned since his brother's death, could be a delightful companion. 'Nothing can be more charming, especially for a sequestered Mountaineer, than to cast eyes over its boundless surface, and hear as I have done almost from the brow of the steep in the Church field at Moresby, the waves chafing and murmuring in a variety of tones below, as a kind of base of harmony to the shrill yet liquid music of the larks above.'

Before he left, he composed several poems, including one, as he had promised Dora, on the new baby. He also wrote a sequel, 'which I fear none of you will like', lamenting the state of the nation. Expediency preferred before principle, cowardly concession feeding the thirst for power in men 'who ne'er concede', a labouring multitude deceived by flatterers into mistaking calamities for wrongs, brooding over fancied usurpations and imagining that universal suffrage was a panacea for all ills; 'Who shall preserve or prop the tottering Realm?' he cried. 'What hand suffice to govern the state-helm?'[3]

It was a poem written for the best of reasons, 'viz. that the author could not help writing it', but he refused to publish it, also for the best of reasons. As he explained to a lady member of the Sheffield Female Anti-Slavery Society, who wrote to solicit a contribution from him for an anthology of anti-slavery poetry and prose, this was not the time to be publishing inflammatory, politically motivated, material. However good the cause – and he thought slavery abhorrent – he was not prepared 'to add to the excitement already existing in the public mind upon these, and so many other points of legislation and government. Poetry if good for any thing, must appeal forcibly to the Imagination and the feelings; but what at this period we want above every thing, is patient examination and sober judgement.' The Wordsworth women were also pushing William to publish, once again hoping, against experience, that, if he cleared his current work, he might make a start on *The Recluse.* Moxon, too, supported the idea, pointing to the success of the *Selections* and offering to print the new volume for him, but William flatly refused. 'Father has written several 100 lines this spring', Dora reported, 'but only "tiresome small poems" as Mother calls them who is vexed that she cannot get him to set down to his long work. *I* don't believe the "Recluse" will ever be finished.'[4]

Dorothy continued to improve very slowly throughout the spring and early summer. The family waited on her devotedly, William no less than anyone else. Twice a day he would come up to her bedroom and massage her swollen feet and ankles, to keep the circulation going; he read to her and, when the weather was fine, even took his turn in pulling her out on the terraces in her invalid carriage. By the beginning of May she was well enough to walk a little, with the aid of two sticks, sew and talk in small doses, eat well, sleep tolerably and, best of all, read voraciously again. By 16 July she had recovered sufficiently, mentally and physically, to resume her journal, though she still had days when she could not see visitors, and rarely sat in company for more than an hour without being exhausted.[5]

This unexpected reprieve allowed the Wordsworths to consider trips away from home. Mary and Dora paid a three-week visit to Stockton, proudly driving themselves there and back in the pony carriage, without even a servant to accompany them. Sara reluctantly left on 2 July to pay her triennial visit to Brinsop Court. 'I have almost a dread not to say horror of the thought of leaving Rydal Mount even to go into Herefordshire lest I should not return & end my Days here', she confessed in a moment of uncharacteristic weakness. It was a fear Dora shared: 'years rob one of ones joyous spirits – & now gloomy forebodings of what may happen before we meet again press upon me sadly & unwisely nay well nigh wickedly'.[6]

Even William was persuaded to take a tour, his companion being Robinson, who took up residence in the Salutation Inn at Ambleside on 14 June, was summoned to Rydal Mount on the 18th, when a bed came free, and then had to kick his heels for a month while William dithered over the weather, his engagements and whether or not he could leave Dorothy. Robinson was an equable soul, happy and proud to be a guest of *Wordsworth* and content to 'lounge agreeably' round Rydal Mount, occupying himself with reading, chat and, when it was fine, walking with William. Their talk, naturally, was almost entirely on politics. The great difference between them, according to Robinson, was that he was a *hoping* alarmist and William a *despairing* one. Though he was convinced that William was 'essentially liberal', he was nevertheless betrayed into a single expression of irritation at William's 'interminable ... political tirades against the Ministry for their Church reforms, etc.' Dorothy also thoroughly enjoyed the company of Robinson, who, in the Hutchinson family terminology, was known as her 'lover', because of his kind attentions to her: he would sit by her bed trying to entertain her, help her on her short rambles into the garden and escort her back to bed when she was tired.[7]

When Robinson had almost given up hope that they would ever get away, William suddenly announced it was time to go. They set off on 13 July, sailing from Whitehaven, where they were joined by John, who left his own wife and child at Rydal Mount. William had also invited Dora, but she declined, thinking she ought to stay behind to look after her aunt and her cousins Tom and George Hutchinson, who spent their Sedbergh school holidays with the Wordsworths. 'I think too I must have died from talk before we had reached the Island –', she added, 'would you believe it Father has no chance with Crabbe [Robinson] – so pent up in a small steam boat what could I have done?' 'Well, Dora, you are a domestic Heroine and a right good Niece to resist their invitation', Quillinan teased, 'though the dread of Crabbe's loquacity takes some little from the heroic part of the credit due to you.'[8]

William's principal object was to visit the islands of Staffa and Iona, which he and Dora had been obliged to miss on their Scottish tour in 1831, because it was then too late in the season. William, John and Robinson began their travels, however, by taking a circuit of the Isle of Man, prompted by Dorothy's journal of her own visit in 1828. In a rare instance of William himself writing a descriptive letter during a tour, we get a tantalizing glimpse of the entertaining and perceptive journal writer he could have been, and the immediate impressions, captured in prose, which would later lead to a whole series of poems celebrating the island. They called on Mr and Mrs Cookson, their friends from Kendal, who had settled in Ballasalla, after the failure of their business in 1830.[9] 'Bala Sala is a little wood-embosomed Village by the side of a stream upon which stands the ruined walls of an old Abbey, a pretty sequestered place – thronged with Blackbirds and thrushes of extraordinary size and power of song –', William enthused; 'the upper part of the old Tower is overgrown with a yellow Lychen which has the appearance of a gleam of perpetual evening sunshine'. From Ballasalla, they followed Dorothy's pedestrian route around the island. At Castletown they admired King William's College, against the backdrop of the 'grand slopes' of South Barule; on the road to St John's they halted under some sycamores by a waterfall and the two elderly travellers took a nap 'to the great delight of the neighbouring cottagers'. At St John's itself they stopped to view Tynwald Hill, and, surrounded by eleven cottage children, were amused by the sight of 'an old Gullion', sitting almost at the top of this 1,000-year-old seat of government, 'with a telescope in his hand through which he peeped occasionally having the advantage of seeing things double, for as he frankly owned he had got a drop too much'. At Peel they took an evening trip round the castle by boat, 'to the great dismay of my Companion though the sea was calm as glass, but it broke unintelligibly with noise and foam over the sharp black rocks on which the Castle stands'. After spending some time with Joanna at Ramsay, the travellers sailed from there to Greenock, ready to begin their tour of the Scottish islands.[10]

'Upon the whole, Dearest D., I liked your Isle of Man better than I expected', William observed, but its subtle delights were lost on the urbane Robinson. 'Mona is hardly worth visiting by a merely curious traveller but it is a cheap residence and Douglas is an agreeable watering place.' Like the good lawyer he was, he had found his greatest amusement in looking over the Manx laws, 'which contain some amusing illustrations of Etymology'. Robinson was equally unimpressed by William's beloved Scotland. 'The greater part of our journey was a threading of the Scotch isles of which I have now had more than enough –', he informed his brother. 'Rocks are pretty in pictures, will do very well in poems, but one does not want them for daily companions.' From Greenock, they travelled by steamboat down the Firth of Clyde (during an eclipse, which their fellow travellers ignored) to Oban, and then through the Inner Hebrides, calling at Mull, Coll, Staffa and Iona. Only the two last were distinguished in Robinson's mind. Staffa he forbore to describe – 'You may consult any book you like' – though it drew from him unexampled praise – 'truly a marvellous sight and well worth a voyage to be seen'. Iona was different. The only reason its ancient monuments were worthy of notice was because they were to be found 'in a spot preeminently desolate & ugly – The whole island has not a tree – Stones are its chief produce – Its population are ragged fishermen who beget numberless children who plague the visitors by tendering little plates of shells & stones'.[11]

William's impressions are not recorded in prose, but this short tour, only a fortnight from start to finish, provided a wealth of material for poems. From them, it is clear that William's own reactions were out of step with his friend's. His first visit to Staffa was a major disappointment. Like many a tourist before and since, he arrived expecting to enjoy silent communion with its isolation and the awesome wonder of Fingal's Cave. Instead, he arrived on a steamboat with the nineteenth-century equivalent of a coach party.

> We saw, but surely, in the motley crowd,
> Not One of us has felt the far-famed sight;
> How *could* we feel it? each the other's blight,
> Hurried and hurrying, volatile and loud.

Unwilling to quit the place with only this memory of it, he became that traditional scourge of the coach party, the One Who is Always Late. 'At the risk of incurring the reasonable displeasure of the master of the steamboat, I returned to the cave,' he explained, 'and explored it under circumstances more favourable to those imaginative impressions which it is so wonderfully fitted to make upon the mind.' Not one, but three more sonnets were the result, which was probably little consolation to those left on board ship, waiting for him to make his reappearance.[12]

The ravaged abbey ruins and lonely Celtic crosses on Iona, sixth-century home of St Columba, and birthplace of Christianity in the north of Britain, could not fail to move William. In one of four sonnets inspired by the place, he checked a lament for the contrast time had wrought between its glorious past and forlorn present: though ruined now, the abbey had fulfilled its purpose in spreading the Word to the heathen.

And when, subjected to a common doom
Of mutability, those far-famed Piles
Shall disappear from both the sister Isles,
Iona's Saints, forgetting not past days,
Garlands shall wear of amaranthine bloom,
While heaven's vast sea of voices chants their praise.

Even the beggar children, who had so irritated Robinson by offering their pathetic array of shells and stones for sale to wealthy tourists, provoked a kindlier response in William. 'How sad a welcome!' he mused, contrasting it with the glory days of Iona's Celtic past.[13]

When they reached Inverary, 'this pleasing little place', Robinson decided that the weather was so gloomy, he could not face travelling on to Loch Lomond and Glasgow with William and John. Instead, he remained there, waiting for better weather, then set off alone to explore eastern Scotland, not forgetting, because of William's poems, to visit the Yarrow, before rejoining them at Rydal Mount. The Wordsworths, meanwhile, returned home through 'Burns Country', Renfrewshire, Ayrshire and Dumfriesshire. A year later, William looked back with fond memories to this pilgrimage. 'It gave me much pleasure to see Kilmarnock, Mauchlin, Mossgeil Farm [Burns's farm], the Air [*sic*], which we crossed where he winds his way most romanticky thro' rocks and woods – and to have a sight of Irwin and Lugar, which naebody sung till he named them in immortal verse.' The only disappointment was the monument to Burns in Dumfries churchyard, which was 'monstrous in conception and clumsy in the execution. It is a disgrace to the Memory of the Poet.' It was perhaps fortunate that William himself had declined to contribute to any memorial of this kind, rejecting a request for a subscription with the comment that Burns had 'raised for himself a Monument so conspicuous, and of such imperishable materials, as to render a local fabric of Stone superfluous'.[14]

William and John arrived, unexpectedly, on 25 July, to find Dorothy improved beyond their wildest dreams. 'Mr Robinson's 40 Lawyer power [conversation] has been of infinite service to our dear Invalid who is so much improved', Dora wrote the day before their return, 'that we can scarcely believe our eyes when we meet her hobbling along the upstairs passage even as far as my Mother's room'. Dorothy drove out in the morning, then, in the afternoon, went into the garden, where her nephews, Tom and George, were her 'dutiful attentive ponies', pulling her along in her little wheeled carriage. To everyone's mortification, the unexpected return of her brother caused her such excitement that she promptly had another relapse that night, undoing much of the good work that had been done.[15]

William had been at home for less than a fortnight when, in his official capacity as Distributor of Stamps, he was summoned to Carlisle to attend a suit for libel brought by the Earl of Lonsdale against several local newspapers. It was an opportunity to pay Willy a visit, so Mary went with him, and, instead of returning by the direct route through Penrith, they made a slight detour to the east, down the lovely Eden valley. Still vibrant with poetry after his Scottish tour, this little excursion was to furnish William with material for seven more sonnets, including one of his most moving, inspired by Nollekens's sculpted monument in the chapel at Wetheral, just outside Carlisle. The antithesis of the Burns monument at Dumfries, it portrayed Maria Howard, whose sole claim to immortality was that of domestic tragedy. She had died giving birth to a still-born son when she was twenty-three.

> Stretched on the dying Mother's lap, lies dead
> Her new-born Babe; dire ending of bright hope!
> But Sculpture here, with the divinest scope
> Of luminous faith, heavenward hath raised that head
> So patiently; and through one hand has spread
> A touch so tender for the insensate Child –
> (Earth's lingering love to parting reconciled,
> Brief parting, for the spirit is all but fled) –
> That we, who contemplate the turns of life
> Through this still medium, are consoled and cheered;
> Feel with the Mother, think the severed Wife
> Is less to be lamented than revered;
> And own that Art, triumphant over strife
> And pain, hath powers to Eternity endeared.[16]

The wide, rust-coloured waters of the Eden itself, flowing slow and deep through woods and blushing rocks, earned its own tribute: its name was 'rightfully borne', since its beauties were indeed those of Paradise. Nunnery Walks, near Penrith, which William had loved since childhood, prompted a sonnet. So did Long Meg and her Daughters, seventy-three standing stones in a circle eighty yards in diameter, with a single larger stone apart from the rest. Because of the lie of the land, they are stumbled across unexpectedly, and, though they crown a small hill, it and they are dwarfed by the surrounding fells, which lower oppressively above and around them.[17] More surprisingly, the railway viaducts spanning the Eden and a neighbouring ravine at Corby also won praise; though trains and steamboats were at war with 'old poetic feeling', and marred the loveliness of nature,

Time,
Pleased with your triumphs o'er his brother Space,
Accepts from your bold hands the proffered crown
Of hope, and smiles on you with cheer sublime.

The Wordsworths ended their little excursion by spending a couple of nights at Lowther Castle (a rare visit by Mary) and three with the Marshalls at Hallsteads, on Ullswater.[18]

They returned to find Rydal Mount in the full throes of the Lakers' season. More than 268 visitors called or stayed this year, among them a young clergyman, Robert Perceval Graves, who was tutor to Mrs Hemans's son, Charles. In a typically flowery letter of introduction, Mrs Hemans had described him as 'one whose long communion with, and true appreciation of your Works, in the study of which he has been my frequent companion, render him well deserving the honour of your acquaintance'. Graves received the usual kind reception, and returned to Dublin determined to exchange the Church of Ireland for the Church of England and secure a curacy in the Lakes. Afraid of appearing to presume on so brief an acquaintance, he persuaded Mrs Hemans to enlist William's assistance in procuring him one. 'I should much rather owe my settlement as a Pastor to your interposition & recommendation than to any other channel of interest which I possess', Graves wrote gratefully, adding that both he and his brother would treasure their memories of their meeting with the poet as 'setting the seal to our knowledge of your Poetry, [which] has become an efficacious influence upon our lives'.[19]

On 28 August, William was visited by a thirty-year-old Bostonian who had just resigned his Unitarian ministry and would later become internationally famous as one of America's most eminent essayists, poets and preachers. When he met William, however, Ralph Waldo Emerson was virtually unknown outside the confines of Boston society. Nevertheless, he brought with him a highly unusual degree of New World and youthful arrogance, which stood in the way of his appreciation of both the man and the poet. William was dismissed (in print, not just a private journal) as 'a plain, elderly, white-haired man, not prepossessing, and disfigured by green goggles', who talked with 'great simplicity'. William spoke at length on his favourite themes, politics and education, assuring Emerson that he did so to impress upon him '& all good Americans, to cultivate the moral, the conservative, &c. &c. & never to call into action the physical strength of the people; as lately had been done in the Reform Bill, &c. in England'. 'He was so benevolently anxious to impress upon me my social duties as an American citizen', Emerson added in a private letter, 'that he accompanied me near a mile from his house talking vehemently & ever & anon stopping short to imprint his words.'

As they walked in the garden along the terraces, William offered to recite the three sonnets on Fingal's Cave he had composed within three days of leaving Staffa, and proceeded to do so with such gravity and power that Emerson was convinced they were more beautiful than anything which had appeared in print. Nevertheless, he found the spectacle amusing.

> This reciting was so unexpected & extraordinary, – he, the old Wordsworth, standing forth & reciting to me in a garden walk, like a schoolboy 'speaking his piece,' – that I at first had nearly laughed; but, recollecting myself, that I had come thus far to see a poet, & he was chaunting poems to me, I saw, that he was right, & I was wrong, & gladly gave myself up to hear.

Emerson went away impressed by William's kindness but 'surprised by the hard limits of his thought. To judge from a single conversation, he made the impression of a narrow and very English mind; of one who paid for his rare elevation by general tameness and conformity. Off his own beat, his opinions were of no value.' This was the opinion he published, together with an account of his visit, the following year, in the book of his tour, *English Traits*.[20] It was hardly a generous return for the time and kindness William had devoted to him, but it was neither the first nor the last time that the privilege of meeting with, and talking to, the poet in the privacy of his own home would be abused. As Dora had remarked, William was always more dove than serpent in these matters, trusting to the good nature of those who sought him out, rather than suspecting their motives.

Another American, the Reverend Orville Dewey, published a far more sympathetic and revealing account of his meeting with William this summer. Unlike Emerson, who thought you should speak to the famous 'as to children or persons of inferior capacity whom it is necessary to humor; adapting our tone & remarks to their known prejudices & not to our knowledge of the truth', Dewey dared to argue with William, and was rewarded with conversation rather than monologue. They discussed politics and poetry literally for hours on end, Dewey noting, as they did so, William's habit, when walking and talking, of stopping every fourth or fifth step and turning round to his companion to enforce what he was saying. Unlike Emerson, Dewey tried to capture a flavour of William's conversation instead of conflating his opinions, and though the same topics were discussed, the slant was very different. Echoing the sentiments of so much of his correspondence, William pronounced himself in favour of gradual reform and, while admitting that hereditary rank and an Established Church were indefensible 'in the broadest views of human rights and interests', argued that they could not be removed without opening the door to anarchy and irreligion. 'Public opinion, the foolish opinion of the depraved, ignorant, and conceited mass, ought not to be the law; it ought not to be expressed in law; it ought not to be represented in government.' Nor was it possible for those in government to act independently, or in the best interests of their country, if they were dependent for their places on 'the ever-wavering breath of popular opinion'. 'He remarked afterwards, that, although he was known to the world only as a poet, he had given twelve hours' thought to the condition and prospects of society for one to poetry.'[21]

By the beginning of October William had composed more than forty sonnets

19. Rydal Water, a pencil and wash drawing by Thomas Chubbard, 1796. Rydal Mount lies just out of sight at the far end of the lake, on the lower slopes of Rydal Fell, which is the mountain on the left.

20. George Webster's architect's drawings for the north elevation of the Wordsworths' new house, which was to be built in the field in front of Rydal Mount if Lady le Fleming ended their tenancy, as she threatened to do in 1826. Note the vernacular round chimney stacks, pillared frontage, symbolic poet's lyre carved into the end gable and grand stone-built terrace.

North Elevation of a Residence.
designed for William Wordsworth Esqr
at Rydal.
Kendal

21. The drawing room at Rydal Mount, drawn by William Westall and published by Edward Moxon in 1840. A crucially important picture in the iconography of the poet, this widely circulated engraving depicts William, aged seventy, standing before his fireside in his favourite pose (his hand tucked into his waistcoat), dictating to his wife. The image is deliberately domestic, but the portraits, busts and, above all, the book-lined shelves testify to the poet's calling. Westall's meretricious use of perspective makes the room appear far larger than it was in reality.

22. William Westall's delightful watercolour of Rydal Mount, painted in 1831 in Dora's sketchbook. Dora herself is in the garden.

23. The garden entrance to Rydal Mount, drawn by K. J. Bennett, one of a family of Quakers who visited the Wordsworths in 1846. The picture was drawn to sell at the Belfast Ladies' Bazaar for the Relief of Irish Destitution and was authenticated by William as 'A most correct Drawing of Rydal Mount'.

24. A highly dramatized painting of the Lower Falls at Rydal, to which all visitors to Rydal Mount, including the dowager Queen Adelaide, were escorted by the Wordsworths. Watercolour of 1780 by C. W. Bampflyde.

25. An early photograph of Rydal Mount, with the terrace steps leading to the overgrown mound, which gave the house its name, on the right.

26. William Wordsworth, aged seventy-two, painted by Benjamin Robert Haydon in 1842 as if the poet were standing on Helvellyn.

27. Mary Wordsworth, aged sixty-nine, miniature painted in oil on ivory by Margaret Gillies in November 1839.

28. Christopher Wordsworth, William's brother, painted as Master of Trinity College in 1824 by George Robson.

29. Henry Crabb Robinson, an undated portrait by J. J. Masquerier.

30. A slightly bizarre image of the tall William Wordsworth walking with short Hartley Coleridge, sketched from life in 1844 by John Peter Mulcaster. This is a watercolour copy by Tom Monkhouse's daughter, Mary Elizabeth; the original is lost.

31. Mary Elizabeth Monkhouse, daughter of Mary Wordsworth's cousin Tom Monkhouse, whose childish beauty and happy disposition inspired William's poem *The Infant M– M–*.

32. The Reverend Owen Lloyd, hard at work on a sermon, observed by Jessy Harden and H. Almack at Brathay Hall, *c.* 1827; an ink and wash drawing by John Harden, whose daughter, Jane, Owen hoped, but failed, to marry.

33. Dorothy Wordsworth, aged sixty-one, painted by Samuel Crosthwaite in 1833, during a period of remission before her final mental and physical collapse. The dog, Miss Belle, was a stray which the family did not have the heart to turn away after it followed William and his son home.

34. Isabella Fenwick, aged fifty-six, painted in 1839 by Margaret Gillies. Miss Fenwick was described by William as 'The star which comes at close of day to shine' and by Dora as her 'good angel'; this picture inspired William's poem *Upon a Portrait*.

35. John Wordsworth's Vicarage at Whitwick, Leicestershire, drawn by his sister, Dora, in August 1828. It was here that Dorothy, living out her dream of keeping house in a country parsonage, caught the illness which eventually led to permanent mental and physical impairment.

36. Samuel Taylor Coleridge, aged about fifty-two, drawn by Charles Robert Leslie, *c*. 1824.

37. Sir Francis Legatt Chantrey's bust of the Poet Laureate, Robert Southey, aged fifty-eight, taken in 1832.

38. A re-creation of the famous visit by William Wordsworth (*standing*) and Sir Walter Scott to the Yarrow in 1831, which inspired William's *Yarrow Revisited*. After a painting by George Cattermole (1800–1868), illustrator of Scott's *Waverley Novels*.

39. Dora Wordsworth, painted by Margaret Gillies in November 1839. Dora later visited Miss Gillies's studio in London 'to have my nose reduced a little'. After Dora's death, at Quillinan's request, Miss Gillies retouched the portrait again to make her appear more 'spiritualized'.

40. (*Below left*) John Wordsworth, the only known portrait of Dora's brother as a young man.

41. (*Below right*) Willy Wordsworth, with his daughter, Mary Louisa, who was born in 1849. Willy's strong resemblance to his father is a family characteristic still in evidence among Wordsworth descendants to this day.

arising from his forays to the Isle of Man and Scotland and down the Eden. It was a level of sustained creativity unparalleled in recent years, and he paid the price with a bout of trachoma so severe that he was temporarily blinded and had to be confined to a darkened room for ten days. Even this could not stem the flow, for as he had told Emerson, he was quite capable of composing several hundred lines of poetry and holding them in his head without writing them down. 'I cannot muster courage to publish them, or any thing else', William told Kenyon. 'I seem to want a definite motive – money would be one, if I could get it, but I cannot.' The print run of the cheap four-volume edition was 2,000, but a year later only 400 had been sold, leaving both author and publisher considerably out of pocket. William circulated copies of the new sonnets privately among his friends and even, with a lack of caution he later regretted, in response to a heartfelt request from a stranger. 'The reason why I withhold such minor pieces as I have written, is not what some have chosen to say – an overweening conceit of their being above the taste of my countrymen:' he explained to this admirer, 'it is no such thing – but a humble sense of their not being of sufficient importance for a separate Publication; and a strong ground of apprehension that either my Publisher or myself might be a loser, by giving them to the world.'[22]

Though Dora and Mary reported that William was 'very, very patient' under his blindness, his progress was so slow that he began to get 'very nervous & very anxious'. For the first time, the seat of the infection was in his eye, rather than the eyelid, and despite the kind attentions of a visiting Liverpool physician, Dr Vose, who applied the ubiquitous leeches and blisters, and forbade him to visit his neighbours, read, think, doze during the day, or walk in the garden when the sun was bright, the air sharp or the wind high, he did not get better. Reports of his blindness began to appear in the newspapers, and though he hastened to contradict them, in his heart of hearts, he feared they might prove true. 'He finds as you may imagine these long fire & candle light evenings distressing & tiresome in the extreme –', Dora wrote to her cousin on 12 November. 'My mother & I read to him a great great deal but as neither her chest nor my throat is of the very strongest we find it fatiguing & he cannot always keep awake & reading aloud is tiresome at best one gets on so slowly.' Even the saintly Mary's patience finally snapped under the strain of looking after so many invalids. In the middle of writing a long tirade to Robinson about the state of the times at her husband's dictation, she stopped mid-sentence and wrote, 'and I M. W. *will not* write another word on this subject'.[23]

The arrival of William's nephew, Chris, on 29 December was greeted with relief and joy by the beleaguered household, yet even he could not lift their spirits. 'My Uncle's eyes are . . . much better,' he told his father, 'indeed they would be quite well, if he did not write verses: but this he *will* do; and therefore it is extremely difficult to prevent him from ruining his eyesight.' Convinced that blindness would be his fate, sooner or later, William consoled himself with the idea of going to Italy, 'to lay in a store of images, poetical and others', to feed his imagination in the darkness to come.[24]

He stood in need of consolation, for he had not just his blindness to contend with but also, in his mid-sixties, he had reached the age when death was reaping a plentiful crop among his friends. As he informed Rogers on 14 January, he had lost no fewer than fourteen relatives, friends or 'valued acquaintance' within the previous three or four months. The most important of these was Jack Hutchinson, Mary's oldest brother, who, at sixty-five, in the wake of his financial ruin and one personal tragedy after another, succumbed to heart disease and died on 31 August 1833. 'I have just lost a very dear & very kind Uncle ... who always made a Pet of me', Dora wrote miserably; 'he is laid in a pretty church yard washed by the river Tees close to the house where my Mother & Aunts & Uncles past their younger days & where already rest four of his own Daughters & a favourite Sister – My poor Mother feels his death deeply, – but she sets us a beautiful example of calm and cheerful resignation to the Will of the Almighty.' Thomas Cookson, one of their oldest friends, died of cholera only a very short time after William had composed the sonnet, supposedly written in his name, celebrating his pretty cottage refuge at Ballasalla in the Isle of Man. Two of William's young Cambridge admirers and friends had also died suddenly, Arthur Hallam (the subject of Tennyson's *In Memoriam*), at the age of twenty-three, and Lionel Fraser (who had shared Ivy Cottage with the Aylings), at the age of twenty-six.[25]

It was a trend that was set to continue throughout the spring and summer. Sara Coleridge gave birth to twins seven weeks prematurely on 14 January; born on the Tuesday, they were baptized on Wednesday, died on Thursday and buried on Saturday. The poor mother herself was in an apparently hopeless state, suffering in mind and body, and ironically, like her father, dependent on opiates. The list seemed endless. William Sotheby, a London friend of more than thirty years' standing; Mary, widow of William Calvert, the Wordsworths' old Keswick friend; Barratt Brydges, Quillinan's kindly brother-in-law; Maria Jane Jewsbury, of cholera, in India, where, against all her friends' advice, she had emigrated on her recent marriage to a chaplain in the East India Company; Mrs Paris Dick, the former Mrs Tom Monkhouse, of typhus, at Clifton, leaving her orphan daughter to the happier fate of informal adoption by the Hutchinson and Monkhouse clan in Herefordshire.[26]

And then there was Coleridge. The Wordsworths had seen so little of him over the previous twenty years, he had survived so many crises, and declined so steadily and slowly, that his death came as a tremendous shock to them all. More than any other, it was a severing of William's poetic ties with the past. By great good luck, both Poole and Sara Hutchinson, who rarely went to London, had visited him several times in the weeks before he died. Though he had then been unwell, no one, except the woman who had carried the oppressive weight of his love so long, guessed dissolution was so close. 'Yesterday I was at Highgate & greatly was I shocked with the changed appearance of my dear old Friend', she confided in Quillinan. '... He will never rise from his bed more I fear tho' this does not seem to be the opinion of his relatives'.

When death came, it came suddenly. He was seized with acute pains in his bowels and difficulty in breathing and speaking. Opium, which had so long been his enemy, proved his friend at last, easing him to a painless death five days later. Even at the end, he still ran from emotional confrontation, as he had done all his life. He refused to see his wife, children or friends, and would allow no one to attend him, except Harriet, his nurse, and Taylor, Gillman's assistant, who had long kept him surreptitiously supplied with opium. He died on 25 July 1834, aged sixty-one. As he had requested, his body was opened after his death, to identify the cause of the internal pains from which he had suffered all his life and for which he blamed his dependency on opium. Nothing was found. His will left what little money he had to his widow, for life, and then to his children; his friend Joseph Henry Green was appointed his literary executor; the Gillmans were to get his pictures and a precious manuscript book; a gold mourning ring, enclosing a lock of his hair, was bequeathed to each of his oldest friends, Lamb, Montagu, Poole, Josiah and Lancelot Wade, and Sara Hutchinson. To William and Southey, who, more than anyone else, had done so much to support him and his family over the years, Coleridge left the 'Gratitude and Reverential Affection' of his children, 'and the sentiments I have left on record in my Literary life and in my Poems, . . . which . . . supersede the necessity of any other Memorial of my Regard and respect'.[27]

If this was an intentional slight, William refused to take it as such. 'I cannot give way to the expression of my feelings upon this mournful occasion; I have not strength of mind to do so –', he confessed to Sara's husband, Henry Nelson Coleridge.

> The last year has thinned off so many of my Friends, young and old, and brought with it so much anxiety, private and public, that it would be no kindness to you were I to yield to the solemn and sad thoughts and remembrances which press upon me. It is nearly 40 years since I first became acquainted with him whom we have just lost; and though with the exception of six weeks when we were on the continent together, along with my Daughter, I have seen little of him for the last 20 years, his mind has been habitually present with me, with an accompanying feeling that he was still in the flesh. That frail tie is broken and I, and most of those who are nearest and dearest to me must prepare and endeavour to follow him.

In private conversation with Robert Graves, Mrs Hemans's protégé, who arrived at Rydal just as the news of Coleridge's death was announced, William was even more generous about his old friend, calling him

> the most <u>wonderful</u> man that he had ever known, wonderful for the originality of his mind & the power he possessed of throwing out in profusion grand central truths from which might be evolved the most comprehensive systems. Wordsworth, as a Poet, regretted that German metaphysics had so much captivated the taste of Coleridge – for he was frequently not intelligible on this subject – whereas if his energy & his originality had been more exerted in the channel of poetry, an instrument of which he had so perfect a mastery, Wordsworth thought he might have done more, permanently, to enrich the literature & to

influence the thought of the nation than any man of the age. As it was, however, he said he believed Coleridge's mind to have been a widely fertilizing one, & that the seed he had so lavishly sown in his conversational discourses & the Sibylline leaves (not the poem so called by him) which he had scattered abroad so extensively covered with his annotations, had done much to form the opinions of the highest-educated men of the day; although this might be an influence not likely to meet with adequate recognition.

William read Henry Nelson Coleridge's moving account of his father-in-law's death to Graves, his voice faltering, and then breaking down completely when he reached the part where Coleridge had expressed the hope, in his final moments, that his end would manifest the depth of his trust in his Saviour, Jesus Christ.[28]

As soon as they learned of Coleridge's death, the Wordsworths immediately sought out Hartley, fearing his reaction to the news. They had an anxious few hours when he did not come, as he had promised Mary he would when she called on him, but he made a belated arrival. 'Poor fellow! in such distress –', Dorothy noted in her journal; '[he] bitterly regrets he has seen so little of his Father except in early childhood.' Only Sara, pardonably, gave way to any bitterness, accusing Coleridge's relations of having more pride in him than love for him: 'at least Pride was the foundation of their Love – & even their Pride did not serve to prevent his being dependent upon the Gillmans for his support since the time when his Pension was withdrawn'.[29] It was her only outburst; thereafter, she kept her feelings about Coleridge to herself, as she had always done.

Sara had returned to Rydal Mount on 21 June, after an absence of almost a year. She was dismayed to find that, while she had been away, most of the fine trees at the entrance had been cut down, and the 'pleasing gloom thro which you passed to the chearful front of the house is gone'. This had been done because the old entrance hall had been converted into a dining room, where light and air were more necessary. Though she understood why it had been done, Sara found it difficult to reconcile herself to the change. She had been escorted home from London by her nephew, 'Keswick' John, and their arrival heralded an influx of visitors. As so often, the Wordsworths had a houseful of children, or rather young people, marshalled under Dora's affectionate care. In addition to 'the quiet John W', who preferred to stay at Rydal Mount rather than with his mother and her new husband, the Keswick attorney John Lightfoot, there were the Sedbergh schoolboys, Tom and George, and, to everyone's delight, the little orphan, Mary Monkhouse. 'Little' was a misnomer, as Dora pointed out, for at twelve years old Mary was already taller than Sara. 'She seems to us very amiable & very interesting & affectionate as possible to us all', Dora enthused, though Sara noted 'something of reserve about her that does not quite please me'.[30]

Despite her occasional tartness, Sara had the kindest of hearts. Just before he was due to return to Sedbergh for his last half-term before going up to university, young Tom broke down and wept, admitting that he feared he would fail dismally, because he had no confidence in his own abilities. While Dora wept with Tom and

William wrote to his headmaster, asking him to encourage the boy, it was Sara who came up with the practical solution, offering to pay for a private tutor at college out of her own purse. She followed it up with some 'trite & prosy' advice: 'I need not tell you that I am most tenderly & deeply interested in your welfare – & to secure your *well doing* there is nothing in my power that should be wanting, if *that would avail* – but it is in your *own* power & *no one's* else'.[31]

Sara also lent her voice to the females' campaign to persuade William to publish another volume of poetry. 'Reluctant as I am, I have at last given way', William wearily informed Moxon, to whom he wished to offer the book, though he felt honour-bound to continue with Longman. He toyed with the idea of including illustrations, as Rogers had done in his latest edition, but, unlike Rogers, he did not have a private fortune and the extra expense was prohibitive. Instead, he settled for a single volume, of the same size and format as the last, 1832, edition, so that former purchasers could buy it to complete their set. The decision was not entirely altruistic: Longman assured him that this edition had sold better than any former one. The choice of title, too, was deliberately popularist. Though it could well have been another *Memorials of a Tour*, this volume was to be called *Yarrow Revisited, and Other Poems*, invoking memories of the two earlier Yarrow poems, which had been widely praised.[32]

As Dora, with characteristic lack of deference, put it, 'a little *stuffing*' would be required to make the volume up to size. Henry Hutchinson's delightful little autobiographical poem, with its refrain 'poor to Sea I went, and poor I still remain', would thus be set among the poems relating to the Isle of Man, duly attributed to 'a Retired Mariner (a Friend of the Author)'. Another 'friend of the author', his sister, was less easily persuaded to contribute. She had always had an antipathy to the idea of appearing in print, resisting considerable pressure from family and friends to publish her tour journals, as well as her poetry. Now, however, William wanted to include a few of her poems in his new volume. She refused, referring to them contemptuously as 'vagrant lines'. Curiously, it was Rogers, to whom *Yarrow Revisited* would be dedicated, who succeeded where everyone else had failed. Visiting Rydal in August, 'He sate a while with me', Dorothy wrote in her current journal, '& determined me not to withhold my consent'. What arguments he used to convince her remain a mystery.[33]

Rogers's visit, the presence of the Arnolds, who had taken up summer residence in their new house, Fox How, and the birth of a first grandson, Henry Curwen Wordsworth, were the only bright spots in the autumn of a year which ended as miserably as it had begun. In September *Tait's Magazine* published the first in what became a series of four 'kiss and tell' articles about Coleridge by de Quincey. Like modern tabloid journalism, they were vastly entertaining to the casual reader, but to Coleridge's family and friends they were utterly abhorrent, not merely because there was what Coleridge's daughter called 'a false colouring' cast over his private life, but especially because one and all regarded it as a breach of trust and friendship. 'Is it not unjustifiable in any man to expose the recesses of a friend's home to the general gaze?' Sara asked. The Wordsworths were up in arms: Aunt Sara burnt with indignation against 'the little Monster – whom she never liked over well' and Dora thought 'such unprincipled wretches do deserve to be shewn up & without mercy'. William, for whom such betrayals of his own confidence were increasing as he grew more famous, was so incensed that he wrote to Green, Coleridge's literary executor, suggesting that he should attempt to stop, or at least contradict, the articles. Hartley threatened to 'give it' to de Quincey, but his sister took a loftier tone. 'It is grievous indeed to see a man of his high order of intellect & gentlemanly education descending to pamper the depraved appetite of the Public for personality & gossip which he ought to have used his best talents & energies to correct.'[34]

At the end of September, Sara Hutchinson received a note from Southey, begging her to go to Keswick immediately. His wife had been increasingly depressed since Edith had married and left home in January; the imminent departure of Cuthbert, her only son, who was going to live with Edith, and be tutored by her husband in preparation for university entrance, triggered a mental crisis. She became so wild and unmanageable that her family were afraid for her safety, as well as their own; by main force she had to be removed to the Retreat at York. 'I have been parted from my wife by something worse than death', Southey wrote on 2 October. 'Forty years has she been the life of my life; and I have left her this day in a lunatic asylum.' 'Miss Hutton', as the young Southeys had called Sara from childhood, went at an hour's notice to care for the afflicted family, and remained with them, not having the heart to leave and they being unwilling to part with her.[35]

At the beginning of November, Dora became very unwell. She had long suffered from want of appetite, indigestion and pains in her neck and shoulders, but Carr now diagnosed an inflammation of the spine and put her on a drastic course of treatment. She was consigned to the sofa, where she was to lie all day and be bled and blistered. Remarkably, she survived, but unremarkably, she grew steadily weaker. Aunt Joanna had to be summoned to assist poor Mary, who had far too much to do. As Dora miserably admitted to her cousin, she was worse than useless; Dorothy could not do much and her father required constant attention. 'We are a bright trio are we not [?]'. The basic problem, as everyone knew, was Dora herself. She had long ago convinced herself that a spare diet was good for her: perhaps she feared that she was too fat (she was certainly tall in an age when this was not fashionable for women), but publicly she would say only that it was necessary for her health. As she now appeared to accept the doctor's diagnosis, her family hoped that she would start to eat properly again, but this she refused to do. She lay on the sofa, read novels and was, to all appearances, perfectly cheerful, complaining only of 'not wellness', rather than illness. 'She persists in living upon *prison fare* – bread & water – ie Tea as weak as water –', Sara told Quillinan two months later, 'though the medical men are of opinion that this spare diet is the cause, in her case, of the complaint – & cannot therefore be the remedy also!'[36] Her family begged and pleaded, to no avail, and it was only a forthright letter of rebuke from an unexpected source which had any effect at all. Quillinan, who was temporarily living in Portugal on business, responded to Sara's letter by writing directly to Dora herself. It was an important letter, and, for reasons which will later become clear, it was a significant intervention.

I long, long ago, perceived that you were destroying your health by that pernicious system of starvation; but you were always so wilful on the subject that I could not presume to venture on anything like repeated remonstrance, which indeed could have produced no effect but irritation, when none better was produced by the interference of those who had a right to remonstrate. But, at this distance, when I learn that you are reduced to serious illness, and that you still persist in your determination to be unable to eat (for that is my construction of the fact) I do take upon myself to implore you to be persuaded into the duty of habituating yourself to a more generous diet. If you continue obstinate, I shall still think of you fifty times a day, but it will always be as Dora Wordsworth the Wilful. – I did hope that your good sense would rid you of your infatuation on this subject. I will say no more; I fear what I have already said may sound harsh if not impertinent; and God knows I am far from intending harshness to a poor sick Girl confined to her sofa . . . God bless you, Dora: make haste and repent of your sin of self-condemnation to 'Prison Fare,' and turn Gourmande.

'I confess I was hurt that you should think so ill of me –', Dora replied; 'if ever we meet again you will have no cause to complain on this head I guess.'[37]

At the beginning of December, it was Dorothy's turn. A severe bilious attack kept her confined to her bed for three long weeks. 'Inside aches constantly but it is bearable, but now & then comes what I call a "piping agony"', she scribbled in her diary. She beguiled much of her time with a pet robin, which, because the weather was unseasonably mild and her windows were left open, would eat crumbs off her window-sill and roosted every night on one of her picture hooks; 'its soft warbling is most delicious, and soothing to her feelings', Mary said.[38]

To cap a bleak year, Lamb, whom William lovingly described as 'a good man if a good man ever was', died on 27 December, aged fifty-nine. The Wordsworths' first thought was for his poor sister, who was suffering one of her periodic fits of insanity, fearing that the eventual realization of her loss would result in permanent madness. It was imperative that she should be well cared for, and, though they rightly suspected that Lamb would have made that provision, William immediately offered to contribute whatever she might need.[39]

This was particularly generous, for William's finances were more than usually under strain. Due to the Stamp Office reforms, his post was now worth only £400 a year. Still blaming himself for the Charterhouse disaster, which had wrecked Willy's chances of a university career, William decided that it was his duty to hand over the Distributorship to his son. It was the only way he could advance Willy's career and secure him enough income to enable him to marry his Mary, to whom he was still devoted. Cupid smiled, in Dora's apt phrase, but Fortune still frowned. It was, of course, impossible for William simply to step down in favour of his son;

the resignation and appointment would have to be made formally, through official channels. Unless the government was inclined to cooperate, there was also the risk that William might resign and his post be given to someone else. When William IV suddenly dismissed Melbourne's Whig administration, on 15 November, and invited Sir Robert Peel to form a government, it was an opportunity which his friends urged William not to miss. He had the support of not only the Lowthers, but also John Thornton, Deputy Chairman of the Board of Stamps and Taxes, who had spent a summer at Grasmere two years before. He hoped to have the support of Peel himself, knowing him to be an admirer of his poetry and that Peel's nephew was serving a farming apprenticeship with the Hutchinsons at Brinsop Court.[40]

What he had reckoned without was the Duke of Wellington's opposition to the appointment of sons as successors to their fathers – not because this was inherently wrong, but because it reduced the range of government patronage. In arguing his case, William revealed just how out of step he was with the times. Now, as in 1813, he sought the post not on the grounds of his own or his son's fitness, but as a reward for his poetical labours:

> I have myself some claim upon my country as a man who in the most disinterested way has devoted his life to the service of sound literature; and now, when the success with which this has been done, is generally acknowledged, and a pecuniary return might be expected to be made to my family, the Law respecting copyright steps in, and declares that the greatest part of my productions, shall be public property the moment I cease to breathe; it would be surely therefore hard, if under these circumstances, my wish to resign in favor of my son were not complied with.[41]

Peel was sincerely committed to the idea of supporting the arts. He had just offered Southey a baronetcy, which was declined, and an additional pension of £300 from the Civil List, which was gratefully accepted. 'It has placed me, as far as relates to the means of subsistence, at ease for the remainder of my days', Southey told William. Peel hoped to do the same for William, but William was still as implacably opposed to the idea of either himself or his wife becoming a government pensioner as he had been over twenty years ago. Besides, a pension for either of them would not help Willy. Nevertheless, Peel's gracious letter, acknowledging the justice of William's claims on men in power and begging him to communicate 'without reserve' if there was any other way he could help, was a consolation. 'I have not the honour of being known to you,' Peel wrote, 'but you must allow the sincerest Respect for your character, & admiration of those works which will secure you lasting Fame, to supply the place of personal acquaintance.' As Sara exclaimed, as she took 'supreme pleasure' in transcribing the letter for Willy, it was 'the most perfect Letter that ever was penned'.[42]

Though it did not solve the problem, Peel's letter was encouraging. Lord Lowther, newly back in office as Treasurer of the Navy and Vice-President of the Board of Trade, was equally positive. 'I think you had better get into the mail coach and come to London when we with other of your friends might decide the specific mode of serving yourself and family, that would be most agreeable to you.' This was advice that could not be ignored. Less than a week after receiving it, William and Mary were in London. The parting from Dorothy, who broke down in tears at the last moment, was traumatic, but she had Dora, Sara, Joanna and little Ebba Hutchinson to comfort her in their absence.[43]

The Wordsworths spent five weeks in town, lobbying everyone they knew. It soon became apparent that they could expect nothing from the Stamp Office, but with the assistance of Christopher, his friends and contacts, they identified a possible opening as a lay Church Commissioner. A new post, to be created as a result of a recommendation that Church rates should be abolished, and the repair and building of churches should be financed by the government, it demanded expertise in arithmetic and business skills. As the bill preparing the way for these changes had not yet been publicly announced, Mary wrote in strictest confidence, and haste, to Willy, telling him to set out his qualifications for the post in a letter which his father could show to the appropriate authorities. Willy panicked, sure that the job was beyond his capabilities (his own ambitions were then turning on being admitted into a bank), but in the end it was irrelevant. The Tory administration fell before any decisions had been taken and the Wordsworths were left exactly where they had been. For the time being, all they could do was urge Willy to economize on his balls and billiards, improve his presentational skills and be happy and hopeful.[44]

William was also anxious to settle another financial matter which had assumed a greater importance since he contemplated giving up the Distributorship. This was the annual payment of £30 to the husband of his French daughter, Caroline, to which he was bound by the terms of her marriage contract. Finding the sum, and the complications arising out of remitting it, had become an increasing problem. What William now wished to do instead was to settle a lump sum of £400 on his daughter, investing it in the French Funds, so that the interest could pay the annuity. It was a perfectly reasonable plan, to which Baudouin at first assented. When he discovered (or claimed to have discovered) that the capital sum was not large enough to produce the equivalent of £30, however, he demanded more. Annette was dragged in, to apply moral pressure on the father of her daughter, and she wrote emotional letters to both William and Dorothy, begging once more for her 'just complaints' to be answered, allowing 'your unhappy Annette' to die in peace. Robinson, who acted as an intermediary in the affair, took a dim view of these proceedings. 'It is quite clear to me that the Baudouins are trying to extort money without any good feeling or excuse whatever'. As a compromise, William offered the £400 outright, in lieu of the annuity, for the Baudouins to do with as they pleased. To Robinson's great relief and pleasure, this was accepted, and, as far as William was concerned, he had fulfilled his duty. 'In this matter as in a hundred others', William wrote to Robinson, 'I feel deeply obliged to your ever-ready Friendship.'[45]

While in town the Wordsworths seized the opportunity to consult two eminent physicians, Sir Henry Holland and Sir Benjamin Brodie, about Dora; though it was a somewhat futile exercise, as the doctors could hardly diagnose or prescribe for a patient they had not seen, it was some comfort to the afflicted parents that at least they were trying to do something for her. At Dora's request, William sat again for his portrait to Pickersgill, so that she could have a smaller copy of the one destined for St John's College. It was, Robinson thought, much better than the larger original.[46]

A fortnight of the Wordsworths' visit was spent staying with Henry Taylor and his step-aunt, Isabella Fenwick, a woman who was to play an increasingly important role in their lives. Taylor was naturally anxious to show off his celebrated guest and at one of his gatherings William had his first encounter with Thomas Carlyle, the great essayist and historian. 'I did not expect much; but got mostly what I expected', Carlyle told his brother. Echoing his American friend Emerson, Carlyle declared William to be, 'A genuine man (which is much) but also essentially a *small* genuine man'. He criticized the poet's handshake, 'feckless, egotistical', his conversation, 'for prolixity, thinness, endless dilution it excels all the other speech I had heard', and his wife, 'the oldest looking woman I ever saw; winking, withered, sleepy-fidgetting, as if she were all dried to a *Kipper* without and within. A silly woman (probably) from the first.'[47] Given the shallowness of his observations, founded upon a single meeting at a party where William was expected 'to perform' by his host, one can only comment that Carlyle got not only what he expected, but also what he deserved.

While the Wordsworths were in London William's new volume of poetry was published. As it was his first collection of new work to appear in thirteen years, it should have been a major event, announced with public and private fanfares. Instead, it crept out almost unnoticed, even by its author. It was to have been published the previous autumn, but there had been delays in printing, which William considered fortunate, as it would have appeared during the political crisis caused by the dismissal of the Melbourne ministry. As he remarked, 'neither Othello, Mackbeth [*sic*] nor the Paradise Lost, if now first produced, would be attended to'. For the same reason, it was withheld from circulation throughout the early part of the year. This unexpected postponement affected the final shape of the volume, for it allowed William to add to it, in response to the pace of political events. Though he had earlier refused to publish the poem, for fear it was too inflammatory, he now decided to include *The Warning*, with its bleak prophecy that the labouring multitudes, deceived by the flattering hopes held out by reformers, would rise 'in marshalled thousands, darkening street and moor' to exact violent revenge for imagined wrongs. 'I felt it due to myself to give this warning to my Countrymen, at this awful Crisis – utterly useless it may prove, but I should have suspected myself of cowardice or selfish caution, if I had suppressed what I had thought and felt'.[48]

Even more important was a lengthy prose postscript on the subject of the Poor Laws which William added in London. Robinson, acting as William's amanuensis, was troubled by it – 'Wordsworth will aggravate antipathies by his polemical notes' – but politics had always been more important than poetry to William, and what he now wrote was as radical as anything he had written in his youth. Returning to a theme he had first publicly espoused in 1798, in *The Old Cumberland Beggar*, he extolled the moral benefits to both recipient and donor of charitable giving to the needy, but now he argued that the poor had a *right* to public support. The principal object of his attack was the Poor Law Amendment Act, passed in August 1834, which had put an end to the old system of 'outdoor relief'. Within two years, no able-bodied persons would be able to claim poor relief, for themselves or their families, except in 'well-regulated' workhouses – 'well-regulated' meaning that husbands, wives and children were separated according to gender, labour on the treadmill was enforced, and food and drink were doled out, not according to need but in predetermined and miserly quantities set out in the act. As William pointed out, the whole basis of the act was punitive. It assumed that it was the labouring man's own fault if he was unable to provide for himself or his family, and took no account of individual circumstances. In the interests of humanity at large, William declared, it was better that ten undeserving poor should have relief than that one worthy man should suffer. In a subsidiary section, he also made an enlightened call, twenty years ahead of its time, for the repeal of the laws governing joint-stock companies, arguing that if workmen were allowed to invest their savings in manufacturing, they would then have a stake in its success.[49]

His sympathy for the plight of the modern labouring poor was articulated most strongly in a poem, *Humanity*, in which he lambasted his countrymen for priding themselves on the abolition of slavery.

> . . . that boast
> Is but a mockery! when from coast to coast,
> Though *fettered* slave be none, her floors and soil
> Groan underneath a weight of slavish toil,
> For the poor Many, measured out by rules
> Fetched with cupidity from heartless schools,
> That to an Idol, falsely called 'the Wealth
> Of Nations', sacrifice a People's health,
> Body and mind and soul; a thirst so keen
> Is ever urging on the vast machine
> Of sleepless Labour, 'mid whose dizzy wheels
> The Power least prized is that which thinks and feels.

If nothing else, William's inclusion of his political poems and his postscript was a public and triumphant answer to Robinson's mock obituary of 1826. He *was* still 'in an active sympathy with the temporary welfare of his fellow creatures', and Southey, for one, wrote to congratulate him for touching upon 'our white slavery' and annexing 'such a postscript'.[50]

Most purchasers of *Yarrow Revisited, and Other Poems*, however, bought it for the quality of the verse, the tour poems in particular appealing to the age of steamboats and trains, and to a growing number of people able to travel faster and more easily to the very places William celebrated in his poetry. And buy it they did, in their hundreds. To William's bemusement and delight, within two months of going on sale *Yarrow Revisited* had sold 900 copies. It was a palpable hit, by anyone's standards. Even the reviews were laudatory. 'As yet we have heard of nought but praise', Dora wrote on 1 June; ' – in truth the way in wh[ich] all the Mag: Newspapers &c puff him is quite absurd'. John's wife, Isabella, however, noted, 'it is extraordinary how he is puffed in all the Whig and Radical publications; and scarcely noticed in the Tory and Conservative Papers'. Was it discreditable to admit, William asked Robinson, that the reviews interested him only so far as they were likely to affect the sale?

> The private testimonies which I receive very frequently of the effect of my writings upon the hearts and minds of men, are indeed very gratifying – because I am sure *they* must be written under *pure* influences – but it is not necessarily or even probably so with strictures intended for the public. The one are *effusions*, the other *compositions*, and liable in various degrees to inter-mixtures that take from their value –

Though he highly valued the private testimonies, William was no more inclined to accept their judgement than that of the professional critics. 'Take care', he wrote to one enthusiastic admirer who had just addressed a letter and a sonnet to him, bewailing the harm the critics had wrought on his works over the years, '. . . that the sense of injustice both to yourself and me, in having neglected, or rather disregarded them so long, does not by a natural reaction of the mind impel you now to overrate them'. For himself, William remained convinced that, irrespective of what any critics thought, his writings would endure only if they truly illustrated the principle he had so long espoused, 'That we have all of us one human heart!' That he should quote now from *The Old Cumberland Beggar* was significant evidence that, as he always claimed, his politics remained fundamentally unaltered, even if he had changed his mind on how they should be implemented.[51]

After the bustle and fatigue of London, William and Mary were glad to go to the comparative peace of Trinity Lodge, Cambridge, where they were 'like ships in harbour after a storm'. The highlight of the visit was an invitation to dine on 4 April with the Master and fellows of St John's College, where William was proud to see his own portrait hanging in the Combination room. Though William had intended to return to London, to be fitted for false teeth, their absence from home was cut short by news that Dorothy had suffered another serious bilious attack. They hurried back to Rydal Mount and were relieved to find that both Dorothy and Dora were, if not better, then better than their own fears had anticipated.[52]

Not long after their return, Sara was seized with lumbago, after bending down to fasten her shoe, which she aggravated by standing in the cold back passage after being in bed all day. All three invalids then caught influenza and, as Anne, the cook who had been with them for twelve years, was also confined to bed with a rheumatic fever, Mary and her niece, fifteen-year-old Ebba, were run off their feet trying to nurse them all. Ebba's mother, Mary Hutchinson, came from Brinsop in answer to their plea for help, and proved invaluable. Dorothy and Sara vied to head the sick-list. It was obvious to them all that Dorothy was dying, as she grew daily weaker and weaker. Sara, though frequently delirious with fever and pain, even in her wanderings could not forget the miseries of the Southey household and begged Mary to explain why she seemed to neglect them. Sara grew better, Dorothy worse. 'Dear Father keeps up his spirits most patiently tho at times I see his heart is well nigh breaking', Dora wrote on 1 June.[53]

And then, as they waited in daily and hourly expectation of Dorothy's demise, Sara slipped quietly away. 'One of our anxieties is over and not that which we thought would first cease', William wrote to Robinson on 24 June; 'on Monday she sunk alarmingly, yesterday at noon a change took place that left no hope of saving her life, and before seven all was over'. Shortly before the end, Dora had asked Carr if anything could be done to ease her, at which Sara had opened her eyes and said 'in a strong and sweet voice . . . "I am quite, I am perfectly comfortable"'. 'O, my dear Southey, we have lost a precious friend', William mourned; 'of the strength of her attachment to you and yours, you can but imperfectly judge. It was deep in her heart.' Informing Christopher of Sara's death, he paid her a tribute that was all the more touching for its simplicity. 'She was to this House an inestimable Friend, disinterested, generous, noble-minded, a sincere and pious Christian, and we trust her Spirit will receive its reward.' To everyone, he described how he had seen her, within an hour after her decease, 'in the silence and peace of death, with as heavenly an expression on her countenance as ever human creature had'. This 'Vision sanctified' would both haunt and comfort William, resulting eventually in a moving poetic tribute to Sara. All traces of pain had been removed, he declared, age smoothed from her brow, and her face revealed 'A loveliness to living youth denied'.

> Oh! if within me hope should e'er decline,
> The lamp of faith, lost Friend! too faintly burn;
> Then may that heaven-revealing smile of thine,
> The bright assurance, visibly return:
> And let my spirit in that power divine
> Rejoice, as, through that power, it ceased to mourn.[54]

The love and respect in which Sara had been so widely held soon became apparent, as tributes flowed in from all over the country. The most significant, given the difficulties of Sara's relationship with Coleridge and all the problems it had caused, was that from his wife and daughter. It is so oddly worded that it can be understood only as making deliberate, if elliptical, reference to the past. 'It is impossible not to regret dear Miss Hutchinson,' Sara wrote,

> who never was anybody's hindrance, and who occupied no place which any other person would be glad to fill . . . She was an excellent kind hearted creature, and possessed a fine clear understanding, which was never put to any but good purposes and was always ready when wanted . . . Her kindness to me I shall ever remember with gratitude. Mama is greatly distressed at this event and keeps saying that she has lost a good friend in Miss Hutchinson and one who has been long tried.[55]

Sara was buried in Grasmere churchyard, close to the two Wordsworth children, on 30 June 1835. It was appropriate that, on the day of her funeral, William was so concerned about the Southey family, to whom Sara had also been a lifelong friend, that he wrote to seek help for them. Mrs Southey had returned from the Retreat a few months earlier but, as Bertha had confided to Dora, she was failing fast, refusing to eat or take her medicines and becoming so violent that sometimes her daughters were obliged to hold her down by brute force. The Wordsworths were convinced that a nurse should be employed to relieve the girls of their heartbreaking work, but it was a delicate situation and they did not wish to interfere. William's solution was to lay the matter confidentially before Southey's younger brother, a London physician, and leave it to him to make the necessary recommendation.[56]

Sara's death had an immediate effect on the remaining invalids at Rydal Mount. Dora 'lost ground considerably' and was fading away before their eyes. Dorothy, who had always been particularly close to Sara, had suffered a shock from which she would never recover. She clung to life with remarkable tenacity, but now began to lose her mind. Though her understanding appeared as good as ever and she could remember events from the past with perfect clarity, even reciting poetry at will, her short-term memory disappeared. She craved food incessantly and, as she stridently maintained that 'She knows best what is good for her', her sickroom became a battleground. 'I fear you cannot read this Letter', William wrote to Robinson. 'I feel my hand-shaking, I have had so much agitation to-day, in attempting to quiet my poor Sister, and from being under the necessity of refusing her things that would be improper for her. She has a great craving for oatmeal porridge principal[ly] for the sake of the butter that she eats along with it and butter is sure to bring on a fit of bile sooner or later.' Convinced at first that this weakening of the mind was a result of the opiates her physical condition required, the Wordsworths gradually weaned her off them, to no avail. A slight improvement in her short-term memory was more than counterbalanced by 'increasing irritability, which when her wishes are necessarily opposed amounts to rage and fury'. She was never happy except when she was eating, she told her brother, a claim that was pitifully substantiated when her old schoolfriend Jane Marshall sent a turkey and two chickens as joint Christmas and birthday presents. Though she had been 'in her disturbed way' when they arrived, the sight of them transformed her:

'she stroked & hugged the Turkey upon her knee like an overjoyed & happy child – exulting in, & blessing over & over again her dear, dearest friend'. When Dora happened to say it was a pity that such beautiful white chickens should have been killed, Dorothy scorned the regret, saying 'what would they do for her alive, her friend knew best what she wanted – & she should eat them every bit herself'.[57] Nothing more clearly illustrates the loss of the sensibility which had been the most striking feature of her character.

Dorothy was to continue in this state for the rest of her life. Unable to walk or retain what she read, though still capable of surprising her nearest and dearest with an occasional brief letter, she alternated between 'mental feebleness', in which she was 'as happy & as amiable as possible', and 'impatient discomfort', when she behaved 'exactly like a very clever, tyrannical spoilt Child'. 'It is some comfort to us that you are spared the pain of witnessing what daily nay indeed hourly we are called upon to witness & without being able in the slightest degree to minister to her comfort or happiness –', Dora told her Cambridge cousins, 'nothing seems to give her pleasure not even the sight of her dear brother – & often & often he comes down from her room his eyes filled with tears – saying "Well all I can do for her now is to heat her night cap I have done it 20 times within the last ¼ of an hour & that seems to give her a momentary pleasure & that is some comfort."' The Wordsworths tried always to remember the better days and lavished love and attention on her. She had constant attendance and companionship from servants and members of the family; she was taken out in her bath-chair whenever the weather permitted and one of the bedrooms was given up to her as an upstairs sitting-room. (When the summer visitors started to arrive, this had to be exchanged for one at the back of the house, as Dorothy had discovered a new amusement in drawing attention to herself by shrieking, and startling the tourists in the house or grounds.)[58]

'Books are to me as a dead Letter, and so must they be for some time', William had written in the summer of 1835, but as the autumn closed in he turned again to poetry. This was partly through necessity. *Yarrow Revisited* had been so successful that a second edition was called for, which he could not allow to go to press without revision. Walking from Lyulph's Tower to Hallsteads, on his way to Lowther Castle in September, he was still capable of finding comfort in the landscape, and throwing off some lovely descriptive lines.

> Not a breath of air
> Ruffles the bosom of this leafy glen,
> From the brook's margin wide around, the trees
> Are stedfast as the rocks; the brook itself
> Following, in patient solitude a course
> Old as the hills that feed it from afar,
> Doth rather deepen than disturb the calm
> Where all things else are still and motionless.[59]

His main preoccupation, however, was to write an epitaph for Lamb, a task which was the sort of request piece he hated, and a troublesome responsibility, because it was Lamb's sister who asked for it. He laboured long and fruitlessly until, at Mary and Dora's suggestion, he took Chiabrera as his model and, on 19 November, composed the entire poem at one sitting. 'By sending it immediately, I have prepared the way, I believe for a speedy repentance – as I dont know that I ever wrote so many lines without some retouching being afterwards necessary.' As Moxon learned to his cost, it was a true prophecy: six months later, William was still sending revisions, and the epitaph, at thirty-eight lines already too long for engraving on the memorial, had swollen to more than 130. This was a pity, for the first version was infinitely the best, a tender and truthful evocation of a man, full of 'Humour, and wild instinctive wit', but also troubled by depression; who had 'humbly earned his bread', but whose genius had triumphed over adversity. The new lines were added because William felt it imperative to write 'a few lines' celebrating the love between Lamb and his sister. Though they certainly do this, at length, the suspicion is inescapable that William would not have felt so compelled to dwell on this aspect of Lamb's life if his own sister had been in health. Death had broken 'the sacred tie' between the Lambs, but Dorothy's descent into senile dementia had effectively done the same for his own relationship with her. It was a lament for the Wordsworths, as much as for the Lambs.

William was extremely anxious that Mary Lamb should like the epitaph and was therefore disappointed to learn that she disapproved of the reference to her brother's lowly occupation and the allusion to the family troubles which had caused him so much grief. She extracted only three lines to be engraved on the monument in Edmonton church, but did allow Moxon, who was married to the Lambs' adopted daughter, to print the poem and circulate it privately.[60]

Eleven days after composing the first version of the epitaph William read in the *Newcastle Journal* that Hogg, the Ettrick Shepherd, had died on 21 November. It was just the latest in a growing list of friends he had lost over the year. Sharp, whose financial advice and touring journals had been invaluable, Tillbrooke of Ivy Cottage, the literary lady Mrs Hemans and, among his oldest and most valued friends, the companion of his walking tour of France and Switzerland in 1790, Robert Jones.[61] Hogg's death was not a personal loss, but it did bring an era to an end. For all the mischief he had created, Hogg was intimately and inextricably connected with one of the most evocative of all William's poetic images, the Yarrow. He had guided William on his first visit to that celebrated spot, just as Scott had been William's companion on his second visit. They, together with Coleridge and Lamb, had all been younger than William, yet he had outlived them all. Within half an hour of reading the notice of Hogg's death, William had composed his great tribute to these friends and fellow poets.

The mighty Minstrel breathes no longer,
'Mid mouldering ruins low he lies;
And death upon the braes of Yarrow,
Has closed the Shepherd-poet's eyes:

Nor has the rolling year twice measured,
From sign to sign, its stedfast course,
Since every mortal power of Coleridge
Was frozen at its marvellous source;

The rapt One, of the godlike forehead,
The heaven-eyed creature sleeps in earth:
And Lamb, the frolic and the gentle,
Has vanished from his lonely hearth.

Like clouds that rake the mountain-summits,
Or waves that own no curbing hand,
How fast has brother followed brother,
From sunshine to the sunless land!

Yet I, whose lids from infant slumber
Were earlier raised, remain to hear
A timid voice, that asks in whispers,
'Who next will drop and disappear?'

Observing her husband's depression of spirits, Mary wrote to Robinson, begging him to come to them for Christmas. She did not attempt to conceal that it could not be a pleasurable visit. 'It must be purely a work of charity – Your presence to W. would be inestimable – he wants such a friend to take him out of himself and to divert his thoughts from the melancholy state in which our poor Sister is *struggling* (to use her own word).' Robinson could not refuse. He arrived at Rydal Mount on Christmas Day and within forty-eight hours was gratified to be told by both Mary and Dora that his presence had already done William great service. He remained at Rydal until 1 February 1836, spending the greater part of the day either at Rydal Mount or walking with William, but lodging at the foot of the hill, an arrangement which suited them all.[62]

Admitted to the intimacy of the Wordsworth household on a daily basis, Robinson soon became aware of the burden they bore, and his admiration for them all increased to the point of veneration. He saw Dorothy only a couple of times, when she was 'in her better way', but even then, she had 'offensive practices' (Mary told Catherine Clarkson that these were the cause of Dorothy's greatest discomforts, but she could not describe them, as it would be too distressing for them both), had a habit of shouting and screaming, without obvious cause, and demanded constant and unbearable heat. The most painful aspect of Dorothy's imbecility was its effect on Dora, who was distressed beyond measure, aggravating her own deplorably weak state of health. 'The poor Aunt is 64 years of age,' William wrote to his nephew, 'but Dora is young enough to have looked forward to years of health and strength, which she will never attain unless it should please God that she should be enabled to quit her present abode, and exist in some quiet of mind, elsewhere.' It says much for the condition of both invalids that Robinson came to the conclusion that Dorothy's death would actually be a comfort, even to her brother.[63]

There was little anyone could do to alleviate these problems, but the Wordsworths consulted Robinson on others, where his legal training and discretion were invaluable. Mary entrusted to him the papers about the settlement for Caroline Baudouin, asking him to keep them sealed in his possession, presumably to avoid any of her own children accidentally discovering that their father had an illegitimate child. William sought his advice both in looking over his late brother's will and settling Richard's affairs. 'Keswick' John, who was then staying at Rydal Mount, would be twenty-one on 29 January 1836, and would therefore come into his own estates, which were heavily encumbered by his father's debts – including one of £2,000 owed to William. A letter from John's stepfather, a prickly Keswick attorney who resented not having been consulted about his stepson's affairs, brought matters to a head. Robinson thought William and Christopher had shown 'indiscreet liberality' towards their nephew, but as he seemed 'perfectly well disposed and honourable', no evil consequences were likely to ensue. It would, however, be necessary to arrange a sale of his lands in order to pay off the debts and, even if a large enough sum could be raised to clear these, and pay his mother's life annuity, John would still have to work to earn his living.[64]

Robinson also advised William on drawing up his own will. He did not have much to leave. His income was now only £450 a year, which, together with his life annuity from Beaumont, would cease at his death. His disposable property, which he could leave to his widow and children, amounted to the £2,000 owed by Richard's estate and a life insurance policy which would realize £7,000 on his death. He also had £4,000 in the hands of Philip Courtenay, an astute financier, who made a fortune for himself and his investors by examining the parish records of remote counties, identifying hale and hearty men of long-lived peasant stock and purchasing annuities on their lives. Whether the scheme had poetic appeal for William or was merely a prudent financial investment, most of his small capital was tied up in it.[65]

Robinson was not merely a valued and trustworthy adviser who could ease William's mind on financial matters. He was also an inveterately cheerful, gossipy, kindly man who listened to, and argued with, his host on politics, religion and literature. Though he occasionally permitted himself a groan when William harped on 'the eternal question – Irish Church Reform', he was ever ready to engage William's intellectual interests and distract him from his melancholy household concerns. When he left, on 1 February, he carried with him the oft-reiterated gratitude of the entire family, though the moment he cherished most was an unsolicited compliment, heard by accident and proudly enshrined in his journal. 'I overheard Wordsworth say last night to the Doctor [Arnold] that I had helped him through the winter and that he should gratefully recollect my kindness as long as he had any memory!'[66]

24. Coming Home

In looking over William's finances, Robinson made a significant discovery. For the last few years (and for the first time in his life), William had been making in the region of £200 a year from his writings. This was due to the increasing popularity of his poetry, his renegotiated terms with his publishers and his recent policy of making his poems available as cheaply as possible. The second edition of *Yarrow Revisited, and Other Poems*, which was published early in the spring of 1836, was a case in point. On Longman's advice, it was printed in stereotype, a form of reverse printing whereby the metal plates were cast from a papier-mâché or plaster of Paris mould poured over the hand-set type. It was a cheap system, used mainly by newspapers, because large quantities could be printed from a single stereotype. The disadvantages were two-fold. The quality of print was not as good as traditional printing methods: as the bibliophile Robinson sourly commented, the result, in the case of *Yarrow Revisited*, was 'the worst-printed book that ever came from the press'. More importantly, especially for an author like William who persisted in making changes until the book was irrevocably bound and could not be 'tinkered' any more, once the plate had been produced, it could not be altered. Any changes necessitated the making of replacement plates, the most expensive part of the process.[1]

William realized the full implication of this only when Longman announced that the last edition of *The Excursion* had sold out, and that just 180 copies of the four-volume *Poetical Works* remained on hand. Longman was anxious to go ahead with a reprint, but William demurred. As always, he was concerned that his purchasers should be able to buy the books individually, but end up with a matching set of volumes; this was now impossible, unless the next edition was also stereotyped. To do so would mean not only that it would be prohibitively expensive to 'tinker' future editions, but also that he was effectively tied permanently to Longman as his publisher. Frustrated that he had failed to anticipate these difficulties when agreeing to *Yarrow Revisited* being stereotyped, he now refused to rush into a decision. He sought advice from his nephews Chris and John, both of whom were experienced authors, and, as he had increasingly done, from Edward Moxon, the young publisher whose name, at William's insistence, had appeared in association with Longman's on the title-page of both *Yarrow Revisited* and the 1835 edition of his *A Guide Through the District of the Lakes*. Rather than enter into complicated negotiations by letter, William decided that he would have to go to London and sort the matter out in person.[2]

His departure was delayed on several counts, most notably by the baptism of his third grandchild, a third William Wordsworth, who made his appearance on 27 December 1835. William was allowed to choose the godparents for his namesake, 'from among *my particular friends*', and the honours fell to Isabella Fenwick, William Rowan Hamilton and Robert Southey. Willy, who was an obvious choice, refused, on the grounds that with Wilson and de Quincey as his own sponsors, he had been so ill-godfathered himself, he would not inflict a similar injury on his nephew. William attended the christening at Workington, where John was acting as locum for his brother-in-law, and returned as delighted with his three grandchildren 'as any fond grandfather ever was since the world begun'.[3]

William's presence was also required in Bowness on 13 April, at a ceremony to mark the foundation of a new free school. The project had been entirely funded by his old friend, 'the Liverpool Croesus', John Bolton of Storrs, who had requested William to stand in for him, as he was too old and ill to attend. Astonishingly, this was the first time William had ever made a speech in public, and he was consumed with nerves. His sister, in one of her rare moments of complete sanity, wrote immediately to her nephew Chris, who had just been appointed Public Orator of Cambridge University, and laid this 'case of distress' before him: 'alas! the poet is no Orator and he knows not what to say on this important occasion. I therefore request *you* the first Orator of the Nation to make a speech for him which I will answer for it he will pronounce verbatim, his diffidence of his own powers being so overwhelming.'[4]

Preceded by a band and the schoolchildren of the neighbourhood, and to the sound of bells ringing and cannons firing, William and his protégé Robert Graves, who was now curate of Bowness, led the procession through the village to the site of the new school. There William buried a time capsule, laid the foundation stone and said his piece. 'The stormy day was unlucky,' he later reported to Bolton's family, 'but nevertheless the thing went off in a manner that gratified everyone, and not the less probably for their escape from the long speech I was disposed to inflict upon them.' It was indeed his own speech, not his nephew's, for it was an opportunity to expound all his pet theories on education, as distinct from tuition, and to impress upon the assembled parents the importance of setting an example to their children outside the classroom.[5]

It was 11 May before William finally arrived in London. He had been bombarded with invitations even before he left Rydal Mount: the Beaumonts, the Marshalls,

Moxon, Taylor, Quillinan, Talfourd, Kenyon, Watson, all fought for the privilege of offering him accommodation. It was an indication of things to come, for there could be no question now that William was leader of the pack where literary lions were concerned. The rarity of his visits to London, his age (he was now sixty-six) and the fact that he was one of the last of his generation combined with his growing poetical reputation to make him the catch of the season. Everyone wanted to meet him. 'I see scores of people that are introduced to me but dont remember the names of one in ten', he admitted in a letter home. There were the usual round of breakfasts, dinners and evening parties, at each of which he was expected to perform for his anxious hosts. He went to concerts and visited the art galleries (but declined to see the Elgin marbles again). He attended, by personal invitation, a lecture on landscape painting by the artist John Constable at the Royal Institution. Sending William a copy of his little work on chiaroscuro as a memento, Constable wrote, 'I shall always reflect with pride that – you – were at one of my lectures'.[6]

He also attended the famous first night at Covent Garden of *Ion*, a play by his friend Talfourd, starring William Macready and Ellen Tree. The play was greeted with huge applause, which gave added zest to the celebratory supper party which followed. William, sitting with the Talfourds, Robinson, Macready and Landor, was placed opposite a twenty-four-year-old poet, Robert Browning. Though this was apparently their first meeting, the conviviality of the occasion prevented any private conversation. 'The happiest day I have spent since I came to London was at Sergeant Talfourd's play and his supper', William told his family. This was ironic, for Landor, in a spiteful satire published soon afterwards, attacked William for remaining unmoved among the general adulation surrounding Talfourd, suggesting that this was because he was incapable of appreciating the merits of his contemporaries. As no one else noted anything of the sort, and Robinson, who had sat close to William throughout the performance, indignantly denied it when he read the satire, Landor's venom can perhaps be attributed to a misunderstanding. Talfourd had sent William a copy of *Ion* in 1835, hoping for endorsement or approval. Arriving, as it did, in the midst of all the Wordsworths' domestic distresses, William had not found heart or time to reply, and Talfourd had taken his silence amiss. When Macready dined with Talfourd in September, he was '*disgusted*' to be told that William had not responded, and this little story he seems to have told to Landor, who was his neighbour at the supper party. What neither man knew was that two months later, in November 1835, William had sent several messages to Talfourd, praising his play liberally. 'If you see Mr Talfourd tell him that we are all delighted with his drama – and which may seem odd – *that* is the very reason why I have put off writing to him – as I wished to do more than merely let him know, with thanks, how much he has pleased us.' And on 28 November, the day after he received a second edition of *Ion*, he wrote immediately to Talfourd, saying he had heard part of it read aloud the night before, and finished it himself that very morning: 'You have most ably fulfilled your own purpose, and your poem is a distinguished contribution to English literature.'[7]

A comparatively minor incident in itself, it is scarcely worth the recounting, except for the all-important fact that it is typical of the way so many of the critical stories about William were circulated. As Robinson pointed out to Landor when he read the satire, Landor had simply absorbed and repeated the prejudices and malicious comments of his friend Byron, which had reinforced his own reasons for disliking William (he wrongly thought William had plagiarized his image of a child holding a seashell to his ear to hear the sound of the sea). The satire gave renewed life and circulation to the stale accusations that William was 'an envious and selfish poet', but, as Rogers observed, it also aimed to poison William's intimacy with both Talfourd and Southey. Fortunately, all three men were above taking notice of such malice; indeed, it had the opposite effect, for it effectively put an end to William and Robinson's friendship with Landor.[8]

William's visit to London was not entirely recreational. 'I have been run off my legs by business, since I arrived', he complained. His priority was to draw up a final legal release from his responsibilities as executor and guardian of 'Keswick' John; this could only be done through Strickland Cookson, the attorney son of his friends from Kendal, who was now in partnership at Richard Wordsworth's old firm. 'Keswick' John, following in the family tradition, had decided that if he had to earn his living, he would like to join the army, once he had finished his apprenticeship with Gardner. Unlike his cousins, his ambition would be fulfilled, his medical training enabling him to join the Army Medical Service.[9]

William was also busy with his brother, Christopher, and their mutual friend Joshua Watson trying to raise a subscription to build a new church in Cockermouth. William had first mooted the idea the previous autumn and it had turned into an obsession. It was never just a purely philanthropic gesture, because to William it represented a practical reverse to the forces of reform, a symbol of hope, planted in his own birthplace. At a time when the Church establishment was everywhere under threat, here he was, extending its influence. There were major obstacles to be overcome. Not just the need to raise enough money to build and endow the fund, but the sullen hostility of the present incumbent, the apathy of the local inhabitants and the fact that, though the population had almost doubled since the beginning of the century, dissent was rife, and even the current church was far from full. In fact, the only person who wanted a second church was William.

It was a campaign that, consciously or unconsciously, he deliberately and publicly associated with himself from the start. The local committee assured him that it had been encouraged to proceed only because it had the assurance of his zealous cooperation and support among his friends. Those friends, whom he inundated with requests for subscriptions, were left in no doubt that they were doing this as much for him as for the church. His letter to Robinson was typical.

> Have you Dissenter as you are, any Friends who would cooperate with a poor Poet, out of their love of his art and his attempts in it, and out of affection to the Church of England, in his endeavour to assist in building a new Church in his *native place* where it is much wanted.

– Sums however small would be acceptable, and I the said Poet should be happy in being the medium of conveying them to the Committee, names mentioned or not – as agreeable –

It was, to say the least, tactless, and many of his friends felt it so. To refuse a donation seemed to imply a rejection of the poet himself. Robinson, who admitted in his private journal that he was annoyed by the application, put his refusal as delicately as he could. 'There are many whom I could ask to subscribe for a monument to you in any church, whom I could not ask to contribute to build a new church in the place of your birth.'[10]

William was more fortunate in London, where he secured a donation of £50 from James Stephen at the Colonial Office and assurances from Christopher and Watson that the Church Building Society would support the project. Stephen, and Henry Taylor, who also worked at the Colonial Office, were anxious to assist William in other ways. They offered, for instance, to act as intermediaries with Thomas Spring-Rice, the Chancellor of the Exchequer, whom William was anxious to lobby about proposed changes to the Stamp Office, which would further reduce his own annual income by £70 and make Willy's position untenable.[11] (It is a measure of William's desperation concerning the family's financial affairs at this time that he actually approached Lord Lonsdale for permission to mine a vein of black lead discovered by a local shoemaker at Troutbeck![12])

Perhaps the most important business of all was to choose the publisher of the next edition of his complete works. The presumptions were all in Longman's favour; his firm had, after all, been William's publisher since 1798, and despite the fact that they had almost lost him over the battle for better terms they still took him for granted. William had become increasingly aware that they were old-fashioned in outlook and had been irritated by the way they had casually sought his permission to stereotype *Yarrow Revisited*, without explaining the consequences. He also strongly suspected that, even now, he was not getting the best financial deal. The final straw came in the midst of their negotiations when, instead of delivering the statement he had promised, Longman simply sent a note, saying that his partner, Rees, was out of town, nothing could be done in his absence and would William kindly call when Rees had returned.[13]

The contrast with Moxon could not have been more pointed. Moxon was not only an innovative publisher but, being an accomplished poet in his own right, had a natural sympathy with his authors. He had been an enthusiast for William's poetry from the start. They had been introduced in 1825 by Lamb, who asked William to 'pat him on the head, ask him a civil question or two about his verses, and favour him with your genuine autograph'. The following year Moxon had visited Rydal Mount and presented William with a copy of his *The Prospect and Other Poems*. Their friendship had blossomed since Moxon's publication of *Selections from the Poems of William Wordsworth*, edited by Hine, in 1831. William had increasingly come to rely on the younger man for advice relating to the publication of his work, and had actually found himself in what must surely be the unique position of having to warn his publisher not to be too generous. 'Take care in respect to the Selections that your liberality to me does not injure yourself', he wrote to Moxon in February.[14]

Moxon's first proposal was disappointing, but William stood firm, and his second was liberal. William was to received £1,000 for an edition of 3,000 copies of his poetical works in six volumes; the books would be printed in stereotype, the copyright and plates remaining in William's hands. Moxon would pay all the expenses of publication, and a further £400 for each future edition. 'So you see dearest Friends there is nothing like standing up for one's self, and one's own legitimate interest', William exulted. His statement of account with Longman showed that the overall profit of his last edition had been £687; the portion he was due to receive at midsummer, with the sum he would also get from the sale of *Yarrow Revisited*, would bring his earnings from poetry this year to £500, 'which may be reckoned as a sort of Godsend'.[15]

The new alliance with Moxon was celebrated with a little excursion to visit Quillinan, at his cottage in Nightingale Vale, in Woolwich. Poet and publisher were accompanied by 'Keswick' John, who had been in regular attendance on his uncle throughout this London visit, and Frank Stone, an artist who had painted Quillinan's daughters. The object of the visit was to persuade Quillinan to assist in preparing the new edition; before the end of June, the two men were both guests at Moxon's house, arranging the distribution of the poems between the six volumes.[16]

Now that all his business was complete, there was nothing to prevent William fulfilling his original intention of accompanying Robinson on a long-dreamt-of tour of Italy. Dora had suggested this in a letter to Robinson before William went to London, and tentative arrangements had been put in place, but it soon became clear that it was the Wordsworth females who were anxious that he should go, rather than William himself. Their reasons were entirely unselfish. They thought he needed a change and a rest from 'the worry & agitating feelings which his poor Sister's state kept him in': her presence at home meant that it could never be 'a place of rest <u>for one</u> who feels so keenly for her'. A tour, they thought, was just the thing to provide him with a stock of images and memories to divert his mind throughout the winter.[17]

For a man usually considered to have 'a domestic divan' of women at his constant beck and call, it is highly amusing to see the way he begged and pleaded to be let out of the engagement. Within three weeks of his arrival in London, William was already getting cold feet: 'tell me sincerely whether you think I ought to go abroad or not –', he wrote home. 'I like the idea less and less every day, I so long to see you, and I feel so fevered.' The longer he stayed in London, the less appealing the idea became, because he needed at least ten weeks for an Italian tour. He tried blackmail, suggesting he might pop home for a visit, selflessly caring nothing for the expense or fatigue, before setting out. 'I feel decided altogether against going, if you don't approve of my coming down.' This too was firmly vetoed from Rydal

Mount. He tried to invite pity, confiding that in a fit of absent-mindedness at one of the Earl of Lonsdale's dinners, he had found himself drinking out of a water decanter, instead of a glass. There was no response. In the end, he had to resort to pathetic special pleading.

> My heart fails – I am so sad in a morning when I wake and think that more than 4 months will elapse before I see you again, if I go to Italy and after an absence of I believe 7 weeks. I cannot bear to think of it[,] having reached the age that we all have except you dearest Dora – I should have thought nothing of it 20 years ago – but now I sicken at the scheme as I draw near to the appointed time. Do let me put it off, and try the events of another year . . .

Realizing that he was 'heartsick and homesick', and 'either is, or thinks himself exhausted by the business and bustle of London', Mary and Dora signed his release. William wrote a shamefaced note of apology to Robinson, explaining that after so long an absence from home, he had not the courage to prepare for a Continental tour. Robinson took his disappointment in such good part, cheerfully assuring William that he thought he was right to defer the trip, that Mary felt obliged to write and tell him 'how much we feel your good-tempered bearing towards your vacillating *fellow-traveller that was to have been.* God bless you!'[18]

Mary also suggested that, having deferred his trip abroad, William should stay a little longer in London, provoking an irritated response from her husband.

> I cannot put off my journey home; for I am quite tired of this mode of life and worn out with it. It is easy for you to say go and spend a quiet day here or there, it is not in my power to spend a quiet day any where. People put so many questions to me, and think it so necessary to endeavour to put me upon something, and to talk to me. You quite forget too my situation and my disposition when you talk to me of quiet and preservation from exhaustion. Should I go to Dr Davy's he would invite his friends to meet me and so on.

Pausing only to visit the dentist and have a set of false teeth fitted (his first), William scuttled happily back to Rydal Mount, arriving there on 7 July. Unusually, he embarked almost immediately on what was normally a winter task, the wholesale revision of his complete poetic works for the new Moxon edition. When Quillinan arrived on 2 August for a visit that would last until 16 September, the work began in earnest.[19]

It was to be the most comprehensive review of his work that William had ever undertaken, because he intended it to be the last he ever did. In his sixty-seventh year, he thought it unlikely that he would live to see another edition through the press, and, in any case, the process of stereotyping effectively meant that it would be extremely difficult to alter in future. With Quillinan as secretary and occasional adviser, he went through all his early poems with a toothcomb. *Descriptive Sketches*, published in 1793, was 'greatly improved' by a careful revision, correction and removal of what Mary called the 'swagger & flourish' and Quillinan the 'corrupt diction' of this juvenile production. *Alice Fell*, on the other hand, which had been removed from William's opus because Coleridge objected to it, was now restored. It was, as William admitted, 'dry and wearisome labour', and Quillinan consoled himself, somewhat wistfully, with the thought that he was 'better employed in helping Mr W to "tinker" as he calls it', than in partridge shooting.[20]

At the beginning of September, there was an unexpected and welcome interruption to their labours. William, Quillinan and Southey were summoned to Lancaster to act as expert witnesses in the infamous case of Wright versus Tatham. The case revolved around a disputed will, in which Admiral Tatham, the heir-at-law, had been disinherited in favour of the testator's steward. The idea of employing expert witnesses of this kind was totally new, even if it owed more to the fact that Tatham's attorney was William's cousin Henry Robinson, than to an attempt to set legal precedent. In his usual conscientious way, William went through all the testator's letters and, on the basis of the discrepancies in style, expression and spelling, convinced himself that they were not all the work of one man. Both Quillinan and Southey agreed, so they were carried off in triumph to give evidence in a crowded courtroom before a judge, who, by an odd twist of fate, turned out to be Coleridge's nephew Sir John Taylor Coleridge.

William and Southey both had a sleepless night and, next morning, William was first to take the stand. Asked if composition had engaged much of his attention, he replied, 'from my youth I may say to this day'. It was his sole contribution to the case. Wright's lawyers objected to his status as an expert witness and, after a three-way legal spat involving both defence lawyers and the judge, it was decided that his evidence was inadmissible. Southey, who had escaped an appearance in the witness box, teased William on his new distinction of being the only 'sworn critic' in England, and remarked that the whole affair seemed like a dream. William, having had no sleep, answered that it was certainly no dream to him.[21]

'Here we are *in the Hall* up to the ears in a muddle of counting lines to fill the *2nd vol* –', Mary wrote to Robinson on 28 September,

> a body of finished sheets from the first [volume], having arrived along with your letter – and their appearance after many changes gives great satisfaction to the Poet and his Clerk – His *Journeyman* in the Person of Mr Quillinan having left us last week, to my great regret, for he supplied my place, which he filled most admirably, and has quite thrown me into the shade. However the Poet is obliged to be thankful for his old helpmate and a busy house we have – working steadily till dinner time – and in a *disorderly* manner the rest of the day:

It was a trying time for both poet and 'clerk', as day after day, for months on end, 'those everlasting Proofs' arrived 'to blind our eyes'. Mary was not prepared to be the passive secretary her husband expected, and she did not always approve of his corrections. 'I must say that he never makes one that he does not *seem* to convince my understanding and judgment – but . . . not always my *feelings*', she admitted after three months of remorseless revision. Half a year later, the work completed and far away from home, William looked back at this time with shame and remorse, and had the grace to make an apology.

Dearest Mary, when I have felt how harshly I often demeaned myself to you, my inestimable fellow-labourer, while correcting the last Edition of my poems, I often pray to God that He would grant us both life, that I may make some amends to you for that, and all my unworthiness. But you know into what an irritable state this timed and overstrained labour often put my nerves. My impatience was ungovernable as I thought *then*, but I now feel that it ought to have been governed. You have forgiven me I know, as you did then, and perhaps that somehow troubles me the more.[22]

It was not surprising that they both looked back wistfully to Quillinan's visit: 'his presence here was a Godsend to me', Mary wrote feelingly at the beginning of November. She would not have felt so kindly towards Quillinan had she known that, while at Rydal Mount, acting on a 'sudden impulse', he had asked her daughter 'a startling question'. 'I had no certain knowledge of what your feelings were and had been for years;' Quillinan later told Dora of this occasion, 'and, when I found that out, I should have been a brute indeed if I had not told you the fact that I had in my heart of hearts held you dearest of all for years too.' This unlikeliest of love affairs, between an ardent, innocent, thirty-two-year-old Anglican and a forty-five-year-old Roman Catholic widower with a reputation as something of a roué, was to remain their secret for some time to come. Though Quillinan wrote to Dora frequently, he knew his letters would be common property at Rydal Mount and he could send her only coded messages. 'Take care of yourself for God's sake, & for many sakes'. Dora's parents suspected nothing, attributing her improved appearance and strength to the kind attentions of Benjamin Brodie, the London physician, who came to Ambleside for a few days in September. Having finally had an opportunity to see his patient, he advised her to leave off her medicines and 'trust altogether to air, & moderate exercise, and nutritious food'.[23]

'Why is it that I feel a sort of awkwardness in telling the Wordsworths (& with no others do I feel it) that we are suddenly going to Portugal?' Quillinan asked his daughter Jemima. 'Because it is a sudden change of mind; & you think more of their good opinion than of any one else's', was Jemima's 'crude, but shrewd' reply. Reporting this exchange in a letter to Rydal Mount at the end of October was Quillinan's subtle way of apologizing to Dora for what would become a year-long absence from England. Quillinan continued to woo Dora industriously through their correspondence. Even if he could not do so overtly, his letters were full of allusions which only Dora would grasp, and, though innocent enough, would naturally foster her parents' later belief that he had been duplicitous in his dealings with them.[24]

The first two volumes of the new edition were published before Christmas. In his anxiety to gratify Moxon, William had relented and allowed an engraving of his portrait by Pickersgill to appear as the frontispiece. It was a decision he regretted immediately. It was a bad engraving of a bad portrait. Reproducing only the head and shoulders, without the reclining attitude of the original, it suggested what William himself called 'an air of decrepitude'. Again, a weakness of expression in the upper lip in the portrait was exaggerated by the engraving into one he aptly described as 'maudlin'. 'If we live to see another Ed:', he remarked grimly to his nephew, 'an engraving from Chantry's Bust shall replace it.' By the end of January, William had completed the revision of all his poems and the printing of the sixth and last volume was about to begin. He had only 'another *tug*' at his postscript on the Poor Laws and a few notes to complete, then he would be ready to set off on his deferred journey to Italy. 'I wish you were here to help –', he told Robinson, adding with obvious feeling, 'Mary wishes it still more'.[25]

On 9 February, he wrote a dignified letter to his friend James Stanger, withdrawing his support for the building of a second church at Cockermouth. It was a project dear to his heart and he had been indefatigable in trying to enlist support. In the end, however, the stumbling block was political antipathy. Lord Lonsdale had offered to endow the living to the value of £150 annually, expecting in return that the appointment of the clergyman would rest with him. In a battle that was being repeated up and down the country, many of the other subscribers threatened to withdraw their donations, unless the appointment was in the hands of either the incumbent or the evangelical Simeon Trustees. As all parties would have agreed to vesting the patronage in the bishop, a compromise should have been possible, but feelings were running so high in Cockermouth that no discussion was possible. Lonsdale suggested a breathing space, but William had had enough.

> Whatever may have been my views at first, I feel so hurt at the manner in which Lord Lonsdale's munificent offer has been received – knowing also, as I do, further dispositions of his regarding the point – that I cannot bring myself to cooperate with Persons who entertain such decisive opinions in opposition to a proceeding which would I am convinced have been beneficial in an eminent degree to the Place.[26]

William was now ready to set off for Italy, but to Robinson's consternation, he suddenly started making excuses again. Dora had been taken ill, Tom Hutchinson had had a serious accident; there were rumours that cholera was sweeping Italy. Robinson duly made inquiries about the cholera and sent back a nicely calculated letter, suggesting that the danger was 'just enough now to justify a wife's fears without ridicule, but not a man's refusal to go without the reproach of cowardice'. It worked a treat. On 10 March William arrived in London, having escorted his wife and daughter as far as Rugby, where Dora would stay with the Arnolds before going on to friends at Leamington, and Mary would travel on to stay with her beleaguered brother's family at Brinsop. Not only was poor Tom completely paralysed, as a result of a fall from his horse, but his oldest daughter, Mary, just twenty years of age, was terminally ill with consumption. With all three Wordsworths absent from Rydal Mount, the care of Dorothy was delegated to

Mary's sister, Joanna, who had been with them since October. They had no qualms about leaving her: she did not notice anyone's absence, had an 'exemplary attendant', another Dorothy, with her constantly and every other member of the household willingly at her beck and call.[27]

For once, this really was to be a short visit to London. William stayed a bare nine days, calling on a few old friends but preoccupied principally with business: purchasing a carriage to take them on their tour, getting passports and calling on the printers. At Moxon's, he learned the astonishing news that almost 2,000 copies of the new edition, out of a print run of only 3,000, had already been sold. This exceeded even Moxon's wildest expectations, as he had calculated that the edition would take two years to sell out – an estimate which William had feared was over-optimistic. Another financial windfall came from an unexpected quarter. Isabella Fenwick, with whom he had been staying, now suggested she would like to invest £400 for her godson, John's second son, William, to pay for his future education once he reached the age of fifteen. William persuaded her that it was not a good idea to put the money in John's name, and that it was better for him to remain in ignorance of it, given his extravagant tendencies and small income. The money was therefore invested in the name of three trustees, Dora, William's nephew Chris, and his solicitor, Strickland Cookson, 'a most excellent man, and a tried Friend'.[28]

Having completed his business affairs, William wrote a series of farewell letters to family and friends. They were cheerful enough, but the unspoken implication was that he might not live to see them all again. There was a particularly urgent reason for writing to Southey. Despite Robinson's best efforts to suppress it, William had just learned from Quillinan, in Portugal, of Landor's malicious satire. Anxious that there should be no bad feeling between himself and Southey, William transcribed a passage from Quillinan's letter to Dora which said it all:

> What of his trying to blow up a flame of discord between your Father and Mr Southey! as if two such long-tried friends could quarrel at this time of day about the opinion that one or the other might or might not entertain as to the value of the other's poetry. Byron or Landor might give up an old Friend for such a cause, but Southey is too right minded to believe that W ever seriously disparaged his talents, or to be very irate if he really had had the bad taste to do so.

'Not a word of all this did I ever see or hear of before', William added.[29]

On 19 March, with Robinson, and Moxon, who was to accompany them as far as Paris, he embarked on a steamboat at the Tower of London and sailed for Calais, on the first stage of the tour of which he had dreamt for so many years. His objective was to get as far as Naples, even Sicily, if possible, but to explore Rome, Florence and Venice, as well as the Roman antiquities in the south of France. 'What shall I say of Paris?' he wrote to Miss Fenwick, in a letter which Taylor uncharitably described as resembling the journal of a schoolgirl on her first visit to foreign parts.

Many splendid edifices and some fine streets have been added since I first saw it at the close of the year -91. But I have had little feeling to spare for novelties, my heart and mind having been awakened everywhere to sad and strange recollections of what was then passing and of subsequent events, which have either occurred in this vast City, or which have flowed from it as their source.[30]

Those recollections were not entirely political, for the first thing William did on arriving in Paris was to seek out the Baudouins. 'I have seen the Baudouins all well, a thousand kind enquiries after you', was William's only recorded comment on their several meetings, made in a letter to Dorothy. While he visited them and accompanied Moxon to the exhibitions, Robinson made himself useful by cultivating Feuillet, head of the Bureau of the Ministry of Foreign Affairs. Though he lived in a modest apartment ninety-two steps up from the street (William counted, a lifelong habit, which always irritated his companions), Feuillet was a passionate bibliophile, who spent vast sums collecting illustrations for rare books and rebinding them. He had embellished Rogers's *Italy* with 100 additional engravings, and was about to do the same with William's poems. Anxious to get their passports dealt with quickly, Robinson presented Feuillet with several literary autographs, then produced his master-stroke, William himself. The passports were immediately forthcoming, though Robinson was rather mortified to find Feuillet had no sense of the 'peculiar charm' of William's poetry.[31]

Having parted with Moxon, whose desire to oblige and good humour had made him an agreeable companion, William and Robinson struck out for the south, passing through Fontainebleau and Nemours, on their way to Avignon. They were unlikely companions, for, despite their long friendship, their interests and habits were diametrically opposed. This became apparent as soon as they reached the south of France, where Robinson proudly showed off the Maison Carrée and the Arena at Nîmes, and was disappointed to find William took more pleasure in the gardens and two pretty little girls near the Arena than in the Roman antiquities. 'I am unable from ignorance to enjoy these sights. I receive an impression, but that is all', was William's rather pompous explanation, confessing, at the same time, that he did not anticipate much pleasure from viewing classical remains on the rest of the tour. Fontaine de Vaucluse, that romantic rocky chasm riven with the beautiful deep, green-hued waters of its river, inspired immediate raptures, not least because of its associations with the exiled poet Petrarch. 'Wordsworth was strongly excited, predetermined to find the charm of interest, and he did.' 'I was enchanted with the power and beauty of the stream,' William wrote home, 'and the wildness and grandeur of the rocks, and several minor beauties which Mr R has not noticed . . . Vaucluse was to me worth 50 perusals'. Writing that letter from Toulon, William mentioned not one of the Roman wonders at Arles, Nîmes, Orange, not even the spectacular Pont du Gard. No part of his tour so far had matched the two hours at Vaucluse and an hour spent at Nîmes, not viewing antiquities but observing the stars 'appearing brighter and at a greater variety of depths, i.e. advancing one before the other more than they do with us'.[32]

By the third week in April they had reached Rome and took up lodgings in the heart of the 'English Colony' in the Piazza di Spagna, just a few doors away from the house where Keats had died. It was an ideal situation. The square, with its characteristic white marble Bernini fountain, lies at the foot of the elegant Spanish Steps, which lead up to the pale, twin-towered church of Trinità dei Monte. From the balconied piazzetta in front of the church unfolds a magnificent panorama of the city, where Roman theatres and temples jostle for elbow room with the thrusting campaniles of countless churches and, in the distance, the dome of St Peter rises serene and authoritative, like a venerable sage surrounded by quarrelling children.

'This has been a very interesting day', Robinson noted after they had walked round the Coliseum, the Forum and the Pantheon. 'To Wordsworth it must have been unparalleled in the number and importance of new impressions.' 'Nothing can exceed the interest of Rome', William observed, 'but though I have seen the Coliseum the Pantheon and all the other boasted things nothing has in the least approached the impressions I received from the inside of St Peter's.' Again, however, his most memorable moment was watching a sunset over the city from the Pincian Hill. Close to the dome of St Peter's, on the glowing horizon, he noted 'one of those broad-topped pines, looking like a little cloud in the sky, with a slender stalk to connect it with its native earth'. His emotion, on being told that this same tree owed its preservation to Sir George Beaumont, who had paid to secure its natural life against the developer's axe, overwhelmed him. 'Oh, what a gush of tenderness was mine!' he would later write in a sonnet commemorating this moment.

> The rescued Pine-tree, with its sky so bright
> And cloud-like beauty, rich in thoughts of home,
> Death-parted friends, and days too swift in flight,
> Supplanted the whole majesty of Rome . . .[33]

Trailing about in the baking-hot streets on the seven hills of Rome, which are so unforgiving to the feet, William soon grew weary of playing the dutiful tourist. 'Of churches and pictures and statues in them I am fairly tired –', he confessed to his family on 6 May; 'in fact I am too old in head, limbs and eyesight for such hard work, such toiling and such straining and so many disappointments either in finding the most celebrated picture covered up with curtains, a service going on so that one cannot ask to have a sight, or the church closed when one arrives at the door.' It was a heartfelt complaint, and one in which every modern tourist in Italy will sympathize, as was his final judgement on the Eternal City. 'But after all it is not particular objects . . . that make the glory of this City; but it is the boun[d]less variety of combinations of old and new caught in ever varying connection with the surrounding country, when you look down from some one or other of the seven hills'.[34]

William was fortunate in being able to explore much of the countryside round

Rome in the more comfortable, lighter carriage of one of Robinson's friends, Frances Mackenzie. She had met his nephews, John and Chris, on their visits to Rome, and was anxious to assist the poet in every way she could. 'You certainly were Wordsworth's good Angel at Rome', Robinson later wrote to her. 'But for you his evenings would have been sad and even his days imperfectly enjoyed.' At her house he had the pleasure of meeting again one of his earliest American visitors, George Ticknor, and many other old friends, including William Collins, the landscape painter, and the two Allen sisters, who had married John and Josiah Wedgwood. He was also reintroduced to the artist Joseph Severn, who had faithfully attended the dying Keats and, after his death, settled in Rome. William sat to Severn for his portrait, which he intended to give to his daughter-in-law, though he feared none of the family would like it. Given the sensitivity with which Severn painted Keats, and the general opinion, even among its critics, that William's portrait was both accurate and 'the most interesting likeness that has been taken', one longs to see it, but it has vanished without trace. William himself thought that it made him look 'at least 4 years older'; Mary complained about the unnatural expression of the mouth, attributing it to his new false teeth, but as she admitted she did not like to look at her husband when he had them in, for the same reason, her complaint seems unjustified; the servants immediately recognized the 'umberella' as the one 'Master took away' and were therefore delighted with it. His grandson William would later describe it as looking 'like an elderly gentleman waiting for a bus'.[35]

Even before they left Rome, William was beginning to feel his age. The constant sightseeing, however pleasurable, gave him 'never-wanting proof that I am rather too old for such *excessive* exertions'. The tour of Italy, he now realized, could not be completed satisfactorily in less than eight months 'unless a person be young and very strong. The country is inexhaustible for those who are well read in antient story and classical Poetry, and its natural beauty tempts you to exertion in every direction.' The south was to be denied them, however, for cholera in Naples and quarantine restrictions made it impractical. Instead, they turned northwards, tracing the River Tiber towards its birthplace in the Apennines, and visited Assisi. Following the River Arno, they now made their way towards Florence, making detours, on horseback, to three of the most evocative of all Italian monasteries, the Franciscan convents at Laverna and Vallombrosa, and the Benedictine house at Camaldoli. Romantically situated, among 'the sternest solitudes of the Appennines', surrounded by rocks, forests and mountain torrents, they were calculated to appeal to Wordsworth. As they struggled up to Laverna, they heard the 'vagrant Voice' of a cuckoo, sounding like that of John the Baptist, 'the voice of him that crieth in the wilderness'. It was a wonderful image, which William wrought up into the only poem he composed while travelling, *The Cuckoo at Laverna*. The cuckoo's call in such a foreign landscape was deeply poignant, not least because William did not actually hear it until Robinson had drawn his attention to it several times; the poet was forced to accept that age had also dulled his hearing.[36]

William told Robinson that he was not interested in places that merely had a connection with a great man, unless they had also influenced his work. He therefore cared nothing for the Pantheon, the burial place of Tasso, but had a deep interest in Vaucluse. Now he was about to see Vallombrosa, the monastery set in the heart of mountainous woodland which had reputedly given refuge to his hero, Milton. As he wrote in the poem which resulted from this visit,

> Vallombrosa! of thee I first heard in the page
> Of that holiest of Bards, and the name for my mind
> Had a musical charm, which the winter of age
> And the changes it brings had no power to unbind.

He was itching to get to Vallombrosa as soon as possible, so that he could fulfil his dream, but Robinson, who had been there before, was not an early riser and had just endured two days of arduous travel and uncomfortable lodging at Laverna and Camaldoli, wanted to defer the visit. They had what Robinson delicately called 'a little quarrel'. William was 'rude' and Robinson, offended, declined to go altogether. It was their first, and only, open disagreement, and as a result William went alone to Vallombrosa, rising at five in the morning and riding up the wooded mountainsides accompanied only by an incompetent guide. This time, his expectations were to be disappointed. The convent stood not in a deep and narrow valley, overshadowed by enclosing hills, but on a shelf on the mountain, surrounded by pines, with chestnut and beech woods above and below. And he did not have time to wander in the monastery grounds to enjoy the views.[37]

Having patched up their quarrel, the two travellers made their way to Florence, but William was already beginning to wish that he was on his way home. In the ten weeks of his absence, he had received only a single letter. He knew that this was his own fault, for not specifying where his family should write poste restante, but his imagination painted every kind of gloomy scenario and he grew increasingly depressed, irritable and unsettled. A letter from Dora, which reached him at Florence, reassured him temporarily, but he was soon agitating to be on the move again. 'Of this be assured', he told his daughter, 'that I never shall go from home for any time again, without a female companion.' Robinson was uncomfortably aware that William was not enjoying Florence as he should, confiding to his journal that his fellow traveller was 'never thoroughly happy but in the country'. 'I have spent my time very pleasantly at Florence; it is so much less fatiguing a place than Rome', William told Dora, 'but even here one has to *waste* a great deal of labour in sight-seeing on account of Churches and Galleries being closed when you expect them to be open.'[38]

After a mere six days at Florence, they took a short nostalgic tour of the Italian Lakes, which brought back painful, as well as pleasing, recollections of his previous tours with Jones, now dead, and Mary and Dorothy, who was no longer the person she had then been. 'I kept much to myself, and very often could I, for my heart's relief, have burst into tears', William confessed to Dora. While Robinson passed the time in reading, William took solitary mountain rambles, at one point thoroughly alarming his companion by disappearing for eight hours at a stretch. On 22 June they arrived in Venice, 'with the wonders of which City I shall consider our Italian tour as concluding', William announced unpromisingly. It was a pity that Venice came at the end rather than the beginning of their journey, for William was not in the mood to appreciate its shimmering waters, palatial buildings and the sharp contrast of shadowed alleyways and brilliant sunlit piazzas. St Mark's Square he admitted was 'a splendid spot!', the Venetian architecture 'wonderfully more splendid than Amsterdam . . . quite unique', and, with the ubiquitous Ticknors, he enjoyed that corniest of tourist gimmicks, which is so embarrassingly magical, an evening trip down the Grand Canal in a flotilla of gondolas while the gondoliers sang national airs and snatches of opera. But he complained of the heat and that his bedroom was too small, making him very uncomfortable, 'endeavouring to sleep while I was actually in an oven'. He was 'so indifferent to mere sights' that Robinson gave up, and they left after only four days, taking the road north towards Salzburg and Munich.[39]

If Robinson had hoped that the alpine scenery and Austrian lakes would restore William's good humour and persuade him to linger over their homeward journey, he was swiftly disabused. William had seen what he wanted to see and, as he wrote grumpily from Munich on 17 July, 'I consider our *Tour* finished'. Four months of living in each other's pockets had exaggerated the differences in their tastes and habits. Robinson was an ardent Germanophile: 'he takes delight in loitering about towns, gossiping, and attending reading-rooms, and going to coffee-houses; and at *table d'hôtes*, etc., gabbling German, or any other tongue, all which places and practices are my abomination', William complained. In the evenings, William had nothing else to do but go to bed, so he was ready to rise early, which Robinson, who retired at midnight, was not. The one time William had given in to his impulse to compose verse, he had suffered several nights of broken rest, upset his stomach and resolved to refrain in future. 'I have nothing to do,' he fretted, 'and as I cannot speak German my time moves very heavily.'[40]

Robinson was equally frustrated. 'I read a chapter in Walter Scott's *Life*, being satiated with beholding fine scenery', he wrote at Hallein. 'After breakfast Wordsworth set out on a boat-excursion for which I had no taste', he noted at Hallstadt. As they neared Munich Robinson re-read *The Excursion*, to remind himself, one imagines, just why he tolerated its author as a travelling companion. Each man was convinced that he was forgoing his own pleasures for the sake of the other, but they had simply reached the point where they were getting on each other's nerves. The root of the problem, as William acknowledged, was that Robinson, a bachelor, had no incentive to hurry home, whereas he was desperate to see his family again. 'I want the sight of your faces and the sound of your voices', he metaphorically shouted at Mary, when she reproached him for hurrying Robinson home. 'Therefore find no more fault, I undertook this journey as a *duty*, I have gone through with it as such'.[41]

On 7 August they landed back on English soil and parted, Robinson returning to his chambers, William to meet Dora and stay with Moxon. Though they met regularly, with no appearance of animosity, their early return had set tongues wagging, and both men were disconcerted when Rogers made pointed remarks about lost tempers and drew attention to the fact that they sat as far from each other as possible. This was intolerable and, to put the seal on the rumour-mill, they agreed to make 'a sort of supplementary journey' and, in a symbolic gesture, explore the Wye together as far as Tintern Abbey. Dora accompanied them, but they got no further than Brinsop. The excursion was thwarted by bad weather and a sudden recurrence of William's trachoma. With the example of John Monkhouse's patient and cheerful endurance of his blindness daily before him, William could not shame to complain, but his condition deteriorated so rapidly that he had no option but to return home as quickly as possible. On 22 September he and Dora took their places in the Liverpool coach and set off for Rydal Mount.[42]

At sixty-seven years of age, William had fulfilled his long-cherished wish of making a tour of Italy, but the whole experience was marred by an abiding sense that it had come too late. 'I have . . . to regret that this journey was not made some years ago, – to regret it, I mean, as a Poet;' he wrote from Salzburg on his way back to England, 'for though we have had a great disappointment in not seeing Naples, etc. . . . my mind has been enriched by innumerable images, which I could have turned to account in verse, and vivified by feelings which earlier in my life would have answered noble purposes, in a way they now are little likely to do.' It was a refrain he would repeat again and again, sometimes with uncharacteristic, if understandable, bitterness, suggesting that the blame lay with Jeffrey, and the other reviewers, who had made him a laughing stock and denied him the profits which would have enabled him to go as a vibrant young man.[43]

William returned to Rydal Mount to find his wife well, his sister 'in her better way' but, unexpectedly, his eldest son's affairs in crisis. On 24 July Isabella had given birth to her fourth child, imaginatively named John Wordsworth. The family were now living at Brigham, John senior having ceded the living of Workington to his brother-in-law, when he came of age. Another child on a restricted income was a problem, but at the beginning of August they were hit by a disaster which would ultimately destroy them. Three of the Curwen coal pits at Workington were swallowed up by the sea. Setting aside the cost in human lives, the financial repercussions on the Curwens were enormous. Isabella's father would lose £3,000 a year by the loss of the pits, but the disaster exposed the fragility of the foundations of the Curwen empire, which was encumbered with debt going back three generations. Isabella's generous allowance, and the expected inheritance, which had made her marriage with John possible, were, quite literally, washed away. The living of Moresby could not support two adults and four children, already indebted beyond their means by building their grand, if ill-fated rectory on the banks of the Derwent. In a touching attempt to make ends meet, and in sharp contrast to the younger generation of the Curwen family, who acted as if nothing had happened, John let it be known that he was looking for pupils. His sister suggested that perhaps the Wordsworths too should cut back on unnecessary expenses, but this Mary was not prepared to do. Their only 'extravagance' was a third maid, dedicated to Dorothy's care, who was absolutely necessary to her comfort. 'No, we must not, at this day – and with Father's triumphs sounding in our ears, be called upon to economize', she told Dora, 'not but I could be as happy *personally* upon £100 a year as when we were in the Cottage at Grasmere.'[44] Dora had welcomed the excuse to return home as her father's escort, but her parents were too afraid of the consequences for her health to allow her to remain at Rydal Mount. At the end of October, when William had re-emerged from the darkened rooms to which he had been confined by the trachoma, she returned to London. Quillinan, newly returned from Portugal, and ever optimistic that he would be able to persuade her to marry him, was waiting to escort her to Dover, where she was to spend the winter with Isabella Fenwick. Miss Fenwick, whom even the grudging Thomas Carlyle thought 'the wisest person male or female I have fallen in with in London', was now to prove her sterling worth. Dora, and possibly Quillinan too, had confided in her, and, under her aegis, the two were not only allowed, but encouraged, to meet. Quillinan was invited to Dover, and Dora, chaperoned by his sister-in-law, was allowed to go to Canterbury, where he had taken a cottage. As if to prove his Roman Catholicism was not a bar to marrying Dora, Quillinan, who had brought his own daughters up in the Anglican faith at their mother's request, assiduously escorted her to the cathedral, noting, with quiet irony, that on one occasion the 'fine anthem' was Mozart's 'Plead Thou my cause'.[45]

William had asked Quillinan, 'as an act of friendship', to go through the latest edition, at his convenience, and compare it with the previous one. 'You know my principles of style better I think than any one else, and I should be glad to learn if anything strikes you as being altered for the worse.' Anxious to please the poet, Quillinan agreed, and at the end of November he went to stay at Rydal Mount, where William was once again 'tinkering' at 'that plaguy poem he has worried so long at'. Quillinan made himself agreeable as only he knew how, talking politics and poetry to the poet, and relieving Mary of the burden of reading the newspapers to him in the evenings. He drove them out to visit their friends, walked with William and accompanied them to church. He even confided in them that he had been obliged to bring Jemima home to put an end to an unsuitable love affair she had begun in Portugal. And all the time, unbeknown to them, he was writing love letters to their daughter, pleading his cause in fantastical accounts of his dreams, in which he depicted her trapped in a Palace of Frozen Tears, with a frozen star instead of a heart. Dora tried hard to keep him at bay, suggesting that her love for him was platonic, and adding that she wished, for his own sake, that he were married to someone else, but her resistance was half-hearted, and they both knew it. 'I look back, now that I understand both you and myself, with deep regret that we were each too proud to be ingenuous to one another', he wrote in December; 'and I am often pained and mortified to think how I have played with your feelings as well as my own, and what an idle butterfly past I have acted in society'. Only one thing had kept him from disaster, and that was Dora. 'Whenever I have been about to surrender myself in desperation & irrevocably to some other [girl: deleted] influence, up sprung the image of the mountain Maiden, and I felt that it was impossible. – There you have as much of the secret of my heart-and-hand loneliness for the last eleven or twelve years as I can venture to expose to you just now.'[46]

Mary's suspicions were first aroused when Quillinan flatly refused to let her see a letter from Dora he was reading. 'I felt ashamed', he admitted to Dora, 'as if I was guilty of some I do not know what to call it, for it is not disingenuousness in its culpable sense – my regard for you is not, cannot be a secret in this house – but it is exactly in this house & to its owners that I could not utter a syllable about it'. Quillinan might have been able to half-persuade himself that he was not deceiving the Wordsworths, but he could not screw up the courage to tell them the truth. This was left to Dora, who was incapable of pretence, especially towards her parents. At the first opportunity, and probably in response to probing by her mother, Dora explained how matters stood. It was only then that Quillinan wrote to William, asking permission to marry his daughter.[47]

The Wordsworths' anger was understandable. They felt that their trust had been betrayed. If Townshend, Hogg and de Quincey had all abused the Wordsworths' hospitality with their journalistic publications, how much more so had Quillinan, who had used his intimacy with the family to win the affections of their only daughter and take her from them? Every aspect of the case put him in a poor light: he was so much older and more worldly than her and he had been neither open nor straightforward in his wooing. They had known him intimately, for almost fifteen years, supported him in his difficulties, indulged and laughed at his flirtations, flippancies and dilettante behaviour. Within the family, he had even been known as Aunt Sara's lover, because they had enjoyed a mutual flirtation. And now he expected them to sanction his marriage to Dora.

William, in particular, was furious, playing the Victorian father as if born to the role. Even his beloved daughter felt his wrath at first, though by 8 February he had calmed down enough to send her a new sonnet 'as a peace-offering, at your dear Mother's request'. Matters were not helped by the fact that, throughout the winter of 1837–8, and indeed until the middle of the year 1838, Dora was away from home, as the doctors had advised, staying principally with Isabella Fenwick, but also visiting the Hoares and Sara Coleridge at Hampstead and her relatives at Cambridge and Brinsop Court. The suspicion that she was reluctant to return to Rydal Mount crossed everyone's minds, and William may even have thought that she was staying away so that she could meet with Quillinan. With or without her father's consent, the lovers considered themselves engaged. Quillinan even thought they were on the brink of marriage, for on 6 April he bought her a ring which he had engraved with lines of his own composition.[48]

When he called to see her, in London, before she left for Brinsop, he was swiftly disillusioned. Dora had just received a vicious letter from her father, which was to prompt a 'really bold speaking-out' response from Dora. Refusing even to allude to Quillinan by name, he had used the analogous situation of thirty-six-year-old Henry Taylor, who had proposed to a girl of seventeen and been rejected, to mount a covert attack on Dora's lover. 'If Men or Women will form engagements so little in accordance with nature and reason, they have no *right* to expect better treatment', he snarled. 'I take no notice of the conclusion of your Letter', he added; '. . . It turns upon a subject which I shall never touch more either by pen or voice. Whether I look back or forward it is depressing and distressing to me, and will for the remainder of my life, continue to be so.'[49]

Both Mary and Miss Fenwick tried to pour oil on troubled waters. Mary assured Dora that her father seemed 'quite a different person' since he had received the assurance that she was on her way home, and he too sent her 'a home-inviting loving message'. 'Well then, what are you to do when you get home?' Quillinan asked.

> Nothing at all: be quiet, my dear Dora, and do not attempt to argue the point. Dutiful to Him I know you will be and dutiful to Her, and gentle, and unquerulous in words as you are in truth affectionate to her, I pray you to be for her sake, your sake, & for my sake. – She has not been very kind to me, but I am sure she has many a heart-ache about you; and who can tell how much kindness even to me is suppres, or how little she really understands, or how much she mistakes, the true nature of this case.

'It is strange', he mused, 'that with all his lucid thought [your father] cannot see that that particular "composition of" your "mind" which has made you so true and tenacious a daughter to him, is the roman cement that also binds you to me.'[50]

William worked off his fury in the garden, symbolically making improvements in the Rash field, which was now known as Dora's field, because he had given it to her. When Dora finally returned home, in June, she did not have to face her parents alone. Miss Fenwick, to whom the lovers already owed so much, accompanied her, and, to all outward appearances, life at Rydal Mount went on as if nothing had occurred. Only Christopher's son John, visiting later in the year, noticed that Dora seemed preoccupied with 'a secret care, which weighs upon the feelings of all here, though they never allude to it in conversation'.[51]

Dora was intimately involved in William's next publication, a single volume containing all his sonnets. It was something which many of his admirers had suggested to him but he had always resisted, fearing that to separate out one element of his work from the rest might injure the sale of the complete editions. The success of Hine's *Selections* had shown that this was not the case. The other objection, that it would give undue importance to one aspect of his work, was less easily overcome, not least because there was still a strong body of opinion which held the sonnet in contempt. Rogers was typical, for instance, in thinking that no ideas of any importance could be expressed or developed within the constraints of the fourteen-line format, making it an unworthy vehicle for serious poetry. William had long championed the sonnet, resting his case on Milton's use of the form. In preparing an edition of his sonnets, William was not just gratifying the wish of those like Robinson and Christopher's son John, whose opinion he respected, but making a public statement about the value he himself attached to this type of poem. As usual in his arrangements with his publisher, he suggested his motives were entirely mercenary. 'I am rather pleased that you approve of the Sonnets in a separate volume,' he informed Moxon, 'not that I care much about it myself, except for the money that it would bring (and that mainly on account of an unfavourable change in the circumstances of my Son)'. When Moxon suggested that only one sonnet should be printed per page, William was surprised and expressed his reservations that the result, selling at 9s, would be 'a book of luxury, and tho' I have no objection to that, yet still my wish is, to be read as widely as is consistent with reasonable pecuniary return'.[52]

William already had over 400 published sonnets in hand, and would add a further twelve new ones while overseeing the volume through the press. Six of these were composed so late that they could not be included in the main body of the text and had to be added as an appendix. One of these was a remodelling, in sonnet form, of a poem he had written after the death of Mrs Southey, in November 1837. William and Mary had visited her on the day she died, peacefully in her bed, having refused food and water for the previous ten days. Though Southey appeared philosophical about his loss, his poor daughters, who had borne the brunt of nursing her, were tormented by regrets 'for unkind things said & done'. Inevitably, the Wordsworths could not help but make comparisons with Dorothy. 'She is an affecting object', Mary had written after a visit to Mrs Southey in August, '– but what a contrast in regard to beautiful neatness and cleanliness to our poor sufferer.' In mental condition, however, they were much the same. Quillinan had not been allowed to see Dorothy during his visit. William, always clutching at straws, had thought a visit from him might be beneficial, but she had been 'in her singing mood', and Mary and the maids thought there was no point in an interview which could only distress Quillinan: 'there is no good done by it –', Mary told Dora, 'only Father fancies every body feels as he does'.[53] In the first version of his poem, 'Oh! what a Wreck! how changed in mien and speech', William had alluded specifically to Dorothy's condition, as well as Mrs Southey's. The revised sonnet cut out these personal references and the comparison with Dorothy, leaving only the kernel of the poem.

> She is not what she seems, a forlorn wretch,
> But delegated Spirits comfort fetch
> To Her from heights that Reason may not win.
> Like Children, She is privileged to hold
> Divine communion;

Mary objected to the inclusion of this sonnet, fearing it would be taken to refer to Dorothy. 'I own I do not see the force of this objection', William told Dora, but he nevertheless sought her opinion, and that of Isabella Fenwick, before including it.[54]

By 21 May William had completed all his part of the book, including the notes, table of contents and a short advertisement, making pointed allusion to Milton, the father of the sonnet. The title was honest, if unmemorable, *The Sonnets of William Wordsworth. Collected in One Volume. With a Few Additional Ones.* Complimentary copies were in the hands of friends a month later, but, to give it a chance of attracting attention, the publication was delayed until after the coronation of Queen Victoria on 25 June. Even then, William was still plagued by doubts whether it would succeed or affect the sale of the six-volume edition, and was grateful for a reassurance from Moxon, at the end of July, that both were selling well.[55]

William had more profound reasons for gratitude to Moxon. He alone, out of all the London publishers, had stood out in favour of a bill to extend the term of author's copyright, which was presented to the House of Commons in April. The bill was the work of William's friend Thomas Noon Talfourd, 'an astonishing man – for talents, Genius, and energy of mind', who had entered Parliament at the end of 1835 as member for Reading. Diametrically opposed to William in politics, his election had nevertheless been welcomed by the poet, who offered his sincere congratulations, adding only a single caveat. 'As you so well know my opinions, which differ I believe in fundamentals from your own, I shall only say, respect them so far, as to think a little more about any course you might be inclined to take as a Member of the House, than you otherwise would have done, if you had not been aware that your notions of prudence and mine might be at variance.'[56]

As an author himself, Talfourd had an interest in extending the term of copyright from twenty-eight to sixty years after publication, but he would not have taken up the cause had it not been for William, who had been lobbying for a change in the law for thirty years. His argument in 1838 was exactly the same as it had been in 1808: 'The law as it now stands merely consults the interest of the useful drudges in Literature, or of flimsy and shallow writers, whose works are upon a level with the taste and knowledge of the age; while men of real power, who go before their age, are deprived of all hope of their families being benefited by their exertions.' As the years had passed, William's own poetic career proved a striking example of the injustice of the copyright laws. By 1835 his rights in *Lyrical Ballads* and *Poems, in Two Volumes* had already lapsed: the moment he died, any publisher could reprint those editions without paying a penny towards his estate. By 1842, the same would be true of *The Excursion* and, the following year, of both the first collected edition of 1815 and *The White Doe of Rylstone.* It had taken thirty years to establish a sale of his works, longer than the term of copyright, and throughout that time he had earned next to nothing. Now, when he was just beginning to reap the financial benefit, his death would mean that his family would be prevented from enjoying the profits of his labours. The example of Burns was always at the forefront of his argument. Burns had died young, leaving his children 'to languish in Poverty and Dependence, while Booksellers are revelling in luxury upon gains derived from Works which are the delight of many Nations'. 'The wrongs of literary men are crying out for redress on all sides', William proclaimed. 'It appears to me that towards no class of his Majesty's Subjects are the laws so unjust and oppressive.'[57]

In recent years, as his own copyrights dwindled and expired in proportion as his sales increased, William had become more urgent in his demands for a reform. He had lobbied hard among his friends in high places and, increasingly, as those friends came from the younger generation, who had been brought up on his works and were his devoted admirers, he had gained an audience. Until he found someone prepared to introduce a bill, however, there was little else he could do. In 1830 he had even seriously considered never publishing anything further in his lifetime, to ensure that his family would have a windfall after his death. The changing market had rightly tempted him to publish again, but he still reserved *The Prelude*, not just because he had not completed *The Recluse*, but because he knew it was likely to be his most marketable commodity after his death.[58]

Talfourd had put a notice in the book of the House of Commons, announcing his intention to bring in a copyright bill, as long ago as November 1836. William having declined his request to petition personally in support of his bill, when it actually came before the Commons, in May 1837, Talfourd had to content himself with making 'honorable mention' of William, who was then in Italy. The bill secured a second reading, but fell victim to the dissolution of Parliament on the death of William IV.[59] Talfourd immediately announced his intention to try again in the new session, and this time, having seen how the booksellers and publishers had petitioned against the bill, and the inference that had been drawn from the silence of authors, William decided he would have to exert himself. Though he still declined to be an individual suppliant for what he considered to be the right of a whole class, and therefore refused to petition, he did write an open letter to Talfourd for him to publish in the *Morning Post*, composed two sonnets pleading the cause for inclusion in the new volume, urged all his literary friends to exert their influence and lobbied indefatigably every Member of Parliament with whom he had even the most tenuous of connections, explaining, cajoling and ultimately asking them to attend the Commons when the bill was reintroduced on 11 April 1838.[60]

By 14 April he could boast that he had written (or rather dictated, since poor Mary did the writing) scarcely fewer than fifty letters on the subject. Among them was a letter to the *Kendal Mercury*, in answer to a petition drawn up by the compositors and printers of Kendal against the bill. William attacked their claim that an extension of copyright would restrict the circulation of books and make them available only to the wealthy, pointing out that the reverse was true in America, where the non-existence of copyright meant that publishers were afraid to venture their capital on standard works, for fear of being undercut by cheaper competitors. Denying the charge that authors were opulently rewarded for their works, he cited Southey, the Coleridges, father and son, and himself as proof that this was not so, and, answering the claim that a longer term of copyright would prevent the publication of school compilations, he again asserted that the reverse was true. He had himself made no objection when Richard Batt, of the Friends' School at Lancaster, had published twenty-five pages of his poems in his *Gleanings in Poetry* without asking his permission. Nor had he complained when the Reverend Robert Housman, in his *A Collection of English Sonnets*, had filled fifty-seven pages, out of 300, with William's poetry; what is more, he had refused to support his own publishers in threatening Housman with an injunction.[61]

The second reading of the bill was passed by thirty-nine votes to thirty-four – and only then because John Ellis, at the instigation of Sir Robert Inglis and Benjamin D'Israeli, went down in a cab to the Carlton Club during the debate 'where I was fortunate enough to persuade one or two to relinquish their claret and go down for the division'. As William remarked, the greatest difficulty in securing the passage of the bill was not so much the united opposition of the booksellers and publishers, but the indifference among members of the Commons to anything but party measures. In the face of mounting opposition from Lord John Russell and Sir Robert Peel, Talfourd decided on a tactical withdrawal of his bill until the next session, to prevent it being voted out altogether.[62]

William would not admit defeat. He could not afford to do so. All his attempts to find his younger son a new and better-paid post had failed: applications to be a Tithe Commissioner and Secretary to the new Birmingham Railway had both come to nothing.[63] His elder son's affairs had gone from bad to worse: having lost all his wife's income and been reduced to living off his salary as rector of Brigham, he had caught typhus visiting his parishioners. So ill that he was unable to perform his duties, he had been bedridden for a couple of months and recovered very slowly; an excursion to Paris did nothing for him, and when he consulted the doctors in London he was advised to spend the winter in the south of France and be careful of doing duty for two years. France was out of the question financially, but he, his wife and youngest child took up their quarters in Leamington and London for the winter and a substitute had to be found for the interval at Brigham. As Mary lamented, 'truly the expences attending this untoward illness is *to us all* a most serious consideration'. The only bright spot, as far as his doting grandparents were concerned, was that John and Isabella left little Willy, who would be three years old on 27 December, at Rydal Mount. His presence 'brought fresh life to this house', Mary observed, and was an additional incentive to William to continue his labours for copyright reform.[64]

William's position as the grand old man of English letters was now firmly established. Honours showered on him from every side. He politely declined, on the grounds of age and inadequacy, invitations to lecture on poetry in a public institution in London and to contribute 'critical reflections' to the *Transactions* of the Royal Irish Academy. He developed a standard reply to the unknown authors who showered him with requests to dedicate their works to him: he refused, but acknowledged at the same time that 'every one is at liberty to dedicate his productions to whom he likes, provided that he makes no declaration, that this is done with the consent of the party to whom he has chosen to inscribe his work'.

The very fact that he had to take this step to avoid appearing to endorse unseen work was an indication that his name and judgement were now respected.[65]

This was also evident from the number of honorary memberships of educational societies that were conferred on him, from the newly founded Kendal Natural History and Scientific Society to the respected Royal Institution of Liverpool. On 21 July 1838 the University of Durham conferred an honorary doctorate on him. It was the first time an honorary graduand had attended the ceremony in person and William was deeply embarrassed that the public oration was not made in Latin, as was customary at Oxford and Cambridge. 'There is . . . some thing very awkward in constraining a Man to hear his own praises, before many listeners, in his Mother tongue', William told Robinson. '– I object to the practice also as lowering the University.' Nevertheless, he was proud of the honour, and, as it was technically a law degree, it allowed him to tease his barrister friend by urging him 'not [to] scruple when a difficult point of Law occurs, to consult me'.[66] In October he was invited by the Secretary of the Wordsworth Committee to stand for election as Rector of the University of Glasgow, an active role which he felt incapable of fulfilling and declined, though sensible of the honour intended, expressing

> the satisfaction which I have derived from this occurrence as an evidence of the sense entertained among the Students in your University of the importance of imaginative Literature. A right understanding upon the subject, and a just feeling is at all times momentous, but especially so in the present state of society, and the opinions now so prevalent respecting the relative values of intellectual pursuits.[67]

With these plaudits ringing in his ears, William now had the confidence to admit publicly that he had failed in the one aspect of his poetic career that mattered most to him. *The Recluse* would never be completed. He had subtly hinted that this was the case in his 1836–7 edition of his *Poetical Works*, where, for the first time, the words 'A Portion of the Recluse' had been dropped from the title-page of *The Excursion.* Only the most sensitive of readers would have picked this up, however, as the preface had remained intact. Inquiries about *The Recluse* had continued unabated over the years, most recently from the poet and critic James Montgomery, who demanded abruptly, 'where is the rest?' When Ticknor, William's American friend, called at Rydal Mount in May, he also asked the all-important request. Significantly, he was prompted not so much by his own curiosity, as by a request from Mary. 'Mrs Wordsworth asked me to talk to him about finishing the Excursion, or the Recluse; saying, that she could not bear to have him occupied constantly in writing sonnets and other trifles, while this great work lay by him untouched'. She herself had ceased to urge him on the subject, because she had done so in vain. William explained that the first part of *The Recluse* was 'partly written in fragments which . . . would be useless and unintelligible in other hands than his own', the second was *The Excursion* and the third was untouched. 'On my asking him why he does not finish it, he turned to me very decidedly, and said, "Why did not Gray finish the long poem he began on a similar subject? Because he found he had undertaken something beyond his powers to accomplish. And that is my case." '[68]

Unable to afford a tour this year, after the expense of going to Italy the previous year, William contented himself with a three-week excursion to Northumberland and County Durham, with Isabella Fenwick, in July, and a three-day excursion to the Duddon in October. On the latter occasion, he was accompanied by quite a party: his nephew 'Cambridge' John, Dora, Ellen, Anna and Letitia Ricketts, her three friends from Dover, and their maid. Newly recovered from a bout of sciatica and determined to protect himself against the cold, William was at his most picturesque in appearance. 'He resembled more the representations of one [of] the Weird Sisters in Macbeth than any thing else I can think of', Ellen recorded in her journal. He wore a cloth cap with neck-protector, like that of a French legionnaire, but made from fur, a Scottish plaid, sewn up two sides, which he threw over his head, forming a conical peak at the top and trailing on the ground behind, which he constantly tripped over as he walked and talked. His sensitive eyes were protected by dark glasses and, whenever there was the least wind, by 'an old weather-beaten faded green Umbrella', with several spokes adrift. 'This completed our Hero's *turn out*,' Ellen noted, 'and a fund of amusement did it occasion us, for we were saucy enough to laugh at him repeatedly, which seemed much to divert him.'[69]

Despite his wife's distaste for such 'trifles', William spent the closing months of the year composing twelve or more new sonnets, some of them arising out of his Italian tour. These he offered to send to Robinson, on condition he did not read them to any '*verse-writers*. We are all in spite of ourselves a parcel of thieves', he told Robinson. 'I had a droll instance of it this morning – for while Mary was writing down for me one of these Sonnets, on coming to a certain line, she cried out somewhat uncourteously "that's a plagiarism" – from whom? "from yourself" was the answer. I believe she is right tho' she could not point out the passage, neither can I.'[70]

The sales of his published work continued to confound all expectations. Only 450 copies remained out of the 3,000 printed for the six-volume edition of 1836–7. A further edition was now necessary and William's nephew 'Cambridge' John, 'the most accurate Man I know', gladly undertook to correct the proofs on his behalf. Evidence that William's reputation was spreading beyond the shore of his native country came from all corners of the globe. The last edition of his poems published in America had a print run of 20,000 copies and the whole of his poetic works were available there in an edition costing less than the modern equivalent of six pence. In a 'highly encomiastic' article in the *New York Review*, written by one of his American editors, Henry Reed, he had been hailed as the successor of Shakespeare, Spenser and Milton. More unexpectedly, an unauthorized edition appeared in Calcutta, giving rise to a controversy about the quality of the poetry in the *Delhi Gazette* of the sort William had thankfully not experienced in twenty years. It too sold for a paltry six rupees.[71]

These successes persuaded William that he would have to overcome his objection to appearing as a petitioner to Parliament on copyright reform. The persistent Talfourd was preparing to try again, and, luckily for William, who was at a loss as to how to proceed, Robinson was paying what had now become almost an annual visit to Rydal. The first version was rejected. 'He is too desirous to express his own impressions and cares, too little about the impressions it will excite in others', Robinson coolly remarked, before amusing himself in rewriting the petition; to his gratification 'a few' of his suggestions were accepted. Adopting a lofty stance, the poet declared that he was on the point of attaining his seventieth year and that his copyrights were now almost all contingent on the duration of his life. He pointed out that he had earned more from his writings in the last four years than in the preceding thirty-four and that this income would have been lost to his family had he died within that period. The main object of the bill, however, was 'to relieve men of letters from the thraldom of being forced to court the living generation, to aid them in rising above degraded taste and slavish prejudice, and to encourage them to rely upon their own impulses, or to leave them with less excuse if they should fail to do so'. Talfourd again got his bill to a second reading, this time with an increased majority, but was thwarted by the unexpected resignation of the ministry in May.[72] Relief for men of letters was not to come for three more years.

25. *Real Greatness*

'I meant to stay here only a month,' Robinson wrote to his brother on 19 January 1839, 'but the Ws seem so unwilling to let me go that I foresee I shall not get away till the end of five weeks.' He was thoroughly enjoying himself, reading, walking, talking and playing evening games of whist (a new pastime) with the Wordsworths, visiting the Arnolds at Fox How, and making the acquaintance of Isabella Fenwick, who was resident for the winter in Ambleside. Like everyone else, male and female, who came within this remarkable lady's ambit, he fell in love with her. Fifty-six years old, with a deformity of the spine 'but otherwise really rather good-looking', in Carlyle's heartless phrase, Miss Fenwick exuded goodness. Henry Taylor, who was the stepson of her cousin, called her 'largely and deeply religious', but she had neither the sickly piety nor abrasive evangelical zeal which was so prevalent in those times. Her sympathies were entirely with repentant sinners rather than 'respectable people', and she had a healthy dislike of the two great Victorian virtues, 'prudential virtue and worldly respectability'. Instinctively attracted to all those in trouble, sorrow, need, sickness, or any other adversity, she was blessed by them as 'an angel upon earth'. Intellectual, without being a blue-stocking, and generous to a fault, her saintly qualities were also spiced with an attractive sense of the ridiculous. And this was an angel who did not fear to tread anywhere.[1]

At the beginning of February, she invited Quillinan to stay with her at Ambleside. Afraid to accept, until reassured by William that he had not forfeited his friendship and that his visit would not be considered an 'intrusion', he arrived on 11 February and was invited to call at Rydal Mount. As Mary said, he came to a gloomy house. William was ill with rheumatics, 'a sad nervous derangement', and a cough. Dora was looking ill, and losing her appetite again. Dorothy was Dorothy. For a week, Quillinan spent every day with Dora, returning at night to Miss Fenwick's. He had no private conversation, directly or indirectly, with William on the subject so close to all their hearts, but by the time he left, they had come to an understanding, which Miss Fenwick summarized to Dora as 'a patient waiting for happier circumstances – your father reconciling himself to all objections – & willing to consent – when there could be any reasonable security of your being provided for – and there being no hinderance [*sic*] to your attachment in the mean time'. Quillinan departed for Ireland, convinced that his visit had removed 'the ill-omened gloom that darkened your house to me', and even William felt that 'we all seemed at ease with each other'.[2]

As soon as Quillinan had gone, William and Mary went to stay with Miss Fenwick at Ambleside, 'for the sake of her society and change of air'. William could not throw off his lumbago, and had convinced himself that it would not be prudent for him to walk between the two houses 'so often as I could wish'. He was now revising his autobiographical poem, *The Prelude*, so that it would be in a fit state for posthumous publication. Miss Fenwick, observing this process for the first time, was astonished at the labour that went into it. William seldom worked fewer than six or seven hours a day, 'or rather one ought to say the whole day, for it seemed always on his mind – quite a possession'. After one such session, he appeared before Miss Fenwick 'radiant with joy' and bursting to tell her that Mary, in the midst of his dictation, had said, 'Well, William, I declare you are cleverer than ever.' With tears in his eyes, he explained why such an apparent commonplace should mean so much to him. 'It is not often I have had such praise; she has always been sparing of it.' As soon as the revision was complete, William gave the poem to Dora and Elizabeth Cookson to be fair-copied. 'Pray do not work *hard*,' he begged, 'I cannot bear you should.' While the two young women stayed at Rydal Mount to make the new transcript, William and Mary accompanied Miss Fenwick and her niece, Isabella, to Bath. They travelled for the first time by train, on the new line from Preston to Birmingham. 'The rail way is charming travelling, but neither *apparently* so rapid, so smooth or like flying as I expected,' Mary commented. Nor was it cheap, costing the thrifty Wordsworths £1 6s 6d '*each*', plus £4 5d for Miss Fenwick's carriage, and 17s for each of the servants.[3]

Their purpose in going to Bath was twofold, to defer a parting from Miss Fenwick, whose family lived in the city, and to take the waters for their rheumatics. Willy, who had joined them at Lancaster, was also of the party. He was in such a delicate state of health that his appearance quite frightened his mother. This, and his recent announcement that he had decided to emigrate to Australia, to try his chances there rather than wait for something to turn up in England, suggest that his long, unhappy engagement to Mary Cust had now been ended by her death. Bertha Southey's marriage to her cousin Herbert Hill the previous month had also stirred up murky waters in Willy's past, so it was not surprising that he was miserable and ill.[4]

The Wordsworths took lodgings at 101 George Street, halfway between the Pump Rooms and Royal Crescent. They bathed, took the waters, visited assiduously and tried unsuccessfully to avoid the '*terrible* Blue Stocking' and 'perfect pest' Mrs

Maltby, who was determined to capture the poet for her salon. They called several times on Mrs de Quincey, who lived nearby at Weston. This was particularly kind, given that the third instalment of her son's revelations about the Wordsworths was published in *Tait's Magazine* that very month. With its unflattering physical descriptions of William, Mary and Dorothy, its gossipy disclosures about their conversation and private lives, and, almost worst of all, its extensive quotation from *The Prelude*, which William himself was deliberately withholding from publication to benefit his children, it was the greatest betrayal of friendship which had yet occurred. In the circumstances, Mary's discretion in reserving the contents of their conversation with Mrs de Quincey 'to be chatted about by Aunty's good fire' seems poignant. William also made contact with another old friend, the seventy-seven-year-old poet William Lisle Bowles, who lived not far away at Chippenham. 'I am truly glad to find your outward Machine, is only a little worse for wear!' Bowles wrote cheerfully to William. 'I am as wizen as a witch, & as Deaf as a Post!', which perhaps explains why he mistook Mary for 'old Dorothy' when they met on 18 April.[5]

The happy atmosphere at Bath was shattered by a letter from Dora, announcing that Quillinan, in contravention of the understanding that had been brought about in February, had written to her, demanding a final answer to his proposal. Did she trust him, he asked? Did she dare to run the risk of marrying him, without any assurance of financial security? Did she have any influence over her father, and would she exert it to make their marriage possible? It was a typically impatient Quillinan gesture, but it angered William deeply: 'that calling upon her in so peremptory a manner to act on so important an occasion *during the absence of her parents*, is, to say the least of it, an ill-judged proceeding', he wrote icily to Quillinan. In the time-honoured fashion, he demanded to know what were his would-be son-in-law's prospects, and, in particular, could he provide for Dora after his death?[6]

Everyone waited on tenterhooks, hoping that Quillinan would be able to provide a satisfactory answer. As he well knew, however, this was impossible. Not only were his current finances in disarray, but what little he had was compromised by securities he had foolishly, if generously, given for his brother's business. Powerless to alter the situation, and notoriously touchy, he chose to respond by taking offence at William's letter. His self-justificatory and accusatory reply made a bad situation worse. 'I do most exceedingly regret the tone of his letter –', Miss Fenwick told Dora, 'for it has disturbed feelings which were certainly very kindly disposed towards him – and which in time would have been all that he could have required – and which still may be – tho' not so soon.' To Dora herself, caught between them, he declared his conviction that they would never marry; 'now that the hopelessness of the case is manifest, I believe in my soul and conscience that you will be the less unhappy for having arrived at the conviction of its hopelessness'.[7]

Though Miss Fenwick had been unstinting in her support for them all throughout this crisis, it actually fell to Willy to heal the breach. Having been in the same situation himself, he understood its difficulties better than anyone. He wrote and called on Quillinan, and persuaded his father to write a generous letter to Dora, stating that he believed Quillinan to be 'a most honorable and upright man, and further that he is most strongly and faithfully attached to you – this I must solemnly declare in justice to you both; and to this I add *my blessing upon you and him*; more I cannot do'. A second letter, from Mary, warned Dora, 'my beloved Daughter', not to agitate the matter further, 'or call upon your *tender Father* (for he *does* deserve that epithet if ever Man did) for more than this passive countenance which he is, I feel, ready to give. And may his and your Mother's blessing be upon you both.'[8]

At the end of April William was summoned to London by Thomas Spring-Rice, then Chancellor of the Exchequer, who wrote that 'it had occurred to him' William might appreciate having his office as Distributor of Stamps transferred to his son. Having battled so long and unsuccessfully to achieve exactly this, it looked as if the gift would now fall, unasked, into Willy's lap. It was too good to be true. On 7 May the resignation of the ministry, which thwarted the progress of the Copyright Bill, also put an end to the transfer. The best Spring-Rice could do was to present William with a memorandum stating his offer and suggest he presented it to his successor in office. Willy gloomily reverted to his idea of emigrating to Australia.[9]

'Father is driving at fine speed from 8oc till 12 at night – either with legs or tongue', Mary informed Dora on 7 May. His eyes continued 'in almost their very best way,' William himself reported, 'notwithstanding lamp light, candle light, late Dinners, late hours . . .' After three weeks, even Miss Fenwick could complain, 'he has been engaged & preoccupied ever since he has been in London and it has only been a chance half hour that I have seen him myself'. During the fortnight he spent at the Marshalls' in Grosvenor Square a grand party was got up every day to meet him. There were visits to Robinson, Rogers, Talfourd, Kenyon, Taylor, the Ricketts, the Clarksons and the Coleridges (where a disgruntled Mary, stuck between a pair of lawyers and forced to listen to Sara's prosing away on literary matters, observed sourly that 'Poor dear Mrs C', who sat opposite her, looked just like 'a *stuffed Turkey*').[10]

In the midst of all this superficial gaiety, the Wordsworths had private griefs to bear. On 24 May Mary's brother Henry died in Douglas, on the Isle of Man. Seventy years old, he had been in ill-health for many years, so his death was not unexpected. Much more shocking was the death, on 10 May, of the wife of their nephew Charles, Charlotte Wordsworth, who was twenty-two and died giving birth to their only child, a second Charlotte. It was a timely reminder of the perils of marriage and child-bearing to which Dora would be exposed. Having briefly visited the widower and his 'most delightful' baby at Winchester, Mary could not stand being parted from her own daughter any longer and returned early to Rydal Mount, leaving William and Willy to finish off their business in town.[11] William and Quillinan had several amicable meetings, at which William gave his permission, if not his approval, for the match. 'I cannot think of parting with you with that complacency, that satisfaction, that hopefulness which I could wish to feel', he wrote sadly to Dora. 'But I must submit, and do submit; and God Almighty bless you, my dear child, and him who is the object of your long and long-tried preference and choice.' More pragmatically, he suggested Quillinan should consider taking on the supervision of a bank of deposit as a way of adding to his earnings. Quillinan succeeded in obtaining the offer of the secretaryship of a new joint stock bank, but he could not fulfil the condition of bringing in 'some good men' as investors, and, to his bitter disappointment, the situation escaped him.[12]

On 10 June Quillinan saw William off on the coach from London to Oxford, for what was to be the greatest accolade of his entire poetic career. The university had decided to bestow an honorary doctorate upon him. This was in itself a matter of pride and pleasure, but what turned it into such a triumph was the reception he received from the Oxford men who packed the Sheldonian Theatre to see him become a Doctor of Civil Law. 'He was most enthusiastically received on entering the Theatre yesterday,' Willy wrote to his mother on 13 June 'such cheering, I never in my life heard, not even at an Election, & I was told by many that, with the exception of the I[n]stallation of the Duke of Wellington, there never was more feeling shown or expressed.' Mary Arnold, who with her husband and daughter, Jane, had come from Rugby to see the ceremony, carried away with her a single striking image:

> that of Mr W with his venerable dignified yet humble look as he advanced to receive the University distinction. His grey hair easily distinguished him nor was he less marked by the deafening shouts of applause & approbation w[hi]ch were heard on all sides from the grave looking body of Masters below, as well as from the more vehement undergraduates above.

Everyone there, she went on, must have contrasted this reception with the neglect and contempt with which his earlier works had been treated; 'yet here was the same man his system & principle unchanged, his own dignified simplicity the same both in himself & in his works & yet having conquered that public opinion w[hi]ch he was content to wait for[,] sure that his principle was true & not over anxious about the early acknowledgment of it. In all this there is real greatness'.[13]

The Reverend John Keble, in his public oration (in Latin this time, to William's relief), declared that he stood out uniquely among all the poets, 'because he alone had placed the customs, pursuits and moral observances of the poor not just in a good light, but even in a heavenly one'. Gratifying though this praise was, it could not match the spontaneous acclamation he received from the crowd, which, like the letters he received from ordinary readers, was voluntarily offered and therefore indisputably sincere. In the unpoetic expression of John Peace, the City Librarian of Bristol who travelled to Oxford for the sole purpose of '*joining in the shout*', it was 'a burst from the central heart of the best men of England at the best period of their lives'. So there he stood, the poet who had championed the poor, with the plaudits of the country's intellectual, political and religious leaders, past, present and future, ringing in his ears: living proof of his own dictum that 'we have all of us one human heart'.[14]

Keble gave the oration in his capacity as Professor of Poetry, but he was better known, then as now, as the author of the immensely popular *Christian Year* and founder of the Oxford Movement. His speech therefore had an added significance, for it went beyond mere praise of William's poetry to venerate the spirit in which it was written. For the first time, the poet who had been variously castigated as an atheist, a pantheist and every other kind of theist (but always doctrinally unsound) was now publicly recognized as a *Christian* poet. This was not lost on those present, John Peace included. 'It was a blessed thing', he wrote to Mary afterwards, '. . . that it fell to the lot of the congenial and heavenly-minded John Keble to avouch before fit audience, not few, that the highest praise which Christian life may utter belonged to the Christian Poet who stood before them.' William had always said that he could not write sacred poetry, protesting that he thought it 'a subject too high for him'.[15] His admirers, however, from all walks of life, had always recognized that his poems were instinctively religious. Many a humble admirer had echoed Sir George Beaumont in declaring that they had received more benefit from reading his works than any other book except the Bible. In John Ruskin's beautiful phrase, William had taught them that, 'A snowdrop was to me, as to Wordsworth, part of the Sermon on the mount.' Keble's oration gave the highest possible sanction to this interpretation, which would once have been regarded as blasphemous. It endorsed the crucial shift in critical and popular opinion, which now recognized as William's greatest strengths what had once been seen as his weaknesses. He had succeeded in educating a whole new generation to believe that Cumberland beggars and daffodils were fit subjects for poetry, that philosophical truths could be found in humble subjects and that religion could and should rise above sectarian difference.[16]

What Keble's oration also did was to claim William for the Oxford Movement, which sought to rise above doctrinal squabbles and regenerate the spiritual heart of the Anglican Church. It was no coincidence that, before he left the city, William breakfasted several times with its leading members, including Keble himself, John Henry Newman, Francis Faber (who had written to ask William if he would accept an honorary degree if conferred) and his brother, the charismatic preacher Frederick William Faber. Nor was it a coincidence that all these men had been disciples of his poetry since youth, so that, in influencing them, he might even be said to have laid the foundations for the Oxford Movement. It was a debt which Newman himself identified, saying he had been central to the 'great progress of the religious mind of our Church to something deeper and truer than satisfied the last century.' The poet whose work had once been castigated by Jeffrey as the 'very paragon of silliness and affectation' was now venerated as sage and seer.[17]

William returned to Rydal Mount, and reality, on 15 June, having requested Keble to send him a copy of the oration for him to keep. Pride coming before a fall, he had also sprained his ankle, a troublesome injury which confined him to the grounds and would cause him much future discomfort.[18] He immediately embarked on corrections for the next edition of his *Poetical Works* in six volumes, delegating the task of proofreading *The Excursion* to his nephew 'Cambridge' John. Always anxious to ensure his readers did not feel themselves unfairly treated, the twelve new sonnets added to the single volume of sonnets were annexed as an appendix to the fifth volume, together with a literary curiosity, translations into Latin of William's two *Odes to May* and the *Somnambulist.* William had received a Latin translation of *Yarrow Visited* (*Arrovia Visa*) from one devoted reader several years earlier, but these were different, for they were by his son John. 'I wish them to be published in this way thinking they may be partly helps to me in getting Pupils, answering as testimonials', John frankly informed Moxon.[19]

This was the last time William was able to call on the invaluable services of his nephew. John, who had never enjoyed robust health, died, aged thirty-four, on New Year's Eve, after a short but painful illness. His father, who had nursed him devotedly day and night, consoled himself with observing John's patient resignation and Christian fortitude, but admitted to his own brother that 'the loss to me and to his Brothers is, irreparable on this side of the grave.' 'The departed was beloved in this House as he deserved to be . . . his life had been as blameless as a man's could well be', William replied. 'He was a pure Spirit and through the goodness of God, is gone to his reward.'[20]

There was also a parting from another nephew this winter. 'Keswick' John had completed his apprenticeship, passed his examinations at Chatham in the Army Medical Department and, due mainly to his uncle's lobbying in the summer, obtained a commission and posting to the Ionian Islands. Having raised £1,500 by selling part of his estate, he sailed for Gibraltar on 7 November, where he was welcomed by the Chief Justice, William's friend Barron Field, before continuing to his station on Corfu.[21]

At the end of October a new visitor came to Rydal Mount. Margaret Gillies was a professional portrait painter in her mid-thirties. A Scotswoman living in London, she was an enthusiastic Wordsworthian who had asked to paint William's portrait. She came garlanded with recommendations from William's friend Thomas Powell, and Leigh Hunt, who lamented as 'a national misfortune that among the various painters who have painted the author of the *Excursion* not one of them seems to have been inspired by the great poet sitting before them'. They 'guaranteed' that Miss Gillies's portrait would be a good likeness. As usual, the Wordsworths seem to have allowed their affection for the artist to cloud their judgement of the portrait, or rather portraits, as both Mary and Dora also ended up sitting to Miss Gillies before she left. 'Every one says that the bust [by Chantrey] only excepted it is much the best thing that has been done of me and if you dearest Mary do not like it we shall be mortified indeed', William wrote to his wife, who was on a visit to Stockton with Miss Fenwick. 'She has worked so carefully and been so anxious and is really for this charming art a person of genius.' The finished portraits, all watercolour miniatures, painted on ivory, show an amiable-looking William seated in a variety of poses, beside an arch through which a lake and mountains can be seen, in profile, swathed in a monastic-looking cloak, and at a table piled high with books. The third version included Mary, quill pen in hand, gazing up at her husband with the expression of sickly adoration usually reserved for bad religious pictures. Only the portrait of Dora gives any impression of the strength of character which all three possessed. Highly romanticized, with masses of gauzy drapery and her arms folded across her breast, she gazes up in the attitude of a virgin saint, but the deep-shadowed eyes, severely swept back hair and large nose form a striking contrast to the superimposed femininity.[22]

While Dora was sitting to Miss Gillies, Quillinan arrived at Rydal Mount. The visit, which lasted two and a half weeks, passed off without any overt unpleasantness, perhaps because Miss Fenwick's presence acted as a restraint. Quillinan was certainly bitter, complaining to Dora of her father's 'undue influence' over her, and his utter aversion to the prospect 'of marriage in old age' and, after he left, pointedly repeating a friend's remark that they had been 'more discreet than wise not to have married sooner'. 'Poor Dora's miserable affairs are as miserable as ever;' Sara Coleridge told their mutual friend Mary Stanger; 'she has had a visit from Mr Q but nothing has been settled. What could they settle unless they could coin a little money. It is quite grievous to think how the whole family suffer in their old age by this most unfortunate affair.'[23]

At the beginning of January 1840 another artist arrived at Rydal Mount. This was the Wordsworths' old friend William Westall, who had come to take some sketches with the idea of illustrating William's poems. Despite his aversion to invasions of his privacy, William was particularly delighted with a drawing of himself and Mary in their sitting room at Rydal Mount. 'It has a most picturesque appearance and I cannot but think would be acceptable to those who take an interest in me or my writings.' Given that Westall's meretricious use of perspective has made the elegant but unquestionably small sitting room look like the library of a stately home, one can understand William's pride and pleasure. With its panelled walls, busts and book-lined shelves, it is every inch the literary gentleman's home – with a tantalizing glimpse through an open door of the folio-laden bookcases of the poet's study.[24]

William was prepared to countenance the publication of Westall's picture, but he absolutely forbade that of Barron Field's critical and biographical memoir of himself. Field had been in Gibraltar since 1829, and had spent seven years in Australia before that, so he was decidedly out of touch with the rise in William's reputation. His memoir was written as a defence of William's poetry, answering the criticisms which had been made twenty years before, but in 1839 it was, as William said, '*superfluous*'. It took William two months to screw up his courage to write the difficult letter to Field:

your wish is, I know, to serve me, and I am grateful for the strength of this feeling in your excellent heart. I am also truly proud of the pains of which you have thought my writings worthy; but I am sure that your intention to benefit me in this way would not be fulfilled. The hostility which you combat so ably is in a great measure passed away, but might in some degree be revived by your recurrence to it, so that in this respect your work would, if published, be either superfluous or injurious ... the notices of me by many others which you have thought it worth while to insert are full of gross mistakes, both as to facts and opinions, and the sooner they are forgotten the better.

On the manuscript itself, William was less restrained, marking errors of fact with 'This is a mistake' and adding his correction, but it was the assertions about his poetic opinions which most annoyed him. 'This is monstrous!' he wrote against a passage where Field had listed his favourite poets, but claimed that he had no 'cordial sympathy' with Shakespeare. 'I extol Chaucer & others because the world at large knows little or nothing of their merits', he added. 'Modesty & deep feeling how superfluous a thing it is to praise Shakespe[a]re have kept me often & almost habitually silent upon that subject. Who thinks it necessary to praise the Sun?'[25]

William's desire to popularize Chaucer found practical expression in the spring of 1840, when he became involved in the publication of *Chaucer's Poems Modernized.* The book was a joint effort, containing contributions by Leigh Hunt, Richard Hengist Horne and Elizabeth Barrett, among others. 'My love and reverence for Chaucer are unbounded', William told Robinson, 'and I should like for the sake of unlearned readers to see the greatest part of his works done in the same way.' His own offering was substantial, *The Prioress's Tale* and the unpublished *Manciple's Tale*, *Cuckoo and the Nightingale* and some stanzas from *Troilus and Cressida*, 'But *beyond this* I do not wish to do any thing', he warned Powell, who had requested his support. 'Little matters in Composition hang about and teaze me awkwardly, and at improper times when I ought to be taking my meals or asleep. On this account, however reluctantly, I must *decline* even *looking over* the Mss either of yourself or your Friends.' Even so, he was unable to resist the temptation to revise his own modernizations, which had been written as long ago as December 1801. When he had completed them, however, he was persuaded (presumably by the combined forces of Mary, Dora and Miss Fenwick) not to send *The Manciple's Tale*, on the grounds that the subject was 'too indelicate for pure taste to be offered to the world at this time'.[26]

Having stipulated that his contribution should appear as unostentatiously as possible, William was not best pleased to learn that his own name featured prominently in the advertisements for *Chaucer's Poems Modernized.* Powell explained that, in seniority alone, William merited top billing, adding that 'nothing would embitter my future life more than that you should imagine I had used your "honoured and farfamed" name for my private purpose'. By then, of course, it was too late. Apart from the editor's 'intolerable' lapse in taste in including *The Reeve's Tale*, however, William did not regret his involvement. He praised the other contributions handsomely, hoped that the book would introduce Chaucer's genius to those who would otherwise know only his name and was genuinely pleased to learn that it was considered a success.[27]

For the second year in succession, William did not go on tour, but stayed quietly at Rydal Mount. Miss Fenwick, who was now in semi-permanent residence at

Ambleside, escorted Dora to London in the middle of February for a series of visits to the Hoares and Sara Coleridge at Hampstead, the Gees at Hendon and the Marshalls in Grosvenor Square. It was an opportunity not just to see old friends, but also to see Quillinan free from the constraints of Rydal Mount. Though not yet official, or public knowledge, her engagement to Quillinan was known and accepted in all these households, enabling him to visit her regularly and accompany her about town. They called together on Moxon and Rogers, and went to Miss Gillies for Dora to have a second sitting 'to have my nose reduced a little'. When she left London, on 24 April, she took Quillinan's elder daughter, Jemima, to spend the summer with her at Rydal Mount.[28]

To celebrate William's seventieth birthday, which fell on 7 April 1840, Miss Fenwick presented him with a cuckoo clock. Surprisingly, the Wordsworths all loved it. 'No children were ever more delighted with a new toy than we are with . . . it', Mary told her. 'Dear Miss Wordsworth was seated before it upon the top of the Stairs the other day – & when the bird had performed its office, & the little door flapped to, I thought she would have dropped from her chair, she laughed so heartily at the sudden exit of the little Mimic.' The Great Poet was equally entranced, hanging it outside his bedroom door so that he could wake to its call and composing a poem in celebration of the gift. The giver herself was more memorably commemorated in a lovely sonnet written just before her departure, which described Miss Fenwick as 'The heart-affianced sister of our love' and compared this late friendship to 'The star which comes at close of day to shine More heavenly bright than when it leads the morn'.[29]

Throughout the spring and summer William produced a crop of poems in a period of more sustained creativity than he had enjoyed in a long time. The poem on the cuckoo clock, for instance, linking in his mind with the *Cuckoo at Laverna*, suggested a sonnet on John the Baptist. Another poem, more unusually, was composed in response to a suggestion from a total stranger but enthusiastic admirer of his verse, Elizabeth Ogle, who wrote describing a scene her mother had witnessed twenty-two years previously in Normandy. Towards the end of December, in a snowstorm, she had seen a small urchin by the roadside, tending a few sheep and goats. He had built himself a crude shelter out of branches and, as she passed, was just fixing to the top a cross he had made from twisted twigs 'as the best means of supplying all deficiencies!' It was an act of simple infant piety which she thought might inspire the poet, and she was right. *The Norman Boy*, incorporating some of her own phrases, was rattled off at speed and sent to her almost by return of post – only to be followed, as a matter of course, by numerous revisions and an even lengthier sequel.[30]

'He has been hard at work for the last 3 or 4 months – and tho' he labours in constant fear of his eyes, and complains of discomfort from them – Yet in reality he has had very little suffering', Mary informed her nephew in June; 'and the work that has principally occupied him, you will imagine to have required deep thought and to be delicately treated, when I tell you that he has written 11 Sonnets "On the punishment of Death!"' Almost half a century earlier, under the influence of Godwin, William had argued the case for transportation, instead of execution, in *The Convict.* Now, as the penal laws were being liberalized and the number of capital crimes reduced by reforming ministries, William argued for the retention of the death penalty on the grounds that it was best for the convict himself. A man condemned to life imprisonment 'needs must eat the heart Out of his own humanity'; a man transported 'In life-long exile on a savage coast' would become hardened to commit more heinous crimes. Hence (by a somewhat obscure logic) William argued that execution was best. The man about to be executed would be sincerely penitent and therefore more likely to earn God's mercy in the Final Judgement. In ending his mortal life, his immortal soul would be saved. 'Strike not from Law's firm hand that awful rod,' he thundered, 'But leave it thence to drop for lack of use'. The *Sonnets Upon the Punishment of Death* are one of William's least appealing productions, but he felt it to be his moral duty to write them and circulate them 'on account of the importance of the subject'.[31]

'Our life here is without incident,' William wrote at the beginning of June, 'except now and then, as the other day, we hear of a Person drowned – mostly by some fault of his own, in one of our Lakes.' He spoke too soon. Summer visitors had poured into the Lakes as usual, more than 300 of them gaining access to Rydal Mount. Among them were some of the most remarkable ones the Wordsworths had ever seen. The Rydal Mount Visitors' Book for July 1840 records among the more familiar names of Faber, Hare, Marshall, Taylor and Southey 'Two Ashan[tee] Princes, Hostages' and 'Adelaide Regina!!'. On 24 July the two African princes, with their tutor, drank tea with the Wordsworths, and were escorted to the waterfalls in Rydal Park by Quillinan, who managed to get their autographs before they left for Keswick. Three days later, they were followed by Queen Adelaide, widow of William IV, her sister, the Duchess of Saxe-Weimar, and a train of grandees. Forewarned by Graves, the curate of Bowness, that she was on her way, William waited to meet her (wearing a new hat) at the lower waterfalls in Rydal Park, and escorted her up to the higher fall. Afterwards, they were greeted by the ubiquitous Tommy Troughton and his band and fifty local children holding the brilliantly coloured garlands of the annual Rush-Bearing ceremony to form an avenue between the park gate and Rydal Mount. 'The world & his wife were assembled on our front to see the cortege', Dora reported excitedly to Willy. 'If you had seen dear Mammy in Miss Fenwick's white satin bonnet this morning & black lace scarf, you would have been proud of her.' William escorted the dowager Queen to each of the viewpoints in his garden, 'particularly to that, through the summer house, which shows the lake of Rydal to such advantage', then took her into the house, where she was shown Beaumont's drawings and introduced to Mary and Dora. 'Do you think Mammy will be able to sleep tonight after having been shaken by the hand at our own door by a Queen – having talked with the Queen in this very room – & her old husband the old Poet having walked side by side & talked with her Majesty a full hour I am sure[?]'[32]

August passed in the usual social whirl. The house was full of young people: Dora and Jemima were joined by Ebba Hutchinson, her brother Tom and their cousin Mary Monkhouse; Miss Fenwick's niece, another Isabella, was with her aunt at Ambleside and Quillinan's nephew Egerton Brydges paid a visit too; Bertha Southey and her husband were living at the foot of Rydal hill; Willy came over from Carlisle. There were picnics, excursions and sailings, culminating, on 31 August, in an ascent of Helvellyn. The seventy-year-old poet led the way, 'mostly poetising by himself', guiding his daughter, on her pony, with Quillinan on foot at her side. 'It was very steep, very hot work, very craggy at times, & in some places worse from being wet & spongy, but we effected the ascent in about two hours & ¼', Quillinan proudly informed Rotha.

I wish you could have seen the Old Poet, seated from time to time, as we paused for breath, on a rock writing down his Waterloo Sonnet – for he composed one as we went up on the visit of Wellington to the Field of Waterloo 20 years after the Battle, as painted lately by Haydon the historical painter, to whom the Duke gave 5 sittings. Haydon sent Mr W a fine print from his painting, urging a request that he would give him a Sonnet on the subject – He complied & composed it on Helvellyn! . . . It is a curious fact, that even on that great steep mountain the Poet was followed by strangers – rather a bore, yet an evidence of the reverence he is held in. – Nobody that is not here can have the least idea how he is hunted, flattered, puffed, carest &c &c. It is enough to spoil any human being.[33]

It was twenty-five years since William had composed his first poetic tribute to Haydon, 'High is our calling, Friend!', and this, his third, showed no sign of diminished power. In measured blank verse, he praised both artist and subject.

By Art's bold privilege Warrior and War-horse stand
On ground yet strewn with their last battle's wreck;
Let the Steed glory while his Master's hand
Lies fixed for ages on his conscious neck;
But by the Chieftain's look, though at his side
Hangs that day's treasured sword, how firm a check
Is given to triumph and all human pride!
Yon trophied Mound shrinks to a shadowy speck
In his calm presence!

'I wished to gratify you by writing a sonnet', William told Haydon on 2 September. 'I now send it, but with an earnest request that it may not be put into circulation for some little time, as it is warm from the brain, and may require, in consequence, some little retouching.' There was much 'retouching', but Haydon was delighted. 'I am spouting the sonnet all day', he declared, and, with William's permission, he sent it to the newspapers, where it appeared with 'such gross blunders' that the poet was deeply irritated. Haydon tried to return the compliment by including William's portrait in a group picture of the Anti-Slavery Society Convention being addressed by Clarkson and by offering to come to Rydal Mount to paint the poet 'on [his] own ground poetically'. The first idea William firmly vetoed: 'Your friendship has misled you. I must on no account be introduced. I was not present at the meeting . . . and tho' from the first I took a lively interest in the Abolition of Slavery, except joining with those who petitioned Parliament, I was too little of a Man of business to have an active part in the work.' The suggestion that Haydon might paint him in the Lakes had more obvious appeal. 'Do not impute this to vanity; I do think you would make of it a fine Picture. But there is one, I fear insurmountable objection, you cannot afford to work without pay, nor can *I* afford to pay you. And I see not how you can expect from any quarter a pecuniary remuneration.'[34]

Unfortunately, it was not Haydon but Pickersgill who was commissioned to paint the next portrait of William. He arrived at Rydal Mount on 5 September and the sitting took place three days later at Ivy Cottage, or Glen Rotha, as William Ball, its new Quaker owner, had renamed it. The new portrait, for Sir Robert Peel's private collection, was a distinct improvement on the one Pickersgill had painted for St John's, and William regretted that Dora's copy of the portrait was taken from the earlier version. Far more robust in stance and expression, this second, three-quarter-length portrait captured the masculine strength that was so absent from the earlier one, but with his hat and gloves in hand, William looks more the polite gentleman than the dishevelled poet. As Quillinan said, the portrait was excellent, but the attitude was crass: William appeared to be holding his cap out like a begging bowl.[35]

While the portrait was being painted, the Wordsworths had a welcome visitor in Rogers, one of the very few living poets who was older than William himself. He arrived in bad weather and with gout, but this did not prevent the two friends spending a week together at Lowther Castle, and making a brief excursion to Drumlanrigg, in Dumfriesshire, at the invitation of the Duke and Duchess of Buccleuch. As Rogers arrived, Quillinan and his daughter left Rydal Mount. After six weeks of daily contact with the Wordsworths, Quillinan's marriage with Dora appeared no closer, but he was making attempts to raise money by publishing a novel, *The Conspirators*, and was not entirely without hope. He confined himself to a few malicious quips to Dora at the expense of the 'Rydal Ravens, and other birds of ill omen, [who] croak that it was a bad match for you', declaring that 'you are the best poetry he ever produced: a bright spark out of two flints'.[36]

At the end of November Mary left for a month's visit to her disabled brother and his family at Brinsop Court, while William visited their sons at Carlisle and Brigham. Driving home in a gig, with his son John, they saw the Kendal to Whitehaven coach approaching on the crest of the hill, and pulled as close into the wall at the side of the road as they could. Instead of slowing his pace down the hill, where there was a narrow bridge just in front of the Wordsworths, the driver continued in full career in the middle of the road and smashed into them. Their gig was forced backwards several yards along the road, through a gap in the wall and into a plantation a yard below the level of the road. With the stones from the road falling on them, William and John scrambled to extricate themselves, while the horse, snapping the traces, took off in fright and galloped seven miles before it was halted at the Grasmere turnpike gate. The coach driver was abject in his apologies and the agent of the company wrote immediately to offer compensation for the damage, but the Wordsworths had had a providential escape. John was unhurt and William had only cuts and bruises, but he was deeply shaken and could not even contemplate going to Brinsop to fetch Mary, as he had promised to do.[37]

Mary made her own way back to Rydal Mount by the beginning of December, and Christmas was spent quietly at home, the family circle including both Isabella Fenwick and Robinson, whose presence at this time of year was now taken for granted. Much to Robinson's surprise, he found Dorothy 'amazingly' improved.

> She can talk for a time rationally enough, but she has no command of herself and has the habit of blowing with her lips very loudly and disagreeably and sometimes of uttering a strange scream, something between the noise of a turkey and a partridge but more shrill than either. She can be withdrawn from this only by being made to repeat verses, which she does with great feeling, quite pathetically.[38]

Robinson passed his time as agreeably as usual, reading Quillinan's novels in the evenings, spending the day with the Wordsworths and calling on all his Ambleside friends, including Mrs Luff, and the Arnolds, who were at Fox How for the holidays. On Christmas Day, Dorothy's sixty-ninth birthday, Dr Arnold preached at Rydal chapel and Bertha and Herbert Hill came for tea. On 5 January the Wordsworths hosted a lively dinner party for twelve, inviting not only the Arnolds and the Ambleside Robinsons, but also James Spedding of Mirehouse, on Lake Bassenthwaite, who was a clerk in the Colonial Office. Despite the fact that virtually all the Wordsworths' guests were Whigs and Spedding a radical, Robinson noted that there was less 'excitement of disputation' than on former visits. 'Ws tone is far more liberal than it used to be. He does not abuse even the Non-cons [Dissenters] except in jest Nor the Whig-rad[ical]s at all – Party animosity seems to be dying away for want of nutriment'. The only sign of age affecting the poet's faculties was that he could not walk as well as he used to – though he could still outpace and outdistance his sons.[39]

It was while he was at Rydal Mount that Robinson was drawn into the tragedy which marred Southey's last years and tore apart his family. Less than a year after his wife's death, Southey had announced to his shocked children that he was going to marry again. His new wife was Caroline, daughter of the poet William Lisle Bowles. Twelve years his junior, she had been his admirer and correspondent for more than twenty years. Initially, the Wordsworths had approved of Southey's remarrying, and successfully persuaded Bertha and Kate to accept it for their father's sake. Gradually, however, it became clear that Southey was losing his mind; he was certainly not in full possession of his mental faculties when he married in June 1839, and may not have been when he became engaged. This was bad enough in itself, but worse still was the deteriorating relationship between the new bride and her stepchildren, especially thirty-one-year-old Kate, who was the only one still living at Greta Hall, and twenty-one-year-old Cuthbert, who had opposed the match from the beginning. As Kate was a frequent visitor to Rydal Mount and Bertha was living at the foot of the hill, the Wordsworths naturally heard more of their side of the story, but they remained open-minded and counselled patience. On 28 July 1839 William called on Mrs Southey to see if he could broker a peace but, realizing that she was implacably hostile to Kate, decided not to intervene, and did not even tell Kate of his visit. Southey himself was in a pitiable state: he did not recognize William, whose efforts to interest him in conversation were in vain. After five minutes William left him as he had found him, 'patting with both hands his books affectionately, like a child'.[40]

When Mrs Southey dismissed Betty, the devoted family servant, who had been with them for many years, refused to allow Kate to see her father for more than a few minutes, once a week, and succeeded in enlisting the support of Edith and her husband, John Warter (who were living far away in the south of England), against her brother and sisters, the Wordsworths could no longer remain neutral. Convinced that no reconciliation was possible which would restore domestic harmony, William reluctantly endorsed Cuthbert's demands for a separate establishment within Greta Hall for Kate and for her to have a daily visit to her father. As Cuthbert inadvertently dated his letter from 'Rydal Mount' rather than 'Rydal Lodge', where he was staying with Bertha, Mrs Southey accused William of instigating the demands and denounced him to her clergyman and the Warters. Refusing to be drawn publicly into the mounting cycle of recrimination and bitterness, William wrote a letter to Robinson, setting out his role in the affair, and urged Kate to do the same, in the hope that ultimately these might serve to reconcile the warring siblings to each other, if not to Mrs Southey. A second sealed letter, defending Cuthbert's conduct and character, was entrusted to Robinson, to be used if needed – the unspoken fear being that Mrs Southey's control over her husband, and her open hostility to her stepson, would lead to his being disinherited. William's own position was now clear: 'I have continued, and shall continue to support, and do all in my power to comfort the Children of my afflicted Friend.' Robinson had seen and heard enough to convince him that his first impression in favour of Mrs Southey was wrong; though he refused to take sides, he willingly became the custodian of the written statements of the opposing parties and was given full discretion to show William's open letter wherever, and whenever, necessary.[41]

The dissensions in the Southey family seem to have been a contributory factor in persuading William to withdraw his veto on Dora's marriage. Nothing had changed financially. Quillinan was still as poor as ever, his estate was encumbered and, at fifty years of age, he had no prospect of ever earning a satisfactory living.

He had shown willing, however, with his publication of his novel and his insistence that Dora's own money, which would normally have become his on their marriage, should be settled on her to be 'absolutely out of reach of any misfortunes that may occur to me'. By the end of February, it was agreed that the marriage should take place before the summer was out. After so many disappointments, Quillinan refused to believe that happiness was within his grasp, but the arrangements went ahead smoothly. At William's suggestion, Willy and Carter were appointed the trustees of Dora's settlement, a choice which again reflected his distrust of his elder son's financial abilities by excluding him. Both Quillinan and Dora were consulted as to the settlement, and it was agreed that Dora's property should pass to her husband for his life but, if she died childless, on his death revert to the Wordsworth family. It was, in any case, little enough: a few small sums she had been bequeathed, which were invested in shares, and the rental of the Rash field.[42]

After so many years of parental opposition to the match, Quillinan had wanted the ceremony to take place at Rydal and William to give his daughter away, so that there could be no doubt that the family not only consented to but approved of the marriage. Mary, Dora and Miss Fenwick, however, knew that this might be asking too much and a compromise was reached. The marriage would take place quietly in Bath, Miss Fenwick's home town, but all the Wordsworth family would attend. In an effort to sugar the pill to William, it was arranged that the wedding party would meet at Tintern Abbey before proceeding to Bath, and that the newlyweds would join William, Mary and Miss Fenwick afterwards for a short tour to Alfoxton, before going their separate ways. Herculean efforts were required to persuade both men to submit to these arrangements, but the females got their way.[43]

On 4 March, Dora and Miss Fenwick left Rydal for London, where Dora was to visit the Gees at Hendon, her cousin Chris at Harrow and Mrs Hoare (another quiet yet indefatigable supporter of her marriage) at Hampstead. At the end of March, William and Mary set off for Brinsop Court, leaving Dorothy in the capable hands of Joanna, who was to stay until their return. After ten days in Herefordshire, the Wordsworths, accompanied by their niece Ebba Hutchinson, went to meet Dora and Miss Fenwick at Tintern Abbey on 13 April. It was a symbolic journey, which William relished, even though it was so different from the ones of his youth: 'We slept at Chepstow, thence by steam to Bristol, and to Bath immediately by rail, just by the Watch 23 minutes!' Dora's looks, her father noted, had not improved since she left home, 'but this is not to be wondered at considering the plunge she is going to make'. They took lodgings at 12 North Parade, an elegant three-storey house in a terrace of pale sandstone, just outside the centre of the city and overlooking the river.[44]

A few days before the marriage took place, William received a confidential letter from his brother, Christopher, announcing his intention of making a gift to Dora, his goddaughter, of £1,000. It was a munificent gift and one which transformed the prospects for the marriage: Dora would have the interest for life, passing to her children after her death; if she died childless, it was to be divided equally between her brothers. 'It may be as well perhaps to keep the matter entirely to yourself, at least for the present, except so far as you would wish to consult her dear Mother', Christopher suggested. William and Mary were 'quite overpowered' by this unexpected act of generosity and almost as much for the way in which it had been done. 'I am truly sensible of the delicacy which induced you, my dear Brother, to abstain entirely from taking any steps connected with this marriage previous to *my opposition* (for it was in truth my *opposition* that held out long after the poor mother's) was withdrawn.' Such was his gratitude to his brother that William readily consented to his request that John and Willy should be the trustees, and the money was invested on Dora's behalf in 3½ per cent bank annuities.[45]

Quillinan arrived at Bath on 8 May and took up residence at the White Hart Inn, on Stall Street, in the shadow of the soaring splendour of the abbey church and close to the colonnaded façade of the Pump Rooms. Apart from John's wife, who had just given birth to a sixth child, and 'old aunty', all the immediate Wordsworth family were there; Quillinan's was represented by his half-brother, John, on whose generosity he was largely dependent. Willy organized the marriage licence. John Quillinan insisted on choosing and buying Dora's wedding ring 'for luck'. At nine-thirty a.m. two carriages rolled up at North Parade, the first for the bride, her parents and Miss Fenwick, the second for Ebba and Miss Fenwick's niece, Miss Tudor, who were to be the bridesmaids. At the last minute, William's nerve failed, just as his sister's had at his own wedding, almost forty years before. He was so distressed by having to bid his daughter farewell that he came to Quillinan and said, 'I have told Dora that I would accompany you to church if you wished it, but this interview with my child has already so upset me that I think I can hardly bear it.' 'We all then begged him not to come,' Quillinan told Rotha, '. . . but he gave us his blessing very affectionately both before & after the wedding: nothing indeed could be kinder than he & all have been.'[46]

At ten o'clock, on Tuesday 11 May 1841, Dora and Edward Quillinan were married in the beautiful Wren-style parish church of St James, at the foot of Stall Street. The bride was either 'very composed', according to Ebba and Mary, or 'in such agitation till it was over – her face was as white as her dress & she tottered so that I thought she would fall', as Quillinan would have it. All were agreed, however, that John Wordsworth conducted the ceremony and Willy gave away the bride, who was dressed in white poplin, with lace collar and cuffs (the latter given by her goddaughter), a silk tippet covered with net and trimmed with lace, and a white silk bonnet, decorated with white orange blossom, and a veil. The two bridesmaids wore lavender silk, with white bonnets, trimmed with pink flowers and pink scarves. Mary and Miss Fennell were dressed 'gravely gay, just as they ought to have been, & had both got everything new for the occasion', but the groom wore an old hat with a new lining, an old pair of boots and white trousers, and a new blue frock coat with velvet collar. 'My Papa', as Dora teasingly called the brother who had given her away, played the Bath dandy to the manner born in a sky blue satin waistcoat.[47]

After the ceremony, which was watched from the gallery by a crowd of curious but uninvited spectators, the little party returned to North Parade for a wedding breakfast. William was waiting for them, calm and cheerful, and embraced both his daughter and son-in-law many times before they were allowed to proceed to cut their cake. At two-thirty the newlyweds set off for Piper's Inn, halfway between Wells and Bridgwater, where, next morning, they were joined by William, Mary, Willy and Miss Fenwick. The whole party then made what Mary herself called a '*pilgrimage*' to Alfoxton, where the now-famous poet received a very different reception from that of forty years before: the whole St Albyn family turned out to welcome him and several hours were spent 'most agreeably' in that most exquisite of places. The Friday after the wedding, Dora, Quillinan and Willy returned to the north; Willy left them at Kendal and the bridal pair went to spend the rest of their honeymoon at Rydal Mount. 'We find dear old Aunty very comfortable & delighted to see us,' Dora wrote soon after her return, '& it is most affecting to me to observe the childlike *fun* & pleasure she makes for herself in addressing me by my new name.' A month later, she wrote to Isabella Fenwick, 'I cannot let this last happy day of four happy weeks pass away from me without one word of deep & heartfelt thanks to you to whom I owe it all.' Her gratitude, she said, would be as constant as Miss Fenwick's own kindness, which had never failed for one second 'since my Good Angel first put me under your Angelic protection at Dover'.[48]

Not the least of Miss Fenwick's thoughtful acts of kindness was to write to Dora soon after she had parted from her father, to assure her that he was perfectly reconciled to the marriage now that the irrevocable step had been taken. She was able to prolong his visit to Somerset by inviting him to stay with her sister, Mrs Popham, who was married to the rector of the tiny church of St Pancras, at West Bagborough, on the south-western slopes of the Quantocks. The Pophams lived in the adjacent rectory, a grand building with an elegant pillared frontage overlooking the woods, parks and undulating hills of Taunton Deane. Having retraced the paths around Alfoxton and Nether Stowey he had explored with Dorothy and Coleridge in his youth, William was carried off by Miss Fenwick and Mary into Devonshire, where they stayed at Devonport, just outside Plymouth, and visited Lyme Regis once more, for old times' sake. One imagines that they at least took a peek at Racedown, but though Wyke Regis and Weymouth Bay were within striking distance, they seem deliberately to have avoided going to see John Wordsworth's grave, even though William himself recognized that 'These were farewell visits for life'.[49]

Instead, having parted from Miss Fenwick at Charmouth, they cut across country to travel once again over Salisbury Plain. Unlike the Quantocks, this was a disappointment, the cultivation taking place on many parts of the Plain greatly detracting 'from the poetical feelings we had so elaborately attached to that region'. At Salisbury, they were to visit William's cousins the Fishers, whose daughter Emmeline was 'a little prodigy of a Poetess'. William had been deeply impressed by the natural poetic gift of this child – not least because, aged eleven, she had succeeded where he had failed in writing a new version of the National Anthem. Afraid that she would become a second Mrs Hemans, however, he had done his best to dissuade Emmie's mother from publishing her daughter's verse and thereby turning her head, as well as possibly extinguishing her talents. This would be their first meeting and the Wordsworths were sufficiently pleased with the child, and confirmed in their judgement of her abilities, to invite her to come back with them to Rydal Mount.[50]

Before they did so, however, William and Mary were to pay a short visit to London. They arrived at the beginning of June and were joined, on the 17th, by the Quillinans. Knowing that, when they left, they would not see Dora again for many months, they prolonged their supposedly short visit almost to the end of July. As usual, they were bombarded with invitations and were constantly on the move, staying with the Marshalls, the Spring-Rices, Rogers, Blomfield (the Bishop of London, at Fulham), Chris at Harrow and the Hoares at Hampstead. While at the Marshalls, it was their fate to be 'Partying every day', and 'tho' the usual murmurings went on in our retirements', William was clearly enjoying himself hugely, much to his wife's relief. In addition to all the usual 'talking' breakfasts and dinners (as distinct from the genuine 'eating' ones), there were social calls on numberless friends, old and new. They called on Margaret Gillies, to have their 'Darby and Joan' picture touched up, and William sat another three hours to Pickersgill to improve that likeness. The Duchess of Sutherland invited him to Stafford House to view the house and pictures. Through Taylor, they obtained tickets to attend the launch of HMS *Trafalgar* at Woolwich, in the presence of the Queen, Prince Albert and 30,000 other spectators. 'I was rather disappointed in the impression made by the mere Launch,' William confessed, 'but the spectacle of the vast crowd upon Land and Water was very striking.'[51]

At Harrow, where they had to endure the 'mighty dull matter' of sitting through the school Speech Day, William found himself 'enthroned in stalls' with his brother (who was there in his capacity as Master of Trinity, rather than father of the Master), Sir Robert Peel, Sir Robert Inglis, the Bishop of Peterborough and an American bishop. William was 'quite reverenced', Robinson noted with pleasure, though in returning thanks to his nephew for his highly complimentary speech he could not make himself heard. William was unfazed, however, using the occasion as an opportunity to seek an interview with Peel so that he could lobby him about the Copyright Bill, which, to William's great indignation, had been lost for another parliamentary session. Peel, like many other members, had been convinced by the specious arguments of the writer Thomas Babington Macaulay (who had been earning £10,000 a year as a member of the Supreme Council of India) that copyright was a form of monopoly which acted against the general interests of the public and should not be extended under any circumstances. 'I made . . . little or no impression,' William reported of his conversation with Peel, 'none indeed to encourage hope that he would support that or a similar measure.' His day was not entirely wasted, however, for he called on Lockhart to give an account of his meeting and persuaded him to write an article for the *Quarterly Review* in support of 'the cause'. William had great hopes for this article. 'Your knowledge ability zeal and the vehicle you have at command, will I am strongly persuaded, bring over many who have either paid little attention to the subject, or entertained inconsiderate prejudices upon it.' He made suggestions as to how Lockhart should tackle the article and supplied him with a copy of the letter he had himself written to the *Kendal Mercury* in 1838, which Lockhart annexed to his article, saying that it anticipated every argument of Macaulay's speech and 'we think conclusively' answered them.[52]

Before the Wordsworths returned home, they paid another of their 'farewell visits' to Coleorton. It was a truly nostalgic visit, for they came as the guests of a Sir George Beaumont (not *their* Sir George, but his nephew and heir) whose loneliness, as a widower of seven years' standing, touched William deeply. He presented them with two pictures by the late Sir George, volunteered the promise that the £100 annuity to William would be continued throughout Mary's life, should he predecease her, and allowed them to wander at will through the house and grounds. The latter were beautifully kept and managed, but William could not altogether conceal his disappointment at the winter garden. The evergreens had been too drastically thinned, an aviary had been introduced which was 'altogether out of character with the place', as well as shutting out some carefully placed views, and the little nook where the pool lay had been overdecorated with shells 'and other pretty ornaments'.[53]

More surprisingly, driving out into Charnwood Forest one day with the Merewethers, they came across the site of Mount St Bernard's Abbey, where the Beaumonts' neighbour Ambrose Phillips de Lisle had commissioned Augustus Pugin to design and build the first Cistercian monastery to be founded in Britain since the Reformation. William was torn between artistic admiration for the choice of location and architecture, 'the effect will be most striking in the midst of that solitude', and his instinctive aversion to anything which smacked of Papist aggrandizement. Ten years earlier (and even more recently) he would have launched into one of those interminable tirades about the threat to the Anglican establishment which Robinson so dreaded. Now, in his seventy-second year, his view was altogether calmer and more fatalistic. 'Perhaps alarm may be needless,' he told Miss Fenwick, 'but surely it is too late in the day for such Institutions to be of much service, in England at least. The whole appearance had in my eyes something of the nature of a dream, and it has often haunted me since'.[54]

William and Mary arrived at Rydal Mount on 22 July, after an absence of almost four months. The concerted plan to keep William from dwelling on the loss of his daughter had worked perfectly and, like the wedding itself, went off 'beyond, far far beyond my expectations', Mary acknowledged. The homecoming could have been difficult, but Joanna and Dorothy were waiting to greet them, as were Mary's cousin and sister-in-law, Mary Hutchinson, and her daughter, Sarah, from Brinsop. The Wordsworths had also brought with them little Emmie Fisher, now a teenager, who, on closer acquaintance, embodied all their worst fears. Her ambitious mother had obviously hoped that Emmie would enjoy one-to-one poetical tuition from the poet; instead, the Wordsworths, shocked by her inability even to dress herself, embarked upon a crash course of re-education. 'I have thought it proper both directly and indirectly to impress Emmie's mind with a conviction that talents and Genius, and intellectual acquirements, are of little worth, compared with the right management of the affections, and sound judgement in the conduct of life', William wrote to her mother; 'that what she may become as a Woman, is of infinitely more importance than what she may grow into as a person of splendid intellect, or an Authoress in any department of Literature.' One would love to know how Mrs Fisher reacted when she learned that the Wordsworths had taught 'the inspired creature' how to knit.[55]

Among the sixty-four visitors who called or stayed at Rydal Mount in August was a sixty-eight-year-old clergyman, Charles Valentine Le Grice. 'I have not for a long time had a visitor in whom I was so much interested', William assured his brother. Le Grice had been not only an undergraduate with Christopher but also a schoolfriend of Lamb and Coleridge, and he was full of fascinating anecdotes about their shared past. William had enjoyed Le Grice's visit, but Le Grice himself was in ecstasies. '*Virgilium vidi*' (I have seen Virgil), he wrote to Robinson, who had provided the letter of introduction. 'The day was beautiful – the Evening beautiful – all was beautiful – I shall never forget the 10th of August.' Le Grice carried away with him a trophy, a walking stick with which William apparently seemed loath to part and was therefore prized the more by its recipient, who addressed a sonnet to the poet, declaring that it was too precious to be used and 'bides, for aye, the glory of my home'.[56]

A clergyman of an altogether different calibre had called a few days earlier. This was George Washington Doane, the Bishop of New Jersey, whom William had met at Harrow and heard preach in London. Doane was a supporter of the Oxford Movement, as well as an admirer of William's poetry, and he added his weight to the request of several other American episcopalians that the poet would write on the subject of the daughter church in America for inclusion in his *Ecclesiastical Sonnets*. William bowed to the pressure, composing three sonnets, *Aspects of Christianity in America*, two on the Pilgrim Fathers, and the third celebrating Bishop White, the first Bishop of Pennsylvania, who had been consecrated in England by the Archbishop of Canterbury, and himself consecrated a further twenty-six American bishops.[57] As with most of his poems written out of duty, they are competent, but uninspired.

Far more attractive were the lines he wrote this summer for Owen Lloyd, the curate of Langdale, whom the Wordsworths had known and loved since birth. The sunny, good-humoured youth, however, who had been a playmate of their own children and lived with them at Rydal Mount, had been afflicted like his unfortunate father. The previous year he had suffered frequent epileptic fits, which had left him so physically weak and mentally confused that, also like his father, he had been sent to the Retreat at York. His brother, Edward, and his wife had then taken him into their own home and there, on 18 April 1841, he had died, having just attained his thirty-eighth birthday. At his own request, his body was brought back to Langdale, where he had been the curate for almost twelve years, and buried under the shade of a yew he had himself planted in the little churchyard under the towering craggs at Chapel Stile. As the coffin was carried up Langdale, hundreds of people, most of them poor farmers and quarrymen, gathered by the roadside to greet the procession and follow their beloved pastor to his final resting place. It had been a particularly moving tribute, carrying with it resonances of *The Excursion*, and William had felt it deeply, even though he had not witnessed it in person. The epitaph he wrote was, he thought, too long to serve its purpose, but others thought differently. It was adopted, in its entirety, and, though it clearly proved a challenge to the local stonemason, it can still be seen today, the humble headstone and crude lettering curiously at odds with the graceful cadences of the verse. The lines found their way into the *Westmorland Gazette* on 12 October, placed there, William suspected, by the redoubtable Troughton, under the alias *Viator* (Wanderer), in yet another subtle allusion to *The Excursion*.[58]

The epitaph for 'poor Owen' was one of only a handful of poems William wrote this year, but poetry was never far from his mind. By the end of 1840 *The Excursion* was out of print, and at William's suggestion the new edition, published this year, was printed in double columns stereotyped. He had two motives for this. First, in response to a number of letters he had received from the newly emerging class of educated labourers and mechanics, asking him to put the price of the book within their range; second, to prove to the opponents of the copyright bill that books would sell cheaply even if the term was extended.[59]

More importantly, he had embarked on what was to be his last new publication in his lifetime. This volume was *Poems, Chiefly of Early and Late Years*, and, as its title suggested, it was a gathering together of all his work which had not been included in previous collections. It would see the first publication of his final version of the Salisbury Plain poem, *Guilt and Sorrow*, and his tragedy *The Borderers*, as well as the hitherto-unseen *Memorials of a Tour in Italy, 1837*, which he was still adding to even as he revised the poems for the press. The decision to publish the early poems was a brave one: he risked drawing attention to, and reviving, all the old controversies about his poetic style and his radical political past. When Robinson, on a visit to Cottle in 1836, had learned for the first time that William had written a tragedy and expressed the hope that it had been preserved, if only as 'a curiosity . . . the *dramatic experiment* of a great philosophic and lyric poet', Mary had replied, 'The Tragedy is in existence – but say nothing about it, lest its destruction should follow.' Looking over his early manuscripts in the summer of 1838, William had been dismissive, suggesting that parts of them might 'perhaps' be thought worthy of publication 'after my death among the "juvenilia" '.[60] Now, in the wake of the latest failure of the Copyright Bill and the insatiable public appetite for 'remains' and 'reminiscences' of literary figures, he realized that the safest way to publish these works was to do it himself. He could control what appeared, alter what he now felt was unacceptable and anticipate criticism in his notes.

By 4 March 1841 he was ready to put out feelers about the possibility of publication. 'By way of *secret* I must let you know, that I have just been copying out about 2000 Lines of miscellaneous Poems, from Mss, some of which date so far back [as] 1793;' he informed Moxon. 'If I could muster a 1000 lines more, there would be enough for another volume, to match pretty well in size with the rest, but this not being the case I am rather averse to publication.' The casual nature of this statement was misleading, for as much effort went into the revision of these poems as into the first edition of his works he had prepared for Moxon. 'I cannot keep my poor brain quiet', he complained to Miss Fenwick in March, before he had plucked up courage even to look at *The Borderers*. 'I could sleep like a top all the afternoon, but in the night or rather morning after 4 o'clock I make poor work of it.' As always, he alternated correction of old poems with composition of new, including *Musings Near Aquapendente*, the gem of *Memorials of a Tour in Italy, 1837*, which he placed first in the series. When William returned from Italy he had composed only a single poem, the *Cuckoo at Laverna*. He had toyed with the idea of writing another, about St Francis, but had been thwarted, he claimed, by his inability to find the particular biography he wanted on his travels. When nothing more was forthcoming, Barron Field spoke for many of William's admirers when he groaned, 'Let not the scorners say that the poet went to Rome to write a Sonnet on the cuckoo.'[61]

It would be more than a year after his return before William began to reap the harvest of Italy. In January 1839 Miss Fenwick reported that he had written 'many' sonnets that winter, 'for the remembrances of Italy seem to have risen on him', and the other Italian sonnets, padded out with a couple of translations from Michelangelo, were added gradually. By the spring of 1841 the process of revising these, and his earliest poems, had prompted *Musings Near Aquapendente*. A rambling blank verse poem, 372 lines long, it was precisely, but misleadingly, dated *April 1837* by its title, even though it was composed almost exactly four years later. It was, as Robinson observed, a happy illustration of the poet's 'peculiar habit' of infusing anticipation and reflection into a single piece, blending all inextricably, but it was more than that. Characteristically, it barely touches upon the waterfall of Aquapendente but, inspired by the familiar golden blossoms of the broom flowering there, moves swiftly into a joyous celebration of the mountains of his native Lakes, which is the most attractive part of the poem. What makes it interesting, however, is that this is consciously an old man's poem. Recalling the dying Scott, for whom Italy had literally been a last journey, William offers a hymn of gratitude for his own health and strength. 'Utter thanks, my Soul!', he cries,

> That I – so near the term to human life
> Appointed by man's common heritage,
> Frail as the frailest, one withal (if that
> Deserve a thought) but little known to fame –

Am free to rove where Nature's loveliest looks,
Art's noblest relics, history's rich bequests,
Failed to reanimate and but feebly cheered
The whole world's Darling – free to rove at will
O'er high and low, and if requiring rest,
Rest from enjoyment only.
Thanks poured forth
For what thus far hath blessed my wanderings, thanks
Fervent but humble as the lips can breathe
Where gladness seems a duty –

The echoes of the young man's poem, *Tintern Abbey*, are deliberate and resonant: *Musings Near Aquapendente* is a joyful affirmation of the power of memory to give 'Abundant recompence' for the lost 'aching joys' and 'dizzy raptures' of youth's instinctive passion for nature.

But where'er my steps
Shall wander, chiefly let me cull with care
Those images of genial beauty, oft
Too lovely to be pensive in themselves
But by reflexion made so, which do best
And fitliest serve to crown with fragment wreaths
Life's cup when almost filled with years, like mine.

While William compiled his new book, the correction of the six-volume edition, which was once more being printed this year, was consigned to Carter, his Stamp Office clerk. Six weeks after the corrections had been sent through, William was fretting because the new edition had not yet appeared. When it was finally published, early in the summer, its sale was unexpectedly slow. Only a quarter of the print run of 1,000 copies had been sold by the middle of November, which, in terms of recent sales, was a significant downturn.[62]

This was not a reflection on William, but an indication of a general malaise in the book trade. Moxon was in particular difficulties. He had just been sued for publishing (against William's advice) a blasphemous libel, Shelley's *Queen Mab*; defended by Talfourd, he had been found guilty, but no sentence had been passed. Nevertheless, rumours 'that Moxon may Crash' percolated to Rydal Mount and, with a new publication in the offing, William felt obliged to take notice of them. The ever-trustworthy Robinson was commissioned to make discreet inquiries and reported back that Moxon's business was bad, 'but not *peculiarly* so'; profits in the whole London book trade were down to a sixth of what they had been only a year before.[63] As he put the finishing touches to the volume over Christmas, William dithered over whether to publish or not. Was there any point if there would be little or no sale?

William hoped that the publication of his *Sonnets Upon the Punishment of Death* would provide a much-needed boost to his sales. He had been in an even greater quandary deciding how to publish these, as he did not want to offer them directly to a newspaper or a periodical. The difficulty was solved by Taylor, who was preparing a general review of William's sonnets for Lockhart's *Quarterly Review*. He included the fourteen sonnets in his article, prefacing them with a summary of contemporary discussion on the death penalty. Though Taylor had done a considerable amount of research, William had his reservations about the whole project. 'I am strongly inclined to think that for many reasons it would be better to leave these Sonnets untouched in your Review,' he wrote on 19 November, 'but I leave the matter to your own judgement.' When the article appeared, in December, critical opinion was sharply divided. Wordsworthian fans, like Robinson, wished that 'the setting was worthy of the gems', and thought Taylor's contribution 'much too preaching and prosy' for the subject. Carlyle, on the other hand, mocked it as 'a very wholesome sermon by Hy Taylor, with Wordsworth's sonnets for text. The Sermon is good; a real Sermon: but the inspired volume of Sonnets – *ach Gott*!'[64]

Christmas at Rydal Mount might have been a sad affair this year, had not Quillinan 'by a special act of generosity', allowed Dora to spend a month there. She arrived on Christmas Eve, escorted by Robinson, after a journey of only sixteen or seventeen hours, compared to the two nights on the road which had been obligatory only a few years earlier. It was a particular comfort to see Dora for themselves, because her health had been causing her parents considerable alarm and distress. Though the gossip among some of her schoolfriends was that she was pregnant, the obvious proof was lacking, and it seems that it was, as her family suspected, simply a recurrence of her old stomach complaints. By the time she arrived at Rydal Mount, however, she was much improved and was able to join in the festivities.[65]

There were the usual dinner and tea parties with the Arnolds, walks in daylight hours, rubbers of whist in the evenings. Robinson accompanied William to pay calls on the Cooksons, who were now living at the Nook in Grasmere, Molly Fisher, the Wordsworths' old servant, and Carr, their physician. Robinson returned several times to see Carr, who, disabled by kidney stones, 'spoke in feeling terms of his destitution as to society'. William was his only intelligent friend in the area and he was no longer as frequent in his visits as he had once been. For this, Carr blamed Miss Fenwick. 'She is a treasure to Wordsworth, and by the resources her society supplies, he is enabled to live without seeking for intercourse out of his own house.' As even Robinson was driven to remark, echoing those comments made so long ago about 'the Concern', 'Two such women as Miss Fenwick and Mrs Wordsworth seem, indeed, enough for any one. Miss Fenwick is a substitute for Mrs Quillinan.'[66]

This Christmas, for the first time, Robinson was introduced to Frederick William Faber, the brilliant young Oxford graduate who was now a tutor in the household of William's cousin Dorothy Harrison. Faber had just returned from a tour of

Greece and Turkey with her son, Matthew, during which a Galignani edition of William's poems had been his constant companion. On the Austrian border, as Faber had written to William at the time, the book was taken from him, tied up with string and sealed 'to silence you, till the Censor's verdict at Vienna'. As only the number of sealed books was noted on his passport, he had slipped off the string and seals on the poems and, with delicious irony, transferred them to a novel by Bulwer-Lytton. A customs official found the poems hidden in Faber's nightshirt, but the Viennese censor decided that, because the books were in English, they must be innocuous and returned them; 'Had he opened you among the Sonnets of Liberty, the consequences might have been different.' Robinson took an immediate dislike to this 'ultra-Puseyite High Churchman', but over dinner, and almost against his will, Faber's charm, intelligence and lively manner won him over. Though he still weakly protested his 'utter dissent' from most of Faber's opinions, the sheer power of the young man's personality had cast its spell.

If Robinson was entranced, William and his family were even more in thrall. Faber had taken the Lakes by storm in the summer of 1837, when, aged twenty-three, he was acting curate of Ambleside. 'When he called upon me, I took him for a Modest Boy', Mary said, but then she heard about his remarkable preaching, 'his simple but beautiful language ... delivered with the calm earnestness of long experience', and how the Ambleside chapel was filled to overflowing. Contrasting it with Fletcher Fleming, who 'prosed over a Congregation of sleepers' so that even 'the artificial flowers nodded during the sleepy looking Preacher's vapid discourse', Mary could not resist the last opportunity to hear Faber for herself before he returned to Oxford and played truant to Ambleside. 'He is an extraordinary creature –', she enthused afterwards, 'to me he is a perfect *model* of what a deacon of our Church ought to be'. Significantly, too, she noted that 'Poetry oozes out of him most gracefully'.[67]

Since then, Faber had been instrumental in securing the honorary doctorate for William at Oxford, paid many visits to Rydal Mount and, particularly after his return from Constantinople with young Matthew Harrison earlier in the year, established himself on intimate terms with the Wordsworths. As with Coleridge and Hamilton, William was dazzled by the younger man's talents. 'He had not only as good an eye for Nature as I have, but even a better one', William freely admitted; 'and he sometimes pointed out to me on the mountains effects which, with all my great experience, I had never detected.' As he walked with the poet, they also conversed, and their talk frequently turned to the subject of religion. The following year, 1842, Faber dedicated his book about his tour, *Sights and Thoughts in Foreign Churches and Among Foreign Peoples*, to William, thanking him not only for personal kindness but also for 'Many Thoughtful Conversations on the Rites, Prerogatives, and Doctrines of the Holy Church'. It was a significant – and double-edged – remark, by which Faber effectively claimed William for the Oxford Movement, just as Keble had done in his oration at Oxford in 1839. It suggested not just the younger man's deference to the older, but also that the poet had impressed *his* views upon the clergyman. This was the opposite of the truth. 'Wordsworth's own religion . . . would not satisfy either a religionist or a sceptic', Robinson had noted in 1836. This was still the case in 1841, and Faber was determined to change it. He wanted to purge all doctrinal unsoundness from William's poetry, particularly the suggestions of pantheism in the early works, and to encourage the poet, in both his life and his work, to become the standard-bearer of the Oxford Movement.

An early indication of the influence he had already obtained over William was that the poet invited him to contribute a note to *Musings Near Aquapendente.* This was not without precedent: de Quincey had written footnotes for the *Convention of Cintra* pamphlet and Robinson had performed the same office for *Memorials of a Tour of the Continent, 1820.* What was different was that their contributions had been factual, whereas Faber's was an expression of opinion which, quite literally, he put into the mouth of the poet himself. And what he made William say was an explicit endorsement of the Oxford Movement 'as likely to restore among us a tone of piety more earnest and real, than that produced by the mere formalities of the understanding'.[68]

More importantly, Faber's influence can also be detected in a significant alteration to one of William's earliest poems. The old Salisbury Plain poem had ended with the sailor giving himself up to be hanged for the murder he had committed, but in a spirit of bitter defiance. In *Guilt and Sorrow,* the heavily revised version of 1841–2, he welcomes execution for ending the pangs of conscience he had suffered since committing his crime, his last words being, 'My trust, Saviour! is in thy name!' The importance of this change cannot be over-estimated. It is not the sentiment that is new: William had argued in his *Sonnets Upon the Punishment of Death* that remorse and penitence would lead the convicted criminal to welcome death. What is new is that this is the first explicit statement of belief in the redemptive powers of Jesus Christ in all William's poetry – and, indeed, in his prose. Coleridge had always said that William was not a Christian, using the term very precisely to mean that his friend did not believe that it was possible for the death of one man, however virtuous, to satisfy God for the sins of the whole world. Robinson had confirmed that this was still the case in more recent years, admitting that William's religion 'falls short of Christianity' and even reporting William's comment that 'perhaps' he did not feel the need for a Redeemer himself.

The sailor's declaration of trust in his Saviour's name was a complete reversal of this position and an acceptance of the single most important tenet of Christianity. Was William simply paying lip-service so as not to offend prevailing opinion or his many powerful clergymen friends? This seems unlikely, as he had never felt it necessary to do so before. The inescapable conclusion is that those 'Thoughtful Conversations' with Faber had led to a profound shift in his thinking. It was not a coincidence that, before the year was out, Faber persuaded William to nail a cedarwood cross above his bedroom window, 'where the good old man's pleased eye rests on it first thing when he wakes'.[69] In doing so he claimed not just the poet, but also the man, and not just for the Oxford Movement, but also for Christ.

'W: is become more companionable being more tolerant than he used to be –', Robinson remarked on 6 January 1842; 'he is now very busy preparing his new Volume'. To Robinson's great delight, William had decided to dedicate to him the *Memorials of a Tour in Italy, 1837*. The problem, as they both acknowledged, was his unpoetic name. 'W: has confessed to me that he has taken much trouble And written some half dozen lines but cannot make the ignoble name endurable in verse – So he has given it up.' Instead, the dedication was titled 'To Henry Crabb Robinson', and he was referred to as 'Companion!' in the verse. When Moxon ventured to give him a sneak preview of the nine dedicatory lines, Robinson was thrilled. 'They do not flatter my vanity,' he explained to Dora, 'but they make me proud.' Neither extravagant nor fulsome in their praise, the simple lines exude the one sentiment that really mattered to Robinson: they were sincere. 'They come from the heart, and the highest praise, after all, that I can receive is that I am an object of regard to such a man.' What is more, they acknowledged what he himself thought had passed unnoticed:

> . . . kindnesses that never ceased to flow,
> And prompt self-sacrifice to which I owe
> Far more than any heart but mine can know.[70]

By 18 January, the day Robinson and Dora returned to London, the whole volume was ready to be sent to press. Despite William's apprehensions about Moxon's stability, he offered it to him, expressing a wish that 2–3,000 copies should be printed, but not stereotyped, as he hoped to incorporate the poems into future editions of his complete works. Perhaps because he was in difficulties, and certainly because he was not hopeful of a good sale, Moxon was disgruntled, indiscreetly complaining to the arch-gossip Moore that 'there never was a more hard, mean and grinding fellow than [Wordsworth] is in making his bargains'. These comments found their way back to Rydal Mount, provoking a stiffly-worded expression of regret that Moxon's connection with William had been 'so unprofitable to you' and pointing out that the labour the poet himself had expended on the new volume was unlikely to earn him wages as high as 2s a day. [71]

William was clearly nervous about the reception of *Poems, Chiefly of Early and Late Years*. 'If I had foreseen the minute Labour which I have had to undergo in correcting these Poems, I never should have gone to Press with them at all', he grumbled. 'I actually detest Publication, and all that belongs to it; and if these Poems do not benefit some minds here and there, I shall reproach myself for playing the Fool at my time of life in such a way.' William had not talked in this way for years, though it had been characteristic of his earlier publications, when he had been on the defensive against what he knew would be a barrage of hostile criticism. That he feared a similar reaction to this volume, which included so much early work, is the only explanation for his absolutely forbidding Moxon to send out any review copies to individual reviewers or editors of any magazine or periodical. 'I cannot tolerate this idea of courting the favour, or seeming to do so, of any critical tribunal in this country', he thundered. If reviewers wanted to puff a book for their own reasons, they would get hold of a copy, so sending them one was unnecessary: 'and if they are hostile, it would only gratify the Editor's or Reviewer's vanity, and set an edge upon his malice'. When poor Moxon protested, he got another tongue-lashing, which Mary, writing at William's dictation, tried to make less offensive by a little wifely ridicule.

Mr W bids me add that he regrets you have nothing more favorable to hold out than that the book is likely to have a 'very *fair* sale['] – cold comfort he says for him who has wasted so much health and strength in minute correction which nobody will either thank him for, nor care any thing about, and which wasted health and strength (I now write from his dictation *observe*) might in part have been recovered if the profts of this volume would have left him free in conscience to take a recreative trip to Paris or elsewhere! such stuff my good husband compels me to write – [72]

Despite Moxon's objections, and a few subtle hints from Robinson, William remained adamant. The volume would have to succeed, or fail, on its own merits.

26. *Poet Laureate*

On 25 February 1842 the historian Lord Mahon wrote to William to inform him that he intended to bring Talfourd's Copyright Bill before the House of Commons on 3 March. The bill had been presented annually since 1836 and had never got beyond a second reading, but William's friends were now determined to secure its passage. Talfourd, Mahon, Lockhart, Milnes and Inglis held a series of pre-emptive meetings with the two most important opponents, Lord John Russell and Sir Robert Peel, and between them they thrashed out a compromise. Instead of the sixty-year term Talfourd had originally proposed, it was agreed to go for twenty-five, with a thirty-year term for posthumous copyright. Knowing this would be a disappointment to William, Mahon softened the blow by pointing out that there was no reason why this period should not be lengthened in future, thereby reconciling him to a 'prudent' but 'inadequate measure'.[1]

On 6 April, the eve of William's seventy-second birthday, the bill which he had fought so long and hard to obtain was passed. The resulting act, though watered down by amendments, received the Royal Assent and became law on 1 July 1842. It transformed the position of authors. The term of copyright was extended from twenty-eight to forty-two years from the date of first publication, or seven years after the author's death, whichever period was longer. Though the act could never have reached the Statute Books without the dogged perseverance of Talfourd, and the support of men like Gladstone, Peel and Mahon himself, it was unquestionably a personal triumph for William. Without his years of sustained lobbying inside and outside Parliament, his contacts, his persistence, even his sheer longevity, which had proved the need for the legislation, there would have been no act.[2]

It was ironic that the act should be passed at a time when the state of the book trade was so poor. 'Pray tell me what you think is the main cause of the great falling off in the Sale of books?' William asked Moxon. Was it, he wondered, that the frenzy of excitement caused by Charles Dickens's novels, published in serial form in the periodicals, was killing off the classics? This was a matter of some moment to William. His *Poems, Chiefly of Early and Late Years* was published in April 1842, but he was also preparing a new and greatly expanded edition of his *Guide Through the District of the Lakes* for the press. With his usual eye for commercial trends, he had noticed that tourists of recent years preferred more detail than his own guide offered, and had sought to remedy this by a complete revision. Unable to do the work himself (he considered it 'very troublesome and *infra dig*'), he turned over the editorship to his publishers, John Hudson and Cornelius Nicholson, of Kendal, stipulating only that what he considered the most important part, his comments on the principles of taste, should be printed in their entirety in a single section. Hudson would revise the guide part of the book, Nicholson offered to compile a glossary of local names (with revisions by Hartley Coleridge and de Quincey) and Thomas Gough, son of the blind naturalist of Kendal, agreed to provide a botanical section. Another friend, Adam Sedgwick, a former pupil at Sedbergh, who was now Professor of Geology at Cambridge, redeemed a twenty-year-old promise by adding 'a short essay' on what he called 'the muscular integuments, ribs and bones of your mountains'. The resulting publication, *A Complete Guide to the Lakes, Comprising Minute Directions for the Tourist, with Mr Wordsworth's Description of the Scenery of the Country, &c. and Three Letters on the Geology of the Lake District, by the Rev. Professor Sedgwick*, appeared later in the year. Though he had resigned the editorship of the book, William by no means resigned his interest: he read the proofs, made suggestions and continued to draw a small income for his contribution.[3]

He did, however, abandon a third, more speculative, venture this spring. Aubrey de Vere, a young Irish poet who was a distant relative of the Spring-Rices and Marshalls, had suggested that he should publish a cheap selection of his poems for the poor. De Vere had written an ardent letter in September 1841, urging the idea 'very earnestly' and begging him to proceed 'without loss of time'. 'This object I have much at heart both as a lover of literature and as a patriot. I am sure that it will tend greatly to the moral health of the English people: and at this moment when all good & bad principles are contending together, who can tell what weight thrown into the scale may not decide the balance?' De Vere had made a selection, very different from that edited by Hine, working on the principle that 'not . . . all the poems fit for the poor are about the poor. We should take a hint from children, who do not wish to hear exclusively stories which relate to children.' William had been sufficiently bowled over by de Vere's eloquence (which, after all, was but an echo of his own views about the scope and purpose of his poetry) to ask Moxon if he would 'dare' to publish such a selection. Assured by Moxon that it would not even cover its own publication costs, William had no option but to thank de Vere for his enthusiasm and quietly veto the idea.[4]

There was also a fourth publication this spring. So insignificant it has been completely ignored by most biographers, even those who have noticed it have misunderstood its importance. The publication was *La Petite Chouannerie, ou Histoire d'un Collège Breton Sous l'Empire*, edited by a Frenchman, Alexis François Rio, and published in Paris by Olivier Fulgence. The book was a celebration of the Breton resistance to Bonaparte, and particularly of the role played by the boys at a college in Brittany who took the lead in the royalist uprising of 1815. It was naturally a subject close to William's heart and, when the author had approached him, the previous summer at a party at the Marshalls' in Grosvenor Square, William had apparently 'promised' to contribute a poem, if provided with sufficient detail. On 11 March 1842 Rio had written to William to call in this 'promise', informing the poet that he had already announced the inclusion of his poem in both England and Brittany 'as the expression of the most honourable sympathy for my countrymen' and hinting darkly that, without it, his favourite chapter on Napoleon and contemporary poets would have to be given up. When William wrote back, as he usually did, saying that he could not write to order, or at such short notice, he received a hysterical and accusatory reply from Rio. The entire book had been printed, except for thirty-two blank pages designated for the chapter 'which I have actually composed as a preface to your poem'. 'I have heard so much about the facility with which those compositions flow from your pen, that I thought it a superfluous precaution to send the materials a long time ago', Rio wailed. Only William and the Italian poet Alessandro Manzoni had let him down and, if necessary, he would have to delay publication till he had received the promised contribution.

William swallowed this story, hook, line and sinker. Tortured by guilt, he sought a way out of his quandary, and found it in the unlikely person of his son-in-law. William had always said that Quillinan knew 'my principles of style better I think than any one else'. Twenty years earlier, he had amended Quillinan's epitaph on his first wife to both's satisfaction. Now he did the same thing again, to fulfil an otherwise impossible engagement. Quillinan wrote the first draft of the poem, *The Eagle and the Dove*, and William corrected it so that it could be passed off as his own. '*He* has done the verses for the *Poet* – which are, or will be, satisfactory – when W. has "tinkered" them', Mary wrote on 10 May, adding the next day, 'Poor Q has been drudging at the Frenchman's Verses – which I hope are finished, tho' I hear the Poet humming at his Washing table.' The ominous humming did not indicate more correction, for the poem was dispatched that day to Moxon, with the command to send it off 'without the delay of a single post'.[5]

In the strictest sense of the word, *The Eagle and the Dove* was, of course, a fraud. It is rather delicious to find, therefore, that it was composed in response to a fraud, for Rio had played exactly the same trick on Moore. 'He spoke to me in the midst of a crowded assembly, and I was not well able to make out his wishes or views on the matter', Moore wrote in his journal. 'Have since received a long letter from him . . . pressing me for the verses which they say I promised'.[6] More seriously, however, the solution to this little difficulty was to be a seductive one for future problems which William would find hard to resist. Though he would refuse to include such hybrid productions in future editions of his poems, as he grew older and demands upon him increased, he was not averse to calling on Quillinan for assistance.

Relations with Quillinan had improved dramatically, once William was assured that his daughter was happy in her choice. Characteristically, William had made the first move, writing an unprompted and generous letter to his son-in-law at the beginning of March. If ever there was a moment when Quillinan might have expected William to round on him, it was then, when he was about to be prosecuted for fraud (financial, rather than poetical) in the highest courts of the land. As a trustee of his first wife's property, he had inadvertently become entangled in the complex business dealings of the Brydges family and was now to be tried for his part in defrauding the estate of some £15,000. 'My motive for writing this short letter is merely to assure you of our sympathy in your vexations and distresses,' William wrote,

> and still more, very much more, to assure you that you need have no anxiety respecting judgment which we are likely to form of your character on these sad proceedings. We have all an entire confidence in your integrity from the first to the last, in your connection with the Brydges family, and the Barrett property, and furthermore are but too well aware of the generous sacrifices which you have made for them who have proved to be so unworthy of them. The confidence you reposed in them, however chargeable it may be with want of discretion, affords itself a strong presumption of your being incapable of joining in any dishonourable practice.

It was a particularly kind gesture, given Quillinan's notorious sensitivity to slights on his character and the very public nature of the proceedings, in which the Wordsworth name was bound to be invoked. Fortunately, Quillinan's friends were all of the same opinion. 'There can be no doubt that he acted most incautiously and weakly in signing deeds, and being an assenting party to transactions which were of a most iniquitous character', the barrister Robinson observed; 'but still I am perfectly convinced of his honour and integrity . . . but it is, after all a melancholy mode of escaping from an imputation on one's honour by allowing that the fault must be transferred to the head.' In April the Vice-Chancellor gave his judgement, clearing Quillinan of any dishonourable proceedings but holding him legally liable, with the other parties to the crime, for repayment of the missing £15,000. In doing so, he effectively ended any chance of Quillinan ever being able to make financial provision for his wife.

'I cannot suffer the morning of my Birth-day to pass without telling you that my heart is full of you and all that concerns you', William wrote to Dora on 7 April, as they waited for the judgement to be delivered. 'Yesterday was lovely, and this morning is not less so. God grant that we may all have like sunshine in our hearts so long as we remain in this transient world.' Even when the verdict became known, he avoided all recrimination, and at the beginning of May he, Mary and Willy went to London to give the Quillinans their full support. As John and his family were all just recovering from scarlet fever and were recuperating in quarantine on Belle Isle, the care of 'old aunty' Dorothy had to be delegated for the first time to Isabella Fenwick, who alone of all their friends could be trusted with such a responsibility.[7] For the first time also, the Wordsworths stayed with the Quillinans, in their relatively humble lodgings at 7 Upper Spring Street, off Baker Street. Their visit to London was supposed to be a profound secret, enabling them to avoid the usual deluge of social invitations, but their presence could not be hidden for long, not least because William's main objective was to persuade the new Tory administration to appoint Willy to a better-paid government office. The Lowthers were the first port of call. Lord Lonsdale was now too old and frail to have the subject raised with him, but his oldest son, Lord Lowther, was Postmaster General and more than willing to help. He quickly quashed any idea of Willy obtaining a post for which he had not spent years in clerkship, but reverted instead to the old idea of William resigning his distributorship of the Stamp Office in favour of his son. This could be justified on the grounds that Willy was already employed in that department and that savings would be made by transferring the office to him at Carlisle. What no one could guarantee was that William's own loss of income (which he put at £400 a year) would be recompensed by an equivalent government pension.[8]

William really had no choice if he wished to assist his son. The letter proposing the transfer to Willy was written and left for the Lowthers to deliver to Peel, the Prime Minister. The pension had to be left to chance. Willy was uncomfortable with the whole arrangement, not wishing to be responsible for his parents losing more than half their income at their time of life, but for William and Mary it was simply a huge relief to have their younger son settled in more suitable and secure employment. They were unconcerned about the prospect of being 'much straitened' and faced the necessity of 'the strictest economy' with perfect equanimity. What they found more difficult to contemplate was the loss of Carter, who was as much part of the family as indispensable Stamp Office clerk. 'I cannot bear the thought of our ever losing him', Mary wrote in distress. 'Whatever comes of us we must never part with him.'[9]

Mary spent most of her time quietly with Dora, who was again far from well. Marriage had not brought her the health they had all hoped for and once again she had subjected herself to her starving regime. 'Doro has just crept off to bed (9oc.)', Mary wrote to Miss Fenwick on 21 May:

> on the whole she has had a better day – but the pain has come on since her poor bit of dinner, about as much bacon as a sparrow might pick, no liquid, for she is afraid of wine, with a little rice. She took no tea – and poor thing, she has retired to hide, or to keep off greater suffering ... really the food she takes is insufficient one would imagine to support life. I am sadly out of heart about her, dear friend ...

William too was worried. 'I cannot but think that she looks worse and worse. What she wants is absolute *tranquillity* and rest of body and mind. Both her temperament and her situation are against her having either one or the other; nor do I see how they are to be attained, so that I cannot but despond as to the issue.' All they could do was consult the physicians, their old friends Dr Davy and Dr Ferguson, urge upon their recalcitrant daughter the need for fresh air and exercise, and hope for the best.[10]

Despite this being a supposedly low-key visit, William kept up a frenetic pace astonishing in a seventy-two-year-old. He had invitations to attend the soirée of the Marquis of Northampton, as President of the Royal Society; 'appeared (as you will perhaps see, mentioned in the Times), among the Stars, at the Marquis of Lansdowne's soiree on Sat. evening, and walked home with Lockhart at 12 oc.'; and on 24 May was one of the 800 personages 'of the haut Ton' including members of the royal family at the Duchess of Sutherland's fancy ball. As Robinson commented with some amusement, except when he condescended to wander into the '*terra incognita*' of Robinson's own lodgings in Russell Square, William 'has dined every day . . . with Bishops & Privy Counsellors, Peers and Archbishops'.[11]

'Every thing here is lost in hurry and distraction', William complained, as he rushed from one gathering to another, lobbying on behalf of his son and helping to get the Copyright Bill through its final stages in the House of Lords. At the beginning of June, they all escaped to Hampstead, to spend a few peaceful days with Mrs Hoare. 'This morning I feel a sort of quietness not unlike the sensation that comes over one when a rattling carriage stops after going over a newly mended road', Mary wrote gratefully, the day after their arrival. Among Mrs Hoare's guests was Christopher, whom the Wordsworths were delighted to find 'the gayest of the gay'. The previous autumn, worn out with the labour and responsibility, he had resigned as Master of Trinity College and now, about to celebrate his sixty-eighth birthday on 9 June, he was enjoying the fruits of a well-earned retirement.[12]

Before they left town, William had to find time for several sittings to the artists who were clamouring to take his portrait. Significantly, two of the three were acts of charity. One was for his old friend, Haydon. Unable to get to the Lakes to paint William *in situ*, Haydon had agreed to make do with some sittings in London, supplying the backdrop from his imagination. The first sitting was a disaster. 'Wordsworth sat and looked venerable, but I was tired with the heat and very heavy, and he had an inflamed lid and could only sit in one light, a light I detest, for it hurts my eyes . . . We talked of our merry dinner with C. Lamb and John Keats. He then fell asleep, and so did I nearly, it was so hot; but I suppose we are getting dozy.' A couple of days later, they had an altogether livelier session, during which Haydon decided he needed to measure William 'to ascertain his real height'. 'I measured him, and found him, to my wonder, eight heads high, or 5ft 9⅞ inches and of very fine, heroic proportions. He made me write them down, in order, he said, to show Mrs Wordsworth my opinion of his proportions.'

The resulting portrait is unquestionably the most striking and memorable image of William ever painted. It purports to show the poet on Helvellyn, composing the sonnet to Haydon. Though it bears no relation whatsoever to Quillinan's description of that event, it is an extraordinarily powerful portrayal of both the man and the poet. William stands, head slightly bowed, arms folded across his chest, deep in concentrated thought. There are no gimmicks to convey the idea that this is a poet at work, and no attempts to refine the features or the stance to something more gracefully approximating the poetic ideal. Put a flat cap on the head and the face beneath it is instantly recognizable as that of a type still seen today: the northern hill farmer of the Lakes, Dales or Pennines, stubborn, forthright and independent. Yet for all its down-to-earth realism, the portrait also conveys its subject's power of thought. Elizabeth Barrett, in a celebratory sonnet which she sent to William, through Haydon, later in the year, sums it up exactly:

No portrait this with academic air!
This is the poet and his poetry.[13]

The second charity portrait was by Mrs Aders, the lady who had played hostess to William, Dora and Coleridge at Godesberg in 1829. Her husband's business and health had failed, and she was attempting to earn a living painting portraits. Robinson begged William to sit to her, arguing that a successful portrait might not make her fortune, but it would lead to other commissions. The result was a profile which even the kindly Robinson was forced to admit was not a good likeness – 'A fierce expression and no character'.[14]

With sittings for these two portraits, and to Pickersgill, William had neither time nor inclination to sit for John Lough, Haydon's friend, a sculptor who wanted to take his bust. Any spare time he had left was dedicated to an attempt to find 'some employment in Book making' for Carter, whom Willy could not afford to retain on the same terms as his father. The Wordsworths had always intended to spend only four or five weeks in town, but the shocking news of the sudden death of their friend Thomas Arnold, on 12 June, sent them hurrying back to Rydal. Arnold was only forty-seven. He had transformed the fortunes of Rugby school, been made Regius Professor of Modern History at Oxford in 1841 and left unfinished his great work, a *History of Rome*, but it was the impact of his death on his large family which everyone feared. 'What a happy house at once broken up!' Robinson exclaimed. William and Mary went over to Fox How to offer what comfort they could to the bereaved family. Always pragmatic at such times, William immediately relieved the afflicted widow of her anxiety about the management of the extensive grounds by offering to undertake it himself. 'We trust that, if we are spared, our society will be of much benefit to her', William wrote before the month was out.[15]

A few days later Mary wrote to Robinson, begging him to come to Rydal Mount to relieve their solitude. They were about to lose Miss Fenwick, who wanted to visit other friends now that her responsibility for Dorothy was at an end; young Anna Ricketts, who had accompanied them from London and was to stay a few weeks, was not old enough to be a companion; Willy and Carter were fully employed in transferring the Stamp Office from Rydal Mount to Carlisle; but most of all, William, especially, felt the loss of Arnold, who had been the constant companion of his walks and an intellectual presence in the neighbourhood every summer and winter for the last dozen years. Robinson did come, at the end of July, but he could spare only a few days, the highlight of which was a four-hour walk with William, a son of Sir Robert Peel, who had won the prize at Harrow the year before, and the latter's tutor. Their path took them round Loughrigg Fell to one of William's favourite places, Loughrigg Tarn, then back by Grasmere, the poet identifying Point Rash Judgement and the Wishing Gate along the way.[16]

Robinson's departure coincided with that of Willy, Carter and the Stamps, a removal which affected the whole household deeply. Even Anne, the cook, commented that it was 'like a funeral going out of the house, when after so much bustle and pulling down in the Office, they had all passed away'. 'Seeing the last of what has been a nearly 30 years interest, could not but be seriously felt by us, at our age –', Mary told Miss Fenwick, 'and it *was* felt, but with thankfulness that what had been so great a benefit to us (in educating our children, and enabling us to live for so many years in the sort of hospitality we liked best), had passed into the hands of our beloved son – and grateful we are to those who have aided us in this object.' No news of a pension having been granted, Willy was still depressed at his father's sacrifice on his behalf – and more selfishly, dreaded the prospect of being tied to the Office by the presence of the Stamps.[17]

The newspapers immediately jumped to the conclusion that William had received a government pension in compensation for his loss of the Stamp Office, but this was very premature. Indeed, it was to avoid just this assumption that Gladstone, who had undertaken to negotiate the pension on William's behalf, had counselled patience. As Gladstone informed William on 28 September, he had not even forwarded the request until a few days after the prorogation of Parliament and it was not until 15 October that Peel himself wrote to tell William that his name had been placed on the Civil List, and he would receive an annual pension of £300 for life. His acceptance of the pension, Peel informed him, would impose no obligations of either a political or a personal nature. 'It will prove a substantial addition to my comforts for the remainder of my life', William replied gratefully;

> and coming as the reward of literary merit from One so eminent in every respect as yourself the gratification is above measure enhanced. Let me add, that the considerate delicacy with which you have stated in your letter every thing bearing upon this Grant, and the terms in which you express yourself towards me personally, have affected me more than I could find words to utter, had I courage to seek for them.

William also wrote to thank Gladstone, repeating that the terms of the offer 'have above measure enhanced the satisfaction I feel upon the occasion'. His letter prompted Gladstone to reply that his own intervention had been purely ministerial and that 'the tribute rendered you has been the sole spontaneous act of the great man from whom it proceeded'. 'It has come later in y[ou]r life than y[ou]r Friends think right', Lady Mary Bentinck wrote on behalf of the Lowthers, 'but still . . . it has come sooner, than we were prepared to expect.' Robinson, having had 'a little chuckling in private' with Dora, also sent his congratulations, but warned Mary, 'you will be troubled now by the looking forward to the execution of old schemes ... And you must submit to the martyrdom of another pilgrimage beyond the Alps.'[18]

In fact the granting of the pension cast only one dark shadow. Caroline's husband, Baudouin, reading the premature reports in the newspapers, wrote immediately to demand more money. Annette had died eighteen months earlier, on 10 January 1841 (an event which passed unnoticed in, or, more likely, expunged from, the Wordsworth correspondence); with her had also died the government pension which the family had relied on to supplement their income. Despite the supposedly final settlement William had negotiated in 1835, Baudouin was constantly on the look out for opportunities to extract more from his father-in-law. Once again it was left to Robinson, advised by Quillinan, to sort the matter out. Baudouin was given to understand, in no uncertain terms, that William had not the means to do anything further and that his own income had been reduced.[19]

On 4 October 1842, the Wordsworths' fortieth wedding anniversary, Mary looked back with 'heart-felt thankfulness' over the years 'of uninterrupted harmony' they had spent together. 'We, like all mortals, have our sorrows, but these have been endeared to us by perfect sympathy, and only drawn us more closely to each other. Then this beautiful region in which we have been permitted to live – and in such home-society!' Even the loss, in different ways, of Sara, Dorothy and Dora, had been compensated for by the blessing of Isabella Fenwick's friendship. To the newly widowed Mary Arnold, the Wordsworths appeared 'as delightful a picture of old age as you can imagine – happy in themselves & by their loving kindness & benevolence ever contributing to the happiness of others'.[20]

To her parents' undisguised joy, Dora returned to Rydal at the beginning of November, bringing her goddaughter, Rotha, with her. The ostensible reason was that the Quillinans' lodgings were being repaired, but Dora, as Robinson observed, 'looked very poorly' and it was obvious that life in London did not suit her. When Quillinan joined them, a few weeks later, what began as a temporary residence in Rydal lodgings soon became permanent. Though she was not under their own roof, Dora had at least rejoined the family circle. The Quillinans, with the indispensable Miss Fenwick, and Robinson, on his annual Christmas visit, were some compensation for the loss of Arnold, but they all felt his absence. Robinson in particular missed his old ally in his religious and political disputes with William – and was clearly rattled by the presence of Faber, whom he called 'a sad fanatic of an opposite character' and 'a flaming zealot for the new doctrines'. 'This Faber is an agreea[bl]e man,' he informed his brother. 'All the young ladies are in love with him And he has high spirits conversational talent & great facility in writing both polemics & poetry'. They had sparred together on every occasion they met, without either man losing his temper, though they had 'exchanged pretty hard knocks'. What disturbed Robinson was not Faber's avowed dislike of Protestantism and predilection for the Church in Rome ('not *of* Rome *yet*', Robinson predicted), but his apparent hold on William. Accompanying the pair on a walk in the new year, he noted, 'Their conversation I was not competent altogether to follow, but certainly Wordsworth's tone was that of deference towards his younger and more consistent friend.'[21]

Earlier in the year, William had agreed that Samuel Wilkinson, editor of a High Church periodical, the *Christian Miscellany*, could publish a selection of his poetry in an article entitled 'Contributions of W. Wordsworth to the Revival of Catholic Truths'. Unusually, however, he asked to see a copy of the article before it was published, indicating that he had unspoken misgivings about the use that would be made of his poems. He was entirely justified. When the article arrived, he found that it included not just a selection from *Ecclesiastical Sonnets*, as he had expected, but extensive quotation from *The Excursion* and even *The Old Cumberland Beggar*. 'There is little I hope in my poetry that does not breathe more or less in a religious atmosphere; as these verses certainly do,' William protested, 'but if you were to take as wide a range as this Ex[tract] leads to, one scarcely sees why it should be selected in preference to many others.'

What Wilkinson was trying to do, as he stated quite explicitly in his preface, was to convince 'any timid Churchman that the doctrines [of the Oxford Movement], which are now branded as Popish, were a few years ago held without persecution, or even without reprehension, by men whose zeal for the Anglican Church none suspect'. Rightly or wrongly, William was now seen as the archetypal Anglican and by including, for instance, Faber's note to *Musings Near Aquapendente* under the heading 'Mr Wordsworth's Opinion of the Oxford Divines', the article sought to give his specific endorsement to the Oxford Movement. 'The poet is a *high* churchman,' Robinson stated, 'but luckily does not go all lengths with the Oxford School – He praises the *reformers* . . . for inspir[in]g the age with deeper reverence for antiquity And a more cordial conformity with ritual observances – As well as a warmer piety – But he goes no further'. But Wilkinson wanted him to go further and nail his colours to the mast. 'I rather think that I should better serve the cause we have in common, were I to abstain from what you recommend', was William's careful response. 'It would seem to enroll me as a partisan'. To the casual reader of 'Contributions of W. Wordsworth to the Revival of Catholic Truths', that is exactly what William had become. 'He is claimed by them as *their* poet', Robinson wrote indignantly. 'And they have published a selection from his works with a dishonest preface from w[hi]ch one might infer he went all lengths with them'.[22]

To Robinson it therefore came as something of a relief when '*Faber* the ultra-catholic – (not *Roman*)' left Ambleside for a Midlands curacy early in January 1843. While acknowledging his gifts, and the fact that he carried with him the affections of all the people, 'having been very zealous & charitable to the poor', Robinson maintained his conviction that 'He may become a nuisance to the world, if he carries out his mischievous principles & acquires distinction'. What he could not, or did not, say was that Faber's departure removed from William's immediate circle a man whose influence he considered both dangerous and insidious.[23]

With both Faber and Robinson gone, and no Arnold to relieve the gloom, Isabella Fenwick hit on a happy idea for keeping the poet amused during the long winter evenings which stretched ahead. She persuaded William to dictate to her a series of notes on his poems, describing when, where and why they were written. The indispensable tool of all future critics and biographers, the Fenwick Notes, as they became known, were intended primarily for the private information of Miss Fenwick and Dora, though, as they expanded in length and importance, William clearly anticipated that they would also be circulated among his friends. What makes them so fascinating to the modern reader is not just the invaluable factual information they contain, but the insights they give into the poet's mind and character. Miss Fenwick made no attempt to polish the conversational style of the dictation into something more approaching a literary essay. The entries range from an abrupt '1799. Germany' for 'A Slumber did my Spirit Seal' to a five-page discourse prompted by *Epistle to Sir George Beaumont.* They include, as conversation does, both personal anecdote and impressions of people and places, together with the occasional digression into diatribe on subjects which aroused his passion. Most of all what they do is make one realize how much we have lost through William's hostility to the whole idea of biography.[24]

The miseries of the Southey family affected the Wordsworths deeply this spring. Sara Coleridge's husband died on 26 January, after a long and painful illness. His death was not unexpected, but they grieved for his young widow. 'She is much beloved in this House, as she must be wherever she is half as well known as we know her'. On 1 February Herbert and Bertha Hill left Rydal for Warwick, where, thanks in part to a glowing reference from William, Herbert had secured the headmastership of the Royal Grammar School. 'They will be much missed in our village,' William wrote sadly, 'and Mr Hill exceedingly both on his own account, and because there will no doubt be a great falling off in his Successor.'[25]

His daughter had barely left the Lakes when Southey had a seizure so violent it left no hope of recovery. He lingered another month, shattered in body as well as mind, only to be carried off by typhus fever. He died on 21 March, aged sixty-eight, fought over to the last by his warring wife and children, but passing away 'as gently as a child falling into slumber'. William was pointedly not invited to the funeral by the widow, but he went anyway. Quillinan drove him over early on the dark stormy morning of the funeral and accompanied him to Crosthwaite churchyard, where they were joined by John, and his seven-year-old son William, who was Southey's godson, so that three generations of Wordsworths attended Southey to the grave. 'Poor Kate', Quillinan remarked. 'Her father will be nearer to her in the Church yard at Keswick than he has been for the last 3 or 4 years'. The good angel, Miss Fenwick, went over to see if she could effect a reconciliation, at least between Southey's children. She succeeded in persuading Kate to write a conciliatory letter to Edith, but not even Miss Fenwick could heal this rift.[26]

William was dragged into the quarrel once again when Southey's literary executor, Henry Taylor, sought his opinion as to the appointment of a suitable editor of Southey's letters. Edith wanted to do it and had the support of Mrs Southey, but she was 'so much under the influence of her wrong-headed and stupid husband' that William advised she should be set aside. William could recommend only that the most appropriate person was Southey's son, Cuthbert, who, despite his youth, had completed the second two volumes of Bell's life for his father, but he suggested that Herbert Hill and the executors should also be involved in a supervisory role to prevent any further unpleasantness. This was the plan adopted, leading ultimately to the bizarre situation where the official *Life and Correspondence of Robert Southey*, edited by Cuthbert, was published in six volumes in 1849–50, but an alternative four volumes, *Selections from the Letters of Robert Southey*, based on Caroline's letters, was put together by Edith's husband, John Warter, and published in 1858.[27]

Southey was barely cold in his grave before rumours began to circulate about who would replace him as Poet Laureate. Southey had held the post since 1813, a thirty-year tenure, during which many finer poets than he had come and gone. Now the London rumour-mill had it that there were only two possible candidates, one old and one new, the sixty-six-year-old Scottish balladeer Tom Campbell and the thirty-four-year-old Alfred Tennyson. Yet on 30 March the Lord Chamberlain, Earl de la Warr, wrote to William, offering him the position. Like the offer of the Civil List pension, it was put in a way that could not fail to touch William personally. 'May I be allowed to add', the Earl wrote, 'that it is with feelings of very peculiar gratification, that I find myself in a position to propose this mark of distinction to an Individual, whose acceptance of it would shed an additional lustre upon an Office in itself highly honorable.' Instead of instantly and gratefully accepting this final accolade as the triumphant vindication of a career dedicated to changing poetic taste and judgement, William turned it down. 'The Appointment I feel . . . imposes Duties which far advanced in life as I am I cannot venture to undertake and I must therefore beg leave to decline the acceptance of an offer that I shall always remember with no unbecoming pride.' 'Had I been several years younger I should have accepted the office with pride and pleasure', he explained to Lord Lonsdale's daughter, but at his age (one might almost add, at any age) he dreaded the obligation to produce verses to order. 'I hope, therefore, that neither you nor Lord Lonsdale, nor any of my friends, will blame me for what I have done.'[28]

In the end, it was a letter from Peel which persuaded William to change his mind. The Prime Minister assured him that the offer had been made only 'in order to pay you that tribute of Respect which is justly due to the first of living Poets' and that it had both his own and the Queen's entire concurrence. 'Do not be deterred by the fear of any obligation which the appointment may be supposed to imply', Peel urged. 'I will undertake that you shall have nothing required from you. But as the Queen can select for this honorable appointment, no one, whose claims for respect and honor on account of Eminence as a Poet, can be placed in "competition with yours" – I trust you will no longer hesitate to accept it.' How could he do otherwise? On 4 April, three days before his seventy-third birthday, William accepted 'with unalloyed pleasure . . . this high Distinction'.[29]

The appointment was drawn up, William took the oath of allegiance before Thomas Dawson, a local magistrate, and Moxon was given power of attorney to collect the annual salary of £70 a year. Despite the assurances to the contrary, however, William felt the pressure to perform. In July he received an invitation to attend the Queen's Ball, which fortunately arrived only the day before, enabling him to plead 'impossibility for non-obedience', but it was only a matter of time before he would have to make a public appearance. Worse still, through his brother, who had stayed overnight with Earl de la Warr, he received a hefty hint that, though nothing was required of him officially, 'yet . . . if your Muse should happen to be in the humour, and could avail herself of any little event which befell the Queen, or any undertaking in which she might happen to engage herself, – he was certain it would be very well taken'. The ever-resourceful Quillinan, disgusted with the idolatrous nature of previous Laureate offerings, suggested that William should compose 'in his own grand way' a hymn invoking 'a blessing on the Queen & Country, or giving thanks for blessings vouchsafed & perils averted'. 'This w[oul]d be a new mode of dealing with the office of laureat[e], & w[oul]d come with dignity & propriety I think, from a Seer of Wordsworth's age & character.' The muse, however, remained stubbornly silent.[30]

William's seventy-third birthday, put off from 7 April to the 20th 'in royal fashion', as Quillinan teased, was celebrated in grand style, as became his new status. Around 130 schoolgirls came to a tea-drinking in Mr North's field and danced to music supplied by a fiddler. The Quillinans organized the event, with the help of the Ambleside Robinsons and Briggses, but it was, of course, Miss Fenwick, who provided the funds for the entertainment.[31]

William's public triumphs were in marked contrast to the private distresses closing in on him. At the beginning of February Willy, who was on a visit to Brinsop, had surprised and delighted his family by announcing his engagement to Mary Monkhouse, the twenty-one-year-old daughter of his mother's cousin Tom. 'Master Willy might have done worse', was Quillinan's laconic comment. 'She is a nice girl enough – just of age, & has a pretty good fortune – I believe not less than £20,000 besides what she will have from her Uncle Monkhouse. In a worldly point of view it is an excellent match for Willia[m] & in every way we are all inclin[ed to] hope & believe not a bad one for e[ither] party.' Unlike Willy's previous engagement, this one met with universal approval: Mary's guardians, John Monkhouse and Samuel Horrocks, both gave their joyful consent and everyone welcomed the idea of the Wordsworths and Monkhouses being drawn closer together. Willy's Uncle Christopher offered £100 as a wedding present and his own services to perform the marriage ceremony at Brinsop.

Then just as suddenly as the engagement had been announced, it was broken off. It had lasted a mere two months and was ended by the disclosure of a letter written by the intended bride to her aunt. Exactly what the letter said is not known, but the Wordsworths were perplexed and indignant. 'I suppose the unhappy girl has become a monomaniac or is fast tending that way – or else I know not what to think – she must be bewitched', was Quillinan's first opinion, but he, like the rest of the family, soon came to think that Willy had had a providential escape. 'The obvious fatuity of the poor Girl, which may still farther degenerate into downright imbecility of mind, if it assume no worse shape, must satisfy him that he has missed a heavy & fearful burthen.' The engagement having been public knowledge, John Monkhouse thought it only proper that the reason for its breaking off 'should be known to be one of pure calamity involving no reproach on W[illy] nor indeed on any one, being a case of undoubted disease'. Diseased or not, Mary Monkhouse broke off a second engagement in 1845 when she decided that her suitor was more interested in her purse than her person (had she suspected this of Willy too?), and ultimately married the Reverend Henry Dew, rector of Whitney in Herefordshire.[32]

While Willy moped at Rydal Mount, his brother's marriage was falling apart. Isabella had been taken seriously ill the previous September: first typhus had been suspected, then it was thought that she was pregnant, and by May, when it was clear she was not, internal inflammation was diagnosed. The London doctors she consulted feared for her lungs, though, as her servants were quick to report to Dora, 'if they could have heard her voice to Mr Wordsworth when he proposed any thing she disliked such as sending away old nurse on account of the heavy expense they would not have thought there was much amiss there'. Clearly, having six children in eight years and the stresses of life on a parson's income were taking their toll on a young woman brought up to expect a life of luxury. Used to dealing with such cases, the doctors recommended that she should spend the winter in Madeira. On 26 October Isabella, her husband, their daughter, Jane, and penultimate child, Charles, who was almost four, embarked for Madeira, leaving their four other sons, aged between nine and two, in the care of the governess at Brigham. John would eventually return to his old life in Cumberland, but his wife, having developed a taste for the life of the leisured invalid traveller, would not.[33]

It was ironic that, as Isabella went abroad to recover her health, William's nephew 'Keswick' John was trying to return home for the same reason. His health had never been good, and in the Ionian Islands he had become seriously ill with what he himself diagnosed as sub-acute bronchitis. Attempts to obtain a transfer elsewhere having failed, he was now sent home on sick leave that would end in his discharge from the army. Unlike Isabella, he had a genuine weakness in his lungs, having contracted the preliminary stages of consumption, and like Keats, his medical training enabled him to observe the progress of his own disease with a morbid fascination which would lead to frequent bouts of depression. Arriving at Rydal Mount in June, he divided his time between his uncle's family there and 'cousin Dorothy' Harrison, at Green Bank, before settling into his own little cottage at Ambleside to await the inevitable.[34]

William and Mary had intended to visit Brinsop Court in the summer, partly to see Mary's crippled brother, Tom, and partly to avoid the influx of Lakers. Their departure was delayed by concerns about Isabella and visits from John and two of his sons, then by the news that Mary's sister Joanna had suffered a paralytic attack while on a visit to their nephew at Elton, near Stockton. 'She is a dear generous singleminded woman, & would be an irreparable loss to her family', Quillinan wrote on learning of her seizure. Early reports were favourable, but a month later, she took a sudden turn for the worse and Mary could bear it no longer. She and William set out immediately for Elton, leaving the Quillinans to take charge of Dorothy and Rydal Mount in their absence. It was an uncomfortable and distressing visit, for though they arrived to find Joanna better than they had expected, her nephew, with whom she was staying, was in a most alarming state. George Sutton, the oldest son of Mary's brother Jack Hutchinson, had been left a vast fortune through his mother's family at a very young age and had taken their name. He had grown up to be wayward and irresponsible, married an elderly heiress for her money and led a life of selfish and careless luxury which had been the despair of his parents and the envy of his brothers. Now, satisfyingly, fate had caught up with him and he was obviously deranged. Instead of simply nursing Joanna, the Wordsworths found themselves arranging lodgings out of his house for her in the village and organizing for Dr Belcombe, who ran a private asylum in York, to send an attendant to confine George within his own home, 'till it shall please God to mitigate the disease of mind under which He is labouring'. As George had determined to accompany them to York, the Wordsworths were obliged to sneak off without his knowledge, knowing that there would be a storm when their absence was discovered.[35]

William and Mary arrived at Brinsop on 20 September, having spent six happy hours exploring York in the company of their Robinson relations and attended a service in the Minster, which was (as it always seems to be) in a state of disrepair following a fire in the nave in 1840. Two days after their arrival, their much-loved maidservant, Jane, who had been with them for many years, was seized with pleurisy. Three days later, on 25 September, Joanna died. She was buried, quietly and simply, as she wished, in the tiny churchyard of the equally tiny church of St John's at Elton, a few hundred yards from the grossly extravagant pile of George Sutton's Elton Hall.[36] The little she possessed in her lifetime had been severely diminished by the decision of the Mississippi State Government to renege on paying interest to its stock-holders, but even that little became a subject of dispute. Her will, written on 5 April 1841, had left the remainder of her personal estate to her brother George, whose misfortunes she had always grieved over, but an improperly executed codicil, dated 27 March 1843, left the money in her savings bank (which was effectively the residue) to her nephew, Jack's son, Henry Hutchinson, who lived in Peel, on the Isle of Man. This was literally a matter of less than £50, but it was an equally important sum to both George and Henry; the latter won, producing inscrutable Manx law as his trump card. One turns with relief from the sordid squabbles over money to Catherine Clarkson's heartfelt tribute. 'I cannot think of the "fair Joanna" as otherwise than young. Her artless dry humour never failed to promote chearfulness & social enjoyment. Many & many a hearty laugh have I had with her – & grieved am I to think that I have nothing to remember of her in later years.'[37]

Robinson, who had joined the Wordsworths at Brinsop in the hope of accompanying William on a tour of Wales, observed the stricken silence as Joanna's death was announced and knew that his excursion was doomed. He left the family to their grief, which was soon to be compounded by the death of 'dear and good and faithful Jane'. As Robinson thoughtfully remarked to Mary, 'The death of an old & attached Servant of her description is one of a very serious character indeed. – And I fear in a degree irreparable – It shews the vanity of our artificial classifications of society. – How indignant you would feel were any one to say by way of consolation or remark on your sorrow that she was *only* your servant'. Jane was buried, next to the Hutchinsons, in the family plot at Brinsop, the Wordsworths testifying to their affection by erecting a headstone in her memory.[38]

'We are most anxious to be at home as if it would be some Shelter from trouble', William wrote on 24 October, 'but there we should have to meet my Nephew John Wordsworth, the only child of my eldest Brother, long since deceased, in I fear a hopeless state of pulmonary consumption.' Too depressed to pay their visits to friends on the way back to the Lakes, William and Mary decided to face up to family responsibilities and went straight to Rydal Mount. They arrived to find John no better, but no worse, and, for the poet, one of those troublesome tasks of duty which he most disliked, a request to write the epitaph for Southey's monument in Crosthwaite church. There was clearly no one more appropriate, but William had written only a handful of poems over the last twelve months. These did include two significant ones. The first was his beautiful sonnet on Wansfell, whose swelling heights formed the horizon of his own Vale of Rydal, written on Christmas Eve, 1842. This William himself declared to be 'one of his most perfect as a work of art'. In it, he reproached himself for never celebrating the mountain before in his verse, 'For all that thou, as if from heaven, hast brought Of glory lavished on our quiet days'.

Bountiful Son of Earth! when we are gone
From every object dear to mortal sight,
As soon we shall be, may these words attest
How oft, to elevate our spirits, shone
Thy visionary majesties of light,
How in thy pensive glooms our hearts found rest.[39]

The importance of these lines lies not in their beauty, but in the sentiment, which Faber would have deplored, since, despite all his efforts to eradicate such pantheism, it comes as close as anything William had written in his early days to worshipping

God in nature. Faber might have imposed the cross upon the poet, but he could not tear out the instinctive heresy in his heart.

The second poem was important for a different reason. *Grace Darling* sang the praises of the daughter of a Farne Island lighthouse-keeper who, in September 1838, with her father, had rowed out to a sinking steamship and rescued nine survivors. Her courage, her sex and her youth (she was only twenty-three at the time of the rescue) had captured the public imagination. For William she was another Lucy, 'Known unto few but prized as far as known'. His tribute came four and a half years after the event – too late for Grace, who had died in 1842 – but it was extraordinary that it came at all, for it cannot have been written without conjuring up visions of the fate of his own brother John.[40]

'Your grief is yet too keen to allow of your treating the Subject in that mitigated tone that *Poetry* requires', he wrote on his return from Brinsop to a man who had sent him some verses on the death of his son. 'And therefore though there are in your verses, many touching passages and profound thoughts, yet as a whole the anguish which is given vent to at such length stands in the way of the general effect. Emotion remembered in a state of mind approaching to tranquillity as I have elsewhere said is more favorable to the production of verses filled to give frequent and general pleasure.' This lesson he now had to apply to himself, in composing the epitaph for one of his oldest friends. Like everything connected with poor Southey's last years, the question of a monument was fraught with difficulties and dissensions; Inglis and Wynn wanted one in Westminster Abbey, Landor was promoting a subscription for a memorial at Bristol and offering his own lines for it, Stanger headed the appeal for one in Crosthwaite church at Keswick, where Southey was buried.[41]

'My verse days are almost over', William had written to Haydon in April. His first impulse then had been to write a prose epitaph, which illustrated perfectly his own dictum that these things were better written after the passage of time. A bare third was devoted to a somewhat anodyne list of Southey's virtues, the rest to the 'slowly-working and inscrutable malady' which had 'prematurely and almost totally obscured' his mind and should serve as a *carpe diem* warning to others. Written less than three months after Southey's death, when the insanity which had afflicted his last five years was painfully uppermost in William's mind, it did not do justice to the vibrant man, poet and scholar of the previous sixty-odd years who was the real Southey. Thankfully, it was rejected, in favour of a far warmer tribute in verse which made only passing allusion to the tragedy of his final years as 'his griefs':

Ye vales and hills whose beauty hither drew
The poet's steps, and fixed him here, on you
His eyes have closed! And ye, loved books, no more
Shall Southey feed upon your precious lore,
To works that ne'er shall forfeit their renown,
Adding immortal labours of his own – ...

His joys, his griefs, have vanished like a cloud
From Skiddaw's top; but he to heaven was vowed
Through his industrious life, and Christian faith
Calmed in his soul the fear of change and death.

The first version of the epitaph was written in November, but was subjected to the usual almost daily revision until it appeared in print on a circular to raise the £1,100 needed to commission John Lough's white marble monument. Southey's widow complained bitterly of William's epitaph, 'was ever such a miserable failure? – or any thing so utterly heartless & spiritless?', but he believed passionately that nothing should appear on a memorial which could not have been said, face to face with the deceased, during life. To eulogize was to offend modesty and the best method of conveying the excellence of the departed was to infer it by expressing either gratitude to the Almighty, by whom he, or she, had been so endowed, or sorrow for premature removal of goodness from this world.[42]

The same year which had seen the revolution in William's reputation so emphatically celebrated by his appointment as Poet Laureate was to see a further confirmation of almost equal significance. Francis Jeffrey, his most virulent critic since the beginning of the century, republished a selection of his articles from the *Edinburgh Review* in a collected edition in 1843. Not only did he omit his more vitriolic reviews of the shorter poems, in which, as Robinson pointed out, his judgement had been reversed by public opinion, but, in a footnote to those of *The Excursion* and *The White Doe*, he confessed that he had often spoken too bitterly and confidently about William's faults as a poet and regretted 'the greater part' of what he was pleased to term his own '*vivacités* of expression'.

And indeed, so strong has been my feeling in this way, that, considering how much I have always loved many of the attributes of his Genius and how entirely I respect his Character, it did at first occur to me whether it was quite fitting that, in my old age and his, I should include in this publication any of those critiques which may have formerly given pain or offence, to him or his admirers.

It was hardly a complete retraction, but, as Robinson said, 'it is something that he has not dared to reprint in utter silence'.[43]

Throughout the year, William continued to give his permission for selections from his work to be published, as he had always done, without asking for any personal remuneration. The Reverend Richard Parkinson, for instance, was allowed to use the memoir of Robert Walker from *The River Duddon* in a booklet for Manchester factory workers; the Reverend Henry Gough, a schoolmaster of St Bees, was permitted to make a selection of William's poems for the use of schoolchildren and, similarly, Robert Chambers, the Edinburgh publisher, for his *Cyclopaedia of English Literature*. In December 1843 it was brought forcibly home to William that he could no longer afford to be so generous. Gough's book turned out to be not the cheap selection for circulation among his own scholars which William had understood the project to be, but a fancy book, with an illustrated title-page, and 233 pages of his poems, printed within an ornamental border, under the imprint of James Burns, a London publisher devoted to the dissemination of materials for the Oxford Movement. Burns obviously knew that he was on dangerous ground. He sent William five complimentary copies of the book, *Select Pieces from the Poems of William Wordsworth*, and a handsome quarto *Book of Common Prayer*, 'by way of I suppose of [*sic*] douceur or hush money'. It was such a flagrant breach of both William and Moxon's trust (William fortunately having referred Gough to Moxon for his permission also), not to mention the provisions of the new Copyright Act, that it could not pass unnoticed. Stiff letters were sent to Gough, who protested his innocence, and Burns, who equivocated, but in a tacit admission of guilt conceded that there would be no second edition and handed over the printing plates to Moxon.[44]

The business with Chambers was even more awkward, because the permission had been sought through the good offices of a mutual friend, Mrs Fletcher, widow of an Edinburgh lawyer, who lived at Lancrigg, in Easedale. William had given his permission for the extracts, subject to Moxon's consent. Chambers not only neglected to secure that consent but, at 1,100 lines, had printed ten times more than William considered either '*moderate*' or '*reasonable*'. As he had neglected to stipulate an amount, he did not feel that he could press a claim for compensation, but he was delighted to learn that Moxon was awarded £50 for what William called 'smoot money', which was apparently printers' slang for casual labour. There was, unfortunately, nothing he could do about the Biographical notices, which were riddled with errors he found deeply offensive: not only was he denominated a member of Coleridge and Southey's Pantisocratic society, but, 'drolly enough', it was suggested that he was married to his own cousin. This second incident, coming so soon after the one with Burns, convinced William that he was out of his depth in granting permissions. 'Every application that shall in future be made to me for leave to print Extracts from my Poems, I shall refer at once to you,' he declared to Moxon, 'and inform the Party that such will be my invariable practise'.[45]

Over the Christmas holidays, William plugged wearily away at his epitaph for Southey. 'I question whether there is a couplet in the whole that has not been objected to, by some one or another', he complained to his nephew Chris, 'and in a way that would surprize you as much . . . as your remarks did me'. Chris, a future Anglican bishop, had taken a dislike to the last four lines, depicting Southey's Christian life: 'I have no notion of an "ordinary Christian"', William responded indignantly; 'a man is a believer with a life conformable to his belief, and if so, all peculiarities of genius, talent and personal character vanish before the sublime position which he occupies with all Brother Christians, Children of One Father and saved by the One Redeemer.'[46]

Christmas was an altogether more sedentary affair this year. There was no Arnold, or Faber, to walk with, and Robinson disabled himself by falling down the stairs of his lodgings on Christmas Eve. The Wordsworths insisted on transferring him to Rydal Mount, where he was nursed with tender care by their manservant, James Dixon. Brought up in a workhouse, James had been thrown out at the age of nine with 2s in his pocket. On the verge of destitution, he had been taken into service by a farmer and had never been out of a place since. 'He is forty-five years of age, and is really a sort of model servant for a country situation like this,' Robinson admired, 'as he is very religious and moral, as well as an excellent servant ... He is a great favourite with the family, and will, I dare say, never leave them.' Not only could he read and write, but he was a musician and artist, with a talent for wood-carving and painting pace eggs. Such was Robinson's gratitude for his care that, on parting, he presented James with a silver watch, a gift which left him literally speechless.[47]

To the Wordsworths Robinson was equally generous. He had always made them a small present after each Christmas visit, but this year was special. 'I never left them with a warmer feeling of gratitude for kindnesses towards all of them', he noted in his journal, before presenting them with a new set of gilt-rimmed tea and breakfast china. 'Never, since we were housekeepers, did we possess a *Company* Tea Service', Mary wrote in high delight and it made its first appearance on what she proudly called 'The *Laureate's* birth Day'. This year Miss Fenwick extended her invitation to the local schoolboys, as well as girls, so over 300 children came to Rydal Mount to celebrate William's seventy-fourth birthday, accompanied by almost half as many adults of all ages and classes. 'The treat went off delightfully with music, choral singing, dancing and chasing each other about, in all directions', William boasted, with pardonable pride. Tea and currant cake were dispensed to all comers. Two sets of 'casual Itinerants', Italian and German, came in to provide entertainment and the children were encouraged to play hide-and-seek through the grounds while the elderly took tea inside the house. Tables were set up on the terrace, covered with moss, laurel leaves and daffodils, and laden with oranges, gingerbread and painted pace eggs, which were presented to the children before they left. Miss Fenwick having provided the feast, she shared the honours with William in getting three cheers from the assembled company. 'I must own I wish that little commemorations of this kind were more common among us', William remarked wistfully. 'One would wish to see the rich mingle with the poor as much as may be upon a footing of fraternal equality. The old feudal dependencies and relations are almost gone from England, and nothing has yet come adequately to supply their place.'[48]

One of the last of those ties had just been broken. On 19 March 'William the Good', Earl of Lonsdale, died in his eighty-seventh year. 'Of my own feelings upon this loss I shall content myself with saying, that as long as I retain consciousness I shall cherish the memory of your father,' William wrote to Lady Mary, 'for his inestimable worth, as one who honoured me with his friendship, and who was to myself and my children the best benefactor.' His son, William, Lord Lowther, for whom William had campaigned in so many elections, succeeded to the Earldom and the Lord Lieutenancy of Cumberland and Westmorland. Fortunately, no epitaph was required or expected of the Poet Laureate, though his advice on an appropriate memorial was sought – and ignored.[49]

Relations with the other local aristocrat, Lady le Fleming, the recluse of Rydal Hall, had not improved over the years. In the autumn of 1843, she, or rather her steward, raised the rent of Rydal Mount by a third to £60 a year, just at a time when William was in reduced circumstances after his resignation from the Stamp Office. Robinson was convinced that she was 'half-crazy'. Though her house was within a stone's throw of William's, she had lived for many years without ever speaking to him, appeared unaware that having a Poet Laureate as a tenant was anything unusual and, through her steward, treated him 'with the utmost indifference'. In the summer of 1844, however, she and the Wordsworths again clashed over William's plans to build. The site was Dora's field, once more, but this time the object was to build a house for Isabella Fenwick, which, after her death, would belong to Dora. Miss Fenwick had more or less made her home permanently in the Lakes, to be near the Wordsworths, but the difficulty of finding long leases of suitable houses, particularly anywhere nearer than Ambleside, had increased, and there was nothing appropriate to buy. Though she occasionally took up residence at Rydal Mount, she preferred to have a home of her own and the idea of building on the Rash seemed the perfect solution, especially as Dora would ultimately benefit. The Wordsworths were prepared to overlook the greatest drawback to them – that the house would cut off access between 'our lovely sequestered Nook' and the terrace – 'we must give up something for the blessing of having you so near'. The indispensable Carter, who now divided his time between Carlisle and Rydal, and was planning to build his own cottage down the valley at Loughrigg Holme, drew up some rough sketches of the available site, but Miss Fenwick wanted to employ her relative Anthony Salvin as her architect. Quite what the flamboyant Salvin, who specialized in restoring, or rather rebuilding, castles and aristocratic mansions in grandiose style, usually with Italianate marble interiors, would have made of a Lakeland cottage remains a mystery, for though expected he never came.[50]

On 14 August, however, the very day that some fifty men assembled in the field to bid for the job of building the house, a letter from Lady le Fleming's solicitor was put into William's hands, informing him that he could not legally build on the field without her express permission, as it was in contravention of the Custom of the Manor; if he persisted, she would take him to court. Afraid that she might end his own tenancy of Rydal Mount if he made too much fuss, William could only make a muted protest about the unchallenged expansion of other houses at Rydal and complain that such claims had not been raised before. Nevertheless, he assured Lady le Fleming that he had no intention of going to court over the matter, taking care to remind her, at the same time, that she had given him an assurance that he would be allowed to remain undisturbed in the possession of his home for the remainder of his days. Dora was vexed to the last degree, but had no doubt who was to blame, Fletcher Fleming, 'the Lord Archbishop of Rydal', who had never forgiven William for helping Graves to the curacy of Bowness: 'his spite is at the bottom of it all'.[51]

Thwarted in the plan to build on Dora's field, William suggested an alternative: would Lady le Fleming exchange it for the Wishing Gate field, overlooking Grasmere lake and village, and a few hundred yards from the cottage at Town End? Though she behaved 'most handsomely' in agreeing to this exchange, Dora's 'stupid marriage settlement' now set another legal obstacle in the way. It was the considered opinion of Talfourd, then a visitor at Rydal, and the other lawyers consulted, that this could be overcome, but they had all reckoned without opposition from an unexpected quarter. Isabella Fenwick was deeply unhappy at the proposal, not because she did not want to live at Rydal, but because she thought it wrong that William was prepared to build a house for her and not one for his daughter, who was also homeless and had a prior and better claim. Dora, generously, did not share this feeling and entered into the schemes with enthusiasm, but Miss Fenwick felt obliged to express herself forcibly on what she considered William's injustice and even unkindness to his daughter. William remained unmoved. 'I must repeat here what I have said to you before,' he wrote to Miss Fenwick, 'that building for Dora, situated as she is, I cannot think of, and if you would not be comfortable in occupation of the House, then there is an end of the matter.' He would not even consider the possibility of giving Dora a fixed allowance. 'I am convinced it would be wrong to do so, as it would only produce in a certain quarter an effect which I should exceedingly deprecate.'[52]

The 'certain quarter' was, of course, Quillinan. Nothing could shake William's conviction that his son-in-law was an idle good-for-nothing. Having swallowed his own pride to seek the Distributorship of Stamps in order to support his family, William found Quillinan's casual attitude towards earning a living immensely irritating. 'Nobody could be kinder or more ready to serve, or more generally amiable', he admitted.

> Neither this nor anything else however reconciles me to his course of life. You say he could not procure employment – I say, that he does not *try*. He has now taken again to hard labour on his translation of Camoens, a work which can not possibly turn to profit of any kind either pecuniary or intellectual. All that ought to be looked to from it is his own amusement at *leisure* hours . . . His inaction mortifies me the more because his talents are greatly superior to those of most men who earn a handsome livelihood by Literature.

To add insult to injury, William felt that his daughter was not well treated by her husband. 'It is not to be doubted that his way of spending his time is little suited to make the day pass pleasantly for others', he complained. 'He never scarcely *converses* with his wife or children; his papers, his books, or a newspaper engross his whole time.' It was simply inexplicable to him why Dora, 'poor Creature', seemed 'very fond' of Quillinan, but he hardened his heart. 'Be assured

I will take care while I live, that she should not *suffer* in mind for scantiness of income', he informed Miss Fenwick. 'That she may be somewhat straightened [*sic*], acting as she has chosen to do with my strongest disapprobation I deem fit and right. – But no more of the subject, nor will I return to it again.'[53]

It was the closest William ever came to a quarrel with Miss Fenwick. She remained convinced that, if a house was to be built, it should be for Dora; he was adamant that she should be the tenant for life and that only after her death should it become Dora's. In the stalemate that followed, the plans to build at Rydal or Grasmere were quietly forgotten. And for the first time in many years Miss Fenwick did not come back to Rydal to spend the autumn and winter with the Wordsworths, remaining instead with her relatives at Leamington. Though she claimed it was for her health, it was an implicit reproof. It did not change William's mind, but it did make him realize how much he owed to his wife. 'I am unworthy of being constantly in your sight', he wrote to Miss Fenwick.

> Your standard is too high for my hourly life . . . Among ten thousand causes which I have to thank God for his goodness towards me is that for more than forty years I have had a Companion who can bear with my offences, who forgets them, and enters upon a new course of love with me when I have done wrong, leaving me to the remorse of my own conscience. Of this chastisement I have had my portion and the feeling seems to be gathering strength daily and hourly; only let me believe that I do not love others less, because I seem to hate myself more.[54]

The Wordsworths were, as usual, inundated with visitors over the summer, more than 270 of them tramping over the black and white tiles of the entrance porch. One of Robinson's Christmas gifts, they spelt out the appropriate Latin message 'SALVE', or 'Welcome'. There was an influx of family: Christopher, and his son Charles; Willy; the Brinsop cousins, Tom, Ebba and Sarah Hutchinson; the ailing 'Keswick' John, 'not worse but not better <u>really</u>'; and from Brigham the three grandsons, Henry, William and John, whose parents had left Madeira and were on their way to spend the summer at the baths at Lucca. Isabella had been ordered to spend a second winter abroad and, as John felt that he could not leave her, they decided to go to Rome, where she could have the benefit of the advice of her favourite doctor. The Quillinans, who had spent a few weeks at Flimby, on the Cumberland coast, in a vain effort to instil some better health into Dora, returned in August to spend three months on Belle Isle, the Curwen-owned island near the Windermere ferry. The island was an excellent alternative venue for visitors to Rydal Mount who wanted to picnic or fish on the lake, though getting there had its hazards, as the seventy-year-old Christopher discovered, when he fell into the water at the boathouse.[55]

On 6 September William led an excursion to his beloved Duddon, fulfilling a two-year-old promise to Mary Fletcher. The party consisted of William and Miss Fletcher, Quillinan, who was the 'charioteer', and Tom and Ebba Hutchinson. They almost turned back at Coniston, because it rained so hard, but a providential break in the clouds allowed them to continue as far as Ulpha Kirk. Early the next morning Miss Fletcher found the poet pacing distractedly in the churchyard; he had not slept well, recollections of former days and people having crowded in on him, particularly those of 'my dear sister; and when I thought of her state, and of those who had passed away, Coleridge, and Southey, and many others, while I am left with all my many infirmities, if not sins, in full consciousness, how could I sleep? and then I took to the alteration of sonnets, and that made the matter worse still.' He could still, however, be stopped in his tracks, mental and physical, by the sheer beauty of a little bunch of harebells and parsley fern, growing out of a wall, which most people would have passed by unobserved. There had to be a benevolent purpose for the inexhaustible beauty of nature, he exclaimed, though the incident which might once have inspired a poem would have passed unrecorded had it not been for Miss Fletcher's journal.[56]

'We have had swarms of Company since you left us,' William wrote to Moxon on 12 September, 'a great part of whom we would willingly have exchanged for a few days more of your society.' Among the visitors had been not only Moxon himself, and Rogers, but an American artist, Henry Inman, who had been commissioned to paint William's portrait by one of his American editors, Professor Henry Reed, of Philadelphia. Reed enjoyed a relationship with the poet unique among foreign editors: William was impressed by his understanding of the poems and the quality of his publications and the two men had kept up a warm correspondence over the years, in which William had often drawn Reed's attention to his latest publications. To the Wordsworths' astonishment, Inman required only half-hour sittings, and completed the portrait in just nine, but, Dora declared, it was 'by far the best painted likeness yet taken – merely the head & neck – large as life an oval form – manly & unaffected & tho not highly poetical in expression perhaps sufficiently so to pass for a Poet – my Mother even is quite satisfied – the likeness as to features is perfect'. A remarkably candid head-and-shoulders portrait, it is indeed so realistic it could easily be mistaken for a photograph.[57]

Another visitor to Rydal Mount in September was Faber, who had just gained William's permission to reprint his *Stanzas Suggested in a Steamboat off Saint Bees' Heads* in his *Life of St Bega.* It was an unexceptionable request – the poem was about St Bega's life – but what Faber did with it was not. He printed it in Newman's *Lives of the English Saints*, with a prefatory note, praising the poem as 'a fresh instance of the remarkable way in which [Wordsworth's] poems ... anticipate the revival of catholic doctrines among us' and proof of William's own 'affectionate reverence for the catholic past'. It was clear, when they met now, that William was beginning to have reservations about Faber. 'He is in the habit of using strong expressions, so that what he says must be taken with some qualification', William told Miss Fenwick. 'This practise in so very pious, good and able a man is deeply to be regretted.' They talked, at length, about Faber's own poetry, which William urged him to give up. 'A man like him cannot serve two Masters. He has vowed himself as a Minister of the Gospel to the service of God. He is of that temperament that if he writes verses the Spirit must *possess* him, and the practise master him, to the great injury of his work as a Priest.'[58]

Entertaining a party of Quakers on the terrace a few days later, he revealed that, whatever tinge of disillusionment had crept over his relationship with Faber, his belief in the central doctrine of redemption, which Faber had brought to him, remained undiminished. Watching the landscape emerge with perfect clearness after a wet morning, William commented, 'It is like the human heart emerging from sorrow, shone on by the grace of God.' When he was asked whether he thought the scenery had any effect on the minds of poorer people, he replied that he believed it did, that it dwelt silently within them, though they could not express it in neat phrases. 'How constantly mountains are mentioned in Scripture as the scene of extraordinary events', he pondered aloud:

> the Law was given on a mountain, Christ was transfigured on a mountain, and on a mountain the great Act of our Redemption was accomplished, and I cannot believe but that when the poor read of these things in their Bibles, and the frequent mention of mountains in the Psalms, their minds glow at the thought of their own mountains, and they realise it all more clearly than others.[59]

When William spoke of the poor in this way, he meant the rural poor, who were natives of the Lakes. His view of the urban poor, from the manufacturing districts, was quite different, as he was about to make clear, very publicly, to the mortification and embarrassment of his friends.

In the latter half of September, the Wordsworths learned that a new company, the Kendal and Windermere Railway, had been formed, with the express intention of linking Kendal with the Lancaster and Carlisle Railway at Oxenholme and carrying the line through as far as Lowwood, on Windermere. There could be no financial justification for extending the line so far merely for the sake of the inhabitants; it was obvious that the developers expected to recoup their costs and make their profits from an influx of working-class tourists from the manufacturing towns of Yorkshire and Lancashire. It was equally obvious to someone as shrewd as William that the railway would not stop just outside Ambleside. A railway was already under construction between Cockermouth and Keswick, which would ultimately link up the great towns of Whitehaven and Workington to the west, and Penrith to the east. All that would be missing, were the line to Lake Windermere completed, would be a link between Lake Windermere and Keswick – which could run, as the road did, only straight through the Vales of Rydal and Grasmere.[60] The view from Rydal Mount, which had been a source of daily pleasure and inspiration to the poet, would never be the same.

William's whole spirit revolted against this desecration of his paradise: once again, as he had done when protesting against local enclosures, he would become the voice of the silent hills. 'Is there no nook of English ground secure From rash assault?' he wrote, in a sonnet composed in response to the threat.

Plead for thy peace, thou beautiful romance
Of nature; and, if human hearts be dead,
Speak, passing winds; ye torrents, with your strong
And constant voice, protest against the wrong.

The sonnet was published in the *Morning Post* on 12 October and was rapidly reprinted in most of the other national and provincial newspapers. There were many other opponents of the scheme, particularly among the proprietors of land over which the railway would run, but William's name, his status as Poet Laureate and his willingness to stand forward publicly, made it seem as if he alone was barring the way of progress. In the age of railway mania, this appeared to be sheer folly. Inevitably, as most defenders of mere beauty are, he was accused of being reactionary, élitist, selfish and even, when his sonnet *Steamboats, Viaducts, and Railways* was quoted, or his reputation as the poet of the poor cited, hypocritical. 'Now that the rail road is coming home to Ambleside, he does not like it. This mere poetical view would equally oppose high-roads', his hitherto loyal disciple Barron Field sneered, in what was the typical response. 'There will always be plenty of nooks for rural retirement.'[61]

Despite his seventy-four years, William flung himself into the campaign with all the vigour of a man half his age. He wrote to Gladstone, who, as President of the Board of Trade, would have to present the Board's report on the bill for the new railway to Parliament, begging him to 'give it more attention than its apparent importance may call for'. He wrote to another old friend, General Charles Pasley, who was now Inspector General of Railways, with the same request:

The traffic will be found quite contemptible, the *staple* of this country is its beauty and that will be destroyed by such a nuisance being carried through these narrow vales. At present nothing is publicly said of its being carried farther than within a mile of Ambleside, but that is all nonsense. Attempts will assuredly be made, and at no distant Period, to carry it on to Keswick, to Maryport, notwithstanding the high ground that parts Westmorland from Cumberland.[62]

William's efforts were interrupted by the necessity of a visit to Leamington to see Isabella Fenwick. He needed to make his peace with her, and that was probably the only motive that could have taken him from home at this time. Dora came over from Belle Isle to take charge of Dorothy and her parents set off for Leamington, where they would pay visits to both Miss Fenwick and Anna Ricketts's family and see Bertha and Herbert Hill in their new home at Warwick. The remainder of their time was divided between Cambridge, where they were invited to stay at Trinity Lodge by their old friends, the new Master William Whewell, and his wife, the former Cordelia Marshall, and at Elton, near Peterborough, where Faber was 'doing a great deal of good, among a flock which had been long neglected'. At Cambridge William was an honoured guest at a meeting of the Camden Society, a High Church group committed to the revival of historic Church principles, particularly in building. Archdeacon Thorp, the president, in welcoming him, claimed that 'He might be considered one of the founders of the Society. He had sown the seed which was breaking out now among them, as in other directions, to the recall of whatever was pure and imaginative, whatever was not merely utilitarian, to the service of both Church and State.' William himself went away delighted to learn that the young men of the university were more interested in religion than before and, more especially, that Low Church views were held in general disrepute and High Church ones were prevailing 'without any tendency to Popery as far as appears'.[63]

The journey home lay through Northampton, where the Wordsworths were unexpectedly detained for two hours by the crowds gathered to greet the Queen, who was passing through the town on her way to Burleigh House. Every village for more than twenty miles around was decked with flowers and triumphal arches and in the town itself the bells were ringing to greet her. These manifestations of loyalty and affection delighted William, who was as anxious as anyone to get a glimpse of the Queen. One wonders what she would have thought had she known that the elderly white-haired gentleman who had climbed on to the roof of the coach to get a better view of her was her Poet Laureate. William saw only 'a woman's face under a black bonnet', but regretted afterwards that it did not strike him at the time to 'throw off my feelings in verse, for I had ample time to have done so, and might perhaps have contrived to present through some of the authorities the tribute to my royal Mistress'.[64]

After a scant month's absence, William and Mary returned to Rydal Mount early in November to find Dora so unwell that she was unable to rejoin the Quillinans on Belle Isle and was again confined to the sofa in her parental home. 'Mr Wordsworth is returned in very good looks, & considerably tranquillized about the Railroad', Mary Arnold observed. The managers of what William called the 'obnoxious' Kendal and Windermere Railway had modified their plans in his absence. The terminus was now to be a mile from Bowness, instead of Lowwood, and it was proposed that a steamer would bring the trippers down Windermere to Ambleside.[65]

Though this decision reduced the immediate threat to the vales of Rydal and Grasmere, it did not remove it altogether and, in any case, the principle remained the same. William was not content to let the matter drop. He wrote two long letters to the *Morning Post* which were published on 11 and 20 December. If his sonnet had roused criticism, this correspondence drew upon him, 'as I knew it would, from the low-minded and ill-bred a torrent of abuse through the Press – both in London Glasgow and elsewhere, but as it has afforded me an opportunity of directing attention to some important truths I care little for such rancorous scurrility, the natural outbreak of self conceit and stupid ignorance'. The strength of his language, however, suggests that some of the barbs had shot home, and it would have been surprising if they had not. The two letters were an honest expression of William's opinion. He did not mince his words, but his turn for the inflammatory phrase, which had been evident throughout his pamphleteering career, now worked against him. His three main arguments against bringing the railway into the heart of the Lakes were simple, effective and, as any visitor today would acknowledge, basically true. The chief attractions of the district were 'its beauty and its character of seclusion and retirement', which a large-scale influx of tourists would destroy. Secondly, anyone who truly wanted to visit the Lakes could already do so easily, whatever his station in life: it cost nothing to walk (as William himself had done many a time) the nine miles from Kendal to Windermere. Thirdly, and more contentiously, he argued that a true appreciation of the scenery was 'neither inherent in mankind, nor a necessary consequence of even a comprehensive education'. Factory hands would gain more benefit from a quiet stroll through the fields near their homes on a Sunday than from being hurtled through the Lakes on cheap railway excursions paid for by their employers. 'Once for all let me declare that it is not against Railways but against the abuse of them that I am contending', he declared towards the end of his second letter. In opposing the undertaking, he spoke not merely for the inhabitants of the Lakes, whose way of life was threatened, but 'for the sake of every one, however humble his condition, who coming hither shall bring with him an eye to perceive, and a heart to feel and worthily enjoy'.

There was nothing new in any of these arguments. William had been making the same points for forty years, complaining about the fashionable Lakers who drove past reading their guide books, or falling asleep in their carriages, instead of walking, looking and genuinely appreciating for themselves. In setting himself against the railway, however, he laid himself open to the charge of being what we would call a snob. Comments about the inevitable increase in wrestling matches, horse and boat races, and pot-houses and beer-shops, catering for the taste of these working-class visitors, did not help. Nor did references to the 'Advance, of the Ten thousand ... We should have the whole of Lancashire, and no small part of Yorkshire, pouring in upon us to meet the men of Durham, and the borderers from Cumberland and Northumberland.' Such remarks played into the hands of his opponents, who summed up his view, in the famous opening line of Horace's ode, *Odi profanum vulgus, et arceo*, 'I loathe the common crowd, and drive them from me.'[66]

William refused to accept such criticism. In January 1845 he reprinted his two letters in Kendal as a pamphlet which he could circulate amongst his friends and acquaintances and send to all those whom he lobbied against this 'vile Gambling Speculation'. He drew up a list of all the land-owners who would be affected and urged Graves, the curate of Bowness, to get them all to sign a petition against the development, warning, as a seasoned campaigner himself, that 'if they sign neuter, in parliamentary construction it will mean favorable'. He attended meetings of Railway Opposition.[67] But he was fighting a lost cause and he knew it. 'I have not the least hope of preventing the Bill being sent to a Committee,' he wrote to Robinson in February, 'but my Letters may prepare an efficient Opposition to another [Bill] which will surely follow this', namely, for a railway from Ambleside to Keswick. In this he was indeed successful. The railway would be carried only as far as Bowness – for which every lover of the Lakes must be forever indebted to him. But it was not without its personal cost. In their recommendation to Parliament, the Board of Trade administered a very public reproof to William.

> We must . . . state that an argument which goes to deprive the artisan of the offered means of occasionally changing his narrow abode, his crowded streets, his wearisome task and unwholesome toil, for the fresh air, and the healthful holiday which sends him back to his work refreshed and invigorated – simply that individuals who object . . . may retain to themselves the exclusive enjoyment of scenes which should be open alike to all . . . appears to us to be an argument wholly untenable.

What is more, because his opposition was misunderstood in this way, there is no doubt that his reputation suffered. It was the eternal dilemma of the artist who destroys the thing he loves best by popularizing it. Barron Field was not alone in asking how the man who had spent almost the last half-century creating a taste for mountains and lakes by extolling them in his poetry could object if the inhabitants of Liverpool and Manchester wanted to see the places he had made famous for themselves? 'I wish he would either complete "The Recluse" or lock up his desk', Field wrote indignantly to Robinson.[68]

27. *Fixed and Irremovable Grief*

The Christmas of 1844–5 was enlivened by the presence of a newcomer to the Lakes, Harriet Martineau, who had overcome deafness to make a name for herself as the authoress of tales of political economy. Robinson was a great admirer of Miss Martineau, as both a writer and a person, having met her for the first time in 1832, and he was determined to effect a meeting between her and William. This would be difficult. She was staying with another political economist, William Rathbone Greg, who had made his fortune in the cotton trade and retired to Ambleside in 1842 for the sake of his wife's health. The Gregs felt that they had been snubbed by the Wordsworths, who had never called during that time, so it would be awkward to meet there. More importantly, the Wordsworths were appalled by Miss Martineau's widely publicized claims to have recovered from an incurable disease by means of a fashionable form of hypnotism, mesmerism. 'The poet entertaining otherwise a very friendly feeling towards her has so bad an opinion of Mesmerism that if he could he would decline seeing her', Robinson confided in his brother.

The meeting eventually took place on 16 January, on neutral ground, at Dr Davy's new house on the Rydal side of Ambleside. Davy hosted a large dinner party, including William, Robinson, Graves, the Gregs, the Davys and the Fletchers. 'By tacit consent the conversation was on purely indifferent matters,' Robinson noted. 'This was better than controversy.' There would have been plenty of opportunity for dispute. Miss Martineau and the Gregs were ardent believers in, and practitioners of, mesmerism; William, Davy and his mother-in-law, Mrs Fletcher, were all scornfully sceptical. William was a High Churchman, a conservative and passionate advocate of the Ten Hours' Bill, which would reduce the daily hours worked by factory hands to a maximum of ten; Greg was a Unitarian, an ultra-radical and, as a cotton-mill owner, opposed any reduction in his workers' hours. In the circumstances, Robinson's comment that 'Any thing like a dispassionate discussion was out of the question' appears an understatement. The two men were civil, but notably cool, towards each other, though William, meeting and liking Mrs Greg, let it be known that his failure to call had been the fault of old age and distance, rather than a deliberate slight. Nevertheless, Robinson realized that there was little likelihood of a warmer relationship developing between the two men.[1]

The same was true of William and Miss Martineau, both of whom carefully refrained from comment on each other before their mutual friend. Robinson rightly took this to mean that they were both afraid of saying what he would not want to hear. Miss Martineau, though her letters of the time were much more favourably disposed, reserved her venom for a snide account in her *Autobiography*, in which, against all the evidence, she claimed that the Wordsworths sought her opinion as to the possibility of mesmerism curing Dora, mocked William's northern accent, frostily misunderstood his attempts at humour and declared that his 'pieces', as she termed his poems, were not enough to make the man a poet. William was more generous, admitting to Isabella Fenwick that he found Miss Martineau's manners 'a little abrupt and peremptory – But it might be that I was mistaken, I mean in not making sufficient allowance first for her being a Dissenter, and next for being what is somewhat vulgarly called a "BLUE" [-stocking] ... for everybody else seems to like her without the least drawback.' Miss Martineau was sufficiently enchanted with the scenery to declare her intention of living in the Lakes for six months, eventually settling permanently in her own house at Ambleside. Robinson predicted that she would not 'become cordial' with the Wordsworths, but even she admitted that they were very kind to her.[2]

The Wordsworths' relations with Robinson himself were more than 'cordial', despite a widening gap between them, particularly on religious grounds. William had been pained by what Robinson proudly called 'my unremitted exertions' to secure the passage of the Dissenters' Chapels Act of 1844, which granted Unitarians legal title to their religious property, including chapels and burial grounds. William's dislike of Unitarianism had not diminished with the years. His first response had been to write a letter of protest, but, unwilling to cause offence to his old friend, he withheld it, reserving his comments for discussion when they next met in person. At Christmas, when they had that discussion, Robinson felt honour-bound to tell William that he was now a member of the Unitarian Association. To Robinson's evident relief, William received the news 'kindly for he really has no bitterness about him'.[3]

'The *beauty* of the season with us has exceeded anything –', William enthused early in January, 'such glorious effects of sunshine and shadow, and skies that are quite heavenly in the evenings especially; with moon and mountain-clouds setting each other off in a way that really has transported us to look upon'. Mary, too, admitted to Miss Martineau that 'the beauty of our valley made us too fond of life, – too little ready to leave it'. The lake was frozen over, so James Dixon, the good-natured 'Skaiting-Master' to all the novices in the vale, and even 'Keswick' John, who was enjoying a brief remission from his consumption, were able to skate several times.[4]

John's fate was inevitable, but Dora's was not. Her family were deeply concerned about her. Throughout the winter and spring she ailed one thing after another, mostly, as her husband and mother suspected, caused by her habit of starving herself. As colds and coughs succeeded one another, each one further wearing down her already fragile frame, Quillinan began to formulate the idea of taking her to Portugal, where the climate and a complete change of lifestyle might restore her. His brother owned a pretty little holiday villa at the mouth of the Douro, three miles from Oporto, and he offered this to the Quillinans for as long as they wished. 'Dr Davy, Miss F[enwick], *Mr* W & even *Mrs* W (though very loth) concur in the prudence of accepting the offer', Quillinan explained to Robinson in April. 'Two great tugs there are "Daddy & Mammy are 75 – says D[ora] & she looks in my face as if her heart would break"'. Apart from the fear of leaving her elderly parents, however, Dora was 'hopeful & eager to go'. Quillinan began to make travel plans, which were abruptly broken off on 7 April, William's seventy-fifth birthday, when they all gathered at Miss Fenwick's lodgings in Ambleside to hold a celebratory dinner. Everyone talked eagerly of the Oporto plan, but one person, Mary, said nothing '& it was too evident that she was very low on the subject'. Dora was immediately flung into uncertainty as to whether she ought to go and Quillinan, with his usual haste, decided to throw up the scheme: 'if she went it could do her no good to be fretting because she would feel that her Mother was fretting. Mrs W's anxiety is natural, & Dora's unwillingness to pain her, & to leave her at 75, is all right – but it is a pity that Mrs W does not take more cheerfully to the only plan likely to restore her daughter's health.'

A week after William had informed Moxon that Dora had 'given up the thought of going to Portugal', there was a complete change of heart. The concerted efforts of William, Miss Fenwick and, especially, Dr Davy, whose professional opinion carried more weight, convinced Mary that she had to accept this temporary parting. Before she had a chance to have second thoughts, the Quillinans set off for London on 23 April, staying with the Hoares while they arranged passports and tickets, and sailing for Oporto during the first week in May. By a happy coincidence, William had received a second invitation from the Lord Chancellor to attend the Queen's Ball on 25 April, so he could accompany his daughter at least as far as London. William had just told Moxon that he could not muster courage to face the fatigues and late dinners of London, but this was an honour he could not again decline. After two years as Poet Laureate, it was only 'right & decent' that he should not defer his formal presentation to the Queen any longer.[5]

William and the Quillinans arrived at Robinson's on 24 April, took an early breakfast with their friend, then went their separate ways, the Quillinans to Mrs Hoare's and William to stay with Moxon. 'I hope he will not get involved in London parties, for he is not very well, & we are all very anxious about him',

Quillinan told Robinson. Neither Mary nor James accompanied the poet, so he would have to fend for himself. He was in a great state of nerves at the thought of his presentation, but both Moxon and Rogers, who was well practised in such affairs, rallied round. Rogers, who was now eighty-two, was remarkably untouched by age, physically or mentally. He coached William through the ceremony, arranged with the Lord Chamberlain that he should not have to pass through the crowds but would be formally noticed, and lent him his own court dress. So, wearing Rogers's bag wig, plum-coloured, high-collared coat with deep cuffs and large silver buttons, shirt with a white jabot falling over a waistcoat, knee breeches, white stockings and flat shoes with silver buckles, and with Sir Humphry Davy's sword buckled to his side, 'science and art being thus fraternally united', William made his way to the Palace. 'The reception given me by the young Queen at her Ball was most gracious', William told everyone. The wife of the American minister Edward Everett was so moved that, as she told Rogers afterwards, she shed tears. 'To see a grey haired Man 75 years of age kneeling down in a large assembly, to kiss the hand of a young Woman is a sight for which institutions essentially democratic do not prepare a spectator of either sex', William intoned to Reed. Less pompously, he admitted in company that the graciousness of the Queen's reception was 'I daresay' to be attributed solely to his years, 'most likely she had not read many of my works'.

Flushed with excitement after this triumph, William, still in the court dress, called on Rogers on his way back to Moxon's. As they walked together, William's attention was arrested by a pretty little girl, sitting alone on the grass, and, as he usually did, he stopped to chat with her. Pleased with her ingenuous answers, he put one hand on her head, delved into his pockets with the other and produced a copy of his *Selections*, which he solemnly presented to her, 'telling her to look well, and note his person; to be sure also to observe well the time of day, and the spot, and to recollect that that little book had been given to her by the author, the celebrated William Wordsworth'.[6]

As the day of Dora's departure approached, William grew steadily more depressed. His eye was inflamed again, he caught a cold and he was filled with apprehensions about his daughter's health and the three-day sea journey she faced. When Robinson dined with him at Mrs Hoare's on 3 May he was 'in wretched spirits And spoke not a word to any one . . . A more uncomfortable dinner I have seldom had.' Perhaps so as not to prolong his agony, the Quillinans left a day earlier than expected. Father and daughter had an emotional parting, neither knowing whether they would ever see the other alive again and, in a final kindly gesture of which Miss Fenwick would have approved, William gave Dora £20, so that she would not be short of money should the need arise. He did not accompany her to Southampton, where, on 7 May, she embarked on the Oporto steam packet with her husband and stepdaughter Rotha. Seasickness hit her straight away and she had to be carried 'like a dead pig' down to her cabin and remain there for the rest of the voyage. Five days later, however, they were all safely installed in John

Quillinan's lovely villa, where he had thoughtfully hung a print of Gillies's portrait of William in Dora's bedroom to welcome her. 'Depend upon it, this "great experiment" will turn out well', Quillinan assured the Wordsworths, while Dora admitted that the only cloud on her happiness was that she knew that her family were anxious about her and could not see the astounding improvement in her appearance that had already taken place.[7]

The day the Quillinans sailed, William was again summoned to court, this time to attend a royal levee. Robinson feared that he would not be fit to go, but it proved a useful, if disappointing, distraction from his grief and anxiety. Prompted by Rogers, Lord Northampton took the poet under his wing and escorted him to the reception. It was 'an idle act him going', Robinson reported, 'for he exchanged not a word with the Queen.' Apart from the court events, it was an unusually quiet visit, William's ill-health providing an excuse to avoid constant socializing. Both at Moxon's and at Mrs Hoare's, however, he was much gratified by the attentions of Tennyson. The two men were fellow guests at a dinner party at Moxon's, with Aubrey de Vere and a small number of other friends. Before they left, Tennyson approached the old poet and, speaking in a low voice so that he could not be overheard but 'with a perceptible emotion', 'expressed in the strongest terms his gratitude to my writings'. De Vere, observing from the sidelines, said, 'The old man looked very much pleased, more so indeed than I ever saw him look on any other occasion; shook hands with him heartily, and thanked him affectionately.' The two poets were aeons apart in their taste and style (Tennyson complained that he 'could not inflame [Wordsworth's] imagination in the least!' with his description of a tropical island where the trees were the colour of blood when they came into leaf), but William had no hesitation in granting the palm to the younger man. 'He is decidedly the first of our living Poets, and I hope will live to give the world still better things.' It was therefore not surprising that William felt 'far from indifferent' to Tennyson's voluntary and obviously sincere compliment.[8]

William did not prolong his stay in London after his daughter's departure, fortuitously sharing a carriage on the north-bound train with General Pasley, whom he no doubt took the opportunity to lobby on the Kendal and Windermere Railway. 'I shall never forget your and Mrs Moxon's kindness to me during my late residence with you, nor Miss Moxon's never ceasing attentions', he wrote from Rydal Mount on 12 May; '. . . Mr Rogers's care and concern for me were you know unbounded and I shall ever remain duly sensible of it.'[9]

While staying with Moxon, William had had much discussion with him about his next publication. A suggestion from Robinson, that Moxon should print a volume containing William's collected prose works, was on the cards, but the need for a new edition of poems was more pressing. William had very decided ideas on how he wanted this to be done. It was to be a single volume, printed in double columns, for cheapness, but it was to have the embellishments which had made the suppressed Burns edition so attractive. Instead of the print of the Pickersgill portrait, of which he had an 'utter dislike . . . It does me and him also great injustice', he wanted an engraving of his bust by Chantrey as the frontispiece. On the title-page, he wanted a vignette of Rydal Mount, for which his neighbour Mary Fletcher was asked to provide a drawing 'from the best point of view'. He also wanted to leave out the prose prefaces and supplement, 'my own wish would be that now the Poems should be left to speak for themselves without them', but Moxon feared such an omission might harm the sale. As a compromise, they agreed that they would be included, but relegated to the back of the volume.[10]

By the beginning of June William and Carter had begun the laborious task of preparing the new edition. *Poems, Chiefly of Early and Late Years* would have to be incorporated for the first time and, as always, every poem would have to be 'tinkered'. Optimistically, William hoped it would be ready in time for the Christmas market. A few weeks later, Robinson was alarmed to learn from Moxon that the new edition would contain 'many alterations'. 'I hope they are merely verbal', he muttered gloomily, but he was right in suspecting that they were not. Taking his cue from Reed's American edition of 1837, William had greatly expanded the number of poems included in the classification of imagination.[11] More importantly, his Christianization of his verse had continued.

William was airily dismissive about Robinson's fears. 'The alterations of which you heard, are almost exclusively confined to a few of the Juvenile Poems', but they included some significant changes to *The Excursion*, one of his best-loved poems, which could hardly be described as 'juvenile'. In the verse preface, which was itself part of *The Recluse*, William had referred to Milton as 'holiest of men'. Faber loathed Milton for denying Christ's divinity: 'accursed be his blasphemous memory', he had raved in a letter to his brother in 1843. Unable to persuade William to suppress his sonnet 'Milton! thou should'st be living at this hour', he succeeded in having 'holiest of men' altered to 'the Bard – In holiest mood'. Even more radically, Margaret's death in *The Ruined Cottage*, which had been absorbed into the second book of *The Excursion*, became an explicitly Christian one. In lines added for the first time, the Pedlar declared that Margaret, 'in her worst distress', had often felt

> The unbounded might of prayer; and learned, with soul
> Fixed on the Cross, that consolation springs,
> From sources deeper far than deepest pain,
> For the meek Sufferer.

In place of the suggestion that 'sorrow and despair' could be overcome by the contemplation of tranquillity, the lines were changed to say that such griefs could never obtain

> . . . .dominion o'er the enlightened spirit
> Whose meditative sympathies repose
> Upon the breast of Faith.

Less radical, but important as an indication of Faber's influence, was the introduction of three new poems in the *Ecclesiastical Sonnets* series: all three were written, specifically at Faber's request, to celebrate 'more explicitly our debt to the papacy'. They did not go as far as Faber hoped, but William intended them 'to qualify or mitigate the condemnation which by conscience I am compelled to pass upon the abuses of the Roman See'.[12]

Now, in his seventy-sixth year, William could still surprise even himself by being prompted to write new poems while he was editing the old. 'It was only a few days ago that I was able to put into Verse the Matter of a short Poem which had been in my mind with a determination and a strong desire to write upon it for more than thirty years', William wrote to a friend on 24 June. The poem rightly belonged in the *Poems on the Naming of Places* series and therefore to the opening years of the nineteenth century. It celebrated the 'twin peaks' between White Moss Common and Bainriggs, where the 'two adventurous Sisters', Mary and Sara Hutchinson, had loved to climb for the view over the merging vales of Rydal and Grasmere. Perhaps because of its subject matter, it shows little diminution in power and the casual reader could be forgiven for not realizing the decades that separated its composition from that of its brethren.[13]

The same could not be said of the sonnet *At Furness Abbey*, written about the same time and inspired by a scene witnessed by Miss Fenwick. She and Kate Southey had taken a party of Arnold and Davy children to Furness Abbey, where a new railway line was being built '*profanely* near this holy pile'. The directors had originally demanded that part of the ruins should be demolished and the line run straight through the abbey, but Lord Burlington had persuaded them to deviate their course slightly, so that it was now being built around the ruins, but so close that passengers on the railway could almost touch the great east window. He '*ought* to have insisted on a still *greater distance*', the indignant Miss Fenwick scolded. The navvies building the line appeared to feel the same, for as William observed in his sonnet, they wandered round the ruins in their lunch break with 'grave demeanour' and seemed 'to feel the spirit of the place'. 'Profane Despoilers', he accused those who had planned and permitted the line,

stand ye not reproved,
While thus these simple-hearted men are moved?

'Sacred as that relic of the devotion of our ancestors deserves to be kept,' William wrote of Furness Abbey, 'there are temples of Nature, temples built by the Almighty, which have a still higher claim to be left unviolated.' He meant, of course, the Vale of Rydal, and one can only imagine his feelings when, a few weeks after writing this sonnet, he saw the railway surveyors at work, planning a line that was to run through Rydal Park and immediately behind Rydal Mount.[14]

William could be under no illusions about the seriousness of this threat. The new railway line about to be built between Cockermouth and Workington would run straight through his son's gardens at Brigham, on an embankment between the parsonage and the river and pass within ten yards of his dining-room window. The ill-fated parsonage, whose site had been chosen with such care for its views, which had cost over £1,200 to build and drained so much of John's income, would be uninhabitable – and John, who was still abroad with his wife, knew nothing of what was planned. Burning with indignation at this injustice, William immediately demanded compensation from the railway company. He soon realized that this would be inadequate, as it would not reimburse all those, including the Church bodies, who had contributed towards the cost. 'The more I think about the Brigham Vicarage as it will be affected by the Railway, the more am I convinced, that justice to the Church and the present Incumbent, requires the Insertion in the Act of a clause enjoining the Erection of a new Parsonage', he wrote to Lord Lonsdale. With the aid of 'Keswick' John's stepfather, the attorney Mr Lightfoot, and Willy, he organized a petition to Parliament to be drawn up to that effect. This was successful and, before the end of the year, William and Willy were back at Brigham to choose a site for John's new vicarage.[15]

John's affairs seemed to be going from bad to worse. With his wife and two children he had spent the winter in Rome, because Isabella insisted on following her favourite doctor there from the baths of Lucca. She then returned to Lucca, with the children, but John's position was becoming untenable. He could not afford to remain abroad, unable to earn his living and yet having to pay a curate to perform his duty. He therefore decided to return to England, prompting Isabella to write a 'strange & disagreeable' letter to Dora, accusing her of deceit and complaining of the rest of her family. Dora was so heart-stricken by such unexpected and unmerited abuse that she promptly suffered her first relapse in months. The 'riddle' of Isabella's choosing to remain abroad seemed inexplicable; Isabella herself claimed she was submitting to the will of others, but, as Dora said, 'when she has a strong desire she will carry it into act & fact depend upon it'.[16]

John had no sooner returned to England, than he was unexpectedly forced to go chasing back to Italy for reasons that are not clear. He left on 18 June, at five in the morning, taking with him all four of his sons who had hitherto remained in England, the youngest of whom had only just celebrated his fourth birthday. Isabella had been variously diagnosed with an ulcer on her womb, haemorrhoids and an inflammation of the lungs, but the children, including the four boys who had not seen her for two years, were to be left in her care. They would spend the remainder of the summer in Lucca, then the two oldest boys would accompany their clergyman tutor to his winter residence in Pisa, while Jane and the younger boys returned to Rome with their mother. In the spring, Isabella said, she hoped to bring them all home. With this John had to be content, returning to England for the second time that year to resume his duties at Plumbland. 'To such matter of fact people as myself these seem strange proceedings,' Mary wrote, 'but we are old-fashioned people and can only submit – I will not say without disturbance of mind.'[17]

William took refuge from these troubles in activity. He advised Miss Martineau on the purchase of the land on which she would build her house, The Knoll, at Ambleside, characteristically throwing himself down among the hazel bushes to find the right orientation to secure the best prospects. He also helped her to lay out her garden and even planted two stone pine trees on the slope beneath her terrace wall, washing his hands in the watering-pot afterwards, then taking her hand in his, wishing her many happy years in her new abode. At seventy-five years of age, however, his ability to labour in his own grounds was diminishing. He caught cold after overexerting himself chopping down and pruning trees and then, having recovered from that, took a second nasty tumble from the Mount which left him bruised and strained.[18]

Then, of course, there was the distraction of the visitors, some 200 of them between the beginning of June and the end of September, including Isabella Fenwick, Kate Southey, Emmie Fisher and her brother Herbert, Charles Wordsworth and his daughter, and blind John Monkhouse from the Stow. There was the usual crop of distinguished Americans, General Williamson of Pennsylvania, the poet William Bryant and, most welcome of all, William's American editor Professor Henry Reed, whom he now met for the first time.[19] William Howitt, the Quaker who had come to Mary's rescue in Nottingham so many years earlier, paid a visit, which he described in *Homes and Haunts of the Most Eminent British Poets*, published in 1849. Howitt ventured to remark that the laurels needed pruning (perhaps prompting William to do so, with such ill effect), and was told that a certain general (Williamson, perhaps), being shown round the grounds by James, had remarked how appropriate it was that laurels should flourish in the Laureate's gardens. 'By this,' William informed Howitt, 'James acquired two new pieces of intelligence; first, that the laurel was a symbol of eminence, and, that his master was an eminent man, of both which facts he had been before very innocently ignorant.' It was fortunate that the laurels grew in such abundance, for they were the object of every souvenir hunter, from the new bride who was overheard telling her husband to 'get on the wall & snatch a sprig of laurel, or anything; we must take something away', to Alan Stevenson, the civil engineer building Skerryvore lighthouse in the Atlantic, thirty miles west of Iona, who framed three laurel leaves from Rydal Mount, a lock of William's hair and his autograph as if they were holy relics and put them in his 'sanctum' to cheer his solitude.[20]

There were so many casual visitors who came bearing letters of introduction which could not be ignored that William often lapsed into auto-pilot. 'I never liked seeing him go the round of his garden and terraces, relating to persons whose very names he had not attended to, particulars about his writing and other affairs which each stranger flattered himself was a confidential communication to himself', Miss Martineau complained, but she in particular had due cause to do so. In August she brought two eminent Educational Commissioners, Seymour Tremenheere and Henry Tufnell, to meet William. Increasingly deaf, the poet had not caught their names, subjected them to the usual tour and bowed them out, wishing them enjoyment of the Lake scenery before they had a chance to mention popular education. That same evening Miss Martineau received a note from Rydal Mount, saying that William had heard the two commissioners were in the district and would much like to meet them! William and Tremenheere came away from the meeting with the impression that the other had been preaching to the converted, but at least they were in agreement.[21]

Sending William some hefty volumes of Privy Council Minutes and Reports on popular education in September, Tremenheere set out his belief, at length, that 'one of the most effective means towards ameliorating even the physical condition of the poor, is to afford them the opportunity of having their minds opened by a more enlarged and useful, as well as their hearts affected, by a religious Education'. 'I am well aware that no one is more alive to these matters than yourself', he wrote, asking William therefore to include 'an addition, however brief, in prose or verse' to his forthcoming volume, 'embodying your present impressions on the subject of elementary education'. The reason why the Educational Commissioner wanted the poet to do this must surely be unique: the poet's opinion

> would be of much value, and would greatly help to increase the growing sense of responsibility, which has been so long in abeyance among those whose positions, whether as Landlords or Manufacturers, make them answerable to a great extent for the condition of the lower classes on their estates or in their neighbourhoods. Happily, your voice is now more and more listened to; and (permit me to add) you may feel conscious that it will be more so yet. A word or two from you, in the present state of public opinion on this subject, would not, I am sure, be in vain.

Tremenheere was convinced he would get a sonnet for his trouble but that William would not bother to read the reports. In fact, William dutifully ploughed through the reports, suggested gently that they set too little value on 'the occupations of Children out of doors, under the direction, or by permission, of their Parents, comparatively with what they do or acquire in school'; objected, as one 'who spent half of his boyhood in running wild among the Mountains', to the suggestion that parents might be reconciled to the expense of schooling by the savings in wear and tear on clothes and shoe-leather; and quietly ignored the suggestion that he might make any sort of new contribution to the education debate.[22]

On 23 September William and Mary left Rydal Mount to pay a farewell visit to Brinsop Court. Tom had never recovered the full use of his limbs after his accident eight years earlier; he knew he would never be able to work the farm again and, as both his sons were now clergymen, there was no one to take over from him. After much soul-searching, he had therefore resigned the lease and he, his wife and two daughters, Ebba and Sarah, hoped to join his younger son, George, who was about to be presented to the living of Mathon, near Malvern, which was in the gift of William's nephew Chris. After viewing the rectory there, and determining to do a little gentle lobbying to raise funds for its improvement, William and Mary set off for home. They returned by York, where William was anxious to see for what was likely to be the last time his oldest surviving cousin, eighty-year-old Mary, the widow of Admiral Robinson, and by Leeds, where they stayed at Headingley with the Marshalls.[23]

The Wordsworths arrived at Rydal Mount on 4 November, after an absence of six weeks, which had inevitably delayed the new volume. There was only one sheet of poetry left to correct in proof, but then the tedious work of the notes and prefaces had to be tackled. Carter proved invaluable in proofreading; he also compiled an index of first lines as William found it impossible to give titles to a third of the poems. The book itself would simply be called *The Poems of William Wordsworth*, but for the first time the title-page would carry the roll-call of his honours: the DCL, Poet Laureateship and, as of this year, honorary membership of the Royal Society of Edinburgh and the Royal Irish Academy. William fussed over the engravings, demanding alterations to both that of Chantrey's bust (nose not curved enough, eyes too small) and that of Rydal Mount (porch too substantial, should only be trelliswork). By the end of November he was happy with the book but gloomy about its prospects. 'We are about to publish this expensive Vol. at a most unfavorable time', he told Moxon. 'Nothing is now thought of but railway shares. The Savings-banks are almost emptied of their old deposits, and scarcely any thing has come into them – all gone to Railway Speculation – a deplorable state of things.'[24]

Robinson, who received one of the first copies, thought it 'A handsome Vol: which makes a beautiful present'. When he came on his annual Christmas visit he suggested to William that it would be an appropriate gesture to have a copy specially got up for presentation to the Queen from her Laureate. Bound in green covers by Westley, the volume was fetched to Rydal Mount by Moxon and inscribed with an unrecognizably Wordsworthian poem, addressed to 'Queen, Wife and Mother', which expressed the hope that it might bring 'Some solace under weight of royal care'. Robinson undertook to convey the book safely back to London, where it was presented to the Queen by the Lord Chamberlain. Her Majesty apparently considered the offering 'very gratifying' and the inscription admirable and was pleased to present her Poet Laureate with an engraving of a portrait of the royal children.[25]

Moxon's arrival, on 27 December, for a week's visit, proved a welcome diversion: he 'very much improved our conversations in vivacity, as he brought with him a good deal of book gossip'. Robinson had enjoyed as hearty a welcome as ever when he came, ten days earlier, but he noticed immediately subtle changes which could have been perceived only by an old friend. The house was emptier than he had ever seen it before – the Quillinans being in Portugal and Miss Fenwick in lodgings at Ambleside. But William was, at last, beginning to show his age. Anxiety and grief at Dora's departure and John's troubles had taken their toll on his appearance, so that he now looked '*very* old'. He had been depressed by the deaths, in quick succession, of Mrs Coleridge, the much-wronged wife of Samuel Taylor; of thirty-four-year-old Julia Myers, only child of his long-dead cousin John Myers; and of his own cousin Sarah Crackanthorpe. 'Link after link is broken,' he wrote to Derwent Coleridge, 'and yet for the most part we do not bear those severings in mind as we ought to do'.[26]

He had also felt deeply the news that Faber had defected from the Church of England and become a Roman Catholic. Conscious that William would feel this as a betrayal, Faber had not even had the courage to write to him personally but had sent him a single-sentence circular letter, written by a clerk, announcing that he had, that day, been received into 'what he calls the Church', as William bitterly described it, and that he hoped to take communion and receive confirmation the following day.[27] Having had so much influence on the new edition, it was particularly galling that Faber's conversion was unintentionally timed almost exactly to coincide with its publication. It appeared to prove what his critics and those of the Oxford Movement had said all along: that far from aiming at a spiritual revival of the Anglican Church, these High Churchmen were not 'catholics', as they claimed, but closet Roman Catholics who wanted to restore the Papacy in England. Robinson, a die-hard Protestant, took care to remind William that he had not carried out his intention of introducing into the new edition 'a note expressing his regret that he had ever uttered a word favourable to Puseyism'. William's justification for this omission, which Robinson thought 'a very insufficient reason', was 'that he was at last quite tired'.[28]

It was a significant admission. After almost fifty years of meticulous, intensive, thoughtful labouring over his poems, William had reached the end of the road. The single-volume edition of 1845 was the last he would revise thoroughly and see personally through the press. When Moxon wrote to him at the end of January 1846, informing him that a new edition of the seven volumes was required, William declined to be involved. 'I really am tired with getting up these Poems, as you witnessed when you were here', he replied. 'When we were together at Rydal we agreed upon what was to be done, and I have no fear of entrusting the work to your superintendence.' If Moxon was reluctant to proceed alone (as well he might be, after long experience of working with the poet), William suggested he send the proof sheets to Carter at Carlisle.[29]

On Christmas Eve, the Wordsworths heard the devastating news that their youngest grandson, four-year-old Edward, had died in Rome. Isabella had not bothered to inform her husband that three of their children were 'in the fever' and her letter informing the Wordsworths of Edward's death on 10 December did not arrive at Rydal Mount until the 24th, by which time the child had been buried in the leafy oasis of the Protestant cemetery in Rome. Terrified for the safety of his remaining children, John decided to return immediately to Italy and bring his family home. Leaving a letter asking William to organize the retrospective permission for absence from his bishop and a curate to take the duty, John set off on New Year's Day, passing by Rydal Mount in the mailcoach without stopping, for fear that his parents might dissuade him. In fact, they were as anxious as he to see the family back in England; they simply doubted his ability to persuade Isabella either to return or to part with her children. Either way, the future for their marriage looked bleak. 'Even if his wife recovers her health, nothing can heal the worse and sorer sicknesses which through her illness have grown up and been fully revealed', Sara Coleridge wrote gloomily to Miss Fenwick; '– nothing, I fear, can turn *her* into a wise woman or *him* into an energetic high-minded man ... A wearisome wasting thing it will be, from year to year, to see that couple wronging each other and mismanaging their children – one pulling this way and the other that.'[30]

'My poor wife has been much shattered by these events,' William observed. He had been able to divert his grief into a sonnet, 'Why should we weep or mourn, Angelic boy', but Mary, who had loved, nurtured and been a second mother to the four boys in their own mother's absence, found it harder to cope. When Miss Martineau came to dinner and, 'having no tact whatever or ability to perceive who believes & who disbelieves in her stories – Or caring nothing about the *Sym*pathy or the *Dis*pathy of her hearers', droned on about the wonder cures effected by mesmerism 'by the hour without intermission', Mary's patience finally snapped. 'According to Miss M: these Mesmerisers can work miracles just as great as Christ & the Apostles', she said, 'in a tone of vexation' to Robinson.[31]

The Wordsworths had barely recovered from the shock of Edward's death when their nephew Charles informed them that his father was in 'a very weak & precarious state of health'. By 27 January, the doctor was preparing them for the worst: Christopher's constitution was in such a collapsed state that there was no hope of recovery. On 2 February Charles wrote to tell them that his father had died that morning. At seventy-one, he was four years younger than William. 'Patience & composure to the utmost of which our poor nature is capable were retained to the end', Charles added. 'You, my dear Uncle, have lost your only surviving Brother – & one whom, I know, you loved & valued most dearly – & whose affectionate admiration of you was unbounded'. Christopher was buried in the churchyard at Buxted, in Sussex, the country parish to which he had retired after resigning the mastership of Trinity College. Charles, who had resigned his post at Winchester school in order to look after his father, was mortified not to be presented to the living, which the Archbishop of Canterbury gave to one of his own relatives. 'I am now quite homeless – & quite uncertain which way to turn.'[32]

Troubles crowded in. 'Keswick' John was now so ill that the doctor expected him to be carried off at any moment. Someone from the family visited him daily at his house in Ambleside. 'Poor Fellow, he is growing weaker and weaker every day, and is quite aware that his dissolution is approaching.' Miss Fenwick was involved in an accident outside Fox How, when her carriage overturned and was dragged several yards along the lane, leaving her deeply shaken. Dreadful reports of Isabella's state prompted her brother and seventy-year-old mother to set off at once for Rome. Mary's niece Margaret Hutchinson, the daughter of her youngest brother, George, 'a young woman of good abilities and well educated', to whom Joanna had been devoted, had become a member of the Mormon sect, and secretly fled to America.[33]

To add to an already difficult situation, William found himself having to contradict all sorts of malicious rumours about his son. It was said that Isabella had died of fatigue at Florence, having been dragged from Rome by her husband, and John was also accused 'most unjustly' of having removed his children from their mother. 'For my own part I shall never be tolerably at ease till they are all back in their own country', William affirmed. The warring couple reached a compromise of sorts. John would take the children home immediately and she would follow at a more leisurely pace with her mother and 'the indispensable Doctor'. By the end of May it was hoped that the whole family would be reunited in England. In the circumstances, it was hardly surprising that when the actor Macready called at Rydal Mount on 25 March William was ill in bed. His family problems had taken their toll on his purse too, for he had sent £75 to Pisa to help John extricate the children and pay for the journey home and had also just sent Dora £50 to enable her to take a short tour of southern Portugal and Spain before returning home. Reminding Moxon to ensure that Burns accounted for any of the recent profits from his illegally printed copy of William's poems, William apologized for pressing the matter, explaining diplomatically, 'I have been hardly drawn upon lately by various causes'.[34]

John and his sons arrived at Rydal Mount on 5 April. At his parents' suggestion, he had left thirteen-year-old Jane with their friend Mrs Gee, who ran a school for girls at Hendon. A clever, bookish child, she preferred reading to any other activity, but 'requires the discipline of a School, which she has never had'. The two oldest boys, Henry and William, were to be sent to the new Church of England school at Rossall, near Fleetwood, on the Lancashire coast. 'They are a little too fond of their own ways and pursuits', their grandfather noted sternly, 'obedient however when necessary, but it requires some urgency and trouble to make them so.' Henry was destined to be a civil engineer, his brighter, more attentive sibling for university. Eight-year-old John, who like his father and namesake was 'slow in book-learning', and the youngest, Charles, who was only six and still delicate after recovering from the fever which had killed his brother, would stay with their grandparents at Rydal Mount until their mother's return.[35]

In the midst of these griefs William appeared to casual observers, like Harriet Martineau, to be taking everything in his stride. 'Ws worldly affairs are most comfortable in his old age', she wrote on 8 February.

His wife is perfectly charm[in]g & the very angel he sho[ul]d have to tend him. his life is a most serene & happy one on the whole & while all goes on methodically he is happy & cheery & courteous & benevolent; so that one co[ul]d almost worship him. But to secure this everybody must be punctual, the fire must be bright & all go orderly as his angel takes care that every thing shall as far as depends on her – he goes every day to Miss Fenwick (he always needs some such daily object) she is the worthiest possible, gives her a smacking kiss, & sits down before her fire to open his mind – Think what she could tell if she survives him –[36]

As William reached and passed his seventy-sixth birthday, however, what he confided in Isabella Fenwick revealed a very different picture. Doing what she loved best, caring for two young children, Mary had thrown off her depression, which had affected her health as well as her spirits, and was now able to keep herself well by 'marvellous activity of mind and body'.

> I wish I could do the same – but many things do not touch her which depress me, public affairs in particular – my contempt for the management of these both in England and Ireland is quite painful . . . My pleasures are among Birds and Flowers, and of these enjoyments, thank God, I retain enough; but my interests in Literature and books in general seem to be dying away unreasonably fast – nor do I look or much care for a revival in them . . . I . . . often think that my life has been in a great measure wasted.

Mary, too, noticed the change in her husband: 'he sits more over the fire in silence etc etc and is sooner tired on his walks – which he is ever unwilling to commence unaccompanied by me'. When he now wrote to Robinson he felt he had nothing of value to say: 'in our course of life one day is just a repetition of its predecessor. Persons we see few except our old Neighbours, and new Books none.' Even his annual day excursion to Hawkshead was depressing: 'how changed!' he lamented. 'In my time we had more than a 100 Boys playing and roaming about the Vale; now not one was to be seen, the School being utterly deserted.'[37]

May produced a crisis in the Hutchinson family. Tom and Mary's son George, newly inducted into his first parish at Mathon, gave a fiery Calvinistic sermon on Ascension Day and, when rebuked by his appalled father and uncle, walked out. In the mental breakdown which followed, he fled his parish and declared his intention of resigning his profession altogether. His family was therefore left in possession of the rectory, but without the rector. They blamed his 'derangement', as he did himself, upon the conflict of religious opinions instilled into him by the woman he had intended to marry and hoped, as that connection was now broken off, he would recover. Until he came to terms with himself, and his faith, however, the future of all the Hutchinsons looked bleak.[38]

By the end of June the Wordsworths heard the glad tidings that Dora and her husband were safely back on English soil. Sara Coleridge, who saw them at the Hoares as they made their way northwards, reported that 'Dora looks like a rose. The improvement in her is marvellous. I have not seen her look so well since her teenish girlhood'. Quillinan, on the other hand, who had suffered a serious attack of pleurisy in Paris, was thin and delicate, though cheerful. They returned to a joyous welcome at Rydal, where, for the first time, they would have a proper home of their own. Carter, who spent most of the year at Carlisle, had built himself a cottage under Loughrigg and offered the tenancy to the Quillinans, with the proviso that he could stay there whenever he was in Rydal. It was the perfect solution for them all, because the cottage, Loughrigg Holme (which Dora poignantly told Carter she would call 'Loughrigg Home'), was within easy walking distance of both

Rydal Mount and Ambleside. Miss Fenwick's strictures had had their desired effect, however, for it was William who was to pay the rent of £80 a year, to include servants' wages, which was more than the total income Quillinan and his daughters had to live on.[39]

In Portugal Dora had said she was selfish enough to hope that she would see her 'child', 'Keswick' John, again before he died. Her wish was granted, but with unforeseen and tragic consequences. He was now, aged thirty-one, in the final stages of consumption, too weak to stand, raise or dress himself: when he was removed from his waterbed to a sofa or easy chair, he had to be carried, wrapped in a blanket. The Wordsworths, Dora now among them, took it in turn to visit him daily. 'He suffers much I grieve to say; yet bears all so patiently that it is affecting to be with him', she declared.[40] On 18 August his long trial ended. 'He expired without any suffering, Nature being quite worn out', William wrote. His mother and his cousin Willy were with him at the end. He was buried in Grasmere churchyard on 22 August with all the ceremony due to the last in the direct line of the Sockbridge Wordsworths. Mourning gloves and scarves were liberally distributed among the Wordsworths, Quillinans, Harrisons, Robinsons and Smiths who attended and the ubiquitous Troughton provided the hearse and driver. By John's death, William became the owner of the Sockbridge estate, which he had administered during his nephew's minority, and of his own brother John's sword, which had been recovered from the wreck of the *Earl of Abergavenny*. John left Willy his gold watch and chain and his sword and Dora nineteen guineas, but nothing to their brother. Once again, John was excluded from family financial arrangements, though the (non-existent) residue of the estate was to go to his son, John, who was 'Keswick' John's godson.[41]

After such a prolonged period of gloom, Willy's announcement that he was engaged to be married was a ray of sunshine. Having betrothed himself to a pauper and an heiress, he now chose the sensible middle course. His fiancée, Fanny Graham, came from a family 'in very moderate circumstances' as Quillinan remarked, with understandable wryness. She was the twenty-six-year-old daughter of a Cumberland stockbroker who had retired to Brighton. Willy had known her for fourteen years and though William and Mary had never met her, Dora and 'cousin Dorothy' Harrison both knew and liked her well. 'Had I not been prepared to love you from the favourable impression you had made upon my daughter, I must now have loved you for the happiness you have conferred upon my dear Son', Mary wrote in one of the effusive letters of congratulation which were dispatched from Rydal to Sussex, as the Wordsworths looked forward eagerly to the prospect of welcoming their new daughter-in-law.[42]

The flow of visitors through Rydal Mount continued unabated throughout the summer and autumn, despite the Wordsworths' private distresses. Miss Martineau brought several parties, Charles Wordsworth visited twice and in July Bertha and Herbert Hill, with their '6 Hillocks', as the Rydal Mount Visitors' Book put it, came from Warwickshire. John and his family were also there as often as not, for

Isabella had taken one look at the bleak parsonage at Plumblands, which was not even properly furnished, and fled, first to Fleetwood, then, for a lengthier period, to Hastings on the south coast, where she was joined by her niece, Clara, and her youngest son. 'He ought to have made the house that is two or three rooms in it really comfortable for his miserable wife', was Dora's forthright opinion, 'not that that would have kept her there – but she would have had no good reason to throw in his face for leaving her home – I pressed this upon him again & again but all in vain'.[43]

In September there were two visitors of particular interest. The first was the Chartist Thomas Cooper, a former apprentice cobbler, who taught himself to read Greek, Latin and Hebrew, and became a schoolmaster and journalist. As editor of a Chartist paper, he had taken part in the strikes of 1842 and been imprisoned for sedition, writing a poem, *The Purgatory of Suicides*, in gaol, which had been published the previous year. A devotee of *The Excursion*, Cooper could not walk past Rydal Mount without at least attempting to see the poet, though he had no introduction and was travelling on foot, staff in hand, and covered with dust. As a 'forlorn hope', he simply scribbled, 'Thomas Cooper, author of "The Purgatory of Suicides," desires to pay his devout regards to Mr Wordsworth' and handed it in at the door. To his utter astonishment, he was shown in and the poet greeted him with a warmth and friendliness that brought tears to Cooper's eyes. Expecting vanity and egotism, Cooper was confounded by William's liberal praise of other poets (apart from his *bête noire*, Byron). 'Mr Tennyson affords the richest promise', he told Cooper. 'He will do great things yet; and ought to have done greater things by this time.' When the inevitable subject of politics came up, Cooper could not believe his ears to hear a hearty endorsement of Chartism from the 'Tory' Wordsworth. '"You were right," he said; "I have always said the people were right in what they asked; but you went the wrong way to get it . . . there is nothing unreasonable in your Charter: it is the foolish attempt at physical force, for which many of you have been blamable."'

As the People's Charter had included demands for universal suffrage, annual ballots and Parliaments, the abolition of the property qualification for, and payment of salaries to, Members of Parliament, Cooper had every right to be amazed. What made the Charter attractive to William, however, was its nostalgic attempt to turn the clock back on the Industrial Revolution. Every working man, it said, should have his own cow and a few acres to cultivate for his family, just like the statesmen of the Lakes, whose virtues William had sung for so long. In an ideal society, where every man was a statesman or Chartist, then democracy was not only possible but desirable. 'I am a Democrat', William had informed Reed three years earlier, and it was as true in the 1840s as it had been in the 1790s. Except that for the last forty years he had also believed that the people had to be capable of exercising power responsibly, which meant having a vested interest in the land. Knowledge was spreading, he told Cooper, and constitutional liberty was sure to follow. '"The people are sure to have the franchise," he said, with emphasis, "as knowledge increases; but you will not get all you seek at once – and you must never seek it again by physical force," he added, turning to me with a smile: "it will only make you longer about it."' Before Cooper took his leave, William introduced him 'as a poet!' to Dorothy, who was being wheeled in her chair along the terrace, walked him to the gate, shook his hand and wished him well. 'I left him', Cooper said, 'with a more intense feeling of having been in the presence of a good and great intelligence, than I had ever felt in any other moments of my life.'[44]

The second visitor of interest was a Quaker, William Bennett, who, with his wife, children and artist friend T. C. Galpin, spent several months in the neighbourhood in the autumn. Like Cooper, he expected William to be 'austere and unapproachable, the cold and haughty aristocrat', and instead found him kind, attentive and expansive. The particular interest of Bennett's account is not his encounters with William, fascinating though they are, but that he gives us a rare glimpse of Dorothy. Strangers were not allowed indiscriminate access to the grounds of Rydal Mount, but were required to get prior permission, so that Dorothy was not subjected to 'the obtrusiveness of mere curiosity'. At William's invitation, the Bennett party came regularly into the gardens to draw and sometimes saw Dorothy being wheeled out on fine days or heard her 'shrill voice' reading or reciting aloud. Knowing of her mental imbecility, they always maintained a discreet distance, but one day they unexpectedly encountered her sitting alone in the shade of an oak tree. 'Won't you speak to me?' she shrieked at them. Pretending they had not heard, they moved on, only to hear repeated pleas and a heartbreaking 'Oh! you're too proud.' Mrs Bennett protested that they had not wanted to intrude, to which they received the unanswerable retort, 'You don't intrude, if I invite you.' Unwillingly drawn in, they were enchanted when Dorothy offered to recite some of her own verses and did so 'in the most clear and beautiful accents, and with that modulation and emphasis which only the poet can give to his own productions'. As she recited, she took off her bonnet,

> exposing clear and striking features, now furrowed and worn down by suffering, surmounted by a noble intellectual forehead quite bare, except where sprinkled over by a few grey hairs; she closed her eyes, and giving herself up to the full feeling of it, threw her whole soul into the poetry. – Even her loss of teeth, interfering with some of the modulations, seemed to add force and impressiveness. – The impression was most solemn and affecting. She paused at the conclusion; then opened her eyes, and looked towards us, her features gilded up with the smile of expected approbation, which indeed was not withheld, but most genuinely awarded.

In the course of the conversation that followed, she appeared completely lucid, telling them about her own illness and the death of her brother John, whose last words she quoted. She then repeated some more verses and, when her attendant returned 'to our no small relief', they were all touched when she took the hand of each of them, including their little girl, in her own 'shrunk and withered hand'.[45]

Bennett remarked several times on William's 'visibly enfeebled step', but Isabella Fenwick was also privately raising doubts about his mental strength. There is no evidence of this in either his conversations with Bennett or his letters of the time, but he was undoubtedly under severe strain due to the deaths, in unprecedented numbers, of so many of those closest to him. Two of these were particularly distressing. Haydon, after years of poverty and rejection, committed suicide at the age of sixty: in a final pathetic gesture, the artist who had cited William's 'High is our calling, Friend!' so often, as if it were a charm to ward off evil, sent his unsold portrait, *Wordsworth on Helvellyn*, to Elizabeth Barrett, the poetess who had written in praise of it, 'to protect' after his death. His suicide, in June, was followed in November by that of Lamb's close friend Thomas Alsager, the scholarly music critic, who, at sixty-seven, cut his own throat when he was dismissed from *The Times*. Coming so close to that of Haydon made it even more shocking.[46] And at the end of September the Wordsworths' beloved old friend Thomas Clarkson, the unsung champion of the abolition of slavery, died. Though he had died peacefully and full of years, his widow was hurt and offended by American abolitionists' attempts to hijack his deathbed reception of their representatives as a public endorsement of their aims. Catherine hinted strongly that, as one of the few left alive who had known her husband intimately as a private man as well as a public figure, William might supply some memorial lines, but, as the poet now freely admitted, his writing days were over.[47]

Plans for Willy's wedding were proceeding apace. At the beginning of October he took the lease on a 'nice thatched ground-floor cottage' at Briscoe, a few miles out of Carlisle, which belonged to William's old friends the Loshes. Miss Fenwick, who had determined not to keep house again, offered him all her plate and Dora agreed to go over to help him choose furniture and prepare the cottage for the arrival of his bride. Fanny had intended to visit Rydal Mount in November, to meet her future in-laws before her marriage, but had been prevented by the serious illness of her sister Matilda. The same reason caused several postponements of the wedding, prompting Mary to write 'a word of Comfort and sympathy [to] mitigate the pain which you must necessarily feel upon the separation from your dear Sister under the present state of her health', but suggesting that, since it was the united wish of both families that the marriage should take place as soon as possible, it would be less painful to everyone concerned if a definite date was fixed.[48]

On 19 January 1847 the Wordsworths held a grand wedding feast to celebrate their youngest son's marriage. Between fifty and sixty of their friends, neighbours and servants were invited to tea at Rydal Mount and the health of the newlyweds was proposed by Thomas Troughton. The Quillinans, including Jemima and Rotha, Mary Hutchinson, who had come from Mathon to help her sister-in-law, and Robinson, who was on his annual visit, were among the guests. As Dora learned afterwards, however, it had all been a little premature. At two o'clock that afternoon Mary had received a letter saying that the wedding had been postponed another day. With only three hours to go before the guests started arriving, some of them from a considerable distance, she consulted with her sister-in-law and they decided to take a chance and go ahead. No one else, not even William or Dora, was in on the secret, lest it should spoil the occasion for them. Though the two 'wily women' 'felt queer' when Troughton proposed his toast, their boldness was vindicated when Thursday's post brought a letter from Willy and Fanny announcing that they were now man and wife. The wedding had taken place on 20 January, at Brighton, and they were on their way to Rydal Mount.[49]

The newlyweds arrived on 30 January and the Wordsworths were delighted with their tall, pretty daughter-in-law, with her quiet, gentle manners and sweet voice, who seemed at once 'quietly at ease' with them. Robinson diplomatically took himself off to the Arnolds' for the day, but before he went he had a long conversation with William about literature. It was worthy of note only because 'I had more talk with Wordsworth than on any day since I came'.

The first six days of his visit had seemed to confirm Miss Fenwick's worst fears. William had been 'quite silent as if the vigour of his mind were gone'. 'He spoke very little to any one And said on one occasion when it was remarked that he was silent – "Yes, the Silence of old age". It was not that his judgement or sense was in any respect impaired, but his activity – He was quite happy quite cordial quite amiable; but not so animated or energetic as he used to be.' The same was true of Mary. 'Perhaps', Robinson mused, 'it is the most graceful form in w[hi]ch old age can manifest itself.'[50]

On 19 February William and Mary set out for Bath, on a long-planned visit to Isabella Fenwick. 'How I wish you were here, instead of our being obliged to go to you', William grumbled. They left Dorothy in the care of Dora, who had been 'wonderfully strong and well' since her return from Portugal, but was now suffering her usual winter cough and cold. 'She looks like a witch for thinness', her mother remarked, but Dora was as cheerful and unconcerned as usual; 'tho' I cough away to make a great disturbance in the house it does not seem to do me any harm.' She was busy putting the final touches to her *Journal of a Few Months' Residence in Portugal and Glimpses of the South of Spain*, which Moxon had agreed to publish, generously offering her two-thirds of any profit, yet taking all the risk to himself. 'Women observe many particulars of manners and opinions which are apt to escape the notice of the Lords of the Creation', William remarked drily, but he had reconciled himself to Dora's decision to publish only because she would do so anonymously.[51]

Mary Hutchinson accompanied William and Mary as far as Mathon, where they were to stay for ten days with Tom, Ebba and Sarah, the afflicted rector still being in London, fleeing from his parish and his crisis of faith. On 3 March they were at last reunited with their beloved Miss Fenwick, who had taken a house at 8 Queen's Square, a large Georgian square overlooking a central garden, on the hill above the Theatre Royal. A few days later they were joined by Robinson, who soon persuaded William to walk with him over the hills to Witcombe, where his mother was buried. 'I was afraid it would be too much for my companion', Robinson noted, 'But he was not so fatigued as I was on our return.' Sara Coleridge and her daughter

Edith, who joined them on 18 March, was not so impressed. 'He can walk seven or eight miles very well', she told her cousin, 'but is always losing his way, and making out *he* is obliged to look sharp after his wife, whose eyesight is grown so bad that she is not to be trusted.'[52]

Sara's purpose in coming to Bath was not just to see the Wordsworths, but also to hear what William had to say about her father. She had just finished editing Coleridge's *Biographia Literaria*, which, despite William's private reservations about the nature of the book, he had allowed her to dedicate to him. Sara, who had not seen William for two years and Mary for even longer, found them both looking 'older in the face' and 'slower and feebler in their movements of body and mind'. Mary was, nevertheless, 'wonderfully active', despite looking frail. On the day appointed for fasting and 'National Humiliation' on account of the Irish famine, she went three times to church 'and would have fasted almost wholly, had not Mr W., in a deep, determined voice, said "Oh, *don't* be so *foolish*, Mary!"' Of William she made the perceptive remark that he seemed 'rather to recontinue his former self, and repeat by habit what he used to think and feel, than to think anything new'.[53]

It was while they were in Bath that William received a request which he felt he could not ignore. Prince Albert was about to be installed as Chancellor of the University of Cambridge and he wanted William to write the words for an Installation Ode which would be set to music and performed at the ceremony. 'His Royal Highness would have felt considerable hesitation in thus breaking in upon your retirement', the private secretary wrote, 'were it not that his Royal Highness felt that he thus might bear testimony to His admiration of your Genius, and might be the means of procuring for the University of Cambridge another valuable work of one of her most distinguished Sons.' Who could resist such flattery? Even though he was opposed to Prince Albert's election and said he personally would have voted against him, William agreed to retouch the harp he thought he had laid aside for good. Robinson undertook to locate Wright's *Inaugural Ode*, which was to be the model, but by 9 April the ode was, as Mary described it, 'unbegun yet!'[54]

The Wordsworths had left Miss Fenwick at Bath the previous day and had now taken up residence at Mrs Hoare's, from where they hoped to go to Playford Hall, to visit the widowed Catherine Clarkson. It was to be a quiet visit to Hampstead, without the frenetic socializing which had characterized earlier trips to London. They made a pilgrimage together to visit Highgate cemetery, where Coleridge's remains had recently been reinterred in a family vault with those of his wife and son-in-law. Friends who knew the Wordsworths' whereabouts came to see them. A recently married Anna Ricketts came to introduce her husband and step-daughter; Charles Wordsworth and his daughter, with his new wife, who was half his age, called to say farewell before departing for Scotland, where he was to found Trinity College at Glenalmond; Robinson brought the book needed for the Installation Ode; Moxon called, with Dora's *Journal of a Few Months' Residence in Portugal*, hot from the press, in two volumes. All the time, however, the Wordsworths were racked with anxiety about their daughter. 'We remain here and in London solely because we think she will do better without than with us', William told Fanny.[55]

Dora had never thrown off the troublesome cough she had acquired the previous November, when she went to Carlisle to help Willy set up his new home. 'Week after week glides by, and I perceive no decided amendment', Quillinan confided in Miss Fenwick. 'Her cough though not so frequent is still troublesome & fitful, & she is feeble & feverish; & no wonder, for she has been a close prisoner for above six weeks and an invalid above four months, ever since that unhappy & needless journey to Carlisle.' He tried to put a brave face on it. 'I am much troubled about my dear wife, but not in the least alarmed, or at least I try to persuade myself so in spite of misgivings that such repeated illnesses must end in woe.' He comforted himself with the thought that he would take Dora abroad again next winter.[56]

On 20 April William and Mary moved to Westminster, to stay with their nephew Chris and his family. They had already abandoned the idea of going to see Mrs Clarkson, so that they could go back home sooner, but William had an engagement to sit to a talented twenty-one-year-old artist, Leonard Wyon, the second engraver at the Royal Mint, who wanted to make a study for a silver medallion. The portrait, in profile, of a dignified but stern-looking William was taken in the cloisters at Westminster, three weeks after his seventy-seventh birthday. As Robinson watched the artist at work, a letter arrived and William was called out of the room. He never returned. The letter was from Quillinan. It said that Dr Fell had examined Dora and, for the first time, 'expressed fears' about her. William and Mary did not hesitate. They left immediately for home and were back at Rydal Mount the next day. The following day, 28 April, they called in the Kendal physician, Dr Gough, for a second opinion. He examined Dora '& gave us no hope', Quillinan bleakly recorded in his diary, '"a question only of time"'.[57]

'You never knew her – perhaps never saw her', Hartley Coleridge wrote on hearing the news.

> I have known her from her infancy. But if you had seen her as I have seen her and seen how a beautiful Soul can make a face not beautiful most beautiful, if you had seen how by the mere strength of affection she entered into the recesses of her Father's Mind and drew him out to gambol with her in the childishness that always hung upon her womanhood, you would feel, as we do, what earth is about to lose and Heaven to gain.

'Dearest Dora!' his sister echoed. 'It seems scarce credible that so much life and love, and such a noble heart, – such a bright open mind should be passing away so soon! She is one of those whom it is scarce possible to think of as thus drawn within the vail [*sic*]'.[58]

The diagnosis was pulmonary consumption, or tuberculosis, which the Wordsworths, like all their contemporaries, believed was inherent, developing out of neglect of or a tendency to coughs and colds. In fact, as has only been discovered in the latter years of the twentieth century, it is purely infective, though most likely to be caught by those who are physically weak. The full extent of the Wordsworths' tragedy becomes clear only with the realization that Dora's death sentence was, unwittingly, the bequest of 'her child', her beloved cousin 'Keswick' John, who had died the previous autumn. Had she not nursed him so devotedly throughout his final weeks, she would not have caught the infection.[59]

Opinion was divided on whether Dora should be told. Miss Fenwick thought she had a right to know, so that she could prepare herself; Sara Coleridge argued that there was no spiritual advantage and that the shock might hasten death. It was Dora herself who settled the question, by quietly insisting that she should be told. She was 'not only resign'd but happy', Hartley informed his sister. 'Her parents bear up like Christians, but are quite absorb'd by their sorrow. I have not seen them – (excepting Mr Wordsworth on the road . . .). I would gladly go, if I could be of any use or comfort, but the Doctor advises me not. They wish to see no one.' Dora was, from the first, nursed at Rydal Mount, where she had been taken ill. Apart from her immediate family and the servants, only Hannah Cookson was admitted to her sickroom. 'H.C. is a treasure to us – being an incomparable nurse – so thoughtful – tender and such presence of mind! as under such circumstances is scarcely to be looked for in one whose heart and affections are so deeply interested.'[60] When Mary Stanger, one of Dora's earliest and closest schoolfriends, called to see her, even she was turned away, for fear that the inevitable emotion of a meeting would disturb the tranquillity Dora was struggling to preserve. 'Dear friend', Mary wrote,

> Excuse my shrinking from seeing you – Dora sends her tenderest love & bids me say she often thinks of you – She would if you much wished it see you – But the close has appeared so near this m[ornin]g that I dare not venture the risk – She has your prayers & those of y[ou]r husband – & you may comfort y[ou]rselves with the thought that she is in a blessed state –
>
> Pray for us who remain
> MW[61]

Dora dealt swiftly with her worldly concerns, jotting down a memo to her father in an unusually untidy hand that she wished to leave £20 to each of her godchildren, Edward Hill, son of Herbert and Bertha, and Priscilla Wordsworth, daughter of Chris and Susan. Her other cash bequests were all to the loyal servants who had been with them so long they seemed part of the family: Mary and Elizabeth, the maids, were to get £5 each, James Dixon £10 and John Carter, who had provided her with her first and only marital home, 'out of gratitude for his affec[tionate] Kindness to my Parents' £100. Her marriage settlement ensured that all her personal property would belong to Quillinan for life and after his death would be divided equally between her brothers. This Dora now varied in a gesture of female solidarity with her goddaughter and only niece, Jane, whose financial prospects did not look promising. After Quillinan's death, she was to receive £300 from Dora's estate.[62]

'She is calm and happy,' Quillinan wrote to Robinson on 19 May, suffers little or no bodily pain, her mind is clear and cheerful, her affections are as much alive as ever, she does not forget a friend, she is prepared to die & willing to live, resigned to departure at any hour, yet hoping, & I think believing with good reason, that she may live many days perhaps several weeks. But it is a treacherous complaint, & she may be snatched away from us in a moment.[63]

As Quillinan had pointed out, it was one of the physiological characteristics of the disease to alternate between rally and relapse, hope and despair. 'Tell her I have more than 7 lives', Dora told her mother, who was writing to Miss Fenwick. And as was so often the case with Victorian deathbeds, she was inundated with well-meant advice which today seems bizarre, if not cruel. William Ball, the Quaker who now owned Ivy Cottage, recommended cod liver oil, 'in the strongest terms as a curative, even in the last stages of Consumption'. Mary and Dora were cynical, but Quillinan, William and John jumped at the chance, rushing off to Kendal to procure some for the invalid, which she took reluctantly, 'as a duty to those who clung to an earthly hope'. She was also offered, and presented with, books intended as spiritual guidance and comfort. 'We have had abundance, perhaps too Many', Mary commented; as they tended to disturb rather than promote Dora's tranquillity, her mother had no hesitation in rejecting them. Instead, they clung to Dora's preferred choice, the simple hymn of absolute trust in the Redeemer, which, Mary said, 'I think in her case is all-sufficient.'

Just as I am – without one plea,
But that thy blood was shed for me
And that thou bidst me come to Thee.
O Lamb of God, I come![64]

Throughout the long dark days of Dora's final illness, mother and daughter revealed a mutual strength and courage that was humbling to behold. Instead of giving way to bitterness or selfish lamentation, they thanked God simply for the fact that they were able to be together and comfort one another. Dora refused to allow her physical sufferings to cow her spirit: 'How mercifully I am dealt with', she would say repeatedly, even finding time and strength of mind to write a farewell letter to Isabella Fenwick. Her mother, who passed every night till two in the morning alone with her daughter in the sickroom, returning to her vigil five or six hours later, was grateful simply for possessing the strength to carry on. 'For myself how thankful I ought to be that such a blessing has been spared to us so long', Mary wrote on 27 May; '– at 77 the separation cannot be long; & how merciful to me is our heavenly Father, that I am yet able to minister to her earthly comforts while I trust I am profitting by the example of her patience, & chearful resignation of all she so intensely loves – & by the humility of her aspirations towards the home whither she is hastening.'[65]

For William there was no such comfort. Lacking Mary's unshakeable faith and unable to assist in nursing his daughter, he was simply helpless. 'I bless God beloved friend that I am able to write to you in so much tranquillity –', Mary told Miss Fenwick. 'O that my dear Husband, the tender Father, had equal self command – he cannot speak without tears except on things wide apart from his heart.' 'Dear Mr Wordsworth comes forth occasionally to see his old friends,' Mrs Arnold told Robinson on 1 June,

> & yesterday morning when I saw him slowly & sadly approaching by our Birch tree, I hastened to meet him, & found that he would prefer, walking with me around our own garden boundary to entering the House, & encountering a larger party – So we wandered about here – & then I accompanied him to Rydal – & he walked back again with me . . . This quiet intercourse gave me an opportunity of seeing how entirely our dear friends are prepared to bow with submission to God's will. No one can tell better than yourself how much they will feel it, for you have had full opportunities of seeing how completely Dora was the joy and sunshine of their lives, but she is herself by her own composure and cheerful submission & willingness to relinquish all earthly hopes & possessions – teaching them to bear the greatest sorrow which could have befallen them . . . I shall always feel with you that these lingering weeks have been most mercifully ordered for them, & are full of present comfort & of consoling memories for the future.[66]

Throughout the ordeal, William was constantly being harassed by Thomas Walmisley, the Professor of Music at Cambridge who had been commissioned to write the music for the Installation Ode. William had written only part of the ode before he left London and he was unusually dismissive about it. 'Miss F says that there is a great deal of thought in it; but he says himself that it is but superficial thought.' His depreciation concealed the embarrassing truth that he had not written the poem at all. Incapable of composing anything suitable in time but unable to get out of the engagement, he resorted to the ploy he had used in the comparable situation with Rio. He asked his son-in-law for help. Quillinan wrote a first draft which William then revised and corrected, so that he could legitimately claim some part in its composition. A second, corrected draft had been sent to Walmisley within a couple of days of William's return to Rydal Mount, but that was not the end of it. First of all Walmisley asked for an additional verse to end the ode on a more joyous note, then he rejected the new lines, 'words of four syllables are extremely difficult to put into musical rhythm' and expressed the hope that the next version 'may not commence with the word "Albert"'. Harried beyond endurance by these details when all he cared about was Dora, William gave Walmisley *carte blanche* to do what he liked with the poem: 'adopt or reject any alterations as they suit you or not'.[67] Nothing could have more clearly indicated his changed priorities than this surrender of control over a poem which would inevitably be the subject of immense public interest. Weighed in the balance against his dying daughter, poetic reputation no longer mattered.

Despite all Dora's 'humility, her repentance resignation faith & hope which is unbounded', there were still occasions when she suffered what she called 'the pangs of death'. One of them was on 1 June. 'A cloud came over her, a fear & cold trembling as if she had lost the support of her Saviour', Quillinan noted sadly. He attributed it to her 'earnestness and over energy in her devout preparations' and 'one of the Spiritual Adversary's most malignant subtleties; an attempt to take advantage of weakness & to substitute despair for peace'. The cloud passed, 'she clung to her Redeemer & he has not deserted her', but it made her realize 'that she must think & wrestle less in order to retain the needful Christian fortitude to the last'. In these crises, Quillinan acknowledged, Mary was the best spiritual comforter Dora could have, but he could not help regretting that the clergyman who attended his wife was her brother John. 'He has shewn more sensibility . . . than I might have given him credit for', Quillinan admitted,

> but, between you and me, I could wish that there were some more influential more really spiritual pastor at hand, for though the poor Mother thinks him very superior to what he is, & though Dora loves him truly & faithfully, I cannot but think that a higher toned mind than his would be more competent to minister to any death-bed doubt or trouble; more in accord with a fine & pure Spirit like Her's.[68]

On 8 June William wrote to James Dawson, asking to borrow again the waterbed which had eased his nephew's sufferings the previous year. On 1 July, during a temporary respite from the continuous diarrhoea which marked her approaching end, Dora could still joke about her 'fat', the tubercles, or glandular swellings, which were now appearing all over her face and body, though she was so emaciated that she was covered in pressure sores. She could even spare a thought from her own sufferings to send her good wishes to her cousin Tom Hutchinson, who was getting married that day. 'It is marvellous how she rallies', her mother wrote. 'Yet she has *at times every day* those sinkings that seem to be the forerunner of immediate dissolution. And dearest Mary, that will be a thankful moment – for nothing but increased suffering can be expected from the sores and weakness. There is no cure for a body exhausted and worn as hers is'.[69]

When Mary Hutchinson offered to come to assist the afflicted family, she was immediately rebuffed. 'By no means think of coming to me,' Mary wrote. 'I shall find my support in the quiet example she has set me.' Dora had insisted that life should go on as normal. 'We are to sit as usual in the room below – the breakfast and dinner bell is to be rung as usual – "No fuss" – is her watchword –'. Her sufferings ended on 9 July. 'At One o'clock A. M. this morning, my precious Dora, your true friend, breathed her last', Quillinan wrote to Robinson. She died, without fuss, in possession of her faculties and a few weeks short of her forty-fourth birthday.

The painful duty of notifying her closest friends and relations fell to her husband and father, their distress of mind being all too evident in the mistakes which crept into their brief formalities. Three days later they shared a second and equally distressing task. Accompanied by Willy, they went to Grasmere churchyard to choose the site of Dora's grave. Logic suggested that she should be placed beside her brother and sister, dead long ago, but husband and father had conflicting claims to be satisfied. The compromise they agreed, which was carried into effect on 14 July, was that she should be buried between her Aunt Sara and Quillinan's first wife, Jemima, enough space being left for 'a Wordsworth' on one side of her and Quillinan on the other.[70]

Out of all the many letters of sympathy which poured into Rydal Mount, two stand out among the mouthings of conventional pieties and platitudes. They came from William's oldest surviving friends. 'Pray forgive me –', one brief note began, 'but write I must, to say how much you are in my thoughts & how much I grieve – not for Her who is at rest but for you who have lost her. May He who alone knows what is best for us – who gives & who takes away, bless & support you! Yours most affectionately Samuel Rogers.' Joseph Cottle also wrote from Bristol to express his shock: 'To lose a Daughter, and an only Daughter, and such a Daughter, must have afflicted you with a poignancy, of which I can but imperfectly conceive.' He alone, out of the many who wrote to congratulate William on the successful performance of his Installation Ode on 6 July, remarked how uncongenial the task of writing it must have been. It was small consolation to the grieving father to learn that it had been greeted with rapturous applause, or to receive a note from Buckingham Palace, written the day Dora died, which, with unconscious irony, declared, 'The force and beauty of the ideas, and the elegance of the Versification fully proved to Her Majesty and the Prince, that Time had been powerless over the Mind or Skill of the Poet.'[71] In other circumstances, one could well imagine that William would have smiled wrily and handed the note to Quillinan.

Miss Fenwick, who had, for her own health's sake, determined not to risk the rigours of a journey to Rydal again, could not abandon her friends in their grief and came immediately to do what she did best, offer hope and consolation in a house of mourning. 'We bear up under our affliction as well as God enables us to do,' William wrote to Moxon, 'but O my dear Friend our loss is immeasurable'. He had been quite convinced that Mary's long vigils would wear her out and that she would quickly follow her daughter to the grave, a fear that had been echoed by their friends, but Mary was made of sterner stuff. She looked 'more aged & feeble', Miss Fenwick reported, '– but she is still able to move about with her accustomed activity'. Her husband 'bears up with firmness, but has paroxysms of great suffering'. He found his chief consolation in constant attendance on his sister, adding to the daily duty he had always performed of pushing her in her chair out on the terrace on fine days. Perhaps her grateful dependence on him was a compensation for his inability to do anything for Dora.[72]

The weeks and months of Dora's final illness had seen a change in the balance of her parents' relationship. Mary's strength of character had seemed to grow in direct proportion as her husband's sank and withered away. Even before Dora fell ill, visitors to William had begun to notice her in a way they had never done before.

Bennett, for instance, said, 'There is a peculiar calm and stillness about this lady, that cannot be conveyed; and her salutation is all benignity.' Harriet Martineau was full of rare praise for her. 'Her excellent sense and womanly devotedness, – (especially when she grew pale and shrunk and dim-eyed under her mute sorrow for the daughter whom *he* mourned aloud, and without apparent consideration for the heart-sufferer by his side) made her by far the more interesting of the two to me.'[73]

When Miss Fenwick left them, Mary tried to divert her husband's grief by focusing his attention on their surviving sons. In September she persuaded him to visit John in his deserted new vicarage, built by the railway company, at Brigham; his wife was now in Paris, with her brother, and already declaring herself remarkably restored in health by her resumption of foreign travel. Mary had hoped that being in a place so strongly connected with his childhood, rather than with Dora, would rekindle her husband's interest, but she was foiled by bad weather that prevented them walking out. She even planned a visit to Carlisle. If she could persuade him to return home by Briscoe, the place indelibly associated in both their minds with the beginning of Dora's fatal illness, she felt that something would be achieved: 'if that trial (which will also be a severe one to *myself*) can be got over, I trust, in God's mercy, that his mind, being more reconciled to itself, he may bear his deep deep sorrow more calmly: otherwise I am sure his bodily health must give way'.[74]

When they got to Carlisle, however, William only complained that the reality was worse than the anticipation. Mary and Willy persuaded him to sit to a local artist, Thomas Carrrick, a famous painter of miniatures on marble. The daily sittings occupied his time but not his mind or heart: the resulting portrait, ineffably sad, depicts the poet staring bleakly from sunken eyes, his mouth unnaturally compressed, as if by force of will. It was a 'striking likeness', Robinson admitted. 'But it is too sad . . . it has an expression of fixed and irremovable grief.'

William was anxious to return home, 'but will he be more at ease here?' Quillinan asked. 'Mrs W with as much feeling, & with a mother's feeling to boot, has a happier method of dealing with her sorrows. – Her remaining children, her grand children & her husband occupy her mind & heart usefully.' If William had felt excluded by the closeness of his wife's relationship with their dying daughter, his son-in-law felt equally shut out by both his wife's parents. 'I have never for a moment felt that I was otherwise than alone', he told Miss Fenwick. 'It is a horrible desolation, & I cannot yet call it anything else.'[75]

'You kindly express a hope that Mr Quillinan and I walk together –', William wrote at the beginning of December, after his return from Carlisle; 'this has not been so, I cannot bear to cross the Bridge and Field that leads to his Abode; and he does not come hither, so that except once on the highway, and once or twice at Church, and one evening when he dined here with Mr Scott, his friend, I have not seen him at all.' When Robinson arrived for his Christmas visit on 18 December, he was deeply perturbed at what he found. 'Both Mr & Mrs Wordsworth have received a blow, the effects of which I fear they will never be able to counteract –', he confided to his brother five days later.

Neither of them has yet ventured to pronounce the name of their beloved daughter – And very few & slight have been the allusions to their loss – Who feels the most intensely – who shall say? But at least Mrs W is able to mix more with her friends And discharge as she has been accustomed the ordinary functions of her domestic life. Mr W keeps very much alone And whichever room I may happen to be in, he goes into the other – All the ordinary occupations in which his daughter took a part are become painful to him – I brought as usual a pack of cards and proposed a hand of Whist to Mrs W: in his absence, but even she rejected it with a shudder – I have been able to draw him out of the house but for a short time – And when I this morning proposed a call on old Mrs Cookson at Grasmere, this produced a flood of tears – This renders it difficult on my part to avoid giving pain – Neither of them go anywhere. And very few of their friends even call ...

The worst consequence of William's inability to face people and places intimately associated with his daughter was that he had never once ventured to set foot in Loughrigg Holme. 'I am sorry indeed to perceive that this is resented by Mr Q: as if it were an insult to his wife's memory', Robinson told Miss Fenwick. '... Q: expresses himself so strongly that I fear the foundation is laid for a lasting estrangement which might widen and lead to an entire alienation.' Before he left Rydal, Robinson made it his business to try to heal the breach, persuading Quillinan to accept his own conviction that William's refusal to enter his house had everything to do with being unable to face his daughter's last home and nothing to do with his son-in-law.[76]

For Robinson, it was a miserable visit. During the three weeks he stayed at Rydal Mount, he noted in his journal almost daily that William was 'very silent'. A kind invitation from Mrs Davy enabled him to escape for Christmas dinner, but he still had to endure the painful sight of William sobbing through the church service on Christmas Day. He succeeded in drawing the poet out on short walks and even to pay a few calls, but on their return William would retire to his room to sit alone '& cry incessantly'. The final evening of his visit was particularly painful. William was 'as moody and silent as on the other evenings', so Robinson read the newspapers, 'which filled up the time'. Rising early the next morning, he had a private conversation with James, lamenting William's inability to submit to the will of providence. 'Ah! Sir And so I took the liberty of saying to Master', James replied. '– He merely said – "Oh she was such a bright creature["] – And then I said "*But Sir don't you think she is brighter now than she ever was,*["] And then Master burst into a flood of tears.' When the time came to part with Robinson, William was again so overcome with emotion that he wept uncontrollably and could not speak to take leave of his friend. Despite all the indications to the contrary, Robinson remained optimistic: 'he has a strong nature in body as well as mind And he may yet rally'. William himself was not so sure. 'I suffer most in head and mind before I leave my bed in a morning –', he wrote to Isabella Fenwick. 'Daily used She to come to my bedside and greet me and her Mother and *now* the blank is terrible. But I must stop. She is ever with me and will be so to the last moment of my life.'[77]

28. *Bowed to the Dust*

The most unfortunate result of the temporary estrangement between Dora's father and husband was that Quillinan was deprived of the opportunity to become William's biographer. Early in November 1847 the Wordsworths were surprised by a letter from their nephew Chris, announcing that he and his wife, Susan, intended to visit Rydal Mount. That there was a purpose behind the visit soon became clear, when Chris offered to prepare some biographical notices of his uncle, after the latter's death. Written by an official family biographer, he argued, such a work might pre-empt gossipy publications of the sort by Cottle, Allsop, Gillman et al., which the Wordsworths felt had done so much to diminish Coleridge's posthumous reputation. William, who had an unjustifiably high opinion of his nephew's talents, gladly agreed, though Mary was uncomfortably aware that Quillinan would be hurt at being passed over, 'for you know he is easily offended'.[1]

Yet Quillinan had just cause for offence, because no one said a word about the arrangement to him. He dined at Rydal Mount when Chris and Susan were there and entertained them to lunch and dinner at Loughrigg Holme, but the subject was not raised. This cannot have been accidental. On the very morning of the day Chris and Susan spent at Quillinan's, William drew up a formal notice, witnessed by his wife, requiring his family and friends to assist his nephew in preparing the biography. What could have been more natural than to discuss this with Quillinan, formally or informally? The kindest interpretation one can put on his being kept in ignorance was a fear of hurting his feelings, but he was bound to find out sooner or later and the conspiracy of silence would then seem more hurtful than the decision itself. When he did find out, several months later, not from any of the Wordsworths but from a casual reference by a close friend, he was mortified. 'In Dora's time, it was perfectly understood by her & by myself (& not by us only) that if I should survive my fatherinlaw, the task of writing his Life would, for many reasons, be confided to me. Every thing was changed when I lost my wife . . .'[2]

Why did William change his mind? There was no question that Quillinan would have made a better biographer. 'Dr CW would do it much better than I in many respects, though perhaps not in all', was Quillinan's own opinion. 'I believe . . . he would be the fittest to discharge the duty which I learn from you is to be cast upon another', Robinson told Miss Fenwick. The biography 'requires critical taste And a wider acquaintance with the history of the poets works And the treatment they have met from the critical part of the world, than he the appointed editor possesses or cares to possess'. Even Mary remarked of Chris that he knew less about William's poetry than almost any person she knew. His appointment over Quillinan, particularly if the latter had a prior claim, seems inexplicable. Chris might not have been the best man for the job, however, but he had other advantages. He had the Wordsworth name, for a start, held a high and influential position in the Church of England and was an indefatigable author of books and pamphlets on Church affairs. If he undertook the task there would be no question that he would complete it and that his work would carry authority. The same could not be said of poor Quillinan, an impoverished, dilettante author of lightweight novels, poems and journalistic criticism. What is more, Chris's offer came at a time when William was so wrapped up in grief for his daughter that he simply did not care about his literary reputation, past, present or future. One gets the impression that he agreed simply to avoid having to think about the matter.

Before his nephew left Rydal Mount, he 'requested Mr Wordsworth to favour him with a brief sketch of the most prominent circumstances in his life'. William therefore began to dictate a series of biographical memoranda to Susan, but his heart was not in it. Compared to the Fenwick Notes, they are flat and dull, a duty task rather than a voluntary outpouring of musings to a dear friend. Poignantly, they limp to a halt with the death of his two children. 'They died in 1812,' he dictated, 'and in 1813 we came to Rydal Mount, where we have since lived with no further sorrow till 1836, when my sister became a confirmed invalid, and our sister Sarah Hutchinson died. She lived alternately with her brother and with us.'[3] He could go no further, for he could not yet speak of his newest and greatest grief.

Miss Fenwick's response to the news that Chris was to be the official biographer was characteristic. Feeling that Quillinan had been unjustly snubbed, she quietly put into his hands the most important material for any potential biographer, the notes she had taken at the poet's dictation in 1843. The letter she sent him, forewarning him of their arrival, was marked 'Private' to ensure that, if he received it in William or Mary's presence, he would not read it to them, 'and that on account of these notes – for on Mr W's being reminded of them – he would immediately wish to see them and you might have some difficulty of getting them again not that there would be any design of keeping them from you but because he would intend to add to them'. This would be desirable, Miss Fenwick added, in which case Quillinan could offer his assistance. Without casting aspersions about the conduct of any of the Wordsworths, Miss Fenwick managed to make it clear that this gift was a gesture of practical support, to ensure that Quillinan could not be entirely excluded in the important decisions that would lie ahead. She told him, quite candidly, that Mary had mentioned the notes in one of her letters, but that she had made no answer: 'now I can say they are yours I always said that what I did was for Dora – and now they fall to you of course!'[4] It was not necessarily an 'of course!' that would be echoed at Rydal Mount.

Relations between William and his son-in-law did improve greatly in the spring, thanks to Robinson's kindly intervention. 'Mr Wordsworth & I walk about together a good deal now, & he seems to seek & to take pleasure in my company', Quillinan reported to his benefactor on 1 February.

> He talks constantly of my beloved Wife, & this suits my feelings, though it is so sad a theme. He comes to this house too occasionally. This is a great step gained, for I could not endure his absenting himself altogether, though I have learnt to respect the feeling that kept him away, or at least to think charitably of it. – Mrs Wordsworth too comes frequently: & this is very gratifying to me.

In one of the most heartening indications that the two men were finding mutual comfort in sharing their sorrow, they were even thinking of a joint publication of all their poems relating to Dora for private circulation among their friends. To Mary, however, her 'beloved Mourner' still seemed 'bowed to the dust . . . His mind and spirits (except for a brief while when, with almost *indifferent* Persons, he can rally a little and appear quite himself) is in the lowest state of *humiliation* and deep sorrow . . . May the Almighty in his mercy see fit to send support ere long.'[5]

One of the 'indifferent Persons' who was brought to Rydal Mount in February by Miss Martineau was the American essayist Ralph Waldo Emerson, paying his second visit to the poet. They found William asleep on the sofa and woke him. Disturbed from his sleep and unaware of who he was even talking to, the poet was, unsurprisingly, 'short & surly'. After spending a hour and a half in conversation, Emerson found all his previous prejudices confirmed. He dismissed William as 'a bitter old Englishman', a view which he toned down only slightly for his published account of the meeting. The article was padded out with a series of anecdotes from the literary circuit to illustrate William's miserly habits; like Chinese whispers, each carried a kernel of truth, but had been distorted and 'improved' in the telling. Harriet Martineau, for instance, said that in his early days William had offered his guests 'bread & plainest fare', telling them that if they wanted more, they would have to pay for it. Greg, the mill-owner, added that Walter Scott had been compelled to sneak out daily when he was the Wordsworths' guest to satisfy his hunger at the Swan Inn. Barry Cornwall, in a particularly venomous account, quite untruthfully claimed intimacy with William in early life and asserted that the poet 'had no personal friend. He was not amiable, & he was stingy. He would receive anything, but he never gave'; when Emerson quoted 'these Westmoreland praises of his exemplary temperance & economy', Cornwall replied, 'Ah, he would spend well enough when Lord Lonsdale came to see him.' Completely insensitive to William's recent loss, of which he cannot have been unaware, though he makes no mention of it, Emerson had few qualms about repeating such malicious gossip in print. It made for an entertaining read, but it was a gross and hurtful caricature of the man whose hospitality he had abused.[6]

At the beginning of April Mary, anticipating the trauma of celebrating William's seventy-eighth birthday at Rydal Mount without Dora, persuaded her husband to spend a month away from home, dividing their time equally between their sons. Willy and Fanny had found it impossible to live at the cottage at Briscoe, where Dora had caught the fateful cold, and at the beginning of the year had bought a house in Carlisle. 'I faintly hope that my poor husband may *possibly* be benefited by the change,' Mary said, though admitting that she herself found the very idea of going to Carlisle painful, even though it was to a new house. The visit to Brigham was less trying to William's spirits and was enlivened by the presence of his granddaughter. Jane was in disgrace. The previous autumn her mother had left her with her cousin Clara in a boarding school at Brighton, while she resumed her Continental travels. It was run by a pair of Evangelical sisters who thought Shakespeare immoral and deprived Jane of her copy of Keble's *Lyra Innocentium*, a High Church book of 'Thoughts in Verse on Christian Children', because it was 'improper reading'. The cousins complained of being 'tyrannised over' and sent to bed early for imaginary faults and, with another girl, decided to run away from school – a Curwen family tradition. Clara did not get away, but the other two girls escaped and got as far as London, before they were recaptured and hauled before Chris, who sent them back to Brighton.[7]

Jane was astute enough to play off her parents' marital differences, declaring that 'her father's friends had never wanted her to be at that school', and she succeeded in persuading her doting father to remove her. Mary thought it 'almost an unpardonable offence – especially in so sensible a Girl', but John and his father were indulgent and Jane rapidly made herself indispensable to him by devoting herself to teaching her two youngest brothers. Even Mary could not find fault with her conduct now, but she regretted the opportunities Jane herself was missing to extend and improve her own education. Her pleas for Jane to be sent to another school fell on deaf ears. Until Isabella returned to England from Italy, where her doctors said she needed to spend another year to renovate her health, Jane would have to take her mother's place at home.[8]

When they returned home, Mary found it difficult to persuade William to leave the house. Even his once favourite walks had become anathema to him, because of their associations with Dora. He still shrank from visiting Loughrigg Holme or even calling on the Cooksons at Grasmere, so that Mary almost despaired. 'Where can we find a place or an object on earth to look upon that is not beset with like hauntings! Could but the thoughts be *fixed* upon that blessed Haven where we trust she now is, we should there find comfort.' Mary's unspoken fear was that her husband's excessive grief would eventually turn his brain and that he would end up like his sister. She noted with foreboding that he had already become, like Dorothy, a lover of a large fire, 'by which he sits close, when within doors'. Rumours of his imbecility were even appearing in the newspapers, spread by a 'trumpery intruder who went one day when Mr W was in one of his silent moods'. Though his family and friends did what they could to combat them, there was clearly cause for concern.[9]

As William found it so hard to go from home but company seemed to be essential to force him to maintain at least a show of spirits, Mary tried to encourage a constant flow of visitors. Kate Southey came to stay in June, followed, in July, when the first anniversary of Dora's death had to be faced, by an influx of relatives and friends. The two youngest grandsons were almost a permanent fixture and as they celebrated their tenth and eighth birthdays on 24 and 25 July, all the children in the neighbourhood were invited to a grand party, the highlight of which was the sending up of a balloon made by the master-of-all-trades, deft-fingered James. Mary's cousin John Monkhouse paid a rare visit from the Stow; almost completely blind, he was cheerful as ever, and had just come fresh from his triumph at the York Agricultural Meeting, where one of his bull calves had won the £20 prize. He won the hearts of both the grandsons, promising ten-year-old John, who had a passion for agricultural matters, that, when he had gone through the proper training, he could come to the Stow 'to finish his education by learning to breed Prize Bulls'.[10]

And this year the Lakers descended in their droves. Few had sought admission the previous summer and fewer still had obtained it; the Rydal Mount Visitors' Book had been abandoned in the wake of Dora's death. This year, however, Mary discreetly encouraged all the strangers who arrived with introductions or 'just happened' to be visiting friends in the area, wisely foreseeing that it would distract her husband from his sorrows to speak to them. 'It seems to me as if America had broken loose, so many, especially from New York, of that country make their way to the Poet', she marvelled.[11]

Among the visitors who called several times at the beginning of September were the Duke and Duchess of Argyll. On each occasion they found the poet seated by the fireside and 'languid and sleepy in manner'. On their first visit he escorted them on the usual tour of the grounds and to the waterfall in Rydal Park, but, 'We went away with no other impression than the vaguest of having seen the man whose writings we knew so well – but with no feeling that we had seen any thing of the mind which spoke through them.' When they called a second time, the family were at church, and they saw only 'a very old, shrivelled, and palsied woman, drawn in a Bath Chair by a servant, whose paralytic countenance, and wandering eye struck us unpleasantly'. Later that evening they caught William at home, and he gave a very different impression from the previous evening. 'His memory seemed clear & unclouded – his remarks forcible & decided'. The Duchess persuaded William to read *Tintern Abbey* to them. 'He read the introductory lines descriptive of the scenery in a low clear voice But when he came to the thoughtful and reflective lines His tones deepened, and he poured them forth with a fervour and almost passion of delivery which was very striking and beautiful.' They were struck by the 'almost unnatural' emphasis he put on the words addressed to his sister, until they realized that 'the old Paralytic, and doited woman' they had seen that morning was that same sister. Mary was visibly affected by the reading, admitting that it was the first time he had read since his daughter's death and that she was thankful to them for making him do it.[12]

In addition to the usual Lakers, however, the Wordsworths were experiencing for the first time the effect of the new railway line from Kendal to Bowness, which had opened on 21 April 1847. Just as William had predicted, hordes of cheap excursionists from the manufacturing towns descended on the Lakes, but instead of demanding beer shops and wrestling, like everyone else, they too wanted to see the poet. 'The Country is strangely changed –', Mary noted; 'think of an Hotel – Omnibus and Carriages running at different hours in the day between Grasmere and the Train! And of numbers pouring in by Monster trains'. 'Yesterday as I happened to be on the Terrace at Rydal Mount,' Quillinan told Robinson on 12 August,

> no less than 50, or 60 (I counted 48 & then left off) Cheap-trainers invaded the poet's premises at once. They walked about all over the terraces & garden, without leave asked, but did no harm; & I was rather pleased at so many humble men & women & lasses having minds high enough to feel interest in Wordsworth. I retreated into the house; but one young lady rang the bell, asked for me, & begged me to give her an autograph of Mr W. – I had none. 'Where could she get one?' I did not know. – Her pretty face looked as sad as if she had lost a lover.

'At this moment', Mary observed a few days earlier, 'a groupe of young Tourists are standing before the window (I am writing in the Hall) and Wm reading a newspaper – and on lifting up his head a profound bow greeted him from each – they look as if come up from the Steamer for the day. I wish you could have seen them.'[13]

As Mary and Dora's joint birthday approached, Mary again persuaded the poet to leave home, taking him on a ten-day nostalgic excursion to their remaining friends and relatives at Penrith, Newbiggin and Hallsteads. 'All were as affectionately kind to us as possible, and we heard and saw much to interest, for the moment, even my husband – but alas! too often "Pleasant thoughts bring sad thoughts to his mind" – and I must plead guilty to the like being *secretly* the case with myself. But we both have much satisfaction of having paid these visits.'[14]

On 24 September news came from Brigham that Isabella Wordsworth had died in Italy. This must have come as something of a surprise, for the family had long since ceased to believe she had any genuine ailment. As Quillinan commented, her loss could not weigh heavily with the Wordsworths in comparison with Dora's, but it was the cause of additional anxiety about John and his children. The two oldest boys, Henry and William, were now at Sedbergh, their father's *alma mater*, having been removed from the unsatisfactory Rossall in the summer, but the three younger ones were effectively being brought up by fifteen-year-old Jane. It had now become much more difficult for the Wordsworths to leave home because William's humouring of his sister since Dora's death had made Dorothy more tyrannical than ever. Deprived of his daily indulgence of her wayward demands, 'which she is much happier without', Mary commented tartly, she fell into a deplorable state, making William doubly miserable and fearful about leaving her.[15]

At the end of November, however, they managed to spend a fortnight at Brigham, where they found the whole household more than ever dependent on Jane, and father and daughter equally determined that she should not be sent off to school again. It was a sign of William's mounting spirits that, on their return journey, he was able to face not only an overnight visit to Mary Stanger, Dora's earliest schoolfriend, at Keswick, but also a trip to Applethwaite, the little estate which Beaumont had given to him and he in turn had passed to Dora. At the beginning of May, he had flatly refused to visit either because the associations were too painful.[16]

'Our return home was most mournful,' William wrote to Isabella Fenwick on 7 December, 'but Mary bears up with a religious resignation, which is in the true spirit of the Gospel of Christ. I wish I could come nearer her excellence in this and every respect'. Robinson had deliberately delayed his annual visit till after Christmas, fearing a repetition of the emotional scenes of the previous year, but when he arrived on 27 December he was relieved and rejoiced to find the Wordsworths 'far more cheerful'. 'In the two days I have spent already here I have had more conversation with the poet than during the whole of my last visit', he crowed to his brother.[17] The house was further enlivened by the presence of Henry and William, on holiday from Sedbergh, and, on 28 December, by that of Derwent Coleridge, making his first visit to the Lakes in many years.

The reason for Derwent's visit was anything but cheerful: he had been summoned to Nab Cottage to attend the death-bed of his fifty-two-year-old brother, Hartley. The two men had barely met since their teenage years, so Derwent was less affected than would otherwise have been the case. His presence relieved Mary of the daily burden of nursing and visiting Hartley, as well as the responsibility for him which she had borne since his mother had left the Lakes in 1829. She had kept an eye on him, paid his bills, organized his clothes and doled out the allowance provided by his family to prevent him spending it all at once on a drunken binge. She had not always been successful and Hartley's fatal illness was the result of his having got drunk and spent five hours in the open air on a wet and windy night trying to find his way home. 'A more worthless life cannot be imagined than his', Robinson wrote disapprovingly, but Hartley was beloved by all in the vales around his home, and by the Wordsworths more than most. As he lay dying, he was tended by four doctors, all of whom gave their services free of charge. 'You should have heard the old man say, "Well! God bless him!" and then turn away in tears', Derwent wrote when Hartley's case was confirmed as hopeless. '"It is a sad thing for me, who have known him so long! He will be a sad loss to us; and let him lie as near to us as possible, leaving room for Mrs Wordsworth and myself. It would have been his wish."' When Hartley died, on 6 January 1849, William was 'dreadfully affected', and could not go in to see his body. Appropriately, it was left to Mary to perform the final rites for the eccentric man to whom she had been a second mother since childhood. She 'kissed the cold face thrice, said it was beautiful, and decked the body with flowers'.[18]

Two days later Robinson accompanied William and Derwent to Grasmere churchyard, to choose where Hartley should lie. As far as William was concerned, there was only one appropriate place. 'When I turned from my daughter's grave', he said of Dora's funeral, 'the first face that met me was Hartley's standing there!' Robinson, who had feared that the visit to the churchyard would overpower William, was pleasantly surprised to find him able to chat on literary subjects, 'a proof of the recovery of a more healthy state of mind'. On 11 January Hartley was buried on a bitter cold day, when the mountains were capped with snow and showers of sleet were interspersed with gleams of sunshine. William and Quillinan attended the funeral, again without ill-effect on the poet's mind, while Robinson remained at Rydal Mount with Mary. He returned to London later that day with the 'comfortable assurance' that his old friend's grief was now 'softened down to an endurable sadness'. 'Whatever his feelings may be,' Robinson told Miss Fenwick, 'the outward expression of them he can repress – I heard no sighs, no moaning – And he never refused to join in any conversation on the topics of the day.' He had not composed a line during the year and, according to Mary, had scarcely written one, 'but it is not to be expected or desired that he should rouse himself to any literary exertions'. Even his long-suffering wife was cautiously optimistic: 'I think I may say, with much thankfulness, that y[ou]r dear Uncle's spirits begin to revive, even when he is not in company.'[19]

'The most agreeable circumstance is that he goes occasionally to Mr Quillinan's', Robinson reported, 'And that they stand in a friendly relation towards each other – Every unpleasant impression on the mind of Mr Qu: is quite removed.' The day after Hartley's funeral William walked through snow and sleet to Loughrigg Holme and sat for an hour 'in his most cheerful mood', talk about his grandchildren leading him to reminisce about his own boyhood and then to talk of Coleridge. 'If I had been inclined to Boswellise, this would have been one of my days for it. He was particularly interesting', Quillinan noted.[20] Visiting Willy at Carlisle a few weeks later, with Mary and their sister-in-law Mary Hutchinson, William was so far his old self as to be drawn into Willy's protest against the latest proposed changes at the Stamp Office, which threatened a further reduction in his income. The first Willy knew of the changes was an advertisement in the newspapers regarding the transfer of former Stamp Office duties to the Excise Office and he was indignant that he had not received prior formal notification. 'After 20 years devotion to the Service – and that the prime of his life [Willy] feels this to be unjust'. So did his father, weighing in with so many letters to the Prime Minister, Sir Robert Peel, and the Chancellor of the Exchequer, Sir Charles Wood, that he clearly tried their patience.[21]

In June the Wordsworths had a reunion with Miss Fenwick, who had taken lodgings at Malvern while they were on a visit to the Hutchinsons at Mathon. On the 21st they were joined by Robinson and Moxon, the former charged with a commission from Quillinan, who had written a sonnet on Cromwell. 'I wish my venerable father-in-law would tinker it right for me; but he won't,' Quillinan explained, 'and asking the author of the political & ecclesiastical sonnets to do such a thing may be almost as presumptuous as scolding Milton for his politics. (Yet if the right words happened to hit Mr Wordsworth he could not help helping me to them. So I hope some of you will provoke him to it. – That's all'[)]. The visit confirmed all Robinson's hopes about William. 'Wordsworth was in good *health*, but the *strength* of his mind has declined – There is no want of intelligence, but of vigour – No delusions but little power – happy but not active. Is not this a comfortable old age?' The day after their arrival, Robinson and Moxon joined the Wordsworths and Hutchinsons on a picnic party at the top of the Camp, a hill about five miles from Malvern. William was soon forced to mount one of the carriages, but he explored the hilltop entrenchments with the best of them and, two days later, aged seventy-nine, 'crossed the Malvern Hill *twice* without suffering any inconvenience'.[22]

At the end of the month there was a sad leave-taking. The Wordsworths made their way to Birmingham, where their kind friend from Lancrigg, Mrs Fletcher, bustled them across the city to the station just in time for the express train to Kendal. They then had a two-hour wait 'at that horrid R. Station', while 'a *Minster* train, 24 Carriages, all close and close packed, passed to Windermere', followed by a special train from Manchester. When their own train arrived, they were almost swamped by the crowd of 'Saturday holiday people'; had it not been for the indispensable James, they would not have found places for themselves or their luggage. Passing one of their nephews, Charles Hutchinson, who was on a pedestrian tour of the Lakes with a friend, on the road from Ambleside, they arrived at Rydal Mount to find Elizabeth and Hannah Cookson waiting to welcome them. 'My dearest Brother,' Mary wrote to Tom that evening, 'I trust to hear a good account of you – and I must hope we may meet again – even in this world – but our prayers must be offered for a heavenly Union that may not be severed. That the Almighty may award us all this blessing is what we now yearn after – satisfied as we ought to be with our earthly blessings – and grateful to be supported under its trials.' For once, William echoed her. 'A mournful return it is to this place, but upon that sorrow I must not dwell. May God give us strength to support our grievous and irreparable loss with resignation to his Will. It is not long that Persons in their 80th year can have to bear these trials.'[23]

The Wordsworths had left Mathon on Saturday morning and reached their home that same evening. At ten o'clock on Monday evening, they were startled by the unexpected arrival of their nephew Tom Hutchinson. He had come, at his mother's request, to break to them, in person and as gently as possible, the news that his father, whom they had left fit and well, had died suddenly and peacefully in the early hours of that morning. 'What a shock for those old people –', Quillinan exclaimed. 'Mrs Wordsworth's favourite brother!' 'He was a beloved friend & Brother to me', Mary mourned, and though she took consolation from the fact that Tom had been twice to church the previous day and received the sacrament from both his sons, she admitted to feeling 'a sorrowful *blank* that I cannot shake off'.[24] Apart from her youngest brother, George, with whom she had never been very intimate, she was the only one of the ten Hutchinson siblings left alive.

The day after Thomas's arrival, the Wordsworths were to have been guests at the wedding of 'Cousin Dorothy' Harrison's daughter, another Dora. James was dispatched to Green Bank to break the news that they could not come, but, on the morning of the wedding, William had a change of heart. Though he declined to attend the festivities afterwards, he did go to church and gave away the bride, as he had promised to do, out of sympathy for her father, Benson Harrison, who, like William himself a few years earlier, had been unequal to the task of parting with his beloved daughter. 'Mr & Mrs Wordsworth are wonderfully well, and *he* is even cheerful, or seems so, to his neighbours & other visitors', Quillinan observed on 12 July. 'I believe it is true "that one great grief makes every other less"'.[25]

Visitors there were a-plenty, including John and all five of his children. Fifteen-year-old Henry had just been removed from Sedbergh and was belatedly swotting for his entrance examinations to the Royal Naval College at Woolwich. Having observed him at work, or rather not at work, his grandfather realized that he was unlikely to pass and wrote to Lord Grey, the Secretary for War, candidly blaming Henry's 'own slackness' for the need to seek a deferral from November to the following May.[26] His place at Sedbergh was to be taken by his ten-year-old brother, Charles, but none of the brothers showed the academic ability of William the third, who was destined for a first-class honours degree at Balliol College, Oxford, and to become a pioneer of Indian education. With the departure of Charles, her youngest charge, Jane, too, was about to be sent to school in Edinburgh, to acquire those ladylike refinements her grandmother thought she needed.[27] The Merewethers paid a fortnight's visit from Coleorton and another face from the past, William Johnson, the former curate of Grasmere who had become headmaster of Dr Bell's Central School in London, returned to the vale, where he had built himself a fine new house on the far shore of the lake. Rydal Mount, Mary declared, echoing her sister's semi-serious complaint of many years before, was more like an inn than a private dwelling.[28]

Mary and Dora's joint birthday, 16 August, passed unmarked. 'Nothing was said about it,' Quillinan told Robinson, 'though they & I well knew that the day was not forgotten.' The Wordsworths did not accompany Quillinan, a month later, to Grasmere churchyard to see the erection of a headstone on Dora's grave. More elaborate than any of the other Wordsworth graves, it was carved with a pattern of ivy leaves round the edge and depicted a lamb, bearing the Cross, at the top. The inscription was simple enough, 'Dora Quillinan 9th Day of July 1847. Him that cometh to me I will in no wise cast out', for Quillinan's original choice of verse had been vetoed by Chris Wordsworth as being 'expressive of, and identified with, a dangerous System of Theology'.[29]

Though Mary protested that William was 'so silent!', Quillinan thought that he was now sustained 'almost as well as his Wife'. 'He is ever ready to receive Strangers & it does him good, – more than he is aware of, for he is always chearful when so called out –', Mary conceded, 'but alas this is required to rouse him from his habitual sad thoughts.' One of those strangers was an American, Ellis Yarnall, who brought a letter of introduction from Professor Henry Reed. He noted William's tall figure, 'a little bent with age, his hair thin and grey, and his face deeply wrinkled. The expression of his countenance was sad, mournful I might say; he seemed one on whom sorrow pressed heavily.' Though the prospects had not looked promising, the two men enjoyed a long conversation lasting most of the afternoon. They discussed recent events in America and France (where the revolutions of 1848 had passed virtually unnoticed at Rydal Mount), talked of Cambridge and the Oxford Movement, which William still defended, despite the defections of so many of its leaders to Rome, and did the tour of the grounds and the lower waterfalls in Rydal Park. As they walked down the hill, Yarnall saw a group of tourists at the church door, talking with the sexton, and fancied their inquiries were about the man by his side. 'One of them caught sight of the venerable man at the moment, and at once seemed to perceive who it was, for she motioned to the others to look, and they watched him with earnest gaze.' Though William was obviously not at the height of his powers, Yarnall was impressed and excited. 'I felt that I had been in the familiar presence of one of the noblest of our race. The sense of Wordsworth's intellectual greatness had been with me during the whole interview. I may speak, too, of the strong perception of his moral elevation which I had at the same time. He seemed to me a man living as in the presence of God by habitual recollection.'[30]

On 1 November, the first two volumes of the six-volume *Poetical Works of William Wordsworth* were published. This was the last edition to appear in the poet's lifetime, but he had played little more than a consultative role in its preparation. He no longer wished to make any substantive changes to his poems and minor corrections of punctuation and proofreading could safely be delegated to Quillinan and Carter. They had also been responsible for this year's new edition of the single volume, double-columned *Poems of William Wordsworth*. Once again, William had been happy to leave the management to Moxon, even countermanding suggestions from Mary and Miss Fenwick that the price should be cheaper: 'Mr W says you know best, & leaves the thing entirely ... to your judgement.' Demand for *The Excursion* still running high, Moxon also published this autumn another reissue of the 1836 stereotype edition. Even excluding the cheap single-volume edition, William estimated that the sale of his poems was running at about 1,000 copies a year, 'which is remarkable as it is upwards of half a century since I began to publish'.[31]

Accolades continued to flow in upon him from every direction. He was invited as a guest of honour to attend the public dinner in Edinburgh to mark the unveiling of the monument to Scott and to the inaugural meeting of a Shakespeare Anniversary festival at Stratford-upon-Avon. To his great pride, he was again proposed as a candidate for the Lord Rectorship of the University of Glasgow, winning a majority of the student votes but, owing to the form of the election, losing to Lord John Russell at the final stage by the casting vote of the then Lord Rector. What was particularly gratifying was that the candidates were almost always drawn from the field of politics, but the students had nominated him 'from a high admiration of your Genius & literary greatness'. The defeat came as a relief, for he feared to cause offence by declining a post which he felt himself too old to accept. Had he known Russell's own sentiments, he would probably have felt the honour even more. 'I should be very sorry to be the cause of preventing the election of Mr Wordsworth', Russell wrote during the contest. '. . . Cannot you represent to the students that I think this would be a good opportunity of making the distinction purely literary? It is a great honour to be thought of for the honour, but I should greatly prefer seeing it conferred on Mr Wordsworth, whose genius has performed so much in which men of all political parties find delight.'[32]

Curiously enough, back in 1841 the literary man had been invited to make a formal entrance into the world of politics when some gentlemen from Glasgow asked him to stand as the Conservative Member of Parliament for the Ayr district of Burgh. That distinction, like the rectorship of the University of Aberdeen, which was offered to him in 1847, he had declined, pleading advanced age as his excuse.[33]

'The time is drawing on for our good friend Mr Robinson's annual visit to us, which we always look forward to with much pleasure', Mary wrote on 29 October. 'You will find your old and faithful friend the poet pretty much as he was on y[ou]r last visit', Quillinan wrote reassuringly. 'The same social cheerfulness – company cheerfulness – the same fixed despondency (uncorrected) I esteem him for both: I love him best for the latter.' For the first time in many years, however, Robinson did not come, being reluctant to face the journey as he had just had a large carbuncle on his back lanced under the new anaesthetic, chloroform. 'Mrs Arnold said, Why, it will be hardly Xmas here without him! – & so we all think', Quillinan replied. 'But what must be must.' It was a decision Robinson was to regret ever after.[34]

Despite Robinson's absence, a large party gathered at Rydal Mount for the double celebration of Christmas Day and Dorothy's seventy-eighth birthday: Quillinan and his two daughters, Hannah Cookson, who had been staying for some time with the Wordsworths, Rolleston, the curate, and three of John's sons. Dorothy herself came down in the evening to join them, as was now her custom. On 2 January William and Mary were invited to Loughrigg Holme. 'Today we are to dine at Mr Quillinans', William told Miss Fenwick, 'a trial which I feel that I am unable to bear as with due submission to God's Will I ought to do. May He have mercy upon me, and upon the Mother of Her whom we have lost.' Both John and Willy came to see their parents over the Christmas period. While the latter was there an officious letter arrived from George Nottage, 'Member of the Comm[itt]ee of Managem[en]t of the City of London Institution'. It complained that their speaker of the night before, the Reverend J. C. Richmond, during a long and rambling discourse on 'the Anglo Saxon Tongue', had regaled his audience with an account of his visit to William on 30 December and a selection of the poet's choicest remarks, including what he described as a passionate denunciation of Francis Jeffrey as 'a coxcomb & a puppy'. 'I humbly conceive that such a retailing in public of conversations held in private must be highly displeasing to you', Nottage sniffed,

> as it certainly involves not only a breach of common politeness but ordinary good feeling and is an act of which no English gentleman [Richmond was American!] can possibly be guilty. I have therefore felt impelled thus to intrude upon you with this unpleasing information, so that you may, if in your judgement it seem prudent, cause a communication to be addressed to Mr Richmond which will prevent the repetition of any such gross violation of confidence in any future lecture.[35]

It had, of course, happened countless times before, and William, though he was reported to be 'disgusted', would have ignored it as he had done in every other instance. Both he and Quillinan, who thought Richmond 'a well-meaning enthusiast', had been rather amused than otherwise by the crassness of the man, who had solemnly informed them that there were only six English poets, Chaucer, Shakespeare, Spenser, Milton, Wordsworth and Martin Farquhar Tupper 'the proverbial Philosopher', whose sole claim to fame was a hugely popular rhythmical setting of commonplace maxims and reflections. Willy, however, was outraged and insisted that *something should be done.* He dispatched Nottage's letter to Robinson, who knew Richmond of old, and Chris Wordsworth, who had supplied the letter of introduction, but there was little either man could do except express their regret and offer to reprimand the offender. It did, however, give Robinson the opportunity for a quiet gloat over holy Chris, who had fallen for Richmond's High Church canting and been the means of introducing the 'blackguard' to Rydal Mount.[36]

The winter of 1850 was long, severe and changeable, alternating between snow and rain, then harsh frosts. The Quillinans were snowed up for several days under Loughrigg and walking was difficult with the snow and slush. William amused himself by the fireside, correcting a memoir of his old friend Westall, written by the artist's son, and regretting that he could not recollect anything further to add to it. On 10 March he attended the morning service at Rydal chapel, as usual, and then in the evening insisted on accompanying Quillinan on his walk to Grasmere churchyard. It was 'very keen cold weather' but he refused to be mollycoddled into wrapping up well. 'I remonstrated with him on being so thinly clad', Quillinan protested, but William simply said, '"I care nothing about it" . . . as if poor man he was invulnerable'. With his niece Ebba Hutchinson, he walked as far as Town End, leaving Quillinan to visit Dora's grave alone. The next day, with Mary, Ebba and her sister, Sarah, he called at Loughrigg Holme to say goodbye to his son-in-law, who was going on a week-long visit to Armathwaite and Carlisle. It was, as Quillinan noted in his diary with a certain grim satisfaction, 'the last house he was ever in except his own'.[37]

On 13 March he went to bed early, complaining of a cold. A week later Mary told Moxon that her husband had suffered a 'severe attack' in consequence of catching cold, but he was much better and they hoped he would be quite well again in a few days' time. On 22 March, Quillinan had every reason to hope that the crisis had passed and there was no longer any danger. William had enjoyed an excellent night and Mary had 'shared the good & sound sleep that has been so beneficial to him'; neither of them had heard Miss Fenwick's cuckoo clock outside their bedroom door between three and seven in the morning. At this stage, Quillinan was more concerned about Mary's 'indefatigable nursing': 'she is very unwilling to accept help, thinking, no doubt quite justly, that her services are more acceptable to her husband than those of anyone else'. Even Dorothy, increasingly immured in her own little world, had done her part while her brother lay sick, 'making little or no noise, which must have been a great effort at self-management on her part'.[38]

'This vile bright keen half-snowy cutting north-easterly weather is not good for any age, least of all for old age', Quillinan complained. It was unfortunate, they all felt, that William's trusted friend Dr Davy was absent. The Ambleside surgeon, Mr Fell, and his assistant, Mr Green, did their best, but they were clearly unhappy at the responsibility of having the life of the elderly and frail Poet Laureate in their hands. 'It is impossible for any medical assistance to be more kindly & anxiously given than that which Mr W receives', Quillinan admitted. 'But unluckily (entre nous) he says he does not like the dolorous face of Green, whom we all understand to be a very able man. I ventured to tell Fell to-day to ask his partner not to look so very solemn.' By the end of the month, William was free from fever, 'but without appetite & very low and weak and inert', and Quillinan was sick of writing bulletins on his father-in-law's health. Mary had wisely tried to keep William's illness a secret from all but their closest friends, knowing that they would be inundated with inquiries, but too many people in Ambleside had too many contacts in London for such news to be suppressed for long. The harassing duty of answering them all devolved on Quillinan. 'I rather submit to the infliction than offend well-meaning though not always considerate, enquirers', he said. 'I answer them *all*! You may suppose I have enough to do, though to some I am very *curt*.' Very few of them even deserved a reply, he thought, only those who valued the man for himself. The rest, two-thirds, he estimated, 'only value Wordsworth for his fame, not from any appreciation of the sterling quality of his mind, nor from even any thing like apprehension of his genius'.[39]

On Easter Sunday, 31 March, Fell assured them all that William was improving. His pulse was steady and his breathing 'free & strong'. Mary was so cheered that she left her husband to attend church and take the sacrament. 'You will be glad to hear that dear William is better', she wrote to Mary Hutchinson, yet I dare say it will be some time before he *thinks* himself as well as he was previous to this ugly attack – which any one who did not know him as I do, would have thought a *frightful* one: to me it has brought back his old habit of exaggerating his *bodily* ailments, which for nearly 3 years he has never seemed conscious of having *one* to complain of, so completely has his mind been engrossed by his sorrows.[40]

William was not better, however. The pleurisy or pneumonia that had threatened his lungs seemed to have been kept at bay by blistering and the application of leeches, but almost all his strength had gone with the fever. He was growing progressively weaker and more lethargic: he would not eat, move nor speak, 'but would have lain on his back motionless, as if in a stupor, till he had sunk from sheer debility'. On 6 April Dr Davy returned from town. Quillinan called on him immediately and Davy went straight up to Rydal Mount. His verdict was hopeful: the patient was in 'a precarious state but not a hopeless one' and he needed strengthening. 'This being so long in bed must be against him, as so contrary to his life-long habits of being much out of doors', Quillinan believed. 'But his constitution was so vigorous & so unabused, that he may yet retain power which w[oul]d fail most men at his age after such an illness.' The next day, William's eightieth birthday, prayers were said for him in Rydal chapel and Davy thought him already improved. 'Since tea he has awaked and so sweetly!' Mary told Miss Fenwick two days later, 'asking me "if I thought he would ever get well?" and upon my expressing my thoughts and explaining why he was so weak and what was to be done to regain lost strength, he jocosely observed – "You preach very nicely" – "Now read to me." This office I turned over to [Ebba], to whom he said "You must excuse me if I fall asleep" – And truly it is even so'. Despite Davy's continuing optimism, Mary was wiser. 'The hopes beloved Friend which lingered about my heart when last Evening I wrote so far,' she continued in a shaking hand, '*have* after a quiet night, passed away, and I feel I must – and I feel I must [*sic*] no longer [no longer: deleted] rest them *here*. I have your prayers and your invaluable love.'[41]

Her unperceptive son John was almost brutal in his assessment of the situation. 'What we have now, I think, most cause to apprehend, is his falling into a condition in some respects similar to our dear Aunt's', he informed his cousin. 'Habitual somnolence, apathy, or paralytic affection is I think to be apprehended.' To prevent it, William was removed from bed and forced to sit in an armchair for an hour every day. 'This is a most painful operation, to all the parties concerned,' John admitted, 'though on his part it arises in a great measure from extreme sensitiveness & nervous apprehension. From the lusty manner in which he screams out when touched he cannot be as weak as he appears to be'. John tried to rally his father with bracing advice, holding up the example of Scott, who had preferred to die of the remedies rather than the disease. 'He on the contrary gives way to the disease in every way – but this in fact is mainly the disease – there is no organic mischief going on.' Out of the blue came a letter from Montagu, which must have wrung Mary's heart. Not having been in contact for several years and knowing nothing of

William's illness, he had written to congratulate him on his eightieth birthday, adding that, if he survived the poet, he expected to hear a clamour raised for him to be buried in Westminster Abbey. 'I think that more good will result from associating the recollection of you, with your native place, than with those groves of stony archwork, where the nation endeavours to preserve the memory of the mighty dead'. 'Pray let me know what your wishes are', the letter asked, unaware of how imminently relevant the question was to become.[42]

John and Willy came as often as they could to Rydal Mount, but the constant daily attendance devolved on Mary, with the devoted assistance of Quillinan, the Hutchinson girls, James and Hannah Holmes, one of the servants, who all took turns at the bedside vigil. Mary, as usual, was a tower of strength. Dorothy, amazingly, seemed 'as much herself as she ever was in her life, & has an absolute *command* of her own will! does not make noises; is not all self; thinks of the feelings of others (Mrs W's for example), is tenderly anxious about her brother; &, in short, but for age & bodily infirmity, is almost *the* Miss Wordsworth we knew in past days.'[43]

By 20 April even John had realized that there was no hope. He gave his father the sacrament for the last time and decreed that he should be left in peace. William lay tranquil and undisturbed in a small bed at the foot of the one he had shared with Mary for almost half a century. 'Poor dear Mother was sadly overcome last night', Willy wrote to his wife and baby daughter at eleven o'clock on the morning of 23 April:

> she went to bed at eleven, & she only got out of her bed once during my stretch to have a look at poor dear Father, & try to wrap up his poor cold feet in a warm flannel shawl, to w[hi]ch he was as averse as ever the moment he felt the clothes being moved – Dear Mother did however gain snatches of sleep & pleased I was whenever I heard her poor sobs subdued by them ... Dear Aunt Hutchinson much to dearest Mother's comfort arrived by mail this morning ... I wish you were both here this lovely day & could hear the glorious thrush that has been singing on the mount ever since day break ...[44]

Before he could sign his name to his letter, Willy was called back to his parents' bedroom and within ten minutes all was over. William had passed away so calmly and so 'very very quietly' that his beloved Miss Fenwick's cuckoo clock could be heard distinctly, shouting the midday hour outside the bedroom door. Across the Vale of Rydal, high up on Loughrigg Fell, Fanny Arnold and her sister watched as the blinds were slowly drawn down at Rydal Mount and they knew that William Wordsworth was dead.[45]

The funeral was held on 27 April. Mary had hoped to keep it as private as possible, so, apart from the immediate family, only Davy was invited. Few were asked, but many came. It was a day, Quillinan said, 'which will long be remembered in these vales, for almost all their population was in the Church & Church-yard of Grasmere'. The Arnolds, Davys and Fletchers were out in force, as they had been for Dora's funeral, not joining the public cortège but quietly waiting in the church to pay their respects. Even so there was still a large procession of carriages and horsemen and, when the family arrived at the church, they found it filled with ladies and gentlemen, all dressed in the deepest mourning. 'When Mrs Wordsworth, supported by her two sons, followed the coffin into the church, I should not have recognized her figure, it was so bowed down with grief', Mrs Fletcher said; 'but she bore it calmly, and I stood opposite to her when she bent over the grave.' William was buried, as he wished to be, beside the daughter he had loved so much. When Mary got into the carriage to go home she almost fainted, but the courage that had borne her through so many trials did not fail her now. By the time she returned to Rydal Mount she had regained her composure so completely that she was able to make tea for all the assembled mourners.[46]

Mrs Fletcher, only a few months older than William herself, who had arrived in the Lakes imbued with the Edinburgh disdain for the poet and the man but, through years of intimacy, had learned to respect both, and owed her home at Lancrigg and its beautiful grounds to his taste and judgement, wrote a touching poem after the funeral. *Thoughts on leaving Grasmere Churchyard, April 27, 1850, after the Funeral of William Wordsworth* is moving on two levels: first, because it is a sincere, if amateur, expression of feeling, but second, and more important, because it could not have been written had there not been a William Wordsworth. Even to its use of blank verse, it is imbued with his spirit, his style, his message, despite the fact that Mrs Fletcher was his diametric opposite in faith and politics. It is a fitting tribute, of the kind William himself would have most appreciated, because it was unsolicited and spoke from the heart.

We saw him laid within the quiet grave,
Near to the yew he had planted. 'Twas a day
Of most rare brightness, and the little birds
Sang no sad requiem o'er the hallowed spot:
'Twas as they welcomed him to his last home.
All Nature glowed instinct with tender love
For him, her fervent worshipper, no more
To chant her praises 'mid her mountain wilds,
Her streams and valleys, 'vocal thro' his song.'
There lives not one whose pilgrimage on earth
Has been more blest, by God's especial grace,
In stirring Heaven-ward thoughts in fellow-men.
His was no narrow creed; he loved mankind
Because God's law is love; and many hearts
In loneliness and grief have felt his power
Work like a charm within them, lifting high
Their thoughts from earthly aims and sordid cares
To life's great purpose for the world to come.

Sweet was the privilege of those who shared
His daily converse, marked his blameless course,
And learned the true philosophy of life
Under his teaching, simple, but sublime.
Peace to his honoured memory; peace to those
Who cherish fervently within their souls
The beautiful realities he taught.[47]

The headstone that was eventually erected over William's grave was, as he wished, stark in its simplicity. A plain piece of Lakeland stone, without ornament of any kind, it simply stated to the curious passer-by, 'William Wordsworth 1850'. As neither of his sons had a grain of poetry in them, it was left to Quillinan, the son-in-law who had so often felt excluded, to pronounce his elegy.

It is said that Shak[e]speare died, on his birthday, April 23, if that be the real date. This great man, Wordsworth, was no Shak[e]speare, and the dramatic power perhaps was not in him. But he had a grand and tender genius of his own that will live in the heart of his country; and these mountains will be his noblest monument. His life was a long & prosperous life, and he was rewarded in the latter part of it at least, for the virtuous use he had made of the great power entrusted to him, with 'honour, love, obedience, troops of friends, & all that should accompany old age.' He has, no doubt, now a higher reward: he is gone to Dora.[48]

Epilogue

The death of William Wordsworth was, as his contemporaries recognized, the end of an era. Sir Robert Peel spoke for the politicians of all parties: 'It is seldom that the Tomb has closed on such a Combination of great Genius, with high Principles and spotless Conduct'. Stanton Biggs, an otherwise anonymous (and inaccurate) obituary writer, spoke for the literary world:

> It would be almost impossible to exaggerate or over-estimate the importance of the influence which Wordsworth, in conjunction with Coleridge, has exercised in the formation of the intellectual characteristics of the present age. These two alone have effected a complete revolution in our modes of thought and of expression . . . the whole of the poetry that has issued from the English press for years, has been tinctured and coloured by the genius of Wordsworth.

Strickland Cookson, the lawyer son of the Wordsworths' old friends the Cooksons of Kendal, and William's hard-nosed legal executor, spoke for all those who had known him intimately over the years: 'I feel that in his death I have lost a friend to whom, all my life, I have been accustomed to look up with reverence and affection, and to whose parental kindness, and interest in my well being, I owe more than it is possible for me to express.'[1]

William himself, however, had planned that his death should not be the end. For half a century he had kept his greatest work under wraps, only to be published after his death. The text of *The Prelude* was ready for publication, all that was lacking being the biographical notice which William had appointed his nephew to prepare. Even Quillinan was prepared to admit that Chris seemed to take up the matter 'in a very good spirit, without any self-interest whatever, beyond the exceeding honour of being his Uncle's biographer', but within days of his uncle's funeral he was already trampling all over the sensitivities of the family. He inserted a paragraph in the newspapers, advertising his appointment as William's biographer but claiming to be his literary executor, which he was not. (The only executors of William's will were Willy, Strickland Cookson and Carter.) At first he said he was writing the biography out of 'pure love' and that he would place all the profits at his aunt's disposal, but less than a month after his uncle's death, he declared that there were 'materials for an ample biography' and that, as this would take more of his time than he had bargained for, he would have to receive proper remuneration from the family or the estate.[2]

Quillinan, who had generously lent Chris his copy of the Fenwick Notes, began to feel understandably annoyed. 'As the Husband & representative of Dora I seem to have been altogether overlooked or set aside in their pecuniary arrangements –', he complained; 'this I conceive to be unjust to the memory of Dora, & unhandsome to myself.' What he did not realize immediately was that Mary was deeply unhappy about the self-expansion of her nephew's remit. For more years than she cared to remember, William had protested against the intrusive nature of contemporary biography, abhorred the publication of private letters and declared that his poems should speak for themselves. Yet here was her nephew, her husband's official biographer, advertising for William's letters and planning a full-scale biography. On 17 May 1850 Mary called a halt. Until she had consulted Isabella Fenwick, who was about to arrive at Rydal Mount, she could not give her sanction to a project which, she felt, ran directly counter to William's intentions. 'He did not desire such a Biography', Quillinan wrote on Mary's behalf. 'On consulting with Miss Fenwick, she finds her scruple not removed but confirmed. Miss F has so often heard your Uncle declare himself about it, that she has no doubt that the Sketch you originally intended will be the proper thing to be done.'[3]

Nevertheless, the biography went ahead. Mary and Miss Fenwick might feel a sentimental attachment to William's wishes, but the more hard-headed members of the family and their friends were all agreed that a full biography, by an officially appointed biographer, was the only way to stem the tide of unofficial and misrepresentative lives that were likely to appear. Mary had to bow to the weight of opinion against her, but, in what might be regarded as a small gesture of defiance, she decided that the publication of *The Prelude* should go ahead without any biographical notice and committed the supervision of the proofs to the spurned biographer. It was Quillinan, therefore, who saw *The Prelude* through the press for Moxon and the poem was published before the end of July.[4]

The progress of the biography, now plodding towards a ponderous two volumes, was much slower. Chris and his family took up residence at Rydal on 11 June and remained there for fifteen weeks, during which he was hard at work. 'He gives all he could', Mrs Fletcher's daughter commented, 'for he did not know much of his Uncle, except by hearsay, and that was not the way to know Wordsworth.' In August they were joined by Robinson and the most contentious subject of the biography was discussed between him, Mary, Miss Fenwick and Chris. Should

William's illegitimate French daughter be mentioned or not? It was a question which would not have arisen had Chris simply prepared a biographical sketch to illustrate *The Prelude*. In a two-volume biography, however, the fact of Caroline's existence had either to be suppressed or explained. The greatest problem was that William's own sons were unaware that they had a half-sister. Understandably, Chris ducked the issue, with a woolly comment about William being 'encompassed with strong temptations' while in revolutionary France and a morally superior remark about the dangers surrounding those 'who in an ardent emotion of enthusiasm put themselves in a position of peril without due consideration of the circumstances which ought to regulate their practice'.[5]

Caroline's husband, however, had seen Chris's announcement of his forthcoming biography and was determined to exact his pound of flesh. Within days of William's funeral he wrote to Mary to establish his claim, and soon he was threatening to come over to England 'to look after his interests if necessary'. The unspoken fear hanging over them all was that 'the price of silence' was a substantial payment to the Baudouin family, otherwise 'a revelation, which will be made as romantic and attractive as French ingenuity in such matters can make it' would be published. The lawyer, Cookson, thought they should get their own version in first, but, by fair means or foul, the more experienced Robinson succeeded in buying the Baudouins' silence.[6]

The French problem might have been settled by Robinson's diplomatic skills, but by the beginning of November Chris had succeeded in alienating both his cousins. A furious letter from the normally quiescent Willy accused him of not only exceeding his brief but also taking financial advantage of his cousins. To Mary's great distress, Chris had insisted on offering his biography to his own publisher, John Murray, William's *bête noire*, instead of to Moxon, the Wordsworths' choice. He had also persuaded Mary to accept an equal division of profits, effectively reducing his cousins to a sixth interest each after their mother's death. In the end, Chris realized he had gone too far. He was acting in opposition to the executors' wishes and, as Moxon offered a better deal than Murray, he was able to transfer publishers without losing face; the spoils remained the same, however, as Mary insisted that Quillinan should be treated equally with his brothers-in-law in the division of her half-share.[7]

The biography, *Memoirs of William Wordsworth*, a dull and unsympathetic cobbling together of poetry and prose, was published in April 1851. A month later the '*insufferable*' Pickersgill portrait of William, 'velvet waistcoat, neat shiny boots – just the sort of dress he would not have worn if you could have hired him', not to mention his 'lackadaisical and mawkishly sentimental expression', had pride of place in the portraits section of the Great Exhibition at Crystal Palace. A more lasting memorial to the poet fell victim to the north–south divide. The Londoners, led by Archdeacon Julius Hare and the Coleridge clan, wanted a life-size statue in Westminster Abbey; the Lakers, headed by Dr Davy and Benson Harrison, were all for an elaborate memorial in Grasmere church, some memorial windows in the new church at Ambleside, which was about to be built, and a 'Wordsworth Library'. Both parties eventually succeeded in getting what they wanted, but neither thought to consult William's widow, who was appalled by all the grandiose schemes, which were so alien to her own and her husband's wishes.[8]

Mary herself remained quietly at Rydal Mount, outliving many of those she cared most about. Edward Quillinan died of pleurisy on 8 July 1851, a day short of the fourth anniversary of Dora's death. Much to Moxon's disappointment, he had failed to produce the edition of William's prose works which they had jointly planned. His last hours were devoted to a vain, delirious, pathetic attempt to read over, and complete, a sentence in the introduction to his translation of Camoens's *Lusiad* from the Portuguese, a task which had occupied him for many years and was left unfinished when he died. Dorothy, whose newly regained self-possession deserted her as soon as her brother died, survived him by almost five years. Mary remained devoted to her, despite the increasing difficulty of managing her as she became more restless and violent. Her death could be regarded as nothing other than a merciful release, even by Mary, who still found the compassion to mourn for the woman her sister-in-law once had been. Dorothy died, aged eighty-four, on 25 January 1855 and was buried in Grasmere churchyard, next to 'her loved Companion' Sara Hutchinson.[9]

Mary found consolation in her family, as she had always done, becoming the much-loved confidante of her grandchildren, whose fortunes in Australia and in the Crimean War she followed with pride, anxiety and simple empathy. 'My belongings', as she referred to them, were the business of her life. In 1853 she braved a final journey from home in the company of her granddaughter Jane, visiting two other remarkable ladies, Isabella Fenwick at East Sheen and Catherine Clarkson at Playford Hall.[10] Though her eyesight gradually failed until she became totally blind, she remained calm, cheerful and uncomplaining. 'She is a model of Christian resignation –', Robinson wrote in admiration. 'Not a syllable of complaint or regret has dropped from her on account of her triple losses in her daughter, her husband & Quillinan'. He could find no more appropriate words to describe her than those William had used half a century before: she was indeed 'a perfect woman'. When she died, aged eighty-eight, in January 1859, her son John declared he had never seen a happier deathbed. She died, as she had lived, contented with her lot, thankful for the kindness shown her, and trusting implicitly in the faith which had upheld her through so many and such long trials. And being the competent organizer that she was, she had quietly arranged the precise spot where she was to be buried. William had wanted to be buried next to Dora. In the crowded Wordsworth corner of Grasmere churchyard there was not enough room between her grave and that of Sara Hutchinson to allow for two separate graves. When William was buried Mary had therefore ordered the grave to be dug deep enough to contain her own coffin as well as her husband's. That way, she said, she had 'the heartfelt satisfaction' of knowing 'that She, as well as the Father, would lie beside their beloved daughter'.[11]

Abbreviations of Names Used in Notes

WW is always taken to refer to William Wordsworth; the following abbreviations refer to his family and friends. In order to distinguish them more easily, I have also given their relationship to WW.

AP	Azariah Pinney (1775–1803), friend
AV	Annette Vallon (1766–1841), French mistress of WW & mother of his daughter
BM	Basil Montagu (1770–1851), friend
BRH	Benjamin Robert Haydon (1786–1846), friend
Capt JW	John Wordsworth (1754–1819), captain of the *Earl of Abergavenny* (ret.1801), cousin
CC	Catherine Clarkson (1772–1856), friend
CCC	Christopher Crackanthorpe Cookson (after 1792 Christopher Crackanthorpe Crackanthorpe) (1745–99), uncle & guardian
Chas W	Charles Wordsworth (1806–92), nephew, son of CW
CL	Charles Lamb (1775–1834), friend
CW	Christopher Wordsworth (1774–1846), brother
CW2	Christopher Wordsworth (1807–85), nephew, son of CW
Dora	Dora Wordsworth (1804–47), daughter
DS	Daniel Stuart (1766–1846), friend & proprietor/editor of the *Morning Post* (1795–1803) & thereafter the *Courier*
DW	Dorothy Wordsworth (1771–1855), sister
EH	Elizabeth (Ebba) Hutchinson (1820–1905), niece, daughter of TH
EIC	East India Company
EIH	East India House
EM	Edward Moxon (1801–58), friend & publisher
EQ	Edward Quillinan (1791–1851), son-in-law
FW	Francis Wrangham (1769–1842), friend
GH	George Hutchinson (1778–1864), brother-in-law
GHG	George Huntly Gordon (1796–1868), friend
HC	Hartley Coleridge (1796–1849), son of STC
HCR	Henry Crabb Robinson (1775–1867), friend
HD	(Sir) Humphry Davy (1778–1829), friend
HH	Henry Hutchinson (1769–1839), brother-in-law
HM	Harriet Martineau (1802–76), friend
HT	Henry Taylor (1800–1886), friend
IF	Isabella Fenwick (1783–1856), friend
IW	Isabella Wordsworth (née Curwen) (1808–48), daughter-in-law, wife of JW3
JC	Joseph Cottle (1770–1853), friend & publisher

JFP	John Frederick Pinney (1773–1845), friend
JH	John (Jack) Hutchinson (1768–1833), brother-in-law
JK	John Kenyon (1784–1856), friend
JL	James Losh (1763–1833), friend
JM	John Monkhouse (1782–1866), cousin of MW
Jo H	Joanna Hutchinson (1780–1843), sister-in-law
JP(M)	Jane Pollard, after 5 Aug 1795, Jane Pollard Marshall (1771–1847) friend of DW
JPP	John Praetor Pinney (1740–1818), father of AP & JFP
JQ	Jemima (Mima) Quillinan (1819–91), stepdaughter of Dora
JR	John ('Jack') Robinson (1727–1802), father's cousin
JW1	John Wordsworth (1741–83), father
JW2	John Wordsworth (1772–1805), brother
JW3	John Wordsworth (1803–75), son
JW4	John Wordsworth (1805–39), nephew, son of CW
KJW	'Keswick' John Wordsworth (1815–46), nephew, son of RW
LL	Sir William Lowther, Lord Lonsdale, after 7 Apl 1807, 1st Earl of Lonsdale (1757–1844), friend & patron
LMB	Lady Margaret Beaumont (1765–1829), friend
MAL	Mary Ann Lamb (1764–1847), friend
MEM	Mary Elizabeth Monkhouse (1821–1900), daughter of TM
MH	Mary Hutchinson, see MW
MJJ	Maria Jane Jewsbury (1800–1833), friend of Dora
MM	Mary Monkhouse (1787–1858), cousin & sister-in-law of MW; after 1 Nov 1812 becomes Mrs TH
Mrs STC	Sarah Coleridge, née Fricker (1770–1845), wife of STC
Mrs TH	Mary Hutchinson, née Monkhouse (1787–1858): see also MM
MW	Mary Wordsworth, née Hutchinson (1770–1859), wife
RC	Raisley Calvert (1773–95), friend
RJ	Robert Jones (1769–1835), friend
RM	Rydal Mount, home of the Ws (1813–59)
RQ	Rotha Quillinan (1821–76), goddaughter & stepdaughter of Dora
RS	Robert Southey (1774–1843), friend
RW	Richard Wordsworth (1768–1816), brother
RWB	Richard Wordsworth of Branthwaite (1752–1816), cousin
RWW	Richard Wordsworth of Whitehaven (1733–94), uncle & guardian
SC	Sara Coleridge (1802–52), daughter of STC
SGB	Sir George Beaumont (1753–1827), friend & patron
SH	Sara Hutchinson (1775–1835), sister-in-law
SJL	Sir James Lowther, after 1784 Earl of Lonsdale (1736–1802), debtor
SR	Samuel Rogers (1763–1855), friend
STC	Samuel Taylor Coleridge (1772–1834), friend
TC	Thomas Clarkson (1760–1846), friend
TdQ	Thomas de Quincey (1785–1859), friend

TH	Thomas (Tom) Hutchinson (1773–1849), brother-in-law
TL	Thomas Longman (1771–1842), publisher
TM	Thomas (Tom) Monkhouse (1783–1825), cousin of MW
TNT	Thomas Noon Talfourd (1795–1854), friend
TP	Thomas (Tom) Poole (1765–1837), friend
TR	Thomas Robinson, brother & correspondent of HCR
VL	William, Viscount Lowther, after 1844, Earl of Lonsdale (1787–1872), friend & patron
W	the Wordsworth family
WC	Rev. Dr William Cookson (1754–1820), uncle
WCal	William Calvert (1770–1829), friend
WG	William Godwin (1756–1836), friend
WM	William Mathews (1769–1801), friend
WRH	William Rowan Hamilton (1805–65), friend
WS	(Sir) Walter Scott (1771–1832), friend
WW	William Wordsworth (1770–1850), himself
WW2	William Wordsworth (1810–83), son

Abbreviations of Sources Used in Notes

The following abbreviations are used for frequently quoted sources. A list of other works cited can be found in the Bibliography; works of minor interest or that are referred to only once are cited in full in the text. All manuscript references are to the Wordsworth Trust at Dove Cottage (DC), unless otherwise stated.

ADL, Orléans	Archives Départementales of Loiret at Orléans
ADL&C, Blois	Archives Départementales of Loir-et-Cher at Blois
Ashton	Rosemary Ashton, *The Life of Samuel Taylor Coleridge* (Oxford, Blackwell, 1996)
Barron Field	Barron Field's *Memoirs of Wordsworth*, edited by Geoffrey Little (Sydney University Press, for the Australian Academy of the Humanities, 1975)
BL	British Library
Blanshard	Frances Blanshard, *Portraits of Wordsworth* (London, George Allen & Unwin, 1959)
BRH, *Autobiography*	Benjamin Robert Haydon, *Autobiography*, with an introduction & epilogue by Edmund Blunden (Oxford University Press, 1927)
– *Diary*	*The Diary of Benjamin Robert Haydon*, edited by William Bissell Pope (Harvard University Press, 1960–63), 5 vols.
CRO	Cumbria Record Office
Cumming	Edward Cumming, *The Wreck of the English East Indiaman, Earl of Abergavenny Weymouth Bay, 1805: Commander John Wordsworth Esq.* (unpublished MS)
Darlington	*The Love Letters of William and Mary Wordsworth*, edited by Beth Darlington (London, Chatto & Windus, 1982)
DC	Dove Cottage, Townend, Grasmere
DWG	Dorothy Wordsworth, *The Grasmere Journals*, edited by Pamela Woof (Oxford University Press, 1991)
DWJ	Dorothy Wordsworth, *Journals*, edited by Ernest de Selincourt (London, Macmillan, 1959), 2 vols.
DWJMS	Dorothy Wordsworth, Journals in manuscript (followed by MS no.)
DWR	Dorothy Wordsworth, *Recollections of a Tour made in Scotland*, introduction, notes & photographs by Carol Kyros Walker (Yale University Press, 1997)
English Witnesses	*English Witnesses of the French Revolution*, edited by J.M. Thompson (Oxford, Blackwell, 1938)
EQD	Edward Quillinan, Diaries in manuscript (followed by MS no.)
EY	*The Letters of William and Dorothy Wordsworth: The Early Years 1787–1805*,

	edited by Ernest de Selincourt, revised by Chester L. Shaver (Oxford, Clarendon Press, 1967)
Farington Diary	*The Diary of Joseph Farington*, edited by Kenneth Garlick, Angus Macintyre et al. (Yale University Press, 1979–), 16 vols.
Gill	Stephen Gill, *William Wordsworth: A Life* (Oxford University Press, 1990)
Guide	William Wordsworth, *A Guide Through the District of the Lakes* (London, Longman, 1822), see *Prose*, ii, 123–465 & Appendix I
Hayden	*Romantic Bards and British Reviewers: A selected edition of the contemporary reviews of the works of Wordsworth, Coleridge, Byron, Keats and Shelley*, edited by John O. Hayden (London, Routledge & Kegan Paul, 1971)
HCRBW	*Henry Crabb Robinson on Books and Their Writers*, edited by Edith J. Morley (London, J.M. Dent, 1938), 3 vols.
HCRD	*Diary, Reminiscences, and Correspondence of Henry Crabb Robinson*, edited by Thomas Sadler (London, Macmillan & Co., 1872), 2 vols.
HCRDMS	Henry Crabb Robinson, Diaries in manuscript, Dr Williams's Library, London
HCRWC	*The Correspondence of Henry Crabb Robinson with the Wordsworth Circle (1808–1866)*, edited by Edith J. Morley (Oxford, Clarendon Press, 1927), 2 vols.
Holmes, i	Richard Holmes, *Coleridge: Early Visions* (Harmondsworth, Penguin Books, 1989)
Holmes, ii	Richard Holmes, *Coleridge: Darker Reflections* (London, HarperCollins, 1998)
IF	[WW dictated to Isabella Fenwick], *The Fenwick notes of William Wordsworth*, edited by Jared Curtis (Bristol Classical Press, 1993)
JL, *Diaries*	James Losh, *The Diaries and Correspondence of James Losh*, edited by Edward Hughes (Durham, Surtees Society, 1962–3), 2 vols.
JLDMS	James Losh, Diaries in manuscript, 26 vols. Reference Library, Carlisle Public Library, The Lanes, Carlisle
Johnston	Kenneth R. Johnston, *The Hidden Wordsworth: Poet, Lover, Rebel, Spy* (New York & London, W.W. Norton & Co., 1998)
Jordan	John E. Jordan, *De Quincey to Wordsworth: A Biography of a Relationship. With the Letters of Thomas de Quincey to the Wordsworth Family* (University of California Press, 1962)
JTM	*The Journal of Thomas Moore*, edited by Wilfred S. Dowden (University of Delaware Press, 1983), 6 vols.
LB	William Wordsworth, *Lyrical Ballads, and Other Poems, 1797–1800*, edited by James Butler & Karen Green (Cornell University Press, 1992)
LCL	*Letters of Charles and Mary Lamb*, edited by Edwin W. Marrs (Cornell University Press, 1975–8), 3 vols.
Legouis	Emile Legouis, *William Wordsworth and Annette Vallon* (London & Toronto, J.M. Dent, 1922)
LHC	*The Letters of Hartley Coleridge*, edited by G.E. and E.L. Griggs (Oxford, 1937, reprinted 1941)

Lindop — Grevel Lindop, *A Literary Guide to the Lake District* (London, Chatto & Windus, 1993)

Lindop, *TdQ* — Grevel Lindop, *The Opium-Eater: A Life of Thomas de Quincey* (London, Weidenfeld, 1993)

LJW — *The Letters of John Wordsworth*, edited by Carl H. Ketcham (Cornell University Press, 1969)

LMW — *The Letters of Mary Wordsworth 1800–1855*, edited by Mary E. Burton (Oxford, Clarendon Press, 1958)

LSH — *The Letters of Sara Hutchinson from 1800 to 1835*, edited by Kathleen Coburn (London, Routledge & Kegan Paul, 1954)

LWS — *The Letters of Sir Walter Scott*, edited by H.J.C. Grierson (London, Constable, 1932–7), 12 vols.

LY, i — *The Letters of William and Dorothy Wordsworth: The Later Years: Part I, 1821–1828*, edited by Ernest de Selincourt, revised by Alan G. Hill (Oxford, Clarendon Press, 1978)

LY, ii — *The Letters of William and Dorothy Wordsworth: The Later Years: Part II, 1829–1834*, edited by Ernest de Selincourt, revised by Alan G. Hill (Oxford, Clarendon Press, 1979)

LY, iii — *The Letters of William and Dorothy Wordsworth: The Later Years: Part III, 1835–1839*, edited by Ernest de Selincourt, revised by Alan G. Hill (Oxford, Clarendon Press, 1982)

LY, iv — *The Letters of William and Dorothy Wordsworth: The Later Years: Part IV, 1840–1853*, edited by Ernest de Selincourt, revised by Alan G. Hill (Oxford, Clarendon Press, 1988)

Memoirs — Christopher Wordsworth, *Memoirs of William Wordsworth* (London, Edward Moxon, 1851), 2 vols.

Moorman — Mary Moorman, *William Wordsworth: A Biography* (Oxford University Press, 1968), 2 vols.

MY, i — *The Letters of William and Dorothy Wordsworth: The Middle Years: Part I, 1806–1811*, edited by Ernest de Selincourt, revised by Mary Moorman (Oxford, Clarendon Press, 1969)

MY, ii — *The Letters of William and Dorothy Wordsworth: The Middle Years: Part II, 1812–20*, edited by Ernest de Selincourt, revised by Mary Moorman & Alan G. Hill (Oxford, Clarendon Press, 1970)

Poems — William Wordsworth, *The Poems*, edited by John O. Hayden (Harmondsworth, Penguin Books, 1977), 2 vols.

PP — Pinney Papers, Special Collections, University of Bristol

Prance — Charles Prance, *Companion to Charles Lamb* (London, Mansell Publishing, 1983)

Prelude — William Wordsworth, *The Prelude: The Four Texts (1798, 1799, 1805, 1850)*, edited by Jonathan Wordsworth (Harmondsworth, Penguin Books, 1995)

Prose — William Wordsworth, *The Prose Works of William Wordsworth*, edited by

	W.J.B. Owen & Jane Worthington Smyser (Oxford, Clarendon Press, 1974), 3 vols.
Reed, i	Mark L. Reed, *Wordsworth: The Chronology of the Early Years 1770–1799* (Harvard University Press, 1967)
Reed, ii	Mark L. Reed, *Wordsworth: The Chronology of the Middle Years 1800–1815* (Harvard University Press, 1975)
Roe	Nicholas Roe, *Wordsworth and Coleridge: The Radical Years* (Oxford, Clarendon Press, 1988)
RMVB	Rydal Mount Visitors' Book, 1830–47: MS DC 166, DC
RSLC	*The Life and Correspondence of Robert Southey*, edited by his son, the Rev. Charles Cuthbert Southey (London, Longman, Brown, Green & Longmans, 1850), 6 vols.
RSNL	*New Letters of Robert Southey*, edited by Kenneth Curry (London & New York, Columbia University Press, 1965), 2 vols.
Sandford	Elizabeth Sandford, *Thomas Poole and His Friends* (Over Stowey, Friarn Press, 1996)
Schneider	Benn Ross Schneider, *Wordsworth's Cambridge Education* (Cambridge University Press, 1957)
SCM	*Memoir and Letters of Sara Coleridge*, edited by Edith Coleridge (London, Henry S. King & Co., 1873), 2 vols.
SJC	St John's College, Cambridge
Smith	Elsie Smith, *An Estimate of William Wordsworth by His Contemporaries 1793–1822* (Oxford, Basil Blackwell, 1932)
STCBL	Samuel Taylor Coleridge, *Biographia Literaria*, edited by James Engell & W. Jackson Bate (Princeton University Press, 1983)
STCL	*Collected Letters of Samuel Taylor Coleridge*, edited by Earl Leslie Griggs (Oxford, Clarendon Press, 1956–71), 6 vols.
STCN	*The Notebooks of Samuel Taylor Coleridge*, edited by Kathleen Coburn (London, Routledge & Kegan Paul, 1957), 4 vols. text & 4 vols. notes
STCP	Samuel Taylor Coleridge, *The Complete Poems*, edited by William Keach (Harmondsworth, Penguin Books, 1997)
Storey	Mark Storey, *Robert Southey: A Life* (Oxford University Press, 1997)
Supp.	*The Letters of William and Dorothy Wordsworth: A Supplement of New Letters*, edited by Alan G. Hill (Oxford, Clarendon Press, 1993)
TdQ, *Recollections*	Thomas de Quincey, *Recollections of the Lakes and the Lake Poets* (Harmondsworth, Penguin Books, 1970, reprinted 1980)
Thompson	T.W. Thompson, *Wordsworth's Hawkshead* (Oxford University Press, 1970)
Venn	J.A. Venn, *Alumni Cantabrigiensis: Part II, from 1752 to 1900* (Cambridge University Press, 1940–54), 6 vols.
WYAS	West Yorkshire Archive Service

Notes

Chapter 1

chapter title: 'The Child is father of the Man', WW, 'My heart leaps up when I behold', l.7 (*Poems*, i, 522).
picture: The Wordsworth House, Cockermouth.
1. *Prelude, 1799*, i, 361–7. WW first described the experience only four years after it occurred in *The Vale of Esthwaite*, ll.425–48 (*Poems*, i, 62). The much elaborated account in the 1799 *Prelude* was carried over, with only minor variants, into both the later versions. Lindop, 390–91, identifies the place as a crag at Outgate, a hamlet 1½ miles from Hawkshead.
2. Wilberforce, *Journey to the Lake District from Cambridge 1779*, 77; Hutchinson, *The History of the County of Cumberland*, ii, 110–19. Wilberforce may have met WW's father on this occasion as his friend and companion was WW's uncle, WC. WW himself was away at school at Hawkshead. Much of Hutchinson's information was provided by the Rev. J. Gilbanks, WW's schoolmaster at Cockermouth.
3. WW and both his sons owed their livelihood to Lowther patronage: see pp. 448, 605, 641, 734, 737.
4. Owen, *The Lowther Family*, 280–84. SJL bribed the under-sheriff conducting the election to ignore the inconvenient fact that he was a minor and therefore ineligible to stand. By 1780 SJL controlled nine parliamentary seats. His nominees were known as 'Sir James' Nine-pins' and included the future prime minister William Pitt, who first entered Parliament as his appointee for Appleby in 1781: ibid., 287–8.
5. A. Carlyle, *Anecdotes and Characters of the Times*, 213. Rev. Alexander Carlyle (1722–1805) was minister of Inveresk, 1748–1805. SJL informed William Lowther on 26 Jan 1782, 'gentlemen who are brought in Parliament by me are not accountable to any person but myself for their conduct'; when his brother Robert defied him, claiming it was his duty to give 'my free vote according to the best of my judgement', SJL compelled him to resign, refused him any other patronage and consigned him to complete oblivion for the rest of his life: Bonsall, *Sir James Lowther and Cumberland and Westmorland Elections*, 61.
6. WW to J. Hunter, 31 Oct 1831 (*LY*, ii, 444). Richard Wordsworth (1690–Jun 1760) had been forced to enter a profession when his father had to sell off the family estates at Normanton, between Wakefield and Castleford, due to an ill-judged speculation in mines. Richard had married in London, but his first wife died without children. WW guessed that his grandfather had come into Westmorland as a Lowther law agent through the influence of the Lowthers of Swillington. Richard's second wife, WW's grandmother, was Mary Robinson (1700–1773) of Appleby.
7. G.G. Wordsworth, 'The Boyhood of Wordsworth', *Cornhill Magazine*, xlviii (1920), 411.
8. WW to J. Hunter, 31 Oct 1831 (*LY*, ii, 444); Bonsall, *Sir James Lowther and Cumberland and Westmorland Elections*, 145–6; Owen, *The Lowther Family*, 285. One of the reputed derivations of the phrase 'before you can say Jack Robinson' is said to be JR's habit of jumping up to ask questions in Parliament almost before the answer to the previous one was given. SJL challenged JR to a duel over his defection which the latter wisely refused. *EY*, 57n.2 wrongly dates to 1770 JR's breach with SJL and his passing of the law agency to his cousin; it is also wrong in attributing the cause of the quarrel to SJL's decision to support the opposition. As JW1's earliest account books for the Lowther estate date from 1765, it is likeliest that JW1 took over the law agency soon after JR became an MP: see MS D Lons/L3/2/191, CRO, Carlisle.
9. See, for example, JW1's account books for 1783, the year he died: MS D Lons/L3/2/236–7, CRO, Carlisle. JW1 was the bailiff and recording officer of the borough of Cockermouth: Reed, i, 38n.

10. Bonsall, *Sir James Lowther and Cumberland and Westmorland Elections*, 103–4, 93–100. Portland's own electioneering expenses in Carlisle and Cumberland in 1767 and 1768 had cost him in the region of £20,000, so SJL's expenditure was not out of line with that of his opponent.

11. The Sockbridge estate was let to a farmer at an annual rental of £70 16s 6d, so that the annuity could be (and was) paid in cash until JW1's mother's death in 1773, when JW1 inherited the estate outright. The complicated financial arrangements were necessary because, in Nov 1763, the merchants were declared bankrupt who held the £500 from the personal estate of Richard Wordsworth which was intended to pay his daughter Ann's legacy. JW1 persuaded his sister and brother to accept his bonds for double the amount of their legacies; these became legally enforceable against him if he failed to pay the legacies on the day of their mother's death. In the days before regulated banking such arrangements were commonplace: JW1, Account Book, *c.*1765–83: WLMS/1/2/3 pp. lv–3.

12. Hudleston, 'Ann Crackanthorpe: Wordsworth's great aunt', 137–46. The Cooksons' shop is wrongly identified by Johnston, 32. It stood on the site of what is now the equally splendid R. Arnison & Sons, 'Draper Costumier and Milliner'; the Cooksons are likely to have lived in Burrowgate, the crooked little street next to the shop, which leads off Market Square.

13. JW1, Account Book, *c.*1765–83: WLMS/1/2/3 p. 10. The marriage settlement was signed on 4 Feb 1766, the day before the marriage. Both Moorman, i, 5 and Johnston, App.A make Ann a year older than she actually was; Johnston, 33 also seriously underestimates the wealth and prestige of the Cooksons.

14. Wordsworth Family Bible, DC; photograph of Register of Marriages, St Andrew's Church, Penrith, exhibited at the Penrith Museum, Robinson's School, Penrith. The marriage was by licence since Ann was under-age. By one of the convoluted relationships in which the Ws specialized, the vicar's wife, Mary Cowper, was great-aunt to MH, WW's future wife, and would become mother-in-law to Ann's brother, WC.

15. Wordsworth Family Bible, DC; Reed, i, 39n. WW and DW were named after their maternal grandparents, JW2 after his father and CW after his maternal uncle. The preponderance of Cookson / Crackanthorpe names in preference to traditional W ones is possibly significant. The six days between WW's birth and baptism was the shortest interval for any of the W children.

16. WW, *Autobiographical Memoranda*, Nov 1847 (*Prose*, iii, 371); *Prelude, 1799*, i, 11–15; *1805*, i, 291–304; WW to JK, 23 Sep [1833] (*LY*, ii, 640). The importance WW attached to the Derwent as a source of poetic influence is reflected in the fact that this eulogy, little altered over the years, opens the first book of each of the four versions of *The Prelude.* In the expanded 1805 version, WW is now five instead of four years old and the silent pools have become a small mill-race severed from the main stream.

17. WW, *Address from the Spirit of Cockermouth Castle* (*Poems*, ii, 747). The sheer horror of this incident stayed with WW for life; the poem describing it was written when he was 73. For a description of the *oubliettes*, see Hutchinson, *The History of the County of Cumberland*, ii, 112.

18. Reed, i, 41. As Reed notices, there are significant gaps in payment to Amy, the maidservant, in JW1's household accounts. She was always paid half-yearly, on Whit Monday (which fell any time in May or Jun) and Martinmas (11 Nov) and was employed from Martinmas 1771 to Martinmas 1778. The omitted payments are for the periods 31 May 1773 to 22 May 1774, 6 Jun 1775 to 26 May 1776 and 11 Nov 1776 to 18 May 1777, suggesting that her services were not required because some or all of the family were at Penrith. This cannot be taken as an absolute rule, however, for Amy was employed at Cockermouth in 1778 even though her mistress and the children were then at Penrith: JW1, Account Book, *c.*1765–83: WLMS/1/2/3 pp. 102v–103. Reed is wrong in assuming that JW1 used Whitsuntide in the legal sense of 15 May, as Whit Monday and Martinmas were the dates of the two great fairs for the hiring of servants in Cockermouth: Hutchinson, *The History of the County of Cumberland*, 115. WW's first meeting with MH at the Penrith Dame School is confirmed by H. Inman to H. Reed, 23 Jun 1845 (Reed, i, 42n).

19. WW told IF, 'I used to pass my summer holydays under the roof of my maternal grand Father', but this may refer only to his schooldays at Hawkshead: *IF*, 54. Ann W (1734–87) married Rev. Thomas Myers (1735–1826) in 1763; their

children were Thomas (1764–1835), who became MP for Harwich in 1802, Mary (1765–1852), who married her mother's cousin Hugh Robinson (brother of JR), and John (1767–1821), who went up to St John's College, Cambridge, with his cousin WW.

20. JW1, Account Book, *c.*1765–83: WLMS/1/2/3 (nn. inside front cover). RWW (1733–94) had married his cousin Elizabeth Favell (1737–1809) in 1751 and, by 1771, had produced five sons and four daughters. Three of the sons, Capt JW, RWB and James, received legacies of £10 each from their grandfather which JW1 paid to them in 1771, 1772 and 1774 respectively, when they left their home at Whitehaven for London. In 1774 JW1 also paid his brother the £300 legacy from their father in full. The gift of £170, which seems to have been made purely from the goodness of JW1's heart, could not be made until JW1 had the legal disposal of his parents' estate: ibid., 4. This gesture is totally at odds with Johnston's portrayal of JW1 as a grasping, self-obsessed villain, for which there is absolutely no evidence.

21. JW1 prevented diminution of the Crackanthorpe estate by enclosure but did not obtain payment of the legacy; his bill for £110 7s 1d was still unpaid when he died in 1783: Hudleston, 'Ann Crackanthorpe: Wordsworth's great aunt', 143. DW considered her uncle's political persuasion a major stumbling block in reaching a settlement with SJL over her father's estate: DW to JP, [late Jul 1787] (*EY*, 4).

22. *The Journals of Caroline Fox*, 129.

23. WW, *Autobiographical Memoranda*, Nov 1847 (*Prose*, iii, 372).

24. *Prelude, 1799*, i, 319–27. Thomas Parker, a butcher from Langwathby, was murdered on the road from Penrith to Edenhall on the night of 18 Nov 1766; his godson, Thomas Nicholson, was executed for the crime at the murder site on 31 Aug 1767 and his body hung in chains there: Furness, *History of Penrith*, 177–8. For James's attitude towards the W children, see DW to JP, [late Jul 1787] (*EY*, 4).

25. WW, *Autobiographical Memoranda*, Nov 1847 (*Prose*, iii, 372).

26. Hutchinson, *The History of the County of Cumberland*, i, 313, 327, 336, 343–5. The town is still remarkable for the friendliness of its people and the wonderful variety and independence of its shops.

27. Ibid., i, 318, 320–21; Anon., *A Short Guide to St Andrew's Church, Penrith*, nd.

28. MW, *Autobiographical Memoranda*, [Nov 1851]: DC 167 pp. 68, 64–5; WW, *Autobiographical Memoranda*, Nov 1847 (*Prose*, iii, 375). Ann's name is usually given as 'Birkett', but she signed her will 'Ann Birkhead' on 1 Oct 1790; she died soon afterwards, the will being proved on 16 Nov 1790: photograph, Penrith Museum.

29. Though it is true that, as Gill, 15, points out, WW moves straight from Cockermouth to Hawkshead in his account of boyish pleasures in *The Prelude*, omitting any reference to Penrith, all these places (except Long Meg and her Daughters, which he did not visit till Jan 1821: WW to SGB, 10 Jan 1821 [*LY*, i, 4–5]) were familiar to WW in childhood and would be celebrated in his other poetry. All these places are open to the public, though the Nunnery Walks are in private hands so a fee is payable for access.

30. WW to E.H. Handley, 18 Apl 1836 (*LY*, iii, 203); E. Ferguson to DW, 21 Mar 1805: WLMS/A/Ferguson p. 1; *IF*, 55.

31. DWJMS: DC 19 p. 21 [14 Mar 1802] (*DWG*, 78); WW, *To a Butterfly* [Stay near me – do not take thy flight!], ll.14–18 (*Poems*, i, 518). White was the colour of the Bourbons, hence the identification of white butterflies with Frenchmen. I am indebted to my son, Edward Barker, flag-expert extraordinaire, for this information.

32. WW, *The Sparrow's Nest*, ll.11–14, 17–20 (*Poems*, i, 530).

33. Moorman, i, 18, suggests Ann W died of pneumonia but WW says his mother died 'of a decline', the lay term for consumption or tuberculosis, brought on by the cold: WW, *Autobiographical Memoranda*, Nov 1847 (*Prose*, iii, 371). The children's removal to Penrith is implied in DW's statement that she last saw the garden terrace at Cockermouth when she was six, a few months before her mother's death; she also says she never spent her birthday, Christmas Day, at home in the interval between her parents' death: DW to LMB, 7 Aug & 25–6 Dec 1805 (*EY*, 616, 663). This suggests the family left for Penrith just after Christmas 1777. The date of Ann's death is not certain but is deduced from the abnormally heavy payments to the Penrith apothecary for the 2½ months ending 8 Mar 1778: Reed, i, 46. The date of burial is taken from the Burial

Register of St Andrew's Church, Penrith: photograph, Penrith Museum.

34. Most of the graves in St Andrew's churchyard are made from the local soft red sandstone and the inscriptions are indecipherable, so it is possible that the same fate befell Ann's.

35. DW to LMB, 18–19 Mar 1805 (*EY*, 568); WW, *Prelude, 1805*, v, 257–90.

36. WW, *Autobiographical Memoranda*, Nov 1847 (*Prose*, iii, 371–2); WW, *Catechizing* (*Poems*, ii, 492–3).

37. RW had entered the grammar school in Oct 1774; WW joined him in Oct 1776: JW1, Account Book, *c.*1765–83: WLMS/1/2/3 pp. 50–51. The obvious partiality of the Cooksons for their two youngest nephews may reflect the fact that they spent more of their early life in Penrith.

38. Ibid., p. 87v. Johnston, 41 is wrong in asserting that DW was 'packed off' to relatives, just after Christmas 1777, in anticipation of her mother's death; he confuses the family departure for Penrith with DW's to Halifax.

39. Wilson, 'Mrs William Rawson and Her Diary', 29–31; DW to JP, *c.*27 Jan 1788 (*EY*, 15–16). Elizabeth (1745–1837) was the daughter of Elizabeth Cookson, sister of WW's grandfather, and Rev. Samuel Threlkeld, a Unitarian minister, who had moved from Penrith to Halifax in 1744.

40. Wilson, 'Mrs William Rawson and Her Diary', 31–2.

41. Ibid., 32; Trigg, 'Dorothy Wordsworth and Her Halifax Friends', 90–91; Hanson, *The Story of Old Halifax*, 199–200, 209.

42. JW1, Account Book, *c.*1765–83: WLMS/1/2/3 pp. 102v–103; JW2 to DW, 10 Mar 1801 (*LJW*, 106).

43. Letters Patent and Founders' Board, Hawkshead Grammar School. I have gleaned a great deal of information from the excellent exhibition at the grammar school.

44. JW1, Account Book, *c.*1765–83: WLMS/1/2/3 p. 86v. WC's name appears in the school records, though his brother's does not: Clarke & Weech, *History of Sedbergh School*, 118.

45. JW1, Account Book, *c.*1765–83: WLMS/1/2/3 p. 86v; Thompson, 5, 12. JW1 paid the Tysons 10 guineas a year for each son, for board alone; extra charges were made for washing, coals, candles and 'cakes': see Hugh & Ann Tyson, Account Book, Hawkshead Old Grammar School; Thompson, 86–8. In 1805, the boys on the charity foundation were allotted only seven guineas per head for their board: Exhibition, Hawkshead Old Grammar School.

46. A drip-course is a projecting stone rim above windows to channel away rain.

47. The restoration was carried out by Lieut.-Col. Myles Sandys of Graythwaite Hall, a descendant of the founder, three years after its tercentenary: Fact Sheet/Guide, Hawkshead Old Grammar School; Marsh & Garbutt, *Wordsworth's Lakeland*.

48. WW, *Autobiographical Memoranda*, Nov 1847 (*Prose*, iii, 372); J. Spedding to WW, 8 Mar 1838: MS 66a p. 3, Spedding Papers. Spedding describes revisiting the school in 1836, contrasting its desolation then with its thriving condition in his youth.

49. WW, *Autobiographical Memoranda*, Nov 1847 (*Prose*, iii, 372); *Prelude, 1805*, v, 58–60, 364–9; *1850*, v, 460–76. *Gil Blas* cost 8s and was purchased from the Penrith bookseller Anthony Soulby on 27 Dec 1781: JW1, Account Book, *c.*1765–83: WLMS/1/2/3 p. 82.

50. *Prelude, 1805*, v, 450–81. The incident, significantly, appears in the section entitled 'Books', rather than in the account of his childhood and schooltime. The schoolmaster, James Jackson, aged 21, drowned on 18 Jun 1779 and was buried in Hawkshead churchyard two days later: Thompson, 33.

51. Ibid., 22, 25–6; *DWR*, 34; *Prelude, 1805*, viii, 253–8; *IF*, 18, 86–7. By a curious coincidence, George Knott's father, Michael, was agent for the le Flemings of Rydal Hall, married a le Fleming and lived at RM, which became WW's home in 1813; like WW, he was a Distributor of Stamps. It is possible Ann may have worked for the Knotts at RM as well as at Coniston Waterhead.

52. Thompson, 348, 350, 362. WCal inherited his father's estates and lived at Keswick, remaining on friendly terms with WW throughout his life. His younger brother RC also had independent means; his legacy to WW was a crucial step in enabling WW to become a poet. John Atkinson (1773–1823) was a particular friend of CW, with whom he attended Trinity College; he went into the Church. John Spedding (1770–1851) went into the army after Oxford; he retired to Mirehouse, near Keswick, where his sisters became friendly

with DW; his brothers were Anthony (1775–1837), a lawyer, and William (1777–1806).

53. Ibid., 41, 71, 78. Both WW's younger brothers had been at Cockermouth Grammar School since Oct 1780: JW2 was at Hawkshead Jan 1782–Dec 1787, CW Aug 1785–91; JW1, Account Book, *c.*1765–83: WLMS/1/2/3 pp. 80v–1, 86v–7. RWW's grandson, Richard (1777–96), came in the latter half of 1787, and his own youngest son, Robinson (1775–1856), in Jan 1789.

54. *Prelude, 1805*, vii, 105–8; Thompson, 37, 43.

55. *Prelude, 1805*, v, 436–40; i, 509–17; WW, *Nutting* (*Poems*, i, 367–9); *IF*, 13.

56. *Prelude, 1805*, ii, 82; *IF*, 30–31; Thompson, 202, 204–7.

57. *Prelude, 1850*, i, 330–39. Thompson, 211–14, quoting Fletcher Raincock's reminiscences.

58. *Prelude, 1805*, i, 329–32.

59. Rawnsley, 'Reminiscences of Wordsworth Among the Peasantry of Westmoreland', 24–5; *Prelude, 1805*, i, 452–89, esp. 484–6.

60. *Prelude, 1850*, i, 562–6. Variant lines on this subject occur as early as the 1798 version. However, as Gill, 5–7 points out, *The Prelude* is a teleological account of WW's formative years and, as such, cannot be regarded as absolute truth.

61. WW, *There was a Boy* (*Poems*, i, 362); *IF*, 61. First published in *LB* (1800), the original version of the MS, dated Oct 1798, is in the first person, confirming that WW was describing a personal experience. He later made the poem impersonal, suggesting that William Raincock was the most successful mimic of the owls; lines added in 1799 indicate that the boy died when he was 12 and was buried at Hawkshead, which have led him to being identified as John Tyson, aged 12, who was buried on 27 Aug 1782: *IF*, 13; Thompson, 56. The poem is actually a composite picture, drawing on all these elements, and was incorporated into *The Prelude, 1805*, v, 389–422.

62. The standard version of this train of events is that JW1 took the inquests just before Xmas 1783 and died after a short illness. This is clearly not the case. There are no records of any inquests in the Lordship of Millom conducted by JW1 later than the ones I describe. The dates I have given for the journey and the inquests themselves appear in a claim for expenses submitted by JW1's executors to the Quarterly Assizes at Epiphany 1783–4; £9 10s was paid. Petitions Epiphany 1783–4, MS Q11 1783–4 Epi 9 & 10, CRO, Carlisle. The identity of the corpses is given in the *Cumberland Pacquet*, 14 Oct 1783, 2.

63. Ibid., 2; JW1, Cumberland Estate Accounts, 1783: D/Lons/L3/2/236 p. 56, CRO, Carlisle; *HCRD*, i, 280.

64. *Cumberland Pacquet*, 18 Nov 1783, 3; Thompson, 92–3. As fees to Mr Mingay for teaching the boys to dance occur only once in the Administrators' Accounts, it may be that they received only a term's lessons, but this seems unlikely.

65. As Moorman, i, 68n. has pointed out, in the first version of this story, written as early as 1787, only four years after the event, WW implies that he already knew his father was dying: 'Long, long, upon yon naked rock / Alone, I bore the bitter shock; / Long, long, my swimming eyes did roam / For little Horse to bear me home, / To bear me – what avails my tear? / To sorrow o'er a Father's bier.': WW, *The Vale of Esthwaite* (*Poems*, i, 62). This seems likely, given the revised date for JW1's attendance at inquests, and explains the anxiety with which he watched.

66. *Cumberland Pacquet*, 6 Jan 1784, 2, 3; DW to CC, 28 Dec 1807 (*MY*, i, 185). According to the parish registers, JW1 died of dropsy, but this was a catch-all term which does not rule out pneumonia or a similar disease: Reed, i, 59n. I have assumed that the boys returned to Penrith on 3 Jan with their uncle, CCC, who received £71 13s as an advance towards housekeeping on that date: see p. 823n.5.

67. *Cumberland Pacquet*, 6 Jan 1784, 3; DW to JP, 6–7 Aug 1787 (*EY*, 7).

68. WW, *Autobiographical Memoranda*, Nov 1847 (*Prose*, iii, 371); JW1, Account Book, *c.*1765–83: WLMS/1/2/3; WW to JL, 16 Mar 1805 (*EY*, 562–3).

69. *Memoirs*, i, 34; RWB, Schedule of Books of the late Mr John Wordsworth of Cockermouth, Oct 1805: WLMS/1/2/10. For the novels, which do not appear on this list, see p. 18. Two examples of youthful poems written by JW1 in 1757 and 1760 survive: WLMS/1/2/1 & 1/2/3.

70. JW1, Account Book, *c.*1765–83: WLMS/1/2/3; the Lowther account books extend to 267 volumes and are preserved in the Lonsdale MSS at CRO, Carlisle.

Chapter 2

chapter title: 'A poor, devoted crew', WW, *Guilt and Sorrow*, l.297 (*Poems*, i, 129).
picture: Possible sketch of WW inside a Hawkshead Grammar School textbook, attributed to John Spedding, 1787.
1. JW1, Letters of Admin., 13 Feb 1784: WLMS/SH/12/15; JW1, Admin. Acct, 1784–6: WLMS/SH/12/23; WW to SGB, *c*.23 Feb 1805 (*EY*, 546); Reed, i, 59n. For the final settlement, see pp. 298, 861n.10.
2. *Cumberland Pacquet*, 27 Apl 1784, 1; JW1, Admin. Acct (Personal Effects), 1783–9: WLMS/SH/12/12. According to this account, JW1 had £224 19s in cash and banknotes in his possession at the time of his death; his gold watch and two rings, sold on 23 Jan, raised £9 15s and £1 8s, the cow £5 2s and the silver coffee pot £10 1s 6d; the sale of furniture raised £149 11s 7d and the rest of the sale £109 ½d. A dozen bottles of Madeira and 53 bottles of port were sold separately for a total of £6 7s 2d: JW1, Admin. Acct, 1784–5: WLMS/SH/12/10.
3. Reed, i, 60–61; DW to LMB, 7 Aug 1805 (*EY*, 616); JW1, Admin. Acct, 1784–5: WLMS/SH/12/10.
4. See, e.g., Johnston, 426. For CCC's debt to the Ws, see pp. 450, 882n.19.
5. JW1, Admin. Acct, Dec 1783–Oct 1788: WLMS/SH/12/12. CCC was advanced £71 13s on 3 Jan 1784 (presumably to cover the cost of having the boys at Penrith until their return to Hawkshead on *c*.19 Jan, but rather more than the rate the Tysons were being paid), £15 3s 5½d on 9 May and £44 4s 8d on 29 May. For the loans to RWB, see ibid., entries under 14 Jun & 18 Oct 1787, and for the only interest paid, on 27 Mar 1789, which had been due in Oct; see also JW1, Admin. Acct, 1788–93: WLMS/SH/12/13 [25 Aug 1791]. RWB had been advertising for a loan of £2,000 on the security of freehold property in Cumberland before JW1 died: see *Cumberland Pacquet*, 4 Nov 1783, 1, 11 Nov 1783, 1, & 18 Nov 1783, 3.
6. RWB, Schedule of Books of the late Mr John Wordsworth of Cockermouth, Oct 1805: WLMS/1/2/10. This list does not reflect the entire contents of the library, so some of the books must have been sold off or distributed among the family. Dorothy thought the Crackanthorpes had the Bible: DW to RW, 25 Aug [1805] (*EY*, 620). As WW did not know what books RWB possessed, Moorman, i, 71 must be wrong in assuming WW pleaded for their preservation.
7. DW to SH, 8 Apl [1815] (*MY*, ii, 224); JW1, Account Book, *c*.1765–83: WLMS/1/2/3 p. 87v. The bills, including £12 a year for board, were paid to 'G. Simpson' by DW's father; Grace Simpson, a widow of Hipperholme-cum-Brighouse, is referred to in 1764–7 and again in 1782, in MS RP 634 & MS Misc 922/62, WYAS, Halifax.
8. Trigg, 'Dorothy Wordsworth and Her Halifax Friends', 92.
9. *Prelude, 1805*, iv, 35–45; viii, 559–61. The identity of the actual cottage is disputed. Beatrix Potter believed it was on a plot of land adjoining the bridge opposite the road to the Friends' Meeting House; others, including Thompson, identify it as Greenend: Lindop, 391–2; Thompson, 56–7, 62–6.
10. Ibid., 56, 61.
11. JW1, Admin. Acct, 1784–5: WLMS/SH/12/2; Reed, i, 64, 66.
12. Thompson, 342. The tablet in Hawkshead Old Grammar School wrongly assigns Christian's assumption of the headmastership to 1781, a date which is followed by Moorman, i, 49–50, 90 & Reed, i, 52, but Thompson's dates, supplied from the records of the Archdeaconry of Richmond, are correct.
13. G. Dyer, *The River Cam*, quoted in Moorman, i, 50; *Prelude, 1805*, x, 492; Schneider, 77.
14. WW, *Resolution and Independence*, ll.43–4 (*Poems*, i, 553); WW to J.F. Mitchell, 21 Apl 1819, to R.P. Gillies, 15 Apl [1816] & to A. Dyce, 12 Jan 1829 (*MY*, ii, 535, 301; *LY*, ii, 3); Peacock, 230, 368.
15. *Prelude, 1805*, v, 577–9. WW claims this happened when he was 13 'or less', but the change seems likely to have come with Taylor's teaching.
16. Ibid., v, 599–601. John Fleming had inherited the Rayrigg estate on Windermere in 1779; it was let 1780–89 to William Wilberforce, MP, who was a friend of WW's uncle WC: Thompson, 117n.
17. WW, *Autobiographical Memoranda*, Nov 1847 (*Prose*, iii, 372); *Lines Written as a School Exercise at Hawkshead, Anno Aetatis 14* (*Poems*, i, 37–40); John Spedding to WW, 8 Mar 1838: MS 66a p. 2, Spedding Papers. Spedding paraphrases the two opening lines and slightly misquotes the next

two: 'Near half a century had been added to the 200 years wch in sunshine have elapsed "Since Science first with all her heavenly train / Beneath that roof began her heavenly reign" '; he must have been quoting from memory, as the lines were unpublished in WW's lifetime. The MS of the verses is now in DC.

18. WW, *Autobiographical Memoranda*, Nov 1847 (*Prose*, iii, 372–3); WW, *Ancreon, The Dog – an Idyllium, [Septimius and Acme], Translation of a Celebrated Greek Song, To Melpomene, The Death of a Starling, Lesbia* (*Poems*, i, 40–45).

19. Peacock, 389; WW, *The Vale of Esthwaite* (*Poems*, i, 50–67); Schneider, 79.

20. WW, *The Vale of Esthwaite*, ll.519–24 (*Poems*, i, 64). The lines would eventually become 'Thus, while the Sun sinks down to rest / Far in the regions of the west, / Though to the vale no parting beam / Be given, not one memorial gleam, / A lingering light he fondly throws / On the dear hills where first he rose': WW, *Extract from the Conclusion of a Poem, Composed in Anticipation of Leaving School* (*Poems*, i, 66–7). This later version, which WW dates to 1786 in *IF*, 6, was actually 'recomposed' for the 1815 edition of his works, when he added the opening stanza 'foretelling' how he would always look back with longing to the Lakes (WW, *Shorter Poems, 1807–1820*, 141–2). The original lines were composed 'while I was resting in a boat along with my companions under the shade of a magnificent row of Sycamores' on Lake Coniston: *IF*, 6; *Prelude, 1850*, viii, 458–75.

21. WW, *Dirge Sung by a Minstrel* and [*A Ballad*] (*Poems*, i, 68–9, 48–50); Thompson, 61–2, 65–9; *IF*, 18; WW, *Peter Bell*, ll.886–915 (*Poems*, i, 343–4); Rachel, wife of Jacob, died giving birth to the son she named Benoni; Jacob renamed him Benjamin: Genesis, ch.35 v.18.

22. WW, *Sonnet on Seeing Miss Helen Maria Williams Weep at a Tale of Distress* (*Poems*, i, 47). There is no indication that Greenwood's poem was published. Johnston, 54 argues implausibly that it was 'To a Gentleman playing very ill on the Flute' attributed to 'Miss Kemble'. 'Axiologus' is not a Latin pun, as he suggests, but Greek. WW, in identifying his sonnet as his only poem published prior to *Evening Walk* (1793), was mistaken in dating it to Jun–Jul 1786: Reed, i, 71n. MW was also wrong in asserting that WW and Greenwood sent their poems to the *Gentleman's Magazine*. MW to CW2, 14 Aug [1853?]: WLL/MW/239 p. 2.

23. A. de Vere to WRH, Jan 1843 (Graves, *Life of Sir W.R. Hamilton* ii, 402). The manuscript notebook was MS Verse 4, DC. Reed, i, 298–301 attempts to impose some chronology on the poems of this period but is unable to come to any decisive conclusions.

24. *Prelude, 1805*, x, 501, 510–14; see also 489–514. Taylor's gravestone can still be seen in the churchyard of Cartmel Priory, Cumbria. His allusion is to the first line of the first stanza of the epitaph in Gray's *Elegy Written in a Country Churchyard*; the whole verse would have made an equally appropriate epitaph for Taylor: 'Here rests his head upon the lap of Earth / A Youth, to Fortune and to Fame unknown; / Fair Science frown'd not on his humble birth, / And Melancholy mark'd him for her own.'

25. Thompson, 342, 344.

26. Ibid., 344, 345; WW to S.C. Hall, 15 Jan 1837 (*LY*, iii, 348); WW, *At the Grave of Burns, 1803*, ll.31–6 (*Poems*, i, 588). Bowman's son also says that WW, in a letter written after his father's death, acknowledged that he first became acquainted with the poetry of Crabbe, Charlotte Smith and the two Wartons in books or periodicals lent by Bowman.

27. *Prelude, 1805*, ii, 321–38.

28. Ibid., ii, 55–78, 145–80. For the firing of cannons from boats or from the lake shores, see Nicholson, *The Lakers*, 55.

29. *Prelude, 1805*, ii, 127–35, 416–18.

30. WW, *The Old Cumberland Beggar* (*Poems*, i, 262–8); *IF*, 56; WW, *The Two Thieves: or, The Last Stage of Avarice* (*Poems*, i, 428–30); *IF*, 57, 79, 36. For some hazy speculation as to the possible identity of WW's Hawkshead pedlar, see Thompson, 239–46.

31. *Prelude, 1805*, i, 372–427; Lindop, 317–18 explains the phenomenon, which a local boatman showed Sir Edward Baines in 1829.

32. DW to CC, 17 [*r*.16] Feb 1807 (*MY*, i, 136); JW1, Admin. Acct, 1783–9: WLMS/SH/12/12 [30 Jan 1788] & JW1, Admin. Acct, 1788–93: WLMS/SH/12/13 [22 Oct 1788].

33. Payments for horsehire and travel expenses for carrying RW, WW, JW2 & CW 'from Branthwaite to Hawkshead school at several different times' appear in JW1, Admin. Acct, 1786–99: WLMS/SH/12/22. In *Prelude, 1850*, v,

57–9 WW records sitting in a cave by the seaside reading *Don Quixote* 'in the stillness of a summer's noon', which suggests a summer visit to Whitehaven. The 1805 version is impersonal, but by 1850 it has become a first-person account.

34. DW to JP, [late Jul 1787] (*EY*, 3). In 1784, less than five days before their first summer vacation after their father's death, the Ws did not know whether they were going to Penrith or Whitehaven, as CCC had not made any arrangements: Thompson, 336.

35. *Prelude, 1805*, vi, 218; DW to JP, [late Jul 1787] (*EY*, 3).

36. Ibid., 3–4.

37. DW to JP, 6 & 7 Aug 1787 (*EY*, 8). Ann Tyson charged WW for nine weeks' board and lodging from 5 Aug, so he must have remained there till *c.*7 Oct: Thompson, 112; Reed, i, 74.

38. WC to D. Cowper, 14 Feb 1781: Cookson/1/3.

39. DW to JP, 6 & 7 Aug & [Nov] 1787 (*EY*, 8, 9–11). Ibid., 10n.2, suggests DW attended Penrith Grammar School, but this was impossible as grammar schools at that time were for boys only, hence DW's scheme of self-education.

40. Ibid., 10. Charlotte Cust (1756–1843) married CCC on 27 Aug 1788 at Penrith; MW, *Autobiographical Memoranda*, [Nov 1851]: DC 167 p. 39.

41. The only son, Rev. William Cowper (1744–1809), was headmaster of a school at Houghton-le-Spring attended by MW's brothers until, in 1786, through the influence of JR, who was second cousin to his wife, he was presented to the livings of Ramsey and Dovercourt, which included JR's constituency of Harwich. The curacy would later be offered to WW: see p. 94. Cowper's sister Mary (1746–71) had married a Mr Airey of Newcastle and died young; her sister Margaret went to look after the Airey children and so was seldom at Penrith. The three youngest sisters still at home were Ann (b.1749), Dorothy (b.1754), who would both marry in 1788, and Julia (1756–93): *EY*, 79n.; MW, *Autobiographical Memoranda*, [Nov 1851]: DC 167 pp. 38–41.

42. Ibid., 66, 32–3. MW's parents' grave lies to the left of the path leading to the door in the tower of St Andrew's Church, Penrith; the inscription, though cracked, is still legible. It commemorates John Hutchinson (15 Mar 1736–19 May 1785), his wife, Mary, daughter of John Monkhouse of Penrith (1744–31 Mar 1783), and their tenth child, William (31 Mar 1783–Jan 1785).

43. MW, *Autobiographical Memoranda*, [Nov 1851]: DC 167 pp. 8, 17–18, 24–5, 65. Bishopton and Whitton are less than 2 miles apart, lying on the escarpment dropping down from Darlington towards Stockton, with the Cleveland Hills in the distance. Bishopton remains exactly as MW describes it, a single line of pretty red-brick and stuccoed cottages with pantiled roofs, and the church at the top of the street. Though the brewery appears to have been in the village, there is a lovely old house, with a duck pond to the front and a large number of barns to the rear, at the foot of the hill at Whitton. As Whitton is only a tiny hamlet and this is called Bishopton Mill, could it have been the Hutchinsons' brewery?

44. Ibid., 26–7, 28–30, 67. MW says the three boys went to County Durham on the death of their father (1785), but she must be confusing this with the death of their mother (1783), as she says elsewhere in the same reminiscences that JH lived at Stockton from his fifteenth year and HH himself says he first went to sea in 1783; MW says HH's first voyage was to China but HH says that his first two voyages were from Stockton to Scandinavia: HH, *The Retrospect of a Retired Mariner*: WLMS/H/1/2/2 pp. v, 1–2.

45. MW, *Autobiographical Memoranda*, [Nov 1851]: DC 167 pp. 36, 73–4, 77. Margaret Monkhouse, née Richardson (1717–88), was Margaret Hutchinson's godmother as well as her grandmother. Her husband, John Monkhouse (1713–96), was often described by WW as 'the most Gentlemanly Man both in look and manner, he ever knew <u>in Penrith</u>': ibid., 73.

46. Ibid., 53. James Patrick would earn immortality as the model for WW's 'intellectual Pedlar' in *The Excursion*, see pp. 283–4, 859n.54. His wife, Margaret Robison (not Robinson, as throughout *EY*), was the daughter of Elizabeth Monkhouse and niece of Aunt Gamage and John Monkhouse.

47. MW, *Autobiographical Memoranda*, [Nov 1851]: DC 167 pp. 57–67.

48. Ibid., 66. Betsy is never mentioned by name in MW's *Autobiographical Memoranda* and rarely in the letters; MW described Aggy Ashburner as being 'only a half-wit – poor Soul very much like our Betsy': MW to WW, 24 Aug 1810 (Darlington, 94). For much of her adult life

she was cared for by a Mrs Elstob, near Stockton: 'she has always been of weak faculties', WW wrote when he learned of her death in 1832, 'and latterly her mind was disordered': *LSH*, 67, 69; WW to CW, 5 May [1832] (*LY*, ii, 522).

49. DW, *Excursion on the Banks of Ullswater*, Nov 1805: DC 51 p. 17 (*DWJ*, i, 421); MW, *Autobiographical Memoranda*, [Nov 1851]: DC 167 p. 68. Margaret was still living with her grandparents at this time, so the three friends had three separate houses.

50. DW to JP, 6 & 7 Aug 1787 (*EY*, 8); TdQ, *Recollections*, 131, 129. MH's extraordinary ability to radiate sheer goodness was constantly remarked upon by all who met her in her later years. Her squint may have been aggravated by prolonged periods of close work, such as copying or writing for William; in her eighties, when she was going blind in her good eye, she found that the sight in her bad eye improved and was better than it had ever been: MW to Mrs CW 2, 28 Jun 1852 (*LMW*, 341).

51. WW, 'She was a Phantom of delight' (*Poems*, i, 603). WW composed this poem in 1803–4, and though the germ of it was originally some lines for *The Highland Girl*, he later told Justice Coleridge that it was developed as a tribute to 'my dear wife': *IF*, 13, 109.

52. *Prelude, 1805*, xi, 317; vi, 233–5.

53. Thompson, 353–4. The books can still be seen at Hawkshead Old Grammar School. Greenwood and Gawthrop had been lodgers at Ann Tyson's since Jan and Jul 1786 respectively: ibid., 72, 74.

54. Reed, i, 73; Ann had purchased silks and velvets for WW's new clothes; Thompson, 112–13; DW was busy making clothes for him in Oct: DW to JP, [Nov 1787] (*EY*, 11).

55. JW1, Admin. Acct, 1785–90: WLMS/SH/12/1; DW to JP, 6 & 16 Dec 1787 (*EY*, 13).

56. The intention in Aug had been that WC would escort his nephews to Cambridge, but there are no references to suggest that he did: DW to JP, 6 & 7 Aug 1787 (*EY*, 7). John Myers was admitted a sizar at St John's College on 30 Jun, WW on 5 Jul, and both took up residence on 30 Oct 1787: Admissions Register 1770–1817: C27.1 nos. 39, 44, SJC.

57. Reed, i, 75n.12. Mary Myers married Hugh Robinson (1735–1802), a widower, on 20 Apl 1787; she sent 'pressing invitations' to DW to visit her, which DW was unable to accept: DW to JP, [Nov 1787] (*EY*, 11 & n.).

58. *Prelude, 1805*, iii, 8–12.

59. Ibid., iii, 28; WW, List of Freshmen at St John's College, 1787: WLMS/1/1/1.

60. *Prelude, 1850*, iii, 46ff., esp. 61–3; *1805*, iii, 28–33; IF to HT, 9 Jun 1838 (Dowden, 123).

61. Schneider, 2; WW, *The Vale of Esthwaite*, l.77.

62. *Prelude, 1805*, iii, 18–19, 23–8, 33–40.

63. Schneider, 7–9.

64. WW held a Foundress Scholarship Nov 1787–Nov 1792, an Allott exhibition, worth £4p.a., Dec 1787–Dec 1790 and a Hare exhibition, worth *c.*£2p.a., Mar 1788–Jan 1790: Accounts of Senior Bursar 1782–1800 & 1787: SB9.13 & SB4.38 p. 41, SJC; Admissions of Scholars from 1775: C3.5 pp. 119, 134, 284, SJC; Examination Register: C15.6 p. 36, SJC.

Chapter 3

chapter title: 'Squandered Abroad', DW to JP, *c.*27 Jan 1788 (*EY*, 16).

picture: St John's College, Cambridge, by R.B. Harraden, from *Harraden's Picturesque Views of Cambridge* (Cambridge, 1800).

1. *LJW*, 10; DW to JP, [*c.*27] Jan 1788 (*EY*, 15); Reed, i, 80; DW to JP, [Nov] & 6 & 16 Dec 1787 (*EY*, 11–12, 13).

2. JR to WW, 6 Apl 1788 (*EY*, 18n.). A fleeting visit by WW to London at this time, even if he did not see JR, would substantiate WW's claim for 1791 that it was three years since he had last been in London: *Prelude, 1850*, vii, 65–8. See Reed, i, 81n. JR's claims to 'most truly wish you well' seem a little hollow when compared with his reluctance to assist the Ws in the Lonsdale suit: see e.g., p. 93.

3. WW, *Autobiographical Memoranda*, Nov 1847 (*Prose*, iii, 373); Schneider, 28; Examination Register: C15.6 pp. 36, 37, SJC.

4. WW to TC, [1816] (*MY*, ii, 351); *Prelude, 1805*, iii, 233–6, 249–58, 508–10, 261–7, 294–328, 669–71. In 1805 WW claimed he drank to Milton's memory 'within my private thoughts', i.e. Milton's name was not actually mentioned by him or his fellow drinkers, who were just having a party. By omitting this line from the 1850 version, which he intended to publish, WW created the impression that the party was an

altogether more intellectual affair and that the drunkenness resulted from his enthusiasm for Milton, rather than wine.

5. WW, Prose Fragment, 8 Jun [1788] (*Prose*, i, 10–11); *IF*, 72–3. The precise date of the Dovedale excursion is unclear. In *The Prelude, 1805*, vi, 208–9 WW implies he visited it from Hawkshead during one of his summer vacations from college, but the prose piece is clearly titled 'Cambridge to Hawkshead' and dated 8 Jun; it refers to arriving in Ashbourne on a Sunday evening and 8 Jun 1788 was a Sunday. In 1789 WW went from Cambridge to Forncett in Norfolk and in 1790 to London and France, leaving the 1788 vacation the only possibility.

6. *Prelude, 1805*, iv, 1–120. Hawkshead Grammar School did not break up until *c.*21 Jun, so CW was more than likely to have been there; he was still lodging with Ann Tyson, as was Richard, son of WW and CW's cousin, RWB: Thompson, 78, 81.

7. *Prelude, 1805*, iv, 127–30, 140–48.

8. RC to WCal, nd [*c.*Mar 1793]: Stanger Albums, ii, 168 p. 1; Pollack, *Wilberforce*, 8; Ashton, 37; for TdQ's frequenting prostitutes I am indebted to a conversation with Grevel Lindop, who is currently editing TdQ's works. Johnston, 127–34 paints a particularly decadent picture of Cambridge at the time and implies WW could not have escaped what he sees as universal prostitution. His evidence, however, like that for his portrayal of London, is almost entirely drawn from satirical sources such as *Gradus ad Cantabrigiam*, which he accepts at face value as fact.

9. *Prelude, 1805*, vii, 412–34; iii, 536–7.

10. Ibid., vi, 13; iv, 272–8, 304–5.

11. Ibid., 319–27, 341–4. Thompson, 125–32 locates the ball to Belle Grange, the summer home on Lake Windermere of John Christian, a wealthy MP, who was cousin to WW's headmaster, Edward Christian, and an active promoter of the early regattas. Moorman, i, 109 has several other suggestions, but, like the story of the old soldier which follows, it is probably not a single specific event but a conflation of several.

12. *Prelude, 1805*, iv, 360–504. This episode was originally the subject of a separate poem, *The Discharged Soldier*, written in Feb 1798, which WW cut and revised for inclusion in *The Prelude.*

13. *Prelude, 1805*, iv, 291–4; Thompson, 344.

14. Ibid., 81, 94, 134n., 342. For the Farishes' poems see ibid., 311–18, 319–21. WW's footnote read, 'From a short MS poem read to me when an undergraduate by my school-fellow and friend, Charles Farish, long since deceased. The verses were by a brother of his, a man of promising genius, who died young': WW, *Guilt and Sorrow*, ll.76–81 (*Poems*, i, 121, 934–5).

15. JW1, Admin. Accts, 1785–90, 1783–88 & 1788–92: WLMS/SH/12/1 [21 Jun 1788], 12 [24 Feb 1788] & 13 [12 Nov 1788]. Moorman, i, 107, Reed, i, 87 & Johnston, 137 all assume WW spent nine weeks at Colthouse this year, but this is based on a misreading of Ann Tyson's 1789 accounts for 1788: Thompson, 134n.

16. WW to MW, 3–4 Jun 1812 (Darlington, 229); *Prelude, 1805*, vi, 208–45. WW was misled by Clarke's *Survey of the Lakes* (1787) into thinking that Sidney had visited Brougham Castle. For DW's dislike of Aunt Gamage (whom MH, always more charitable, forgave because she remembered her earlier kindness to her mother and herself), see MW, *Autobiographical Memoranda*, [Nov 1851]: DC 167 pp. 67–8.

17. Reed, i, 89–90; *LJW*, 10–11; JW1, Admin. Acct, 1783–8: WLMS/SH/12/12 [28 Aug 1788].

18. DW to JP, 7 & 8 Dec 1788 (*EY*, 18); JW1, Admin. Acct, 1785–90: WLMS/SH/12/1. DW does not mention WW's presence in Penrith in her letters of this period, but not all are extant.

19. DW to JP, 7 & 8 Dec 1788 (*EY*, 18–19).

20. *Prelude, 1805*, vi, 32–48.

21. RC to WCal, nd [*c.*Mar 1793]: Stanger Albums, ii, 168 p. 2. According to Venn, i, 494, RC was admitted a pensioner at Magdalene College on 14 Feb 1793, but there is no further university record of him; in his letter to his brother he says his residency was 'not above a week'.

22. RS to J. White, 25 Oct 1811 (*RSLC*, iii, 318).

23. Examination Register: C15.6 pp. 36–40, SJC; RS to G. Bedford, 20 Jul 1794 (*RSLC*, i, 215).

24. *Prelude, 1805*, iii, 414ff.; 65–72, 531–9, 630–31, 635–43, 318.

25. Schneider, 42–3. There were 28 pensioners and 14 sizars in WW's year: Admissions Register 1770–1817: C27.1 p. 19, SJC.

26. Schneider, 43–4, does not appear to realize that CL is describing STC, for whose adventures in the 15th Light Dragoons and subsequent ignominious return to Cambridge, after being discharged on the grounds of insanity, see Ashton 41–2; Holmes, i, 53–8.

27. *Prelude, 1805*, vi, 22–9, 55ff., esp.64–9; Examination Register: C15.6 pp. 38–9, SJC; Schneider, 95, 105.
28. WW, *Autobiographical Memoranda*, Nov 1847 (*Prose*, iii, 373). For Isola, see Prance, 166. The *Vision of Mirza* was an allegorical tale by Addison, published in the *Spectator*.
29. WW to SGB, 17 & 24 Oct 1805 (*EY*, 628); T. Moore, *Diary*, 1835 (Peacock, 169).
30. Schneider, 102; DW to JP, 26 Jun [1791] (*EY*, 52); WW to A. Dyce, 10 May [1830] (*LY*, ii, 259–60).
31. For WW's translations of Virgil and Horace dating from this period, see *Poems*, i, 72–6, 91–3. See also Reed, i, 302–6.
32. *Prelude, 1805*, vi, 67–9.
33. *IF*, 6–7. For the 1793 version of *An Evening Walk*, see *Poems*, i, 77–87. For a putative chronology of the various fragments which went towards the final version of the poem, see Reed, i, 302–6.
34. WW to BM, 1 Oct 1844 (*LY*, iv, 610); Schneider, 5, 66, 156, 172, 189; Prance, 232–3. In the two years after William left Cambridge, Hawkshead boys continued to lead the field. Thomas Jack and John Rudd were Fourth and Tenth Wranglers respectively in 1792 and John Harrison was First Wrangler in 1793.
35. WW, *Autobiographical Memoranda*, Nov 1847 (*Prose*, iii, 373).
36. DW to JP, 28 Dec 1788 & 30 Apl 1790 (*EY*, 22–3).
37. *Prelude, 1805*, iv, 213–21. See n.24.
38. MW, *Autobiographical Memoranda*, [Nov 1851]: DC 167 pp. 67, 80. MW's own account of her departure from Penrith makes it clear she could not have been there in the summer of 1789, so William could not have walked with her as so often suggested, e.g. Reed, i, 93. There is no indication in the Administrators' Accounts that WW visited Penrith before Oct 1789: see n.40..
39. *Prelude, 1805*, vi, 208–9. Moorman, i, 122, Reed, i, 93 & Johnston, 161 state that WW spent time this summer with his cousin Mary W and her husband, John Smith, at Broughton-in-Furness: though WW says he spent time here 'During my college vacation, and two or three years afterwards, before [*sic*] taking my Bachelor's Degree' (*IF*, 31), he could not have done so *this* summer because the Smiths were not married until 10 Nov 1789: RWB to RW, 31 Oct 1789: WLMS/SH/16/1. There is no evidence at all to support the suggestion in Moorman, i, 122 that WW visited Sockburn this summer.
40. CCC to RW, 22 Oct 1789: WLMS/SH/11/11. Reed, i, 95n. is wrong in stating that 21 and 14 Oct 1789 were Fridays, so wrong in assuming WW called on the 14th; CCC's letter was written on Thursday 22nd, so can refer only to the previous Friday, which was the 16th.
41. CCC to RW, 22 Mar 1789: WLMS/SH/11/3. In response to the Administrators' bill and summons against SJL in Jan/Feb 1788, the latter had obtained an injunction in the Court of Exchequer preventing the Administrators proceeding against him on the grounds that JW1 had agreed to do all his business for an annual salary of £100. This was patently untrue, and SJL could provide no evidence, so the Administrators were able to get the injunction set aside in May 1788, but a series of delaying tactics by SJL's lawyers prevented this taking effect for another three years.
42. RW to CCC, 5 Sep 1789: WLMS/SH/11/9. For CCC's handling of the estate, see the correspondence between him and RW, Aug 1789–*c.*5 Jan 1790: WLMS/SH/11/5–15. CCC eventually let the estate for £70 p.a. for a term of seven years, which effectively prevented RW returning to live on the estate until the expiry of the lease.
43. Examination Register: C15.6 p. 40, SJC; Schneider, 156–60.
44. RW to CCC, 29 Nov 1789: WLMS/SH/11/12 p. 2. The only reference to JW2's visit is a passing remark in CCC to RW, 10 Oct 1789: WLMS/SH/11/10 p. 1.
45. CCC to RW, 18 Dec 1789 & 6 Jan 1790: WLMS/SH/11/13 p. 2 & 14.
46. Dyce (ed.), *Recollections of the Table-talk of Samuel Rogers*, 258n.; RW to CCC, [*c.*5 Jan] & 21 Apl 1790: WLMS/SH/11/15 p. 2 & 19; DW to JP, 25 & 26 Jan [1790] (*EY*, 25). Ibid., n.3 confuses author and recipient in quoting from this last letter: JW2 had written to RW, not CCC.
47. DW to JP, 25 & 26 Jan [1790] (*EY*, 25).
48. Ibid., 26–7; DW to JP, 30 Apl 1790 (*EY*, 28, 30–31).
49. JW1, Admin. Acct, 1785–90: WLMS/SH/12/1 [24 Sep 1790]; CCC to RW, 26 Feb 1790: WLMS/SH/11/16 p. 1; DW to JP, 30 Apl 1790 (*EY*, 29).
50. Examination Register: C15.6 p. 41, SJC; Schneider, 167, 172. RJ, Myers and Gawthrop also

took only part of the examination and, like WW, did 'well in the subjects which they undertook'.

51. *Prelude, 1805*, vi, 342–5; v, 277; DW to JP, 6 Oct [1790] (*EY*, 39). While on his tour WW suffered from considerable uneasiness, knowing how anxious DW would be about him: WW to DW, 6 [& 16] Sep [1790] (*EY*, 35).

52. For fascinating eyewitness accounts of these events, see *English Witnesses*, 77–9, 81–6.

53. Gill, 45 & n.

54. WW, *A Character*, ll.1–2, 17–20 and *Dedication to Descriptive Sketches* (*Poems*, i, 261, 94); WW to DW, 6 [& 16] Sep [1790] (*EY*, 37); WW, *Autobiographical Memoranda*, Nov 1847 (*Prose*, iii, 373).

55. C.B. Wollaston, 18 Jul 1790 (*English Witnesses*, 83–4). WW's only traceable comment on his attendance at the *Fête de la Fédération* is that it was 'solemnised with due pomp at Calais' and that they left in the afternoon to sleep at Ardres: WW, *Autobiographical Memoranda*, Nov 1847 (*Prose*, iii, 373). See also WW to DW, 6 [& 16] Sep [1790] (*EY*, 32).

56. *Prelude, 1805*, vi, 694–6, 352–3, 355–70.

57. Ibid., vi, 401–13; WW to DW, 6 [& 16] Sep [1790] (*EY*, 36).

58. Ibid., 32–4; WW, *Descriptive Sketches, 1793*, ll.80–175 (*Poems*, i, 899–901); *Prelude, 1805*, vi, 590–661.

59. Ibid., 424, 466–8; WW to DW, 6 [& 16] Sep [1790] (*EY*, 3–4); Gill, 48. WW was often sarcastic at the expense of Lake tourists who drove past reading their guidebooks instead of looking at the scenery; though he cannot have been said to have done this himself in 1790, his realization that he had become trapped by his own reading influenced his later hatred of such practices.

60. *Prelude, 1805*, vi, 494–572; esp.556–72; WW to DW, 6 [& 16] Sep [1790] (*EY*, 35–6).

61. 'There is nothing I have more feeling of having regretted than that I could not accept your friendly invitation of joining your Party. It would have been a singular and a memorable incident in our Lives to have gone over the same ground again together after an interval of 30 years.' Recalling having walked to the hospital at Dijon with WW in 1790, he demanded to know all the details of the route and WW's impressions of the scenes they had seen before, adding, 'Did you revisit the Grand Chartreuse? I hope you did': RJ to WW, 28 Feb 1821: WLMS/A/Jones, R./2 pp. 1–4. See pp. 536–41 for an account of the tour.

62. WW to DW, 6 [& 16] Sep [1790] (*EY*, 32); *Memoirs*, i, 57n.; WW, *Author's voyage down the Rhine (Thirty Years Ago)* (*Poems*, ii, 446). I assume WW travelled through Brabant (now part of Belgium) as he refers to seeing the revolutionary army massing there in *Prelude, 1805*, vi, 691–2. He may have returned via Ostend, but there is no evidence to suggest which was his port of departure.

63. RJ to WW, 28 Feb 1821: WLMS/A/Jones, R./2 p. 2.

64. *Prelude, 1805*, vi, 453–7, 621–58; WW to DW, 6 [& 16] Sep [1790] (*EY*, 35); *DWJ*, ii, 219–20, 243–5. The two incidents may both have happened on the same night as DW says WW and RJ were separated by a thunderstorm at night and became lost in the woods near Gravedona and that WW describes this incident in *The Prelude*. *The Prelude* does describe WW and RJ being lost in the woods at night after being misled by the Gravedona clock chimes, but does not imply any separation; as this account concentrates on their attempts to sleep on the rock overlooking the lake, it is not impossible that they had indeed become briefly separated during a thunderstorm. For WW's escapade at Lauterbrunnen, see *Prose*, i, 9, 14; Reed, i, 111–12 misdates and misplaces the incident due to a misreading of 'head of the valley' in the MS which he takes to be 'heart'.

65. WW to DW, 6 [& 16] Sep [1790] (*EY*, 37); *Prelude, 1805*, vi, 342–3.

Chapter 4

chapter title: 'A vital interest', WW, *Prelude, 1805*, ix, 108.

picture: Miniature, said to be of AV, artist and date unknown.

1. JW1, Admin. Acct, 1788–93: WLMS/SH/12/12 [19 Oct 1790]. RW, Acct of sums granted & not included in former accts for WW & DW, 1790–1810: WLMS/2/1 [6 Nov 1790]. RW also lent WW five guineas on 7 Mar 1790.

2. DW to JP, 23 May [1791] & 16 Jun & [10 & 12 Jul] 1793 (*EY*, 47, 95–6, 97–8).

3. *Memoirs*, i, 48; Scott (ed.), *Admissions to the College of St John the Evangelist in the University of*

Cambridge, iv, 571. Besides his residency requirement, WW needed only to show a competent understanding of the first book of Euclid, arithmetic, vulgar and decimal fractions, simple and quadratic equations, and the Cambridge moral texts to qualify for his BA: Schneider, 189. The date of WW's admission to his BA degree is wrongly given as 27 Jan 1791 in Moorman, i, 153. For Mary Myers's comment, see Reed, i, 75n.

4. WW to RW, 10 Oct [1794] (*EY*, 130). The income on JW1's estate was £4,845 7s 3½d for the period 1783–9; expenditure was £4,782 4s 6d over the same time. In the period 1790–92 the expenditure rose to £6,452 9s 8½d, a rise of £1,607 2s 5d, of which £525 15s 6d was contributed as a loan by the executors to make up the shortfall in income. From these figures (which may not be complete) I hesitantly conclude that the young Ws should have each had access to about £100 p.a.: JW1, Admin. Accts, 1783–9 & 1790–92; WLMS/SH/12/12 & 13. Sockbridge produced £70 p.a. in rent alone, with additional income from the sale of hay, wood, etc., but I have erred on the cautious side and not taken this additional income into account. DW estimates the total income of Sockbridge as £100 p.a.: DW to JP, 7 Dec [1791] (*EY*, 66).

5. Barker, *The Brontës*, 4, 10–11.

6. Schneider, 191; H.K. White, *Remains of Henry Kirke White* (London, Longman & Co., 1823), i, 222. White was told by his tutor, 'We make it a rule (he said) of providing for a clever man, whose fortune is small; and you may therefore rest assured . . . that after you have taken your degree, you will be provided for with a genteel competency by the college': ibid., i, 194. It was this sort of patronage WW forfeited by his refusal to become part of the system.

7. Ashton, 40; RC to WCal, [Feb/Mar 1793]: MS Stanger Albums, ii, 168.

8. Venn, iii, 607; ii, 518; v, 87; iii, 26, 139; vi, 142; iv, 508; v, 234.

9. JW1, Admin. Acct, 1788–93: WLMS/SH/12/13 [28 Jan 1791].

10. *Prelude, 1805*, vii, 157–8, 161–7, 174–5; CL to WW, 30 Jan 1801 (*LCL*, i, 267).

11. WW to WM, 17 Jun [1791] (*EY*, 49); Roe, 23; Gill, 54–5. For Mathews, see Venn, iv, 360.

12. DW to JP, 23 May [1791] (*EY*, 44–5); Porritt, 'The Rawson Family', 27–52. It is unclear from DW's account whether her 'aunt' met WW and RW together or independently.

13. Roe, 23–4, 27–31. Roe offers evidence only that Nicholson was active in 1784–6. Though he dates WW's friendship with Nicholson to 1791, he does not make the connection with Mrs Rawson's bridal visit, which seems to me to be the obvious occasion of a first meeting and, indeed, the only evidence tending to support any connection between the two at this time.

14. *IF*, 80; Roe, 24–5 points out that Hazlitt's view of Fawcett as a man destroyed by the French Revolution is 'somewhat at odds with what is known of his life'. Nevertheless, it is Hazlitt's view that WW adopts for the Solitary, suggesting that WW's own knowledge of Fawcett was as perfunctory as the *IF* note indicates.

15. *Prelude, 1805*, vii, 60–62, 76.

16. *Prelude, 1805*, vii, 284ff. For Dora Jordan, see Tomalin, *Mrs Jordan's Profession*.

17. *Prelude, 1805*, vii, 69–72; ix, 96–7, 108; vii, 520–28; *IF*, 54.

18. Roe, 17; Gill, 53; Pollack, *Wilberforce*, 106, 108; Cobhan (ed.), *The Debate on the French Revolution*, 77; *Prelude, 1805*, vii, 539–42.

19. DW to JP, 23 May & 26 Jun [1791] (*EY*, 45, 51); JW1, Admin. Acct, 1788–93: WLMS/SH/12/13. DW was hoping to persuade WW to call on JP at Halifax 'on his way into Cumberland'. WW had been in regular contact with CW, who eventually undertook the walking tour with two friends: Fink (ed.), *The Early Wordsworthian Milieu*, 11–12.

20. WW to WM, 17 Jun & 3 Aug [1791] (*EY*, 49, 56).

21. WW to WM, 17 Jun & DW to JP, 26 Jun [1791] (*EY*, 50, 51). The oldest sister, Anne, was twenty-three, the youngest, Elizabeth, only twelve; apart from Mary, aged sixteen, it is not known which of the sisters was at home during WW's visit.

22. *Poems*, i, 94–5.

23. WW to WM, 3 Aug [1791] (*EY*, 55); *Guide*, 174.

24. *Prelude, 1805*, xiii, 1–84, esp.29–32, 41–51. Gill, 50–51 & n. points out how closely *The Prelude* follows Pennant's account in his *A Tour in Wales* and uses other literary sources to underpin WW's own experience.

25. WW to GHG, 14 May 1829 (*LY*, ii, 77–9).

Pennant had written *A Tour in Scotland, 1769* (1771), *A Tour in Wales, 1770* (1778–81) and a *History of Quadrupeds* (1781). Of the projected 14 volumes of *Outlines of the Globe*, he published only two in his lifetime; two more were published posthumously.

26. RW to CCC, [Aug 1790]: WLMS/SH/11/23; CCC to RW, 26 Apl & 15 Jun 1791: WLMS/SH/11/36 & 37.

27. RW to Mrs Cookson, 29 Aug 1791: WLMS/SH/14/2; DW to JP, 26 Jun [1791] (*EY*, 52–3); Anon., [Advice to the estate of JW1 on the case against the Earl of Lonsdale], [Aug] 1791, WLMS/SH/14/5. For JR's involvement, see Reed, i, 80–81, 83–4; *EY*, 57n.2.

28. RW to RWB, 21 Sep 1791: WLMS/SH/14/1; RW to RWW, 7 Nov 1791: WLMS 2/45. Burrow was the second choice of arbiter stipulated by the agreement; the first, Thomas Harrison, a Kendal solicitor, wisely refused to accept the position. Burrow was Surveyor General of the Customs in London and a political protégé of Lonsdale: see DW to JP, 7 Dec [1791] (*EY*, 64 & n.2). The £5,000 approved by the court was never paid to the Ws.

29. JW1, Admin. Acct, 1788–93: WLMS/SH/12/1 [27 Aug 1791 & 1 Aug 1792]. Anthony Parkin (1745/6–1827) was a cousin of JW1; in *c.*1777 he became Solicitor to the General Post Office.

30. MW, *Autobiographical Memoranda*, [Nov 1851]: DC 167 p.41; *EY*, 79n.1.

31. WW to WM, 23 Sep, DW to JP, 9 Oct & WW to WM, 23 Nov 1791 (*EY*, 58–9, 60–61, 62).

32. DW to JP, 9 Oct 1791 (*EY*, 60); CCC to RW, 16 Nov 1791: WLMS/SH/11/40.

33. WW to WM, 23 Nov & DW to JP, 7 Dec [1791] (*EY*, 62, 66). These letters confirm that WW originally intended to spend the winter in France, not a year, as suggested by Johnston, 281.

34. WW to WM, 23 Nov [1791] (*EY*, 61–2); RW to RWW, 7 Nov 1791; MS WLMS 2/45; JW1, Admin. Acct, 1788–93: WLMS/SH/12/13 [10 Nov 1791]. RW had returned to London only the night before he wrote to RWW and explained WW 'wish[es] to set off immediately'.

35. J. Lough, *An Introduction to Eighteenth Century France* (New York, 1960), 64. WW knew where he would be staying in Orléans before he left England: WW to WM, 23 Nov [1791] (*EY*, 62–3).

36. WW to RW, 19 Dec [1791] (*EY*, 68–9); Reed, i, 123n.13. Johnston, 282 and, to a lesser extent, *EY*, 68n.2, assume that the meeting with Charlotte Smith occurred through JR, who was brother-in-law and trustee of the husband from whom she was separated, but the implication of WW's letter is that Capt JW and his wife were responsible. Through JW2, WW had met them and other officers of the *Earl of Abergavenny* in London before setting off for France.

37. WW to RW, 19 Dec [1791] (*EY*, 68).

38. *English Witnesses*, 129–30, 137, 138–40.

39. *Prelude, 1805*, ix, 40–3. See also Clayden, *The Early Life of Samuel Rogers*, 137, 141; *English Witnesses*, 113, 133.

40. *Prelude, 1805*, ix, 46–9; WW to RW, 19 Dec [1791] (*EY*, 71). WW's contact in the National Assembly is unidentified, though Jacques Pierre Brissot (1754–93) is parroted with monotonous regularity. Johnston, 287–9 accepts this identification without question and elaborates at length upon their connection. Other biographers, e.g. Gill, 57 & Moorman, i, 172–3, have rightly been more cautious. The only evidence linking WW and Brissot is supplied by the anonymous author of the biographical preface to the 1828 Galignani edition of WW's poems, who says that WW and Brissot stayed in the same house in Paris. This statement was repeated by Barron Field, 26, but WW crossed it through when reading the MS and wrote above it 'a mistake'. In this context it is significant that WW also crossed through Barron Field's next statement, that he had been driven from Paris by the horrors of the reign of Robespierre, but did not correct the earlier claim that 'he is said to have become acquainted with many of the leaders of the revolutionary party'. See also Reed, i, 126, 137. In the circumstances, I see no reason to identify the anonymous member as Brissot.

41. Clayden, *The Early Life of Samuel Rogers*, 128–30; *Prelude, 1805*, ix, 55–62; William Hunter, [Feb 1792] (*English Witnesses*, 152).

42. *Prelude, 1805*, ix, 63–80, 92–5, 108–11. The portrait, which hung in the chapel of the Carmelite convent in the Rue d'Enfer, was part of the regular tourist itinerary. SR also made a special trip to see it on 9 Feb 1791: Clayden, *The Early Life of Samuel Rogers*, 145.

43. *Nouveau Plan d'Orléans*, 1778 & *Plan Général de la Ville d'Orléans*, 1779: MSS in the ADL, Orléans; Barbour, *France: The Loire*, 69–88; M.W. Labarge, *Gascony, England's First Colony, 1204–1453* (London,

Hamish Hamilton, 1980), 93, 97–8. Most of the city was flattened by German and American bombing in World War II; though many of the finest buildings and streets, including the Rue Royale, where WW lived, have been restored, the Archives Départementales du Loiret were almost entirely destroyed. This is an irreparable loss, as G. Lefebvre, *Etudes Orléanaises, I: Contributions à l'Etude des Structures Sociales à la fin du XIIIème siècle* (Paris, 1962), 7, points out. Much of the evidence for the period of William's residence in the area has been lost and, despite careful trawling through all the relevant archives by my highly efficient assistant, Marcus Ackroyd, little new information of substance has turned up.

44. Roe, 46. For Vaughan's radicalism, see Schneider, 144–5, 200, 202, 214.

45. WW to RW, 19 Dec [1791] (*EY*, 68–70).

46. MS 45/11/2 J 1941 no.1224 & 19 Dec 1789, ADL, Orléans. Gellet-Duvivier is usually described by biographers as a hosier and hatter, but here he is listed as a '*marchand de bas*'. For the Bourdon incident, see pp.128–9.

47. WW to RW, 19 Dec [1791] (*EY*, 70). For the dragoons, see ibid., 69n.1. In *The Prelude* WW does not distinguish between his residences at Orléans and Blois, but the military officers stationed 'in the city', who were his 'chief associates' and royalist to a man, were more likely these soldiers than the Bassigny regiment at Blois.

48. WW to RW, 19 Dec [1791] (*EY*, 69); *Prelude, 1805*, ix, 113–22. Foxlow's half-brother Francis (1771–1841) was an undergraduate at St John's, 1789–94, and may have been known to WW.

49. Legouis, 8–9, 12. Legouis's sentimental and novelistic approach to the story of WW and AV sticks in the craw; while his interpretations cannot be relied on, his sources are generally supported by other evidence.

50. The Dufours were probably the 'very agreeable' family with whom WW passed some evenings in Orléans after rejecting their lodgings as too dear: WW to RW, 19 Dec [1791] (*EY*, 70). Legouis, 12, says that they lived in the Rue du Poirier, but a widowed Mme Dufour lived in the more appropriately named Rue des Pensées in 1789: MS 45/11/2 J 1941, no.1178, ADL, Orléans. Caroline was born at Orléans on 15 Dec 1792; assuming a normal 40-week gestation, she must have been conceived on or around 10 Mar.

51. DW to JP, 16 Feb & [10 & 12 Jul] [1793] (*EY*, 87, 98).

52. Legouis, 110. See p.82: this miniature is assumed to be of AV, but its provenance is not beyond doubt. The original is in DC.

53. Bouis, *A verser au dossier d'Annette Vallon*, 4; RS to J. Rickman, 17 Jan 1800 (*RSNL*, i, 218); by a curious coincidence, RS here suggests that the ideal cross-cultural mating to improve the human species was a French mother and an English father.

54. Legouis, 55. Françoise Vallon (b.1762) gave birth to her son, whom she named after his father, Toussaint Décadi, on 1 Nov 1798: he was handed over to the Hôtel-Dieu, the hospital at Blois where her brother was the surgeon, and not acknowledged by Françoise as her child until she was living in Paris in 1819. Paul Vallon (1763–1835), AV's lawyer brother, had a liaison with the notorious courtesan Mme Bonneuil, who passed him off as her 'secretary', 1795–1803: ibid., 78–81.

55. Tom Myers was a civil servant in the EIC from 1781, became Accountant-General of Bengal in 1796 and returned to England in 1798. He married his cousin Lady Mary Neville in Jan 1802. DW hoped to be given care of the child, who was three or four, when she came over to England to be educated; though she was expected to arrive *c.*Nov 1795, *EY*, 147n.2 wrongly says there is no evidence she ever left India. She may have been the 'young person, an Indian by half-blood,' sobbing at her uncle John Myers's funeral in 1821: WW to SGB, 10 Jan 1821 (*LY*, i, 4).

56. Two letters of 1793 are in the ADL&C, Blois; the third, of 1835, is in DC, where it was discovered inside the binding of a book. The absence of any letters from WW and DW to AV and Caroline suggests that these were acquired by the Ws, possibly in 1850: see p.809.

57. AV to WW, 20 Mar [1793]: MS L 2060, Comité de surveillance de la commune de Blois, pp.1–2, ADL&C, Blois (Legouis, 127). Legouis's version of AV's letters standardizes her erratic spelling and punctuation. Her meaning is not always clear, but one assumes the 'mon petit' she kisses and loves always is WW's penis: I am grateful to Marcus Ackroyd and Mme H. Shovelar for confirming this.

58. Ibid., p.1 (Legouis, 125). Legouis guesses '*au*

voyage' for the words obliterated by a tear in the MS, but this is too long and does not fit what is visible. I have suggested 'the danger' simply because this is clearly AV's general meaning, though I do not think it is the actual missing word. AV's ignorance of the fact that France had already declared war against England on 1 Feb 1793 strikingly bears out WW's assertion that Londoners would be better informed of French events than those living in 'a petty provincial town in the heart of the kingd[om] itself': WW to WM, 19 May [1792] (*EY*, 77).

59. The precise date of WW's removal to Blois is not known but the consensus of opinion is that he left no later than Mar and possibly as early as Feb: Reed, i, 129–30. In either case, Caroline was probably conceived in Blois.

60. Cosperec, *Blois*, 310–11; Denis, *Histoire de Blois et sa Région*; Barbour, *France: The Loire*, 138–42, 144–59, 161–6. Henri Grégoire (1750–1831) was also a member of the States General and Constituent Assembly (1789), the National Convention (1792), the Council of Five Hundred (1795) and the Senate (1801).

61. WW to WM, 19 May [1792] (*EY*, 76, 77–8). France and Austria were at war by Apl 1792. The Austrian army invaded in support of the counter-revolutionary movement and the Queen, Marie Antoinette, herself an Austrian. The French were ill-armed, ill-trained and taken so completely by surprise that they suspected their leader, General Dillon, of treachery. He was therefore brutally murdered by his own troops after their defeat; they put his body on a bonfire in the main square at Lille and danced around it like savages: *English Witnesses*, 155–7.

62. *Prelude, 1805*, ix, 313–20; Obituary of Michel Beaupuy, *Moniteur*, xxix, 168 (Roe, 55–6). My information about Beaupuy is taken principally from Roe, but for a more detailed study of his career see G. Bussière & E. Legouis, *Le Général Michel Beaupuy* (Paris & Périgueux, 1891).

63. *Prelude, 1805*, ix, 482–511. WW mentions visiting the Château de Romorantin-Lanthenay and the more famous Chambord. WW scholars, from de Selincourt to the present day, remain convinced that the 'rural castle' where François I's mistress lived whose name is now 'slipped from my remembrance' is Beauregard. In fact it does not exist. WW either invented the story or, more probably, elaborated on the legend that François I chose to build at Chambord, rather than Romorantin-Lanthenay, because his mistress, the Countess of Thoury, lived nearby. For WW's association of the district with Arthurian scenes, mentioning specifically Ariosto's Angelica and Tasso's Erminia, see ibid., ix, 445–68.

64. Ibid., ix, 328ff., esp.354–6, 392–6.

65. Ibid., ix, 518–26. Beaupuy's position was more ambivalent than this anecdote suggests. In Mar 1792 his regiment spilt blood when punishing the starving villagers of d'Onzain, St-Dye and Muides for stealing a consignment of grain: Roe, 59n.22.

66. Ibid., 55–6, 58n.21.

67. *English Witnesses*, 157–80; Roe, 66.

68. DW to JP, [8] May [1792] (*EY*, 73).

69. Roe, 49, 50, 68. Grégoire's speech was printed and published by Les Amis at Blois.

70. *Prelude, 1805*, ix, 289. WW implies that Beaupuy was isolated from the rest of his regiment who were all royalist, but, as Roe says, many of them were members of Les Amis, so were active pro-revolutionaries.

71. DW to JP, [8] May & WW to RW, 3 Sep 1792 (*EY*, 73, 80–81).

72. 'The king was dethroned when I was at Blois, and the massacres of September took place when I was at Orleans': WW, *Autobiographical Memoranda*, Nov 1847 (*Prose*, iii, 374); 'At the time of the September massacres he was at Orléans': E. Yarnall to H. Reed, Sep 1850 (*Memoirs*, ii, 491).

73. WW's letter to RW of 3 Sep was postmarked on arrival in London on 10 Sep, so RW could not have received it, or put arrangements in place for WW to receive the money in Blois, before that date.

74. The evidence that this decision was taken suddenly and that AV was hurried away 'by night And unforewarned' rests solely on WW's fictional story of Vaudracour and Julia, in *The Prelude, 1805*, ix, 613–25, where it purports to be a story told by Beaupuy, though WW told IF he heard it from a French lady 'who had been an eye and ear-witness of all that was done & said': *IF*, 10. The story had obvious parallels with WW's affair with AV and its inclusion at such length in *The Prelude* suggests that the autobiographical implications were intentional. There are so many significant differences, however, that I do not feel able to quote it as a

source for this period of WW's life. WW himself omitted the story from the final version of *The Prelude* prepared for posthumous publication.
75. *English Witnesses*, 189–201; Roe, 70–71; Browning (ed.), *The Despatches of Earl Gower*, 255; WW, *Autobiographical Memoranda*, Nov 1847 (*Prose*, iii, 374).
76. Roe, 66.
77. Denis, 'William Wordsworth et l'Orléanais', 255; *IF*, 7; WW, *Descriptive Sketches* [1793], ll.760ff. (*Poems*, i, 917); WW to WM, 19 May [1792] (*EY*, 76–7).
78. WW to RW, 3 Sep [1792] (*EY*, 81); WW, *Descriptive Sketches* [1793], ll.774–85 (*Poems*, i, 917–18). WW has often been accused of betraying his revolutionary principles; the 1849–50 version of these lines proves otherwise, increasing the contrast between them and the preceding lines and making the 'battle hymn' theme more emphatic. '– But foes are gathering – Liberty must raise / Red on the hills her beacon's far-seen blaze; / Must bid the tocsin ring from tower to tower! – / Nearer and nearer comes the trying hour! / Rejoice, brave Land, though pride's perverted ire / Rouse hell's own aid, and wrap thy fields in fire: / Lo, from the flames a great and glorious birth; / As if a new-made heaven were hailing a new earth!': ibid., ll.638–45 (*Poems*, i, 113).
79. Legouis, 25; Harper, *Wordsworth's French Daughter*, 28–9. In *Vaudracour and Julia*, the lovers consummate their passion either 'through effect Of some delirious hour', or because Vaudracour saw so many bars to their marrying that he decided to ignore 'law and custom, and entrust himself To nature'. This may (or may not) have implications for WW's own reasoning with regard to AV: *Prelude, 1805*, ix, 596–604.
80. AV's brother Charles married in a civil ceremony in 1794 that was secretly blessed two years later by a non-juring priest: Legouis, 51.
81. AV signed the register of a secret RC marriage on 14 Jul 1795 as 'William Wordsworth Vallon' and in police documents of 31 Jan 1800 is described as '*veuve* Williams': Legouis, 50–51, 54. In a letter to the *préfet* of Blois on 13 Dec 1801 she signs herself '*f*[*emme*] William' and in documents supporting her claim to a pension in 1818 she is described as 'Mme Williams': Bouis, *A verser au dossier d'Annette Vallon*, 3–5. For her letter to WW asking to 'pass as William's wife' see MW to SH, 19 Jun 1812 (*Supp.*, 133).
82. AV to DW, 20 Mar 1793: MS 2060 p.3 (Legouis, 130).
83. WW to RW, 19 Dec [1791] (*EY*, 70–71); William Cobbett (*English Witnesses*, 152–3).
84. *Prelude, 1805*, x, 38ff. For an eyewitness account of the occasion, see John Moore, 3 Nov 1792 (*English Witnesses*, 210–12).
85. Ibid., 207–8; Roe, 66, 78. In his copy of *The Works of Edmund Burke*, vii, 305, now in DC, WW wrote in the margin against the name of Gorsas, 'I knew this man. W.W.' For Brissot, see p.831n.40.
86. *Prelude, 1805*, x, 130–36; Roe, 39–42. Roe's own suggestion, p.79, that WW intended to become a speaker in the National Convention, was not an option open to WW as an Englishman. Johnston, 323 ludicrously contemplates WW becoming a spy, agitator or assassin.
87. *Prelude, 1805*, x, 190–91. Caroline's baptismal certificate is reproduced in Harper, *Wordsworth's French Daughter*, 28–9. WW is also referred to there as 'Williams Wordworsth' and 'Williams Wordsodsth'.

Chapter 5

chapter title: 'A patriot of the world', *Prelude, 1850*, x, 242.
picture: Silhouette of DW, artist unknown, *c.*1806.
1. WW, *An Evening Walk*, ll.250–78 (*Poems*, i, 84, 928n.).
2. Roe, 27–8.
3. WW to WM, 23 May [1794] (*EY*, 120).
4. *Critical Review*, viii (Jul–Aug 1793) & *Monthly Review*, xii (Oct 1793) (Smith, 7–11).
5. DW to JP, 16 Feb [1793] (*EY*, 89, 87); CW diary (Smith, 12); *STCBL*, i, 77.
6. DW to JP, 16 Feb [1793] (*EY*, 89).
7. WW to A. Taylor, 9 Apl 1801 (*EY*, 327–8); trunks were traditionally lined with paper from discontinued books.
8. Clayden, *The Early Life of Samuel Rogers*, 211–12, 214, 216, 217; the 5th–19th editions alone sold 22,350 copies. The 1st edition (500 copies) of WW's *Excursion*, one of his most successful works, published in 1814, lasted till 1820; the 2nd edition (also 500 copies) lasted seven years; from 1837, however, WW sold 1,000 copies a year of his collected poems.
9. CCC to RW, 14 Jun 1792; WLMS/SH/11/47; DW to JP, 7 Dec [1791] (*EY*, 65); WW to CW, 12

Jan [1816] (*MY*, ii, 271–2). WW complains in this letter of CCC's injustice 'in having permitted his Mother in her feeble state of Health to make a present to his Wife of £500, when he had the certainty of succeeding to the estate at her Death'. Moorman, i, 75 & Johnston, 150 assume this was a wedding gift, but CCC's mother was not then in feeble health. It seems more likely that this large sum was not given till Mrs Cookson inherited the Crackanthorpe estate.

10. CCC to RW, [spring 1792]: WLMS/SH/11/43. DW lent her £100 to JW2 to invest in trade on his voyage the following year: JW2 to CCC, 26 Apl 1793 (*LJW*, 70); CCC to RW, 30 Apl 1793: WLMS/SH/11/51; RW, Accts for JW2, Jun 1792–Apl 1797 [May 1793]: WLMS/3/16; the banknote transferring the money, dated 16 May 1793, is WLMS/3/20.

11. WW to [?R. Addison], [*c.*Jun 1816] (*MY*, ii, 326–7). As WW noticed, according to RW's accounts, only £136 of the intended £150 was paid. In 1794 CCC paid over a further £143 13s 4d, being the Ws' third share in his mother's personal estate: see pp.139, 837n 69

12. CCC to RW, 5 Jan 1792: WLMS/SH/11/41; CCC to RW, [spring 1792]: WLMS/SH/11/43.

13. DW to JP, [10 & 12 Jul 1793] & WW to RW, 3 Sep [1792] (*EY*, 100, 81 & n.2).

14. R. Watson, DD, Bishop of Llandaff, *A Sermon Preached before the Stewards of the Westminster Dispensary at their Anniversary Meeting, in Charlotte-Street Chapel, April 1785. With an Appendix* (London, T. Cadell & T. Evans, 1793).

15. WW, *A Letter to the Bishop of L[l]andaff* (Prose, i, 31).

16. *Prelude, 1805*, x, 233–7.

17. Ibid., 135.

18. WW, *A Letter to the Bishop of L[l]andaff* (*Prose*, i, 29). The only surviving MS of this work is undated. Moorman, i, 226 suggests spring 1793, Johnston, 333–4 (following Reed, i, 142) dates it to Jun 1793 and argues from this that it was inspired by his uncle's refusal to let him have the curacy Johnston believes WW actually wanted. The editors in *Prose*, i, 20–21, however, convincingly date it, on internal evidence, to Feb–Mar 1793 and it seems much more likely that this avowal of republicanism helped precipitate the rift with WC rather than resulted from it.

19. WW, *A Letter to the Bishop of L[l]andaff* (*Prose*, i, 32).

20. Ibid., 43. This paragraph appears to support the supposition that the 'absolute want of funds' which forced WW back to England also prevented his marriage to AV. For WW's attack on the courts, see ibid., 47.

21. Ibid., 38, 33–4. WW's argument is similar to that of James Mackintosh in *Vindiciae Galliciae* (London, 1792), 162–4, a copy of which WW possessed: ibid., 54.

22. Ibid., 24, 56.

23. *Prelude, 1805*, x, 637.

24. DW to JP, [10 & 12 Jul 1793] (*EY*, 101). It is unclear whether WC knew about AV, though WW did not keep the affair a secret except (possibly) from his own children by MW. WC later claimed he and WW had quarrelled over WW's support for 'French principles': *Farington Diary*, vi, 2303. AV's admonitions to DW in Mar 1793 to 'say nothing to your uncle' because 'that would be a painful confrontation which she could not win' and urging her to hide the reason for her tears from her aunt and uncle, suggest that WC was still ignorant of the affair at this time, but could be interpreted as counselling her not to cause renewed recriminations: AV to WW & AV to DW, 20 Mar 1793: MSS L 2060 pp.2, 4, ADL&C, Blois (Legouis, 126, 132).

25. DW to JP, [10 & 12 Jul 1793] & to RW, [28 May 1792] (*EY*, 103, 79).

26. DW to JP, 16 Oct [1792] (*EY*, 82–4, esp.83). DW's association with royalty at this period became a matter of family legend: MW, *Autobiographical Memoranda*, [Nov 1851]: DC 167 pp.39–40.

27. DW to JP, 16 Feb [1793] & to unidentified, 22 Dec 1892 (*EY*, 87–8, 86).

28. AV to DW, 20 Mar 1793: MS L 2060 pp.1–2, ADL&C, Blois (Legouis, 127–9).

29. Moorman, i, 180–81. Gill, 66 is rightly sceptical.

30. AV to WW, 20 Mar 1793: MS L 2060 p.1, ADL&C, Blois (Legouis, 125).

31. AV to DW, 20 Mar 1793: MS L 2060 pp.2–4, ADL&C, Blois (Legouis, pp.129–32).

32. See p.113.

33. D'Illiers, *L'Histoire d'Orléans Raconté par un Orléanais*, 310. For Bourdon's version of events, as given to the tribunal and reflected in the charges, see *Bulletin du Tribunal Criminel Révolutionnaire*, [16 Jun 1793], nos.61–4: Serie L1(1): Microfilm 745, ADL, Orléans. Legouis, 39–45 has a not entirely accurate account. For Bourdon, see Jones, *The*

Longman Companion to the French Revolution, 325.

34. MSS BB 30/87 & AF II 107/1344 items 149 & 157, Archives Nationales, Paris. Six more suspects are named in the *Bulletin du Tribunal Criminel Révolutionnaire*, 62, 249–50. Legouis, 42 is wrong in noting only 30.

35. MSS BB 30/87 & AF II 107/1344 items 149 & 157, Archives Nationales, Paris; *Bulletin du Tribunal Criminel Révolutionnaire*, 62, 250; 63, 255. According to Caroline's birth certificate, Dufours was '*greffier du tribunal du district d'Orléans*'; a *secretaire greffier* was one of the officials sacked by the two commissioners from the National Convention sent to sort out the city after the attack: MS AF II 1371 item 3, Archives Nationales, Paris.

36. P. Gellet-Duvivier, *Mémoire pour le citoyen Gellet Duvivier, d'Orléans, accusé dans l'affaire du citoyen Léonard Bourdon* [1793]: Ref 2J 1973: Microfilm 3104, ADL, Orléans; Legouis, 45.

37. Legouis is the main culprit but Johnston runs him a close second; curiously, AV's sister-in-law Marie Catherine Puzela, who married Paul Vallon, is described in similar terms: see Trouillard, *Mémoires de Madame Vallon*; Denis, *Histoire de Blois et sa Région*, 186.

38. Legouis, 54; MS F 7/6410/dossier no.8171, Archives Nationales, Paris.

39. Bouis, *A verser au dossier d'Annette Vallon*, 4–7. A good example of AV's method is her successful plea to the *préfet* of Blois on 13 Dec 1801 that the émigré René Fontenay be allowed to transfer his place of residence under surveillance from Blois to Vendôme, which is an extraordinary mixture of determination, flattery and threat: ibid., 2–3.

40. DW to JP, [10 & 12 Jul 1793] (*EY*, 103). DW told TdQ that WW 'had all but resolved . . . to take pupils' after his return from France and before RC died; this seems as good a time as any for him to have done so: TdQ, *Recollections*, 191.

41. DW to JP, [10 & 12 Jul 1793] (*EY*, 97–102).

42. DW to JP, [5 Jun] & [10 & 12 Jul] [1793] (*EY*, 91, 102). The quote is from WW, *An Evening Walk*, l.28.

43. DW to RW, [9 Aug] & DW to JP, 30 Aug [1793] (*EY*, 105–7, 109). RW sent her £10 as she had only 1½guineas left to see her through till Jan: DW to RW, 12 Aug [1793] (*EY*, 107).

44. WW, [*At the Isle of Wight. 1793*], (*Poems*, i, 116); *Prelude, 1805*, x, 291–4. The first poem was unpublished in WW's lifetime, but the ideas and images were incorporated into ibid., 290–306.

45. WW, *Advertisement, Prefixed to the First Edition of [Guilt and Sorrow]*, 1842 (*Poems*, i, 118). Legouis, 35 & Johnston, 343 posit that WW was on the island to reconnoitre a return to France. This is not credible: as Moorman, i, 231 sensibly points out, the fleet headquarters was the last place anyone wanting to make an illicit trip to France would choose as a port of departure.

46. WW, *A Letter to the Bishop of L[l]andaff* (*Prose*, i, 49); JW2 to CCC, 26 Apl 1793 (*LJW*, 70); TP to Mr Gutteridge, 23 Feb 1793 (Sandford, 44). Like WW, TP had divided loyalties about the war: 'If the French conquer, will licentiousness instead of liberty prevail? If the French are conquered, Europe is enslaved. I had rather run the risque of the former, than bear the burden of the latter': TP to Mr Gutteridge, 7 Jun 1793: ibid., 60.

47. DW to JP, 30 Aug [1793] [*EY*, 109]; RW, WW in acct with RW, 1794–99: WLMS/2/8.

48. *Prelude, 1805*, xii, 316–18. Here WW says he spent three days on Salisbury Plain but in WW, *Advertisement . . . to . . . [Guilt and Sorrow]* (*Poems*, i, 118) he says he spent only two.

49. *IF*, 62–3; *WW, Advertisement . . . to . . . [Guilt and Sorrow]* (*Poems*, i, 118–19).

50. WW to JK, [summer 1838] (*LY*, iii, 616); WW to FW, 20 Nov [1795] (*EY*, 159). In assigning the poem to 1793–4, WW claimed that much of this story had been written 'at least two years before' and that 'All that relates to her sufferings as a Soldier's wife in America & her condition of mind during her voyage home were faithfully taken from the report made to me of her own case by a friend who had been subjected to the same trials & affected in the same way': *IF*, 62.

51. WW published part of this poem as *The Female Vagrant* in 1798, then fleshed it out for republication as *Guilt and Sorrow* in 1842. For an accurate text of the versions and commentary see Gill (ed.), *The Salisbury Plain Poems of William Wordsworth*. In May 1793 William Frend was expelled from Cambridge for publishing an anti-war pamphlet and John Frost was sentenced to six months' imprisonment for sedition. For the same offence Thomas Muir and Thomas Fysshe Palmer were transported for 14 and seven years respectively in Aug and Sep; in Jan 1794 Maurice Margarot and William Skirving were also transported for 14 years: Gill, 76–7.

52. Clayden, *The Early Life of Samuel Rogers*, 177, 192–200; Humphries, *On the Trail of Turner in North and South Wales*.
53. WW, 'In vain did Time and Nature . . .' and 'The western clouds a deepening gloom display' (*Poems*, i, 116–17).
54. WW, *We are Seven*, Preface to *Lyrical Ballads, 1802*, and *Peter Bell* (ibid., i, 298–300, 871, 315–51); *IF*, 2–4, 17–18. The oddity of WW's statement that he walked *downwards* from Builth to Hay has often been remarked upon and remains unresolved. Johnston, 357ff. argues that this is evidence of WW's walking back down the Wye from North Wales to make a secret return trip to France in Sep. As I do not believe such a return took place (see pp.136–8) I can only assume WW was either mistaken (as he was about spending college vacations with the Smiths at Broughton) or, more likely, that he retraced his steps to accompany the 'wild rover', as he did in his Wye tour of 1798: see p.217.
55. WW, *Tintern* ll.50–57 (*Poems*, i, 358–9).
56. Ibid., ll.67–83 (*Poems*, i, 359–60).
57. DW to JP, 30 Aug 1793 (*EY*, 108–9).
58. Ibid., 110; CCC to RW, 14 Aug 1793: WLMS/SH/11/52; *LJW*, 15–16. JW2 had spent the interval between voyages visiting relatives. Though barely noticed by DW, he had spent four months at Forncett with her and the Cooksons at the beginning of 1792, then visited RWW, his mother's cousins the Griffiths in Newcastle, CCC and Uncle Tom Myers in Penrith (which is where he was when his grandmother died). In the summer vacation, he joined CW on a walking tour of the Lakes, taking in visits to his Wordsworth cousins at Broughton and Rampside. He may have sailed to the Azores from Whitehaven before returning to London by Mar 1793, ready for the *Earl of Abergavenny*'s next voyage: ibid., 14–15.
59. Carlyle, *Reminiscences*, 405.
60. Johnston, 357–400 leads the field in imagining a glamorously novelesque return to France but fails to offer any valid motive or argument to prove it. Moorman, i, 239–42 and Gill, 77-8 are sceptical, but ultimately bow to Carlyle's infallibility.
61. *Prelude, 1805*, x, 272–3.
62. I am indebted to Jonathan Wordsworth for making this point in conversation at Grasmere. For a typical English reaction to witnessing a guillotine execution, see *English Witnesses*, 250–52.
63. WW and Carlyle met at HT's in 1835 and then again in 1836, before the publication of *The French Revolution* in 1837. These were intimate breakfasts at which the type of conversation Carlyle records could not have taken place. Neither man took to the other, but both were happy to talk together quietly in a corner when they met in the 1840s on grand social occasions at the Marshalls', Spring-Rices' and Lord Stanley's. The conversation more likely dates from this period, but does not appear in extant letters. Carlyle describes the execution of Gorsas and his final words, but not WW's alleged presence or comments, in Carlyle, *The French Revolution*, ii, 275–6. He wrote his account of WW in Feb–Mar 1867, 17 years after WW's death: Carlyle, *Reminiscences*, xxx.
64. DW to JP, 30 Aug [1793] (*EY*, 108).
65. This was WW's first trip to Cumberland since Mary's marriage on 10 Nov 1789, which is why I place this visit then: see p.828n.39.
66. JW1, Admin. Acct, 1788–92: WLMS/SH/12/13 [26 Dec 1793 & 11 Jan 1794]. Neither cash nor hat was a gift; both were charged to the estate. The bill was paid on 11 Jan 1794, but the hat may have been a much earlier purchase.
67. WW to WM, 17 Feb & DW to JP [21 Apl] [1794] (*EY*, 111, 115).
68. WW to WM, 17 Feb [1794] (*EY*, 112–13).
69. JW1, Admin. Acct, 1788–92: WLMS/SH/12/13 [10 Mar 1794]; RW, WW & DW in account with RW, [1793–1803]: WLMS/2/5 & 2/6 [1 Mar 1793] [*r.*1794]; CCC to RW, 23 Feb 1794, WLMS/SH/11/42, forwards £143 13s 4d as the Ws' third share in their grandmother's personal estate. WW and DW each got £28 14s 8d, being a fifth share of this sum; it remained in RW's hands, earning interest at the rate of 50 per cent over 10 years.
70. *DWJ*, i, 104, 182; *IF*, 19. 'In recollection of that happy ramble, that most happy day & hour', WW wrote a poem some six years afterwards: WW, 'There is a little unpretending Rill' (*Poems*, i, 565).
71. DW to unidentified, [Apl] & to JP, [21 Apl] [1794] (*EY*, 113, 114–16).

72. DW to Mrs CCC, 21 Apl [1794] (*EY*, 116–18, esp.117).
73. RW to WW, 23 May 1794: WLMS/2/47 (*EY*, 120–21); Reed, i, 153; WW to WM, 23 May [1794] (*EY*, 120); WW, *Inscription for a Seat by the Pathway Side Ascending to Windy Brow* (*Poems*, i, 141). For an excellent summary of the importance of WW's revisions and the evolution of his philosophy, see Gill, 81–3.
74. WW to WM, [8] Jun [1794] & to SGB, [*c.*23] Feb 1805 (*EY*, 127, 546).
75. *Prelude, 1805*, x, 431–2. In addition to those guillotined in Paris, 3,000 were executed in Nantes, 2,000 in Angers and 2,000 in Lyons: Barraclough (ed.), *The Times Atlas of World History* (London, Guild Publishing, 1984), 203, fig.2. For a discussion of WG's influence see Roe, *passim.*
76. WW to WM, [8] Jun [1794] (*EY*, 124).
77. RS to G. Bedford, 8 Feb 1795 (*RSLC*, i, 231). The magazine was to be mainly a vehicle for their poetry, but would include essays expressing their political 'sentiments'.
78. WW to WM, 23 May [1794] (*EY*, 118–19).
79. RW to WW, 23 May 1794: WLMS/2/47 (*EY*, 121).
80. DW to LB, 7 Aug [1805] (*EY*, 616).
81. RW to WW, 23 May 1794: WLMS/2/47 (*EY*, 120–21); DW to RW, 28 May [1794] (*EY*, 121, 123). RWW's symptoms suggest heart disease. Reed, i, 156 wrongly gives his age at death as 51 instead of 61.
82. DW to RW, 28 May [1794] (*EY*, 122–3). The revival of interest in the Ws' claim was probably stimulated by the news that, on 26 May, Henry Littledale of Whitehaven had been awarded more than £4,000 against SJL in the House of Lords, as damages for a property destroyed in Jan 1791 by subsidence caused by Lowther coal mines. The Ws had personal links with Littledale as JW1 had lent him £900, which, with interest, was finally repaid to his estate on 14 Jun 1787: JW1, Admin. Accts, 1783–9: WLMS/SH/12/12.
83. RW to WW, 13 Oct 1794: WLMS/2/90 p.2 (*EY*, 132n.1).
84. DW to RW, 28 May & WW to WCal, 1 Oct [1794] (*EY*, 122–3, 129). Calvert was commissioned an ensign in the 1st West Riding Regiment of Yorkshire Militia on 1 Jan 1794 and promoted Lieutenant on 25 Feb 1795. He was still a serving officer in 1797 but does not appear in army lists after 1799: *Lists of the Officers of the Several Regiments and Corps of Fencible Cavalry and Infantry; of the Officers of the Militia; of the Corps and Troops of Gentlemen and Yeomanry; and of the Corps and Companies of Volunteer Infantry* (War Office, 1794ff., 1798 volume lacking). I am indebted to Michael Ball of the National Army Museum for this information.
85. WW to WM, [8] Jun [1794] (*EY*, 125–6).
86. Ibid., 126, 128; DW to RW, 28 May [1784] (*EY*, 121).
87. WW to WM, [8] Jun [1794] (*EY*, 123–5).

Chapter 6

chapter title: 'Benighted heart and mind', *Prelude, 1805*, xii, 21.
picture: Racedown, by S.L. May, date unknown.
1. *Prelude, 1805*, x, 466–566, esp.539–52. Maximilien Robespierre (1758–94) was guillotined in Paris on 28 Jul 1794, but WW is unlikely to have heard the news before 21 Aug: Reed, i, 158n.
2. WW, *Elegiac Stanzas suggested by a Picture of Peele Castle, in a Storm*, ll.1–12, and *The River Duddon*, Sonnet xxi, l.3 (*Poems*, i, 694; ii, 391); *IF*, 31.
3. WW to WCal, 1 Oct [1794]: Stanger Albums, ii, 168, no.43 p.1 (*EY*, 129).
4. WW to RW, 10 Oct [1794] (*EY*, 131).
5. WW to WCal, 1 Oct [1794]: Stanger Albums, ii, 168, no.43 pp.1–2 (*EY*, 129–30).
6. Johnston, 401–26 puts the worst possible interpretation on all WW's connections with RC, describing them as cynical 'legacy-hunting'. WW's anxiety to get the will signed is not edifying, but does not justify such an interpretation.
7. WW to RW, 10 Oct [1794] (*EY*, 131–3). RW records a payment in 1794 of 10 guineas to WW 'by Joseph Lough of Penrith': RW in account with WW, 1794–9: WLMS/2/8 [1794].
8. RW to WW, 13 Oct 1794: WLMS/2/90 pp.1–3 (*EY*, 132n.1).
9. WW to RW, [*c.*17 Oct 1794] (*EY*, 133–4); RC, Last Will & Testament, with Codicil, 23 Oct 1794: WLMS/2/95. For RW's bond for £400, dated 21 Oct 1794, leaving WW 'free and clear of and from any claim or demand' by RWW's executors, see WLMS/2/97.
10. WW, *To the Memory of Raisley Calvert*, ll.9–14 (*Poems*, i, 569). For RC's death see Reed, i, 161. A

search in Greystoke churchyard failed to locate RC's grave.

11. WW to WM, 7 Nov & *c.*24 Dec 1794 & 7 Jan 1795 (*EY*, 134–6, 136–9). STC considered becoming a reporter for the *Telegraph* in Jan 1795; RS was a contributor by Feb and hoped to become Bristol correspondent. It was taken over by the *Morning Post* in Mar 1797 (*EY*, 139n.2).

12. WW to WM, 7 Nov 1794 (*EY*, 136).

13. DW to RW, 16 Jan & to JP, Apl [1795] (*EY*, 140, 143). The tone of DW's account, and her references to having 'seen' CCC and had 'a meeting', all imply that this took place away from Newbiggin. DW says he had expressed 'so much affection for me and my brothers' to the Misses Griffith that she 'could not resist' a meeting, suggesting the Griffiths brokered it.

14. DW to JP, Apl [1795] (*EY*, 142).

15. The whole Sockburn peninsula, including the ruins of the now deconsecrated church, is private property and cannot be entered without the prior permission of the owners. I am indebted to the Misses Gatheral and Mrs Joyce Cracknell for the privilege of a visit. Sarah Hutchinson (1710–86) had lived with her brother, Thomas, at Sockburn. Jane Hutchinson (1767–93), first wife of JH, was the daughter of Isaac and Elizabeth Wilkinson of Penrith: both her daughters died in 1827 and their barely legible tombstone was erected by their 'afflicted Father' close to that of their mother. A full history and description of the place, including transcripts of some of the gravestones, can be found in R. Surtees, *The History and Antiquities of the County Palatine of Durham* (EP Publishing, 1972, repr. of Nichols, Son & Bentley edn of 1816–40), iii, 243–51.

16. DW to JP, Apl [1795] (*EY*, 141–2).

17. *LJW*, 16–17; Cumming and Carter, 'The *Earl of Abergavenny* (1805)', 31. JW2's promotion cost him eight guineas for new uniform, though the entire voyage earned him only £51 11s 3d.

18. WW's name and address are noted in another hand on STC to G. Dyer, *p.m.*10 Mar 1795 (*STCL*, i, 154). The address is Chalton, not Charlton, Street, as in Johnston, 449.

19. Schneider, 222; Reed, i, 164; for Holcroft's review, see Smith, 10–12, & p.118.

20. Schneider, 222.

21. WG's diaries record calls by or on WW on 28 Feb, 10, 25 & 31 Mar, 9 & 22 Apl, 14 & 29 Jul & 15 & 18 Aug: Reed, i, 164–6.

22. BM, *Autobiography*: WLMS/A/Montagu/26 pp.1–3, esp.p.3.

23. Schneider, 66, 164–5, 209–10; M. Belfitt, 'Wordsworth Evening at Brompton Church', *[Scarborough?] Mercury*, 27 Oct 1984, 4.

24. WW, [*Imitation of Juvenal – Satire VIII*], ll.9–13 (*Poems*, i, 142–7). The first two lines, which WW considered the best, were contributed by RS: WW to FW, 20 Nov [1795] (*EY*, 158). His Majesty George III (1738–1820) had already suffered two attacks of mental illness, the latest in 1788–9; His Grace the 11th Duke of Norfolk (1746–1815) was a Catholic peer of notoriously slovenly appearance; His Excellency William Eden (1744–1814) had been ambassador to The Hague before the Low Countries were invaded by France; SJL held the Honour of Lonsdale among many other titles.

25. Ibid., ll.100–104. Sir Thomas More (1478–1535), saint, philosopher and statesman (not necessarily in that order), was executed by Henry VIII (1491–1547) for refusing to accept the King as head of the Anglican Church. Sir Walter Raleigh (*c.*1552–1618), historian, poet, explorer and New World colonizer, was executed by James I (1566–1625) after returning from a failed expedition on the King's behalf to find gold along the Orinoco river.

26. DW to JPM, 2 Sep [1795] (*EY*, 149). The satire was still unfinished at the end of Nov, for which WW blamed 'my procrastinating spirit' and 'indolence': WW to FW, 20 Nov [1795] (*EY*, 156–7).

27. For the Pinney family background generally, see Pares, *A West India Fortune* and *EY*, 148n2; for JFP in Paris, see MSS Box S/4/15 (typescript) & Box 34, Letters of JFP II, folder ii, no.1, PP. For AP's radicalism, see Roe, 154–5, 226, 240.

28. DW to JPM, 2 Sep [1795] (*EY*, 147–8). For details of the alterations, including plans, and the handwritten advertisement, see MS Folder xviii, PP. The £42 p.a. rent was not to include the furnishings.

29. Johnston, 430–67 argues unconvincingly that WW and WM's monthly miscellany was published as the *Philanthropist*, which ran for 11 months from Mar 1795 to Jan 1796. Beyond the fact that it shared the same title, derived from WG, and a radical agenda, there is nothing to suggest any link; in any case, WW and WM had

abandoned the project almost six months earlier: WW to WM, 7 Nov 1794 (*EY*, 134–5).

30. WW, *The Birth of Love* (*Poems*, i, 114–16); Reed, i, 24 & n. The poem was sent in, and had an introductory note, by FW.

31. Reed, i, 169–70; DW to JPM, 2 Sep [1795] (*EY*, 147); a friend of BM's offered WW a rent charge on his landed estate for £500; WCal had told WW he would 'do his utmost to procure the money as soon as possible': WW to RW, [14 Sep 1795] (*EY*, 152).

32. DW to JPM, 2 Sep [1795] (*EY*, 146–7).

33. Ibid., 146–51.

34. Ibid., 151; JPP to JFP, 15 Aug 1795: Box S/3/4 no.6 p.1, PP (Reed, i, 167n.); WW to WM, 24 Oct [1795] (*EY*, 153).

35. JPP to JFP, 15 Aug 1795: Box S/3/4 no.6 pp.1–2, PP.

36. RS to H.W. Bedford, 22 Aug 1794 (*RSNL*, i, 72).

37. RS to C. Danvers, 15 Jun 1809 (ibid., i, 511).

38. WW to WM, 24 Oct [1795] (*EY*, 153).

39. *Farington Diary*, x, 3628, quoting a conversation with LMB on 7 Apl 1810; MW & WW to SC, [7 Nov 1845] (*LY*, iv, 719).

40. WW to WM, 24 Oct [1795] (*EY*, 153–4).

41. JC said he was introduced to WW at Nether Stowey in 1798, a statement repeated in Barron Field, 28 but crossed through as incorrect by WW: JC, *Reminiscences*, 174–5; Reed, i, 168n. JC was notoriously inaccurate but it seems likely that WW's reading of his Salisbury Plain poem to STC, which is usually assigned to this period, did not take place till later. In the absence of other evidence, and half-persuaded by Reed, i, 185n.11, I have placed it here.

42. *STCBL*, i, 78–9; *IF*, p.62.

43. RS was apparently in Bath by 1 Sep, STC in Nether Stowey by 19 Sep and possibly as early as 12 Sep: Reed, i, 168n.

44. E. Pinney to JJP, 23 Sep 1795: Box S/3/4 no.1 p.2, PP; Evans & Pinney, 'Racedown and the Wordsworths', 15.

45. WW to WM, [20 &] 24 Oct [1795] (*EY*, 155–6); CL to STC, 4 Nov 1802 (*LCL*, ii, 84).

46. WW to WM, [20 &] 24 Oct & DW to JPM, 30 Nov [1795] (*EY*, 154, 162). The eight naval vessels retired safely into Portland Roads harbour but 10 of the 200 merchantmen and transports were wrecked attempting to join them; the Dorset coast from Weymouth to Abbotsbury (all clearly visible from Pilsdon Pen) was strewn with bodies (over 300 men drowned) and wreckage: Attwooll, *Shipwrecks*, 18–21.

47. Advertisement for the letting of Racedown Lodge, 31 May 1793: Folder xviii, PP; Inventory of Racedown, 7 Sep 1795: Folder i, no.4, PP; DW to JPM, 30 Nov [1795] (*EY*, 161). The inventory reveals that the piano in the breakfast room/library was to be removed before the Ws took up residence. The room also had a mahogany tea chest, reading stand and table desk, a satinwood tea caddy and a picture of the Piazzetta in Venice. See Mayberry, *Coleridge & Wordsworth in the West Country*, 81, for a photograph.

48. DW to JPM, 30 Nov [1795] (*EY*, 160); Mayberry, *Coleridge & Wordsworth in the West Country*, 82; Pares, *A West India Fortune*, 142–3.

49. DW to JPM, 30 Nov & 2 Sep [1795] (*EY*, 160, 147 & n., 149). For Myers's child, see pp.104, 832n.55.

50. DW to JPM, [7 Mar 1796] & 19 Mar [1797] (*EY*, 166, 180–81). DW wanted 'a strong girl' as a servant who could 'cook plain victuals tolerably well' because they would occasionally have BM and JFP staying with them: DW to JPM, 2 Sep [1795] (*EY*, 149).

51. WW to FW, 7 Mar [1796] (*EY*, 168); BM, *Autobiography*. WLMS/A/Montagu/26 pp.7–10, 16, 19, 27–9, 41, 43–4. Mr Lane, an early patron of BM's, with whom Basil lived in the 1800s, was 'obliged to dismiss him from his house as his kindness had been returned by [ingratitude: del] contumacy which he could never forget.' He asked never to see Basil again.

52. WW to RW, 7 May & to F. Wrangham, [*c*.25 Feb] [1797] (*EY*, 184, 178). WW bought £1 12s of 'fine Souchong Tea' from Edward Allen, Wholesale & Retail Tea Dealer & Grocer of Bristol, on 12 Nov 1795; in settling this and a bill of £1 3s for yarn bought at the same time, AP had to add 2s 6d to make up the shortfall: WW Receipts, Misc. Vols, Scrapbook 1791, DM 3, PP.

53. DW to JPM, 2 Sep [1795] (*EY*, 147). For WW's financial arrangements with BM and Douglas, see WW to RW, 7 May [1797] (*EY*, 183–4). WW's arrangements, particularly with Douglas, were informal and legally unenforceable because there was no consideration for the loan. WW jokingly claimed this laid him open to prosecution for usury, but it was a common practice in the days before a

regulated banking system. It did, however, mean that WW was trusting to BM's and Douglas's sense of honour for repayment of the loans and interest. WW could not afford to buy a conventional annuity for himself or DW until he had the full legacy from RC, hence his need to make temporary and informal arrangements to secure an income.

54. DW to JPM, 2 Sep [1795] (*EY*, 149); *LJW*, 17; Venn, vi, 579.

55. DW to JPM, 30 Nov & [7 Mar 1796]; WW to WM, 24 Oct & WW to FW, 20 Nov [1795] (*EY*, 161, 165, 154–5, 159). Leader (1773–1836) was an Irish barrister, member of the Middle Temple and, like WW, a friend of WM, BM, John and James Tobin, as well as a disciple of WG.

56. WW to FW, 20 Nov [1795] & 7 Mar [1796] (*EY*, 159, 168). Gill records lending the paper to WW in his diary: Evans & Pinney, 'Racedown and the Wordsworths', 17.

57. AP to WW, 26 Nov 1795: Letter Book 13, pp.3–4, PP.

58. WW to JC, [Jan 1796] (*EY*, 163). The first issue of the *Watchman* was published on 1 Mar 1796, the 10th and last on 13 May 1796; its stated objectives were to agitate against the gagging acts and call for suffrage 'general and frequent': Ashton, 81–2; Holmes, i, 116.

59. WW to WM, 24 Oct [1795] (*EY*, 153–4). 'The peasants are miserably poor; their cottages are shapeless structures (I may almost say) of wood and clay – indeed they are not at all beyond what might be expected in savage life': DW to JPM, 30 Nov [1795] (*EY*, 162).

60. DW to JPM, [7 Mar 1796] (*EY*, 166). For Dr John Moore (1729–1802), Mme Roland (1754–93) and Louvet (1760–97), see *Oxford Companion to English Literature*, 556, 704–5; *Webster's Biographical Dictionary*, 1049, 1276, 923. Part of Moore's journal is reproduced in *English Witnesses*, 162–3, 167–70, 174–84, 187–8, 203–12, 213–15. Miss Williams's affecting account of visiting Mme Roland in prison is ibid., 239–40.

61. DW to JPM, [7 Mar 1796] & 30 Nov [1795] (*EY*, 166, 161); WW, 'The hour-bell sounds, and I must go' (*Poems*, i, 147, 937); AP to WW, 26 Nov 1795: Letter Book 13, p.5, PP. AP sent the Louvet with his letter, but brought the Mme Roland and Miss Williams with him at Christmas.

62. WW to JC, [Jan] & to WM, 21 Mar [1796] (*EY*, 163, 169); RS's preface attracted much hostile comment from reviewers: see Madden (ed.), *Robert Southey: The Critical Heritage*, 40–50.

63. AP to Jas Tobin, 12 Apl 1796: Letter Book 13, p.9, PP; HH, *Retrospect of a Retired Mariner*. WLMS/H/1/2/3 pp.44–8. The first occasion a man-o'-war, *The Argonaut*, boarded HH's ship as it lay off Cork and ordered all hands to serve the king. HH found the conditions better than on his previous ship and was made a midshipman, but received no wages for the two-year voyage. The second time, operating on a privateer off Santa Cruz, he was 'rescued' by and pressed into service on the English frigate, the *Fortunee*, thereby losing all his prizes.

64. WW, *Adventures on Salisbury Plain*, [1795–9], ll.820–4 (WW, *The Salisbury Plain Poems*, 154).

65. WW to WM, 21 Mar [1796] (*EY*, 170–71); CL to T. Manning, 3 Nov 1800 (*LCL*, i, 244); STC to J. Thelwall, 13 May 1796 (*STCL*, i, 215). STC always quarrelled with WG's atheism and defence of promiscuity.

66. AP to Jas Tobin, 12 Apl 1796: Letter Book 13, p.9, PP.

67. DW to JPM, [7 Mar 1796] (*EY*, 164–5); AP to Jas Tobin, 12 Apl 1796: Letter Book 13, p.9, PP.

68. AP to Jas Tobin, 12 Apl & to WW, 25 Mar 1796: Letter Book 13, pp.9, 6–7, PP.

69. Ibid., pp.7–8. See also JPP to J. Russell, 22 Apl & to S. Praetor, 18 Feb 1796: Letter Book 12, pp.150, 135, PP. Johnston, 489–90 misinterprets the reference to sending in Perkins as a threat to sue WW for 'borrowing, or otherwise making use of, the petty cash at Racedown'. This is untenable. The 'shortfall' obviously refers to the Racedown rent which was missing from all other rents due on 25 Mar 1796. There is, in any case, no suggestion that the Pinneys ever kept any cash at Racedown, because Perkins was responsible for all the administration and finances.

70. JJP to J. Gill, 16 Sep & to J. Perkins, 27 Jun 1796: Letter Book 12, pp.169, 183; Advertisement for the letting of Racedown Lodge, 31 May 1793: Folder xviii, PP; DW to unidentified, [Dec 1795–Jan 1796] (*EY*, 163).

71. JPP to AP, 29 May & to J. Gill, 16 Sep 1796: Letter Book 12, pp.155–6, 183, PP.

72. DW to JPM, [7 Mar] & WW to WM, 21 Mar [1796] (*EY*, 165, 169).

73. WW, 'The road extended o'er a heath', 'No spade for leagues had won a rood of earth',

Address to the Ocean and *Argument for Suicide* (*Poems*, i, 147–51, 160–61, 161–2); STC, *Lines Written at Shurton Bars* (*STCP*, 88–91, 465). WW was imitating J.B. Farish's metrical games, see pp.99, 827n.14. RS and Charlotte Smith also contributed verse to the *Weekly Entertainer*, where WW published his poem: Moorman, i, 299.

74. STC to J. Thelwall, 13 May 1796 (*STCL*, i, 215–16).

75. CL to STC, 30–31 May 1796 (*LCL*, i, 9, 11).

76. DW to JPM, 2 Sep [1795] (*EY*, 149). WG's diary records meetings on 7, 18, 19 & 25 Jun: Reed, i, 182–4.

77. For James (1767–1814) and John Tobin (1770–1804), see *EY*, 210n.1 & Prance, 332; for Robert Allen (1772–1805) and John Stoddart (1773–1856) see ibid., 6, 315–16. The Tobins and Stoddart are mentioned frequently in correspondence in the PP.

78. WW, Preface to *The Borderers* (*Prose*, i, 78–9).

79. WW, *[Fragment of a 'Gothic' Tale]*, (*Poems*, i, 153–60); *IF*, 77; WW, *The Borderers*, iii, v, 81–8 (pp.214, 216). All references cited are to the 1797 text.

80. Ibid., iii, v, 23, 26–33; v, iii, 264–75; iv, ii, 134–5; ii, iii, 289–91 (pp.210, 294, 238, 168). For WW at Cockermouth Castle, see pp.7, 819n.17.

81. WW, Preface to *The Borderers* (*Prose*, i, 76–80); *IF*, 78.

82. WW, *Prelude, 1805*, x, 818–29, 897–900. WW is deliberately quoting Rivers's words, see p.172.

83. WW, *Preface to The Borderers* (*Prose*, i, 77).

Chapter 7

chapter title: 'A Sett of Violent Democrats', J. Walsh to J. King, 16 Aug 1797 (Roe, 260).

picture: Alfoxton House and Park, by Miss Sweeting, engraved by R. Pocock.

1. WW to the *Weekly Entertainer*, 23 Oct 1796 (*EY*, 171). The letter was published on 7 Nov 1796, followed, on 21 Nov, by WW's poem, *Address to the Ocean*, signed 'WW'; DW to unidentified, 24 Oct 1796 (*EY*, 172). WW had good reason to claim the 'best authority' for his statement: Fletcher Christian had briefly been one of his fellow pupils at Cockermouth Grammar School; Edward Christian was WW's headmaster at Hawkshead and legal adviser on the Lonsdale suit; WC and Capt JW were signatories to Edward Christian's pamphlet defending his brother in 1794: R. Hough, *Captain Bligh and Mr Christian* (London, Arrow Books Ltd, 1972), 56.

2. HH, *Retrospect of a Retired Mariner.* WLMS/1/2/3 pp.66–70. HH claimed that he arrived to find Ball had sailed without him and that his replacement was killed at the battle of the Nile. Margaret Hutchinson died on 28 Mar 1796, aged 24; she is buried at the old All Saints' Church, Sockburn, where there is a memorial stone in the churchyard to her and her sister-in-law, Jane, wife of their oldest brother, John, who died on 15 Jun 1793. Moorman, i, 308, wrongly dates MH's arrival to spring 1797.

3. DW to RW & to JPM, 19 Mar [1797] (*EY*, 178, 181); WW, 'She was a Phantom of delight', ll.3, 11–12 (*Poems*, i, 603); *Prelude, 1850*, xii, 153–62, 171–3. In the 1805 version the last phrase is the more appropriate 'her life is blessedness'.

4. *Prelude, 1805*, v, 276–7; iv, 214.

5. WW to FW, [*c*.25 Feb 1797] (*EY*, 177); WW, *[Fragment: The Baker's Cart]*, *Animal Tranquillity and Decay* and *Inscription for a Seat by a Roadside, Half Way up a Steep Hill, Facing the South* (*Poems*, i, 242–4). WW later claimed *Animal Tranquillity and Decay* was 'If I recollect right . . . an over-flowing from the old Cumberland Beggar', but the MS suggests it anticipates the poem: *IF*, 57; Reed, i, 27, 342–3. For the Windy Brow version of *Inscription for a Seat*, see *Poems*, i, 141.

6. Rawnsley, 'Reminiscences of Wordsworth among the Peasantry of Westmoreland', 13, 19, 22, 28, 31, 24, 36; *Prelude, 1805*, xii, 145, 161–8.

7. WW to J. Wilson, [7 Jun 1802] (*EY*, 355).

8. WW, *Lines Left upon a Seat in a Yew-tree*, ll.50–57 (*Poems*, i, 255). WW began the poem at school; the builder of the seat was Rev. William Braithwaite of Satterhow (1753–1800), a former Hawkshead schoolboy and graduate of St John's College, Cambridge, but his misanthropy is WW's invention. Yew trees, because they were traditionally grown in churchyards, have melancholy associations in literature: *IF*, 36; Thompson, 256–65, 299.

9. *Prelude, 1805*, xii, 168ff., esp.231–37, 240; WW to FW, [*c*.25 Feb 1797] (*EY*, 177).

10. For variant texts of this poem see WW, *The Ruined Cottage and The Pedlar.* The poem was never published in its originally conceived form, but was absorbed into, and became, the climax of

the 1st book of *The Excursion*, published in 1814 (*Poems*, ii, 53–66).
11. DW to JPM & to RW, 19 Mar [1797] (*EY*, 181, 178–9).
12. JL, *Diaries*, i, xii–xiii; ii, 36 [24 Sep 1824]; *RSNL*, i, 118; *STCL*, i, 308.
13. JLDMS, vii [n. inside back cover, 20 Mar 1797]. JL was recovering fast and would return to Cumberland on 6 Jun, which may be a partial explanation for his generosity in supplying WW with so many books.
14. JLDMS, vii [27 & 28 Mar 1797]; WW, *Written on the Thames near Richmond*, in JC, Commonplace Book (Reed, i, 195).
15. STC to C. Lloyd Snr, 15 Oct 1796 & to J. Thelwall, 6 Feb 1797 (*STCL*, i, 240, 308). The cottage at Nether Stowey, much enlarged and gentrified by the addition of a raised, pantiled roof (instead of a low thatch) when it became an inn, is now a museum belonging to the National Trust. I am indebted to the kindness of the curator, Derrick Woolf, for allowing me (and my family) to pay an extended visit after hours. His three leaflets, *Walking with Coleridge in the Quantocks*, co-written with R. Watters, are an essential guide to the district.
16. STC to JC, [early Apl 1797] (*STCL*, i, 319–320). Lloyd spent his life in and out of asylums. He published two volumes of poems in 1795 and 1796 and contributed, with CL, to STC's *Poems* (1797): Prance, 206. STC & RS had quarrelled over STC's reluctance to marry Sarah Fricker and RS's insistence that he was honour-bound to do so. In Sep 1796 RS had instigated a reconciliation, but their friendship was never so close again: Ashton, 90–91.
17. STC to J. Wade & to W.L. Bowles, 16 Mar 1797 (*STCL*, i, 316, 318).
18. C. Poole, 15 Mar 1796 (Sandford, 85). TP tried to help the starving rural population by devising a method of making bread out of wheat, barley, beans and potatoes or turnips.
19. Ibid., 275–6; Mayberry, *Coleridge & Wordsworth in the West Country*, 196–8, 208. Walford's Gibbet is still marked on the OS map and the walk to it from Nether Stowey is featured in Watters & Woolf, *Walking with Coleridge in the Quantocks*, no.1. TP said he wrote his narrative in Mar 1797 at the request of WW and RS, but RS's presence seems unlikely: Reed, i, 195n.
20. DW to RW, 28 May [1797] (*EY*, 186).
21. RW to WW, 3 May 1797: WLMS/2/48 pp.1–3 (*EY*, 182n.1); WW to RW, 7 May [1797] (*EY*, 184). JW2's return to England from his previous voyage was too late for him to secure a berth on the *Earl of Abergavenny*, which sailed from Portsmouth on 18 Mar 1797; he needed to make another voyage immediately, so as to be back before the *Abergavenny* sailed again: *EY*, 179n.1; *LJW*, 17–19.
22. DW to RW, 28 May & WW to RW, 12 Jun [1797] (*EY*, 185–6, 188). Similar letters were written to RW on 4 Jun and 11 Nov, without success: ibid., 187, 193.
23. WW to RW, 7 May, DW to RW, 28 May & WW & DW to RW, 5 [*r*.4] Jun [1797] (*EY*, 185, 186, 187). MH arrived in London the day after setting out, but did not find RW at home; she left the shirts at the porter's lodge with a message to say she would be at the George & Blue Boar Inn, Holborn (awaiting her coach connection to the north) till 7 p.m.: ibid., 187n.2.
24. WW to MW, 11 Aug 1810 (Darlington, 61–2).
25. MW & WW to SC, [7 Nov 1845] (*LY*, iv, 719).
26. DW to MH, [Jun 1797] (*EY*, 189); STC to J.P. Estlin, [10 Jun] & to JC, [8 Jun] 1797 (*STCL*, i, 326, 325).
27. DW to MH, [Jun 1797] (*EY*, 188–9). The quotation is from Shakespeare's, *A Midsummer Night's Dream*, Act v, Scene i, l.12.
28. STC to JC, [*c*.3 Jul 1797] (*STCL*, i, 330–31). The quote was from STC's lines on Joan of Arc, intended for inclusion in RS's poem, but eventually published separately as *Destiny of Nations* (1817).
29. STC to J.P. Estlin, [9 & 10 Jun], to JC, 29 Jun & to RS, [*c*.17 Jul] 1797 (*STCL*, i, 326, 327–8, 334, 336).
30. DW to MH, [4 Jul 1797] (*EY*, 189); STC to RS, [*c*.17 Jul 1797] (*STCL*, i, 334). Confined to TP's garden by his injury, STC composed *This Lime-Tree Bower My Prison* while WW, DW and CL were out walking one evening: *STCP*, 138–40.
31. CL to STC, [27 Sep], 3 Oct & 14 Nov 1796 (*LCL*, i, 44–5, 48, 63); *The Journals of Caroline Fox*, 128.
32. CL to STC, [19 or 26 Jul 1797] (*LCL*, i, 117–18).
33. STC to RS, [*c*.17 Jul 1797] (*STCL*, i, 334); DW to MH, [4 Jul] & 14 Aug 1797 (*EY*, 189, 190); the

Memorandum of Agreement is dated 14 Jul 1797 and is for one year, but the tenancy is backdated to Midsummer (24 Jun): Sandford, 127.

34. The name of the house has always been subject to variant spellings. The lease called it 'Allfoxen', WW and DW usually (but not always) Alfoxden. I have called it by the correct name, Alfoxton, in my text, but kept the variants in quotation. Today it is known as Alfoxton Park and it is a privately owned hotel of much charm.

35. DW to MH, 14 Aug 1797 (*EY*, 190).

36. For Thelwall's career, see the introduction to Claeys (ed.), *The Politics of English Jacobinism.*

37. J. Thelwall to his wife, 18 Jul 1797 (Sandford, 130); *IF*, 4; Coleridge (ed.), *Specimens of the Table Talk of Samuel Taylor Coleridge*, i, 190–91. In 1838 WW said Thelwall's words were, 'Nay to make one forget the world altogether': WW to Mrs Thelwall, 16 Nov [1838] (*LY*, iii, 640).

38. C. Poole, Journal, 23 Jul 1797 (Sandford, 131); *STCBL*, i, 193–5 gives a typically embroidered account, making STC himself the main object of the spy's interest. Recycling a favourite pun, STC claimed that his frequent mentions in conversation to 'one Spy Nozy' were mistaken by the spy as references to himself, until he realized that Spinoza was 'the name of a man who had made a book and lived long ago'.

39. J. Walsh to J. King, 11 Aug 1797 (Roe, 249–50).

40. Dr D. Lysons to the Duke of Portland, 11 Aug 1797 (ibid., 248). Lysons's first letter, of 8 Aug 1797, is missing; presumably Walsh carried it with him to Somerset.

41. Roe, 252–6. On learning the news of this invasion, JPP wrote immediately to his London bankers, demanding a certificate of the stock he held in the no.42 India Bonds: JPP to Nat Martin Bank, 2 Mar 1797: Letter Book 12, p.283, PP.

42. J. Walsh to J. King, 11 Aug & J. King to J. Walsh, 12 Aug 1797 (Roe, 250–51).

43. J. Walsh to J. King, 15 Aug 1797 (Roe, 258); see also ibid., 258–60.

44. Reed, i, 203; STC to TP, [*c*.17 (*r.c*.22) Jul 1797] (*STCL*, i, 332). No other guests can be identified, despite Johnston, 525.

45. J. Walsh to J. King, 16 Aug 1797 (Roe, 261); STC to J. Wade, 1 Aug 1797 (*STCL*, i, 339).

46. J. Walsh to J. King, 16 Aug 1797 (Roe, 261); JPP to J. Perkins, 15 Aug 1797: Letter Book 12, p.328, PP. Peggy Marsh described BM and AP as 'a Great Counsellor from London' and 'a Gentleman from Bristol'; JFP was, according to his father's letter, in Scotland at this time, so the Bristol gentleman must have been AP.

47. J. Walsh to J. King, 16 Aug 1797 (Roe, 260–61); *STCBL*, i, 195.

48. Roe, 261–2 raises these questions but it is Johnston, 528–36 who takes them to their most extreme conclusion, ludicrously suggesting WW was 'our man in Somerset', spying on STC for the government.

49. Roe, 261.

50. RS to T. Southey, 22 Aug 1805 (*RSLC*, ii, 343).

51. STC to J. Thelwall, [19 Aug 1797] (*STCL*, i, 341); TP to Mrs St Albyn, 16 Sep 1797 (Sandford, 133–4).

52. STC to J. Thelwall, [21 Aug 1797] (*STCL*, i, 343–4).

53. J. Thelwall, *Lines written at Bridgewater, in Somersetshire, on the 27th of July, 1797* (*STCL*, i, 339n.1); Claeys (ed.), *The Politics of English Jacobinism*, p.xxxiii.

54. C. Lloyd to RS, [15 Sep 1797] (*STCL*, i, 345–6). I agree with Reed, i, 207n.30, that this letter indicates that Tom Wedgwood's companion was his brother John, not, as Moorman, i, 333 asserts, James Tobin. The latter was at Bridgwater on 30 Aug 1797 and may have visited STC and WW then: STC to TP, [30 Aug 1797] (*STCL*, i, 345).

55. See p.180. For Tom Wedgwood's treatment at Dr Beddoes's lung disease clinic, the Pneumatic Institution (where JL had also been treated), see Sandford, 139.

56. WG, *An Enquiry Concerning Political Justice*, i, 16–17, 24, esp.17.

57. Ibid., 14, 26; T. Wedgwood to WG, nd (Moorman, i, 334–5).

58. *Prelude, 1805*, v, 295–8, 337–40, 350–52. For DW's review of the effect of Basil's education upon him, see DW to Mrs Rawson, 15 Jun [1798] (*EY*, 221–2).

59. Moorman, i, 333; Hazlitt, *Selected Writings*, p.50; STC to J.P. Estlin, [16 Jan] & to Jos. Wedgwood, 17 Jan 1798 (*STCL*, i, 370–74).

60. DW to ?MH, Nov 1797 (*EY*, 194); RS to J. May, Aug 1799 (*RSLC*, ii, 22–3). The Valley of Rocks was then known as the Valley of Stones and the desolation of the scene has eroded in inverse proportion to the aggrandizement of its name. There is no evidence to support the claim in Reed, i, 208 & n.33 that it was on this trip that

STC parted from the Ws between Linton and Porlock and took opium to stem dysentery, leading to the writing of *Kubla Khan.* He was clearly with them when they arrived at the Valley of Rocks.

61. STC, Prefatory Note to *The Wanderings of Cain* (*STCP*, 218); Hazlitt, *Selected Writings*, p.62.

62. DW to ?MH, 20 Nov 1797 (*EY*, 194); *IF*, 2–3; *STCP*, 498. Both WW and STC dated the trip to the spring of 1798, though the poems were clearly written before that time.

63. STC to W.L. Bowles, 16 Oct, to JC, [*c.*20 Nov] & to TP, [2 Dec] 1797 (*STCL*, i, 355, 357–8); DW to ?MH, 20 Nov & to CW, 8 Dec 1797 (*EY*, 194, 195). Thomas Knight, an actor in Bath, Bristol and Covent Garden, and a friend of TP's brother, forwarded the play to Covent Garden: *IF*, 78.

64. E. Threlkeld to S. Ferguson, 14 Feb 1798; DW to RW, 11 Nov & to CW, 8 Dec [1797] (*EY*, 197n.1, 193, 195); *LJW*, 17–19.

65. E. Threlkeld to S. Ferguson, 14 Feb 1798, WW to JC, 13 Dec [1797] & M. Ferguson to S. Ferguson, 13 Feb 1798 (*EY*, 196, 197n.1)

66. DW to CW, 8 Dec [1797] (*EY*, 196 & n.1). For a wonderful insight into theatrical life in the late 18th and early 19th centuries, see Tomalin, *Mrs Jordan's Profession.*

67. E. Threlkeld to S. Ferguson, 14 Feb 1798 (*EY*, 197n.1). WW's disdain for theatrical depravity did not prevent him using his Covent Garden and Drury Lane contacts to attend a number of plays, including *Isabella, or the Fatal Marriage* and *The Merchant of Venice* starring Sarah Siddons (1755–1831): DW to CW, 8 Dec [1797] (*EY*, 196).

68. STC, *Sonnets Attempted in the Manner of Contemporary Writers* (*STCP*, 144–5, 495–6); STC to JC, [*c.*20 Nov] & to RS, [7 Dec 1797] (*STCL*, i, 357–8, 359).

69. *STCN*, 3, 4006; *STCL*, 404n.; *STCBL*, i, 29n.; DW to Mrs Rawson, 13 Jun 1798 (*EY*, 223). Lloyd was so angry that he refused JC permission to reprint his poems in the 2nd edition of the joint volume with STC and CL and wrote a novel, *Edmund Oliver*, drawing on anecdotes of STC's early life, which JC published in Apl 1798: Gill, 149. WW and DW's loyalty to STC annoyed RS, who declared their conduct towards Lloyd 'very unhandsome': RS to JC, 19 Jan 1798 (*RSNL*, i, 158).

70. RW records the payment of 5s to Mr Tweddell for Mrs WG in his accounts for Sep 1797; WW and Tobin visited WG on 13 Dec 1797: Reed, i, 206, 211.

71. *Morning Post*, 14 Dec 1797; Reed, i, 212, 334; WW, *The Convict* (*Poems*, i, 152–3); Moorman, i, 351–2. STC was paid a guinea a week for his contributions to the *Morning Post* but found the deadlines difficult to meet: STC to Jos. Wedgwood, 5 Jan 1798 (*STCL*, i, 365). STC cribbed more of WW's poems for the *Morning Post*: see pp.219, 848n.34, 855n.4.

72. WW to JC, 13 Dec [1797] & DW to RW, 6 Jan [1798] (*EY*, 196, 198); Jos. & T. Wedgwood to STC, 10 Jan; STC to Jos. Wedgwood, 17 Jan & to WW, [23] Jan 1798 (*STCL*, i, 373–4, 377–8).

73. The MS of DW's Alfoxton journal has long been lost. Local legend has it that Professor Knight, the first editor and last person to see the MS, dropped it in Grasmere Lake after a convivial night out. Knight was a careless and censorious editor: his transcripts of the journals which survive are unreliable and idiosyncratic. As Reed, ii, 217n.7, points out, even the phases of the moon reported do not always tie in with known facts, to which could be added that, even accounting for the mild climate of Somerset, there is a similarly unseasonal description of flowers. And how do we explain the young lasses wearing their summer holiday clothes on 4 Feb 1798? As the Alfoxton journal exists only in his transcript, we cannot even be sure that the journal begins on 20 Jan 1798, particularly as DW usually began with an opening statement, missing from this version.

74. Rawnsley, 'Reminiscences of Wordsworth among the Peasantry of Westmoreland', 32, 13: see also 18, 19, 22, 27, 30–31, 36. For a good example of a coincidence of vocabulary and imagery between DW's Alfoxton journal and WW's poetry, see *DWJ*, i, 4 [25 Jan 1798] and WW, *A Night-Piece* (*Poems*, i, 262). A striking instance of DW's picking up her companion's phraseology occurs in the Alfoxton journal: walking with STC, she remarks she has never seen 'such a union of earth, sky, and sea', which is derived from his 'one life' theory: *DWJ*, i, 6. For STC's description of DW as 'a perfect electrometer', see p.184.

75. DW's unpublished journals of 1824–9 are DC 104; those of 1830–35 are DC 118.

76. *DWJ*, i, 3–4, 7; Sandford, 135.

77. TdQ, *Reminiscences*, 54. For a sympathetic life of the unfortunate Mrs STC, see Lefebure, *The Bondage of Love*. The apt phrase 'calculated provocation' is hers, p.93.
78. STC, *Religious Musings*, ll.130–31 (*STCP*, 110). WW explicitly adopted STC's words in a description of the Pedlar omitted in the final version: 'for in all things He saw one life, & felt that it was joy': WW, *The Ruined Cottage and The Pedlar*, ll.176–7.
79. DW to MH, 5 Mar [1798] (*EY*, 199); WW, *The Ruined Cottage and The Pedlar*, 46.
80. See, e.g., the lines on the power of sound and the soul retaining an obscure sense of possible sublimity (ibid., 118–19) which appear in the Alfoxton notebook among the lines for *The Ruined Cottage*, but became *Prelude, 1799*, ii, 351–71; DW to MH, 5 Mar [1798] (*EY*, 200).
81. *Prelude, 1805*, xii, 20–21; x, 914–15, 918–20.
82. STC to JC, [early Apl 1797] (*STCL*, i, 320–21). STC's projected poem, *The Brook*, tracing a stream from its source to the sea, was an attempt at this scheme; it had been the cause of the activities which brought him, WW and DW to the attention of the Home Office in Aug.
83. STC to J.P. Estlin [30 Dec 1797] (*STCL*, i, 361–3). Hazlitt, *Selected Writings*, 50. STC and BM intended to finance their scheme by taking eight pupils at £100 p.a., excluding board and lodging; they themselves would be both teachers and 'managing students'. The Wedgwoods actively supported the scheme as likely to be 'of general Benefit'.
84. WW to JL, 11 Mar [1798] (*EY*, 214); CL to STC, 7–10 Jan 1797 (*LCL*, i, 87). CL addressed these remarks to STC, saying, 'I want you to write an epic poem.'
85. WW to Jas Tobin, 6 Mar & to JL, 11 Mar [1798] (*EY*, 212, 214).
86. STC to JC, [7 Mar 1798] (*STCL*, i, 391).
87. WW to JC, [28 Feb or 7 Mar] & to Jas Tobin, 6 Mar [1798] (*EY*, 199, 212).
88. Gill, 145.

Chapter 8

chapter title: 'The Giant Wordsworth', STC to JC, [7 Mar 1798] (*STCL*, i, 391).
picture: The Market Place, Goslar, Germany.
1. DW to MH, 5 Mar [1798] & WW to Jas Tobin, 6 Mar [1798] (*EY*, 199, 211). That she was aware of WW's love for MH is evident from DW's '*our* wishes will turn to Sockburn' (my italics) and valedictory 'William's very best Love'. WW indignantly denied STC's claims that he had been forced to leave Alfoxton by harassment and the spy incident and that he had applied for a renewal of his lease: STC to JC, [early Apl 1798] (*STCL*, i, 403); Barron Field, 29.
2. WW to JL, 1 Mar [1798] (*EY*, 213). STC, his wife and son stayed at Alfoxton 9–18 Mar 1798; *DWJ*, i, 12.
3. STC to JC, [*c*.20 Nov 1797] (*STCL*, i, 357). WW, in later life, regretted that German metaphysics had so captivated STC's taste, 'for he was frequently not intelligible on the subject', and they had diverted him from poetry, which was his true métier: Peacock, 223.
4. WW to JL, 4 Dec 1821 (*LY*, i, 97). WW would later mourn the conquest of the Swiss in *Thought of a Briton on the Subjugation of Switzerland* (*Poems*, i, 725).
5. DW to Mrs Rawson, 13 Jun [& 3 Jul] 1798 (*EY*, 224). BM's default also affected the repayment of Douglas's £200 loan, due on 1 Jan 1798, because BM had taken over half of it himself in Dec 1796: Moorman, i, 297, 350.
6. WW to Jas Tobin, 6 Mar [1798] (*EY*, 211); STC to JC, [*c*.13 Mar 1798] & [early Apl 1798] (*STCL*, i, 399–400, 402–3). It is not clear whether JC refused the tragedies or WW and STC withdrew them from the proposal. WW was very unwilling to publish his.
7. WW to JC, 12 Apl & DW to RW, 30 Apl [1798] (*EY*, 215, 216).
8. WW, *Simon Lee* and *The Last of the Flock* (*LB*, 67, 85–8); *IF*, 9, 37. WW transferred Trickie's story to Cardiganshire. In his 1800 preface to *LB*, WW said the purpose of *Simon Lee* was to place the reader 'in the way of receiving from ordinary moral sensations another and more salutary impression than we are accustomed to receive from them'. This confirms his implicit rejection, in the last stanza, of WG's tenet that gratitude was a degrading sentiment born of inequality. *The Last of the Flock* also challenges WG's theory that property is the source of all vice; WW later admitted he had not personally witnessed the incident, but 'a friend of mine' had: *LB*, 745–6, 346, 353.
9. WW, *The Idiot Boy* (ibid., 91–104); *IF*, 10.

10. WW, *The Female Vagrant* and *The Complaint of a Forsaken Indian Woman* (*LB*, 50–58, 111–13). *The Female Vagrant* was the section from the Salisbury Plain poem telling the beggarwoman's story.
11. WW, *Lines written at a small distance from my House...*, ll.1, 24–8, *Expostulation and Reply* and *The Tables Turned*, ll.21–4, 29–32 (*LB*, 63–4, 107–9).
12. WW, *Goody Blake and Harry Gill* and *The Complaint of a Forsaken Indian Woman* (*LB*, 59–62, 344, 111–13, 356–7). The original story, which Darwin gathered from newspapers, was set in Warwickshire. To emphasize its moral message, WW subtitled the poem 'A True Story.' Darwin's *Zoönomia* (1794–6) influenced at least two other poems. *The Mad Mother's* madness is quieted by suckling her child, as described in *Zoönomia*, ii, 360. Darwin also cited the murder of BM's mother, Martha Ray, by Rev. James Hackman as an example of the 'furious and melancholy insanity' of the spurned lover: this no doubt explains WW's tactless decision to call the crazed, jilted woman in *The Thorn* Martha Ray. Her suicidal madness may also have been informed by WW's reading of WG's life of his wife, *Memoirs of the Author of a Vindication of the Rights of Woman* (1798): the infidelity of her American lover, by whom she had a daughter, had twice driven her to attempt suicide: *LB*, 77–85, 352.
13. *DWJ*, i, 16 [16 & 22 (*r.*17) May 1798]; the latter, misdated, entry is the last in Knight's transcript of the Alfoxton journal. Berkeley Coleridge was born on 14 May: STC to TP & to G. Coleridge, 14 May 1798 (*STCL*, i, 408–9).
14. STC to J.P. Estlin, [18] May [1798] (ibid., 410).
15. Hazlitt, *Selected Writings*, 56–8.
16. STC to G. Coleridge, 10 Mar 1798 (*STCL*, i, 397).
17. Hazlitt, *Selected Writings*, 58–9. WW indignantly denied having a 'narrow' forehead, substituting the word 'broad' (breadth signifying intellect) in Barron Field, 27.
18. Blanshard, 41–3, 140–42 & pl.s 1, 2; *DWJ*, i, 16 [26 Apl & 6 May 1798] mentions WW going to have his picture taken and the painter being expected. I presume the oddly sinister bulge beneath WW's heart in the Hancock portrait is his hand. Hazlitt's choice of BRH's portrayal of WW, in his *Christ's Entry into Jerusalem*, as 'the most like' tends to confirm that he was relying on later memories of WW's appearance: WW was then 47.
19. Hazlitt, *Selected Writings*, 59; WW to SGB, [Feb 1808] (*MY*, i, 194). See also WW, advertisement to *LB* (*LB*, 738).
20. Hazlitt, *Selected Writings*, 59–60.
21. WW to JC, 9 May 1798 (*EY*, 218); JC, *Reminiscences*, 182–4.
22. STC to JC, [28 May 1798] (*STCL*, i, 411–12); *LB*, 12. In Jul 1798 STC would be satirized in the *Anti-Jacobin* as an apologist for French atheism: 'C-dge, and S-th-y, Ll-d and L-be and Co. Tune all our mystic harps to praise Lepaux!': the 'and Co.' may refer to WW but, given his anonymity at this period, was probably introduced simply to rhyme with Lepaux.
23. Ibid.; JC, *Reminiscences*, 178.
24. DW to RW, 30 Apl & WW to RW, 5 May 1798 (*EY*, 216–17); RW, Calculation of interest due on RC legacy, 2 Aug 1798: WLMS/2/92. WW asked RW to send him £30 in six weeks' time, the rest a month later. WCal accepted RW's calculations, deducted £16 for legacy tax and forwarded the sum of £367 in bills and banknotes: only £366 17s 3d was actually due, leaving RW 2s 9d (not the half a crown [2s 6d] WCal suggested) in credit for the postage, which was then paid on receipt of a letter: WCal to RW, 10 Aug 1798: WLMS/2/93. For the correspondence between WCal and RW relating to the final payment of the legacy, see WLMS/2/91–4 (*EY*, App.iii). For RW's purchase of £500 worth of 3 per cent consols, at a cost of £267 2s 6d, see RW, Acct. of Payments made for WW by RW, 1794–9: WLMS/2/8 [4 Dec 1798] & RW to WW, 15 May 1799: WLMS/2/49 p.1 (*EY*, 674).
25. DW to Mrs Rawson, 13 Jun [& 3 Jul] 1798 (*EY*, 221).
26. RS to J. May, 8 Jul 1798 (*RSNL*, i, 170); STC to TP, 16 Jun & 3 Aug 1798 (*STCL*, i, 413, 414). DW to Mrs Rawson, 13 Jun [& 3 Jul] 1798 (*EY*, 221).
27. WW, advertisement to *LB, 1798* (*Prose*, i, 117); DW to RW, [14] Jun [1798] (*EY*, 225–6); JL, *Diaries*, i, 162; JLDMS, viii [12 Jun 1798].
28. DW to RW, [14] Jun [1798] (*EY*, 225–6); BM, *Autobiography*: WLMS/A/Montagu/26 p.5; DW to Mrs Rawson, 13 Jun [& 3 Jul] 1798 (*EY*, 221). Peggy Marsh had married the previous year and was now pregnant, so she could not have

accompanied the Ws to Germany; the Ws stayed in touch with her for many years, often sending her small sums of money: *Memoirs*, i, 116–17. DW dates the departure to Monday 26 Jun, but Monday was the 25th.

29. DW to Mrs Rawson, 13 Jun [& 3 Jul] 1798 (*EY*, 223).

30. JL, *Diaries*, i, 162; JLDMS, viii [8 & 9 Jul 1798]; *Memoirs*, i, 116–17. Rev. Richard Warner (1763–1857) had published his *A Walk through Wales in 1797* in Feb 1798; the frontispiece was an aquatint of Tintern Abbey: *EY*, 222n.1.

31. STC to G. Coleridge, [*c.*10 Mar 1798] (*STCL*, i, 396).

32. WW, *Tintern Abbey . . . July 13, 1798*, ll.116–22, 90–112 (*LB*, 118–19). WW rarely dated his poems so emphatically, confirming his claim that it had been composed and written in its final form during the tour: the date appears to be that of completion. STC was not alone in being disturbed by the pantheism of these lines. 'On one subject we are habitually silent –', he wrote in May, 'we found our data dissimilar, & never renewed the subject.' The subject was Christianity, which was central to STC's beliefs but not, as yet, to William's; '– he loves & venerates Christ & Christianity – I wish he did more . . . [we must accept that] not being against us he is for us': STC to J.P. Estlin, [18] May [1798] (*STCL*, i, 410). CW2 also tied himself in knots attempting to prove that the lines were subliminally Christian: *Memoirs*, i, 117–18.

33. *IF*, 15. WW's remarkable memory for poetry meant he was able to compose, and recall, all 160 lines of the poem without writing anything down.

34. For STC's contribution see *LB*, App.iv. In order to fulfil his contract, STC sent seven of WW's poems to the *Morning Post*, using the pseudonyms given in brackets: *The Convict* (Mortimer), 14 Dec 1797; 'If Grief dismiss me not to them that rest' (WW) and *Translation of a Celebrated Greek Song* (Publicosa), 13 Feb 1798; *The Old Man of the Alps* (Nicias Erythraeus), 8 Mar 1798; *Lines Imitated from Catullus* (Mortimer), 11 Apl 1798; *Lewti [Beauty and Moonlight]* (Nicias Erythraeus), 13 Apl 1798; 'The Hour Bell Sounds and I Must Go' (Mortimer), 10 May 1798: Reed, i, 212, 219, 224, 231, 232, 236.

35. WW, advertisement to *LB* (*Prose*, i, 116).

36. See p.216.

37. *IF*, 3–4.

38. STC to TP, 3 Aug 1798 (*STCL*, i, 414); WW to H. Gardiner, 3 Oct 1798 (*EY*, 232); *IF*, 4; WW to Mrs Thelwall, 16 Nov [1838] (*LY*, iii, 640).

39. STC to TP, 3 Aug 1798 (*STCL*, i, 414); WW to JC, 28 [Aug 1798] (*EY*, 226–7). The journey to London cost them £1 18s 6d each. Young Basil may have accompanied them, but given the nature of this journey, it seems likely that they parted with him earlier. TL had formed a partnership in *c.*1794 with JC's neighbour Owen Rees (1770–1837), a Bristol bookseller; they bought up JC's stock when he went out of business in 1800. TL was based in Paternoster Row, where he was both a publisher and a bookseller: *EY*, 227n.3.

40. DW to unidentified, 13 Sep 1798 (*EY*, 227); *LB*, 14–15.

41. STC to Mrs STC, 18 Sep & 3 Oct 1798 (*STCL*, ii, 417, 420). Johnson published a quarto pamphlet containing *Fears in Solitude*, *France: An Ode* and *Frost at Midnight* before the end of the year. The three poems did not fit the categories prescribed by the advertisement to *LB*, but it is odd that STC should have withheld his best work from the volume.

42. JC to J. Johnson, 2 Oct 1798 & to Jas Tobin, [8 Feb 1799]: WLMS/A/Cottle/1 & 2, & (RW copies of same) WLMS/2/49 p.3 (*EY*, 675–6); WW to J. Johnson, 14 Sep [17]98, to RW, 23 May [1799] & to H. Gardiner, 3 Oct 1798 (*EY*, 228, 260, 232). WW's original letter to JC does not survive but is described in WW to JC, [*c.*20 May 1799] (*EY*, 259).

43. *LB*, 15. Copies were circulating in Bristol and among JC's circle in Sep.

44. WW to JC, 28 [Aug 1798] (*EY*, 227); RW, WW in account with RW, 1794–9: WLMS/2/8 [14 Sep 1798]; RW, Memos on my Brother WW, 14 Sep 1798: WLMS/2/9. Instructions included paying Jos. Wedgwood £20 on WW's account in a fortnight's time, dealing with the loans to Douglas and BM and inquiring about a receipt for RC's legacy. RW was told to receive the sales money from Johnson and reimburse JC the £9 11s he had already paid WW. For WW's sending the Wedgwoods a copy of *The Borderers* prior to departure, see STC to TP, 3 Aug & to Mrs STC, 18 Sep 1798 (*STCL*, i, 415, 417).

45. Hazlitt, *Selected Writings*, 60–61; *DWJ*, i, 19; *STCN*, 335; STC to Mrs STC, 18 Sep 1798

(*STCL*, i, 416). In his letter STC drew symbols beside every passenger on his list, indicating how ill they had been. Sickest of all was the French émigré M. de Leutre.

46. *DWJ*, i, 19. Despite DW's skills as a diarist, STC's journal, recorded in *STCN*, 335ff. is a far more acute and poetic response to, and evocation of, this Continental trip.

47. STC to TP, 26 Oct 1798 (*STCL*, i, 431, 433); *STCBL*, ii, 175–7, 180–81; WW, *Descriptive Sketches*, 112. Johnston, ch.25 argues that de Leutre (whom he confuses with Baron de Lenthe) 'recruited' WW as a British government spy in Germany. His whole argument rests on a single piece of evidence: an entry on 13 Jun 1799 in the Duke of Portland's Secret Services Account Book, Oct 1793–Dec 1801 (DC 1994.125), which reads 'To paid Mr Wordsworth's Dra[ft] £92 12'. Durey, 'The spy who never was', 14–15 conclusively demolishes Johnston's thesis and proves the payment was to Robinson W for arresting and conveying to London two men charged with high treason.

48. *DWJ*, i, 10–11; *STCN*, 336; *STCL*, i, 431–3. Baldwin was JL's brother-in-law; WW had presumably been given his address by JL.

49. *DWJ*, i, 22; *STCN*, 337; STC to Mrs STC, 8 Nov & to TP, 20 Nov 1798 (*STCL*, i, 436–7, 441–5).

50. WW, *Conversations with Klopstock*: DC 19 pp.4–5v (*Prose*, i, 91–2); *STCN*, 339. Ironically, many of WW's visitors, on meeting him for the first time in his old age, came to the same conclusion about him as WW did of the elderly Klopstock.

51. WW, *Conversations with Klopstock*: DC 19 pp.4–5v (*Prose*, i, 91–2). WW had remembered that the *Analytical Review*, xiii (Jun 1792), 121–38, contained a review, with lengthy quotation, of Richard Cumberland's *Calvary: or, The Death of Christ* (1792), which Klopstock had expressed a wish to see.

52. WW, *Conversations with Klopstock*: DC 19 pp.6–13 (*Prose*, i, 92–5); *DWJ*, i, 24–5; STC to TP, 20 Nov 1798 (*STCL*, i, 441–5). Both WW and DW refer to having dinner with the Klopstocks, using the word in its northern sense of a midday meal. Misunderstanding this point has caused confusion as to when WW actually met the poet on the second and third occasion.

53. STC to Mrs STC, 26 Nov 1798 (*STCL*, i, 446); *STCN*, 342, 344; *STCBL*, ii, 191–3.

54. Ibid.; *STCN*, 340; STC to Mrs STC, 26 Nov 1798 (*STCL*, i, 446); *DWJ*, i, 27, 29. WW was so indignant that he took the pen from DW to record these incidents himself. STC noted that the Jews 'are horribly, unnaturally oppressed & persecuted all throughout Germany': STC to Mrs STC, 12 [*r.*10] Mar 1799 (*STCL*, i, 473).

55. *STCN*, 346; *DWJ*, i, 28.

56. CL to RS, Nov 1798 (*LCL*, i, 152); TP to STC, 8 Oct 1798 (Sandford, 150, 153); STC to TP, 4 Jan 1799 (*STCL*, i, 454).

57. *DWJ*, i, 28–31; WW, *Conversations with Klopstock* (*Prose*, i, 93); Reed, i, 253; WW to TP & to H. Gardiner, 3 Oct 1798 (*EY*, 229–31, 231–2).

58. *DWJ*, i, 31–4; STC to Mrs STC, 12 Mar 1799 (*STCL*, i, 471); DW to unidentified, [mid-Oct or Nov 1798] (*EY*, 232–3).

59. Ibid., WW to Jos. Wedgwood, 5 Feb 1799 (*EY*, 249).

60. STC to Mrs STC, 14 Jan 1799 (*STCL*, i, 459); DW to CW, 3 Feb & WW to Jos. Wedgwood, 5 Feb 1799 (*EY*, 245, 246, 249).

61. STC to Mrs STC, 8 Nov & to TP, 20 Nov 1798 (*STCL*, i, 440, 445).

62. DW to CW, 3 Feb 1799 & WW & DW to STC, [14 or 21 Dec 1798] (*EY*, 243–4, 242); *IF*, 38.

63. WW to STC, [late Nov–early Dec 1798] (*EY*, 234). WW used the metre of Bürger's *Leonora* for his *Ellen Irwin*, written this winter in Germany: WW, *Ellen Irwin* (*Poems*, i, 397–9); *IF*, 26.

64. WW & DW to STC, [14 or 21 Dec 1798] (*EY*, 236); STC to TP, 20 Nov 1798 (*STCL*, i, 445).

65. WW, *Ruth* (*Poems*, i, 371–9); *IF*, 14.

66. This first version of 'She dwelt among the untrodden ways' is taken from WW & DW to STC, [14 or 21 Dec 1798] (*EY*, 236–7). WW links this poem with 'Strange fits of passion have I known' and 'I travelled among unknown men', in *IF*, 8. For the origins of *Lucy Gray*, see *IF*, 1.

67. This early version of 'A slumber did my spirit seal', entitled *Epitaph*, is quoted in STC to TP, 6 Apl 1799 (*STCL*, i, 480), on learning of the death of Berkeley on 10 Feb 1799: Gill, 159; Lefebure, *The Bondage of Love*, 111–17.

68. The trend for psychosexual interpretation of WW's poetry was started by Frederick Bateson, *Wordsworth: A Re-interpretation* (London, Longmans, Green, 1954), but remains principally the domain of literary critics rather than

biographers. Johnston, 633–5, 644–53 is desperate to believe there was an incestuous relationship but, unable to convince even himself, falls back on suggesting that it is 'hard to believe that the possibility was not often on their minds, whether as a temptation or a threat'. The apt description of STC's 'cuckoo in the nest mentality' was coined by Holmes.

69. STC to WW, 10 Dec 1798 (*STCL*, i, 453).

70. WW & DW to STC, [14 or 21 Dec 1798] (*EY*, 238, 240–41).

71. STC to Mrs STC, 12 [*r.*10] Mar & [Mar], & to TP, 4 Jan 1799 (*STCL*, i, 476, 477, 454); DW to CW, 3 Feb 1799 (*EY*, 245).

72. DW & WW to STC, 27 Feb [1799] (*EY*, 254–5). WW's definition of learning a language explains his frustration in Goslar: 'having your mind in such a state that the several German idioms and phrases without any act of thought or consideration shall immediately excite feelings analogous to those which are excited in the breasts of the natives. Unless our minds *are* in this state, what we call knowledge of languages is a wretched self-delusion; words are a mere dead letter in the mind': WW to Jos. Wedgwood, 5 Feb 1799 (*EY*, 249–50).

73. DW to CW, 3 Feb 1799 (*EY*, 244).

74. WW to Jos. Wedgwood & WW & DW to RW, 5 Feb 1799 (*EY*, 247–9).

75. DW & WW to STC, 27 Feb [1799] (*EY*, 250–57). WW refers to having discovered a new invention in Germany which 'would render only one washing bason necessary for the largest family in the kingdom'. He intended to patent it for importation to England but details could not be entrusted to a letter. What this invention was, and what became of the patenting plan, remains a mystery. Johnston, 662 naturally believes it to be a coded message, but cannot explain why WW would wish to send coded messages to STC.

76. STC to TL, 15 Dec 1800 (*STCL*, i, 654).

77. The ludicrous thesis that WW 'disappeared' on a mission as a spy for the British government (Johnston, 656–70) is demolished by Durey, 'The spy who never was'.

78. Peacock, 264–5. WW's opinion of Goethe remained consistent, much to the annoyance of HCR, a devoted Germanist, who declared WW prejudiced and ignorant on the subject.

79. STC to Mrs STC, 23 Apl 1799 (*STCL*, i, 484).

80. STC to TP, 6 May 1799 (ibid., 490–91).

81. DW & WW to STC, [14 or 21 Dec 1798] & DW to unidentified, [*c.*3 Feb 1799] (*EY*, 236, 247); STC to TP, 6 May 1799 (*STCL*, i, 490–91).

82. STC to Mrs STC, 14 Jan 1799 (ibid., 459).

83. WW and DW may have paid a brief visit to STC at Göttingen in Mar, but the sources are unreliable and appear to confuse different events: Carlyon, *Early Years and Late Reflections*, i, 196–7, 35–8; Howitt, *Homes and Haunts of the Most Eminent British Poets*, ii, 257–8; STC to C. Parry, 25 Jun 1799 (*STCL*, i, 520); *STCN*, 502, 1586.

Chapter 9

chapter title: 'The Concern' (STC's description of the W circle), *STCN*, ii, 2537.

picture: WW, by Robert Hancock, 1798.

1. Jo H to JM, 12 May & JH to JM, [18 May] 1799: WLMS/H/1/8/1 p.2 & WLMS/H/1/1/2 p.1. GH was the family poet, hence the nickname 'Poet George'.

2. The visit to CW is inferred from WW to RW, 13 May [1799] (*EY*, 257). CW had met Priscilla, seven years his junior, through Charles Lloyd, whom he had been tutoring at Cambridge: 'her miseries were one of the things which first made me love her'. She made an astonishing mental and physical recovery at the Clarksons': CW to J. Walton, 31 Jan, 5 Mar & 22 Apl 1799: WLL/CW/4 p.3, 6 p.2 & 5 p.2. CW was elected fellow of Trinity College, Cambridge, on 1 Oct 1798: Reed, i, 253.

3. WW to RW & to Jos. Wedgwood, 13 May [1799] (*EY*, 257–8); RW to WW, 15 May 1799: WLMS/2/49 (ibid., 673–8). RW threatened BM with legal action, saying, 'there are persons in affluent circumstances with whom you have been long and intimately acquainted to whom you should apply to render the pecuniary assistance which it is not in my power to afford'.

4. WW to JC, 27 Jul [1799] (ibid., 267). See also WW to JC, 2 & 24 Jun [1799] (ibid., 262–5). JC owed WW £21 10s, having paid him only £10 out of the £30 due for the copyright of *LB*.

5. WW to JC, 27 Jul [1799] (ibid., 267); RS to Mrs RS, 9 May 1799 (*RSLC*, ii, 16).

6. *Critical Review*, xxiv (Oct 1798), 197–204 (Hayden, 3–5); WW to JC, [summer] 1799 (*EY*, 267–8). RS's sarcasm was in keeping with his

reviewing style, but was exacerbated by his recent quarrel with STC.

7. *Analytical Review*, xxviii (Dec 1798) & *Monthly Review*, xxix (Jun 1799) (Smith, 33–7).

8. WW to JC, 24 Jun & 27 Jul [1799] (*EY*, 264, 267). See also WW to JC, 2 Jun [1799] (ibid., 263). For WW's comment to Klopstock, see p.225.

9. WW & DW to RW, 20 Aug & DW to RW, 3 Sep [1799] (ibid., 268, 270); *Prelude*, xxviii–xxix, xlviii. DW and MH both made complete fair copies of the 1799 two-part *Prelude* in the autumn of 1799.

10. STC to WW, [*c.*10 Sep] & 12 Oct 1799 (*STCL*, i, 527, 538).

11. STC to RS, 30 Sep [1799] (ibid., 533–4); ibid., 542n.1; Holmes, i, 243–4; Lefebure, *The Bondage of Love*, 123–4.

12. *STCN*, 571, 1537. I have assumed STC's cryptic remarks refer to sensitivity about his personal appearance: at first sight, DW thought him 'very plain', but changed her mind on hearing him speak: see p.184. STC and JC arrived at Sockburn *c.*25–6 Oct 1799.

13. Ibid., 495; WW to DW, [8 Nov 1799] (*EY*, 271); JC, *Reminiscences*, 258–9.

14. WW to DW, [8 Nov 1799] (*EY*, 271); CW to J. Walton, 9 Oct [1799]: WLL/CW/9 pp.1–2; Reed, i, 273.

15. WW to DW, [8 Nov 1799] (*EY*, 271); *LJW*, 20–21; STC & WW to DW [*c.*10 Nov 1799] (*STCL*, i, 543). This last is the same as WW to DW, [8 Nov 1799], though *EY* omits STC's contributions. Only an extract made by MW survives, hence the disparity in presumed datings.

16. WW to DW, [8 Nov 1799] (*EY*, 271); *STCN*, 510. Myers's wife, WW's aunt, was also buried in Barton church in 1787; there is a memorial plaque to her on the chancel wall.

17. WW to DW, [8 Nov 1799] (*EY*, 271–2); *STCN*, 511–14. Newton's inn is now Church Stile, housing a National Trust shop and an art gallery: Lindop, 91–2. JW2 had made a profit of £400 on his last voyage, but in offering WW £40 of his capital, he was substantially reducing his own ability to invest in his next voyage: *LJW*, 20.

18. STC to DW, [*c.*10 Nov 1799] (*EY*, 543). Holmes, i, 248 is wrong in asserting JW2 had to leave early for his next voyage and that the climbing of Helvellyn was a pledge for the future: it was the quickest route on foot to Penrith, where John was returning to Newbiggin. He did not sail again until the spring of 1801.

19. WW to DW, [8 Nov 1799] (*EY*, 271–2); *STCN*, 540–55; *Prelude, 1805*, vii, 328ff.

20. CC to P. Lloyd, 12 Jan 1800 (Reed, i, 280n.24); *STCN*, 555.

21. SC to E. Coleridge, 8 Sep 1851 (*SCM*, i, 19–20).

22. *STCN*, 578, 1575, 1576. Given the propriety of SH's later conduct to STC, it seems hard to believe she actively flirted with him, unless she did not know he was married.

23. STC to JC, [*c.*1 Dec 1799] (*STCL*, i, 547). STC justified his jaunt to the north by blaming 'alarming' accounts of WW's health: STC to RS, 10 Nov [1799] (ibid., 545).

24. Mrs Rawson to S. Ferguson, 1 Jun & DW to TP, 4 Jul [1799] (*EY*, 265n.1, 266); STC to TP, 10 Sep 1799 (*STCL*, i, 526–7). Cruikshank, the tenant of Alfoxtón, had got into serious financial difficulties; when WW decided he could not afford the rent there, even should it become vacant, STC attempted to secure it for himself.

25. WW & DW to STC, 24 [& 27] Dec & DW to RW, 14 Dec [1799] (*EY*, 277–80, 272–3); WW, Promissory Note to JH, 11 Dec 1799: WLMS/2/21. DW anticipates travelling by coach and post chaise to Grasmere; the decision to walk must have been made at the last minute.

26. WW, *A Farewell*, ll.1, 5–6 (*Poems*, i, 572); TdeQ, *Recollections*, 128, 134; DW to JPM, 10 [& 12] Sep [1800], WW & DW to STC, 24 [& 27] Dec [1799] & DW to CC, 25 Dec 1805 (*EY*, 295–6, 274, 275, 661). Today it is difficult to imagine the vista from the cottage, which has been obstructed by the building between it and the lake of the new road (1830) and the disproportionately large Prince of Wales Hotel (1843) and Lake Terrace (1860). The cottage did not become known as Dove Cottage until it was acquired by the Wordsworth Trust in 1890; it is now a museum open to the public. Early photographs of the interior and exterior can be seen in Marsh & Garbutt, *Wordsworth's Lakeland*, 23–33.

27. DW to CC, 21 Dec 1815 (*MY*, ii, 259); DW to CC, 25 Dec 1805 (*EY*, 661). The time of arrival given varies between 4.30 and 6 p.m.: 'laal' is northern dialect for 'little'.

28. WW & DW to STC, 24 [& 27] Dec [1799] (ibid., 275, 277); *LB*, 566.
29. *STCN*, 579; WW, *To M.H.*, esp.ll.15–24 (*LB*, 250–51, 278–9). In the MS, which is dated 'Sat. Decbr.28 99', the trees in the last line are poplars, not beeches.
30. WW to JL, 16 Mar 1805 & to DW, [*c.*late May 1800] (*EY*, 563, 282 & n.2). *DWJ*, i, 41 & 43 note receipt of two letters, now lost, from WW on 24 & 30 May. RW records paying postage for 'a French letter for you' on 2 Nov 1799 and for 'a foreign letter for you' on 22 Mar & 8 Apl 1800; it is unclear whether he was paying to send or receive letters, but AV had WW's address as c/o RW at Staple Inn, which suggests these were letters from France: RW, WW's Debits & Credits, 1799–1800: WLMS/2/11. It is worth entering the caveat here that a lapse in *records* of a correspondence does not necessarily mean that there was a lapse in the actual *correspondence.*
31. WW to DW, [8 Nov 1799] (*EY*, 271); RW, WW & DW in Acct with RW, 1792–1815: WLMS/2/4 [1 Jan 1800]. For CCC paying CW's university expenses (as a pensioner, not a sizar like WW) and loaning JW2 £100, see WW to CW, 12 & 31 Jan [1816] (*MY*, ii, 271, 279); *LJW*, 17–18.
32. DW to LMB, 29 Nov [1805] (*EY*, 649).
33. WW to SGB, [*c.*23] Feb; DW to LMB, 29 Nov & DW to JPM, [15 & 17] Mar [1805] (ibid., 547–8, 649, 559–60). See also MW to CC, 7 Mar [1805]: WLL/MW/2 (*LMW*, 3).
34. WW, *The Brothers*, esp.ll.41–6, 58–62 (*LB*, 142–59, 566–77, 580–85, 590–97); WW, preface to *LB* (1800) (ibid., 746).
35. WW to SGB, [*c.*23 Feb 1805] (*EY*, 547).
36. Jo H to JM, [*p.m.*9 Apl 1800]: WLMS/H/1/8/3 p.2. The date of MH's visit to Penrith is unclear. On 20 Jan 1800 she and Jo H were on a week's visit from Penrith to Sebergham; they were back at Penrith by 23 Jan: Jo H to TM, [*c.*early Jan] & to JM, [*p.m.*9 Apl] 1800: WLMS/H/1/8/5 p.1 & 3 p.2; JH to JM, 20 Jan 1800: WLMS/H/1/1/6 p.2; Jo H to JM, [27 (*r.c.*12–18) Apl 1800]: WLMS/H/1/8/4 p.1.
37. DW to JPM, [15 & 17] Mar [1805] (*EY*, 560); MW to CC, 7 Mar [1805]: WLL/MW/2 (*LMW*, 3).
38. JW2 to MH, [25 & 26 Feb 1801] (*LJW*, 95–6).
39. JW2 to MH, [12 Sep 1802]: WLL/DW/83 p.2 (*LJW*, 125–6). This letter is written as a postscript on DW to MH, [12] Sep [1802] (*EY*, 375–6). For JW2 as a '*silent* Poet' see WW, 'When to the attractions of the busy world', l.80 (*Poems*, i, 450). Moorman, i, 473–4 & Holmes, i, 342; ii, 40, 60, 76 accept uncritically, as fact, STC's notebook fantasies that JW2 might have married SH, but, as Moorman herself points out, JW2 had very little opportunity, if any, to meet her: it is obvious from the context of these suggestions that STC was simply fantasizing about increasing the ties between the W circle.
40. STC to TP, [21 Mar 1800] (*STCL*, i, 582). TP accused STC of 'prostration in regard to Wordsworth', but STC defended himself by asking, 'What if you had known Milton at the age of thirty, and believed all you now know of him?': STC to TP, 31 Mar 1800 (ibid., 584).
41. CL to T. Manning, 5 Apl 1800 (*LCL*, i, 191); Jo H to JM, [*p.m.*9 Apl 1800]: WLMS/H/1/8/3 p.2. MH left Penrith for Sockburn on 11 Apl 1800 with her cousin, MM, after a visit of five or possibly six weeks: G. Monkhouse to JM, 11 Apl 1800: WLMS/H/1/13/7 p.2; DW to RW, 11 Apl [1800] & to JPM, [15 & 17] Mar [1805] (*EY*, 282, 560).
42. STC to RS, [10] Apl, to S. Purkiss [*p.m.*27 Mar] & to WG, 21 May 1800 (*STCL*, i, 585, 583, 587); WW, note to *The Brothers* (*LB*, 142).
43. STC to WG, 21 May 1800 (*STCL*, i, 588). STC had already seen Greta Hall, with its 'sublime & beautiful' views over Derwentwater, and contemplated inviting WG and HD to join him and WW there.
44. JH to JM, 20 Jan 1800: WLMS/H/1/1/6 p.2; G. Monkhouse to JM, [*p.m.*?12 May 1800]: WLMS/H/1/13/11 p.1. MH became 'well acquainted' with Cayley: DW to JPM, 19 Nov 1809 (*MY*, i, 378). For the remarkable Sir George Cayley (1773–1857), see J.H. Rushton, *The Snainton Story* (typescript, Scarborough Reference Library), 54, 64, 67, 74.
45. SH to JM, 12 Jul 1800 (*LSH*, 3–4). The farm, considerably enlarged at the turn of the 20th century, and now known as Gallows Hill, still stands just off the A170, a mile east of Brompton-by-Sawdon. It is now in private hands, though a permanent exhibition on WW and STC and an excellent tea-room in the barns are open to the public.
46. DWJMS, [14 May 1800]: DC 20 pp.7–7v, 8v, 9 (*DWG*, 1–2). My reading of the MS differs in several points from that of *DWG*.

47. DWJMS, [19 (*r.*18) May–7 Jun 1800]: DC 20 pp.11–21 (*DWG*, 3–9). The Sympson family consisted of Rev. Joseph (1715–1807), his wife, Mary (1725–1806), their son Bartholomew (1757–1832) and daughter Elizabeth (1767–1803). Another daughter, Mary or Margaret (b.1765), was married to Thomas Jameson (d.23 Jun 1800); their son Tommy (1789–1827) was also a frequent visitor: *EY*, 299n.1; *DWG*, 153.

48. DWJMS, [7 Jun 1800]: DC 20 pp.20–21v (*DWG*, 8–9). JW2 had left WW at Greta Bridge 'to see the country in that neighbourhood': WW to RW, 8 [Jun] 1800 (*EY*, 284).

49. DW to JPM, 10 [& 12] Sep [1800] (*EY*, 298). WW incorporates a description of these caves in *Prelude, 1805*, viii, 711ff. and drew on memories of this tour in his rather dull trilogy uninspired by William Westall's *Views of the Caves near Ingleton, Gordale Scar, and Malham Cove in Yorkshire* (1818), 'Pure element of waters! wheresoe'er', *Malham Cove* and *Gordale* (*Poems*, ii, 376-8).

50. Jo H to JM, 21 May 1800: WLMS/H/1/8/7 p.3. It is usually assumed SH was there too, but there is no indication of her presence in this, or other sources, so she cannot have met JW2 again: see n.39. She was probably with other relatives at Penrith or Stockton, but not at Bishop Middleham with GH, as Johnston, 714 asserts, following Moorman, i, 476, as GH had not yet taken this farm. He went with TH and MH to Gallow Hill, but returned to Sockburn in Aug 1800 to harvest the crops there, which still belonged to TH, and spent the winter with his brother JH at Stockton, marketing them. SH was at Gallow Hill by 12 Jul: SH to JM, 8 & 23 Aug & 12 Jul 1800 (*LSH*, 5, 6, 7, 3).

51. JW2 to MH [16 Feb], to DW, 3 May & to MH, 8 Jan [*r.*Feb] [1801] (*LJW*, 90, 124, 89); WW to FW, [late Feb 1801] (*EY*, 317–18). Richard Langley (1762–1817) lived at Wykeham Abbey; his wife, Dorothy (1758–1824), was the oldest daughter of Henry Willoughby, 5th Lord Middleton; his cousin, who died 9 Mar 1800, was FW's first wife. When MH became a 'great favourite' of the Langleys, JW2 told her he liked the Langleys 'better than any rich people I know' because they allowed the poor to graze their cattle in their Park: JW2 to MH, [9 Mar 1801] (*LJW*, 102).

52. RW, WW's Debits & Credits since 1799: WLMS/2/11 [24 May & 4 Jun 1800]; WW to RW, 8 [Jun] 1800, DW to RW, 14 Dec [1799] & WW to RW, 11 Mar [1800] (*EY*, 283, 273, 281); STC to Jos. Wedgwood, [4 Feb 1800] (*STCL*, i, 567–8). Richard Cooke, who had been involved in a complicated financial transaction with RW on behalf of Douglas, visited WW at Grasmere for three days in Apl; perhaps as a result of this, he paid £10 into WW's account with RW on 4 Jun: DW to RW, 11 Apl [1800] (*EY*, 282).

53. WW to Jos. Wedgwood, 13 Jul [1800] (*EY*, 283–4). *EY* is wrong in suggesting that the debt was not repaid. In Nov 1800, when JW2 was fund-raising for his next voyage, WW discovered that it was still outstanding and authorized JW2 to insist that it was 'paid immediately'. JW2 then wrote to DW on 17 Nov to say that it had been paid: JW2 to DW, 10 & 17 Nov 1800 (*LJW*, 74, 75).

54. JC, *Reminiscences*, 259–60. WW to RW, 8 [Jun] & to TL & Rees, 18 Dec 1800 (*EY*, 283, 310). JC claimed the copyright in *LB* was independently valued '*as nothing*' during the sale to TL, so he reclaimed it and gave it to WW.

55. *STCN*, 749; *DWG*, 7, 8 [2, 4 & 5 Jun 1800]; STC to HD, 15 [*r.*16] Jul & to TP, 24 Jul 1800 (*STCL*, i, 604, 607).

56. Barron Field, 62.

57. Tables of Contents for 1798 & 1800 editions, *LB*, 46, 130–32. The order for the first volume was established by mid-Jul, when STC wrote twice to the printers with a table of contents, the text of *Love* and his alterations to his own poems, particularly the extensive revision of the *Ancient Mariner*. WW wrote at the same time with additional lines to *Lines left upon a seat in a Yew-Tree* and other minor emendations: STC & WW to Biggs & Cottle, [mid-Jul 1800] (*STCL*, i, 593–602; *EY*, 285–8). The new edition of the 1st volume contained 24 poems, rather than 23, because WW, at STC's suggestion, divided his *Lines written near Richmond, upon the Thames, at Evening* into two poems, *Lines Written when sailing in a Boat at Evening* and *Lines Written near Richmond, upon the Thames*: *LB*, 106–7.

58. STC to HD, 15 [*r.*16] Jul 1800 (*STCL*, i, 606).

59. *LB*, 23–4; STC to DS, 15 Jul & to WG, 22 Sep 1800 (*STCL*, i, 603, 624); Reed, i, 73. WW could not sell his copyright to TL until the 1st edition, published by Arch, sold out. DW and JW2 (despite his execrable hand) made a copy of WW's preface to *The Borderers* in anticipation of

sending the MS to Sheridan, but WW abandoned the idea by 1 Nov: Reed, i, 72n.26; STC to Jos. Wedgwood, 1 Nov 1800 (*STCL*, i, 646). Sheridan's interest in staging a play by WW may well have been inspired by his lead actress, Dora Jordan, who had announced her intention of singing stanzas from WW's *The Mad Mother* when she played Cora again in Sheridan's own play *Pizarro*: Tomalin, *Mrs Jordan's Profession*, 179–80.

60. WW to HD, [29] Jul [1800] (*EY*, 289); STC to HD, 25 Jul 1800 (*STCL*, i, 612); *STCN*, 758. DW spent one morning 'unpacking our Somersetshire goods', which presumably arrived with STC's. She records STC's anecdote as two separate events, taking tea on the island on Friday 18 Jul, and making a great fire and taking tea with the Sympsons at Bainriggs, on the edge of the lake, on Sunday 20 Jul: DWJMS [25 Jun 1800]: DC 20 pp.30v–31 (*DWG*, 14).

61. STC to TP, 24 Jul, to HD & to Jas Tobin, 25 Jul 1800 (*STCL*, i, 608, 610, 613).

62. WW to HD, [29] Jul [1800] (*EY*, 289–90). Humphry Davy (1778–1829) became Professor of Chemistry at the Royal Institution in London (1802) and President of the Royal Society (1820); he had written poetry since childhood and retained an interest in literary matters throughout his life. He is most famous for inventing the miner's safety lamp, named after him, and his seminal *Elements of Chemical Philosophy* (1812). His brother, John Davy, MD, later settled with his family in Ambleside and became the Ws' family doctor.

63. See, e.g., WW's two letters, both *p.m.*16 Aug from Keswick: WW to Biggs & JC [*c.*13 Aug 1800] (*EY*, 291–3).

64. DWJMS [9 Aug–(14) Sep 1800]: DC 20 pp.35–35v, 38v–9v, 43v–6v (*DWG*, 16–22); JLDMS, x [4–5 Sep 1800]; DW to JPM, 10 [& 12] Sept [1800] (*EY*, 293–5, 300–301). JL had spent the previous day with WCal and STC at Keswick, noting that STC 'perhaps always talks rather too much but so well that one readily forgives him': STC told him WW was 'engaged in a great moral work in verse' and was 'the first Poet now living'. RJ brought with him John Palmer (1769–1840), a Whitehaven-born contemporary of RJ and WW at St John's, who was senior Wangler and fellow of the college, and would become Professor of Arabic (1804–19) and President of St John's (1815–19): Venn, v, 14; *DWG*, 168.

65. DWJMS [29 Sep 1800]: DC 20 pp.46v–7 (*DWG*, 23); Gordon, '*Christopher North*', i, 133–5. This latter account, describing the outline of an intended poem by John Wilson, draws heavily on WW's description of his final parting from JW2. It is impossible to tell whether the laying of a foundation stone for a fishing hut provided the idea for *Michael* or whether Wilson drew on that poem for an analogy. WW describes the parting in *Elegiac Verses in Memory of My Brother, John Wordsworth* (*Poems*, i, 644–6). Lines 21–4 and 61–4 were carved into a rock just below the lip of Grisedale Tarn in 1882, as a memorial to the brothers' parting, but have weathered to virtual illegibility. JW2 was heading for Penrith to see Mr Parkin, co-owner of the *Earl of Abergavenny*, and to Newbiggin Hall. He sent his apologies to MH for not calling on her or her Penrith relatives in the rush: JW2 to MH, [4 Oct 1800] (*LJW*, 71–2).

Chapter 10

chapter title: 'Home at Grasmere', WW, *Home at Grasmere* (*Poems*, i, 697–717).

picture: The Ws' cottage at Town End, by Dora, undated.

1. WW, *The Childless Father*, ll.17–20 (*LB*, 227).

2. WW, *To Joanna*, 'It was an April morning: fresh and clear' and 'A narrow girdle of rough stones and crags' (*LB*, 244–6, 242–3, 247–50); *IF*, 18; *STCN*, 761; *DWR*, 66. WW believed *To Joanna*, a particular favourite of JW2, revealed 'the greatest genious of any poems in the 2d Vol': JW2 to MH, [25–6] & [24] [Feb 1801] (*LJW*, 96, 93–4). Significantly, bearing in mind WW's obsession with the order of his poems when publishing, he opened the series with DW's and ended with MH's. Oddly, the poem for JW2, 'When, to the attractions of the busy world', was not completed in time for inclusion.

3. WW, 'There is an Eminence' (*LB*, 247). WW identified the eminence as Stone Arthur and admitted that it could not really be seen from the orchard seat at Town End: *IF*, 18.

4. WW, preface to *LB* (*LB*, 741); STC to TP [*c.*11 Oct], to WG, 13 Oct & to Jos. Wedgwood, 1 Nov 1800 (*STCL*, i, 634, 635, 643). The *Morning Post*

published three of WW's poems this summer and autumn, all sent by STC as part of his contract with DS. WW's *The Farmer of Tilsbury Vale* and his new poem, *The Seven Sisters* (as *The Solitude of Binnorie*), written in Aug 1800, were published anonymously on 21 Jul and 14 Oct 1800; a revised version of the Windy Brow inscription appeared as *Inscription for a Seat by a Road Side* under the pseudonym 'Ventrifrons', a Latin translation of 'Windy Brow': Reed, i, 73, 95, 96.

5. STC to TP, [*c.*11 Oct] & 14 Aug 1800 (*STCL*, i, 634, 618); *STCP*, 507; DW to JPM, 10 [& 12] Sep & WW to Biggs & JC, 15 Sep & [*c.*2 Oct] [1800] (*EY*, 297, 302, 303); *DWG*, i, 61–2. Only 677 lines of *Christabel* were ever printed, so STC probably exaggerated in telling TP he had written 1,400.

6. WW & DW to STC, 25 [& 27] Dec [1799] (*EY*, 281); Ashton, 51, 97; Prance, 184.

7. DWJMS [4–6 Oct 1800]: DC 20 pp.50–51 (*DWG*, 24); *STCP*, 507; STC to HD, 9 Oct 1800 (*STCL*, i, 631). WW cancelled all references to *Christabel* 'whatever the expence may be, which I hereby take upon myself', and assured his printers that they could '*depend*' on future copy being supplied without intermission in WW to Biggs & JC, [*c.*6 or 7 Oct 1800] (*EY*, 304–5). STC was under pressure from *Morning Post* deadlines and expecting the imminent death of his son Derwent (1800–1883), born on 14 September. Having named his first two sons after philosophers, STC named this one in conscious tribute to the river and, perhaps, unconscious tribute to his friend, who had grown up by its side at Cockermouth: STC to WG, 16 Sep, to DS, [23 Sep] & to HD, 9 Oct 1800 (*STCL*, i, 622, 626, 632).

8. DWJMS [11–12 Oct 1800]: DC 20 pp.54–5 (*DWG*, 26). John Fisher observed 'that in a short time there would be only two ranks of people, the very rich & the very poor, for those who have small estates . . . are forced to sell – & all the land goes into one hand': DWJMS [18 May 1800]: DC 20 p.12 (*DWG*, 3). Greenhead Ghyll lies only a mile from Town End, behind the famous Swan Inn. There is a heart-shaped sheepfold at the foot of Sour Milk Ghyll, or Churn Milk Force, Easedale.

9. WW, *Michael*, esp.ll.420–22, 485–91 (*LB*, 252–68, esp.266, 268). WW said that the poem was based on two separate local stories, of a dissolute son who ran away from elderly parents, and of an old shepherd taking seven years to build a sheepfold in a remote valley: *Memoirs*, ii, 305; *IF*, 10.

10. WW to TP, 9 Apl 1801 (*EY*, 322). WW 'sometimes thought I was delineating such a man as you yourself would have been under the same circumstances'. For WW's struggle in writing the poem, see *DWG* [12 Oct–9 Dec 1800], 26–35. The entry 'W burnt the sheep fold', i.e. *Michael*, occurs on 9 Nov 1800. For extant lines of the early ballad version, see *LB*, 319–20, 464–5. WW reiterated many times his insistence that *Michael* should complete the volume, even offering to send more poems to insert before it if the book was too short: WW to Biggs & Cottle, [18 Dec 1800] (*EY*, 307–8).

11. WW, preface to *LB* (*LB*, 741–65). Gray was 'at the head of those who by their reasonings have attempted to widen the space of separation betwixt Prose and Metrical composition, and was more than any other man curiously elaborate in the structure of his own poetic diction': ibid., 749.

12. WW described those capable of enjoying his poetry and its message as being 'in a healthful state of association': ibid., 745. The other phrase habitually used by WW's admirers is that his works ranked second only to the Bible in bringing them solace: see, e.g., E.F. Ogle to WW, [*p.m.*16 May 1840]: WLMS/A/Ogle/1 pp.2–3; E. Peabody to WW, 29 Mar 1829: WLMS/A/Peabody/2 p.5; W.P. Atkinson to WW, 25 May 1845: WLMS/A/Atkinson/1 p.3; SC to A de Vere, 1846 (*SCM*, ii, 56).

13. STC to TL, 15 Dec 1800 & to TP, 19 Jan 1801 (*STCL*, i, 654; ii, 665–7); Tomalin, *Mrs Jordan's Profession*, 179–80. STC knew Anna Letitia Barbauld (1743–1825), who wrote poems, prose essays on natural studies and *Hymns in Prose for Children*. Georgiana, Duchess of Devonshire (1757–1806), was a friend of Fox, Sheridan, Selwyn and Dr Johnson; Sir James Bland Burges (1752–1824) had published in 1798 an 18-book poem, *Richard Coeur de Lion* (1798), written in 'a pure and unmixed vein of native English', which was the reason for his inclusion: WW [*r.*STC] to Sir J.B. Burges, 14 Jan 1801 (*EY*, 683). Wilberforce was included, not because he was an acquaintance of DW and a friend of WW's uncle WC (this was not mentioned in the accompanying letter), but because he had

published *A Practical View of the Prevailing Religious System of Professed Christians* (1797).

14. WW to C.J. Fox, 14 Jan 1801 (*EY*, 312–15). The letters accompanying gifts of *LB* were delivered to Longman by JW2, who was 'much entertain'd with the reading of them I could not help thinking that Wm was becoming a most accomplish'd Courtier': JW2 to MH, [31 Jan 1801] (*LJW*, 85).

15. *LB*, 31; RS to STC, 25 Jul [1801] (*RSLC*, ii, 153); JW2 to DW, 21 Feb [1801] (*LJW*, 92). JW2 boasted jokingly to DW, 'I am a great man with Mr Arch tho' he does not know my name – I talk knowin[g]ly of Col[e]rid[g]e Southey. Wordsworth. Lamb &c'.

16. *British Critic*, xvii (Feb 1801) and *Monthly Review*, xxxviii (Jun 1802) (Smith, 46–51); JW2 to WW, [30 Jan 1801] (*LJW*, 82). JW2 summarized Stoddart's review for WW on the day it appeared in the *British Critic*: JW2 to DW [2 Mar 1801] (*LJW*, 99–100). For Stoddart, see p.171. He had visited the Ws in Apl and 29 Oct–4 Nov 1800: Reed, ii, 60, 96–8.

17. JW2 to MH, [9–10 Mar] & [25–6 Feb] [1801] (*LJW*, 103, 95). JW2 thought TL was 'a vile abominable and impudent Jew for only giving Wm 80£ for the 2 Editions he will clear at least 400£ or perhaps 500£. They are sure of a good and steady sale'.

18. CL to WW, [30 Jan 1801] & to T. Manning, [15 Feb 1801], (*LCL*, ii, 265–9, 272–4). CL objected strongly to the didactic element in *LB* and having the message 'ramm'd down one's throat'. *The Old Cumberland Beggar*, e.g., was too 'like a lecture . . . An intelligent reader finds a sort of insult in being told, I will teach you how to think upon this subject.'

19. C.J. Fox to WW, 25 May [1801] (*Memoirs*, i, 171–2).

20. DW & WW to SH, [late Feb–early Mar 1801] (*EY*, 319–20). 'I think Stoddart a very poor judge of Poetry': JW2 to WW, [30 Jan 1801] (*LJW*, 83). CW preferred the 2nd volume of *LB* to the 1st as being 'much humaner & gentler . . . and consequently much better calculated for general favour . . . I have no doubt of their being exceedingly popular. Nor do I think that I am mistaken in saying that they mark out my Brother as decidedly the first of living English Poets': they were of 'very great moral value': CW to J. Walton, 16 Feb [1801] & 16 Apl 1801: WLL/CW/18 p.3 & 19 p.4.

21. *LB*, 31; the new edition was published in April: Reed, ii, 157; DW to RW, 6 Apl 1802 (*EY*, 345–6).

22. JW2 to DW, [10 Mar 1801] (*LJW*, 106); C. Lloyd to T. Manning, 26 Jan 1801 (Reed, ii, 107n.70). The indefinable 'something' observed by JW2 was probably Priscilla's mental instability; he found her very talkative, adding ironically, 'but *I* was *most eloquent*'.

23. DWJMS [14–17 Nov, 28 Nov–2 Dec & 18–20 Dec 1800]: DC 20 pp.68v–71v, 75–75v & 79 (*DWG*, 32, 33–4, 35); *STCN*, 848; STC to HD, 11 Jan & to TP, 19 Jan 1801 (*STCL*, ii, 662–5). STC often had dreams of being pursued by menacing female figures; as in this instance, he usually woke with swollen eyelids.

24. STC to TP, 7 [*r.*6] Jan 1801 (*STCL*, ii, 661–2, 665n.3); DW & WW to MH, [29] Apl [1801] (*EY*, 330–31).

25. WW to TL & Rees, 27 Mar 1801 (*EY*, 321); STC to WG, 25 Mar 1801 (*STCL*, ii, 714). WW did not lend STC the £30 in cash, but asked TL to transfer the debt from STC's account to his own, reducing his earnings from *LB* from £80 to £50.

26. STC to TL, 26 [*r.*27] Mar 1801 (*STCL*, ii, 716). This letter was written on the same sheet as WW's asking TL to transfer STC's debt to his account: see n.25. TL wisely declined another Coleridgean prospectus, but William Bulmer (1757–1830), founder of the Shakespeare Press, who produced illustrated folio editions of Milton (3 vols., 1793–7) and Shakespeare (9 vols., 1791–1805), accepted the proposal, complete with vignettes. 'I long to have the book in my hand', WW wrote, 'it will be such a Beauty': WW to TP, 9 Apl [1801] (*EY*, 324). It did not appear as Coleridge did not complete the poem.

27. STC to TP, [23 Mar] & to HD, 4 May & 3 Feb 1801 (*STCL*, ii, 710, 726, 670–71); Reed, ii, 77; WW to TL & Rees, 27 Mar 1801 (*EY*, 321); JW2 to MH, [25–6 Feb 1801] (*LJW*, 96); WW to WCal, [late Mar 1801]: Stanger Albums, ii, 170 (*Supp.*, 3). My reading of the MS of WW's letter to WCal differs in several important respects to the published version.

28. CC to Rev. R.E. Garnham, 12 Feb 1801 (*HCRWC*, i, 41); T. Wilkinson to M. Leadbeater, 15 Feb 1801 (Reed, ii, 110n.3). Wilkinson also

learned from William that he 'writes in what he conceives to be the language of Nature in opposition to the finery of our present poetry'.

29. JW2 to WW, [6 Feb 1801] (*LJW*, 87); Jo H to JM, 2 May 1801; WLMS/H/1/8/9 pp.3–4.

30. JW2 to MH, 10 Jan & to WW, [6 Feb] [1801] (*LJW*, 80–81, 87); CW to J. Walton, 16 Feb [1801]: WLL/CW/18 p.2. One of JW2's first disappointments was his inability to secure a safe merchant shipping berth for MH's sailor brother, HH, because it was too late in the season: JW2 to MH, 5 & 12 Dec 1800 & 10 Jan 1801 (*LJW*, 76–9, 81).

31. JW2 to DW, [26 Feb 1801] (*LJW*, 97); DW to RW, 6 Apl [1802] (*EY*, 345 & n.1). DW had difficulty in getting the money in JW2's absence; RW loaned JW2 £1,650 of his own money. WW's loan was secured by a bond for £555; he was to receive 5 per cent interest on his capital, which, like all the loans, was repayable in 18 months' time; JW2, Bond to WW, 19 May 1801: WLMS/2/13. Robert Griffith, JW2's mother's cousin, based in Philadelphia but in partnership with the Threlkelds of Halifax, was applied to for £500 but could afford to lend only £200: R.E. Griffith to W. Threlkeld, 12 Aug 1801: WLMS/SH/16/2 pp.1–2. JW2 expected to make £6,000 by the voyage but a series of mishaps beyond his control left him with a loss: JW2 to DW, 21 & [26 Feb 1801] (*LJW*, 93, 97–8, 32–3).

32. WW to WCal, [late Mar 1801] (*Supp.*, 3). The visit, which occupied CW's Easter vacation, may have put CW in a difficult position, as it appears Lloyd lied to his father about CW's presence: JW2 to DW, 22 [& 23] Apl [1801] (*LJW*, 119). CW returned to Cambridge on 15 Apl: CW to J. Walton, 16 Apl 1801: WLL/CW/19 p.1.

33. JW2 to MH, [9–10 Mar 1801] (*LJW*, 104). SH's last act at Grasmere was to copy out WW's latest poems and revisions to *The Prelude* for JW2 to take with him on his voyage to China: GH was at Bishop Middleham by 8 Feb: JW2 to MH, 8 Jan [*r.*Feb] & [*c.*9 Apl] & to DW, [10 Mar] [1801] (*LJW*, 89, 116, 107). Jo H described the house as a 'very beautifull place indeed . . . extremely large' but 'almost in ruins': Jo H to JM, 20 Jul & 23 Jun 1801: WLMS/H/1/8/11 p.1 & 10 pp.1–2.

34. WW, 'I travell'd among unknown men' in DW & WW to MH, [29] Apl & to STC, [22 May] [1801] (*EY*, 332–3, 335).

35. WW & DW to RW, [*c.*23 Jun] & WW to TP, [early Jul] [1801] (*EY*, 336, 339–40); JW2 to DW, 22 [& 23] Apl & 3 May [1801] (*LJW*, 117-18, 123–4).

36. TP to STC, 21 Jul 1801 (Sandford, 194–5). STC was 'vexed' and 'almost irritated' that WW had applied to TP on his behalf, accusing WW of acting '*erroneously* but not wrongly': STC to TP, 5 Oct & 7 Sep 1801 (*STCL*, ii, 765–6, 756).

37. STC to RS, 22 & 25 Jul 1801 (*STCL*, ii, 746–7). Jo H noted the arrival of STC 'today', declaring 'he is a nice man but William for my money': Jo H to JM, 20 Jul 1801: WLMS/H/1/8/11 pp.2–3, but see *STCN*, 970; GH to JM, 29 Jul 1801: WLMS/H/1/7/1 p.1.

38. STC to RS, 1 & 11 Aug 1801 (*STCL*, ii, 748–9, 751); *STCN*, 974, 980, 784–6. STC imagines a spring, with a tiny cone of loose sand ever rising and sinking at the bottom, but its surface without a wrinkle, adding immediately after it the initials WW. MH. DW. SH. He reports learning the art of making 'the abstrusest Truths intelligible; & interesting even to the unlearned' so that 'the infinitely beloved Darling' (SH) could understand his knowledge. There is no evidence to suggest he succeeded.

39. WW & DW to RW, [*c.*23 Jun 1801] (*EY*, 336); Reed, ii, 123. Moorman, i, 514 is wrong in stating that BM was now regularly paying WW's annuity: according to WW, he was still 'considerably in arrears with the payment'.

40. The route is inferred from the speed of the journey to Glasgow and references to earlier visits by WW in *DWJ*, i, 217, 229–31 and *IF*, 27. STC said WW was 'in the Scotch Lakes': STC to TP, 7 Sep & to WG, 22 Sep 1801 (*STCL*, ii, 757, 763). From the Trossachs, the usual tourist route to Northumberland would be through Stirling and Edinburgh, passing through Alnwick to Morpeth and Newcastle, where they saw JL: JLDMS, x, [16 Sep 1801].

41. STC to RS, 21 Oct 1801 (*STCL*, ii, 767); DWJMS [10 Oct 1801]: DC 25; *DWG*, 35, 182. This is the first entry in DW's second attempt at a Grasmere journal.

42. *DWG*, 35–7; *STCN*, 999. TH had left Town End by 9 Nov, when the Ws walked to Keswick to say goodbye to STC. *DWG*, 183 and Reed, ii, 127 both suggest MH accompanied STC to Grasmere on 6 Nov, but offer no evidence.

Though the relevant page is torn out of DWJMS (see n.43), there is no indication that MH left Keswick until she returned with the Ws to Grasmere on 10 Nov.

43. DWJMS [5–9 Nov 1801]: DC 25 (*DWG*, 37); *Memoirs*, i, 177. The words 'left us' at the top left-hand corner of the stub presumably apply to the entry for 5 Nov. DW usually wrote *c.*10 lines (roughly 100 words when each entry is more than one line) per side, leaving some 18 lines (*c.*180 words) unaccounted for.

44. DWJMS [9–10 Nov 1801]: DC 25 (*DWG*, 37). John Stanley was landlord of the King's Head at Thirlspot, at the foot of Helvellyn, on the road between Grasmere and Keswick: it was a convenient place to stop for refreshment and was often used by the Ws and their friends. Aquafortis is nitric acid, used in chemical experiments for dissolving gold and platinum; DW surely means aqua vitae, i.e. brandy.

45. STC to WG, [19 Nov] & to TP, [24 Dec] [1801]; STC to WG, 22 Jan 1802 (*STCL*, ii, 775, 777, 782).

46. DWJMS [12–16 Nov 1801]: DC 25 (*DWG*, 38). After this weekend, DW records several times WW and MH taking walks together and returning 'chearful blooming & happy' or 'fresh & well', something she had not done before: ibid. [25 Nov & 2 Dec 1801] (*DWG*, 42, 44). It is tempting to see the sudden expansion of DW's journal from staccato daily entries of who did what when into long lyrical descriptive passages as a (hopefully) subconscious attempt to stake her own claim to the most important part of WW's life.

47. DWJMS [27 Nov & 21 Dec 1801]: DC 25 (*DWG*, 43, 50); WW to RW [*c.*21 Nov 1801] (*EY*, 341). I assume the letter from AV was in response to one from WW informing her of his intention to marry.

48. WW, *Repentance: A Pastoral Ballad*, ll.35–6 (*Poems*, i, 476–7); *IF*, 9, 22; DWJMS [24 Nov 1801]: DC 25 (*DWG*, 40–41). STC said he and WW regarded the peace as 'necessary; but the Terms as most alarming': STC to RS, 21 Oct 1801 (*STCL*, ii, 771). DW's journal notes in Nov–Dec 1801 widows of two soldiers [27 Nov], a soldier, his wife and child [28 Nov], two drunken soldiers [1 Dec], a pensionless sailor who had been 57 years at sea [22 Dec] and a 'broken soldier begging' [23 Dec]. WW was working on the 'poem for Coleridge' (*The Prelude*) on 26 Dec and MH copied some lines 'of the 3rd part' the following day. For WW's Chaucerian translations, see 15 and 24 Nov, 2 & 4–9 Dec 1801 (*DWG*, 38, 40, 44, 45–7) and *Poems*, i, 478–510.

49. DWJMS [28 Dec 1801]: DC 25 (*DWG*, 53). The Ws and MH had been reading Spenser on 6 Dec [*DWG*, 45), but DW probably meant a spencer, i.e. a short woollen jacket (see ibid., 40). Unable to get the £10 from STC, WW obtained it as an advance from DS for supplying poems to that value to the *Morning Post*: WW to DS, 21 Dec [1801] (*EY*, 342).

50. DWJMS [28 Dec 1801]: DC 25 (*DWG*, 53). Mrs Harcourt was the wife of General William Harcourt (1743–1830), who had commanded a regiment in the American War of Independence and captured General Charles Lee (1776). They were intimate friends of the royal family, to whose attention *LB* had undoubtedly been brought by WW's uncle WC. JW2 sent WC a copy of *LB*, only to discover he had already bought one of his own volition: JW2 to DW, 21 Feb [1801] (*LJW*, 91–2).

51. DWJMS [29 Dec 1801–24 (*r.*22) Jan 1802]: DC 25 (*DWG*, 54–5); MM to JM, 10 Jan & Jo H to JM, 13 Jan 1802: WLMS/H/1/5/10 pp.1–2 & WLMS/H/1/8/14 p.1.

52. DWJMS [23 & 27 Jan & 8 Feb 1802]: DC 25 (*DWG*, 57–9, 63–4); WW, *To a Young Lady Who Had Been Reproached for Taking Long Walks in the Country* and *Louisa After Accompanying Her on a Mountain Excursion* (*Poems*, i, 511–12). Three men had recently died crossing by Grisedale Tarn one night and the Greens would die in similar conditions in 1808: see p.372. WW divided the original poem into two: *IF*, 8, 16.

53. WW's translation from Petrarch, 'If Grief Dismiss Me Not to Them That Rest' (which had already appeared in the *Morning Post* on 13 Feb 1798, sent in by STC) was published on 2 Feb 1802; *To a Young Lady*, retitled *To a Beautiful Young Lady, who had been harshly spoken of on account of her fondness for taking long walks in the country*, on 12 Feb 1802; and *Written in Very Early Youth* ('Calm is all nature as resting wheel'), retitled *Sonnet*, on 13 Feb 1802. All three were printed without name or initials. For WW's agreement with DS, see n.49.

54. DWJMS [27 Jan 1802]: DC 25 (*DWG*, 59); *IF*, 79; MW, *Autobiographical Memoranda*, [Nov 1851]:

DC 167 p.53. See also pp.44, 825n.46. Margaret's own mother had been cut off by her family for marrying Alex Robison, 'one of those Itinerant Merchants from Scotland, the Pedlars of former days', in 1715. The breach was eventually made up, and Robison founded a highly successful hardware shop in Penrith: ibid., pp.50–52.

55. DWJMS [29 Jan, 2 & 6 Feb 1802]: DC 25 (*DWG*, 59, 62–3); RS to C. Danvers, 6 Feb 1802 (*RSNL*, i, 272). On 8 Feb the Ws were 'somewhat damped' by receiving a letter from STC speaking 'with less confidence about France': *DWG*, 64.

56. DWJMS [14–16 Feb 1802]: DC 25 & DC 19 p.26v (*DWG*, 68–9); STC to Mrs STC, 24 Feb [1802] (*STCL*, ii, 788).

57. DWJMS [13 & 24 Feb 1802]: DC 25 & DC 19 p.30v (*DWG*, 68, 72); Paul Vallon was in London for three months in 1802, but probably too late to be 'the Frenchman': Legouis, 77; MH's cousin JM, who was working in London at the time, mixed chiefly with French émigrés '& very good company they are': JM to Jo H, [Jan 1801]: WLMS/H/1/14/5 p.3.

58. WW to MW, 22 Jul & 11 Aug 1810 & 1 Jun 1812 (Darlington, 38, 63, 210–11).

59. DW's journal records letters to and from AV on 21 Dec 1801, 26 Jan, 15, 22 & 24 Feb, 22 & 26 Mar, 14 May, 7, 12 & 14 Jun, 3 Jul (a letter from AV dated Blois, 23 Jun) & 5 Jul. She does *not* record WW writing to AV before 21 Dec, but neither does she record the engagement itself.

60. DWJMS [28 & 19–21 Mar 1802]: DC 19 pp.51, 48–9 (*DWG*, 83, 81–2); *STCN*, 1120, 1151, 3383. STC stayed at Gallow Hill 2–13 Mar: DW's spirits were 'agitated very much' by receiving a letter from SH the day STC arrived.

61. DWJMS [28 Mar–5 Apl 1802]: DC 19 pp.51–2 (*DWG*, 83); STC to TP, 7 May & to SH, 4 Apl 1802 (*STCL*, ii, 799, 790–98).

62. *STCN*, 3304. The notes to this entry claim this conversation is 'well-substantiated' and took place on 3 Apl 1802; this is repeated by other biographers, but the dating seems inherently unlikely. STC claims he was ill in bed, yet on 3 Apl, according to *DWG*, he climbed Skiddaw with WW; he is more likely to have been ill after writing *Dejection* and to have urged WW to 'conclude on marrying' the night before WW left to see Mary, both of which point to the night of 4 Apl.

63. DWJMS [5–15 Apl 1802]: DC 19 pp.52–4 (*DWG*, 83–4); WW & DW to STC & DW to MH, 16 Apl [1802] (*EY*, 346–7, 350). WW went to Bishop Middleham from Eusemere on his birthday, 7 Apl, and returned there on 13 Apl.

64. STC to RS, 29 Jul 1802 (*STCL*, ii, 830). STC had 'lately some little controversy on this subject' with WW and they agreed to differ, STC believing metre and new combinations of language were essential to poetry: STC to W. Sotheby, 13 Jul 1802 (*STCL*, ii, 812).

65. WW, *Resolution and Independence* (*Poems*, i, 551–6); DW & WW to MH & SH, 14 Jun [1802] (*EY*, 366–7). Lewis Carroll's Ballad of the White Knight in *Through the Looking-Glass* was a parody of WW's poem, 'that has always amused me a good deal ... by the absurd way in which the poet goes on questioning the poor old leech-gatherer, making him tell his history over and over again, and never attending to what he says': C. Dodgson to H. Dodgson, 14 May 1872 (*The Letters of Lewis Carroll*, edited by M.N. Cohen [Macmillan, 1979] i, 177).

66. WW to J. Wilson, [7 Jun 1802] (*EY*, 358).

67. DWJMS [3 Oct (*r.*26 Sep) 1800]: DC 20 pp.48v–50 (*DWG*, 23–4); *IF*, 14.

68. DWJMS [13 Mar 1802]: DC 19 p.40 (*DWG*, 77). For DW's original account, see ibid. [10 Jun 1800]: DC 20 pp.23–4v (*DWG*, 9–10).

69. WW, *To the Same Flower [The Small Celandine]*, ll.33–6 (*Poems*, i, 550).

70. Capt JW to RW, 25 May 1802: WLMS/SH/33/4; WC to RW, 22 Jun 1802: WLMS/SH/33/2 p.2; CW to J. Walton, [*c.*15 Jun 1802]: WLL/CW/24 pp.1–2; DW & WW to RW, 10 Jun [1802] (*EY*, 360–61). Fearing RW would be dilatory, WW wrote to WC asking him to use his influence on RW to get matters moving: DW & WW to MH & SH, 14 Jun [1802] (*EY*, 368); WC's letter to RW was in response to this.

71. DWJMS [18 Jun 1802]: DC 31 (*DWG*, 111); [TC], Memorandum re. Lonsdale suit, [*c.*16–17 Jun 1802]: WLMS/SH/14/6 pp.1–4; WW to RW, [18 Jun 1802] (*EY*, 368–9).

72. DWJMS [21 Jun 1802]: MS DC 31 (*DWG*, 112); WW to RW, 24 Jun [1802] (*EY*, 369–71). RW had CW's approval, if not WW's, in claiming interest: CW to RW, 23 Jun 1802: WLL/CW/25.

73. DW & WW to RW, 3 Jul 1802 (*EY*, 371–2); RW to J. Richardson, 26 Jun & to WW, 9 Jul 1802: WLMS/SH/14/4 & 16/5 (*EY*, 686–7).

74. In Dec 1801 it was simply known as Sara's Rock, though MH had also carved her initials on it, which WW, after their engagement, deepened with his knife; STC added the other initials later: DWJMS [28 Dec 1801, 13 Jan, 4 May & 9 Jul 1802]: DC 25 & 31 (*DWG*, 112, 53, 61, 95, 112); *STCN*, 1163. The rock was a convenient meeting place between Grasmere and Keswick. Blown up when Thirlmere reservoir was created, the fragments were preserved by Canon Rawnsley and can now be seen in the garden at DC.
75. DW & WW to MH & SH, 14 Jun [1802] (*EY*, 362–3); DWJMS [11 (*r*.12) Jul 1802]: DC 31 (*DWG*, 119).
76. DWJMS [13 (*r*.14) Jul–29 Aug 1802]: DC 31 (*DWG*, 119–25); WW, 'It is a beautous evening, calm and free' (*Poems*, i, 576–7).
77. WW, *Composed by the Sea-Side, near Calais, August, 1802*, ll.11–14 (*Poems*, i, 576).
78. CW to J. Walton, 13 Sep 1802: WLL/CW/29 p.1; DW to MH, [12] Sep [1802] (*EY*, 375–6); CL to STC [8 Sep 1802] (*LCL*, ii, 66).
79. DW & JW2 to MH, [12] Sep [1802] (*EY*, 375–6; *LJW*, 125–6). I suspect RW confused recipients in debiting JW2 for a dress for DW at the same time: JW2, in account with RW, Apl 1802–Jun 1803: WLMS/3/18 [28 Sep 1802]. The Ws later made a joke of the fact that they received no wedding presents and MH's 'blasted expectations': MW, *Autobiographical Memoranda*, [Nov 1851]: DC 167 pp.3–4.
80. WW to MW, 9–13 May 1812 (Darlington, 142); DWJMS [24 Sep, 1 Oct, 4, 7 & 23 Mar]: DC 31 & 19 pp.34, 44 & 49v (*DWG*, 125–6, 79, 82, 74); DW to JPM, 29 Sep 1802 (*EY*, 377).
81. WW, Marriage Affidavit, 2 Oct 1802: WLMS/1/1/3; WW & TH, Marriage Bond, 2 Oct 1802: WLMS/1/1/2. A licence was necessary as WW was not resident in the parish of Brompton-by-Sawdon; if any impediments were found to exist, then WW and TH were liable to a fine of £200, payable to the Archbishop of York.
82. DWJMS [4 Oct 1802]: DC 31 (*DWG*, 126); WW & MH, Copy of Marriage Register Entry, 4 Oct 1802: WLMS/1/1/6a. The marriage appeared in several newspapers, including the *York Courant*, 11 Oct 1802: WLMS/1/1/49 (photo). For the joke appearance in the *Morning Post* on 9 Oct 1802, see p.860n.3.

Chapter 11

chapter title: 'The set is now broken', WW to RW, 11 Feb 1805 (*EY*, 540).
picture: The rescue of survivors from the wreck of the *Earl of Abergavenny*, published by Thomas Tegg, 24 Dec 1808, as the frontispiece to the anonymous pamphlet *Correct Statement of the Loss of the Earl of Abergavenny*.
1. DWJMS [4–8, 13 & 17 Oct 1802]: DC 31 (*DWG*, 126–32, 133).
2. WW to SGB, [*c*.23] Feb & to RW, 15 Nov 1805 (*EY*, 547, 644).
3. *STCN*, 1250; STC, *Dejection: An Ode* (*STCP*, 307–11, 553–7); STC, *Spots in the Sun* (Gill, 206). STC may also have been responsible for the silly notice of WW's marriage in the *Morning Post* on 9 Oct 1802 (Moorman, i, 574–5) which gave more than half the entry to a description of STC's house; CL was also a possible culprit.
4. STC to T. Wedgwood, 20 Oct & to Mrs STC, 22 [*r*.23] Nov & 13 Dec 1802 (*STCL*, ii, 876, 887–8, 894); DWJMS [13 Oct 1802]: DC 31 (*DWG*, 132); *STCN*, 1261. I assume WW's involvement in STC's affairs from his repeated trips to Keswick which resulted in his being 'oppressed' & 'not well': DWJMS [13–16, 19, 23 Oct & 2 Nov 1802]: DC 31 (*DWG*, 132–4).
5. The date of SH's arrival at Grasmere is not known: she was possibly there early in Nov, but left 7 Jan 1803: see ibid. [7–8 Nov & 24 Dec 1802, 7 Jan 1803]: DC 31 (*DWG*, 134, 135, 136); JW2 to DW, 7 Nov [1802] (*LJW*, 129).
6. DW to RW & JW2, 25 Dec 1802 (*EY*, 381); JW2 to DW, [22 Oct], 7 Nov & 1 Dec [1802] (*LJW*, 126 & n., 128–30, 130–32). JW2 was fined £210 on 21 Dec 1802 for importing 'camblets', cloth made from silk and wool, as part of his personal trade. The EIC had a monopoly on the sale, but in 1801 7,861 of the 19,733 pieces exported had been sold privately by the company's officers; the EIC now decided to clamp down on the practice and enforce its monopoly for the first time. JW2 was unlucky in being among the first officers to be made an example of and fined. A second offence would lead to dismissal.
7. JW2 to DW, 1 Dec [1802] (*LJW*, 132–4). RW's letter was a response to one from the Lowther solicitor requesting a statement of account 'which he some time ago desired' but had not

received; RW's claim was the equivalent of £351,125.55 today: J. Graham to RW, 6 Oct 1802: WLMS/SH/15/8; RW to J. Graham & to J. Richardson, 8 Oct 1802: WLMS/SH/15/7 & WLMS/SH/14/3.

8. DW to RW & JW2, 25 Dec 1802 (*EY*, 379–81); JW2 to DW, 7 Nov & 1 Dec [1802] (*LJW*, 128, 130–31). DW made no entries in her journal from, and including, 9 to 23 Dec.

9. RW to LL, 4 Feb, to J. Graham, 12 Feb & to WW, 14 Feb 1803 (*EY*, 689–92); WW, Memos on Accts with RW, 1803–4: WLMS/2/16 [21 Jan 1803].

10. WW to RW, 23 Feb 1803 (*EY*, 382); JW1, Letters of Admin., 21 Feb 1803: WLMS/SH/2/12; RW, General Release on Settlement of Lowther Debt, 7 Jul 1803: WLMS/SH/15/1. RW claimed the maximum possible, including interest on law bills delivered after JW1's death for which there was 'no pretence in *Law*', he admitted, 'it must be supported on ye score of liberality and generosity'. RW records payments into WW and DW's joint account of £1,305 on 1 Mar 1803, £657 on 30 Jul 1803 and £1,845 on 7 Jul 1804; on 27 Jul 1803 RW purchased £2,500 worth of 3 per cent annuities for £1,300 on behalf of WW and DW, which can only represent the £1,305 they had received from LL, indicating that this sum was not invested in JW2's voyage: WW & DW, in account with RW, 1792–1815: WLMS/2/4; R Dover, Receipt to RW, 27 Jul 1803: WLMS/SH/15/16.

11. JW2 to DW, [21 Feb] & to WW, 16 Apl [1803] (*LJW*, 136–8, 138–40); DW to RW, 22 Apl & 30 Apl–1 May [1803] (*EY*, 386, 388–90).

12. JW2 to Capt JW, [8 Aug 1804] (*LJW*, 141, 37–40). JW2's sword is now on display at RM. One of JW2's fellow captains in this action was Christopher Rawson (1777–1849), the nephew by marriage of Mrs Rawson (the former 'Aunt' Threlkeld). He claimed to have been offered a knighthood by George III, which he refused, and put his commemorative silverware on show at the Halifax Exhibition of 1840: Porritt, 'The Rawson Family', 31. Photographs of pictures of the action are in the Bankfield Museum, Halifax.

13. DW & WW to RW, 10 Jun, DW to RW, 15 [& 19] Jun & to CC, [7 or 14 Jun 1803] (*EY*, 359–60, 394, 392); STC to RS, 12 Mar [1803] (*STCL*, ii, 937).

14. DW to RW, 15 [& 19] Jun [1802] (*EY*, 395); *STCN*, 1404. Dora W was born on 17 Aug 1804, but at the beginning of Jun the Ws believed she was due in Sep: by 18 Jul they expected the birth in the 1st, 2nd or 3rd week in Sep: DW to CC, [*c*.1 Jun] & 18 Jul 1804 (*EY*, 480, 488).

15. DW to RW, 15 [& 19] Jun & to CC, 26 Jun [1803] (*EY*, 395). DW enclosed a lock of JW3's hair for CC.

16. Ibid., 396–7; WW & DW to RW, [17 Jul] 1803 & DW to RW & JW2, 25 Dec 1802 (*EY*, 398–9, 381). SC was born at 6.30 a.m. on 23 Dec 1802: *STCN*, 1310. JW2 was reluctant to take STC: 'I think I shall be blamed for taking him from his Wife and family': JW2 to DW, [21 Feb 1803] (*LJW*, 138).

17. WW, *Composed Upon Westminster Bridge, September 3, 1802* (*Poems*, i, 574–5).

18. WW, *Calais, August, 1802*, ll.6–8, 14, and *To Toussaint L'Ouverture*, ll.9–14 (ibid., 575–6, 577).

19. WW, *London, 1802*, ll.1–8 (ibid., 579–80). See also WW, *Composed near Calais, on the Road Leading to Ardres, August 7, 1802*, *September 1, 1802*, *Calais, August 15, 1802* and *Composed in the Valley, near Dover* (ibid., 575, 577–9).

20. DWJMS [7–8 Nov 1802, 11 Jan 1803]: DC 31 (*DWJ*, 134, 137); STC to WG, 10 Jun 1803 (*STCL*, ii, 950). On 11 Jan, according to DW, WW had been working on 'the poem to C', but this is the only reference to renewed activity on *The Recluse*.

21. WW's poems in the *Morning Post* in 1803 were *Calais, August 1802* (13 Jan); *Epitaph in – Church, Wiltshire* (14 Jan); 'I grieved for Buonaparté' and *Calais, August 1802* (29 Jan); *To Toussaint L'Ouverture* (2 Feb); *Banished Negros [September 1, 1803]* (11 Feb); *Calais, August 15, 1802* (26 Feb); 'It is Not to Be Thought of That the Flood' (16 Apl); there was then a break till 'When I Have Borne in Memory' (17 Sep); *Translated from the Italian of Milton* ['A Plain Youth, Lady, and a Simple Lover'] (5 Oct); 'I Find it Written of Simonides' (10 Oct); 'Laura, Farewell My Laura' (17 Oct); 'To the Grove, the Meadow, the Well' (22 Oct); 'The Swallow, That Hath Lost' (2 Nov); 'Gentle Zephyr' (15 Nov); 'Oh! Bless'd All Bliss above' (12 Dec). Another poem, *Anticipation*, appeared under WW's own name in the *Courier* on 28 Oct: Reed, ii, 207–12, 234, 238–9, 242–4; *DWG*, 197.

22. STC to WW, [23 Jul] & to RS, 14 Aug 1803 (*STCL*, ii, 957–8, 975); Dyce, *Recollections of the Table-talk of Samuel Rogers*, 209; DW to CC, 15

[*r*.17] Jul & 13 Nov 1803 (*EY*, 397, 418); STC to TP, 13 Feb & to WG, 23 Jun 1801, to SGB & LMB, 12 Aug & to RS, 14 Aug 1803 (*STCL*, ii, 675, 737, 964, 974). RW had no spare cash, having loaned JW2 £2,000, so to finance the tour WW borrowed £60 from DS of the *Morning Post*: STC to DS, [8] May 1807 (ibid., iii, 17).

23. STC to RS, 14 Aug 1803 & to DS, [8] May 1807 (ibid., ii, 975 & n.1; iii, 17). DW claimed she took no notes on the journey and therefore had to compile 'recollections', rather than a journal, after her return (DW to LMB, 22 [*r*.19] Dec 1806 [*MY*, i, 111]), but this is belied by the detail in *Recollections* and the existence of pencilled notes in DC 43. There are several MSS of *Recollections* (including DC 43, 50, 54, 55, 97), but there is no satisfactory collated printed text: I have used the edition by Carol Kyros Walker (cited as *DWR*) simply because it has a wonderful set of photographs illustrating the progress of the tour.

24. *DWR* [16 Aug 1803], 40, 219–20; *STCN*, 1432.

25. *DWR* [16–17 Aug 1803], 40–41; Dyce, *Recollections of the Table-talk of Samuel Rogers*, 209–10. SR was wrong; their route and most of their lodging places were determined by WW, who followed the recommendations of the ostlers at the inns: *DWR* [22 Aug 1803], 73.

26. Ibid., [18, 20 & 21–2 Aug 1803], 41–5, 55, 62–5, 69–70; *STCN*, 1434, 1449.

27. *DWR* [29 Aug 1803], 115, 117; STC to Mrs STC, [2] Sep [1803] (*STCL*, ii, 978); *IF*, 26.

28. STC to A. Welles, 13 [Sep] 1803 (*STCL*, ii, 987); WW, *Tintern Abbey*, ll.81–3 (*Poems*, i, 360); *DWR* [11 Sep 1803], 181.

29. Ibid., [17 Sep 1803], 199–200; Lockhart, *Narrative of the Life of Sir Walter Scott*, 117.

30. Ibid., 117–18; *DWR* [19–20 Sep 1803], 206–10; DW to LMB, 27 Oct 1805 (*EY*, 632–3); Dyce, *Recollections of the Table-talk of Samuel Rogers*, 209n.2. STC had given Stoddart an MS copy of *Christabel*, which he frequently read in Edinburgh circles.

31. *DWR* [22–5 Sep 1803], 215–18; DW to LMB, 4 May 1805 (*EY*, 590–91).

32. WW to SGB, 14 Oct 18[03] (*EY*, 409–10). WW, *Address to Kilchurn Castle, upon Loch Awe* and *Sonnet Composed at [Neidpath] Castle* (*Poems*, i, 592–3); *IF*, 26–7. WS was sent a copy of the latter for telling WW who had cut the trees at Neidpath. DW 'was spared any regret for the fallen woods when we were there, not then knowing the history of them': WW to WS, 16 Oct 1803 (*EY*, 414); *DWR* [18 Sep 1803], 201.

33. Ibid., [18 Sep 1803], 202; DW to CC, 9 Oct [1803] (*EY*, 403). There is no evidence to suggest WW took part in any military exercises.

34. WW to SGB, 14 Oct 18[03] (*EY*, 410–11 & n.2); WW, *To the Men of Kent. October, 1803* and *Anticipation. October, 1803* (*Poems*, i, 594–5, 1000). Acting under a strong hint from WW, SGB sent the poems to several publications: *Anticipation* appeared in the *Courier* 28 Oct 1803, the *Poetical Register* of 1803 and the *Anti-Gallican* of 1804.

35. STC to WW, [23 Jul 1803] (*STCL*, ii, 957); DW & WW to RW, 12 Dec 1803 (*EY*, 427); SGB to WW, 24 Oct 1803: WLMS/A/Beaumont/1 pp.1–2. WW met the Beaumonts before they left Keswick on 12 Aug 1803 but when is not clear.

36. WW to SGB, 14 Oct 18[03] (*EY*, 408); SGB to WW, 24 Oct 1803: WLMS/A/Beaumont/1 p.2.

37. STC to TP, 14 Oct 1803 (*STCL*, ii, 1013). According to STC, WW had 'yielded to my urgent & repeated – almost unremitting – requests & remonstrances' and 'made a Beginning to his Recluse'.

38. DW to CC, 9 Oct & 13 Nov [1803] (*EY*, 404, 417); *STCN*, 1608. The house, on the north-east banks of Ullswater, is now an inaccessible ruin on private land, virtually surrounded by a large residential caravan site.

39. WW to SGB, 3 Jun 1805 (*EY*, 594); STC to WW, [23 Jul] & to T. Wedgwood, 16 Sep [1803] (*STCL*, ii, 957–8), 990; RS to R. Duppa, 14 Dec 1803 (*RSLC*, ii, 238). RS undoubtedly made the comment himself, though he attributes it to a friend. WW's portrait was burnt because Hazlitt and WW's friends were not happy with it: WW to CL, 21 Nov 1818 (*Supp.*, 161).

40. CL to WW, 28 Dec 1814 (*LCL*, iii, 125 & n.); STC to J. Perry, [5 Feb 1818]; (*STCL*, iv, 831); *HCRBW*, i, 169–70. Hazlitt's clothes and box had to be left behind but, as late as the following Mar, 'No body durst venture to seize' them. When Hazlitt attacked *The Excursion* in the *Examiner*, noting among the deficiencies of country life the absence of 'courtesans', MW observed ironically, 'A pretty comment upon these opinions would be to relate the story of the critics departure for this unaccommodating country': WW to W. Hazlitt, 5 Mar [1804] (*EY*, 447); MW to DW, [29 Oct 1814] (*LMW*, 24).

41. STC to Mrs J. Thelwall, [22 Nov], to J.

Thelwall, [26 (*r.*25) Nov] & to M. Coates, 5 Dec 1803 (*STCL*, ii, 1017–21). The Southeys and Mrs Lovell, who was the sister of both Mrs STC and Mrs RS, were at Greta Hall by 13 Sep, lodging in the smaller part of the house with Mr Jackson; on 24 Nov the two families exchanged houses: *STCN*, 1682.

42. DW & WW to STC [9 Dec] & to RW, 12 Dec 1803; WW to W. Sotheby, 12 Mar 1804 (*EY*, 424, 427, 455–7). The college debt was for £10 15s 3½d. For WW's complex loan to STC see STC to T. Wedgwood [25] Jan, to SGB, 30 Jan & to W. Sotheby, 13 Mar 1804 (*STCL*, ii, 1040, 1049, 1087).

43. *STCN*, 1761; STC to TP, 15 Jan, to T. Wedgwood, [25] Jan & to R. Sharp, 15 Jan 1804 (*STCL*, ii, 1035, 1040, 1032); DW to CC, 15 Jan 1804 (*EY*, 428–30).

44. *STCN*, 1776, 1782, 1801, 1843; DW to CC, 15 Jan 1804 (*EY*, 429). For STC at Grasmere, see *STCN*, 1761–1844. Derwent went home on 3 Feb, in the company of Sally Ashburner: DW to CC, 13 Feb 1804 (*EY*, 441).

45. STC to R. Sharp, 15 Jan 1804 (*STCL*, ii, 1032–4).

46. DW to CC, 13 Feb, WW to W. Hazlitt, 5 Mar & DW & WW to STC, 6 Mar 1804 (*EY*, 440, 447, 452). WW repeated the plea for the notes, saying he would give three-quarters of his possessions for them: WW & DW to STC, 29 Mar [1804] (*EY*, 464). They never came.

47. STC to Ws, 8 Feb 1804 (*STCL*, ii, 1060); DW to CC, [25] Mar & WW & DW to STC, 29 Mar 1804 (*EY*, 458–9, 464–5). On specific instructions from STC, the Ws forwarded the MSS under cover to John Rickman, to avoid postal charges. When Rickman discovered this had been done without his knowledge, STC flatly denied the instruction and blamed the Ws: STC to Ws, 8 Feb & to J. Rickman, 17 & 18 Mar 1804 (*STCL*, ii, 1060, 1094–6, 1096–7).

48. WW, 'She was a Phantom of delight', ll.27–30 (*Poems*, i, 603). *Yarrow Unvisited* was sent to WS in the New Year: WW to WS, 16 Jan [1805] (*EY*, 531–2).

49. WW, 'I wandered lonely as a cloud', ll.19–24 (*Poems*, i, 620); *IF*, 14; Reed, ii, 259–60. It is usually claimed that WW was inspired by DW's description in *DWG*, 85 [15 Apl 1802] but there is little verbal similarity and the daffodils at Gowbarrow Park had been celebrated in guidebooks since WW's youth. CW had noted them in 1791 and WW must have seen them many times before: Fink, *The Early Wordsworthian Milieu*, 64–6, 81. MW's contribution was the lines 'They flash upon that inward eye Which is the bliss of solitude'.

50. RS to J. Rickman, 30 Mar 1804 (*RSLC*, ii, 277); STC to Ws, 8 Feb 1804 (*STCL*, ii, 1060); WW, *Ode to Duty*, ll.29–32 (*Poems*, i, 606); *IF*, 40.

51. WW, *Ode: Intimations of Immortality from Recollections of Early Childhood* (*Poems*, i, 523–9); *IF*, 61–2.

52. WW to R. Sharp, 29 Apl 1804 & to WS, 16 Oct 1803 (*EY*, 470, 412–13); RS to J. Rickman, 18 Oct 1802 (*RSNL*, i, 294).

53. [F. Jeffrey], review of *Thalaba*, *Edinburgh Review*, i (Oct 1802), 63–83 (Madden [ed.], *Robert Southey*, 68, 71, 72–3); WW to J. Thelwall, [mid-Jan 1804] (*EY*, 432). By 1813 more than 12,000 people subscribed to the *Edinburgh Review* (*The Times* had only 8,000), and Jeffrey estimated each issue was read by at least 50,000 within a month of publication: Greig, *Francis Jeffrey of The Edinburgh Review*, 10.

54. DW to CC, 3 & 9 May [1804] & to LMB, 25 May & 20 Jun 1804 (*EY*, 471, 473–4, 475–6, 482–4). Jo H came to live at Park House because GH, having failed to make a success of the farm at Bishop Middleham, had taken a job in a Newcastle counting house.

55. DW to CC, [*c.*1 Jun], 24 Jun & 18 Jul & to LMB, 20 Jun 1804 (*EY*, 480, 486, 488, 482–4). Sarah Weir (1762–1834) was a friend of the Hutchinsons who ran a boarding school for girls at Stockton: MW's cousin MM was a pupil there in 1801, and JH's two daughters by his first wife were there now: Jo H to JM, 2 May 1801: WLMS/H/1/8/9 p.2.

56. DW to CC, 3 May, to LMB, 25 May & to CC, [*c.*1 Jun 1804] (*EY*, 471, 476, 479–80).

57. DW to LMB, 24 Aug & 23 Aug [*r.*Sep] 1804 (*EY*, 496, 503); *Memoirs*, i, 367.

58. DW to LMB, 23 Aug [*r.*Sep] & to CC, [15] Oct [1804] (*EY*, 501–2, 510–11). CW was Dora's godfather: CW to WW, 20 Feb 1805: WLL/CW/39 p.2.

59. Storey, 169; DW to LMB, 7 [& 10] Oct & to CC, [15] Oct [1804] (*EY*, 507–8, 511); WW, *Yew-Trees* (*Poems*, i, 622–3); *IF*, 13.

60. Reed, ii, n.10; DW to CC, [15] Oct & WW & DW to RW, [*c.*1 or 8 Oct] [1804] (*EY*, 511,

504–5); WW described RWB's claims as 'a very Jesuitical performance': WW to RW, 22 Sep [1804] (ibid., 500). For the final payments of the promissory notes from LL, see RW to LL, Jun 1804 & LL to RW, 2 Jul 1804: WLMS/SH/16/8 & 33/6. CW's wedding was attended by only Priscilla's sisters; it was preceded by the baptism of the bride (on her 23rd birthday) into the Anglican Church. The marriage was made possible by CW's appointment to the joint livings of Ashby and Oby-cum-Thyrne, worth £400 p.a., in the diocese of Norwich: Priscilla W, Diary: WLMS/1/8/3 [1 & 6 Oct 1804]; Overton & Wordsworth, *Christopher Wordsworth, Bishop of Lincoln*, 7.

61. JW2 to Capt JW, [8], 15 & 22 Aug & 15 Sep & to DW, 15 Sep 1804 (*LJW*, 140–47, 148); WW & DW to JW2 & RW, 27 Dec [1804] (*EY*, 523).

62. WW to SGB, 25 Dec 1804 (*EY*, 517). Richard Duppa (1770–1831) had called with the artist Henry Edridge (1769–1821), probably in Oct 1804: Reed, ii, 270n.46. Duppa's *Life of Michelangelo* (1806) included contributions from WW & RS: *RSNL*, ii, 488–9.

63. DW to CC, 9 Dec & WW to SGB/DW to LMB, 25 Dec 1804 (*EY*, 516, 518, 520–21).

64. DW to LMB, 5 Jan, to CC, 6 Jan & WW to R. Sharp [*c*.7 Feb] [1805] (*EY*, 524–7, 527–8, 533). GH had left the Newcastle counting house after six months; WW asked Sharp if he knew any corn or wine merchants wanting a clerk, as GH had 'lost his own little property by a series of misfortunes, some of them I know unmerited'. WW blamed his lifelong problems with his eyes to this winter crossing of Kirkstone Pass: *IF*, 42.

65. JW2 to WW, 24 Jan [1805] (*LJW*, 155); T. Evans to WW, 9 Apl 1805: WLMS/3/10 p.2; Cumming & Carter, 'The *Earl of Abergavenny* (1805)', 31; J. Braithwaite, *Journal of the 'Endeavour'*, 1805–7: MS in private hands, photocopy in Weymouth Reference Library; JW2 received £1,534 15s, after payment of a 5s stamp, from EIH for his passengers: JW2, in account with RW, Dec 1804–Apl 1805: WLMS/3/20 [31 Jan 1805]. This may refer only to the military officers of the EIC, not to the nine civilian passengers, who would have made their own terms with JW2 as captain of the ship.

66. JW2 to Capt JW, 28 Jan 1804 [*r*.1805] (*LJW*, 157). The numbers vary, but must be roughly those quoted by official sources, e.g. *An Authentic Narrative of the Earl of Abergavenny*, 5, 33–52.

67. JW2 to Capt JW, [23] & 28 Jan, & to WW, 24 Jan 1805 (*LJW*, 152–8); Jerdan, *Autobiography*, i, 99. For William Jerdan (1782–1869), see Prance, 171.

68. JW2 to Capt JW, 31 Jan 1804 [*r*.1805] & to C.T. Coggan of EIH, 1 Feb. 1805 (*LJW*, 159–60, 161); *An Authentic Narrative of the Earl of Abergavenny*, 7–10; Cumming, ch.5 p.2.

69. T. Gilpin (*An Authentic Narrative of the Earl of Abergavenny*, 10–11, 12–14); *Correct Statement of the Loss of the Earl of Abergavenny*, 11; T. Evans to WW, 9 Apl 1805: WLMS/3/10 p.4.

70. *An Authentic Narrative of the Earl of Abergavenny*, 11–25; *Correct Statement of the Loss of the Earl of Abergavenny*, 11, 13; *St James's Chronicle*, 7–9 Feb 1805, 3; T. Gilpin to WW, 25 Apl 1805: WLMS/3/11 p.1.

Chapter 12

chapter title: Acquiring the Quiet Mind, see *Tintern Abbey*, ll.121–34 (*Poems*, i, 361).

picture: Brathay Hall, Ambleside, with Langdale Pikes beyond, seen across Windermere, by John Harden, 1808.

1. RW to WW & CW, 7 Feb 1805: WLMS/2/52 & 2/53.

2. DW to CC, 10 Feb, WW to RW & to SGB, 11 Feb & to CC, 16 Feb 1805 (*EY*, 538–41, 544); Jo H to TM, 27 Feb 1805: WLMS/H/1/8/15 p.2.

3. RS to WW, [11 or 12 Feb 1805]: WLMS/A/RS/1; WW to RS, [12 Feb] & to TC, 16 Feb & DW to LMB, 11 Apl 1805 (*EY*, 542, 544, 577). RS told a friend, 'I have . . . never witnessed such affliction as his and his sister's': Reed, ii, 284n.12.

4. WW to TC, 16 Feb & DW to CW, [27] Feb 1805 (*EY*, 544–5, 550).

5. TC to WW, 1 Mar 1805: WLMS/3/8 pp.1–3; CL to WW, [18 Feb 1805] (*LCL*, ii, 151–2). Wilberforce had heard the news direct from EIH and TC called on him that evening. 'He called to mind your Brothers modest and unaffected manner; he considered himself as the Patron of a young man who was lost: and his Grief continued with[out?] Intermission for the three days I was with him.' TC was so affected by his own grief that he could not attend to his abolitionist labours.

6. *STCN*, 2517 [31 Mar 1805], 2527 [6 Apl 1805]. STC later exaggerated his reaction for his wife's benefit: STC to Mrs STC, 21 Jul 1805 (*STCL*, ii, 1170).
7. Evans refers to 'your late much lamented Brother whose Conduct towards my family & self endeared him to us when living, & whose memory, when no more, is, & ever will be dear to us'. By a terrible irony, his daughter or niece, who survived this shipwreck, was drowned in that of the *Calcutta* in 1809: T. Evans to WW, 9 Apl 1805: WLMS/3/10 p.1; Cumming, ch.6 p.8. James Gilpin greatly deplored 'the untimely end of my old and respectable shipmate'; his son, Thomas, who had sailed twice before with JW2, spoke 'in grateful terms' of his kindness and called him 'a humane good Man & his loss I shall ever regret': J. Gilpin to Capt JW, 14 Feb & T. Gilpin to WW, 25 Apl 1805: WLMS/A/Gilpin pp.1–2 & WLMS/3/11 p.4.
8. A. Henstock (ed.), *The Diary of Abigail Gawthern of Nottingham 1751–1810*, Thoroton Society, xxxiii (1980), 116–17 [8 & 19 Jun & 14 Jul 1805].
9. DW to JPM, [15 & 17] Mar, WW to RW, 11 Feb, DW to RW, 27 Feb & DW & WW to RW, 4 Mar 1805 (*EY*, 560, 540, 549, 551–2); RW to DW, 8 Mar 1805: WLMS/2/54 p.1. 'Poor Mrs Robinson has loss'd her only son, they tell me she has neither eat slept nor shed a tear since she heard the news. indeed this news seems to have thrown a damp upon every body in Penrith': Jo H to TM, 27 Feb 1805: WLMS/H/1/8/15 p.2. Fifteen-year-old Christopher Robinson was buried in St Ann's Churchyard, Radipole, Weymouth, and is one of the few victims to have a gravestone: Cumming, epilogue, p.2.
10. CL to WW, [18 & 19 Feb 1805] (*LCL*, ii, 152, 153); T. Gilpin to WW, 25 Apl 1805: WLMS/3/11 p.1. WW chose to ignore midshipman Benjamin Yates's statement that he had a 'certain belief in my own mind he never had a wish to survive the loss of his property': B. Yates to B. Yates of EIH, Mar [1805]: WLMS/3/15 p.3 (*LCL*, ii, 163).
11. Committee of Shipping, Report to the Court of Directors, EIC, 15 Feb 1805; India Office Records, (Cumming, ch.6 p.15); *Sherbourne Mercury*, 25 Feb 1805 (ibid., ch.6 p.11). Complaints that Weymouth residents ignored the pleas of victims in their haste to plunder the wrecks had been made throughout the 18th century, including 1795, when the West Indies fleet sank: Attwoll, *Shipwrecks*, 14–21.
12. *Sherbourne Mercury*, 4 Mar 1805 (Cumming, ch.6 p.12); C.H. Stewart to Capt JW, 22 Mar 1805: WLMS/3/13 pp.1–2; Buxton, *Memoirs of Sir Thomas Fowell Buxton*, 2–3, 7, 37. Stewart's own son was among the dead; he was also required to identify Mrs Blair's remains, which were washed ashore on 23 Apl, and those of Baggot, which were recovered on 19 Jul: *Gentleman's Magazine* (Cumming, ch.6 pp.12–13).
13. D. Hollings, *A History of Wyke Regis* (privately printed, 1997), 38; Mrs King-Warry to Miss C.M. Maclean, 27 May 1932: WLMS/3/27; WW to C. Haviland, 28 Oct [1846] (*LY*, iv, 810). A stone tablet in the churchyard records the burial of 17 officers and 26 men lost in the wreck of the West India Fleet in 1795; 80 of the dead from the *Earl of Abergavenny* were also buried here in a mass, unmarked grave. Most of the legends on the tombstones in the oldest part of the churchyard have been worn away by sea winds and are largely illegible.
14. WW to JL, 16 Mar 1805 (*EY*, 565). See also WW to SGB, [c.23] Feb 1805 (*EY*, 547).
15. DW to LMB, 11 Apl & WW to SGB, 1 May 1805 (*EY*, 576, 586–7).
16. WW to SGB, 3 Jun 1805 (*EY*, 594–5).
17. STC to Ws, 19 Jan & 1 May & to Mrs STC, 21 Jul 1805 (*STCL*, ii, 1159, 1169). WW to SGB, [*c*.23] Feb & DW to LMB, 11 Jun 1805 (*EY*, 548, 599); Holmes, ii, 50–61. STC's story may be true: Major Ralph Adye (1764–1804) did die of plague in Gibraltar on 22 Oct 1804, but, taken with STC's claim that, on a second occasion, another packet of his papers was thrown overboard to prevent capture by French privateers, it all sounds too convenient an excuse for his inability to produce what was expected of him.
18. Jo H to TM, 27 Feb 1805: WLMS/H/1/8/15 p.2; DW to CC, 18 Mar & [*c*.16 Apl], to LMB, 15 Apl & 4 May & WW to SGB, 3 Jun 1805 (*EY*, 570, 582, 585, 590, 595).
19. DW to CC, 8 Jun [1805] (*EY*, 596–7). Sally Ashburner (b.1790) had assisted old Molly Fisher, but when the unnamed servant who replaced her in May 1804 left to care for her dying sister, Sally took her place: DW to CC, 10 Feb 1805 (*EY*, 538).
20. WW, *Elegiac Verses in Memory of My Brother, John Wordsworth*, ll.61–70 (*Poems*, i, 646); *IF*, 63; DW to LMB, 11 Jun 1805 (*EY*, 598–9).

21. WW, *To the Daisy* ('Sweet Flower!'), ll.50–70, and 'Distressful gift! this Book receives', ll.38–42 (*Poems*, i, 642–3, 640–44); JW2 had described the Isle of Wight where 'the daisy's [*sic*] after sunset are like little *white* stars upon the dark green fields': JW2 to DW, 2 Apl 1801 (*LJW*, 112).
22. WW to SGB, 12 Mar & to RW, 16 Apl 1805 (*EY*, 556, 583).
23. SGB to WW, 17 Feb & 3 Mar 1805: WLMS/Beaumont/5 p.2 & 8 pp.2–3; WW to SGB, [*c*.23] Feb 1805 (*EY*, 546–7); RW to DW, 8 Mar 1805: WLMS/2/54 p.1. In replying to SGB's query, WW states that JW2 had the £1,200 which was his and DW's share of the first payment of the Lowther debt, but this does not appear in RW's accounts for JW2's estate: RW records as debts to WW only the 1801 bond for £270 and to DW the £100 loan of 1793 and a further £80 in 1801: JW2 in account with RW, Apl 1805–Jun 1806: WLMS/3/21. The insurance paid out 18s in the pound.
24. DW to LMB, 14 Jul, E. Ferguson to S. Ferguson, 28 Jul & Mrs Rawson to [unidentified], 1 Dec 1805 (*EY*, 608, 618n.1, 619n.1). DW had a lifelong antipathy to SC, possibly caused by WW's admiration of her beauty and intellect. As a baby, he said, she had 'the most truly celestial expression of countenance, I ever beheld in a human Face'; later he would call her 'the Celestial Blue': STC to RS, 14 Aug 1803 (*STCL*, ii, 977).
25. WW & DW to LMB, 7 Aug [1805] (*EY*, 615–16).
26. TC to J. Wadkin, 23 & 26 Jul 1805: WLMS/A/Clarkson/3 & 4; WW to SGB, 29 Jul [1805] (*EY*, 611–12); WW, *Fidelity* (*Poems*, ii, 646–8); *IF*, 39–40; T. Wilkinson to M. Leadbeater, 30 Aug 1805: WLMS/A/Wilkinson, T./2.
27. Reed, ii, 296–8; WW, *Musings near Aquapendente April, 1837*, ll.63–5 (*Poems*, ii, 841); *IF*, 69; DW to LMB, 26 Aug [1805] (*EY*, 621); W. Scott to A. Seward, 10 Apl 1806 (*LWS*, i, 287). WS's poem was *Helvellyn*. Gough's fate was also celebrated by TdQ, Wilkinson and John Wilson: Lindop, 113–14.
28. DW to RW, [11] & 25 Aug & to LMB, 27 Oct 1805 (*EY*, 618-19, 620, 631).
29. WW to SGB, 17 [& 24] Oct 1805 (*EY*, 628–9). The last to leave were CC and SH, who had arrived on 25 Aug.
30. Reed, ii, 301; WW, *Incident Characteristic of a Favourite Dog*, *Tribute to the Memory of the Same Dog*, *Rob Roy's Grave* and *To the Sons of Burns, after Visiting the Grave of their Father* (*Poems*, i, 648–9, 650–51, 651–7); *IF*, 39, 143, 26–7; *DWR*, 41–2, 99 & n.2, 100, 187. WW was later embarrassed to discover Rob Roy was not buried at Portnellan, as he supposed, but at Balquhidder, though this did not affect the sentiment of his poem.
31. WW, *The Solitary Reaper* (*Poems*, i, 657–8); *DWR*, 193–4. The description by Wilkinson was eventually published in his *Tours to the British Mountains* (London, Taylor & Hessey, 1824), 12: 'Passed a female who was reaping alone: she sung in Erse as she bended over her sickle; the sweetest human voice I ever heard: her strains were tenderly melancholy, and felt delicious, long after they were heard no more.' WW always acknowledged the debt to Wilkinson in a published note to the poem.
32. DW to LMB, 4 Nov [1805] (*EY*, 635).
33. WW to R. Sharp, [*c*.7 Feb] & DW to LMB, 26 Aug & [7 Nov] [1805] (*EY*, 534, 621, 637); DW, [*Ullswater Excursion*], 7–13 [*r*.6–12] Nov 1805 (*Prose*, ii, 368–78). A large Victorian house now stands on the site.
34. Ibid., 375–6; DW to LMB, 29 Nov & WW to SGB, 17 [& 24] Oct 1805 (*EY*, 649–50, 626). DW's days or dates are one out throughout the journal, making precise dating difficult.
35. DW, [*Ullswater Excursion*], 12 [*r*.11] Nov 1805 (*Prose*, ii, 376–78); DW to CC, 24 [& 26] Nov & to LMB, 29 Nov [1805] (*EY*, 647, 651). After their riverside walk, the Ws and SH spent several hours in Penrith, visiting MW's relations and friends; WW also read Admiral Collingwood's account of the battle of Trafalgar in the newspapers.
36. DW to CC, 24 [& 25] Nov & to LMB, 29 Nov [1805] (*EY*, 646–7, 648–9).
37. DW to CC, [14] & 25 Dec & to LMB, 25 (& 26] Dec 1805 (*EY*, 653–4, 658–61, 664).
38. DW to LMB, 25 [& 26] Dec [1805] (*EY*, 664); CL to WW, [13 Oct 1804] (*LCL*, ii, 147); RWB, Schedule of books of the late Mr John Wordsworth, Oct 1805: WLMS/1/2/10. See pp.25–6 for a brief summary of the contents of JW1's library, or Reed, ii, 301n.38 for a detailed list. DW also commissioned MAL to buy editions of Milton, Shakespeare, Chaucer and Spenser for her: DW to RW, [Jan 1806] (*MY*, i, 4–5); MAL to RW, [*end*.30 Jan 1806] & CL to

WW, 1 Feb 1806 (*LCL*, ii, 203–4, 204–5); CL, Receipt, [*end*.30 Jan 1806]: WLMS/A/Lamb/5.

39. WW to SGB, 11 Feb [1806] (*MY*, i, 7); WW, *Character of the Happy Warrior*, ll.1–2 (*Poems*, i, 660 & n.); *IF*, 40–41. WW drew the comparison with JW2 explicitly in the *IF* note, saying that he had not wished to link the poem expressly to Nelson because the latter's public life was 'stained with one great crime', his summary court martial and hanging of the Neapolitan Jacobin Admiral Prince Francesco Caracciolo (1752–99), in contravention of the terms of a capitulation, signed by his subordinate, which Nelson considered *ultra vires*. SGB, who greatly admired Nelson, urged WW to address Nelson more particularly in his poem and mention his name: SGB to WW, 5 Mar 1806: WLMS/A/Beaumont/13 p.2.

40. WW to SGB, 11 Feb [1806] (*MY*, i, 6–7); HM, *Autobiography*, ii, 237.

41. *Memoirs*, ii, 310; *IF*, 11; WW to H. Busk, 6 Jul 1819 (*MY*, ii, 547); Reed, ii, 311n.1; WW, *Benjamin the Waggoner* (*Poems*, i, 665–89); *HCRBW*, i, 101.

42. DW to CC, 2 Mar [1806] (*MY*, i, 8); WW to SGB, 11 Feb & DW to CC, 2 Mar [1806] (*MY*, i, 7, 11).

43. DW to CC, 2 Mar [1806] (*MY*, i, 10).

44. WW to BM, [*end*.7 Mar, *p.m.*27 Mar 1806] (*MY*, i, 15–16); RS to Mrs RS, 5 Apl 1806 (*RSNL*, i, 424).

45. DW & WW to CC, 28 Mar [& *c*.4 Apl 1806] (*MY*, i, 19). For CW's appointment in Feb 1805, see Mrs CW to DW, 23 Feb [1805]: WLMS/1/8/1 p.2. CW's oldest son, John, was born on 1 Jul 1805, his second, Charles, on 22 Aug 1806.

46. WW to CC, [Apl] & DW to LMB, 20 Apl [1806] (*MY*, i, 22, 24–5); Reed, ii, 320–23. That WW stayed with BM and CL is implied from his redirecting his mail to BM's after leaving CW's, and leaving clothing at BM's & CL's: WW to CC, [Apl] & DW to CC, [*c*.27 Jun 1806] (*MY*, i, 22, 48).

47. *Farington Diary*, vii, 2785, 2736, 2741, 2767 [17 Jun, 26 Apl, 1 & 20 May 1806]; DW to LMB, 20 Apl [1806] (*MY*, i, 24–5).

48. *Farington Diary*, vii, 2741 [1 May 1806]; SGB to WW, 29 Jun 1806: WLMS/A/Beaumont/14 p.1; WW, *Elegiac Stanzas suggested by a Picture of Peele Castle, in a Storm, Painted by Sir George Beaumont*, ll.35–40 (*Poems*, i, 695).

49. Blanshard, 46–7, 142–4, pl.3. The original is now at DC.

50. Dyce, *Recollections of the Table-talk of Samuel Rogers*, 90; Warter (ed.), *Selections from the Letters of Robert Southey*, i, 386–7. WW's undoubtedly better version of the conversation is usually printed: Fox said, 'I am glad to see Mr Wordsworth, though we differ as much in our views of politics as we do in our views of poetry', to which WW rejoined, 'But in poetry you must admit that I am the Whig and you the Tory': Mrs J. Davy, *Memories of William Wordsworth* (Harper, *William Wordsworth*, ii, 113n.). This cannot be true, however, as in 1806 WW was still a radical and had, on this same London visit, been called a republican: see p.343.

51. WW to FW, 7 Nov & to LMB, 3 Jun 1806; DW to CC, 28 Mar, to JPM, 2 Jun & to CC, [*c*.27 Jun 1806] (*MY*, i, 89, 34, 18–19, 30–31, 50).

52. DW to RW, 2 Jun & WW to CC, [Apl] & to TH, [*c*.6 May] 1806 (*MY*, i, 33–4, 22, 27).

53. WW to CW, 15 Jun, DW to LMB, 17 Jun & to CC, 23 Jul [1806] (*MY*, i, 42, 43–5, 60, 66); MW to Mrs Cookson, 3 Aug [1806]: WLL/MW/3 pp.1–3.

54. DW to CC, 9 Jun & [*c*.27 Jun], WW to WS, [*pre* 15 Jun] & 4 Jul [1806] (*MY*, i, 37–8, 49–50, 40–41, 51–2); WW was also expecting the imminent arrival of TdQ and the Beaumonts, none of whom came. Laura Montagu died on 17 Jun, leaving BM with three small children, in addition to his son by his first marriage. BM did not come to Grasmere till the end of the summer.

55. MW to Mrs Cookson, 3 Aug [1806]: WLL/MW/3 pp.2–3; DW to LMB & to CC, 23 Jul [1806] (*MY*, i, 55–6, 58–60). JM had married Isabella Addison in Jun 1806: DW to CC, 9 Jun [1806] (ibid., 39).

56. T. Wilkinson to WW, 29 Jul 1806: WLMS/A/Wilkinson, T./3; WW to T. Wilkinson, [29 Mar] & to SGB, 5 & 21 Aug 1806 (*MY*, i, 20, 67–9, 75–7); SGB to WW, 10 Aug 1806: WLMS/A/Beaumont/16 pp.1–3. WW assured SGB that he hoped Applethwaite would remain in the W family 'for generations'; he later gave it to Dora.

57. WW to LL, 19 & 21 Aug 1806 (*MY*, i, 74–5, 76–7). This visit to Yanwath resulted in WW's obliquely addressed encomium on Wilkinson's character: WW, *To the Spade of a Friend* (*Poems*, i, 719–20); *IF*, 38–9.

58. WW to SGB, 1 Aug & WW & DW to SGB & LMB, 5 Aug 1806 (*MY*, i, 64, 70). By 8 Sep WW had completed one book of 1,000 lines and written 300 lines of another, 'I hope all tolerably well, and certainly with good views': WW to SGB, 8 Sep [1806] (*MY*, i, 79).

59. DW to CC & to LMB, 15 Aug [1806] (*MY*, i, 71, 72); STC to RS, 19 [*r*.20] Aug & to Mrs STC, 16 Sep 1806 (*STCL*, ii, 1177, 1180–82); MAL to DW, [29 Aug] & to STC [Sep] [1806] (*LCL*, ii, 238–9, 240–41).

60. WW to STC, 18 Sep & to SGB, 8 Sep & DW to LMB [late Sep] [1806] (*MY*, i, 80, 78–9, 84–5); Jos. Wedgwood to TP, Oct 1806 (Sandford, 248). WW had responded to a similar request from Wedgwood: WW to Jos. Wedgwood, [Sep 1806] (*Supp.*, 7–8). SGB said it was impossible for him to be angry with STC but he was 'rather hurt' at not having received a line from him: SGB to WW, 17 Oct 1806: WLMS/A/Beaumont/19 p.1.

61. S. Lloyd to CW, 27 Aug 1806 (Reed, ii, 334n.40); SGB to WW, 6 Aug 1806: WLMS/A/Beaumont/15 p.2.

62. WW, 'Lines ['Loud is the Vale! the Voice is up'], ll.17–24 (*Poems*, i, 721).

63. DW to CC, 5–6 Nov 1806 (*MY*, i, 85–7).

64. Ibid., 87–8; MW to Mrs T. Cookson, 1 Nov [1806] (Reed, ii, 710–11); DW to RW, 7 Nov, WW to STC, 7 Nov & to SGB, 10 Nov 1806 (*MY*, i, 91, 90–91, 94); SGB to WW, 6 Nov 1806: WLMS/A/Beaumont/20 pp.1, 3–4.

65. WW to SGB, 17 [& 24] Oct 1805 (*EY*, 625–7).

66. WW to SGB, 10 Nov & to LMB [*c*.Dec] 1806 (*MY*, i, 94, 112–20).

67. WW to WS, [*pre* 15 Jun] & 10 Nov 1806 & DW to LMB, 15 Nov [1806] (ibid., 41, 96, 100).

68. WW, *The Horn of Egremont Castle* and *Song at the Feast of Brougham Castle* (*Poems*, i, 721–4, 726–30); *IF*, 15, 28.

69. WW, *November, 1806*, ll.1–8, 12–14 and *Thought of a Briton on the Subjugation of Switzerland*, ll.1–4 (*Poems*, i, 725). 'What deplorable accounts from the Continent! I hope and pray that the struggle we shall have will invigorate us as it ought to do; then all will be well; and it will be a blessing; if otherwise we shall fall, a thing that would break my heart but for this, that we shall deserve it': WW to WS, 10 Nov 1806 (*MY*, i, 97).

70. WW to FW, 7 Nov 1806 (ibid., 89).

71. STC to Mrs STC, [25 Dec 1806] (*STCL*, ii, 1204); DW to LMB, 7 Nov [*r*.Dec], [19] & 23 [Dec 1806] (*MY*, i, 106–7, 109, 121). DW's letter of Friday evening, i.e. 19 Dec, is wrongly printed as [22 Dec] in *MY*, i, 109. STC intended to have custody of both sons, but Derwent was too ill to travel.

72. WW to STC, 7 Nov & DW to CC, 5–6 Nov & to LMB, [19 Dec] 1806 (*MY*, i, 90, 87, 110).

73. Ibid., 110; DW to LMB, [24 Jan 1807] (ibid., 128); *STCN*, 2001, , 2861, 2938, 3231.

74. Ibid., 2975, 3328, 4537, 3547; Johnston, 829–31; Holmes, ii, 82–5.

75. STC, *To William Wordsworth, Composed on the night after his recitation of a poem on the growth of an individual mind*, ll.102–12 (*STCP*, 341–2).

Chapter 13

chapter title: WW, *The Convention of Cintra* (*Prose*, i, 193–415).

picture: WW, by Henry Edridge, 1806.

1. DW to CC, 24 Nov & WW to T. Wilkinson, Nov [1806]; WW to WS, 20 Jan [1807] (*MY*, i, 104, 105, 122–3).

2. SGB to STC, 8 Feb 1807: WLMS/A/Beaumont/21 pp.3–4; DW to LMB, [24 Jan], WW to LMB, [Jan] & DW to LMB, [15 Feb 1807] (*MY*, i, 128, 130–31, 135). One of WW's efforts in Feb 1807 was a sonnet about the winter garden addressed to LMB: WW, *To Lady Beaumont* (*Poems*, i, 734–5).

3. RS to J. Rickman, [mid-Apl, 1807] (*RSNL*, i, 449). RS was prepared to allow Mrs STC and SC to remain part of his family, but was anxious 'to get rid of' Derwent, 'who is by no means an amiable child': RS to C. Danvers, 25 May 1807 (*RSNL*, i, 450–51).

4. DW to CC, 20 Jan & 17 [*r*.16] Feb, WW to RW, 7 Mar & DW to RW, 18 Mar [1807] (*MY*, i, 125, 137, 140–41, 141–2); STC to RS, [*c*.16 Feb 1807] (*STCL*, iii, 3–5). SGB generously dismissed WW's concerns about the cost to the Beaumonts of their prolonged occupation of the Hall farm as a trifle compared to the daily expense of entertaining friends 'one cares not three farthings for': SGB to WW, 15 Mar 1807: WLMS/A/Beaumont/23 pp.1–2.

5. WW to R. Sharp, [*c*.7 Feb] & DW to CC, 10 Feb 1805 (*EY*, 539, 534); DW to LMB, 20 Apl [1806] & WW to J.G. Crump, 27 Apl [1807] (*MY*,

i, 23, 144). When the Crumps eventually took up residence at Allan Bank, they became close friends of the Ws.

6. WW to WG, [21 Apl 1807] (*Supp.*, 8); WW to TdQ, 28 Apl [1807] (*MY*, i, 144); *LWS*, xii, 111, 115; *Farington Diary*, viii, 3033–4, 3037 (28 Apl & 3 May 1807]; STC to G. Coleridge, 2 Apl & to W. Sotheby, [5 May 1807] (*STCL*, iii, 6–8, 15).

7. Gill, 258–9; STC to TP, 14 Oct 1803 (*STCL*, ii, 1013). The title was the one WW had proposed, and TL rejected, for the 1800 edition of *LB*: see p.266.

8. Reed, ii, 352–3. Of the 100 gns WW received from TL, £60 was immediately used to repay DS for his loan which had financed the Scottish tour of 1803: ibid., 353n.15.

9. WW to LMB, 21 May 1807 (*MY*, i, 145–7, 150); *Farington Diary*, viii, 3044 [13 May 1807].

10. *Eclectic Review*, iv (Jan 1808) and *Annual Review*, vi (1808) (Hayden, 32, 37); ibid., 17, 19, 37, 23, 31, 19.

11. *Critical Review*, xi (Aug 1807) (Smith, 74). Ironically, WW had feared a hostile review in the *Critical Review* from Charles Le Grice (1773–1858), a former schoolfriend of STC, and had asked FW to secure a critic with a less 'malignant Spirit'; this was the result: WW to FW, 12 Jul [1807] (*MY*, i, 155).

12. *Edinburgh Review*, xi (Oct 1807) (Hayden, 23, 25); ibid., 25, 37–8; Smith, 74.

13. DW to WS, 30 May & 13 Jun 1825 (*LY*, i, 358, 366–7); *LWS*, ix, 128–9, 141–3. DW was convinced she and WW had visited Anna Seward (1747–1809) with WS, but in order to catch their return coach they had only 15 minutes in Lichfield and were thus deprived of the visit and more than a cursory glimpse of the cathedral.

14. WW to LMB, 21 May & DW to CC, 7 Jun 1807 (*MY*, i, 150–51, 152); WW, *Inscription in the Grounds of Coleorton* (*Poems*, i, 852).

15. DW to CC, 19 Jul [1807] (*MY*, i, 157–8). The Rawsons moved from Mill House, Triangle, to Saville Green, Halifax, in 1806: DW to JPM, 2 Jun 1806 (ibid., 32).

16. DW to CC, 19 Jul [1807] (ibid., 158); WW, unpublished draft advertisement for *White Doe*, in WW, *The White Doe of Rylstone*, edited by K. Dugas (Cornell UP, 1988), 198–9.

17. MM & Jo H to TM, 23 May 1807: WLMS/H/1/5/12; DW to CC, 19 Jul [1807] (*MY*, i, 156–7, 158–9).

18. WW was with the Beaumonts at Keswick 13–16 Jul; DW spent 12 days with them after his return: ibid., i, 159; DW to CC, 30 Aug [1807] (ibid., 160–62).

19. *The Journal of Elizabeth, Lady Holland (1791–1811)*, ii, 231; Granville (ed.), *Lord Granville Leveson Gower (First Earl Granville)*, ii, 280. Henry Fox, 3rd Baron Holland (1773–1840), was Lord Privy Seal at the time of his visit to Grasmere; his wife (1770–1845) had been divorced by her former husband for adultery with Holland. The party also called on RS at Keswick and found him more to their taste, 'full of genius and poetical enthusiasm'.

20. DW to CC, 30 Aug, to JPM, 19 Sep & to RW, 2 Oct [1807] (*MY*, i, 161, 164–5, 167); Granville (ed.), *Lord Granville Leveson Gower (First Earl Granville)*, ii, 280. The Ws were later mortified to discover RW had been at Sockbridge while they were at Eusemere; illness and a riding accident prevented him from coming to Grasmere, so WW went to Penrith to see him: DW to CC, 4 Nov [1807] (*MY*, i, 171).

21. DW to JPM, 19 Sep [1807] (ibid., 164–5). WW had earlier accepted the terms of a settlement, adding that he thought interest should be paid if the delay had 'originated with us'. RWW's widow had been receiving the rents of some of RW's properties in partial payment: WW to RW, 5 Feb 1807 (ibid., 132).

22. WW, *The White Doe of Rylstone; or, The Fate of the Nortons*, ll.1069–72 (*Poems*, i, 774); *IF*, 32–3; WW to STC, 19 Apl 1808 (*MY*, i, 221–2).

23. DW to JPM, 18 Oct 1807 & WW to WS, 18 Jan 1808 (ibid., 167–8, 191).

24. TdQ to WW, 31 May & 6 Aug 1803 (Jordan, 30, 34); WW to TdQ, 29 Jul 1803 & 6 Mar [1804] (*EY*, 400–401, 454).

25. TdQ to WW, 6 Apl 1806 (Jordan, 42–3). Richard de Quincey (1789–*c.*1815) turned up safely on this occasion, but eventually 'disappeared' during a hunting expedition with a shipboard party on Haiti in the 1820s: Lindop, *TdQ*, 276. Learning of STC's financial difficulties, TdQ presented him with £300 through JC; the gift was supposedly anonymous, but STC was left in no doubt where it had come from: STC to J. Wade, [Aug 1807] (*STCL*, iii, 24–5); Lindop, *TdQ*, 146–8.

26. TdQ, *Recollections*, 128, 129, 131–2.

27. Ibid., 134–42, 129–31; SGB to WW, 15 Mar 1807: WLMS/A/Beaumont/23 p.2.

28. TdQ, *Recollections*, 131–4; Lindop, *TdQ*, 181.
29. DW to CC, 4 Nov & 2 Dec [1807] (*MY*, i, 173, 177–9); STC to DW, 24 Nov 1807 (*STCL*, iii, 39); *STCN*, 3146, 3148.
30. TdQ, *Recollections*, 210–16, 225–6; DW to LMB, 6 Dec [1807] (*MY*, i, 180). TdQ said WW and RS entertained 'a mutual esteem, but did not cordially like each other'.
31. WW to RS, [Jan 1808], DW to LMB, 6 Dec & to CC, 28 Dec [1807] & WW to FW, 4 Nov [1807] (ibid., 162, 180–82, 186, 174).
32. WS to RS, 1 Oct 1807 (*LWS*, i, 387); DW to LMB, 3 Jan & [*c*.20 Feb] & to CC, 5 Feb 1808 (*MY*, i, 188, 196, 192). Archibald Constable (1774–1827) founded the *Edinburgh Review* (1802) and published WS's *Lay of the Last Minstrel* (1805) and *Marmion* (1808).
33. RS to WS, 11 Feb 1808 (*RSLC*, iii, 131–2); DW to JPM, [23] & 24 Feb [1808] (*MY*, i, 198, 200); CL to C. Manning, 26 Feb 1808 (*LCL*, i, 274).
34. STC to SGB, 18 Feb, to DS, [18 Feb], to TC, [3 Mar] & to the Morgans, [29 Mar] 1808 (*STCL*, iii, 74–5, 76–7, 78–9, 82); HH, *Retrospect of a Retired Mariner*, 24 Dec 1834: WLMS/H/1/2/2 pp.96–163.
35. STC to CC, 9 Mar 1808 (*STCL*, iii, 79); Ashton, 246; WW to SGB, 8 Apl [1808] & DW to CC, 16 Jun 1811 (*MY*, i, 208, 495).
36. Ibid., 208; Reed, ii, 376–7; WW to WS, 14 May 1808 (*MY*, i, 237–8); STC to RS, [24 Mar 1808] (*STCL*, iii, 80); Mrs CW, Diary, 1808 [6, 27 & 29–31 Mar, 1 & 10 Apl]: WLMS/1/8/4. WW had earlier expressed a wish to see the renowned collection of John Julius Angerstein (1735–1823), which later became the nucleus of the National Gallery, mainly through the advocacy of SGB: WW to SGB, 25 Dec 1804 (*EY*, 517 & n.2).
37. WW to STC, 19 Apl 1808 (*MY*, i, 221–3).
38. RS to M. Barker, 2 Feb 1808 (Reed, ii, 372n.4); Hazlitt, *Selected Writings*, 230.
39. HCR to TR, [Mar 1808] (*HCRWC*, i, 54). HCR met WW at breakfast at CL's on 15 Mar and accompanied him to and from a visit to CC at Deptford: Reed, ii, 378.
40. WW to SGB, [Feb 1808] (*MY*, i, 195).
41. WW to DW, [25 Mar 1808] (*Supp.*, 13); STC to WW, [21 May 1808] (*STCL*, iii, 108). Most of STC's criticisms are invalid for the poem as published in 1815, suggesting WW took them to heart and revised accordingly.
42. STC to TL, [23 May 1808] (*STCL*, vi, 1021); WW to DW, [25 Mar] & DW to WW, 31 Mar [1808] (*Supp.*, 11; *MY*, i, 207).
43. WW to SGB, 8 Apl [1808] (ibid., 207–9); WW, 'Pressed with conflicting thoughts of love and fear' (*Poems*, i, 798–9). WW had to cancel a planned trip to visit TdQ at Oxford. SH, who had been living with the Ws since mid-Jan, had 'burst a small blood vessel' in her lungs and coughed up blood, giving rise to fears of consumption; she remained unwell for eighteen months: DW to CC, 22 Apl [1808] (*MY*, i, 227).
44. WW to R. Sharp, 13 Apl & to FW, 17 Apl & DW to CC, [*c*.18 Apl] [1808] (*MY*, i, 211, 212–13, 214–16).
45. DW to CC, 28 Mar & to WW, 23 Mar & WW to FW, 17 Apl [1808] (ibid., 204–6, 201–3, 213–14).
46. WW to FW, 17 Apl & DW to CC, 10 May & to JPM, 11 May 1808 (ibid., 211–12, 232–3, 234–5). For the sums contributed see WW to FW, 2 Oct & [Oct] 1808 (ibid., 269; *Supp.*, 14); MW, Green Family Account Book, 1808–29: DC 45; Moorman, ii, 128n.3. All eight younger children were found homes in Grasmere Vale, except the boy who went to live with his older brother at Ambleside: DW, *A Narrative Concerning George and Sarah Green of the Parish of Grasmere*, 4 May 1808: DC 64 pp.14–15, 19–21; Moorman, ii, 128n.2.
47. WW, *Elegiac Stanzas Composed in the Churchyard of Grasmere* (*Poems*, i, 817–18); WW to STC, 19 Apl & [late May–early Jun] & to R. Sharp, 13 Apl [1808] (*MY*, i, 218–21, 239–40, 211). The poem was never published by WW, but was included in TdQ's article on the Greens in *Tait's Edinburgh Magazine*, Jul 1839 (TdQ, *Recollections*, 248–71). DW's *A Narrative Concerning George and Sarah Green* was not intended for publication, but as a family record of the tragedy: DW to JPM, 11 May 1808 (*MY*, i, 235–6). No satisfactory collated text of the two surviving MSS (DC 64 & Add. MS 41, 267A fos. 12–31, BL) exists; the unreliable edition by E. de Selincourt (Oxford, 1936) was reissued with additional material as *The Greens of Grasmere*, edited by Hilary Clark (Wolverhampton, 1987).
48. HH, *Retrospect of a Retired Mariner*, 168–72; DW to CC, 10 May, 5 Jun & 3 Jul [1808] (*MY*, i, 231–2, 252, 256); JM to TM, 18 May 1808: WLMS/H/1/14/12 p.3.
49. Allan Bank belongs to the National Trust but remains a private house. I am indebted to the

Hunt family for allowing me access to the house and gardens.

50. Jo H and 'Aunt' Monkhouse, not MM, as suggested by *MY*, i, 255n.1, were at Allan Bank by 3 Jul; JM and MM came together *c.*14 Jul. SH and Jo H were considering living in the Ws' cottage at Town End or buying a little estate at Grasmere: DW to CC, 3 Jul, to TdQ, 7 Jul & to CC, 3 Aug [1808] (ibid., i, 255, 257, 259, 262); MM to TM, 1 May & 24 Jul 1808: WLMS/H/1/5/13 & 14 pp.1–2.

51. MM to TM, 24 Jul 1808: WLMS/H/1/5/14 p.2; DW to CC, 28 Mar & 3 Aug [1808] (*MY*, i, 206, 260–63); J. Wilson to WW, 24 May 1802 (Gordon, '*Christopher North*', i, 39–48]; WW to J. Wilson, [7 Jun 1802] (*EY*, 352–8). John Wilson (1785–1854) became first editor of *Blackwood's Magazine* (1817), writing under the pen-name 'Christopher North'.

52. Reed, ii, 388–9; Rev. J. Pering, Journal of a Tour of the Lakes of Cumberland & Westmoreland, 20 Jun–1 Jul 1808: WLMS/A/Pering/1 pp.95–123; WW to Rev. J. Pering, 2 Oct 1808 (*MY*, i, 271–2); see also WW to R. Sharp, 27 Sep [1808] (ibid., 266). Having failed to get a description of the lakes from WW, Pering copied WW's letter and his account of the Greens into his journal.

53. *STCN*, 3357; Holmes, ii, 141–6; DW to CC, 28 Dec [1807] (*MY*, i, 184).

54. DW to LMB, 20 Apl, to CC, 22 Apl, to STC, 1 May & to JPM, 11 May 1808 (ibid., 225, 228, 230, 236). See also STC to WW, [21 May] & to TL, [23 May] [1808] (*STCL*, iii, 107–15, 115–16).

55. *STCN*, 3304; WW to STC, [late May–early Jun 1808] (*MY*, i, 239–45). The day before writing to WW, STC had written a similarly hysterical and accusatory letter to his brother, declaring it would be his last: STC to G. Coleridge, 11 May 1808 (*STCL*, iii, 102–5).

56. WW to STC, [late May–early Jun 1808] (*MY*, i, 239–45, 239n.1). This letter exists in two drafts, both incomplete, suggesting that no final version was sent.

57. Holmes, ii, 143–6; STC to T.G. Street, 19 Sep & to J.P. Estlin, 3 Dec 1808 (*STCL*, iii, 124–6, 127–9); WW to FW, 2 Oct 1808 (*MY*, i, 270); *STCN*, 3358. WW set off to see STC when he heard he was ill at Leeds, but was recalled by two letters from TC's Quaker friends saying that STC had left on the Kendal coach and then that he had delayed at Settle to visit Malham and Gordale Scar: J. Broadhead & I. Wilson to WW, 25–7 Aug 1808: WLMS/A/Broadhead/1.

58. STC to Mrs STC, [9 & *c.*18 Sep 1808] (*STCL*, iii, 120–21, 122); *SCM*, i, 17–19.

59. *Memoirs*, i, 367; DW to CC, 8 Dec [1808] (*MY*, i, 283). Catherine was baptized at Grasmere church on 2 Oct 1808: Reed, ii, 398.

60. SH to MM, [Oct] & [30 Nov] [1808] (*LSH*, 9–10, 12); DW to CC, 8 Dec [1808] (*MY*, i, 282). DW included the three servants (a cook, a maid and a 'little girl') in her numbers. WW had written to TdQ saying that they did not have a bed available for him to stay at Allan Bank, but DW's numbers indicate that one was found: WW to TdQ, [*c.*late Oct] (ibid., 272).

61. SH to MM, [Oct] & [30 Nov] [1808] (*LSH*, 9, 11–13); DW to CC, 4 & 8 Dec [1808] (*MY*, i, 280, 281–2).

62. WW to R. Sharp, 27 Sep [1808] (ibid., 267); *SCM*, i, 19. RS had earlier found himself and WW alone in disapproving of the British pre-emptive attack on neutral Denmark, which had resulted in the capture of the Danish fleet: RS to WS, 22 Apl 1808 (*RSLC*, iii, 141). In his letter to Sharp, WW modified his opposition because the Danes had subsequently behaved 'infamously' towards anti-Gallic Spaniards.

63. RS to H. Senhouse, 19 Oct [1808] (*RSNL*, ii, 483–5); RS to T. Southey, 30 Oct & 22 Nov, to WS, 6 Nov, & to W.S. Landor, 26 Nov 1808 (*Prose*, i, 196–7). WW and RS had the support of J.C. Curwen, MP, but were reluctant to allow him to present a county petition because it would align them with his radical politics: WW's letter declining an invitation to visit is almost certainly addressed to Curwen: WW to unidentified, 25 Nov [1808] (*MY*, i, 274–5).

64. WW to FW, 3 Dec [1808] (ibid., 278); STC to DS, [*c.*6 Dec 1808] (*STCL*, iii, 134); DS to STC, 16 Dec 1808: WLMS/A/Stuart/1 pp.2–3.

65. TdQ, *Recollections*, 159–60; DW to JPM, 4 Dec 1808 (*MY*, i, 280); STC to DS, 28 Dec 1808, to BM, [7 Jan] & to DS, [Jan] 1809 (*STCL*, iii, 151, 161, 164); WW, *Convention of Cintra* (*Prose*, ii, 223, 224–9, 229–38, 372). Both parts were signed 'G[rasmere?]' and ended with '(*To be continued*)'. STC claimed to have rewritten the second essay when it was lost, and that the 'two last Columns ... excepting the concluding Paragraph, were

written all but a few sentences by me': STC to TP, 3 Feb 1809 (*STCL*, iii, 174).

66. WW to DS, [5 Feb] & 25 May 1809 (*MY*, i, 289, 344); TdQ to DW, 21 Mar [1809] (Jordan, 116); STC to DS, [3 Jan 1809] (*STCL*, iii, 160).

67. TdQ to DW, [2] & 5 Mar 1809 (Jordan, 91–6, 96–104). TdQ continued to write to DW every few days (sometimes twice daily) with news and fussy queries on the proofs throughout his residence in London: ibid., 109–202.

68. As instances of the difficulties on both sides, TdQ was ordered to '*Stop the Press*' on 7 Mar when WW could not transcribe some additions in time for the post; on 11 Mar he admitted that he had not allowed any *final* printing to proceed since he came to London because he had wanted instructions from Grasmere on a single dubious reading: DW to TdQ, [7 Mar 1809] (*MY*, i, 294); TdQ to DW, 11 Mar [1809] (Jordan, 107).

69. TdQ to DW, 21 Mar & 1 Apl 1809 (Jordan, 116–17, 132-3); WW to TdQ, 29 Mar, DW to TdQ, 5 Apl & WW to TdQ, [7 Apl] [1809] (*MY*, ii, 305–9, 314–15, 317–19). Lindop, *TdQ*, 168 perceptively points out that TdQ's mortification at having his note on Saragossa cancelled was due to the fact that this removed his own reference to himself as 'the friend of the author', which echoed his very first letter to WW and was 'pathetic proof of his longing to be admitted to Wordsworth's friendship'. WW made amends by suggesting TdQ write a footnote on Moore, saying it was 'by a Friend of the Author upon his suggestion'. This note was included in the final text and was greatly approved by WW: WW to TdQ, 29 Mar & 26 May [1809] (*MY*, i, 309, 347).

70. TdQ to DW, 25 Apl [1809] (Jordan, 144–6); DS to STC, 26 Apl 1809: WLMS/A/Stuart/9 pp.1–3; STC to DS, 2 May 1809 (*STCL*, iii, 205). STC also attacked, unjustifiably, TdQ's 'strange & most mistaken System of punctuation': STC to DS, 13 Jun 1809 (ibid., 214).

71. WW to DS, [3 May], to TdQ, 5 May & to STC, [5 May] [1809] (*MY*, i, 327–8, 329–30, 332–4); TdQ to DW, 12 May & to WW, 16 May [1809] (Jordan, 162–3, 164–5). The passage WW particularly feared was libellous said that Wellesley and his fellow generals had earned 'the unremovable hatred and contempt of their countrymen' by signing the Convention.

72. WW to DS, 25 & [*c*.28] May, to TdQ, 24 & 26 May [1809] (*MY*, i, 344, 349–50, 341–2, 347–8); TdQ, *Recollections*, 145. TdQ associated John Wilson with himself in his remarks on WW's poor return for proffered friendship.

73. TdQ to DW, 25 May & 7 Jul [1809] (Jordan, 182–3, 238); WW to FW, [*end*.Mar 1809] (*MY*, i, 312). See also WW to DS, [26 Mar 1809] (ibid., 296).

74. WW, *Convention of Cintra* (*Prose*, i, 284, 303, 316, 318).

75. Ibid., 222; WW to FW, [*end*.Mar 1809] (*MY*, i, 312).

76. STC to DS, 13 Jun 1809 (*STCL*, iii, 214); WW, *Convention of Cintra* (*Prose*, i, 265, 300). Ironically, the 'porch' about which STC complained was the part in which he had had most input; once he had left Allan Bank, WW reverted to the passionate style, which is both more idiosyncratically his and more readable. The 'porch' prevented many of WW's friends reading any further: LL read only a dozen pages before declaring it 'written in a very bad taste, not with plainness & simplicity such [as] is proper to a political subject, but in a style inflated & ill suited to it'; HT also thought it 'a very poor performance; too heavy to be read through'. Even SGB seems to have had his doubts, rebuking his wife's publicly expressed enthusiasm by the dry comment that she spoke of the pamphlet 'as if she was *employed to sell it*': *Farington Diary*, ix, 3478; x, 3511; ix, 3482.

77. *Eclectic Review*, v, pt.ii (Jul 1809), *British Critic*, xxxiv (Sep 1809) & *London Review*, ii, no.4 (1 Nov 1809) (Smith, 115, 118, 119).

78. DS to STC, 27 May 1809: WLMS/A/Stuart/11 pp.1–2; *Prose*, i, 214. TL's partner, Orme, told TdQ that out of 20 political pamphlets published, only one ever cleared its expenses.

Chapter 14

chapter title: 'The blessedest of men!', WW to MW, [30 May 1812] (Darlington, 201).

picture: View of Grasmere Vale and Helm Crag from White Moss Common, by WW's niece Sarah Hutchinson, 1853.

1. STC to BM, [7 Jan 1809] (*STCL*, iii, 161). Two sonnets were dedicated to Don José de Palafox y Melzi (1775–1847), who led the defence of Saragossa and, after its fall (the subject of a third sonnet), was taken to France, where he spent five

years in captivity: WW, *1810* ['Ah! where is Palafox? Nor tongue nor pen'], 'Is there a power that can sustain and cheer' and 'Hail, Zaragoza! If with unwet eye' (*Poems*, i, 822–3). WW intended to publish *The White Doe, Peter Bell* and *Benjamin the Waggoner* in the winter of 1810: DW to TdQ, 1 May [1809] (*MY*, i, 325).

2. DW to CC, 22 Apl [1808], to TdQ, [7 Mar] & 5 Apl & WW to TdQ, [7 Apl] [1809] (*MY*, i, 226, 292, 315, 317); Jo H to MM, 22 Feb [1809]: WLMS/H/1/8/19 p.1; SH to MM, 27 Mar [1809] (*LSH*, 15); MW to JM, 16 Mar [1809] (*LMW*, 6–7). Reed, ii, 409 and, more especially, Gittings & Manton, 178–9, and Jones, *A Passionate Sisterhood*, 168–9, misinterpret this expedition from home as 'an exile' to 'boarding school': as MW's letter makes clear, she was not a pupil in the formal sense, but was visiting her cousins. There is no evidence for Gittings & Manton's claim, repeated by Jones, that Dora travelled alone on the coach to Appleby.

3. MM to TM, 2 Sep 1808: WLMS/H/1/5/15 pp.1–2; TH to JM, 12, 14 & 21 Oct, 10 & 15 Nov 1808: WLMS/H/1/5/1–5; JM to TM, 17 Nov & to MM, 9 Dec 1808: WLMS/H/1/14/18 & 20; SH to MM, 27 Mar & 19 Apl [1809] (*LSH*, 16, 18–21). Hindwell had been taken by 10 Feb 1809 when DW wrote to RW (*MY*, i, 290), but Jo H and JM remained in Penrith throughout Mar; SH's letter to MM of 19 Apl is addressed to her at Hindwell, and is the first indication that the cousins had all arrived there.

4. STC to DS, [*c*.14 Dec 1808] (*STCL*, iii, 141); DW to CC, 8 Dec [1808] (*MY*, i, 282); MAL & CL to CC, [10 Dec 1808] (*LCL*, ii, 290); R. Sharp to STC, 12 Dec 1808: WLMS/A/Sharp/1 p.1. STC even sent a bundle of prospectuses to Jeffrey, of the *Edinburgh Review*. F. Jeffrey to STC, 28 Dec 1808: WLMS/A/Jeffrey/4 pp.1–3.

5. MAL & CL to CC, [10 Dec 1808] (*LCL*, ii, 290); STC to BM, [28 Mar 1809] (*STCL*, iii, 184); WW to TP, 30 Mar & [*c*.30 May] [1809] (*MY*, i, 310, 352–3).

6. DW to CC, 15 [*r*.14] Jun & WW to DS, [14 Jun] [1809] (ibid., 355–6, 358–9).

7. Holmes, ii, 163ff.; Ashton, 250–57; TdQ to MW & JW3, 30 Sep–18 Oct 1809 (Jordan, 250–51).

8. DW to TdQ, 1 May [1809] (*MY*, i, 325); WS to RS, 1 Mar 1809 (*LWS*, ii, 172). Both WS and RS regularly contributed literary and political commentary to periodicals.

9. WW to DS, [26 Mar] & 25 May [1809] (*MY*, i, 296, 345); BRH, *Autobiography*, 126. WW argued that in countries, like Britain, with 'a considerable portion of practical liberty', governments were more afraid of dissenting opinion than in those under arbitrary rule, because the latter were confident of their own security and therefore saw no probable connection between opinion and action: WW to DS, 26 Apl [1809] (*MY*, i, 322).

10. WW to DS, [26 Mar 1809] (ibid., 296); WW to TP, 13 Mar 1815 (ibid., ii, 210); Ashton, 247–8; Holmes, ii, 131–3. Both systems were widely adopted. Dr Andrew Bell (1753–1832) became a personal friend of the Ws; Joseph Lancaster (1778–1838) emigrated to America in 1818.

11. J.H. Thom to S. Brooke, 8 Jul 1890: WLMS/A/Thom/1 p.2; Reed, i, 324n.2. Thom refers to a Presbyterian meeting house, which may be a confusion with the Quaker one at Colthouse.

12. E.M. Taylor, *William Wordsworth and St Oswald's Church, Grasmere* (Grasmere Church Publications, 3rd edn, 1991), 3–5; *IF*, 64–5.

13. DW to CC, 17 [*r*.16] Feb [1807] & WW to SGB, 10 Nov 1806 (*MY*, i, 136, 94); J.H. Thom to S. Brooke, 8 Jul 1890: WLMS/A/Thom/1 p.2; *Guide*, 171.

14. MW to JM, 16 Mar [1809] (*LMW*, 6); SH to MM, 27 Mar [1809] (*LSH*, 15). TdQ was genuinely attached to the W children and wrote a wonderful letter to JW3 from London, describing the workings of the press there and encouraging his efforts to be a better scholar: TdQ to JW3, [28 Mar 1809] (Jordan, 125–30).

15. DW to CC, 15 Jun & to TdQ, 25 [*r*.22] Jun [1809] (*MY*, i, 357, 360); E. Monkhouse to JM, 17 Jun 1809: WLMS/H/1/12/2 p.3.

16. Ibid., p.3; WW to T. Wilkinson, 7 Jul [1809] (*MY*, i, 362); MM & JM to TM, 6 Aug 1809: WLMS/H/1/5/21 p.2. Curwen had become friendly with WW through their mutual opposition to the Convention of Cintra: see p.871n.63. RW was at Sockbridge for several weeks but did not call or contact the Ws at Grasmere, causing DW to remark, 'he is a curious brother': DW to CC, 26 or 27 Aug [1809] (*MY*, i, 371).

17. DW to TdQ, 1 Aug, to CC, 26 or 27 Aug & to RW, 20 Aug [1809] (ibid., 364, 368–9, 367); TdQ to DW, 25 May 1809 (Jordan, 180).

18. DW to TdQ, 25 [*r*.22] Jun, MW to TdQ, [12 Sep] & DW to LMB, 28 Dec 1809 (*MY*, i, 360,

371–2, 378–9); Gordon, '*Christopher North*', i, 129–30. Wilson, who admired MM and was teasingly called her 'lover' by the Ws, celebrated the expedition in his poem *The Angler's Tent*: J. Wilson, *Isle of Palms* (Edinburgh, 1812), 200.

19. DW to TdQ, 1 May, WW & SH to TdQ, 5 May & DW to TdQ, 1 Aug 1809 (*MY*, i, 326, 330, 366); MM to TM, 22 May 1809: WLMS/H/1/5/19 p.5. MM and JM were still expecting WW and SH 'in a month at least' on 6 Aug, but the scheme had been abandoned by 12 Sep when the Ws were at Elleray: MM & JM to TM, 6 Aug 1809: WLMS/H/1/5/21 p.2; MW to TdQ, [12 Sep 1809] (*MY*, i, 371).

20. SH to MM, 27 Mar [1809] (*LSH*, 17–18); DW to TdQ, 5 Apl & to CC, 18 Nov [1809] (*MY*, i, 316, 374).

21. DW to CC, 18 Nov & to JPM, 19 Nov 1809 (ibid., 373, 375–6).

22. 'Tell our friend Wordsworth – that no two works, descriptive of the same country can be more different, or less likely to interfere with each other, than his [Green's] and mine'. J. Wilkinson to STC, [Jun 1809]: WLMS/A/Wilkinson, J./1 pp.1–2; *Prose*, ii, 123–5. William Green (1760–1823), a Manchester surveyor and artist, lived in Market Square, Ambleside, from 1800. He had published *Forty-eight Views of the Lake District and Four Views of Wales* (1795) and *Series of Picturesque Views of the North of England* (1796) and was preparing *The Tourist's New Guide to the Lake District* (1819): Burkett & Sloss, *William Green of Ambleside*, 16–21.

23. See p.375. WW told Lady Holland in Aug 1807 that he was 'preparing a manual to guide travellers in their tour amongst the Lakes': *The Journal of Elizabeth, Lady Holland*, ii, 231. WW rejected Pering's proposal because, as the latter makes clear in his journal (p.123), he wanted it purely as a favour and for inclusion in that same private journal; he was not requesting WW to write and publish a description of the Lakes for general circulation as Moorman, ii, 157 and *Prose*, ii, 123–4 assume.

24. J. Wilkinson to STC, [Jun 1809]: WLMS/A/Wilkinson, J./1 p.2. The detailed commission he intended to send later does not appear to have survived.

25. DW to CC, 18 Nov [1809] (*MY*, i, 372); *Guide*, 206, 200–201, 203, 206, 207, 409–10. The analogy does not hold entirely, as the 3rd edition, published in WW's own *Guide* in 1823, is the one referring to the last 60 years.

26. WW to LMB, 10 May 1810 (*MY*, i, 404); *Guide*, 171. The originality of WW's simile was questioned by Moorman, ii, 160 and Nicholson, *The Lakers*, 7 but the editors of *Guide* prove conclusively that they are mistaken: *Prose*, ii, 388–9.

27. Nicholson, *The Lakers*, 47–8; Thomas, *Man and the Natural World*, 266. The Claude-glasses were also known as Lorrain-glasses, for obvious reasons.

28. Ibid.; *Guide*, 236, 230, 232.

29. Ibid., 210–11, 218, 219–21. One wonders what WW would have made of the Forestry Commission's plantations which currently deface (exactly as he described) large areas of Grizedale, Ennerdale and Thirlmere.

30. Ibid., 213, 212, 211–12, 214, 217, 225; Gill, *Wordsworth and the Victorians*, 235–60.

31. DW to CC, 18 Nov [1809] (*MY*, i, 372).

32. WW, *Epitaphs Translated from Chiabrera, Hofer*, l.12, and *On the Final Submission of the Tyrolese*, ll.6–8, 12–14 (*Poems*, i, 830–36, 829–30); *IF*, 57. The *Friend* (1809) published WW's 'Advance – come forth from thy Tyrolean ground' and *Hofer* (26 Oct); 'Alas! What boots the long laborious quest' (16 Nov); 'And is it among rude untutored Dales', *Feelings of the Tyrolese*, 'O'er the wide earth, on mountain and on plain' and *On the Final Submission of the Tyrolese* (21 Dec) (*Poems*, i, 826–30, 1035–6). Gabriello Chiabrera (1552–1637) was a lyric poet, sometimes known as the 'Italian Pindar', who introduced innovations in metrical form which were adopted by later poets. Andreas Hofer (1767–1810) was betrayed to the French, tried by martial law and shot on 20 Feb 1810.

33. 'Mathetes' to the *Friend* (14 Dec 1809) (*Prose*, ii, 33).

34. CL to T. Manning, 2 Jan 1810 (*LCL*, iii, 36); WW, *Reply to Mathetes* (*Prose*, ii, 13, 9, 23, 13, 18). The first 158 lines of WW's essay were published on 14 Dec 1809, the remaining 490 on 4 Jan 1810.

35. DW to LMB, 28 Dec 1809 & to JPM, [1 Jan 1810] (*MY*, i, 379, 382–3); SH to MM, 3 Jan 1810 (*LSH*, 22–3).

36. STC to LMB, 21 Jan & to TP, 28 Jan 1810 (*STCL*, iii, 275, 280); DW to CC, 12 Apl & to LMB, 28 Feb [1810] (*MY*, i, 398–9, 390–91); WW, *Essays upon Epitaphs, I* (*Prose*, ii, 53). The more interesting 2nd and 3rd essays attacked Alexander Pope (1688–1744) for writing epitaphs as 'a metrical Wit' and championed simplicity, sincerity and heartfelt sentiment in the writer. WW reprinted the first essay as a note to *The Excursion*, suggesting he may have written the essay for *The Recluse*.

37. DW to LMB, 28 Feb & to CC, 12 Apl [1810] (*MY*, i, 391, 399).

38. *STCN*, 3547, 3552. My italics represent enciphered words. The second passage, with its reference to STC's demand for 'all but [love's] utmost', endorses the implication of the first that his love remained unconsummated.

39. STC to Mrs STC, [*c*.19 Feb 1810] (*STCL*, iii, 284); DW to LMB, 28 Feb [1810] (*MY*, i, 389–90). Reed, ii, 448, 450 dates the departure to *c*.14 Mar, 39, but STC heads an entry in his notebook '4 March 1810, Monday Night (the night before the day of Sara's Departure for Wales!)'. Though Monday night was actually 5 Mar, it seems unlikely that STC would have misdated SH's departure by more than a week. Henry Addison, who was the brother of RW's business partner Richard, as well as brother-in-law of JM, had joined them a few days earlier at Allan Bank: *STCN*, 3724; SH to MM, 3 Jan 1810 (*LSH*, 23); DW to LMB, 28 Feb [1810] (*MY*, i, 390).

40. DW to CC, 12 Apl [1810] (ibid., 398–400). See also MW to WW, 14 Aug [1810] (Darlington, 71). WW maintained a tight-lipped discretion on the subject of STC, apologizing to SGB for his long silence: 'I could not write without opening my heart; and that would have led to painful subjects, which, knowing his [SGB's] state of health and spirits, I thought it better to avoid': WW & DW to LMB, 10 May [1810] (*MY*, i, 405).

41. DW to RW, 9 Jan, 9 Feb, 2 & 23 Mar & to CC, 12 Apl 1810 (ibid., 385–6, 392–3, 397); STC to TP, 12 Jan 1810 (*STCL*, iii, 273). The Ws spent as much annually on tea as on rent, owing Twining £29 12s for tea bought in Oct 1808 & Aug 1809: DW to RW, 9 May 1810 (*MY*, i, 403). Their annual drawings were *1804* – £166 4s 10d; *1805* – £82 10s 6d; *1806* – £392 15s; *1807* – £332 10s 6d; *1808* – £199 13s 6d; *1809* – £407 10s 6d. The economies of 1810 paid off, for in that year they managed to reduce this to £225 13s 6d: RW, in account with WW & DW, 1804–10: WLMS/2/4.

42. DW to CC, 12 Apl & to JPM, 13 Apl [1810] (*MY*, i, 395–7, 401–2); SH to TH, [*c*.5 Jun 1812]: G1/10/1 p.3.

43. DW to CC, 11 May & 12 Apl [1810] (*MY*, i, 407–8, 398); *STCN*, 3912.

44. DW to LMB, 10–12 May, to CC, 11–12 May & to RW, [*c*.20 May] [1810] & WW & MW to SH, [Sep 1811] (*MY*, i, 406, 408–9, 410, 511); Reed, ii, 452, 454. The earliest reference to the baby as WW2 appears in DW to CC, 2 Jun [1810] (*MY*, i, 411).

45. WW to J. Wilkinson, [*c*.Mar 1810] (*Supp*., 20); DW to CC, 12 Apl & 11 May, to RW, 19 Jun & to CC, [9 Jul] [1810] (*MY*, i, 399, 408, 415–17); MW to WW, 1 Aug [1810] (Darlington, 51).

46. DW to Mrs Cookson, 29 Aug [1810] & WW to J. Edwards, 27 Mar [1811] (*MY*, i, 431–2, 471); WW to MW, [22 Jul 1810] (Darlington, 36). John Edwards (1772–1845) thought WW's *Convention of Cintra* 'exceeds all that has been written since Burke's on the french revolution. It is excellent in argument, beautiful in metaphors & similes, and sublime in its moral & philosophical strains': J. Edwards to STC, 28 Oct 1809: WLMS/A/Edwards/2.

47. WW to MW, [22 Jul 1810] (Darlington, 34–42). The prospect of seeing MW again soon made him better able to 'bear my longings': WW to MW, 19 Aug [1810] (ibid., 89).

48. MW to WW, 1 Aug [1810] (ibid., 46–56). Her 'our uncomfortableness' is obscure, but would appear to refer to her pregnancy, and probably the painful mouth complaint which regularly afflicted her after giving birth: 'sometimes I have fancied that I was caressing thee, and thou couldst not meet me with kindred delight and rapture from the interrupted [*sic*] of this distressing pain': WW to MW, 11 Aug [1810] (ibid., 62).

49. DW to CC, 4 Aug [1810] (*MY*, i, 419); WW to MW, 11 Aug & [22 Jul] [1810] (Darlington, 60–61, 36); SGB to WW, 13 Nov 1810: WLMS/A/Beaumont/33 p.2. William Shenstone (1714–63) had created a celebrated estate at the Leasowes, near Halesowen. *Venice Preserv'd* was a blank-verse tragedy by the dramatist Thomas Otway (1652–85).

50. STC to HCR, [12 Mar 1811] (*STCL*, iii, 305); WW to MW, 11 & 19 Aug & MW to WW, 15 Aug [1810] (Darlington, 60, 62, 86–7, 64, 60, 79–80, 77–8, 90). WW had admired MW's 'dusky hair' in 'She was a Phantom of delight', l.6 (*Poems*, i, 603).

51. DW to LMB, 14 Aug, to WW & SH, 14 Aug & to Mrs Cookson, 29 Aug [1810] (*MY*, i, 420–23, 423–7, 431–5), but see MW to WW, 24 Aug [1810] (Darlington, 95–6).
52. Reed, ii, 461; DW to Mrs Cookson, 29 Aug & to HCR, 6 Nov 1810 (*MY*, i, 434, 442–3); CL to TC, 18 [*r.*17] Sep, to WW, 19 Oct & to W. Hazlitt, 28 Nov 1810 (*LCL*, iii, 55, 57, 68–9); *HCRBW*, i, 16.
53. DW to CC, 15 & 30 Oct [1810] (*MY*, i, 437–8, 439); JM to TM, 26 Sep 1810: WLMS/H/1/14/26 p.1. MM obtained a consultation, through STC, with his physician, Anthony Carlisle, and returned to Hindwell on 22 Nov with his prescriptions and in good health: MAL & CL to DW, 23 Nov 1810 (*LCL*, iii, 64); STC to JM, [1 Nov 1810] (*STCL*, iii, 298–9).
54. DW to CC, 30 Oct [1810] (*MY*, i, 440).
55. Ibid., 441; DW to CC, 12 Nov 1810 (ibid., 447–8). MW, DW and the children remained only four days at High Hacket, returning to Allan Bank on 29 Oct.
56. Ibid., 448–9; DW to CC, 23 Feb [1811] (ibid., 464–5). MW gave up binding Catherine's good arm when a door closed on the child's left hand, cutting her fingers so badly that the wound had to be dressed by Scambler: MW to WW, 15 Aug [1810] (Darlington, 75–7).
57. WW to RW, [*c.*Apl/May] & DW to RW, 1 Jun 1810 (*MY*, i, 402, 410); MW, Cash Book, 1811–12: WLMS/2/18 pp.1–4, 9–10. The accounts for Algernon Montagu's lodgings open on 1 May 1810.
58. Mrs BM to STC, 18 Dec 1808 & 1 Oct 1809: WLMS/A/Montagu, A.S./1 p.1 & 17, p.2; WW to MW, 19 Aug [1810] (Darlington, 85).
59. Ibid., *STCN*, 3995; RS to J. Rickman, 1 Aug 1810 (*RSNL*, i, 537).
60. DW to CC, [9 Dec 1810] (*MY*, i, 454); Mrs BM to STC, 1 Oct 1809: WLMS/A/Montagu, A.S./17, p.3; DW to CC, 12 May [1811] (*MY*, i, 488).
61. WW to DW, [13] & 15 May [1812] (*Supp.*, 69–70, 75); DW to CC, 12 May & 27 Dec [1811] (*MY*, i, 490, 523). STC had stayed at Harrison's while supervising the printing of the *Friend* at Penrith. DW thought STC's consultation of Carlisle was 'quite a farce . . . For my part I am hopeless of him, and I dismiss him as much as possible from my thoughts': DW to CC, 12 Nov [1810] (ibid., 450).
62. Ibid., 488–9; WW to DW, [13 May 1812] (*Supp.*, 69–71).
63. *STCN*, 3991, 3997. The appearance of these first two key phrases in STC's notebooks as early as 26–8 Oct 1810, within 10 days of his departure from Grasmere, bears out his claim that these were BM's own words, not his own later gloss on what BM had said.
64. DW to CC, 12 Nov 1810 & 12 May [1811] (*MY*, i, 450, 489); MAL & CL to DW, 13 Nov 1810 (*LCL*, iii, 61, 62). See also HCR to DW, 23 Dec 1810 (*HCRWC*, i, 63–4, 65). The Ws were puzzled by reports of STC's good health, for he had been 'bloated and swollen up with fat' when he left Grasmere for London: DW to CC, 9 Dec [1810] (*MY*, i, 454).
65. DW to CC, 30 Dec [1810] (ibid., 455–8). The rubbing treatment had been suggested by Mrs Rawson, who had broken her hip a year earlier and, though not expected ever to do so, had recovered the use of her own legs by its means: WW & DW to LMB, 10 May [1810] (ibid., 406).
66. DW to RW, 10 Feb & to CC, 23 Feb 1811 (ibid., 461, 465–6).
67. DW to CC, 12 May [1811] (ibid., 486). The book she read was Philip Beaver's *African Memoranda: relative to an Attempt to establish a British Settlement on the Western Coast of Africa in the Year 1792* (London, 1805).
68. *Prose*, ii, 125–6; WW to MW, 22 Jul [1810] (Darlington, 42); DW to CC, 12 Nov 1810 (*MY*, i, 449). As some of the later sections of the manuscript are in SH's hand, they must have been completed before her departure in Mar 1810.
69. WG to WW, [*c.*1] & WW to WG, 9 Mar 1811 (ibid., 467n.2, 468–9). CL and MAL both contributed to WG's *Juvenile Tales*, most famously their tales from Shakespeare, though CL also undertook a prose version of 'Beauty and the Beast'.
70. DW to RW, 10 Feb 1811 & to CC, 30 Dec [1810] (ibid., 461–2, 460).
71. WW to J. Edwards, 27 Mar [1811] (ibid., 471).

Chapter 15

chapter title: 'Suffer the little children', Matthew 19:4; Mark 10:14; Luke 18:16. Inscription on Catherine Wordsworth's gravestone.
picture: Undated miniatures, said to be of Thomas and Catherine W.

1. TdQ to RS, 31 May 1811: Stanger Albums, ii, 188; TdQ, *Recollections*, 159–60; *IF*, 28–9.
2. WW to C. Pasley & to R. Sharp, 28 Mar 1811 (*MY*, i, 477, 478–82; ii, 660–61; i, 483). The two sonnets were *On a Celebrated Event in Ancient History* and *Upon the Same Event* (*Poems*, i, 840). Charles Pasley (1780–1861), a friend of STC, pioneered instruction in military engineering for non-commissioned officers and became director at Chatham in 1812.
3. DW to CC, 23 Feb [1811] (*MY*, i, 462–5); Jo H to TM, [*c.*Feb 1811]: WLMS/H/1/8/20 pp.1–2; TH to JM, 18 & 29 Mar 1811: WLMS/H/1/5/6 pp.2–3 & 7 pp.1–3; MM to TM, [*p.m.*30 Mar 1811]: WLMS/H/1/5/23 p.2. The farm at Stockton was managed by JH for the Ws: it is this to which WW refers in WW & MW to SH, 4 Oct 1813 (*MY*, ii, 118), and not a new purchase by himself as assumed in the footnote.
4. WW & DW to LMB, 10 May, DW to CC, 11 May & 30 Dec [1810] (ibid., i, 406, 408, 455). Jo H left Allan Bank, probably with her aunt, on 11 May: DW to CC, 12 May [1811] (ibid., 487).
5. DW to CC, 11 May [1810], 16 Jun & 27 Dec 1811 (ibid., 408, 493–4, 496, 524). The Parsonage is now the Rectory, a private house, and much changed: a new façade and wing were added in the 1890s, giving access to the views up Silver Howe. More recently, the floor level has been raised 5 feet because of continuing problems with flooding. I am grateful to Rev. Bob Wilkinson and his wife, Celia, for giving me a conducted tour of their lovely house and gardens.
6. DW to CC, 12 May & 16 Jun 1811 (*MY*, i, 486, 493, 497). DW said that they had 'just got into' the new house in DW to RW, 11 Jun [1811] (ibid., 492).
7. WW to J. Edwards, 27 Mar [1811] (ibid., 470); RS to G.C. Bedford, 14 Jan 1811 (*RSNL*, ii, 3–4). 'It would pity any body's heart to look at Hartley when he enquires as if hopelessly if there has been any news of his Father': DW to CC, 23 Feb [1811] (ibid., 466).
8. DW to CC, 12 May [1811] (ibid., 489); STC to M. Betham, [14 Mar 1811], to J.J. Morgan, [23 Feb] & to WW, 4 May 1812 (*STCL*, iii, 309, 376, 399, 402).
9. DW to CC, 12 May & 27 Dec [1811] (*MY*, i, 490, 524).
10. DW to CC, 16 Jun & [14 Aug] [1811] (ibid., 497, 501–2); SH to MM, 3 Dec [1811] (*LSH*, 34–5). Miss Weir's teacher, Miss Jameson, who accompanied Dora to Appleby, was probably one of the Ambleside Jamesons and therefore a sister-in-law of DW's friend Mrs Jameson, daughter of Rev. Joseph Sympson of Wythburn.
11. DW to CC, [14 Aug], WW to SGB, 28 Aug & WW & MW to SH, [Sep 1811] (*MY*, i, 499–500, 503, 507–8, 511). Bootle lies between Ravenglass and Millom, on the Cumbrian coast; it should not be confused with the Bootle in Merseyside. James Satterthwaite (1773–1827) was a fellow of Jesus College; in 1813 he became rector of Lowther, a post which he held till his death.
12. WW to SGB, 28 Aug & DW to CC, 12 May & [14 Aug] 1811 (ibid., 506–7, 490, 502); WW, *Upon the Sight of a Beautiful Picture*, *Epistle to Sir George Howland Beaumont*, *View from the Top of Black Comb* and *Written with a Slate Pencil* (*Poems*, i, 841–52); *IF*, 19–20, 64–6, 16, 29.
13. WW & MW to SH, [Sep 1811] (*MY*, i, 509–11); MM to SH, [late Sep]: WLMS/H/1/5/24 p.1; SH to MM, [27] Oct [1811] (*LSH*, 26–33, esp.33, 28). The grave of 'Wonderful' Walker (1709–1802) lies to the side of the path between the churchyard gate and the church porch. WW admired his saintly life, celebrated him in *The Excursion*, vii, and wrote a long prose note on him to accompany his *River Duddon* sonnets.
14. MW to WW, 1–3 Aug [1810] (Darlington, 46–8); SH to MM, [27] Oct [1811] (*LSH*, 28, 30, 31); WW to SGB, [Nov 1811] & to A. Bell, [Jan] & [Mar] [1812] (*MY*, i, 514–15; ii, 661–2); WW, *The Excursion*, note to ix, 299 (*Poems*, ii, 967). Rev. William Johnson (1786–1864) left Grasmere by the end of Mar 1812. Jo H evidently took the family interest in Johnson one step further by angling for him as a husband: SH to JM, 28 Mar [1812] (*LSH*, 44).
15. MW and DW took it in turns to teach at the school every afternoon or evening; SH, who had once said, 'Of all Trades keep me from being a School mistress!!' taught there every morning: DW to CC, 27 Dec [1811] (*MY*, i, 525); SH to MM, [27] Oct [1811] (*LSH*, 30).
16. WW to SGB, [Nov] & 16 Nov 1811 (*MY*, i, 514, 516–17); SGB to WW, 28 Oct, 4 Nov & [late Nov] 1811: WLMS/A/Beaumont 34 pp.1–2, 35 pp.1–3 & 36 p.2; LMB to WW, 27 [Nov 1811]: WLMS/A/Beaumont 37. BRH had similar problems when painting a picture for SGB: BRH, *Autobiography*, 164–5.

17. WW to SGB, [Nov 1811] (*MY*, i, 514); WW, *Essays upon Epitaphs*, ii, 572–83 (*Prose*, ii, 78); WW, *Inscription in a Garden of the Same [Coleorton]*, ll.3–13 (*Poems*, i, 853–4). WW also write *Inscription in the Grounds of Coleorton, Written . . . for an Urn* and *For a Seat in the Groves of Coleorton* (ibid., 952–4). All but the inscription for the niche in the winter garden were engraved *in situ* as intended: *John Constable's Correspondence*, vi, 143; *IF*, 29.
18. WW to SGB, 16 Nov 1811 (*MY*, i, 518–19); SGB to WW, [late Nov] & 6 Dec 1811: WLMS/A/Beaumont/36 p.1 & 38 pp.1–3. SGB urged WW to keep the money to finance a future tour. WW may have done this, as he told MW he had 'money for that purpose [i.e. a tour] and for no other': WW & MW to DW & SH, [19 Jun 1812] (*Supp.*, 133).
19. SH to MM, 3 Dec [1811] (*LSH*, 35, 39–40); DW to CC, 27 Dec [1811] (*MY*, i, 524–5). HH, who had given up his sailing career earlier in the year, stayed with the Ws at Grasmere *c.*20 Oct–20 Dec 1811, then returned to Stockton, where he had acquired a house: SH to MM, [27] Oct & 3 Dec [1811] (*LSH*, 32, 39).
20. DW to CC, 12 Nov 1810 & 27 Dec [1811] (*MY*, i, 449, 524–7).
21. RS to J. Burney, 19 Jan & to G.C. Bedford, 17 Jan 1812 (*RSNL*, ii, 23; *RSLC*, iii, 326–7).
22. WW to LL, 6 Feb 1812 (*MY*, ii, 2–3); LL to WW, 25 Feb 1812: WLMS/A/Lonsdale/2 pp.1–2. In May WW called on LL in London and told him that the Distributorship of Stamps was the sort of office he was looking for: WW to MW, [1 Jun 1812] (Darlington, 215–16).
23. SH to JM, 28 Mar [1812] (*LSH*, 46–7); WW to MW, [30 May] & [3–4 Jun] [1812] (Darlington, 202, 232); HCRDMS, 1812, 93 (*HCRBW*, i, 93).
24. SH to MM, 3 Dec [1811] & to JM, 28 Mar [1812] (*LSH*, 36, 46). Unwilling to risk any of his small capital, to which his own family as well as AV and Caroline had a better claim, WW refused Luff a loan of £100 without security: DW to CC, 27 Dec [1811] (*MY*, i, 526); MW to WW, 18 May & WW to MW, [3–4 Jun] [1812] (Darlington, 166–7, 230–31).
25. STC to J.J. Morgan, [23 Feb] & [24 Mar] [1812] (*STCL*, iii, 376, 380); Mrs STC to TP, 30 Oct 1812 (Ashton, 278). These sources prove that correspondence passed between the two households in an effort to secure a reconciliation, contrary to the usual claim that WW and STC remained obstinately incommunicado throughout STC's visit to Greta Hall.
26. STC to J.J. Morgan, [27 Mar 1812] (*STCL*, iii, 381–2); RS to WW, Sunday morning [Apl 1812]: WLMS/A/Southey/2 pp.1–2; SH to JM, 28 Mar [1812] (*LSH*, 45–6). Everyone, including his family, thought he had left for London, but he had gone to earth for a month at the inn at Penrith; RS eventually located him through Anthony Harrison: CC to HCR, 22 Apl 1812 (*HCRWC*, i, 68).
27. Ibid., 45; WW to CC, 6 May, to DW, [24 (*r.*23) Apl] & to MW, 29 Apl [1812] (*MY*, ii, 16; *Supp.*, 43–7; Darlington, 108). WW's intention of going to London in April was mentioned in DW to RW, 2 Feb 1812 (*MY*, ii, 1).
28. STC to R. Sharp, 24 Apl [1812] (*STCL*, iii, 389); DW to WW & MW, 3 May [1812] (*MY*, ii, 16); WW to MW, 29 Apl & [2 May] [1812] (Darlington, 109–10, 123). STC assumed WW would have told SGB of the quarrel and referred to it, 'not in the slightest degree suspecting that he was ignorant of it': STC to WW, 4 May 1812 (*STCL*, iii, 400).
29. HCRDMS, 1812, pp.72, 53–4 (*HCRBW*, i, 77, 67–8). HCR deleted Mrs WG's comments in the MS, p.67, but the following words, which are not in *HCRBW*, can be made out beneath the cancellation: 'I [understood?] on Saty from Mrs G that M bro[ugh]t C to London under [pretence? pretext?] of C having medical advice but in reality by W's desire in order to get rid of C and that at the last stage before they reached Ms – M told C that he had been commissioned by W to say that C c[oul]d no longer remain with him!!!'
30. CC to WW, [*c.*27 Apl 1812]: WLMS/A/Clarkson/16 pp.1–2; WW to MW, 29 Apl [1812] (Darlington, 109).
31. STC to CL, 2 May 1812 (*STCL*, iii, 394–6); HCRDMS, 1812, pp.66–7 (*HCRBW*, i, 70–72); WW to CC, 6 May [1812] (*MY*, ii, 16–17). STC's friend and patron Jos. Wedgwood was suggested as an arbiter and agreed to act, but was rejected by STC. A few months later, claiming business losses, Wedgwood ended the payments of his half of the annuity to STC. It is reasonable to assume that his knowledge of the quarrel, added to the fact that he had never forgiven STC for failing to write a memoir of his brother, now led him to sever the connection: HCRDMS, 1812,

p.66 (*HCRBW*, i, 71); WW to MW, [9–13 May 1812] (Darlington, 148); Ashton, 281.

32. STC to CL, 2 May 1812 (*STCL*, iii, 395); DW to WW & MW, 3 May [1812] (*MY*, ii, 14); HCRDMS, 1812, pp.74, 75, 66–7, 70–71 (*HCRBW*, i, 79, 80, 70–72, 74–7).

33. HCRDMS, 1812, pp.66–7, 70–71 (*HCRBW*, i, 70–72, 74–7).

34. HCRDMS, 1812, pp.73, 74–5 (*HCRBW*, i, 78, 79–81). In admiring WW's 'coolness', HCR was privately reiterating his rebuke to CL, who on 9 May had complained that WW was 'cold': HCR had replied, 'It may be so; healthful coolness is preferable to the heat of disease': HCRDMS, 1812, p.73 (*HCRBW*, i, 78).

35. HCRDMS, 1812, pp.75, 79 (*HCRBW*, i, 81, 84); HCR to TR, 20 May 1812 (*HCRWC*, i, 70); STC to RS, [12 May 1812] (*STCL*, iii, 410–11). The two drafts, one by WW, the other a revision by HCR, are given ibid., 404–6; a copy of the final statement, which is identical to HCR's revision, is included in WW to DW, [13 May 1812] (*Supp.*, 69–71). The most important omissions are the suggestion that STC might have been confused, through agitation, about what he heard from BM; and an entreaty that, if STC did not give the '<u>perfect consent of his whole soul</u>' to WW's assertions, then they should fall back on the original idea of a meeting between STC, WW and BM, in the presence of an arbiter. STC's acceptance is far more guarded than he implies to RS: STC to WW, 11 May 1812 (*STCL*, iii, 407–8).

36. WW to DW, [13] & [15 May] [1812] (*Supp.*, 69, 71–2); HCRDMS, 1812, p.79 (*HCRBW*, i, 84). WW had expected an emotional scene and had earlier informed HCR he would rather not see STC alone for that reason: HCRDMS, 1812, p.71 (*HCRBW*, i, 76–9).

37. WW to MW, [9–13] & [2 May] [1812] (Darlington, 147–8, 123–4); HCRDMS, 1812, p.78 (*HCRBW*, i, 83–4).

38. WW to MW, [9–13 May 1812] (Darlington, 147); HCRDMS, 1812, p.78 (*HCRBW*, i, 83–4); WW to DW, [15 May 1812] (*Supp.*, 76). Byron franked WW's letter to MW.

39. Ibid., 72, 74; HCRDMS, 1812, p.75 (*HCRBW*, i, 83); WW to MW, [7–9 May] & [1 Jun] [1812] (Darlington, 135–7, 213–15).

40. WW to HCR, [15 May 1812] (*MY*, ii, 18); WW to MW, [30] & [17–18] [May 1812] (Darlington, 202, 160).

41. WW to MW, [2], [9–13] & 23 May [1812] (Darlington, 125, 146, 179); WW to C.W. Pasley, [*c*.25 May 1812] (*MY*, ii, 20); C.W. Pasley to WW, 27 May 1812: WLMS/A/Pasley/2 pp.1–4.

42. MW to WW, 23 Apl [1812] (Darlington, 103–4); DW to WW, 17 May [1812] (*MY*, ii, 18–19). DW summarized the contents of Baudouin's letter because she thought it had gone astray; WW had, in fact, received it: WW to MW, 29 Apl [1812] (Darlington, 109).

43. MW to WW, 20 May, WW to MW [17–18] & [16] [May 1812] (Darlington, 169, 161, 157); WW to DS, 13 Oct 1812 (*MY*, ii, 47–8); WW & MW to DW & SH, [19 Jun 1812] (*Supp.*, 133). It is not clear whether the £20 was for AV or Baudouin.

44. MW to WW, 2 & 18 May & 6 Jun; WW to MW, [9–13 May] & [3–4 Jun] [1812] (Darlington, 120, 142, 167, 239, 237, 231); WW & MW to DW & SH, [19 Jun 1812] (*Supp.*, 133). AV's letter is reconstructed from references in the Ws' letters cited here. The correspondence to and from AV passed through TM's merchant contacts: see WW to MW, [7–8 Jun] (Darlington, 240–41). The last letter from AV in this sequence known to survive indicates that Caroline had 'great expectations' from her uncles, but AV wished to pass herself off as WW's wife to secure these advantages; AV had herself given up a legacy from her own uncle to its rightful heirs; and Caroline had begun to learn English: WW & MW to DW & SH, [19 Jun 1812] (*Supp.*, 133).

45. WW to MW, [9–13 May], MW to WW, 23 May & WW to MW, [30 May] [1812] (Darlington, 148, 183, 201).

46. MW to WW, 2 Jun & WW to MW, [3–4 Jun] [1812] (Darlington, 219, 229–30). MW accidentally set fire to WW's letter when re-reading it by candlelight in bed, hence the gaps in transcription: MW to WW, 8 Jun [1812] (Darlington, 246).

47. WW to MW, [3–4 Jun 1812] (Darlington, 227–8); DW to CC, 23 Jun [1812] (*MY*, ii, 32); SH to TH, [4 Jun 1812]: G1/10/1 p.1.

48. Ibid., pp.1–3.

49. Ibid., p.4; DW to WW & MW, 13 Jun [1812] (*Supp.*, 126); DW to CC, 23 Jun 1812 (*MY*, ii, 33). DW mistakenly tells CC the grave was in the south-west corner of the churchyard. JW3 helped DW and SH choose the site. The trauma of his siblings' death stayed with him for life. He would never allow his own wife to leave home

when he was absent, 'for fear of anything going wrong in the household in the absence of us both': IW to M. Stanger, 5 Oct [1841]: Moorsom 62/2/5 p.7.

50. DW to WW, 4 Jun [1812] (*Supp.*, 116); R. Scambler to WW, 4 Jun 1812: G1/11/1 p.3; SH to TH, [4 Jun 1812]: G1/10/1.

51. WW to CC, 11 [*r.*10] Jun [1812] (*MY*, ii, 24–5); WW to TH, [11 Jun 1812] (*Supp.*, 123–4); MW to WW, 8 Jun [1812] (Darlington, 245, 250). MW later wrote on this letter, 'Our Child had been 4 days dead!': it was probably written as Catherine was being buried.

52. WW to TH, [11 Jun 1812] (*Supp.*, 124); WW to CW, [(*r.*18) Jun 1812] (*MY*, ii, 26–7).

53. DW to WW & MW, 13 Jun & [*r.*SH &] DW to WW, 17 Jun [1812] (*Supp.*, 125, 127–9); DW to JPM, 21 Jun & to CC, 23 Jun; WW to CC, 18 Jun & to TdQ, [20 Jun] [1812] (*MY*, ii, 29, 32, 25–6, 27–8); WW & MW to DW & SH, [19 Jun 1812] (*Supp.*, 131).

54. MW to WW, 29 May [1812] (Darlington, 195); DW to WW, 13 & [22] Jun [1812] (*Supp.*, 125, 139); DW to CC, 23 Jun [1812] (*MY*, ii, 33–4).

55. DW to JPM, 26 Jul, to RW, 31 Jul & to CC, 16 Aug [1812] (ibid., 36, 38, 44); TM to JM, 10 Aug 1812: WLMS/H/1/15/5b p.2. The Marshalls had bought Watermillock, against DW's advice, in the spring of 1810: DW to JPM, 13 Apl [1810] (*MY*, i, 400–401).

56. DW to JPM, 26 Jul & to CC, 31 Jul, 10 & 16 Aug [1812] (*MY*, ii, 37, 39–40, 41–2, 45).

57. DW to CC, 31 Jul & 16 Aug 1812 (ibid., 39–40, 45). See also WW to RW, 12 Aug 1812 (ibid., 43).

58. MM to TM, [31 Oct] & 7 Nov 1812: WLMS/H/1/5/27 p.1 & 28 pp.1–2; WW, *Composed on the Eve of the Marriage of a Friend in the Vale of Grasmere, 1812* (*Poems*, ii, 857–8). TM, TH & Jo H met at Grasmere in early Oct and took MM and SH to the annual races at Penrith before the wedding: DW to R. Addison, 12 Oct 1812 (*MY*, ii, 47).

59. SGB to WW, 31 Aug 1812: WLMS/A/Beaumont/40 pp.1–3.

60. WW to LL, 14 Sep & to DS, 13 Oct 1812 (*MY*, ii, 46, 48); SGB to WW, 2 Oct 1812: WLMS/A/Beaumont/41 pp.1–2. WW's letter rejecting LL's offer is not known to survive; it was reluctantly forwarded by SGB.

61. LL to WW, 12 Dec 1812: WLMS/A/Lonsdale/1 p.1; SH to Mrs TH, 19 [Nov 1812] (*LSH*, 48, 51).

62. SH to MM, [27] Oct [1811] (ibid., 27); DW to CC, 5 Jan [1813] (*MY*, ii, 63). WW2 may have had measles in Jun, for DW refers to his spots being mended: DW to WW & MW, 13 Jun [1812] (*Supp.*, 125). Thomas seems to have died from pneumonia, a secondary infection commonly arising from the measles.

63. DW to CC, 5 Jan [1813] & WW to RS, [2 Dec 1812] (*MY*, ii, 60, 62–4, 51–2).

64. WW to E. Monkhouse, 6 Dec [1812] (*Supp.*, 140–41); DW to CC, 5 Jan [1813] (*MY*, ii, 63).

65. Ibid., 60; WW to LL, 17 & 27 Dec & to BM, 27 Dec 1812 (ibid., 52–3, 58, 55–6).

66. LL to WW, 12 Dec 1812: WLMS/A/Lonsdale/1 pp.1–3; WW to LL, 17 Dec & to DS, 22 Dec 1812 (*MY*, ii, 53, 54–5).

67. DS to WW, 25 Dec 1812: WLMS/A/Stuart/15 pp.1–2; SGB to WW, 23 Dec 1812: WLMS/A/Beaumont/42 p.2.

68. WW to LL, 27 Dec 1812 (*MY*, ii, 57). The letter is written as from Grasmere, but WW was still at Ambleside.

69. DW to CC, 5 Jan & to JPM, 24 Jan [1813]; DW to Mrs Cookson, [31 Dec 1812] (*MY*, ii, 60, 59, 76, 60). WW, MW & WW3 apparently returned to Grasmere on 2 Jan 1813.

Chapter 16

chapter title: *The Excursion* (*Poems*, ii, 35–289).
picture: Blea Tarn, home of the Solitary in *The Excursion*, undated.

1. WW to LL, 8 Jan, DW to JPM, 24 Jan & to CC, 5 Jan 1813 (*MY*, ii, 66, 76, 61, 63–4); LL to WW, 2 Jan 1813: WLMS/A/Lonsdale/3 p.3.

2. WW to LL, 8 Jan & to SR, 12 Jan 1813 (*MY*, ii, 66–7, 69); SR to WW, 9 Jan 1813: WLMS/A/Rogers/1 p.1.

3. WW, *Characteristics of a Child Three Years Old*, ll.1–6, 11–14 (*Poems*, i, 858). Despite WW's claim (*IF*, 1) that the poem was written at Allan Bank, it would more appropriately post-date the holiday at Bootle, before which Catherine was too much of an invalid to exhibit the traits described; she was also not three until 6 Sep 1811.

4. WW, *The Excursion*, iii, 659–61, 666–77, 678–9, *Maternal Grief*, ll.49–58 (*Poems*, ii, 111; i, 861); *IF*, 67–8. It is tempting to identify the boy as Thomas, particularly as WW said of him, explaining his heart-rending fear of death, that

'he was of an age to have thought much upon death a subject to which his mind was daily led by the grave of his Sister': WW to RS, [2 Dec 1812] (*MY*, ii, 51).

5. HCRDMS, 1812, pp.99, 71 (*HCRBW*, i, 103, 77); Lindop, *TdQ*, 199–202; WW, 'Surprised by joy – impatient as the Wind' (*Poems*, i, 863); A. de Vere, quoted in Gill, 294. It took WW several years to compose the epitaph for Thomas's headstone, which can still be seen today: 'Six months to six years added, he remained / Upon this sinful earth, by sin unstain'd; / O blessed Lord, whose mercy then removed / A Child whom every eye that look'd on loved, / Support us – teach us calmly to resign / What we possess'd – and now is wholly Thine!': WW to BRH, 20 Jan 1817 (*MY*, ii, 361).

6. DW to RW, 11 Jan & to Mrs TH, 1 Feb 1813; WW to BM, 27 Dec [1812] (ibid., 68–9, 80, 56); SH to Jo H, 24 Nov 1815 (*LSH*, 87). It seems curiously insensitive to have sent JW3 and Dora now to the school where Thomas had been a star pupil, particularly as DW could not face going into the building after his death and therefore gave up teaching there.

7. See, e.g., 'John and [Dora] are opposites – Thomas was between them – he had not the faults of either. Willy is a very quick and spirited child – I wish he – I wish any one of them was more like Thomas. Yet if it were so perhaps they would not be so fit for this world – *his* were heavenly graces – and Catherine's temper was as sweet as his – in *her* temper too there was no seed of evil': DW to CC, 5 Jan [1813] (*MY*, ii, 64–5).

8. STC to WW, 7 Dec 1813 (*STCL*, iii, 423); DW to CC, 5 Jan & 6 [*r.*8] Apl [1813] (*MY*, ii, 65, 90); CC to HCR, [*end.*10] & [29] [Mar 1813] (*HCRWC*, i, 71, 74–5). As late as 2 Jul, TdQ saw STC in London and invited him to accompany him north, but received no answer: TdQ to WW, 3 Jul 1813 (Jordan, 273). Jo H and JM saw *Remorse* in Mar 1813: 'I was very much entertained with the play it acts much better than I expected it would from reading it – & Mrs Glover in my opinion performed her part to admiration as to Miss Smith, she was very bad indeed, she appeared as if she was thinking of something else all the time, & had no int[e]rest or feeling in the part she performed': Jo H to Mrs TH, 3 & 25 Mar 1813: WLMS/H/1/8/22 p.3 & 23 p.1.

9. CC to HCR, [29 Mar 1813] (*HCRWC*, i, 76–7); DW to CC, 5 Jan & to R. Addison, 27 Apl [1813] (*MY*, ii, 64, 94); Reed, ii, 529 & n.16.

10. RM was substantially altered by the Ws and later inhabitants. Both house and grounds are now privately owned and still used by the W family, but are open daily to the public. I am indebted to the curators, Peter and Marion Elkington, for much personal kindness and access to private areas of the house out of hours.

11. DW to JPM, [2 (*r.*13) May 1813] (*MY*, ii, 95); SH to TM, 23 Jun [1813] (*LSH*, 55).

12. DW to CC, [*c.*14 Sep] & to SH, [11 Sep] [1813] (*MY*, ii, 114, 109–13); SH to JM, 27 Aug [1813] (*LSH*, 64). See also SH to TM, [16 May] & 23 Jun & to Mrs TH, 1 Aug & 29 Sep [1813] (ibid., 53, 55, 60, 69). WW paid TM £53 6d for the carpets and other soft furnishings purchased through him in London: WW & DW in Account with RW, 1813: WLMS/2/2/4 [6 Aug 1813].

13. DW to CC, 6 [*r.*8] Apl [1813] (*MY*, ii, 89); C. Arbuthnot to LL, 27 Mar 1813: WLMS/A/Arbuthnot/1; WW, Distributor's Bond, 26 Apl 1813: WLMS/1/1/6a, b & c. For the triangular arrangements between WW, LL and Wilkin concerning the appointment, see LL to WW, 28 Feb & 18 Mar 1813: WLMS/A/Lonsdale/4 pp.1–2 & 5 pp.1–2; WW to LL, 6 & 14 Mar 1813 (*MY*, ii, 83, 86). For the securities, see SGB to WW, 15 Apl 1813: WLMS/A/Beaumont/43 p.1; LL to WW, 16 Apl 1813: WLMS/A/Lonsdale/6; WW to RW, [Apl] & to LL, 19 Apl 1813 (*MY*, ii, 92, 93).

14. John Carter (d.1863, not 1856 as *MY*, ii, 83n.) served as Stamp Office clerk to WW and WW2 after him.

15. WW to LL, 6 Mar & DW to CC, 6 [*r.*8] Apl 1813 (*MY*, ii, 83, 88); SH to MW, 16 Aug [1820] (*LSH*, 187); WW to CW, [13 Mar 1829] & to VL, 7 Feb 1821 (*LY*, ii, 50; i, 25).

16. WW to FW, 26 Apl [1814] (*MY*, ii, 144).

17. WW to TNT, [*c.*14 Jun 1838] (*LY*, iii, 598); Jo H to Mrs TH, 25 Mar [1813]: WLMS/H/1/8/23 p.3; CC to HCR, [29 Mar 1813] (*HCRWC*, i, 77). Jo H agreed 'it will enable them to have many comforts, & be able to take many little Jaunts without being anxious about money matters . . .'

18. WW to BM, 30 May & DW to CC, [*c.*14 Sep] & to SH, 10 Oct 1813 (*MY*, ii, 97, 117, 126); SH to TM, 23 Jun & to Mrs TH, [1] & 27 Aug [1813] (*LSH*, 56, 57–8, 60, 62–3); MW to SH, 4 Oct 1813

(*LMW*, 8–9). Crosthwaite's Museum at Keswick proudly advertised 'many Hundred Natural and Artificial Curiosities, from every Quarter of the World' and was immensely popular with tourists: Nicholson, *The Lakers*, 193.

19. SH to Mrs TH, [1 Aug 1813] (*LSH*, 59); WW to RW, 2 Aug & DW to RW, 3 Aug 1813 (*MY*, ii, 103, 104); RW to WW, 20 Aug 1813: WLMS/2/44 pp.1–2. The sum sought in full settlement was £984 4s 5d, of which RW was due £665 15s 2½d for rent for Sockbridge, plus 20 years' interest. The remaining £318 9s 2½d was due to the estate and therefore belonged to the Ws equally: DW & WW were credited their ²⁄₅ share (£127 7s 8d) in 1813: WW & DW in Account with RW, 1816: WLMS/2/4.

20. DW to SH, [11 Sep] & to CC, 4 Oct [1813] & DW to RW, 23 Jan 1814 (*MY*, ii, 112, 123, 130–31). WW went to Branthwaite to see his cousin's family on learning of the loss of the *Peacock*: SH to TM, [16 May 1813] (*LSH*, 53–4), DW to E. Cookson, [17 May 1813] (*MY*, ii, 96–7). The family had been particularly unfortunate: in addition to the *Peacock* disaster, their oldest son, Joseph, whom JW2 had saved from the wreck of the *Earl of Abergavenny*, was disabled mentally and physically by a paralytic stroke; a second son died of yellow fever and a daughter of hydrophobia; another daughter had just become pregnant by a servant and eloped to marry him; and RWB himself had long been 'helpless from corpulency' and 'subject to the most frantic passions': DW to CC, 4 Oct [1813] (ibid., 123).

21. WW to FW, 28 Aug & DW to CC, 4 Oct 1813 (ibid., 108, 122); SH to JM, 27 Aug [1813] (*LSH*, 64).

22. DW to CC, 4 Oct 1813 (*MY*, ii, 122); MW to SH, [Oct 1813] (*LMW*, 12); BM, *Autobiography*: WLMS/A/Montagu/26 pp.19, 42–4, 48. See also five letters of BM Jnr, Dec 1813, at the end of this MS.

23. DW to CC, 5 Jan & WW & MW to SH, 4 Oct 1813 (*MY*, ii, 63, 119); SH to JM, 27 Aug & to Mrs TH, 29 Sep [1813] (*LSH*, 64, 65). See also DW to E. Threlkeld & JPM, 19 Jan 1813 (*MY*, ii, 73).

24. BM Jnr to Mrs BM, 5 & 25 Dec 1813: BM, *Autobiography*, WLMS/A/Montagu/26 pp.85–6, 92–3.

25. BM Jnr to Mrs BM, 5, 19 & 25 Dec 1813: ibid., pp.59–61, 77, 90; WW to BM, 20 Jan, DW to RW, 23 Jan & DW to CC, 24 Apl [1814] (*MY*, ii, 129–30, 130, 137–9).

26. DW to CC, 24 Apl [1814] (ibid., 139–40).

27. Jeffrey's most recent attack on WW had been in his review of Wilson's *Isle of Palms* in Feb 1812, in which he scathingly pointed out that the prosperity of WS, Campbell and Crabbe had not been won by 'ecstacies about spades or sparrow's eggs – or men gathering leeches – or women in duffle coats – or plates and porringers – or washing tubs': Gill, 301; Greig, *Francis Jeffrey of The Edinburgh Review*, 131–2. A review of RS's *Carmen Triumphale* in the aptly named *Scourge* (Feb 1814) referred incidentally to 'the disgusting affectation of the school of Wordsworth': Madden (ed.), *Robert Southey*, 196.

28. DW to CC, 24 Apl [1814] (*MY*, ii, 140). DW had seen some of the alterations to the manuscript during a week's visit to RM from Keswick, probably in mid-March, but had not been involved in any other stage of the project. She gives the impression that the decision to publish was also taken in her absence.

29. Ibid. See also, e.g., WW to FW, 28 Aug 1813 & to TP, 28 Apl 1814 (ibid., 108, 146).

30. WW to SR, 5 May 1814 (ibid., 148).

31. DW to CC, 24 Apl [1814] & WW to J. Edwards, [*c*.20 Mar 1815] (ibid., 140; *Supp.*, 157). The title was still in doubt the month before publication: BRH saw the sheets in the press and told SGB that it was to be called 'The Wanderer'. LMB did not approve of the substitution of *The Excursion* for *The Recluse*: SGB & LMB to WW, 2 Jun & 4 Jul 1814: WLMS/A/Beaumont/46 p.4 & 47 p.3.

32. WW, [Dedicatory Sonnet to] *The Excursion*, ll.9–11 (*Poems*, ii, 35); WW to LL, 4 Jun & to SGB, 23 Jun 1814 (*MY*, ii, 148–9; *Supp.*, 144); RW to WW, 26 Mar [1803] (*EY*, 384n.1). The sonnet was dated 29 Jul, but as WW was in Scotland then this is probably a mistake for 29 Jun, a few days after WW learned LL had accepted the dedication.

33. WW, Preface to *The Excursion* (*Prose*, iii, 5–6, 8, 6–7).

34. WW, *The Excursion*, iv, 10–21, 1141–50, 1207–17, 1223–4 (*Poems*, ii, 121, 152, 154).

35. WW to SR, 5 May & to SGB, 23 Jun 1814 (*MY*, ii, 148; *Supp.*, 145–6).

36. Reed, ii, 562; WW & MW to DW, 19 or 20 [*r*.21] Aug [1814] (*Supp.*, 149).

37. WW to FW, 26 Apl & 16 Jul & to SR, 5 May 1814 (*MY*, ii, 144, 149–50, 148); MW to WW, [1 Aug 1810] (Darlington, 49); WW to SGB, 23 Jun [1814] (*Supp.*, 143–4). WW's sonnet *November, 1813*, written in response to the Allied victory at Leipzig, was published in the *Courier* on 1 Jan 1814 (*Poems*, i, 862, 1045).
38. DW to CC, 24 Apl [1814] (*MY*, ii, 142); RS to J. Rickman, 16 Jun & to T. Southey, 10 Jul 1814 (*RSLC*, iv, 79; *RSNL*, ii, 101–2).
39. WW to RW, [Jul], to FW, 16 Jul & to LL, 18 Jul [1814] (*MY*, ii, 149, 150–51); SH, Notes for a Tour of Scotland, 1814: DC 77 p.1; SH to Mrs TH, [3 Aug 1814] (*LSH*, 72); Reed, ii, 556 & n.19; JL, *Diaries*, i, 37 [19 Jul 1814]. BM had repaid the £200 outstanding on the capital of his loan from WW on 17 May, though the debt would not be finally cleared until 27 Dec 1817: Reed, ii, 553.
40. SH, Notes for a Tour of Scotland, 1814: DC 77 pp.3, 8, 20. The route is derived from SH's Notes & SH to Mrs TH, 2 Sep [1814] (*LSH*, 78–9).
41. SH, Notes for a Tour of Scotland, 1814: DC 77 pp.6, 10, 11–12, 34; WW & MW to DW, 19 or 20 [*r.*21] Aug [1814] (*Supp.*, 149); SH to Mrs TH, [3 Aug 1814] (*LSH*, 72).
42. Ibid.; SH, Notes for a Tour of Scotland, 1814: DC 77 p.15.
43. Ibid., p.35; SH to Mrs TH, 2 Sep [1814] (*LSH*, 79); Gillies, *Memoirs of a Literary Veteran*, ii, 142–4; WW, 'From the dark chambers of dejection freed', ll.13–14 (*Poems*, ii, 299); *IF*, 2; WW to R.P. Gillies, 12 Nov 1814 (*MY*, ii, 168). In 1813 Robert Pearce Gillies (1788–1858) published *Childe Alarique, a poet's reverie with other poems* and a series of essays in the *Ruminator*, written with Sir Egerton Brydges (1762–1832).
44. Hogg, *Memoir of the Author's Life*, 68–70; WW to R.P. Gillies, 22 Dec 1814 (*MY*, ii, 180); *IF*, 59.
45. *IF*, 27–8; Hogg, *Memoirs of the Author's Life*, 69; SH, Notes for a Tour of Scotland, 1814: DC 77 pp.35–6; SH to Mrs TH, 2 Sep [1814] (*LSH*, 79). HCR, who met Robert Anderson (1750–1830) in 1821, described him as 'a lively old man, small and insignificant in his person, with the manner one should expect in a Scotch bookmaker': *HCRBW*, i, 269. WW's copy of Anderson's edition is at DC.
46. SH to Mrs TH, 2 Sep [1814] (*LSH*, 78); WW to J.G. Lockhart, 27 Apl [1838] (*LY*, iii, 562).
47. SH to Mrs TH, [3 Aug 1814] (*LSH*, 77).
48. Hogg, *Memoir of the Author's Life*, 70–71. Hogg's autobiography is notoriously unreliable. He relates this incident (which also appeared in the *Noctes Ambrosianae* of the *Edinburgh Review*) as his justification for parodying WW in his *Poetic Mirror* (1816). Even Hogg, who admitted he had 'never met with any thing but the most genuine kindness' from WW, casts doubt on its veracity by his admission, 'I have always some hopes that de Quincey [who reported supposed words] was *leeing*, for I did not myself hear Wordsworth utter the words.' WW himself dismissed it as a 'silly story' and pointed out that Hogg's memory was at fault: there had been no evening party and Wilson and Hogg had returned to RM from Grasmere, having observed the phenomenon, to draw it to the Ws attention. WW never used the word 'fellow' in any circumstances, but admitted it was 'possible and not improbable' that he might have used a contemptuous expression, having been irritated by Hogg's conceited remarks on subjects he knew nothing about. WW to EQ, [14 Apl 1832] (*LY*, ii, 517–18).
49. Hogg, *Memoir of the Author's Life*, 37; WW to R.P. Gillies, 12 & 23 Nov 1814 (*MY*, ii, 167; *Supp.*, 156). Hogg claimed WW's recalling his poem (to which he added four new stanzas) was one of the reasons for abandoning his original project. This is untrue. WW told Gillies that *Yarrow Visited* would no longer serve Hogg's purpose, as it would be published in *Poems 1815* before Hogg's anthology was ready, but offered to send a substitute.
50. WW to R. Anderson, 17 Sep 1814 & 4 Jan [*r.*Feb] 1815 (*MY*, ii, 151–5, 193).
51. *HCRBW*, ii, 147 [13 Aug 1814]. Longman accounts for *The Excursion* opened on 4 Aug: Reed, ii, 562.
52. Hazlitt, *Examiner*, 21 & 28 Aug & 2 Oct 1814 (Smith, 147–9); CL to WW, [19 Sep 1814] (*LCL*, iii, 112). Hazlitt's 'detention' of CL's copy delayed CL's reading and reviewing it.
53. Jeffrey, *Edinburgh Review*, Nov 1814 (Hayden, 39–52); DW to CC, 16 Mar [1814] (*MY*, ii, 213). Sydney Smith, who found WW 'uninteresting' and had not read the review, asked Jeffrey, 'was it worth while to take any more notice of a man respecting whom the public opinion is so completely made up? and do not such repeated attacks upon the man wear in some little degree the shape of persecution?': *The Letters of Sydney*

Smith, edited by Nowell C. Smith (Oxford, Clarendon Press, 1953), i, 250.

54. Anon. reviews in *Monthly Review*, Feb 1815 & *British Critic*, May 1815 (Smith, 186, 194–5).

55. *HCRBW*, ii, 481; *British Critic*, May 1815 & James Montgomery, *Eclectic Review*, Jan 1815 (Smith, 195, 177, 175). See Gill, *Wordsworth and the Victorians*, ch.2 for a fascinating account of how those with as disparate beliefs as Quakers and Roman Catholics claimed WW for their own.

56. CL to WW, [19 Sep] & [28 Dec] [1814] & [7 Jan 1815] (*LCL*, iii, 112, 125, 129–30). CL made the comparison with Piers Plowman to vindicate WW's choice of a pedlar as his philosophical mouthpiece: CL, *Quarterly Review*, Oct 1814 (Hayden, 60).

57. WW to RS & to CC, [Jan 1815] (*MY*, ii, 187, 188–91); *HCRBW*, i, 159. WW told HCR in private conversation in 1812 that 'he cd not feel with the Unitarians in any way. Their religion allows no room for Imagination & satisfies none of the cravings of the Soul – I can feel more sympathy with the Orthodox believer who needs a Redeemer & who sensible of his own demerits flies for refuge to him (though perhaps I do not want one for myself) than with the cold & rational notions of the Unitarian': ibid., 87.

58. RS to B. Barton, 19 Dec, to WS & J. Hogg, 24 Dec 1814 (*RSLC*, 97, 91; *RSNL*, ii, 112); WW & DW to CC, 31 Dec [1814] & DW to SH, 18 Feb [1815] (*MY*, ii, 182, 202). SGB warned Farington in 1809 that 'Lady B was as intolerant in Her opinion [on WW's poems] as Bishop Bonner on religious matters'; when she eulogized WW's *Convention of Cintra*, SGB commented 'drily', that she 'spoke of the Book as if she was *employed to sell it*': *Farington Diary*, ix, 4325–6, 3482.

59. WW & DW to CC, 31 Dec [1814] (*MY*, ii, 182); WW to A. Hodgson, 26 Sep 1814 (*Supp.*, 153–4); W. Cookson to WW, 20 Aug 1814: WLMS/A/Cookson/2 p.1. The editor of *Supp.* does not make the connection between WW's reply to Abigail Hodgson, of 21 Great Street, Liverpool, and the Liverpool Quakeress referred to in WW's letter to CC, but the two would appear to be the same person.

60. CL to WW, [19 Sep] & [28 Dec] [1814] (*LCL*, iii, 112–13, 125); WW & DW to CC, 31 Dec 1814 (*MY*, ii, 182).

61. STC to LMB, 3 Apl 1815 (*STCL*, iv, 564). STC's letter sought the return of a copy of his verses written in 1806 at Coleorton after hearing WW's recitation of *The Prelude*, so that he could publish it. LMB showed WW this letter when he was in London in May, prompting WW's letter of 22 May 1815 (see n.62), begging STC 'out of kindness' not to publish the poem because the commendation would be injurious to them both 'and my work when it appears, would labour under a great disadvantage in consequence of such a precursorship of Praise'. STC disregarded this plea, publishing the poem in 1817 (*STCP*, 572).

62. WW to STC, 22 May 1815 (*MY*, ii, 238).

63. STC to WW, 30 May 1815 (*STCL*, iv, 574–5).

64. Only three months before receiving STC's letter, WW had 'one of his weeks of rest' prior to resuming work on *The Recluse*: 'he intends completely to plan the first part of the Recluse before he begins the composition, he must read many Books before he will fairly set to labour again': DW to SH, 18 Feb [1815] (*MY*, ii, 200). WW would often announce his intention to make a start on *The Recluse* throughout the coming years, but would never actually do so.

Chapter 17

chapter title: 'Increasing influence', R.P. Gillies to WW, 15 Oct 1816: WLMS/A/Gillies, RP/5 p.2.

picture: CL by Robert Hancock, 1798.

1. WW to TdQ, [late Oct 1814] (*MY*, ii, 163–4). The copy belonged to SH, who was on a visit to Hindwell: MW to DW, 22 Oct [1814] (*LMW*, 18). Longman still had 230 copies of WW's *Poems, in Two Volumes* (1807) in stock, so there was no real need for a new edition: *Prose*, iii, 57.

2. MW to DW, [29 Oct 1814] (*LMW*, 22–3, 25); WW, *Laodamia* (*Poems*, ii, 302–7). The poem was written very quickly, but, years later, WW changed the ending and, as a result, 'it cost me more trouble than almost anything of equal length I have ever written': *IF*, 16.

3. DW to CC, 9 Oct [1814] (*MY*, ii, 157, 160–61); Mrs TH to TM, 27 Nov & 27 Oct [1814]: WLMS/H/1/5/33 pp.1–2, 4 & 32 p.2. TH's new estate was near Presteigne and cost him £10,200. JM had moved to the Stow after the marriage of his sister to TH and lived there alone till his death in 1866; he regularly stayed at Hindwell with the

Hutchinsons and they with him. The house he built, now Stowe Farm, can still be seen above Stowe on the A438 between Whitney-on-Wye and Winforton; SH stayed with him at Xmas 1814 to design his pleasure gardens: JM to TM, 17 Dec 1814: WLMS/H/1/14/29 pp.1–3.

4. WW to DW, [4], to SH [6] & [10], to RW, 15 & WW & DW to CC, 31 Dec 1814 (*MY*, ii, 172–6, 183).

5. WW to CW, 26 Nov & DW to CC, 24 Apl [1814] (ibid., 171–2, 141); SH to Mrs TH, [1 Aug 1813] (*LSH*, 58); MW to DW, [29 Oct 1814] (*LMW*, 24). SH declared Miss Fletcher 'so deaf that Music is the only way in which you can hold communion with her': SH to Jo H, 24 Nov 1815 (*LSH*, 87).

6. WW to R.P. Gillies, 23 Nov & to CW, 26 Nov [1814] (*Supp.*, 156; *MY*, ii, 171); SGB to WW, 20 & 30 Nov 1814: WLMS/A/Beaumont/49 p.3 & 50 pp.2–3. WW had offered to dedicate *Poems, 1815* to SGB in Jun, adding that he could have *The White Doe* or *Peter Bell* instead, if he preferred. SGB chose the last, but WW persuaded him to accept *Poems*, because the publication was imminent: WW to SGB, 23 Jun [1814] (*Supp.*, 146); SGB to WW, 4 & 19 Jul 1814: WLMS/A/Beaumont/47 pp.1–2 & 48 p.1.

7. WW to R.P. Gillies, 22 Dec 1814 & to STC, [5 May 1809] (*MY*, ii, 180; i, 334–6); *HCRBW*, i, 89, 93.

8. WW, Preface to *Poems, in Two Volumes, 1815* (*Prose*, iii, 26–9).

9. Anon., *Monthly Review*, Nov 1815 (Smith, 216).

10. WW & DW to CC, 31 Dec [1814] & to DS, [Jan or Feb 1815] (*MY*, ii, 181, 198). No letters from TdQ were published in the *Courier*.

11. WW, 'Essay Supplementary to the Preface, 1815' (*Prose*, iii, 64–5, 66, 83, 84). TdQ, who supervised the printing of the preface and essay in London, persuaded WW to leave out some direct attacks on Jeffrey: WW to TdQ, [*c*.5 Feb 1815] (*MY*, ii, 195); *HCRBW*, i, 161.

12. Ibid., 165, 166; W.R. Lyall, *Quarterly Review*, Oct 1815 (Hayden, 73); Anon., *Monthly Review*, Nov 1815 (Smith, 217).

13. DW to Mrs CW, [27 Feb] & to SH, 8 Apl [1815] (*MY*, ii, 206–7, 226); MW to DW, [29 Oct 1814] (*LMW*, 26).

14. DW to CC, 11 Apl [1815] & 9 Oct [1814] & to SH, 8 Apl [1815] (*MY*, ii, 229, 158, 227).

15. MW to DW, [29 Oct 1814] (*LMW*, 25–6); WW & DW to CC, [31 Dec 1814] & DW to SH, 18 Feb & 8 Apl & to CC, 16 Mar [1815] (*MY*, ii, 185–6, 199, 227–8, 211–12). AV had not dared to write openly of Baudouin's return, but underlined 'Messieurs B send their regard' to make the Ws understand. It is not clear whether Baudouin returned of his own accord or with Bonaparte's troops.

16. MW to TM, 28 Mar [1815] (*LMW*, 30); DW to SH, 8 Apl [1815] (*MY*, ii, 226). MW enclosed a letter to AV for TM to forward.

17. MW, WW & DW to SH, 2 May [1815] (ibid., 233–4); RS to JC, 17 Apl & to G.C. Bedford, 4 Nov 1814 (*RSNL*, ii, 93–5, 109); RS to J.T. Coleridge, 14 Mar 1814 (Ashton, 288). WW truly remarked that RS had 'a little world dependent upon his industry': WW to TP, 28 Apl 1814 (*MY*, ii, 146).

18. WW to TP, 28 Apl 1814 & 13 Mar 1815 (ibid., 145–6, 209–10); RS to JC, 27 Oct 1814 (*RSNL*, ii, 107–8). DW had written to Wade, on behalf of Mrs STC, as long ago as 27 Mar 1814, asking how STC planned to provide for HC's education: DW to J. Wade, 27 Mar 1814 (*MY*, ii, 133).

19. WW to J.T. Coleridge, 9 [May] & to LL, 6 May [1815] (ibid., 235); MW to TM, [*p.m.*8 May 1816 (*r.*1815)] (*LMW*, 30–31); RS to H.H. Southey, 16 May 1815 (*RSNL*, ii, 122); SH to Mrs TH, [29 (*r.*28) Jun 1815] (*LSH*, 81–2). The Ws did not pre-book their lodgings, but took the first empty ones they found.

20. WW to J.T. Coleridge, 9 [May] & to WS, [*c.*23 May] [1815] (*MY*, ii, 235–6, 239); WS to RS, 20 Jun & to WW, [Apl/Jun] 1815 (*LWS*, iv, 70; *HCRWC*, ii, 845). The portrait had been purchased from a pawnbroker by CL's brother: CL to WW, [16 & 28 Apl 1815] (*LCL*, iii, 140, 148).

21. WW to W. Wilberforce, 20 May & WW & DW to SH, 16 Mar [1815] (*Supp.*, 158; *MY*, ii, 219); W. Wilberforce to WW, 23 May 1815: WLMS/A/Wilberforce/1; Pollock, *Wilberforce*, 255–6; Moorman, ii, 282. JM was thinking of selling his farm, by which he had lost £3,000; in Jul he secured a rent reduction from £980 to £800 p.a. in recognition of his genuine difficulties. GH, who had also taken a farm of his own, the Porth, at New Radnor, had to sell his cattle to pay the rent: JM to TM, 24 Mar, 4 Apl, 26 May & 12 Jul 1815: WLMS/H/1/14/31–5.

22. *HCRBW*, i, 165–6, 166, 168, 167; CL to WW, [?16 May 1815] (*LCL*, iii, 158 & n.2). Eliza O'Neill

(1791–1872), an Irish actress, made her sensational début as Juliet at Covent Garden on 6 Oct 1814; it was said that men were carried from her tragic performances in a dead faint.

23. *HCRBW*, ii, 167; B. Field to WW, 10 Apl 1828: WLMS/A/Field/1. Thomas Massa Alsager (1779–1846) was an intimate friend of CL and HCR; he owned the copy of Chapman's *Homer* which inspired Keats's famous sonnet; Thomas Noon Talfourd (1795–1854) was introduced by CL to WW as 'my only admirer', became CL's biographer and, as an MP, agitated for the reform of copyright law with WW's backing; Barron Field (1786–1846), a future Judge of the Supreme Court in NSW, Australia, and Chief Justice of Gibraltar, wrote a memoir of WW which WW persuaded him not to publish (Prance, 8, 320, 116–17).

24. *HCRBW*, i, 169–70; MW to DW, [29 Oct 1814] (*LMW*, 24); BRH to WW, 15 Apl 1817: WLMS/A/Haydon/9 p.2. Bonaparte's defeat at Waterloo in Jun 'prostrated' Hazlitt in mind and body: 'he walked about, unwashed, unshaved, hardly sober by day, and always intoxicated by night, literally, without exaggeration, for weeks': BRH, *Autobiography*, 283.

25. BRH to WW, 15 Apl 1817: WLMS/A/Haydon/9 p.2; WW to L. Hunt, 12 Feb 1815 & to SGB, 23 Jun [1814] (*MY*, ii, 195; *Supp.*, 144–5 & n.5); James Henry Leigh Hunt (1784–1859) was editor of the *Examiner* from 1808 and had recently been released from prison for publishing animadversions on the Prince Regent. Moorman, ii, 278, is mistaken in thinking WW *sent* Hunt a copy of *Poems, 1815* with his letter of 12 Feb 1815 pasted inside: copies were not sent out till Apl.

26. L. Hunt to WW, 28 May 1815 (*Supp.*, 144n.5); BRH, *Diary*, i, 451; *The Autobiography of Leigh Hunt*, ii, 20. WW and Hunt did not meet again for 30 years. When they did, Hunt found WW's manner greatly superior to that of their first meeting and noticed he no longer uttered scornful criticisms of other authors.

27. BRH to WW, [1804]: WLMS/A/Haydon/1; BRH, *Diary*, i, 446; BRH, *Autobiography*, 279. Benjamin Robert Haydon (1786–1846) championed the Elgin marbles as a model for anatomical study and campaigned for their purchase by the British Museum.

28. BRH, *Diary*, i, 45; BRH to WW, 18 Nov 1816: WLMS/A/Haydon/7 p.2. BRH took a life-mask of Keats the following year: Motion, *Keats*, 140.

29. WW to SGB, 23 Jun [1814] & to J. Scott, 14 May 1815 (*Supp.*, 145; *MY*, ii, 237); J. Scott, review in the *Champion*, 25 Jun 1815 (Hayden, 65, 66); WW, *A Poet's Epitaph*, ll.45–52 (*Poems*, i, 397). John Scott (1783–1821) was editor of the *Champion* (1815–17) and the *London Magazine* (1820–21).

30. BRH to WW, 18 Nov 1816: WLMS/A/Haydon/7 p.3. The phrase 'creating the taste by which he is to be enjoyed' had been coined by STC, but WW quoted it frequently, most recently in his 'Essay, Supplementary to the Preface' (*Prose*, iii, 80).

31. WW, *The White Doe* (*Poems*, i, 741–97). After the second edition in 1820, WW replaced the opening sonnet, 'Weak is the will of Man, his judgement blind' (ibid., 738), with a quotation from *The Borderers*. Much to WW's annoyance, his dedicatory poem, 'In trellised shed with clustering roses gay' (ibid., 742–3), appeared in the *Courier* on 17 May 1815, without his permission and with 'vile incorrectness': WW to STC, 22 May 1815 (*MY*, ii, 238–9); Reed, ii, 602. WW claimed that the expensive format was intended to show the world his own opinion of the poem's value: *JTM*, i, 362 [27 Oct 1820].

32. Anon., *New British Lady's Magazine* (Jul 1815) (Hayden, 67, 68, 70).

33. F. Jeffrey, *Edinburgh Review* (Oct 1815), Anon., *Eclectic Review* (Jan 1816), *Monthly Review* (Nov 1815) & *Gentleman's Magazine* (Dec 1815) (Smith, 226–7, 238, 232, 233).

34. DW to CC, 28 Jun [1815] (*MY*, ii, 239–40); SH to Mrs TH, [29 (*r.*28) Jun 1815] (*LSH*, 80, 82); Mrs CW, *Diary*, 1815: WLMS/1/8/7 26–7th week. According to Mrs CW, the Ws arrived on 28 Jun and left on 3 Jul; her baby was due at the end of Sep.

35. DW to CC, 28 Jun [1815] (*MY*, ii, 240–41).

36. Ibid.; DW to CC, 15 Aug [1815] (ibid., 245). HCR was asked to escort DW's 'friend' to England, but his tour, from 6 Aug to 2 Sep 1815, took him only through Belgium and Holland: CC to MW, 29 Jul 1815: WLMS/A/Clarkson/19 p.2; *HCRD*, i, 258–62.

37. RS to H.H. Southey, 23 Aug 1815 (*RSLC*, iv, 121–3).

38. H. Parry to WW, 29 Jul 1815: WLMS/A/Parry/2; *HCRBW*, i, 169. WW's objection, like HCR's, was that going to see the portrait implied an act of homage 'to the shadow of a

villain'; DW also declared herself sick of 'the adulation, the folly, the idle Curiosity which was gathered together round the ship that held the dastardly spirit', which does not imply a favourable reception for Parry's gift: DW to CC, 15 Aug [1815] (*MY*, ii, 244).

39. Ibid., 245; SH to TM, [15 Oct 1815] (*LSH*, 84–5). For Tillbrooke's accident, see SH to Mrs TH, 29 Sep [1813] (ibid., 67).

40. DW to JPM, 13 [*r.*15] Oct & WW to CW, [13 Oct] [1815] (*MY*, ii, 250–3); CW to WW, 7 Oct [1815]: WLL/CW/41; Overton & Wordsworth, *Christopher Wordsworth*, 13.

41. DW to JPM, 13 [*r.*15] Oct & to CC, 31 Dec [1815] (*MY*, ii, 253, 266); CW to DW, 30 Oct 1815 & to WW, 20 Mar 1816: WLL/CW/42 & 43. Francis Merewether reported that CW's resolution was 'wonderful'; if he was overpowered by his grief for a few minutes, he recovered himself and felt it his duty to resist giving way. He 'even seemed' to enjoy the presence of his sons: SGB to WW, 19 Nov 1815: WLMS/A/Beaumont/56 p.1.

42. CL to SH, 19 Oct 1815 (*LCL*, iii, 202–3); WW to CC, 25 Nov 1815 (*MY*, ii, 256–7). CC sent the Ws Luff's unpublished journal, written during his years in Mauritius: DW to CC, 23 Dec [1815] (ibid., 259–60).

43. DW to CC, 16 Mar & 15 Aug [1815] & WW & DW to CC, 31 Dec [1814] (ibid., 213, 247, 184); LMB to WW, 29 Apl 1815: WLMS/A/Beaumont/53 p.2. One of the Ws' neighbours, Mrs Green, a blue-stocking widow with £1,500 p.a. refused to spend two guineas for a part of a work, saying she would borrow *The Excursion* from a circulating library.

44. MW to DW, 22 Oct 1814 (*LMW*, 19); J.H. Reynolds to WW, 12 Nov 1814: WLMS/A/Reynolds/1; B. Barton to WW, 22 Dec 1815: WLMS/A/Barton/1; WW to B. Barton, 12 Jan 1816 (*MY*, ii, 269–70). John Hamilton Reynolds (1796–1852) published two volumes of verse (1814), sent WW his poem *The Naiad* (1816) and published a parody of WW's *Peter Bell* (1819). Bernard Barton (1784–1849), a bank clerk, published *Metrical Effusion* (1812).

45. BRH to WW, 15 Apl 1817, 27 Nov & 29 Dec 1815: WLMS/A/Haydon/9 p.4, 2 p.2 & 3 pp.1, 4; WW to BRH, 12 Sep 1815 (*MY*, ii, 248–9); WW, *To B.R. Haydon* (*Poems*, ii, 317–18). See also BRH, *Diary*, i, 491–2.

46. WW to BRH, 13 Jan [1816] & 21 Dec 1815 (*MY*, ii, 273, 257); WW, *September, 1815*, ll.12–14 (*Poems*, ii, 318–19). *To B.R. Haydon* was published in the *Champion* (4 Feb) and in the *Examiner* (31 Mar), *November I* in the *Examiner* and the *Champion* (28 Jan) and *September, 1815* in the *Examiner* (11 Feb). Despite their titles, WW states that all three were written the day after receiving BRH's letter and the following day: WW to BRH, 21 Dec 1815 (*MY*, ii, 258).

47. SH to Mrs TH [29 Jun 1815] (*LSH*, 81); DW to CC, 24 Apl & WW to CW, 26 Nov [1814]; DW to CW, 23 Dec [1815] (*MY*, ii, 143, 171, 261–2). They had married on 9 Feb 1814 at Addingham, Cumberland (Reed, ii, 549) but apparently the Ws did not find out till two months later; KJW was born on 29 Jan 1815.

48. DW to CC, 31 Dec & 15 Aug [1815] & WW to CW, 31 Jan [1816] (*MY*, ii, 263–7, 246, 279). WW & DW returned to RM on 14 Dec. In Mar 1816 Lloyd was placed in the Retreat, the famous Quaker asylum at York: WW to CW, 31 Jan & 25 Mar 1816 (ibid., 279, 292).

49. WW to CW, 12 & 31 Jan [1816] (ibid., 271–2, 278–9). WW turned down RW's offer of a £4,000 bond, accepting one for £3,000 instead: WW to BM, 29 Apl 1816 (ibid., 307).

50. WW to J. Scott, 29 Jan 1816 (ibid., 277); WW, *Occasioned by the Battle of Waterloo*, ll.9–14 (*Poems*, ii, 334); J. Scott to WW, 7 Feb 1816: WLMS/A/Scott, J/1 p.1. The two other sonnets were *Siege of Vienna Raised by John Sobieski February, 1816* and 'The Bard – whose soul is meek as dawning day' (ibid., 326, 333); all three were published in the *Champion* on 4 Feb 1816 (not 14 Feb, as *MY*, ii, 277n.).

51. WW, *Ode: The Morning of the Day Appointed for a General Thanksgiving. January 18, 1816*, ll.57–8, 91 (*Poems*, ii, 320–21).

52. WW to RS, [*c.*Jun 1816] (*MY*, ii, 324); WW, advertisement to *Thanksgiving Ode, January 18, 1816: With Other Short Pieces, Chiefly Referring to Recent Public Events* (Longman, 1816), iii–iv (Gill, 317).

53. WW to J. Scott, 11 & 21 Mar, to CW, 12 Mar & to R.P. Gillies, [*p.m.*9 Apl] 1816 (*MY*, ii, 284, 290, 287, 299).

54. WW to HCR, 2 Aug 1816 (ibid., 334). For the reviews in *Eclectic Review* (Jul 1816), *British Critic* (Sep 1816) and *Monthly Review* (Jan 1817), see Smith, 261–6. The 'Other Short Pieces' were *Ode:*

1814, Ode ['Who rises on the banks of Seine'], *Invocation to the Earth, February, 1816, The French Army in Russia 1812–13, On the Same Occasion, Ode: 1815, Feelings of a French Royalist, on the Disinterment of the Remains of the Duke D'Enghien*, the three sonnets sent to BRH in Dec 1815 and the three sonnets sent to Scott in Jan 1816. The book was published at WW's own cost.

55. WW to J. Scott, 22 Feb 1816 (*MY*, ii, 280); J. Gray to WW, 28 Nov 1815: WLMS/A/Gray/1 pp.3–4. The date of Gray's visit to RM is not known. Though not intending to solicit anything other than a private letter, Gray and Burns happily acquiesced in WW's decision to publish it: J. Gray to WW, 18 Mar 1816: WLMS/A/Gray/3.

56. WW, *A Letter To A Friend of Robert Burns* (*Prose*, iii, 121, 122, 127, 128, 112n.3). Aristarchus was a celebrated critic in charge of the Alexandrian Library in the second century BC. The *Letter* was seen through the press by CL, who let many errors slip through: CL to WW, 26 Apl & 23 Sep 1816 (*LCL*, iii, 214, 225).

57. J. Wilson, *Blackwood's Magazine*, Jun 1817 (Smith, 250); *HCRBW*, i, 220 [24 Feb 1818]. Wilson, while retaining good relations with WW personally, took every opportunity to snipe at him anonymously in the Edinburgh periodicals; unable to resist his own cleverness, he composed not only this review but a letter in defence of WW and a reply attacking the defence, all published in Jun, Oct & Nov 1817: Smith, 248–53.

58. DW to CC, 4 Apl [1816] (*MY*, ii, 293–4).

59. Caroline W, Marriage Certificate, 6 & 15 Mar 1816 (Legouis, 134–6). Legouis, 100, says the wedding took place on 28 Feb; the marriage contract was dated 16 Feb 1816.

60. DW to CC, 4 Apl [1816] (*MY*, ii, 296); Petition to Louis XVIII on behalf of AV, Mar–Apl 1816 (Legouis, 137–40). Twenty witnesses signed the petition, including the Marquis d'Avaray and the Comte de Salaberry, who attended the wedding. The latter, and his fellow guests Jean Marie Pardessus, a professor at the Ecole de Droit and member of the Chamber of Deputies, and the Baron de Tardif, also appended three personal letters witnessing AV's loyalty and active service to the royalist cause. Caroline's daughter, Louise Marie Caroline Dorothée Baudouin, the first of three, was born on 27 Dec 1816. WW was her godfather as well as her grandfather: Legouis, 106–7.

61. WW to CW, 12 Mar, DW to RW, 15 Mar & to CC, 26 May & WW to BM, 29 Apl & 3 May 1816 (*MY*, ii, 287, 288–9, 318, 307–8).

62. WW to CW, 3 May 1816 (ibid., 309–10); CW to WW, 4 May 1816: WLL/CW/44 pp.1–3; RW, Last Will & Testament, 6 May 1816: G18/1/1. Though RW's will empowered his executors to sell all his recent land purchases to clear his debts, WW rightly feared they would prove insufficient. RW's customary freeholds in Cumberland and Westmorland were to be held in trust for KJW till the age of 21, subject to an annual payment of £150 to his widow for life. Sockbridge, which KJW was to inherit, was to remain in trust for her until she remarried or died, when it would pass to WW; other properties were left in trust for DW and CW.

63. DW to CW, 14 [May], WW to CW, [20 May] & DW to CC, 26 May 1816 (*MY*, ii, 312–13, 315–16, 318); CW to WW, 15, 17, 18, 19 & 23 May 1816: WLL/CW/46–50, esp.46 p.2, 49 p.3 & 50 pp.1–2. CW conducted the funeral; the mourners were Mrs RW, Richard Addison (RW's business partner) and Curwen Gale (Capt JW's brother-in-law).

64. WW to CW, [20] & 23 May & 1 & 2 Jun & DW to WW, [19 Jul] 1816 (*MY*, ii, 315, 316–17, 321, 663, 329); CW to WW, 23 May 1816: WLL/CW/50 p.3. WW was still entreating Wilkinson to be a trustee in Nov, but by Dec was approaching Capt JW: WW to T. Hutton, 25 Nov, 6 Dec & [*c*.11 Dec] 1816 (*MY*, ii, 344–5, 347–8, 348).

65. WW to T. Hutton, 18 & 24 Jan, 13 & 17 Feb 1817 (ibid., 359, 363, 365, 366). The sale at Sockbridge was on 3 Mar 1817: WW to R. Lumb, 24 Feb & DW to CC, 2 Mar 1817 (ibid., 368, 372). HCR attended sales of RW's lands at Cockermouth and Ravenglass in Sep 1816, but their titles were still in dispute the following Feb, so the money cannot have been paid immediately: *HCRBW*, i, 191–2; WW to T. Hutton, 13 Feb 1817 (*MY*, ii, 365).

66. CW to WW, 24 & 27 Feb, 8 Mar & 4 Apl 1817: WLL/CW,54–7; WW to T. Hutton, 24 Feb & DW to CC, 2 Mar 1817 (*MY*, ii, 369, 372).

67. CW to WW, 4 & 30 Oct, 13 Nov 1817: WLL/CW/59, 60, 62. For the probate date, see CW to WW, 7 May 1819: WLL/CW/67 p.3. The Ws did make efforts to secure payment of small debts to those in need, such as Mary Ley, RW's London servant, who was owed £12: CW to WW, 4 Oct

1817: WLL/CW/59 p.2; E. Ley to RW, nd: WLMS/2/28. WW and DW were personally owed £2,766 by RW's estate: CW to WW, 24 Sep 1816: WLL/CW/53 p.1.

68. SH to TM, 14 Jul [1816] (*LSH*, 92–3); WW to LL, 28 Jul 1816 (*MY*, ii, 331). Ironically, the bishop's widow sent WW the customary mourning scarf and hat-band 'as a Mark of her respect': DW to WW, [19 Jul 1816] (ibid., 330).

69. WW to LL, 28 Jul 1816 (*MY*, ii, 331); SH to TM, 1 Nov & 14 Jul [1816] (*LSH*, 95, 93); S. Tilbrooke, *The Ivied Cot*, in SH to JM, [6–11 Aug 1816]: WLL/SH/27a pp.3–4; R.P. Gillies to WW, 15 Oct 1816: WLMS/A/Gillies/5 p.2.

70. SH to JM, [6–11 Aug 1816]: WLL/SH/27a pp.1–2; Blanshard, 60–61, pl.7a; RS to H.H. Southey, [17 Apl 1816] (*RSNL*, ii, 137). When Herbert died, SH brought Edith Southey and SC to RM to stay a week; WW offered to go over as and when needed or wanted: RS to G. Bedford, 18 Apl 1816 (*RSLC*, iv, 141); WW to RS, [21] & 26 Apl & DW to CC, 26 May [1816] (*MY*, ii, 305–6, 306–7, 319–20).

71. SH to JM, [6–11 Aug 1816]: WLL/SH/27a pp.1–2; WW to CW, 25 Mar 1816 (*MY*, ii, 291). George Hutchinson (b.1801) almost certainly boarded with Jackson, as DW had unsuccessfully solicited Tom Clarkson for him as a pupil on these terms: DW to CC, 28 Jun [1815] (ibid., 242).

72. WW to HCR, 2 Aug 1816 (ibid., 333–4); *HCRD*, i, 275–81; HCR to TR, 29 Sep 1816 (*HCRWC*, i, 89–90); WW to Revd W. Carr, 23 Sep 1816 (*MY*, ii, 335); *HCRBW*, i, 195; MAL to SH, [Nov 1816] (*LCL*, iii, 233).

73. *HCRBW*, i, 187, 195–6; MW to DW, [29 Oct 1814] (*LMW*, 24–5); SH to Jo H, 24 Nov 1815 (*LSH*, 88). The date the estrangement began is unclear but TdQ believed WW had alerted his mother in the autumn of 1815 that he was about to make an unsuitable marriage: Lindop, *TdQ*, 215–16.

74. WW to CL, 21 Nov [1816] (*Supp.*, 162); DW to CC, 2 Mar [1817] (*MY*, ii, 372). DW's remark that the newlyweds 'with their infant son are now spending their honeymoon in *our* cottage at Grasmere' (my italics) seems redolent of sexual jealousy.

75. WW to CL, 21 Nov [1816] (*Supp.*, 163–4, 163n.2).

76. J. Keats to BRH, 20 & [21] Nov [1816] (*The Letters of John Keats*, i, 117, 118–19). See also Motion, *Keats*, 128–9.

Chapter 18

chapter title: 'Bombastes Furioso', Nickname for WW during 1818 general election campaign: *MY*, ii, 471n.2.

picture: Lowther Castle and Park, Westmorland, engraved by Thomas Allom, after J. Thomas.

1. DW to CC, 10 Jan & 2 Mar 1817 (*MY*, ii, 353, 370). DW returned to RM on 17 Feb.

2. SH to TM, 5 Jan & to JM, 17 Feb 1817 (*LSH*, 97, 100, 103). SH returned to RM on 10 Feb.

3. SH to TM, 5 Jan & 21 Feb 1817 (ibid., 98, 108); WW to H. Parry, 17 Jan & to T. Hutton, 18 & 24 Jan & 17 Feb 1817 (*MY*, ii, 356–7, 359–60, 364, 366).

4. SH to TM, 21 Feb 1817 (*LSH*, 108); WW to BRH, 20 Jan & 7 Apl 1817 (*MY*, ii, 362, 376–7). For BRH's vignette of WW in the finished portrait (with a disembodied Keats perched on top of his head like a malevolent parrot), see Blanshard, pls.6a, 6b.

5. DW to CC, 13 Apl & 16 Oct [1817] (*MY*, ii, 380, 402); SH to TM, 15 May 1817 (*LSH*, 109); RS to Mrs RS, 17 May 1817 (*RSNL*, ii, 160–61). It seems improbable that RS failed to write his impressions directly to the Ws, but DW's brief account of the visit appears to be based on this letter to Mrs RS; one assumes a more detailed account was not entrusted to a letter but given in person on RS's return.

6. WW to BRH, 7 Apl & 20 Jan 1817 (*MY*, ii, 377 & n.2, 361). Scott's son had died while his parents were on their way to Italy, so there were close parallels with Catherine's death.

7. DW to CC, 13 Apl [1817] (ibid., 379); WW, *Vernal Ode*, ll.133–5 (*Poems*, ii, 352). DW claimed this was WW's first poem in 'more than a year and a half', but this is an exaggeration, as the poems published in *Thanksgiving Ode* were demonstrably written in Jan–Mar 1816.

8. WW, *Composed upon an Evening of Extraordinary Splendour and Beauty*, ll.61–80 (ibid., 358–9). It is an interesting insight into WW's changing religious views that this poem rejects the implicit pantheism of *Intimations of Immortality* and explicitly invokes the Deity.

9. WW, *Ode to Lycoris, May 1817*, *Ode to Lycoris* and *Sequel to 'Beggars' Composed Many Years After* (ibid.,

352–4, 367–8, 365–6); *IF*, 41–2; DW to JPM, 25 Jun [1817] (*MY*, ii, 394); Moorman, i, 521n.1 & ii, 304–5. A similar awareness of mortality runs through WW's *The Longest Day. Addressed to My Daughter, Dora* (*Poems*, ii, 359–62).

10. DW to CC, 16 Oct [1817] (*MY*, ii, 402); JM to TM, 26 Apl 1817: WLMS/H/1/14/41 p.2; Mrs TH to TM, 4 May [1817]: WLMS/H/1/5/42 pp.1–4; SH to TM, 15 May 1817 (*LSH*, 109). GH had taken the Porth in 1815; the rent reduction of 32½ per cent was made in Oct 1816: Mrs TH to TM, 27 Nov [1817]: WLMS/H/1/5/33 p.2; JM to TM, 24 Oct 1816: WLMS/H/1/14/40 p.2. For GH's amorous adventures, see Jo H to E. Monkhouse, 5 Sep 1815: WLMS/H/1/8/30 p.2; JM to TM, 26 Apl 1817: WLMS/H/1/14/41 p.2.

11. JM to TM, 24 Oct 1816 & 4 May 1815: WLMS/H/1/14/40 p.3 & 34 pp.2–3; Mrs TH, to SH, 25 May 1816: WLMS/H/1/5/36 pp.4–5; SH to Jo H, 24 Nov 1815 & to TM, 15 May 1817 (*LSH*, 89, 109); DW to CC, 13 Apl [1817] (*MY*, ii, 380).

12. SH to TM, 15 May & 28 Aug 1817 (*LSH*, 109, 110–11); DW to JPM, 25 Jun [1817] (*MY*, ii, 395); Jo H & SH to JM, 16 Sep [1817]: WLMS/H/1/8/33 pp.1–2.

13. Ibid., p.2.

14. Ibid., p.1; SH to TM, 28 Aug [1817] (*LSH*, 111); DW to JPM, 25 Jun & to CC, 16 Oct [1817] (*MY*, ii, 394–5, 401); Jo H & SH to JM, 16 Sep [1817]: WLMS/H/1/8/33 p.2. Capt JW, a widower, had married Elizabeth Littledale at Whitehaven on 16 Sep 1816: C. Stanger to J. Stanger [*p.m.*8 Sep] 1816: Moorsom Papers, 36/11 p.2.

15. WW to HCR, 24 Jun & to R.P. Gillies, 19 [Sep] 1817 (*MY*, ii, 392, 399); Jo H & SH to JM, 16 Sep [1817]: WLMS/H/1/8/33 pp.1–2, 4.

16. Blanshard, 35–6, 54–6 & pl.5; SH to TM, 28 Aug [1817] (*LSH*, 111); Jo H & SH to JM, 16 Sep [1817]: WLMS/H/1/8/33 pp.3–4. Richard Carruthers (1792–1876) gave up painting soon after completing this portrait, became a businessman in Lisbon and, having made a small fortune, returned to live at Carlisle. WW said of the engraving of this portrait that it was 'very quizzical – it looked like a man with a headache': J. Keymer, Conversation with WW, [Apl 1831]: WLMS/A/Keymer p.4.

17. CW to WW, 30 Oct & 13 Nov 1817: WLL/CW/60 p.3 & 62 p.4; SH to TM, [10 Dec 1817] (*LSH*, 112–13). 'Sundridge is a sweet place, I think the sweetest thing of the kind I ever saw. Perhaps a little too ornamental you would think for that purpose – but in no other respect unworthy of the exquisite picture in your Excursion. To have such a Place for occasional retirement from fatigue or disappointment, seemed to strengthen my hands greatly': CW to WW, 20 Mar 1816: WLL/CW/43 p.3.

18. *HCRBW*, i, 213; Jo H & SH to JM, 16 Sep [1817]: WLMS/H/1/8/33 p.4.

19. *HCRBW*, i, 210–11; BM, Memo, 27 Dec 1817: WLMS/A/Montagu/21; WW to BM, 11 May 1816 & to RW, 19 Aug [1813] (*MY*, ii, 311, 104–5).

20. Jo H to JM, 6 Aug [1813] & to Mrs TH, 30 Dec [1814]: WLMS/H/1/8/26 pp.3–4 & 27 p.5; WW to TP, 13 Mar 1815 (*MY*, ii, 210); CL to WW, 26 Apl 1816 (*LCL*, iii, 215); Ashton, 297. Jo H succeeded in finding out that STC had talked about HC going to college as if he expected it to happen, enabling WW and RS to proceed with their plans for HC's assistance.

21. *HCRBW*, i, 213; STC to W. Mudford, [18 Feb 1818] (*STCL*, iv, 839).

22. *HCRBW*, i, 214–16. William Hone (1780–1842) had written and published parodies of the Church Catechism, Athenasian Creed and the Litany. The Ws were ardently in favour of his prosecution, but STC and HCR (the latter a dissenter and, as a barrister, defender of a bookseller prosecuted for selling the works) both thought it mistaken. Hone's three separate trials for the offences, which HCR attended, were held on 18, 19 and 20 December, while the Ws were in London. Hone conducted his own defence and was acquitted on each charge by the jury: see *HCRD*, i, 302–7. DW said that Hone's acquittal was 'enough to make one out of love with English Juries': DW to TM, [*c.*5] Jan 1818 (*MY*, ii, 410); see also WW to DS, 7 Apl 1817 (ibid., 375).

23. CC to HCR, 15 Jan 1818 (*HCRWC*, i, 94); WW to J.P. Collier, Wednesday [Dec 1817/Jan 1818] (*MY*, ii, 664). John Payne Collier (1789–1883) was a reporter on *The Times*, literary critic and editor of Shakespeare and the Elizabethan poets: Prance, 76.

24. SH to Dora, 4 Jan & to TM, 25 Jan 1818 (*LSH*, 115, 119); *HCRBW*, i, 217; Blanshard, 59–61, pls.7a, 7b; WW & DW to WRH & E. Hamilton, 13 Jun 1831 (*LY*, ii, 400). Nash's picture is undated. BRH's is dated 19 Jan 1818 and was drawn for and presented to MW: according to BRH, his friends

thought it 'the best sketch I had ever made of any one': BRH to WW, 12 Sep [1818]: WLMS/A/Haydon/10 p.3.

25. BRH, *Autobiography*, 359–62; J. Keats to G. & T. Keats, 5 Jan 1818 (*The Letters of John Keats*, i, 198). In Nov 1818 Kingston was promoted to be one of the seven Commissioners of the Stamp Office.

26. J. Keats to G. & T. Keats, 5 Jan & to BRH, 21 Mar 1818 (ibid., 197, 251); Motion, *Keats*, 223. The incident sparked Keats's later sarcasm at the infallibility of WW's 'fireside Divan': J. Keats to BRH, 8 Apl 1818 (*The Letters of John Keats*, i, 265). His description of MW and SH suggests greater familiarity with WW's poetry than powers of observation; he seems to have thought SH was DW, a mistake he repeated later in the year: see pp.519, 893n.26.

27. J. Keats to J. Taylor, 10 Jan, to B. Bailey, 23 Jan, to G. & T. Keats, 21 Feb & to BRH, 10 Jan 1818 (ibid., 202, 212, 237, 203). BRH's famous rejoinder was, 'allow me to add sincerely a fourth to be proud of – *John Keats' genius!*': ibid., 203.

28. WW to LL, 13 Dec [1817], 1, 4, 21 & 23 Jan 1818 (*MY*, ii, 404, 407, 408, 414, 415–16). In his eagerness to secure the post, WW was even prepared to take the responsibility and do all the business, while granting Ramshay the whole of the profits, if he would resign.

29. Owen, *The Lowther Family*, 390–91, 395. William, Viscount Lowther (1787–1872), was MP for Cockermouth, 1808–13, then MP for Westmorland, 1813–31 and 1832–41. He was unmarried, but had three illegitimate children by different opera singers, the first born in 1818 in Paris (poignantly for WW, named Marie Caroline): all three were acknowledged and supported by him. He was succeeded by his nephew, son of his brother, Henry Cecil Lowther (1790–1867), who had married Lady Lucy Sherard in 1817.

30. WW to LL, 13 & 20 Dec [1817] & DW to TM, [*c*.5 Jan 1818] (*MY*, ii, 404–5, 404n.3, 406, 410).

31. WW to J. Scott, 25 Feb [1816] & to JL, 4 Dec 1821 (ibid., 283; *LY*, i, 97).

32. DW to CC, 26 May 1816 & 10 Jan 1817 (*MY*, ii, 319, 355); SH to TM, 14 Jul [1816] (*LSH*, 93); see also SH to TM, 1 Nov [1816] (ibid., 96]; DW to CC, 13 Apl 1817 (*MY*, ii, 380).

33. WW to DS, 7 Apl 1817, to FW, 19 Feb 1819 & to LL, 21 Jan 1818 (ibid., 375–6, 523, 413).

34. MW to TM, 23 Jan [1818] (*LMW*, 32–3); WW to LL, 18 [*r*.17] & 29 Jan 1818 (*MY*, ii, 410–11, 417–18). The Ws left London for Coleorton on 19 Jan, and Coleorton for Kendal on 27 Jan: WW to LL, 21 & 23 Jan 1818 (ibid., 412, 414–15, 416). SH remained at Playford Hall till the end of May: SH to TM, [17 Jan] & 21 [May] [1818] (*LSH*, 116–17, 138–9).

35. MW to TM, 3 Mar [1818] (*LMW*, 36); WW to LL, 10 Feb 1818 (*MY*, ii, 425).

36. WW to LL, 14 Mar, 13 Feb & [24 Mar] & DW to SH, [24 Mar] 1818 (ibid., 439, 426–7, 443–4, 448).

37. WW to LL, 6 Apl, 1 Jan & 14 Mar 1818 (ibid., 462, 407, 439). 'Every sentence almost in it reminds me of what I used to read in France, in the year 1792, when the Revolution was advancing towards the zenith of its horrors': WW to VL, 16 Mar 1818 (ibid., 440).

38. WW to LL, 10 & 13 Feb & [*c*.3 Aug] 1818 (ibid., 424–5, 427, 478); MW to TM, 3 Mar [1818] (*LMW*, 36–7); DS to WW, 9 Mar 1818: WLMS/A/Stuart/19 p.2; TdQ to WW, 14 Apl 1818 (Jordan, 319). For TdQ's wider role, see Lindop, *TdQ*, 224–31; Jordan, 278–333.

39. WW to LL, 31 Jan & [*c*.19] Feb 1818 (*MY*, ii, 420n.4, 434 & n.2). WW's 1st letter, dated 30 Jan, was published in the *Kendal Chronicle* on 31 Jan 1818, the 2nd and 3rd, dated 16 and 17 Feb, on 21 Feb 1818, and the 4th, dated 10 Mar, on 14 Mar 1818. A 5th undated letter, signed 'An Enemy to Detraction', appeared in the *Westmorland Gazette* on 31 Dec 1818 (*Prose*, iii, 202–4). WW wrote two articles as 'Anti-Janus', attacking Whig claims that the militia was a conscription and that the yeomanry were being unfairly taxed; these were also published in the *Westmorland Gazette*, on 23 May and 6 Jun 1818, and circulated as handbills: WW, *Deception Exposed* (*Supp.*, 263–74).

40. WW to LL, 10 Feb, to TM, [14 Feb] & to VL, 4 Apl 1818 (*MY*, ii, 425, 430, 459); WW, *Two Addresses to the Freeholders of Westmorland* (*Prose*, iii, 149–93). The prefatory advertisement is dated 26 Mar 1818 and 'To the Reader' 4 Apl 1818, but WW's letter to VL asks him to approve the text so that it can be put into immediate circulation.

41. WW to LL, 18 Feb & 2 May 1818 (*MY*, ii, 431, 469). WW's public defence of the indefensible

was that there were no other Tory candidates willing or able to stand forward, so the Lowthers were candidates by default: WW, *Two Addresses to the Freeholders of Westmorland* (*Prose*, iii, 155–6). Prince Leopold of Saxe-Coburg (1790–1865) had been granted an annuity of £50,000 p.a. on his marriage in 1816 to Princess Charlotte; she died the following year.

42. WW to LL, [*c.*25 Jan] & [*c.*11 May] [1818] (*MY*, ii, 416, 471). WW also refused to ask permission for JM's friends to shoot on Lowther land as 'it might seem as if one was setting a price upon one's services': WW to JM, 23 Jul 1818 (ibid., 477).

43. WW to LL, [*c.*19] Feb 1818 (ibid., 434, 471n.2); SH to TM, 22 Feb & 13 Apl [1818] (*LSH*, 125, 132). Bombastes Furioso was the hero of a burlesque of that name by William Barnes Rhodes (1772–1826), published in 1810; the name was applied to anyone speaking pompously. Crackanthorpe had boasted that TC's support would bring 50 votes to Brougham: WW to LL, 18 Feb & 11 Mar & to VL, [27 Mar] 1818 (*MY*, ii, 432, 437, 451).

44. DW to TM, 3 Mar, WW to VL, 16 Mar & to LL, [24 Mar] & DW to SH, [24 Mar] 1818 (ibid., 436, 441–5, 445–9); SH to TM, 13 Apl [1818] (*LSH*, 132); MW to TM, [24 Mar 1818] (*LMW*, 38, 39).

45. Jo H to SH, 15 Jul 1818: WLMS/H/1/8/35 p.2; DW to CC, 18 Sep & WW to VL, 18 Jul [1818] (*MY*, ii, 481, 475 & n.2).

46. TdQ to WW, 27 Sep [1818] (Jordan, 323–5); WW to VL, 6 & 23 Oct, 8 Nov, 6 & 8 Dec 1818, 2 & 10 Jan 1819 (*MY*, ii, 489, 503–4, 506–7, 511, 512, 515, 516–17); VL to WW, 22 & 29 Oct [1818]: WLMS/A/Lowther/53 p.2 & 54 p.4. Before this incident with Fleming, DW believed they had lost no old friends, but gained some new ones (including the Norths) by their advocacy of the Lowther cause: DW to CC, 18 Sep 1818 (*MY*, ii, 481).

47. WW to VL, 18 Jul, to LL, [*c.*3 Aug] & to TM, 4 Dec 1818 (ibid., 476, 478, 509 & n.5); MW to TM, 15 Nov [1818] (*LMW*, 40). Betty and Jonathan Yewdale, parents of the Ws' former maid, had spent Christmas at RM: DW to TM, [*c.*5] Jan 1818 (*MY*, ii, 409). A new freehold could be created from a customary tenancy, if the landlord consented.

48. CW to WW, 6 Feb 1819: WLL/CW/65 pp.1–2; WW to LL, 28 Nov 1818 (*MY*, ii, 508). CW had just sat next to Brougham at a parliamentary dinner; though 'mutually civil . . . I was much struck with the disagreeableness of his countenance – and remarked that his left cheek, and his nose was in a sort of convulsive twitch, the whole of the afternoon. I do not know whether this is habitual to him; or that he may be in a greater degree of irritable excitement than usual – but the effect was exceedingly unpleasant.'

49. J. Keats to T. Keats, 25–7 & 29 Jun & to G. & G. Keats, 27–8 Jun 1818 (*The Letters of John Keats*, i, 299, 300, 306, 302–3). Did Keats again confuse SH with DW? See pp.511, 891n.26.

50. WW to LL, 23 Aug & DW to CC, 18 Sep 1818 (*MY*, ii, 479, 482–3); W. Wilberforce to DW, 1 Jul & 10 Aug 1818: WLMS/A/Wilberforce/2 & 3.

51. T. Arnold to S. Arnold, 5 Sep 1818: WLMS/A/Arnold/1 pp.1–3; DW to CC, 18 Sep 1818 (*MY*, ii, 481–2). Thomas Arnold (1795–1842) would later become a close friend of WW and build a house, Fox How, on Loughrigg, overlooking Rydal.

52. MW to SH, [1 Dec 1818] (*LMW*, 41).

53. *STCBL*, i, 196; WW, *The River Duddon, A Series of Sonnets* (London, Longman et al., 1820), 38.

54. BRH to WW, 12 Sep [1818]: WLMS/A/Haydon/10 pp.4–5; CW to WW, 17 Apl 1819: WLL/CW/66 p.4; DW to CC, 12 Jan [1819] (*MY*, ii, 520).

55. WW to TM, 4 Dec 1818 (ibid., 509); CW to WW, 14 Dec 1818: WLL/CW/63 pp.1–3; MW to TM, 18 Dec [1818] (*LMW*, 44–6); RS to W. Browne, 31 Dec 1818 (*RSNL*, ii, 194); SH to TM, 16 Jan [1819] (*LSH*, 149). Derwent Coleridge, ambitious to go to Cambridge and become a clergyman, had found himself a place as a private tutor near Ulverston so that he could study privately to prepare himself; he called at RM on 6 Dec and tried to encourage JW3, without much success: DW to CC, 12 Jan [1819] (*MY*, ii, 520).

56. MW to TM, 6 & 18 Dec [1818] & 12 Jan [1819] (*LMW*, 42–3, 45, 48); WW to CW, 1 Jan 1819 (*MY*, ii, 513–14); SH to TM, 16 Jan [1819] (*LSH*, 149). See also DW to CC, 12 Jan [1819] (*MY*, ii, 519).

57. SH to TM, 16 Jan [1819] (*LSH*, 149); CW to WW, 6 Feb 1819: WLL/CW/65 p.4; DW to CC, 12 Jan [1819] (*MY*, ii, 519). 'Really your time is too

valuable for such occupations': CW to WW, 17 Apl 1819: WLL/CW/66 p.4.

58. RS to W. Browne, 31 Dec 1818 (*RSNL*, ii, 192); SH to TM, 13 Apl [1818] (*LSH*, 133); DW to JPM, [14] Oct [1818] & to CC, 12 Jan [1819] (*MY*, ii, 496, 519); SC to E. Crump, 27 Feb 1819: WLMS/A/SC/1 p.3.

59. Mrs STC to TP, [1818 (*r*.1819)] (Sandford, 283); WW to LL, 13 Jan 1819 (*MY*, ii, 521); SGB to WW, 23 Mar 1819: WLMS/A/Beaumont/65 p.3; CW to WW, 17 Apl 1819: WLL/CW/66 p.4. WW had his name removed from the list of magistrates (though he had never been sworn in, so could not act) in Nov 1828: WW to LL, [mid-Nov 1828] (*LY*, i, 660).

60. E.g. WW asked Spedding, as executor of WW's old college friend John Baldwin (brother-in-law of JL), to pay the legacy duties through his district rather than direct to head office; he also sought the registration of the new Kendal–Ambleside coach at Ambleside rather than Kendal: WW to J. Spedding, [1 Mar] & to Mr White, 3 Apl 1819 (*MY*, ii, 525–6, 531).

61. MW to SH, [1 Dec 1818] (*LMW*, 41); WW, 'Pure element of waters!', *Malham Cove* and *Gordale* (*Poems*, ii, 376–8); WW to the *Westmorland Gazette*, 3 Feb & to FW, 19 Feb 1819 (*MY*, ii, 522–3). WW added a fourth sonnet which he had just completed: WW, *Composed during a Storm* (*Poems*, ii, 397).

62. Blanshard, 57–8, pl.42a; SH to TM, 3 May [1819] (*LSH*, 152); MW to TM, 12 Jan [1819] (*LMW*, 50). The magazine had approached TM for biographical details, but the Ws had asked him not to deal with them, because being related to WW might give 'a sort of sanction to any absurdities which it may contain': MW to TM, 6 Dec [1818] (ibid., 43).

63. Ticknor, *Life, Letters and Journals*, i, 237–8. George Ticknor (1791–1871) was Professor of Belles Lettres, French and Spanish at Harvard University (1819–35) and a friend of the American painter Washington Allston. Another American, the Quaker scientist John Griscom (1774–1852), called at RM on 21 Apl 1819: *Supp.*, 169n3.

64. *Selected Prose of J.H. Reynolds*, 259; SH to JM, 7 May [1819] (*LSH*, 154). WW did not agree, thinking Hazlitt 'could *not* write anything so foolish'.

65. STC to Taylor & Hessey, 16 & [22] Apl 1819 (*STCL*, iv, 934–5, 938–9); for Taylor & Hessey's reply, see ibid., iv, 935n.1; *Selected Prose of J.H. Reynolds*, 465. Shelley, one of WW's bitterest critics, wrote another satire, *Peter Bell the Third*, in Oct 1819; lacking Reynolds's light touch, it is a savage, personal and unfunny attack on the poet himself for what Shelley considered his abandonment of the poetry and politics of his youth. Shelley sent it to Hunt for immediate publication, but it did not appear until 1839, 17 years after Shelley's own death: R. Holmes, *Shelley: The Pursuit* (London, Quartet Books, 1976), 551–6.

66. Anon., *Eclectic Review*, xi (May) & xii (Jul) 1819 (Smith, 294, 302); L. Hunt, *Examiner*, 2 May 1819 (Hayden, 88); Anon., *Monthly Review*, 89 (Aug 1819) (Smith, 303).

67. Anon., *British Critic*, xi (Jun 1819) (Hayden, 99, 107).

68. WW to LL, 22 May [1819] (*MY*, ii, 542); SH to JM, 7 May [1819] (*LSH*, 154). See also WW to H. Busk, 6 Jul 1819 (*MY*, ii, 547). WW responded to the criticisms by composing a sonnet in defence of *Peter Bell*: WW, *On the Detraction Which Followed the Publication of a Certain Poem* (*Poems*, ii, 445–6).

69. CL to WW, [7 Jun 1819] (Lucas, ii, 250); Anon., *Monthly Review*, xc (Sep 1819) (Hayden, 108–11). See also Smith, 307–14.

70. TdQ to WW, 14 Jun 1819 (Jordan, 326); W. Pearson to WW, 30 Jul 1819: WLMS/A/Pearson/1. Pearson enclosed a sonnet he had written, 'Wordsworth! to thee what praises shall I bring Or how convey the high respect I feel'.

71. DW to Jo H, 5 Sep 1819 (*MY*, ii, 554, 556–7). SH had gone to Hindwell from the Clarksons in Jun 1818, to take care of the children, Thomas (1815–1903) and Mary Monkhouse (1817–37), in anticipation of the birth of George (1818–76) on 10 Oct 1818. The Hutchinsons left Hindwell on 16 Apl 1819, were joined towards the end of their visit by TH, and left RM on 21 Jul: SH to TM, 3 May & 25 Jul [1819] (*LSH*, 150, 157).

72. S. R. Pattison (ed.), *The Brothers Wiffen: Memoirs and Miscellanies* (London, Hodder & Stoughton, 1880), 32–42. Wiffen mistook Mrs TH, an 'elegant lady in white . . . much younger than he, [who] has a figure of symmetry', for DW. WW always referred to his sisters-in-law as his sisters, hence the confusion.

73. SH to TM, 4 Aug & 3 May [1819] (*LSH*, 159, 152); WW to LL, 19 Sep [1819] (*MY*, ii, 557–8);

SH to TM, 26 Sep [1819]: WLL/SH/55a pp.1–2. When the problem recurred is unclear, but Wiffen saw WW's green eyeshade, which he used when he had eye problems, on the table at RM on 6 Jul: Pattison (ed.), *The Brothers Wiffen*, 34.

74. Westall, who stayed at RM in Aug, had come direct from Sedbergh, where he had been staying with the headmaster when his wife died: SH to TM, 4 Aug [1819] (*LSH*, 160); MW to TM, [*p.m.*8 Nov 1819] (*LMW*, 52); Clarke & Weech, *History of Sedbergh School*, 80, 118; *Sedbergh School Register*, 206–7. The Old Grammar School in the centre of the town, which housed the whole school from 1719 to 1879, is now the library; the more modern buildings of Sedbergh, which is now a public school, are on a site on the outskirts of the town.

75. WW to FW, 17 Dec & DW to CC, 19 Dec 1819 (*Supp.*, 174; *MY*, ii, 571); SH to JM, [Nov–Dec 1819] (*LSH*, 166–7); MW to TM, [*p.m.*11] & 16 Dec [1819] (*LMW*, 53, 54). William Crackanthorpe, a former pupil of Stephens, subscribed £50. WW advised against a public subscription, fearing it would not succeed because Stephens had notoriously become an alcoholic in later years. 'You may depend upon it that I will do every thing in my slender power to serve his poor family, for whose condition I assure you I feel much': WW to W. Westall, 22 Nov [1819] (*Supp.*, 173).

76. WW to LL, 11 Nov 1819 (*MY*, ii, 565–6); LL to WW, 15 Nov 1819: WLMS/A/Lonsdale/12 pp.1–2; Clarke & Weech, *History of Sedbergh School*, 80–83; SH to Mrs TH, 27 Feb 1820 [*LSH*, 176]. According to the Admissions Register, JW3 entered Sedbergh on 17 Apl 1820. Wilkinson transformed the fortunes of the school and JW3 was the first of many Ws and Hutchinsons to attend in the first half of the 19th century.

77. Ibid.; WW to LL, 14 Oct 1819 (*MY*, ii, 562–3); WW2 to Dora, 26 Nov–3 Dec 1819: WLL/WW2/3 pp.3–4.

78. WW2 to MW, 12 Nov 1819: WLL/WW2/2; SH to JM, [Nov–Dec 1819] & to TM, 10 Apl [1820] (*LSH*, 169, 165, 179); SH to TM, [Nov–Dec 1819]: WLL/SH/58a pp.2–3; WW2 & W. Johnson to MW, 24 Mar 1820: WLL/WW2/7 pp.1–3.

79. WW to VL, [mid-Jan] & 4 Feb 1820 (*MY*, ii, 575–6, 582). The estate WW sold is unidentified, but may have been the one at Patterdale.

80. CL to WW, 7 Jun 1819 (Lucas [ed.]), *The Letters of Charles Lamb*, ii, 250); DW to CC, 1 Aug [1819] (*MY*, ii, 552).

81. SH to JM, [Nov–Dec 1819] (*LSH*, 165). See also WW to J. Edwards, [autumn 1819] (*MY*, ii, 562).

Chapter 19

chapter title: 'A Tour of the Continent', WW, *Memorials of a Tour of the Continent, 1820* (*Poems*, ii, 408–46).

picture: Cascade de la Folie, Chamonix, France, by John Ruskin, 1849.

1. WW, *On the Death of His Majesty*, ll.1–2 (*Poems*, ii, 405); WW2 to Dora, 28 Jan–2 Feb 1820: WLL/WW2/5 pp.2–3.

2. WW to LL, 2, 4, 5 & 6 Feb & to VL, 4 Feb 1820 & DW to Jo H, 5 Sep 1819 (*MY*, ii, 579–80, 580n.1, 581–4, 555); SH to JM, [Nov–Dec 1819] (*LSH*, 168).

3. SH to Mrs TH, 27 Feb 1820 (ibid., 174–5); DW to Mrs TH, 5 May [1820] (*MY*, ii, 595–6); JM to TM, 9 Feb & [*p.m.*17 Apl] 1820: WLMS/H/1/14/46 pp.1–2 & 47 pp.1–2. GH's marriage seems to have taken place mid-1819: JM to SH, 23 May & to TM, [*p.m.*17 Jul] [1819]: WLMS/H/1/14/43 p.2 & 44 p.4. TH too was in difficulties: the birth of a 4th child, Elizabeth, on 3 Apl 1820 threatened them with, in JM's farming metaphor, 'more stock of the biped species than the pasture will carry': Jo H to TM, 4 Apl [1820]: WLMS/H/1/8/37 p.1; JM to TM, [*p.m.*17 Jul] [1819]: WLMS/H/1/14/44 p.3.

4. SH to Mrs TH, 27 Feb 1820 (*LSH*, 175–6); WW to VL, 23 Aug & to LL, 19 Sep 1819 (*MY*, ii, 553–4, 558); WW to VL, [mid-Oct 1819] (*Supp.*, 171). WW signed the *Westmorland Address* to the Prince Regent, which expressed general confidence in the government while deploring the hardships of the poor, but had strong reservations about its tone and content: as 'An Enemy to Detraction', he wrote to the *Westmorland Gazette*, defending VL's support for the act allowing magistrates to search for weapons: WW to VL, 27 Oct & 31 Dec 1819 (*MY*, ii, 564 & n.2, 574); SH to TM, [28 Oct 1819] (*LSH*, 163).

5. Jordan, 290; SH to TM, 10 Apl 1820 (*LSH*, 180). The Ws gave up their subscription to the paper when TdQ resigned.

6. WW, *To the Rev. Dr Wordsworth*, ll.55–6, 59–60, and *After-Thought* (*Poems*, ii, 382, 396–7). *The River Duddon* also included 32 'other poems', many with no Lakeland connection.

7. WW to BRH, [?late Apl 1820] (*MY*, ii, 593–4); *Eclectic Review*, xiv (Aug 1820) (Smith, 322); SH to JM, 7 Sep [1820] (*LSH*, 197); Gill, 336–7. WW's decision to go from a reprint in three volumes of the same size as the 1815 edition to four in a smaller size was taken after DW's departure for London and without her knowledge: WW to TL, 11 Apl [1820] (*Supp.*, 175–6).

8. WW to HCR, [late Jan 1820] (*MY*, ii, 579); MW to SH, 30 May 1820 (*LMW*, 55); SH to Mrs TH, 27 Feb & to TM, 30 Apl 1820 (*LSH*, 176, 181).

9. DW to CC, 19 Dec [1819], to Mrs TH, 5 May & to TM, [9 May] [1820] (*MY*, ii, 572, 597–8, 602).

10. MW to SH, 30 May 1820 (*LMW*, 55–8); RJ to WW, 28 Feb 1821: WLMS/A/Jones/2 p.2. See also WW, *A Parsonage in Oxfordshire* (*Poems*, ii, 408).

11. DW to TM, [16 May], to J. Watson, [20], 23, 25 & 27 May & to Dora, [23 Jun] 1820 (*MY*, ii, 604, 605–6, 609, 612); DW to C. Lloyd Snr, 26 & 30 May 1820 (*Supp.*, 177–8, 179); SH to TM, [Jun 1820] (*LSH*, 183).

12. SH to Mrs TH, 27 Feb & to TM, [Jun] 1820 (*LSH*, 176, 182–3, 184); Jo H to SH, 10 Jun [1820]: WLMS/H/1/8/38 p.5; Mrs TH to TM, 12 Jun 1820: WLMS/H/1/5/49 p.1; JM to TM, 15 Jun 1820: WLMS/H/1/14/48 p.1; *HCRBW*, i, 254, 239–43.

13. J. Keats to C. Brown, [*c.*21 Jun 1820] (*The Letters of John Keats*, ii, 299); BRH to WW, 28 Apl 1820: WLMS/A/Haydon/11 p.3. Keats's caution was justified; he suffered a lung haemorrhage the day after he should have met WW.

14. WW to BRH, [?late Apl 1820] (*MY*, ii, 593); *HCRBW*, ii, 241–2. WW knew BRH already owed TM money which he could not repay: see MW to TM [*p.m.*8 Nov 1819], which is written on BRH to TM, 1 Nov 1819, pleading for an extension of credit: WLL/MW/24. WW wanted to raise £2,000. The picture was on display at the Egyptian Hall in London from 25 Mar to 4 Nov 1820, earning BRH £1,298, but the following year it was sold to a creditor for £240: Blanshard, 148.

15. Ibid., 61–4, 151, pl.8b; HT, *Autobiography*, i, 182. WW blamed the sittings to Sir Francis Leggatt Chantrey (1781–1842) for his inability to see more of STC during this London visit: WW to STC, [8 Jul 1820] (*MY*, ii, 614–15).

16. *HCRBW*, i, 241; CW to DW [*p.m.*7 Jul 1820]: WLL/CW/67a p.3.

17. DW to Dora, [23 Jun 1820] (*MY*, ii, 611); *DWJ*, ii, 7–9; DW's journal is published in full, if inaccurately, in *DWJ*, ii, 1–336: the MS is DC 90; heavily edited selections from HCR's journal, the MS of which is in Dr Williams's Library, appear in *HCRBW*, i, 243–55 & *HCRD*, i, 351–64: MW's contemporaneous notes for her journal are DC 91, and the finished version DC, 92–5, all at DC.

18. MW & DW to SH & Dora, 13 Jul 1820 (*MY*, ii, 621, 616); *DWJ*, ii, 29; WW, *After Visiting the Field of Waterloo*, ll.6–14 (*Poems*, ii, 411). See also DW to CC, 23 Jul [1820] (*MY*, ii, 624).

19. *DWJ*, ii, 72, 23; MW to SH, 1 Aug [1820] (*LMW*, 60–61). MW had to forfeit a further trip round the Schaffhausen falls to escort Mrs TM back to the inn. 'Head very bad' was MW's terse comment: ibid., 63. At Herzogenbuchsee, where they refused to pay the landlord's extortionate rates, they took only one room, which Mrs TM shared with her sister and maid, while her husband and the Ws slept in the carriages: *DWJ*, ii, 98–100.

20. Ibid., 86, 45; MW & DW to SH & Dora, 13 Jul & DW to HCR, 6 Aug 1820 (*MY*, ii, 619, 627). HH & W. Jackson both expressed their disapproval of this parting of bride and groom and a complete stranger, 'Muley Mulock', a lecturer on English literature at Geneva, told TM five minutes after meeting him 'that the world made comments on his having left Mrs Monkhouse and Miss Horrocks at Geneva, and very seriously advised him as to his duty as a married man': SH to MW, 16 Aug [1820] (*LSH*, 189); *HCRBW*, i, 246.

21. *DWJ*, ii, 103, 117, 151–3, 134, 91, 219–24, 225, 241–6; *HCRBW*, i, 246, 253. 'The Ws had before talked abo[u]t going back to see the lake of Como again M & I had from the first declared that we were not inclined to go again to Como And certainly they wo[ul]d not have gone alone, when Mr Graham & a Mr Sharpe (an Invalid) offering themselves as Companions to supply our place – the party was formed and M & I were left behind. [We could not afterwards go with them as that would have compromised our

consistency. M was with reason offended, principally with Miss W by whose pertinacity this was carried into effect.: deleted in MS]': HCRDMS, 1820. HCR took a certain malign pleasure in discovering that Graham was a convicted forger who was later killed in a duel: he tried to dun the Ws, HCR and TM for money, and the Ws were glad to part with him: *HCRD*, i, 358–9.

22. Ibid., 359–60; *HCRWB*, i, 253; *DWJ*, ii, 239–40. On seeing da Vinci's drawings WW said it was instructive to see how the great man had prepared himself for producing his sublime and beautiful art works by intense and laborious study of 'mere science in which there was nothing but mathematical proportion': HCRDMS, 1820, p.91. Was WW thinking of his own necessary preparations for *The Recluse*?

23. *DWJ*, ii, 255–61, 263, 280.

24. MW to SH, 22 Sep [1820] (*LMW*, 66–7); *DWJ*, ii, 303–30; *HCRBW*, ii, 249, 254–5; DW, Notes for a Journal of a tour of the continent: DC 91 [9 & 2 Oct 1820]. WW wrote a poem on Goddard's death, *Elegiac Stanzas*, for the *Memorials*, with a long head-note by HCR explaining the circumstances (*Poems*, ii, 437–8).

25. DW, Notes for a Journal: DC 91 [15 Oct 1820]; *HCRBW*, i, 248; HCRDMS, 1820, pp.134, 136, 137.

26. Ibid., pp.136–41; DW, Notes for a Journal: DC 91 [9 & 2–19 Oct 1820]; WW to LL, 7 Oct [1820] (*MY*, ii, 642); *HCRBW*, i, 248; H.M. Williams to WW, [10 Oct 1820]: WLMS/A/Williams/2. Miss Williams promised to return to town from the country 'solely for the purpose of receiving so distinguished a visitor as Mr Wordsworth': H.M. Williams to WW, [11 Oct 1820]: WLMS/A/Williams/1. See also WW & MW to H.M. Williams, [11 & 15 Oct] & DW to CC, 14 Oct [1820] (*MY*, ii, 643–4, 646, 646–7).

27. *JTM*, i, 354, 355, 355–6. Lady Mary Lowther (1785–1862) married Lord William Frederick Cavendish-Bentinck (1781–1828) in 1820. George Canning (1770–1827) was Foreign Secretary (1807–10), infamously fought a duel with Castlereagh in a disagreement over the prosecution of the war against France, became Foreign Secretary (1822) and Prime Minister (1827). Thomas Moore (1779–1852), Irish poet and satirist, published, most famously, *Irish Melodies* (1807) and *Lalla Rookh* (1817). Byron entrusted his memoirs to Moore, who destroyed them.

28. SH to TM, 4 Aug [1819] (*LSH*, 159–60); SC to E. Crump, 12 Nov 1820: WLMS/A/SC/2 p.5; *DWJ*, ii, 331–4.

29. MW to TM, 5 Nov [1820] (*LMW*, 68–9); *DWJ*, ii, 333–5; WW, *After Landing – the Valley of Dover, November, 1820* and *At Dover* (*Poems*, ii, 441–2). WW also commemorated their shipwreck in *On being stranded near the harbour of Boulogne* (ibid., 441).

30. *DWJ*, ii, 209–10; HCRDMS, 1820, pp.64–5; Blanshard, 64–5, 152, pls.9, 10a. The last day of the trial was 10 Nov but the date of the Ws' arrival in London is unclear. MW expected to be there on the evening of 8 Nov; WW's letter, saying he arrived 'this morng' is dated 'Thursday Nov 8th' but Thursday was 9 Nov and HCR says on 11 Nov that WW arrived in town 'yesterday night': MW to TM, 5 Nov [1820] (*LMW*, 69); WW to F.L. Chantrey, 8 [*r.*9] Nov [1820] (*Supp.*, 181–2); *HCRBW*, i, 256.

31. Smith, 317–37, esp.327; TNT to WW, 1 Dec 1820: WLMS/A/Talfourd/2 pp.1–2.

32. MW to TM, 5 Nov [1820] (*LMW*, 68); SH to TM, 7 Nov [1820] (*LSH*, 214); *HCRBW*, i, 256–7.

33. MW to TM, 1 Dec [1820] (*LMW*, 69–70); WW to LL, 4 & 11 Dec 1820 (*MY*, ii, 648, 653); WW to HCR, [*c.*12 Mar 1821] (*LY*, i, 45). CW's appointment as Master of Trinity had been almost a certainty before the Ws left Lambeth for the Continent: WW to CW, [28 Jun 1820] (*MY*, ii, 614). CW discussed his plans for reforming the syllabus with WW: CW to WW, 5 Aug 1821: WLL/CW/68 pp.1–2.

34. DW to TM [5 (*r.*3–4) Dec], WW to LL, 4 & 18 Dec & WW2 & DW to TM, 14 Dec 1820 (*MY*, ii, 648–50, 657, 655). WW2 joined DW at Playford Hall and Cambridge for his Christmas holidays: CW2 & DW to TM, 2 Jan 1821 (*LY*, ii, 20–21). For the replanting of the winter garden, see SH to MW, 19 Sep [1820] (*LSH*, 206); LMB to DW, 19 Mar 1821: WLMS/A/Beaumont/71 p.1.

35. SH to MW, 11 & 19 Sep & to JM, 7 Sep [1820] (*LSH*, 199–203, 208–9, 193); SH to Jo H, 7 Aug [1820]: WLL/MW [*sic*]/30 p.1; DW to Dora, [23 Jun 1820] (*MY*, ii, 612). JM was amused at SH's naïvety in allowing Mary Bell 'a short half year to heal the Wounds of Love. You maiden ladies seem to think that Cupid and his Quiver are so little to be dreaded as a scratch': JM to SH, 3 Sep 1820: WLMS/H/1/14/49 p.3.

36. MW to TM, 3 Jan [1821] (*LMW*, 72); WW to

Commissioners of Stamps, 19 Jan, to T. Myers, [5 Jan], to SGB, 10 Jan, & DW to CC, [19 Jan] & 15 Feb [1821] (*LY*, i, 14, 2–3, 3–4, 17, 33–4). Myers's wife, Rachel Philips, had died in 1816; Julia (1811–45) was her father's heir but much of his property was entailed, so passed out of her hands. Myers followed the family tradition in dying intestate. For the sale, see WW to W. Myers, [7 Mar], to VL, [*c.*10 Mar] & DW to TM, 16 Mar [1821] (*LY*, i, 40–41, 41, 47). WW's difficulties in getting a warrant to bury the body caused him to urge LL to appoint a coroner for Millom, the office then being in abeyance: WW to LL, [*c.*12 Jan 1821] (ibid., 12).

37. DW to CC, 19 Dec [1819] (*MY*, ii, 572); SH to Mrs TH, 27 Feb 1820 (*LSH*, 178).

38. MW to TM and Mrs TM, 9 Apl [1821] (*LMW*, 79); WW to BRH, 16 Jan 1820 (*MY*, ii, 578); WW to HCR, [*c.*12 Mar 1821] (*LY*, i, 43–4 & 44n.). Scott had left his widow and two children penniless; the man who killed him, J.H. Christie, and his second, were prosecuted for murder but acquitted. Scott's second, P.G. Patmore (1786–1855), a friend of CL from 1826, fled to France after the duel but returned after the acquittal. His failure to halt the duel after the first shot was widely believed to have been the cause of Scott's death: Prance, 254–5.

39. *Prose*, ii, 132; RS to W. Westall, 8 Dec 1820 (*RSLC*, v, 50); DW to TM, 15 Feb [1821] (*LY*, i, 37).

40. DW to CC, 27 Mar [1821] (ibid., 50–51); RS to G.C. Bedford, 15 Apl 1821 (*RSLC*, v, 65). RS had proposed his *Book of the Church* in 1811; it was not completed and published till 1824: Storey, 212, 386.

41. WW to VL, [*c.*10], [28] & 30 Mar [1821] (*LY*, i, 42, 55, 58).

42. *HCRBW*, i, 90; ii, 482. HCR adds that W 'allowed us to laugh at this droll concession from a staunch advocate for the establishment'. William Blake (1757–1827), who had some pretty odd views on religion himself, was convinced WW was not 'a Bible Christian', so HCR sent him the *Ecclesiastical Sketches* to see if they changed his mind: ibid., i, 335.

43. WW, *Catechizing* and 'I saw the figure of a lovely maid' (*Poems*, ii, 492–3, 483–4); *IF*, 35.

44. WW to R. Sharp, 16 Apl & to W.S. Landor, 20 Apl [1822] (*LY*, i, 119, 126).

45. WW to VL, [28] & 30 Mar [1821] (ibid., 54n, 56–7, 58); MW to TM & Mrs TM, 9 Apl [1821] (*LMW*, 79–80). Hume obtained the abolition of the Receiver-General's office, but his plan to offer the local collection of duties to the lowest bidder foundered. 'It is impossible that the present administration should be so imbecile as to give way to this extent to a vulgar Demagogue like Hume, were not his plans supported by influences that do not appear', WW raged: WW to VL, [Jun–Jul, 1821] (*LY*, i, 66).

46. SH to Mrs TH, 27 Sep [1821] (*LSH*, 222–3). HH visited in Mar and again in Sep: DW to CC, 27 Mar [1821] (*LY*, i, 50); SH to Mrs TH, 27 Sep [1821] (*LSH*, 224).

47. JM to TM, 21 Jul 1821, 8 Mar & 30 Jul 1822: WLMS/H/1/14/54, p.1, 60 pp.1–3 & 62 pp.2–3; DW to CC, 27 Mar [1821] (*LY*, i, 49–50); Mrs TH to SH, 6 Nov 1820 & to TM, 14 Mar 1821: WLMS/H/1/5/50 p.3 & 52 pp.1–2. TH had sunk much of his £14,000 fortune into improvements at Hindwell, from which he had not gained the expected benefit, due to the harsh times: WW to VL, 19 Apl 1822 (*LY*, i, 120–21).

48. DW to CC, 27 Mar & 25 Aug [1821] (ibid., 52, 75); Mrs TM to TM, 14 Jul & 6 Aug 1821: WLMS/H/1/16/2 & 4; Mrs TH to TM, 2 Aug & [*p.m.*6 Aug] 1821: WLMS/H/1/5/55 pp.1–2 & 56 p.1.

49. HH, *Retrospect of a Retired Mariner*: WLMS/H/1/2/2 p.87; JM to TM, 26 Jun 1809: WLMS/H/1/14/24 p.3; E. Monkhouse to JM, 17 Jun 1809: WLMS/H/1/12/2 p.2; Mrs TH to SH, 25 May 1816: WLMS/H/1/5/36 p.1; Joe Monkhouse to TM, 16 Mar 1810: WLMS/H/1/18/2 pp.1–2.

50. Joe Monkhouse to TM, 21 Apl 1821: WLMS/H/1/18/4 pp.1–2; JM to TM, 25 Oct 1821: WLMS/H/1/14/56 p.3; Mrs TH to SH, 26 Jun & 12 Oct & to TM, 6 Aug 1821: WLMS/H/1/5/54 pp.4–5, 58 pp.1–2 & 56 p.2.

51. TM to JM, 5 Nov & 9 Dec 1822: WLMS/H/1/15/6f pp.1–3 & 6g pp.2–3. TM refused later requests to purchase the freedom of another of Joe's sons by a different mother: 'I have replied it is not in my power to recognise any more of his children – it cannot be expected that we should – there might be no termination of such appeals': TM to JM, 4 Jul 1823: WLMS/H/1/15/7a p.3.

52. DW to CC, 25 Aug [1821] (*LY*, i, 74–6). KJW eventually went to Hawkshead Grammar

School, rather than Sedbergh, and the Ws continued to complain of his rustic accent.

53. Ibid., 75; *HCRBW*, i, 271–3; DW to CC, 24 Oct [1821] (*LY*, i, 89); JK to WW, 11 Sep 1821: WLMS/A/Kenyon/1 pp.1–2; JL, *Diaries*, i, 138; CW to WW, 5 Aug 1821: WLL/CW/68 p.1. The Ws first met John Kenyon (1784–1856), poet, philanthropist and friend of RS, when he spent four days at RM with RS in Nov 1819: SH to JM, [Nov–Dec, 1819] (*LSH*, 167). William Whewell (1794–1866) married JPM's daughter, Cordelia Marshall, and succeeded CW as Master of Trinity.

54. EQ, *First Visit to the Lakes*, [May 1821]: WLMS/13/1/5a pp.13–15.

55. WW to R.P. Gillies, 15 Apl [1816] (*MY*, ii, 300); SH to Mrs TH, 27 Sep [1821] (*LSH*, 223); DW to CC, 25 Aug & WW to JK, 23 Jul 1821 (*LY*, i, 76–7, 68); EQ, *Excursion with WW to Yorkshire*, 3–6 Nov 1821: WLMS/13/1/5b. DW says they saw 'the Caves, Studley Park, Knaresborough and York': DW to HCR, 24 Nov [1821] (*LY*, i, 92).

56. SH to Mrs TH, 27 Sep [1821] & to TM, 11 Jan [1822] (*LSH*, 224, 229); DW to HCR, 24 Nov [1821] (*LY*, i, 92); *HCRBW*, i, 272. Rotha was 'new-born' in WW & MW to JK, 22 Sep 1821 (*LY*, i, 83), so she cannot have been born in the spring as ibid., 92n.

57. MW to TM & Mrs TM, 9 Apl [1821] (*LMW*, 78); SH to TM, 23 Nov [1821] (*LSH*, 225); DW to CC, 24 Oct [1821] (*LY*, i, 89); *HCRBW*, i, 271–2. HCR was particularly struck by MW's descriptions of objects before her 'as in a panorama . . . These were written on the spot, and I recollect her often sitting on the grass, not aware what kind of employment she had.'

58. DW to CC, [31 May], to TM, [2 Jan] & WW to JK, 5 Feb 1821 (*LY*, i, 64–5, 2, 25).

59. MW to TM, 5 Nov [1821] (*LMW*, 81); DW to CC, 16 Jan [1822] & 24 Oct [1821] (*LY*, i, 104, 89); SH to TM, 23 Nov [1821] (*LSH*, 225–7). WW asked HCR to send the *Elegiac Stanzas* on Goddard, the American drowned on Lake Zurich, to the young man's mother.

60. DW to CC, 16 Jan [1822] & MW to JK, 28 Dec [1821] (*LY*, i, 104, 100); *HCRBW*, i, 272; HCR to DW, 25 Feb 1822 (*HCRWC*, i, 110–12).

61. WW to SR, [16 Sep] & to R. Sharp, 3 Oct 1822; DW to SR, 3 Jan 1823 (*LY*, i, 152–3, 155–6, 180–82); SR to WW, Sep 1822 & to DW, [*c.*Jan 1824]: WLMS/A/Rogers/2 pp.1–2 & 3 pp.1–2; SR happily undertook the commission but advised DW to raise the money any other way than the way proposed.

62. SH to TM, 11 Jan, [5] & 24 Feb, to JM, 22 Feb 1822 (*LSH*, 229, 231, 239, 237); HCR to DW, 25 Feb 1822 (*HCRWC*, i, 111); DW to HCR, 3 Mar & WW to R. Sharp, 16 Apl 1822 (*LY*, i, 113, 118).

63. DW to HCR, 21 Apl [1822] (*LY*, i, 127 & n.); *Edinburgh Review*, cccvii (Nov 1822) (Smith, 352–3). See also ibid., 341–58.

64. *Prose*, ii, 133–4. *A Description of the Scenery of the Lakes* . . . was 'in the press' in Apl: WW to R. Sharp, 16 Apl [1822] (*LY*, i, 120).

65. WW to W.S. Landor, 20 Apl [1822] (ibid., 126).

66. MW to JK, 28 Dec [1821] (ibid., 100–101); CW to WW, 4 Jan 1822: WLL/CW/70 pp.2–5; SH to TM, 11 Jan & [5 Feb] & to JM, 22 Feb 1822 (*LSH*, 230, 232, 238).

67. WW to LL, 18 Jul & DW to EQ, 6 Aug 1822 (*LY*, i, 142, 147–8). WW2 entered Sedbergh on 6 May & left in Jun 1822: Sedbergh School Admissions Register.

68. DW to JPM, 13 Jun 1822 (*LY*, i, 139–40).

69. Ibid., 139, 141; DW to EQ, [22 May 1822] (ibid., 133); J. Satterthwaite to CW, 21 May 1822: WLMS/A/Satterthwaite pp.1–3. EQ, thinking that his wife was recovering, was in London on business when she died. MW accompanied EQ, JQ and RQ as far as Matlock on the first stage of their journey to Kent: MW to EQ, [*p.m.*25 Jun 1822] (*MWL*, 85); EQ to MW, 3 Sep 1822: WLL/EQ/3.

70. TC to WW, 16 May 1822: WLMS/A/Clarkson/21 pp.1–2; Dora & WW to CW, 29 May & DW to JPM, 13 Jun 1822 (*LY*, i, 136, 141); CC to HCR, [6] Dec 1822 & 31 Mar 1821 (*HCRWC*, i, 119–20, 101). The identity of the parson is not clear. Thomas Jackson, rector of Grasmere since 1806, died in Dec 1821; Sir Richard le Fleming took charge in Jun 1822, but his notoriety makes it impossible for him to have been WW's 'model parish priest'. The most likely candidate was the former curate, William Jackson, rector of Whitehaven since Jan 1821, who was the Ws' friend: WW to LL, 20 Jan 1821 (*LY*, i, 19 & n.).

71. TM to JM, 14 Mar 1822: WLMS/H/1/15/6d pp.1–2; DW to HCR, 21 Apl & to EQ, 6 Aug [1822] (*LY*, i, 126–7, 148); Mrs TH to Mrs TM, 19 Jun [1822]: WLMS/H/1/5/64 pp.1–4.

72. DW to EQ, 6 Aug & to HCR, 21 Dec 1822 (*LY*, i, 148, 177); Chas W to Dora, [*p.m.*21 Oct 1822]: WLMS/1/10/1 p.1; MW to EQ, 19 Sep [1822] (*LMW*, 87); CW to J. Watson, 5 Sep 1822: 1990.1.5.9 pp.1–4.
73. SH to JM, 12 Sep [1822] (*LSH*, 242–3); MW to EQ, 19 Sep [1822] (*LMW*, 87). Charles Hutchinson (b.1805) entered Sedbergh in Aug 1822, aged 17, joining his younger brother, Henry (1807–50), who had been there since Feb 1822. Both boys left in 1823, Charles in Jun, Henry in Dec: *Sedbergh School Register*, 221.
74. MW to EQ, 19 Sep [1822] (*LMW*, 87–8). There is no complete and accurate published text of DW's journal of this tour, only the unsatisfactory edition in *DWJ*, ii, 339–97.
75. Ibid., 357, 354.
76. Ibid., 396–7; WW to R. Sharp, [mid-Oct] & 12 Nov [1822] (*LY*, i, 157, 159).
77. SH to JM, 12 Sep [1822] (*LSH*, 242); MW to EQ, 19 Sep [1822] (*LMW*, 89); WW to LL, 3 Nov, to R. Sharp, 12 Nov, DW & WW to M. & D. Laing, [13–16 Nov] & DW to EQ, 19 Nov[1822] (*LY*, i, 158, 159, 161, 164–5).
78. Ibid., 169–70; MW to EQ, 19 Sep, 19 Oct & 21 Dec 1822 (*LMW*, 88, 92, 96); EQ to MW, 13 Nov & 5–15 Dec 1822: WLL/EQ/5 p.3 & 4 p.1; MW to EQ, 29 Nov [1822]: WLL/MW/49 pp.1–2.
79. DW to HCR, 21 Dec 1822 (*LY*, i, 178). The two other poems he wrote this December were *To the Lady Fleming on Seeing the Foundation Preparing for the Erection of Rydal Chapel* and 'By Moscow self-devoted to a blaze' (*Poems*, ii, 510–13).

Chapter 20

chapter title: 'Idle Mount', CW's name for RM: DW to TM, 20 May 1824 (*LY*, i, 268).
picture: Rydal Mount, by Dora, undated.
1. WW to Lady Ann le Fleming, 3 May [1822] (*LY*, i, 129–30); SH to TM, 3 Mar [1822]: WLL/SH/80a p.1.
2. LL to WW, 18 Dec 1824: WLMS/A/Lonsdale/24 p.3; MW to EQ, 21 Dec 1822 & to LMB, 5 Feb 1823 (*LMW*, 97; *Supp.*, 183). SGB had recently built a new church at Coleorton, inspiring three sonnets by WW, which, according to his preface to *Ecclesiastical Sketches*, prompted him to begin that collection: WW, *Church to be erected*, *Continued* and *New church-yard*: *Ecclesiastical Sketches*, xxxix, xl, xli (*Poems*, ii, 500–501).
3. WW, *To the Lady Fleming on Seeing the Foundation Preparing for the Erection of Rydal Chapel, Westmoreland*, ll.21–4 (ibid., 511). The 'le' in the Fleming name was optional: LL to WW, 31 Jan 1823: WLMS/A/Lonsdale/22 pp.2–3.
4. MW to LMB, 5 Feb 1823 (*Supp.*, 183); Lady le Fleming to WW, 29 Jan, Tues a.m. & [31 Mar] 1823: WLMS/A/Fleming/1–3; WW to Lady le Fleming [late Jan 1823] (*LY*, i, 186). The poem was not published until 1827, when it was added to WW's new edition of his poetry.
5. DW to SR, 17 Feb 1823 (ibid., 189); MW to LMB, 5 Feb 1823 & to TM, 25 Jun [1824] (*Supp.*, 182–3; *LMW*, 108).
6. MW to EQ, 3 Mar [1823] (ibid., 98); WW to J. Keble, 18 Dec [1822] & [17 Feb 1823] (*LY*, i, 174–5, 187–8). John Keble (1792–1866), poet and founder of the Tractarian and Oxford Movements, became Professor of Poetry at Oxford (1831–41) and dedicated his poetry lectures of 1841 to WW.
7. WW to J. Keble, [17] & 24 Feb & 5 Mar [1823] (ibid., 188, 190–91, 191–2); A. Hare to WW, [13 Mar] & [?20 Dec] [1823]: WLMS/A/Hare, A/1 pp.1–2 & 2 pp.1–3. HC to D. Coleridge, 2 May [1823] (*LHC*, 80); CW2, Diary, 31 Oct 1825 (Overton & Wordsworth, *Christopher Wordsworth*, 38). Augustus Hare (1792–1834) had been a fellow and tutor at New College since 1818; his brother Julius Charles (1795–1855) was a lecturer in classics at Trinity College, Cambridge. CW2 put WW's income at *c.*£600 p.a. and said JW3's education had cost £300 p.a. for the last three years, rising, at Oxford, to £400 p.a.
8. TM to JM, 20 Mar 1823: WLMS/H/1/15/6h p.2; *HCRBW*, i, 291–3. Henry Hallam (1777–1859), author of *A View of the State of Europe during the Middle Ages* (1818) and *Constitutional History of England* (1827), whose post as a Commissioner for Stamps had been axed in the recent reforms, was father of Tennyson's friend Arthur Hallam (1811–33), whose early death inspired *In Memoriam*. Henry Francis Cary (1772–1844) published translations of Dante's *Inferno* (1805–6) and *Purgatorio* and *Paradiso* (1814) and was appointed assistant librarian of the British Museum (1826–37), partly due to lobbying by WW, RS, CL, SR and STC.
9. King, *The Translator of Dante*, 157–8; *JTM*, ii, 622. Attending a musical party four nights later,

WW proved his lack of appreciation by declaring himself perfectly delighted, but sitting alone, covering his face, 'and – as was generally supposed – asleep': *HCRBW*, i, 293.

10. TM to Miss Horrocks, [22 (*r.*5) Apl 1823] (*HCRWC*, i, 125); *JTM*, ii, 623–4; *HCRBW*, i, 292–3. HCR says that he, MW, SH and STC's minder, James Gillman, were the only other guests present; Moore does not mention Gillman's presence, and believed SH to be MAL.

11. TM to Miss Horrocks, [22 (*r.*5) Apl 1823] (*HCRWC*, i, 125); WW to JK, 16 May [1823] (*LY*, i, 198); SH to EQ, [25 May 1823]: WLL/SH/85a pp.1–2; MW, *Journal of a Tour of Holland*, 1823: DC 102 pp.5–8. MW's journal of this tour is unpublished. They followed a route suggested by SR and HCR, whose journals they consulted before leaving London, and used a guidebook lent them by EQ's brother-in-law: *HCRBW*, i, 293.

12. MW, *Journal of a Tour of Holland*, 1823: DC 102 pp.21, 37. See also ibid. p.8. The recurrent image of scenes being suitable for a Dutch picture may have come from WW: in thanking LL for a gift of game in Nov, he wrote, 'it would have made a charming Picture in the hands of a Dutch Artist': WW to LL, 9 Nov [1823] (*LY*, i, 227).

13. MW, *Journal of a Tour of Holland*, 1823: DC 102 pp.65–6, 127, 131.

14. Ibid., pp.12–13, 61, 75, 87–9, 133, 143. The phrase 'A cheap Excursion!' appears to have been added later, and the sum of £24 has been substituted for a deleted £25. The Ws returned via Calais, rather than encounter the longer crossing from Ostend. They reached England on 11 Jun and by nightfall were at Lee Priory, where they stayed several days before returning to London: ibid., p.143; SH to EQ, [25 May 1823]: WLL/SH/85a p.2.

15. *HCRBW*, i, 295–6; DW to EQ, 17 Jun & 4 Jul & to E. Crump, [17 Jul] 1823 (*LY*, ii, 200, 202, 204); MW to Jo H, 20 Jul [1823] (*LMW*, 99–100). Dora spent several weeks at Harrogate with Julia Myers and the Robinsons of York; the Ws took adjoining lodgings for their stay.

16. HC to Derwent Coleridge, [*p.m.*24 Jun 1823] (*LHC*, 84); DW to E. Crump, [17 Jul] & 12 Nov [1823] (*LY*, i, 204–5, 232). For HC's deprivation of his Oriel fellowship in May 1820, see Ashton, 326–7, 338–9; Holmes, ii, 511–18.

17. MW to Jo H, 20 Jul [1823] (*LMW*, 99–100); SH to TM, [28 Jun], 22 Jul & [Sep–Oct], & to Jo H, 12 Jul [1823] (*LSH*, 248–51, 257–60, 260–61, 252–6); TM to JM, 4 Jul 1823: WLMS/H/1/15/7a pp.1–2; DW to E. Crump, 31 Aug [1823] (*LY*, i, 217).

18. SH to EQ, [13 Oct] & to TM, 14 & [18] Oct [1823] (*LSH*, 262–3, 264, 266–7); Mrs TM to TM, [*p.m.*21] & [?31] [Oct] [1823]: WLMS/H/1/16/7 pp.3–4 & 8 p.4; *STCNB*, 5003–19, 5032–3, 5037. TM was in treaty to buy the Fox Ghyll estate in Aug 1823: DW to E. Crump, 31 Aug [1823] (*LY*, i, 218).

19. Macready, *Reminiscences*, 216. William Charles Macready (1793–1873), a leading actor of his day, became manager of Covent Garden (1837–9) and Drury Lane (1841–3).

20. DW to CC, 12 Nov [1823] (*LY*, i, 230); WW & DW to TC & CC, 20 Mar [1824] (*Supp.*, 186). CW signed the petition, a fact which Brougham commented on in Parliament: Overton & Wordsworth, *Christopher Wordsworth*, 46.

21. SH to EQ, 1 Nov [1823] (*LSH*, 267); DW to CC, 12 Nov, WW to LL, 9 Nov & DW to M. Laing, 25 Nov 1823 (*LY*, i, 230–31, 228, 234).

22. WW to LL, 9 Nov & [early Dec] [1823], DW to EQ, 7 Jan & WW to LL, 17 Feb 1824 (*LY*, i, 228, 235, 242, 253).

23. WW to LL, 23 Jan & 5 Feb 1824 (ibid., 247, 250); HC to STC, 12 Mar 1824 (*LHC*, 87); WW to J.C. Hare, [late 1831 or early 1832] (*LY*, ii, 471). Hare was the editor of the *Philological Museum*, a scholarly journal dedicated to classical scholarship. WW never included the translation in any of his editions of his works, a sure sign he thought it a failure.

24. WW to LL, 5 Feb & DW to JK, 23 Mar [1824], to M. Laing, 26 Aug & 10 Oct & to E. Crump, 31 Aug & 10 Oct [1823] (ibid., 253, 256, 214, 222, 216–17, 221); Dora to EQ, [*p.m.*22 Mar 1824]: WLL/Dora/4 p.1.

25. TM to Mrs TH, 26 Mar [1823 (*r.*1824)]: WLMS/H/1/15/7 pp.2–3. TM was now hoping to reprise the dinner party of 4 Apl 1823: DW to EQ, 29 Mar [1824] (*LY*, i, 258).

26. *HCRBW*, i, 303–5; SC to E. Crump, 17 Apl 1824: WLMS/A/SC/6 p.4; DW to EQ, 29 Mar & to JM, 16 Apl [1824] (*LY*, i, 257–8, 260–62); Dora to EQ, [22 Mar 1824]: WLL/Dora/4 pp.1–2.

27. Ibid., p.4; SH to EQ, 15 Apl [1824] (*LSH*, 275);

DW to JM, 16 Apl 1824 (*LY*, i, 259). SH, who was in Wales, repeatedly but tactfully offered to come to TM 'whenever you wish for my company': SH to TM, 29 Apl [1824] (*LSH*, 278).

28. DW to EQ, [19 Apl], to JM, 16 Apl, to TM, 20 May & to HCR, 23 May 1824 (*LY*, i, 264, 263, 267–8, 270–72); SH to EQ, 15 Apl [1824] (*LSH*, 276); EQ to SH, 3 May 1824: WLL/EQ/10 p.1; Dora to EQ, 11 May [1824]: WLL/Dora/5 p.4; MW to E. Crump, 11 Jun [1824]: WLL/MW/60 p.1.

29. MW to TM, 25 Jun [1824] (*LMW*, 110–11); SH to TM, [Jun–Jul 1824] (*LSH*, 285); M. Calvert, *Journal*, 1824–9: Moorsom 49/8 [3 Aug 1824]; SC to E. Crump, 19 Oct 1825: WLMS/A/SC/10 p.7. The Miss Aylings were former pupils of Charlotte Lockier, a relative of the Gees, hence their introduction to RM. Frances Ayling was to marry William Ashburnham when they left Rydal for London in Jul: MW to TM, 14 Jul [1824] (*LMW*, 113).

30. WW to RJ, 3 Nov 1823 & to SGB, 20 Sep [1824]; DW to JK, 4 Oct & to LMB, 18 Sep [1824] (*LY*, i, 226, 275–6, 281, 274); SH to EQ, [10 Sep 1824] (*LSH*, 288).

31. WW to SGB, 20 Sep [1824] (*LY*, i, 275–6); J.H. Hobart to WW, 1 Sep 1825: WLMS/A/Hobart/1 p.1. Hobart invited WW to New York, an invitation he surprisingly never took up, despite his many American friends and acquaintances.

32. WW to CW, 4 Jan 1825 & to SGB, 20 Sep [1824] (*LY*, i, 297, 278).

33. MW to EQ, 27 Sep & 26 Oct [1824] (*LMW*, 116, 119); WW to SGB, 20 Sep [1824] (*LY*, i, 277); WW, *To the Lady E.B. and the Hon. Miss P.* (*Poems*, ii, 602). Though WW privately viewed the 'Ladies' with cynicism (*IF*, 24), his sonnet panders to their view of themselves.

34. WW, *Composed among the Ruins of a Castle in North Wales*, ll.9–14, and *To the Torrent at the Devil's Bridge, North Wales, 1824* (*Poems*, ii, 603); WW to SGB, 20 Sep [1824], and to CW, 4 Jan 1825 (*LY*, i, 278–9, 297).

35. MW to EQ, 27 Sep [1824] (*LMW*, 116); SH to TM, 12 Jun and [Jun–Jul] [1824] (*LSH*, 282, 287); JM to TM, 3 Jul 1824: WLMS/H/1/14/65 pp.2–3. A Grade I listed building, Brinsop Court dates mainly from the 14th century, though wings added in 1913 enclose what is now the central courtyard. I am grateful to Messrs Knight Frank for sending me particulars when the estate (then valued at £4 million) was offered for sale in 1998. It remains in private hands.

36. SH to EQ, 15 Apl & SH to TM, 12 Jun [1824] (*LSH*, 276, 281). The phrase 'useful as well as ornamental' was Jo H's, but borrowed by SH.

37. DW to JK, 4 Oct [1824] (*LY*, i, 281); SH to EQ, [10 Sep], [3 Nov] & [10 Sep] [1824] (*LSH*, 288, 290–91, 288–9); MW to E. Crump, 22 Nov [1824]: WLL/MW/63 p.1.

38. MW to EQ, 26 Oct [1824] (*LMW*, 118–19); DW to HCR, 13 Dec [1824] (*LY*, i, 292).

39. MW to EQ, 27 Sep [1824] (*LMW*, 117); WW, *The Contrast: The Parrot and the Wren*, ll.25–8, 30, 41–6 (*Poems*, ii, 611–13); *IF*, 11–12.

40. TM to Mrs TH, 26 Mar [1823 (*r.*1824)]: WLMS/H/1/15/7 p.2; DW to JM, 16 Apl & to HCR, 13 Dec 1824 (*LY*, i, 262–3, 292, 294); WW, *The Infant M– M–* (*Poems*, ii, 604). TM was 'extremely affected' by the poem: MW to EQ, 10 Dec [1824]: WLL/MW/64 p.3.

41. WW, *To –* (*Poems*, ii, 606–7); *IF*, 9. WW also wrote another poem about MW at this time, 'How rich that forehead's calm expanse!' (ibid., 601); *IF*, 9. The re-emergence of MW's doubts about her lack of conventional beauty were probably raised by Mrs TM, who was famously beautiful: WW, *To –* ['Look at the fate of summer flowers'] (*Poems*, ii, 607); *IF*, 8.

42. *HCRBW*, i, 304; ii, 482.

43. SH to EQ, [8 Dec 1824] (*LSH*, 292); WW to CW, 4 Jan 1825 (*LY*, i, 297); WW, *To –* ['O dearer far than light and life are dear'], ll.3–6, 11–16 (*Poems*, ii, 610); *IF*, 9. The italics in the penultimate line are mine.

44. WW to T.B. Barrett, 19 Nov [1824] (*LY*, i, 286); MW to E. Crump, 22 Nov [1824]: WLL/MW/63 p.3. JW3, who weighed 13 stones, had been lifted off his feet a yard from the ground during the storm on 12 Oct 1824: MW to EQ, 26 Oct [1824] (*LMW*, 119).

45. WW to LL, 6 Dec 1824 (*Supp.*, 188–9); MW to EQ, 18 Dec [1824] (*LMW*, 120); DWJMS, 1824–5: DC 104/1 [4 Dec 1824]; Dora to E. Crump, 27 Dec 1824: WLL/Dora/6 p.1. LL sent his solicitor, Anthony Harrison, and his agent, William Nicholson, to attend the second meeting at which a proposal for converting the common into stinted pasture, without division or enclosure, was accepted: LL to WW, 18 Dec

1824: WLMS/A/Lonsdale/24 p.1; WW to LL, 21 Jan [1825] (*LY*, i, 304–5).

46. Dora to E. Crump, 27 Dec 1824: WLL/Dora/6 p.2; WW to F. Merewether, 10 Jan 1825 (*LY*, i, 301); MW to EQ, 12 Nov [1823] (*LMW*, 104); DW to CC, 12 Nov [1823] (*LY*, i, 233). Fletcher Fleming (1795–1876) was perpetual curate of Rydal and Loughrigg, 1825–57, and rector of Grasmere from 1857.

47. SH to EQ, 11 Feb [1825]: WW/SH/106a pp.1–2; SH to EQ, 28 Feb [1825] (*LSH*, 301); DW to CC, 10 Mar & to HCR, 12 Apl [1825] (*LY*, i, 325, 336).

48. WW to W.B. Bleamire, 28 Feb [1825]: MS 1990.1.3.2; WW to SR, 23 Mar & 21 Jan 1825 (*LY*, i, 329, 308). TM was mourned in similar terms by HCR: *HCRBW*, i, 314.

49. DW to CC, 10 Mar & to HCR, 12 Apl [1825] (*LY*, i, 326, 336–7); SH to EQ, 28 Feb & 29 Mar [1825] (*LSH*, 301, 302–3). The Sebergham estate passed to TM's daughter instead of JM, as TM intended.

50. WW to SR, 19 Feb [1825] (*LY*, i, 320), reiterating one of 21 Jan 1825 (ibid., 306 & n.) which WW feared had not reached its destination. Even WW's most successful publication, *A Guide to the Lakes*, earned him only £9 8s 2d for the 1st edition, while he was charged £27 2s 3d for advertising; TL had already charged him £30 7s 2d for advertising the 2nd edition, though he had not yet received any profit. 'Thus my throat is cut': WW to SR, 23 Mar [1825] (ibid., 328).

51. WW to SR, 23 Mar 1825 & to A.A. Watts, 16 Nov 1824 (ibid., 328–9, 284–5).

52. Within the previous year WW had rejected at least three requests: from his old friend Stoddart, who wanted as a 'real kindness, & essential utility' a letter once or twice a year from WW, or even DW, for his *New Times*; from Lupton Relfe for poems for *Friendship's Offering*; from Thomas Kibble Hervey for poems for an unspecified publication, probably *Friendship's Offering* again: J. Stoddart to WW, Dec 1824: WLMS/A/Stoddart/4; WW to L. Relfe, 26 Feb 1825 (*Supp.*, 190–91); WW to T.K. Hervey [late 1825] (*LY*, i, 419–20). The letter to Relfe mentions having recently rejected an application 'from an old friend the Conductor of a London Journal, so strongly urged that I could not have refused to comply with it, however averse, except upon the ground of my having invariably declined entering upon this field of literature': this must be Stoddart rather than Watts, as suggested by *Supp.*, 191n.1.

53. WW to SR, 23 Mar [1825] (*LY*, i, 327).

54. SR to WW, 22 Apl 1825: WLMS/A/Rogers/4; WW to SR, [3 May] & 15 Aug, to J. Murray, 6 Aug [1825] & to HCR, 27 Apl [1826] (*LY*, i, 341–2, 381, 379, 443–4). For Byron's profanities about WW, see *Byron's Letters and Journals*, vi, 47, vii, 158, 167, 168, 253; viii, 66, 68, 207; xi, 198.

55. WW to J. Fletcher, 17 Jan & 25 Feb 1825 (*LY*, i, 303, 322).

56. SH to EQ, 2 Jun [1825] (*LSH*, 305). SH did not return to RM till 5 Aug 1825, having been absent since 18 Feb 1823: DWJMS, 1824–5: DC 104/1 [5 Aug 1825].

57. SGB to WW, 10 Dec 1824 & 25 May 1825; WLMS/A/Beaumont/80 p.4 & 83 p.3; WW, *Elegiac Stanzas (Addressed to Sir G.H.B. upon the Death of his Sister-in-Law)* and *Cenotaph* (*Poems*, ii, 604–6, 609–10); WW to SGB, 28 May [1825] (*LY*, i, 350).

58. DW to HCR, 2 Jul [1825] (ibid., 350, 373–4).

59. DW to HCR, 26 Nov & WW to MJJ, 4 May 1825 (ibid., 405, 343–4); MJJ to WW, [*end.* Apl 1825]: WLMS/A/Jewsbury/1 pp.1–2. Maria Jane Jewsbury (1800–1833) was the older sister of the more famous Geraldine (1812–80), authoress of *Zoe* (1845), *Marian Withers* (1851) and *Right or Wrong* (1859), and friend of the Carlyles, Mrs Gaskell and Charlotte Brontë.

60. DWJMS, 1824–5: DC 104/1 [23 & 31 May 1825]; Dora to E. Crump, [*c.*1 Jun 1825]: WLL/Dora/2 p.3; SH to JM, [7 Aug 1825]: WLL/SH/110a p.2.

61. MJJ, *Kents Bank Mercury*, 19 Jul 1825: WLMS/A/Jewsbury/52 pp.3–7v; WW to A.A. Watts, 5 Aug 1825 (*LY*, i, 377). Mambrino was a Moorish king with a golden helmet which made him invincible; MJJ's mocking reference is to the barber in *Don Quixote* who put his brass basin on his head during a rain shower and was mistaken by the knight for Mambrino.

62. A.A. Watts to WW, 30 Aug & 22 Oct 1825: WLMS/A/Watts/3 p.5 & 5 pp.1–2; WW & Dora to MJJ, [6 Aug 1825] (*LY*, i, 378). Alaric Alexander Watts (1797–1864) was editor of the *Leeds Intelligencer* and the *Literary Souvenir* when he sent WW a copy of his *Poetical Sketches* (1824), acknowledging his debt to WW for 'the

regeneration of my taste . . . effected by the perusal of your compositions': A.A. Watts to WW, 23 Jul 1824: WLMS/A/1 p.2.
63. WW & Dora W to MJJ, [6 Aug 1825] (*LY*, i, 378); Lockhart, *Narrative of the Life of Sir Walter Scott*, 478. Wilson had asked WW for a letter supporting his candidature for the post of Professor of Moral Philosophy: WW's response was 'Jesuitical', according to SH, because it claimed ignorance of the qualities necessary for the post, referred only to Wilson's intellectual abilities, energy of character and industry, and made no mention of his lack of personal morality. Wilson's public drunkenness, cock-fighting and wrestling had made him notorious in the Lakes, and his covert attacks on WW, through *Blackwood's Magazine*, had deeply hurt and annoyed the Ws. SH opposed giving Wilson any sort of reference, but WW said Wilson was beneath his resentment: J. Wilson to WW, [Apl–May 1820]: WLMS/A/Wilson/3; WW to J. Wilson, 5 May 1820 (*MY*, ii, 594–5); SH to JM, 7 Sep [1820] (*LSH*, 194).
64. Lockhart, *Narrative of the Life of Sir Walter Scott*, 478–9; WS to Mrs Scott of Lochore, [22 Aug], to J.B.S. Morritt, 25 Aug & to SGB, 28 Aug 1825 (*LWS*, ix, 208, 211n.1 & 215–16); SC to E. Crump, 19 Oct 1825: WLMS/SC/10 p.6; DWJMS, 1824–5: MS DC 104/1 [7 Oct 1825]. For Blomfield, see pp. 436–7.
65. DW to CC, 18 Oct & to RJ, 7 Oct, Dora & DW to EQ, 17 Oct & DW to M. Laing, 3 Nov 1825 (*LY*, i, 392, 387, 388–9, 395); Dora to M. Stanger, 7 Oct [1825]: Moorsom 62/4/1 p.2; MW to EQ, 5 [Oct 1825] (*LMW*, 122–3); SH to EQ, [24] Oct [1825] (*LSH*, 307); Overton & Wordsworth, *Christopher Wordsworth*, 38. CW's oldest son, John, had just won the first prize for Latin verse at Trinity.
66. Dora & DW to EQ, 17 Oct [1825] (*LY*, i, 389); SH to EQ, 21 Nov [1825] (*LSH*, 309–11); Watts, *Alaric Watts*, i, 238–40. Priscilla Watts, a Quaker poetess and writer, was the youngest sister of Jeremiah and Benjamin Wiffen, who had visited WW at RM in 1819: see p.527.
67. Dora to M. Stanger, 7 Oct [1825]: Moorsom 62/4/1 pp.2–3; DWJMS, 1824–5: DC 104/1 [21 Oct–4 Nov 1825]; DW to M. Laing, 3 Nov 1825 (*LY*, i, 395).
68. Lieutenant Thomas Robinson (1794–1838) was the grandson of WW's aunt Anne W, and nephew of WW's friend and cousin the late John Myers; he was the son of Hugh Robinson (1735–1802) and his much younger wife, Mary Myers (1765–1852). DWJMS records his presence twenty times between 8 Oct and 23 Nov, but it is clear he was there more often: DWJMS, 1824–5, DC, 104/1.
69. MW to EQ, 5 Oct [1825] (*LMW*, 122); B. Hill to M. Stanger, 6 Mar [1874]: Moorsom 59/1/13 pp.1–2; WW to [T. Robinson], 17 Jan 1826 (*LY*, i, 423–4); SC to E. Crump, 19 Oct 1825: WLMS/A/SC/10 p.7. JW3 confirmed that Robinson's proposal could not be entertained because of his want of means, and that Dora was not 'interested' in her suitor: Mrs JW3 to M. Stanger, 3 Mar [1874]: Moorsom 62/3/1 pp.2–3.
70. MW to LMB, 9 Dec [1825] (*LY*, i, 413).
71. WW to R. Heber, 21 Nov, to LL, 29 Nov & MW to LMB, 9 Dec 1825 (*LY*, i, 398–9, 407–8, 412–13); R. Heber to WW, 9 Dec 1825: WLMS/A/Heber/1; G. Canning to WW, 26 Nov 1825: WLMS/A/Canning/1; W. Howley to WW, 25 Nov 1825: WLMS/A/Howley/1.
72. DW to HCR, 13 Dec [1824] & WW to unidentified, 22 Dec [1825] (*LY*, i, 293, 414); W. Howley to WW, 6 Dec 1825: WLMS/A/Howley/2 pp.2–3.
73. MW to LMB, 9 Dec & DW to JPM, 23 Dec 1825 (*LY*, i, 412, 416).
74. CC to DW, 25 Dec 1825: WLMS/A/Clarkson/22 p.4; SH to EQ, 25 Jan & to JM, 28 Jan 1826 (*LSH*, 313, 315–16). The Tees Bank failure was caused by admitting a partner, Mr Perce, whose securities turned out to be worthless. The Marshalls' bank at Halifax was also affected by the run, but its losses, like those of the Kendal Bank, were not serious: DW to JPM, 23 Dec [1825] (*LY*, i, 417). WW's friend the barrister JL acted on behalf of some of the partners in the Tees Bank: JL, *Diaries*, ii, 41.
75. A.A. Watts to WW, 30 Dec 1825 & 21 Jan 1826: WLMS/A/Watts/7 & 8; WW to A.A. Watts, 19 & 23 Jan [1826] (*LY*, i, 424–6). Watts said (and the Ws believed him) that his arrangements with Hurst & Robinson protected WW from loss or future claim, but the non-delivery of the MS was undoubtedly crucial in preventing his involvement. The collapse of Constable's publishing house in Edinburgh ruined their London agent, Hurst & Robinson, and James Ballantyne & Co. As a partner in the last, WS

was personally liable for debts of £114,000, which were paid in full on his death.

76. DW to HCR, 25 Feb & WW to HCR, 27 Apl & [late May] [1826] (ibid., 428, 444, 450).

77. DW to JPM, 23 Dec [1825] & to G. Webster, 18 Feb 1826 (ibid., 417; *Supp.*, 191–2); G. Webster, Plans for WW, 1826; SH to EQ, 25 Jan [1826] (*LSH*, 314). George Webster (1797–1864), architect and monumental sculptor, designed many public buildings and private mansions in the Lakes; he became Mayor of Kendal in 1829.

78. WW to RJ, 18 May [1826] (*LY*, ii, 448); WW, *Composed When a Probability Existed of Our Being Obliged to Quit Rydal Mount as a Residence*, ll.1–8, and WW, 'The massy Ways, carried across these heights', ll.6–22 (*Poems*, ii, 625, 623).

Chapter 21

chapter title: 'Shades of the prison-house', *Ode: Intimations of Immortality*, l.67 (*Poems*, i, 525).
picture: Silhouette of WW by MJJ from her *Kents Bank Mercury*, 19 Jul 1825.

1. HCR to WW, [20 Feb 1826] (*HCRWC*, i, 153–4).

2. WW to HCR, 6 Apl & MW & WW to JK, 25 Jul [1826] (*LY*, i, 440, 473). For WW's comment to MJJ, see p.577.

3. DW to M. Laing, 29 Mar & to CC, 1 Apl & WW to RJ, 18 May & to CW, 9 Apl 1826 (ibid., 431, 434–5, 448, 442); JW4 & CW to WW, 4 Apl [1826]: WLL/CW/74 p.5. The italics in the quotation are mine.

4. VL to WW, 1 May 1826: WLMS/A/Lowther/66a; WW to LL, [*c.*15 May], 22, 26, 28, 29 & 30 Jun, 2, 5 & 7 Jul 1826 (*LY*, i, 445–7, 455–71); ibid., 466n.1. WW had vehemently opposed the founding of a non-denominational university in London, of which Brougham was a leading proponent: WW to LL, 15 Jun [1825] (ibid., 371–2).

5. WW to RJ, 18 May & to LL, 7 Jul 1826 (ibid., 448, 471). The Lowther brothers polled 1,925 and 1,851 votes to Brougham's 1,353. RJ's arrival at RM was expected at the end of Sep: Dora to RJ, 18 Sep [1826]: WLMS/A/Jones/9 p.1; SH to JM, 19 Sep [1826] (*LSH*, 324).

6. DWJMS: DC 104/2 [22 Jun & 8 Jul 1826]; RS to H.H. Southey, 8 Jul & to G.C. Bedford, 16 & 19 Jul 1826 (*RSNL*, ii, 306; *RSLC*, v, 252–3); SC to E. Crump, 18 Jul 1826: WLMS/A/SC/13 pp.1–3. *LY*, i, 475n.2, is wrong in identifying Isabel's 'twin-like' sister as Bertha; Kate, born in Aug 1810, was the sister in question.

7. WW & MW to JK, 25 Jul [1826] (ibid., 474); WW, 'Once I could hail (howe'er serene the sky)' (*Poems*, ii, 622–3).

8. SH to EQ, 22 May & 23 Aug & to JM, 19 Sep [1826] (*LSH*, 318, 320–22, 326); WW to HCR, [late May 1826] (*LY*, i, 452). Jo H and HH sailed from Whitehaven on 16 Aug and went into lodgings in Douglas: DW to JM, [24 Aug 1826] (ibid., 482).

9. LMB to MW, [early Dec 1825]: WLMS/A/Beaumont/85 pp.1–2; SH to EQ, 22 May [1826] (*LSH*, 318).

10. SH to JM, 19 Sep & to EQ, [28] Sep [1826] (ibid., 324, 329); WW to JPM, [22 Sep] & to JK, [*c.*29 Oct] [1826] (*LY*, i, 484–5, 491); *HCRBW*, i, 339–41.

11. SH to JM, 19 Sep & to EQ, [28] Sep & [11 (*r.*9) Nov] [1826] (*LSH*, 324–5, 328–9, 333); B. Hill to M. Stanger, 6 Mar [1874]: Moorsom 59/1/13 p.2. Bertha's impression that Dora's 'feelings were not interested' in Ayling is confirmed by JW3: Mrs JW3 to M. Stanger, 3 Mar [1874]: Moorsom 62/3/1 pp.2–3. The Ws called Ivy Cottage '*the Rydal Wife-Trap*', as Tillbrooke was known to be on the lookout for a bride: *HCRBW*, i, 339; MW to JM, 17 Jul [1827]: WLMS/H/1/3/1 pp.1–2. *LY*, ii, 429n.2, following Venn, vi, 192, identifies Tillbrooke's bride as Frances but the Ws and Bertha all identify her as her sister Emma.

12. DWJMS: DC 104/3/2 [26, 28 & 30 Nov, 2, 3, & 4 Dec]; B. Hill to M. Stanger, 6 Mar [1874]: Moorsom 59/1/13 p.2; DW to CC, 9 Sep [1831] (*LY*, ii, 429–30). WW2 met Fraser in Cambridge in May 1829 and learned that he had had nothing to do with the Aylings, or Tillbrooke, since leaving RM: 'he says Mr Ayling has behaved to him like a mad man abusing him wherever he goes': WW2 to MW, 20 May [1829]: WLL/WW2/9 p.2. According to Bertha, Ayling later took a living in Sussex, went out of his mind and starved himself to death: this was 'many years ago'.

13. DW to HCR, 18 Dec [1826] & WW to W. Jackson, 26 Jan [1827] (*LY*, i, 499, 509); Dora to RJ, 19 Sep [1826]: WLMS/A/Jones/9; for JW3's wish to join the army (shared by WW2) see 582, 596.

14. MJJ to Dora, 2 Oct [1826]: WLMS/A/

Jewsbury/7 pp.2–3; DWJMS: DC 104/3/1 [1–30 Oct 1826].

15. SH to EQ, [28] Sep [1826] (*LSH*, 329); WW to F.M. Reynolds, 24 Oct, DW to HCR, 18 Dec & MW to JK, 27 Oct [1826] (*LY*, i, 489, 500, 490).

16. WW to A.A. Watts, 22 Oct & to J. Murray, 4 Dec & DW to HCR, 18 Dec 1826; WW to TL, 2 Jan, DW to HCR, 6 Jan & WW & DW to HCR, 29 Jan 1827 (*LY*, i, 487, 496, 500, 502, 504, 510–11); DWJMS: DC 104/3/2 [12 Jan 1827]. WW had the gratification of turning down Murray's belated agreement to his terms on 29 Jan 1827 and again in Feb 1829: WW & DW to HCR, 29 Jan 1827 (*LY*, i, 510–11); B. Field to WW, 26 Feb 1829: WLMS/A/Field/5 p.1.

17. MW to W. Jackson, 15 Jan 1827 (*LY*, i, 502n.3); HCR to DW, [20 Feb 1826] (*HCRBW*, i, 151). HCR, like CL, particularly disapproved of WW's classifications, suggesting groupings, roughly based on Nature, Human Life, The Age (i.e. Politics) and Religion (ibid., 153–4).

18. WW to HCR, 6 Apl & to L. Relfe, 25 Jul 1826 (*LY*, i, 440, 476).

19. WW to TL, 10 May [1827] (ibid., 526–7). A.A. Watts to WW, 14 May 1827: WLMS/A/Watts/10; HCR to DW, [21 May 1827] (*HCRBW*, i, 183–4); LMB to MW, 28 Jun [1827]: WLMS/A/Beaumont/89; MJJ to Dora, 10 Jul 1827: WLMS/A/Jewsbury/11; SR to WW, 14 Jul 1827: WLMS/A/Rogers/8; F. Hemans to WW, 25 Jul 1827: WLMS/A/Hemans/3. The 3rd volume was 455 pages long, the rest were around 400 pages each.

20. LMB to WW, 8 [Feb 1827]: WLMS/A/Beaumont/87; SH to Mrs TH, 11 Feb [1827] (*LSH*, 337–8); *The Journal of Sir Walter Scott*, 270. WW denied that he had been present, saying that he had merely agreed with SGB's sentiments when SGB related the story to him: WW to J.G. Lockhart, 27 Apl [1838] (*LY*, iii, 560–61).

21. LMB to MW, 20 Jul 1827: WLMS/A/Beaumont/90 p.3; SGB, Extract from Will, 26 Aug 1824: WLMS/A/Beaumont/88.

22. Dora to M. Stanger, 8 Jan 1827: Moorsom 62/4/3 p.6; SH to JM, 6 Feb & to EQ, 21 Apl [1827] (*LSH*, 335, 338). Jane died in March, Bessy in April. JH's poem 'When five and twenty years around her head', was written at Sockburn on the day of Jane's funeral, 21 Mar 1827: WLMS/H/1/1/29. Their joint gravestone in the churchyard of the old All Saints' Church, Sockburn, is now so heavily weathered and worn that it is barely legible. All that remains of the inscription is 'Erected by an afflicted Father to the Memory of Two beloved daughters whose Lives w[ere . . .] hearts sincere . . . the . . . in'.

23. SH to EQ, 15 Mar [1827]: WLL/SH/123a p.2; SH to JM, 18 Mar [1827] (*LSH*, 340 & n.); Dora to M. Stanger, 8 Jan 1827: Moorsom 62/4/3 p.3. *The Ephesian Matron* (1796) was a 'Comic Serenata, after the manner of the Italian' by Isaac Bickerstaffe, the Irish dramatist.

24. Ibid., p.2. Dora's claim that she had only once been beyond the threshold of RM since September is contradicted by the regular rides recorded in DWJMS: DC 104/3/2.

25. RS to H. Hill, 5 Apl 1827 (*RSNL*, ii, 311); SH to EQ, 10 Apl [1827] (*LSH*, 343); DW to JW4, 6 Jun & to CW2, 23 Jun [1827] (*LY*, i, 530–32, 536); MW to JM, 17 Jul [1827]: WLMS/H/1/3/1 pp.1–2. JW4 and CW2 were at Cambridge, Chas W at Oxford: for their prizes, see Overton & Wordsworth, *Christopher Wordsworth*, 54–5.

26. EQD, 1827: WLMS/13/1/9 [15–28 Aug 1827]; MW to JK, 28 Aug 1827 (*LY*, i, 538–9).

27. DWJMS: DC 104/3/3 [3–5 Sep 1827]; SH to EQ, 12 Sep [1827] (*LSH*, 350).

28. Ibid., 351; WW to H. Douglas, [early Sep 1827] (*LY*, i, 541–2). *Hic*, *haec* and *hoc* are the male, female and neuter cases of the Latin pronoun meaning 'this'; *coelebs* is a reference to a novel by Hannah More with the self-explanatory title, *Coelebs in Search of a Wife* (1809).

29. SH to EQ, 12 Sep [1827] (*LSH*, 351–2); MW to JM, 17 Jul [1827]: WLMS/H/1/3/1 p.2; MW to LMB, 9 Dec [1825] & WW to LL, [early Dec 1827] (*LY*, i, 413, 559–60). Satterthwaite died on 8 Nov 1827.

30. WW to LL, 25 Jan, to W. Jackson, [early Mar], to SR, [17 Apl] & DW to MJJ, 21 May 1828 (ibid., 575, 588, 603, 607); CW to WW, 3 Feb 1828: WLL/CW/77 p.1.

31. DW & WW to WS, 13 Jun 1825, DW to EQ, 2 Nov, WW to W. Jackson, 26 Nov & to SR, [*c*.30 Nov] 1827 (*LY*, i, 368, 551, 554, 556).

32. DW to W. Jackson, 12 Feb & WW & DW to H. Douglas, 29 Feb [1828] (ibid., 582, 585); SH to EQ, 27 Jan & 4 Mar [1828] (*LSH*, 358, 360). DW had known of WW2's intention and had not forbidden it, hoping that the result would be a rejection.

33. DWJMS: DC 104/3/3 [12 Nov 1827]; WW to CW & CW2, [*c.*30 Nov 1827] (*LY*, i, 556–7); C. & S. Lloyd to WW & MW, 3 Dec 1827: WLMS/A/Lloyd, C./2. Charles Lloyd Snr died only a few weeks after WW's visit, leaving £20,000 to each of his oldest sons (including Charles Jnr) and £4,000 each to all his other children. CW was bequeathed a house and estate worth £4,000, to be passed to his sons: CW to WW, 3 Feb 1828: WLL/CW/77 pp.2–3.

34. WW to LL, [early Dec 1827] & DW to M. Laing, 21 Jan 1828 (*LY*, i, 560, 572–3); Dora to CW2, 3 Dec & to EQ, [20 Dec] 1827: WLL/Dora/9 p.3 & 10 p.2. Elizabeth Monkhouse, who had lived for many years with TH, died on 12 Feb 1828 and was buried in the churchyard of the enchantingly pretty and tiny Brinsop church, where her grave can still be seen, together with those of several Hutchinsons.

35. DWJMS: DC 104/3/4 [29 Jan 1828]; CW to WW, 3 Feb 1828: WLL/CW/77 p.4; WW to MW & Dora, [early Mar 1828] (*LY*, i, 589–90). The furniture for JW3's rectory cost a further £84: SH to JM, 28 Apl [1828] (*LSH*, 363).

36. WW to unidentified, 30 Jan & to A. Cunningham, 7 Mar 1828 (*LY*, i, 578, 593); Dora to MJJ, 21 May [1828] (ibid., 580n.1). WW, *A Gravestone upon the Floor in the Cloisters of Worcester Cathedral* (*Poems*, ii, 672), was written at Brinsop, *The Country Girl* (later known as *The Gleaner*) and *The Wishing Gate* (ibid., 646–9) after WW's return to RM: SH to EQ, 27 Jan [1828] (*LSH*, 358); WW to MW & Dora, [early Mar] [1828] (*LY*, i, 590). A fourth poem was composed 'on the roof of the Coach upon the first sight of my native mountains'; WW described it as 'not worth sending', then as 'too personal for general interest': WW to B. Field, 16 Apl 1828 & to unidentified, [1828–9] (ibid., 602, 699).

37. WW, *A Tradition of Oker Hill in Darley Dale, Derbyshire* (*Poems*, ii, 671).

38. DW to W. Jackson, 12 Feb, WW to MW & Dora, [early Mar], WW to GHG, 15 Dec, to HCR [15 Dec] & to B. Field, 20 Dec 1828 (*LY*, i, 582, 590, 689, 691, 695). In Mar, the poem was called *The Promise*; it was changed to *The Triad* for publication in Nov.

39. WW to B. Field, 16 Apl, to SR, [17 Apl], to W. Jackson, [late Mar], & DW to MJJ, 21 May & to M. Laing, 3 Jun 1828 (ibid., 602, 603, 597, 607, 611). WW said JW3 had 'a good voice, not ill managed, which is of great importance in a Northerner, an excellent and easy pronunciation'.

40. SH to JM, 28 Apl & to EQ, 4 Mar [1828] (*LSH*, 363, 360); WW to SR, [17 Apl] & to F. Merewether, 5 May [1828] (*LY*, i, 603, 604). MW wrote to EQ saying they would arrive on 10 May, EQ's diary notes their arrival on 6 May and DW says they arrived on 11 May: MW to EQ, 5 May [1828]: WLL/MW/67; EQD, 1828: WLMS/13/2/1 [6 May 1828]; DW to MJJ, 21 May [1828] (*LY*, i, 607).

41. Dora to CW2, [*p.m.*14 May 1828] (Overton & Wordsworth, *Christopher Wordsworth*, 64–5); *HCRBW*, i, 355–8; EQD, 1828: WLMS/13/2/1 [6–28 May 1828]; *Journal of Sir Walter Scott*, 475–6, 481–2; WS to SR, 16 May & to Major WS, 18 May 1828 (*LWS*, x, 420, 422); *JTM*, iii, 1138; Dora to CW2, [*p.m.*26 May 1828]; WLL/Dora/11.

42. *HCRBW*, i, 358; DW to M. Laing, 3 Jun [1828] (*LY*, i, 611–12); Dora to Mrs Hoare, 16 Jun [1828]: WLL/Dora/12 p.1.

43. WW to HCR, [16 Jun], to STC, 17 [Jun] & to F.M. Reynolds, [21 (*r.*20) Jun] [1828] (*LY*, i, 613, 614, 616); MW to EQ, 23 Jun [1828] (*LMW*, 124). Dora's delightful journal, now at DC, is unpublished. After 1 Jul, Dora's dating is out by a day or two. She also took sketches at every opportunity: these are also now at DC.

44. Dora, *Journal of a Tour of the Continent*, 1828: DC 110 pp.4, 7, 12, 13, 46/48 & 18/20 [22, 23, 26 Jun, 14 (*r.*12) Jul & 28 Jun 1828].

45. T.C. Grattan, *Beaten Paths; and those who trod them* (Knight, *The Life of William Wordsworth*, iii, 131–2). Thomas Colley Grattan (1792–1864) lived for some years in France and Belgium, where he was now resident: he sent a copy of his first series of *Highways and Byways* (1823) to CL; a second and third series appeared in 1825 and 1827: Prance, 132–3. Dora described him as a 'most entertaining good-humoured creature', teasing her mother that, were he not married, MW ran the risk of having 'one of the ugliest men in the world' for a son-in-law: SC to E. Wardell, 10 Jul 1828: WLMS/SC/22 p.3.

46. Young, *A Memoir of Charles Mayne Young*, i, 173, 175–7; Dyce, *Recollections of the Table-talk of Samuel Rogers*, 207.

47. Young, *A Memoir of Charles Mayne Young*, i, 178–9, 173–5, 180; C. Aders to HCR, [Aug 1828] (*HCRWC*, i, 190); *HCRBW*, ii, 361. Barthold

Georg Niebuhr (1776–1831), historian, statesman and philologist, was a former Prussian Ambassador to Rome (1816–23); Augustus Wilhelm von Schlegel (1767–1845), Professor at Bonn (1818–45), was co-founder, with his brother, of the literary journal *Athenaeum*, the mouthpiece of the German romantic school, and author of translations of Shakespeare and a tragedy, *Ion* (1803).

48. MW to EQ, 26 Jul [1828] (*LMW*, 126); STC, unpublished passage in *STCN*, quoted by Ashton, 383.

49. *DWJ*, ii, 404, 408, 410–13; DW to W. Jackson, 12 Feb [1828] (*LY*, i, 583); for Jo H's accident, which lamed her for life, see DW to M. Laing, 23 Jan 1827 (ibid., 507).

50. Dora & WW to EQ, 1 Aug [*r.*31 Jul], WW to C. Aders & to HCR, [7 Aug], to C.J. Blomfield, 9 Aug & to W. Jerdan, 9 Aug & 7 Oct 1828 (*LY*, i, 620–21, 622, 624, 624–5, 625n.1, 632).

51. WW to CW, [mid-Oct], to WS, 28 Aug & to EQ, [11 Nov] [1828] (ibid., 634, 627, 656); DWJMS: DC 104/4/1 [25 Sep 1828]; WW to H.J. Rose, 11 Dec 1828 (*LY*, i, 685–6).

52. WW to H.J. Rose [late Jan 1829] (ibid., ii, 18–23).

53. WW to W. Jackson, [early Oct], to CW, [mid-Oct] & to CW2, 27 Nov [1828] (ibid., i, 629–30, 634–5, 669–70). WW asked Jackson, who had done so much to help JW3, to tutor WW2, but, newly installed as rector of Lowther, he was reluctant to take on any pupils.

54. WW to GHG, 15 Dec 1828 & 24 Jan 1829 (ibid., 687–8; ii, 6–7); Dora to EQ, 30 Dec 1828–8 Jan 1829: WLL/Dora/17 pp.7–8.

55. WW to LL, 6 & 23 Dec, DW to JPM, 26 Dec 1828 (*LY*, i, 683–4, 696, 697–8); MW to EQ, 25 Dec [1828] (*LMW*, 129). JW3 was ordained priest at Cambridge just before Christmas. DW left RM for Whitwick on 7 Nov, travelling via Manchester, where she stayed with MJJ and visited not only churches and museums but also a cotton factory, infant school and Deaf and Dumb Institution: DWJMS: DC 104/4/1 [12–15 Nov 1828]; MJJ to Dora, [*p.m.*18 Nov 1828]: WLMS/A/Jewsbury/16 p.2.

56. WW to EQ, 17 Oct & [11 Nov] 1828 (*LY*, i, 638, 656). HH visited RM in Sep, leaving on 1 Oct; Jo H arrived in the last week of Oct: DWJMS: DC 104/4/1 [1 Oct 1828]; Jo H to EH, 6 Nov 1828: WLMS/H/1/8/44 p.3.

57. WW to EQ, [11 Nov], to F.M. Reynolds, 19 Dec 1828 & to MJJ, [late Jan 1829] (*LY*, i, 656, 692; ii, 28); HCR to WW, [17 Nov 1828] (*HCRWC*, i, 191); JW4 to Dora, [*p.m.*6 or 8] Feb 1829: WLMS/1/9/1 p.4. *The Poetical Works of William Wordsworth. In Four Volumes* (Boston, Mass., Cummings, Hilliard & Co., 1824) boasted 'the latest English edition has been carefully followed; and whatever is peculiar in Orthography, Punctuation, and the Use of Capital Letters is copied from the same without change': Broughton, *The Wordsworth Collection*, 5.

58. WW to HCR, [15 Dec 1828] (*LY*, i, 690–91). 'I have not noticed a single error that I am not myself answerable for', WW said of the Galignani edition.

59. WW to A. Cunningham, [early Dec] & to F.M. Reynolds, 19 Dec 1828 & [*c.*27 Jan 1829] (ibid., 680, 692–3; ii, 14–15]. The only rejected sonnet identifiable with certainty was WW, *Roman Antiquities* (*Poems*, ii, 724–5).

60. MW & WW to JK, 25 Jul & WW to A.A. Watts, 18 Jun 1826 (*LY*, i, 473, 474, 455); SC to E. Wardell, 2 Feb 1828 [*r.*1829]; WLMS/A/SC/20 p.3. SC's letter is obviously misdated, as it refers to JW3's acceptance of Moresby and WW2's trip to Bremen, neither of which can be dated before Dec 1828. WW was therefore advising HC from experience, not acting against his own advice, as suggested in *LY*, ii, 15n.1.

61. WW to GHG, 25 Dec 1828 (*LY*, i, 689); WW, *The Egyptian Maid; or, The Romance of the Water Lily* (*Poems*, ii, 652–63); *IF*, 30.

62. WW to GHG, 15 Nov 1828 (*LY*, i, 668); WW, *On the Power of Sound* (*Poems*, ii, 664–71); *IF*, 17; Dora to EQ, 30 Dec 1828–8 Jan 1829: WLL/Dora/17 p.10. Among the 1,000 lines were 350 belonging to *The Russian Fugitive* (*Poems*, ii, 672–83), which WW refers to in WW to GHG, 29 Jan 1829 (*LY*, ii, 26).

63. Dora to EQ, 30 Dec 1828–8 Jan 1829: WLL/Dora/17 pp.11–12.

64. WW to A. Dyce, 12 Jan & 16 Oct & to D. Lardner, 12 Jan 1829 (*LY*, ii, 3, 157, 4–5). WW suggested the book on poetesses to Dionysius Lardner (1793–1859), Professor of Natural Philosophy and Astronomy in the new University of London, in London in May–Jun 1828, probably for Lardner's *Cabinet Cyclopaedia of Eminent Literary and Scientific Men* (1829–49). WW welcomed the discovery that Dyce had already

written *Specimens of British Poetesses* (1825): WW to A. Dyce, 16 Oct [1829] (ibid., 157).

65. B. Field to WW, 19 & 24 Dec 1828: WLMS/A/Field/3 & 4; WW to B. Field, 19 Jan 1829 (*LY*, ii, 5–6); E. Peabody to WW, 9 Dec 1825 & 29 Mar 1829: WLMS/A/Peabody/1 & 2. *Lalla Rookh* (1817) was Moore's highly successful series of Oriental tales in verse. Elizabeth Peabody (1804–94), a leading American educationalist, published elementary textbooks and opened the first American kindergarten in Boston. A parishioner of WW's visitor of 1822, William Ellery Channing, she did not find courage to send her first letter to WW till 17 Jun 1827.

66. WW to J. Dyer, 3 Apl, to unidentified, 30 Jan & to A. Cunningham, 9 Jan, [11 Nov] & [early Dec] 1828 (*LY*, i, 597–8, 578, 568, 653–4, 680). The publisher was Oliver & Boyd of Edinburgh. For Cunningham's suggested preface, which he thought RS should rewrite, and his table of contents, see ibid., 703–4.

67. WW to CW, [13 Mar] & to C. Blomfield, 3 Mar 1829 (ibid., ii, 52, 40–41, 36–7); WW to Sir R. Inglis, 11 Jun 1825 (ibid., i, 360–61). The proposal to pay the salaries of Irish Catholic priests was dropped before the bill passed into law.

68. WW to R. Inglis, 11 Jun 1825 (ibid., 361–5). Sir Robert Inglis (1786–1855), an ardent defender of the Anglican establishment, opposed all attempts to reform Church or state throughout his parliamentary career.

69. WW to C. Blomfield, 3 Mar, to W. Jackson, 10 Apl, to F. Merewether, 22 Jun & to BM, 29 Jul 1829 (ibid., ii, 36–46, 63–4, 87–8, 99); EQ to SH, 25 Apl 1829: WLL/EQ/24 p.2. Much of WW's letter to Blomfield is based on his earlier one to Inglis: see n.68.

70. SC to M. Stanger, 29 Jan 1829: Moorsom 55/1/5 p.3; SC to E. Wardell, 2 Feb [1828 (*r.*1829)]: WLMS/A/SC/20 pp.3–4; WW to HCR, 26 Apl & to F.M. Reynolds, 9 May 1829 (*LY*, ii, 67, 74). The first attack occurred in Mar.

71. WW to W. Jackson, 10 Apl, DW to HCR, 2 May & to CC, 18 Oct & WW to HCR, 26 Apl 1829 (ibid., 63, 71, 159, 69); DWJMS: DC 104/4/4 [28 Mar & summary of 3 Apl 1829].

72. WW to W. Jackson, 10 Apl & 10 Mar [*r.*May] 1829 (*LY*, ii, 63, 76); MW arrived at Whitwick on 10 Apl and remained there till 11 May; WW2 left the day before his mother: DWJMS: DC 104/4/4 (summary of 3 Apl, 10 & 11 May 1829).

73. WW2 to MW, 23 & [*p.m.*25] May, to WW, MW & Dora, 4–6 Jun, to SH, 26–7 Jun, to Dora, 14 Jul & to MW, 19 Aug 1829: WLL/WW2/10 p.3, 11 pp.1–3, 12 pp.9–10, 13 pp.2, 4, 14 p.4 & 16 pp.2–3. WW2's expenses were despite gifts of three pairs of trouses and two waistcoats by JW4, £5 from CW and three sovereigns from SH.

74. DWJMS: DC 104/4/4 [22–4 Jun, 31 Jul–7 Aug 1829]; LMB to WW [*c.*Jun 1829]: WLMS/A/104; Dora to CW2, 27 Aug [1829]: WLL/Dora/22 pp.3–4; DW to JPM, 15 Sep [1829] (*LY*, ii, 131).

75. WW to SGB Jnr, 19 Jul & to F. Merewether, [mid-Nov] 1829 (ibid., 92, 167–8). SGB and LMB were childless; their heir was SGB's cousin, Sir George Beaumont (1799–1845), who married Mary Anne (d.1834), oldest daughter of CW and WW's friend William Howley, Bishop of London. LMB left DW a legacy of £20: Lady Beaumont Jnr to DW, 18 Jul [1830]: WLMS/A/Beaumont/108, note at top of p.1. WW's tribute to SGB was composed in Nov 1830: WW, *Elegiac Musings in the Grounds of Coleorton Hall, the Seat of the Late Sir G.H. Beaumont, Bart.* (*Poems*, ii, 696–8).

76. DWJMS: DC 104/4/4 [8 Sep 1829]; Dora & DW to MJJ, 11 Sep & DW to D. Coleridge, 27 Sep 1829 (*LY*, ii, 127–9, 152–3); *LHC*, 99.

77. DW to CC, 18 [*r.*19]–27 Oct [1829] (*LY*, ii, 159). DW became ill on 9 Oct; she stopped writing entries in her diary on 16 Oct and did not resume until 23 Nov: DWJMS: DC 104/4/4 [9 Oct–23 Nov 1829].

Chapter 22

chapter title: 'Furiously Alarmist', Tennyson, *Alfred Lord Tennyson: A Memoir*, i, 72.

picture: Chalk drawing of WW, by Henry Pickersgill; a preparatory study for the portrait commissioned by St John's College, 1832.

1. WW to RJ, 27 Jan, to GHG, 20 Mar & 9 Apl, & to HCR, 26 Apl 1829 (*LY*, ii, 12, 56, 60, 68). WW had been contemplating a tour of Ireland since at least 1824: DW to HCR, 13 Dec [1824] (ibid., i, 293).

2. WW to RS, [15 Sep] & to WRH, 24 Sep 1827 (ibid., 542–3, 545–7); WRH, 'It haunts me yet, that dream of earthly love': WLMS/Hamilton/1; WRH to E. Hamilton, 16 Sep 1827 (Graves, *Life of*

Hamilton, i, 262). William Rowan Hamilton (1805–65) was appointed Professor of Astronomy at Trinity College, Dublin, in 1827, while still an undergraduate, and knighted in 1837. He and his sister Eliza (1807–51), a poetess, became lifelong friends of the Ws.

3. WW to WRH, 24 Jul & to DW, [5 Aug] & DW to CW2, 28 Aug 1829 (*LY*, ii, 96, 105, 113); Dora to CW2, 27 Aug [1829]: WLL/Dora/22 p.2. Dora did not accompany her father but went to Moresby and Whitehaven with MW for the sea-bathing, as her health continued poor.

4. Ibid.; WW to MW & Dora, [29 Aug], [30 Aug] & [4 Sep] & to CW, 5 Sep [1829] (*LY*, ii, 114–16, 116, 117–18, 121).

5. WW to MW & Dora, [4 Sep 1829] (ibid., 120). For E. Hamilton's account of WW's visit see Graves, *Life of Hamilton*, i, 311–14.

6. WW to CW, 5 & 17 Sep, to the Ws, 18 Sep & to DW, 24 [Sep] [1829] (*LY*, ii, 121–4, 139–40, 143, 145).

7. Dora & WW to EQ, [11 Oct] & WW to CW, 17 [Sep] & to GHG, 1 Dec 1829 (ibid., 154, 140, 181); WW, *Eagles*, ll.4–9 (*Poems*, ii, 715); *IF*, 48–9.

8. WW to F.M. Reynolds, 9 May, WW to GHG, 1 Dec, 4 & 29 Jul & [12 *or* 13 Oct] 1829 (*LY*, ii, 74–5, 182, 90, 98, 156); Dora to EQ, 25 Jul 1829: WLL/Dora/21 p.1.

9. WW to GHG, 29 Jul & 14 Nov, to DW, [5 Aug], MW to GHG, 28 Oct 1829 & WW to SR, 5 Jun [1830] (*LY*, ii, 98, 165–6, 105, 165, 275–6).

10. EQD: WLMS 13/2/2 [15 Oct–3 Nov 1829]; DW to JW4 & CW2, 18 Nov [1829] (*LY*, ii, 169).

11. Dora to EQ, 21 Nov & [*p.m.*19 Dec] 1829: WLL/Dora/23 p.5 & 25 pp.3–4; DW to MAL, 9 Jan 1830 (*LY*, ii, 191).

12. Dora to EQ, [*p.m.*19 Dec] 1829: WLL/Dora/25 p.3; DWJMS: DC 118/1/1 [summary of 21 Jan 1830]; WW2 to Dora & to WW, 16 Dec 1829: WLL/WW2/23 pp.1–2 & 22 pp.1–2; G.E. Papendick to WW, 16 Dec 1829: WLL/WW2/24 pp.1–4. On WW's birthday, WW2 bought *himself* a horse as a birthday present, saying he needed to ride for his health: WW2 to MW, 17 Apl 1830: WLL/WW2/34 pp.1–2.

13. DW to MJJ, 22 Mar, WW to GHG, 6 Apl & to CW2, 13 Apl 1830 (*LY*, ii, 219, 227–8, 229).

14. WW to Dora, Tues [late Apl/early May] & DW to CW2, 13 Apl [1830] (ibid., 257, 229).

15. Dora to EQ, 21 Nov 1829: WLL/Dora/23 p.1; WW & Dora to EQ, 11 Feb & WW to EQ, 18 Feb [1830] (ibid., 203–4, 206). EQ had been charged with negotiating terms for the single volume with Longman.

16. RS to A. Cunningham, 21 Dec 1828 (*RSLC*, v, 339); WW to J. Gardner, 5 Apl & 19 May 1830 (*LY*, ii, 224–6, 264). The Ws knew, and repeated, RS's witticism. John Gardner (1804–80), a London physician, later founded the Royal College of Chemistry.

17. WW to J. Gardner, 19 May & 5 Apl, WW to EM, 2 Jun 1830 (ibid., 264, 225–6, 273–4). WW envisaged an edition selling at under £1 instead of the current 45s.

18. WW to CW, [12 Jun] & DW to J & JPM, 13 Jul [1830] (ibid., 282, 298). Isabella Curwen (1808–49), daughter of Henry Curwen (1783–1861), was five years younger than JW3; her brother Henry (1812–94) was a pupil of Owen Lloyd. For JW3's extravagance, see DW to CW2, 13 Apl [1830] (ibid., 229); DWJMS: DC 118/1/1 p.1.

19. WW to CW, [12 Jun 1830] (*LY*, ii, 282–3); DWJMS: DC 118/1/1 [8–11 Jun 1830].

20. DW to J & JPM, 13 Jul [1830] (*LY*, ii, 299); SH to EQ, 31 Jul [1830] (*LSH*, 370); RMVB, pp.1–8. See also DW to RJ, 7 Oct 1825 (*LY*, i, 387). The numbers cannot be calculated with complete accuracy, as names often include 'and party'.

21. RMVB, pp.2–7; DW to W. Pearson, 22 Jun & to J & JPM, 13 Jul, WW to EQ, [*c.*27 Apl], DW & WW to CW, 27 Apl [1830] (*LY*, ii, 293, 300–301, 250, 252). WW to F. Hemans, [11 Jul 1830] (*Supp.*, 205–6); DWJMS: DC 104/4/4 [23 Aug 1830]; WRH to S. Hamilton, 30 Jul 1830: WLMS/Hamilton/2 pp.1–2.

22. SH to EQ, 31 Jul [1830] (*LSH*, 370–71); DWJMS: DC 104/4/4 [2 Jul 1830]; WW to WRH, [late Jun (*r.*2 Jul) 1830] (*LY*, ii, 295); Mrs Hemans to unidentified, copied from undated *Athenaeum*: WLMS/A/Hemans/14; *IF*, 60; WW to GHG, [1 (*r.*21) Jul 1830] (*LY*, ii, 296). WW did share SH's opinion of Mrs Hemans: see WW to GHG, [early Aug 1830] (ibid., 311). The bride was presumably SC.

23. J. Ruskin, *A Tour to the Lakes in Cumberland: John Ruskin's Diary for 1830*, edited by J.S. Dearden (Aldershot & Vermont, Scolar Press, 1990), 46. The Ruskins had used the same subterfuge at Crosthwaite Church, Keswick, to see RS, who, unlike WW, seemed 'extremely attentive' and 'very pious', had a 'very keen eye & looks extremely like – a poet': ibid., 42.

24. DW to CW, 6 Aug & to CW, 6 Oct, WW to SGB2, 19 Oct & DW to Mrs STC, [8 Nov] [1830] (*LY*, ii, 314; *Supp.*, 207; *LY*, ii, 329, 342–3); MW to Mrs TH, 26 Nov [1830] (*LMW*, ii, 131). The delay in procuring a house meant that JW3 had to begin married life at Workington Hall, living with his parents-in-law.

25. WW to GHG, 30 May, DW & WW to H. Douglas, 12 Jun, DW to CC, [*c.*5 Nov], DW to JPM, [12 Nov] & WW to WRH, 26 Nov 1830 (*LY*, ii, 268, 284, 335, 347–8, 353).

26. WW to DW, [8 Nov] & to WRH, 26 Nov & MW to Lady Beaumont Jnr, 21 Dec 1830 (ibid., 340–41, 353, 357). WW, 'Chatsworth! thy stately mansion, and the pride' and *Elegiac Musings in the Grounds of Coleorton Hall* (*Poems*, ii, 695–6, 696–8).

27. WW to WRH, 26 Nov 1830 (*LY*, ii, 354). Agricultural labourers were rioting, smashing machinery and committing arson, in protest at the desperate state of the rural economy.

28. Dora to CW2, 7 Mar [1831]: WLL/Dora/33 pp.3–4; Tennyson, *Alfred Lord Tennyson: A Memoir*, i, 71–2. Tennyson missed this chance of a meeting with WW, though he was a friend of Spedding and admirer of WW's poetry. When the young men said they had enjoyed WW's conversation but that he had not said anything profound, Tennyson defended him, saying, 'How can you expect a great man to say anything "very profound" when he *knows* it is expected of him?' WW had noted that Trinity had a 'respectable show of blossom in poetry. Two brothers of the name of Tennyson in particular, are not a little promising': WW to WRH, 26 Nov 1830 (*LY*, ii, 354).

29. EQD: WLMS 13/2/4 [1 Jan, 28 Feb, 1 & 12 Mar 1831]; WW to JK, [late Jan–early Feb 1831] (*LY*, ii, 366). The 'Prince' was probably William Frederick, Duke of Gloucester, who was Chancellor of Cambridge University.

30. WW to LL, 24 Feb 1832 (ibid., 499); HT, *Autobiography*, i, 83; Mill, *Additional Letters*, 12; *The Greville Memoirs*, ii, 122–3.

31. EQD: WLMS/13/2/4 [4 Apl 1831]; BRH to WW, 28 Jun 1831: WLMS/A/Haydon/13 p.3; WW to BRH, [*c.*8 Jul 1831] (*LY*, ii, 407–8).

32. WW to J.K. Miller, 17 Dec 1831, to CW, 1 Apl [1832] & to HCR, 5 Feb 1833 (ibid., 464, 517, 588). See also WW to LL, 24 Feb 1832 (ibid., 500).

33. WW to J.K. Miller, 17 Dec 1831 (ibid., 464); ibid., 366n.2; Dora to CW2, 4 Feb [1831]: WLL/Dora/30 p.3.

34. WW to R. Lawrence, 2 Mar [1832] & DW to CC, 9 Sep [1831] (*LY*, ii, 506, 428); EQD: WLMS 13/2/4 [30 Mar 1831]; HT, *Autobiography*, i, 181; Blanshard, 68–70, 153–4, pl.11a. Francis Wilkin (1791–1842) also produced a much less sensitively drawn lithograph of the portrait (ibid., pl.11b) which was widely circulated and was the subject of the comments.

35. EQD: WLMS 13/2/4 [6 Apl 1831]; J. Keymer, 'WW interview with my father', [Apl 1831]: WLMS/A/Keymer p.3; WW to J. Gardner, [late 1832 or early 1833] & to EQ, 23 Feb [1833] (*LY*, ii, 578, 594–5); EQ to Dora, 29 Nov 1834: WLL/EQ/53 p.6; Blanshard, 70–71, 154–5, pl.12a, 12b.

36. Dora to MJJ, 21 Jul 1831 (Blanshard, 68, 156). Gardner breakfasted with WW on 28 Feb, but painting his portrait probably required several sittings: EQD: WLMS 13/2/4 [28 Feb 1831].

37. Ibid. [11, 25 & 26 Mar, 6 Apl 1831]; WW to DW & SH, [1 Apl 1831] (*LY*, ii, 373); Blanshard, 68, 155–6, pl.38b. Lawrence Macdonald (1799–1878), a Scottish sculptor, made a bust of WS in 1830 and exhibited in London in 1832. He later helped to found the British Academy of Arts in Rome.

38. EQ to DW, [*p.m.*3 Mar 1831]: WLL/EQ/28 pp.1–3. Hine was invited to breakfast on 4 Mar. On 7 Apl WW & WW2 dined and slept at Brixton, when, presumably, *Selections from the Poems of William Wordsworth, Esq., chiefly for the Use of Schools and Young Persons* (London, Moxon, 1831) was discussed further: EQD: WLMS 13/2/4 [1 Mar & 7 Apl 1831].

39. WW to EM, 13 & [*c.*9] Jun, WW, Dora & DW to Chas W, 6 Jun & WW & DW to WRH & E. Hamilton, 13 Jun 1831 (*LY*, ii, 401, 395–6, 389, 399); SR to WW, 25 Jun 1831: WLMS/A/Rogers/20 pp.3–4; RS to J. May, 1 Oct 1831 (*RSLC*, vi, 161).

40. WW to EQ, [29 Apl 1831] (*LY*, ii, 380–81); Dora to E. Hamilton, 1 Jun & to CW2, 29 Apl [1831]: WLL/Dora/35 pp.1–2 & 34 pp.1–3; M. Howitt to Dora, 17 Jun 1831: WLMS/A/Howitt/1. Howitt's sonnet addressed to Dora, 'Go get thee to thy native hills', was included in his wife's letter.

41. Dora to CW2, 7 Mar & 26 [*r.*27] Feb [1831]: WLL/Dora/33 p.3 & 31 p.1. WW echoed Dora's opinion more calmly: WW to RJ, 7 Jun [1831] (*LY*, ii, 393).

42. WW2 to WW, 14 May 1830: WLL/WW2/36

p.3. See also WW2 to WW, 1 May, 23 Jun, 18 Sep & 20 Oct 1830: WLL/WW2/35 pp.3–4, 38, 43, 44; WW to GHG, [31 May], DW to JW4, 1 Jun [1830] (*LY*, ii, 269–70, 271–2). Papendick chose his words with care when reporting that WW2's improvements in German, 'I think I may safely venture to assure you have kept pace with the time he has devoted to them under my roof': G.E. Papendick to WW, 25 May 1830: WLL/WW2/37 p.1.

43. M. Stanger to J. Stanger, [*p.m.*21 Apl 1831]: Moorsom 46/6, p.4; DWJMS: DC 118/1/3 [1 May 1831]; JW3 & DW to F. Merewether, 6 Jun & 9 Sep [1831] (*LY*, ii, 390, 428–9). WW2 took up office on 20 Oct 1831. Carter had given up gardening duties when he decided to become a clergyman, and did not resume them when the Bishop of Chester ruled him ineligible for ordination, because he had been to neither university nor St Bees: MW to EQ, 10 Dec [1824]: WLL/MW/64 p.4; MW to LMB, 9 Dec [1825] (*LY*, i, 413).

44. WW & DW to CW2, 9 May [1831] (ibid., ii, 383); SH to EQ, 10 May [1831] (*LSH*, 381). William Crackanthorpe stood against the Lowthers in Westmorland, but withdrew in the pre-poll agreement.

45. Dora to E. Hamilton, 1 Jun 1831: WLL/Dora/35 p.3; JW & DW to F. Merewether, 6 Jun [1831] (*LY*, ii, 392).

46. WW to BRH, 23 Apl & 11 Jun & to EM, 21 Jul 1831 (ibid., 378, 396, 410–11); BRH to WW, 28 Jun 1831: WLMS/A/Haydon/13 p.1; WW, *To B.R. Haydon, On Seeing his Picture of Napoleon Buonaparte on the Island of St Helena* (*Poems*, ii, 707); *IF*, 26. WW was anxious to cement his recent reconciliation with BRH after a seven-year estrangement, but the sonnet was a genuine tribute to a picture he had seen and admired in London in the spring.

47. WW to JK, 9 Sep [1831] (*LY*, ii, 425–6); WW, 'In these fair Vales, hath many a tree' (*Poems*, ii, 695); DWJMS: DC 118/1/3 [27 Jul, 1, 5 & 16 Aug 1831]. The poem was engraved on a brass plaque inserted into the stone in WW's absence on his Italian tour of 1837: *IF*, 29.

48. Mill, *Autobiography*, 89; Mill, *Journals and Speeches*, xxvii, 555. In a rejected first draft of his autobiography, Mill wrote: 'At present my estimate of Wordsworth as a poet is very far indeed below that which I then formed [in 1828]; but poetry of deeper and loftier feeling could not have done for me at that time what this did. I wanted to be made to feel that there was happiness in tranquil contemplation': *Autobiography & Literary Essays*, 150.

49. DWJMS: DC 118/1/3 [13 Sep 1831]; SH to EH, [11 Oct 1831] (*LSH*, 394); WW to J. Gardner, 27 Dec, to EQ, 23 Aug & to WS, 16 Sep [1831] (*LY*, ii, 470, 421, 434).

50. *IF*, 50–51; WW, *Yarrow Revisited*, ll.65–72 and *On the Departure of Sir Walter Scott from Abbotsford, for Naples*, ll.5, 8–9 (*Poems*, ii, 708–11, 711–12).

51. *Journal of Sir Walter Scott*, 660; *IF*, 50–51; Lockhart, *Narrative of the Life of Sir Walter Scott*, 614–16; J.G. Lockhart to WW, 27 Dec 1831: WLMS/A/Lockhart/1 p.2; WW to EM, 21 Jul & to A. Watts, [early Dec] [1831] (*LY*, ii, 410, 462–3). WW had always said that if ever he published anything in the annuals again, his first obligation was to Watts, as a return for his assistance in trying to find him a new publisher.

52. *IF*, 51; WS to Capt. B. Hall, 26 Oct 1831 (*LWS*, xii, 35); *Journal of Sir Walter Scott*, 661. WS returned to Scotland, dying at Abbotsford on 21 Sep 1832.

53. Dora to MW, 7 Oct [1831]: WLL/Dora/37 p.3; WW to SR, 7 Nov [1831] (*LY*, ii, 447). The burial ground probably inspired WW's *A Place of Burial in the South of Scotland* (*Poems*, ii, 712). Chas W left the Ws at Callander on 29 Sep, arriving at RM on 1 Oct: SH to EQ, 1 Oct [1831]: WLL/SH/143a p.1; Dora to MW, 7 Oct [1831]: WLL/Dora/37 p.3.

54. WW to Lady F. Bentinck, 9 Nov [1831] (*LY*, ii, 448–9); Dora to MW, 7 Oct [1831]: WLL/Dora/37 pp.1–2, note in margin on p.2. The six poems included in this letter were *On the Departure of Sir Walter Scott from Abbotsford, for Naples*, *Composed in Roslin Chapel, During a Storm*, *A Place of Burial in the South of Scotland*, *The Trosachs* [*sic*], *Composed in the Glen of Loch Etive* and [*Composed in the Same Place*] (*Poems*, ii, 711–14).

55. WW to WRH, 27 Oct & to BM, [19 Oct] & Dora to Mrs Fletcher (née MJJ), 20 Oct [1831] (*LY*, ii, 440–41, 439 & n.1); WW, *Yarrow Revisited* and *Eagles* (*Poems*, ii, 708–11, 714–15). WW variously calls the castle 'Dunally', 'Donollie' and 'Dunolly', but his identification of it as 'a ruin seated at the tip of one of the horns of the bay of Oban', and Dora's references to visiting Dunstaffanage Castle, suggest that the last might

be the correct place: Dora to MW, 7 Oct [1831]: WLL/Dora/37 p.4.

56. CW to CW2, 18 Apl 1832 & WW to J.K. Miller, 17 Dec 1831 (*LY*, ii, 443n.1, 463); Dora to M. Kinnaird, 18 Feb 1832 (*Prelude*, xlv). JW4 arrived at RM on 6 Nov 1831 and left on 6 Mar 1832: DWJMS: DC 118/1/3 [6 Nov 1831]; EQD: WLMS 13/2/4a [6 Mar 1832].

57. M. & T. Arnold to S. Arnold, [*p.m.* 4 Jan 1832]: WLMS/A/Arnold/4 p.1. The Arnolds arrived on 19 Dec 1831 and left on 23 Jan 1832: T. Arnold to G. Cornish, 23 Dec 1831 (*The Letters of Matthew Arnold*, i, 8); M.M. Hutchinson to her family, 19 Jan 1832: WLMS/H2/3/2 pp.1–2.

58. T. Arnold to J.T. Coleridge, 5 Apl 1832 (*The Letters of Matthew Arnold*, i, 8–9); M. & T. Arnold to S. Arnold, [*p.m.*4 Jan 1832] & T. Arnold to WW, [early 1832]: WLMS/A/Arnold/4 p.4 & 5. In his letter of 4 Jan, Arnold describes going up to RM to 'tempt' WW to the walk up Greenhead Ghyll: 'He was at Work also on his Poems, and he cast a divided look at the bright Sun without, and what I doubt not was the bright Poetry within, – but his wife & Daughter reminded him that he would not have me to walk with next Week, so he arose vigorously, & put on his Clogs, and out we sallied to see the Sheepfold . . .'

59. SH to EQ, 6 Jan 1832 (*LSH*, 386–7); WW to CW, 1 Apl [1832] (*LY*, ii, 516). Capt Thomas Hamilton (1789–1842), a veteran of the Peninsular War and friend of WS, published *Cyril Thornton* (1829), *Annals of the Peninsula Campaign* (1829) and *Men and Manners in America* (1833). In 1834 he married the Ws' friend Lady Farquhar.

60. DWJMS: DC 118/1/3 [14 Dec 1831 & 16 Jul 1833]. That the second series of entries does belong to 1833 is proved beyond doubt, both on internal evidence and from other unconnected, but confirmatory, sources, even though the '1833' has been added in the margin in pencil in a different hand. It is possible that the removed section was irrelevant to the journal, as DW often had to end entries abruptly when she ran into other material recorded in the same notebooks. However, the size of writing and spacing of the lines on the stubs is consistent with the rest of the journal.

61. MW to Dora, [8 Apl 1839]: WLL/MW/123 pp.3–4 (omitted from *LMW*, 222); Dora & WW to EQ, 12 Apl, Dora to JQ & RQ, 27 Apl & to EQ, 3 [*r*.4] Oct [1832]: WLL/Dora/38 pp.7–8, 39 p.10 & 44 p.5. WW's uncle CCC had married Charlotte Cust of Penrith, whom DW loathed, in 1788: see p.60. MW and WW2 accidentally encountered Mary's mother in Penrith in April 1838, 'W & she cool – he considering himself ill-used by her & the sister – but I suppose still feels himself bound to the Girl': MW to Dora, 4[–8] Apl [1838]: WLL/MW/117 p.5 (omitted from *LMW*, 207).

62. Dora to EQ, 22 Feb 1833 & 1 Oct 1834: WLL/Dora/42 pp.2–3 & 60 p.2; SC to J.T. Coleridge, 22 Mar 1843 (*LY*, iv, 402n.4).

63. WW to LL, 17 & 24 Feb 1832 (ibid., ii, 491, 500–501). WW's analogy was carefully thought out. The invincible Hercules was destroyed when his wife gave him a shirt poisoned with the blood of a centaur he had killed; she had been tricked into thinking it would make him faithful to her, but it clung to him, causing such agonies of pain, that he voluntarily ended his sufferings by placing himself on a funeral pyre.

64. WW to R. Inglis, [*c*.19] Feb & to F. Merewether, 18 Jun 1832 (ibid., 491–2, 530); DWJMS: DC 118/1/3 [25 & 26 Oct 1831]; RS to C.W.W. Wynn, 29 Mar 1832 (*RSNL*, ii, 374); Dora & WW to EQ, 12 Apl [1832]: WLL/Dora/38 pp.3–4; WW, *Upon the Late General Fast. March, 1832* (*Poems*, ii, 729). The General Fast had been declared as a penitential gesture in the face of a cholera epidemic then sweeping the country.

65. Dora & WW to EQ, 12 Apl [1832]: WLL/Dora/38 pp.3, 9–10.

66. WW to CW, 5 & 19 May [1832] (*LY*, ii, 521, 525); DW lines in Dora to EQ, 25 May [1832]: WLL/Dora/40 pp.3–4. DW refers to the closing stanzas of *Tintern Abbey*, which speak of her memory being a consolation, 'If solitude, or fear, or pain, or grief/Should be thy portion'.

67. WW to CW, 5 May [1832] (*LY*, ii, 522). SH and Jo H had both left RM six weeks earlier to tend their sister, but Jo H's poem of 21 Jun 1832, 'Why was I absent at that hour/When pious thoughts did overpower/Thy week [*sic*] enfeebled mind?' (WLMS/H/1/8/46) suggests she was not present when Betsy actually died.

68. WW to J. Gardner, 12 Mar & 22 Jun 1832 (*LY*, ii, 511, 533). HCR reported that TL had sold out

the five-volume edition in HCR to DW, 6 Mar 1832 (*HCRBW*, i, 228). Though no unpublished poems appeared in *The Poetical Works of William Wordsworth* (London, Longman Rees, Orme, Brown, Green & Longman, 1832), it did contain the small number of new poems which had already appeared in the *Keepsake* and other periodicals.

69. WW to J. Gardner, 4 Jan [*c*.2 & *c*.20 Feb], 22 Jun & 16 Jul 1832 (*LY*, ii, 472, 486, 492–3, 532–3, 542); CW to WW, 7 Jun 1832: WLL/CW/82 p.3; EQ to WW, 26–7 Mar 1832: WLL/EQ/33 p.4.

70. LL to WW, 12 & 19 May 1832: WLMS/A/Lonsdale/31 p.2 & 32 pp.1–2; WW to F. Merewether, 18 Jun 1832 (*LY*, ii, 531).

71. WW to WRH, 25 Jun 1832 (ibid., 535).

72. WW to HCR, 21 Jul & to J.C. Hare, 28 or 29 Aug [1832] (ibid., 546; *Supp*., 215); T. Arnold to J.T. Coleridge, 17 Sep 1832 (*The Letters of Matthew Arnold*, 11–12). See also WW to RJ, 22 Jul [1832] (*LY*, ii, 548–9). Davy had died in 1829; in 1831 WW was asked to assist his brother, John Davy, MD, in preparing a memoir: J. Stoddart to WW, 7 Apl 1831: WLMS/A/Stoddart/5 pp.1–2.

73. RMVB, pp.13–20; Dora to EQ, 3 Oct [*r*.4] [1832]: WLL/Dora/44 pp.5–6 (1 & 2 crossed).

74. The Americans included Harriet Douglas, 'as vain as ever', paying a farewell visit before returning to New York: ibid., p.7 (3 crossed). Among the relations were TH's daughter Mary, who was still a permanent resident, attending Miss Dowling's school at Ambleside, and Jo H, who stayed most of the summer.

75. J. Wood to WW, 8 Jun 1831: WLMS/A/Wood/1; DWJMS: DC 118/1/3 [11 Jun 1831].

76. WW to SR, 14 Jun [1831] to H.W. Pickersgill, [23 Aug 1832] (*LY*, ii, 402, 552); Dora to EQ, 3 [*r*.4] Oct [1832]: WLL/Dora/44 pp.3–4; Dora to M. Kinnaird, 15 Oct 1832 (Blanshard, 75–6); Blanshard, 74–9, 157–60, pls.14a, 14b.

77. WW & MW to T. & M. Arnold, 19 [*r*.18] Sep [1832] (*The Letters of Matthew Arnold*, i, 15); EQ to Dora, 12 Oct 1832: WLL/EQ/40 p.1; Dora to EQ, 23 Oct 1832: WLL/Dora/45 p.1. The reference to kingdoms melting before the breath of change was altered from this earliest version, given to the Arnolds, when published in 1835: WW, *To the Author's Portrait* (*Poems*, ii, 729).

78. WW to R.E. Griffith, 6 Oct & to JW4, 7 Dec [1832] (*LY*, ii, 557, 572). According to the RMVB, p.20, CW, HH, TH and JM all came to RM in response to this request: JW3 and WW2 also came.

79. WW to E. Hamilton, 10 Jan 1833 (*LY*, ii, 581).

Chapter 23

chapter title: 'Among my friends the yellow leaf has been falling and the green leaf swept off lately in an appalling way', WW to HT, [Feb 1825] (*LY*, iii, 22).

picture: Silhouette of SH, artist unknown, *c*.1827.

1. WW to CW, 29 Jan [1833] (*LY*, ii, 583); Dora to Miss Marshall, [early Feb] & WW, DW & Dora to EQ, 23 Feb 1833: WLL/Dora/46 pp.1–3 & 42 pp.1–2; SH to Mrs STC, [9] Feb [1833] (*LSH*, 391–2).

2. WW to CW, 29 Jan [1833] & to J. Gardner, [late 1832 or early 1833] (*LY*, ii, 583, 577); J. Dick to R. Addison, 2 Oct & 11 Dec [1832]: WLMS/H/1/17/14 & 18; R. Addison to JM, 28 Nov & 4 Dec 1832: WLMS/H/1/17/15 & 16; WW, DW & Dora to EQ, 23 Feb 1833: WLL/Dora/42 p.4 (crossed). The invitation, again at the suggestion of Mrs Dick's own solicitor, who was clearly worried about the child, was backed up with a threat of an application to the chancellor, if it was refused. By May, however, the Ws heard rumours that MEM had not gone to school after all: SH to EQ, 27 May [1833] (*LSH*, 395).

3. Dora to JQ & RQ, 23 Mar 1833: WLL/Dora/47 p.2; WW to B. Dockray, 25 Apl & to his family, [1 Apl] [1833] (*LY*, ii, 605, 599–601); WW, *To – Upon the Birth of Her First-Born Child, March, 1833* and *The Warning A Sequel to the Foregoing*, ll.87–8 (*Poems*, ii, 734–41); *IF*, 45. As a result of or during this visit to Moresby, WW also composed *By the Sea-Side, Composed by the Sea-Shore* and *On a High Part of the Coast of Cumberland* (ibid., 741–4); *IF*, 74, 55.

4. *Poems*, ii, 1041; WW to M.A. Rawson, [?May] & to EM, 14 May [1833] (*LY*, ii, 614–15, 616–17); Dora to EM, [*p.m.*11 Feb] & to EQ, 17 May 1833: Stanger Album, ii, 172 & WLL/Dora/48 p.7.

5. Dora & WW to CW2, 17 Jun & WW to CL, 17 May 1833 (*LY*, ii, 625, 620); DWJMS: DC 118/1/3 [16 & 18 Jul 1833].

6. SH to EQ, 27 May [1833]: WLL/SH/149 p.1 (omitted from *LSH*, 392); ibid., 395; Dora & WW to CW2, 17 Jun & to EQ, 27 Jun 1833 (*LY*, ii, 626 & WLL/Dora/49 p.3). SH took Mary, TH's daughter, back to Brinsop.

7. *HCRBW*, i, 427–33, esp.429; HCR to TR, 4 Jul 1833 (*HCRWC*, i, 243–4); Dora & WW to CW2, 17 Jun 1833 (*LY*, ii, 625); DWJMS: DC 118/1/3 [16 Jul 1833].

8. *HCRBW*, i, 433; Dora to EQ, 27 Jun 1833: WLL/Dora/49 p.3; EQ to Dora, 12 Jul 1833: WLL/EQ/44 p.1.

9. WW to CW, JW4 & CW2, [Mar 1830] & to HCR, 5 Jun 1833 (*LY*, ii, 214, 624); *HCRBW*, ii, 495. The Cooksons' many children had remained in England, securing their own livelihood in various humble occupations. Elizabeth and her sister set up school in Ambleside, where Henry Wilkinson, the headmaster of Sedbergh, anonymously paid the first two years' rent on their cottage for them through WW: SH to Mrs TH, 6 Jan [1831] (*LSH*, 377–8); H. Wilkinson to WW, 30 Mar 1830: WLMS/A/Wilkinson/2 pp.1–2.

10. WW to his family, [17 Jul 1833] (*LY*, ii, 629–32). The image of the lichen was incorporated (less successfully) into the sonnet WW wrote, in the person of Cookson, *At Bala-Sala, Isle of Man* (*Poems*, ii, 757); *IF*, 52. The tipsy 'Gullion' provided material for WW, *Tynwald Hill* (*Poems*, ii, 757–8); *IF*, 52.

11. WW to his family, [17 Jul 1833] (*LY*, ii, 631); HCR to TR, 23 Jul 1833 (*HCRWC*, i, 245–6). The eclipse, on 17 Jul, inspired WW, *In the Firth of Clyde, Ailsa Crag* (*Poems*, ii, 758–9); *IF*, 52–3.

12. WW, *Cave of Staffa*, ll.1–4. See also WW, *Cave of Staffa (After the Crowd had departed)*, *Cave of Staffa* ('Ye shadowy Beings, that have rights and claims') and *Flowers on the Top of the Pillars at the Entrance of the Cave* (*Poems*, ii, 762–4, 1046).

13. WW, *Iona*, ll.9–14 and *Iona (Upon Landing)*, l.1 (ibid., 764, 765). See also *The Black Stones of Iona* and 'Homeward we turn. Isle of Columba's Cell' (ibid., 765–6). The abbey on Iona was not reroofed and restored until the beginning of this century, so the holy site was more desolate when WW visited it.

14. *HCRD*, ii, 141–2; *HCRBW*, i, 434; WW to GHG, 24 Aug 1833 & A. Cunningham, 14 Jun [1834] (*LY*, ii, 639, 722). For WW's refusal to subscribe to a monument for Burns in Edinburgh, see WW to J.F. Mitchell, 21 Apl 1819 (*MY*, ii, 534).

15. DWJMS: DC 118/1/3 [25–7 Jul 1833]; Dora to JQ & RQ, 24 Jul 1833: WLL/A/Dora/50 p.2.

16. WW to EM, [*c*.10 Aug] & to CW, 25 [Sep] [1833] (*LY*, ii, 633 & n.4, 645); WW, *Monument of Mrs Howard (by Nollekens)* (*Poems*, ii, 767–8); *IF*, 54. Joseph Nollekens (1737–1823), son of a Flemish painter, was celebrated for his busts of leading politicians of the day. WW had seen this monument in preparation in Nollekens's London studio many years earlier.

17. WW, *The River Eden, Cumberland, Nunnery* and *The Monument Commonly Called Long Meg and her Daughters, Near the River Eden* (*Poems*, ii, 767–9); *IF*, 54.

18. WW, *Steamboats, Viaducts, and Railways*, ll.11–14 (*Poems*, ii, 769 & n.); WW to RJ, 11 Aug & to CW, 25 [Sep] [1833] (*LY*, ii, 635, 645). The visit to Lowther and LL's victory in the libel suit, which vindicated his personal character, prompted WW, *Lowther* and *To the Earl of Lonsdale* (*Poems*, ii, 769–70 & nn.); *IF*, 54–5; that to Hallsteads, a sonnet addressed to JPM's daughter, who was wearing a necklace made from silver mined from Helvellyn: WW, *To Cordelia M[arshall]* (*Poems*, ii, 775).

19. Mrs Hemans to WW, 21 Jul & 12 Sep 1833: WLMS/A/Hemans/6 pp.1–2 & 7 pp.2–3; WW to Mrs Hemans, 20 Aug [1833] (*LY*, ii, 637); R.P. Graves to WW, 12 Oct 1833: WLMS/A/Graves/1 pp.3–4. Graves's use of the word 'Pastor' was a deliberate evocation of *The Excursion*. WW recommended Graves to the curacy of Bowness (vacated by the death of WW's schoolfriend John Fleming), on the proviso that Fleming's sons had a prior claim. Much to the Ws' distress, one of those sons, their own chaplain at Rydal, Fletcher Fleming, chose to be offended with them for 'their interference' when Graves was appointed: WW to R.P. Graves, 20 Jan & to FW, 2 Feb 1835 (*LY*, iii, 12–13, 17–18). Graves proved a conscientious pastor and held the curacy for the rest of his life. His letters describing the RM circle, dated 12 & 18 Aug, are from a second visit, in 1834, not from 1833, as suggested ibid., ii, 637n.1.

20. Emerson, *English Traits*, 19, 24; Emerson, *Journals and Miscellaneous Notebooks*, x, 556–7; R.W. Emerson to A. Ireland, 30 Aug 1833 (*The Letters of Ralph Waldo Emerson*, i, 395). Ralph Waldo Emerson (1803–82) was touring Europe and sought out Carlyle, Landor, STC, RS and WW; he formed an intimate acquaintance with the first, lasting 40 years (which perhaps explains why he lacked sympathy with WW), but declared that he had not met a single first-class

mind or one with insight into religious truth: Emerson, *Journals and Miscellaneous Notebooks*, iv, 78–9.

21. Ibid., 79; Rev. Orville Dewey, *The Old World and the New* (New York, 1836), 2 vols., quoted in Knight, *Life of William Wordsworth*, iii, 238–42.

22. Dora to CW, 5 Oct 1833: WLL/Dora/53 pp.1–2; Emerson, *Journals and Miscellaneous Notebooks*, x, 555; WW to JK, 23 Sep & to T.F. Kelsall, [*c*.30 Oct] [1833] (*LY*, ii, 641, 656). When WW had not received an acknowledgement from Kelsall a fortnight later, he began to suspect a hoax to get a poem from him for a periodical, but was reassured by a grateful if dilatory response: WW to HCR, [*c*.14 Nov] & MW to HCR, 23 Nov [1833] (ibid., 658, 660).

23. Dora to CW2, 5 Oct & to JQ & RQ, 6 Oct & MW & Dora to EQ, 8 Nov 1833: WLL/Dora/53 pp.1–2, 54 pp.4 & 3 margin & 55 pp.1–2, 6–7; WW to RJ & to F. Merewether, 29 Oct & to HCR [*c*.14 Nov] [1833] (*LY*, ii, 650, 652, 657); Dora to CW2, 12 Nov 1833: WLL/Dora/56 pp.3–4.

24. DW to WW2 & CW2 to CW, 2 Jan 1834 (*LY*, ii, 677, 676n.2). CW left on 14 Jan 1834: DW to LMB, 13 Jan [1834] (ibid., 683).

25. WW to SR, 14 Jan [1834] & to RJ, 29 Oct [1833] (ibid., 688, 651); Dora to RQ, 10 Sep 1833 & to EQ, 20 Feb [1834]: WLL/Dora/51 pp.3 & 4 (p.2 crossed) & 57 p.4. JH's grave at Sockburn is not identifiable.

26. Mrs STC to E. Wardell, 19 Jan 1834: WLMS/Coleridge, S/1 p.1; SH to EQ, 17 Mar & to CC, 28 Jun [1834] (*LSH*, 407–8, 419–20); WW to SR, 14 Jan & to EQ, 11 Jun [1834] (*LY*, ii, 688, 718–19); IW to M. Stanger, 28 Jan [1834]: Moorsom 62/2/2; EQ to Dora, 8 Jun 1834: WLL/EQ/49 pp.1–2; DWJMS: DC 118/2/1 [15 Jun 1834]. Another friend from WW's youth, JL, had died on 23 Sep 1833: WW to FW, 2 Feb [1835] (*LY*, iii, 19 & n.3).

27. SC to Dora, 16–24 [Jul 1834]: WLMS/SC/33 pp.5–7; SH to EQ, [9 May] & to CC, 28 Jun [1834] (*LSH*, 414, 421); SC to Mrs Plummer, Oct 1834 (*SCM*, ii, 109–11); STC, Last Will & Testament, 17 Sep 1829: G1/16/1.

28. WW to H.N. Coleridge, 29 Jul [1834] (*LY*, ii, 728); R.P. Graves to Mrs Hemans, 12 & 16 Aug [1834]: WLMS/A/Graves/4 pp.1–3.

29. WW to HC, 29 Jul [1834] (*LY*, ii, 728); DWJMS: DC 118/2/1 [27–8 Jul 1834]; SH to Mrs TH, [3 or 10 Aug 1834] (*LSH*, 428).

30. SH to CC, 28 Jun & to EQ, 20 Jul [1834] (ibid., 419–20, 423); Dora to RQ, 19 Jul [1834]: WLL/Dora/59 pp.2–4. MEM stayed a week, from 14 Jul, before returning, via Brinsop, to school at Clapham; it was her first visit to RM.

31. SH to Mrs TH, 3 or 10 Aug & to TH Jnr, 15 Oct [1834] (*LSH*, 425–9, 433). The private tutor appointed was Henry Cookson, son of the Kendal Cooksons, who had been 7th Wrangler in 1832, was now a fellow and would become Master of Peterhouse, Cambridge.

32. WW to EM, 17 Jul & Dora & DW to HCR, [*c*.24 Jul] [1834] (*LY*, ii, 724, 725); SH to EQ, 20 Jul [1834] (*LSH*, 424). WW had been given a complimentary copy of SR's *Poems* (Moxon, 1834) and been delighted with it: the illustrations were by J.M.W. Turner and Thomas Stothard: WW to SR, 14 Jan [1834] (*LY*, ii, 688).

33. Dora & DW to HCR, [*c*.24 Jul] [1834] (ibid., 725); HH, *By a Retired Mariner (A Friend of the Author)* (*Poems*, ii, 757); DWJMS: DC 118/2/1 [13 Aug 1834].

34. SC to W. Wardell, Oct 1834: WLMS/A/34 p.2; Dora to EQ, 1 Oct 1834: WLL/Dora/60 p.4; WW to J.H. Green, [mid-Sep 1834] (*LY*, ii, 739); SC to M. Stanger, 25 Oct 1834: Moorsom 55/1/9 p.5. TdQ's 'allusions to Mrs Coleridge are utterly inexcuseable [*sic*]': EQ to Dora, 29 Nov 1834: WLL/EQ/53 p.5. Henry Curwen Wordsworth (1834–65) was born in Jul, 'at 5 months old', as the Ws said, IW having totally miscalculated her dates: SH to Mrs TH, [3 or 8 Aug 1834] (*LSH*, 427).

35. SH to Mrs STC, [28 Sep (*r*.5 Oct) 1834] (ibid., 430–32); Dora to EQ, 1 Oct 1834: WLL/Dora/60 p.1; RS to G.C. Bedford, 2 Oct 1834 (*RSLC*, vi, 244). SH's letter is dated only Sunday. As it relates the events described by Dora and RS, it must post-date their letters. SH returned to RM on 23 Nov: DWJMS: DC 118/2/2 [23 Nov 1834].

36. Dora to CW2, 10 Nov 1834 & to EQ, 8 Jan 1835: WLL/Dora/61 pp.1, 3 & 62 p.1; MW to JPM, 27 Dec [1834] (*LMW*, 136); SH to EQ, 8 Jan 1835 (*LSH*, 437).

37. EQ to Dora, 10 Mar 1835: WLL/EQ/54 pp.1–2; Dora to EQ, 1 Jun 1835: WLL/Dora/64 p.12.

38. MW to JPM, 27 Dec [1834] (*LMW*, 135–6); DWJMS: DC 118/2/2 [3 & 9 Dec 1834].

39. *HCRBW*, ii, 453; WW to TNT, 1 Jan 1835

(*LY*, iii, 2). HCR paid a duty-visit to MAL on 12 Jan and found her aware, but insensible, of her loss. She talked much 'utterly wild and groundless' nonsense of old friends, including the allegation that DW was 'ill-treated by her sister-in-law and the family – "all treat her ill; old maids are of no great use in the world, but it is a pity when they are cut off before their time"': *HCRBW*, ii, 455.

40. *JTM*, iv, 1661; Dora to EQ, 20 Feb 1834: WLL/Dora/57 p.4; TNT to WW, 29 Dec 1834: WLMS/A/Talfourd/3 p.3; WW to LL & to J. Thornton, 13 Jan 1835 (*LY*, iii, 9, 10–11). After the dissolution of Parliament on 29 Dec, and a general election in Jan, at which both Lowthers were returned for Westmorland, Peel headed a minority Tory government until forced to resign on 8 Apl 1835.

41. WW to LL, 24 Jan 1835 (ibid., 16).

42. RS to WW, 9 May 1835 (*RSLC*, vi, 267); WW to VL, 14 Feb [1835] (*LY*, iii, 27); SH to WW2, [5 Feb 1835]: WLMS/A/Peel/2 p.1. For the correspondence relating to RS's baronetcy and Civil List pension, Feb–Apl 1835, see *RSLC*, vi, 254–65.

43. VL to WW, 12 Feb 1835: WLMS/A/Lowther/67 p.2; DWJMS: DC 118/2/2 [17 Feb 1835].

44. WW to WW2, [9 Mar 1835] (*LY*, iii, 29–30); W. Howley to WW, 14 Mar 1835: WLMS/A/Howley/7; MW to WW2, 15 & 28 Mar [1835]: WLL/MW/80 pp.1–3 & *LMW*, 139–40.

45. *HCRBW*, i, 452; ii, 454, 461–3; AV to DW, 2 Apl 1835: WLMS/4/1 (*Supp.*, 275–7); WW to HCR, [*c.*27 Apl 1835] (*LY*, iii, 42–3). AV's letter to WW has not survived; her letter to DW was discovered inside the binding of a book at the DC library.

46. WW to RJ, 30 Mar [1835] (*LY*, iii, 35–6); SC to M. Stanger, 25 Mar 1835: Moorsom 55/1/10 p.7; *HCRBW*, ii, 457–9; Blanshard, 158–9. Sir Benjamin Brodie (1783–1862) opposed homoeopathy and promoted a conservative treatment of diseases in the joints, resulting in reduced numbers of amputations. For Holland and his visit to RM in 1821, see p.548.

47. Dora to EQ, 6 Apl 1835: WLL/Dora/63 p.1; T. Carlyle to J.A. Carlyle, 17 Mar 1835 (*Collected Letters of Thomas and Jane Welch Carlyle*, viii, 80–81 & 80n.16).

48. WW, MW & DW to HCR, 21 Nov [1834] & WW to TNT, 1 Jan 1835 (*LY*, ii, 747–8; ibid., iii, 3); SH to EQ, 8 Jan 1835 (*LSH*, 438); WW, *The Warning*, l.122 (*Poems*, ii, 740).

49. *HCRBW*, ii, 459–60; WW, *Postscript, 1835* (*Prose*, iii, 240–74, esp.246, 248–9). HCR (wrongly) thought WW was 'accustomed to an amanuensis thoroughly patient and unpresuming to criticise – I could not be so patient and my interference was not always in vain'.

50. WW, *Humanity*, ll.83–94 (*Poems*, ii, 691–2); RS to WW, 9 May 1835 (*RSLC*, vi, 266).

51. WW to J. Watson, 16 Jun, DW & IW to CW2, [*c.*18 May], WW to HCR, [*c.*27 Apl] & to E. Simms, 27 Apl 1835 (*LY*, iii, 62, 52, 43–4, 45); Dora to EQ, 1 Jun 1835: WLL/Dora/64 p.8; WW, *The Old Cumberland Beggar*, l.153 (*Poems*, i, 267).

52. WW to RJ, 30 Mar, to J. Wood, 1 Apl & to HT, [*c.*26 Jun] [1835] (*LY*, iii, 34–5, 40, 71); MW to IF, 25 Apl [1835] (*LMW*, 141–2); Dora to EQ, 1 Jun 1835; WLL/Dora/64 p.9. WW said his portrait 'looks well, but is of too large a size for the room'. CW2 had been present at its unveiling some months earlier: CW2 to Dora, 1 Jan 1835: WLMS/1/11/9 pp.8–9.

53. SH to Mrs TH, [30–31 May 1835] (*LSH*, 443, 445–6); WW to HCR, [May–Jun], WW & MW to RS, 7 Jun & WW to J. Watson, 16 Jun 1835 (*LY*, iii, 53, 57–8, 62); MW to IF, 16 Jun [1835] (*LMW*, 147); Dora to EQ, 1 Jun 1835: WLL/Dora/64 pp.1–2, 9, 12, 14.

54. WW to HCR, to RS & to CW, 24 Jun [1835] (*LY*, iii, 65, 66, 67); WW, *November, 1836*, ll.9–14 (*Poems*, ii, 810).

55. SC to Dora, [Jun 1835]: WLMS/A/SC/38 pp.2, 4. 'I & my daughters have lost in her one of the persons in the world whom we loved best': RS to KJW, 25 Jun 1835: WLMS/A/RS/20.

56. B. Southey to Dora, 29 [Jun 1835]: WLMS/A/Southey, B/1 pp.1–2; WW to H.H. Southey, 30 Jun [1835] (*LY*, iii, 75–6); H.H. Southey to WW, 8 Jul 1835: WLMS/A/Southey, H.H./1.

57. WW to HCR, 6 Jul, to CC, 6 Aug & to CW, [26 Sep] 1835 (*LY*, iii, 78–9, 83, 96–7); EH & MW to Mrs TH, 5 [Aug 1835]: WLMS/H/2/5/1 p.4; MW & DW to JPM, [Dec 1835]: WLL/MW/85 pp.1–2.

58. MW to JPM, [Jan], to M.A. Marshall, 4 May & to JPM, 28 Jun [1836]: WLL/MW/86 pp.1–3, 91 pp.4–5 & 92 pp.2–3; Dora to CW2, 7 Jan [1836]: WLL/Dora/65a p.1.

59. WW to J. Anster, 21 Jul, to TL & Co., 17 Sep,

to EM, [*c*.25 Sep] & to J. Watson, 5 Oct [1835] (*LY*, iii, 81, 91, 93, 104). The poem was published, with alterations, as WW, *Airey-Force Valley* (*Poems*, ii, 796).

60. WW to EM, 20, 23, 24 Nov & [mid-Dec], to HCR, [15 Dec] 1835 & to EM, [4 Jan 1836] (*LY*, iii, 114–15, 119, 120, 143, 145, 147–8); MW to JPM, [Jan 1836]: WLL/MW/86 pp.6–7; *HCRBW*, ii, 468; HCR to WW, 8 Dec 1835 (*HCRWC*, i, 286–7); WW, *Written After the Death of Charles Lamb* (*Poems*, ii, 797–800). The lines chosen for the monument were 'Still, at the centre of his being, lodged/A soul by resignation sanctified:/O, he was good, if e'er a good Man lived!': ibid., ll.30–31, 38.

61. WW to SR, 5 Apl & to E. Hughes, 16 Aug [1835] (*LY*, iii, 41, 86–7); Dora to EQ, 1 Jun 1835: WLL/Dora/64 pp.5, 12.

62. WW, *Extempore Effusion upon the Death of James Hogg*, ll.9–28 (*Poems*, ii, 801); MW to HCR, [*c*.20 Nov 1835] (*LY*, iii, 117); *HCRBW*, ii, 466, 471. The poem was published in the *Newcastle Journal*, 5 Dec, *Athenaeum*, 12 Dec 1835, and thereafter in other newspapers: WW to J. Hernaman, [30 Nov] & 1 Dec, to EM, 6 Dec [1835] (*LY*, iii, 127 & n.2, 128–31, 130n.1).

63. *HCRBW*, ii, 474, 477, 487; MW to CC, [Jun 1837] (*LMW*, 157); WW to CW2, 8 Feb [1836] (*LY*, iii, 166).

64. *HCRBW*, ii, 480, 483, 484–5; J. Lightfoot to WW, 9 Jan 1836: G1/6/7; WW to J. Lightfoot, 11 & 29 Jan & to CW2, 8 Feb 1836 (*LY*, iii, 153–4, 161–2, 165); MW to Mrs TH, 30 Jan [1836] (*LMW*, 148–9) & WLL/MW/87 p.2 for omitted paragraph. There were no purchasers at the Sockbridge sale on 9 Mar 1836, which WW attended with KJW, but some land was sold by private treaty afterwards, raising £140, and the house at Sockbridge was relet: MW to HCR, 20 Feb, WW & MW to HCR, 16 [*r*.17] Mar & DW, MW & WW to CW2, [late Mar] [1836] (*LY*, ii, 175, 184, 192); MW to KJW, [*c*.20 Mar 1836]: WLL/MW/90 p.2.

65. *HCRBW*, ii, 486. HCR had himself purchased some of WW's shares from Courtenay at a generous premium in 1834: ibid., i, 450–51.

66. Ibid., ii, 485, 487; WW & MW to IF, 18 Jan & WW to EM, 30 Jan [1836] (*LY*, ii, 159, 162).

Chapter 24

picture: Informal sketch of WW, probably drawn from memory, by Daniel Maclise (as 'Alfred Croquis') and published in *Fraser's Magazine*, Oct 1832.

1. *HCRBW*, ii, 486, 489.

2. WW to EM, [4 Jan] & [?5 Feb] & DW, MW & WW to CW2, [late Mar] [1836] (*LY*, iii, 148–9, 163, 190–91). When TL allowed WW's *Guide* to go out of print, WW offered it to the Kendal booksellers and publishers Hudson & Nicholson, who republished it, with additions, in 1835: TL and EM appeared on the title-page as the London agents: WW to Hudson & Nicholson, 7 May & to EM, 2 Aug 1835 (ibid., 48, 81–2).

3. WW to KJW, 12 Jan, WW & MW to IF, 18 Jan, WW to WRH, 26 Jan, MW & WW to G. Hutchinson & Mrs TH, [9 Feb] & WW & MW to HCR, 16 [*r*.17] Mar 1836 (ibid., 155, 157, 160–61, 169, 185). JW3 resigned Moresby but kept Brigham when he agreed to hold the living of Workington for three years until his brother-in-law, Henry Curwen, was old enough to be legally presented to it; JW3 and his family lived at Workington from Easter 1834: Dora to EQ, 20 Feb [1834]: WLL/Dora/57 p.3.

4. J. Bolton to WW, Mar 1836: WLMS/A/Bolton/1; DW, MW & WW to CW2, [late Mar 1836] (*LY*, iii, 188–9). WW advised CW2 to keep DW's letter as 'a great curiosity'. It was a perfect illustration of her mental condition, which so puzzled her family: she went on to say that she was now as well as she had ever been in her life, except that she had not recovered the use of her legs. 'My Arms have been active enough as the torn caps of my nurses and the heavy blows I have given their heads and faces will testify . . . I intend, God willing, to see you all at Cambridge in the summer.'

5. WW & MW to S. & M. Staniforth, 16 Apl [1836] (ibid., 198); WW, *Speech at the Laying of the Foundation Stone of the New School in the Village of Bowness* (*Prose*, iii, 287–99). WW's speech was printed in the *Westmorland Gazette* on 16 Apl 1836.

6. WW to his family, [11] & [?20] [May 1836] (*LY*, iii, 214, 222); *HCRBW*, ii, 492–7; HT to IF, 24 May 1836 (*LY*, iii, 210n.2); *John Constable's Correspondence*, ii, 139; J. Constable to WW, 15 Jun

1836: G1/13/4. Constable, like WW, had been an early protégé of SGB.

7. *HCRBW*, ii, 494; *The Diaries of William Charles Macready*, i, 318–19, 284; WW to EM, 20 Nov & to TNT, 28 Nov 1835 & to his family [*c*.28 May 1836] (*LY*, iii, 115, 125–6, 226); TNT to WW, 28 Oct 1835: WLMS/A/Talfourd/5. TNT was anxious for a response because his preface was laudatory of WW and his influence.

8. *HCRBW*, ii, 506–9; HCR to W.S. Landor, 7 & 17 Dec [1836] (*HCRWC*, ii, 326–9, 329–33). HCR considered Landor's *A Satire on Satirists and An Admonition to Detractors* (1836) 'a most unwarrantable publication which makes me quite indifferent now to the continuance of his acquaintance'. He did his best to prevent WW's finding out about it, earning WW's gratitude for his discretion: *HCRBW*, ii, 514–16.

9. WW to TNT [*c*.13 May], to S. Cookson, [31 May] & to KJW, [?15 Jun] & [15 Jun] [1836] (*LY*, iii, 216, 231–2, 251, 252).

10. WW to J. Watson, 5 Oct [1835] & 9 Feb 1836 & to HCR, [mid-Apl 1836] (ibid., 104, 170–71, 202); W. Wood to WW, 9 Apl 1836: WLMS/A/Wood, W./2 p.2; *HCRBW*, ii, 490; HCR to WW, 22 Apl 1836 (*HCRWC*, i, 300). HCR regretted sending the letter, fearing it might cause offence, and was relieved to get a reply from WW beginning, 'My dear Friend, Offended! what could you be dreaming about!': *HCRBW*, ii, 490–91; WW to HCR, 27 Apl [1836] (*LY*, iii, 207). As a result of HCR's letter, WW retracted his application to TNT, whose friends were also chiefly dissenters: TNT to WW, 27 Apl 1836: WLMS/A/Talfourd/6.

11. WW to his family, [13 May] & WW & MW to HCR, 16 [*r*.17] Mar [1836] (*LY*, iii, 214–15, 184); *HCRBW*, ii, 492. Stephen's donation was matched only by those from CW and WW himself: *Cockermouth New Church, Friends of WW Subscription Book*, Apl 1836: WLMS/A/Wood, W./3. WW was already having to subsidize WW2 to the tune of £10 p.a.

12. WW to LL, 29 Mar 1836 (*Supp.*, 223–4). The shoemaker, Henry Lancaster, had lost the specimen he had discovered, but evidently succeeded in convincing WW that there was the potential for open-cast mining. Nothing came of the application.

13. WW to his family, [?20 & 22 May] [1836] (*LY*, iii, 221, 223–4).

14. WW to EM, [*c*.7 Dec 1826] & [?5 Feb 1836] (ibid., i, 497 & nn; iii, 163). In 1826 WW told EM, 'I always feel some apprehension for the destiny of those who in Youth addict themselves to the Composition of verse. It is a very seducing employment . . . Fix your eye upon acquiring Independence by honorable business, and let the Muses come after rather than go before.'

15. WW to his family, [late May, early Jun & 4 Jun] & to TL & Co., 6 Jun 1836 (ibid., 232–3, 239, 241, 242). WW's expected earnings from TL are not entirely clear; a few days later he said he would get £450 for *Yarrow Revisited* alone: WW to his family, 6 Jun 1836 (ibid., 245). TL & Co. were convinced that EM would lose by his 'speculation on Wordsworth': *JTM*, v, 1908.

16. WW to his family, 6, [13] & [27] Jun 1836 (*LY*, iii, 243, 248, 266).

17. WW & Dora to HCR, 27 Apl [1836] (ibid., 208); *HCRBW*, ii, 492; MW to JPM, 28 Jun [1836]: WLL/MW/92 pp.1–2.

18. WW to his family, [?22 & 25 May] & [*c*.17, 27 & ?29 Jun], to HCR, [24 Jun] & MW to HCR, 4 Jul [1836] (*LY*, iii, 224–5, 226–8, 253, 266, 269, 258, 276); *HCRBW*, ii, 497.

19. WW to his family, [30 Jun] & to EM, [*c*.9 Jul] [1836] (*LY*, iii, 271–2, 279); EQD: WLMS/13/3/2 [2 Aug–20 Sep 1836]. EQ left RM on 16 Aug, but visited Brigham and Cockermouth with WW before sailing to London from Whitehaven on 20 Sep.

20. WW to H. Reed, 19 Aug 1837 & to JK, [*c*.24 Sep 1836] (*LY*, iii, 445, 292–3); EQD: WLMS/13/3/2 [4 & 5 Aug, 1 Sep 1836].

21. Ibid., [3–7 Sep 1836]; WW to RS, [3 Sep 1836] (*LY*, iii, 288 & n.); RS to HT, 10 Sep 1836 (*RSLC*, vi, 298). Robert Shelton Mackenzie (1809–80), editor of the *Liverpool Echo* and correspondent for the *New York Evening Star*, who met WW, RS & EQ at the trial, published an account of it in the US papers, part of which is given in *RSLC*, vi, 299–305. After completing his circuit, Coleridge leased Fox How from Arnold and spent six weeks in daily contact with the Ws: see *Memoirs*, ii, 300–315.

22. MW to HCR, 28 Sep & 19 Dec, DW & MW to JPM, 24 Dec [1836] & WW to his family, [5 Jul 1837] (*LY*, iii, 297–8, 330, 332, 423–4).

23. MW to HCR, 1 Nov 1836 (ibid., 315); EQ to Dora, 22–3 Apl 1838 & 13 Oct 1836: WLL/EQ/79 p.2 & 63 p.2; WW to B.C. Brodie, [6 Sep] & MW

to HCR, 1 Nov [1836] (*LY*, iii, 289, 316). B.C. Brodie to WW, 5 Nov 1836: WLMS/A/Brodie/1 p.2. Brodie added that his visit to the Lakes had enabled him to understand better 'those Lyrical Ballads which I learned to admire when I was yet a boy, and to which I have continued faithful, in however much I may have been altered otherwise by thirty years of active engagements in the unpoetical world'.

24. EQ to the Ws, 29 Oct 1836: WLL/EQ/65 p.4. See, e.g., JQ 'wants a Governess or a Stepmother: can you recommend me the latter?': EQ to Dora, 7 Mar 1837: WLL/EQ/68 p.3.

25. WW to EM, 10 Oct & to HT, 4 Nov [1836]; WW to CW2, 9 Jan & to HCR, 28 Jan [1837] (*LY*, iii, 304, 319, 343–4, 355). Graves thought that the frontispiece 'conveying a false impression of the poet, has even conduced with many to a misinterpretation of his poetry': Blanshard, 78.

26. [Copies of] W. Wood to WW, 31 Jan 1837 & J. Stanger to WW, 23 Jan 1837: WLMS/A/Wood, W./4 pp.1–3; LL to WW, 5 Jan & 6 Feb 1837: WLMS/A/Lonsdale/45 pp.1–2 & 43 pp.1–2; WW to J. Stanger, 9 & 15 Feb & to J. Watson, [14 Feb] [1837] (*Supp.*, 232; *LY*, iii, 233, 360–61). The new church at Cockermouth was not built until 1865.

27. *HCRBW*, ii, 512–13; WW to HCR, [*c*.17] & 20 [Feb], Dora to HCR, 27 Feb & WW to MW, [13 Mar] [1837] (*LY*, iii, 363–4, 367, 370); HCR to WW, [24 Feb 1837] (*HCRWC*, i, 340–41); MW to IF, 16 Feb [1837] (*LMW*, 154–5); HC to Mrs STC, 28 Oct 1836 (*LHC*, 201). Mary Monkhouse Hutchinson died on 27 Apl 1837, aged 20; her grave, next to that of Elizabeth Monkhouse, can still be seen in Brinsop churchyard.

28. WW to Dora, [13] & [*c*.15] Mar & to CW2, 23 Mar [1837] (*LY*, iii, 371, 372, 377–8); *HCRBW*, ii, 514–15. WW told Dora the sum was £400, but CW2 it was £500. All three trustees were enjoined to secrecy. This, and the implied distrust of JW3's probity, caused JW3 much bitterness and resentment when the trust matured and was revealed to him.

29. WW to RS, [18 Mar 1837] (*LY*, iii, 375). See also WW to DW, [17 Mar] & to LL, [19] Mar [1837] (ibid., 373, 375–6).

30. WW to DW, [17 Mar] [1837] (ibid., 373); J. Spedding to R.M. Milnes, 4 Apl 1837 (Reid, *The Life, Letters and Friendships of Richard Monckton Milnes*, i, 192); WW to IF, 24 Mar [1837] (*LY*, ii, 380–81).

31. WW to DW, 25 Mar & to IF, 24 Mar [1837] (ibid., 385, 381–2); HCRDMS, 1837, pp.3–4 [22, 23–6 Mar 1837].

32. WW to his family, 8 Apl [1837] (*LY*, iii, 388–9); *HCRBW*, ii, 517.

33. Ibid., 519; WW to DW, MW & Dora, [29] Apl [1837] (*LY*, iii, 394–6); WW, *The Pine of Monte Mario at Rome*, ll.8–12 (*Poems*, ii, 850).

34. WW to MW & Dora, [6 May 1837] (*LY*, iii, 399–400).

35. Ibid., 398; WW & HCR to F. Mackenzie, 11 Aug & 17 Nov 1837 (ibid., 437); Ticknor, *Life, Letters and Journals*, ii, 85–6; WW to DW, MW & Dora, [29] Apl & [6 & 19 May] [1837] (*LY*, iii, 394–5, 399, 402); MW to Dora, 31 Aug [1837] (*LMW*, 177); *HCRBW*, ii, 520; Blanshard, 83. WW had met Joseph Severn (1793–1879) at BRH's in 1817, in company with Keats and Hunt.

36. WW to MW & Dora, [19 May] & to Dora, 30 [*r*.31] May [1837] (*LY*, iii, 401–3, 407); *HCRD*, ii, 193–4; WW, *The Cuckoo at Laverna, May 25, 1837* (*Poems*, ii, 855–8); *IF*, 71–2. See also WW to Dora & MW, 21 Jun [1837] (*LY*, iii, 417).

37. *HCRBW*, ii, 519, 523; WW, *At Vallombrosa*, ll.25–8 (*Poems*, ii, 860); WW to Dora, 30 [*r*.31] May [1837] (*LY*, iii, 406); *IF*, 72.

38. WW to Dora, 4 Jun [1837] (*LY*, iii, 409–12); *HCRD*, ii, 194.

39. WW to Dora & MW, 21 Jun [1837] (*LY*, iii, 416–19); *HCRD*, ii, 196–7; Ticknor, *Life, Letters and Journals*, ii, 98; *HCRBW*, ii, 528. HCR declined to accompany the gondola party, having 'no curiosity' to hear 'Tasso chanted by gondoliers'. WW & HCR had met the Ticknors at Como and Bergamo, and would meet them again at Munich: WW & HCR to F. Mackenzie, 11 Aug [1837] (*LY*, iii, 438).

40. WW to MW, 17 Jul [1837] (ibid., 425–30).

41. *HCRBW*, ii, 528–30; WW to MW, 17 Jul [1837] (*LY*, iii, 426).

42. *HCRBW*, ii, 533–4, 535; WW to EM, 13 Sep, to EQ, 20 Sep, to CW2, 5 Oct & WW & HCR to F. Mackenzie, 11 Aug & 17 Nov 1837 (*LY*, iii, 462–3, 464, 468–9, 437); *HCRBW*, ii, 536–9. Dora was allowed to accompany WW only on condition that she left RM before the end of Oct to spend the winter in the south, as recommended by Brodie.

43. WW to his family, [5 Jul 1837] (*LY*, iii, 423); *HCRBW*, ii, 535. See also WW & HCR to F.

Mackenzie, 11 Aug & 17 Nov, & to LL, 27 Sep [1837]; WW to J. Kenyon, [summer 1838] (*LY*, iii, 438, 466, 617).
44. MW to Dora, 28 Jul, 14 Aug & [Aug], & to WW, [28 Aug] [1837] (*LMW*, 158, 164–5, 169, 170); MW to Dora & WW, 14–16 Aug [1837]: WLL/MW/100 pp.1–2.MW tried to help raise a subscription for the 15 widows and 50 orphans, and urged Dora to do the same.
45. EQD: WLMS/13/3/3 [2–7 & 10–15 Nov 1837]; T. Carlyle to M. Carlyle, 25 Mar 1825 (*Collected Letters of Thomas and Jane Welch Carlyle*, viii, 85); EQ & JQ had returned from Portugal on 8 Oct and had expected to meet WW & Dora at Brinsop, but were prevented by the Ws' early departure.
46. WW to EQ, 20 Sep [1837] (*LY*, iii, 464–5); EQ to WW, 25 Oct & to Dora, 7, 8, 24 & 27 Dec 1837: WLL/EQ/70 p.3 & 72–5; MW to Dora, 9–11 & [29–30] Nov 1837 (*LMW*, 191 & WLL/EQ/113 p.3); EQD: WLMS 13/3/3 [28 Nov–19 Dec 1837].
47. EQ to Dora, 8 Dec 1837 & 19 Jan [1838]: WLL/EQ/73 p.3 & 77 p.2. EQ later admitted that when he had refused to read Dora's letter to MW, he had felt 'painfully conscious that I might be suspected of evasive conduct': EQ to Dora, 22–3 Apl 1838: WLL/EQ/79 p.2.
48. WW to Dora, 8 Feb [1838] (*Supp.*, 239); EQD: WLMS/13/4/1 [6–12 Apl 1838].
49. Dora to IF, 19 [Apl 1838]: WLL/Dora/68 p.4 crossed; WW to Dora, [*c*.5 Apl 1838] (*LY*, iii, 548–9).
50. MW to Dora, [20 Apl 1838] (*LMW*, 210); EQ to Dora, 22–3 Apl 1838: WLL/EQ/79 pp.2, 1.
51. MW to IF, 3 May [1838] (*LMW*, 212); Dora to RQ, 2 Jul [1838]: WLL/Dora/69 p.1; JW4 to CW2, 7 Oct 1838: 1990.1.6.13 pp.4–5.
52. WW to EM, [*c*.3 Feb 1838] (*LY*, iii, 518). See also WW to T. Powell, 9 Jan, to HCR [Feb] & to JW4, 10 Mar [1838] (ibid., 514–15, 521–2, 530). WW told EM to send a sample to Dora for her approval 'as Father told him the thing was done chiefly at your suggestion and he wished you to be pleased': MW to Dora, [25 (*p.m.*30) Mar 1838] (*LMW*, 202).
53. WW to EM, 21 May & to Dora, [Feb–Mar] [1838] (*LY*, iii, 591, 524–5); MW to Dora, [14–16] Nov [1837]: WLL/MW/111 p.2; B. Southey to Dora, 9 Dec 1837: WLMS/A/Southey, B./2 p.2; MW to Dora [Aug] & 8 [Dec] [1837] (*LMW*, 168, 201). Mrs RS died on 16 Nov and was buried at Crosthwaite church on 19 Nov 1837.
54. WW, 'Oh! what a Wreck! how changed in mien and speech', ll.6–10 (*Poems*, ii, 812); WW to Dora, [Feb–Mar 1838] (*LY*, iii, 524–5). In the *IF* note, WW alluded only to Mrs RS's condition having prompted the poem, and made no reference to DW: *IF*, 77.
55. WW to EM, 21 May, 4 & 28 Jul [1838] (*LY*, iii, 591, 618, 621); Dora to RQ, 2 Jul [1838]: WLL/Dora/69 p.5.
56. WW to EM, 28 Jul [1838] & to TNT, 13 Jan [1836] (*LY*, iii, 592, 156).
57. WW to R. Sharp, 27 Sep [1808] & to J.F. Mitchell, 21 Apl 1819 (*MY*, i, 266; ii, 534–5). The term of copyright in 1808 was 14 years; in 1814 it was extended to 28 years, or the term of the author's life, whichever was longer.
58. WW to J. Gardner, 19 May 1830 (*LY*, ii, 264–5). DW thought this the preferable solution: see p.620.
59. TNT to WW, 12 Nov 1836: WLMS/A/Talfourd/9; WW to TNT, 16 Nov [1836], to Dora, 30 [*r*.31] May [1837] & to TNT, 18 Apl 1838 (*LY*, iii, 323, 407 & n.1, 556). TNT also asked WW to sign a petition to the US Congress, seeking copyright protection for English authors. WW declined, because he said the allegations that American publishers 'garbled' English works for sordid purposes was untrue, in his own case, and that he thought such emotive language impolitic when the publishers were not actually breaking any law: WW to TNT, 16 Nov [1837] & to HCR, 15 Dec [1837] (ibid., 321–2, 493); HCR to WW, 11 Dec 1837 (*HCRWC*, i, 348).
60. WW, *A Plea for Authors* and *A Poet to his Grandchild: Sequel to 'A Plea for Authors'* (*Poems*, ii, 818); WW to TNT, [18 Apl 1838] (*LY*, iii, 556–8); MW to TH & Mrs TH, [18 Apl 1838] (*LMW*, 209). WW's letter to TNT was published in the *Morning Post* on 23 Apl 1838 (*Prose*, iii, 313–14). For examples of some of the letters, written between 23 Mar and 14 Apl, including ones to Gladstone, Peel and the Cumberland and Westmorland MPs, see *LY*, iii, 535–80.
61. WW to TNT, [14 Apl 1838] (ibid., 553); WW to the *Kendal Mercury* (*Prose*, iii, 309–12). See also WW to R.F. Housman, 15 Dec [*r*.Jan 1836] (*Supp.*, 222).
62. J. Ellis to WW, 28 Apl & WW to J.G. Lockhart, 4 May 1838 (*LY*, iii, 562n.1 & 577). Peel

was reluctant to endorse the bill, believing copyright to be analogous to patent, thereby raising the spectre of restricting mercantile activity; WW tried, but failed, to convince him otherwise: WW to TNT, [2 May] & to R. Peel, 3 May 1838 (ibid., 568–9, 572–4).

63. WW to J. Watson, 28 Feb, to unidentified, 10 Sep, MW to HCR, [28 Sep] & 1 Nov 1836 (ibid., 178–9, 291, 299, 315). WW2's application for the railway post and his supposed success were reported in the London press: CC to HCR, [6 Oct] & HCR to MW, 27 Oct 1836 (*HCRWC*, i, 320). WW2 still considered himself bound to Mary Cust and ill-used by her mother; his cousin, Dorothy Harrison, who had seen Mary and her sister at the Carlisle ball, described them as 'the two plainest – sickliest looking, & awkwardest Girls in the Ball room': MW to Dora, 4 Apl [1838]: WLL/MW/117 p.5, omitted from *LMW*, 207.

64. SC to M. Stanger, 1 Mar 1838: Moorsom 55/1/14 p.6; WW to EM, 13 Mar [1838] (*LY*, iii, 531); MW to Mrs TH, 8 Oct & 3 May [1838] (*LMW*, 215–16, 212).

65. WW to WRH, 21 Dec [1837] & 4 Jan [1838], & to unidentified, 12 Feb 1840 (*LY*, iii, 501, 508–9; iv, 16–17).

66. WW to C. Nicholson, 7 Oct 1835, to unidentified, 10 Jan 1837 & to HCR, 28 Jul & [*c*.5 Dec] & to CW2, [16 Aug] [1838] (ibid., iii, 106, 345, 622, 644, 630). WW was on a three-week tour of County Durham and Northumberland with IF when the DCL was conferred, enabling him to attend the ceremony.

67. J. Hutcheson to WW, 29 Oct 1838: WLMS/A/Hutcheson/1; WW to J. Hutcheson, [*c*.30 Oct 1838]: WLMS/A/Hutcheson/2. WW's reply, which MW copied and sent to WW2, is wrongly ascribed to Oct 1846, and printed as WW's answer to his second nomination that year in *LY*, iv, 807–8. For the later nomination, see p.800.

68. J. Montgomery to WW, 12 Jan 1838: WLMS/A/Montgomery/4 p.2; Ticknor, *Life, Letters and Journals*, ii, 167.

69. MW to Mrs TH, 8 Oct [1838] (*LMW*, 218); E. Ricketts, *Recollections of our 3 Days Excursion at the Lakes with Mr Wordsworth, 1838* (*LY*, iii, 761–2). Ellen was unable to recollect any of WW's conversation, though she remembered he talked about Ireland, and that he confessed to feeling sensitive if ignored by those around him, a consequence, he thought, of having been spoilt by living so much in the society of ladies.

70. WW to HCR, [*c*.5 Dec 1838] & to M.F. Howley, [early Feb 1839] (ibid., 644, 658); *HCRBW*, ii, 567; HCR to Dora, [Mar 1839] (*HCRWC*, i, 382).

71. WW to EM, 11 Dec & to CW2, 18 Dec [1838], to HCR, 28 Jan [1837] & to H. Reed, 22 Feb 1839 (*LY*, iii, 647–8 & n.1, 649–50, 355, 667). EM suggested publishing a stereotyped edition of WW's works in a single volume, costing £1; the proposal lapsed when EM admitted such an edition was likely to damage sales of the six-volume edition.

72. *HCRBW*, ii, 566–7; WW to TNT, [26 Jan] & WW to RS, 18 Feb [1839] (*LY*, iii, 657, 662–3); MW to Dora, [9 May 1839] (*LMW*, 238). The final version of the petition is in WW, Petition to Parliament: Appendix to the Seventh Report on Public Petitions (27 Feb–1 Mar 1839): WLMS/A/Talfourd/11 no.2324. Among the other petitioners were Arnold, Baillie, Browning, Campbell, Carlyle, HC, Cunningham, Dickens, Hood, Horne, Hunt, Lockhart, HM, SR, HT & Wilson; RS alone declined, despite WW's pleas.

Chapter 25

chapter title: 'Real Greatness', M. Arnold, Family Notebook: WLMS/A/Arnold item 7.
picture: DW in her wheelchair, by John Harden after a visit to her in 1842.

1. HCR to TR, 19 Jan 1839 (*HCRWC*, i, 376); *HCRBW*, ii, 560–68; T. Carlyle to M. Carlyle, 25 Mar 1835 (*Collected Letters of Thomas and Jane Welch Carlyle*, viii, 85); HT, *Autobiography*, i, 52–4; SC to A. de Vere, 1 Oct 1851: *SCM*, ii, 455.

2. EQD: WLMS/13/4/2 [11–18 Feb 1839]; WW & MW to EQ, [early Feb] & to RS, 18 Feb [1839] (*LY*, iii, 659–60, 663); IF to Dora, 18 Apl 1839: WLMS/A/Fenwick/2 p.3; EQ to Dora, 20 Feb & 17 Apl 1839: WLL/EQ/83 p.1 & 85 p.2. HCR did his part for the romance by engineering a reconciliation between JW3 and EQ on 7 Feb, persuading the latter that JW3 was 'not unfriendly towards his pretensions with Dora': *HCRBW*, ii, 568.

3. WW to HCR, 19 Feb, to Dora, 1 May & MW & WW to Dora, [3 Apl] [1839] (*LY*, iii, 664, 691, 672–3); IF to HT, 28 Mar 1839 (Dowden, 117–18).

4. MW & WW to Dora, [3 Apl] [1839] (*LY*, iii, 672–3); MW to Dora, [8 Apl 1839] (*LMW*, 220) & WLL/MW/123 pp.3–4 for omissions; CW to WW, 7 Mar 1839: WLL/CW/97 p.2. Herbert Hill (1810–92) married Bertha Southey on 12 Mar 1839: HC to SC, 23 Feb 1839 (*LHC*, 228).
5. MW to Dora, [8 & 16 Apl 1839] (*LMW*, 219–22, 226); W.L. Bowles to WW, 15 Apl [1839]: WLMS/A/Bowles/2 p.3; WW to W.L. Bowles, 23 Apl [1839] (*LY*, iii, 685–6); W.L. Bowles to T. Moore, 19 Apl 1839 (R. Russell [ed.], *Early Correspondence of Lord John Russell 1805–40* [London, T. Fisher Unwin, 1913], ii, 248–9). TdQ's articles on WW appeared in *Tait's Magazine* in Jan, Feb & Apl 1839; further ones, on WW & RS and RS, WW & STC, appeared in Jul & Aug, followed by *Recollections of Grasmere* in Sep 1839.
6. EQ to Dora, 17 Apl 1839: WLL/EQ/85 p.3; WW to EQ, 13 Apl [1839] (*LY*, iii, 681–2).
7. MW to Dora, 13 Apl 1839 (*LMW*, 224); EQD: WLMS/13/4/2 [7, 16 & 17 Apl 1839]; IF to Dora, 18 Apl 1839: WLMS/A/Fenwick/2; EQ to Dora, 17 Apl 1839: WLL/EQ/85 p.3. EQ's angry letter to WW, which his diary says he sent on 16 Apl, is not extant.
8. WW to Dora, [*c.*24 Apl 1839] (*LY*, iii, 686–7); MW to Dora, 19 [Apl 1839] (*LMW*, 231); EQD: WLMS/13/4/2 [7 Jun 1839].
9. T. Spring-Rice to WW, 18 Apl & 9 May 1839: WLMS/A/Spring-Rice/1, 6 & 7; WW to T. Spring-Rice, 19, 21 & 28 Apl & to Dora & DW, [*c.*9 May] 1839 (*LY*, iii, 683–4, 684–5, 689–90, 692); R. Bourke to WW, 20 Apl 1839: WLMS/A/Spring-Rice/2; MW to Dora, [*franked* 29 Apl 1839]: WLL/MW/131 p.3.
10. MW to Dora, [7 & 9 May 1839] (*LMW*, 237, 238); WW to Dora & DW, [*c.*9 May 1839] (*LY*, iii, 693); IF to I. Fenwick, 20 May 1839: E462.2.1 pp.2–3.
11. Ibid., p.3; *HCRBW*, iii, 571; WW to Chas W, [16 May], to CW, [26 May] & MW, 8 Jun [1839] (*LY*, iii, 695–6, 698, 700); Manx *Advertiser*, 28 May 1839. Charlotte W was buried in the cloisters of Winchester College, where her husband was Second Master: Chas W, *Annals of My Early Life*, 238–9. HH was buried in the old churchyard of Kirk Braddan, just outside Douglas. Mary Arnold found the grave in 1845 and sent MW some grasses picked from it, but it is no longer identifiable: Braddan Parish Burial Register, ii, 1800–1849, Manx Museum, Douglas; M. Arnold to MW, 29 Jul 1845: WLMS/A/Arnold/13. See also *Prose*, ii, 99.
12. EQD: WLMS/13/4/2 [7–10, 25, 26 & 29 Jun 1839]; WW to Dora, [9 Jun 1839] (*LY*, iii, 702–3); *HCRBW*, ii, 573.
13. F.A. Faber to WW, 17 Apl 1839: WLMS/A/Faber/1; WW2 to MW, [13 Jun 1839]: WLL/WW2/49 pp.1–2; M. Arnold, Family Notebook: WLMS/A/Arnold item 7. Dr Arnold also remarked, 'it was striking to witness the thunders of applause, repeated over and over again, with which he was greeted in the theatre, by the undergraduates and masters of arts alike': Barron Field, 35.
14. *Memoirs*, ii, 355; J. Peace to MW, 12 Aug 1839: WLMS/A/Peace/2 p.2; WW, *The Old Cumberland Beggar*, l.153 (*Poems*, i, 267).
15. J. Peace to MW, 12 Aug 1839: WLMS/A/Peace/2 p.2; R.P. Graves to Mrs Hemans, 16 Aug 1834: WLMS/A/Graves/4 p.4. See also WW to H. Alford, [*c.*20 Feb 1840] (*LY*, iv, 23–4).
16. SGB, 21 Mar 1804 (*Farington Diary*, vi, 2174); J. Ruskin, *Praeterita* (OUP, 1978), 205. Coincidentally, after receiving his honorary doctorate, WW presented the Newdigate Poetry Prize to Ruskin, then a 20-year-old student at Christ Church: Gill, 396. For WW's ability to appeal across the sectarian divide and his influence on the next generation, see Gill, *Wordsworth and the Victorians*, esp.40–80.
17. Ibid., 63; F. Jeffrey, *Edinburgh Review*, xi (Oct 1807) (Hayden, 18).
18. WW to J. Keble, [14 Jun 1839] (*LY*, iii, 706); MW to EM, 22 Jun [1839]: WLL/MW/133 pp.1–2.
19. WW to JW4, [early Apl], to EM, [late Jun] & 1 Nov, & JW & WW to EM, 8 Nov [1839] (*LY*, iii, 675–6, 711, 732, 738–9); JW4 to WW, 22 Apl & 26 Oct 1839: WLMS/1/9/9 pp.1–2 & 10 p.1; F.T. Price to WW, 28 May 1836: WLMS/A/Price, F./1. WW insisted that JW3's translations were checked by CW2 before inclusion, even though this delayed publication: JW & WW to EM, 8 Nov, WW to HCR, 7 Dec & to CW2, 22 Dec [1839] (*LY*, iii, 738–9, 745, 748–9).
20. CW to WW, 31 Dec 1839: WLL/CW/100; WW to CW, 3 Jan [1840] (*LY*, iv, 1); Mrs CW2 to KJW, 10 Jan 1840: G11/4/1 pp.1–2; JW4, Obituary in the *Cambridge Chronicle*, 11 Jan 1840: WLMS/1/21/1.
21. Army Medical Dept to KJW, 7 Jan & 16 Jul 1839: G11/3/1 & 2; WW to J. Davy, 21 Aug, to Mrs

CW2, 21 Oct, to Sir W.M. Gomm, 29 Oct & to MW & IF, [3 Nov] [1839] (*LY*, iii, 719, 729, 731, 737); EQ to Dora, 24 Sep 1839: WLL/EQ/90 p.2; KJW to CW, 7 Nov 1839: WLL/CW/99. KJW's letter is dated 'London' and says he is sailing that afternoon, so WW's sailing 'from Gibraltar' [3 Nov] should be 'for Gibraltar'.

22. T. Powell to WW, 20 Jul & 3 Aug 1839: WLMS/A/Powell/5 p.1 & 6 pp.1–3; WW to T. Powell, [13 Oct] & to MW & IF, [3 Nov] [1839] & to C. Marshall, 19 Feb 1840 (*LY*, iii, 727, 736; iv, 22); Blanshard, 86–7, 163–6, pls.16, 17, 18, 20 & 47. Margaret Gillies (1803–87) studied in Edinburgh and Paris; she also painted Leigh Hunt, HM and Charles Dickens. HCR was disappointed by all the Gillies portraits, 'only Mrs Wordsworth at all like and hers by no means excellent': *HCRBW*, ii, 582. MW's inspired two WW sonnets both entitled *To a Painter* (*Poems*, ii, 867–8).

23. EQ to Dora, 24 Sep & 5 Dec 1839: WLL/EQ/90 p.2 & 92 pp.3–4; SC to M. Stanger, [*p.m.*11 Dec 1839]: Moorsom 55/1/22 p.2; EQD: WLMS/13/4/2 [17 Nov–3 Dec 1839].

24. WW to EM, 10 Jan 1840 (*LY*, iv, 5); Blanshard, pl.21.

25. WW to EM, 10 Jan & to B. Field, 16 Jan 1840 (*LY*, iv, 5, 6–7). B. Field to WW, 21 Nov 1839: WLMS/A/Field/8; Barron Field, 36n.40. WW's corrections to Field's text give it its only importance as a biographical source: Field's own sources were chiefly Galignani's biographical preface, TdQ's articles in *Tait's Magazine*, Hazlitt's essays and JC's *Early Recollections*.

26. WW to T. Powell, 18 Jan, to HCR, [23 Jan], to EM, [?18 Feb] & to EQ, 9 Mar 1840; WW to H. Reed, 13 Jan 1841 (*LY*, iv, 8, 11, 19–20, 42, 165). WW did not acknowledge the force of the objections to its inclusion, but yielded to his females' judgement; Hunt's modernization of the tale appeared instead.

27. WW to T. Powell, 16 Oct & [late Oct] 1840, to H. Reed, 13 Jan & to T. Powell, [Mar] 1841 (ibid., 129, 134, 165–6, 185); T. Powell to WW, 23 Oct 1840: WLMS/A/Powell/9 p.3.

28. EQD: WLMS/13/4/3 [14 Feb–24 Apl 1840]; Dora to IF, nd (Blanshard, 87); EQ to Dora, 24 Apl 1840: WLL/EQ/98 pp.1–2. Dora's letter cannot be August, as Blanshard suggests, as she was not in London then: EQ met Dora at Miss Gillies's on 21 Feb 1840, which therefore seems the likeliest date for the sitting.

29. MW to IF, 10 Apl [1840]: WLL/MW/136 pp.2–3; WW, *The Cuckoo Clock* and [*To IF*], ll.1–2, 14 (*Poems*, ii, 830–31, 829). See also WW, *Upon a Portrait* (ibid., 828–9), addressed to Gillies's portrait of IF.

30. MW to IF, Apl [1840] (*LMW*, 243); WW, *Before the Picture of the Baptist, by Raphael, in the Gallery at Florence*, *The Norman Boy* and *The Poet's Dream: Sequel to the Norman Boy* (*Poems*, ii, 861–2, 832–8); *IF*, 73, 74–5; E.F. Ogle to WW, [*p.m.*16], 26 & 28 May 1840: WLMS/A/Ogle/1, 2 & 3; WW to E.F. Ogle, 20 May 1840 (*LY*, iv, 73–5). Two days after composing the *Norman Boy*, WW rejected a request for a similar poem celebrating youthful piety, because the circumstances (the death of a daughter) were too painful for him to contemplate after his own loss of Catherine and Thomas: WW to C.H. Parry, 21 May 1840 (ibid., 75–6).

31. MW to CW2, 24 Jun [1840] (*LMW*, 244); WW, *Sonnets Upon the Punishment of Death*, esp.nos.xi–xiii (*Poems*, ii, 822–8); WW to EM, 27 Jan 1840 (*LY*, iv, 14).

32. RMVB, pp 72–81, esp.75–6; EQD: WLMS/13/4/3 [24–5 & 27 Jul 1840]; R.P. Graves to WW, [21 Jul 1840]: WLMS/A/Graves/10; WW to HCR, 3 Jun & to Lady F. Bentinck, [30 Jul 1840] (*LY*, iv, 80, 96–7); Dora to WW2, [27 Jul 1840]: WLL/Dora/72 pp.1–2. Lady le Fleming apparently 'shammed sick' during the visit, out of pique that the Queen visited WW rather than herself: EQ to Dora, [?29 Sep, 13 Oct or 1 Dec 1840]: WLL/EQ/110 p.3.

33. EQD: WLMS/13/4/3 [30 Jul–31 Aug 1840]; WW to HCR, 4 [*r.*3] Sep [18]40 (*LY*, iv, 106–7); EQ to RQ, 1 Sep 1840: WLL/EQ/101 pp.3–4. EQ arrived at RM on 1 Jul and left, with JQ, on 11 Sep.

34. WW, *On a Portrait of the Duke of Wellington upon the Field of Waterloo, by Haydon*, ll.1–9 (*Poems*, ii, 839); BRH to WW, 9 [Sep] 1840: WLMS/A/Haydon/21; WW to BRH, 2, 7, 10 & 11 Sep [*bis*] & 24 [Oct] & to H. Reed, 14 Sep 1840 (*LY*, iv, 100, 107–12, 131, 117).

35. EQD: WLMS/13/4/3 [5 & 8 Sep 1840]; WW to BRH, 10 & [17] Sep [1840] (*LY*, iv, 109, 120); Blanshard, pl.22; EQ to Dora, 7 Dec 1840: WLL/EQ/109 p.1.

36. WW to SR, [11], [early (*r.*14)] & [17] [Sep], & to Dora & to IF, [14 Sep] [1840] (*LY*, iv, 111, 108, 119, 113, 114); EQ to RQ, 17 Nov & to Dora, 28 &

30 Sep 1840: WLL/EQ/108 pp.1–2, 102 p.4 & 103 p.9.

37. WW to HCR, 27 Oct, to IF, [3 Nov], to unidentified [?P. Fisher], 12 Nov & to IF, 14 Nov 1840 (*LY*, iv, 132, 135–6, 137–8, 139–41); P. Fisher to WW, 11 Nov 1840: WLMS/A/Fisher, P./1. The accident was widely reported in the newspapers; Queen Adelaide was one of many who wrote to express their concern: Lord Howe pp.Queen Adelaide to WW, 13 Nov 1840: WLMS/A/Howe/1.

38. *HCRBW*, ii, 588. HCR arrived on 24 Dec 1840, stayed in his usual lodgings at the foot of the hill, and left on 21 Jan 1841: ibid., 587, 590; WW to HCR, 17 Dec [18]40 (*LY*, iv, 156). IF stayed at RM, arriving by 14 Dec 1840 and leaving with Dora on 4 Mar 1841: IF to I. Fenwick, 14 Dec 1840: E462.2.6 p.1; WW to EM, 4 Mar 1841 (*LY*, iv, 183).

39. *HCRBW*, ii, 587–90; WW to Jas Spedding, 28 Dec 1840 (*LY*, iv, 157); HCR to TR, 12 Jan & to J. Masquerier, 18 Jan 1841 (*HCRWC*, i, 422 [*bis*]). For an example of WW outwalking his son, see WW to IF, [3 Nov 1840] (*LY*, iv, 135).

40. EQ to Dora, 12 Aug 1839: WLL/EQ/89 p.2; WW to Lady F. Bentinck, 30 Jul 1840 & to HCR, 26 Jan 1841 (*LY*, iv, 97, 169–72); Storey, 340ff.

41. WW to HCR, 26 Jan 1841 (*LY*, iv, 172–4); HCR to TR, 12 Jan 1841 (*HCRWC*, i, 422); *HCRBW*, i, 590; Dora to HCR, 2 Feb [1841] (*LY*, iv, 175–6). As late as Nov 1840, WW cautioned IF that 'poor dear K[ate] is too apt to put unwarrantably an unfavorable construction upon some of Mrs S's proceedings', adding that this was 'very pardonable considering K's position', but sympathy for her should not be allowed to condone injustice to Mrs RS. IF, like HCR, was also recruited to the Southey children's cause: WW to IF, [30 Nov 1840] (ibid., 151); IF to I. Fenwick, 20 Jan 1841: E462.2.8.

42. EQ to Dora, 10 Jun 1839, 26 Feb & 25 Mar 1841: WLL/EQ/88 p.8 & 111 p.1; G1/12/1 pp.1–2; Dora to WW2, 26 Mar 1841: G1/App.2/2 p.1; WW to EQ, 27 Mar 1841: G1/12/2 pp.1–2. The marriage settlement was signed the day before the wedding: Dora, Marriage Settlement, 10 May 1841: G2/20/1.

43. *HCRBW*, ii, 580–81; IF to I. Fenwick, 6 Apl 1841: E462.2.13. EQ remained sensitive to rumours that WW did not approve of the match and objected to accompanying the Ws on a tour after his marriage: SC to M. Stanger, [*franked* 12 Apl 1841]: Moorsom 55/1/24 pp.3–4; EQ to Dora, 26 Feb 1841: WLL/EQ/111 p.2.

44. WW to EM, 4 Mar, to HCR, 18 Apl & to J. Peace, 19 Mar 1841 (*LY*, iv, 183, 189–90, 192–3). The Ws date their Bath letters from 12 North Parade, though the plaque is placed at no.9; most of the terrace is now part of the Parade Park Hotel.

45. CW to WW, 1 May 1841: WLL/CW/101 pp.1–3; WW to CW, [3–4 May 1841] (*LY*, iv, 195–6); CW, Deed of Trust, 12 May 1841: G2/21/3. Like the marriage settlement, this deed ensured that Dora received the money in her own right, so that it could not be appropriated by EQ or his creditors.

46. EQD: WLMS/13/4/5(a) [8–11 May 1841]; EQ to RQ, 12 May 1841: WLL/EQ/114 p.1. *The Bath Directory, 1841* (Bath, H. Silverthorne, 1841). JW's 5th son and 6th child, Edward, was born on 5 Apl 1841: *Carlisle Patriot*, 10 Apl 1841: WLMS/1/4/5.

47. EH to JQ, [*c.*12 May 1841]: WLMS/H2/5/15; MW to Mrs CW2, 15 May 1841 (*LMW*, 245); EQ to RQ, 12 May & to JQ, 21 May 1841: WLL/EQ/114 p.1 & 116 pp.1–6. St James's Church was destroyed by incendiary bombs during the blitz in World War II: pictures survive in the newspaper clippings file at Bath Reference Library.

48. EH to JQ, [*c.*12 May 1841]: WLMS/H2/5/15 p.4; EQ to RQ, 12 May & to JQ, 21 May 1841: WLL/EQ/114 pp.1–3 & 116 pp.4–8; MW to Mrs CW2, 15 May 1841 (*LMW*, 245); Dora to HCR, 19 May 1841 (*HCRWC*, i, 434); Dora to IF, 8 Jun [1841]: WLL/Dora/74 p.1.

49. Ibid., p.3; WW to [?T.H. Cornish], 20 May, MW to HCR, 22 May & WW to J. Peace, 4 Sep [1841] (*Supp.*, 244; *LY*, iv, 200, 242); the Church of St Pancras, West Bagborough, is full of monuments to the Popham family, including a brass plaque to IF's sister, Susannah Popham (d.23 Jan 1865).

50. MW to IF, 2 Jun [1841]: WLL/MW/138 pp.3–4; WW to T. Spring-Rice, 17 Oct, to E. Fisher, 15 Dec [1837] & to IF, [4 *or* 5 Jun 1841] (*LY*, iii, 474, 490–91; iv, 202–3); E. Fisher to WW, 2 Dec 1837: WLMS/A/Fisher, E/3. Emmie's mother, Elizabeth Fisher, was the daughter of WW's uncle WC: 'the Spirit of Poetry contained in the "Lyrical Ballads" (which have been perpetually under the pillow, or in [Emmie's] hands, since she

was four years old) has been the fostering Genius under which her love and taste for poetry have grown': E. Fisher to WW, 28 Nov 1837: WLMS/A/Fisher, E./2 pp.1–2.

51. WW to T. Powell, [?11 Jun], to J.C. Hare, 15 Jun & to IF, 29 Jun [1841] (*LY*, iv, 204–5, 206–7, 209); MW to IF, 18 Jun 1841: WLL/MW/139 pp.1–2; Dora to IF, 28 Jun [1841]: WLL/Dora/75 p.9; The Quillinans left RM on 16 Jun and London, for Canterbury, on 31 Aug: EQD: WLMS/13/4/5(a) [16 Jun–31 Aug 1841].

52. HCR to TR, 12 Jul 1841 (*HCRWC*, i, 439–40); WW to IF, 10 Jul & to J.G. Lockhart, [early Nov] 1841 (*LY*, iv, 214, 259–60, 259n.2). Lockhart's 'The Copyright Question' appeared in the *Quarterly Review*, lxix (Dec 1841). TNT had introduced his Copyright Bill again in Jan and carried it with another increased majority, but at the 2nd reading debate was deferred for six months: WW told TNT, 'Indignation stifles every other emotion but gratitude towards you, for the noble and persevering exertions which you have made so long': WW to TNT, 8 Feb [1841] (*LY*, iv, 178 & n.1).

53. WW to IF, 24 [Jul] & to M.F. Howley, 23 Aug 1841 (ibid., 217, 233–4). The Ws left London on 13 Jul: EQD: WLMS/13/4/5(a).

54. WW to IF, 24 [Jul 1841] (*LY*, iv, 217–18). Augustus Welby Northmore Pugin (1812–52), a leader of the Gothic revival in English architecture, was currently employed by Sir Charles Barry in detail drawing for the new Houses of Parliament. Mount St Bernard's was founded in 1835, but the building were not completed until 1844.

55. WW to IF, 24 [Jul], [5 Aug] & 30 [Aug]; W to E. Fisher, [?autumn] [1841] (ibid., 217, 221–2, 235, 245); MW to Mrs CW2, 15 May 1841 (*LMW*, 245).

56. RMVB, pp.83–4; WW to CW, 11 Aug [1841] (*LY*, iv, 225–7): C.V. Le Grice to HCR, 14 Aug 1841 & to unidentified, 9 Sep 1850 (*HCRBW*, i, 441–2 & WLMS/A/Le Grice/5); C.V. Le Grice, 'Wordsworth, Bard of the heart!', nd: WLMS/A/Le Grice/7.

57. WW to G.W. Doane & to H. Reed, 16 Aug 1841 (*LY*, iv, 228–9, 229–30); WW, *Ecclesiastical Sonnets*, xiii–xv (*Poems*, ii, 488–90, 1012–13). To the Ws' disgust, George Washington Doane (1799–1859) published an account of his meeting with WW and WW's private letters to him: MW to IF, [Aug 1842] (*LMW*, 262); HCR to WW, 27 Aug 1842 (*HCRWC*, i, 468).

58. WW to HCR, 3 Jun 1840, to CW, 11 Aug & to CW2, 5 Nov 1841 (*LY*, iv, 83, 225, 257); Dora to WW2, 26 Mar 1841: G1/App.2/2 p.4; *IF*, 76; Owen Lloyd, Gravestone in Holy Trinity churchyard, Chapel Stile; Viator to the *Westmoreland Gazette*, 12 Oct 1841: WLMS/A/Lloyd, O./6. The epitaph was published by WW, with corrected punctuation, in 1842: WW, *Epitaph in the Chapel-Yard of Langdale, Westmoreland* (*Poems*, ii, 872–3).

59. WW to W.F. Hook, 7 Dec & to EM, 17 Dec 1840 & 17 Jan 1841 (*LY*, iv, 153, 155, 167).

60. HCR to WW, 12 Sep 1836 (*HCRWC*, ii, 316); MW to HCR, 1 Nov [18]36 & WW to JK, [summer 1838] (*LY*, iii, 314, 616).

61. WW to EM, 4 Mar & to IF, [Mar] [1841] (ibid., iv, 183–4, 187); Barron Field, 15.

62. IF to HT, 4 Jan 1839 (Dowden, 110); HCR to MW, 22 Apl 1842 (*HCRWC*, i, 458–9); WW, *Musings near Aquapendente*, ll.88, 91–103, 198–204 (*Poems*, ii, 842, 845); WW to EM, 4 Mar, 19 Apl & 24 Dec, DW & WW to Dora, [mid-Nov] [1841] (*LY*, iv, 183, 192, 277, 261).

63. HC to H.N. Coleridge, 10 Jul 1840 (*LHC*, 243); WW to HCR, [late Nov 1841] (*LY*, iv, 265); HCR to WW, 15 Dec 1841 (*HCRWC*, i, 449–50); *HCRBW*, ii, 603.

64. WW to EM, 4 Feb & to HT, [19 Nov] [1841] (*LY*, iv, 176, 263); HCR to TR, 6 Jan 1842 (*HCRWC*, i, 452); *HCRBW*, ii, 606; T. Carlyle to J. Sterling, 12 Jan 1842 (*Collected Letters of Thomas and Jane Welch Carlyle*, xiv, 11). WW thanked both HT and Lockhart for publishing the article: an 'anonymous quarrelsome Admirer of mine', he told HT, had 'inflicted upon me no less than 19 of his – in refutation, and abuse of us both': WW to J.G. Lockhart & HT, 17 Jan [18]42 (*LY*, iv, 284, 284–5).

65. *HCRBW*, ii, 603; SC to M. Stanger, 4 Jan [1842] & 6 Dec [1841]: Moorsom 55/1/29 p.4 & 55/1/28; HCR to J. Masquerier, 5 Jan 1842 (*HCRWC*, i, 450); WW to Dora [Nov/Dec] & 7 Dec [1841] (*LY*, iv, 266, 269).

66. *HCRBW*, ii, 603–11, esp.610–11.

67. Ibid., 605; F.W. Faber to WW, 26 Jun 1841: WLMS/A/Faber, F.W./1 pp.1–2; MW to WW, [28 Aug], to WW, Dora, TH & Mrs TH, 18 Sep & to Dora, 21 Sep [1837] (*LMW*, 176, 188 & WLL/MW/108 p.3 (omitted from *LMW*, 190).

68. Gill, *Wordsworth and the Victorians*, 72–4; *HCRBW*, ii, 481; *IF*, 70. Gill, 70–80 gives an illuminating account of Faber's remarkable influence on WW.
69. WW, *Guilt and Sorrow*, l.657 (*Poems*, i, 140); STC to J.P. Estlin, [18] May [1798] (*STCL*, i, 410); *HCRBW*, ii, 550, 490; i, 87; F.W. Faber to J.B. Morris, 25 Nov 1842 (Gill, *Wordsworth and the Victorians*, 80).
70. *HCRBW*, ii, 603, 612; HCR to TR, 6 Jan, to MW, 21 Feb & to Dora, 7 Mar 1842 (*HCRWC*, i, 451, 453, 454); WW, *To Henry Crabb Robinson*, ll.6–9 (*Poems*, ii, 839).
71. WW to EM, 18 Jan & 3 Feb 1842 (*LY*, iv, 285–6, 289–90); HCR to WW, [22 Jan] & 8 Feb 1842 (*HCRWC*, i, 452–3); *JTM*, v, 2225. 'Mr' Quillinan in WW's letter of 18 Jan should be 'Mrs': see *HCRBW*, ii, 611.
72. WW to EM, 23 Mar, 3 Apl, 27 Mar & 1 Apl 1842 (*LY*, iv, 307–8, 318, 308–9, 313).

Chapter 26

picture: WW, by Jane Pasley, etched by John Bull, 1845.
1. Lord Mahon to WW, 25 Feb, 2 & 7 Mar & to Lord J. Russell, 28 Feb 1842: WLMS/A/Mahon/1–4; R. Inglis to WW, 28 Feb 1842: WLMS/A/Inglis/1 pp.2–4; WW to Lord Mahon, 28 Feb & 4 Mar 1842 (*LY*, iv, 293–4, 299–301). Philip Henry Stanhope, Lord Mahon (1805–75), author of *History of the War of the Succession in Spain* (1832) and *History of England from the Peace of Utrecht to the Peace of Versailles* (1836–53), later founded the National Portrait Gallery and the Historical Manuscripts Commission.
2. Lord Mahon to WW, 7 Apl & 1 Jul 1842: WLMS/A/Mahon/5 & 6. Copyright in posthumously published works would also last for 42 years after the date of first publication.
3. MW & WW to EM, [1 Apl], to J. Hudson, 13 Mar & [early Apl] & to A. Sedgwick, [late Mar] 1842 (*LY*, iv, 314, 304–5, 317–18, 309–10); A. Sedgwick to WW, 26 Mar 1842: WLMS/A/Sedgwick/1 p.1; P. Bicknell (ed.), *The Illustrated Wordsworth's Guide to the Lakes* (Webb & Bower, 1984), 21–2. *A Complete Guide to the Lakes* would be published twice more in WW's lifetime, in 1843 and 1846.
4. A. de Vere to WW, 3 Sep 1841: WLMS/A/de Vere/1 pp.3–5; WW to EM, [5 Nov 1841] & to Sir A. de Vere, 31 Mar [18]42 (*LY*, iv, 255–6, 311–12). Aubrey de Vere (1814–1902), a devotee of WW's verse, had stayed at the foot of Rydal Hill in the spring of 1841: taken ill there, he had been looked after by the Ws with great kindness: WW to IF, [?Mar 1841] (ibid., 187); A. de Vere, *Recollections*, 120–22.
5. A Rio to WW, 11 & 20 Mar 1842: WLMS/A/Rio/1 & 2; WW to EQ, 20 Sep [1837] & to EM, 11 May 1842 (*LY*, iii, 465; iv, 335); MW to IF, 10–11 May [1842] (*LMW*, 250–51).
6. *JTM*, v, 2241–2. Unlike WW, Moore declined to contribute. HCR 'hastily looked over' the newly published *La Petite Chouannerie* on 26 Jun 1842, 'Rio is a writer of some talent, but I could not sympathise with the book': *HCRBW*, ii, 618–19.
7. WW to EQ, 1 Mar & to Dora, 7 Apl 1842 (*LY*, iv, 294–5, 319); *HCRBW*, ii, 613, 614; IF to I. Fenwick, 4 May 1842: E462.2.18 pp.2–4. For similar reactions, see SC to M. Stanger, [*p.m.*4 Mar 1842]: Moorsom 55/1/31; S. Cookson to Dora, 20 Apl 1842: G2/21/4.
8. HCR to MW, 22 Apl 1842 (*HCRWC*, i, 459); WW to CW, 6 May, to IF, [7 May] & to W.E. Gladstone, 28 Jun [1842] (*LY*, iv, 330, 332, 345); VL to WW, 7 & 14 May 1842: WLMS/A/Lowther/68 & 69. The arrangement reached with Spring-Rice in 1839 was quoted as precedent, but actually provoked a backlash instead of helping WW's claim: T. Spring-Rice, Memo re WW, 13 Jun 1842: WLMS/A/Spring-Rice/11; W.E. Gladstone, 11 Oct 1842: WLMS/A/Gladstone/3.
9. *HCRBW*, ii, 617; WW to DW & IF, [24 May 1842] (*LY*, iv, 338); MW to IF, [9 (*r.*16) May 1842] (*LMW*, 248–9).
10. MW to IF, [21 May 1842] (ibid., 252); WW to DW & IF, [24 May 1842] (*LY*, iv, 338).
11. WW to IF, [7] & [24 May 1842] (ibid., 332, 338); MW to IF, [9 (*r.*16) May 1842] (*LMW*, 247); HCR to TR, 21 May 1842 (*HCRWC*, i, 462).
12. WW to DW & IF, [24 May 1842] (*LY*, iv, 337); MW to IF, [2 Jun 1842] (*LMW*, 259).
13. Blanshard, 89–90, pl.23. E. Barrett [Browning], *Wordsworth upon Helvellyn!* in BRH to WW, 19 Sep 1842: WLMS/A/Haydon/25 p.1. WW wrote to thank Miss Barrett for her sonnet (suggesting corrections) on 26 Oct 1842 (*LY*, iv, 384–5).
14. Blanshard, 91–2, 168; *HCRBW*, ii, 618. Mrs Aders made two copies of the portrait which

HCR gave to Dora; none has been identified.
15. WW to HCR, [4 Jun] & to Lady Monteagle, 28 Jun [1842] (*LY*, iv, 342–3, 346–7); *HCRBW*, ii, 618. The Ws left London for RM on 16 Jun, having learned of Arnold's death on the 13th or 14th: WW to W.E. Gladstone, 28 Jun [1842] (*LY*, iv, 344).
16. HCR to TR, 2 & 21 Jul 1842 (*HCRWC*, i, 466, 467); *HCRBW*, ii, 621–2; WW to R. Peel, 25 Jul 1842 (*LY*, iv, 357).
17. MW to IF, [Aug 1842] (*LMW*, 261–2). The formal notification of WW2's appointment arrived on 24 Jul: WW wrote next day to thank Peel, who sent a gracious reply: 'It is some compensation for the severe toil and Anxiety of public Life to have occasionally the opportunity of serving or gratifying those – who are an Honour to their Country': MW & WW to IF, 28 Jul & WW to R. Peel, 25 Jul 1842 (*LY*, iv, 358, 356–7); R. Peel to WW, 7 Aug 1842: WLMS/A/Peel/3.
18. WW to W.E. Gladstone, 11 Jul & 17 Oct & to R. Peel, 17 Oct 1842 (*LY*, iv, 352, 379, 378); W.E. Gladstone to WW, 28 Sep & 18 Oct 1842: WLMS/A/Gladstone/2 & 4; R. Peel to WW, 15 Oct 1842: WLMS/A/Peel/4; Lady F. Bentinck, 18 Oct 1842: G1/14/5 pp.1–2; HCR to MW, 19 Oct 1842 (*HCRWC*, i, 468–9).
19. *HCRBW*, ii, 623; EQD: WLMS/13/5/1 [8 Aug 1842]; J. Jaffray to HCR, 18 Aug 1842 (*HCRWC*, i, 467). AV had died, aged 75, at the Boulevard des Filles du Calvaire in Paris: the death register gave her name as 'Marie Anne Vallon, known as William' and her status as 'employee' and 'spinster'. She was buried in the Père Lachaise cemetery, but her remains were exhumed and reburied (1846), with those of her granddaughter, Anne Léonide Baudouin (1819–25), in the Baudouin family vault at St Firmin: Legouis, 110–11.
20. MW to IF, 4 Oct 1842 (*LMW*, 266); M. Arnold to Miss Trevenell, 9 Dec 1842: WLMS/A/Arnold/48.
21. *HCRBW*, ii, 626, 628; EQD:/WLMS 13/5/1 [31 Oct, 1 & 24 Nov 1842]; HCR to TR, 29 [Dec 1842] (*HCRWC*, i, 472–3).
22. Ibid.; WW to S. Wilkinson, 11 Jul & 21 Sep 1842 (*LY*, iv, 353–4, 370–72); Gill, *Wordsworth and the Victorians*, 63–6.
23. HCR to TR, 12 Jan 1843 (*HCRWC*, ii, 473–4); IF to I. Fenwick, 24 Jan 1843: E462.2.20 p.3. Having seen much of Faber during 1842, IF admitted that 'this nearer sight has led to admiration & esteem & I may say also affection'.
24. *IF*, xiii, 14, 64–6; IF to HCR, 9 Mar 1843 (*HCRWC*, i, 479).
25. WW to J.T. Coleridge, 29 Jan 1843 & to the Governors of Warwick School, 15 Sep 1842 (*LY*, iv, 398, 368–9).
26. EQ to HCR, 15 Feb, HCR to TR, 29 Mar & EQ to HCR, 5 & 19 Apl 1843 (*HCRWC*, i, 477, 479, 485, 494); WW to TNT, [22 Mar] & to J.T. Coleridge, 17 Apl 1843 (*LY*, iv, 405, 431); EQ to EM, 22 Mar 1843: WLL/EQ/122 p.2.
27. WW to HT, 31 Mar [1843] (*LY*, iv, 419–20); HT to WW, 1 Apl 1843: WLMS/A/Taylor, H/10. RS's brother, Dr Henry Southey, was HT's co-executor, but declined to act, so his duties devolved on Cuthbert: WW to EM, [29 Mar 1843] (*LY*, iv, 418).
28. HCR to WW, [late Mar 1843] (*HCRWC*, i, 537); Earl de la Warr to WW, 30 Mar 1843: WLMS/A/De la Warr/1 p.2; WW to Earl de la Warr & to Lady F. Bentinck, 1 Apl 1843 (*LY*, iv, 421, 422). Alfred Tennyson (1809–92) succeeded WW as Poet Laureate in 1850.
29. R. Peel to WW, 3 Apl 1843: WLMS/A/Peel/5 pp.2, 3–4; WW to Earl de la Warr, 4 Apl 1833 (*LY*, iv, 424). The Lord Chamberlain also asked WW to reconsider, offering the same assurances: Earl de la Warr to WW, 3 Apl 1843: WLMS/A/De la Warr/2.
30. Sir W. Martins to WW, 22 Apl 1843: WLMS/A/Martins/2; WW, Oath of Allegiance, 24 Apl 1843: WLMS/1/1/6c; WW to EM, [26 May 1843] (*LY*, iv, 444); Dora to Mrs CW2, 27 Jul [1843]: WLL/Dora/81 pp.6–7; CW to WW, 27 Nov 1843: WLL/CW/111 p.4; EQ to HCR, 23–8 Jul 1843 (*HCRWC*, i, 507). A similar strong hint was given by the official responsible for dispensing the annual salary: W. Nichol to WW, 7 Mar 1844: WLMS/A/Nichol/2 pp.3–4.
31. EQ to HCR, 9 [*r*.19] Apl 1843 (*HCRWC*, i, 495–6).
32. EQ to HCR, 15 & 7 Feb & 5 & 9 [*r*.19] Apl 1843 (ibid., 478, 476–7, 484, 493); CW to WW2, 20 Feb & to WW, 4 Apl 1843: WLL/CW/109 & 110 pp.1–2; WW to CW, 20 Mar [1843] & to IF, [early Jan 1845] (*LY*, iv, 402–3, 648); HCR to MW, 10 Apl 1843 (*HCRWC*, i, 492).
33. Dora to M. Stanger, 22 Sep [1842]: Moorsom 62/4/10 pp.1–3; MW to M. Stanger, 14 Mar

[1843]: Moorsom 61/2/1 pp.3–4; EQ to HCR, 9 & 9 [r.19] Apl & 1 Jun 1843 (*HCRWC*, i, 490, 493, 500); WW to SC, 2 May, to A. Hook, 24 Oct & to Mrs Harrison, [13 Nov] 1843 (*LY*, iv, 441, 490, 497); Jo H to M. Monkhouse, 8 Jul 1843: WLMS/H/1/8/50 p.1; Dora to MW, 26 Aug [1843]: WLL/Dora/80 pp.1–2. JW3 had held the living of Plumbland, worth £420 p.a., jointly with Brigham, since 1840, but without the Curwen fortune to back him he was in financial difficulties, exacerbated by the medical bills and cost of going to Madeira: JPM's sisters each offered JW3 £50 to help him: WW to EQ, 9 Mar 1840 & to Dora, 14 [Oct 1843] (*LY*, iv, 44, 485).

34. KJW to Dora, 1 Jan 1843: WLMS/1/7/5 p.2; WW to Sir J. McGrigor, 16 Apl & to IF, 2 Aug 1843 (*LY*, iv, 428–9, 462); Dora to Mrs CW2, 27 Jul [1843]: WLL/Dora/81 pp.1–2; RMVB, p.97.

35. Jo H to M. Monkhouse, 8 Jul 1843: WLMS/H/1/8/50 p.1; HCR to TR, 21–2 Jul & EQ to HCR, 23 Jul & 1 Sep 1843 (*HCRWC*, i, 505, 506, 520); WW to KJW, [27 Aug], to IF, 21 Sep & to CW2, 25 Sep 1843 (*LY*, iv, 473, 476; *Supp.*, 246–7). Dr Henry Belcombe ran a private asylum at Clifton in York on the same principles as the Retreat: B. Hutton, *Clifton and its People in the Nineteenth Century. A North Riding Township now part of York City* (Yorkshire Philosophical Society, 1969), 17; Barker, *The Brontës*, 512, 625).

36. WW to IF, 21 Sep & to CW2, 25 Sep 1843 (*LY*, iv, 476–7; *Supp.*, 247). Jo H's grave lies next to at least three other Hutchinson graves. The legend on her gravestone reads, 'Here rest the Remains of Joanna Hutchinson who died Sepr 25 1843 aged 62 years also of John Hutchinson late of Stockton esq who died at Seton Carew Augst 31st 1833 Aged 65 years and buried at Sockburn in this county.' Were JH's remains reinterred with those of his sister? It seems more likely that this inscription is simply a carelessly composed 'in memory of' JH.

37. Jo H, Last Will & Testament, 5 Apl 1841: WLMS/H/1/8/51; Jo H, Memo/Codicil, 24 Mar 1843: G3/3/11; JM to WW2, 15 Jun 1843: G3/1/5; H. Hutchinson to WW2, 15 Nov & 29 Dec 1843: G3/1/7 & G3/2/5; GH to WW2, 23 Dec 1843: G3/2/4; CC to HCR, quoted in HCR to MW, 24 Oct 1843 (*HCRWC*, i, 530). The position was further complicated by the fact that Henry Hutchinson, with WW2, was Jo H's executor.

38. HCR to TR, 28 Sep & to MW, 24 Oct 1843 (*HCRWC*, i, 528–9, 529–30); WW to WW2, [17 Oct 1843] (*LY*, iv, 485–6). The inscription on Jane Winder's headstone, in Brinsop churchyard, includes, 'This stone is erected by William and Mary Wordsworth in affectionate & grateful remembrance of her faithful services continued through fifteen years.'

39. WW to A. Hook, 24 Oct & to CW, 20 Dec & [?mid-Dec] & MW to J. Stanger, [mid-Nov] [1843] (*LY*, iv, 490, 511, 507–8, 498–9); WW, 'Wansfell! this Household has a favoured lot', ll.7–14 (*Poems*, ii, 876); *HCRBW*, ii, 628.

40. WW, *Grace Darling*, l.7 (*Poems*, ii, 885). The poem was written in Feb/Mar 1843, privately printed in Carlisle and circulated by WW among his friends. It was written then, he said, as a contrast to the cruel treatment received by survivors of a recent wreck on the French coast: WW to CW, 20 Mar [1843] (*LY*, iv, 404).

41. WW to unidentified [?Sir J.T. Coleridge], 4 [Nov] & to Sir J.T. Coleridge, 27 Jun 1843 (ibid., 492–3, 451). Landor's espousal of the Bristol scheme seems to have been, in part at least, a perverse response to WW's connection with that for Keswick. For his attack on WW in *Blackwood's Magazine* and EQ's response to it, see WW to WRH, Apl 1843 (ibid., 438); EQ to HCR, 7 Feb & 5 Apl & HCR to EQ, [3] & 7 Apl 1843 (*HCRWC*, ii, 475–6, 482–4, 480–81, 487–8).

42. WW to BRH, [6 Apl], to Sir J.T. Coleridge, 27 Jun 1843 & to unidentified, 13 Jan 1844 (*LY*, iv, 426, 452, 517); WW, *Inscription for a Monument in Crosthwaite Church, in the Vale of Keswick*, ll.1–6, 15–18 (*Poems*, ii, 887–8); Storey, 344. The whole epitaph is inscribed on the base of the monument to RS in Crosthwaite church; WW contributed £5 to the subscription: RS, Subscription Appeal, 20 Dec 1843: WLMS/A/RS/28 p.3.

43. Greig, *Francis Jeffrey of The Edinburgh Review*, 222; HCR to MW, 4 Dec 1843 (*HCRWC*, i, 532).

44. R. Parkinson to WW, 14 Mar 1843: WLMS/A/Parkinson/1; WW to R. Parkinson, 17 Mar, WW to R. Chambers, 4 Aug, to CW, 20 Dec & to EM, 4, [c.6], 20 & [23] Dec 1843 (*LY*, iv, 400–401, 465, 509–10, 504–5, 507, 508–9, 512).

45. WW to EM, 20 & [29] Apl [1844] (ibid., 547–8, 549).

46. WW to CW2, [16 Jan 1844] (ibid., 518–19).

47. *HCRD*, ii, 251–2; *HCRBW*, ii, 637–40; MW & DW to HCR, 5 Feb [1844] (*LY*, iv, 522–3); HCR

to MW, 11 Feb 1844 (*HCRWC*, ii, 544–5). See also DW to M.A. Marshall, 19 Nov [1829] (*LY*, ii, 175) & EQD: WLMS/13/5/2 [13 Nov 1843]. A dozen of Dixon's exquisitely painted pace eggs are on display at DC.

48. *HCRBW*, ii, 639; MW to HCR, 6 Feb & 7 Apl & WW to EM, 15 Apl & to H. Reed, 5 Jul 1844 (*LY*, iv, 525, 541, 543, 546, 560–61); IF to HCR, 7 Apl 1844 (*HCRWC*, ii, 549). See also, *Memoirs*, ii, 446–7.

49. WW to Lady F. Bentinck, 31 Mar & to W. Jackson, [?11 Jul] 1844 (*LY*, iv, 539, 566–7); Owen, *The Lowther Family*, 388, 392.

50. WW & MW to IF, [?9] Aug [1843] & WW to HCR, 14 Jul & to IF, [17 & 22 Jul] 1844 (*LY*, iv, 466, 570–71, 574, 578); HCR to TR, 2 Jan 1845 (*HCRWC*, ii, 582); MW to IF, 12 Jun [1844] (*LMW*, 269–70 & omitted paragraph from WLL/MW/149 p.8); Dora to IF, [7 Aug 1844]: WLL/Dora/85 pp.1–2. As the Ws paid only £55 p.a. rent in 1850, WW must have been successful in his personal appeal to Lady le Fleming: T. Jackson, Receipt, 3 Jun 1850: G2/8/18. Anthony Salvin (1799–1881) 'restored' Windsor Castle, the Tower of London and Alnwick Castle; he had, however, also built St John's Church at Keswick and would rebuild the little church at Patterdale, so perhaps his designs would not have been out of keeping.

51. WW to Lady le Fleming, 17 Aug 1844 (*LY*, iv, 584–7); Dora to IF, [21 Aug 1844]: WLL/Dora/87 pp.2–4. The identity of 'the Lord Archbishop of Rydal' is not spelt out: it may refer to Thomas Jackson, Lady le Fleming's agent, though theepithet suggests a clergyman.

52. Ibid., pp.4–5; WW to R. Moser, 18 Aug, 18 & 19 Sep & to IF, [17 Jul], [19 Sep], [22 Jul] 1844 (*LY*, iv, 588, 594, 599–600, 574–5, 596, 579); Dora to IF, [12 Sep 1844]: WLL/Dora/88 pp.1–2.

53. WW to IF, [19 Sep] & [17 & 22 Jul] [1844] (*LY*, iv, 597, 576, 579).

54. WW to IF, [17 Jul 1844] (ibid., 575).

55. Dora to IF, [7 & 21 Aug 1844]: WLL/Dora/85 pp.3–4 & 87 p.1; WW to EM, 15 Apl & [21 Jun], WW & MW to Dora, [*c*.28 Jun] & MW to HCR, 9 Jul & 23 Sep 1844 (*LY*, iv, 546, 557, 558, 563–4, 601); Mrs Fletcher to HCR, 4 Jul 1844 (*HCRWC*, ii, 561); EQD: WLMS/13/5/3 [Aug–Dec 1844, esp.17 & 26 Aug]. For the Quillinans' visit to Flimby, see also ibid., [3 May–20 Jul 1844].

56. [Mary Fletcher], Journal, 6–7 Sep 1844 (*Memoirs*, ii, 451); WW & MW to IF, [19 Sep 1844] (*LY*, iv, 597); EQD: WLMS/13/5/3 [6 & 7 Sep 1844].

57. WW to EM, 12 Sep, to HCR & to H. Inman, 14 Jul, & MW to HCR, 23 Sep 1844 (*LY*, iv, 592, 570, 568–9, 602–3); Dora to IF, [21 Aug] & [12 Sep] [1844]: WLL/Dora/87 pp.7–8 & 88 p.6; Blanshard, 170–71, pl.27. Henry Inman (1801–46) also painted the frontage of RM, including himself at work, and WW standing before him.

58. WW to F.W. Faber, 6 Aug & to IF, 5 Oct [1844] (*LY*, iv, 582–3, 613–14); WW, *Stanzas Suggested in a Steamboat off Saint Bees' Heads, on the Coast of Cumberland* (*Poems*, ii, 749–53); *IF*, 176.

59. *The Journals of Caroline Fox*, 157–8 [6 Oct 1844]; the visit of 'Mr Mrs & Miss Fox, Truro' is recorded in RMVB, p.114.

60. *Prose*, iii, 331; W to unidentified, 17 Nov 1844 (*Supp.*, 249). The first mention of the proposed railway occurs in MW to HCR, 23 Sep [1844] (*LY*, iv, 603).

61. WW, *On the Projected Kendal and Windermere Railway*, ll.1–2, 11–14 (*Poems*, ii, 889); B. Field to HCR, 21 Oct 1844 (*HCRWC*, ii, 575). WW did receive one or two letters of support, notably one from the Quaker poet Bernard Barton: B. Barton to WW, 21 Nov 1844: WLMS/A/Barton/5 pp.1–2.

62. WW to W.E. Gladstone & to C.W. Pasley, 15 Oct 1844 (*LY*, iv, 616, 617). Both men replied sympathetically but noncommittally, Gladstone adding the surprisingly silly comment that thanks were owed to the scheme indirectly for making WW produce the sonnet: W.E. Gladstone to WW, 19 Oct 1844: WLMS/A/Gladstone/6 pp.2–3.

63. MW to M. Stanger, 10 Oct [1844]: Moorsom 61/2/2; W. Whewell to WW, 19 Oct 1844: WLMS/A/Whewell/5 pp.1–2; WW to Mrs Harrison, 17 Nov & to H. Reed, 18 Nov 1844 (*LY*, iv, 625, 626 & n.); Gill, *Wordsworth and the Victorians*, 23.

64. WW to Mrs Harrison, 17 Nov & to H. Reed, 18 Nov 1844 (*LY*, iv, 624–5, 626–7).

65. MW to HCR, 4 Nov & to C.W. Pasley, 16 Nov 1844 (ibid., 620, 624); Mrs Arnold to HCR, 27 Nov 1844 (*HCRWC*, ii, 577). WW was dismayed when the new Lord Lonsdale consented to the steamer, 'because it never occurred to me that it would be looked upon as any thing else than a general advantage': LL to

WW, 8 Jan 1845: WLMS/A/Lowther/71 p.3.
66. WW to IF, [early Jan 1845] (*LY*, iv, 647); WW, *To the Morning Post*, 9 & 17 Dec 1844 (*Prose*, iii, 341, 343, 345, 355, 346, 350–51, 333n.3).
67. Ibid., 333–4; WW to R.P. Graves, 19 Dec [1844] & to CW, 24 Jan 1845 (*LY*, iv, 641–2, 652–3).
68. WW to HCR, 2 Feb [1845] (ibid., 658–9); Report of the Board of Trade on the proposed Kendal and Windermere Railway, 16 Apl 1845 (*Prose*, iii, 334); B. Field to HCR, 16 Feb 1845 (*HCRWC*, ii, 591). It is doubly ironic that the line from Oxenholme to Bowness was axed by Beeching in the 1960s for want of use and that its removal has since added to the problems of the Lake District by increasing congestion on the roads.

Chapter 27

chapter title: 'Fixed and irremovable grief', *HCRWB*, ii, 674.
picture: Dora as bridesmaid to SC, by Miss Rainbeck, 1829.
1. MW & WW to IF, 14 Dec [1844] (*LY*, iv, 638–9); *HCRBW*, ii, 650; HCR to TR, 9 & 16 Jan 1845 (*HCRWC*, ii, 583, 584).
2. HCR to TR, 24 Jan & to IF, 27 Jan 1845 (ibid., 585, 587–8); HM, *Autobiography*, ii, 232ff., esp. 236–7; WW to IF, 25 Jan 1845 (*LY*, iv, 654).
3. *HCRD*, ii, 261; HCR to TR, 13 Jul & 27 Dec & to WW, 24 Jul 1844 (*HCRWC*, ii, 563, 580–81, 566); WW to HCR, 14 Jul 1844 (*LY*, iv, 569–70). See also *HCRD*, ii, 258–62 for fuller versions of HCR's letters.
4. WW to IF, [early Jan 1845] (*LY*, iv, 646); HM, *Autobiography*, ii, 434.
5. EQ to HCR, 4, 7, 8 & 18 Apl 1845 (*HCRWC*, ii, 594, 595, 597, 598–9); WW to EM, 10 Apl 1845 (*LY*, iv, 666). EQ told HCR, 'The scheme does not originate with me', so it was probably concocted by IF; with or without Dora, EQ was expected to go to Portugal to attend his brother's marriage: WW to EM, 18 Apl [1845] (ibid., 669).
6. EQ to HCR, 18 & 21 Apl 1845 (*HCRWC*, ii, 598–9); *HCRD*, ii, 265; WW to EM, 18 Apl & to H. Reed, 1 Jul 1845 (*LY*, iv, 669 & n.3, 686–7); Brookfield, *Mrs Brookfield and Her Circle*, i, 150; Young, *A Memoir of Charles Mayne Young*, i, 184. SR's court dress was also borrowed by the next Poet Laureate, Alfred Tennyson, for his presentation at court in 1851: J.O. Hoge (ed.), *Lady Tennyson's Journal* (University of Virginia Press, 1981), 24. SR promised to donate it to WW's heirs: faded to an inelegant brown, it is now on display at DC.
7. *HCRBW*, ii, 653; HCR to TR, 5 [*r.*3?] May 1845 (*HCRWC*, ii, 599–600); Dora to MW, 24 Aug [1845]: WLL/Dora2/13 p.1; EQ & Dora to WW & MW, 12 May 1845: G1/12/4 pp.2–3.
8. HCR to TR, 5 [*r.*3?] May 1845 (*HCRWC*, ii, 600); WW to Lord Northampton, [5 (*r.*6) May] & to H. Reed, 1 Jul 1845 (*Supp.*, 250; *LY*, iv, 687–8); *HCRBW*, ii, 653; Tennyson, *Alfred Lord Tennyson: A Memoir*, i, 208–11. HCR dates the levee to the same day as the Quillinans' sailing, which two sources put at 7 May, suggesting that the dating of HCR's and WW's letters is a day adrift.
9. WW to EM, 12 May [1845] (*LY*, iv, 672).
10. WW to EM, 23 Jan, [Jun] & 10 Apl & to H. Reed, 27 Sep 1845 (ibid., 650, 675, 676, 665, 708–9). Nothing came of the proposed prose edition, though EM was apparently intending to publish one 'soon' according to WW to unidentified, 30 Oct 1846 (ibid., 811), and EQ was anxious to undertake the editorship.
11. WW to EM, 2 Jun & 14 Jul, WW to H. Reed, 31 Jul 1845 (ibid., 674-5, 689, 694); HCR to IF, 17 Jul 1845 (*HCRWC*, ii, 605).
12. WW to HCR, 7 Aug 1845 (*LY*, iv, 697); Gill, *Wordsworth and the Victorians*, 74–9; WW, Preface to *The Excursion*, ll.24–5; *The Excursion*, ii, 935–9, 953–6 (*Poems*, ii, 38, 66, 67); WW, *Ecclesiastical Sonnets*, ii, 2, 9 & 10 (ibid., 464, 467–8). WW added a further six sonnets to this series, on Church rites, see ibid., iii, 26–31 (ibid., ii, 494–6).
13. WW to GHG, 24 Jun 1845 (*LY*, iv, 680); WW, 'Forth from a jutting ridge, around whose base' (*Poems*, ii, 895–6).
14. MW & WW to HCR, 21 Jun & WW to CW2, [*c.*8 Aug] [1845] (*LY*, iv, 679, 700); IF to HCR, 1 Jul 1845 (*HCRWC*, ii, 603); WW, *At Furness Abbey*, esp.ll.13–14 (*Poems*, ii, 894–5); WW, *To the Editor of the Morning Post*, 17 Dec 1844 (*Prose*, iii, 353).
15. WW to W. Jackson, 12 & 15 Dec & to unidentified, 18 & [late] Dec 1844, to LL, 28 Jan, to EM, [5 Mar] & MW to HCR, 16 Sep 1845 (*LY*, iv, 635, 639–40, 640–41, 643–4, 657, 662, 705); J. Lightfoot to KJW, 3 Mar 1845: G11/1/9; Dora to WW & MW, 9 Jul [1845]: WLL/Dora2/9 pp.1–2.

16. WW to W. Jackson, 12 Dec [1844] (*LY*, iv, 635); Dora to WW & EQ to MW, 27 May & Dora to MW, 18 Jun 1845: WLL/Dora2/6 pp.1–2 & 7 pp.1–2.
17. MW & WW to HCR, 21 Jun, WW to CW2, [30 Jun] & MW to HCR, 16 Sep [1845] (*LY*, iv, 678, 684, 705); MW to M. Stanger, 20 Jan [1845]: Moorsom 61/2/3 pp.1–2; Dora to WW & MW, 9 Jul [1845]: WLL/Dora2/9 p.2; MW to CC, 7 Sep [1845] (*LMW*, 273–4). Dora could not see why the two oldest boys should not have returned to school in England, where their father could see them. 'I feel so very much for John in the separation that is about to take place & which seems to me a necessary one. I don't believe Isabella will care much about it & that is a sort of comfort tho' not a pleasant sort': Dora to MW, 1 & 29 Oct [1845]: WLL/Dora2/17 p.9 & 20 pp.3–4.
18. HM, *Autobiography*, ii, 226–35; WW to HCR, 7 Aug [1845] (*LY*, iv, 697); CW to WW, 2 Sep 1845: WLL/CW/116.
19. RMVB, pp.115–23, esp.117–19; MW to HCR, [7 Aug 1845] (*LY*, iv, 698–9). WW presented Reed with a valuable gift, an illustrated, two-volume *Glossary of Terms used in Grecian, Roman, Italian, and Gothic Architecture* by J.H. Parker (Oxford, 1845): WW to H. Reed, 31 Jul & to HCR, 7 Aug 1845 (*LY*, iv, 693, 696).
20. Howitt, *Homes and Haunts of the Most Eminent British Poets*, ii, 288–9; EQD: WLMS/13/3/2 [1 Sep 1836]; Jas Wilson to MW, 6 Dec 1842: WLMS/A/Wilson, Jas/1. Alan Stevenson, uncle of Robert Louis, had spent three or four seasons at the Skerryvore with only workmen for companions: 'Many were the moments in my solitude, during which I have felt my common place labours ennobled by the Poet's views of duty and perseverance'.
21. HM, *Autobiography*, ii, 241–3; RMVB, p.121. Hugh Seymour Tremenheere (1804–93) was a fellow of New College, Oxford (1824–56), an Inspector of Schools from 1840 and sat on a number of commissions on education, child labour and working practices; Henry Tufnell (1805–54) was MP for Devonport and Secretary to the Treasury under Lord John Russell: (*LY*, iv, 732n.1).
22. S. Tremenheere to WW, 19 Sep 1845: WLMS/A/Tremenheere/1 pp.3, 4, 5–6; WW to S. Tremenheere, 16 Dec 1845 (*LY*, iv, 733).
23. WW to EM, 20 Sep & to H. Reed, 27 Sep 1845 (ibid., 709–10); MW to CC, 7 Sep & to Rev. J. Meakin, 22 Sep 1845 (*LMW*, 274, 275). For WW's efforts on George's behalf, including a gift of £16 from himself, see WW to CW2, 13, 24 & 31 Oct & [Dec] 1845 (*LY*, iv, 712–16, 727–8); CW to WW, 4 Nov 1845: WLL/CW/117 p.3.
24. WW to EM, [4], [5], 17, 19 & 25 Nov 1845 (*LY*, iv, 716–17, 717, 723, 725, 726). WW had been elected an honorary fellow of the Royal Society of Edinburgh in Mar and received confirmation of his election to the Royal Irish Academy in Dec: WW to J.D. Forbes, Mar & to EM, 9 Dec [1845]; to WRH, 14 Mar 1846 (ibid., 662–3, 730, 766).
25. HCR to TR, 13 Dec 1845 (*HCRWC*, ii, 615); WW to EM, 22 Dec & to F. Westley, 22 Dec 1845 & [*c.*9 Jan 1846] (*LY*, iv, 736, 736–7, 744–5); Earl de la Warr to WW, 16 Jan & 20 Feb 1846: WLMS/A/De la Warr/3 & 4; *HCRBW*, ii, 657. For the inscription see WW, 'Deign, Sovereign Mistress! to accept a Lay', esp.ll.5, 23 (*Poems*, ii, 897–8).
26. *HCRBW*, ii, 655–6; HM to HCR, 24 Jun [1845] (*HCRWC*, ii, 602); WW to D. Coleridge, 29 Sep 1845 (*LY*, iv, 711). The Ws had been informed that Julia Meakin (née Myers) was dying in Sep: MW to Rev. J. Meakin, 22 Sep 1845 (*LMW*, 274–5); Mrs STC died suddenly on 24 Sep: Lefebure, *The Bondage of Love*, 259–60; Sarah Crackanthorpe, who had been due to visit the Ws on her return home, died suddenly in Edinburgh in Dec: Dora to MW, 19 Dec [1845]: WLL/Dora2/23 p.3; WW to H. Hill, 22 Jan 1846 (*LY*, iv, 748).
27. F.W. Faber to WW, 17 Nov 1845: WLMS/A/Faber, F.W./3; WW to EM, 19 Nov [1845] (*LY*, iv, 725). Only the 'Mr Wordsworth' was in Faber's own hand. In Feb 1846 WW was further saddened by the conversion to Roman Catholicism of Rev. George Burder, curate to STC's nephew Rev. James Coleridge. While holidaying at Nab Cottage, Burder had sought rebaptism, fearing his first was invalid. WW and MW had stood as his godparents at his earnest request: 'I am already, as to my Intellectual & Moral Being, a child of yours – how deep & pure would be the joy of feeling bound to you by still stronger & holier ties!': G. Burder to WW, [early Jul 1842]: WLMS/A/Burder/1 p.4; WW to G. Burder, [early Jul 1842] (*LY*, iv, 351–2); *HCRBW*, ii, 657.
28. Ibid., 655. WW was even tired of politics:

'The indifference of Wordsworth to the results of the present political party arrangements is remarkable. He seems to expect no good from the success of any one': ibid., 656.

29. WW to EM, [1] & 23 Feb [1846] (*LY*, iv, 753, 760). The only proof sheets WW requested to see were those of the eight poems which were to be published in this form for the first time: WW to EM, [late Feb 1846] (ibid., 761).

30. *HCRBW*, ii, 656; MW to M. Stanger, 29 Dec [*r.*Nov?] [1845]: Moorsom 61/2/7; WW to W. Jackson, 2 & 8 Jan & to H. Hill, 22 Jan 1846 (*LY*, iv, 741–2, 743, 748–9); Dora to MW, 18 Jan [1846]: WLL/Dora2/25 p.3; SC to IF, nd (*LY*, iv, 754n.2). Edward's grave lies in the more crowded modern section of the cemetery; the headstone was presumably erected by JW3, as it makes no mention of IW: 'Sacred to the memory of Edward Christopher Wordsworth who died at Rome December 10th 1845 aged 4 years youngest son of the Revd John Wordsworth of Brigham Vicarage Cumberland – "Suffer the little children to come unto me, and forbid them not for of such is the kingdom of God" Mark 10ch 14v.' The text is the same as that on the headstone of JW3's sister Catherine.

31. *HCRBW*, ii, 656; WW to W. Jackson, 8 Jan & to CW2, [*c.*10 Jan] 1846 (*LY*, iv, 743, 746); WW, 'Why should we weep or mourn, Angelic boy' (*Poems*, ii, 895); HCR to TR, 2 Jan 1846 (*HCRWC*, ii, 618).

32. Chas W to WW, 15 & 27 Jan, 2 Feb & 1 Mar 1846: WLMS/1/10/5, p.1, 7 pp.1–2, 8 p.4 & 9 p.7. As Chas W forgot to mention the date of the funeral in his letter to RM, none of WW's family were able to attend. CW had given 'an express injunction' for a private funeral, so only his curates and five or six clergymen were present: ibid., pp.1–3.

33. WW to HCR, 2 Feb, to W. Jackson, [Mar] & to H. Reed, 3 Feb 1846 (*LY*, iv, 754–5, 763, 756).

34. WW to M. Stanger, 2 Mar, to IF, 13 May & to W. Jackson, 28 Apl 1846 (*Supp.*, 251–2; *LY*, iv, 774–5, 772); *The Diaries of William Charles Macready*, ii, 330; WW, Cheque Book, 1846: G2/3/8 [17 Apl & 23 Mar 1846]; WW to EM, 23 Feb [1846] (*LY*, iv, 760). EM sent WW a cheque for £65 5s, as his share of the Burns profits: WW to EM, 2 Apl 1846 (ibid., 768).

35. WW to E. Girdlestone, 6 Apl, to IF, 7 Apl & to CW2, 17 May 1846 (ibid., 769–70, 770–71; *Supp.*, 255). The date of Mrs JW3's return is uncertain, but she was at RM with the rest of her family on 22 Jun: WW to HCR, 22 Jun 1846 (*LY*, iv, 787).

36. HM, extract from letter copied by HCR, 8 Feb 1846 (*HCRWC*, ii, 621–2).

37. WW to IF, 7 Apl, WW & MW to IF, [13 May] & WW to HCR, [20] May 1846 (*LY*, iv, 771, 775–6, 777, 779). HCR noted of this letter, 'I am sorry to remark that his hand is becoming illegible': *HCRBW*, ii, 658. WW's depression was not helped by IF's absence. She had gone to Bagborough, on the way to France, and did not intend to return to the Lakes until the summer of 1847: WW to HCR, [20] May 1846 (*LY*, iv, 779).

38. WW to CW2, [late May], 11 Jun & [late Jul] & WW & MW to T. Hutchinson & Mrs TH, [24] Sep 1846 (ibid., 784–5, 784n3, 786–7, 800).

39. SC to HCR, 27 Jun 1846 (*HCRWC*, ii, 631); Dora to WW & MW, 7 Mar [1846]: WLL/Dora2/26 pp.1–2; MW to Mrs TH, [early Apl 1848] (*LMW*, 296). The Quillinans left Oporto on 31 Mar, returning via Cintra, Cadiz, Seville, Gibraltar and France. For EQ's pleurisy, see Dora to MW, 31 May [1846]: WLL/Dora2/30.

40. Dora to IF, 28 Mar & to M. Stanger, 13 Jul [1846]: WLL/Dora/90 pp.7–8 & Moorsom 62/4/12 p.2. The waterbed had been borrowed from James Dawson of Wray Castle: WW to J. Dawson, 20 Aug 1846 (*LY*, iv, 798). Joiner's bills reveal the bleak details of KJW's sufferings, including a 'crook and handle for raising Mr W': J. Atkinson, invoice, 25 May–18 Aug 1846: G11/19/3.

41. WW to Mrs Harrison, [19 Aug 1846] (*LY*, iv,797); KJW, Death certificate, 18 Aug 1846: G11/21/2; KJW, Last Will & Testament, 10 Feb 1846: G11/22/1. For Troughton's bills, see G11/19/6–9 & G11/21/3. KJW's headstone, among the W graves in Grasmere churchyard, describes him as 'Staff Assistant Surgeon to her Majesty's forces in the Ionian Islands, only son of the late Richard Wordsworth, of Sockbridge . . . and nephew of William Wordsworth, of Rydal Mount' and 'much lamented'.

42. EQ to SC, 15 Aug [*r.*Sep] 1846: WLL/EQ/129a p.7; MW to WW2, [Sep] & to F. Graham, 8 Sep 1846 (*LMW*, 275, 276); Dora to F. Graham & to WW2, 13 Sep [1846]: WLL/Dora/95 & 96 p.1; WW to R. Graham, 14 Sep 1846 (*LY*, iv, 799 & n.1). Fanny Elizabeth Graham (1820–88) was ten years younger than WW2.

43. RMVB, pp. 126–7, 129–30; MW to WW2, [Sep 1846] (*LMW*, 276); Dora to WW2, [15 Oct 1846]: WLL/Dora/93 p.2; WW to IF, 5 Feb 1847 (*LY*, iv, 833). The RMVB, and references in the Ws' letters and diaries of EQ and HCR, disprove conclusively HM's claim that she 'refused, from the first, to introduce any of my visitors at Rydal Mount, because there were far too many already': HM, *Autobiography*, ii, 241.

44. *The Life of Thomas Cooper, written by himself* (London, Hodder & Stoughton, 1872), 287–95; WW to H. Reed, [10 Nov 1843] (*LY*, iv, 496). WW told HCR, 'I have a great deal of the Chartist in me'; HCR agreed: HCR to MW, 7 Mar 1848 (*HCRWC*, ii, 665).

45. W. Bennett, Reminiscences, 18 Sep 1846: WLMS/A/Bennett/2a esp.pp.10–14. Bennett had sent WW a sonnet, *To Wm Wordsworth – On Visiting Rydal Mount*, 4 Sep 1846 and on 11 Nov invited him to tea, during which they had a wide-ranging discussion on poetry; on 24 Nov he called at RM to get WW to sign his children's drawings of RM for sale at the Belfast Bazaar in aid of Irish famine relief: WLMS/A/Bennett/1, 2b & 2c; WW to W. & Mrs Bennett, [late Nov (*r.*10 Nov) 1846] (*LY*, iv, 822).

46. WLMS/A/Bennett/2a p.5 & 2b p.6; *HCRBW*, ii, 659; Blanshard, 90; WW to EM, 23 Nov 1846 (*LY*, iv, 821). WW subscribed £5 to the fund for BRH's widow and daughter: WW to O. Hyman, 1 Jul & to EM, 18 Jul 1846 (ibid., 789, 790). WW was offered the portrait, but declined it chiefly on account of its size; it was eventually bought by his Kendal publisher, Cornelius Nicholson: WW to C. Marks, 29 Nov 1846 (ibid., 823 & n.2).

47. WW to CC, 2 Oct 1846 (ibid., 804); CC to WW, 11 Oct, to MW, 2 Nov, to WW, 19 Nov & to MW, 28 Dec 1846: WLMS/A/Clarkson/30 pp.5–6, 31 pp.3–4, 33 & 34; WW to T.A. Walmisley, 26 Mar 1847 (*LY*, iv, 840).

48. MW to Mrs TH, 10 Oct [1846]: 1990.1.3.4 p.1; *HCRBW*, ii, 659; Dora to WW2, [18 Oct 1846]: WLL/Dora/94 p.1; MW to F. Graham, [14 Jan 1847] (*LMW*, 277).

49. *HCRBW*, ii, 660; Dora to IF, 24 Jan [1847]: WLL/Dora/97 pp.1–3. Matilda Graham died the following month, the day WW2 and his wife left RM to visit her: MW & WW to CW2, 27 Feb [1847] (*LY*, iv, 836).

50. WW to SC, [*c.*4 Feb 1847] (ibid., 832); Dora to M. Stanger, 1 Feb [1847]: Moorsom 62/4/13 p.2; *HCRBW*, ii, 660–61; HCR to TR, 5 Feb & 17 Jan 1847 (*HCRWC*, ii, 639–40, 639).

51. WW to IF, 5 Feb 1847 & 19 Oct 1846, to EM, 1 & 12 Oct & WW to IF, [14 Dec] 1846 (*LY*, iv, 833, 808–9, 803–4, 805, 825); MW to WW2, [15 Jan 1847]: WLL/MW/159 pp.6–7; Dora to M. Stanger, 1 Feb [1847]: Moorsom 62/4/13.

52. MW to IF, 25 Feb [1847]: WLL/MW/160/pp.1–2; *HCRBW*, ii, 662; SC to J.T. Coleridge, 29 Mar 1846 (*LY*, iv, 837n.2).

53. SC had forwarded her request and some queries on STC's sources to WW through HCR: *HCRBW*, ii, 661; SC to IF, [end Jan] & to A. de Vere, Apl 1847 (*SCM*, ii, 98–9, 106–7); WW to SC, [*c.*4 Feb] & to IF, 5 Feb 1847 (*LY*, iv, 831–2, 833–4).

54. C.B. Phipps to WW, 12 Mar 1847: WLMS/A/Phipps/1; WW to C.B. Phipps, 15 Mar & WW & MW to DW, 9 Apl 1847 (*LY*, iv, 839, 842); *HCRBW*, ii, 663–4; Yarnall, *Wordsworth and the Coleridges*, 38.

55. WW & MW to DW, 9 Apl 1847 (*LY*, iv, 841); MW to IF, 9 Apl [1847]: WLL/MW/161 pp.2–4; *HCRBW*, ii, 664; HCR to TR, [Apl 1847] (*HCRWC*, ii, 646).

56. Dora to M. Stanger, 1 Feb [1847]: Moorsom 62/4/13 p.4; EQ to IF, 21 Apl 1847: WLL/EQ/130 pp.1–2.

57. WW to HCR, 24 Apl 1847 (*LY*, iv, 844–5); *HCRBW*, ii, 664–5; HCR to TR, 1 May 1847 (*HCRWC*, ii, 646); EQD: WLMS/13/5/5 [23, 27 & 28 Apl 1847]. Leonard Charles Wyon (1826–91), oldest son of the chief engraver of the Royal Mint, was cousin of Edward William Wyon (1811–85), who had made wax medallions of WW & RS in 1835. The silver medallion is less successful than the brooding and powerful presence of the portrait: Blanshard, 160–61, 173–4, pls.30a & 30b.

58. HC to T. Blackburne, [spring] 1847 (*LHC*, 293); SC to EQ, [*c.*1 May 1847]: WLMS/A/SC/45 pp.2–3.

59. For a history of the diagnosis and treatment of tuberculosis and the myths surrounding it, see Dormandy, *The White Death*.

60. SC to IF, 3 May 1847 (*SCM*, ii, 112–16); HC to SC, 18 May 1847 (*LHC*, 294); MW to SC, 25 May 1847 (*LY*, iv, 848–9). Hannah was one of the Kendal Cooksons. She had lived for some time with her mother and sister, Elizabeth, in the Ws'

former home at Town End, before moving into How Foot, the house they built a few yards up the lane at Grasmere: WW to IF, [13 May 1846] (ibid., 775).

61. MW to SC, 25 May 1847 (ibid., 848); MW to M. Stanger, [15 May 1847]: Moorsom 61/2/10.

62. Dora, Memo to WW, 12 May 1847: WLL/Dora/2/31; J. Carter, Memo, 13 May 1847: G2/21/5. The Hutchinsons had a family tradition of leaving large bequests to the daughters of the family: Dora herself had benefited from similar ones, especially from SH.

63. EQ to HCR, 19 May 1847 (*HCRWC*, ii, 647). HCR commented that it was 'a remarkable letter under such circumstances' and responded with a farewell letter addressed to Dora which she found so moving she kept it beside her and asked EQ to preserve it after her death: *HCRBW*, ii, 665; EQ to HCR, 24 May 1847 (*HCRWC*, ii, 647).

64. MW to IF, [24 May] & to Mrs TH, [Apl–Jun 1847] (*LMW*, 278, 280). Anne Brontë described cod liver oil as smelling and tasting like train oil: Barker, *The Brontës*, 581.

65. MW to SC, 25 May & to M. Stanger, 27 May 1847 (*LY*, iv, 849 & Moorsom 61/2/11 p.3); Dora to IF, 24 May 1847: WLL/Dora/1/99: 'I received your farewell note with deep deep emotion, it will be precious to me as long as I have life . . . May the almighty enable me to meet my end as you are meeting yours': IF to Dora, 27 May 1847: WLMS/A/IF/4 p.1.

66. MW to [?Lady Monteagle], 1 Jun [1847]: WLL/MW/164 p.3; MW to IF, [24 May 1847] (*LMW*, 279); Mrs Arnold to HCR, 1 Jun 1847 (*HCRWC*, ii, 648).

67. SC to IF, 26 Apl 1847 (*SCM*, ii, 112); WW to T.A. Walmisley, 29 Apl & 5 May 1847 (*LY*, iv, 845, 846); T. Walmisley to WW, 3 & 20 May 1847: WLMS/A/Walmisley/2 & 3 pp.1–2. Ironically, Walmisley preferred the first version of many of the readings, which were presumably EQ's.

68. MW to IF, 1 Jun [1847]: WLL/MW/160 pp.1–2; EQ to IF, 2 Jun 1847: WLL/EQ/131 pp.1–3.

69. WW to J. Dawson, [8 Jun 1847] (*LY*, iv, 850–51); MW to Mrs TH, [1 Jul 1847] (*LMW*, 281–2).

70. MW to Mrs TH, [7] Jul 1847 (ibid., 284); EQ to HCR, 9 Jul 1847 (*HCRWC*, ii, 651); WW to Chas W & to CW2, 9 Jul 1847 (*LY*, iv, 851, 852); EQD: WLMS/13/5/5 [12 & 14 Jul 1847]. The cramped nature of the final arrangement of the graves indicates that this was a triumph of diplomacy over common sense.

71. SR to MW, [14 Jul 1847]: WLMS/A/Rogers/31a; JC to WW, 19 Jul 1847: MS pp.1 & 3, University of Bristol; CW2 to WW, 8 Jul 1847: WLMS/1/11/21 pp.1–3; A. Sedgwick to WW, 10 Aug 1847: WLMS/A/Sedgwick/2 p.1; C.B. Phipps to WW, 9 Jul 1847: WLMS/A/Phipps/2 pp.1–2.

72. WW & MW, [Jul] & WW to EM, 9 Aug 1847 (*LY*, iv, 853, 854); *HCRBW*, ii, 665, 667; IF to HCR, 12 Aug & HCR to TR, 9–10 Sep 1847 (*HCRWC*, ii, 652, 653).

73. W. Bennett, Reminiscences, 18 Sep 1846: WLMS/A/Bennett/2a p.5; HM, *Autobiography*, ii, 240.

74. MW to IF, 21 Sep [1847] (*LMW*, 286).

75. EQ to IF, 13 Oct 1847: WLL/EQ/132 pp.1–2 & 5; MW to IF, 18 Oct [1847] (*LMW*, 288–9); Blanshard, pl.31; *HCRBW*, ii, 674. WW paid Carrick £31 10s for the portrait: WW, Cheque Book, 1849–50: G2/3/10 [17 Mar 1849].

76. WW to IF, 6 Dec 1847 (*LY*, iv, 859); HCR to TR, 23 Dec to IF, 24 Dec 1847 & 10 Jan 1848 (*HCRWC*, ii, 654, 655–6, 658); *HCRBW*, ii, 671–2. This is one of the few instances where I disagree with Gill, 420, who suggests WW's resentment of EQ's fecklessness, which he believed had hastened Dora's end, was the cause of the estrangement.

77. *HCRBW*, ii, 670–73; HCR to IF, 10 & 24 Jan & to TR, 14–15 Jan 1848 (*HCRWC*, ii, 657–8, 661, 659); WW to IF, 6 Dec [1847] (*LY*, iv, 860).

Chapter 28

chapter title: 'Bowed to the dust', MW to IF, 2 Feb [1848] (*LMW*, 293).

picture: Portrait of WW, by Henry Inman, 1844. Photograph by Professor Henry Reed's grandson.

1. MW to Mrs WW2, 10 Nov [1847]: WLL/MW/171 pp.3 & 5; MW to IF, 27 Dec [1847] (*LMW*, 291). CW2 disingenuously claimed that 'he would not of his own accord, have ventured on this task' and did so only because his uncle had put such a request in writing, but MW

explicitly told IF that CW2 'who had been talking with Willy on the subject offered his service': *Memoirs*, i, 5–6.

2. EQD: WLMS/13/5/5 [12 & 16 Nov 1847]; WW, Memo, 16 Nov 1847 (*HCRWC*, ii, 728); EQ to IF, 25 Jul [1848]: WLL/EQ/134/ p.6. EQ told IF his informant was 'closely connected by friendship, but neither by blood nor marriage with the Wordsworth family'.

3. Ibid., p.6; HCR to IF, 24 Jan 1848 (*HCRWC*, ii, 661); EQD: WLMS/13/5/8 [11 Jul 1850]; *Memoirs*, i, 6; WW, *Autobiographical Memoranda*, Nov 1847 (*Prose*, iii, 371–5).

4. IF to EQ, 11 Feb 1848: WLMS/A/IF/5 pp.1–3. IF had intended to bequeath the notes to EQ but decided to make the gift now: 'I would rather on any *direct* application for the sight of them from Dr CW – say that I had given them to Mr Q': IF to HCR, 5 Feb 1848 (*HCRWC*, ii, 665).

5. EQ to HCR, 1 Feb 1847 [*r.*1848] (ibid., 663); MW to IF, 2 Feb [1848] (*LMW*, 293).

6. EQ to IF, 19 Mar 1848: WLL/EQ/133 p.4; SC to IF, 3 Apl 1848 (*LY*, iv, 864n.1); Emerson, *Journals and Miscellaneous Notebooks*, x, 558–60; *The Letters of Ralph Waldo Emerson*, iv, 23, 25, 26–7, 30; Emerson, *English Traits*, 294–8.

7. EQ to IF, 19 Mar & to HCR, 15 Apl 1848: WLL/EQ/133 p.2 & *HCRWC*, ii, 665; MW to Mrs TH, [early Apl 1848] & to IF, 21 Sep [1847] & 2 Feb [1848] (*LMW*, 296, 287–8, 293); SC to M. Stanger, [*p.m.*6 Apl 1848]: Moorsom 55/1/59 pp.5–7. IW had deliberately chosen an Evangelical school, having an 'utter horror' of the Oxford Movement as 'the worst kind of Popery viz Popery in disguise': IW to M. Stanger, 2 Jun 1848: Moorsom 62/2/11 p.2.

8. SC to M. Stanger, *p.m.* 6 Apl 1848: Moorsom 55/1/59 p.7; MW to IF, [May 1848] (*LMW*, 297–8). Jane's other grandmother, Mrs Curwen, refused to see her, being 'justly offended' with her, as the Curwens had paid her school fees. IW blamed this loss of contact and Jane's removal from the school on the Ws 'as the principles of this lost one [i.e. IW] are not in accordance with the views of her Father's family': IW to M. Stanger, 2 Jun 1848: Moorsom 62/2/11 pp.2–3.

9. MW to IF, [May 1848] (*LMW*, 296–7, 298); MW to HCR, 7 Jun 1848 (*LY*, iv, 869); HM to HCR, 8 Jun [1848] (*HCRWC*, ii, 671).

10. EQ to HCR, 6 Jun & 23 Jul 1848 (ibid., 666, 675); MW to HCR, 22 Jul [1848] (*LY*, iv, 872). The Hills were also regular visitors, though they stayed in Keswick.

11. EQ to HCR, 23 Jul 1848 (*HCRWC*, ii, 673–4); MW to IF, 2 Aug 1848 (*LMW*, 299).

12. Duke of Argyll to Rev. J.G. Howson, 8 Sep 1848: WLMS/A/Argyll/1 pp.2–9. 'You have lived to see the birth & growth of a generation whose mind has been widely & deeply influenced by y[ou]r own. This is given to few: But it is given to fewer still to feel, as assuredly you may feel, that that influence has been as <u>good</u> as it has been powerful': Duke of Argyll to WW, 7 Apl 1849: WLMS/A/Argyll/3 pp.2–3.

13. MW to IF, 29 Aug 1848 (*LMW*, 304); EQ to HCR, 12 Aug 1848 (*HCRWC*, ii, 677); MW to IF, 2 Aug 1848 (*LY*, iv, 300).

14. EQD: WLMS/13/5/6 [7 Aug 1848]; MW to IF, 29 Aug & to E. Hutchinson, 19 Aug 1848 (*LMW*, 303, 301–2). The Ws were absent 7–17 Aug.

15. EQD: WLMS/13/5/6 [24 Sep 1848]; EQ to HCR, 2 Oct & 12 Aug 1848 (*HCRWC*, ii, 678–9, 676); WW to IF, [mid-Nov 1848] (*LY*, iv, 877); MW to Mr & Mrs TH, [Nov 1848] (*LMW*, 305–6). IW died at Lucca, where she had spent the summer, not Pisa, as in *LY*, iv, 875n.3, and in Sep, not Oct, as in Moorman, ii, 598: JW3 to M. Stanger, [Apl 1867]: Moorsom 62/1/3 p.3. Henry and William were admitted to Sedbergh on 7 Aug 1848: Register of Admissions, Sedbergh School.

16. EQ to HCR, 13 Nov 1848 (*HCRWC*, ii, 679); MW to E. & S. Hutchinson, 4 Nov [*r.*Dec] [1848]: WLL/MW/186 pp.2–3; MW to M. Stanger, 1 Dec & 9 May [1848]: Moorsom 61/2/14 pp.1–3 & 61/2/13; WW & MW to IF, 7 Dec [1848] (*LY*, iv, 879).

17. WW & MW to IF, 7 Dec [1848] (ibid., 880]; *HCRBW*, ii, 682–3; HCR to TR, 28 Dec 1848 (*HCRWC*, ii, 680).

18. *HCRBW*, ii, 683; MW to Mrs CW2, 28 Dec 1848: WLL/MW/187 pp.2–3; HCR to TR, 12 Jan & [4–5 Jan] 1849 (*HCRWC*, ii, 684, 680–81); WW to Sir J.T. Coleridge, 19 Feb 1849 (*LY*, iv, 886); SC to Rev. E. Coleridge, quoting Derwent, Jan 1849 (*SCM*, ii, 211).

19. Hainton, *The Unknown Coleridge*, 226, 227; *HCRBW*, ii, 685–6; HCR to TR, 12 Jan 1849 & to IF, 15 Jan 1848 [*r.*1849] (*HCRWC*, ii, 683–4, 685); MW to Mrs CW2, 28 Dec 1848: WLL/MW/187 p.6.

20. HCR to IF, 15 Jan 1848 [*r.*1849] & EQ to

HCR, 12 Jan 1849 (*HCRWC*, ii, 685, 682). But MW said, 'His memory, as regards present things merely, is sadly failed – or perhaps it is rather, that his thoughts being elsewhere, it is absence & not a lack of memory – but so it is, hourly occurences make no impression on his mind': MW to Mrs CW2, 28 Dec 1848: WLL/MW/187 p.6.

21. MW to HCR, 28 Mar [1849] (*LY*, iv, 894); R. Peel to WW, 5 & 9 Apl & 9 & 12 Jun 1849: WLMS/A/Peel/6, 7, 8, 9; WW to R. Peel, 7 & 13 Apl, 7 Jun 1849 (*LY*, iv, 897–8, 898–9, 900); C. Wood to WW, 8 Apl & 24 May 1849: WLMS/A/Wood/1 & 2. The Ws and Mrs TH were at Brigham 6–14 Mar, Carlisle 14–26 Mar and spent the night of 26 Mar at Penrith; Mrs TH arrived in Feb and left at the end of Easter week: MW to IF, 7 [*r.*17] Mar [1849] (*LMW*, 308–9); MW to HCR, 24 Feb [1849] (*LY*, iv, 889).

22. R. Fenwick to I. Fenwick, 10 Jun 1849: E462.1.18 p.3; HCR to TR, [16 & 27 Jun] & EQ to HCR, 20 Jun 1849 (*HCRWC*, ii, 694, 698, 697); *HCRBW*, ii, 690.

23. MW to TH & family, [30 Jun 1849] (*LMW*, 311–12); WW to JK, 1 Jul 1849 (*LY*, iv, 903).

24. MW to Mrs CW2, 3 Jul [1849]: WLL/MW/192 pp.1–8; WW [& MW] to EM, 7 Jul 1849 (*LY*, iv, 904); EQ to HCR, 9 Jul 1849 (*HCRBW*, ii, 698); MW to Mrs TH, [6 Jul 1849] (*LMW*, 312). TH died at 3 a.m. on 2 Jul 1849; he was 76.

25. MW to Mrs CW2, 3 Jul [1849]: WLL/MW/192 pp.6–7; EQ to HCR, 9 Jul 1849 (*HCRBW*, ii, 699). The wedding was on 3 Jul 1849.

26. MW to Mrs TH, 16 or 18 Aug [1849]: WLL/MW/196 p.4; WW to Earl Grey, 7 Sep 1849 (*LY*, iv, 907). The deferral was granted and Henry passed his examination, entering the Woolwich Academy: he was offered a commission but emigrated to Australia, where he became an unsuccessful sheep farmer and, eventually, a government-appointed Crown Lands Ranger: *Sedbergh School Register*, 228.

27. MW to Mrs TH, 16 or 18 Aug & WW to IF, [autumn] [1849]: WLL/MW/196 pp.1–2 & *LY*, iv, 908. Charles was at Sedbergh Aug 1849–53; he joined the P&O Company and was involved in action in the Crimean War; he emigrated to Melbourne, Australia: Admissions Register [7 Aug 1849], Sedbergh School; *Sedbergh School Register*, 231. William left Sedbergh for Balliol (Dec 1854) and took a first-class honours in Law and History (1859); he became Vice-Chancellor and Honorary DCL of the University of Bombay and Principal of Elphinstone College, Bombay: ibid., 228. He died in 1917 and was buried close to his brother Edward in the Protestant cemetery, Rome, where his headstone describes him as 'Pioneer of Indian Education Wise, Magnanimous, Tenderhearted'.

28. MW to Mrs TH, 16 or 18 Aug [1849]: WLL/MW/196 pp.2–3 & 5; EQ to HCR, 17 Aug 1849 (*HCRWC*, ii, 702–3); WW to IF, [autumn 1849] (*LY*, iv, 909); MW to Mrs CW2, [Sep? 1849]: WLL/MW/197 pp.5–6 (*nb* first 4pp. of MS missing).

29. EQ to HCR, 17 Aug 1849: *HCRWC*, ii, 703; EQD: WLMS/13/5/7 [22 Sep 1849]; CW2 to EQ, 24 Mar 1849: WLMS/1/11/25. EQ's first choice of inscription remains a mystery, but CW2 thought it 'very undesirable that the name of your wife and my uncle's daughter should be associated with such teaching, and be liable to be cited by its advocates in its behalf'.

30. MW to Mrs TH, 16 or 18 Aug & to Mrs CW2, [Sep] [1849]: WLL/MW/196 p.6 & 197 pp.6–7; EQ to HCR, 17 Aug 1849 (*HCRWC*, ii, 703); Yarnall, *Wordsworth and the Coleridges*, 33–51, esp.35, 42, 50.

31. MW to EM, 30 Jul 1849: WLL/MW/195 p.2; WW to IF, [autumn], MW to EM, 29 Oct & WW to EM, 31 Oct 1849 (*LY*, iv, 908, 910, 911). For WW's estimate of his annual sales, which refers to the period 1837–46, thereby excluding the single volume in double columns, see WW to unidentified, 30 Oct 1846 (ibid., 811–12).

32. J. Ballantine to WW, 5 Aug 1846: WLMS/A/Ballantine/1; WW to C. Wren-Hoskins, 19 Apl 1847 (*LY*, iv, 842–3). WW declined both invitations. G. Colville to WW, 16 Nov 1846: WLMS/A/Colville/1 pp.1–2; WW to IF, [early Nov] & to Sir W. Gomm, 23 Nov 1846 (*LY*, iv, 812–13, 821–2); S. Walpole, *The Life of Lord John Russell* (London, Longman, Green & Co., 1891), ii, 145–6. WW's undated letter to James Hutcheson, which *LY*, iv, 807, prints as [Oct 1846], does not belong to this election, but to the one of 1838: see pp. 698, 921n.67.

33. D. McCorkindale to WW, 3 Jun 1841: WLMS/A/McCorkindale/1; WW to D. McCorkindale, 7 Jun 1841 & to J. Cumming, 18 Jun 1849 (*LY*, iv, 204, 901); J. Reid to WW, 8 Feb 1847: WLMS/A/Reid/1.

34. MW to EM, 29 Oct 1849 (*LY*, iv, 911); EQ to HCR, 14 Oct & 16 Dec 1849 (*HCRWC*, ii, 706, 709–10); MW to EH, 17 Dec 1849: WLL/MW/198 p.2; *HCRBW*, ii, 694. *Despondency Corrected* is the title of the 4th book of *The Excursion.*

35. EQ to HCR, 25 Dec 1849 (*HCRWC*, ii, 713); WW to IF, 2 Jan 1850 (*LY*, iv, 914); G. Nottage to WW, 17 Jan 1850 (*HCRWC*, ii, 716–17). Matthew Arnold and his wife were fellow guests with the Ws: EQ to HCR, 2 Jan 1850 (ibid., 715).

36. EQ to HCR, 16 Feb & 2 Jan, WW2 to HCR, 18 Jan, CW2 to HCR, 24 Jan & HCR to TR, 26 Jan 1850 (ibid., 720, 715, 717, 719[*bis*]). Martin Farquhar Tupper (1810–89), author of *Proverbial Philosophy* (1838–42). See also EQ to HCR, 20 Jan 1850 (*HCRWC*, ii, 718).

37. Ibid.; MW to Mrs TH, 14 Feb [1850]: WLL/MW/199 p.3; EQD: WLMS/13/5/8 [10–12 Mar 1850].

38. Ibid. [13 Mar 1850]; MW to EM, 21 Mar 1850: WLL/MW/201/ p.2; EQ to IF, 22 Mar 1850: WLL/EQ/136 pp.1–4.

39. EQ to Lady Richardson, 24 Mar 1850: WLL/EQ/136 p.2; EQD: WLMS/13/5/8 [scrawled across the week 24–30 Mar 1850]; EQ to SC, 28 Mar 1850: WLL/EQ/136a pp.1–2; EQ to HCR, 23 Apl 1850 (*HCRWC*, ii, 726). A 'stupid paragraph' in the *Westmorland Gazette*, which was copied into most other papers, started the avalanche.

40. EQD: WLMS/13/5/8 [31 Mar 1850]; EQ to Miss Taylor, [31 Mar 1850]: WLL/EQ/137 pp.1–2; MW to Mrs TH, [early spring (*r.*?31 Mar) 1850] (*LMW*, 315–16). MW says WW had risen from his bed while she was at church; 31 Mar is the only date her attendance there was noted and EQ's diary notes an improvement in WW around that time, so I have assumed that is the date of her letter: it may, however, date from Sunday 17 Mar, though not 24 Mar, when he was worse.

41. EQD: WLMS/13/5/8 [6–9 Apl 1850]; EQ to Mrs CW2, 9 Apl 1850: WLL/EQ/139 pp.1, 3–4 & 6; MW to IF, [6–7 (*r.*7–8) Apl 1850] (*LMW*, 318).

42. JW3 to CW2, [11 Apl 1850]: WLMS/1/41 pp.2–3; BM to WW, 11 Apl 1850: WLMS/A/Montagu/25 p.3.

43. EQ to HCR, 23 Apl 1850 (*HCRWC*, ii, 725).

44. JW3 to EM, [20 Apl 1850]: Moorsom 62/1/1; WW2 to Mrs WW2, 23 Apl 1850: WLL/WW2/51 pp.2–3.

45. Ibid., p.4; EQ to SC, 23 Apl 1850: WLL/EQ/141a p.1; Yarnall, *Wordsworth and the Coleridges*, 81–2; F. Arnold, Obituary from *The Times*, 11 Sep 1923: WLMS/A/Arnold/37. There is some confusion about the actual time of death. EQ comments on the cuckoo clock and says that it was 12 o'clock, but both WW2 and JW3 said it was a quarter to 12: EQD: WLMS/13/5/8 [23 Apl 1850]; EQ to SC, 23 Apl 1850: WLL/EQ/141a p.1; WW2 to Mrs WW2, 23 Apl 1850: WLL/WW2/51 p.4; JW2 to CW2, 23 Apl 1850: WLMS/1/4/2 p.1.

46. EQ to SC, 28 Apl 1850: WLL/EQ/141b p.1; Mrs Davy to Mrs Arnold, [26 Apl 1850]: WLMS/A/Arnold/43; *Leeds Intelligencer*, 11 May 1850; Mrs Fletcher to Lady Richardson, 1 May 1850 (*Autobiography of Mrs Fletcher*, 283).

47. Ibid., 284. MW was 'much affected and much gratified' by this poem: EQ to HCR, 16 Jan 1851 (*HCRWC*, ii, 769).

48. EQ to SC, 23 Apl 1850: WLL/EQ/141a p.3. The quotation is a pastiche from *Macbeth*, Act v, Scene iii, ll.24–5.

Epilogue

picture: The Wordsworth graves in Grasmere churchyard. Photograph by Abraham's of Keswick, *c.*1910.

1. R. Peel to WW2, 24 Apl 1850: WLMS/A/Peel/10 p.2; J. Stanton Biggs, Obituary of WW, *Soulby's Ulverston Advertiser*, 25 Apl 1850 p.3; W.S. Cookson to WW2, 24 Apl 1850: G9/3/2 p.1.

2. EQ to HCR, 30 Apl 1850 (*HCRWC*, ii, 727); W.S. Cookson to WW2, 1 & 4 May 1850: G9/3/4 p.2 & 5 p.2; EQ, Memo of meeting re Memoir of WW, 16 May 1850: WLL/EQ/142 p.1.

3. Ibid., p.3; MW to CW2, 17 May [1850]: WLL/MW/204 pp.1–2; EQ to CW2, 18 May 1850: WLL/EQ/143 pp.1–2. MW suspected CW2 had been persuaded to do the longer biography by his brother, Chas W: EQ, Memo of meeting re Memoir of WW, 16 May 1850: WLL/EQ/142 p.2.

4. J. Carter to WW2, 23 May 1850: G6/1/5; W.S. Cookson to WW2, 25 May 1850: G9/3/10 p.3; EQD: WLMS/13/5/8 [10 Jun & 9 Jul 1850]; *HCRBW*, ii, 702. Carter also overlooked the proofs of *The Prelude*: J. Carter to WW2, 8 Jun 1850: G6/1/9 p.3. For CW2's argument for the full biography, see CW2 to MW, 18 May 1850: G2/15/4. Carter lived on at the cottage he had built, Loughrigg Holme, with a generous

pension from WW2 augmenting what he had been left by WW; he died in Jan 1863.

5. CW2 note on MW to CW2, 17 May [1850]: WLL/MW/204 p.4; Lady Richardson to HCR, 20 Apl 1853 (*HCRWC*, ii, 793); *HCRBW*, ii, 703; *Memoirs*, i, 74–5. CW2 was convinced of the 'certainty that the truth will out' and only doubted whether he should have been more explicit: CW2 to EQ, 21 Mar 1851: WLMS/4/7 p.1.

6. *HCRBW*, ii, 697, 703; HCR to TR, 3–4 May & W.S. Cookson to HCR, 31 Aug 1850 (*HCRWC*, ii, 729, 756). HCR received Baudouin's first letter, forwarded by MW, on 4 May and replied immediately, demanding that all future correspondence should be carried on through him. The fact that no W letters to AV survive suggests he managed to acquire and destroy them, perhaps in return for a payment. HCR continued to visit MW after WW's death and died on 5 Feb 1867.

7. WW2 to CW2, 21 Oct, 4, 8 & 14 Nov 1850: WLL/WW2/52 pp.1–2, 53, 54 & 55; CW2 to MW, 3 Sep & CW2 to WW2, 6 & 9 Nov 1850: WLMS/1/11/31 pp.2–3, 43 & 46; EQ to CW2, 9 Nov 1850; WLL/EQ/149; MW to WW2, [Sep 1850] (*LMW*, 321).

8. HCR to TR, 11 Apl 1851, EQ to HCR, 30 Jun 1850 & W. Boxall to HCR, 24 Sep 1851 (*HCRWC*, ii, 776, 751, 782); SC to IF, 25 May 1851 (*SCM*, ii, 416); J. Davy to EQ, 6 Apl 1851: WLMS/A/Davy/1. MW disapproved of Keble's wording for the plaque in Grasmere church, which described WW first as a philosopher, then as a poet, and was, she thought, too much of an encomium. The memorial windows in Ambleside church were effectively paid for by American subscriptions raised by Reed: B. Harrison to HCR, [30 Jun 1853] (*HCRWC*, ii, 794).

9. EQ to EM, [Oct 1850]: WLL/EQ/146; EH, *Diary*: H2/3/5 [8 Jul 1851]; WW2 to EM, 10 Jul 1851: G4/1/8 pp.2–3; MW to Mrs TH, 26 Jan & to Mrs CW2, 7 Feb 1855 (*LMW*, 352–4).

10. MW to Mrs CW2, 28 Jun 1852 (ibid., 342); J. Wordsworth to HCR, 30 Sep & HCR to TR, 12 Nov 1853 (*HCRWC*, ii, 795, 796–7). CC died on 31 Jan 1856; IF in Dec 1856: Mrs Dickenson to HCR, 31 Jan 1853 & Lord Monteagle to HCR, [Dec] 1856 (ibid., 807, 816).

11. HCR to TR, 22 Sep 1851, 9 Sep 1852 & JW3 to HCR, 15 Jan [1859] (ibid., 781, 789, 827); EQ to SC, 28 Apl 1850: WLL/EQ/141b p.2.

Bibliography

This bibliography contains only those printed sources which are cited more than once; details of works of minor or local importance are given in full in the notes. More frequently cited sources are listed under the heading 'Abbreviations': see p. 814. All manuscripts are cited in full throughout the notes and refer to the holdings of the Wordsworth Trust at Dove Cottage, Grasmere, unless otherwise stated.

An Authentic Narrative of the Earl of Abergavenny East Indiaman . . . by a Gentleman in the East-India House (London, Minerva Press, 1805)

[Arnold, Matthew,] *The Letters of Matthew Arnold*, edited by C.Y. Lang (Charlottesville, University Press of Virginia, 1996–7), 2 vols.

Attwooll, Maureen, *Shipwrecks* (Discover Dorset series, Dovecote Press, Wimborne, 1998)

Barker, Juliet, *The Brontës* (London, Weidenfeld & Nicolson, 1994)

Bonsall, Brian, *Sir James Lowther and Cumberland and Westmorland Elections 1754–1775* (Manchester University Press, 1960)

Bouis, Regis, *A verser au dossier d'Annette Vallon* (Blois, 1944), pp.1–8 of Brochure 59, ADL&C, Blois

Brookfield, C. & F., *Mrs Brookfield and Her Circle* (London, Pitman & Sons, 1905), 2 vols.

Broughton, Leslie Nathan, *The Wordsworth Collection: A Catalogue* (New York, Cornell University Library, 1931)

Browning, Oscar (ed.), *The Despatches of Earl Gower* (Cambridge University Press, 1885)

Bulletin du Tribunal Criminel Révolutionnaire, nos. 61–4, [16 Jun 1793,] Microfilm 745, Série L1(1), ADL, Orléans

Burkett, M.E. & Sloss, J.D.G., *William Green of Ambleside: A Lake District Artist (1760–1823)* (Abbot Hall Art Gallery, Kendal, 1984)

Buxton, Charles (ed.), *Memoirs of Sir Thomas Fowell Buxton, Bart* (London, John Murray, 1848)

[Byron, George Gordon, Lord,] *Byron's Letters and Journals*, edited by Leslie A. Marchand (London, John Murray, 1973–94), 12 vols., with a supplementary vol.

Carlyle, Reverend Alexander, *Anecdotes and Characters of the Times*, edited by James Kinsey (Oxford University Press, 1973)

[Carlyle, Thomas,] *Collected Letters of Thomas and Jane Welch Carlyle*, edited by C.R. Sanders (Durham, NC, Duke University Press, 1970–97), 25 vols. to date.

Carlyle, Thomas, *The French Revolution* (London, Chapman & Hall, 1888), 2 vols.

– *Reminiscences*, edited by K.J. Fielding & Ian Campbell (Oxford University Press, 1997)

Carlyon, Clement, *Early Years and Late Reflections* (London, Whittaker & Co., 1843), 2 vols.

[Carroll, Lewis,] *The Letters of Lewis Carroll*, edited by M.N. Cohen (London, Macmillan, 1979), 2 vols.

Claeys, G. (ed.), *The Politics of English Jacobinism: Writings of John Thelwall* (Pennsylvania State University Press, 1995)

Clarke, H.L. & Weech, W.N., *History of Sedbergh School, 1525–1925* (Sedbergh, 1925)

Clayden, P.W., *The Early Life of Samuel Rogers* (London, Smith, Elder & Co., 1887)

Cobhan, Alfred (ed.), *The Debate on the French Revolution 1789–1800* (London, Nicholas Kaye, 1950)

Coleridge, H.N. (ed.), *Specimens of the Table Talk of Samuel Taylor Coleridge* (London, 1835), 2 vols.

[Constable, John,] *John Constable's Correspondence*, edited by R.B. Beckett (Suffolk Records Society, 1964), 6 vols.

Correct Statement of the Loss of the Earl of Abergavenny (London, Thomas Tegg, 1808)

Cosperec, Annie, *Blois: La Forme d'une Ville* (Paris, 1994)

Cottle, Joseph, *Reminiscences of Samuel Taylor Coleridge and Robert Southey* (Highgate, Lime Tree Bower Press, 1970, repr. of 1st edn, London, Houlston & Stoneman, 1847)

Cumming, Edward M. & Carter, David J., 'The *Earl of Abergavenny* (1805), an outward-bound English East Indiaman', *The International Journal of Nautical Archaeology and Underwater Exploration*, 19, 1 (1990), 31–3

Denis, Serge, 'William Wordsworth et l'Orléanais', *Extrait du Bulletin de la Société Archéologique et Historique de l'Orléanais*, xxii, 232 (1933), 251–61

Denis, Yves, *Histoire de Blois et sa Région* (Toulouse, 1988)

D'Illiers, Louis, *L'Histoire d'Orléans Raconté par un Orléanais* (Orléans, 1954)

Dormandy, Thomas, *The White Death: A History of Tuberculosis* (London, The Hambledon Press, 1999)

Dowden, Edward (ed.), *The Correspondence of Henry Taylor* (London, 1888)

Durey, Michael, 'The spy who never was', *Times Literary Supplement*, 10 Mar 2000, 14–15

Dyce, Alexander (ed.), *Recollections of the Table-talk of Samuel Rogers* (London, Edward Moxon, 1856)

Edwards, David L., *Christian England. Vol.3: From the 18th Century to the First World War* (London, William Collins, 1984)

Emerson, Ralph Waldo, *English Traits* (Boston, Houghton Mifflin Co., 1903)

– *Journals and Miscellaneous Notebooks*, edited by M.M. Sealts (Harvard University Press, 1973), vols. iv, x

– *The Letters of Ralph Waldo Emerson*, edited by R.L. Rusk (Columbia University Press, 1939), 6 vols.

Evans, Bergen & Pinney, Hester, 'Racedown and the Wordsworths', reprint from *The Review of English Studies*, viii, 29 (Jan 1832) (London, Smith & Jackson, [1935])

Fink, Z.W., *The Early Wordsworthian Milieu: A Notebook of Christopher Wordsworth with a few entries by William Wordsworth* (Oxford, Clarendon Press, 1958)

Fitzgerald, Percy H., *The Royal Dukes and Princesses of the Family of George III: A View of Court Life and Manners for Seventy Years, 1760–1830* (London, Tinsley Brothers, 1882), 2 vols.

[Fletcher, Mrs,] *Autobiography of Mrs Fletcher*, edited by the survivor of her family [Lady Richardson] (Edinburgh, Edmonston & Douglas, 1875)

[Fox, Caroline,] *The Journals of Caroline Fox 1835–71*, edited by Wendy Monk (London, Elek Books Ltd, 1972)

Furness, William, *History of Penrith* (1894)

Gellet-Duvivier, Pauline, *Memoire pour le citoyen Gellet Duvivier, d'Orléans, accusé dans l'affaire du citoyen Léonard Bourdon*, Ref. 2 J 1973, Microfilm 3104, ADL, Orléans

Gill, Stephen, *Wordsworth and the Victorians* (Oxford, Clarendon Press, 1998)

Gillies, Robert Pearce, *Memoirs of a Literary Veteran* (London, 1851), 3 vols.

Gittings, Robert & Manton, Jo, *Dorothy Wordsworth* (Oxford, Clarendon Press, 1985)

Godwin, William, *An Enquiry Concerning Political Justice*, facsimile of the 1793 edition, with an introduction by Jonathan Wordsworth (Oxford & New York, Woodstock Books, 1992), 2 vols.

Gordon, Mary, *'Christopher North': a Memoir of John Wilson by his Daughter* (Edinburgh, 1862), 2 vols.

Granville, Castalia, Countess (ed.), *Lord Granville Leveson Gower (First Earl Granville): Private Correspondence 1781–1821* (London, John Murray, 1917), 2 vols.

Graves, R.P., *The Life of Sir W.R. Hamilton* (Dublin & London, 1882–9), 3 vols.

[Gray, Thomas,] *The Correspondence of Thomas Gray*, edited by Paget Toynbee & Leonard Whibley (Oxford, Clarendon Press, 1935), 3 vols.

Greig, James A., *Francis Jeffrey of The Edinburgh Review* (Edinburgh & London, Oliver & Boyd, 1948)

Greville, Charles Cavendish Fulke, *The Greville Memoirs, 1814–60*, edited by Lytton Strachey & Roger Fulford (London, Macmillan & Co., 1938), 8 vols.

Hainton, R. & G., *The Unknown Coleridge: The Life and Times of Derwent Coleridge 1800–1883* (London, Janus Publishing Co., 1996)

Hanson, T.W., *The Story of Old Halifax* (Wakefield, Chantry Press, 1986)

Harper, George Maclean, *William Wordsworth: His Life, Works and Influence* (London, John Murray, 1916), 2 vols.

– *Wordsworth's French Daughter* (Princeton, 1916)

Hazlitt, William, *Selected Writings*, edited, with an introduction by Ronald Blythe (Harmondsworth, Penguin Books, 1970)

Hogg, James, *Memoir of the Author's Life*, edited by Douglas S. Mack (Edinburgh & London, Scottish Academic Press, 1972)

[Holland, Elizabeth, Lady,] *The Journal of Elizabeth, Lady Holland (1791–1811)*, edited by the Earl of Ilchester (Longmans, Green & Co., 1909), 2 vols.

Howitt, William, *Homes and Haunts of the Most Eminent British Poets: The Early Years, 1770–1803* (London, Richard Bentley, 1849), 2 vols.

Hudleston, C. Roy, 'Ann Crackanthorpe: Wordsworth's great-aunt', *Transactions of the Cumberland and Westmorland Antiquarian and Archaeological Society*, NS, vol.lx (Kendal, 1960), pp.137–46

Humphries, Peter, *On the Trail of Turner in North and South Wales* (Cardiff, Cadw, 1997)

[Hunt, Leigh,] *The Autobiography of Leigh Hunt*, edited by Roger Ingpen (London, Archibald, Constable & Co., 1903), 2 vols.

Hutchinson, William, *The History of the County of Cumberland* (Carlisle, 1794), 2 vols.

Jerdan, William, *Autobiography* (London, Arthur Hall, Virtue & Co., 1852), 4 vols.

Jones, Colin, *The Longman Companion to the French Revolution* (London & New York, Longman, 1988)

Jones, Katherine, *A Passionate Sisterhood* (London, Constable & Co., 1997)

[Keats, John,] *The Letters of John Keats, 1814–1821*, edited by H.E. Rollins (Cambridge, Mass., 1958), 2 vols.

King, R.W., *The Translator of Dante: The Life, World and Friendships of Henry Francis Cary (1772–1844)* (London, Martin Secker, 1925)

Knight, W., *The Life of William Wordsworth* (Edinburgh, William Paterson, 1889)

Lefebure, Molly, *The Bondage of Love* (London, Victor Gollancz, 1986)

Lockhart, J.G., *Narrative of the Life of Sir Walter Scott, Bart, Begun by Himself, and Continued by J.G. Lockhart* (London, J.M. Dent, 1905)

Lucas, E.V. (ed.), *The Letters of Charles Lamb, to which are added those of his Sister Mary Lamb* (London, 1935), 3 vols.

[Macready, William Charles], *The Diaries of William Charles Macready 1833–1851*, edited by William Toynbee (London, Chapman & Hall, 1912), 2 vols.

– *Reminiscences*, edited by F. Pollock (London, Macmillan, 1876)

Madden, Lionel (ed.), *Robert Southey: The Critical Heritage* (London, Routledge & Kegan Paul, 1972)

Marsh, John & Garbutt, John, *Wordsworth's Lakeland: Britain in Old Photographs* (Sutton Publishing, 1997)

Martineau, Harriet, *Autobiography*, with a new introduction by Gaby Weiner (London, Virago, 1983, repr. of 3rd edn of 1877), 2 vols.

Mayberry, Tom, *Coleridge & Wordsworth in the West Country* (Stroud, Alan Sutton Publishing, 1992)

Mill, John Stuart, *Additional Letters*, edited by M. Filipiuk, M. Laine & J.M. Robson, from *Collected Works of John Stuart Mill* (University of Toronto Press, 1991), vol. xxii

– *Autobiography*, edited by J. Stillinger (Oxford University Press, 1971)

– *Autobiography and Literary Essays*, edited by J.M. Robson & J. Stillinger, from *Collected Works of John Stuart Mill* (University of Toronto Press, 1981), vol. i

– *Journals and Speeches*, edited by J.M. Robson from *Collected Works of John Stuart Mill* (University of Toronto Press, 1988), vol. xxvii

Mitchell, Harvey, *The Underground War Against Revolutionary France: The Missions of William Wickham, 1794–1800* (Oxford, Clarendon Press, 1965)

Motion, Andrew, *Keats* (London, Faber & Faber, 1997)

Nicholson, Norman, *The Lakers* (Milnthorpe, Cicerone Press, 1995)

Overton, John Henry & Wordsworth, Elizabeth, *Christopher Wordsworth, Bishop of Lincoln 1807–1885* (London, Rivingtons, 1888)

Owen, Hugh, *The Lowther Family: Eight Hundred Years of 'A Family of Ancient Gentry and Worship'* (Sussex, Phillimore & Co., 1990)

Pares, Richard, *A West India Fortune* (London, Longmans, Green & Co., 1950)

Peacock, Markham L., *The Critical Opinions of William Wordsworth* (New York, Octagon Books, 1969)

Pollock, John, *Wilberforce* (Lion Publishing plc, repr. 1986)

Porritt, Arthur, 'The Rawson Family', *Transactions of the Halifax Antiquarian Society* (1966), pp. 27–52

Prance, Charles A., *Companion to Charles Lamb* (London, Mansell Publishing, 1983)

Quillinan, Edward, *Poems, with a memoir by William Johnston* (London, Edward Moxon, 1853)

Rawnsley, H.D., 'Reminiscences of Wordsworth among the Peasantry of Westmoreland', with an introduction by Geoffrey Tillotson (London, Dillon's, 1968)

Reid, T. Wemyss, *The Life, Letters and Friendships of Richard Monckton Milnes, first Lord Houghton* (London, Cassell & Co., 1890), 2 vols.

[Reynolds J.H.,] *Selected Prose of J.H. Reynolds*, edited by Leonidas Jones (Harvard University Press, 1966)

[Rickman, John,] *Life and Letters of John Rickman*, edited by Orlo Williams (London, Constable & Co., 1911)

Scott, R.F. (ed.), *Admissions to the College of St John the Evangelist in the University of Cambridge* (Cambridge, 1903 & 1931), vols. iii & iv

[Scott, Walter,] *The Journal of Sir Walter Scott*, edited by W.E.K. Anderson (Oxford, Clarendon Press, 1972)

Taylor, Henry, *Autobiography 1800–1875* (London, Longmans, Green & Co., 1885), 2 vols.

Tennyson, Hallam, *Alfred Lord Tennyson: A Memoir, by his Son* (London, Macmillan & Co., 1897), 2 vols.

Thomas, Keith, *Man and the Natural World: Changing Attitudes in England 1500–1800* (Harmondsworth, Penguin Books, 1984)

Ticknor, George, *Life, Letters and Journals*, edited by George S. Hillard (Sampson Low, Marston, Searle & Rivington, 1876), 2 vols.

Tomalin, Claire, *Mrs Jordan's Profession* (Harmondsworth, Penguin Books, 1995)

Trigg, W.B., 'Dorothy Wordsworth and Her Halifax Friends', *Transactions of the Halifax Antiquarian Society* (1951), pp.89–98

Trouillard, G., *Mémoires de Madame Vallon. Souvenirs de la Révolution dans le département de Loir-et-Cher publiés par G. Trouillard* (Paris, 1913)

Warter, J.W. (ed.), *Selections from the Letters of Robert Southey* (London, 1849–50), 4 vols.

Watters, Reggie & Woolf, Derrick, *Walking with Coleridge in the Quantocks* (privately printed, Coleridge Cottage, 1998), nos. 1. Stowey, 2. Alfoxton, 3. Kilve

Watts, Alaric Alfred, *Alaric Watts, a Narrative of his Life* (London, Richard Bentley & Son, 1884), 2 vols.

Wilberforce, William, *Journey to the Lake District from Cambridge 1779*, edited by C.E. Wrangham (Oriel Press, 1983)

Wilson, John, 'Mrs William Rawson and Her Diary', *Transactions of the Halifax Antiquarian Society* (1958), pp.29–50

Wordsworth, Charles, *Annals of My Early Life 1806–46* (London, Longman, Green & Co., 1891)

Wordsworth, Dorothy, *A Narrative Concerning George and Sarah Green*, edited by E. de Selincourt (Oxford, 1936)

– *The Greens of Grasmere*, edited by Hilary Clark (Wolverhampton, 1987)

Wordsworth, William, *The Borderers*, edited by Robert Osborn (Cornell University Press, 1982)

– *Descriptive Sketches*, edited by E. Birdsall (Cornell University Press, 1984)

– *Lyrical Ballads, and Other Poems, 1797–1800*, edited by James Butler & Karen Green (Cornell University Press, 1992)

– *The Ruined Cottage and The Pedlar*, edited by James Butler (Cornell University Press, 1979)

– *The Salisbury Plain Poems*, edited by Stephen Gill (Cornell University Press, 1975)

– *The Shorter Poems*, edited by C.H. Ketcham (Cornell University Press, 1989)

Yarnall, Ellis, *Wordsworth and the Coleridges* (New York & London, Macmillan, 1899)

Young, Julian Charles, *A Memoir of Charles Mayne Young, tragedian, with extracts from his son's journal* (London, Macmillan & Co., 1871), 2 vols.

Index